AUTOMOTIVE TUNEUP

Books and Instructional Materials by William H. Crouse and * Donald L. Anglin

Automotive Air Conditioning*
  Workbook for Automotive Air Conditioning*
Automotive Chassis and Body*
  Workbook for Automotive Chassis and Body*
Automotive Electrical Equipment
  Workbook for Automotive Electrical Equipment*
Automotive Emission Control*
  Workbook for Automotive Emission Control*
Automotive Engines*
  Workbook for Automotive Engines*
Automotive Fuel, Lubricating, and Cooling Systems*
  Workbook for Automotive Fuel, Lubricating, and Cooling Systems*
Automotive Tools, Fasteners, and Measurements—A Text-Workbook*
Automotive Transmissions and Power Trains*
  Workbook for Automotive Transmissions and Power Trains*
  Transparencies for Automatic-Transmissions Hydraulic Circuits*
Automotive Tuneup*
  Workbook for Automotive Tuneup*
Automotive Service Business: Operation and Management
Automotive Engine Design
Workbook for Automotive Service and Trouble Diagnosis
Automotive Mechanics
  Study Guide for Automotive Mechanics
  Testbook for Automotive Mechanics*
  Workbook for Automotive Mechanics*
  Automotive Engines—Sound Filmstrip Program
    Set 1 and Set 2
    Preview-Review Exercises
  Automotive Room Chart Series
    Automotive Electrical Equipment Charts
    Automotive Engines Charts
    Automotive Fuel Systems Charts
    Automotive Emissions Controls Charts
    Automotive Engines Cooling Systems, Heating, and Air Conditioning Charts
    Automotive Suspension, Steering, and Tires Charts
    Automotive Transmissions and Power Trains Charts
    Automotive Brakes Charts
  Automotive Troubleshooting Cards
The Auto Book
  Auto Shop Workbook*
  Auto Study Guide
  Auto Test Book*
  Auto Cassette Series
Pocket Automotive Dictionary*
General Power Mechanics (with Robert Worthington and Morton Margules*)
Small Engines: Operation and Maintenance
  Workbook for Small Engines: Operation and Maintenance

Automotive Transparencies by William H. Crouse and Jay D. Helsel

Automotive Air Conditioning†
Automotive Brakes
Automotive Electrical Systems
Automotive Emission Control†
Automotive Engine Systems
Automotive Transmissions and Power Trains
Automotive Steering Systems
Automotive Suspension Systems
Engines and Fuel Systems

†*In production.*

AUTOMOTIVE TUNEUP

William H. Crouse
Donald L. Anglin

McGRAW-HILL BOOK COMPANY
Gregg Division

NEW YORK
ST. LOUIS
DALLAS
SAN FRANCISCO
AUCKLAND
BOGOTÁ
DÜSSELDORF
JOHANNESBURG
LONDON
MADRID
MEXICO
MONTREAL
NEW DELHI
PANAMA
PARIS
SÃO PAULO
SINGAPORE
SYDNEY
TOKYO
TORONTO

ABOUT THE AUTHORS

William H. Crouse

Behind William H. Crouse's clear technical writing is a background of sound mechanical engineering training as well as a variety of practical industrial experience. After finishing high school, he spent a year working in a tinplate mill. Summers, while still in school, he worked in General Motors plants, and for three years he worked in the Delco-Remy Division shops. Later he became Director of Field Education in the Delco-Remy Division of General Motors Corporation for which he prepared service bulletins and educational literature.

During the war years, he wrote a number of technical manuals for the Armed Forces. After the war, he became Editor of Technical Education Books for the McGraw-Hill Book Company. He has contributed numerous articles to automotive and engineering magazines and has written many outstanding books about science and technology. He was the first Editor-in-Chief of the 15-volume McGraw-Hill Encyclopedia of Science and Technology. In addition, he has authored more than fifty technical books including *Automotive Mechanics,* which has sold over a million copies. His books have been widely translated and used in automotive mechanics training throughout the world.

William H. Crouse's outstanding work in the automotive field has earned for him membership in the Society of Automotive Engineers and in the American Society of Engineering Education.

Donald L. Anglin

Trained in the automotive and diesel service field, Donald L. Anglin has worked both as a mechanic and as a service manager. He has taught automotive courses in high school, trade schools, community colleges, and universities. He has also worked as curriculum supervisior and school administrator for an automotive trade school. Interested in all types of vehicle performance, he has served as a racing-car mechanic and as a consultant to truck fleets on maintenance problems.

Currently he serves as editorial assistant to William H. Crouse, visiting automotive instructors and service shops. Together they have coauthored magazine articles on automotive education and several books in the McGraw-Hill Automotive Technology Series.

Donald L. Anglin is a Certified General Automotive Mechanic and holds many other licenses and certificates in heavy duty truck mechanics, automotive education, service, and related areas. His work in the automotive service field has earned for him membership in the American Society of Mechanical Engineers and the Society of Automotive Engineers.

Library of Congress Cataloging in Publication Data

Crouse, William Harry, (date)
Automotive tuneup.

Includes index.
1. Automobiles—Maintenance and repair. I. Anglin, Donald L., joint author. II. Title.
TL152.C694 629.28'7'22 76-50083
ISBN 0-07-014810-4

AUTOMOTIVE TUNEUP

1 2 3 4 5 6 7 8 9 0 WBWB 7 8 3 2 1 0 9 8 7

The editors for this book were Ardelle Cleverdon and Myrna W. Breskin, the designer was Dennis Purdy, the art supervisor was George T. Resch, and the production supervisor was Rena Shindelman. It was set in Melior by York Graphic Services, Inc.
Printed and bound by Webcrafters, Incorporated.

CONTENTS

	Preface	vii
	To the Student	ix
	Acknowledgments	x
1.	ENGINE FUNDAMENTALS	1
2.	ENGINE OPERATION	8
3.	ENGINE MEASUREMENTS	19
4.	ENGINE TYPES	28
5.	SAFETY IN THE SHOP	45
6.	ADJUSTING VALVES	50
7.	ENGINE LUBRICATING-SYSTEM OPERATION AND SERVICE	53
8.	ENGINE COOLING SYSTEMS	66
9.	COOLING-SYSTEM SERVICE	74
10.	AUTOMOTIVE-ENGINE FUELS	84
11.	AUTOMOTIVE FUEL SYSTEMS	91
12.	AUTOMOTIVE CARBURETORS	108
13.	DIAGNOSING FUEL-SYSTEM TROUBLES	129
14.	FUEL-SYSTEM SERVICE	139
15.	CARBURETOR SERVICE	149
16.	FUEL-INJECTION OPERATION AND SERVICE	170
17.	AIR POLLUTION, SMOG, AND THE AUTOMOBILE	187
18.	CLEANING UP THE EXHAUST GAS	198
19.	SERVICING EMISSION-CONTROL SYSTEMS	212
20.	FUNDAMENTALS OF ELECTRICITY	219
21.	AUTOMOTIVE BATTERIES	231
22.	BATTERY SERVICE	238
23.	STARTING MOTORS	249
24.	STARTING-MOTOR TROUBLE DIAGNOSIS	258
25.	STARTING-MOTOR SERVICE	262
26.	AUTOMOTIVE CHARGING SYSTEMS	267
27.	CHARGING-SYSTEM SERVICE	278
28.	IGNITION SYSTEMS	297
29.	IGNITION-SYSTEM TROUBLE DIAGNOSIS	311
30.	IGNITION-SYSTEM SERVICE	319
31.	IGNITION-DISTRIBUTOR SERVICE	332
32.	AUTOMOTIVE ELECTRONICS	349

33. ENGINE TESTING PROCEDURES AND TOOLS 355
34. DIAGNOSING ENGINE TROUBLES 362
35. ENGINE TUNE-UP 376
Glossary 386
Index 401
Answers to Questions 405

PREFACE

What is a tuneup? To some people, a tuneup means replacing spark plugs, distributor points, and condenser. To others, a tuneup includes almost all operations that are performed without disassembling the engine. Today, in many automotive service departments and repair shops, the tuneup technician is counted on to do much more than just change points and adjust the carburetor. The car has changed. More importantly, so have the laws affecting it.

During the past few years, federal, state, and local laws limiting automotive emissions have made it very important that an engine be properly tuned. This has placed an added responsibility on the tuneup technician. Now, changing parts is not enough. When tuneup work is performed, it must be done accurately and completely. Today's tuneup technician is being held to higher standards of competency and performance than ever before.

The National Institute for Automotive Service Excellence (NIASE) requires that for certification in engine tuneup, a technician must have two or more years of appropriate hands-on work experience. In addition the technician must pass a test covering starting and charging systems, ignition and fuel systems, manifold and exhaust systems, engine tuneup, and emission control systems. *Automotive Tuneup* covers in depth the subjects tested by NIASE in the mechanic certification test *Engine Tuneup*. (The NIASE Tests are used for certifying general automotive mechanics and specialists in other areas under the NIASE voluntary mechanic testing and certification program.)

Many schools offer courses in automotive tuneup. However, none of the available textbooks covered all the subject matter in the depth required to train a tuneup technician properly. It was to meet this need that *Automotive Tuneup* was prepared.

One feature of *Automotive Tuneup* is that it has the metric equivalents of all United States Customary (USC) measurements. The metric equivalent follows each USC measurement given. Instructors will recognize the importance of this feature.

Automotive Tuneup is printed in an $8\frac{1}{2} \times 11$ inch [215.9×279.4 mm] format to permit large illustrations for easy understanding of details. The text has been carefully prepared using simple explanations and short sentences to enhance readability.

Several ancillary materials have been developed for use with *Automotive Tuneup*. These include a shop workbook and an instructor's guide and answer key. Also the following sets of the McGraw-Hill *Automotive Room Charts Series* cover automotive tuneup subjects.

1. Automotive Electrical Equipment Charts
2. Automotive Engines Charts
3. Automotive Fuel Systems Charts
4. Automotive Emissions Controls Charts
5. Automotive Engines Cooling Systems, Heating, and Air Conditioning Charts

In addition, the *Automotive Troubleshooting Cards* and the twelve *Automotive Engines Sound Filmstrips* can be used effectively.

The *Workbook for Automotive Tuneup* already mentioned includes the basic tuneup service jobs as proposed in the latest recommendations of the Motor Vehicle Manufacturers Association—American Vocational Association Industry Planning Council. Taken together, *Automotive Tuneup* and the *Workbook for Automotive Tuneup* supply the student with the background information and "hands-on" experience needed to become a qualified and certified automotive tuneup technician.

To assist the automotive instructor, the *Instructor's Planning Guide for Automotive Tuneup* is available only to instructors from McGraw-Hill. The Instructor's Guide was prepared to help the automotive instructor do the best possible job of teaching by most effectively utilizing the textbook, workbook, and the other related instructional materials. The instructor's guide contains suggestions on classroom instruction and related shop activities, automotive curriculum, and much more. It also includes the answer key for the tests at the end of each jobsheet in the *Workbook for Automotive Tuneup*.

Also in the instructor's guide is a list of various related textbooks and ancillary instructional materials available from McGraw-Hill. Used singly or together, these items form a comprehensive student learning and activity package. They provide the student with meaningful learning experiences and help the student develop job competencies in automotive mechanics and related fields. The instructor's guide explains how the various available materials can be used, either singly or in combination, to satisfy any teaching requirement.

With the book, they add up to an instructional program that will fit any teaching situation in high school, trade school, and community college classes. The program is flexible. It will fit classroom instruction, shop activities, individual instruction, or "do it yourself" courses for hobbyists and consumers. The automotive technician who wishes to master another specialty area in the automotive-service field can do so by using this book.

The authors are very grateful to the many people, both in industry and in education, whose contributions and comments helped shape this book. They share, with the authors, a hope that this program will help achieve the aims of all who work in the field of automotive mechanics instruction, namely, to train high-caliber automotive mechanics and technicians who are capable of taking their proper place in the automotive-servicing profession.

WILLIAM H. CROUSE
DONALD L. ANGLIN

ACKNOWLEDGMENTS

During the preparation of *Automotive Tuneup,* the authors were given invaluable aid and inspiration by many people in the automotive industry and in the field of education. The authors gratefully acknowledge their indebtedness and offer their sincere thanks to these people. All cooperated with the aim of providing accurate and complete information that would be useful in training automotive mechanics.

Special thanks are owed to the following organizations for information and illustrations that they supplied: AC Spark Plug Division of General Motors Corporation; American Motors Corporation; Autoscan, Inc., Black & Decker Manufacturing Company; Buick Motor Division of General Motors Corporation; Cadillac Motor Car Division of General Motors Corporation; Caterpillar Tractor Company; Champion Spark Plug Company; Chevrolet Motor Division of General Motors Corporation; Chrysler Corporation; Delco-Remy Division of General Motors Corporation; Detroit Diesel Allison Division of General Motors Corporation; Digital Equipment Corporation; Fluidyne Instrumentation; Ford Motor Company; Ford Motor Company of Germany; GMC Truck and Coach Division of General Motors Corporation; General Motors Corporation; Hamilton Standard Division of United Aircraft Corporation; Harrison Radiator Division of General Motors Corporation; Hillman Motor Car Company, Limited; Honda; Inter-Industry Emission Control Program; Johnson Motors; Los Angeles County Air Pollution Control District; Mercedes-Benz; Mercer County Area Vocational-Technical School; Motor Vehicle Manufacturers Association; NSU of Germany; Oldsmobile Division of General Motors Corporation; Pontiac Motor Division of General Motors Corporation; Robert Bosch GmbH; Snap-on Tools Corporation; Standard Motor Products, Inc.; Sun Electric Corporation; Tecumseh Products Company; Teledyne Wisconsin Motor; Texaco Incorporated; Toyo Kogyo Company, Ltd.; Toyota Motor Sales, Limited; Union Carbide Corporation; Universal Testproducts, Inc.; Volkswagen; and Waukesha Motor Company. To all these organizations and the people who represent them, sincere thanks.

WILLIAM H. CROUSE
DONALD L. ANGLIN

TO THE STUDENT

Automotive Tuneup is one of nine books in the McGraw-Hill Automotive Technology Series. These books cover in detail the construction, operation, and maintenance of automotive vehicles. They are designed to give up the complete background of information you need to become successful in the automotive service business. The books satisfy the recommendations of the Motor Vehicle Manufacturers Association—American Vocational Association Industry Planning Council. The books also meet the requirements for automotive mechanics certification and state vocational educational programs, and recommendations for automotive trade apprenticeship training. Furthermore, the comprehensive coverage of the subject matter makes the books valuable additions to the library of anyone interested in automotive engineering, manufacturing, sales, service, and operation.

Meeting the Standards

The nine books in the McGraw Hill Automotive Technology Series meet the standards of the Motor Vehicle Manufacturers Association (MVMA) for associate degrees in automotive servicing and automotive service management. These standards are described in the MVMA booklet "Community College Guide for Associate Degree Programs in Auto and Truck Service and Management." The books also cover the subjects recommended by the American National Standards Institute in their detailed standard D18.1-1972, "American National Standard for Training of Automotive Mechanics for Passenger Cars and Light Trucks."

In addition, the books cover the subject matter tested by the National Institute for Automotive Service Excellence (NIASE). The tests given by NIASE are used for certifying general automotive mechanics and automotive technicians working in specific areas of specialization under the NIASE voluntary mechanic testing and certification program.

Getting Practical Experience

At the same time that you study the books in the McGraw-Hill Automotive Technology Series, you should be getting practical experience in the shop. You should handle automotive parts, automotive tools, and automotive servicing equipment, and you should perform actual servicing jobs. This is what is meant by getting practical experience. To assist you in your shop work, there are workbooks for each book in the series. For example, the *Workbook for Automotive Tuneup* includes the jobs that cover the basic servicing procedures in automotive tuneup. If you do every job covered in the workbook, you will have had "hands-on" experience with the basic jobs in tuning a technician is expected to perform.

If you are taking an automotive mechanics course in school, you will have an instructor to guide you in your classroom and shop activities. But even if you are not taking a course, the workbook can act as an instructor. It tells you, step by step, how to do the various servicing jobs. Perhaps you can meet others who are taking a school course in automotive mechanics and can talk over any problems you have with them. A local garage or service station is a good source of information. If you can get acquainted with the automotive mechanics there, you will find they have a great deal of practical information. Watch them at their work if you can. Make notes of important points for filing in your notebook.

Service Publications

While you are in the service shop, study the various publications received at the shop. Automobile manufacturers, as well as suppliers of parts, accessories, and tools, publish shop manuals, service bulletins, and parts catalogs. All these help service personnel do better jobs. In addition, numerous automotive magazines are published which deal with problems and methods of automotive service. All these publications will be of great value to you; study them carefully.

These activities will help you obtain practical experience in automotive mechanics. Sooner or later this experience, plus the knowledge that you have gained in studying the books in the McGraw-Hill Automotive Technology Series, will permit you to step into the automotive shop on a full-time basis. Or, if you are already in the shop, you will be equipped to step up to a better or more responsible job.

Checking Up on Yourself

You can check up on your progress in your studies by answering the questions given every few pages in the book. There are two types of tests, progress quizzes and chapter checkups, the answers to which are given at the back of the book. Each progress quiz should be taken just after you have completed the pages preceding it. These quizzes allow you to check yourself as you finish a lesson. On the other hand, the chapter checkup may cover several lessons, since it is a review test of the entire chapter. Because it is a review test, you should review the entire chapter by rereading it or at least glancing through it to check important points before trying the test. If any of the questions stump you, reread the pages in the book that will give you the answer. This sort of review is valuable. It will help you to remember the information you need when you work in an automotive shop.

Keeping a Notebook

Keeping a notebook is a valuable part of your training. Start it now, at the beginning of your studies of automotive tuneup. Your notebook will help you in many ways; it will be a record of your progress; it will become a storehouse of valuable information you will refer to time after time; it will help you learn; and it will help you organize your training program so that it will do you the most good.

When you study a lesson in the book, have your notebook open in front of you. Start with a fresh notebook page at the beginning of each lesson. Write the lesson or textbook page number and date at the top of the page. As you read your lesson, jot down the important points.

In the shop, use a small scratch pad or cards to jot down important points. You can transfer your notes to your notebook later.

You can also make sketches in your notebook showing wiring or hose diagrams, fuel circuits, and so on. Save articles and illustrations from technical and hot-rod magazines. File them in your notebook. Also, save instruction sheets that come with service parts. Carburetor kits, for example, have instruction sheets explaining how to make the proper adjustments. Glue or tape these to sheets of paper, if necessary, and file them in your notebook.

As you can see, your notebook will become a valued possession—a continuing record of what you have learned and are learning about automotive tuneup.

Glossary and Index

A glossary (a definition list) of automotive terms is given in the back of the book. Whenever you have any doubt about the meaning of a term or what purpose some automotive part has, you should refer to this list. Also, there is an index at the back of the book. This index will steer you to the page in the book where you will find the information you are seeking.

And now, good luck to you. You are studying a fascinating, complex, and admirable machine—the automobile. Your studies can lead you to success in the automotive field, a field where opportunities are nearly unlimited.

chapter 1

ENGINE FUNDAMENTALS

In this chapter, we discuss the engine—the power plant of the automobile. A mixture of gasoline and air is burned inside the engine. It is the burning, or combustion, that produces the power that makes the engine run.

⊘ **1-1 Internal-Combustion and External-Combustion Engines** There are two kinds of engines: internal-combustion engines and external-combustion engines. *Internal-combustion engines* burn fuel *inside* the engines. The engines in automobiles are internal-combustion engines.

External-combustion engines burn fuel *outside* the engine. Steam engines are external-combustion engines. Fuel burned outside the engine boils water and produces steam. The engine runs on the steam.

⊘ **1-2 Internal-Combustion Engines** Internal-combustion, or IC, engines are of two types. The type used in almost all automobiles is the *piston engine*. In this engine, the pistons move up and down—or reciprocate—in the engine cylinders. The word "reciprocate" means to move back and forth along a line. Since its pistons move up and down, the piston engine is also called a *reciprocating engine*.

The other IC engine is a newcomer, but you may hear a lot about it in the future. It is the *rotary engine*. The Wankel engine and the gas turbine are two kinds of rotary engines. Both are gaining in popularity, and you may see many rotary engines in the years to come. In rotary engines, the power of the burning fuel makes rotors spin. Rotary engines are discussed in Chap. 3.

⊘ **1-3 The Engine Cylinder** We shall now describe the piston engine in detail, and see how it works. Most automobiles have engines with four, six, or eight cylinders. The same action takes place in each cylinder. Thus, by studying just one cylinder, you can learn about the whole engine. Figure 1-1 is a six-cylinder engine, partly cut away to show the pistons and other inside parts.

Let's simplify our study by taking away all the parts except one piston and one cylinder. What you see in Fig. 1-2 looks like two beverage cans, one a little smaller than the other. The larger can is open at the bottom, so it is filled with air. The smaller can fits into the larger can, as shown in Fig. 1-3. If you push the smaller can up into the larger can, you squeeze the air into a smaller volume. That is, you compress the air. Now let's call the cans by their right names. The bigger can is the engine *cylinder*. The smaller one is the *piston*.

When the piston is pushed up into the cylinder, the air in the cylinder is compressed. Suppose there were some gasoline vapor in the compressed air. If a spark got into the cylinder, the mixture of air and gasoline would explode. The explosion would blow the piston out of the cylinder, as shown in Fig. 1-4.

⊘ **1-4 The Connecting Rod and Crankshaft** Blowing a piston out of a cylinder just once is not enough to make a car move. The piston must move up and down rapidly in the cylinder. Then this up-and-down, or reciprocating, motion must be changed into rotating motion to rotate the car wheels. The connecting rod and crankshaft do the job of changing the reciprocating motion of the piston into rotary motion.

Figure 1-5 is a picture of a piston. The piston is about 4 in (inches) [101.6 mm (millimeters)] in diameter. It weighs about 1 lb (pound) [0.454 kg (kilogram)]. Figure 1-6 shows the piston with the connecting rod attached. Figure 1-7 shows a crankshaft. The part of the crankshaft that changes the reciprocating motion of the piston into the rotary motion of the wheels is the *crank*. Figure 1-8 shows how the piston, connecting rod, and crankshaft work together. Only part of the crankshaft is shown in Fig. 1-8. The connecting rod is attached to the piston by a piston pin. The piston pin goes through two holes in the piston and one hole in the connecting rod. This is shown in Fig. 1-9. The other end of the connecting rod is attached to a crankpin on the crankshaft (see Fig. 1-9). Now let's see how this combination changes reciprocating motion into rotary motion.

⊘ **1-5 The Crankpin** First note how the crankpin swings around the crankshaft in a circle as the crankshaft rotates (Fig. 1-10). Look at the cutaway

Fig. 1-1. Six-cylinder, in-line engine with overhead valves, partly cut away to show its internal construction. (*Ford Motor Company*)

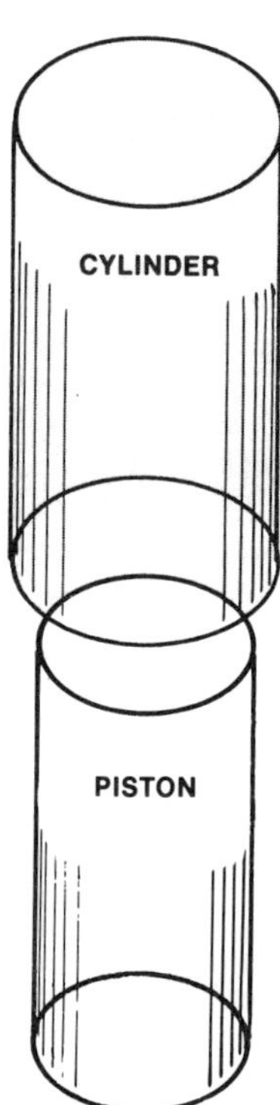

Fig. 1-2. The piston is a metal plug that fits snugly into the cylinder.

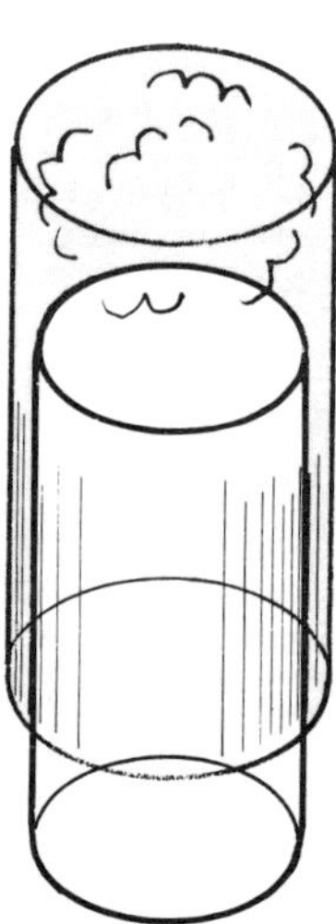

Fig. 1-3. When the piston is pushed up into the cylinder, air is trapped above the piston and compressed. The cylinder is drawn as though it were transparent, so that the piston can be seen.

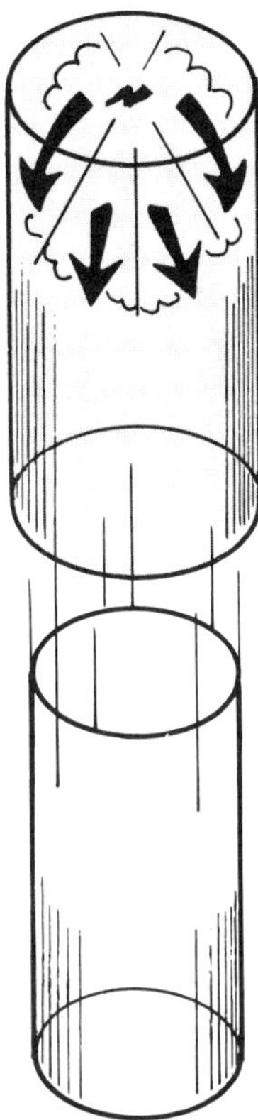

Fig. 1-4. If gasoline vapor were mixed with the air, and if a spark occurred in the cylinder, the explosion would blow the piston out of the cylinder.

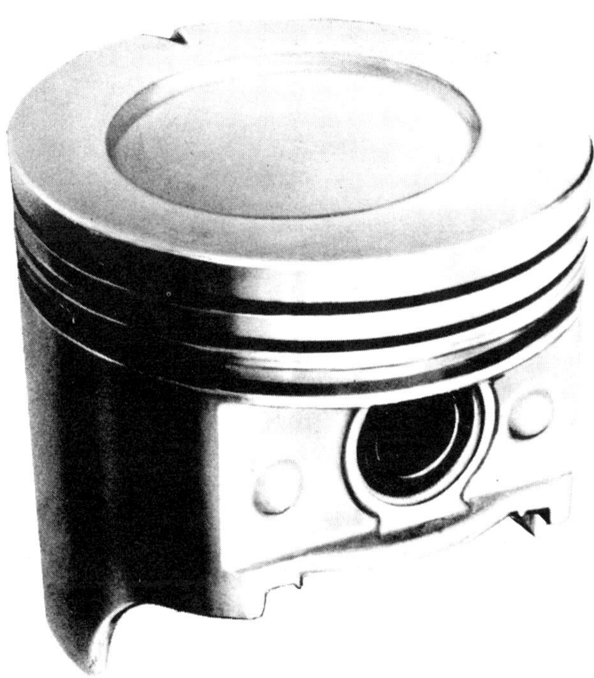

Fig. 1-5. Engine piston.

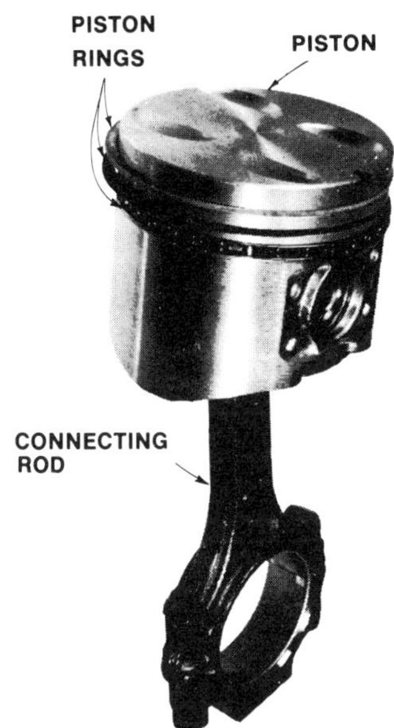

Fig. 1-6. Typical piston, with connecting rod attached and piston rings installed. (*Chrysler Corporation*)

view of an engine cylinder in Fig. 1-11. Find the piston, the connecting rod, the crankpin, and the crankshaft. Compare these parts with the same parts shown in Figs. 1-5 to 1-7.

When the piston moves up and down in the cylinder, the piston, the connecting rod, and the crankpin go through the eight positions shown in Fig. 1-12. The crankpin moves in a circle. The connecting rod tilts first in one direction and then in the other. The lower end of the connecting rod moves in a circle with the crankpin. Study the eight pictures in Fig. 1-12 to see how the up-and-down, or reciprocating, motion is changed into rotary motion.

⊘ 1-6 Cranks There are many cranks and connecting rods around you. Look at a bicycle. (See Fig. 1-13.) The pedal and its support form a crank. Your lower leg is the connecting rod. As you pump the pedal, your knee acts as the piston pin and moves up

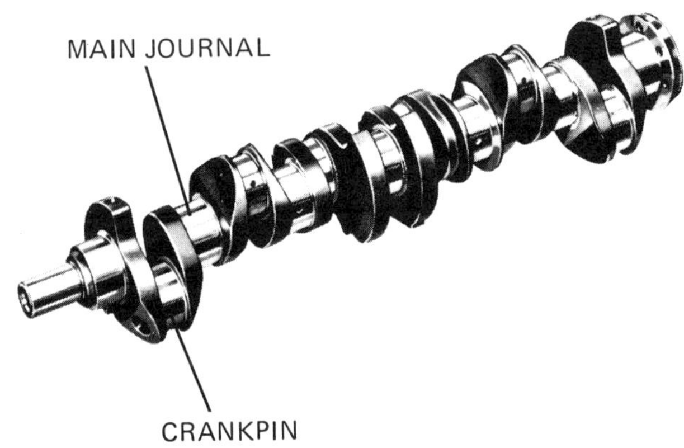

Fig. 1-7. Crankshaft for a six-cylinder engine. (*Ford Motor Company*)

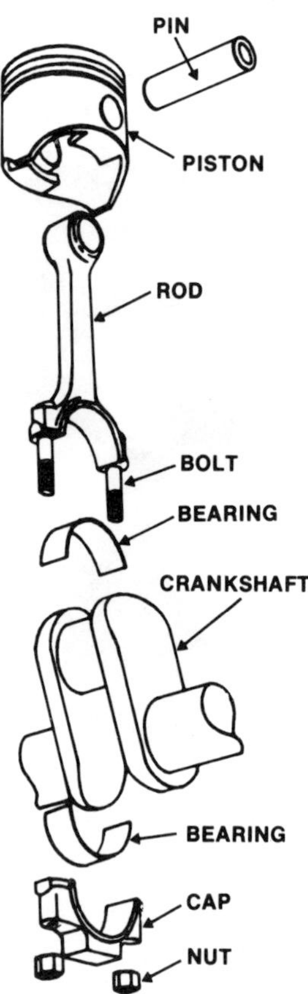

Fig. 1-8. Piston, connecting rod, piston pin, and crank in disassembled view. (*Chrysler Corporation*)

and down. Your foot is the lower end of the connecting rod. It moves in a circle as it follows the crank (the bicycle pedal and support).

⊘ 1-7 Piston Stroke When the piston moves from top to bottom, or from bottom to top, it completes one *stroke*. The piston completes *two strokes* as it goes through the eight positions shown in Fig. 1-12. In position 1, the piston is at the top. It moves down through positions 2, 3, and 4 to arrive at the bottom position 5. This is one piston stroke. Then the piston starts back up, moving through positions 6, 7, and 8 and back to 1. This is the second piston stroke.

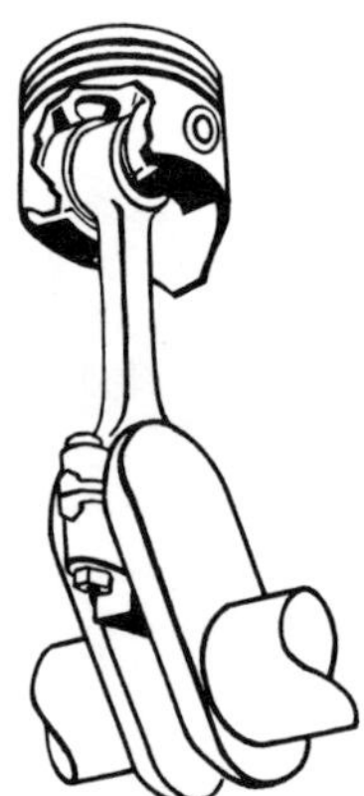

Fig. 1-9. Piston and connecting-rod assembly, attached to the crankpin on the crankshaft.

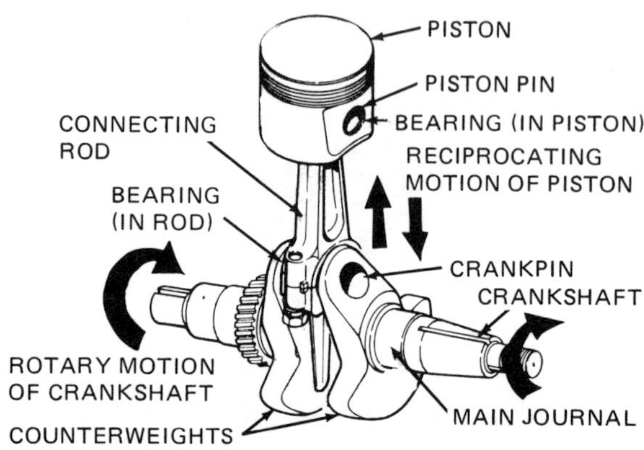

Fig. 1-10. The crankpin moves in a circle around the crankshaft while the piston moves up and down.

When the piston is at the top position, it is said to be at top dead center (TDC). When it is at the bottom position, it is said to be at bottom dead center (BDC). You will see many mentions of TDC and BDC in this book and in shop manuals. They are the reference points for setting valve and ignition timing.

⊘ 1-8 Four Strokes You may have heard someone call automobile engines "four-cycle engines." What this means is that the engines are *four-stroke-cycle engines*. In other words, it takes each engine piston four strokes or two revolutions of the crankshaft to go through a complete cycle. We shall explain what this means later.

⊘ 1-9 Making the Engine Run The piston moves up and down, and the crankshaft rotates (usually clockwise rotation as you face the front of the engine). But what makes the piston move? As you probably know, burning of gasoline in the engine does this job.

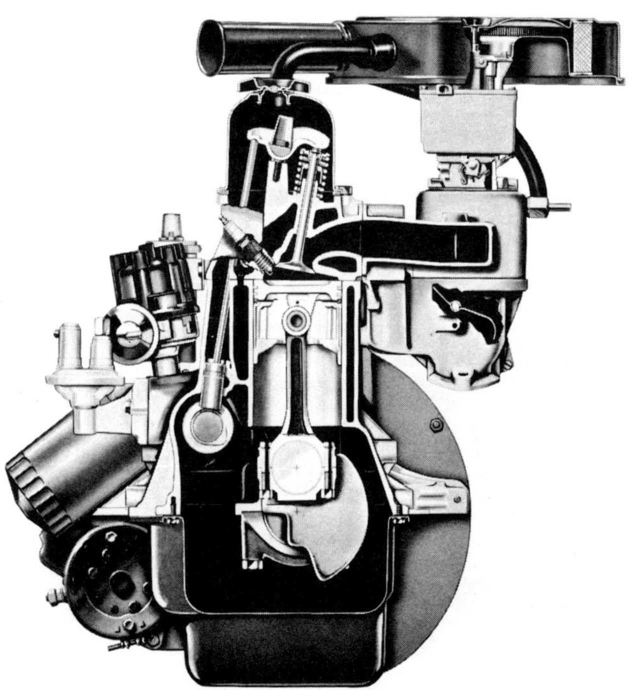

Fig. 1-11. Sectional view of a six-cylinder engine. (*American Motors Corporation*)

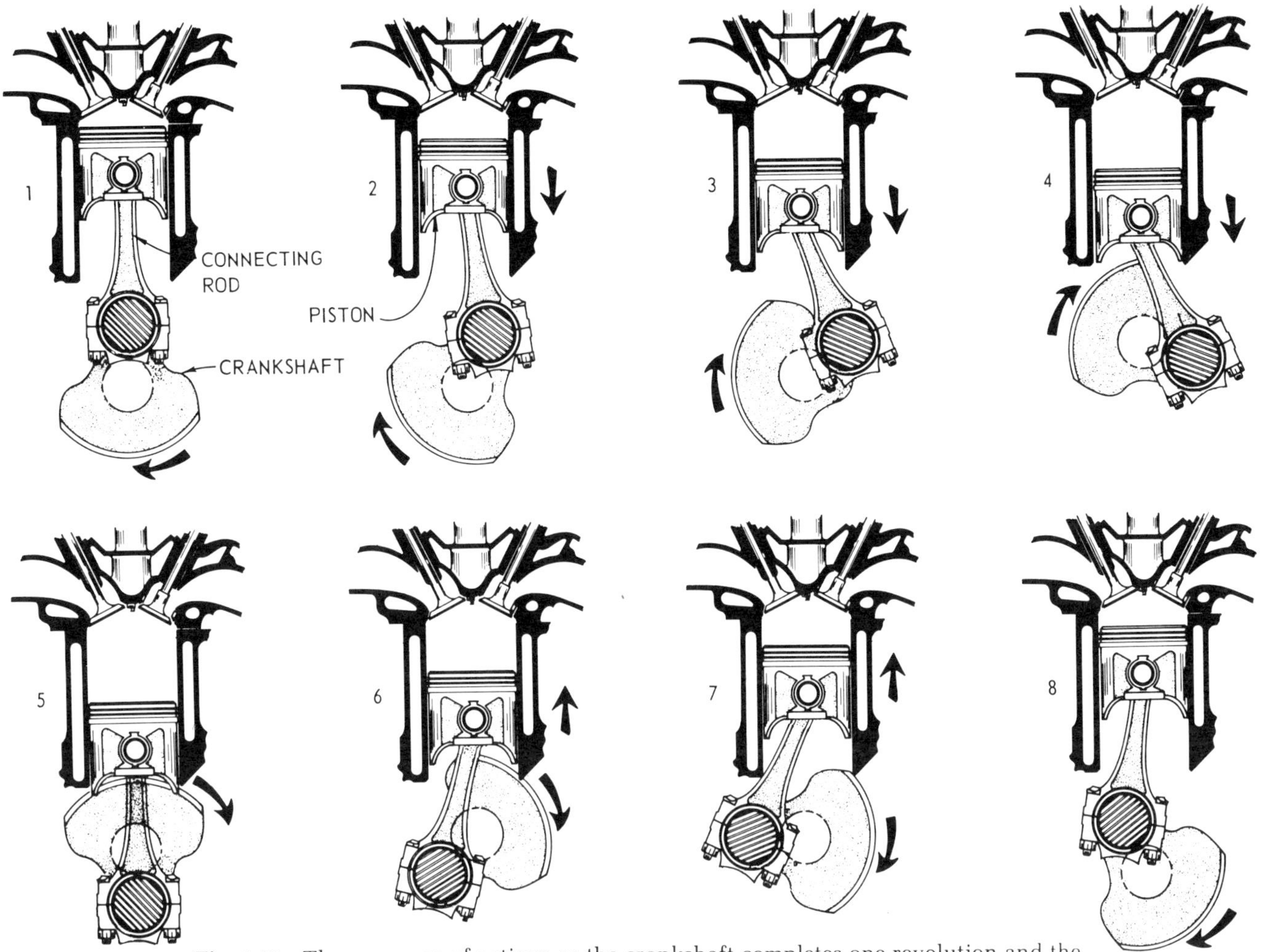

Fig. 1-12. The sequence of actions as the crankshaft completes one revolution and the piston moves from top to bottom to top again.

First, a mixture of gasoline vapor and air goes into the cylinder. Then the piston is pushed up to compress the mixture. Next a spark occurs in the cylinder. This spark ignites the mixture and it burns rapidly, pushing the piston down. It is this push that makes the crankshaft turn and the car wheels rotate. Then the piston must be pushed up to get the burned gases out of the cylinder.

⊘ 1-10 The Valves There must be an opening in the top of the cylinder so that the air-fuel mixture can get into the cylinder. A second opening is needed to get rid of the burned gases. That means there must be two openings. However, these openings cannot remain open all the time. They must be open when they are needed, and closed the rest of the time. *Valves* are used to open and close the openings. The valves let the air-fuel mixture into the cylinder, and let the burned gases out.

An engine valve is a long metal stem on which there is a flat top. It looks so much like a mushroom (Fig. 1-14) that engine valves are called "mushroom valves." They are also called "poppet valves" because they "pop" up and down.

Each valve moves up and down in a *valve guide* (Fig. 1-15), which is a round hole in the cylinder head. The guide keeps the valve moving up and down in a straight line. When the valve moves up, the valve head fits into a round opening in the cylin-

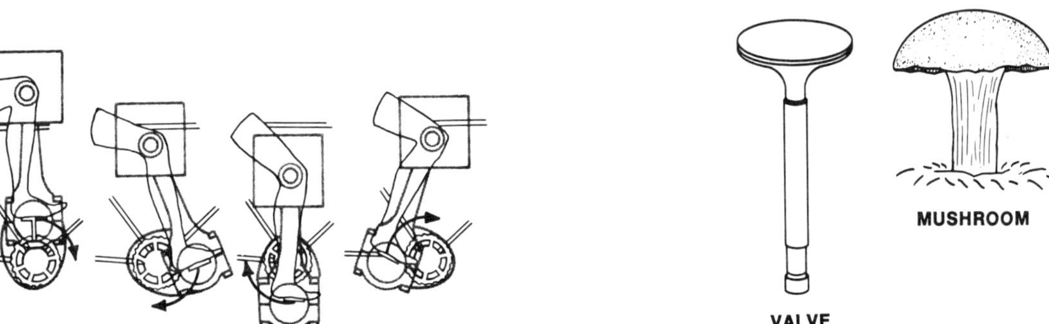

Fig. 1-13. The bicycle pedal, and the lever to which it is attached, form a crank.

Fig. 1-14. Engine valve (called a *mushroom* valve because it is shaped somewhat like a mushroom).

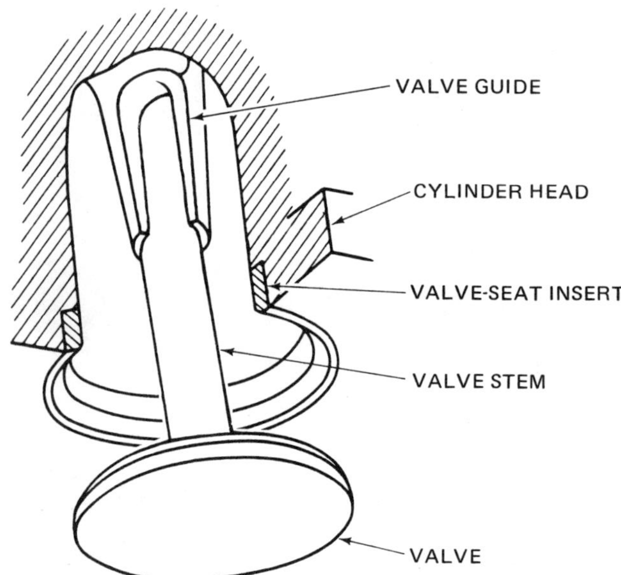

Fig. 1-15. Valve, valve guide, and valve seat. The cylinder head and valve guide have been partly cut away so that the valve stem can be seen.

der head. This opening is called the *valve port*. When the valve is up, the valve port is closed. The valve head is tight against the edge of the port, and the opening is closed off.

Check Your Progress[1]

Progress Quiz 1-1 The following exercises will help you find out how well you understand what you are studying. If you have trouble answering any of the questions, study the chapter again. Most successful students read and study their assignments several times, to make sure they understand them. Don't be discouraged if you cannot answer all the questions the first time. The material you are studying is not as easy to remember as the plot of a novel or a movie. So, if you run into trouble as you do the exercises, just restudy the chapter and try the questions again. As you practice this technique of read and restudy, you will learn how to pick out the important facts you should remember. The book will become much easier to read and understand; and you will be better able to sort out and retain the essential facts. This will mean that you are becoming an expert student. And the expert student, the person who can recall the facts, is headed for success in any line of work. So being an expert student is a big step toward being an expert—and successful—automotive tuneup technician.

Purpose and Operation of Components The following questions ask for the purpose and operation of some engine components discussed in this chapter. Write the answers in your notebook. If you have any difficulty, turn back in the chapter and reread the pages that give you the answer. Then write the required explanation. Do not copy directly from the book; instead, try to tell it in your own words. This is a good way to fix the explanation firmly in your mind.

1. What is an engine cylinder?
2. What is the purpose of the piston?
3. How is the up-and-down motion of the piston changed to rotary, or circular, motion?
4. What is a crankpin?
5. What does the piston do during one complete stroke?
6. How many "strokes" are there in the operating cycle of an automobile engine?
7. What is the job of the engine valves?

Matching In the left column below are 10 words or phrases used in the chapter you just studied. In the right column are 10 other words or phrases. Each of these means the same, or nearly the same, as a word or phrase in the left column. Match each item in the right column with an item from the left column. Then write the combined list in your notebook. When you have finished, turn to the answers at the end of the book to check your work. If you missed any, restudy the pages in the chapter that give you the correct answer.

internal-combustion engine	top dead center
external-combustion engine	burns fuel inside engine
reciprocating	attaches piston to crankpin
piston	opened and closed by valve
connecting rod and crankshaft	fits in cylinder
TDC	moves up and down in valve guide
valve	burns fuel outside engine
valve port	bottom dead center
BDC	up-and-down motion
connecting rod	
convert reciprocating to rotary motion	

CHAPTER 1 CHECKUP

NOTE: Since the following is a chapter review test, you should review the chapter before taking the test.

You have completed one chapter of the book and have taken an important step toward a better future for yourself. The general principles of engine operation are often harder to understand and remember than the details. But these general principles are important to you. Once you do understand them, you will find that you can answer many puzzling questions about how an engine wears and why

[1] Answers to questions in the quizzes and chapter checkups are given at the end of the book.

it needs a tuneup. The following questions will give you a chance to check up on how well you understand and remember these fundamentals. They will also help you to remember the fundamentals.

Write your answers in your notebook. The act of writing will fix the facts more firmly in your mind. And, later, your notebook will be filled with valuable information to which you can refer quickly.

Completing the Sentences The sentences below are incomplete. After each sentence there are several words or phrases, but only one of them correctly completes the sentence. Write each sentence in your notebook, ending it with the one word or phrase that completes it correctly.

1. The two types of engines are: (*a*) internal-combustion and heat engines, (*b*) explosion and external-combustion engines, (*c*) internal- and external-combustion engines.
2. An engine in which pistons move up and down is called a: (*a*) reciprocating engine, (*b*) rotary engine, (*c*) Wankel engine.
3. The reciprocating motion of the piston is changed to rotary motion by a: (*a*) flywheel, (*b*) connecting rod and crankshaft, (*c*) valve train.
4. The typical piston in an engine is about 4 in [101.6 mm] in diameter and weighs about: (*a*) 1 pound, (*b*) 1 gram, (*c*) 1 kilogram.
5. The letters TDC stand for: (*a*) top dead center, (*b*) turning direction clockwise, (*c*) transient direct current.
6. Each valve moves up and down in a: (*a*) valve spring, (*b*) valve seat, (*c*) valve guide.
7. The round opening in the cylinder head that is opened and closed by the valve is: (*a*) a valve port, (*b*) a valve guide, (*c*) neither (*a*) nor (*b*).

Definitions In the following, you are asked to define certain terms. Write the definitions in your notebook. This will help you remember them. It will also provide you with a quick way to locate the meanings, when you need the information again. If you cannot remember the meanings of the terms, look them up in the text or in the glossary at the back of the book.

1. What is a piston engine?
2. Define "reciprocating engine."
3. What is a crankshaft?
4. Define "connecting rod."
5. Define "reciprocate."
6. Define "piston."
7. Define "piston stroke."
8. What is a crank?
9. What is a four-stroke-cycle engine?
10. Define "valve."

SUGGESTIONS FOR FURTHER STUDY

The subject of automotive tuneup receives a great deal of publicity in newspapers and magazines, and on radio and television. When you see an informative article dealing with the subject (or with a related subject such as emission control), cut out the article and add it to your notebook. Also, if you have a chance, talk about engine operation with your friends, local service technicians, and your automotive tuneup instructor. Ask especially about points that might not be clear to you.

chapter 2

ENGINE OPERATION

We noted, in the previous chapter, that pistons move up and down in the engine cylinders. This reciprocating motion is turned into rotary motion by the connecting rods and the cranks on the crankshaft. Valves in the cylinders open and close to admit air-fuel mixture and to allow the burned gases to escape. First, one of the valves opens to let the air-fuel mixture into the cylinder. Later, the other valve opens to let the burned gases out. In this chapter we shall follow this train of events through a complete engine cycle.

A cycle is a series of events that repeat themselves. For example, the four seasons—spring, summer, fall, and winter—form a cycle. In an engine, the four-stroke cycle includes the intake stroke, the compression stroke, the power stroke, and the exhaust stroke.

⊘ 2-1 The Intake Stroke We start with the piston moving down, as shown in Fig. 2-1. As the piston moves down, it produces a vacuum in the cylinder. A *vacuum* is the partial absence of air or any other substance. Where there is a vacuum, substances outside the vacuum tend to rush in to fill it. For example, when you drink liquid through a straw, you produce a vacuum in the straw. Since the straw is open to the liquid in the glass, the liquid rushes up the straw and into your mouth. When the liquid is gone, air rushes into the straw to fill the vacuum.

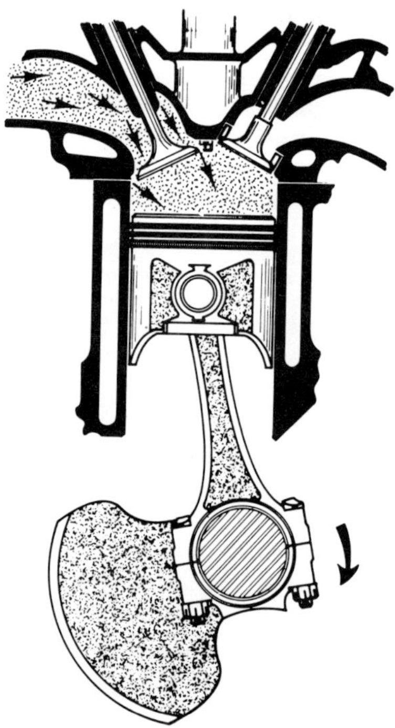

Fig. 2-1. The intake stroke. The intake valve, at left, has opened. The piston is moving downward, drawing air and gasoline vapor into the cylinder.

During this downward piston stroke, one of the valves (the intake valve) is open. That is, the valve is down off its seat. This allows air-fuel mixture to enter the cylinder. The air-fuel mixture fills the vacuum produced by the downward movement of the piston. This downward piston movement is called the *intake stroke*, because the cylinder is *taking in* a mixture of fuel and air. The air-fuel mixture has moved to the cylinder from the carburetor. The *carburetor*—sometimes called the "pot"—sits on top of the engine. It has the job of mixing gasoline vapor with air passing through it. Carburetor actions are explained in Chap. 12.

The piston moves all the way down to BDC on the intake stroke. During this time, the intake valve is open. The air-fuel mixture pours into the cylinder. At the end of the intake stroke, the intake valve closes. We shall discuss later what makes the valve close.

⊘ 2-2 The Compression Stroke After the piston reaches BDC at the end of the intake stroke, it starts to move up. Both valves are closed, so the air-fuel mixture has no place to go. It is pushed, or *compressed*, into a smaller space (Fig. 2-2). The amount by which the mixture is compressed is called the *compression ratio*.

In a modern engine, the air-fuel mixture is com-

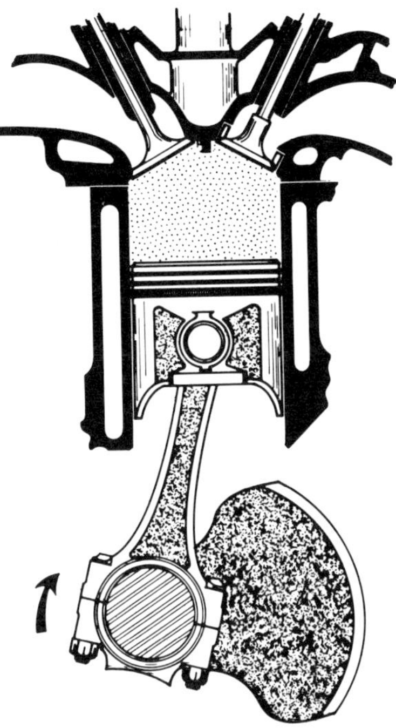

Fig. 2-2. The compression stroke. The intake valve has closed. The piston is moving upward, compressing the mixture.

pressed to one-ninth or one-tenth of its original volume. That is like taking a quart of air and squeezing it down to less than half a cup (Fig. 2-3).

If you squeeze a quart of mixture to half a cup, you have a compression ratio of 8 to 1. There are 8 half-cups in a quart. Thus, when you compress the quart, you compress 8 half-cups into 1 half-cup. That is, you compress the mixture down from 8 to 1. So, the compression ratio is 8 to 1. Usually, the ratio is shown as 8:1. You read this as "8 to 1."

We are going to discuss compression ratios again in Chap. 3. But first we have to go through the rest of the piston actions. As we said, the piston moves up from BDC, compressing the mixture. This stroke is called the *compression stroke.*

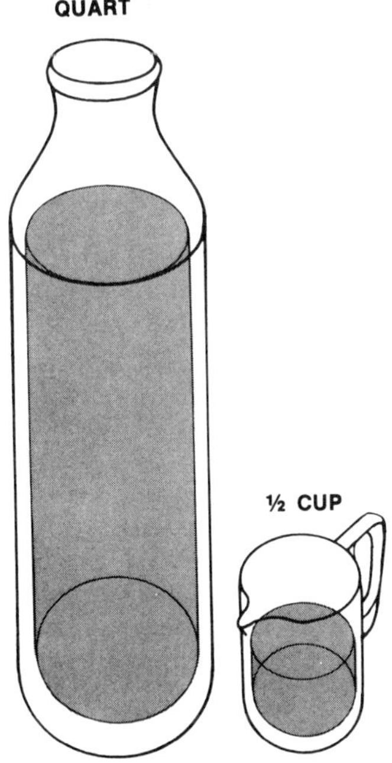

Fig. 2-3. If you compressed a quart of air to half a cup, you would compress it to one-eighth of its original volume.

⊘ 2-3 The Power Stroke

As the piston nears TDC at the end of the compression stroke, a spark occurs in the top of the cylinder. (You probably know that a spark plug makes the spark.) When the spark occurs in the compressed air-fuel mixture, there is a rapid burning and expansion of the mixture. The pressure and temperature of the mixture increase tremendously. Every square inch of the piston head gets a push of 600 lb [272 kg] or more. That adds up to as much as 4,000 lb [1,814 kg] pushing down on the piston. And that is several hundred pounds more than the weight of the whole New York Jets defensive football team! (See Fig. 2-4.)

The 4,000 lb [1,814 kg] pushes the piston downward. This downward movement is called the *power stroke* (Fig. 2-5). The powerful push on the piston is carried through the connecting rod to the crank on the crankshaft. The crankshaft turns this downward movement into rotary motion. The rotary motion is carried through gears and shafts to the car wheels, so that the car moves.

NOTE: The *combustion chamber* is the space at the top of the cylinder (above the piston) in which the air-fuel mixture burns (Fig. 2-5). Combustion chambers vary in shape.

⊘ 2-4 The Exhaust Stroke

As the piston reaches BDC on the power stroke, the exhaust valve opens. The piston moves up again, and it pushes the burned

Fig. 2-4. At the start of the power stroke, as much as 2 tons of pressure is applied to the piston head.

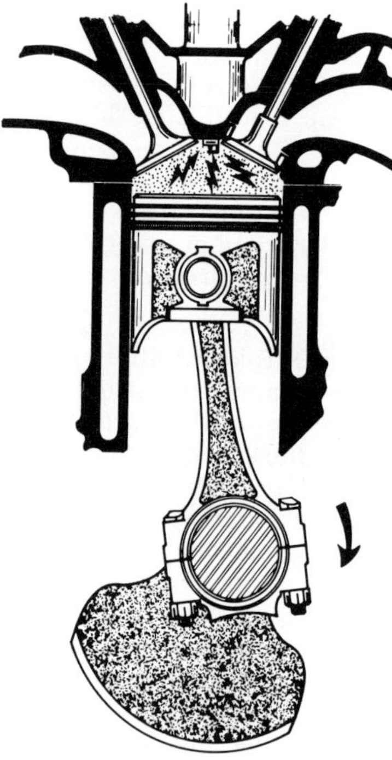

Fig. 2-5. The power stroke. The ignition system produces a spark that ignites the mixture. As the mixture burns, high pressure is created, pushing the piston down.

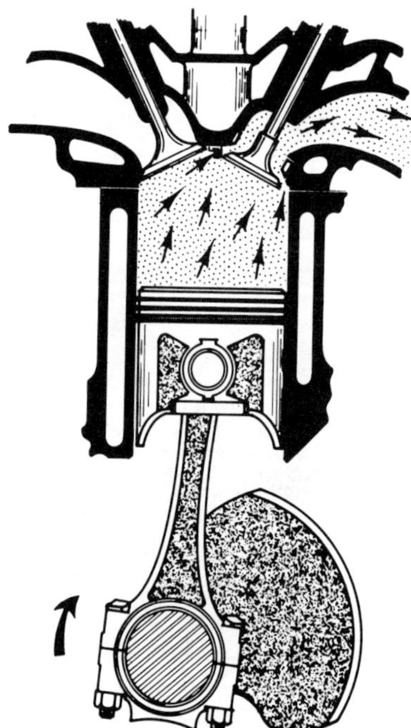

Fig. 2-6. The exhaust stroke. The exhaust valve, at right, has opened. The piston is moving upward, pushing the burned gases out of the cylinder.

gases out through the exhaust port. This upward movement of the piston is called the *exhaust stroke* because the burned gases are pushed out, or exhausted, from the engine cylinder (Fig. 2-6). Finally, as the piston reaches TDC on the exhaust stroke, the exhaust valve closes and the intake valve opens. The piston moves down once more on another intake stroke. The cycle of events in the cylinder is then repeated: intake stroke, compression stroke, power stroke, exhaust stroke. And this cycle continues to repeat as long as the engine runs.

⊘ **2-5 Piston Rings** Piston rings are essential to the operation of the engine. They are metal rings that fit into grooves in the pistons. You can see these piston grooves in Fig. 1-5. You can see piston rings installed on a piston in Fig. 1-6. The piston rings form a tight seal between the piston and the cylinder wall. As we have seen, there is great pressure above the piston during the compression and power strokes. The piston cannot be made to fit very tightly in the cylinder. So this pressure could leak past the piston. Such leakage could mean serious power loss. The rings, however, do press tightly against the cylinder wall and the sides of the piston grooves. They seal the pressure above the piston. The rings are covered with oil by the engine lubricating system. This allows them to slide up and down easily on the cylinder wall.

⊘ **2-6 The Four-Stroke Cycle** Since it takes four piston strokes to complete one cycle, the engine is called a *four-stroke-cycle engine*. The name is usually shortened to *four-cycle engine*.

⊘ **2-7 Multiple-Cylinder Engines** A single cylinder, with a single piston working in it, cannot produce enough power to run an automobile. Also, with one cylinder there would be only one power stroke for every two revolutions of the crankshaft. This would make for a very rough ride. So automobiles have engines with four, six, or eight cylinders. In these engines, there are one or more power strokes going on all the time. The engine produces a continuous flow of power, and the automobile moves along smoothly.

Valve Operation

⊘ **2-8 The Valve Train** So far, we have looked at the four strokes of the four-stroke cycle. We saw that the intake valve is open during the intake stroke, and the exhaust valve is open during the exhaust stroke. Typical valves are shown in Fig. 2-7. Note that the intake valve and the exhaust valve are different from each other. The intake valve is larger.

The assembly of parts that make the valves open and close is called the *valve train*. There are three

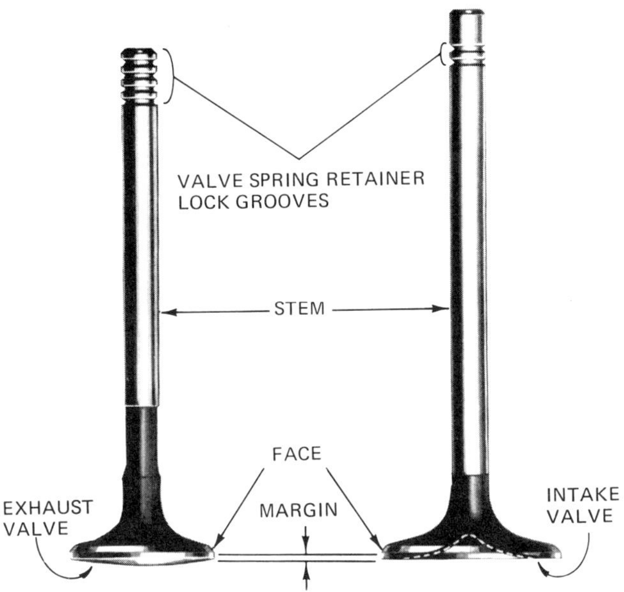

Fig. 2-7. Typical engine valves. (*Chrysler Corporation*)

basic kinds of valve trains: L-head, I-head or overhead-valve, and overhead-camshaft.

NOTE: One way of classifying engines is by the arrangement of the valves in the cylinder head or cylinder block. The arrangements get their names from their likeness to letters of the alphabet. (See the illustrations in Fig. 4-11.) In most engines today, the valves are arranged in the shape of an I.

⊘ 2-9 L-Head Valve Train The L-head valve train is the simplest valve train. It is used in many one-cylinder engines, such as those in lawn mowers and edgers. Years ago, nearly all automobile engines had L-head valve trains, but not any more.

Figure 2-8 shows the valve train for an L-head engine. The valve moves up and down in a valve guide, which is installed in the cylinder block. The *cylinder block* is the large block of cast iron that encloses the cylinders. All the other engine parts are installed in or on the cylinder block.

When the valve is down, its head seals off the valve port, so no air can get into or out of the cylinder. But when it is pushed up, the valve is raised off the valve seat, so air or gas can pass through. About three-quarters of the time, the valve is held down in the closed position by the valve spring.

The stem end of the valve has one or more grooves cut in it. You can see these grooves in Fig. 2-7. When a valve is installed in the engine, the spring is put in place and compressed with a special tool. Then a spring retainer, which is a large washer, is installed. Next, a spring-retainer lock is installed. The lock fits into the grooves in the valve stem. When the spring is released, spring pressure forces the spring retainer down on the lock. The lock is thus held in the grooves in the valve stem.

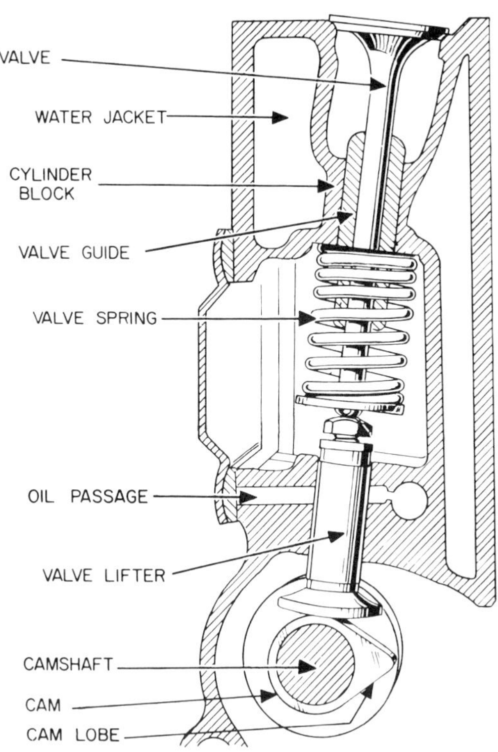

Fig. 2-8. Valve train for an L-head engine. The valve is raised off the valve seat with every camshaft rotation.

Figure 2-9 shows the parts of the valve train for a one-cylinder L-head engine. The parts are in their proper order of assembly. Notice the cams on the camshaft. Each cam is a round collar with a high spot, called the *cam lobe*. The lobe opens the valve, as we shall see in a moment.

Spring pressure keeps the valve closed most of the time. Meanwhile, the camshaft rotates. It is driven by a gear that is meshed with a gear on the crankshaft. As the camshaft rotates, the cam lobe comes around under the valve lifter. As the lobe moves up under the lifter, it pushes the lifter upward. (See Fig. 2-10.) This, in turn, pushes the valve up so that it opens. Notice that the lifter is between the cam and the end of the valve stem. The lifter takes all the wear caused by the cam rubbing against it. In many engines, the lifter has a screw which provides a means of valve-clearance adjustment.

As the camshaft continues to rotate, the cam lobe moves out from under the valve lifter. The spring then pulls the valve back down on its seat.

NOTE: The valve lifter is often called the *valve tappet* by many automotive mechanics.

⊘ 2-10 Flat-Head The L-head engine is also called the "flat-head" engine because the cylinder head is flat on top. Figure 2-11 is a cutaway view of one cylinder of a flat-head engine. Study the picture, and find the valves, the piston, and the combustion

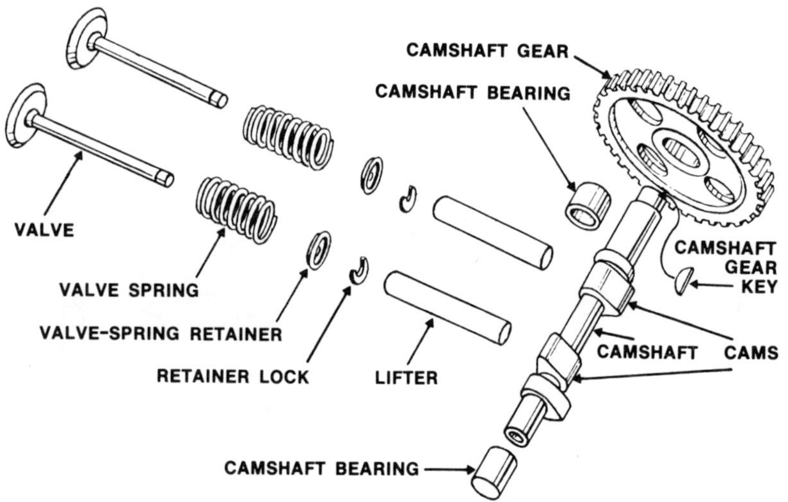

Fig. 2-9. Complete valve trains for a one-cylinder engine. (*Cushman Motor Works*)

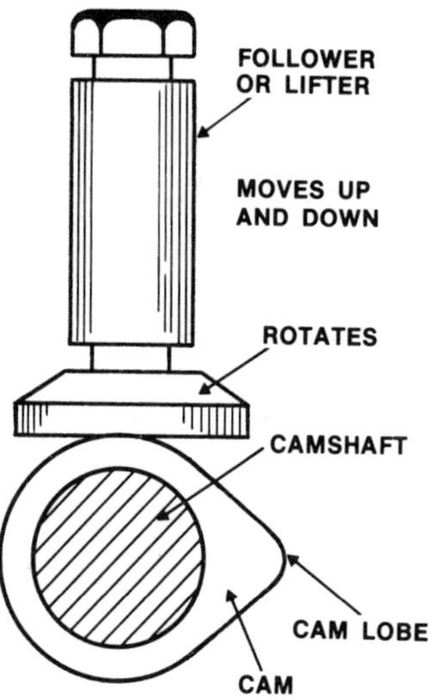

Fig. 2-10. Every time the cam lobe comes under the valve lifter, the lifter is raised.

chamber. Figure 2-12 shows why the engine is called an L-head engine. Note that the combustion chamber and cylinder are in the shape of an upside-down L.

⊘ 2-11 I-Head In recent years, automotive manufacturers have stopped making L-head engines and have switched to overhead-valve engines. There are several reasons for this change, which are explained later. First, let's look at the I-head engine, which is also called the *overhead-valve* engine or the *valve-in-head* engine. As the name implies, the valves are in the cylinder head instead of in the cylinder block.

Figure 2-13 shows the essential parts of the valve train for one cylinder in an overhead-valve engine. The parts that have been added are the pushrods and the rocker arms. The valve springs are not shown here, but they are used, just as in the L-head engine. When the cam lobe moves under the valve lifter, it pushes the valve lifter up. This pushes up on the

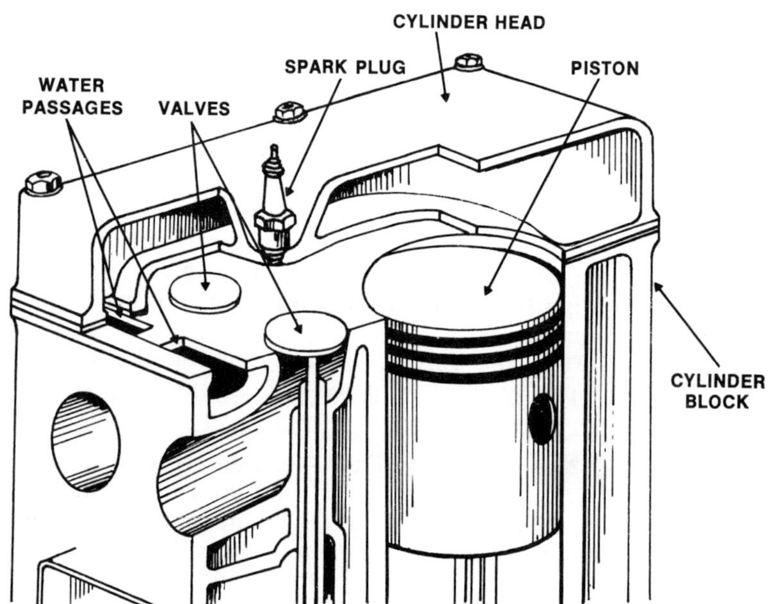

Fig. 2-11. Cutaway view of an L-head engine.

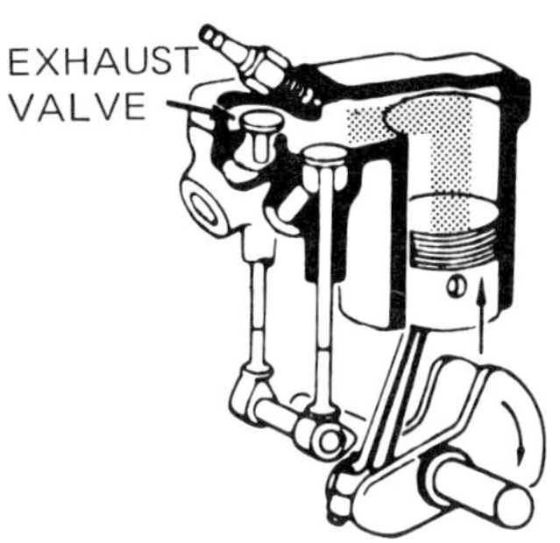

Fig. 2-12. The combustion chamber and cylinder of the L-head engine are shaped like an upside-down L; that gives the engine its name.

pushrod. The pushrod moves up, pushing up on one end of the rocker arm. The rocker arm is mounted on a shaft so that it can rock back and forth, like a seesaw. When one end of the rocker arm is pushed up by the pushrod, the other end pushes down on the end of the valve stem. The valve is pushed down off its seat, and it opens.

Take a moment to study Fig. 2-14, which is a

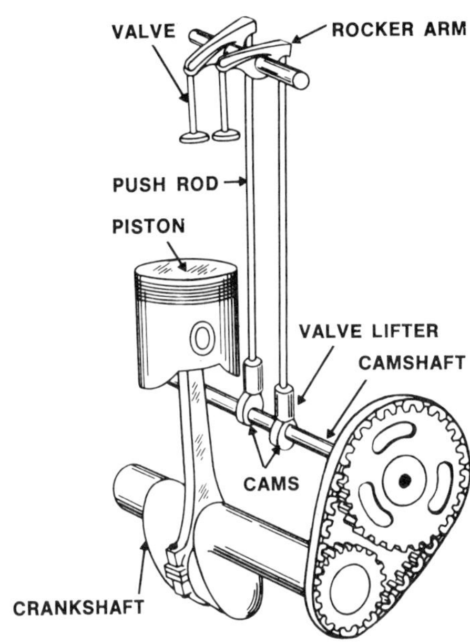

Fig. 2-13. Valve-operating mechanisms for one cylinder of an overhead-valve engine. Only the essential moving parts are shown.

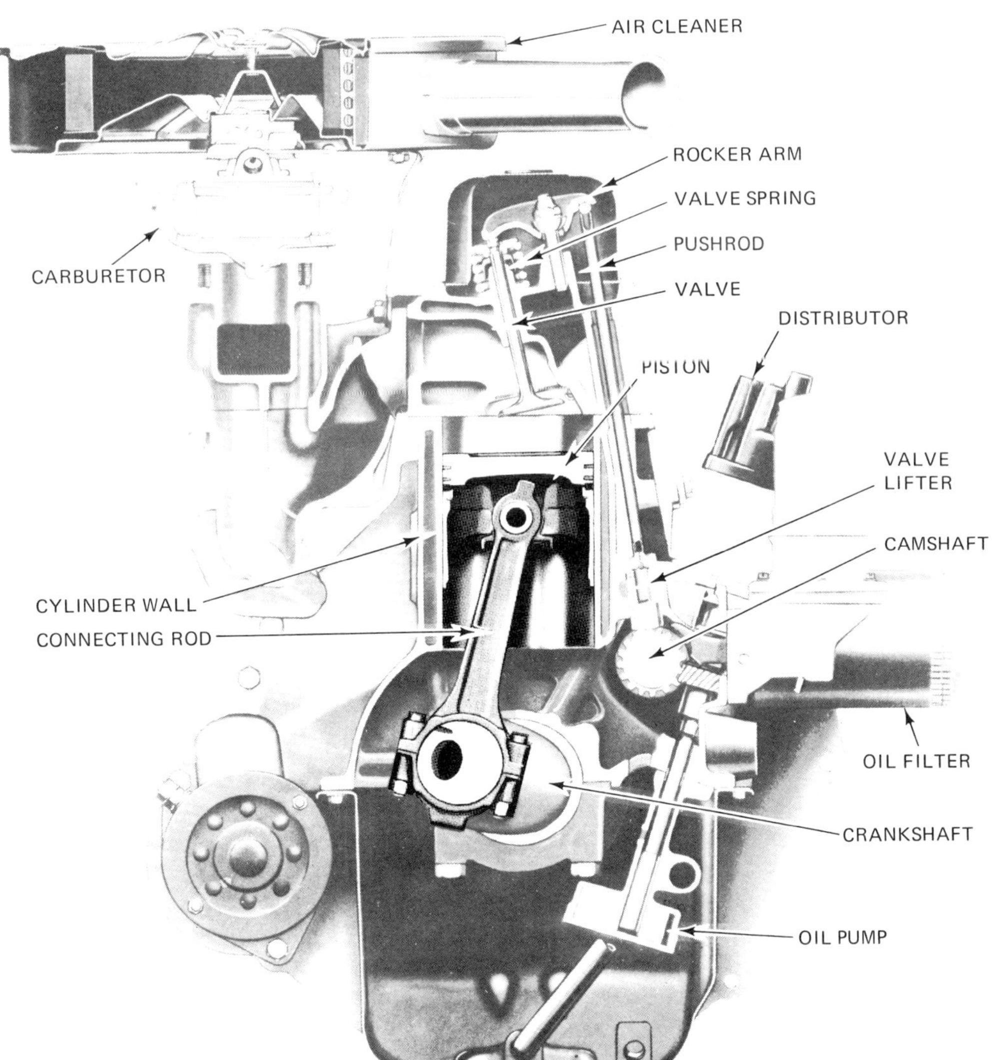

Fig. 2-14. Sectional view of an engine from the end, showing the piston in one of the cylinders. (*Ford Motor Company*)

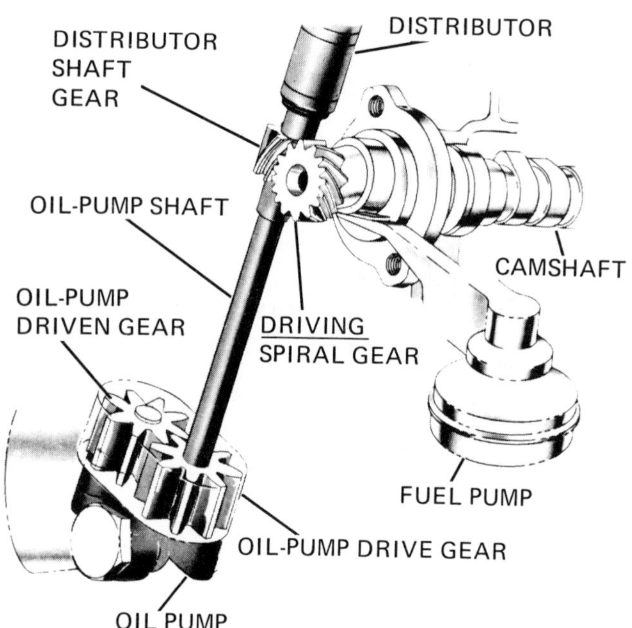

Fig. 2-15. Oil-pump, distributor, and fuel-pump drives. The oil pump is of the gear type. A gear on the end of the camshaft drives the ignition distributor. An extension of the distributor shaft drives the oil pump. The fuel pump is driven by an eccentric on the camshaft. *(Buick Motor Division of General Motors Corporation)*

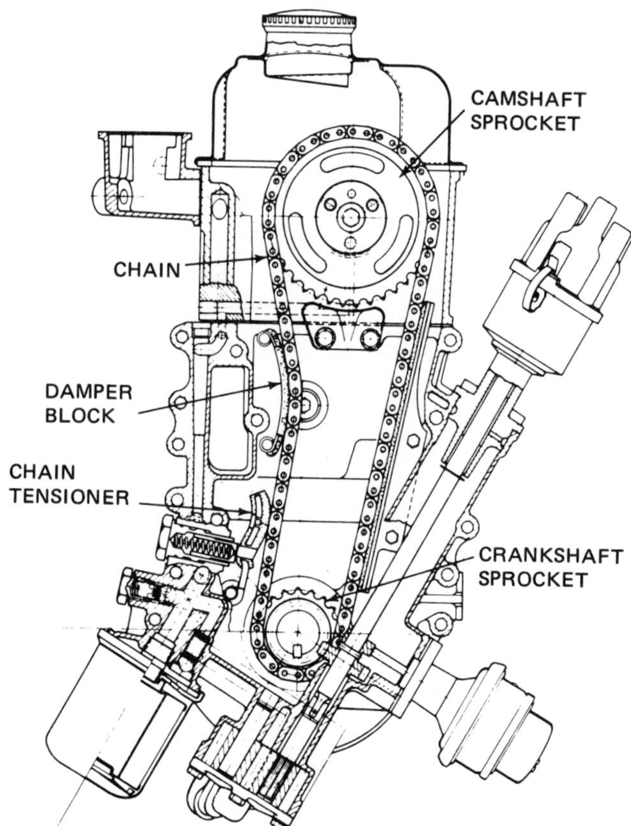

Fig. 2-16. Camshaft drive arrangement for the Opel overhead-camshaft engine. *(Buick Motor Division of General Motors Corporation)*

sectional view from the end of an engine cylinder. Find the valve, the valve spring, the rocker arm, the pushrod, the valve lifter, and the cam on the camshaft. Notice that the rocker arm is mounted on a ball pivot instead of a shaft. The action is the same, however. When the valve lifter is pushed up by the cam lobe, the pushrod moves up. It then pushes on the rocker arm. The rocker arm rocks, and the valve is pushed down off its seat.

In most engines, the camshaft has a gear that drives the ignition distributor and the lubricating-system oil pump. This arrangement is shown in Fig. 2-15.

⊘ 2-12 Overhead-Camshaft Engine

In the overhead-camshaft engine, the camshaft is located in the cylinder head. This eliminates the pushrod and puts the cams closer to the valves. With this setup, the valves respond quicker to the cam lobes, and the engine is more responsive. That is, the engine accelerates faster and can have a higher speed (in revolutions per minute, or rpm).

Overhead-camshaft (OHC) engines may have one camshaft per cylinder bank or two camshafts per cylinder bank. They are called single-overhead-camshaft (SOHC) and double-overhead-camshaft (DOHC) engines, respectively. A camshaft may be driven by sprockets and a chain (Fig. 2-16), or by a neoprene belt (Fig. 2-17). The belt is reinforced with fiber-glass cords and has a facing of woven nylon fabric on the toothed side. The teeth in the belt fit the teeth on the drive pulley and driven pulley. In some engines, the cam-lobe motion is carried directly to the valve stem through the valve tappet. This arrangement is shown in Figure 2-17. In other OHC engines, the cam action is carried through a rocker arm, as shown in Fig. 2-18.

The upper right of Fig. 2-17 shows the distributor drive arrangement in an overhead-camshaft engine. We describe the ignition system and the lubricating system in later chapters.

⊘ 2-13 Valve Timing

Valve timing refers to the relationship between valve movement and piston movement. The valves must move "in time" with the piston. That is, the intake valve must be open during the intake stroke. The exhaust valve must be open during the exhaust stroke. Both valves must be closed during the compression and power strokes.

The crankshaft rotates twice during each four-stroke cycle. One-half rotation [or 180° (degrees)] is needed for each piston stroke. For four piston strokes, the crankshaft must rotate two full turns, or 720°. Now how about the camshaft? Remember, each time the camshaft rotates, both valves open and close. Thus, the camshaft should rotate only once per cycle. So the camshaft must rotate once while the crankshaft rotates twice.

In other words, the gear on the camshaft must turn once while the gear on the crankshaft turns twice. How can the camshaft gear be made to rotate half as fast as the crankshaft gear? By using a cam-

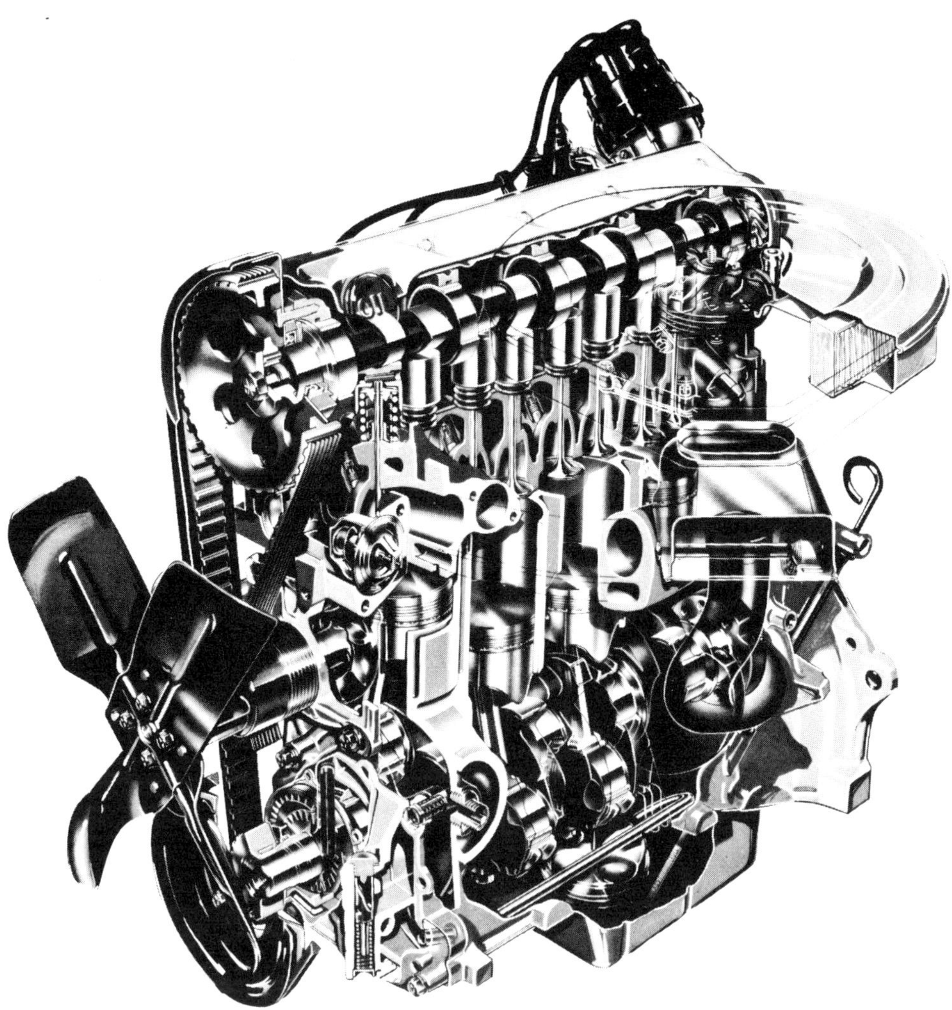

Fig. 2-17. Cutaway view of the Vega four-cylinder engine. This is an overhead-valve engine with the camshaft in the cylinder head. (*Chevrolet Motor Division of General Motors Corporation*)

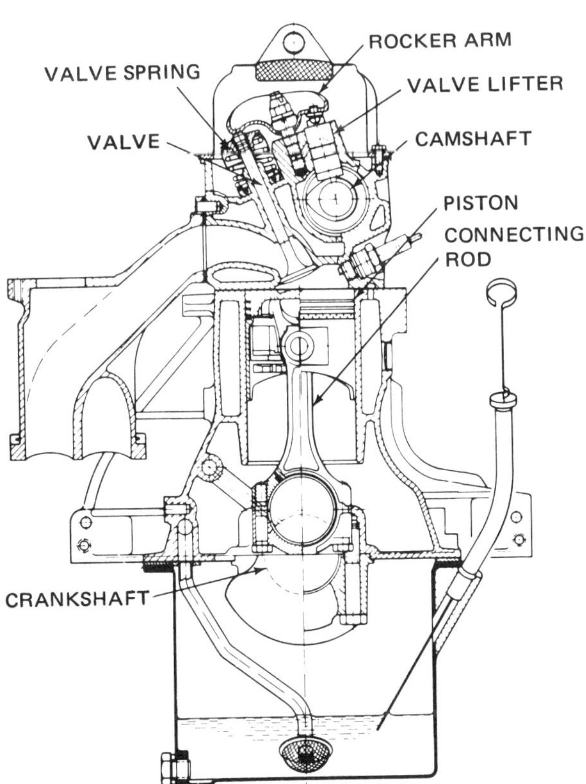

Fig. 2-18. Sectional view from the end of the Opel overhead-camshaft engine. (*Buick Motor Division of General Motors Corpoation*)

shaft gear that is twice as big as the crankshaft gear (Figs. 2-19 and 2-20).

In Fig. 2-19, the lobe on the cam has moved under the valve lifter, causing the exhaust valve to open. At the same time, the piston is moving up on the exhaust stroke. It is forcing the burned gases out through the exhaust port. Further rotation of the crankshaft turns the camshaft so that the lobe moves out from under the valve lifter. This allows the valve spring to close the valve. The actions of the crankshaft and valves during the four piston strokes are shown in Figs. 2-1, 2-2, 2-5, and 2-6.

Figure 2-21 shows crankshaft and camshaft gears for a six-cylinder engine. Note the timing marks on the gears. These timing marks must be lined up when the engine is assembled. Otherwise, the timing between the valves and the piston will not be correct.

⊘ 2-14 Timing Chain Figure 2-22 shows the timing chain and sprockets used in an overhead-valve engine. Most engines use timing chains and sprockets instead of the gears shown in Fig. 2-21. The chain is made of metal links that fit the teeth on the two sprockets. The upper sprocket is on the camshaft, and the lower sprocket is on the crankshaft. Note the timing marks on the two sprockets. Again, these must be lined up when the engine is assembled, to time the valves to the piston.

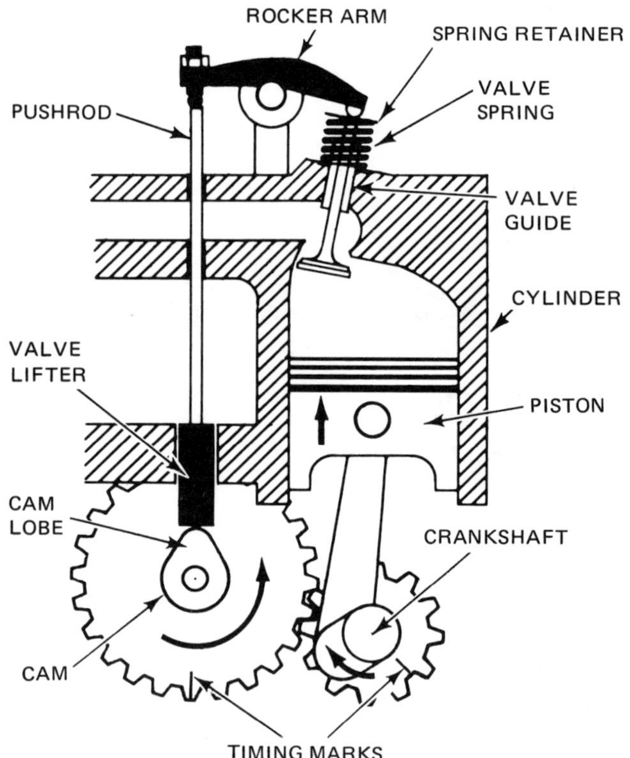

Fig. 2-19. Simplified drawing of an overhead valve train. The lobe on the cam has moved under the lifter, raising the lifter and opening the valve. At the same time, the piston is moving up, pushing the burned gases out of the cylinder.

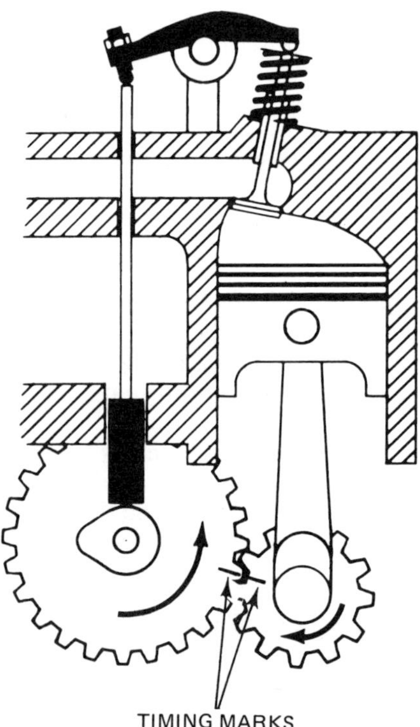

Fig. 2-20. Here, the piston has reached the end of the exhaust stroke. The cam lobe has moved out from under the valve lifter, and the valve spring has pulled the valve closed. The other cam on the camshaft (not shown) is opening the intake valve. The piston is ready to move down on the intake stroke.

Fig. 2-21. Crankshaft and camshaft gears for a six-cylinder engine. Note the timing marks on the gears. (*Buick Motor Division of General Motors Corporation*)

⊘ 2-15 Hydraulic Valve Lifter Many automotive engines use hydraulic valve lifters. The valve lifter, you will recall, is a round cylinder that rides on the cam. It moves up and down as the cam lobe passes under it. The motion of the valve lifter moves the pushrod up and down. The pushrod motion causes the rocker arm to rock, and the valve to open and close. Hydraulic valve lifters take up any clearance in the valve train. They thus reduce both noise in the valve train and wear of valve-train parts.

Figure 2-23 shows the details of a hydraulic valve lifter used in a V-8 I-head engine. Oil is fed into the valve lifter by the oil pump. The oil travels through an oil gallery that runs the length of the

Fig. 2-22. Crankshaft and camshaft sprockets, with chain drive, for a V-8 engine. (*Chrysler Corporation*)

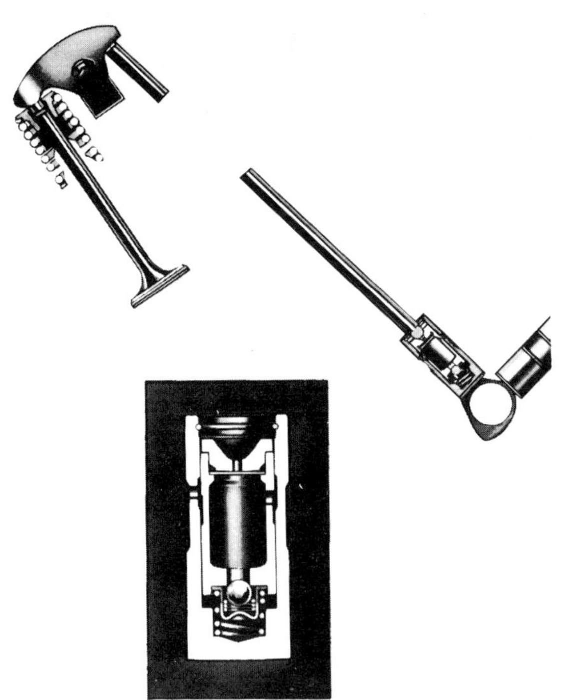

Fig. 2-23. Sectional view of a V-8 I-head engine, showing the location of the hydraulic valve lifter in the valve train. The inset shows the construction and operation of the lifter. (*Cadillac Motor Car Division of General Motors Corporation*)

engine. When the valve is closed, oil from the pump is forced into the valve lifter through oil holes in the lifter body and plunger. The oil pressure opens the ball-check valve in the plunger. Oil then passes the ball-check valve and enters the space under the plunger. The plunger is forced upward until it touches the valve pushrod. This takes up any clearance in the system.

Now, when the cam lobe comes around under the lifter body, the lifter is raised. Since there is no clearance, there is no tappet noise. The raising of the lifter and the valve suddenly increases the pressure in the body chamber under the plunger. This causes the ball-check valve to seat (close). Oil is therefore trapped in the chamber. Thus, the lifter acts just like a solid lifter. It moves up as an assembly, and causes the valve to open. Then, when the cam lobe has passed out from under the valve lifter, the lifter moves down. The valve spring closes the valve. If any oil has leaked out from the chamber under the plunger, the oil pressure again opens the ball-check valve. Engine oil then refills the chamber, as noted above.

Check Your Progress

Progress Quiz 2-1 The following quiz will help you check how well you understand this chapter. If you have difficulty with the questions, reread the chapter. Remember, most students read their lessons several times; don't be discouraged if you don't remember everything the first or second time. The questions usually refer to the most important facts and details. They will pinpoint these important details and help you remember them. That is, the questions are for your benefit, to allow you to check up on yourself. If you are not sure about the answer to any question, reread the pages that deal with the topic.

Correcting Lists The purpose of this exercise is to give you practice in spotting unrelated items in a list. For example, look through the list "cylinder, piston, rings, brake shoe, connecting rod." You should see that "brake shoe" does not belong. It is the only item that is not in an engine. Each of the following lists contains one unrelated item. Write each list in your notebook, but do not write the item that does not belong.

1. The four piston strokes are intake, exhaust, reverse, compression, and power.
2. The valve train includes the camshaft, valve lifter, valve, flywheel, valve spring, and valve guide.
3. Basic kinds of valve train are the L-head, I-head, overhead camshaft, and underhung camshaft.
4. In automobile engines, valves may be located in the cylinder head, intake manifold, and cylinder block.
5. Camshafts may be driven by an electric motor, gears, chain and sprockets, and sprockets and toothed belt.

Completing the Sentences The sentences below are incomplete. After each sentence there are several words or phrases, but only one of them correctly completes the sentence. Write each sentence in your notebook, ending it with the one word or phrase that completes it correctly.

1. In the standard engine each cylinder has: (*a*) one valve, (*b*) two valves, (*c*) three valves, (*d*) four valves.
2. The four strokes in a four-stroke-cycle engine are, in order: (*a*) intake, power, exhaust, and compression, (*b*) intake, exhaust, compression and power, (*c*) intake, compression, power, and exhaust.
3. The two types of engine valves are: (*a*) intake and port, (*b*) intake and inlet, (*c*) intake and exhaust.
4. The valve is opened when the cam lobe on the cam raises the: (*a*) valve lifter, (*b*) bearing, (*c*) piston pin, (*d*) valve guide.
5. The camshaft has a separate cam for each: (*a*) engine valve, (*b*) piston, (*c*) cylinder, (*d*) crankpin.

CHAPTER 2 CHECKUP

NOTE: Since the following is a chapter review test, you should review the chapter before taking the test.

Here is another chance to check yourself on the chapter you have just completed. The questions that follow have two purposes. One is to test your knowledge. The other is to help you to review the chapter and fix the facts firmly in your mind. If you cannot answer any question, turn back and reread the pages that give you the answer. For instance, under "Listing Parts" you are asked to list the parts in the valve mechanism. If you cannot remember them all, turn back to the illustration of the valve mechanism in the chapter; refer to it while writing your list. The act of writing the names of the parts will help you to remember them.

NOTE: Write all your answers in your notebook. Then later, when you finish *Automotive Tuneup,* your notebook will be filled with valuable information to which you can quickly refer.

Completing the Sentences The sentences below are incomplete. After each sentence there are several words or phrases, but only one of them correctly completes the sentence. Write each sentence in your notebook, ending it with the one word or phrase that completes it correctly.

1. The parts that must be added to the piston to ensure a good seal with the cylinder wall are the: (*a*) piston pins, (*b*) connecting rods, (*c*) piston rings, (*d*) gaskets.
2. The part that tends to keep the valve closed is called the: (*a*) guide, (*b*) lifter, (*c*) spring, (*d*) cam, (*e*) retainer.
3. For each crankshaft revolution, the camshaft revolves: (*a*) one-half turn, (*b*) one turn, (*c*) two turns.
4. To reduce valve-train noise, many engines use: (*a*) mechanical valve lifters, (*b*) hydraulic valve lifters, (*c*) solid camshafts, (*d*) solid tappets.
5. A typical engine compression ratio would be: (*a*) 8:1, (*b*) 15:1, (*c*) 18:1, (*d*) 2:1.

Listing Parts In the following, you are asked to list engine parts and operations. Write the lists in your notebook.

1. List the four piston strokes in the four-cycle engine.
2. List the parts that move up and down in the engine cylinder.
3. List the parts in the valve mechanism.
4. List the parts through which and past which the air moves as it passes from outside the engine into the engine cylinder.
5. List the different basic valve-train arrangements.

Definitions In the following, you are asked to define certain terms. Write the definitions in your notebook. This will help you remember them. It will also provide you with a quick way to locate the meanings, when you need the information again. If you cannot remember the meanings of the terms, look them up in the chapter or in the glossary at the back of the book.

1. Define "cycle."
2. What is a vacuum?
3. Define "carburetor."
4. Define "compression ratio."
5. What is a power stroke?
6. Define "piston rings."
7. What is a four-cycle engine?
8. Define "valve train."
9. What is an overhead-camshaft engine?
10. What is valve timing?

SUGGESTIONS FOR FURTHER STUDY

There are several ways to do some further studying about automotive engines. First, you can inspect your own and your friends' cars. Do not, however, get out your toolbox and start tearing them apart. You are not quite ready for that yet.

Also, you can go into your school automotive shop or to a friendly service shop where automotive-engine work is done. By watching what goes on in a service shop you can learn a lot about the types of engines, how to identify them, and how to service them.

You may be able to borrow for study a manufacturer's service manual from a dealer service shop or from your school automotive-shop library. These manuals are sometimes available, for a price, from manufacturers. Your school automotive shop may have cutaway parts and engines which are used as teaching aids. Study these to see how automotive engines are constructed and how they work.

For further information on the construction and operation of automotive engines and their accessories, refer to the following books, all published by the McGraw-Hill Book Company:

The Auto Book
Automotive Electrical Equipment
Automotive Engines
Automotive Engine Design
Automotive Fuel, Lubricating and Cooling Systems
Automotive Emission Control
Automotive Mechanics

chapter 3

ENGINE MEASUREMENTS

To compare one engine with another, you have to take various measurements. It is not very helpful to say that a big engine puts out a lot of power, and a little engine "hasn't got it." To compare engines, you have to know what is meant by phrases like "a high-compression job with 300 horses and 284 cubes." In this chapter, you will find out what all this means.

⊘ 3-1 Bore and Stroke We start our study of engine measurement by looking at the engine cylinder. There are two basic cylinder measurements—bore and stroke. The *bore* is the diameter of the cylinder. The *stroke* is the distance the piston moves from BDC to TDC. (See Fig. 3-1.)

When the measurements of an engine cylinder are given, the bore is always mentioned first. For example, a 4- by 3.5-in cylinder has a bore of 4 in [102 mm] and a stroke of 3.5 in [89 mm].

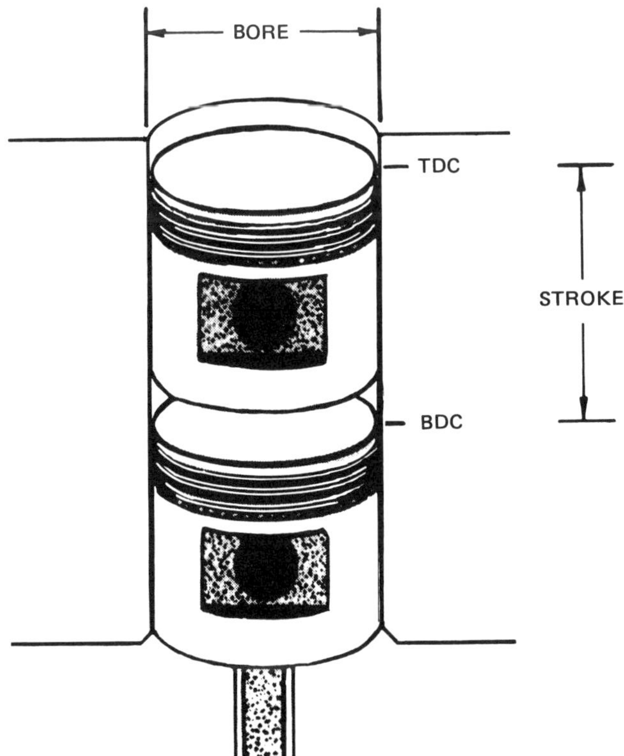

Fig. 3-1. Bore and stroke of an engine cylinder.

When you listen to the experts, you may hear them talk about an oversquare engine. *Oversquare* means that the bore is greater than the stroke. A 4- by 3.5-in [102- by 89-mm] engine cylinder is oversquare. A 4- by 4-in [102- by 102-mm] cylinder is square. Most modern engines are oversquare. With a shorter stroke, the piston and rings don't have to move as far. There is less wear and less loss of power through friction. The bigger the piston, the more powerful the power strokes. A bigger piston has more area for the high-pressure gases to push down on.

⊘ 3-2 Piston Displacement When the piston moves up from BDC to TDC, it pushes away, or *displaces*, a certain volume. You can picture this volume as the diameter of a cylinder, with the top and bottom being the piston head at TDC and at BDC (see Fig. 3-2).

Now let's talk figures. Suppose, for example, an engine cylinder measures 4 in [102 mm] in diameter. And suppose that the distance the piston moves from BDC to TDC is 3.5 in [89 mm]. The displacement of this engine cylinder is the volume of a cylinder 4 in [102 mm] in diameter and 3.5 in [89 mm] in length. To calculate the volume, let D stand for diameter, and L for length. The symbol π is called "pi," and it is equal to 3.1416. The calculation is:

$$\text{Displacement} = \frac{\pi \times D^2 \times L}{4} = \frac{3.1416 \times 4^2 \times 3.50}{4}$$

$$= \frac{3.1416 \times 16 \times 3.50}{4}$$

$$= 43.98 \text{ cubic inches}$$

The displacement of one cylinder of the engine is 43.98 in^3 (cubic inches) [720.1 cm^3 (cubic centimeters)]. What does 43.98 in^3 look like? For comparison, 1 quart contains about 60 in^3 and 1 pint about

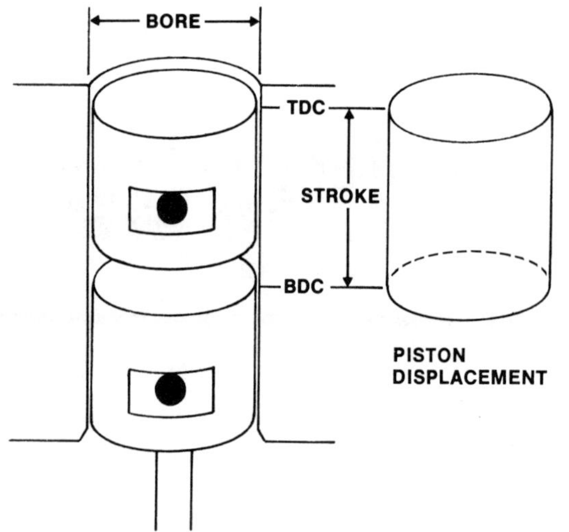

Fig. 3-2. The piston displacement is the volume the piston displaces, or takes the place of, as it moves from BDC to TDC.

30 in^3. (Actually, a pint is 28.4 in^3 [473.2 cm^3].) So 43.98 in^3 is equal to about 1½ pints (actually 1.52 pints [720.1 cm^3]). (See Fig. 3-3.) That's for one cylinder. To find the displacement of an eight-cylinder engine, we multiply 43.98 in^3 [720.1 cm^3] by 8, to get 351.84 in^3 [5,765.6 cu cm]. That's about 1½ gallons, or 6 quarts [5.76 liters]. Many people don't say "cubic inches." Instead, they say "cubes." For example, they will say "It's a 350-cube engine," meaning the engine has a displacement of 350 in^3.

When you talk with hot-rodders and the people who build and race cars, they will tell you that limits are set for engine displacements in most races. In a 500-mile race at Indianapolis (the "Indy 500"), the maximum allowable displacement for nonsupercharged engines was 305.1 in^3 [5,000 cu cm^3, or 5 liters].

In many races, especially those in Europe, the displacement is given in *liters,* a metric measurement. One liter equals 61.02 in^3, or 1.057 quarts. Thus, as noted above, the Indy-500 spec of 305.1 in^3 limited engine displacement to 5 liters (305.1 divided by 61.02 is exactly 5 liters).

Do you see why racing authorities must limit displacement in the money races? If they didn't, somebody would show up with a huge, powerful engine of perhaps 1,000 cubes. The car would be a runaway winner. There would be no contest.

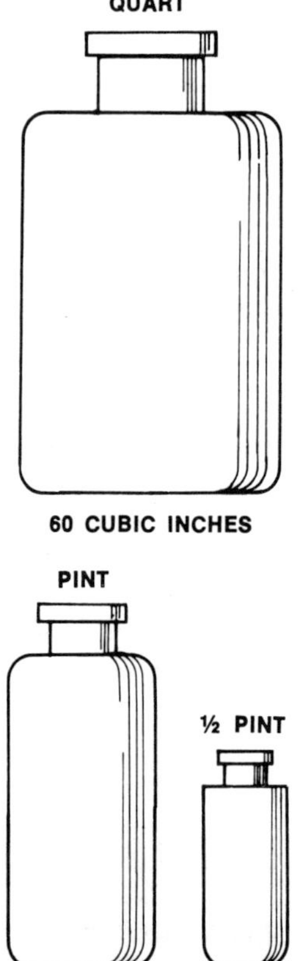

Fig. 3-3. One quart contains about 60 in^3 [946.4 cm^3]. A pint and a half is about 45 in^3 [759.8 cm^3].

⊘ 3-3 Compression Ratio Let's have another look at compression ratio. In Chap. 2 we mentioned that the piston squeezes the air-fuel mixture into a smaller volume, or space. When the volume goes from a quart to a half-cup, the compression ratio is 8:1. That is, the volume is reduced to one-eighth of the original volume. In terms of cubic inches, the volume goes from 60 in^3 (1 quart) to 7.5 in^3 (a half-cup). This is a ratio of 60:7.5, or 8:1. In metric measurements, the volume goes from 984 cm^3 to 123 cm^3. This is a ratio of 984:123, or, again, 8:1.

Figure 3-4 shows an engine cylinder twice—once with the piston at BDC and once with the piston at TDC. It shows what compression ratio means inside an engine. The cylinder volume is reduced from *A* to *B* when the piston moves from BDC to TDC. In other words, the compression ratio is *A* divided by *B*.

As an example, suppose *A* is 45 cubes (cubic inches) and *B* is 5 cubes. Then the ratio between *A* and *B*—which is the compression ratio—is 45 di-

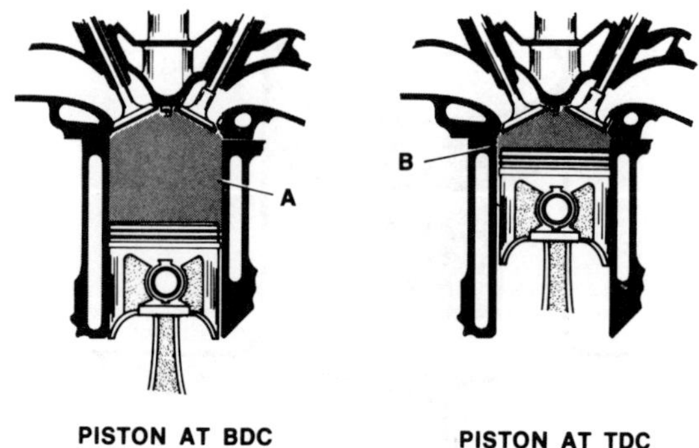

Fig. 3-4. The compression ratio is the volume in a cylinder with the piston at BDC, divided by the volume with the piston at TDC. That is, *A* divided by *B*.

vided by 5, or 9. Thus, the compression ratio is 9:1. The volume *B* above the piston when it is at TDC is called the *clearance volume*. The volume *A*, with the piston at BDC, is the *air volume*. As you can see, carbon buildup in the combustion chamber increases the effective compression ratio.

⊘ 3-4 Importance of High Compression You should know two important facts about compression ratio. First, when compression ratio goes up, engine power goes up. A car with a higher-compression engine has more getaway, can pass more quickly on the highway, and can go faster. This is because more push is exerted on the piston during the power stroke due to higher pressure within the combustion chamber. Second, a high-compression engine needs "high-octane" gasoline. If the engine does not get it, the engine will "ping," or detonate. Detonation or spark knock is the sudden explosion of the remaining compressed air-fuel mixture after the spark occurs at the spark plug. The result is a loss of power, engine overheating, and a characteristic rattling sound called pinging. You can ruin a high-compression engine with low-octane gas. The engine could detonate so hard that engine parts actually break! What's more, the settings and adjustments on a high-compression engine must be just right if the engine is to give top performance.

The high-compression engine has been blamed for a lot of the air pollution that comes from automobiles. Chapter 17 explains air pollution; how the automobile adds to this pollution; and what the automotive mechanic can do to reduce automobile air pollution. This will be one of your jobs as an automotive expert: To help keep the air clean by seeing that the cars you work on are properly serviced.

⊘ 3-5 Engine Power Now we come to the most talked-about subject on engines—horsepower. "How many horses?" is what people want to know about the engines that move automobiles along the highway and around the oval racetrack. The question means, "How many horses would it take to equal the maximum power output of the engine?" But first, let's see what horsepower is. *Horsepower* (hp) is a measure of how hard an engine can work.

⊘ 3-6 Work What is work? You can say that sitting at a desk to figure out an engine repair bill is work. And it is work, because it is part of your job. But it is not what engineers mean when they talk about work.

Engineers have a special meaning for the word "work." To them, it means *changing the position of an object against an opposing force*. Put another way, work means moving an object with a force that overcomes some other force. For example, gravity tends to pull objects down. So when you lift an object against the opposing force of gravity, you are doing work on the object. If you lift a 10-lb [4.54-kg] weight a distance of 5 ft (feet) [1.5 m (meters)], you are doing 50 ft-lb (foot-pounds) [6.81 m-kg (meter-kilograms)] of work on the weight (Fig. 3-5). The weight will "give back" the work if you drop it.

Fig. 3-5. When you lift an object against the opposing force of gravity, you are doing work on the object.

⊘ 3-7 Adding Up the Power Strokes Let's go over work again. During a power stroke in the engine, the high-pressure gas pushes on the piston head with a force of up to 2 tons (4,000 lb [1,814 kg]). The automobile is the opposing force. The 2-ton [1,814-kg] force must overcome the opposing force of the automobile to move it along. This is work. The repeated power strokes in all the engine cylinders provide the work necessary to keep the car moving. Thus, engine power results from the work done on the pistons by the burning gases in the cylinders.

As a simple example, let's say the 2 tons [1,814 kg] of pressure push the piston down 3 in or $\frac{1}{4}$ ft [76.2 mm]. See Fig. 3-6. This means the push has produced $\frac{1}{4} \times 4{,}000 = 1{,}000$ ft-lb [138.2 m-kg] of work.

When the power strokes follow one another very rapidly, the engine is working hard. It is producing a lot of work in a given amount of time. The engine is putting out a lot of *power*, and the car is moving fast. When there are fewer power strokes per minute, the engine is producing less work in the same amount of time. It is putting out less power.

Now you have it. Power is the rate, or the speed,

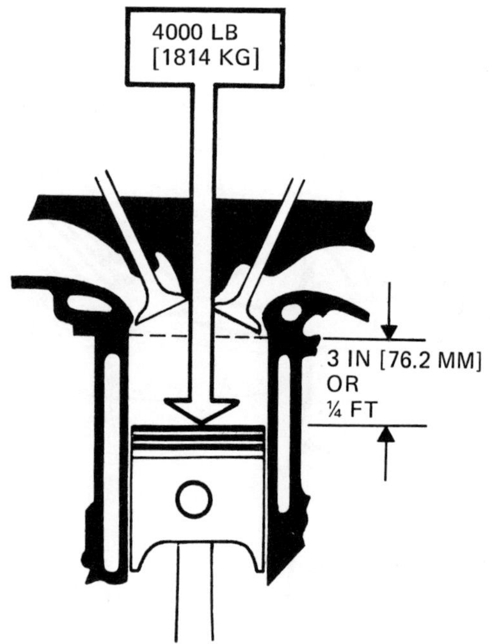

Fig. 3-6. To move the piston, the pressure on top of the piston must overcome the opposing force of the automobile. This is work.

at which work is done. If an engine can do work fast, it is called a *high-powered engine.*

⊘ 3-8 Engine Horsepower Engine performance is measured in horsepower. One horsepower is the amount of work one horse can do in 1 minute. The average horse can raise a 200-lb [90.76-kg] weight a distance of 165 ft [50.29 m] in 1 minute. Figure 3-7 shows how this measurement can be made. The horse walks 165 ft [50.29 m] in 1 minute. The cable, running over the pulley, raises the 200-lb [90.76-kg] weight 165 ft [50.29 m]. The amount of work done in 1 minute is 165 × 200 = 33,000 ft-lb [4,560 m-kg]. In other words, 1 hp is 33,000 ft-lb per minute.

If the horse took 2 minutes to do the same amount of work (33,000 ft-lb), it would be working only half as hard. It would thus be putting out only ½ hp. Three horses would be needed to raise 600 lb [272.16 kg] a distance of 165 ft [50.29 m] in 1 minute. Why? The work required would be 600 × 165 = 99,000 ft-lb, and this work would have to be done in 1 minute.

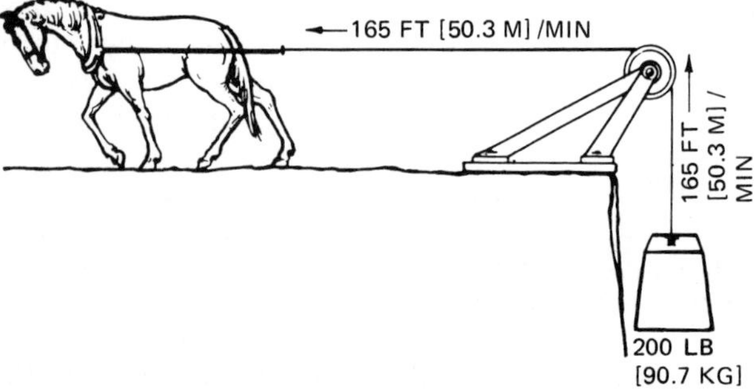

Fig. 3-7. One horse can do 33,000 ft-lb [4,562.25 m-kg] of work in 1 min.

You may be interested to know how engineers figure horsepower. Here is the formula they use:

$$\text{HP} = \frac{\text{ft-lb/min}}{33{,}000} = \frac{L \times W}{33{,}000 \times t}$$

where HP = horsepower
L = distance moved, ft
W = push or pull exerted, lb
t = time required, min

PROBLEM: How many horsepower would it take to raise 3,000 lb a distance of 220 ft in 1 minute?

SOLUTION

$$\text{HP} = \frac{L \times W}{33{,}000 \times t} = \frac{220 \times 3{,}000}{33{,}000 \times 1} = 20 \text{ hp}$$

There is a second formula that uses engine torque as one of the measurements instead of *W* and *L*. It is described in ⊘ 3-12.

Other Engine Measurements

You can now talk with hot-rodders and engine experts about horsepower, engine displacement, and compression ratio. Some other engine measurements the experts discuss are volumetric efficiency, torque, friction horsepower, and engine efficiency. We look at these engine measurements in the remainder of this chapter.

⊘ 3-9 Volumetric Efficiency The word "volumetric" means "having to do with volume." "Efficiency" generally refers to how well a job is done. The two words used together refer to how well the engine cylinder fills up on the intake stroke. Remember, the piston moves down on the intake stroke. The air-fuel mixture pours in to fill the vacuum left by the downward movement of the piston. The mixture doesn't pour in instantly. It needs time to flow through the carburetor and past the intake valve.

The same thing happens when you drink through a straw. The liquid doesn't come up into your mouth the instant you start sucking. It takes a fraction of a second to reach your mouth.

There isn't much time for the air-fuel mixture to get into the engine cylinder on the intake stroke. At high engine speed, or high rpm (revolution per minute), the intake stroke takes less than a hundredth of a second. The piston moves very fast! So, before the cylinder fills up completely, the intake valve closes and the compression stroke starts. If the cylinder fills up almost completely, then the volumetric efficiency is high. If the cylinder fills up only partly, then the volumetric efficiency is low.

The key idea is this: The less time the mixture has to fill the cylinder, the lower the volumetric efficiency will be. At low engine speed, such as idle, when the intake stroke takes as long as one-tenth of a second, the cylinder can almost fill up. The volumetric efficiency is high. This means there is more air-fuel mixture to be compressed and burned. As a result, the power stroke is stronger.

At high engine speed, the intake stroke takes such a short time that the cylinder gets much less air-fuel mixture. The volumetric efficiency is low. There is less air-fuel mixture to be compressed and burned, and the power stroke is weaker.

That is why engine speed cannot be increased indefinitely. As engine speed increases, the intake-stroke time gets shorter and shorter. So the volumetric efficiency gets lower and lower. Less and less air-fuel mixture gets in, and the power output of the engine falls lower and lower. Finally, the power strokes become so weak that they cannot increase the speed any further.

Here is the formula for volumetric efficiency:

$$\text{VE} = \frac{\text{Amount of air-fuel mixture entering cylinder}}{\text{Amount entering under ideal conditions}}$$

Suppose that at a certain speed 40 in^3 [656 cc] of mixture enter the cylinder. However, under ideal conditions, 50 in^3 [819 cc] could enter. The volumetric efficiency is 40 divided by 50, which is 0.8 or 80 percent.

⊘ 3-10 Improving Volumetric Efficiency The volumetric efficiency can be improved by increasing the size of the passages through which the air-fuel mixture travels. If the intake valve, the valve port, and the passages through the carburetor are made larger, the air-fuel mixture can get into the cylinder more easily. This is done in modern engines. Engineers call it "improving the engine's breathing." They point out that an engine "breathes" just as you do. It takes in air and then blows it out.

With improved engine breathing, the engine can put out more power at higher speeds. For example, when engineers assemble a racing engine, they open up the air-fuel passages as much as possible. This allows the engine to breathe better at high speed. This, in turn, improves the volumetric efficiency of the engine. Suppose an engine has a volumetric efficiency of 80 percent at high speeds. Modifying the engine might raise the actual amount of air-fuel mixture taken in from 40 in^3 [656 cc] to 45 in^3 [737 cc]. The VE would then be increased to 90 percent.

You have heard of "two-barrel" and "four-barrel" carburetors. These carburetors are used on high-horsepower engines. The extra barrels are additional air passages that let the engine breathe easier. They give the engine higher volumetric efficiency. The higher volumetric efficiency allows the engine to put out more horsepower, especially at high speeds.

⊘ 3-11 Torque *Torque* is twisting, or turning, effort (Fig. 3-8). You apply torque to the steering wheel when you take a car around a turn. The engine applies torque to the car wheels to make them rotate.

Torque, however, must not be confused with power. Torque is twisting, or turning, effort which may or may not result in motion. In other words, torque is the ability to cause something to rotate.

Torque is measured in pound-feet (lb-ft) or in kilogram-meters (kg-m). Do not confuse this with work, which is measured in foot-pounds (ft-lb) or meter-kilograms (m-kg). For example, suppose you pushed on a crank with a 20-lb [9.07-kg] push. If the crank were $1\frac{1}{2}$ ft [0.457 m] long, you would be applying $20 \times 1\frac{1}{2} = 30$ lb-ft [4.15 kg-m] of torque to the crank (Fig. 3-9). You would be applying this amount of torque *whether or not* the crank was turning.

⊘ 3-12 Engine Torque Engine torque comes from the pressure of the burning gases in the cylinders. This pressure pushes down on the pistons and causes the crankshaft to turn. The harder the push on the piston, the greater the torque. *Engine torque is not engine power.* Torque is the twisting effort that

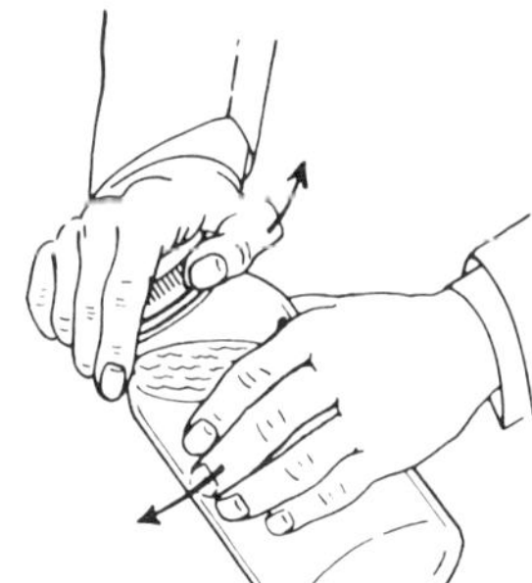

Fig. 3-8. Torque, or twisting effort, must be applied to loosen and remove the top from a screw-top jar.

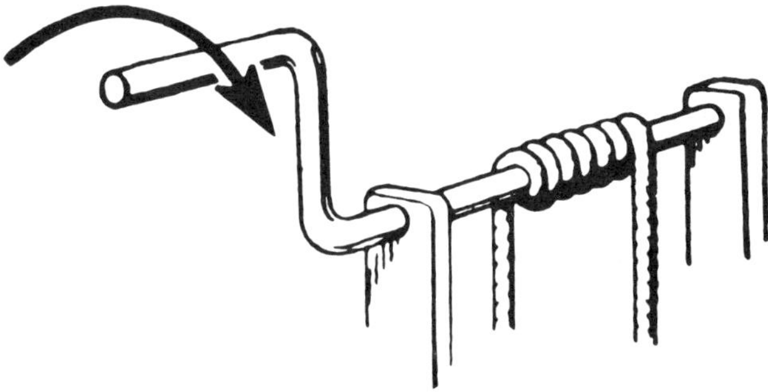

Fig. 3-9 Torque is measured in pound-feet (lb-ft) or kilogram-meters (kg-m). It is calculated by multiplying the push by the crank offset—that is, the distance of the push from the rotating shaft.

the engine applies to the crankshaft. Power is the rate at which the engine is working.

Engine torque varies with the speed of the engine. An engine develops more torque at intermediate speed (with open throttle) than at high speed. Here's the reason: At intermediate speed, there is more time for the air-fuel mixture to enter the cylinder. In other words, the volumetric efficiency is high. This means that more air-fuel mixture enters the cylinder, the combustion pressure goes up, and there is a stronger push on the piston. In other words, more torque is applied to the crankshaft.

At higher speeds, there is less time for the air-fuel mixture to get into the cylinder. Volumetric efficiency drops off. There is less air-fuel mixture to burn, and the combustion pressure is lower. There is less push on the piston, and the engine torque is lower.

The fact that torque drops at high speed is shown in Fig. 3-10. At low speed, about 500 rpm (revolutions per minute), the torque is about 180 lb-ft [24.9 kg-m]. Find this point on the graph by moving up the 500-rpm line until it crosses the curved line. From this point, move across to the left. You should see that the torque is slightly above 175 lb-ft [24.2 kg-m], or about 180 lb-ft [24.9 kg-m]. As engine speed increases, the torque goes up. Torque reaches a peak in the 1,500- to 2,000-rpm range. Then it begins to drop; at about 4,000 rpm, the torque is less than 125 lb-ft [17.29 kg-m].

This explains why an engine performs better at intermediate speed than at high speed. It is the torque of the engine that gives acceleration and "performance."

Here is another formula for calculating horsepower. It uses the torque developed by the engine.

$$\text{HP} = \frac{\text{torque} \times \text{rpm}}{5{,}252}$$

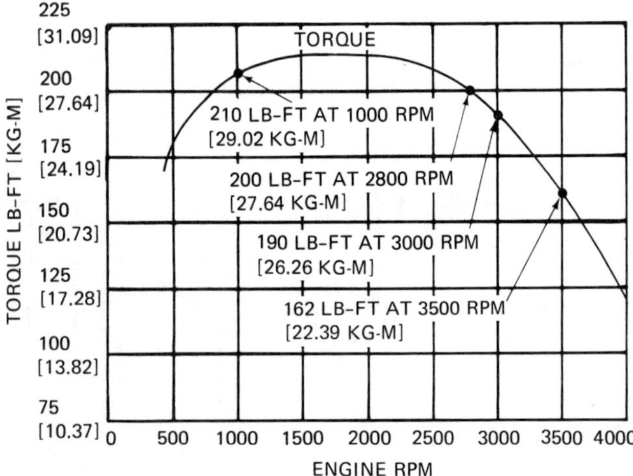

Fig. 3-10. Torque curve of an engine, showing the relationship between torque and speed.

When you work in the shop and use the shop dynamometer to measure engine output, you will see why this formula is more convenient than the one in ⊘ 3-8. You can measure torque and rpm, as well as horsepower, with the dynamometer.

PROBLEM: How many horsepower are produced by an engine that develops 210 lb-ft of torque at 2,400 rpm?

SOLUTION

$$\text{HP} = \frac{\text{torque} \times \text{rpm}}{5{,}252} = \frac{210 \times 2{,}400}{5{,}252} = 96 \text{ hp}$$

⊘ 3-13 Friction Horsepower Another important engine measurement is friction horsepower. *Friction* is the resistance to motion between two objects in contact with each other. For example, suppose you put a book on a table and push it (Fig. 3-11). Some effort is required to move the book. If you put a lot of oil on the table, the book would slide on the oil. You could move the book much more easily, because the oil reduces the friction between the book and the table.

In the engine, all moving parts are covered with oil, or lubricated, so that they will easily slip over one another. Even so, some power is used up just to make them move—to overcome the friction. The power that is used to overcome friction is called *friction horsepower* and abbreviated fhp.

Friction horsepower goes up as engine speed goes up. The graph in Fig. 3-12 shows this. At low speeds, it takes only a few horsepower to overcome the friction in the engine. But as speed increases, the friction loss goes up until, at 4,000 rpm, friction is using up 40 hp.

⊘ 3-14 Brake Horsepower The *brake horsepower* (bhp) of an engine is the actual horsepower that the engine is producing. It is called "brake" horsepower because, when engineers first started measuring engine performance, they used a type of brake to measure this power. Today, engine power is meas-

Fig. 3-11. Friction resists the push on the book.

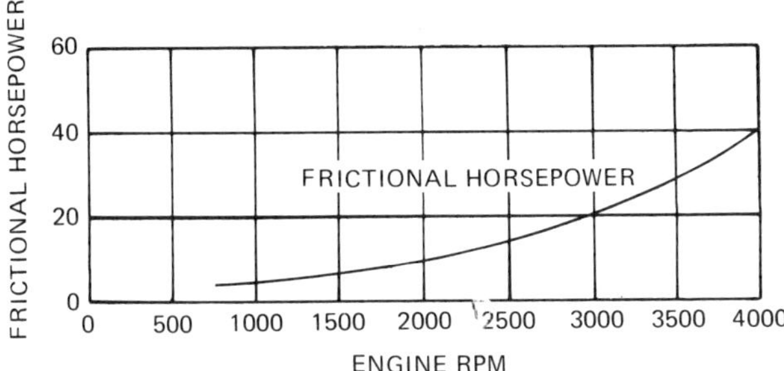

Fig. 3-12. Friction-horsepower curve, showing the relationship between friction horsepower and engine speed.

ured by a dynamometer. This word comes from "dynamo" and "meter." Originally, the dynamometer was an electric generator with a meter to measure the amount of electricity the generator produced. Today, the term "dynamometer" is applied to several types of power-measuring devices. In use, an engine drives the dynamometer, which measures the amount of power the engine produces. The more power the engine produces, the more power is absorbed by the dynamometer and the higher the meter reads. Thus, engine output is measured as the amount of power the dynamometer is absorbing.

The amount of power that an engine puts out depends on its torque and speed (rpm). As speed goes up, horsepower goes up. And, as torque goes up, horsepower goes up. You can see this in the formula in ⊘ 3-12. The horsepower calculated by that formula is actually brake horsepower (bhp).

The graph of horsepower output for an engine is shown in Fig. 3-13. Note that the horsepower starts out low at low speed and builds up to about 110 hp at 3,500 rpm. After that, as speed increases further, the horsepower output drops off.

The dropoff of horsepower output results from the decrease in torque and the increase in friction horsepower at higher speeds. So the decrease in

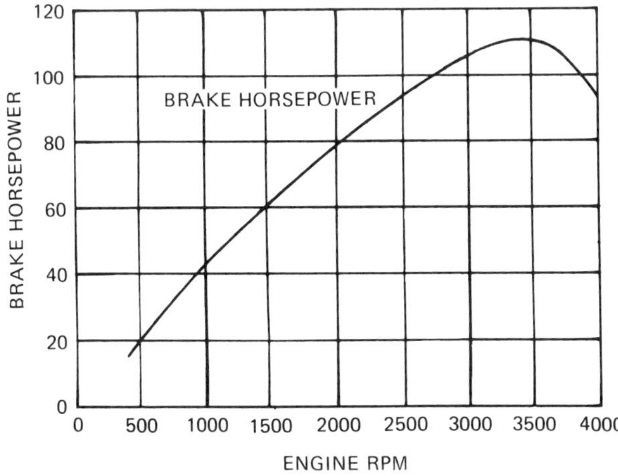

Fig. 3-13. Curve showing the relationship between brake horsepower and engine speed.

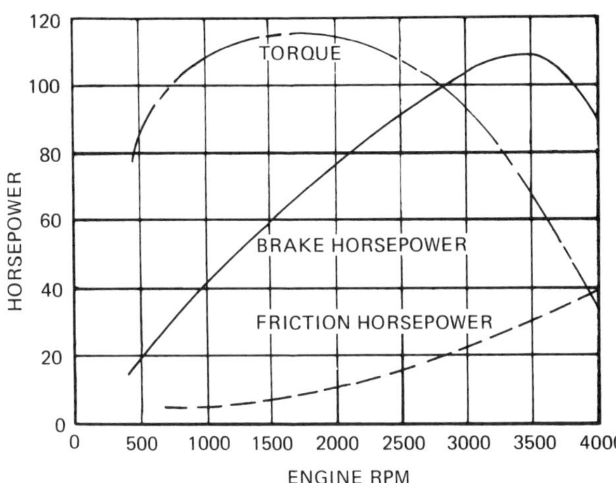

Fig. 3-14. Comparison of the torque, friction-horsepower, and brake-horsepower curves of an engine.

torque and the increase in friction horsepower keep the engine horsepower from increasing with further increases in rpm.

The graph in Fig. 3-14 combines the three graphs we have been discussing.

NOTE: The four graphs (Figs. 3-10 and 3-12 to 3-14) are for one particular engine only. Different engines have different torque, friction-horsepower, and brake-horsepower curves. The peaks may be at higher or lower speeds. The relationships may not be quite the same as those shown in our graphs.

⊘ **3-15 Engine Efficiency** We noted that the word "efficiency" refers to how well a job is done. In an engine, it is the relationship between the effort exerted and the results obtained. Engine efficiency is the ratio of the power actually delivered to the power that could be delivered if the engine operated without any power loss.

Unfortunately, there is considerable power loss in an engine. Power is lost because of friction, and because only part of the energy in gasoline is converted to power. A good deal of the potential power in gasoline is lost as heat. The engine cooling system, which is described in Chap. 8, removes about a third of the heat energy of the gasoline. Another third is lost because the exhaust gases are very hot when they leave the engine. More power is lost because of friction. The result is that only about 15 to 20 percent of the energy in the fuel is actually used to move the car.

Check Your Progress

Progress Quiz 3-1 Once again you have the chance to check up on yourself—to find out how well you remember and understand what you are reading. The material you have just covered is different from the material in previous chapters; it describes some of the ways in which engine performance is measured. This is valuable information. Anyone interested in automotive engines should know how engine output is measured, what "compression ratio" means, and so on. Find out how efficiently you have studied this material, by taking the following quiz.

Completing the Sentences The sentences that follow are incomplete. After each sentence there are several words or phrases, but only one of them correctly completes the sentence. Write each sentence in your notebook, ending it with the one word or phrase that completes it correctly.

1. The size of an engine cylinder is given by its: (*a*) bore and width, (*b*) bore and stroke, (*c*) diameter and bore.
2. Piston displacement is calculated from the: (*a*) bore and stroke, (*b*) piston length and diameter, (*c*) cylinder diameter and length.
3. The air volume above the piston with the piston at TDC is called the: (*a*) compression ratio, (*b*) clearance volume, (*c*) piston displacement, (*d*) bore.
4. The air volume in the cylinder with the piston at BDC divided by the clearance volume is called the: (*a*) piston displacement, (*b*) cylinder ratio, (*c*) compression ratio.
5. As carbon accumulates in a cylinder, it causes an increase in the: (*a*) clearance volume, (*b*) effective compression ratio, (*c*) piston displacement.
6. The amount of air-fuel mixture taken in by the engine on the intake stroke is a measure of the engine's: (*a*) clearance volume, (*b*) compression ratio, (*c*) volumetric efficiency.
7. A volumetric efficiency of 80 percent for an engine running at fairly high speed is: (*a*) good, (*b*) impossible, (*c*) poor.
8. The more easily an engine can breathe, the higher is its: (*a*) volumetric efficiency, (*b*) piston displacement, (*c*) compression ratio.
9. The dynamometer is used to determine: (*a*) compression ratio, (*b*) bhp, (*c*) volumetric efficiency.
10. Friction horsepower increases as the engine: (*a*) speed increases, (*b*) speed decreases, (*c*) idles.

Problems Work out the following problems in your notebook. Refer back to the formulas in the chapter if you are not sure of them.

1. What is the piston displacement in a 3- by 4-in [76.2 by 101.6 mm] cylinder?
2. What is the compression ratio of an engine that has a clearance volume of 5.3 in^3 [86.8 cm^3] (piston at TDC) and an air volume of 45.05 in^3 [738.2 cm^3] with the piston at BDC?
3. An engine has a compression ratio of 8:1. It has a clearance volume of 5 in^3 [81.9 cm^3], and an air volume of 40 in^3 [655.5 cm^3] with the piston at BDC. After some months of service, about 1 in^3 [16.4 cm^3] of carbon has accumulated in each cylinder. What is the effective compression ratio?

CHAPTER 3 CHECKUP

NOTE: Since the following is a chapter review test, you should review the chapter before taking the test.

You are making good progress in your study of the automobile engine. The chapter you just completed gives you a good background on the ways in which engines and engine performance are measured. When someone talks to you about piston displacement, compression ratio, or brake horsepower, you will know what is meant. The following questions will help you remember the important points covered in the chapter. Reread the chapter before taking the test. If the questions seem hard to answer, review the chapter again.

Completing the Sentences The sentences that follow are incomplete. After each sentence there are several words or phrases, but only one of them correctly completes the sentence. Write each sentence in your notebook, ending it with the one word or phrase that completes it correctly.

1. The power used in overcoming friction in the engine is called: (*a*) ihp, (*b*) fhp, (*c*) bhp.
2. Engine torque is highest at: (*a*) low speed, (*b*) intermediate speed, (*c*) high speed.
3. One reason why torque drops off at high speed is that at high speed: (*a*) volumetric efficiency is lower, (*b*) the engine breathes better, (*c*) the fuel mixture is richer.
4. Of the energy in the gasoline burned in the engine, the percentage that is actually used to move the car may be as low as: (*a*) 15 percent, (*b*) 25 percent, (*c*) 35 percent, (*d*) 70 percent.
5. Knowing the bore and stroke, you can calculate the: (*a*) compression ratio, (*b*) piston displacement, (*c*) volumetric efficiency.
6. Knowing the clearance volume and the air volume in the cylinder with the piston at BDC, you can figure the: (*a*) compression ratio, (*b*) volumetric efficiency, (*c*) bhp, (*d*) ihp.
7. Knowing the speed at which an engine is running and the torque it is developing, you can figure the: (*a*) bhp, (*b*) ihp, (*c*) fhp.

Definitions In the following, you are asked to define certain terms. Write the definitions in your notebook. This will help you remember them. It will also provide you with a place where you can quickly locate the meanings, if you need the information again. If you cannot remember the meaning of a term, look it up in the chapter you have just studied, or in the glossary at the back of the book.

1. What is piston displacement?
2. Define "bore."
3. What is oversquare?
4. Define "stroke."
5. What is compression ratio?
6. What is volumetric efficiency?
7. Define "horsepower."
8. What is torque?
9. What is a dynamometer?
10. Define "friction horsepower."

SUGGESTIONS FOR FURTHER STUDY

There are a number of engineering books with additional information on engine measurements and engine testing. If you are interested in learning more about these topics, go to your local library. The librarian will help you find the proper books. Your automotive instructor or physics teacher may also be able to help you. The operating instructions for dynamometers usually contain a review of basic engine-performance measurements and how to obtain them.

chapter 4

ENGINE TYPES

We have already mentioned some of the different types of automotive engines—L-head, I-head, reciprocating, and rotary. Now we are going to look at the classifications of engines. Automotive piston, or reciprocating, engines can be classified in at least seven different ways. They are:

1. *By number of cylinders*
2. *By the arrangement of cylinders*
3. *By the arrangement of valves*
4. *By type of cooling systems*
5. *By the number of piston strokes per cycle*
6. *By type of fuel burned*
7. *By firing order*

This is not a complete list, but it gives you an idea of the ways in which engines can be classified.

⊘ **4-1 Number and Arrangement of Cylinders** Almost all piston engines have either four, six, or eight cylinders. Usually, the cylinders in four-cylinder and six-cylinder engines are arranged in a single row, or line. Some V-4 and V-6 engines have been made. In these, the cylinders are placed in two rows set at an angle to each other. Flat four-cylinder and flat six-cylinder engines have also been made. In these, the cylinders are in two rows, across from each other. Eight-cylinder engines are all of the V type. The two rows of cylinders are set at an angle to each other. Figure 4-1 shows the various arrangements. Now let's look at the different engines in detail.

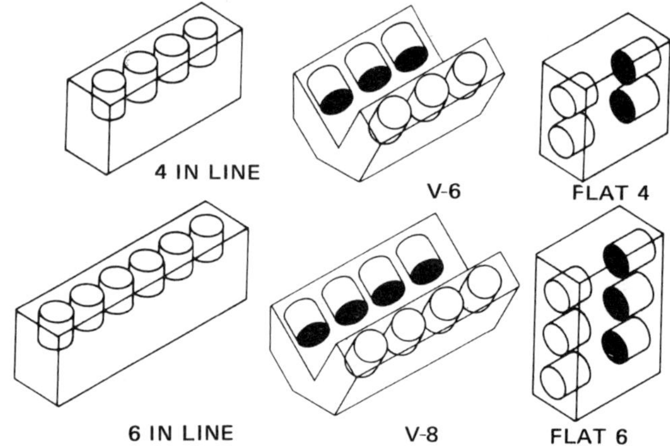

Fig. 4-1. Several cylinder arrangements.

⊘ **4-2 Four-Cylinder, In-Line Engines** As already mentioned, the cylinders in a four-cylinder engine can be arranged in a single line, in pairs set at an angle to form a V, or in pairs set opposite each other. A typical four-cylinder, in-line engine is shown in Fig. 4-2. Note that this engine has overhead valves operated by pushrods and rocker arms. Study the figure, and locate the pistons, connecting rod (one is shown), camshaft, camshaft drive gear, spark plugs, pushrods, rocker arms, and valves. If you look carefully, you will see a spiral gear on the camshaft; it is meshed with another spiral gear on a nearly vertical shaft. The purpose of these gears is to drive the oil pump that lubricates the engine. They also drive the ignition distributor, which is not shown in the picture. See also Fig. 2-15. Part of the oil pump is shown at the bottom of Fig. 2-15. See Chap. 7 for descriptions of oil pumps, and Chap. 28 for pictures of ignition distributors.

NOTE: A great deal of the information in this book is contained in the pictures. It is important that you study them carefully.

⊘ **4-3 V-4 Engines** Not very many V-4 engines have been built, but there are a few in this country. Figure 4-3 is a phantom view of a V-4 engine, showing the working parts. You can see the crankshaft, pistons, connecting rods, camshaft, and valve train. The extra shaft with a gear (near the bottom of the picture) is a special balance shaft that is needed to

Fig. 4-2. Partial cutaway view of a four-cylinder, in-line, overhead-valve engine. (*Chevrolet Motor Division of General Motors Corporation*)

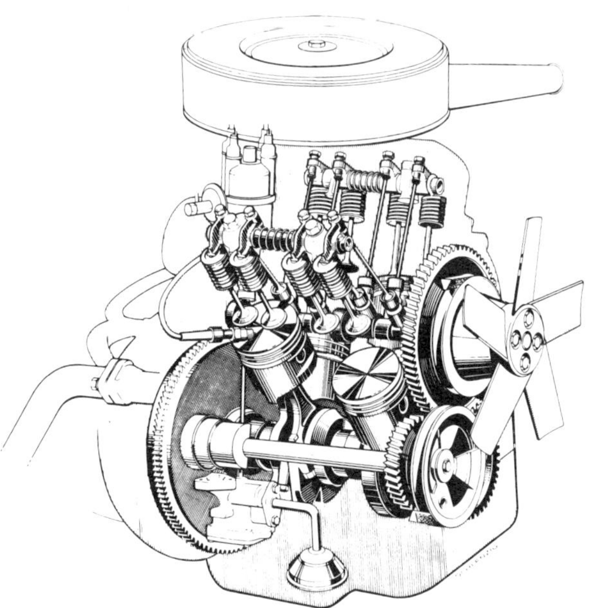

Fig. 4-3. Phantom view of a V-4 engine, showing the major moving parts in the engine. (*Ford Motor Company of Germany*)

balance the engine. A balanced engine runs smoothly and does not vibrate. The difficulty of balancing a V-4 engine is one reason why very few of them have been built.

⊘ 4-4 Flat-Four Engines The best example of the flat-four engine is the Volkswagen engine, which is shown in sectional view in Fig. 4-4. The four cylinders are arranged in two opposing rows of two cylinders each. If you study this picture, you will see pistons, connecting rods, cylinders, rocker arms, valves, and pushrods. You will also notice something different about the engine. The cylinders are surrounded by flat metal rings, or metal fins. These fins provide large surfaces from which heat can leave the engine. The fins are needed because the engine is air-cooled. That is, heat from the combustion of the air-fuel mixture passes from the cylinders to the fins. The fins radiate the heat into the surrounding air. In most automobiles, the engines are liquid-cooled. We look more closely at these two kinds of cooling systems later in this chapter.

Fig. 4-4. Flat four-cylinder engine with two banks of two cylinders each, opposing each other. This is an air-cooled engine. (*Volkswagen*)

Another interesting thing about the Volkswagen engine is that the pushrods are carried in hollow tubes between the cylinder heads and crankcase. There are four long studs per cylinder. They hold the cylinder heads, tubes, and cylinders to the crankcase.

Figure 4-5 shows how the Volkswagen engine is mounted at the rear of the car. This picture was taken from the back of the car with the hood raised.

⊘ 4-5 Six-Cylinder, In-Line Engines Most six-cylinder engines are of the in-line type. In these engines, the six cylinders are arranged in a single row, or line. Figure 4-6 is a partial cutaway view of a six-cylinder, in-line engine. As you can see, it is an overhead-valve engine. The picture is especially good because you can see so many different parts. Find the crankshaft, camshaft, valves, rocker arms, pushrods, pistons, connecting rods, and other parts. You can see the oil pump and the ignition distributor in this picture, as well as the drive gears. They are located front and center in the picture. The oil pump is located at the bottom in the oil pan. As previously mentioned, the oil pump supplies oil to the moving parts in the engine, to keep them well lubricated. The ignition distributor works with other parts in the ignition system to produce sparks at the spark plugs.

Fig. 4-5. Mounting arrangement for the flat four-cylinder engine at the rear of the automobile. (*Volkswagen*)

Another six-cylinder, in-line engine is shown partly cut away in Fig. 4-7. This engine is especially interesting because the cylinders are slanted to one side. Thus it is often called a "slant-six." The engine has been built in two styles, one with a cast-iron cylinder block and the other with a cast-aluminum cylinder block. Cylinder blocks are discussed in more detail in Chap. 10. Figure 4-7 is another good picture that shows many of the internal engine parts. Locate as many of the parts as you can.

⊘ 4-6 V-6 Engines Several companies have built V-6 engines. These have two rows of three cylinders each, set at an angle to form a V. Figure 4-8 is a cutaway view of a V-6 engine. It shows many engine parts and construction details.

⊘ 4-7 Flat-Six Engines The flat-six engine is very similar to the flat-four engine, except that one more

Fig. 4-6. Six-cylinder, in-line engine with overhead valves, partly cut away to show the internal parts. (*Ford Motor Company*)

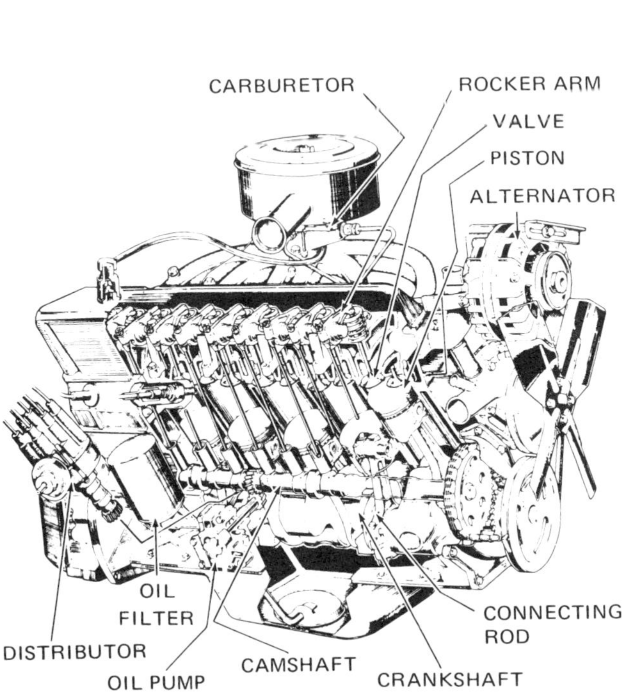

Fig. 4-7. Slant-six, in-line, overhead-valve engine, cut away to show the internal parts. The cylinders are slanted to permit a lower hood line. (*Chrysler Corporation*)

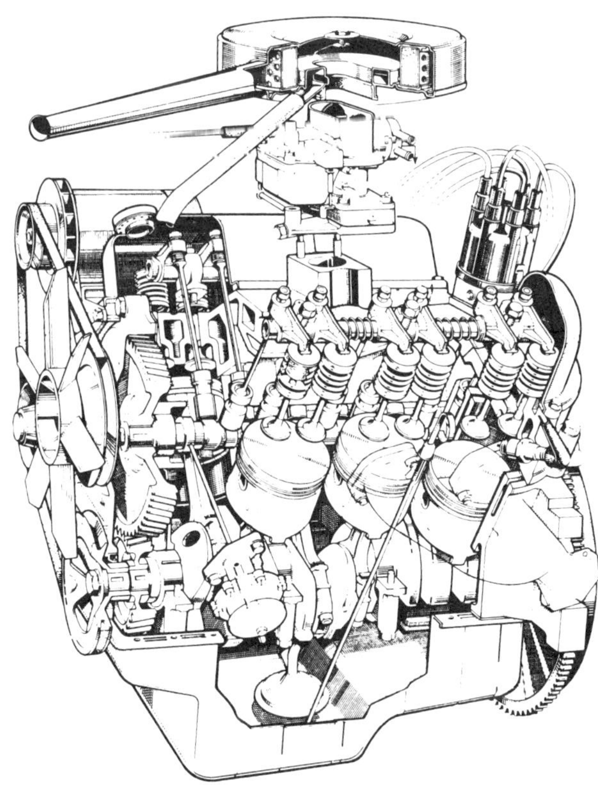

Fig. 4-8. Cutaway view of a V-6 overhead-valve engine. (*Ford Motor Company of Germany*)

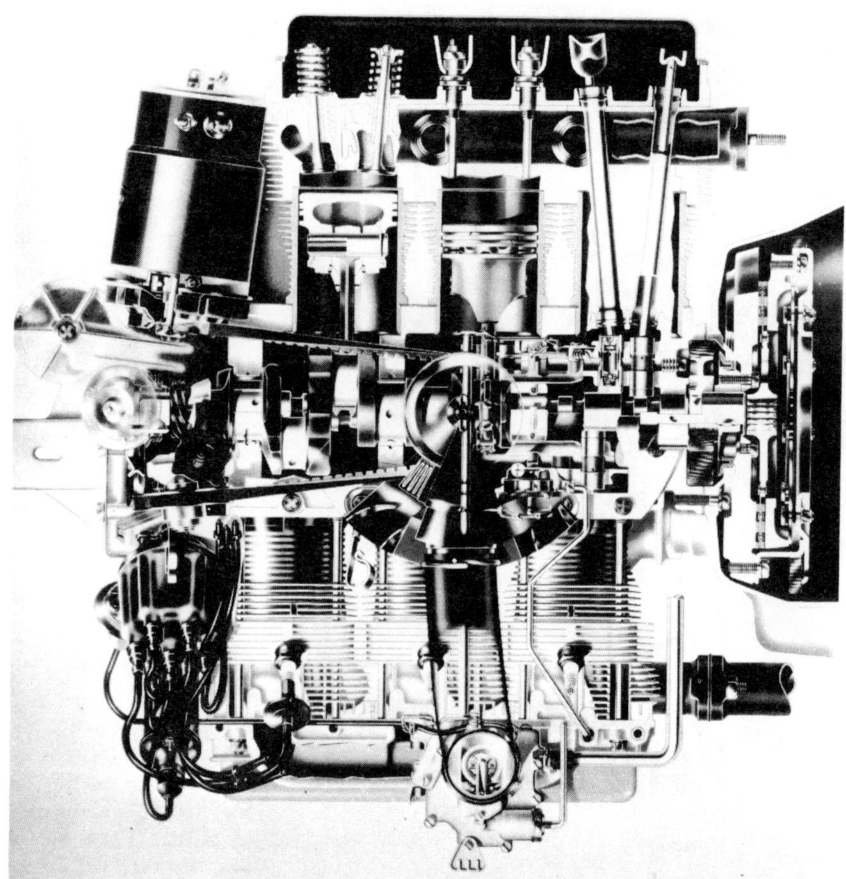

Fig. 4-9. Sectional view from the top of a flat, six-cylinder, overhead-valve, air-cooled engine. Flat engines are sometimes called "pancake" engines. (*Chevrolet Motor Division of General Motors Corporation*)

cylinder is added to each bank. Figure 4-9 is a cutaway view (from the top) of the flat-six engine used in the Chevrolet Corvair. This engine is air-cooled and is mounted at the rear of the car.

⊘ 4-8 V-8 Engines All eight-cylinder automotive engines made today are of the V type. They have two rows of cylinders, with four cylinders in each row. The two rows are set at an angle to form a V. Figure 4-10 is a cutaway view of one model of V-8 engine. Study the picture for a moment, and then pick out the various internal parts.

At one time, eight-cylinder, in-line engines were common. Today, V-8 engines have taken their place. The V-8 is a shorter and more rigid engine. The cylinders are closer together, and have a better chance of getting their share of air-fuel mixture from the carburetor. The more rigid engine permits higher running speeds and higher compression pressures, with less difficulty from bending of the block and crankshaft. The shorter engine also allows more passenger space on the same wheelbase.

⊘ 4-9 Arrangement of Valves Another way to classify engines is according to the arrangement of the valves and valve trains. In Chap. 2 we mentioned the L-head (or flat-head), the I-head (or overhead-valve), and the overhead-camshaft arrangements. These arrangements are shown in Fig. 4-11.

⊘ 4-10 Cooling Methods There are two methods of engine cooling: liquid cooling and air cooling. Almost all automotive engines are liquid-cooled. The liquid is a mixture of water and an antifreeze solution. The antifreeze solution prevents the water from freezing when the temperature falls below 32°F (degrees Fahrenheit) [0°C (degrees Celsius)]. Another fact not widely known is that the antifreeze also helps to protect the engine from overheating in hot weather.

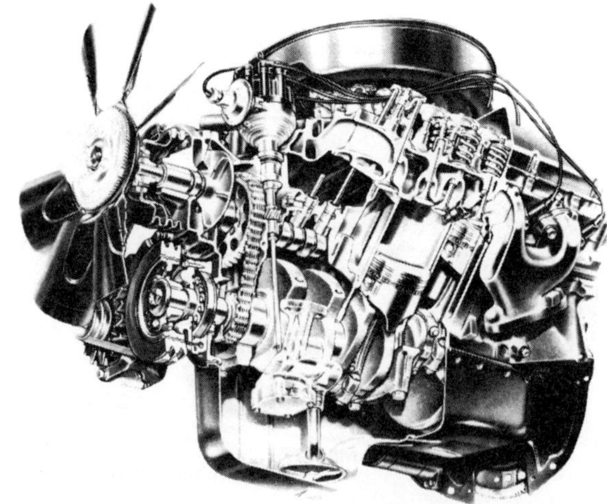

Fig. 4-10. Cutaway view of a 365-hp V-8 engine. (*Ford Motor Company*)

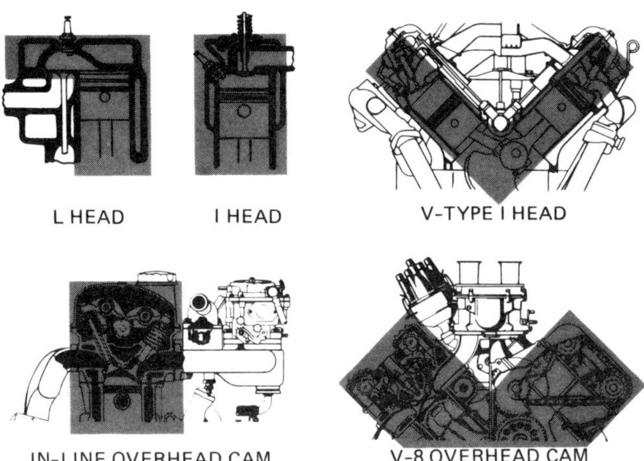

Fig. 4-11. Various valve arrangements. Compare these drawings with the pictures of engines shown throughout the book.

⊘ 4-11 Air-Cooled Engines

The Volkswagen and Corvair engines, shown in Figs. 4-4 and 4-9, are both air-cooled. Also, almost all the small engines used in power mowers and other garden equipment are air-cooled. Figure 4-12 shows a one-cylinder, air-cooled engine. Note the fins that circle the cylinder block and head. These fins have large surface areas that allow heat to radiate from the cylinders. Many air-cooled engines are equipped with *shrouds*. These are metal shields that direct air from a fan attached to the crankshaft. The air is directed past the fins and helps to keep the engine cool. Figure 4-13 shows how the air flows over and around the fins. Figure 4-14 shows the temperatures of the very hot combustion area, the cylinder wall, and the cooling fins. Note the differences. The heat is carried away from the fins as fast as it arrives.

The multiple-cylinder air-cooled engine uses a similar air circulating system, with shrouds. Air is directed around the cooling fins on the cylinders and cylinder heads. You can see the fins and shrouds in Figs. 4-4 and 4-9.

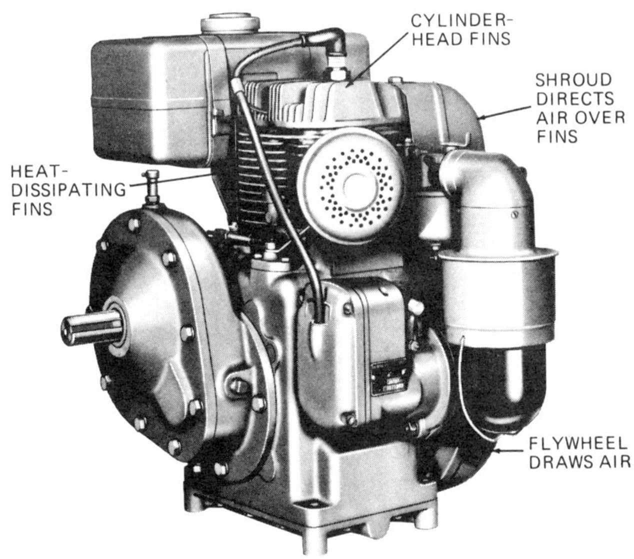

Fig. 4-12. One-cylinder, air-cooled engine. (*Teledyne Wisconsin Motor*)

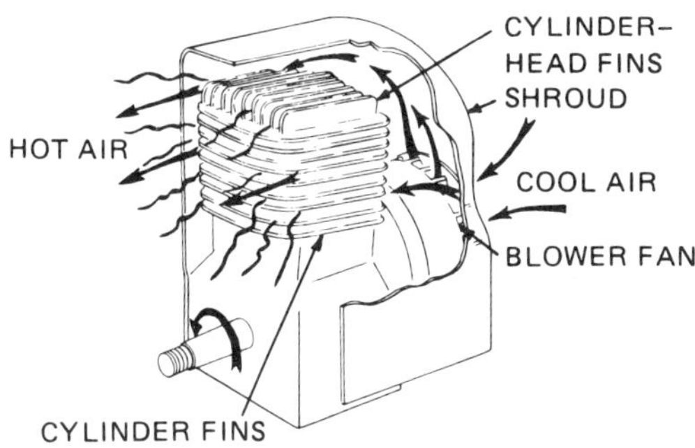

Fig. 4-13. Circulation of air around the cylinder fins.

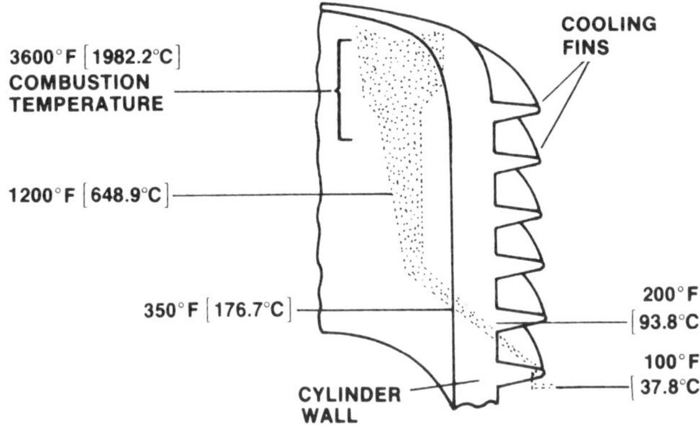

Fig. 4-14. Temperature differences in a cylinder of an air-cooled engine.

⊘ 4-12 Liquid-Cooled Engines

As we mentioned, most automobile engines are liquid-cooled. The coolant is a mixture of water and antifreeze. In liquid-cooled engines, the cylinder block and cylinder head have *water jackets* through which the coolant circulates. Water jackets are spaces that surround the cylinders and the combustion chamber. You can see them in many of the cutaway views of engines on previous pages.

Figure 4-15 is a cutaway view of a six-cylinder engine. The arrows show how the coolant circulates. The coolant is pumped through the engine water jackets by a water pump mounted on the front of the engine. As the coolant flows through the water jackets, it picks up heat. It gets very hot, almost to the boiling point. Then it flows into the top of the radiator. The radiator has a series of coolant passages and a series of air passages. The coolant moves down through the radiator and loses heat to air passing through the radiator. The engine fan helps the movement of the air. It pulls a strong blast of air through the radiator air passages. The water pump then draws cooled coolant from the bottom of the radiator and sends it back to the water jackets. This circulation of the coolant between the engine and

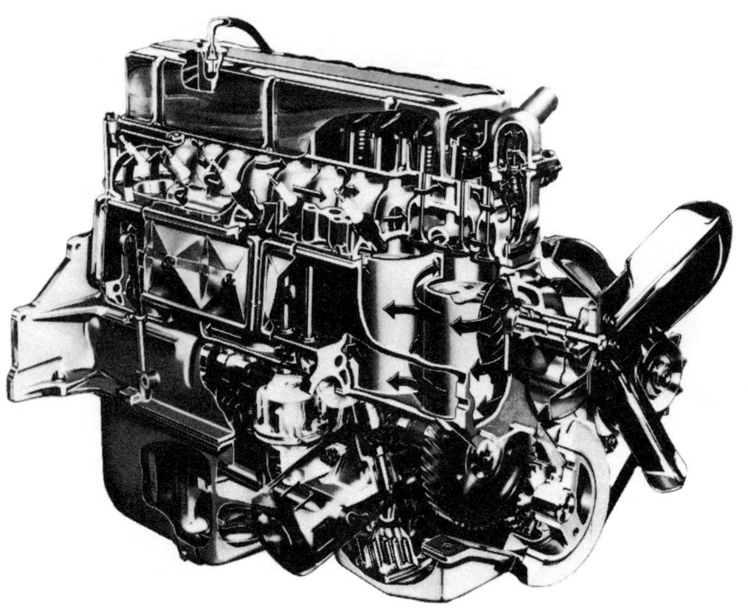

Fig. 4-15. Six-cylinder, in-line engine, partly cut away to show the engine cooling system. The arrows show the direction of water flow through the engine water jackets. *(Oldsmobile Division of General Motors Corporation)*

the radiator removes excess heat from the engine. The engine is thereby protected from overheating.

A cooling system for a V-8 engine is shown in Fig. 4-16. The engine has been partly cut away to show the circulation of the coolant through the engine, as well as the water pump and fan. There is more about cooling systems in Chap. 8.

⊘ 4-13 Classification by Piston Strokes Engines can be classified according to the number of piston strokes needed to complete one engine cycle. We have already mentioned the four-stroke-cycle engine (see Chap. 1), also known as the four-cycle engine. This engine requires four piston strokes to complete a cycle. There is also a two-stroke-cycle, or two-cycle engine. In the two-cycle engine, the whole cycle takes place in only two piston strokes.

⊘ 4-14 Two-Cycle Engines The two-cycle engine usually has no valves. The piston itself acts as a valve. The intake and exhaust ports are located in the cylinder wall. As the piston moves down, it

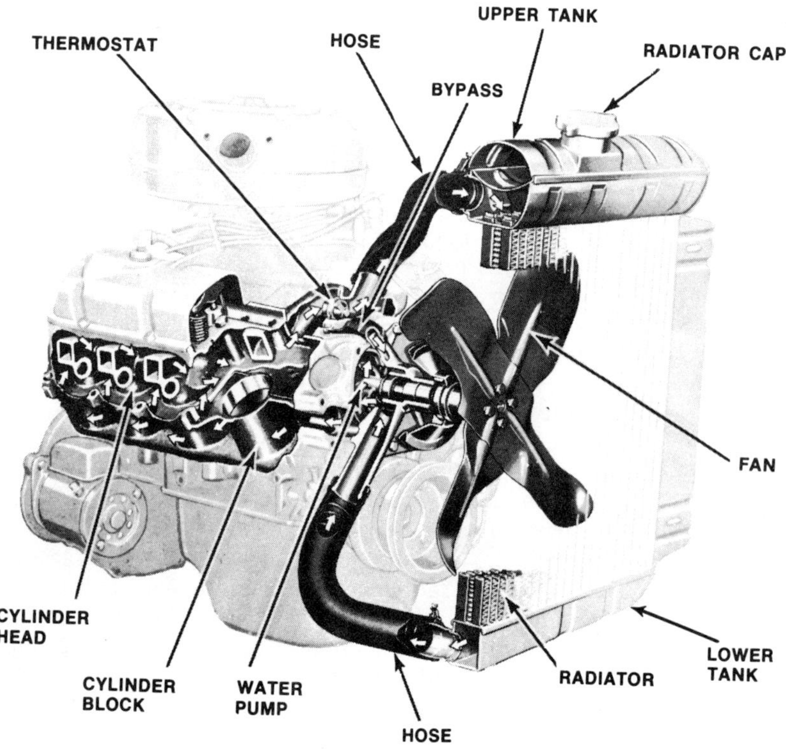

Fig. 4-16. Cutaway view of a V-8 engine, showing the cooling system. The arrows show the direction of water flow through the engine water jackets. *(Ford Motor Company)*

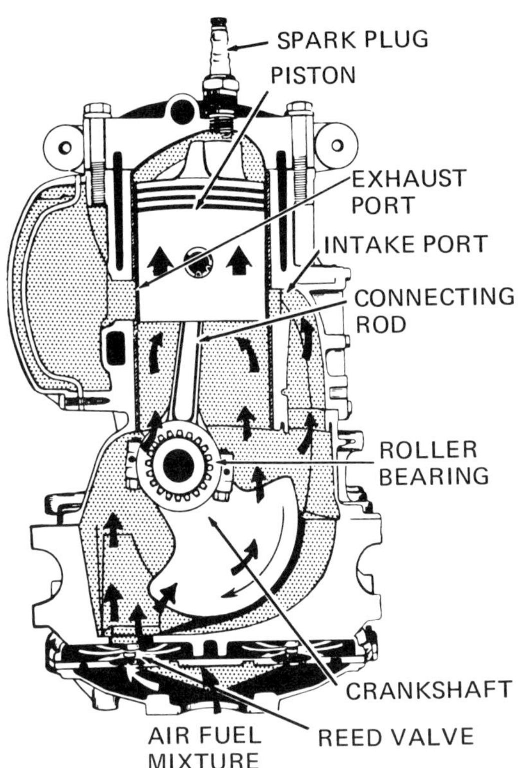

Fig. 4-17. Sectional view of a two-cycle engine with the piston nearing TDC. Ignition of the compressed air-fuel mixture occurs at about this point. (*Johnson Motors*)

clears these ports. This permits the exhaust gases to leave and a fresh charge of air-fuel mixture to enter at the same time.

Let's go over this series of events. We shall start with the piston nearing TDC and with ignition having taken place (Fig. 4-17). The compressed air-fuel mixture burns, the pressure goes up, and the piston is pushed down on the power stroke. As it nears BDC, the piston uncovers the intake and exhaust ports in the side of the cylinder (Fig. 4-18). Burned gases, still under some pressure, begin to stream out through the exhaust port. At the same time, the fresh charge of air-fuel mixture begins to flow into the cylinder through the intake port (arrows in Fig. 4-18). Note that the top of the piston is shaped to give this incoming air-fuel mixture an upward movement. This helps to push the exhaust gases out through the exhaust port.

As the piston passes through BDC and starts up again, it covers the intake and exhaust ports. This seals the air-fuel mixture above the piston (Fig. 4-19). The piston compresses the mixture as it moves up toward TDC, and the compressed mixture is then ignited. The piston is pushed down by the high pressure of the burning gases. The whole cycle is repeated as long as the engine runs.

We mentioned that the air-fuel mixture flows into the cylinder after the piston passes the intake port on its way down toward BDC. The air-fuel mixture has to be under pressure in order to flow into the cylinder. It is put under pressure in the

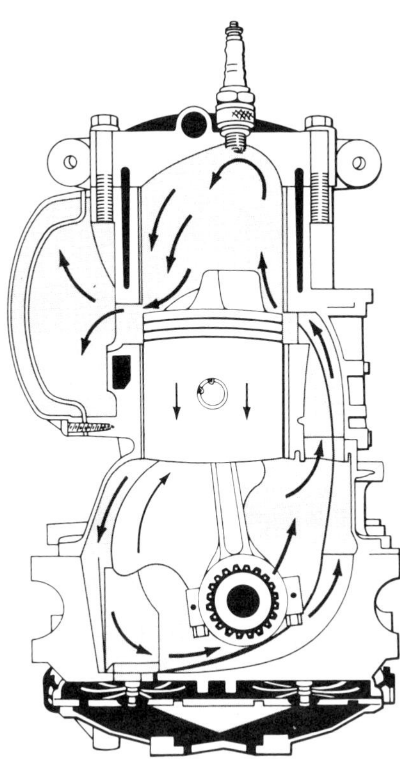

Fig. 4-18. As the piston approaches BDC, it uncovers the intake and exhaust ports. Burned gases stream out through the exhaust port. A fresh charge of air-fuel mixture enters through the intake port. This is shown by the arrows. (*Johnson Motors*)

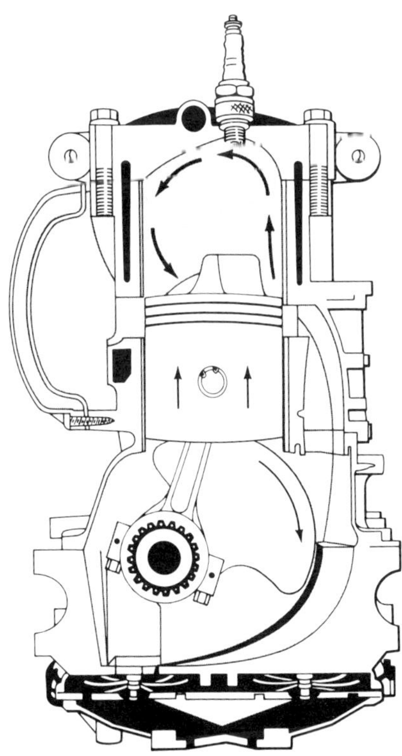

Fig. 4-19. After the piston passes BDC and moves up again, it covers the intake and exhaust ports. Further upward movement of the piston traps and compresses the air-fuel mixture. (*Johnson Motors*)

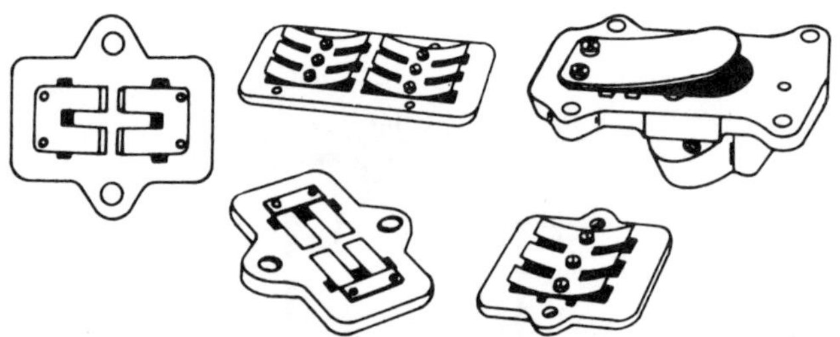

Fig. 4-20. Various types of reed valves. (*Tecumseh Products Company*)

crankcase. Figure 4-17 shows the piston moving up toward TDC. As the piston moves up, it produces a vacuum in the crankcase. The crankcase is sealed except for a reed valve. The reed valve is a flat strip of metal that rests on the floor of the crankcase, over a hole (Fig. 4-20). This hole is connected to the carburetor.

As the piston moves up and a vacuum develops in the crankcase, the reed valve is lifted off the hole by the vacuum. The vacuum causes the air-fuel mixture to flow from the carburetor into the crankcase. Next, as the piston starts to move down, the pressure in the crankcase increases. This increasing pressure pushes the reed valve down and closes the hole. As the piston moves further down, the air-fuel mixture in the crankcase is compressed. When the piston passes the intake port on its downward stroke, the compressed air-fuel mixture flows from the crankcase into the cylinder (see Fig. 4-18).

⊘ 4-15 Transfer Port There is another type of two-cycle engine. It uses a transfer port instead of a reed valve. The transfer port is a third port in the cylinder wall (Fig. 4-21). In this engine, the intake port is cleared by the piston as it moves up toward TDC. When this happens, the air-fuel mixture flows into the crankcase. It flows in because the upward movement of the piston has created a vacuum in the crankcase. Then, when the piston moves down, it covers the intake port. The mixture in the crankcase is compressed.

At the same time, the piston clears the exhaust port and the burned gases begin to exhaust from the cylinder. With further downward movement, the piston clears the transfer port. Now, the compressed air-fuel mixture begins to flow from the crankcase, through the transfer port, into the cylinder. Then, as the piston moves up, it seals off all the ports. The mixture is trapped above the piston. It is compressed, ignited, and the whole cycle takes place again.

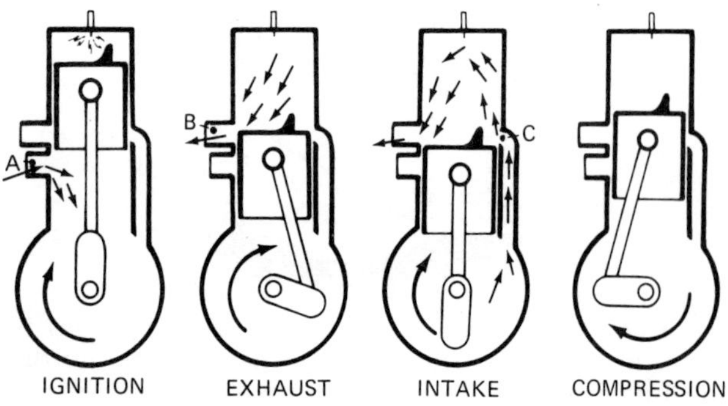

Fig. 4-21. Actions in a three-port, two-cycle engine.

⊘ 4-16 Comparison of Two-Cycle and Four-Cycle Engines The four-cycle engine requires four piston strokes (intake, compression, power, exhaust) to complete one cycle of events. The two-cycle engine does the job in two piston strokes. In the four-cycle engine, only one of every four piston strokes is a power stroke. That is one power stroke for *every two* crankshaft revolutions. In the two-cycle engine, every other piston stroke is a power stroke. That is a power stroke for *each* crankshaft rotation. Figure 4-22 compares the operating cycles of the two types of engines.

You might think that the two-cycle engine is twice as powerful as the four-cycle engine, because it produces twice as many power strokes. This is not so. Here's the reason: In the two-cycle engine, intake and exhaust take place during the same piston stroke. Thus, there is always some mixing of the fresh charge and the burned gases. Not all the burned gases get out, and this prevents a full charge of fresh air-fuel mixture from entering. In addition, only part of a piston stroke is used to draw the air-fuel mixture into the cylinder, so less gets in.

In the four-cycle engine, nearly all the burned gases are forced out of the cylinder by the piston on the exhaust stroke. Also, more air-fuel mixture can then enter. This is because a complete piston stroke is used to get the air-fuel mixture into the cylinder. The result is a more powerful piston stroke. So the power stroke of the two-cycle engine is weaker than the power stroke of the four-cycle engine.

Even though the power stroke of the two-cycle engine is comparatively weak, it is powerful enough for many jobs. Two-cycle engines are widely used as power plants for lawn mowers, motor boats, snow removers, motor scooters, power saws, and other such equipment. These engines are usually air-cooled. Because two-cycle engines have no valve train or liquid cooling system, they are lightweight, simple in construction, and easy to service. These are desirable characteristics for engines on equipment that must be handled and moved about.

⊘ 4-17 Diesel Engines Until now, we have been talking about gasoline engines. All gasoline engines have this in common: The fuel is mixed with air before the air goes into the cylinder. Then the mixture is compressed, and it is ignited by an electric spark at the spark plug.

In the diesel engine, air alone enters the cylinder. The air is compressed and becomes very hot. (The heat results from the compressing and is called *heat of compression*.) Then, as the piston nears TDC

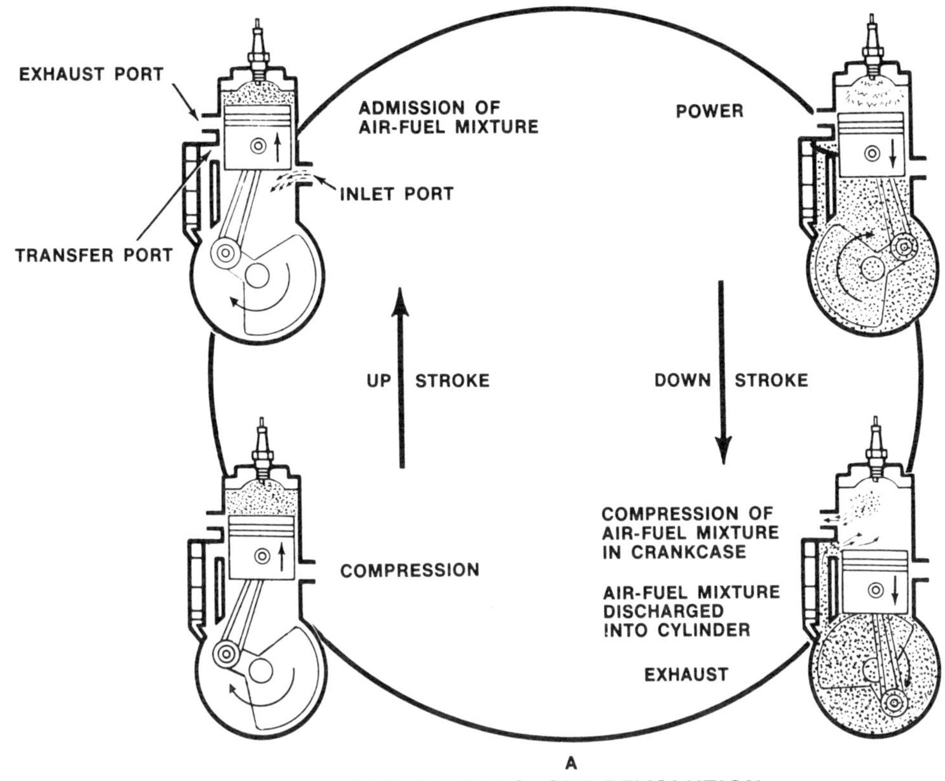

A
TWO STROKES—ONE REVOLUTION

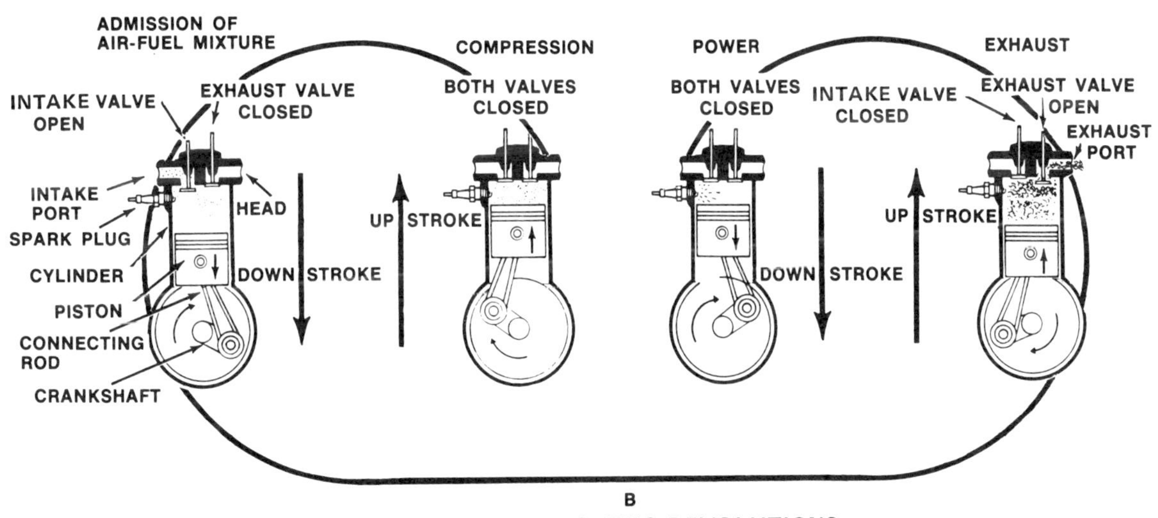

B
FOUR STROKES—TWO REVOLUTIONS

Fig. 4-22. Comparison of the operation of a two-cycle and a four-cycle engine.

on the compression stroke, the fuel is injected, or sprayed, into the compressed air. The air is so hot that it ignites the fuel.

As we said, when air is compressed, it gets hot. The more it is compressed, the hotter it gets. In a diesel engine, the compression ratio may be as high as 21:1. This means that the air is compressed to only $\frac{1}{21}$ of its original volume. This is like compressing a quart into less than one-fourth of a cup (less than 2 fluid ounces [60 cc]). When air is compressed this much, its temperature can go up to 1,000°F [538.7°C]. Water boils at 212°F [100°C], so you can see that 1,000°F [538.7°C] is very hot! This temperature is high enough to ignite the fuel as it is sprayed into the compressed air.

The fuel used in diesel engines is normally a light oil. It is special in several ways. It ignites easily when sprayed into high-temperature air, and it burns cleanly, leaving little residue such as carbon.

There are two-cycle and four-cycle diesel engines, as with gasoline engines. The four-cycle diesel engine requires the usual four piston strokes—

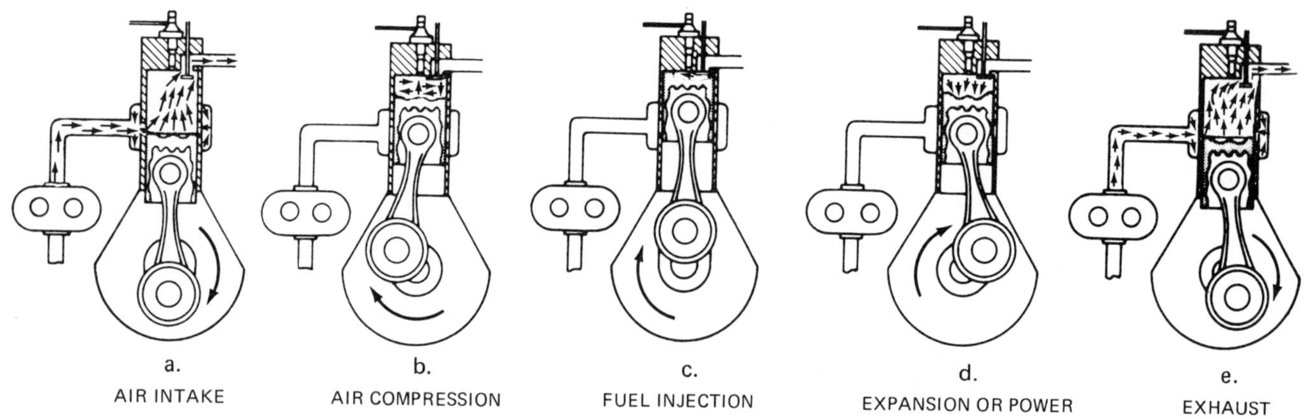

Fig. 4-23. Sequence of events in the two-stroke-cycle diesel engine. (*Detroit Diesel Allison Division of General Motors Corporation*)

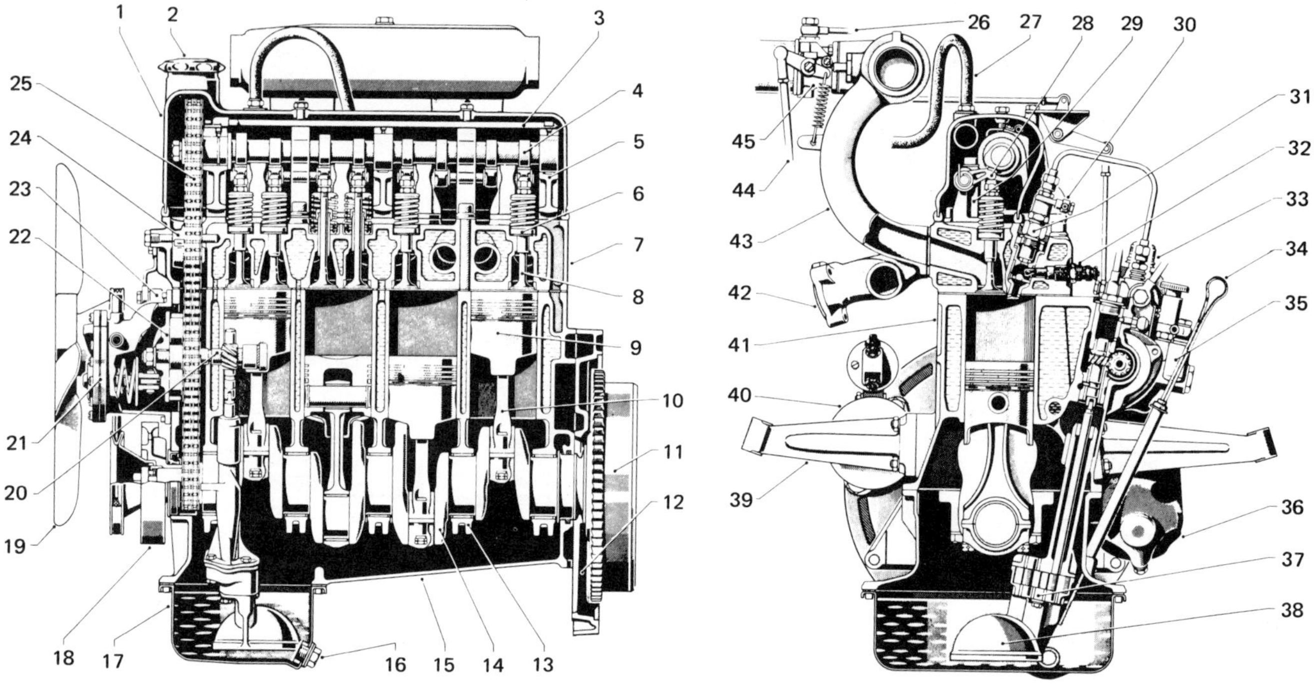

1. Cylinder-head cover
2. Oil-filler neck
3. Oil pipe (camshaft lubrication)
4. Camshaft
5. Camshaft bearing
6. Rotocap (valve turning device)
7. Cylinder head
8. Exhaust valve
9. Piston
10. Connecting rod
11. Flywheel
12. Intermediate flange
13. Crankshaft bearing cover
14. Crankshaft
15. Oil sump, upper part
16. Oil drain plug
17. Oil sump, lower part
18. Counterweight
19. Fan
20. Drive shaft (injection pump—oil pump)
21. Vacuum pump
22. Injection timer
23. Water pump
24. Timing-chain sprocket bearing
25. Double roller chain
26. Vacuum line
27. Breather line
28. Rocker arm
29. Rocker-arm support
30. Fuel-overflow line
31. Injection nozzle
32. Glow plug
33. Injection pump
34. Oil dipstick
35. Fuel-feed pump
36. Oil filter
37. Oil pump
38. Strainer
39. Engine bracket
40. Starter
41. Cylinder crankcase
42. Exhaust manifold
43. Ram manifold
44. Control linkage
45. Mixture controller

Fig. 4-24. Sectional views of a four-cylinder diesel engine for passenger cars. (*Mercedes-Benz*)

intake, compression, power, and exhaust. The main difference between the gasoline engine and the diesel engine is in the way the fuel is put into the cylinder and ignited.

The two-cycle diesel engine uses a blower, or high-pressure air pump, to ensure fast entry of air and fast exit of the exhaust gases. One type of two-cycle diesel engine has a valve in the cylinder head, shown in Fig. 4-23. This is an exhaust valve. Air under pressure is delivered to the cylinder through a series of intake ports in the cylinder wall. This action is shown in Fig. 4-23*a*. As we noted, the air is delivered by an air pump, or blower. As the air pours in, the exhaust valve opens. The fresh air sweeps the burned gases out of the cylinder past the open exhaust valve. Next, as the piston moves up, it closes off the intake ports (Fig. 4-23*b*). Meanwhile, the exhaust valve has closed. The air is compressed; the fuel is sprayed in and ignited (Fig. 4-23*c*); and the power stroke (Fig. 4-23*d*) and the exhaust stroke (Fig. 4-23*e*) follow.

Diesel engines are used mostly in buses and trucks. However, several foreign manufacturers produce passenger cars with diesel engines (Fig. 4-24). Some American manufacturers are planning to produce cars with diesel engines. Stationary diesel engines are also used to drive electric generators and to operate machinery.

⊘ 4-18 Diesel-Engine Fuel System The compressed air in a diesel engine is under high pressure. Thus, the fuel must be at a still higher pressure to be injected into the compressed air. The diesel-engine fuel system includes a high-pressure pump or similar arrangement, to inject the fuel into the cylinders. A variety of systems have been used. In one system, a central high-pressure pump feeds all the cylinders. In another system, a relatively low-pressure pump delivers fuel to injectors at the cylinders. Each injector has a plunger that is operated by a cam on a camshaft. At the proper time, the cam lobe forces the plunger down, and the plunger sprays fuel into the cylinder.

Diesel engines and diesel-engine fuel systems are special. If you get a chance to work on them, you will be given the special instructions required.

⊘ 4-19 Firing Order Another way of classifying piston engines is by their firing order—the order in which the cylinders deliver their power strokes. Engines are designed to deliver the power strokes to the crankshaft in a particular pattern. The pattern ensures that two cylinders close together do not fire one after the other. When an end cylinder fires, the next cylinder to fire should be near the center or the other end of the crankshaft. The power strokes are spread out along the crankshaft to avoid large stresses on any one part of the crankshaft. If two or three nearby cylinders are fired one after the other, the shocks could add and overstress that part of the crankshaft. A proper firing order prevents this.

However, in four-cylinder engines, adjoining cylinders must fire one after another. This is because there are only two reasonable firing orders: 1-3-4-2 and 1-2-4-3. In the 1-3-4-2 firing order, cylinder 1 fires first, followed in order by cylinders 3, 4, and 2. Cylinders are numbered from front to back.

It is easier to keep the power strokes scattered in a six-cylinder in-line engine. Two firing orders used in these engines are 1-5-3-6-2-4 (Fig. 4-25) and 1-4-2-6-3-5.

In both four-cylinder and six-cylinder engines, the cylinders are numbered from front to back. The cylinders in V-8 engines are numbered in various ways. One engine manufacturer numbers them from front to back in this way:

Left bank	*Right bank*
①	②
③	④
⑤	⑥
⑦	⑧

The right bank is the right-hand row as viewed from the driver's seat. The firing order for this engine is 1-8-4-3-6-5-7-2.

NOTE: In almost all engines, the firing order is built in by the manufacturer. It cannot be changed without major engine rebuilding. However, in some engines the firing order can be changed by installing a different camshaft and rewiring the ignition.

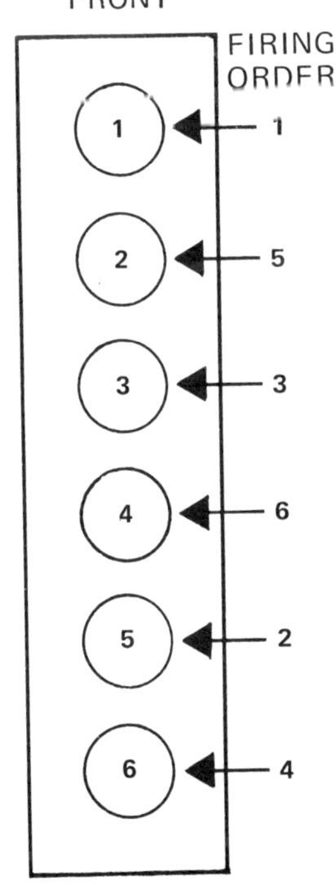

Fig. 4-25. One six-cylinder firing order. The firing order is 1-5-3-6-2-4, which is used on almost all in-line, six-cylinder engines.

Rotary Engines

⊘ 4-20 Rotary Engines Until now, we have been talking about reciprocating engines. These engines have pistons that move up and down, or reciprocate, in cylinders. There is another type of engine, called the *rotary engine,* that has no pistons. Instead, it has a rotor that is spun by the burning of the fuel in the engine. There are two general types of rotary engines: the *gas turbine* and the *Wankel.* We shall look at the gas turbine first.

⊘ 4-21 Gas Turbines Gas turbines are used in some buses and trucks; and some experts say we may never see them used as the main power plant for cars. However, you are probably interested in this kind of engine, and should know how it works. Figure 4-26 is a simplified sectional view of a gas turbine. Figure 4-27 is a cutaway of an actual unit. There are two sections to the gas turbine: the gasifier section, where the fuel is burned, and the power section, where the power from the burned fuel is produced. The turbine can use gasoline, kerosene, or oil for fuel.

The compressor in the gasifier section has an air-intake rotor with a series of blades on it. When the air-intake rotor spins, it acts as an air pump and supplies the burner with high-pressure air (shown by the arrows at the left in Fig. 4-26). In the burner, fuel is sprayed into the compressed air and ignited by a special type of spark plug called an ignitor.) The burned gases then flow, at still higher pressures, through the blades of the gasifier section of the turbine. This causes the turbine rotor to spin. The gasifier turbine rotor is mounted on the same shaft as the

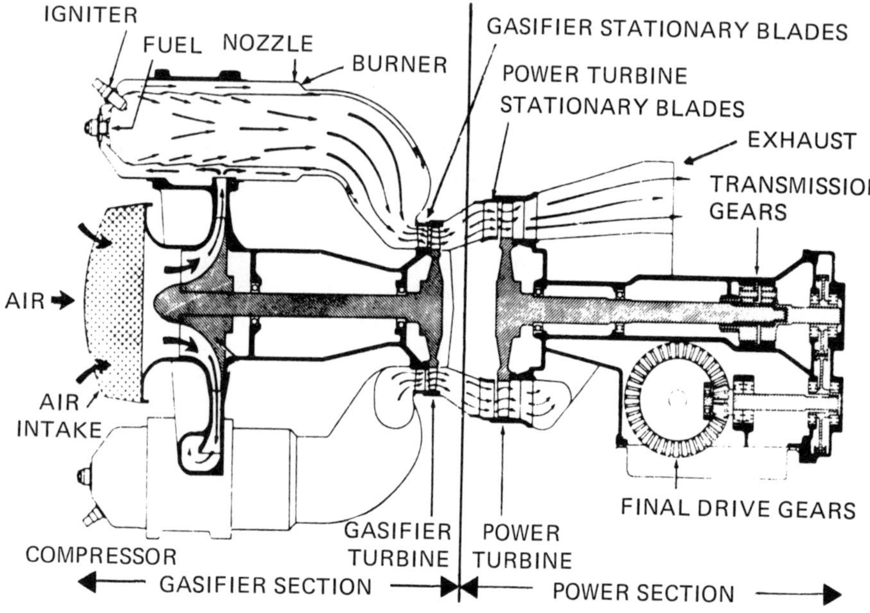

Fig. 4-26. Simplified drawing of a gas turbine. The gasifier section burns fuel and delivers the resulting high-pressure gas to the power section. There, it spins the power turbine. (*General Motors Corporation*)

Fig. 4-27. Cutaway view of a gas turbine. (*Caterpillar Tractor Company*)

air-intake rotor. This shaft spins the air-intake rotor and supplies the burner with compressed air.

After passing through the gasifier section, the burned gases pass through the power section, causing the power-turbine rotor to spin. This rotary motion is carried through shafts and gears to the vehicle's wheels.

⊘ 4-22 Wankel Engine The Wankel engine is new on the automotive scene. It is also called a rotary-combustion, or RC, engine because the combustion chambers rotate, or move in somewhat circular paths. Some engineers say that the Wankel will become a widely used engine in the next few years.

The Wankel engine uses a three-lobe rotor that rotates eccentrically in an oval housing (Figs. 4-28 to 4-30). The three lobes are always in contact with the oval housing, and they form a tight seal (Fig. 4-31). This seal is like the seal formed by the piston rings and the cylinder wall in a reciprocating engine. The rotor is positioned on the crankshaft by external and internal gears.

The four engine actions—intake, compression, power, and exhaust—go on at the same time when the engine is running. However, they take place at different locations around the rotor. Figure 4-32 gives you an idea of how the engine works. The rotor lobes A, B, and C seal tightly against the side of the oval housing. The rotor has recesses in its three faces, between the lobes. The dashed lines on the rotors in Fig. 4-32 show the locations of the recesses and how deep they are. It is in these recesses that combustion actually starts. The spaces between the rotor lobes are where intake, compression, power, and exhaust take place.

Let us follow the rotor around as it goes through a complete cycle—intake, compression, power, and exhaust. At I (upper left), lobe A has passed the

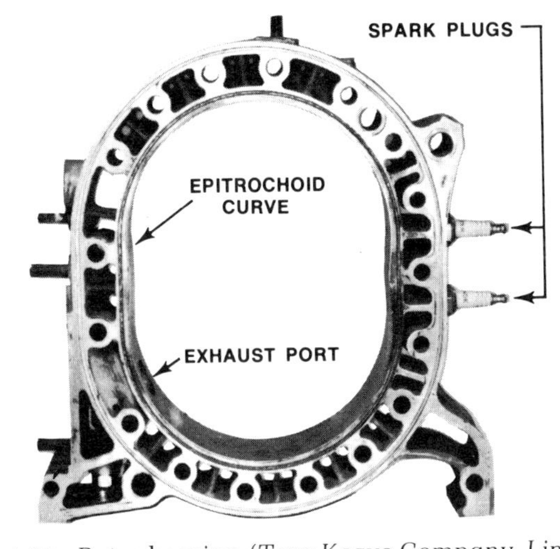

Fig. 4-29. Rotor housing. (*Toyo Kogyo Company, Limited*)

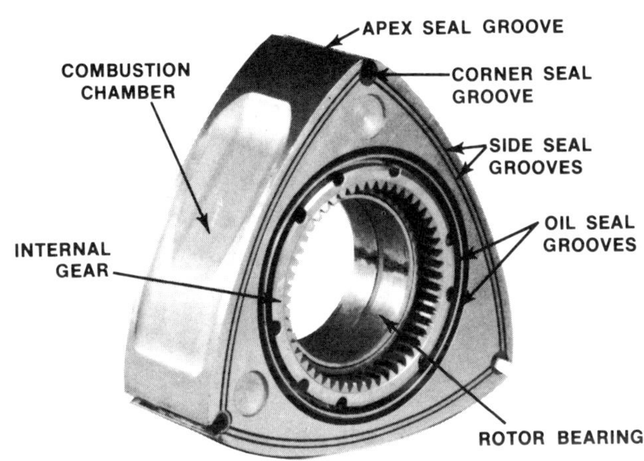

Fig. 4-30. Rotor for a Mazda Wankel engine. (*Toyo Kogyo Company, Limited*)

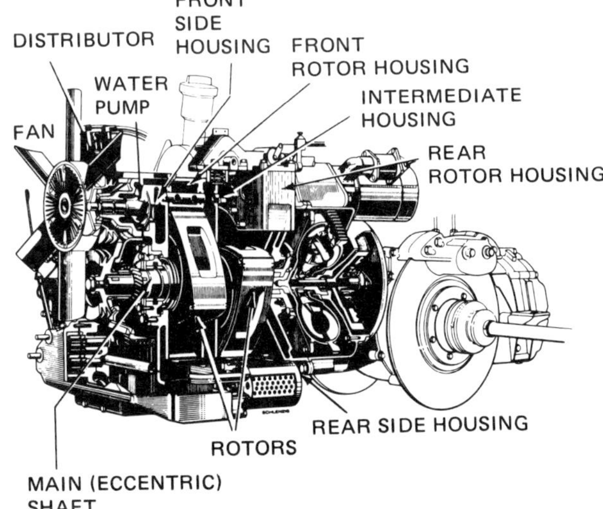

Fig. 4-28. Cutaway view of a two-rotor Wankel engine with attached torque converter and transmission. (*NSU of Germany*)

Fig. 4-31. How the rotor fits into the rotor housing. (*Toyo Kogyo Company, Limited*)

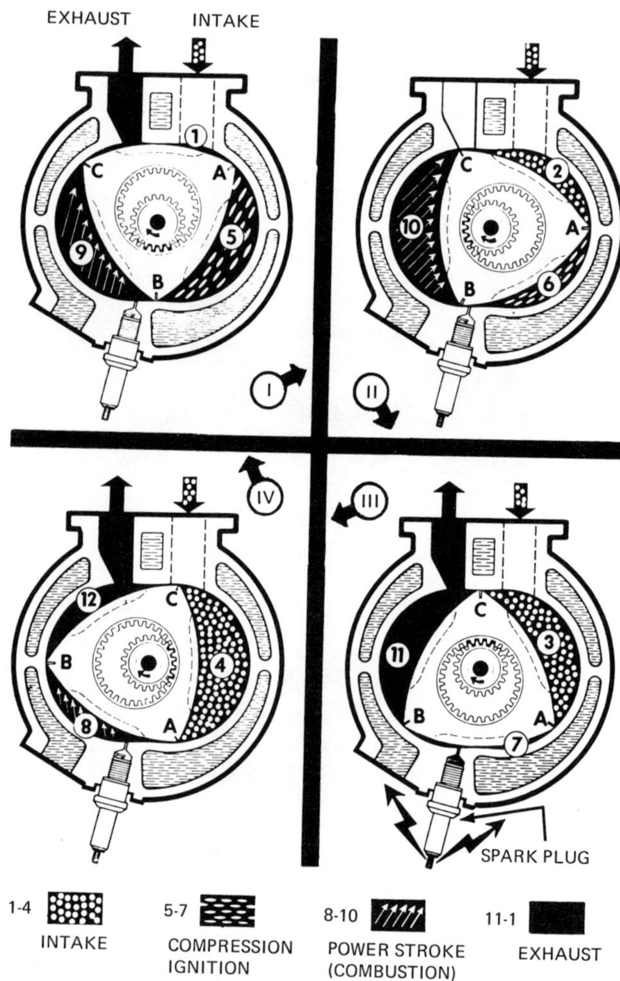

Fig. 4-32. Actions in a Wankel engine during one complete revolution of the rotor.

intake port, and the air-fuel mixture is starting to enter. This is shown by the circled 1. As the rotor moves around (see II at the upper right), the space between lobes A and C increases, as shown by the circled 2. This produces a vacuum, which causes the air-fuel mixture to enter. This action compares with the intake stroke of the piston in a reciprocating engine. At III (lower right), the air-fuel mixture continues to enter as the space between lobes A and C continues to increase. This is shown by the circled 3. Then lobe C starts to move past the intake port, as shown in IV (lower left). Further rotor movement carries lobe C past the intake port, so the air-fuel mixture is sealed between lobes A and C, as shown by the circled 4.

To see what happens to the air-fuel mixture, let us go back to I (upper left) again. Here the air-fuel mixture has been trapped between lobes A and B, as shown by the circled 5. Further rotation of the rotor decreases the space between lobes A and B. By the time the rotor reaches the position shown in III, the space (circled 7) is at a minimum. This action is the same as the piston reaching TDC on the compression stroke in a reciprocating engine. Now the spark plug fires and ignites the compressed mixture. Pressure is exerted on the side of the rotor; this forces the rotor to move around. See IV (lower left). This action is the same as the power stroke in a reciprocating engine.

At IV, the high pressure of the burned air-fuel mixture (circled 8) forces the rotor around to position I again. Continued expansion of the burned gases continues to rotate the rotor until the leading lobe passes the exhaust port. Then the burned gases begin to exhaust from between the lobes, as shown by the circled 11 and 12 in III and IV. As the rotor continues to rotate, the space between the lobes decreases and the gases are exhausted. This action is the same as the exhaust stroke in a reciprocating engine.

Following the exhaust stroke, the leading lobe passes the intake port, and the whole cycle is repeated. Note that there are three lobes and three spaces between the lobes. That means that there are three complete cycles of intake, compression, power, and exhaust going on at the same time. The engine is delivering power almost continuously. In a way, the engine is equivalent to a three-cylinder piston engine. A two-rotor Wankel engine would, then, be equivalent to a six-cylinder piston engine. A leading manufacturer of Wankel and Wankel-powered passenger cars is Toyo Kogyo of Japan. This company has manufactured several hundred thousand Wankel-powered Mazda cars.

Check Your Progress

Progress Quiz 4-1 Here is an opportunity to find out how well you remember the material covered in the last few pages. If a question stumps you, turn back and reread the pages that give you the answer.

Completing the Sentences The sentences that follow are incomplete. After each sentence there are several words or phrases, but only one of them correctly completes the sentence. Write each sentence in your notebook, ending it with the one word or phrase that completes it correctly.

1. The smallest number of cylinders in use in American automobile engines is: (*a*) two, (*b*) four, (*c*) six, (*d*) eight.
2. The most common type of V engine is the: (*a*) V-4, (*b*) V-6, (*c*) V-8, (*d*) V-12.
3. One firing order for six-cylinder engines is: (*a*) 1-3-2-6-5-4, (*b*) 1-4-3-2-6-5, (*c*) 1-5-3-6-2-4, (*d*) 1-2-3-5-4-6.
4. By type of cooling system, engines are classified as: (*a*) air-cooled and liquid-cooled, (*b*) water-cooled and liquid-cooled, (*c*) air-cooled and oil-cooled.
5. Two piston strokes are needed to complete an operating cycle in a: (*a*) four-cycle engine, (*b*) two-cycle engine, (*c*) overhead-camshaft engine, (*d*) V-8 automobile engine.

Lists In the following, you are asked for certain lists. Write the lists in your notebook. The act of writing will help to fix the information in your mind. More than that, you will have the information in your notebook, where you can quickly refer to it.

1. List the various cylinder arrangements given in the book.
2. List the various valve arrangements given in the book.
3. List the differences between the two-cycle and four-cycle engines.
4. List the differences between four-cycle automobile engines and diesel engines.
5. List the differences between air-cooled and liquid-cooled engines.

CHAPTER 4 CHECKUP

NOTE: Since the following is a chapter review test, you should review the chapter before taking the test.

You are making real progress in your study of the automobile engine. The four chapters you have read cover a great deal of necessary background information. This information will be of considerable help to you in the chapters that deal with such practical topics as engine tuneup and tuneup procedures. The following questions will allow you to check how well you remember and understand the facts discussed in this chapter.

Completing the Sentences The sentences that follow are incomplete. After each sentence there are several words or phrases, but only one of them correctly completes the sentence. Write each sentence in your notebook, ending it with the one word or phrase that completes it correctly.

1. The two classifications of engine by cycle are: (*a*) one-cycle and two-cycle, (*b*) two-cycle and three-cycle, (*c*) two-cycle and four-cycle.
2. The two-cycle engine produces a power stroke every: (*a*) crankshaft revolution, (*b*) two crankshaft revolutions, (*c*) four crankshaft revolutions.
3. The two-cycle engine has valve ports in the: (*a*) pistons, (*b*) cylinder walls, (*c*) piston rings.
4. For fuel, diesel engines use: (*a*) LPG, (*b*) gasoline, (*c*) fuel oil.
5. In the diesel engine, fuel is injected into the cylinder at the end of the: (*a*) intake stroke, (*b*) compression stroke, (*c*) power stroke, (*d*) exhaust stroke.
6. In the diesel engine, rapid compression of the air produces an air temperature of about: (*a*) 100°F [37.8°C], (*b*) 1,000°F [537.8°C], (*c*) 2,000°F [1,093.3°C], (*d*) 5,000°F [2,760°C].
7. Compression ratios in diesel engines are as high as: (*a*) 5:1, (*b*) 10:1, (*c*) 15:1, (*d*) 21:1.
8. The two major parts of the gas turbine are the: (*a*) gasifier and combustion sections, (*b*) gasifier and power sections, (*c*) power and turbine sections.
9. A rotary engine you can buy in some cars is the: (*a*) diesel, (*b*) two-stroke, (*c*) Wankel, (*d*) four-stroke.
10. The order in which the cylinders deliver their power strokes is the: (*a*) firing order, (*b*) cylinder numbering, (*c*) valve timing, (*d*) crankshaft rotation.

Questions Here are questions that deal with the types of engines and the differences between them. In your notebook, write the answer to each question in your own words. If you do not know the answer, turn back through the pages in the chapter covering that type of engine. Be sure to refer to the illustrations. It is often said that "a picture is worth a thousand words." Studying the illustrations will help you understand the various engines and how they operate.

1. What is the most usual cylinder arrangement for four-cylinder and six-cylinder engines?
2. In what car is the flat-four engine most widely used?
3. What is the name for the metal shields that direct air around the fins of an air-cooled engine?
4. What causes the coolant to circulate in a liquid-cooled engine?
5. What is the name for the passages through which coolant circulates in liquid-cooled engines?
6. How many piston strokes are needed to complete one cycle in a four-cycle engine?
7. What opens and closes the intake and exhaust ports in the two-cycle engine?
8. Why is the power stroke stronger in a four-cycle engine than in a two-cycle engine?
9. When the air in a diesel-engine cylinder is compressed, how hot does it get?
10. What ignites the fuel in a diesel engine?
11. What are two kinds of rotary engines?
12. What are the two sections in a gas turbine?
13. In a gas turbine, what causes the power turbine to spin?
14. In the Wankel engine, how many lobes does the rotor have?
15. In what way are the two-cycle and Wankel engines similar?

Definitions In the following, you are asked to define certain terms. Write the definitions in your notebook. This will help you remember them. It will also provide you with a place where you can quickly locate the meanings, if you need the information again. If you cannot remember the meaning of a term, look it up in the chapter you have just studied, or in the glossary at the back of the book.

1. What is a diesel engine?
2. Define "fuel injection."
3. What is coolant?
4. Define "rotary engine."
5. What is an eccentric shaft?
6. Define "two-cycle engine."
7. What is a gas-turbine engine?
8. Define "firing order."
9. Define "Wankel engine."
10. What is a flat-four engine?

SUGGESTIONS FOR FURTHER STUDY

If you would like to learn more about diesel engines, you can probably find books about them in your local public or school library. In addition, your automotive instructor may have books or manuals on diesel engines. Find out if a diesel-engine manufacturer has a branch or a dealership in your area. You can probably find out a good deal about diesel engines from the various people who work there. You might also try to visit a local trucking company or a bus system that operates a fleet of diesel-engine vehicles.

chapter 5

SAFETY IN THE SHOP

Shopwork is varied and interesting. The shop is where you learn how to do all sorts of automotive jobs, including adjusting front-end alignment, checking charging systems, pulling an engine from a car and tearing it down, grinding valves, and performing an engine tuneup. Engine tuneup and related automotive service jobs are discussed in this book.

Before you work in the shop, you should know about safety. Safety in the shop means protecting yourself and your fellow workers from possible danger and injury. This chapter describes the rules you should follow in the shop to protect yourself from harm. Remember this: When everybody obeys the rules, the shop is a much safer place than your home! Many more people are hurt in the home than in the shop.

⊘ 5-1 Safety is your Job Safety is your job. In the shop, you are "safe" when you protect your eyes, your fingers, your hands—all of yourself—from danger. And, just as important, when you look out for the safety of those around you.

The rules of safety are listed and discussed in the next few pages. Follow the rules for your protection, and for the protection of your fellow workers.

⊘ 5-2 Shop Layouts The term "shop layout" means the locations of workbenches, car lifts, machine tools, and so on. Shop layouts vary (Fig. 5-1). So the first thing you should do in a shop is find out where everything is located. This includes the different machine tools and the workbenches, car lifts, and work areas. Many shops have painted lines on the floor to mark off work areas. These lines guide customers and workers away from danger zones where machines are being operated. The lines also remind workers to keep their tools and equipment inside work-area lines.

Many shops have warning signs posted around machinery. These signs are there to remind you about safety, and about how to use machines safely. Follow the posted instructions at all times. The most common cause of accidents in the shop is failure to follow instructions.

Fig. 5-1. Typical shop layout. (*Motor Vehicle Manufacturers Association*)

⊘ 5-3 What to Do in Emergencies If there is an accident and someone gets hurt, notify your instructor at once. Your instructor will know what to do. He or she may try first aid, or phone the school nurse, a doctor, or an ambulance. Be very careful in attempting first aid. You must know what you are doing. Trying first aid on an injured person can do more harm than good if it is done wrong. For example, a serious back injury could be made worse if the injured person is moved. On the other hand, quick mouth-to-mouth resuscitation may save the life of a person who has suffered an electric shock. Talk to your instructor if you have any questions about this.

And remember this about fires: The quicker you get at them, the easier it is to control them. But you have to use the right kind of fire extinguisher, and use it correctly. Again, ask your instructor if you have any questions.

⊘ 5-4 Fire Prevention

⊘ 5-4 Fire Prevention Gasoline is used so much in the shop that people forget it is very dangerous if not handled properly. In a closed place filled with gasoline vapor, a spark or lighted match can cause an explosion. Even the spark from a light switch can set off an explosion. So you must always be careful with gasoline. Here are some hints.

Suppose there are gasoline vapors around, because someone spilled gasoline or a fuel line is leaking. Then you should keep the shop doors open or keep the ventilating system going. Wipe up the spilled gasoline at once, and put the rags outside to dry. Never smoke or light cigarettes around gasoline. When you work on a leaky fuel line, carburetor, or fuel pump, catch the leaking gasoline in a container or with rags. Put the soaked rags outside to dry. Fix the leak as quickly as possible. And don't make sparks around the car, for instance by connecting a trouble light to the battery.

Store gasoline in an approved safety container (Fig. 5-2). Never, *never* store gasoline in a glass jug. The jug could be broken and could cause a terrible explosion or fire.

Fig. 5-2. Safety container for gasoline and other flammable substances.

Oily rags can also be a source of fire. They can catch fire without a spark or flame. Oily rags and waste should be put into special closed metal containers where they can do no harm (Fig. 5-3).

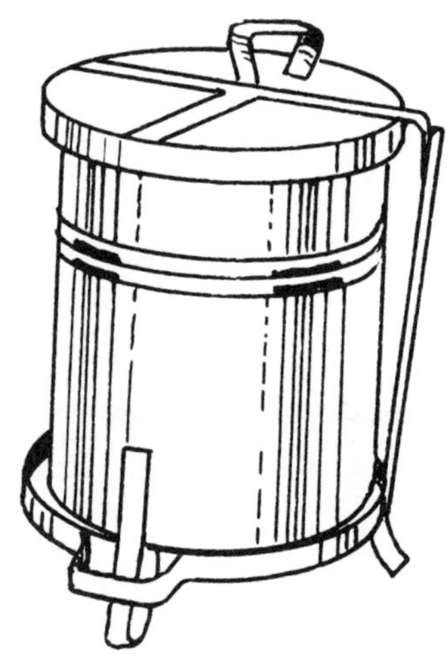

Fig. 5-3. Safety container for oily rags.

⊘ 5-5 The Safety Rules Some people say, "Accidents will happen!" But safety experts do not agree. They say, "Accidents are caused: They are caused by careless actions, by inattention to the job at hand, by using damaged or incorrect tools. And sometimes accidents are caused by just plain stupidity!"

To keep accidents from happening, follow these simple rules:

1. Work quietly, and give the job your full attention.
2. Keep your tools and equipment under control (Fig. 5-4).

Fig. 5-4. Keep your tools within convenient reach, neatly arranged. Do not scatter them around. (*Mercer County Area Vocational-Technical School*)

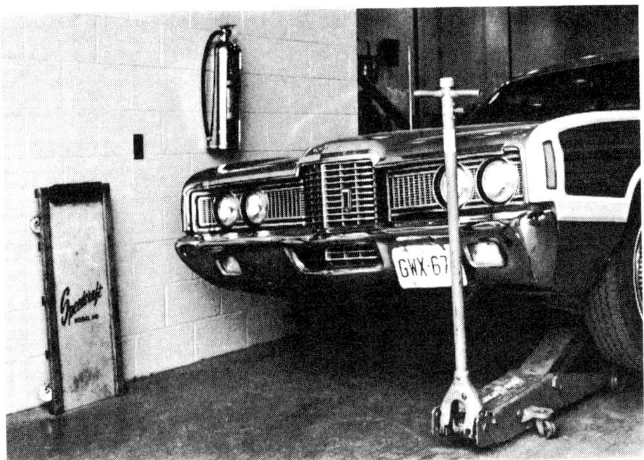
Fig. 5-5. Jack handles should be kept up. Creepers should be stood against the wall, out of the way.

3. Keep jack handles out of the way. Stand creepers against the wall when they are not in use (Fig. 5-5).
4. Never indulge in horseplay or other foolish activities. You could cause someone to get seriously hurt.
5. Don't put sharp objects, such as screwdrivers, in your pocket. You could cut yourself or get stabbed. Or you could ruin the upholstery in a car.
6. Make sure your clothes are right for the job. Dangling sleeves or ties can get caught in machinery and cause serious injuries. Do not wear sandals or open-toe shoes. Wear full leather shoes with nonskid rubber heels and soles. Steel-toe safety shoes are best for shop work. Keep long hair out of machinery by wearing a cap.
7. If you spill oil, grease, or any liquid on the floor, clean it up so that no one will slip and fall.
8. Never use compressed air to blow dirt from your clothes. Never point a compressed-air hose at another person. Flying particles could put out an eye.
9. Always wear goggles or a face shield when there are particles flying about. Always wear eye protection when using a grinding wheel or machine that can throw chips (Fig. 5-6).
10. Watch out for sparks flying from a grinding wheel or welding equipment. The sparks can set your clothes on fire.
11. To protect your eyes, wear goggles when using chemicals, such as solvents. If you get a chemical in your eyes, wash them with water at once. Then see the school nurse or a doctor as soon as possible.
12. When using a car jack, make sure it is centered so that it won't slip. And never, *never* jack up a car while someone is working under it! People have been killed when the jack slipped and fell on them! Always use car stands or supports, properly placed, when going under a car (Fig. 5-7).
13. Always use the right tool for the job. The wrong tool could damage the part being worked on and could cause you to get hurt.

CAUTION: Never run an engine in a closed garage that does not have a ventilating system. The exhaust gases contain carbon monoxide. Carbon monoxide is a colorless, odorless, tasteless, poisonous gas that can kill you! In a closed one-car garage, enough carbon monoxide to kill you can collect in only 3 minutes.

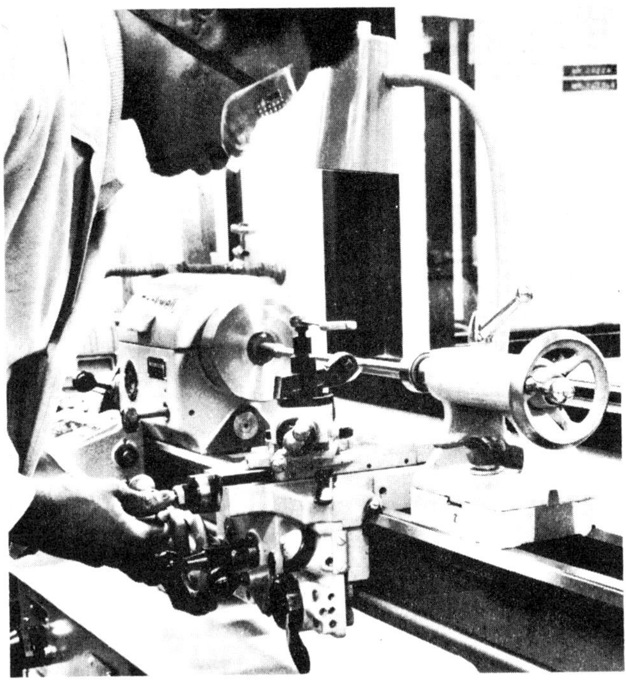
Fig. 5-6. Always wear goggles or a face mask when using a machine that can throw chips or sparks.

Fig. 5-7. Car stands should be properly placed before you go under a car.

⊘ 5-6 Taking Care of Your Tools Tools should be clean and in good condition. Greasy and oily tools are hard to hold and use. Always wipe them off before trying to use them. Do not use a hardened hammer or punch on a hardened surface. Hardened steel is brittle, almost like glass, and may shatter from heavy blows. Slivers may fly out and become embedded in your hand or, worse, in your eye. Use a soft hammer or punch on hardened parts.

⊘ 5-7 Using Power-Driven Equipment A lot of power-driven equipment is used in the automobile shop. The instructions for using any equipment should be studied carefully before the equipment is operated. Hands and clothes should be kept away from moving machinery. Keep your hands out of the way when using any cutting device, such as a drum lathe. Do not attempt to feel the finish while the machine is in operation. There may be slivers of metal that will cut your hands badly. When using grinding equipment, keep your hands away from rotating parts. Do not try to feel the finish with the machine in operation. Sometimes you will work on a device with compressed springs, such as a clutch or valves. Use great care to prevent the springs from slipping and jumping loose. If this happens, the spring may take off at high speed and hurt someone.

Never attempt to adjust or oil moving machinery unless the instructions tell you that this should be done.

⊘ 5-8 Driving Cars in the Shop Cars have to be moved in the shop. They must be brought in for service, and may have to be moved from one work area to another. When the job is finished, they have to be moved out of the work area. You must be extremely careful when you drive a car in the shop. Make sure the way is clear. Make sure no one is under a nearby car. Someone might suddenly stick out an arm or a leg. Make sure there are no tools on the ground that you could run over.

When you take a car out for a road test, *fasten your seat belt*, even though you're going only a short distance.

CAUTION: Always fasten your safety belt in a moving car, whether you are the driver or a passenger. Seat belts save lives. Your seat belt could save yours. Buckle up for safety!

CHAPTER 5 CHECKUP

NOTE: Since this is a chapter review test, you should review the chapter before taking the test.

Safety in the shop is a subject that you cannot know too much about. Every year some people are injured in accidents that happen while they are working on cars. In this chapter, we try to point out some of the danger areas in automobile service work. As you learned from the chapter, you must be very careful when working on, around, and under the car.

Now find out how well you understand safety in the shop by taking the test that follows. If you cannot answer all the questions, or if you are confused about the proper action to take in any situation, study the chapter again. If you still are not sure about something, ask your instructor for further safety instructions.

Completing the Sentences The sentences below are incomplete. After each sentence there are several words or phrases, but only one of them correctly completes the sentence. Write each sentence in your notebook, ending it with the one word or phrase that completes it correctly.

1. Safety in the shop means protecting, from danger or harm, yourself and: (*a*) no one else, (*b*) those around you, (*c*) your boss.
2. One of the most common causes of accidents in the shop is: (*a*) failure to follow instructions, (*b*) following instructions, (*c*) following the wrong instructions.
3. If there is an accident in the shop, you should: (*a*) ignore it, (*b*) notify your parents, (*c*) notify your instructor at once.
4. One liquid that is used so much in the shop that people forget it is very dangerous if not handled properly is: (*a*) engine oil, (*b*) carburetor cleaner, (*c*) gasoline.
5. You should never store gasoline in: (*a*) an approved safety container, (*b*) a glass jug, (*c*) a metal tank.
6. Oily rags must be stored in: (*a*) a closed metal container, (*b*) piles under the workbench, (*c*) the corner of the shop.
7. A compressed-air hose must never be: (*a*) used in the automotive shop, (*b*) pointed at someone else, (*c*) left pressurized overnight, (*d*) kept on a reel.
8. The right time to jack up a car is when: (*a*) someone is working under it, (*b*) never, (*c*) you are working under it, (*d*) no one is working under it.
9. Before you get under a car to work on it, you must be sure that: (*a*) the jack handle is up, (*b*) you use a creeper, (*c*) the tires are inflated, (*d*) the car is supported on stands.
10. Safety goggles should be worn: (*a*) when doing any job that could endanger your eyes, (*b*) when you are told to wear them by the instructor, (*c*) only if you do not wear glasses, (*d*) while welding.

Questions Write each of the following questions, and then the answer, in your notebook. If you have trouble recalling the answer to a question, turn back to the pages that cover the material and study them again.

1. What is "shop safety?"
2. What do the lines painted on the shop floor mean?
3. What should you do if someone nearby is injured in the shop?
4. What is the proper procedure to follow when you walk into a shop and smell a strong odor of gasoline?
5. Explain why horseplay is forbidden in the shop.
6. What dangers are there in using compressed air to blow off your clothes?
7. Describe how to jack up a car properly.
8. Describe the dangers of running an engine in a closed garage.
9. Why must proper clothing be worn in the automotive shop?

Definitions In the following, you are asked for several definitions. Write them in your notebook. The act of writing the definitions does two things: It tests your knowledge, and it helps fix the information more firmly in your mind. Turn back into the chapter if you are not sure of a definition, or look it up in the glossary at the back of the book.

1. Define "safety."
2. What are safety glasses? Goggles?
3. Define "approved safety container."
4. What is carbon monoxide?
5. Define "power-driven equipment."

SUGGESTIONS FOR FURTHER STUDY

Study the various safety charts, posters, and signs placed around the shop. Then make a safety inspection of your shop and your work area. Notice the locations of the fire extinguishers, first-aid kits, telephones, and fire exits. Inspect each fire extinguisher to be sure that it has been checked recently. Make sure the pressure gauge shows it is still charged and ready for use.

chapter 6

ADJUSTING VALVES

Many automotive engines have hydraulic valve lifters, as described in ⊘ 2-15. These generally need no adjustment. However, valve trains using the solid, one-piece valve lifter do require periodic adjustment to compensate for wear of the valve-train parts. When valve-train parts wear, excessive clearances appear in the valve train. This results in tappet noise. This noise is heard as the valve-train parts come together, each time the cam lobe moves under the valve lifter to open the valve. The noise is annoying, and the action can cause increased wear of valve-train parts. Therefore, the clearance should be adjusted to the specified value.

⊘ 6-1 Safety Cautions in Engine Work There are two special cautions you should observe when working on engines that can run:

1. Keep your hands and clothing away from the fan and fan belt. You could be seriously injured by the fan or belt when the engine is running.
2. Avoid touching the hot exhaust manifold. It can give you a nasty burn.

You must, of course, also observe the general safety cautions given in Chap. 5.

⊘ 6-2 Tools and Supplies Needed You will need feeler gauges, basic hand tools, a fender cover, and an oil can filled with light engine oil. You may also need a new valve-cover gasket, if you damage the old one when you remove the valve cover. You should also have the manufacturer's shop manual for the vehicle you are working on. If this is not available, you should look up the specifications in a publication that prints them for all makes of cars.

⊘ 6-3 Adjusting procedure Here is a typical procedure for adjusting the valves on an overhead-valve engine which has mechanical valve lifters. No valve adjustment can be made on many engines equipped with hydraulic valve lifters.

1. Put fender covers on the fenders.
2. Start the engine. Run it at fast idle until it reaches normal operating temperature. Then shut off the engine to make the checks and adjustments.
3. Remove the valve cover. On some engines, the PCV hoses and the air cleaner must be removed first.
4. Make a quick inspection for broken valve springs and valve-stem oil seals. Note the amount of sludge on the cylinder head. Be sure the oil-drain passages in the cylinder head are open.
5. Squirt a liberal amount of light engine oil on all valve stems.
6. Check the manufacturer's service manual for the proper positioning of the crankshaft. Also check which valves to adjust in each crankshaft position. Adjust the valves, following the procedure in the manufacturer's service manual. If the manufacturer's valve-adjusting procedure is not available, the following procedure may be used.
7. Adjust the exhaust valves first (Fig. 6-1). Bump the engine with the starting motor until No. 1 piston is at

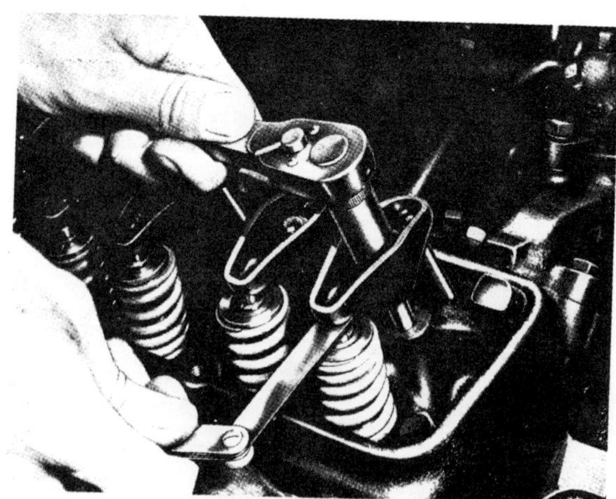

Fig. 6-1. Adjusting valve-tappet clearance on an engine with rocker arms independently mounted on ball studs. Backing the stud nut out increases the clearance. (*Chevrolet Motor Division of General Motors Corporation*)

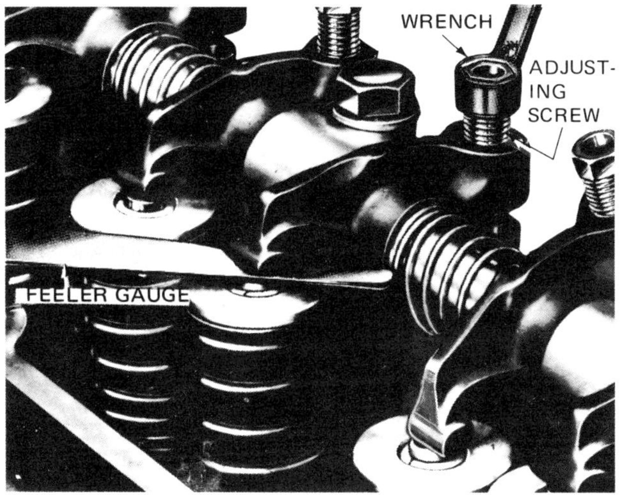

Fig. 6-2. Adjusting valve-tappet clearance on an I-head engine. (*Ford Motor Company*)

TDC on the compression stroke. Adjust the exhaust valve for No. 1 cylinder by inserting a feeler gauge of the specified thickness between the valve stem and the end of its rocker arm. Make the adjustment according to the type of rocker arm (shaft-supported or ball-pivoted).

8. The shaft-supported rocker arm has an adjusting screw at the pushrod end (Fig. 6-2). Back the adjusting screw off enough to allow the gauge to slip in between the valve stem and the end of the rocker-arm.

9. To adjust the screw, first turn it in until the feeler gauge is gripped firmly between the valve stem and the end of the rocker arm. Then back the screw out until the feeler gauge can be moved in and out with a slight drag. The valve-tappet clearance is now properly adjusted.

NOTE: Some rocker-arm adjusting screws are locked in place with a locknut.

10. To adjust the ball-pivoted rocker arm, turn the self-locking nut on the stud. Adjust for the proper clearance between the rocker arm and the valve stem. Figure 6-1 shows the valve clearance being adjusted on this type of rocker arm.

11. Adjust the rest of the exhaust valves in the same manner, following the engine firing order. Remember to first bring each piston to TDC on the compression stroke.

12. Select a feeler gauge of the proper thickness for the intake valves. Adjust the intake valves, following the same procedure.

13. After all the valves are adjusted, replace the valve cover. Use a new gasket if the old one is damaged.

14. Replace the air cleaner and the PCV hoses, if they were removed.

⊘ 6-4 Other Valve Service Jobs There are several other valve service jobs. However, they require special shop equipment, such as a valve-refacing machine (Fig. 6-3) and a valve-seat grinder (Fig. 6-4). For information on these machines and other valve jobs, refer to *Automotive Engines*, another book in the McGraw-Hill Automotive Technology Series.

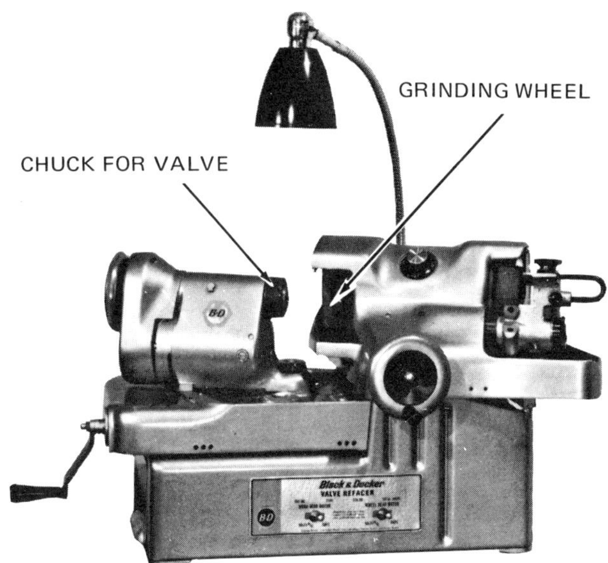

Fig. 6-3. Valve-refacing machine. (*Black and Decker Manufacturing Company*)

Fig. 6-4. Concentric valve-seat grinder. The stone is rotated at high speed. About once every revolution, it is automatically lifted off the valve seat so it can throw off loosened grit and grindings. (*Black and Decker Manufacturing Company*)

CHAPTER 6 CHECKUP

NOTE: Since the following is a chapter review test, you should review the chapter before taking the test.

You are now in the part of the book that is designed to guide you in actual work on automotive engines. Nearly all servicing procedures on modern engines are discussed in this part. You should, of course, remember the essential steps of these procedures. Then, when you are in the shop, you will have a good idea of what to do and why you should do it. The following checkup will give you a chance to see how well you remember the procedures.

Completing the Sentences The sentences that follow are incomplete. After each sentence there are several words or phrases, but only one of them correctly completes the sentence. Write each sentence in your notebook, ending it with the one word or phrase that completes it correctly.

1. To adjust the tappet clearance on the ball-pivot type of rocker arm, you (*a*) turn the adjusting screw, (*b*) turn the adjusting nut, (*c*) install or remove shims, (*d*) grind the end of the valve stem.
2. When adjusting the screw in the rocker arm, you turn it in to get: (*a*) zero clearance, (*b*) a few thousandths clearance, (*c*) tight fit of "go no-go" gauge, (*d*) a clicking noise.
3. To adjust the tappet clearance on the shaft-supported type of rocker arm, you (*a*) turn the adjusting nut, (*b*) grind the end of the valve stem, (*c*) install or remove shims, (*d*) turn the adjusting screw.
4. The adjusting nut used to adjust the ball-pivot type of rocker arm is: (*a*) self-locking, (*b*) locked with a locknut, (*c*) locked with a lockscrew, (*d*) locked with a cotter pin.
5. The adjusting screw used on the shaft-supported type of rocker arm is: (*a*) locked with a cotter pin, (*b*) locked with a lockscrew, (*c*) self-locking or locked with a locknut, (*d*) locked with a rivet.

Service Procedures In the following, you are asked for certain procedures. Write them in your notebook. Do not copy from the book; instead, write each procedure in your own words, just as you would explain it to another person. Give a step-by-step story. This will help you remember the procedures later when you go into the shop. In addition, you will fill your notebook with valuable information to which you can easily refer.

1. Explain how to prepare an engine for a valve-clearance adjustment.
2. Describe how to adjust the valve clearance on an engine with shaft-supported rocker arms.
3. Describe how to adjust the valve clearance on an engine with ball-pivoted rocker arms.
4. Discuss the differences in the valve-clearance adjusting procedures when using a "go no-go" type of feeler gauge.
5. Describe the procedure you followed in checking and adjusting valve-tappet clearance on the I-head engine you are servicing.

SUGGESTIONS FOR FURTHER STUDY

When you are in the engine service shop, keep your eyes and ears open. Learn all you can about how various engine jobs are done. Study the operating manuals supplied by service-equipment manufacturers, to learn how to operate valve-refacing machines, seat grinders, and so on. Also carefully study the shop manuals issued by automobile manufacturers. These manuals supply a great deal of specific information on how to do various service jobs.

Keep a notebook. Jot down every important fact you learn in the shop or when you are reading the manuals. You will find that this helps you remember the facts. At the same time, your notebook will become an increasingly valuable reference for you.

chapter 7

ENGINE LUBRICATING-SYSTEM OPERATION AND SERVICE

All the moving parts in the engine must be lubricated. That is, they must be coated with oil so they can move easily, without actual metal-to-metal contact. If moving metal parts contact and rub against each other, they wear very rapidly and soon fail. Figure 7-1 shows the metal parts of a V-8 engine that require lubrication. (Only one piston and rod and one set of valves are shown. To show them all would clutter up the picture.) The engine lubricating system floods the engine parts with oil to keep them properly lubricated.

⊘ 7-1 Engine Oil Before we explain the lubricating system, let's take a look at oil. Oil is the liquid used in the lubricating system. Oil was formed underground, millions of years ago, in locations around the world. To get the oil, deep holes—wells—must be drilled into underground pools of "crude" oil. Then the crude oil must be refined before it can be used. In the refining process, gasoline, kerosene, lubricating oil, and many other petroleum products are made.

All lubricating oil is not the same. There are several grades of oil, and several ratings. Oil made for automobiles contains a number of *additives* (chemical compounds that are *added* to the oil). The additives improve the performance of the oil. Let's take a look at these ratings and additives.

⊘ 7-2 Oil Viscosity and Service Ratings Viscosity refers to the ability of a liquid to flow. An oil with high viscosity is very thick and flows slowly. An oil with low viscosity flows easily. Oil gets thicker as it becomes colder. The cold increases the viscosity of the oil. Therefore, starting a car in cold weather is more difficult than starting it in warm weather.

Oil viscosity is rated in two ways by the Society of Automotive Engineers (SAE). It is rated for (1) winter driving and (2) summer driving. Winter oils come in three grades: SAE5W, SAE10W, and SAE20W. The "W" stands for winter grade. For other than winter use, the grades are SAE20, SAE30, SAE40, and SAE50. The higher the number, the higher the viscosity (the thicker the oil). All these grades apply to single-viscosity oils.

Some oils have multiple-viscosity ratings. For example, SAE10W-30 oil has the same viscosity as SAE10W oil when it is cold, and the same viscosity as SAE30 oil when it is hot.

Car manufacturers specify the viscosity of the oil to be used in their engines. For example, a recent Ford shop manual recommended the following:

MULTIPLE-VISCOSITY OILS

OUTSIDE TEMPERATURE CONSISTENTLY	USE SAE VISCOSITY
Below 32°F [0°C]	5W-30*
−10°F to 90°F [−23.3°C to 32.2°C]	10W-30
−10°F to above 90°F [−23.3°C to above 32.2°C]	10W-40
Above +10°F [−12.2°C]	20W-40

*For sustained high-speed driving, use 10W-30 or 10W-40.

If you study the table, you will see that the higher the outside temperature, the higher the specified viscosity rating. The 10W-30 oil, for example, is good for starting and driving in very low outside temperatures. It works very well in outside temperatures consistently around 90°F [32.2°C]. If higher temperatures are expected, 10W-40 oil should be used because it holds its viscosity in the higher temperatures. In other words, 10W-40 oil does not thin out too much when it heats up.

The service rating of an oil indicates the type of service for which it is best suited. For gasoline engines the service ratings are SA, SB, SC, SD, and SE. Here is a brief description of each of these ratings:

- SA Acceptable for engines operated under the mildest conditions
- SB Acceptable for minimum-duty engines operated under mild conditions
- SC Meets requirements of gasoline engines in 1964–1967 model passenger cars and trucks

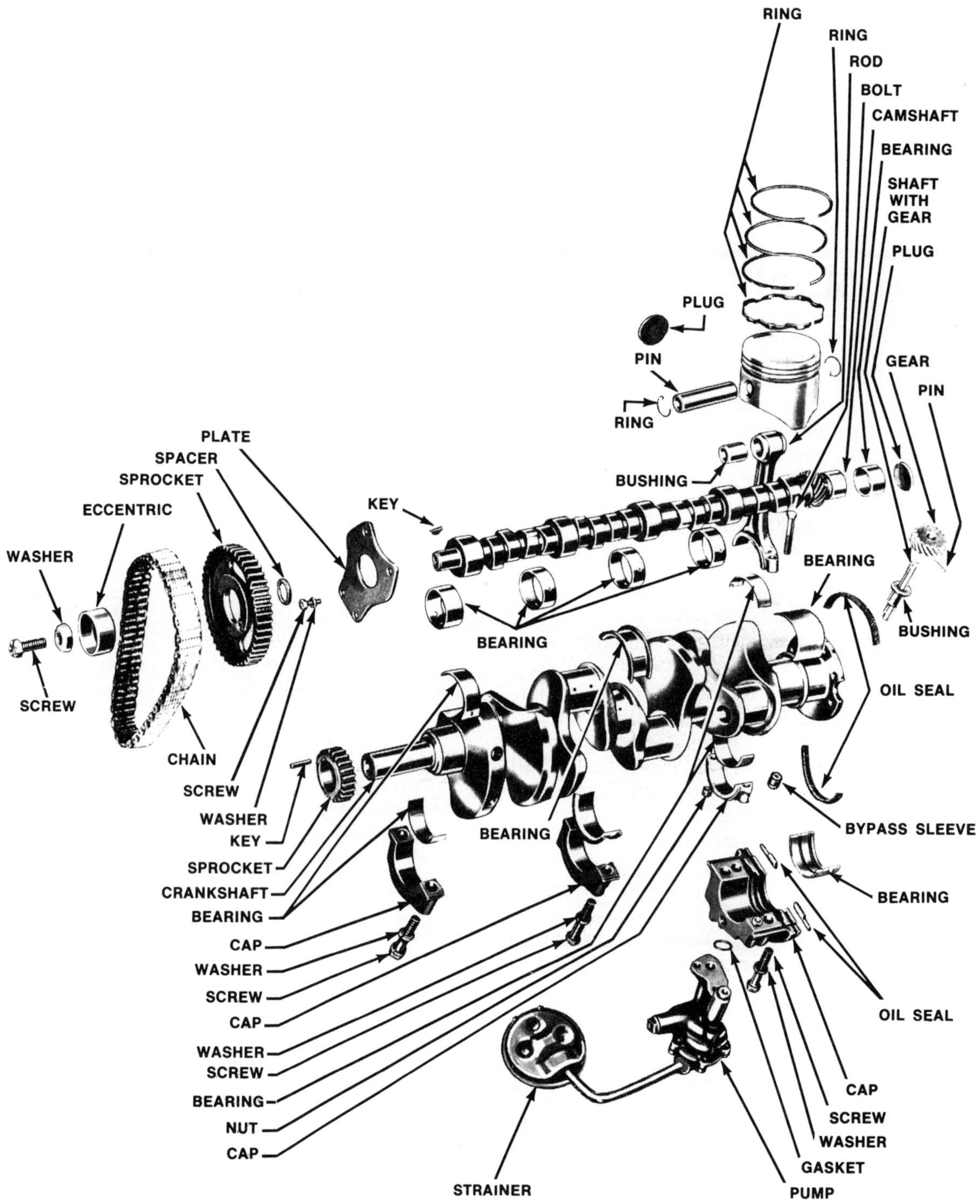

Fig. 7-1. These are the moving parts in a V-8 engine that must be lubricated. (*Chrysler Corporation*)

SD Meets requirements of gasoline engines in 1968–1970 model passenger cars and some trucks

SE Meets requirements of gasoline engines in 1972 and later cars and certain 1971 model passenger cars and trucks

Notice that this is an "open-end" series. That is, if car manufacturers and oil producers see the need for other types of oil, they can bring out oils rated SF, SG, and so on.

Diesel engines require different types of oils; they are service-rated CA, CB, CC, and CD. CD oil is for diesel-engine operation under the most severe conditions.

⊘ 7-3 Oil Additives We mentioned that chemical compounds, called *additives*, are added to engine oil. These additives give the oil certain properties that it does not have in its original refined state. The refining process determines the viscosity and other basic properties of the oil. The additives give the oil other desirable properties. Let's take a look at the additives and what they do.

1. *VISCOSITY IMPROVER* The viscosity improver reduces the tendency of the oil to thin out as it gets hot. Without this additive, oil might become too thin for high-temperature operation. For example, let's look at a 10W oil that does not contain this additive. Ford says that this oil can be used when the outside temperature is consistently between −10°F and +32°F [−23.3°C and 0°C]. The oil would not be safe for high-temperature, high-speed operation because it might thin out too much. However, a 10W-40 oil (improved-viscosity type) could be used in outside temperatures of −10°F to 90°F [−23.3°C to 32.2°C].

The multiple-viscosity oils are obtained by adding a viscosity improver.

2. *POUR-POINT DEPRESSANTS* Pour-point depressants help prevent the oil from getting too thick at low temperatures. These additives keep the oil flowing at low temperatures. In other words, they depress the tendency of the oil to thicken.

3. *INHIBITORS* Inhibitors help prevent oil and lubricating-system troubles. Several inhibitors are used in engine oil. Some fight corrosion and rust. Others fight oxidation of the oil. Oil oxidation takes place because, at fairly high temperatures, the oil is constantly agitated, or stirred up, in the engine crankcase. The crankcase is the space (between the cylinder block and oil pan) in which the crankshaft rotates. The oil does not get hot enough to burn. But it does get hot enough to react with oxygen in the air. When this happens, oxidation occurs. Oil oxidation results in the formation of compounds that are harmful to the engine. One compound formed by oil oxidation is a sticky, tarlike material called sludge that can clog oil lines. It also causes valves and piston rings to hang up and not work properly. Another compound formed by oil oxidation is similar to varnish. This compound can also cause trouble in the engine.

Another oil additive—an antifoaming compound—helps to prevent the oil from foaming. As oil is stirred up in the crankcase, by the rotating crankshaft, the oil tends to foam. The action is the same as an egg beater causing egg whites to foam. Foaming prevents normal oil circulation and results in loss of lubrication and engine damage.

4. *DETERGENT-DISPERSANTS* A detergent is similar to soap. When you wash your hands with soap, the soap surrounds and loosens the particles of dirt. You can then rinse off the dirt with water. Similarly, the detergent in the oil loosens particles of carbon, gum, and dirt on engine parts. The oil carries them away. Some of the particles drop to the bottom of the crankcase, where they are drained away when the oil is changed. Other particles are trapped in the oil filter.

The dispersant action *disperses*, or scatters, the particles. This prevents the particles from clotting, or forming clumps, which could clog oil passages and bearings.

5. *EXTREME-PRESSURE COMPOUNDS* Today's engines are built with heavy valve springs that put a lot of pressure on the valve-train parts. Combustion pressures are also higher. The extreme-pressure compounds added to oil help to resist the very high pressures between engine parts. Extreme-pressure additives fight "squeezing out" by furnishing lubrication even under extreme pressures.

⊘ 7-4 Purpose of Engine Oil Oil flows onto the engine parts and forms slippery layers that prevent metal-to-metal contact. Figure 7-2 gives you an idea of how the oil works. The picture shows two surfaces, highly magnified. If you looked at a very "smooth" metal part (such as a crankpin) under a microscope, you would see tiny rough edges sticking up from the surface. If two such surfaces rub against each other, without oil, the irregular edges catch each other. The rough particles of metal are worn off, but this requires a considerable push and, hence, wastes power.

What is worse is that the rubbing and tearing action (that is, the friction) produces heat. When you rub your hands together very fast and hard, they get warm. Imagine what would happen in the engine if it ran without oil. Metal parts would be rubbing against each other with hundreds, even thousands, of pounds of pressure. Without oil, these parts would quickly get so hot that the metal would melt. The whole engine would become a pile of junk.

The oil prevents this by covering the metal surfaces, as shown in Fig. 7-2. Thin layers of oil keep the metal surfaces away from each other. So only the oil layers touch as the metal parts move. The oil thus greatly reduces power loss and wearing of moving metal parts. The oil does other jobs as well.

⊘ 7-5 Other Jobs for Oil Besides reducing friction and wear, engine oil does the following jobs:

1. Removes heat from the engine
2. Absorbs shocks between bearings and other engine parts

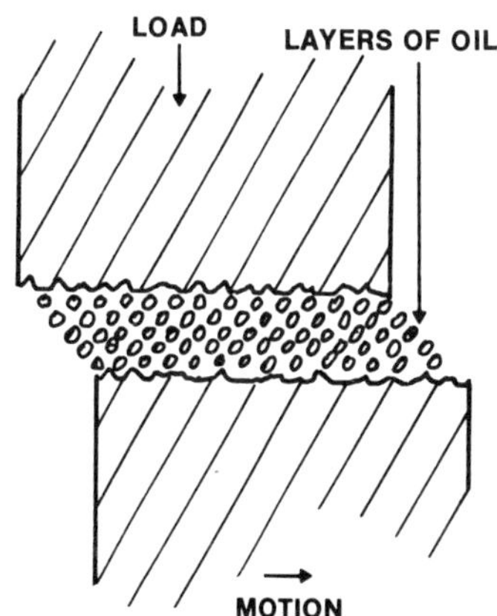

Fig. 7-2. These two highly magnified surfaces show irregularities that you could not see without a microscope. When the surfaces move relative to each other, the layers of oil prevent metal-to-metal contact.

3. Forms a seal between the piston rings and the cylinder wall.
4. Acts as a cleaning agent

Let's look at each of these in detail.

⊘ 7-6 Removing Heat Engine oil is pumped up from the oil pan at the bottom of the engine, through various oil passages, to the moving engine parts. As the oil circulates through the engine, it gets hot. That is, it takes heat out of the engine. Then the oil flows back down into the oil pan. The oil pan is much cooler than the engine. It is below the engine and in the path of air sweeping under the moving car. The hot oil therefore loses heat to air passing under the oil pan. The cooled oil then recirculates between the engine and the oil pan. It thus continues to take heat away from the engine. This helps keep the engine cool.

⊘ 7-7 Oil Coolers In some high-performance engines, the oil does not lose enough heat in the oil pan. Because these engines require additional cooling, a separate radiator, or heat exchanger, is used. The heat exchanger is similar to the radiator used in the engine cooling system. It has a series of passages through which the hot oil can flow. It has another series of passages through which coolant from the engine cooling system can flow. The coolant picks up heat from the oil, thus cooling the oil. The heated coolant then passes through the engine cooling-system radiator. There, it gives up its heat to air passing through the radiator. Meanwhile, the cooled oil returns to the engine.

In other engines, a small section of the engine radiator is used to cool the engine oil. Engine oil flows through this small section of the radiator, where it is cooled by the air passing through.

⊘ 7-8 Absorbing Shocks The layers of oil between moving engine parts help to absorb shocks. For example, consider the bearing in the big end of the connecting rod. This bearing rests on a crankpin of the crankshaft. When the compressed air-fuel mixture ignites, a load of up to 4,000 lb [1,814 kg] is suddenly put on the rod. This load is carried through the rod bearing to the crank journal. The only thing that prevents metal-to-metal contact is a layer of oil between the bearing and the journal. The layer of oil resists "squeezing out." It acts as a cushion between the parts, to absorb the sudden shock of the combustion load (see Fig. 7-3).

⊘ 7-9 Forming a Seal Between Rings and Wall The cylinder walls are covered with oil. (We shall explain later how the oil gets on the cylinder walls.) The oil on the cylinder walls lubricates the piston rings as they slide up and down. If you put a drop of oil between your finger and thumb, you can feel how slippery it is. But notice, also, how sticky it is. Note how the oil tends to resist your attempts to separate your finger and thumb. It is this "stickiness" that allows the oil to form a seal between the piston rings and the cylinder wall. The layer of oil on the cylinder wall fills in all irregularities so that there is a good seal.

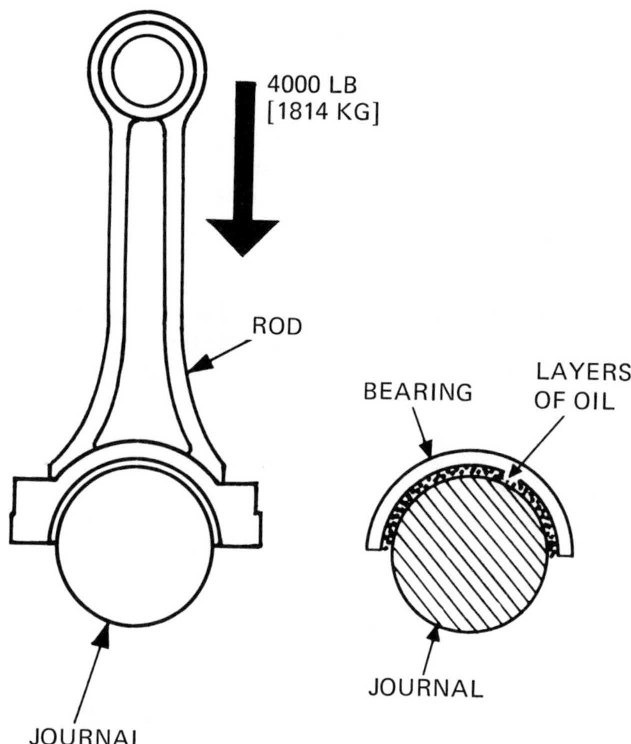

Fig. 7-3. The layer of oil between the bearing and the journal acts as a cushion. It absorbs the sudden shock of the load as combustion takes place.

⊘ 7-10 Acting as a Cleaning Agent The oil circulates through the engine and then flows back down into the oil pan. As the oil passes through the engine, it picks up particles of carbon, metal, and dirt. The oil carries all these particles back down to the oil pan. The larger particles fall out. Smaller particles are filtered out by the oil filter.

Engine Lubricating Systems

⊘ 7-11 Oil Pump The main purpose of an engine lubricating system, no matter what type, is to get engine oil to all the moving parts in the engine. The oil pump does this job. It sits in the engine oil pan and pumps oil from the pan up to the engine parts. In Chap. 4 there are several cutaway pictures of engines, showing the location of the oil pump and the gears that drive it. Figure 7-4 is a simplified drawing of a lubricating system used in a V-8 engine. Near the bottom is a pair of gears. The gears represent the oil pump.

The pump sends oil from the oil pan through the oil filter, as shown by the arrows. We explain the oil

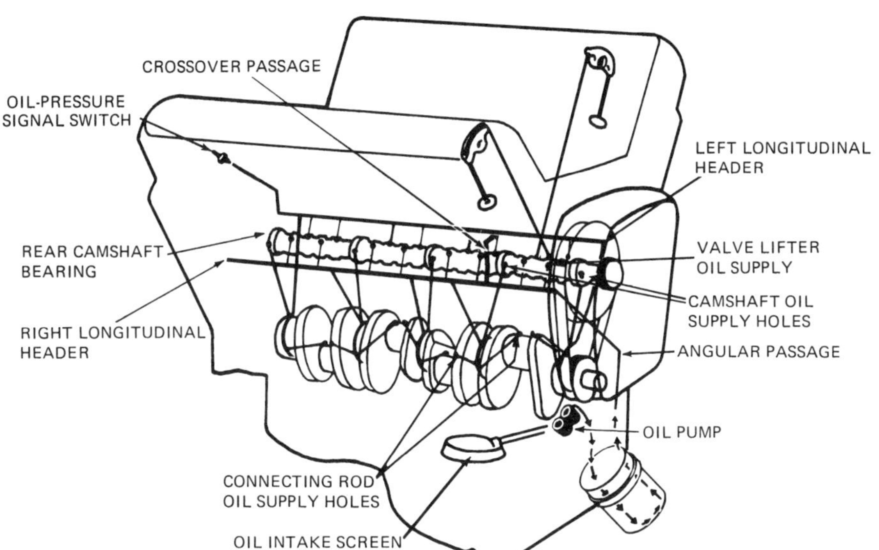

Fig. 7-4. Simplified drawing of the lubricating system for a V-8 engine.

filter later. The oil then passes through oil lines to the crankshaft bearings, camshaft bearings, valve lifters, pushrods, rocker arms, and valves. These circuits are shown by lines in the picture. Then the oil drains off and flows back down to the oil pan.

⊘ 7-12 Oil-Pump Operation The two common types of oil pumps are the gear-type pump and the rotor-type pump. We discuss the gear type first. This type of oil pump is driven by a pair of spiral gears (Fig. 2-15). In the arrangement shown, the spiral driving gear is on the end of the engine camshaft. This gear drives a spiral gear on the ignition-distributor shaft. The oil-pump shaft, which is an extension of the distributor shaft, drives the oil pump.

As the gears are turned in the oil pump, the drive gear drives the driven gear (Figs. 2-15 and 7-5). The spaces between the gear teeth are filled with oil from the oil inlet of the pump. As the gear teeth mesh, the oil is forced out through the oil outlet. Figure 7-5 is a disassembled view of a gear-type oil pump. Larger dirt particles are screened out by a pickup screen, which is submerged in the oil.

The other type of oil pump used in engines is the rotor type. It has a pair of rotors, as shown in Fig. 7-6.

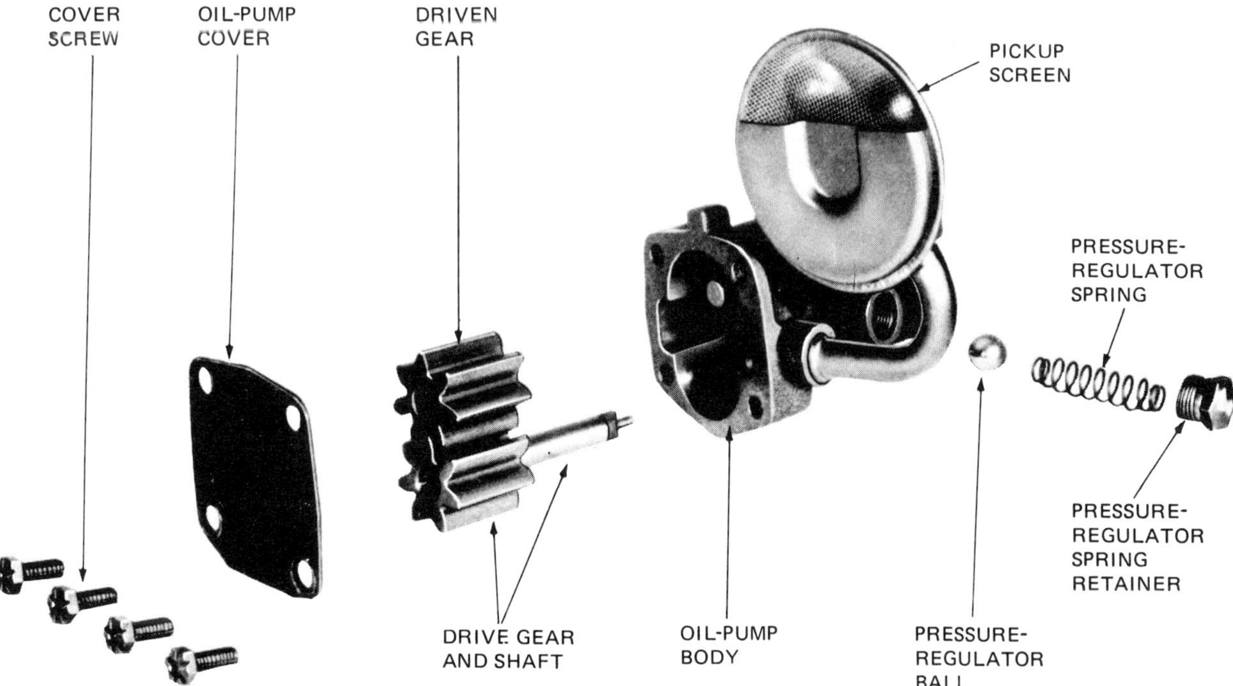

Fig. 7-5. Disassembled view of a gear-type oil pump. (*Pontiac Motor Division of General Motors Corporation*)

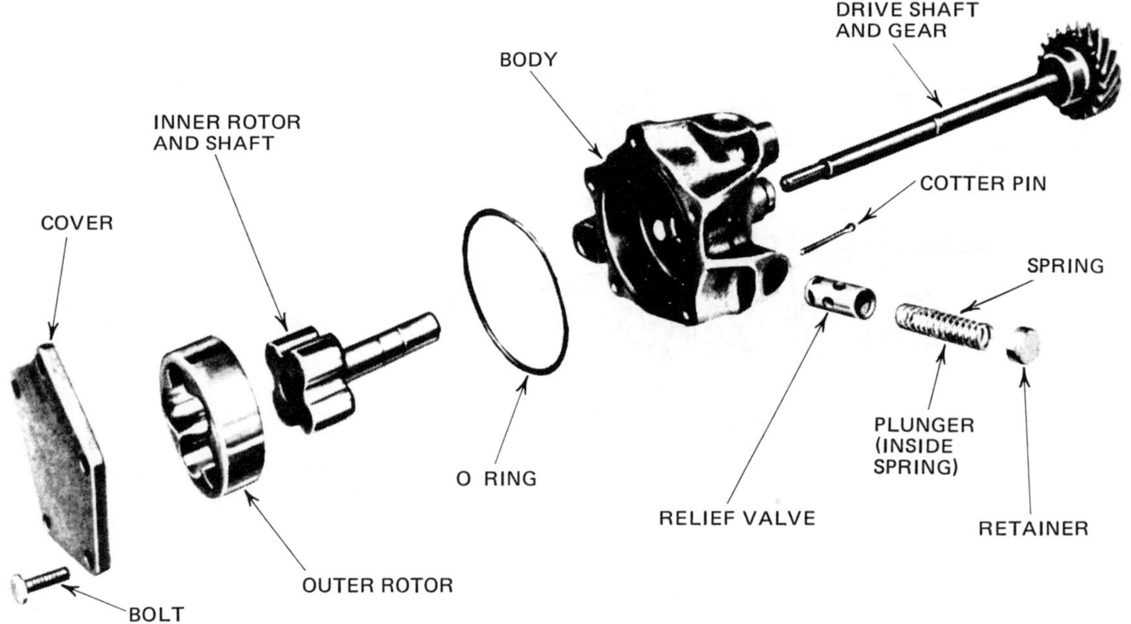

Fig. 7-6. Disassembled view of a rotor-type oil pump. (*Chrysler Corporation*)

The inner rotor has four lobes. The outer rotor has four recesses into which the four lobes fit. The outer rotor is offset so that, on one side, there is space between the lobes of the inner rotor and the recesses of the outer rotor. The inner rotor is driven by the camshaft. As the inner rotor turns, it forces the outer rotor to turn. The spaces between the lobes and the recesses fill with oil from the oil inlet. Then, as the lobes move into the recesses, the oil is forced out through the pump outlet.

⊘ 7-13 Relief Valves The faster an engine runs, the faster the gears or rotors turn in the oil pump. This means that the oil pressure could become very high. To prevent excessive pressure, oil pumps contain a relief valve. This valve contains a ball (Fig. 7-5) or a plunger (Fig. 7-6), which is held in place by a spring. When the pressure starts to get too high, the ball or the plunger is pushed back against the spring tension. This opens up a relief hole, which allows part of the oil to flow back down into the oil pan. Thus the pressure is relieved so it does not go too high.

⊘ 7-14 Oil Filters Oil leaving the oil pump must pass through an oil filter before it goes up to the engine. The oil filter is the engine's protection against dirt. The filter removes particles of carbon and dirt. This keeps them out of the engine, where they could damage engine bearings and other parts. The filter contains a filtering element made of pleated paper or fibrous material. As the oil passes through the filter, the paper or fiber traps the dirt particles.

Figure 7-7 is a cutaway view of a filter. The filter element is housed in a replaceable can. The entire filter is discarded when the element becomes clog-

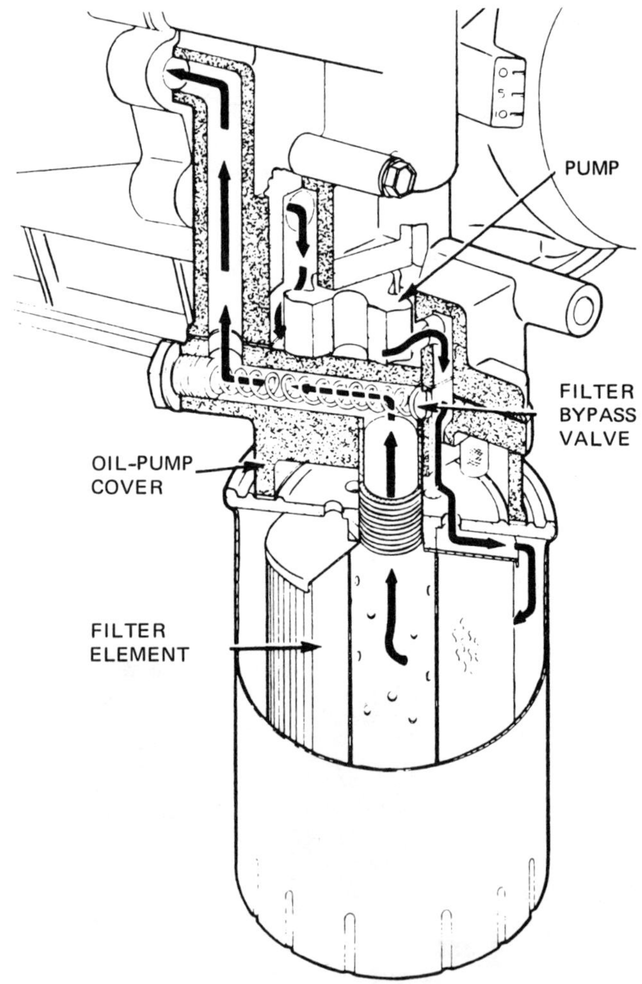

Fig. 7-7. Cutaway view of a full-flow oil filter with bypass valve. (*Buick Motor Division of General Motors Corporation*)

ged with dirt. The filter has a bypass relief valve, which consists of a spring-loaded ball. If the filter element becomes so clogged that sufficient oil cannot pass through the filter, the increased pressure in the filter causes the valve to open. This allows oil from the pump to bypass the filter and go directly to the engine.

Of course, the filter element should be replaced before it stops working properly. Car manufacturers recommend that oil filters be replaced periodically. A typical recommendation is to replace the filter every *other* time the oil is changed (see ⊘ 7-22).

⊘ 7-15 Oil-Pressure Indicators Every car is equipped with some means of showing the driver the oil pressure in the engine. If the pressure drops too low, the engine is not being properly lubricated. Continued operation at low oil pressure will ruin the engine. Thus, the driver must be warned of low pressure so that the car can be serviced at once.

There are two general types of oil-pressure indicators. In one, a dial on the car instrument panel shows the oil pressure. In the other, a light comes on if the oil pressure drops too low.

⊘ 7-16 Oil-Level Indicators A dipstick is used to check the level of the oil in the oil pan (Fig. 7-8). To use the dipstick, pull it out, wipe it off, and put it back in place. Then pull it out again and check the level of the oil shown on the dipstick.

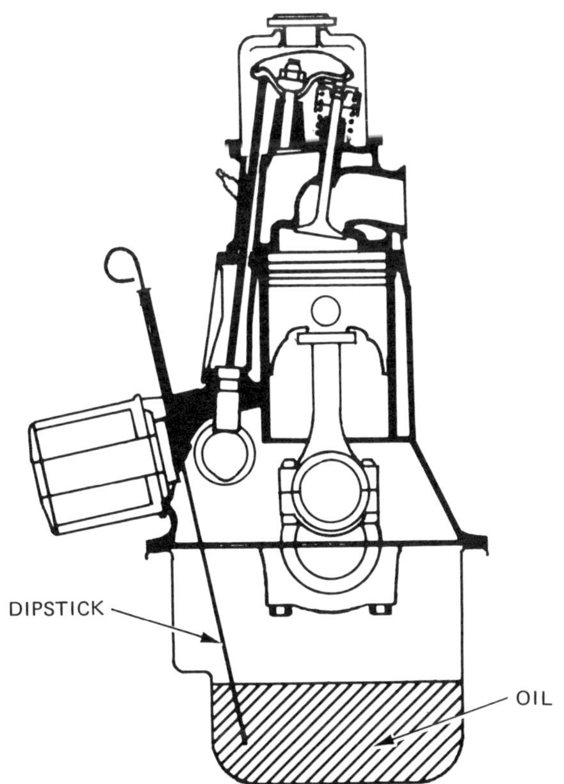

Fig. 7-8. Location of the oil-level stick, or dipstick, in the engine.

NOTE: In the positive crankcase ventilating (PCV) system used in modern engines, the dipstick has a seal to prevent crankcase gases from escaping through the dipstick tube.

⊘ 7-17 How the Engine Lubricating System Works Figure 7-9 shows the circuits through which oil gets to the parts of a V-8 engine. Let's examine this picture in detail. Start at Fig. 7-9*a*, which is a cutaway view of the engine from the side. Oil is picked up from the oil pan by the oil pump. The oil is sent through the oil filter (shown in Fig. 7-9*d*), and then to an oil passage that branches off into two parts. One part directs oil to the crankshaft; the other part sends oil to the valve trains.

The oil sent to the crankshaft lubricates (1) the main bearings in which the crankshaft turns, (2) the connecting-rod bearings, (3) the camshaft bearings, and (4) the cylinder walls. Let's see how the oil gets to all these parts.

In the engine shown in Fig. 7-9, the oil enters an oil gallery (or passage) drilled in the cylinder block. From there, it flows to the crankshaft bearing supports. These supports are ribs in the bottom of the cylinder block (see Fig. 7-10). The oil flows through holes drilled in these bearing-support ribs and through holes in the bearings to reach the crankshaft main journals. Rotation of the journal carries the oil around to the lower bearing half. Thus the entire bearing is lubricated. Oil flows from the center of the bearing to the edges, where it drops off and returns to the oil pan. This action not only oils the bearings, but also cleans them. That is, the oil carries away any dirt particles trapped between the crankshaft journal and the bearing.

Part of the oil flowing to the bearing takes an additional circuit. It goes through holes drilled in the crankshaft to reach the connecting-rod bearings. A crankshaft with holes drilled in it is shown in Fig. 7-11. Every time the hole in the crankshaft main journal passes the hole in the main bearing, a spurt of oil flows through the drilled hole to the crankpin. The oil flows over the crankpin to lubricate the connecting-rod bearing. The oil flows out from the center to the edges of the bearing and then drops back into the oil pan. Here, too, the oil lubricates and cleans.

Some of the oil has still not finished its trip through the engine. In many engines, oil thrown off the connecting-rod bearings covers the cylinder walls. There, it provides lubrication for the pistons, piston rings, and piston pins (see Fig. 7-9*c*).

Some engines ensure adequate lubrication of the pistons, piston rings, and piston pins by means of *spit holes* in the connecting rod. Some of the oil feeding through the crankshaft holes to the connecting-rod bearings spurts through these spit holes and onto the cylinder walls. You can see this action in Fig. 7-12. Oil spurts out every time the hole in the connecting rod aligns with the hole in the crankpin. This supplies the pistons, piston rings, and piston pins with the oil they need.

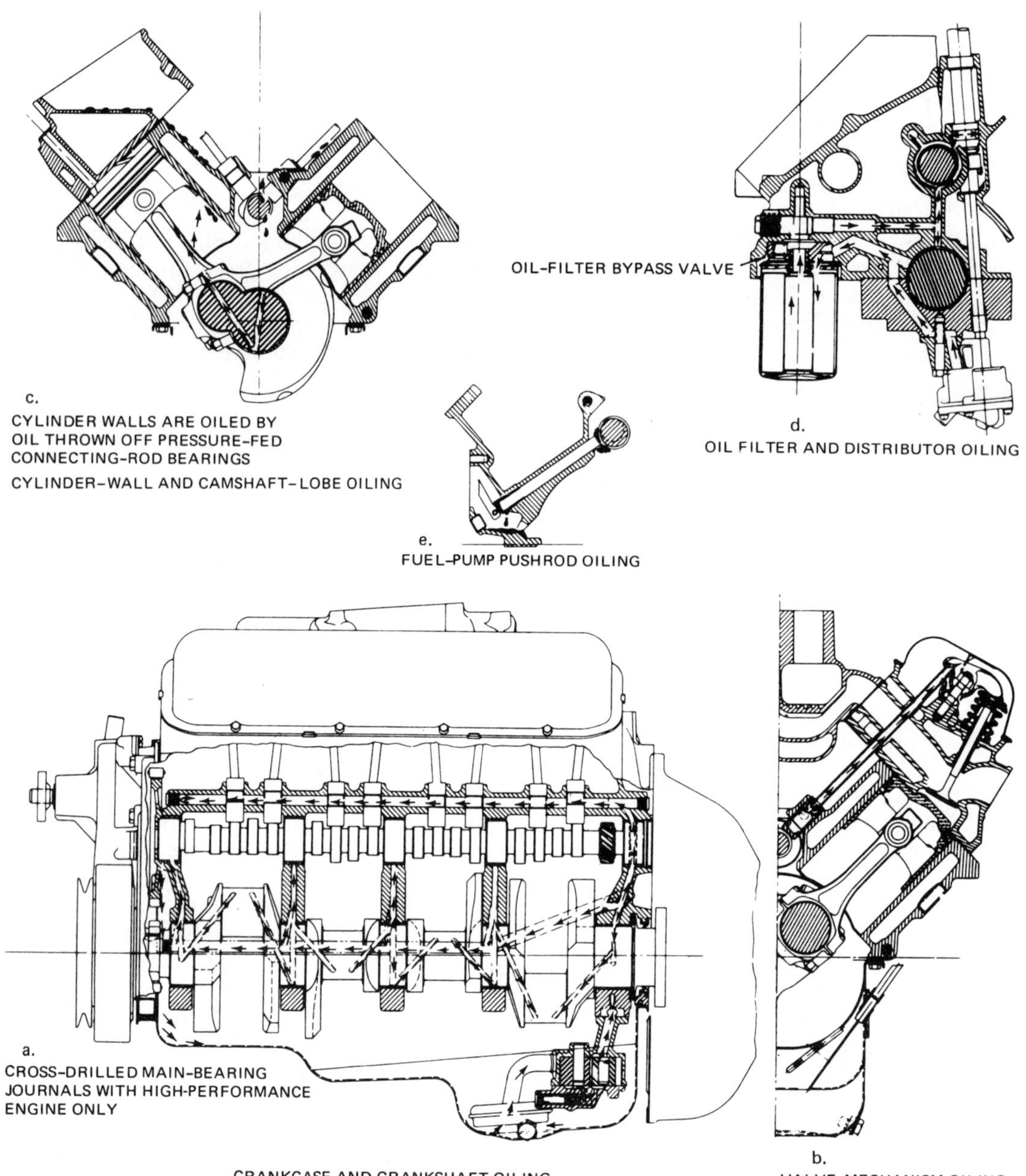

Fig. 7-9. Lubrication system of a V-8 engine. The arrows show the flow of oil to the moving parts in the engine. (*Chevrolet Motor Division of General Motors Corporation*)

Some of the oil flowing to the main-bearing supports flows upward, through holes drilled in these supports, to the camshaft bearings. You can see this flow in Fig. 7-9*a*. The camshaft cams are lubricated by oil thrown off the connecting-rod bearings (see Fig. 7-9*c*).

⊘ 7-18 Valve-Train Lubrication The valve-oiling arrangement is shown in Fig. 7-9*b*. Some of the oil from the oil pump flows through an oil gallery to all the valve lifters (Fig. 7-9*a*). This oil lubricates the valve lifters. Some of the oil flows from the lifters up through the pushrods, which are hollow. You can see this in Fig. 7-9*b*. As the oil reaches the top of the pushrods, it spills out and lubricates the rocker arms, the rocker-arm shaft or ball supports, and the valve stems. Drain holes allow the oil to pass back down into the oil pan.

⊘ 7-19 Six-Cylinder Lubricating System Figure 7-13 shows, in end sectional view, the lubricating system for a six-cylinder engine.,The principle here is the same as for a V-8 engine. Oil flows to the main and camshaft bearings through oil galleries drilled in the cylinder block. Oil flows up the hollow pushrods to the rocker arms and valves. Note in Fig. 7-13 that the valve has an oil shield. This shield keeps excessive oil away from the valve stem. Excessive oil

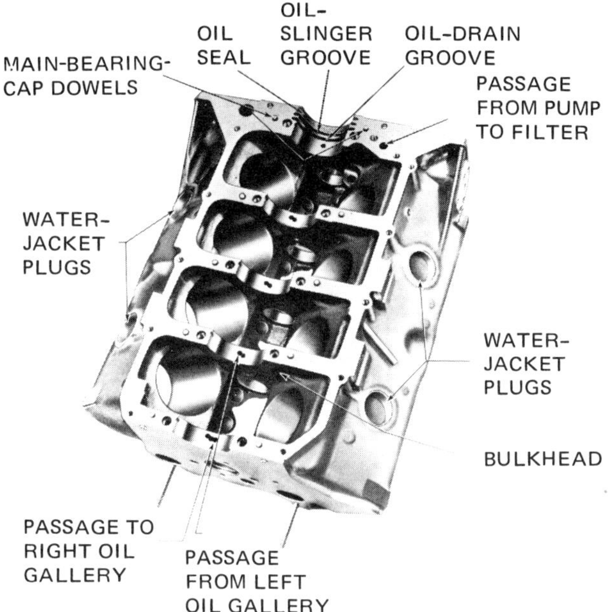

Fig. 7-10. Bottom view of a cylinder block for a V-8 engine, showing the oil passages drilled in the block. (*Pontiac Motor Division of General Motors Corporation*)

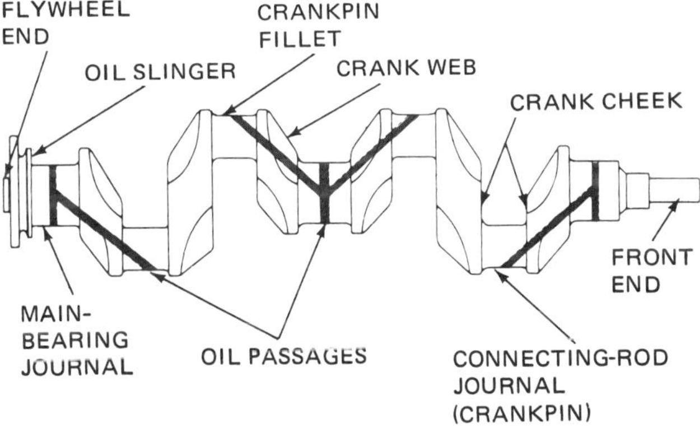

Fig. 7-11. This drawing of a crankshaft shows the oil passages drilled in the crankshaft.

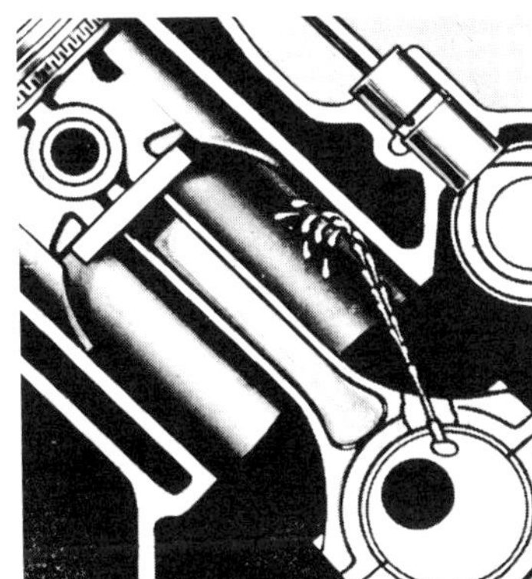

Fig. 7-12. When a hole in the connecting rod aligns with a hole in the crankpin, a spurt of oil is sprayed onto the cylinder wall, as shown. This lubricates the piston and rings. (*Ford Motor Company*)

could work its way down the valve stem, through the valve guide, and into the combustion chamber. There, it would burn and cause carbon buildup and other troubles.

⊘ 7-20 Lubricating-System Service The three lubricating-system services are changing the oil, changing the oil filter, and servicing the oil pump. Oil-pump service is rarely required. The pump is designed to run for many miles without trouble and, in fact, often lasts the life of the engine. We cover oil changing and oil-filter changing in following sections.

⊘ 7-21 Reason for Changing Oil and Filter From the day that fresh oil is put into the engine crankcase, it begins to lose its effectiveness as an engine lubricant. This gradual loss of effectiveness is largely due to the depletion, or "wearing out" of the additives. The oxidation inhibitor becomes used up, and this allows gum and varnish to form. The corrosion and rust inhibitors are gradually depleted, so that corrosion and rust can begin. In addition, during engine operation, carbon tends to form in the combustion chambers. Some of this carbon gets into the oil and reduces its effectiveness. Also, the air that enters the engine (in the air-fuel mixture) carries a certain amount of dust. Even though the air filter may be operating efficiently, it cannot remove all the dust. Then, too, the engine releases fine metal particles as it wears.

All these substances tend to circulate with the oil. As the mileage piles up, the oil accumulates more and more of these contaminants. Even though the engine has an oil filter, some of these contaminants remain in the oil. Finally, after many miles of operation, the oil is so loaded with contaminants that it is not safe to use. If it is not drained and replaced with clean oil, engine wear increases rapidly. Low-speed, short-trip operation contributes to oil contamination.

Different automotive manufacturers have different recommendations as to how often engine oil should be changed. Chrysler recommends that in normal service the oil should be changed every 3 months or 4,000 mi [6,437 km], whichever comes first. For severe service (extended periods of idling and short-trip operation, dusty driving conditions, towing trailers, and so on), the oil should be changed more often—every 2 months or 2,000 mi [3,219 km].

Ford recommends, for normal service, changing the oil every 4 months or 4,000 mi [6,437 km], whichever comes first. For severe service, they recommend an oil change every 2 months or 2,000 mi [3,219 km].

General Motors recommends, for normal service, changing the oil every 4 months or 6,000 mi [9,656 km], whichever comes first. For severe service, they recommend an oil change every 2 months or 3,000 mi [4,828 km].

The oil filter should be changed at the first oil change on a new engine, and at *every other* oil

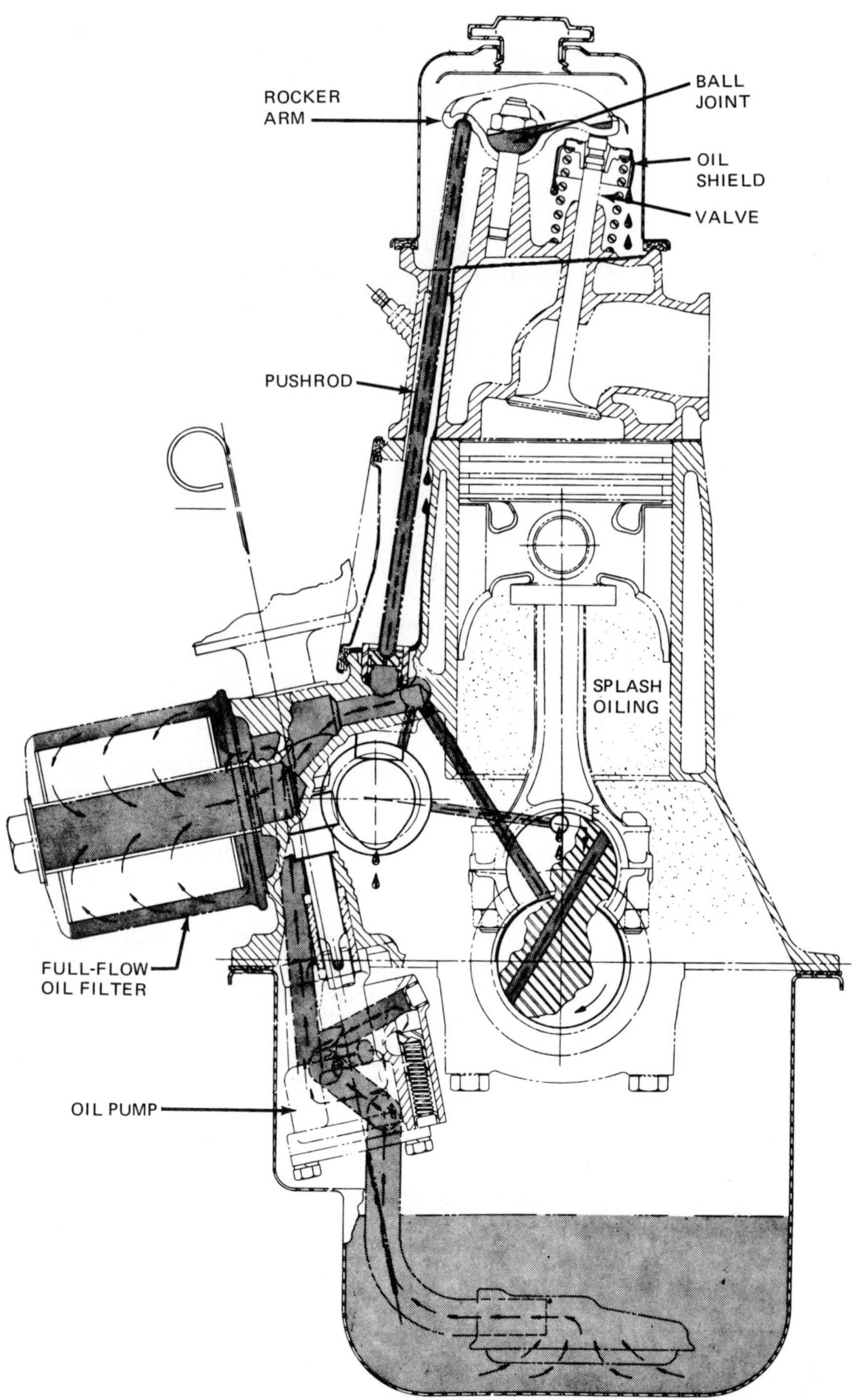

Fig. 7-13. Valve-train lubrication in a six-cylinder, in-line engine. (*Chevrolet Motor Division of General Motors Corporation*)

change after that. However, for severe service, when the oil is being changed more frequently, the oil filter should be changed at *every* oil change.

⊘ 7-22 Changing Oil and Oil Filter Whenever the oil is changed, an oil-change (or lubrication) sticker is placed on the left front door jamb or edge. The sticker indicates the mileage and date of the oil change. The driver can thus determine when the next oil and filter change should be made. To change the oil and filter, you need an oil-filter tool (to remove the old filter), a drain pan, and basic hand tools. You also need fresh oil and a new oil filter. Proceed as follows:

NOTE: You will need the amount of oil (quarts or liters) listed in the manufacturer's specifications for an engine-oil refill with a filter change. Be sure the oil is of the correct type and grade.

1. Run the engine for about 5 minutes to warm up the oil. Then shut off the engine.

CAUTION: Operate the engine only in a well-ventilated area. Remember, exhaust gas contains carbon monoxide, which can be deadly in closed areas.

2. Raise the car on a hoist (Fig. 7-14), or use a jack to raise the front end of the car. If you use a jack, place stands under the front end, and let the car down on the stands. On many vehicles, you do not need to raise the car to change the oil. You can reach the oil drain plug by lying under the front of the car. Many trucks do not need to be raised for an oil change, because of their high road clearance.
3. Using the proper size wrench (or an adjustable wrench), loosen the drain plug slightly until you can turn it with your fingers.
4. Remove the wrench, and place a drain pan under the plug to catch the oil. Be sure the pan will hold the amount of oil in the crankcase. Remember, the oil will flow outward at first, rather than straight down. Be sure to set the pan in the right place to catch the draining oil.
5. Remove the plug with your fingers, and let the oil drain into the pan. While removing the plug, keep your arm above the plug; otherwise, the oil will run down your arm. While the oil is draining, check the drain-plug gasket.
6. After the oil has drained, start the plug into the threads in the drain hole. Then move the drain pan under the oil filter.
7. Tighten the plug securely, but be careful not to overtighten it.
8. Use the oil-filter tool (Fig. 7-15) to turn the filter one or two turns counterclockwise, but do not unscrew the filter from the engine. Allow any oil to drain from the filter into the drain pan.
9. Unscrew the filter. Place the filter in the drain pan, with the gasket end facing up. Make sure that the old filter gasket is not on the engine. Clean any sludge out of the filter mounting recess on the engine. Clean the engine oil-filter gasket surface.
10. Compare the new filter with the old filter. If the new filter is a different size, be sure it has sufficient clearance from the frame and suspension after installation. Check the gasket end of the new filter. The gasket surface should be the same size as that of the old filter. The threads for screwing the filter onto the engine must be the same on both filters.

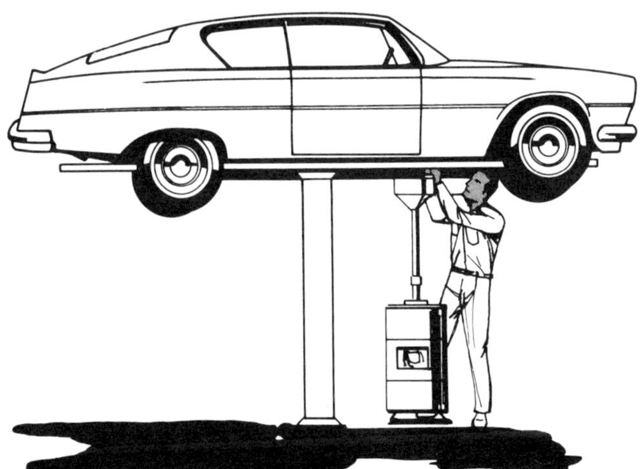

Fig. 7-14. Engine oil is changed by placing the container under the oil-pan drain hole and then removing the drain plug.

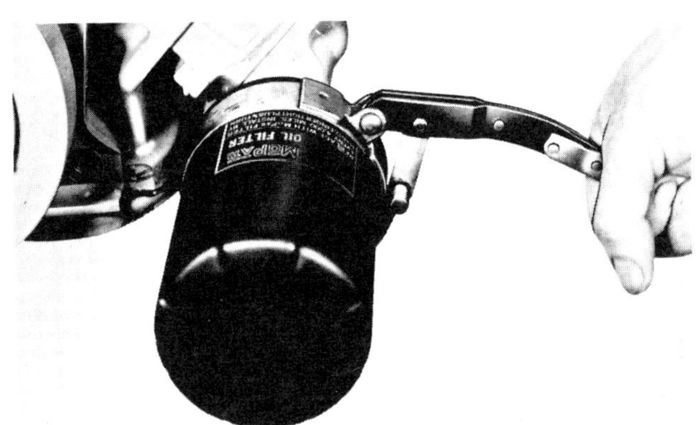

Fig. 7-15. Removing an oil filter. It is usually necessary to use a tool, as shown, to loosen the filter. (*Chrysler Corporation*)

11. Coat the gasket on the new filter with clean oil. If the filter mounts in a position that permits it to be filled with oil before installation, fill the filter with fresh oil. Position the filter on the engine. Hand-tighten the filter until the gasket contacts the engine gasket surface. Be sure the new oil-filter gasket is properly positioned on the filter. Then turn the filter by hand an additional one-half turn, or the amount specified in the filter-installation instructions. Wipe the filter and mounting area clean.

NOTE: Do not tighten the filter with a wrench. Always tighten an oil filter with your hands. Be careful not to cross-thread the filter during installation.

12. Wrap a shop towel around the engine oil-filler neck to catch any spilled oil. Remove the oil-filler cap. Fill the crankcase to the required level with the proper type and grade of engine oil.
13. Reinstall the oil-filler cap. Clean the area, and start the engine.
14. Watch the oil light or gauge on the instrument panel. The light should not glow red for more than 30 seconds, while the oil filter fills up. If there is no oil pressure, or if there is a leak at the filter, shut off the engine. Remove the filter, and make sure the threads and gasket are not damaged. Reinstall the filter, and start the engine. If the oil light continues to remain on, stop the engine and determine the cause.
15. Run the engine for about 5 minutes. Then shut off the engine. Check around and under the oil filter and the drain plug for leaks.
16. Fill out a new lubrication sticker, and attach it to the vehicle. Be sure to enter the mileage (or number of kilometers) shown on the odometer and the date.
17. Check the crankcase oil level with the dipstick. Be sure the crankcase is full before returning the car to the customer.

Check Your Progress

Progress Quiz 7-1 Here is your chance to check how well you remember the material you have just finished studying. The questions that follow will help you review the material and fix it more firmly in your mind.

Completing the Sentences The sentences below are incomplete. After each sentence there are several words or phrases, but only one of them correctly completes the sentence. Write each sentence in your notebook, ending it with the one word or phrase that completes it correctly.

1. Oil is: (*a*) not all the same, (*b*) all the same, (*c*) all the same except for color.
2. Chemical compounds that are added to oil to improve its performance are called: (*a*) crude oil, (*b*) oil additives, (*c*) lubricating systems.
3. An oil with high viscosity is: (*a*) very thick and flows slowly, (*b*) very thin and flows quickly, (*c*) very thin and flows slowly.
4. A multiple-viscosity oil with the rating SAE10W-30 has the same viscosity as (*a*) SAE10W and SAE30 when each is cold, (*b*) SAE10W when it is cold, and SAE30 when it is hot.
5. Of the following, the oil that makes an engine easiest to start in cold weather is (*a*) SAE10W-40, (*b*) SAE20W, (*c*) SAE30.
6. The oil used in a 1974 passenger-car engine should have a service rating of: (*a*) SA, (*b*) SE, (*c*) SB.
7. An oil additive that combats the tendency of oil to thin out as it gets hot is: (*a*) a viscosity improver, (*b*) a pour-point depressant, (*c*) an inhibitor.
8. Besides reducing friction and wear, oil also: (*a*) removes heat from the engine, absorbs shocks between bearings and other engine parts, forms a seal between bearings and other engine parts, forms a seal between the piston rings and the cylinder wall, and acts as a cleaning agent, (*b*) removes heat from the radiator, absorbs road shocks, prevents blowby, and is used in the automatic transmission.
9. The main purpose of an engine lubricating system is to (*a*) provide a seal between the piston rings and the cylinder wall, (*b*) get engine oil to all the moving parts in the engine, (*c*) cool the engine oil pan.
10. The oil pump is driven by the: (*a*) camshaft, (*b*) crankshaft, (*c*) fan belt.

CHAPTER 7 CHECKUP

NOTE: Since the following is a chapter review test, you should review the chapter before taking the test.

You are making fine progress. The material you have just studied will be of great help to you when you go into the shop. Complete the checkup below to see how well you remember the material on engine lubricating systems. If you are not sure of an answer, reread the pages that give it to you. Reviewing the chapter and writing down the answers will help you remember the important points.

Completing the Sentences The sentences below are incomplete. After each sentence there are several words or phrases, but only one of them correctly completes the sentence. Write each sentence in your notebook, ending it with the one word or phrase that completes it correctly.

1. Oil pumps are of: (*a*) the gear type, (*b*) the rotor type, (*c*) both the gear and rotor types.
2. In the gear-type pump, the oil travels from the inlet side to the outlet side: (*a*) outside the meshing gear teeth, (*b*) in the spaces between the gear teeth, (*c*) in the space between the oil-pump cover and the gears.
3. To prevent excessive pressure, oil pumps contain a: (*a*) pressure valve, (*b*) poppet valve, (*c*) relief valve.
4. If the oil-filter element becomes so clogged that all the oil needed by the engine cannot pass through the filter, the: (*a*) engine is seriously damaged, (*b*) oil-filter bypass valve opens to allow oil to flow directly to the engine, (*c*) oil-pressure relief valve closes to raise the oil-pump pressure and increase the oil flow.
5. The indicator used to check the level of oil in the crankcase is the: (*a*) instrument-panel warning light, (*b*) dipstick, (*c*) door-jamb lubrication sticker.
6. The indicator used most often to notify the driver of low oil pressure in the engine is the: (*a*) instrument-panel warning light, (*b*) dipstick, (*c*) door-jamb lubrication sticker.
7. The five service ratings of lubricating oil for gasoline engines are: (*a*) SAE5, 10, 15, 20, 30, (*b*) DA, DB, DC, DD, DE, (*c*) SA, SB, SC, SD, SE.
8. A typical recommendation for a late-model car operating under favorable conditions is that the oil be changed every: (*a*) 1,000 mi [1,609 km], (*b*) 2,000 mi [3,219 km], (*c*) 4,000 mi [6,437 km].
9. Two ways in which oil might be lost from the engine are by: (*a*) burning and leakage, (*b*) dilution and mixing, (*c*) splash and pressure.
10. If you use your car during the winter for short-trip, start-and-stop service, you should use: (*a*) SE oil, (*b*) CE oil, (*c*) DE oil.

Unscrambling the Purposes of Oil When the two lists below are unscrambled and combined, they form a list of the jobs that oil does in the engine and the reasons why these jobs must be done. To unscramble the lists, find the item in the "Reasons" list that goes with each item in the "Jobs" list. Combine each pair of items, and write the combined list in your notebook.

Jobs	*Reasons*
Lubricate	To absorb shock loads in bearings
Lubricate	To serve as a cleaning agent
Act as a cooling agent	To minimize power loss

Resist squeezing out	To form a seal between rings and wall
Cover rings	To minimize wear
Pick up dirt	To remove heat from engine parts

Lubricating-System Review In the following, you are asked about lubricating oil and lubrication-system components. Write your answers in your notebook. The act of writing will help you remember the facts. It will also fill your notebook with valuable information to which you can refer as necessary.

1. List the purposes of engine oil. Explain how the oil accomplishes these purposes.
2. Explain how viscosity and service ratings indicate the actions of lubricating oil in the engine.
3. Name the properties that a good lubricating oil must have. Explain what these properties mean, in terms of engine operation.
4. List the ways in which oil may be lost from the engine.
5. Name and describe the operation of the two most widely used types of automotive oil pumps.
6. What is the purpose of the relief valve?
7. What is the purpose of the oil filter?
8. Name and describe the operation of the two types of oil-pressure indicators.
9. Where are oil-level indicators usually located, and how are they used?
10. How often should the engine oil and oil filter be changed?

SUGGESTIONS FOR FURTHER STUDY

Examine various engines, oil pumps, filters, and other lubrication-system components. Work toward understanding how the oil is circulated from the crankcase to the various engine parts. Study the illustrations and descriptions of lubrication systems in all the automotive shop manuals you can find. At your local library, read whatever you can find on the subject of lubricating oils, greases, and petroleum refining methods. Write, in your notebook, any important facts that you want to remember.

chapter 8

ENGINE COOLING SYSTEMS

The burning of fuel in the engine produces a great deal of heat. Part of this heat is removed by the lubricating system, as explained in Chap. 7. Some heat leaves the engine with the exhaust gases. The rest of the excess heat is removed from the engine by the engine cooling system.

⊘ 8-1 Purpose of the Cooling System The cooling system must remove the right amount of heat from the engine. If the cooling system cools the engine too much, gasoline will be wasted and the engine will lose power. If the cooling system does not cool the engine enough, the engine will overheat. Overheating can burn the film of lubricating oil off the cylinder walls. This will damage the cylinder walls, pistons, and piston rings. The result could be a ruined engine.

An overheated engine loses power also. Let's take a look at engine heat. Combustion temperatures in the cylinders can reach 4,500°F [2,482°C]. That's a high enough temperature to melt the cylinder block. The heat must be taken away from the engine before it causes damage. Part of the heat leaves the engine with the hot exhaust gases. The rest of the heat travels into the metal parts around the combustion chamber: the cylinder heads, the cylinder block, and the pistons. As we noted, some of this heat is carried away by the engine oil. Most of the heat, however, is removed by the cooling system.

Not all the heat should be carried away. Some heat must be left, so that the engine stays just hot enough to run efficiently.

⊘ 8-2 Types of Cooling Systems There are two kinds of cooling systems: air cooling and liquid, or water, cooling. In an air-cooled engine, air passing over the cooling fins on the cylinders and cylinder heads carries away the excess heat. In a liquid-cooled engine, water mixed with antifreeze circulates around the combustion chambers and carries away the excess heat. The mixture of water and antifreeze—called the *coolant*—cools the engine. Air-cooled and water-cooled engines are shown in Chap. 4. In this chapter we discuss liquid-cooled engines.

⊘ 8-3 Liquid-Cooled Engines Figure 8-1 is a simplified cutaway view of a liquid cooling system for an engine. The coolant is pumped from the engine to the top of the radiator. It flows down through the radiator, losing heat to air passing through. Then the coolant is pumped back through the engine by the water pump. Now let's look at each part of the system, to see exactly how it works.

⊘ 8-4 Water Jackets Water jackets are the spaces that surround the combustion chamber and the cylinder walls. Figure 8-2 shows one bank of a V-6 engine, partly cut away to show the water jackets. In the cylinder block, the water jackets are formed by the inner shells of the cylinders and the outer shell of the cylinder block. Remember that the water jackets are watertight, and that a mixture of water and antifreeze circulates through them. As we noted, the mixture is called the coolant; we shall use that term from now on.

The coolant passes through the cylinder-block water jackets and then through the cylinder-head water jackets. It picks up heat from the engine. Then the hot coolant flows into the radiator. As it flows through the radiator, the coolant loses heat. The cooled coolant then flows back into the bottom of the cylinder-block water jackets to start another trip through the engine.

⊘ 8-5 Water Pump The water pump forces the coolant to flow through the cooling system. The water pump is mounted at the front end of the engine. It is driven by a pulley and a belt, from a pulley on the front end of the crankshaft. Figure 8-1 shows the location of the pump in the engine. Figure 8-3 is a cutaway view of a V-8 engine. The pictures give you another view of the water-pump location. Note that the pulley that drives the pump also carries the engine fan. The fan is described later.

The *impeller* type of water pump is used in automobile-engine cooling systems. The impeller is a flat plate with a series of curved blades, or vanes. When the impeller spins, any coolant between the

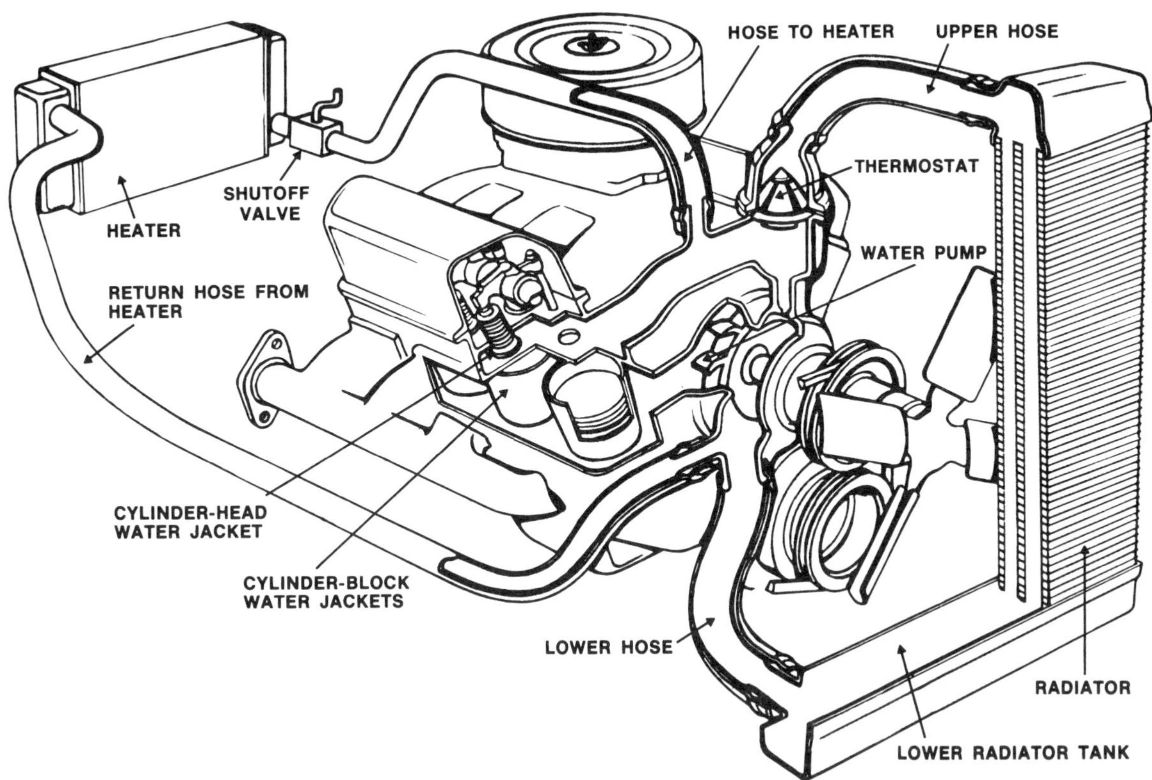

Fig. 8-1. Cutaway view of a V-8 engine, showing the cooling system.

blades is thrown outward and forced through the cooling system. Figure 8-4 shows a disassembled water pump.

A sectional view of a water pump is shown in Fig. 8-5. The shaft that holds the impeller and pulley is supported by a double-row ball bearing. This is a ball bearing with two rows of balls. A seal holds the coolant in the system and prevents it from leaking out past the shaft or the bearing.

The arrows in Fig. 8-3 show how the coolant circulates. It leaves the bottom of the radiator and goes up to the water pump. It is forced through the engine water jackets by the water pump. The coolant then leaves the water jackets and moves to the top of the radiator.

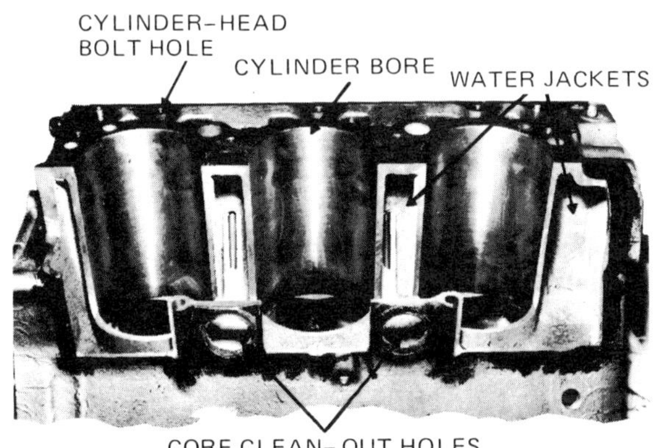

Fig. 8-2. One bank of a V-6 engine, cut away so the water jackets can be seen. (*Truck and Coach Division of General Motors Corporation*)

⊘ 8-6 Radiators The radiator has two separate circuits: a coolant circuit and an air circuit. The coolant circuit carries the coolant from a tank at the top of the radiator to a tank at the bottom of the radiator. The air circuit allows air to flow through the radiator from front to back.

Two kinds of radiators are the tube-and-fin radiator (Fig. 8-6) and the ribbon-cellular radiator (Fig. 8-7). Both are shown cut away, so that you can see how they are made.

The tube-and-fin radiator (Fig. 8-6) is easiest to understand. It has a series of coolant tubes that connect the top tank to the bottom tank of the radiator. Air fins surround these tubes and are fastened to them. Coolant passing through the tubes gives off heat to the tubes and fins. Air passing around the outside of the coolant tubes and between the fins absorbs this heat.

The ribbon-cellular radiator (Fig. 8-7) is made of a series of metal ribbons. The ribbons are soldered together along their edges to form two sets of passages. One set is formed by the coolant tubes, which go from the top tank of the radiator to the bottom tank. The other set of passages allows air to pass from the front of the radiator to the back.

The effect is the same in both types of radiator. The coolant enters the radiator hot and comes out comparatively cool. The heat is transferred from the coolant to air passing through the radiator.

⊘ 8-7 Engine Fan The engine fan (Fig. 8-8) helps pull air through the radiator. You can see the loca-

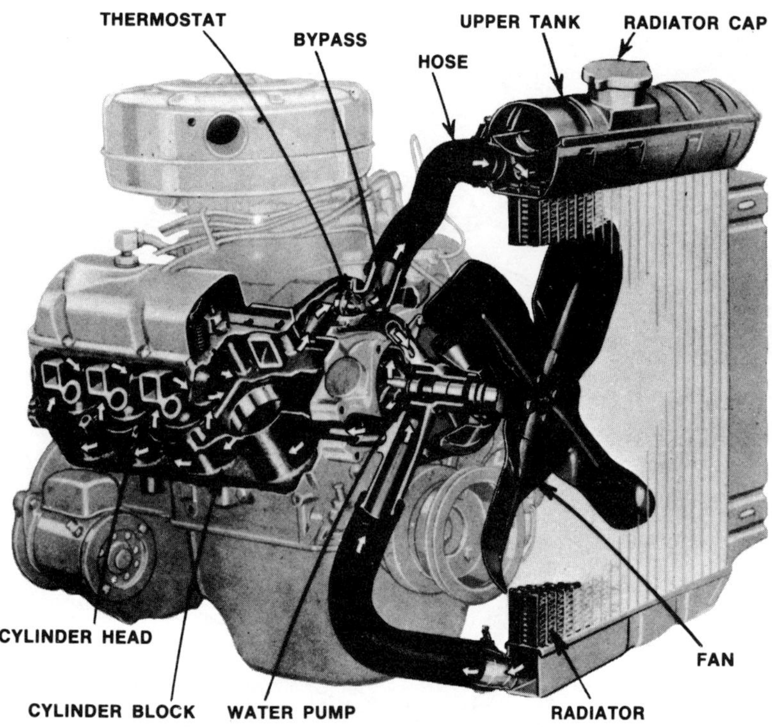

Fig. 8-3. Cutaway view of a V-8 engine, showing the cooling system. The arrows show the direction of coolant flow through the engine water jackets. (*Ford Motor Company*)

tion and shape of the engine fan in several of the pictures in this chapter—for example, Figs. 8-3 and 8-5. The fan is located behind the radiator. It has four or more curved blades. The fan is driven by the belt from the pulley on the engine crankshaft. When the curved blades rotate, they "scoop up" air and push it back toward the engine. This action pulls air through the radiator.

⊘ 8-8 Variable-Speed Fan Drive Many engines have a variable-speed fan drive. This drive increases the speed of the fan when the engine gets hot, and reduces the speed of the fan when the engine gets cooler. The advantage of variable speed is the saving of horsepower when the fan is run at low speed. Also, the fan is quieter when it runs slower.

The variable-speed fan drive has a small fluid coupling. The driving force passes through a fluid in the coupling. When the engine gets hot, more fluid is forced into the coupling, and the fan runs faster. When the engine is cool, less fluid goes into the coupling, and the fan runs slower.

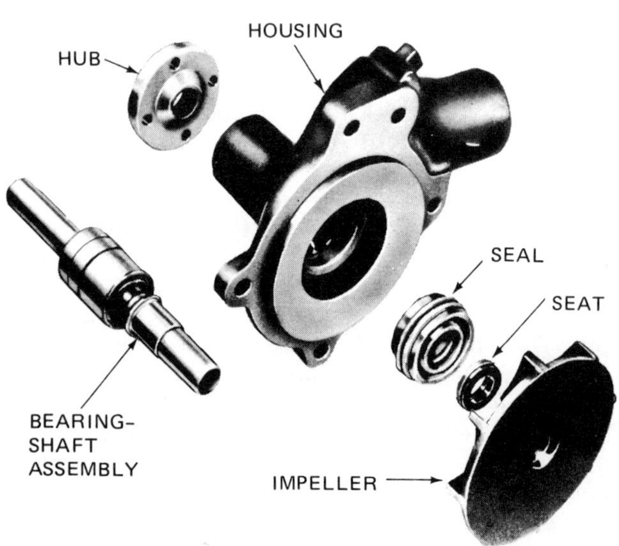

Fig. 8-4. Disassembled view of a water pump. (*Pontiac Motor Division of General Motors Corporation*)

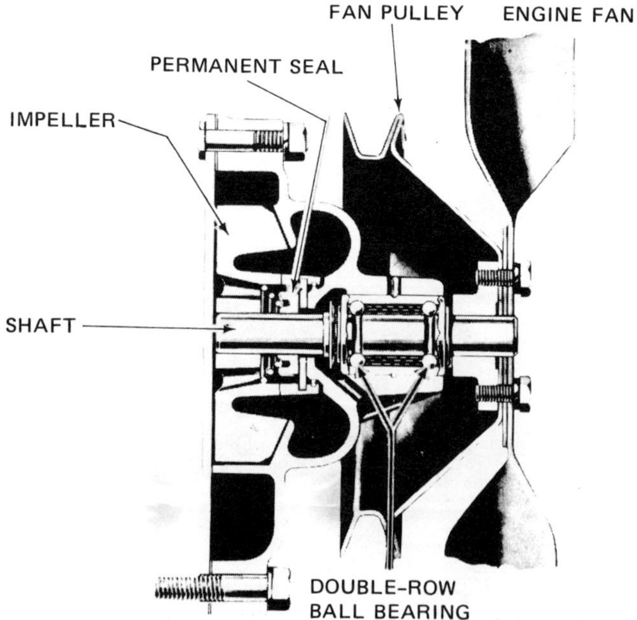

Fig. 8-5. Sectional view of a water pump, showing how the shaft is supported on a double-row ball bearing.

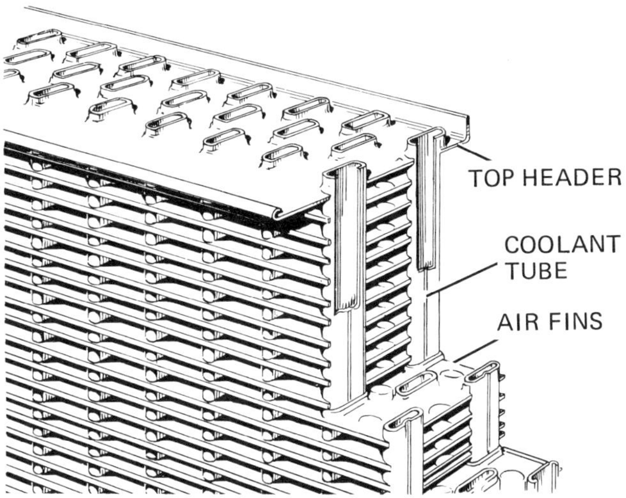

Fig. 8-6. Construction of a tube-and-fin radiator core.

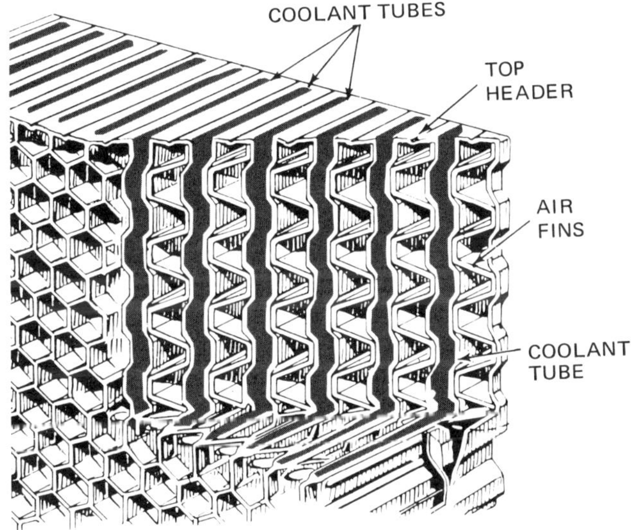

Fig. 8-7. Construction of a ribbon-cellular radiator core.

Fig. 8-8. The engine fan helps pull air through the radiator.

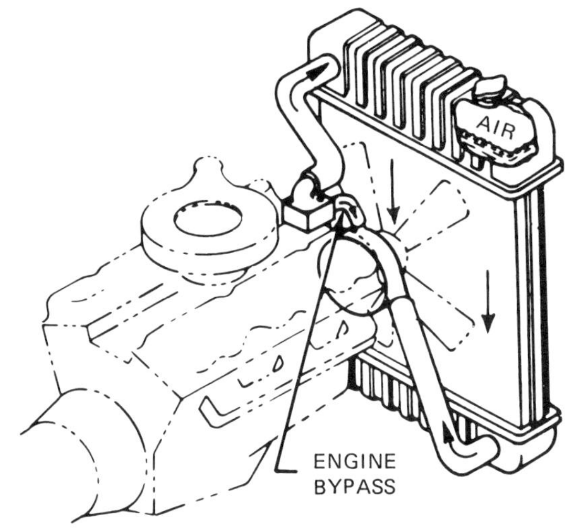

Fig. 8-9. Cooling system using a down-flow radiator. (*Harrison Radiator Division of General Motors Corporation*)

⊘ 8-9 Down-Flow and Cross-Flow Radiators The radiators we have been talking about are all down-flow radiators. That is, the coolant flows down from a tank at the top to a tank at the bottom. This system is shown in Fig. 8-9.

In a cross-flow radiator, the coolant flows across the radiator, as shown by the arrows in Fig. 8-10. The advantage here is that the radiator can be made shorter from top to bottom. Many late-model cars use cross-flow radiators because they take up less height under the hood. This allows car manufacturers to design lower hood lines.

⊘ 8-10 Thermostat When the engine is cold, it must be warmed up as fast as possible, because a cold engine wears quickly and operates poorly. Why does a cold engine wear fast? When an engine stops and cools off, most of the oil on the cylinder walls

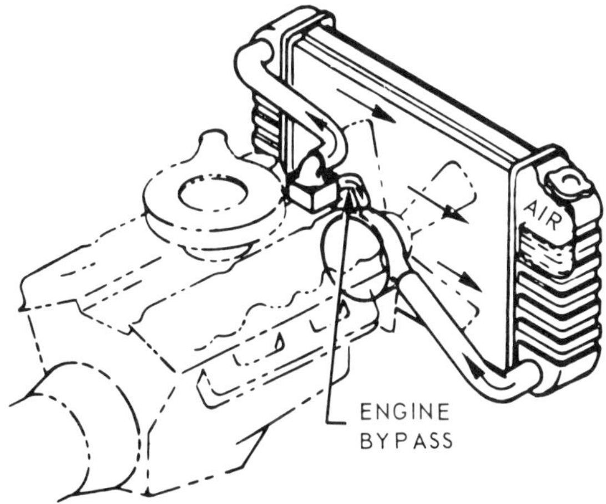

Fig. 8-10. Cooling system using a cross-flow radiator. (*Harrison Radiator Division of General Motors Corporation*)

and bearings drains back down into the oil pan. When the engine is started again, the oil takes a little while to start circulating. Therefore, for a few moments the engine runs without enough oil on its moving parts. The result is rapid wear. As the engine begins to warm up, the oil begins to thin out and circulate to the moving parts.

NOTE: This is one good reason why you should never race a cold engine. Give it a chance to warm up, so that the oil can get to all the moving parts.

A cold engine operates poorly because the gasoline does not evaporate very well when it is cold. The air-fuel mixture getting to the cylinders is not right for good combustion. The result is poor engine operation.

The thermostat is a device located in the cooling system. It shuts off the circulation of coolant to the radiator when the engine is cold. Thus, when the engine is cold, no coolant can flow to the radiator. Instead, it flows through a bypass and back into the engine. This means that the radiator cannot take any heat out of the engine. The heat stays in the engine and warms it up faster. This shortens the time during which the engine operates without proper lubrication and without the proper air-fuel mixture. Then, when the engine gets hot enough, the thermostat opens the circuit to the radiator. The cooling system can then go to work, taking heat out of the engine.

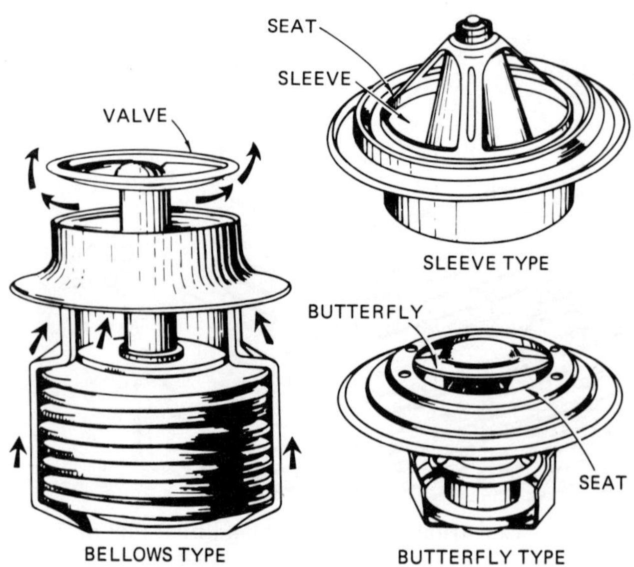

Fig. 8-11. Various thermostats for engine cooling systems. The bellows type (no longer widely used) is shown open, with arrows indicating the water flow past the valve. *(Chrysler Corporation)*

⊘ 8-11 Types of Thermostats The thermostat is located at the top of the cylinder head (Figs. 8-1 and 8-3). There are several types of thermostats, as shown in Fig. 8-11.

All thermostats operate in the same way. When the engine is cold, a valve in the thermostat is closed. This blocks off the coolant passage to the radiator. As the engine warms up, the valve starts to open. This allows coolant to flow to the radiator so that the cooling system can take heat out of the engine.

Most thermostats contain a wax pellet that expands with heat. This forces the valve to open so that the circulation of coolant to the radiator can start. Some thermostats have a metal bellows that is partly filled with a liquid. When the operating temperature is reached, the liquid starts to evaporate. This forces the bellows to expand and raise the valve. The bellows type of thermostat is shown to the left in Fig. 8-11.

If you look at Figs. 8-3, 8-9, and 8-10, you will see an engine bypass. This bypass allows the pump to circulate coolant through the engine when the engine is cold. Of course, when the engine is hot, the coolant circulates between the engine and the radiator.

Two types of thermostats that control both the bypass and the circuit to the radiator are shown in Fig. 8-12. They are called *blocking bypass thermostats,* and they work as follows: There are two valves in the thermostat, a primary valve and a secondary valve. The primary valve controls the flow of coolant to the radiator. When the engine is cold, the primary valve is closed and coolant cannot flow to the radiator.

The secondary valve controls coolant flow through the bypass. When the primary valve is closed, the secondary valve is open. With the sec-

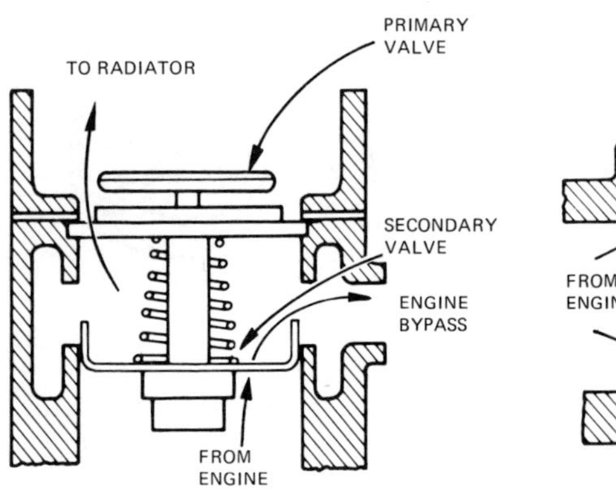

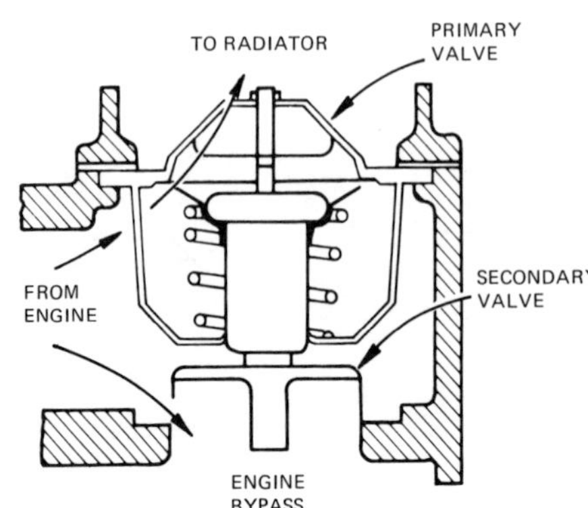

Fig. 8-12. Blocking bypass thermostats.

ondary valve open, coolant flows through the bypass. When the engine warms up, the primary valve opens and the secondary valve closes. The coolant begins to flow to the radiator. Note that the valves work together. As the primary valve opens the passage to the radiator, the secondary valve closes the bypass.

⊘ 8-12 Radiator Pressure Cap The cooling systems of most modern engines are sealed. When the engine gets hot, pressure develops in the cooling system. The increasing pressure increases the boiling point of the coolant.

At normal air pressure, water boils at 212°F [100°C]. If the air pressure is increased, the temperature at which water boils is also increased. For example, if the pressure is raised 15 psi (pounds per square inch) [1.05 kg/cm² (kilograms per square centimeter)] over normal pressure, the boiling point is raised to about 260°F [126.6°C].

This is what happens in the sealed cooling system: As the pressure goes up, the boiling point goes up. Thus, the coolant can be safely run at a temperature higher than 212°F [100°C] without boiling. This is very important. The higher the coolant temperature, the greater the difference between the coolant temperature and the air temperature. The difference in temperatures is what causes the cooling system to work. The hotter the coolant, the faster the heat moves from the radiator to the cooler passing air. Thus the pressurized, sealed cooling system can take heat away from the engine faster. That is, the cooling system works more efficiently under higher pressure.

However, the cooling system can be pressurized too much. If the pressure in the system gets too high, it can blow out the radiator. To prevent this, the radiator cap has a pressure-relief valve (Fig. 8-13). When the pressure gets too high, it raises the valve so that the excess pressure can escape.

The radiator cap also has a vacuum valve. This valve lets air into the cooling system if the pressure falls too low. For example, when the engine stops and cools off, the pressure in the cooling system falls. It can fall below normal air pressure, so that a vacuum forms in the system. If this happens, the outside air pressure could cause a partial collapse of the radiator. To prevent this, the vacuum valve opens just enough to allow some air to get into the system.

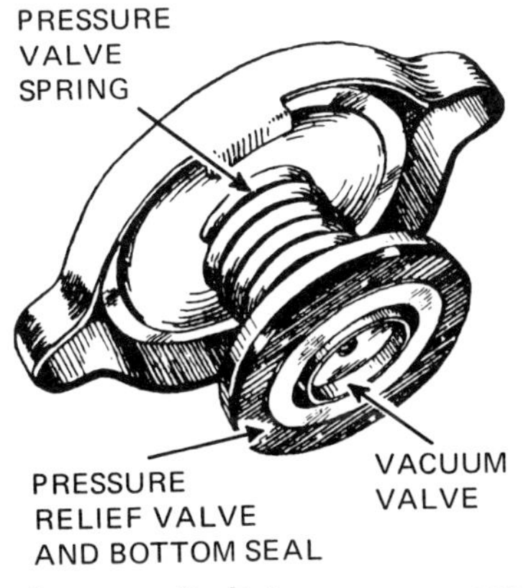

Fig. 8-13. Radiator pressure cap.

⊘ 8-13 Cooling System With Expansion Tank Some cooling systems have a separate, translucent, expansion tank, as shown in Fig. 8-14. The expansion tank, also called a *reservoir*, is partly filled with coolant and is connected to the radiator cap. As the coolant is heated, it expands; part of the coolant flows into the expansion tank. Then, when the engine approaches operating temperature, a valve in the radiator cap closes. The cooling system is now sealed. The pressure in the cooling system increases and thus prevents boiling. Then, when the engine cools off, the coolant in the cooling system contracts. Contraction of the coolant produces a vacuum in the cooling system. The vacuum draws coolant, from the reservoir, back into the radiator. The entire operation works to keep the cooling system filled with coolant at all times. Figure 8-15 shows how the expansion tank looks in one application.

⊘ 8-14 Car Heater Heat from the coolant is used to heat the car interior. The simplest version of a car heating system is shown in Fig. 8-1. It consists of a heater radiator, located in the passenger compartment and connected by two hoses to the engine cooling system. Hot coolant flows through the hoses and the heater radiator. A small electric fan forces air through the heater radiator. The air absorbs heat from the heater radiator and warms the passenger compartment.

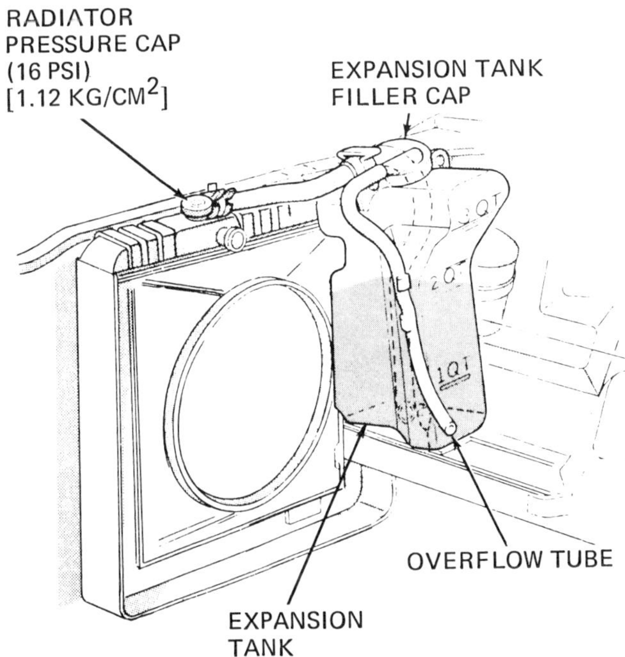

Fig. 8-14. Radiator and expansion tank. (*Chrysler Corporation*)

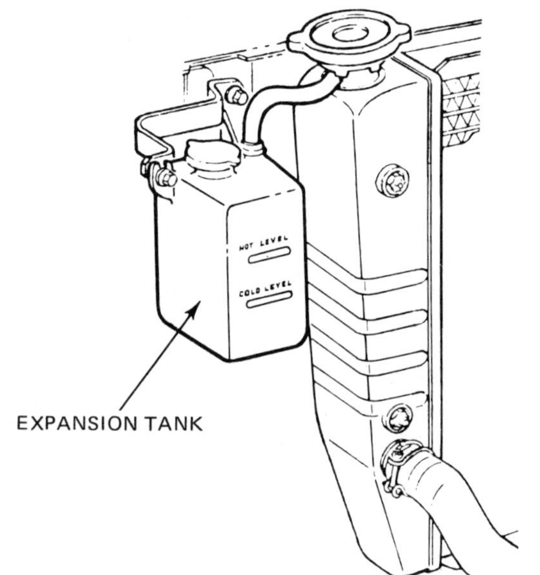

Fig. 8-15. Expansion tank (also called a *constant-full reservoir*) for a cooling system.

A more complex car heater is shown in Fig. 8-16. The operating principle is the same as that described above. Hot coolant from the engine circulates through a small heater radiator. An electric fan circulates air from the passenger compartment through the heater radiator. The system shown in Fig. 8-16 also includes a defrosting arrangement. Driver-operated controls direct the heated air either into the passenger compartment or against the windshield. The heat melts frost or evaporates mist that has formed on the windshield.

In some cars, the heating system is automatically controlled. Automatic controls turn the system on when the passenger compartment is cold, and turn the system off when the passenger compartment is warm. Some heating systems work with an air-

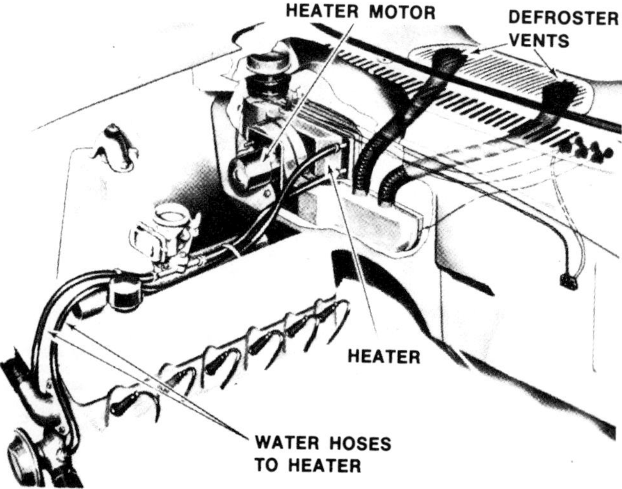

Fig. 8-16. Car heater system. Hot water from engine cooling system circulates through a small radiator. The fan blows air through the radiator.

conditioning system to maintain the desired temperature in summer or winter.

⊘ 8-15 Antifreeze Solutions Water freezes at 32°F [0°C]. If water freezes in the engine cooling system, it stops coolant circulation. Some parts of the engine will overheat, and this could seriously damage the engine. What is worse, when water freezes, it expands. Water freezing in the cylinder block could expand enough to crack the block. Water freezing in the radiator could split the radiator seams. Both conditions are serious. A cracked cylinder block cannot be repaired satisfactorily. A split radiator is also hard to repair.

As you can see, a freeze-up in the cooling system can completely ruin the engine. To prevent freeze-up, antifreeze is added to the water. A mixture that is about one-half water and one-half antifreeze will not freeze even if the temperature drops to −34°F [−36.7°C]. This is 34° below zero, and it seldom gets that cold anywhere in the United States. Higher concentrations of antifreeze in water will prevent freeze-up of the coolant at temperatures as low as −84°F [−64.4°C]. The most commonly used antifreeze is ethylene glycol.

Some antifreeze compounds also fight small leaks in the cooling-system radiator. These antifreeze compounds contain tiny plastic beads or inorganic fibers. They circulate freely with the coolant. If a leak develops, the beads or fibers jam in the leak and plug it. Of course, they will not help if the holes are too large.

NOTE: The beads or fibers will not stop leaks in hoses, cylinder-head gaskets, or pump seals.

Corrosion protection is also "built into" antifreeze solutions. Compounds are added to fight corrosion inside the engine water jackets and the radiator.

Many people have the idea that antifreeze solutions are good only for cold-weather protection. This is not so. They are also good for hot-weather operation. Car manufacturers recommend that cooling systems be periodically drained, flushed out, and refilled with a fresh mixture of water and antifreeze. One company recommends that this be done every two years. Another says it should be done every year, preferably in late fall, before freezing weather sets in.

⊘ 8-16 Temperature Indicators There are two kinds of temperature indicators: lights and a dial. The light system includes a light that comes on when the engine temperature gets too high. This is a warning to the driver that something is wrong, so the engine can be stopped before serious damage occurs. The other system includes a dial on the instrument panel. A needle or pointer moves across the dial to show the actual temperature of the coolant in the engine.

CHAPTER 8 CHECKUP

NOTE: Since the following is a chapter review test, you should review the chapter before taking the test.

You should now have a good understanding of how the engine cooling system operates. The questions that follow will help you check how well you remember what you have been reading. If a question stumps you, reread the pages that contain the information you need.

Completing the Sentences The sentences that follow are incomplete. After each sentence there are several words or phrases, but only one of them correctly completes the sentence. Write each sentence in your notebook, ending it with the one word or phrase that completes it correctly.

1. The pump part that rotates to cause water circulation between the radiator and engine water jackets is called the: (*a*) impeller, (*b*) fan, (*c*) body, (*d*) bypass.
2. The two types of radiators discussed in the chapter are the: (*a*) zigzag and fan-cooled, (*b*) horizontal and vertical, (*c*) tube-and-fin and ribbon-cellular.
3. In normal operation, coolant in a down-flow radiator circulates: (*a*) from top to bottom, (*b*) from bottom to top, (*c*) in a circular path in the radiator.
4. The part of the cooling-system thermostat that opens and closes the valve is called the: (*a*) seater, (*b*) bellows or wax pellet, (*c*) pressure valve, (*d*) vacuum valve.
5. The device in the cooling system that raises the boiling point of the coolant in the system is called the: (*a*) pressure cap, (*b*) vacuum valve, (*c*) radiator, (*d*) water jacket.
6. The two valves in the pressure cap are the: (*a*) pressure valve and blow-off valve, (*b*) atmospheric valve and vacuum valve, (*c*) pressure valve and vacuum valve.
7. The most commonly used antifreeze is: (*a*) alcohol base, (*b*) ethylene glycol, (*c*) iso-octane.
8. In terms of the direction of coolant flow, radiators can be classified as: (*a*) down-flow and up-flow, (*b*) right-flow and left-flow, (*c*) direct-flow and cross-flow, (*d*) down-flow and cross-flow.
9. In the blocking bypass thermostat, when the primary valve is opened, the secondary valve: (*a*) permits circulation to the radiator, (*b*) blocks off water flow to the radiator, (*c*) blocks off the engine bypass.
10. Coolant is a mixture of: (*a*) water and oil, (*b*) water and antifreeze, (*c*) oil and antifreeze.

Review Questions Write each of the following questions, and then the answer, in your notebook.

1. What is the purpose of the cooling system?
2. How does the cooling system operate?
3. How does the water pump operate?
4. Describe the operation of the variable-speed engine fan.
5. In what two general ways can radiators be classified? Describe each classification.
6. Describe the operation of a cooling-system thermostat.
7. Describe the operation of a cooling-system radiator pressure cap.
8. Describe a sealed cooling system.
9. Describe the indicator-light system discussed in the chapter.
10. What is the purpose of the expansion tank?

SUGGESTIONS FOR FURTHER STUDY

Automotive Fuel, Lubricating and Cooling Systems, another book in the McGraw-Hill Automotive Technology Series, contains additional information on cooling system operation, troubles, and servicing. You can also find out a good deal about the cooling system and its components in a friendly service shop or your school shop. Examine water-pump parts and thermostats. Note how the radiator is mounted and connected with hoses to the engine and water pump. Write, in your notebook, any interesting facts you learn.

chapter 9

COOLING-SYSTEM SERVICE

In this chapter, we cover cooling-system troubles and discuss how to service the cooling system.

⊘ 9-1 Cooling-System Trouble Diagnosis Two common complaints related to the engine cooling system are engine overheating and cooling-system leaks. If the engine is slow to warm up, the problem could also be in the cooling system. Possible causes of these complaints are discussed in following sections. Detailed testing of the system is covered later in the chapter.

⊘ 9-2 Overheating The driver may notice that the red light stays on, or the temperature gauge registers in the overheating zone. Or, the driver may complain that the engine boiled over. Possible causes of engine overheating include:

1. Low coolant level due to leakage of coolant from the system, as described in ⊘ 9-3.
2. Accumulations of rust and scale in the system, preventing normal circulation of coolant. This is less common today, because modern antifreeze compounds contain agents that fight rust.
3. Collapsed hoses, preventing normal coolant circulation.
4. A defective thermostat, which does not open normally and thus blocks the circulation of coolant. If the engine overheats without the radiator becoming normally warm, and the fan belt is properly tightened, then the thermostat is probably at fault. Sometimes, on new cars, a few grains of sand from the engine block or head core will lodge behind the thermostat, preventing it from opening.
5. A defective water pump, which does not circulate enough coolant through the engine. To check the water-pump efficiency, install a clear plastic pipe in place of the upper radiator hose. Then run the engine. You will be able to see how much coolant is circulating. Note that one of the more common causes of water-pump bearing failure is an overtight fan belt. Fan belts should always be tightened correctly with a belt-tension gauge (Fig. 9-12). Bearing failure is usually obvious, because it is noisy. A quick check of the bearing can be made (with the engine off!) by grasping the tips of two fan blades. Try to move the fan toward and away from the radiator. Any movement indicates a worn bearing.
6. A loose or worn fan belt will not drive the water pump fast enough. It should be tightened or replaced. Where a pair of belts is used, both should be replaced at the same time. If you replace only one belt, the new belt will do all the work; it will wear rapidly. If both belts are replaced, then each new belt will handle half the job.
7. The trouble may be due to afterboil. That is, the coolant may start to boil after the engine has been turned off. This could happen, for example, after a long, hard drive. The engine has so much heat in it that, after the engine is turned off, the coolant starts to boil.
8. Boiling can also occur if the radiator is frozen. This slows or stops the circulation of coolant. Then the coolant in the engine becomes so hot that it boils. Freezing of the coolant in the radiator, engine block, or head may crack the block or head, or open seams in the radiator. A frozen engine may be damaged seriously.

NOTE: There are other causes of engine overheating which have nothing to do with conditions in the cooling system. These causes of overheating include high-altitude operation, insufficient oil, overloading of the engine, hot-climate operation, improperly timed ignition, and long periods of slow-speed or idling operation.

⊘ 9-3 Loss of Coolant Leakage of coolant from the cooling system is somewhat more common now than it used to be. This is because modern engines have pressurized cooling systems. Leaks are usually obvious, for two reasons. First, the system requires frequent refilling with water or coolant. Second, the point of the leak is usually indicated by telltale scale or water marks below the leak. A leaky gasket (at the cylinder head or water pump) may require replacement. The attaching bolts should be tightened to the correct tension.

If the leak is in the radiator, the radiator should be removed and either repaired (⊘ 9-17) or replaced.

If the leak is at a hose connection, the hose connection should be tightened. If a hose is leaking, the hose should be replaced.

In ⊘ 9-12 we describe the procedure for pressure-testing the cooling system to locate leaks. See Fig. 9-11 for possible locations of leaks in the system.

⊘ 9-4 Slow Warm-up The probable cause of slow engine warm-up is a thermostat that is stuck open. This open position allows the coolant to circulate between the engine and the radiator even though the engine is cold. The engine therefore has to run longer to reach operating temperature. As a result, engine wear is greater, because the engine operates cold for a longer time. The driver's complaint here would be that it takes a long time for the car heater to start putting out heat. If you get this complaint, you should suspect that the thermostat is stuck open (see ⊘ 9-8).

⊘ 9-5 Cooling-System Tests Cooling-system tests include:

1. Checking the coolant level
2. Checking the coolant strength
3. Testing the thermostat
4. Checking the hose and hose connections
5. Testing the water pump
6. Checking for exhaust-gas leakage into the system
7. Pressure-testing the system and cap
8. Checking the fan belt or belts for wear and tension
9. Checking the system for accumulations of rust and scale

These are covered in detail in following sections.

⊘ 9-6 Checking the Coolant Level On cooling systems with a separate expansion tank, it is not necessary to remove the radiator cap to check the coolant level. In fact, car manufacturers warn against removing the radiator cap except for major service. The coolant level can be checked by looking at the expansion tank, which is plastic so that you can see the level of the coolant (Fig. 9-1).

On cooling systems without an expansion tank, you remove the radiator cap to check the coolant level.

CAUTION: Use care when removing a pressure-type radiator cap, especially when the engine is hot. Cover the cap with a cloth to protect your hand, and turn the cap only to the first stop. Any pressure in the system will be released through the overflow tube. Then turn the cap further to remove it. Some manufacturers warn against taking the cap off when the engine is hot and there is pressure in the cooling system. They state that you should turn the cap slightly and listen. If you hear a hissing sound, retighten the cap at once. Leave the cap on tight until the engine has cooled and the pressure has dropped. They also say that the coolant level should not need checking unless the engine has been overheating.

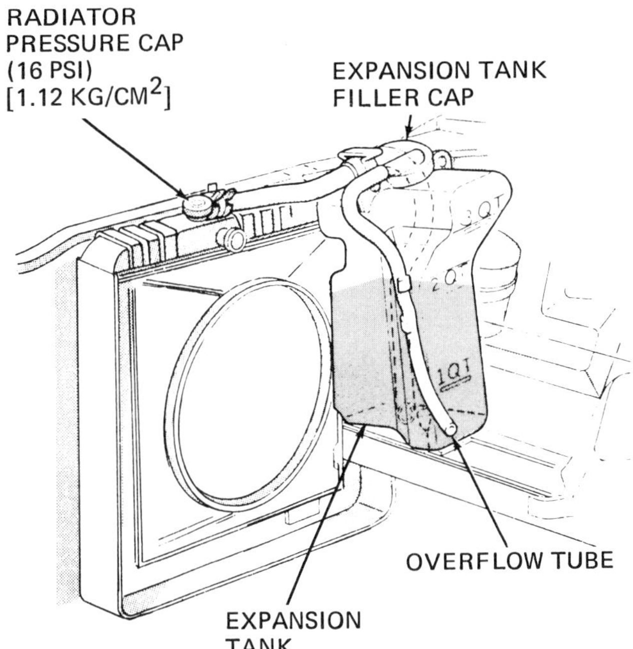

Fig. 9-1. Radiator and expansion tank. (*Chrysler Corporation*)

CAUTION: Keep your hands away from the revolving engine fan. You can be seriously cut by the whirling blades.

⊘ 9-7 Testing the Coolant Strength The strength of the coolant must be great enough to protect against freeze-up at the lowest expected temperature. The strength of the coolant can be checked with any of three testers. One is the hydrometer (Fig. 9-2). The higher the float rises in the coolant, the higher the percentage of antifreeze in the coolant, and the greater its strength. To use the hydrometer, put the rubber tube into the coolant, and then squeeze and release the rubber bulb. Note how high the float rises in the coolant. Check the lower scale, which shows the temperature of the coolant and the lowest temperature at which the coolant will protect against freeze-up.

A second tester has several balls in a glass tube. Coolant is sucked into the tube by squeezing and releasing a rubber bulb. The stronger the solution, the more balls will float.

A third tester, called a *refractometer,* uses the principle of light refraction (bending of light rays) as light passes through a drop of the coolant. To use the refractometer, open the plastic cover at the slanted end of the tester (Fig. 9-3). Wipe the measuring window and the bottom of the plastic cover, as shown, with a tissue or a clean cloth.

Close the plastic cover. Release the tip of the

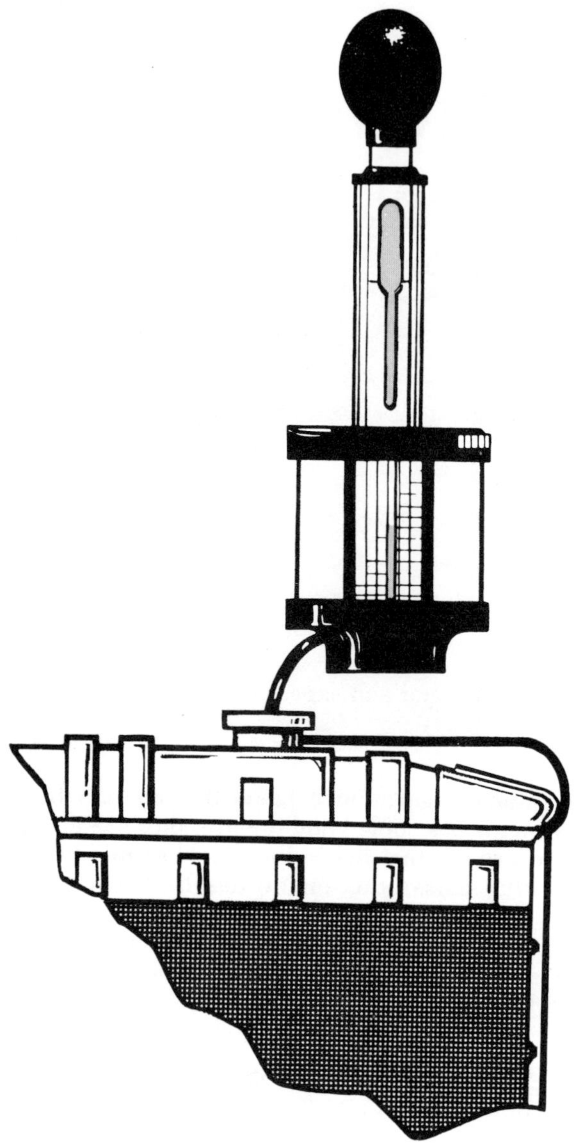

Fig. 9-2. Cooling-system hydrometer, used to check coolant freeze-up protection. (*Ford Motor Company*)

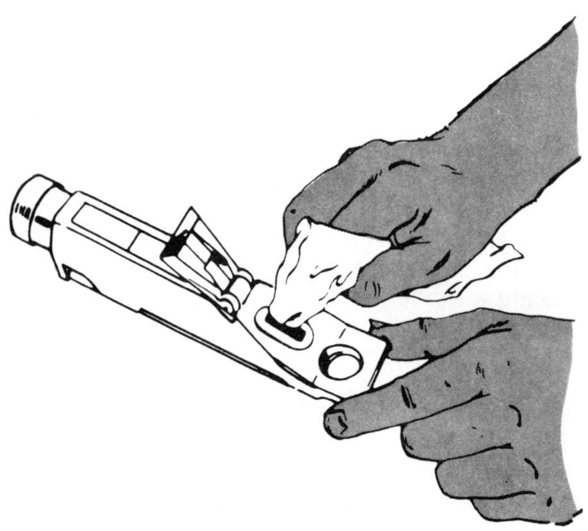

Fig. 9-3. Cleaning the refractometer measuring window.

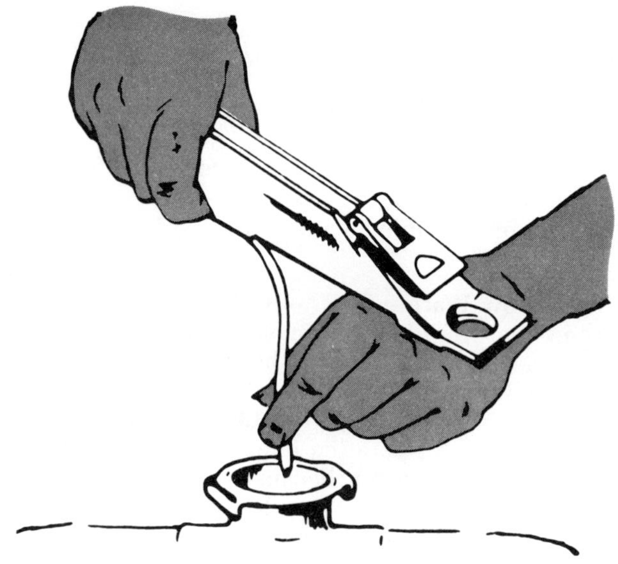

Fig. 9-4. Collecting a sample of coolant from the radiator.

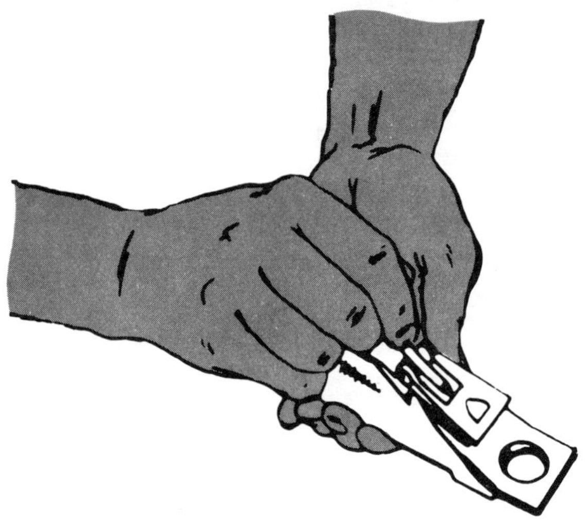

Fig. 9-5. Dropping the sample of coolant on the measuring window.

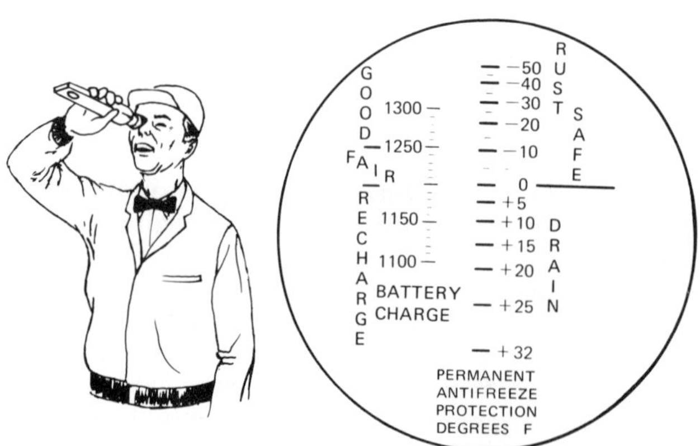

Fig. 9-6. Reading the refractometer.

pump from the tester housing. Insert the tip of the tube into the radiator filler neck (Fig. 9-4). Be sure the end of the tube is well below the level of the coolant. Now press and release the bulb, so that a sample of the coolant is sucked up. Bend the tube around, as shown in Fig. 9-5, so that the tip can be inserted into the cover-plate opening. Squeeze the bulb to put a few drops of coolant into the measuring surface.

Now point the tester toward the light, and look into the eyepiece (Fig. 9-6). The antifreeze-protection reading is where the dividing line between light and dark (the edge of the shadow) crosses the scale. Readings on the lower half of the scale indicate solutions without sufficient antifreeze protection.

NOTE: The refractometer can also be used to check battery electrolyte, to determine the battery state of charge.

CAUTION: The coolant is poisonous! It can cause serious illness and even death if it is swallowed!

⊘ 9-8 Testing the Thermostat Different car manufacturers have different testing procedures for thermostats. Three different manufacturers' procedures are given below.

Chevrolet Procedure

1. To remove the thermostat, partly drain the cooling system so that the coolant level is below the thermostat. If the cooling system contains good antifreeze, catch the drained coolant in a drain pan. The coolant can then be put back in the radiator after the thermostat is replaced.
2. Remove the thermostat housing bolts or nuts, and then remove the housing and gasket.
3. Examine the thermostat for damage such as a cracked bellows, or a sticking valve or valve plunger.
4. Note the thermostat opening temperature, which is usually stamped on the thermostat. If necessary, look up the specification in the service manual.
5. Pour a mixture of one-third antifreeze and two-thirds water in a pan. Place a thermometer in the pan. Heat the mixture until it is 25°F [14°C] *above* the temperature stamped on the thermostat.
6. Submerge the thermostat completely in the mixture, as shown in Fig. 9-7. Then agitate the mixture with the thermostat. If the thermostat is good, the thermostat valve should open fully.
7. Remove the thermostat. Submerge it in a mixture of one-third antifreeze and two thirds water that is heated to a temperature 10°F [5.6°C] *below* the temperature stamped on the thermostat. If the thermostat is good, it should close completely.
8. If the thermostat checks okay, reinstall it. Use a new housing gasket. If the thermostat does not open and close as specified, replace it.

Be sure that all of the old gasket is removed and that the new gasket is properly installed. Install the thermostat with the pellets or bellows end toward

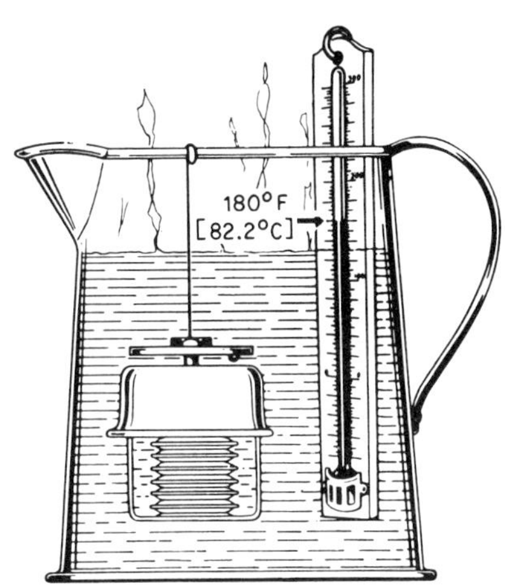

Fig. 9-7. Testing a cooling-system thermostat.

the engine. Otherwise, overheating will result. Do not overtighten the housing nuts or bolts. The thermostat housing may break if it is overtightened or not tightened properly.

9. Refill the radiator, and start the engine. Check for leaks. Be sure the radiator is full before returning the car to the customer.

Plymouth Procedure

Plymouth recommends testing the thermostat in the system. With the cooling system filled to the proper level, warm the engine by driving the car for about 10 min. Remove the radiator cap, observing proper safety precautions. Insert a thermometer into the coolant. Idle the engine with the hood raised. The coolant temperature should stabilize at no lower than 8°F [4.4°C] *below* the thermostat opening temperature.

Ford Procedure

Ford recommends immersing the thermostat in boiling water, as shown in Fig. 9-7. If it does not open, it is defective. If the problem is slow warm-up, the thermostat may be leaking. Hold the thermostat up to the light to see if the valve is closing completely. If there is a gap between the valve and seat with the thermostat at room temperature, replace the thermostat.

⊘ 9-9 Checking the Hose and Hose Connections The appearance of the hose and hose connections usually indicates their condition. If a hose is rotten and soft and collapses easily when squeezed, it should be replaced. Figure 9-8 shows a badly decayed section of hose, split open so that you can see its internal appearance. To avoid leaks, the hose must be in good condition, and connections should be properly tightened.

⊘ 9-10 Testing the Water Pump The test for water-pump efficiency is described in ⊘ 9-2 and 9-5. To make this test, substitute a clear plastic pipe for

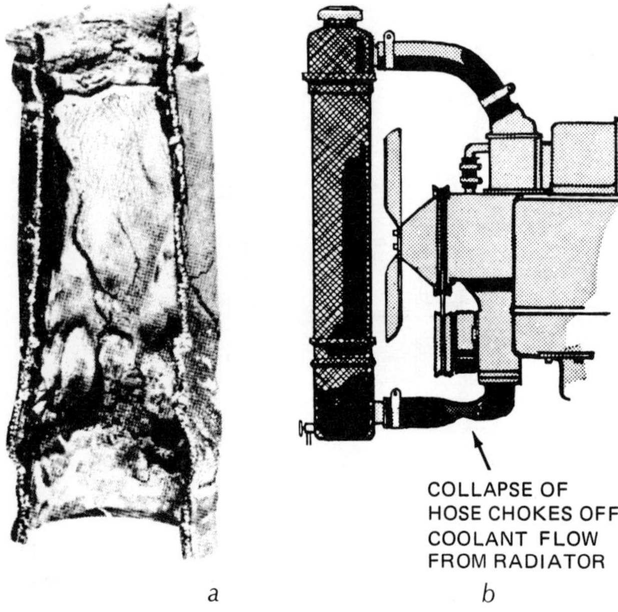

Fig. 9-8. Defective water hose: (*a*) appearance when slit open; (*b*) how the collapsed hose restricts coolant flow.

the upper radiator hose. Then, when the engine is running, you can see how much coolant is circulating. Always be careful when checking and tightening fan belts. Overtightening fan belts can greatly shorten water-pump bearing life (see ⊘ 9-2, item 5).

⊘ 9-11 Checking for Exhaust-Gas Leakage into the System A defective cylinder-head gasket may allow exhaust gas to leak into the cooling system. This is very damaging. Strong acids can form as the gas unites with the water in the coolant. These acids corrode the radiator and other cooling-system parts. A test for exhaust-gas leakage can be made with a Bloc-Chek tester. Install the tester in the radiator filler opening (Fig. 9-9) with the engine running. Then squeeze and release the bulb. This draws an air sample from the cooling system up through the test fluid. The test fluid is ordinarily blue. However, if combustion gas is leaking into the cooling system, the test-fluid color changes to yellow. If a leak is indicated, the exact location can be found by removing one spark-plug wire at a time and retesting. When a leaking cylinder is firing, the liquid color changes to yellow. When only nonleaking cylinders are firing, the liquid remains blue.

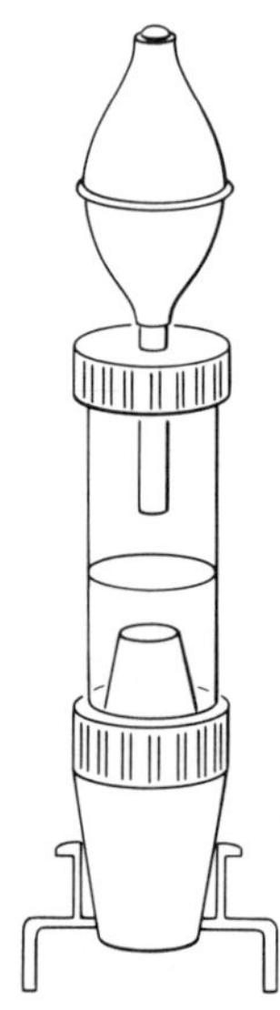

Fig. 9-9. Checking for exhaust-gas leakage into the system with a Bloc-Chek.

NOTE: On cars equipped with a catalytic converter, make this test as quickly as possible. Prolonged operation with the spark-plug cable disconnected may damage the catalytic converter.

Undetected combustion leaks in the valve areas can cause cracked valve seats and cylinder heads. During heavy acceleration, the combustion gases seeping through the leak force coolant away from the leak area. This causes excessive heat buildup. When acceleration stops, the coolant rushes back to the overheated area. The sudden cooling of the area can crack the cylinder head and valve seat.

⊘ 9-12 Pressure-Testing the System To pressure-test the system, apply pressure with a special tester (Fig. 9-10). The tester quickly shows a leaky cooling system. To use the tester, remove the radiator cap and fill the radiator to within ½ in [12.7 mm] of the filler neck. Wipe the neck sealing surface, and attach the tester. Then operate the pump to apply a pressure of not more than 3 psi [0.210 kg/cm^2] *above* the manufacturer's specification. If the pressure holds steady, the system is not leaking. If the pressure drops, there are leaks. Look for external leaks at hose connections, hose, engine expansion plugs, water-pump and cylinder-head gaskets, the water-pump drive shaft, and the radiator (see Fig. 9-11).

If no external leaks are visible, remove the tester and start the engine. Run the engine until the engine

Fig. 9-10. Using the pressure tester to check a cooling system for leaks. (*Texaco Incorporated*)

Fig. 9-11. Places in the cooling system where leaks might develop. (*Union Carbide Corporation*)

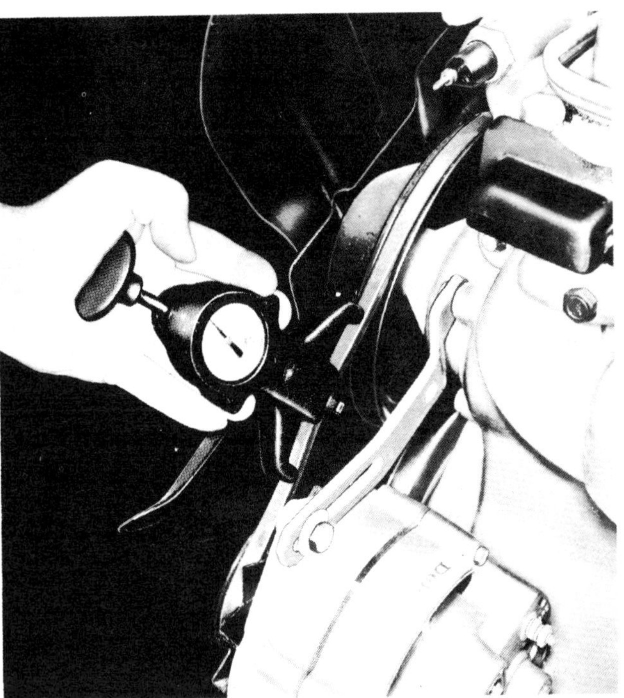

Fig. 9-12. Using a special belt-tension gauge to check fan-belt tension. (*Chevrolet Motor Division of General Motors Corporation*)

operating temperature is reached. Reattach the tester, and apply a pressure of 15 psi [1.055 kg/cm^2]. Increase the engine speed to about half throttle. If the needle of the pressure gauge fluctuates, it indicates an exhaust-gas leak, probably through a cylinder-head gasket. On a V-8 engine, you can determine which bank is at fault by grounding the spark plugs in one bank.

If the needle does not fluctuate, sharply accelerate the engine several times. Check for an abnormal discharge of water through the tail pipe. This indicates a cracked block or head or a defective head gasket.

⊘ 9-13 Pressure-Testing the Radiator Cap The pressure tester shown in Fig. 9-10 can be used to check the radiator pressure cap. If the cap will not hold its rated pressure, it should be replaced.

⊘ 9-14 Testing the Fan Belt Fan belts should be checked for wear and tension. If worn, fan belts should be replaced. On cars with two fan belts running in parallel, if one is worn and requires replacement, then both should be replaced. They come in matched sets. If only one is replaced, the new belt will take most of the wear because it is not stretched like the old belt. This means the new belt will wear rapidly, while the old belt may slip, overheat, and also wear rapidly.

You should always use a tension gauge, such as shown in Fig. 9-12, to check and adjust fan-belt tension.

The fan belt should be checked every few thousand miles to make sure it is still in good condition. A fan belt that has become worn or frayed, or has separated plies, should be discarded. Remember that a faulty belt cannot only cause engine overheating, but may also cause a run-down battery. The faulty belt cannot drive the water pump or alternator fast enough for normal operation.

⊘ 9-15 Testing the System for Accumulations of Rust and Scale At one time, it was common practice to use only water in the cooling system during the summer months. However, with pressurized systems and the use of antifreeze all year round, less rust collects in the cooling system. Some scale may collect from minerals in the water. This is why many manufacturers recommend periodic cleaning of the cooling system. The cooling systems of modern high-temperature engines are very sensitive to accumulations of scale and rust.

There is no easy way to determine the actual amount of scale and rust in the system. The approximate amount of deposits can be found, however, if you know the original capacity of the cooling system. You drain the system and refill it, measuring the amount of water you add. Then you compare the amount of water you added with the capacity of the system. The difference is the amount of rust and scale that has collected.

⊘ 9-16 Cleaning the Cooling System The cooling system should be cleaned periodically. The cleaning removes collected rust and scale, and restores the system to top operating conditions. Recommenda-

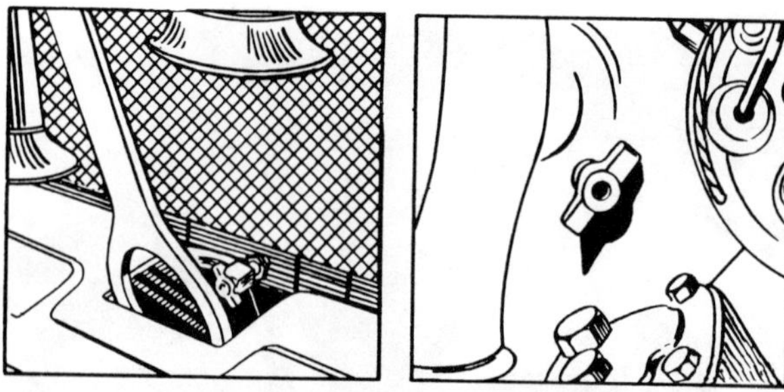

Fig. 9-13. Locations of drain cocks in the radiator and the engine block on one car. (*Chrysler Corporation*)

tions vary. Chevrolet, for example, recommends that the system be drained and flushed with plain water every 2 years. Coolant with new antifreeze should be put in at that time. Here is the procedure that Chevrolet recommends for use in heavily rusted and scaled cooling systems:

1. Drain the cooling system (Fig. 9-13). Remove the thermostat housing and the thermostat. Reinstall the thermostat housing. Close the drain cocks, and add the liquid part of the cooling-system cleaner. Fill the system with water to about 3 in [76.2 mm] below the top of the overflow pipe.
2. Cover the radiator. Run the engine at moderate speed until the water reaches 180°F [82.2°C]. Remove the cover from the radiator, and run the engine for another 20 min. Stop the engine if the water begins to boil.
3. With the engine running, add the powder part of the cooling-system cleaner. Run the engine for another 10 min.

CAUTION: Do not scald your hands.

4. Stop the engine, and wait for it to cool. Then open the drain cocks again to drain the system. Remove the lower hose connection from the radiator.
5. Blow any dirt and bugs from the radiator fins with compressed air, blowing from the engine side. Do not bend the radiator fins, because this decreases the cooling-system efficiency.
6. Reverse-flush the radiator and engine block. In reverse-flushing, water is forced through the system in the direction opposite to normal flow. The water gets behind the scale and rust, loosens it, and flushes it away.
7. To reverse-flush the radiator, remove the radiator's upper and lower hoses. Then replace the radiator cap.
8. Connect a leadaway hose to the inlet at the top of the radiator. Connect a new hose to the radiator outlet at the bottom of the radiator (Fig. 9-14). Connect the water hose of the flushing gun to a water outlet, and the air hose to an air line, as shown. Connect the flushing gun to the new hose at the bottom of the radiator.
9. Turn on the water. When the radiator is full, turn

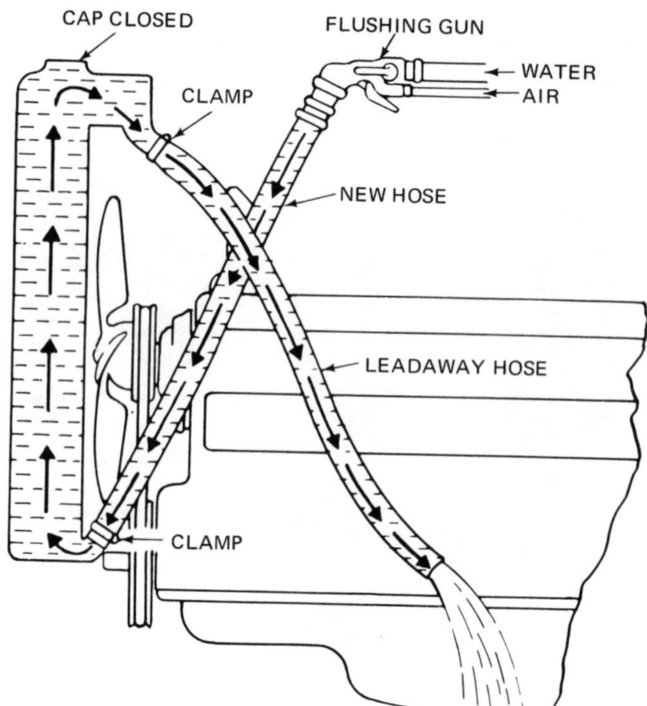

Fig. 9-14. Reverse-flushing a radiator.

on the air in short blasts. Allow the radiator to fill with water between blasts of air.

CAUTION: Apply the air gradually, because the radiator will stand only about 20 psi [1.406 kg/cm^2].

10. Continue until the water leaving the leadaway hose runs clear.
11. To reverse-flush the cylinder block and head, first disconnect the heater hose. Cap the connections at the engine. With the radiator hose removed, attach a leadaway hose to the water-pump inlet. Connect a length of new hose to the coolant outlet at the top of the engine (Fig. 9-15). Connect the flushing gun to the new hose at the top of the engine.
12. Turn on the water. When the engine water jacket is full, turn on the air in short blasts.

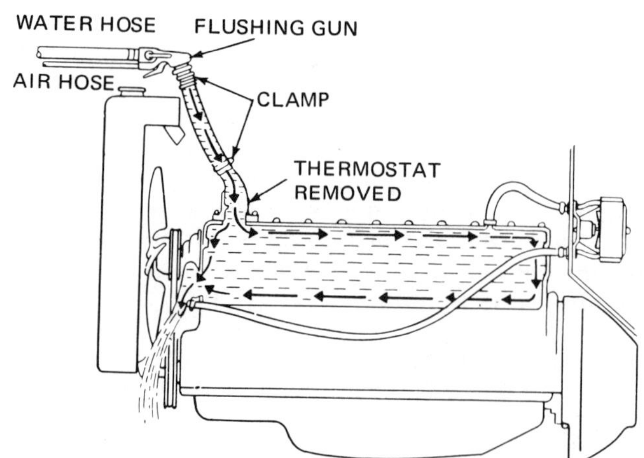

Fig. 9-15. Reverse-flushing the engine water jackets.

CAUTION: Excessive pressure can blow out the cylinder-block freeze plugs (also called the *expansion-core plugs* or *water-jacket plugs*). Servicing of these plugs is covered in ⊘ 9-19.

13. Continue flushing until the water leaving the leadaway hose runs clear.
14. The heater radiator core should also be reverse-flushed. Take care to avoid too much air pressure. The core can be damaged by excessive air pressure.
15. Replace the thermostat and the radiator's upper and lower hoses. Use new hoses if the old hoses are worn or damaged in any way. Make sure the hoses are fully engaged on the tubes, and that the clamps are properly tightened.
16. Add enough antifreeze to give full protection against freeze-up at the lowest temperature expected. Fill the system with water. Since the water is cold, the thermostat will close and prevent quick filling. Air will be trapped in back of the closed thermostat (Fig. 9-16). The thermostat has a small hole that permits air to leak out, but this takes some time. You may have to wait and refill the radiator a couple of times. The engine can be started and run for a few moments until the thermostat heats up and opens. Then completely fill the radiator with water.
17. Check the system for leaks after running the engine for a few minutes.

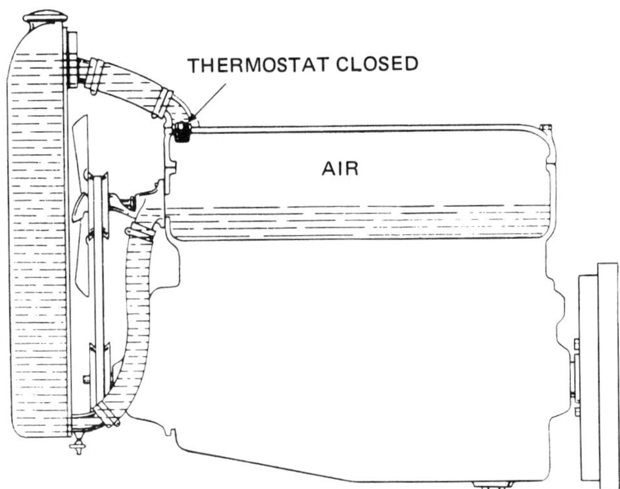

Fig. 9-16. Air is trapped behind a closed thermostat as the engine cooling system is filled.

⊘ 9-17 Locating and Repairing Radiator Leaks Figure 9-17 shows the radiator for a V-8 engine. Leaks in a radiator are usually obvious. Telltale scale marks or water marks form on the outside of the core, below the leaks. An accurate way to locate radiator leaks is to remove the radiator from the car and drain out all the coolant. Then close the openings at top and bottom, and immerse the radiator in water. Air bubbles will escape from the radiator through any leaks. Small leaks can sometimes be repaired without removing the radiator from the car. Certain liquid compounds, when poured into the radiator, seep through the leaks. They harden on contact with the air, sealing off the openings. A more effective way of repairing leaks is to solder them. If there are several leaks at various places in the radiator, it may not be worthwhile to repair them. The radiator is probably corroded to a point where other leaks will soon develop.

NOTE: Radiator repairs are usually performed in a shop that specializes in radiator service.

Removing a radiator is a simple job, although it takes a considerable amount of work. The procedure

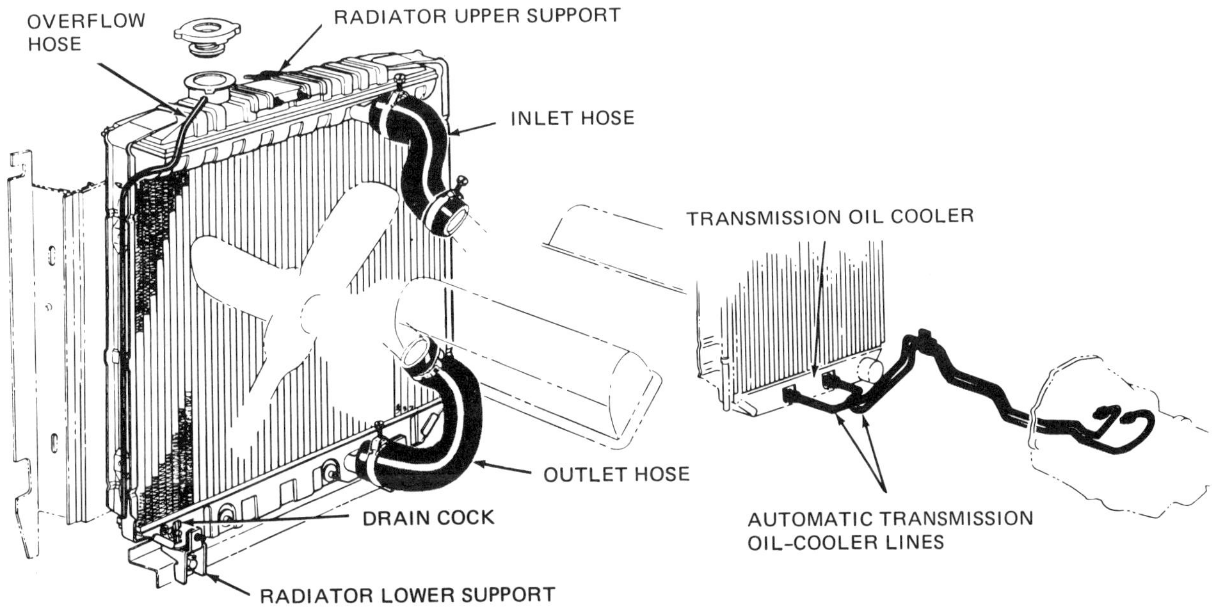

Fig. 9-17. Radiator installation on a V-8 engine. (*Ford Motor Company*)

varies somewhat from car to car but, in general, is as follows:

1. Drain the engine and radiator by opening the drain cocks in the radiator and engine block.
2. Detach the upper and lower radiator hoses.
3. Remove any support bolts, horns, wiring harnesses, and other components that might interfere with radiator removal.
4. With these parts out of the way and the radiator loose, lift it straight up and off the car.

⊘ 9-18 Water-Pump Service The water pump is a relatively simple mechanism which requires little service in normal operation. Some pumps require periodic lubrication; others, with sealed ball bearings, require no lubrication. If the pump develops a noise or leaks or becomes otherwise defective, it must be removed for repair. The removal and replacement procedures vary for different cars. Here is a typical procedure.

The water pump for a V-8 engine is shown disassembled in Fig. 9-18. To remove the pump, drain the cooling system. Then remove the water-inlet hose and the heater hose from the pump. Remove the fan belt and attaching bolts, and take off the pump.

CAUTION: On six-cylinder engines, you must pull the pump straight out to avoid damaging the impeller and shaft.

When reinstalling the pump on the engine, adjust the fan belt to the proper tension (⊘ 9-14).

⊘ 9-19 Expansion-Core Plugs You might have to remove an expansion-core plug from an engine block (because of coolant leakage, for example). To do this, place the pointed end of a pry bar against the center of the plug. Tap the end of the bar with a hammer until the point goes through the plug. Then press the pry bar to one side to pop the plug out. Another method is to drill a small hole in the center of the plug and then pry the plug out.

CAUTION: Do not drive the pry bar or drill past the plug. On some engines the plug is only about $^3/_8$ in [9.52 mm] from a cylinder wall. You can damage the cylinder wall if you drive the pry bar or drill too far in. Do not drive the plug into the water jacket. You will have trouble getting it out, and it may block coolant circulation if it is left in.

Inspect the bore for roughness or damage that would prevent proper sealing of a new plug. If necessary, bore out the bore to take the next larger size of plug. Before installing the new plug, coat it with the proper sealer (water-resistant for cooling systems; oil-resistant for oil galleries). Use the proper installation tool, and proceed as follows, depending on the type of plug (Fig. 9-19):

1. *CUP TYPE* The cup-type plug is installed with the flanged edge outward. A tool of the proper size must be used. It must not contact the flange; the tool must drive against the internal cup. The flange must be brought down below the chamfered edge of the bore.
2. *EXPANSION TYPE* The expansion-type plug is installed with the flanged edge inward, as shown. Again, the proper tool must be used. The crowned center part must not be touched when the plug is

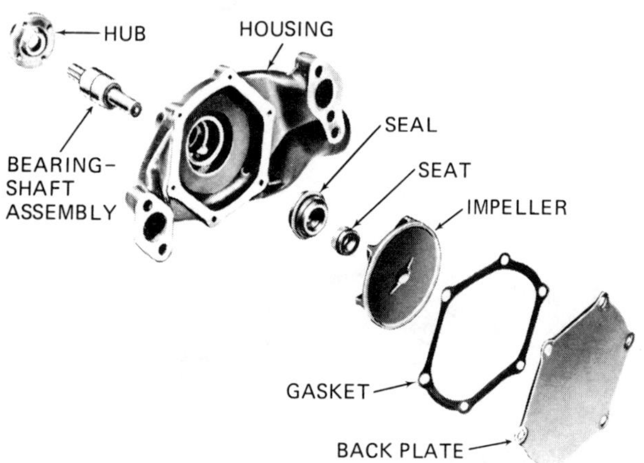

Fig. 9-18. Disassembled view of a water pump for a V-8 engine. (*Chevrolet Motor Division of General Motors Corporation*)

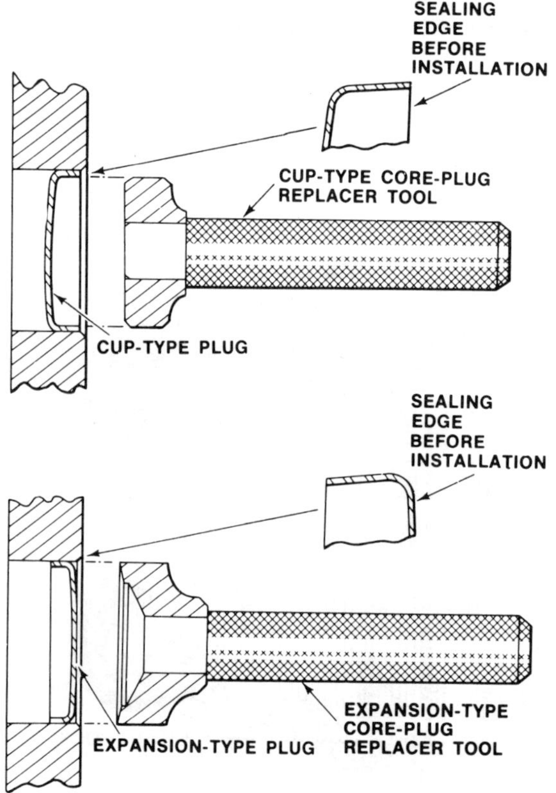

Fig. 9-19. Expansion-core plugs and installation tools. (*Ford Motor Company*)

driven in. Instead, the tool must drive against the outer part of the plug, as shown. The plug should be driven until the top of the crown is below the chamfered edge of the bore.

CHAPTER 9 CHECKUP

NOTE: Since the following is a chapter review test, you should review the chapter before taking the test.

You have made good progress in your studies. The information you learned in the last two chapters gives you the basic background you need to become a specialist in engine tuneup, or to become a good all-around automotive mechanic. Work through this checkup on cooling-system service, to make sure you have grasped the essential facts. Write your answers in your notebook.

Completing the Sentences The sentences below are incomplete. After each sentence there are several words or phrases, but only one of them correctly completes the sentence. Write each sentence in your notebook, ending it with the one word or phrase that completes it correctly.

1. Accumulations of rust and scale in the engine cooling system cause: (*a*) slow warm-up, (*b*) reduced heating capacity, (*c*) overheating.
2. If the thermostat is stuck closed, the engine will: (*a*) warm up slowly, (*b*) overheat, (*c*) fail to start.
3. If the thermostat is stuck open, the engine will: (*a*) warm up slowly, (*b*) overheat, (*c*) fail to start.
4. The strength of the coolant in the cooling system is checked with a: (*a*) micrometer, (*b*) hydrometer, (*c*) barometer, (*d*) thermometer.
5. Exhaust-gas leakage into the cooling system is most likely to be due to a defective: (*a*) cylinder-head gasket, (*b*) manifold gasket, (*c*) water pump.
6. Air will be drawn into the cooling system if there are leaks at any point between the: (*a*) water pump and jackets, (*b*) radiator and water pump, (*c*) thermostat and radiator.
7. When the coolant boils after the engine has been turned off after a hard run, the condition is known as: (*a*) overheating, (*b*) hard running, (*c*) a clogged radiator, (*d*) afterboiling.
8. When reverse-flushing the radiator, you connect the flushing gun to the: (*a*) upper tank, (*b*) pump inlet, (*c*) lower tank.
9. When reverse-flushing the engine water jackets, you connect the flushing gun to the: (*a*) upper tank, (*b*) lower tank, (*c*) thermostat housing, (*d*) pump inlet.
10. When refilling the system with cold water causes the engine to cool down, air may be trapped: (*a*) back of the thermostat, (*b*) above the thermostat, (*c*) in the radiator.

Correcting Lists Each of the lists below contains one item that does not belong. Write each list in your notebook, but do not write the item that does not belong.

1. Engine overheating can be caused by: accumulations of rust and scale, thermostat stuck closed, thermostat stuck open, loose fan belt, defective hose, and defective water pump.
2. Slow engine warm-up can be caused by: thermostat stuck open, manifold heat-control valve stuck, and thermostat stuck closed.
3. The cooling-system tests include tests of the: thermostat, radiator (for restrictions), hose and hose connections, water pump, fuel pump, fan belt, and coolant strength.
4. Items in the cooling system that can be flushed with the flushing gun include the: radiator, engine water jackets, filter, and car heater.
5. Boiling of the coolant can occur because of: radiator freezing, afterboil, thermostat stuck closed, high-altitude operation, broken fan belt, and thermostat stuck open.

Procedures In the following, you are asked about certain servicing procedures and troubles. Write the answers in your notebook. The act of writing helps you remember the important points. It also makes your notebook a very valuable reference, where you can look up things that have escaped your memory for the moment.

1. How is the thermostat tested?
2. How can the cooling system be tested for rust and scale?
3. How can you check the radiator for restrictions?
4. How can the water pump be checked on the car?
5. How can the cooling system be tested for exhaust-gas leakage?
6. How is the fan belt adjusted?
7. How is the strength of the coolant tested?
8. What conditions in the cooling system cause engine overheating?
9. What condition in the cooling system would cause slow engine warm-up?
10. Describe how a cooling system is flushed out.
11. Describe how to remove a radiator core, locate a leak, and repair the leak.
12. Describe, step by step, how to remove and replace a water pump on a car.

SUGGESTIONS FOR FURTHER STUDY

Watch how the mechanics at an automotive service shop clean out cooling systems and take off radiators and water pumps. Notice how they service water pumps, and what special equipment they need for this job. Study the shop manuals for various makes of cars, and notice the different repair methods these manuals recommend. Write in your notebook any important facts you run across in the manuals or in the shop.

chapter 10

AUTOMOTIVE-ENGINE FUELS

This chapter discusses the fuels used in automotive-type engines: gasoline, LPG (liquified petroleum gas), and diesel-engine fuel oil.

⊘ 10-1 Gasoline Gasoline is a hydrocarbon (abbreviated HC) made up of hydrogen and carbon. These two elements unite readily with oxygen, a common element which makes up about 20 percent of our air. When hydrogen unites with oxygen, water (H_2O) is formed. When carbon unites with oxygen, carbon monoxide (CO) and carbon dioxide (CO_2) are formed. If all the gasoline burned completely in the engine, only water (H_2O) and carbon dioxide (CO_2) would leave the tail pipe. However, perfect combustion is not achieved in the engine. So some CO and HC are present in the exhaust gases. These two compounds, plus nitrogen oxides (NO_x), are the pollutants emitted from automobiles. Later in the book, we explain in detail how these emissions are controlled.

NOTE: Gasoline is often referred to as "gas," which can cause some confusion. The sort of gas you burn in a gas stove or use to heat a house is actually in the gaseous state. It is delivered through gas lines or pipes. So there is gas that is actually a gas, and "gas" that is a slang expression for the liquid fuel gasoline. Don't get confused on this.

⊘ 10-2 Source of Gasoline Gasoline is made from crude oil, or petroleum. No one knows exactly how crude oil was originally formed. It is found in "pools" or reservoirs in the ground. A well is drilled down into a reservoir. Underground pressure (or pressure artificially applied from above ground) forces the oil up and out of the well. The crude oil is then put through a refining process. From this process come gasoline, lubricating oil, greases, fuel oil, and many other products.

In the refining process, several compounds, called *additives*, are put into the gasoline. These additives give the gasoline the properties a good fuel should have. They are described in ⊘ 10-15.

⊘ 10-3 Volatility of Gasoline Actually, gasoline is not a simple substance. It is a mixture of a number of different hydrocarbons. Each has its own characteristics. Aside from its combustibility, one of the important properties of gasoline is *volatility*.

Volatility refers to the ease with which a liquid boils, or vaporizes. A liquid that boils at a low temperature has a high volatility; it evaporates readily. If its boiling point is high, its volatility is low. A heavy oil with a boiling point of 600°F [315.5°C] is considered to have a low volatility. Water has a high volatility; it boils at 212°F [100°C] at atmospheric pressure.

Gasoline is a blend of different hydrocarbon compounds. Each compound has a different volatility, or boiling point. The proportions of high-volatility and low-volatility hydrocarbons in gasoline must be correct for engine operating requirements. These requirements include:

1. Easy starting. For easy starting with a cold engine, gasoline must vaporize readily at a low temperature. Thus, a percentage of the gasoline must be highly volatile. This percentage must be higher for the colder northern states than for the warmer south.
2. Freedom from vapor lock. If the gasoline is too volatile, engine heat will cause it to vaporize in the fuel pump. This can cause vapor lock. Vapor lock prevents normal fuel delivery to the carburetor and usually stalls the engine. Thus, the percentage of highly volatile gasoline must be kept low to prevent vapor lock. The use of a vapor-return line to return vaporized fuel from the fuel pump to the fuel tank is discussed in ⊘ 11-7.
3. Quick warm-up. The speed with which the engine warms up depends in part on how much gasoline vaporizes immediately after the engine starts. Volatility does not have to be quite so high for this purpose as for easy starting. But, all the same, it must be fairly high.
4. Smooth acceleration. When the throttle is opened for acceleration, there is a sudden increase in the amount of air passing through the throttle valve. At the same time, the accelerator pump delivers extra gasoline. If this gasoline does not vaporize quickly, the air-fuel mixture is too lean for a few seconds.

This causes the engine to hesitate, or stumble. Then, when the gasoline begins to evaporate, the mixture becomes too rich. Here again, there is poor combustion, and the engine tends to hesitate. Enough of the gasoline must be highly volatile to assure adequate vaporization for smooth acceleration.

5. Good economy. For good fuel economy, or maximum miles per gallon, the fuel must have high heat content, or energy, and low volatility. High overall volatility tends to reduce economy. It may produce an overrich mixture under many operating conditions. On the other hand, lower-volatility fuels tend to burn more efficiently. They have a higher heat content. However, the lower-volatility fuels increase starting difficulty. They reduce the speed of warm-up, and do not give quite as good acceleration. Thus, only a limited percentage of the gasoline can be of low volatility.

6. Freedom from crankcase dilution. Crankcase dilution results when part of the gasoline is not vaporized and it enters the engine cylinders as a liquid. The liquid gasoline does not burn. It runs down the cylinder walls and enters the oil pan, where it dilutes the oil. This washes lubricating oil from the cylinder walls (thus increasing the wear of walls, rings, and pistons). Also, diluted oil is less able to lubricate other engine parts, such as the bearings. To avoid damage from crankcase dilution, the gasoline must be volatile enough to vaporize before it enters the cylinders.

As you can see, no one volatility satisfies all engine operating requirements. The fuel must be of high volatility for easy starting and good acceleration. But it must also be of low volatility to give good fuel economy and combat vapor lock. Thus, gasoline is blended from different hydrocarbons having different volatilities. Such a blend satisfies the various operating requirements.

⊘ 10-4 Antiknock Value During normal combustion in the engine cylinder, the pressure increases evenly. Under some conditions, the last part of the compressed air-fuel mixture explodes, or detonates. This produces a sudden and sharp pressure increase that may cause a pinging or rattling noise. This noise is called spark knock, or detonation. It sounds almost as though the piston head was hit with a hammer. Actually, the sudden pressure increase does put a sudden heavy load on the piston, almost like a hammer blow. This can be very damaging to the engine. It can wear moving parts rapidly, and even cause parts to break. Also, some of the energy in the gasoline is wasted. The sudden pressure increase does not permit best use of the fuel energy.

Some types of gasoline produce much more detonation than others. Because detonation is so undesirable, gasoline producers try to reduce detonation tendencies. Certain chemicals have been found to reduce detonation when added to gasoline. The actual antiknock tendency of a gasoline is given as its *octane number* (ON).

⊘ 10-5 Heat of Compression To understand why detonation occurs, remember what happens to air or any other gas when it is compressed. The diesel engine compresses air to about $\frac{1}{20}$ of its original volume. This increases the air temperature to about 1,000°F [537.8°C]. The temperature rise is called the *heat of compression*. The gasoline engine does not compress the air-fuel as much as the diesel engine. However, it does compress the mixture enough to raise its temperature several hundred degrees. Let's see how this heat of compression affects detonation.

⊘ 10-6 Cause of Spark Knock or Detonation Normally, the spark at the spark plug starts the fuel burning in the combustion chamber. A wall of flame spreads out in all directions from the spark. (It moves outward almost like a rubber balloon being blown up.) The flame travels rapidly through the compressed mixture, until all the charge is burned. The speed with which the flame travels is called the *rate of flame propagation*. The movement of the flame wall during normal combustion is shown in the row of pictures at the top in Fig. 10-1. During combustion, the pressure increases to several hundred pounds per square inch. It may exceed 1,000 psi [70.3 kg/cm^2] in modern high-compression engines.

Under certain conditions, the last part of the compressed air-fuel mixture, the *end gas*, explodes before the flame front reaches it (Fig. 10-1, bottom). The unburned mixture is subject to increasing pressure as the flame moves through the combustion chamber. This increases the temperature of the end gas (because of heat of compression and heat from the combustion process). If the temperature gets high enough, this end gas explodes before the flame front arrives. The effect on the piston head is almost the same as a heavy hammer blow. In fact, it sounds as though this had happened. The sudden shock load due to detonation of the end gas increases wear on bearings. It may actually break engine parts if the detonation is severe enough.

⊘ 10-7 Compression Ratio versus Detonation As compression ratios of engines have gone up, so has the tendency for engines to detonate. Here is the reason. With a higher compression ratio, the mixture is more highly compressed at TDC (top dead center). *It is thus at a higher initial temperature*. With higher initial pressure and temperature, the detonation temperature is reached sooner. Thus, high-compression engines have a greater tendency to detonate. However, special fuels which burn slower have been developed for higher-compression engines. These fuels have a greater resistance to being ignited suddenly by the heat of compression. They are less apt to explode suddenly. They depend, for ignition, only on the wall of flame traveling through the air-fuel mixture.

⊘ 10-8 Measuring Antiknock Values There are several methods of measuring the antiknock value of

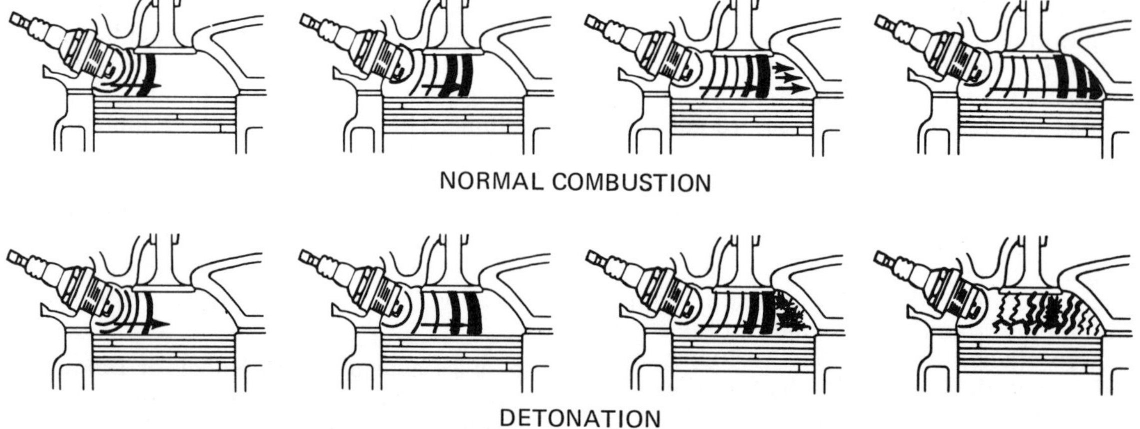

Fig. 10-1. Normal combustion without detonation is shown in the top row. The fuel charge burns smoothly from beginning to end, providing an even, powerful thrust to the piston. Detonation is shown in the bottom row. The last part of the fuel explodes, or burns, almost all at once, producing detonation, or spark knock. (*General Motors Corporation*)

a fuel. The antiknock rating is given as an octane number (ON). A high-octane (high-ON) gasoline is highly resistant to detonation. A low-octane fuel detonates rather easily. For example, one fuel, called *iso-octane* is very resistant to detonation. It is given an octane number of 100. Another fuel, called *heptane,* detonates very easily. It has an ON of zero. A mixture of half iso-octane and half heptane (by volume) would have an ON of 50. A mixture of 90 percent iso-octane and 10 percent heptane would have an ON of 90.

Actually, iso-octane and heptane are reference fuels, used only to test and rate unknown fuels. The test is made approximately as follows: The fuel to be tested is used in an engine under various conditions and compression ratios. Its tolerance to detonation is noted. Then the two reference fuels are mixed in varying proportions and used to run the engine under identical conditions. For example, suppose a mixture of 88 percent iso-octane and 12 percent heptane produces the same detonation as the fuel being tested. Then the fuel being tested is considered to have an ON of 88.

One test method, called the *modified borderline procedure,* rates the fuel at various speeds. The engine is run at various speeds on a dynamometer. The amount of ignition spark advance the fuel can tolerate without detonation is determined for each speed. (If the spark is advanced too much at any particular speed, detonation will occur.) The test results give a curve that shows, at every engine speed, the detonation characteristics of the fuel being tested (Fig. 10-2). Any spark advance above the curve causes detonation.

We should note, however, that some fuels detonate at high speeds, and others detonate at low speeds. For an example, refer to Fig. 10-3. This shows the curves of two fuels, *A* and *B*. Curve *C* is the amount of spark advance the distributor pro-

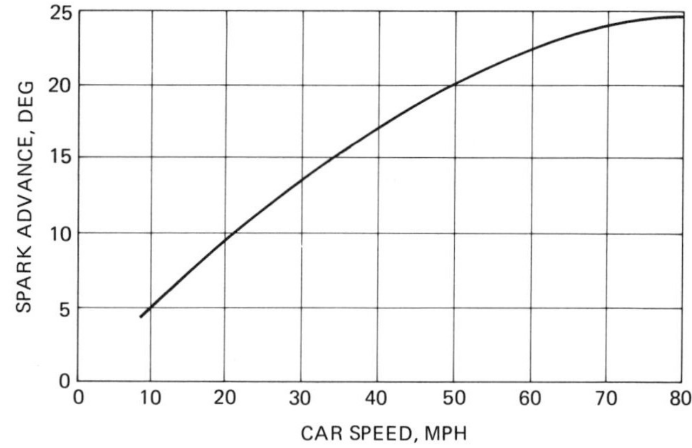

Fig. 10-2. Borderline detonation curve. The fuel being tested will detonate, or ping, if the ignition spark is advanced to any value above the curve at any speed.

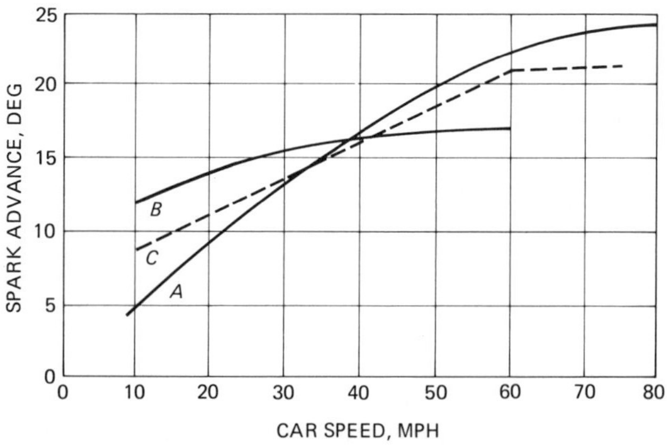

Fig. 10-3. Comparison of borderline detonation curves of two fuels (*A* and *B*). Curve *C* is the spark advance actually provided by the ignition distributor on the engine.

vides on the engine used in the test. (See ⊘ 28-20 to 28-25 for a discussion of spark-advance mechanisms.) At any particular speed, if the distributor advances the spark more than the fuel can tolerate, the fuel will detonate. Thus fuel *A* will detonate at low speed, since the spark advance is more than the fuel can tolerate. (That is, curve *C* is above curve *A* at low speed.) On the other hand, fuel *A* will not detonate at high speed. The spark advance is less than what the fuel can tolerate at high speed. But fuel *B* shows a different picture. It will not detonate at low speed but will detonate at high speed, with the spark-advance curve shown. The curves in Fig. 10-3 apply only to fuels *A* and *B*. However, they show that different fuels act differently at different speeds and in different engines.

⊘ 10-9 Detonation versus Preignition Let us define these two terms: *Detonation* is a secondary explosion that occurs *after* the spark at the spark plug. *Preignition* is ignition of the air-fuel mixture *before* the spark occurs at the spark plug.

Thus far, we have discussed the type of spark knock that results from detonation, or sudden explosion, of the last part of the fuel charge. This type of noise is usually regular in character. It is most noticeable when the engine is accelerating or is under heavy load, as when climbing a hill. Under these conditions, the throttle valve is nearly or fully wide open. The engine is taking in a full air-fuel charge on every intake stroke. This means the compression pressures in the cylinders are maximal. The detonation pressure is more likely to be reached, once the mixture is ignited.

There are other types of abnormal combustion, however, including surface ignition, preignition, and rumble. Surface ignition can start at hot spots in the combustion chamber. The hot spot may be a hot exhaust valve or spark plug, or a combustion-chamber deposit. In some cases, deposits break loose; the particles float free and become hot enough to produce ignition. Surface ignition can occur before (preignition) or after the spark occurs at the spark plug. It can cause engine rumble and rough operation, or mild to severe noise. In some cases, the hot spots act as substitutes for the spark plugs. Then the engine continues to run even after the ignition switch is turned off. This can cause serious engine damage.

Preignition, surface ignition, and rumble are usually service problems. They result from inadequate servicing of the engine and from installation of the wrong spark plugs (which run too hot). They may also result from the use of incorrect fuels and lubricating oils.

Incorrect fuel or oil may cause engine deposits, which lead to surface ignition and rumble. Engine deposits also increase the compression ratio, so the engine tends to detonate more.

⊘ 10-10 Chemical Control of Detonation Several chemicals, when added to gasoline, tend to prevent detonation of the end gas during combustion. One theory is that the chemical increases the reaction time of the fuel. That is, it increases the time required for the end gas to explode. This gives the flame front more time to reach the end gas. The result is that the end gas ignites normally, instead of exploding. One of the compounds most successful in preventing detonation is tetraethyl lead, commonly called *ethyl* or *tel*. A small amount added to gasoline raises the ON of the gasoline.

Special *scavengers* are also added. These prevent the lead in the tel from depositing in the combustion chambers (on plugs, valves, cylinder walls, and pistons). These compounds (ethylene dibromide and ethylene dichloride, for example) change the lead into compounds which vaporize and exit with the exhaust gases.

⊘ 10-11 Octane Ratings The antiknock values of gasoline, or octane ratings, are measured and given in different ways (⊘ 10-8). The research octane number (RON) is a measure of the antiknock properties under relatively mild operating conditions. The engine octane, given by the motor octane number (MON), is measured under more severe operating conditions. A third octane rating, now in widespread use, is the *antiknock index*, which is related to the actual road antiknock characteristics of car engines. This is the rating you find on the white circular stickers posted on gasoline pumps at service stations. The antiknock index is actually the average of the research-octane and motor-octane numbers. That is, antiknock index = $\frac{1}{2}$(RON + MON). Generally, the antiknock index is 87 for unleaded regular gasoline, 90 for leaded regular gasoline, and 95 for leaded premium gasoline.

⊘ 10-12 Tetraethyl Lead Tetraethyl lead raises the ON rating of gasoline and thus reduces detonation tendencies. It also increases valve and valve-seat life. The lead coats the valve and valve seat and thus provides lubrication. However, lead in gasoline has a bad effect on the catalysts used in catalytic converters. These converters are connected into the exhaust system; they convert certain pollutants in the exhaust gases to harmless compounds. (There is more on this in ⊘ 18-17.) Lead from the gasoline deposits on the catalysts and stops them from doing their job. That is why some gasolines today have little or no lead. And, because there is less lead in gasoline, the compression ratios of automotive engines have been reduced in recent years.

The lack of lead in gasoline can also have a harmful effect on valves and valve seats. Without the lubrication provided by the lead, the valve and valve seat can wear more rapidly. To prevent this, modern automotive-engine valves have special coatings, or facings, on their faces. Also, many engines use valve-seat inserts or have valve seats that are induction-hardened.

⊘ 10-13 Mechanical Factors Affecting Detonation The shape of the combustion chamber has a great effect on engine detonation. The top of the combustion chamber of an I-head engine is formed by the cylinder head, intake and exhaust valves, and spark plug. The bottom is formed by the piston head and top compression ring (Fig. 10-4). There are two general combustion-chamber shapes, wedge and hemispheric (Fig. 10-5). The shape determines the amount of turbulence, squish, and quench. These three factors affect detonation.

1. *TURBULENCE* When you stir coffee, you produce movement, or turbulence. The turbulence causes the cream and sugar to mix with the coffee. In the same way, turbulence in the air-fuel mixture entering the combustion chamber assures more even mixing. This makes the combustion more even. Turbulence also reduces the time required for the flame front to sweep through the compressed mixture.

2. *SQUISH* In some combustion chambers, the piston squishes, or squeezes, part of the air-fuel mixture at the end of the compression stroke. Figure 10-5 (left) shows the squish area in a combustion chamber. As the piston nears TDC, the mixture is squished, or pushed, out of the squish area. As it moves out, it increases turbulence and mixing of the air-fuel mixture.

3. *QUENCH* We noted that detonation results when the end-gas temperature goes too high. The end gas explodes before the flame front reaches it. However, if some heat is taken from the end gas, then its temperature drops. It does not reach the detonation temperature. In the cylinder shown to the left in Fig. 10-5, the squish area is also a quench (heat-removal) area. The cylinder head is close to the piston. Both these metallic surfaces are cooler than the end gas. They remove heat from the end gas and "quench" its tendency to detonate. However, this causes a problem with exhaust emissions (⊘ 18-6).

4. *THE HEMISPHERIC COMBUSTION CHAMBER* In a hemispheric combustion chamber, the spark plug can be located near the center of the dome (Fig. 10-5, right). Then, when combustion starts, the flame front has a shorter distance to travel. There are no distant pockets of end gas to detonate. The chamber has no squish or quench areas. However, there is relatively little turbulence.

5. *THE WEDGE COMBUSTION CHAMBER* In a wedge combustion chamber, the spark plug is located to one side. The flame front must travel a greater distance to reach the end of the wedge (Fig. 10-5, left). The end of the wedge has a squish and quench area which cools the end gas to prevent detonation. At the same time it causes turbulence in the mixture.

6. *SMOG* The shape of the combustion chamber also affects the amount of pollutants in the exhaust gases. The cooler metal surfaces of the cylinder head and piston top slow combustion. Therefore, the layers of air-fuel mixture next to these metal surfaces do not burn completely. Incomplete burning means more pollutants. The wedge combustion chamber has a larger surface area. It thus produces a greater percentage of pollutants than the hemispheric combustion chamber (see ⊘ 18-6 and 18-7).

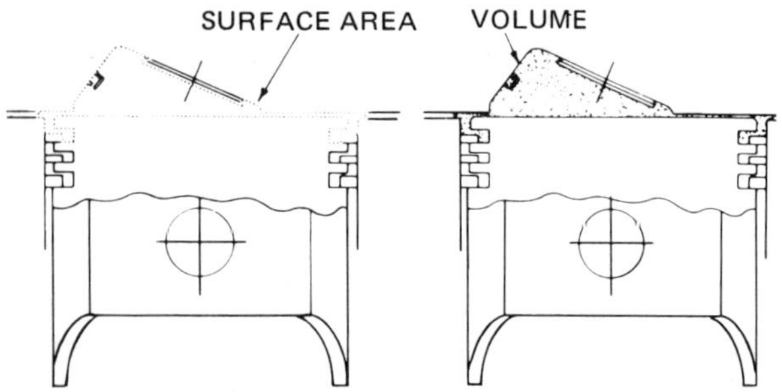

Fig. 10-4. Combustion chamber. The surface area is shown by the dotted line.

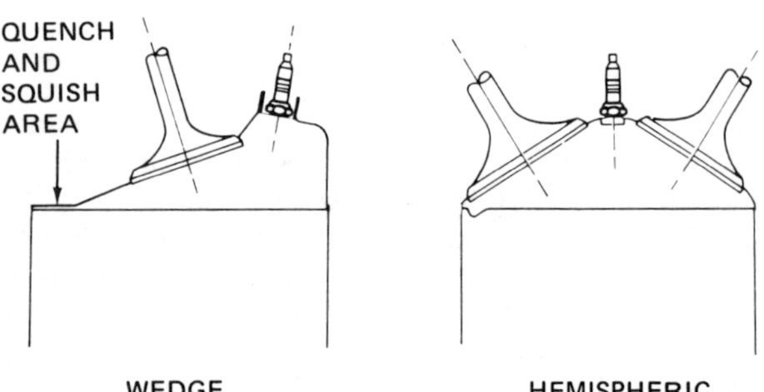

Fig. 10-5. Wedge and hemispheric combustion chambers. (*General Motors Corporation*)

⊘ 10-14 Other Factors Affecting Detonation Many operating conditions in an engine affect detonation. For example, higher air temperatures increase the tendency to detonate. Higher humidity (damper air) and higher altitudes (lower-density air) reduce the tendency to detonate. Engine deposits (carbon in the combustion chamber) increase detonation tendency. Advancing the spark increases the tendency to detonate. Less fuel in the air-fuel mixture increases the tendency of the engine to detonate.

All these factors show the need for good maintenance of the modern high-compression engine. Buildups of scale in the cooling system reduce cooling efficiency. Clogged fuel lines or nozzles in the carburetor lean out the mixture. These increase detonation in the engine, as do improper ignition timing and engine deposits.

⊘ 10-15 Other Gasoline Additives Antiknock compounds and lead-vaporizing substances are put into gasoline to raise its octane rating (⊘ 10-10). Other additives are also used. These include:

1. Oxidation inhibitors, to help prevent the formation of gum while the gasoline is in storage.

2. Metal deactivators, to protect the gasoline from the harmful effects of certain metals. Such metals can be picked up in the refining process or in the vehicle fuel system.
3. Antirust agents, to protect the vehicle fuel system.
4. Anti-icers, to combat carburetor icing and fuel-line freeze.
5. Detergents, to keep the carburetor clean.
6. Phosphorous compounds, to combat surface ignition and spark-plug fouling.
7. Dye, for identification.

In addition, the refining process is carefully controlled to keep sulfur compounds and gum-forming substances to a minimum. Sulfur compounds, in excess, form acids which seriously damage metal parts and bearings. They also contribute to air pollution as they burn with the fuel. Gum-forming substances form deposits in carburetor systems and intake manifolds, and on valves, pistons, and rings. Proper refining minimizes the amounts of these harmful substances in gasoline.

⊘ 10-16 Chemistry of Combustion We noted (⊘ 10-1) that gasoline forms water (H_2O) and carbon dioxide (CO_2) when it burns completely. *This occurs only when enough oxygen is present to combine with all the hydrogen and carbon atoms.* However, there is usually not enough oxygen in the gasoline engine. As a result, the carbon does not burn completely. Some atoms of carbon unite with only one atom of oxygen (instead of two). This produces carbon monoxide (CO). Carbon monoxide is a dangerously poisonous gas. It has no color, is tasteless, and has practically no odor. But 15 parts of carbon monoxide in 10,000 parts of air makes the air dangerous to breathe. Larger amounts may cause quick paralysis and death. Thus, an engine should never be operated in a closed space without some means of directing the exhaust gas to the outside. Remember this fact: In 3 minutes, an automobile engine running in a closed one-car garage produces enough CO to cause paralysis and death. *Never operate an engine with the garage doors closed!*

When there is incomplete combustion, the exhaust gases contain unburned hydrocarbons. These contribute to smog, which is a health hazard in populous areas. Automotive companies are working on exhaust-system devices that convert these compounds to harmless gases. Also, cars are equipped with positive crankcase ventilating (PCV) systems, to prevent the escape of blowby gases from the engine. Of course, with perfect combustion, there would be no problem. See Chaps. 17 to 19 for the details of automotive emission controls.

⊘ 10-17 Diesel-Engine Fuels Diesel engines use fuel oil. The fuel oil is sprayed into the compressed air in the combustion chamber, at the end of the compression stroke. The heat of compression ignites the fuel oil, and the combustion stroke follows. Diesel oil is light, with a low viscosity and high cetane number (⊘ 10-19).

⊘ 10-18 Diesel-Fuel Viscosity Viscosity refers to the tendency of a liquid to resist flowing. The higher its viscosity, the slower the liquid flows. Water has a low viscosity; it flows easily. A light oil is more viscous than water, but it still flows easily. It too has a low viscosity. Heavy oil has a high viscosity; it flows slowly. The fuel oil used in diesel engines must have low viscosity so that it flows easily through the fuel system. But it must have sufficient viscosity to lubricate the moving parts in the fuel system. However, if the viscosity is too high, the fuel will not spray, or atomize, easily. It will not burn well.

⊘ 10-19 Cetane Number of Diesel Fuel The cetane number of diesel fuel refers to the ease with which the fuel ignites. A high-cetane-number fuel ignites easily (or at a relatively low temperature). The lower the cetane number, the higher the temperature needed to ignite the fuel. A fuel with a lower cetane number is more likely to knock. The fuel being sprayed into the cylinder does not ignite quickly. Instead, it tends to collect in the cylinder. Then, when ignition does take place, there is a combustion knock as the fuel suddenly burns. On the other hand, if the cetane number is high enough, the fuel ignites and burns as soon as it enters the cylinder. There is thus an even pressure rise, and no knock.

⊘ 10-20 Liquified Petroleum Gas (LPG) This fuel requires a special fuel system (⊘ 11-22). Actually, two types of LPG, *propane* and *butane*, have been used as automotive-engine fuels. Of these, propane is the more widely used. Sometimes, small amounts of butane are added to the propane. Propane boils at −44°F [−42.2°C] at atmospheric pressure. Thus, it can be used in any climate where the temperature stays above this value. Butane cannot be used in temperatures below 32°F [0°C], since it is liquid below that temperature. If it remains a liquid, it will not vaporize in the fuel system. It will never reach the engine.

CHAPTER 10 CHECKUP

NOTE: Since the following is a chapter review test, you should review the chapter before taking the test.

The automotive tuneup specialist should know what engine fuel is, and how it burns in the engine. That is what we have been discussing in this chapter. To find out how well you remember and understand the material, take the test that follows.

Completing the Sentences The sentences below are incomplete. After each sentence there are several words or phrases, but only one of them correctly completes the sentence. Write each sentence in your notebook, ending it with the one word or phrase that completes it correctly.

1. Gasoline is made up of: (*a*) hydrogen and carbon, (*b*) hydrogen and oxygen, (*c*) hydrocarbon and carbon monoxide.
2. Hydrocarbon (HC) is another name that can be used for: (*a*) water, (*b*) gasoline, (*c*) air.
3. If gasoline burns completely, all that remains is: (*a*) water and carbon monoxide, (*b*) carbon monoxide and hydrocarbon, (*c*) water and carbon dioxide.
4. The ease with which a gasoline vaporizes is called its: (*a*) volatility, (*b*) oxidation, (*c*) octane rating.
5. If a gasoline is too volatile, it vaporizes in the fuel pump, causing: (*a*) oxidation, (*b*) vapor lock, (*c*) engine runaway.
6. When the last part of the air-fuel mixture in the combustion chamber explodes before being ignited by the flame front, the condition is called: (*a*) detonation, (*b*) preignition, (*c*) vaporization.
7. A gasoline that detonates easily is called a: (*a*) high-octane gasoline, (*b*) low-octane gasoline, (*c*) blended gasoline.
8. Two ways to increase the octane rating of gasoline are: (*a*) changing the refining process and adding tetraethyl lead, (*b*) take more water out of gasoline and add less lubricating oil, (*c*) neither (*a*) nor (*b*).
9. A high compression ratio can cause a problem because it increases: (*a*) the temperature of the air-fuel mixture, (*b*) the strain on the cylinder-head bolts, (*c*) crankshaft-bearing wear.
10. To prevent preignition, the compression ratio must be kept low or: (*a*) a low-octane gasoline must be used, (*b*) a high-octane gasoline must be used, (*c*) gasoline cannot be used as the fuel.

Definitions and Review Questions In the following, you are asked for some definitions and explanations. Write them in your notebook. The act of writing helps you remember the information. It also increases the value of your notebook. Turn back into the chapter if you are not sure of an answer.

1. With perfect combustion, what two compounds are formed when gasoline burns?
2. Name three pollutants that are emitted from automobiles.
3. What is volatility? Why is it important in gasoline?
4. What does the term "antiknock value" mean?
5. What is heat of compression?
6. Explain how detonation is produced by the heat of compression.
7. What effect does increasing the compression ratio have on detonation? Why?
8. Explain one method of measuring the antiknock value of a gasoline.
9. What does octane number mean?
10. What is the difference between detonation and preignition?
11. What effect does lead have on valves and valve seats?
12. Why has lead been removed from gasoline?
13. What is quench?
14. What is squish?
15. What are the two basic combustion-chamber shapes?
16. Name six gasoline additives.
17. Why is CO dangerous?
18. Can you tell by the odor whether or not CO is present in a garage?
19. What does cetane number mean?
20. What does LPG mean?

SUGGESTIONS FOR FURTHER STUDY

Find out how gasoline is made. In your local library, check an encyclopedia for information on oil and gasoline. Make notes on how engineers prospect for oil in the earth. Find out how the crude oil is carried to refineries, and what is done to the oil when it gets there. Make notes on the important points, and file them in your notebook.

chapter 11

AUTOMOTIVE FUEL SYSTEMS

This chapter describes automotive fuel systems, including all fuel-system components except carburetors. Carburetors are covered in detail in the next chapter. In this chapter, we discuss fuel tanks, filters, gauges, pumps, and vapor-return lines. We also briefly cover emission controls in the fuel system, such as vapor-recovery systems, exhaust-gas recirculation, and positive crankcase ventilation.

⊘ **11-1 Purpose of the Fuel System** The fuel system supplies a combustible mixture of air and fuel to the engine. It must change the proportions of air and fuel for different operating conditions. When the engine is cold, for example, the mixture must be rich (have a high proportion of fuel). This is because the fuel does not vaporize readily at low temperatures. The extra fuel is added so that enough fuel vaporizes to form a combustible mixture.

⊘ **11-2 Fuel-System Components** The fuel system consists of the fuel tank, fuel pump, fuel filter, carburetor, intake manifold, and fuel lines. The fuel lines are tubes connecting the tank, pump, and carburetor (Figs. 11-1 and 11-2). Some gasoline engines use a fuel-injection system. In this system, a fuel-injection pump replaces the carburetor.

⊘ **11-3 Fuel Tank** The fuel tank (Fig. 11-3) is normally located at the rear of the vehicle. It is usually made of sheet metal and attached to the car frame. The filler opening of the tank is closed by a cap. The fuel line is attached at or near the bottom of the tank. In some tanks, there is a filter at the fuel-line con-

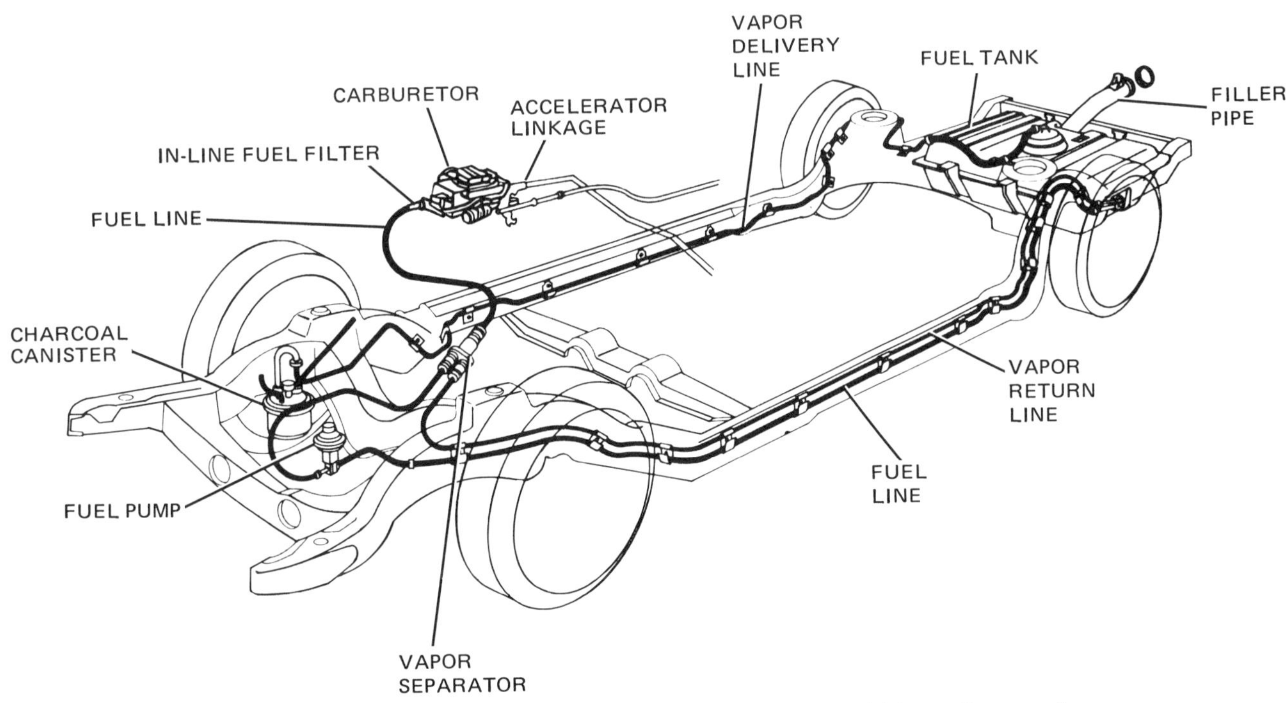

Fig. 11-1. Fuel system for a car with a V-8 engine. (*Ford Motor Company*)

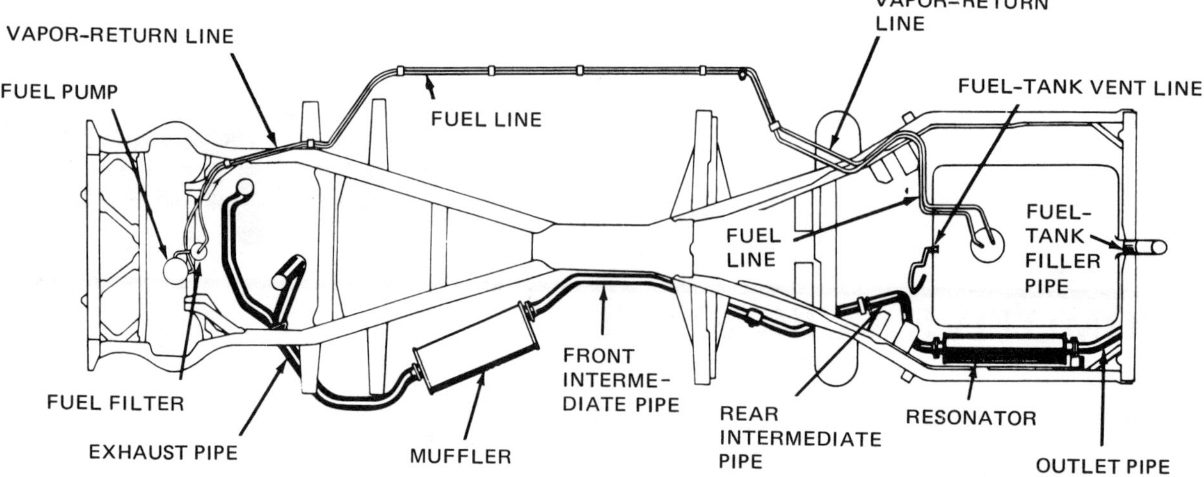

Fig. 11-2. Fuel and exhaust systems in place on a car frame. The carburetor and the engine are not shown. (*Cadillac Motor Car Division of General Motors Corporation*)

nection. The tank also contains the sending unit of the fuel gauge. The tank may also have a vent pipe to allow air to escape when the tank is being filled (Fig. 11-2).

Vaporized gasoline can escape from the fuel tank through the vent pipe. It then contributes to the formation of smog. To prevent this, cars manufactured since 1970 are equipped with a vehicle vapor-recovery system. In this system, the fuel-tank vent pipe is connected to a charcoal canister. The canister holds the vapor and prevents it from escaping into the air (⊘ 11-8).

⊘ 11-4 Fuel Filters and Screens Fuel systems have filters and screens to keep dirt in the fuel from entering the fuel pump and carburetor. Dirt could prevent normal operation of these units and cause poor engine performance. One type of filter is part of the fuel pump (Fig. 11-8). The filter may also be a separate unit, connected into the fuel line between the tank and fuel pump. Or, it may be located between the fuel pump and the carburetor (Fig. 11-1). It may also be in or on the carburetor itself. Figure 11-4 shows the type that is outside the carburetor but mounted on it. The screw threads enter a tapped hole in the carburetor. The fuel line fits on the opposite end of the filter. Figure 11-5 shows the type that is installed in the carburetor. This filter has an element made of pleated paper.

⊘ 11-5 Fuel Gauges There are two types of fuel gauge—*balancing-coil* and *thermostatic*. Each of these gauges has a tank unit and a dash unit.

1. *BALANCING-COIL (FIG. 11-6)* The tank unit in this fuel gauge contains a sliding contact. The contact slides back and forth on a resistor as the float moves up and down in the fuel tank. This changes the electric resistance of the tank unit. As the tank empties, the float drops, and the sliding contact moves to reduce the resistance.

The dash unit contains two coils, as shown in Fig. 11-6. When the ignition switch is turned on, current from the battery flows through the two coils. This produces a magnetic pattern that acts on the

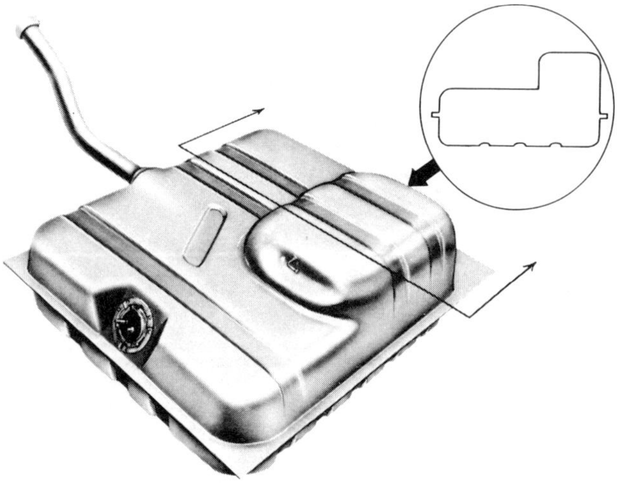

Fig. 11-3. Domed fuel tank of the type used with vapor-recovery systems. (*Chrysler Corporation*)

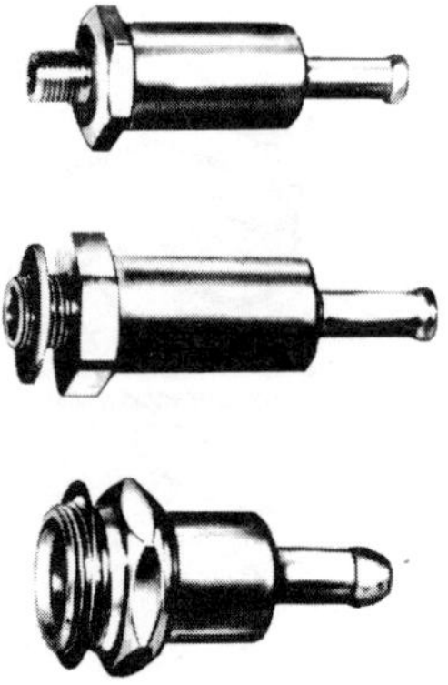

Fig. 11-4. In-line fuel filters. (*Ford Motor Company*)

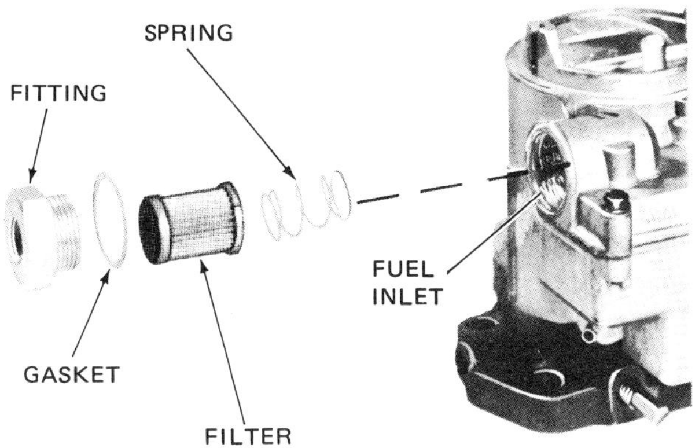

Fig. 11-5. Fuel filter located in the carburetor. (*Buick Motor Division of General Motors Corporation*)

armature. The dial pointer is attached to the armature. When the tank is filled and the float is up, resistance of the tank unit is high. The current through the E (empty) coil also flows through the F (full) coil. The armature is pulled to the right, and the pointer is on the F (full) side of the dial. When the tank begins to empty, the resistance of the tank unit drops. More of the current flowing through the E coil passes through the tank unit. Since less current flows through the F coil, its magnetic pull is weaker. The armature is pulled to the left. The pointer swings toward the E (empty) side of the dial.

2. *THERMOSTATIC* Figure 11-7 is the wiring diagram for a thermostatic fuel gauge. It has a fuel-tank unit much like that in the balancing-coil system. That is, the tank unit has a float and a sliding contact that moves on a resistor. Current from the battery flows through a heater wire in the dash unit, and through the resistance in the tank unit. When the fuel is low in the tank, most of the resistance is in the circuit. Very little current can flow. When the tank is filled, the float moves up. The sliding contact cuts most of the resistance out of the circuit, and more current flows. As the current flows through the heater in the dash unit, it heats the thermostat. The thermostat blade bends because of the heat. This moves the needle to the right, toward the F (full) mark.

Note that the system in Fig. 11-7 has an instrument voltage regulator. This device is thermostatic; its purpose is to keep the voltage to the fuel-gauge system low.

3. *LOW FUEL-LEVEL INDICATOR* The system in Fig. 11-7 also has a low-fuel-level indicator. It includes a thermistor assembly in the fuel tank, a warning light, and a warning relay. A *thermistor* is a special resistor that loses resistance as it gets hot. As long as there are more than a few gallons of fuel in the tank, the thermistor is submerged and is kept cool. However, when the fuel level is low, the thermistor is exposed to air. It gets hotter. Its resistance decreases, and more current flows. The increased current flow is sufficient to activate the warning relay. It connects the warning light to the battery. The light comes on to warn the driver that the fuel is getting low.

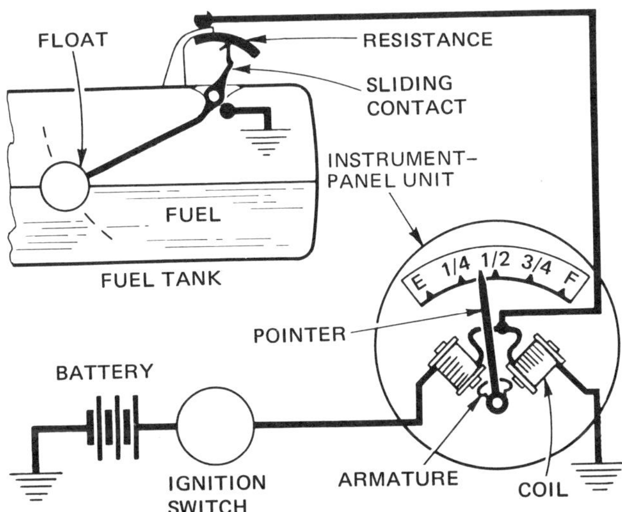

Fig. 11-6. Schematic wiring diagram for a balancing-coil fuel-gauge indicating system.

⊘ 11-6 Fuel Pumps The fuel system contains a fuel pump to deliver fuel from the tank to the carburetor. There are two types of fuel pump—mechanical and electric. Electric fuel pumps are discussed in ⊘ 11-9. The mechanical fuel pump is operated by an eccentric (an off-center section) on the engine camshaft (see Fig. 2-15). The mechanical fuel pump is mounted on the side of the cylinder block in an in-line engine. In some V-8 engines, the pump is mounted between the two cylinder banks. Most modern V-8 engines have the fuel pump on the side of the cylinder block, at the front of the engine.

The mechanical fuel pump has a rocker arm whose end rests on the camshaft eccentric. Many V-8 engines also use a pushrod from the eccentric to the rocker arm.

As the camshaft rotates, the eccentric rocks the rocker arm back and forth. The inner end of the rocker arm is linked to a flexible diaphragm. The diaphragm is clamped between the upper and lower pump housings (Fig. 11-8). There is a spring under the diaphragm that keeps tension on it. As the rocker arm rocks, it pulls the diaphragm down and then releases it. The spring then forces the diaphragm up. Thus, the diaphragm moves up and down as the rocker arm rocks.

This diaphragm movement produces partial vacuums and pressures in the space above the diaphragm. When the diaphragm moves down, a partial vacuum is produced. This allows atmospheric pressure, acting on the fuel in the tank, to force fuel through the fuel line and into the pump. The inlet valve in the pump opens to admit fuel, as shown by the arrows in Fig. 11-8. Note that the fuel first passes through a filter bowl and screen.

When the diaphragm is released by the rocker arm, the spring forces the diaphragm upward. This

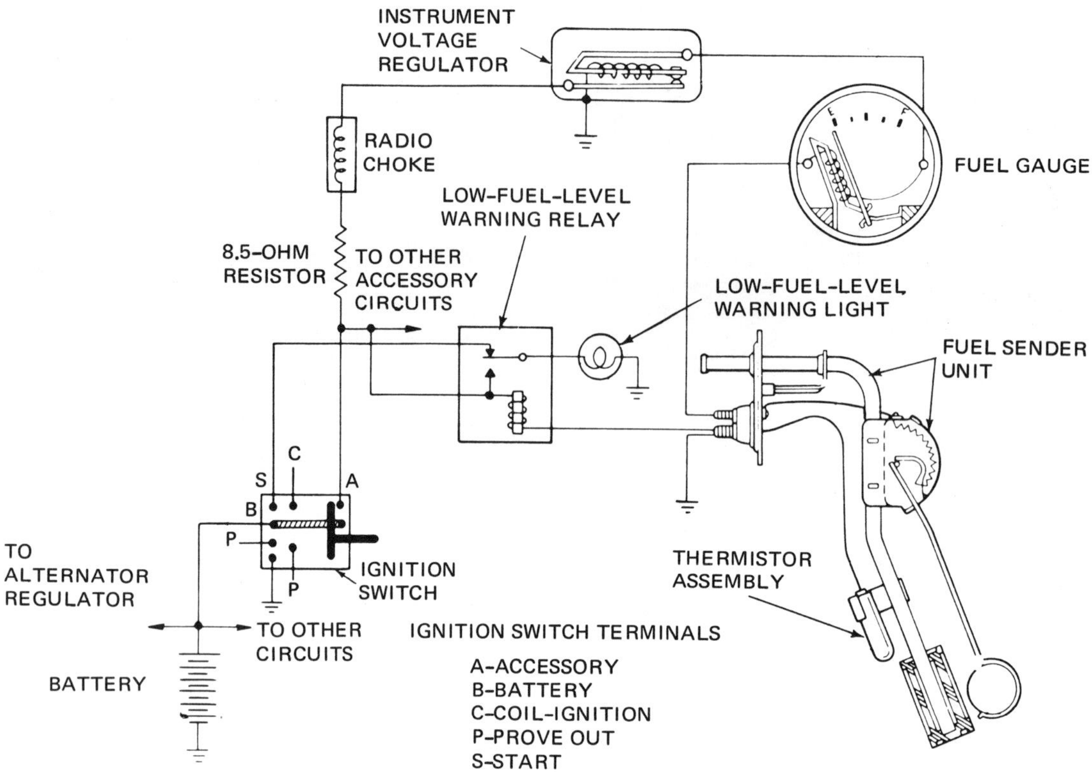

Fig. 11-7. Schematic wiring diagram for a thermostatic fuel-gauge indicating system. This system uses a variable-resistance tank unit and a thermostatic dash unit. (*Ford Motor Company*)

produces pressure in the space above the diaphragm. The pressure closes the inlet valve and opens the outlet valve. Now the fuel pump forces fuel through the fuel line to the carburetor. The actions in the pump are shown in Figs. 11-9 and 11-10.

Fuel from the fuel pump enters the carburetor through a needle valve in the float bowl. When the bowl is full, the needle valve is closed. No fuel can enter. When this happens, the fuel pump cannot deliver fuel to the carburetor. The rocker arm continues to rock, but the diaphragm stays down. The spring cannot force the diaphragm up as long as the carburetor does not accept fuel. However, as the carburetor uses up fuel, the needle valve opens. Fuel is admitted to the float bowl. Now the diaphragm can move up (on the rocker-arm return stroke) to force fuel to the carburetor.

⊘ 11-7 Vapor-Return Line The fuel system in Fig. 11-2 has a vapor-return line running from the fuel

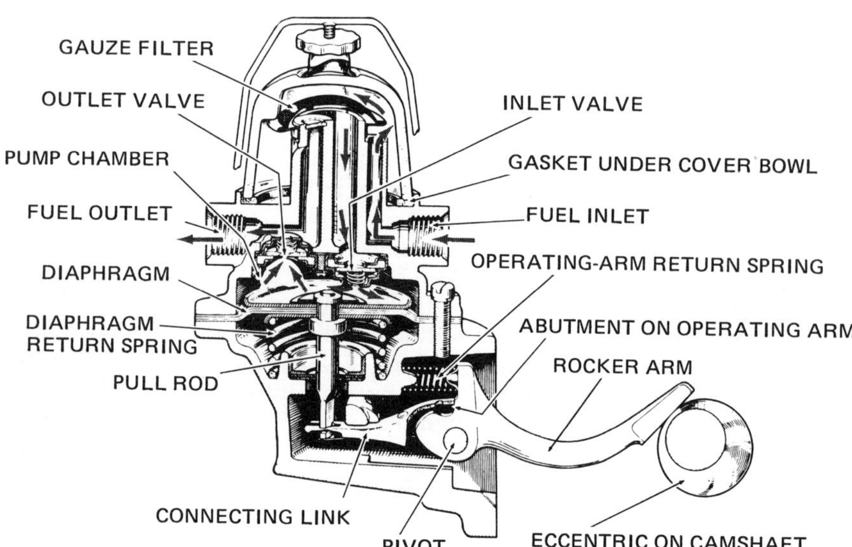

Fig. 11-8. Sectional view of a fuel pump. (*Hillman Motor Car Company, Limited*)

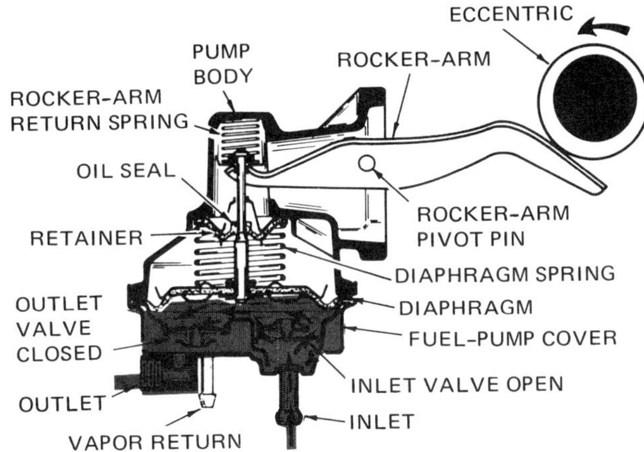

Fig. 11-9. When the eccentric rotates so as to push the rocker arm down, the arm pulls the diaphragm up. The inlet valve opens to admit fuel into the space under the diaphragm.

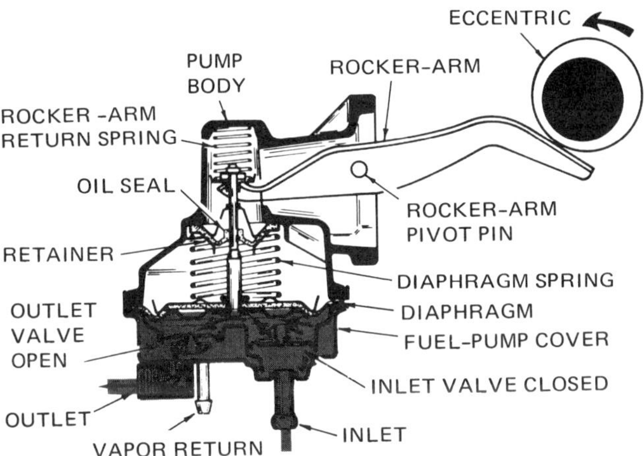

Fig. 11-10. When the eccentric rotates, the rocker arm moves up under it. The diaphragm is then released so it can move down, producing pressure under it. This pressure closes the inlet valve and opens the outlet valve, so fuel flows to the carburetor.

pump to the fuel tank. This line is installed on many cars with air conditioning. The air-conditioning system increases the under-the-hood temperature. It "dumps" heat in the engine compartment. Also, during idling, the engine cooling system is not very efficient. This allows the under-the-hood temperature to increase. The higher temperature tends to cause vapor to form in the fuel pump.

To understand how vapor can form in the fuel pump, note that the pump alternately produces vacuum and pressure. During the vacuum phases, the boiling (or vaporizing) temperature of the fuel goes down. The lower the pressure, the lower the temperature at which any liquid vaporizes. For example, water boils at 212°F [100°C] at sea-level atmospheric pressure, which is 14.7 psi [1.078 kg/cm^2]. See ⊘ 8-12. But at an altitude of 16,000 ft [4,876 m], where the pressure is around 7 psi [0.492 kg/cm^2], water boils at 185°F [85°C].

The combination of increased temperature and partial vacuum in the fuel pump can cause the fuel to vaporize. This produces vapor lock, a condition that prevents normal delivery of fuel to the carburetor. The engine can stall.

The vapor-return line is connected to a special outlet in the fuel pump. It allows the vapor to return to the fuel tank. The vapor-return line also permits excess fuel being pumped by the fuel pump to return to the fuel tank. This excess fuel, in constant circulation, helps keep the fuel pump cool. It thus prevents vapor from forming.

Some cars have a vapor separator connected between the fuel pump and the carburetor (Fig. 11-11). It consists of a sealed can, a filter screen, an inlet and outlet fitting, and a metered orifice, or outlet, for the return line to the fuel tank. Any fuel vapor that the fuel pump produces enters the vapor separator (as bubbles) along with fuel. The bubbles of vapor rise to the top of the vapor separator. The fuel-pump

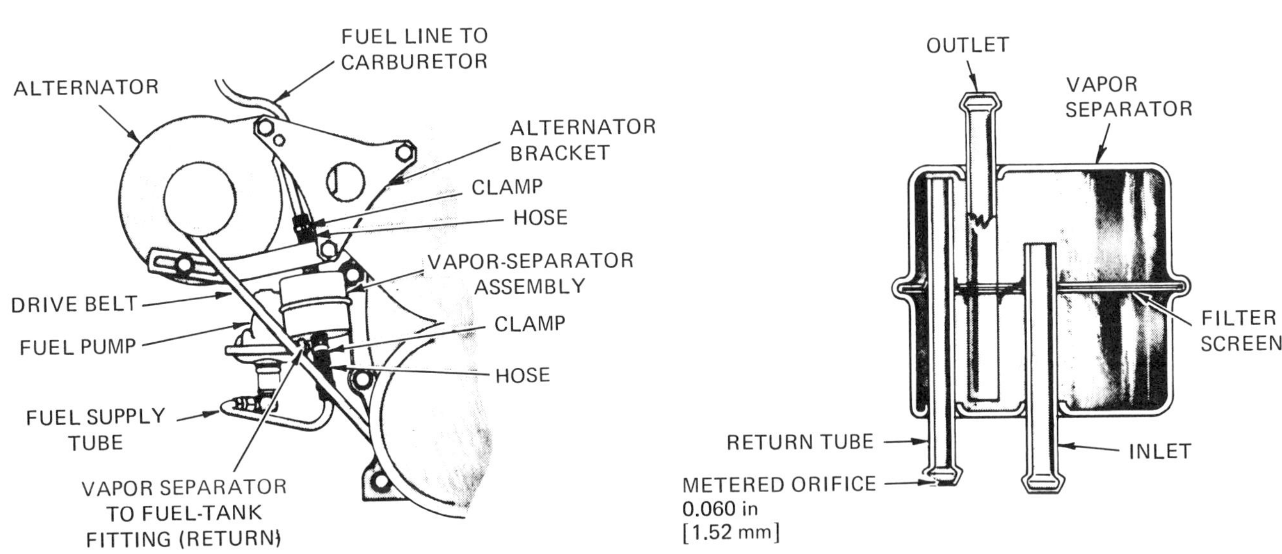

Fig. 11-11. *Left:* Location of the vapor separator, in the line between the fuel pump and carburetor, on V-8 engine. *Right:* Enlarged sectional view of the fuel-vapor separator. (*Chrysler Corporation*)

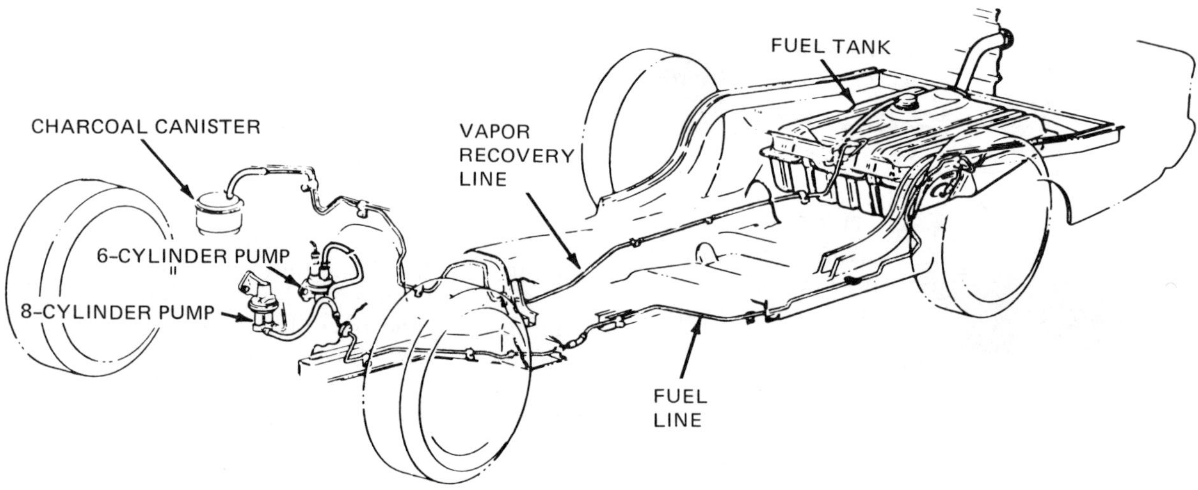

Fig. 11-12. Fuel-vapor recovery system. (*Ford Motor Company*)

pressure then forces the vapor back to the fuel tank through the fuel-return line. In the tank, it condenses into liquid fuel.

⊘ 11-8 Fuel-Vapor Recovery System Gasoline vapor can escape from uncontrolled fuel tanks and carburetors. This happens when the car is sitting idle and the engine is not running. When the engine *is* running, gasoline is being pumped from the fuel tank and drawn from the carburetor, so gasoline vapor does not escape.

Large quantities of gasoline vapor (HC) can escape from parked cars without vapor controls. The vapor adds to atmospheric pollution. To prevent the loss of gasoline vapor, modern automobiles are equipped with vapor-recovery systems. Figure 11-12 shows one system. The fuel tank is sealed. Escaping gasoline vapor has to flow through the vapor-recovery line to the charcoal canister. Gasoline vapor from the carburetor float bowl also flows to the charcoal canister. There, the charcoal particles pick up (or adsorb) and hold the gasoline vapor. Then, when the engine is started and running, air flows through the charcoal canister on its way to the carburetor. This air picks up the gasoline vapor from the canister and carries it to the carburetor. There, it mixes with the air-fuel mixture and enters the engine. It is thus burned, instead of being allowed to enter the atmosphere as HC. Chapter 17, on emission controls, describes vapor-recovery systems in detail.

⊘ 11-9 Electric Fuel Pumps Electric fuel pumps have certain advantages over mechanical fuel pumps. Fuel is at the carburetor as soon as the ignition is turned on. The pump can deliver more fuel than the engine requires, even under maximum operating conditions. Thus, the engine is never starved for fuel. Electric fuel pumps are therefore used in many high-performance and heavy-duty applications.

There are various types of electric fuel pumps. One of the latest is mounted in the fuel tank (Fig. 11-13). It contains an impeller driven by an electric motor (Fig. 11-14). This pushes fuel through the fuel line to the carburetor. Other types of electric fuel pumps are mounted in the engine compartment. One design is shown in Fig. 11-15. It contains a flexible metal bellows that is operated by an electromagnet. The electromagnet is connected to the battery when the ignition switch is turned on. It pulls down the armature and extends the bellows. This produces a vacuum in the bellows. Fuel from the fuel tank enters the bellows through the inlet valve. Then, as the armature reaches its lower limit of travel, it opens a set of contact points. This disconnects the electromagnet from the battery. The return spring pushes the armature up and collapses the bellows. This forces fuel from the bellows, through the outlet valve, and to the carburetor. As the armature reaches the upper limit of its travel, it closes the contacts. The electromagnet is again energized and

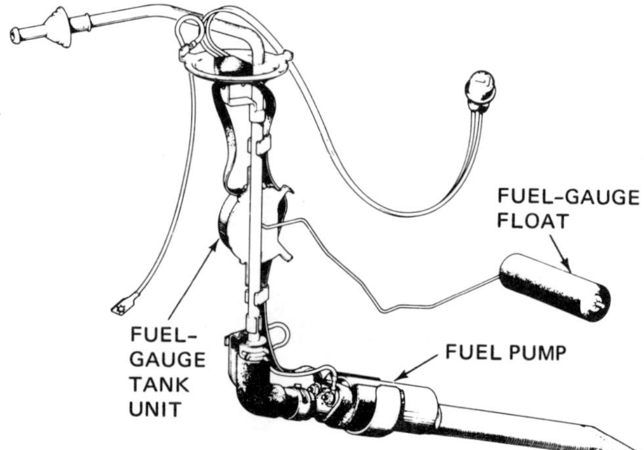

Fig. 11-13. Location of the electric fuel pump in the fuel tank. It is mounted on the same support as the fuel-gauge tank unit. (*Buick Motor Division of General Motors Corporation*)

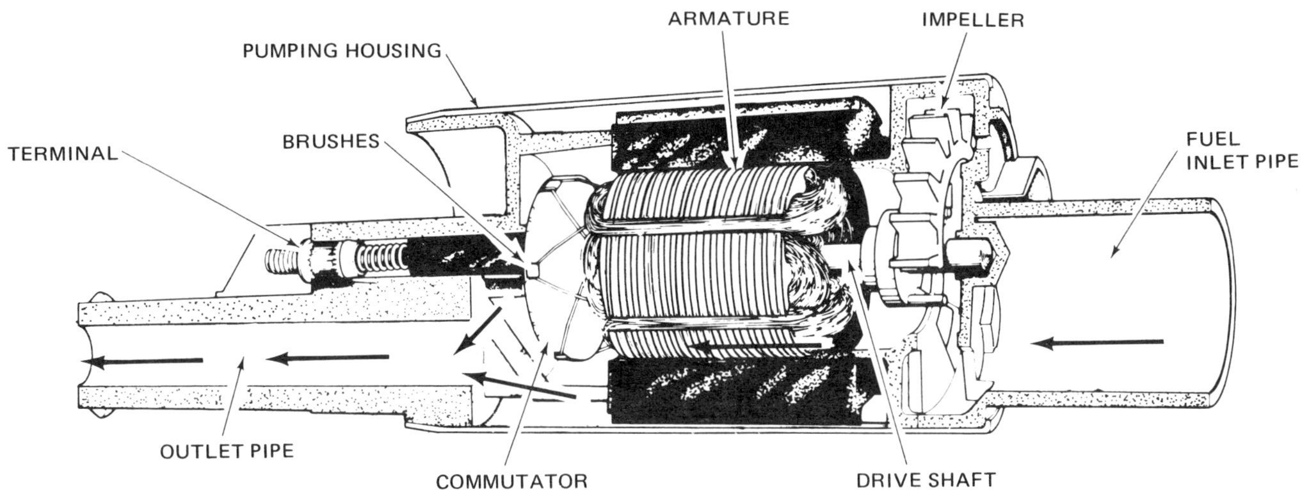

Fig. 11-14. Cutaway view of a tank-mounted electric fuel pump. (*Buick Motor Division of General Motors Corporation*)

again pulls the armature down. These actions are repeated as long as the ignition is on.

NOTE: Electric fuel gauges and fuel pumps mounted in the fuel tank are designed with safety in mind. Their operation does not create sparks that could cause the gasoline in the tank to ignite or explode.

⊘ 11-10 Air Cleaners As already noted, the fuel system mixes air and fuel to produces a combustible mixture. A great deal of air passes through the carburetor and engine—as much as 100,000 ft^3 (cubic feet) [2831.7 m^3 (cubic meters)] of air every 1,000 car miles [1609.3 km]. This is a lot of air, and it probably contains a lot of floating dust and grit. The grit and dust could cause serious damage if they entered the engine. Therefore, an air cleaner is mounted on the air horn, or entrance, of the carburetor, to keep out the dirt (Fig. 11-16).

All air entering the engine through the carburetor must first pass through the air cleaner. The upper part of the air cleaner contains a ring of filter material. (It is composed of fine-mesh metal threads or ribbons, special paper, cellulose fiber, or polyurethane.) The air must pass through this ring, which traps most of the dust particles. Some air cleaners also have an oil bath, a reservoir of oil. The incoming air flows past the oil bath. The moving air picks up particles of oil and carries them up into the filter. There, the oil washes any dust back down into the reservoir. The oiliness of the filter material also improves the filtering action.

The air cleaner also muffles the noise of the intake of air through the carburetor, manifold, and valve ports. This noise would be quite noticeable if it were not for the air cleaner. In addition, the air cleaner acts as a flame arrester, in case the engine

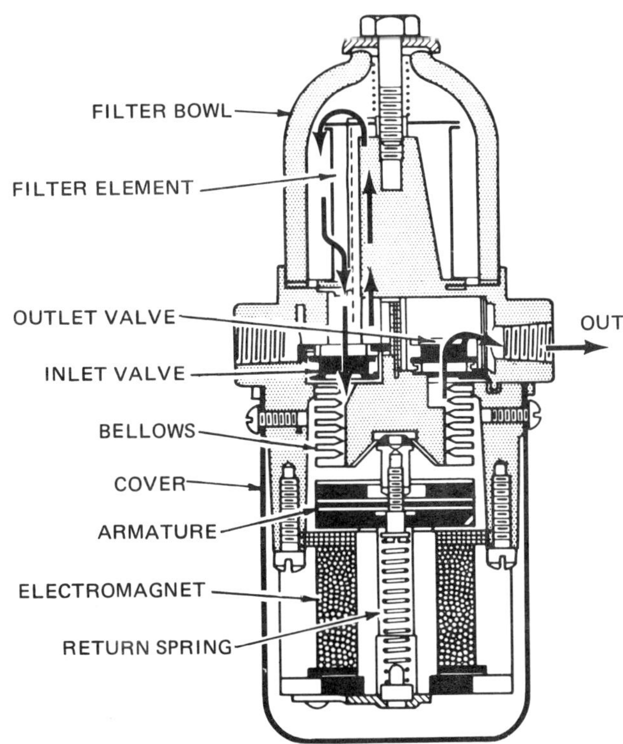

Fig. 11-15. Sectional view of an electric fuel pump.

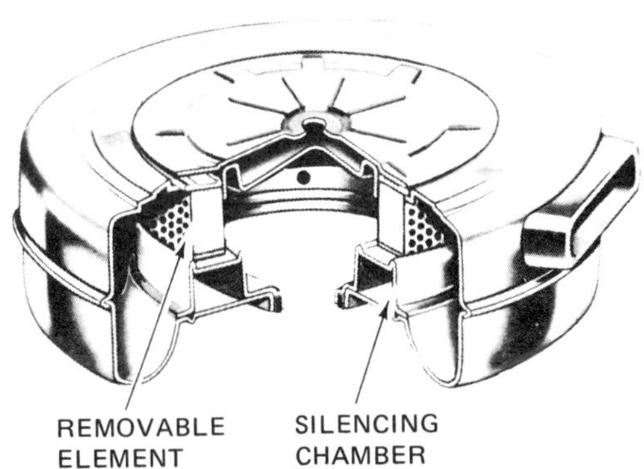

Fig. 11-16. Typical air cleaner, partly cut away to show the filter element. (*Ford Motor Company*)

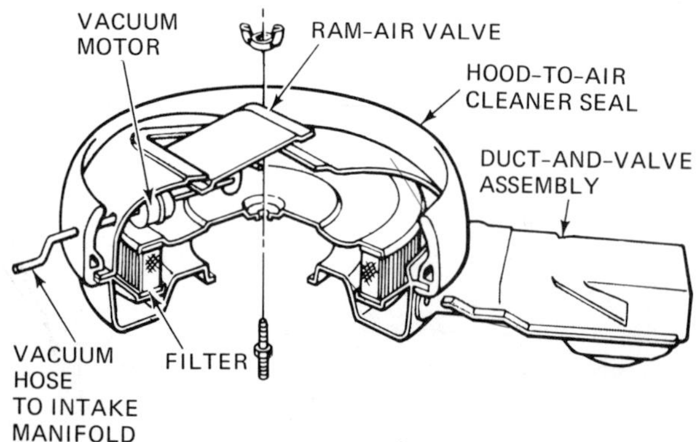

Fig. 11-17. Ram-air air cleaner, with ram-air valve shown open. (*Ford Motor Company*)

backfires through the carburetor. Backfiring may occur if the air-fuel mixture is ignited in a cylinder before the intake valve closes. When this happens, there is a momentary flashback of flame through the carburetor. The air cleaner keeps the flame from leaving the carburetor and igniting gasoline fumes outside the engine.

Some late-model cars have a ram-air air cleaner (Fig. 11-17). It allows extra air to be forced into the air cleaner during open-throttle or heavy-load operation. A vacuum motor, connected to the intake manifold by a vacuum hose, opens a ram-air valve, as shown in Fig. 11-17. This valve is in line with the air scoop on the engine hood. When the valve opens, extra air from the air scoop is forced into the carburetor. This improves engine performance under heavy-load conditions. At other times, the manifold vacuum is not great enough to hold the ram-air valve open. Then, air enters the filter through the snorkel tube or duct-and-valve assembly (⊘ 11-11) in the normal manner.

⊘ 11-11 Thermostatically Controlled Air Cleaner The thermostatically controlled air cleaner is part of a controlled-combustion system used on late-model cars. It is one component of the emission-control equipment discussed in detail in Chaps. 17 and 18. To reduce engine emissions, carburetors are adjusted to give leaner mixtures at idle and part-throttle. That is, the amount of gasoline in the air-fuel mixture is reduced. The leaner mixtures assure more complete burning of the gasoline. This results in less HC coming out the tail pipe.

However, these leaner mixtures can reduce engine performance when the engine is cold. To correct this, a thermostatically controlled air cleaner is used. The system is called the *heated-air system* (HAS) by General Motors. It sends heated air to the carburetor during cold weather, when the engine is cold (Fig. 11-18). This improves engine performance after a cold start and during engine warm-up. It allows leaner mixtures to be used, to reduce smog without affecting cold-engine performance.

One air cleaner of this type is shown in Fig. 11-19. It contains a sensing spring which reacts to the

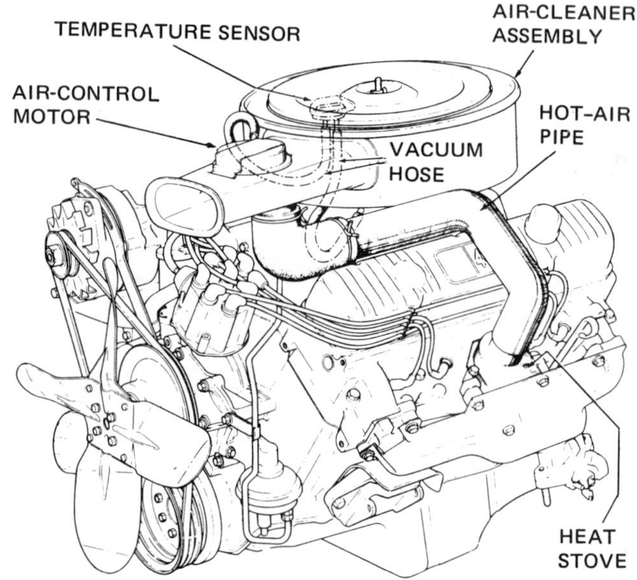

Fig. 11-18. Heated-air system installed on a V-8 engine. (*Buick Motor Division of General Motors Corporation*)

temperature of the air entering the carburetor through the air cleaner. This spring controls an air-bleed valve (see Fig. 11-20). When the entering air is cold, the sensing spring holds the bleed valve closed. Now, intake-manifold vacuum is applied to the vacuum chamber. The diaphragm is pushed upward by atmospheric pressure, and the diaphragm spring is compressed. In this position, a linkage from the diaphragm raises the control-damper assembly. The snorkel tube is blocked off. All air now has to enter from the hot-air pipe (Fig. 11-20B). This pipe is connected to the heat stove on the exhaust manifold. Thus, as soon as the exhaust manifold begins to warm up, hot air is delivered to the carburetor and engine. This improves cold operation and warm-up operation.

As the engine begins to warm up, the underhood temperature increases. If the underhood temperature goes above 128°F [53.3°C] (in the application

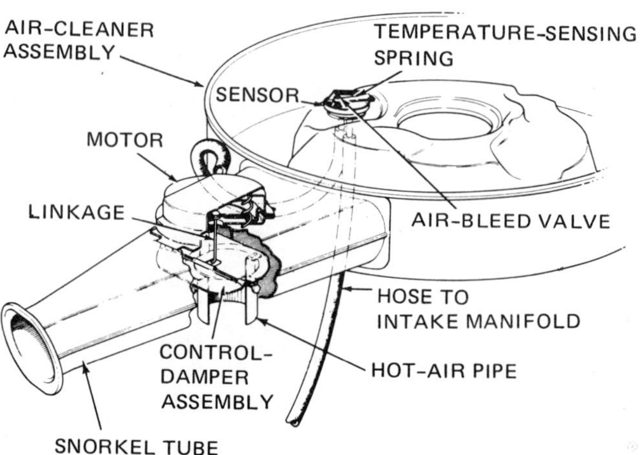

Fig. 11-19. Air cleaner with thermostatic control. (*Chevrolet Motor Division of General Motors Corporation*)

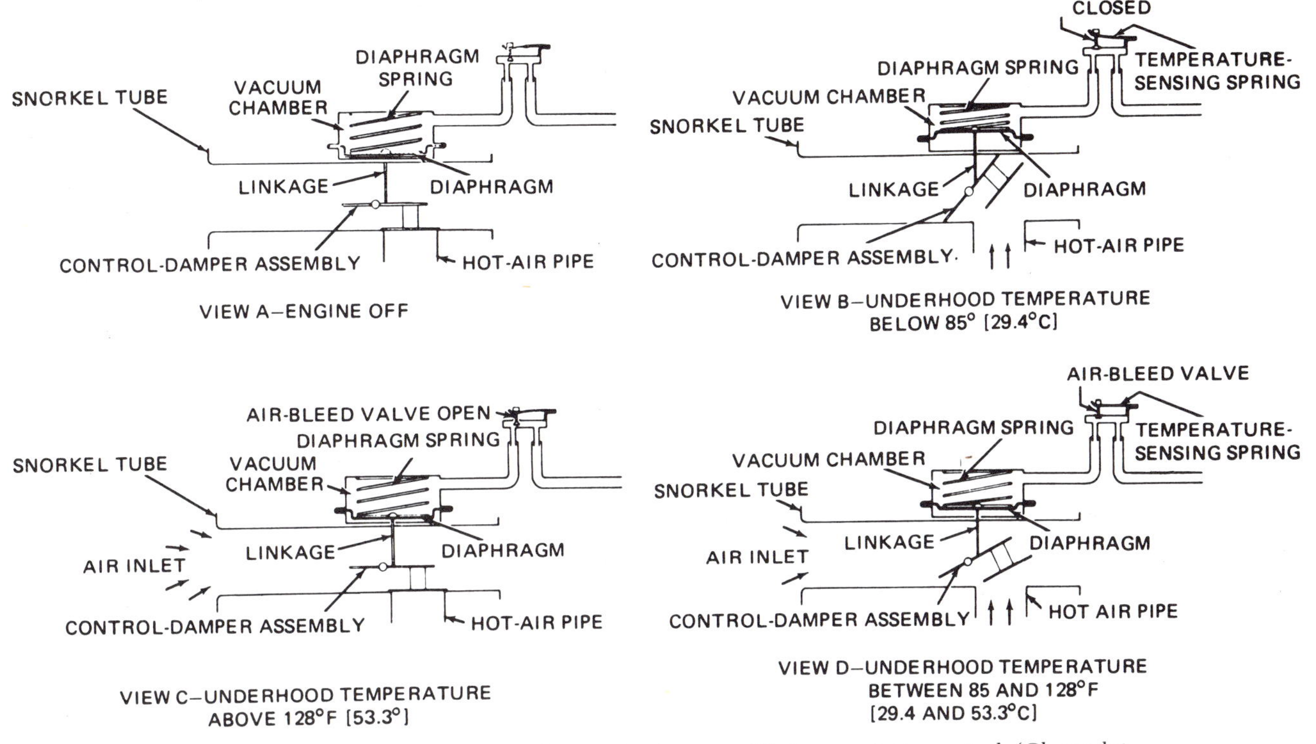

Fig. 11-20. Operational modes for an air cleaner with thermostatic control. (*Chevrolet Motor Division of General Motors Corporation*)

shown), the conditions are as shown in Fig. 11-20C. The temperature-sensing spring has bent enough to open the air bleed valve. This reduces the vacuum above the diaphragm so that the diaphragm spring pushes the control damper all the way down. Now all air entering the carburetor comes from under the hood, and none comes from the hot-air pipe.

If the temperature under the hood stabilizes at somewhere between 85 and 128°F [29.4 and 53.3°C], conditions will be as shown in Fig. 11-20D. The temperature-sensing spring will hold the air-bleed valve partly open. Some vacuum will therefore get to the vacuum chamber above the diaphragm. This vacuum will hold the control damper partly open, as shown. In this position, some air enters from under the hood, and some comes up through the hot-air pipe from the heat stove around the exhaust manifold.

A similar thermostatically controlled air cleaner is shown in Figs. 11-21 and 11-22. This design has a thermostatic bulb that acts directly on the valve plate. When the engine is cold, the thermostatic bulb positions the valve plate as shown in Fig. 11-22. Now, all incoming air must come from the hot-air duct, which is connected to a shroud around the exhaust manifold. As the engine warms up, the hotter air from the shroud causes the thermostatic bulb to move the valve plate. Thus, some air begins to enter from the engine compartment. With further increases in temperature, the valve plate moves farther. More engine-compartment air enters. When the engine compartment becomes hot, most or all of incoming air comes from the engine compartment.

The design shown in Figs. 11-21 and 11-22 includes a vacuum override motor. This motor operates on intake-manifold vacuum. During cold-engine acceleration, when additional air is needed, the motor overrides the thermostatic control. This opens the system to both engine-compartment and heated air, so that adequate air is delivered to the carburetor.

⊘ 11-12 Exhaust-Gas Recirculation The higher the combustion temperature, the more nitrogen oxides are formed during combustion. Nitrogen oxides (NO_x) contribute to smog, so changes have been

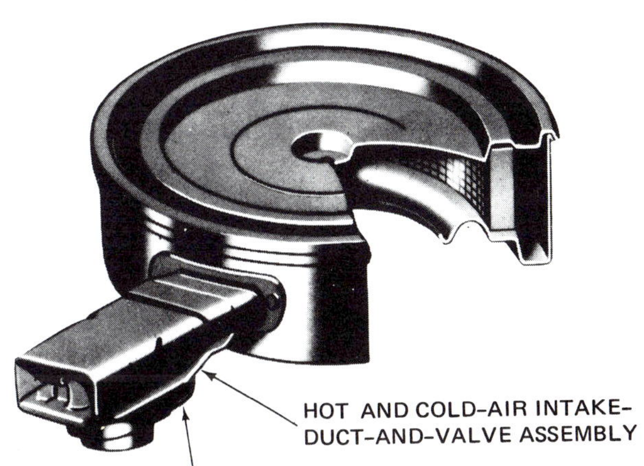

Fig. 11-21. Air cleaner with thermostatic control. (*Ford Motor Company*)

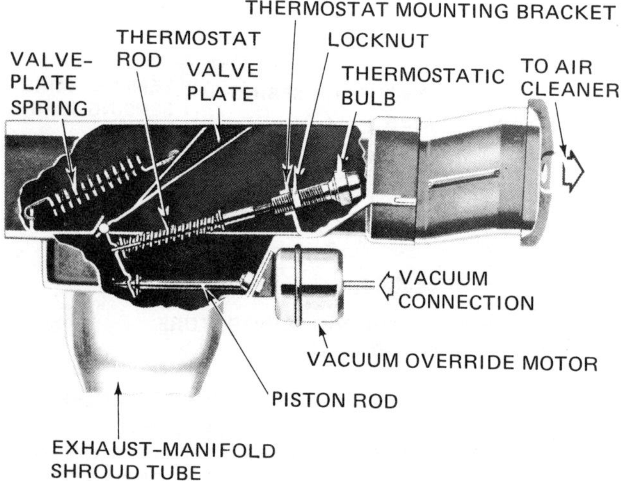

Fig. 11-22. Cutaway view of the hot- and cold-air intake ducts and valve assembly for the air cleaner in Fig. 11-21. (*Ford Motor Company*)

made in engines and fuel systems to reduce NO_x. One method is to use an exhaust-gas recirculation (EGR) system. The system sends part of the exhaust gas back through the engine. The exhaust gas reduces the combustion temperature and, thus, the amount of NO_x coming out the tail pipe. Figure 11-23 shows one system for sending some of the exhaust gas back through the engine. The system has an exhaust-gas-recirculation valve that is controlled by engine vacuum. During part-throttle operation, the vacuum causes the valve to raise its diaphragm and open the port. This allows some of the exhaust gas to enter the intake manifold.

Another system uses high valve overlap. That is, the camshaft cams allow the exhaust and intake valves to be open together for a longer time. This allows more exhaust gas to remain in the cylinders and mix with the incoming air-fuel mixture. Chapters 17 and 18 describe these systems in detail.

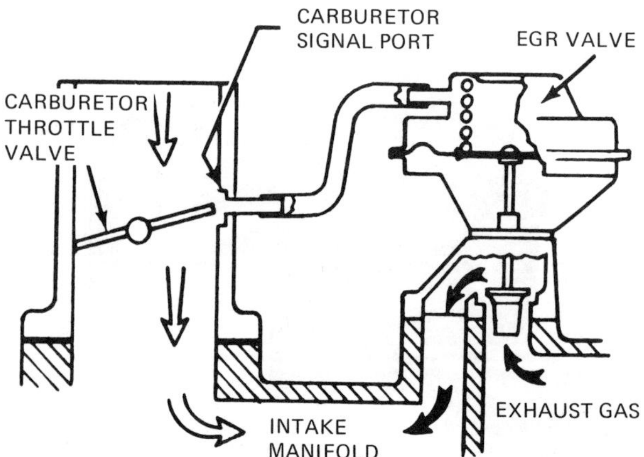

Fig. 11-23. Schematic drawing of an exhaust-gas recirculation system. (*Chevrolet Motor Division of General Motors Corporation*)

⊘ 11-13 Crankcase Ventilation Crankcases must be ventilated. Some blowby always gets past the piston rings and enters the crankcase. In addition, water and liquid fuel collect in the crankcase during cold-engine operation. These must be cleared from the crankcase before they cause trouble. In earlier engines, the crankcase was ventilated by an opening at the front of the engine and a vent tube at the back or lower side of the crankcase. The forward motion of the car, plus the rotation of the crankshaft, caused air to flow through and remove the blowby, water, and fuel. Today, however, positive crankcase ventilating (PCV) systems are used on all cars. Air circulates through the crankcase, as before. But the air then enters the carburetor and intake manifold. Any blowby, water vapor, or unburned fuel is sent back through the engine, instead of being emitted into the atmosphere. Positive crankcase ventilating systems are covered in ⊘ 17-6.

⊘ 11-14 Exhaust System The exhaust system includes the exhaust manifold, exhaust pipe, muffler, and tail pipe (Figs. 11-24 and 11-2). Some V-8 engines have a crossover pipe to connect their two exhaust manifolds. Other V-8 engines use two separate exhaust systems (a dual system), one for each cylinder bank (Fig. 11-24). This improves the "breathing" ability of the engine. It exhausts more freely, and its power output increases somewhat.

Exhaust manifolds have heat-control valves. These valves close when the engine is cold; this sends heat to the intake manifold. The heat helps vaporize the ingoing gasoline, and thus improves cold-engine operation. Manifold heat-control valves are covered in detail in ⊘ 12-25.

Some engines have exhaust manifolds equipped with an air-injection system. The system includes an air pump and a series of injection tubes in the exhaust manifold. In operation, the air pump sends a flow of air into the exhaust manifold, opposite the exhaust valves. This extra air helps to burn any HC or CO in the exhaust gases. The air-injection system is covered in Chap. 18.

⊘ 11-15 Muffler The muffler (Fig. 11-25) contains a series of holes, passages, and resonance chambers. They absorb and damp out the high-pressure surges that enter the exhaust system when the exhaust valves open. This quiets the exhaust. Some new exhaust systems do not use a muffler. Instead, the exhaust pipe contains a series of scientifically shaped restrictions. The restrictions damp out the exhaust noises without interfering with the flow of exhaust gases.

To further reduce exhaust noises, many exhaust pipes are made of a three-ply laminate. The laminate consists of a plastic film sandwiched between two metal skins. The laminate has very good sound-deadening properties.

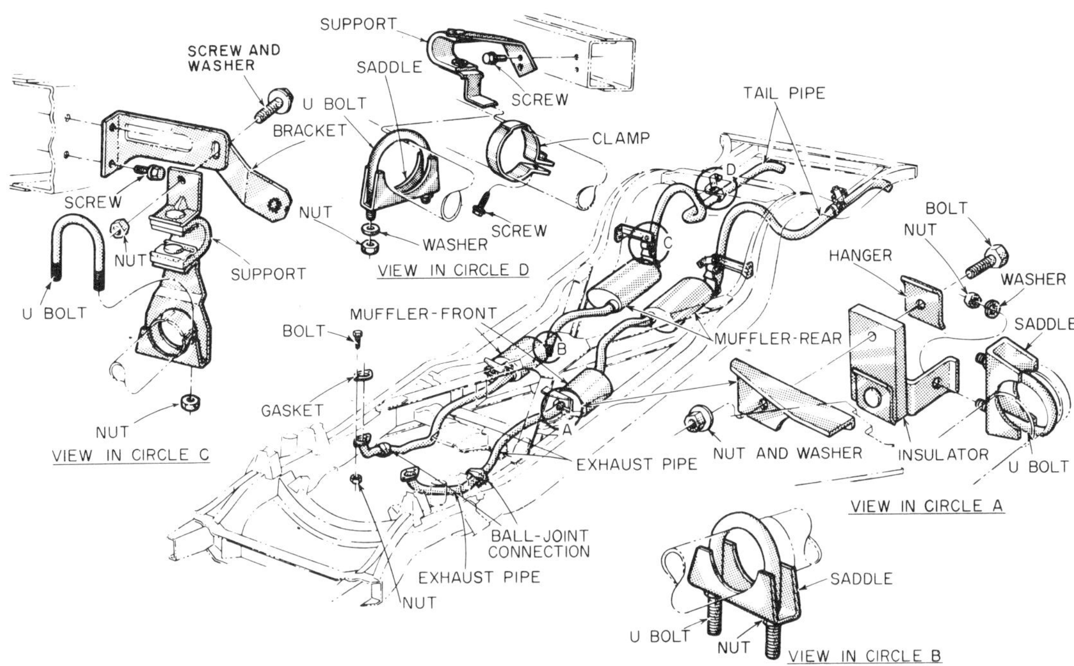

Fig. 11-24. Dual-exhaust system for a V-8 engine. Each bank of cylinders has its own exhaust system. The circles show assembly and attachment details. (*Ford Motor Company*)

⊘ 11-16 Catalysts Late-model cars have catalytic converters in the exhaust system. These are muffler-like containers filled with catalysts. The catalysts convert the pollutants coming from the engine into harmless gases (see Chap. 18).

⊘ 11-17 Diesel-Engine Fuel System In the diesel engine, air alone is compressed. Then, at the end of the compression stroke, the fuel system injects fuel oil into the cylinder. A typical diesel-engine fuel system is shown in Fig. 11-26. The system includes a fuel tank, filters, fuel lines, a fuel-injection pump assembly, and fuel-injection nozzles at each cylinder. The fuel-injection pump assembly includes a fuel supply pump, the hydraulic head assembly, a timing-advance mechanism, a governor and fuel-control unit, and an excess-fuel device for starting.

In operation, the fuel-supply pump sends fuel from the fuel tank to the hydraulic head assembly.

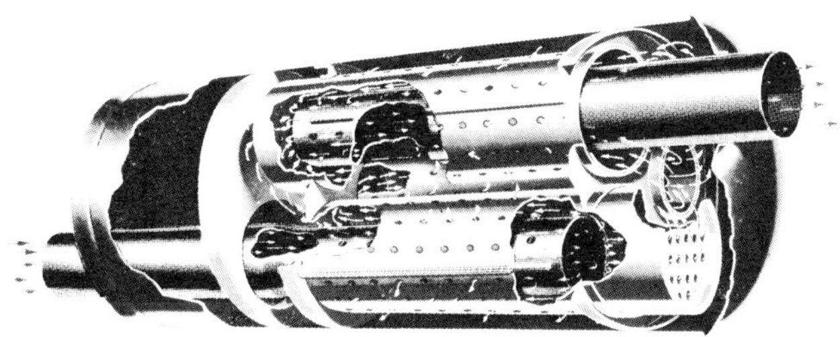

Fig. 11-25. Exhaust muffler in cutaway view. The arrows show the path of exhaust-gas flow through the muffler. (*Chevrolet Motor Division of General Motors Corporation*)

The hydraulic head assembly includes a pump which sends fuel at high pressure to the fuel nozzles in the proper firing order. This is much like the ignition distributor on gasoline engines, which sends sparks to the cylinders in the proper firing order. The diesel engine, however, fires from the heat of compression, as previously explained.

The fuel-injection pump assembly includes a timing-advance mechanism. This is a form of governor. It works against a sleeve to push the pump-drive shaft ahead as speed increases. This gets the fuel to the cylinders earlier at higher speeds. The fuel thus has enough time to ignite and burn.

The fuel-injection pump assembly also includes a fuel-control unit. This unit varies the amount of fuel injected, according to throttle position. When the throttle is pushed down, calling for more engine power, the fuel-control unit raises a metering sleeve. This allows the pump plunger to send more fuel to the fuel nozzles.

⊘ 11-18 Fuel Injection for Gasoline Engines The carburetor fuel system is the most common in automotive engines. In this system, the fuel is mixed with ingoing air in the carburetor. In the fuel-injection system, air alone enters the intake manifold. Fuel nozzles are located in the intake manifold. At the proper time, they inject fuel into the air. Figure 11-27 shows, in a simplified view, how the system works. In the system shown, the nozzle is just back of the intake valve. This is different from the diesel-engine fuel-injection system. There, the fuel is injected directly into the engine cylinder near TDC on the compression stroke (Fig. 11-28).

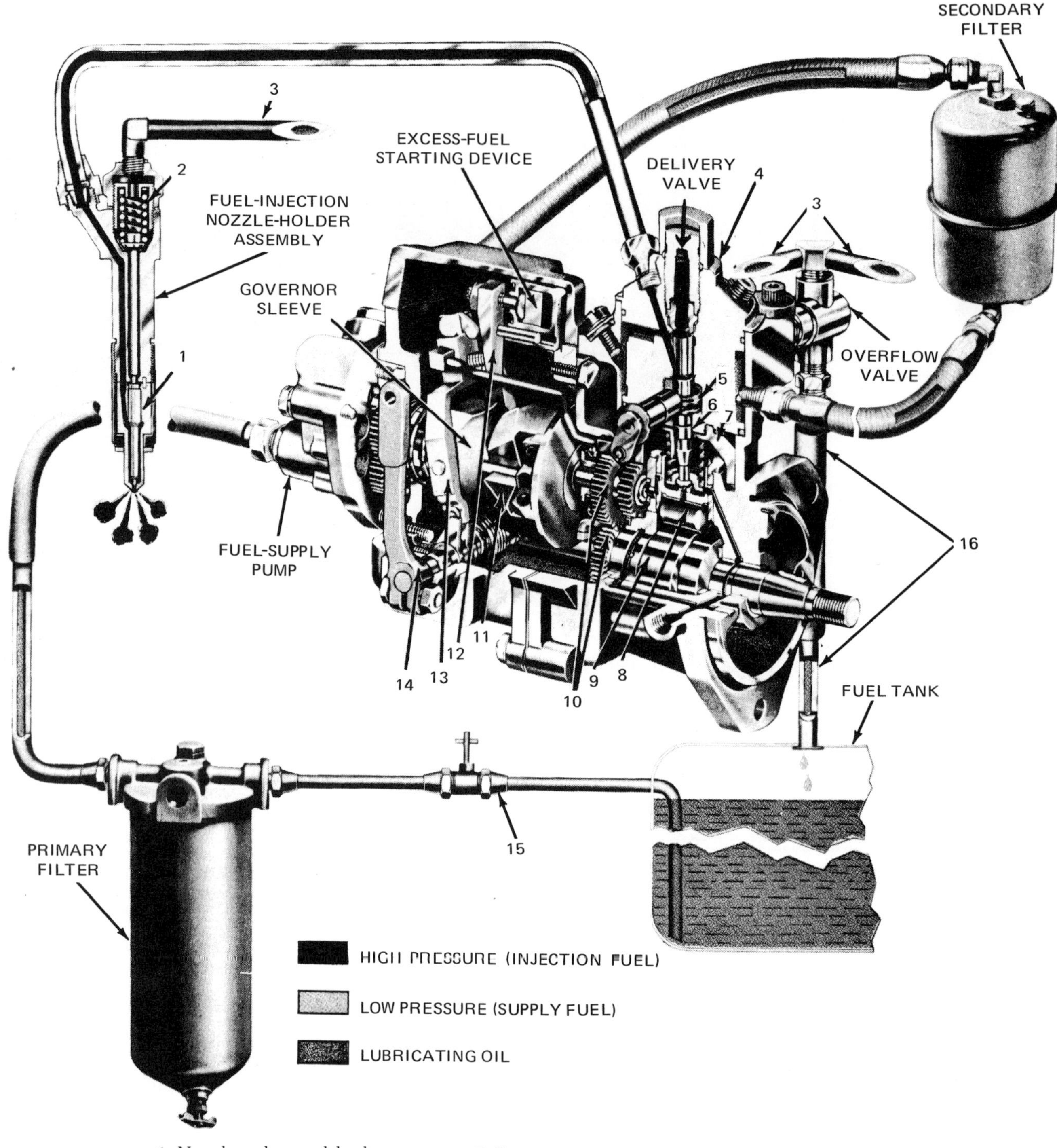

1. Nozzle valve and body
2. Nozzle valve spring
3. Leak-off lines
4. Hydraulic head assembly
5. Fuel-metering sleeve
6. Pump plunger
7. Face gear
8. Tappet and roller
9. Cam
10. Governor gears
11. Governor weights
12. Governor stop plate
13. Fulcrum lever
14. Stop lever
15. Shutoff valve
16. Fuel-return line

Fig. 11-26. Diesel-engine fuel-injection system. (*Chevrolet Motor Division of General Motors Corporation*)

The fuel-injection system must supply varying amounts of fuel. The amount required changes with engine speed and throttle opening, and for cold starts, warm-up, and full-power running. The fuel is supplied through a pump system, including a metering unit that controls the amount of fuel injected. Figure 11-29 illustrates one fuel-injection system for a six-cylinder engine. The injection pump (5 in Fig. 11-29) supplies the fuel-metering units (7) with fuel at high pressure. The fuel is injected through the

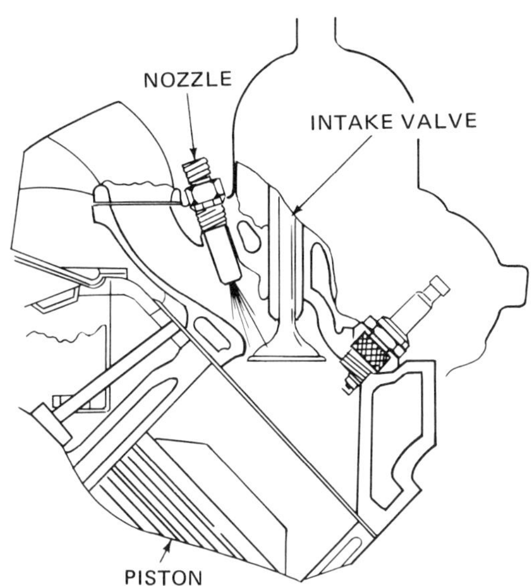

Fig. 11-27. Simplified view showing the method of injecting fuel into the intake manifold just back of the intake valve.

injection valves (8) at the proper time and in the proper amount.

⊘ 11-19 Electronic Fuel-Injection System A fuel-injection system that is controlled by electronic means is illustrated in Figs. 11-30 and 11-31. This system was designed for the Volkswagen flat-four air-cooled engine. The basic ideas apply to all electronically controlled fuel-injection systems. The fuel is injected into the intake manifolds behind the intake valves. The injection is timed to coincide with valve opening, by triggering contacts in the ignition distributor. The amount of fuel injected is controlled by the length of time the fuel injectors are open.

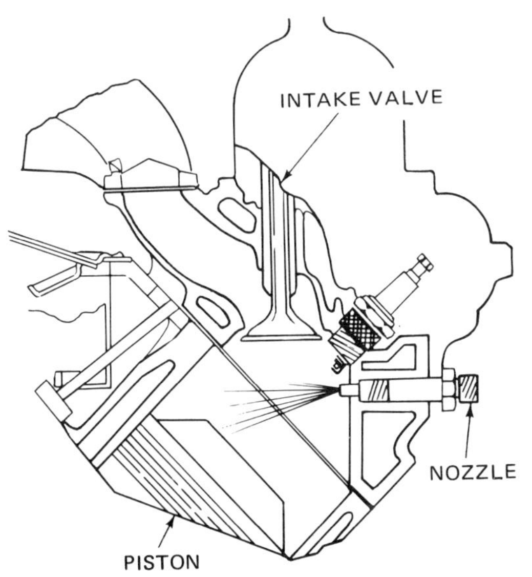

Fig. 11-28. Simplified view showing the method of injecting fuel directly into the combustion chamber of the engine.

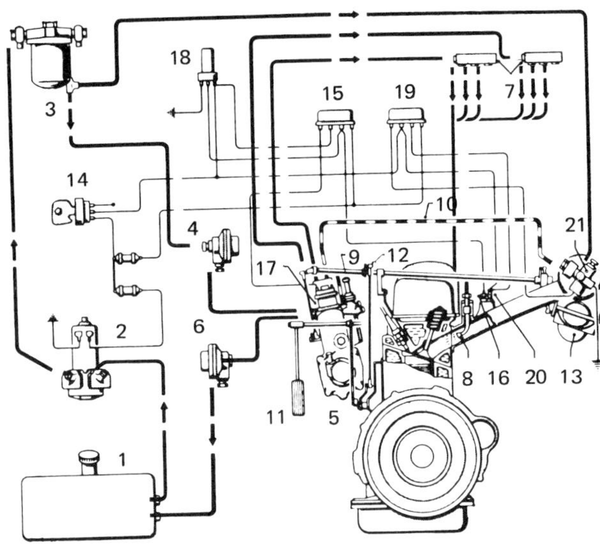

1. Fuel tank
2. Fuel-feed pump
3. Fuel filter
4. Damper container (inlet)
5. Injection pump
6. Damper container (outlet)
7. Fuel-metering units
8. Injection valves
9. Cooling-water thermostat
10. Additional air duct
11. Accelerator
12. Control linkage
13. Throttle connector
14. Ignition-starter switch
15. Relay
16. Thermo switch in cooling-water circuit
17. Magnetic switch for mixture control
18. Time switch
19. Relay
20. Thermo time switch in cooling-water circuit
21. Electromagnetic starter valve with atomizing jet

Fig. 11-29. Schematic layout of a fuel-injection system for a six-cylinder engine. (*Mercedes-Benz, Daimler-Benz Aktiengesellschaft*)

This, in turn, is determined by sensors which send electric signals to the transistorized control unit (Fig. 11-30). Figure 11-31 shows the air-supply system and its controls. Figure 11-32 shows the fuel-supply system.

⊘ 11-20 Superchargers and Turbochargers The word "supercharger" tells you what the device is. It is a mechanism for supplying the engine with a "super" charge of air-fuel mixture. The idea is simple. A centrifugal pump, similar to the engine water pump, is located between the carburetor and the engine cylinders (Fig. 11-33). It is driven at high speed. It compresses the air-fuel mixture from the carburetor and delivers it to the cylinders. A greater amount of air-fuel mixture therefore enters the cylinders, and the power strokes are stronger. That is, the engine can deliver more horsepower. The supercharger can increase the pressure on the mixture as much as 16 psi [1.125 kg/cm^2] above normal air pressure. An increase in engine horsepower of up to 50 percent is possible with supercharging.

The problem with the early supercharger was in the drive arrangement. It was driven by a belt, by

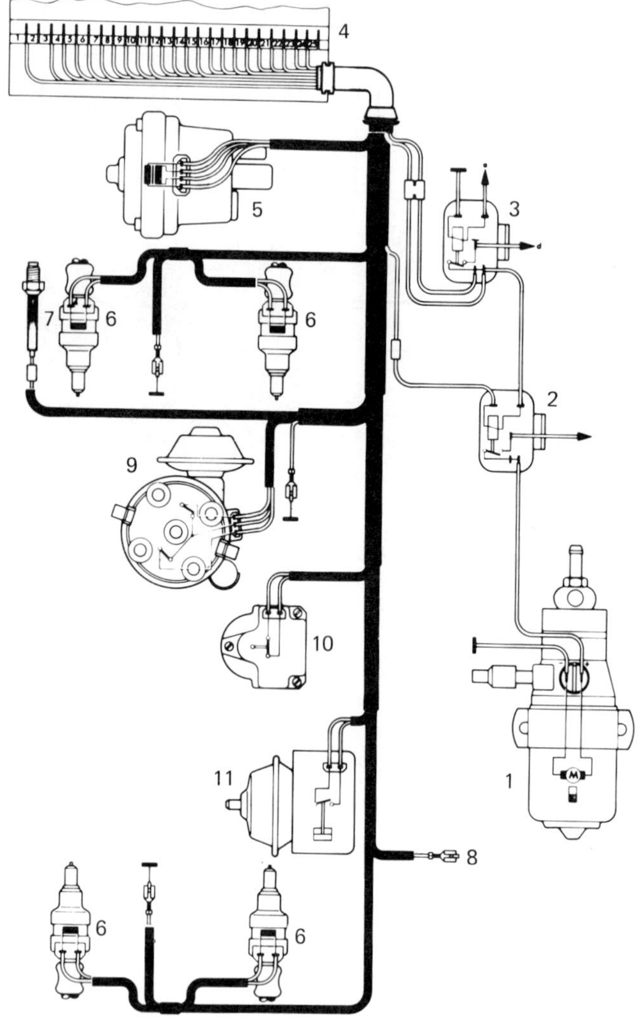

1. Fuel pump
2. Pump relay
3. Main relay
4. Control unit
5. Intake-manifold pressure sensor
6. Injector
7. Cylinder-head temperature sensor
8. Crankcase sensor
9. Ignition distributor
10. Throttle switch
11. Full-load pressure switch

Fig. 11-30. Schematic layout of the control system for the Volkswagen electronic fuel-injection system. The electronic control unit (4) receives signals from various sensors and integrates them to determine the amount of fuel to be injected. (*Volkswagen*)

gears, or by a chain and sprockets. These mechanical drives were put through great stress and sometimes caused trouble. Today, the supercharger is driven by the exhaust gas and carries the name "turbosupercharger," or simply "turbocharger." Figure 11-34 shows the arrangement. The exhaust gas, still under some pressure as it leaves the engine cylinders, is directed into a turbine. The turbine wheel is spun by the exhaust gas. The turbine wheel is on the same shaft as the centrifugal-pump rotor. It drives the pump rotor, which pressurizes the ingoing air-fuel mixture.

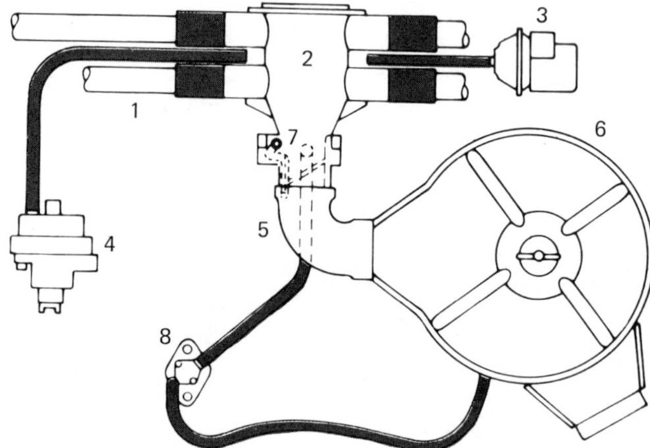

1. Air pipes to cylinders
2. Air distributor
3. Pressure switch
4. Pressure sensor
5. Idling circuit
6. Air cleaner
7. Adjusting screw
8. Auxiliary air regulator (rotary valve)

Fig. 11-31. Air-supply control for the Volkswagen electronic fuel-injection system. (*Volkswagen*)

⊘ 11-21 Stratified Charge In the stratified-charge engine, there is a layer of rich mixture within the compressed air-fuel charge (Fig. 11-35). During combustion, the rich mixture ignites first. It then spreads outward into areas where the mixture is lean and harder to ignite. With stratified charging, a much leaner air-fuel mixture (on the average) can be used. The combustion takes place largely in and around

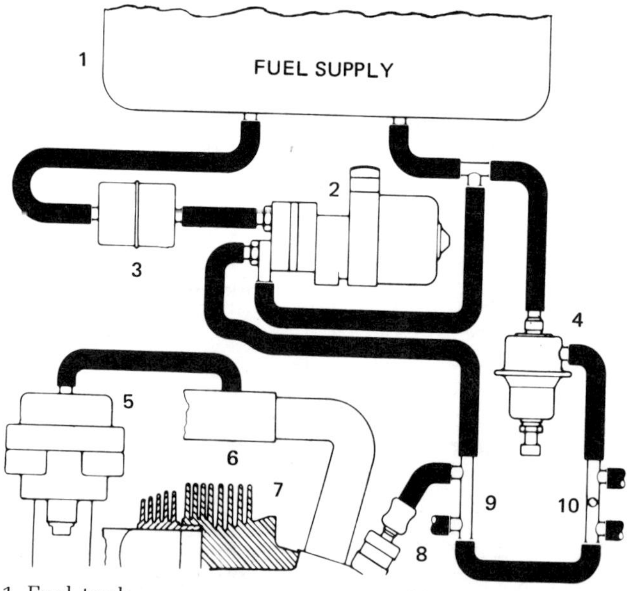

1. Fuel tank
2. Electric fuel pump
3. Filter
4. Pressure regulator
5. Intake-manifold pressure sensor
6. Air pipe
7. Cylinder head
8. Fuel injector
9–10. Distributor pipes to injector

Fig. 11-32. Fuel-supply system for the Volkswagen electronic fuel-injection system. (*Volkswagen*)

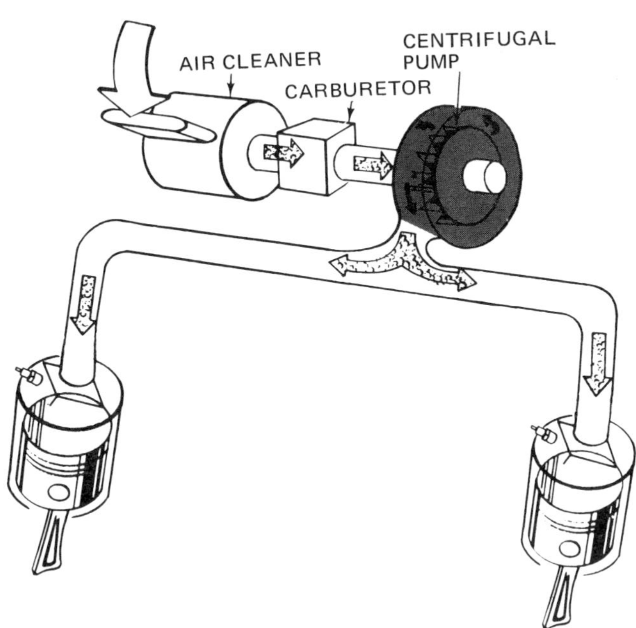

Fig. 11-33. Schematic diagram showing the principle of the supercharger.

the concentration of rich mixture. This means that the fuel is more completely burned. The amount of pollutants, such as carbon monoxide, unburned gasoline, and nitrogen oxides, is reduced.

One way to achieve stratified charging is to give the air-fuel mixture a swirling motion as it enters the cylinder. This can be done by careful placement of the intake port.

Another method is the so-called Honda system. Here, a separate small precombustion chamber is

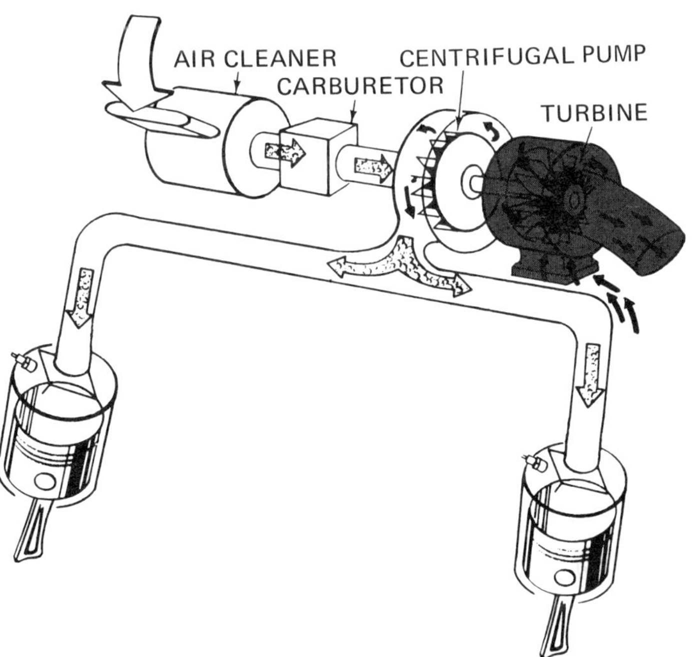

Fig. 11-34. Schematic diagram showing the principle of the turbocharger.

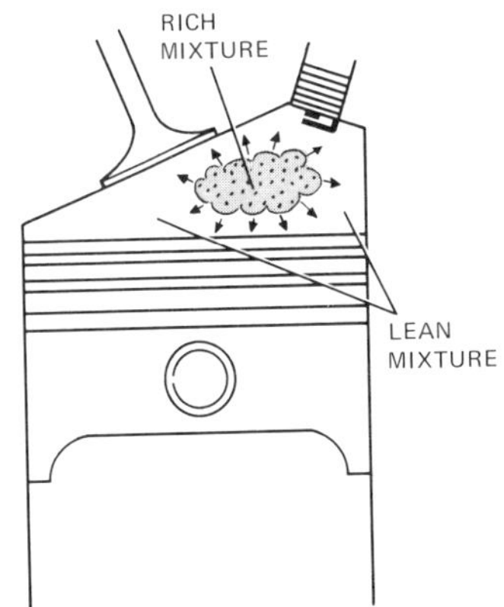

Fig. 11-35. Principle of stratified charging.

used. This precombustion chamber has the spark plug and its own intake valve. Figure 11-36 is an outline view of the engine showing the valves, spark plug, and pistons for one cylinder. Figure 11-37 shows how the arrangement works. In operation, the carburetor delivers a very lean mixture to the main combustion chamber. It delivers a very rich mixture to the precombustion chamber. Ignition takes place in the precombustion chamber. The rich mixture, under the high pressure of combustion, streams out into the main combustion chamber, as shown in 3 and 4 of Fig. 11-37. There, it mixes with the lean mixture, and combustion continues. This assures good burning of the fuel so that pollutants are kept to a low level. Study Fig. 11-37 to see the sequence of actions in the engine.

⊘ 11-22 LPG Fuel System Liquified petroleum gas (LPG) is a fuel that is liquid only under pressure (see ⊘ 10-20). When the pressure is reduced, the fuel vaporizes. Thus, the fuel system must include a pressure-tight fuel tank in which to store the fuel at high pressure. A typical LPG fuel system is shown in Fig. 11-38. Pressure forces fuel through the filter, high-pressure regulator, and vaporizer. The high-pressure regulator reduces the pressure so that the fuel starts to turn to vapor. This vaporizing process is completed in the vaporizer. The vaporizer has an inner tank surrounded by a water jacket. Coolant from the cooling-system flows through the water jacket. The coolant adds heat to the fuel so that it is well vaporized. It then passes through the low-pressure regulator, where the pressure is further reduced. It then enters the carburetor. The carburetor is simply a mixing valve that mixes the vaporized fuel with air. The low-pressure regulator reduces the pressure to slightly *below* atmospheric pressure. This prevents it from flowing into the carburetor when the engine is off. Fuel flows only when the engine is running and there is a vacuum in the carburetor venturi (or air horn).

LPG fuel systems have been used on some cars, trucks, buses, and fork-lift and platform trucks. The

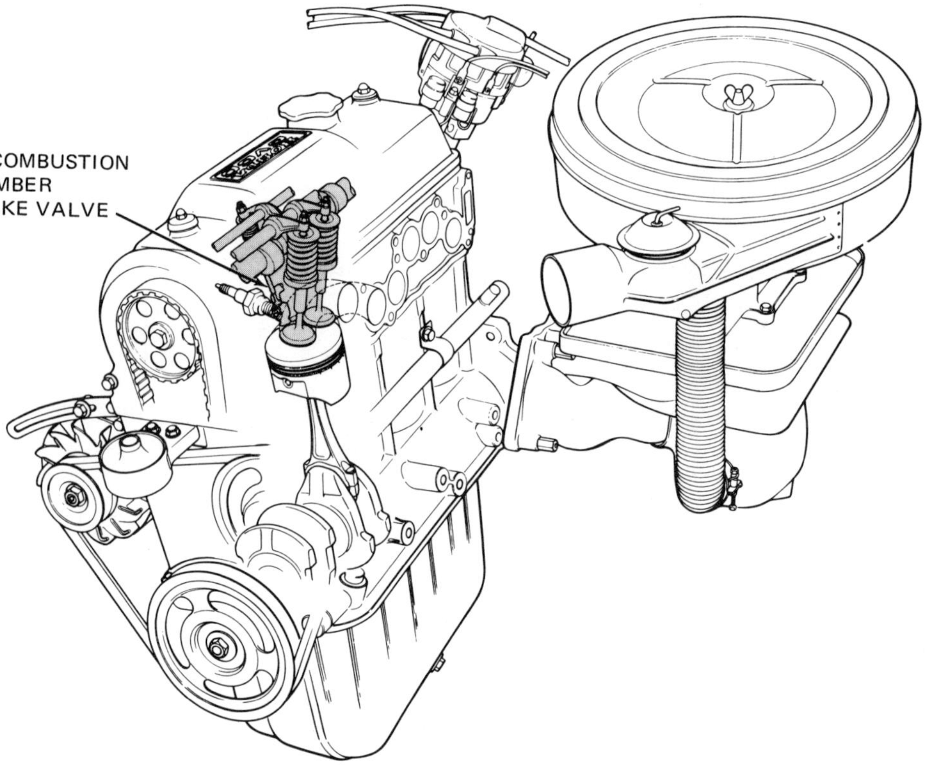

PRECOMBUSTION
CHAMBER
INTAKE VALVE

Fig. 11-36. Outline view of the Honda four-cylinder engine, showing the essential working parts of one cylinder. (*Honda*)

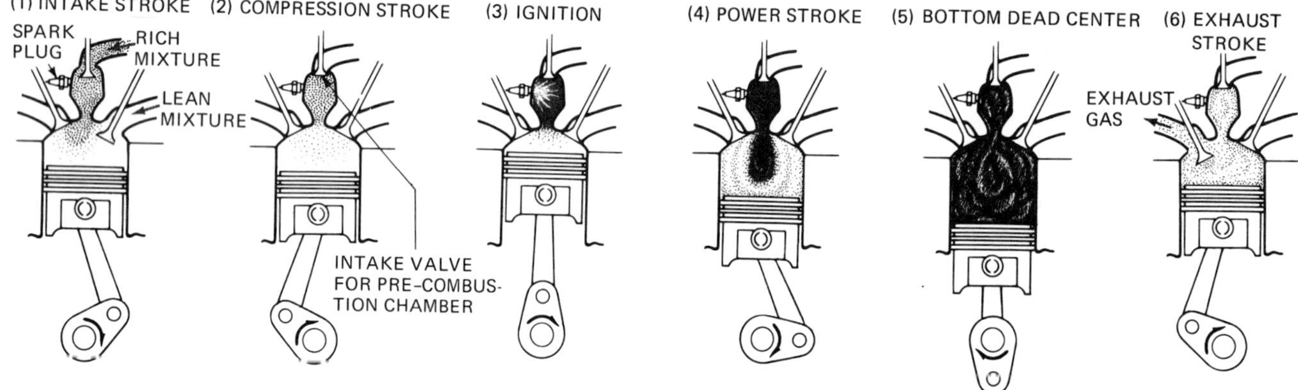

Fig. 11-37. Sequence of actions in the Honda system. (*Honda*)

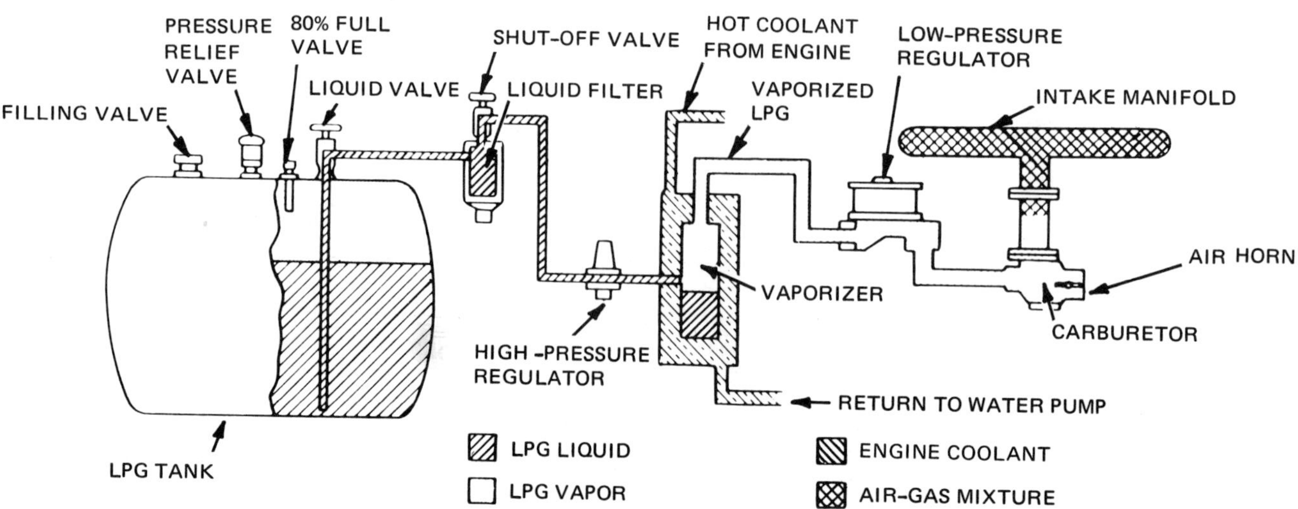

Fig. 11-38. LPG fuel system, shown schematically.

system is well suited for such applications, since the fuel burns clean. The exhaust gases contain very few contaminants.

CHAPTER 11 CHECKUP

NOTE: Since this is a chapter review test, you should review the chapter before taking the test.

You are making good progress in your study of automotive fuels and fuel systems. Now check up on yourself by taking the test that follows. If any of the questions seem difficult, turn back into the chapter. Reread the pages that give you the information you need.

Completing the Sentences The sentences that follow are incomplete. After each sentence there are several words or phrases, but only one of them correctly completes the sentence. Write each sentence in your notebook, ending it with the one word or phrase that completes it correctly.

1. The fuel system consists of the fuel tank, fuel lines, fuel filter, fuel pump, and the: (*a*) carburetor and electric pump, (*b*) intake manifold and carburetor, (*c*) carburetor and combustion chamber.
2. The low-fuel-level indicator is attached to the: (*a*) tank unit of the fuel gauge, (*b*) instrument-panel unit of the fuel gauge, (*c*) fuel tank.
3. The filtering element in an air cleaner is made of: (*a*) fiber, special paper, or polyurethane, (*b*) steel wool or wood chips.
4. The air cleaner sits on top of the: (*a*) fuel tank, (*b*) carburetor, (*c*) fuel pump.
5. When the engine is cold, all air entering the thermostatically controlled air cleaner comes from the: (*a*) intake manifold, (*b*) exhaust manifold, (*c*) heat stove on the exhaust manifold.
6. The purpose of the EGR system is to: (*a*) reduce engine temperatures, (*b*) reduce NO_x in the exhaust gas, (*c*) improve the combustion of HC.
7. The purpose of the crankcase ventilation system is to: (*a*) remove exhaust gases from the crankcase, (*b*) remove blow-by from the crankcase, (*c*) improve engine cooling.
8. In the fuel-injection system for gasoline engines, the fuel injector: (*a*) injects fuel into the cylinders, (*b*) replaces the carburetor, (*c*) supplies an unvarying amount of gasoline.
9. The purpose of the thermostatically controlled air cleaner is to: (*a*) reduce the noise of the air entering the carburetor, (*b*) send heated air to the carburetor during cold weather, when the engine is cold, (*c*) prevent engine backfire.
10. In an engine, the higher the combustion temperature, the greater the formation of: (*a*) nitrogen oxides, (*b*) hydrocarbons, (*c*) carbon monoxide.

Definitions and Explanations In the following, you are asked for definitions, lists, and explanations relating to the fuel system. Write them in your notebook.

1. Name four of the components of the fuel system.
2. What are the two types of fuel gauges?
3. Explain how a fuel pump works.
4. What is the purpose of the vapor-return line?
5. What is the purpose of the fuel-vapor recovery system?
6. Describe the operation of two types of electric fuel pumps.
7. What is the purpose of the air cleaner?
8. What is the purpose of the thermostatically controlled air cleaner? How does it work?
9. What is the purpose of the EGR system? How does it work?
10. Why does high valve overlap reduce NO_x?
11. What is the purpose of the crankcase ventilation?
12. Describe an exhaust system.
13. What is the purpose of the catalytic converter in the exhaust system?
14. What is the purpose of the muffler?
15. Explain how a diesel-engine fuel system works.
16. How does the supercharger work?
17. How is the turbocharger driven?
18. What is meant by stratified charge?
19. Explain how the Honda system works.
20. Describe how the LPG fuel system works.

SUGGESTIONS FOR FURTHER STUDY

Keep your eyes open for articles in automotive magazines about stratified-charge engines, superchargers, and fuel-injection systems. Some engineers say that these will be part of the automotive engines of the future. In fact, some of these ideas are already being used in present-day automobiles. To keep up with new developments in automotive engineering, you should have a good understanding of the concepts behind them. That way, you will be able to understand and handle any new developments.

chapter 12

AUTOMOTIVE CARBURETORS

In previous chapters, we discussed automotive fuels and fuel systems. In this chapter, we look at automotive carburetors. We discuss the various systems in carburetors, and how they work.

⊘ **12-1 Carburetion** Carburetion is the mixing of gasoline with air to obtain a combustible mixture. The carburetor performs this job. It supplies a combustible mixture of varying richness, to suit engine operating conditions. The mixture must be rich (have a higher percentage of fuel) for starting, acceleration, and high-speed operation. A less rich (leaner) mixture is desirable at intermediate speeds with a warm engine. The carburetor has several systems through which air-fuel mixture flows during different operating conditions. These systems produce the varying mixture richness required for varying operating conditions. All this is explained in the sections that follow.

⊘ **12-2 Vaporization** When a liquid changes to a vapor, it is said to evaporate, or vaporize. Water placed in an open pan will evaporate: It changes from a liquid to a vapor. Wet clothes hung on a line become dry because the water evaporates out of the clothes. When the clothes are spread out, they dry more rapidly than when they are bunched together. This illustrates an important fact about evaporation. The greater the surface exposed, the more rapidly evaporation takes place. A pint of water in a tall glass takes quite a while to evaporate. But a pint of water in a shallow pan evaporates much more quickly (Fig. 12-1).

Fig. 12-1. Water evaporates from the shallow pan faster than from the glass. The greater the area exposed to air, the faster the evaporation.

⊘ **12-3 Atomization** To vaporize the liquid gasoline more quickly, it is sprayed into the air passing through the carburetor. Spraying the liquid turns it into many fine droplets. This effect is called *atomization*, because the liquid is broken up into small droplets. (But it is not actually broken into atoms, as the name implies.) Each droplet is exposed to air on all sides. With so much surface exposed, it vaporizes very quickly. During normal engine operation, the gasoline vaporizes almost as soon as it is sprayed into the carburetor air.

⊘ **12-4 Carburetor Fundamentals** A simple carburetor could be made from a round cylinder with a constricted section, a fuel nozzle, and a round disk, or valve (Fig. 12-2). The round cylinder is called the *air horn;* the constricted section is the *venturi;* and the valve is the *throttle valve*. The throttle valve can be tilted more or less to open or close the air horn (Fig. 12-3). In the horizontal position, it shuts off, or *throttles*, the airflow through the air horn. When the throttle is turned away from this position, air can flow through the air horn.

⊘ **12-5 Venturi Effect** As air flows through the constriction, or venturi, a partial vacuum is produced at the venturi. This vacuum causes the fuel nozzle to deliver a spray of gasoline into the passing airstream. The venturi effect (of producing a vacuum) can be illustrated with the setup in Fig. 12-4. Three dishes of mercury (a very heavy metallic liquid) are connected by tubes to an air horn with a venturi. The greater the vacuum, the higher the mercury is pushed up in the tubes by atmospheric pressure. Note that the greatest vacuum is right at the venturi. Also, the faster the air flows through the venturi, the greater the vacuum will be.

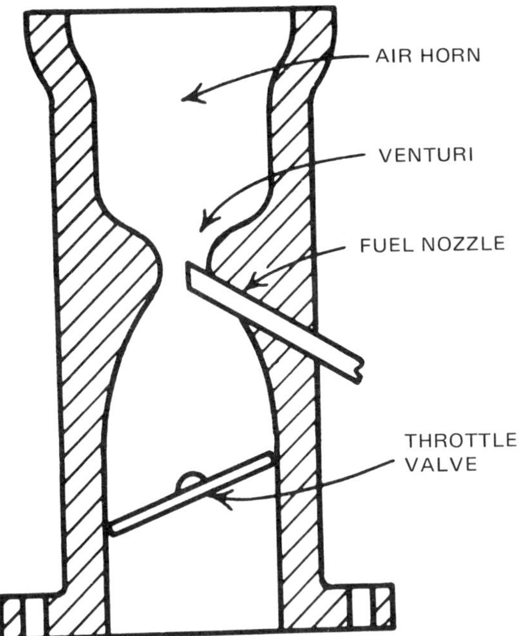

Fig. 12-2. Simple carburetor consisting of an air horn, a fuel nozzle, and a throttle valve.

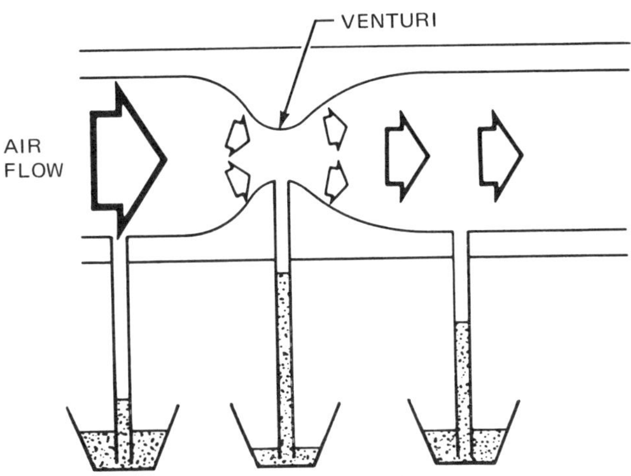

Fig. 12-4. Three dishes of mercury, with tubes connected to an air horn. Differences in vacuum are shown by the distances the mercury rises in the tubes. The venturi has the highest vacuum.

Why is there a vacuum at the venturi? A simple explanation might be as follows: The air is made up of countless molecules. As air flows into the top of the air horn, all the air molecules move at the same speed. But if all the molecules are to get through the venturi, they must speed up as they enter it. Now consider two molecules, one behind the other. As the first molecule enters the venturi, it speeds up, tending to leave the second molecule behind. The second molecule also speeds up as it enters the venturi. But the first molecule has, in effect, a head start. Thus, the two molecules are farther apart in the venturi than they were before they entered it. Now imagine a great number of molecules going through the same action. The molecules are all farther apart in the venturi than they were before they entered it. This is just what a partial vacuum is: a thinning out of the air, a greater-than-normal distance between molecules.

⊘ 12-6 Fuel-Nozzle Action The partial vacuum occurs in the venturi, where one end of the fuel nozzle is located. The other end of the fuel nozzle is in a fuel reservoir (the float bowl), as shown in Fig. 12-5. Atmospheric pressure pushes on the fuel through a vent in the float-bowl cover. So there is a vacuum at one end of the nozzle, and atmospheric pressure at the other end. Because of this pressure difference, fuel is pushed up through the nozzle. The fuel enters the passing airstream as a fine spray. It quickly turns to vapor as the droplets of fuel evaporate. The more air that flows through the air horn, the greater the

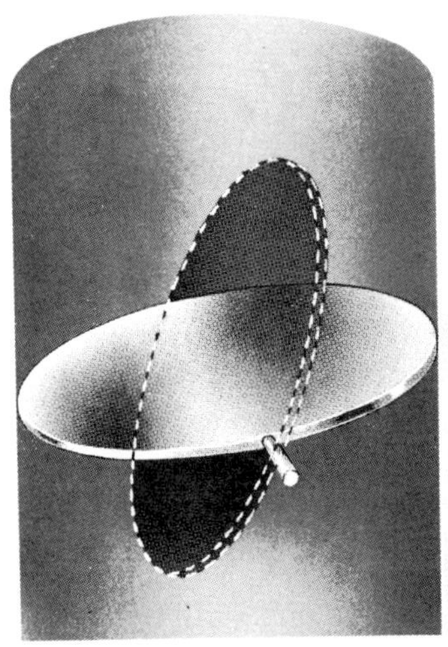

Fig. 12-3. Throttle valve in the air horn of a carburetor. When the throttle is closed, as shown, little air can pass through. But when the throttle is opened, as shown dashed, there is little throttling effect.

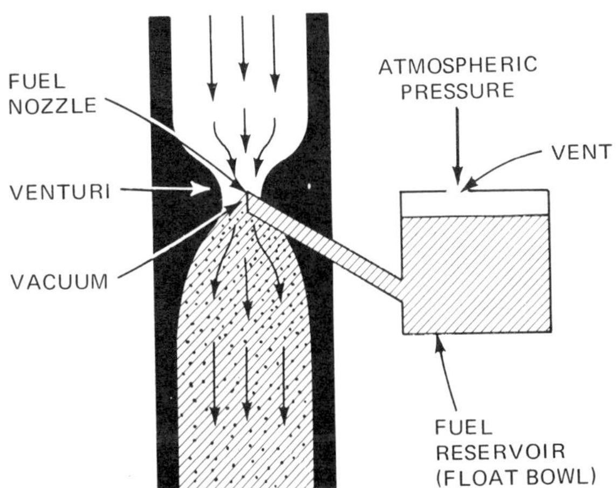

Fig. 12-5. A venturi, or constriction, causes a vacuum to develop in the airstream just below the constriction. Then atmospheric pressure pushes fuel up and out the fuel nozzle.

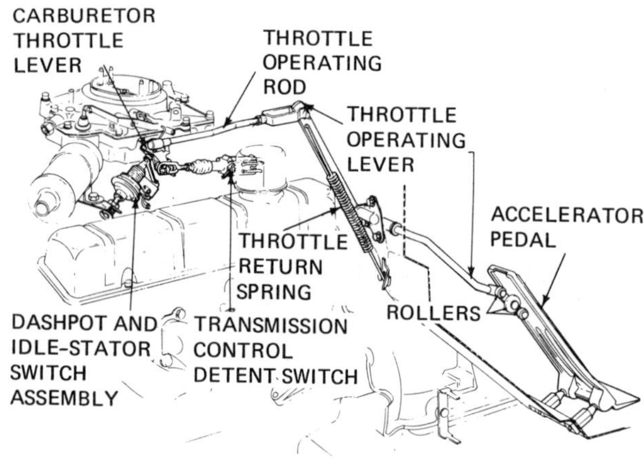

Fig. 12-6. Linkage between the accelerator pedal and the carburetor throttle lever. (*Buick Motor Division of General Motors Corporation*)

vacuum in the venturi. The greater the vacuum, the more fuel is delivered.

⊘ 12-7 Throttle-Valve Action

The throttle valve can be tilted in the air horn to allow more or less air to flow through (Fig. 12-3). When it is tilted to allow more air to flow, larger amounts of air-fuel mixture are delivered to the engine. The engine develops more power and tends to run faster. But if the throttle valve is tilted to throttle off most of the air, then only small amounts of air-fuel mixture are delivered. The engine produces less power and tends to slow down. The throttle valve is linked to an accelerator pedal in the driver's compartment. It permits the driver to position the throttle valve as required (Fig. 12-6).

⊘ 12-8 Air-Fuel-Ratio Requirements

As already noted, the fuel system must vary the air-fuel ratio to suit different operating conditions. The mixture must be rich (have a high proportion of fuel) for starting. It must be leaner (have a lower proportion of fuel) for part-throttle medium-speed operation.

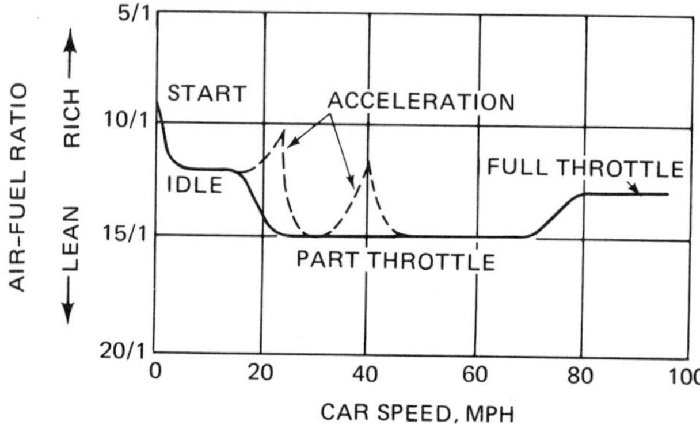

Fig. 12-7. Graph of air-fuel ratios for different car speeds. The graph is typical. The speeds at which the various ratios are obtained may vary with different cars. Also, there may be some variation in the ratios.

Figure 12-7 is a graph showing typical air-fuel ratios for various car speeds. The ratios, and the speeds at which they are obtained, vary with different cars. In the example shown, a rich mixture of about 9:1 (9 lb [4.082 kg] of air for each 1 lb [0.454 kg] of fuel) is supplied for starting. Then, during idle, the mixture leans out to about 12:1. At medium speeds, the mixture leans out further, to about 15:1. But at higher speeds, with a wide-open throttle, the mixture is enriched to about 13:1. Opening the throttle for acceleration at any speed causes a momentary enrichment of the mixture. This results from special carburetor systems which we shall study later. Two examples are shown in Fig. 12-7—at about 20 mph (miles per hour) [32.18 km/h (kilometers per hour)] and about 30 mph [48.27 km/h].

You might think that the engine itself needs different air-fuel ratios for different operating conditions. This is not quite true. For example, we noted that the mixture must be very rich for starting. This is because fuel vaporizes very poorly under starting conditions. The engine and carburetor are cold, the air speed is low, and much of the fuel does not vaporize. Thus, extra fuel must be delivered by the carburetor, so that enough will vaporize for starting. Likewise, sudden opening of the throttle for acceleration allows a sudden inrush of air. Extra fuel must enter at the same time (that is, the mixture must be enriched). This is because only part of the fuel vaporizes and mixes with the ingoing air. Again, the additional fuel is needed to provide the proper proportions of air and fuel in the engine.

The following sections describe the various systems in the carburetor. These systems supply the air-fuel mixtures required for different operating conditions.

⊘ 12-9 Carburetor Systems

The systems (or "circuits," as they are sometimes called) in the carburetor are:

1. Float system
2. Idle system
3. Main metering system
4. Power system
5. Accelerator-pump system
6. Choke system

These systems are discussed in detail in ⊘ 12-10 to 12-24.

⊘ 12-10 Float System

The float system includes the float bowl and a float-and-needle-valve arrangement. The float and the needle valve maintain a constant level of fuel in the float bowl. If the level is too high, then too much fuel will feed from the fuel nozzle. If it is too low, too little fuel will feed. In either case, poor engine performance will result. Figure 12-8 is a simplified drawing of the float system. If fuel enters the float bowl faster than it is withdrawn, the fuel level rises. This causes the float to move up and push the needle valve into the valve seat. This, in turn,

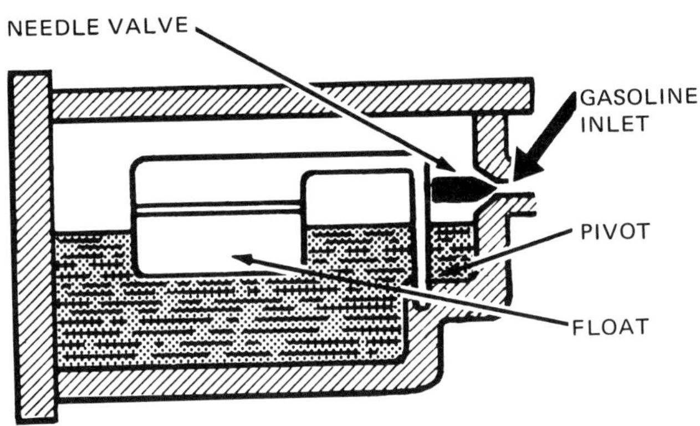

Fig. 12-8. Simplified drawing of a carburetor float system.

shuts off the fuel inlet so that no fuel can enter. Then, if the fuel level drops, the float moves down and releases the needle. This opens the fuel inlet so that fuel can enter. In actual operation, the fuel is kept at an almost constant level. The float tends to hold the needle valve partly closed. Just enough fuel enters the float bowl to make up for the fuel being withdrawn.

Figure 12-9 shows an actual carburetor with a dual float assembly. The carburetor is partly cut away so that the two floats can be seen. The float bowl partly surrounds the carburetor air horn. The two floats are attached by a U-shaped lever and operate a single needle valve. Some carburetors have an auxiliary fuel valve and inlet, as shown in Fig. 12-10. During heavy-load or high-speed operation, fuel may leave the float bowl faster than it can enter through the main fuel inlet. If this happens, the fuel level drops. The end of the float lever presses against the auxiliary valve, pushing it upward. This opens the auxiliary fuel inlet so additional fuel can enter.

A number of years ago, some four-barrel carburetors had two sets of floats (Fig. 12-11). The four-barrel carburetor is, in effect, two two-barrel carburetors. As will be explained later, the primary barrels supply the engine during most operating conditions. But the secondary barrels come into operation during acceleration and high speed, for improved performance. The idea of using two sets of floats was to provide, in effect, a separate float system for each pair of barrels. However, more recent four-barrel carburetors have a single, centrally located float. The two-float system requires a large float bowl; it has other disadvantages that single and dual-float systems do not have. For example, single and dual floats are more centrally located, so they respond more accurately to fuel needs. Also, the float bowl is smaller. There is thus less of a problem with fuel evaporation and atmospheric pollution by escaping HC.

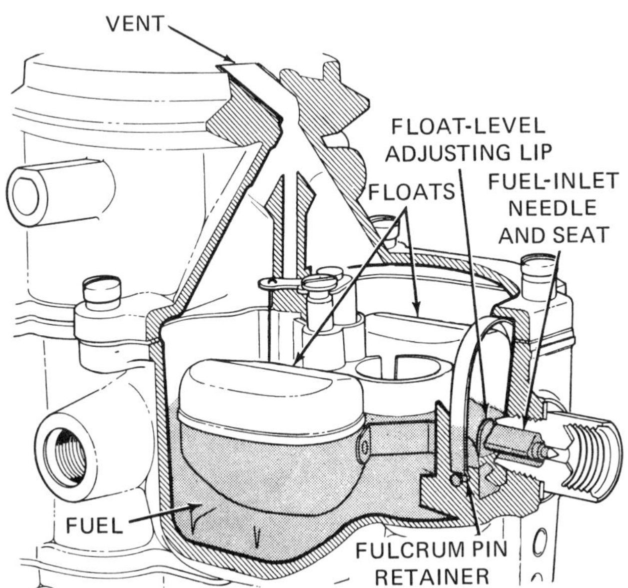

Fig. 12-9. Carburetor, partly cut away to show the float system. (*Chrysler Corporation*)

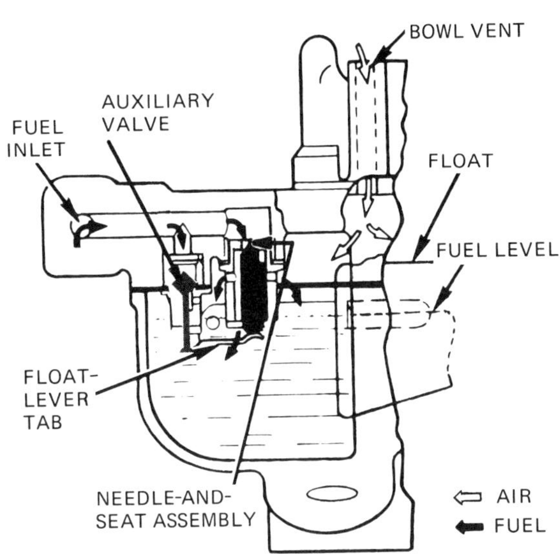

Fig. 12-10. Float system using auxiliary fuel valve and inlet. (*American Motors Corporation*)

⊘ 12-11 Float-Bowl Vents

The float bowls of carburetors are vented into the carburetor air horn at a point above the choke valve (see upper left in Fig. 12-9; upper left in Fig. 12-12). The purpose of the vent is to equalize the effect of a clogged air cleaner. Here's how it works: Suppose the air cleaner does become clogged with dirt. The passage of air through the air cleaner is then restricted. As a result, a partial vacuum develops in the carburetor air horn. Therefore, a somewhat greater vacuum is applied to the venturi end of the fuel nozzle (since this vacuum is added to the venturi vacuum). However, the partial vacuum resulting from the clogged air cleaner is also applied to the float bowl (through the vent). So the same additional vacuum is applied to both ends of the nozzle. The driving force that pushes fuel from the fuel nozzle is still the air pressure in the air cleaner. Thus, the vent "cancels" the effect of a clogged air cleaner.

If the float bowl were vented to the atmosphere,

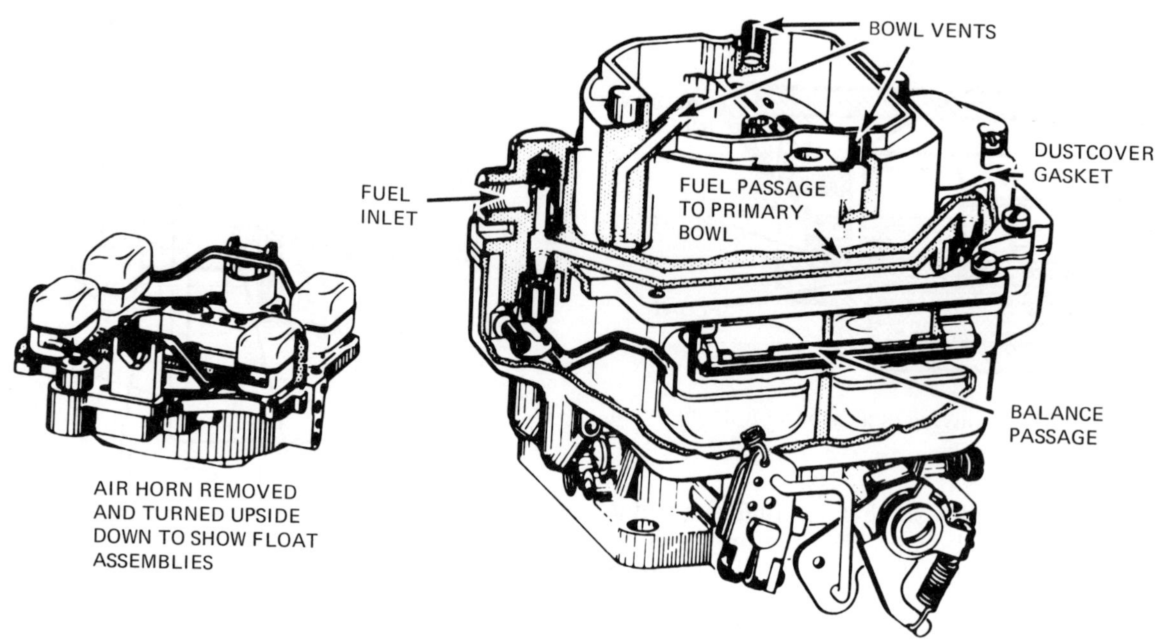

Fig. 12-11. Float system for a four-barrel carburetor, using two sets of floats. (*Chevrolet Motor Division of General Motors Corporation*)

then atmospheric pressure would force fuel through the nozzle. This would produce a greater fuel flow from the fuel nozzle, and the mixture would be too rich.

The float bowl has another vent, shown to the upper right in Fig. 12-12. This vent is connected by a tube to the charcoal canister which is part of the fuel-vapor recovery system (⊘ 17-8). In the carburetor in Fig. 12-12, the float bowl has a pressure-relief valve. The valve opens when the vapor pressure in the float bowl increases. This allows the fuel vapor to flow to the charcoal canister. In other carburetors the vent to the charcoal canister has a valve operated by the accelerator-pump lever. The valve is opened when the engine is idling or when it has been turned off.

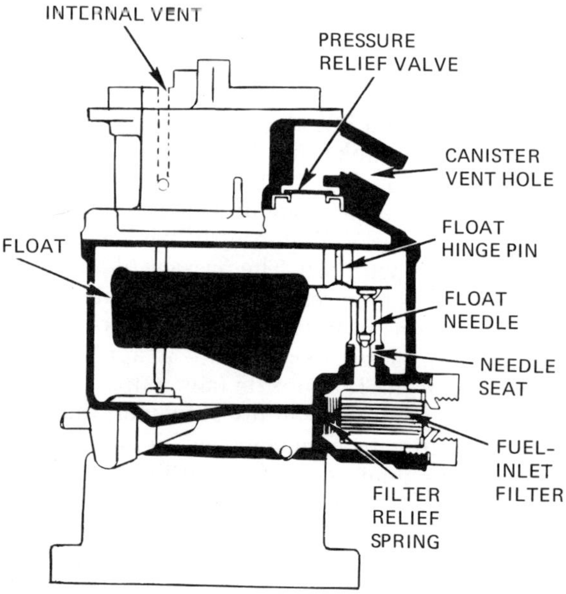

Fig. 12-12. Float system, showing the two vents—one internal, and the other to the charcoal canister. (*Chevrolet Motor Division of General Motors Corporation*)

⊘ 12-12 Hot-Idle Compensator Valve The internal vent could be a problem during idling or low-speed operation, especially in hot weather. Gasoline vapor from the float bowl could pass through the internal vent in sufficient amounts to upset the air-fuel ratio. That is, the gasoline vapor could add to the normal air-fuel mixture, and the mixture would become too rich. To solve this problem, some carburetors have a hot-idle compensator valve (left, in Fig. 12-13). The valve is operated by a thermostatic blade. When the temperature reaches a preset value, the blade bends enough to open the valve port. Now additional air can flow through the auxiliary air passage. This additional air bypasses the idle system. It leans out the mixture enough to make up for the added gasoline vapor coming from the float bowl.

⊘ 12-13 Idle System When the throttle is closed or slightly open, only a small amount of air can pass through the air horn. The airspeed is low, and very little vacuum develops in the venturi. This means that the fuel nozzle cannot feed fuel. The carburetor must have another system to supply fuel when the throttle is closed or slightly open.

This system, called the *idle* system, is shown in operation in Fig. 12-14. It includes passages through which air and fuel can flow. The air passage is called the *air bleed*. With the throttle closed as shown, there is a high vacuum below the throttle valve (from the intake manifold). Atmospheric pressure pushes air and fuel through the passages as shown.

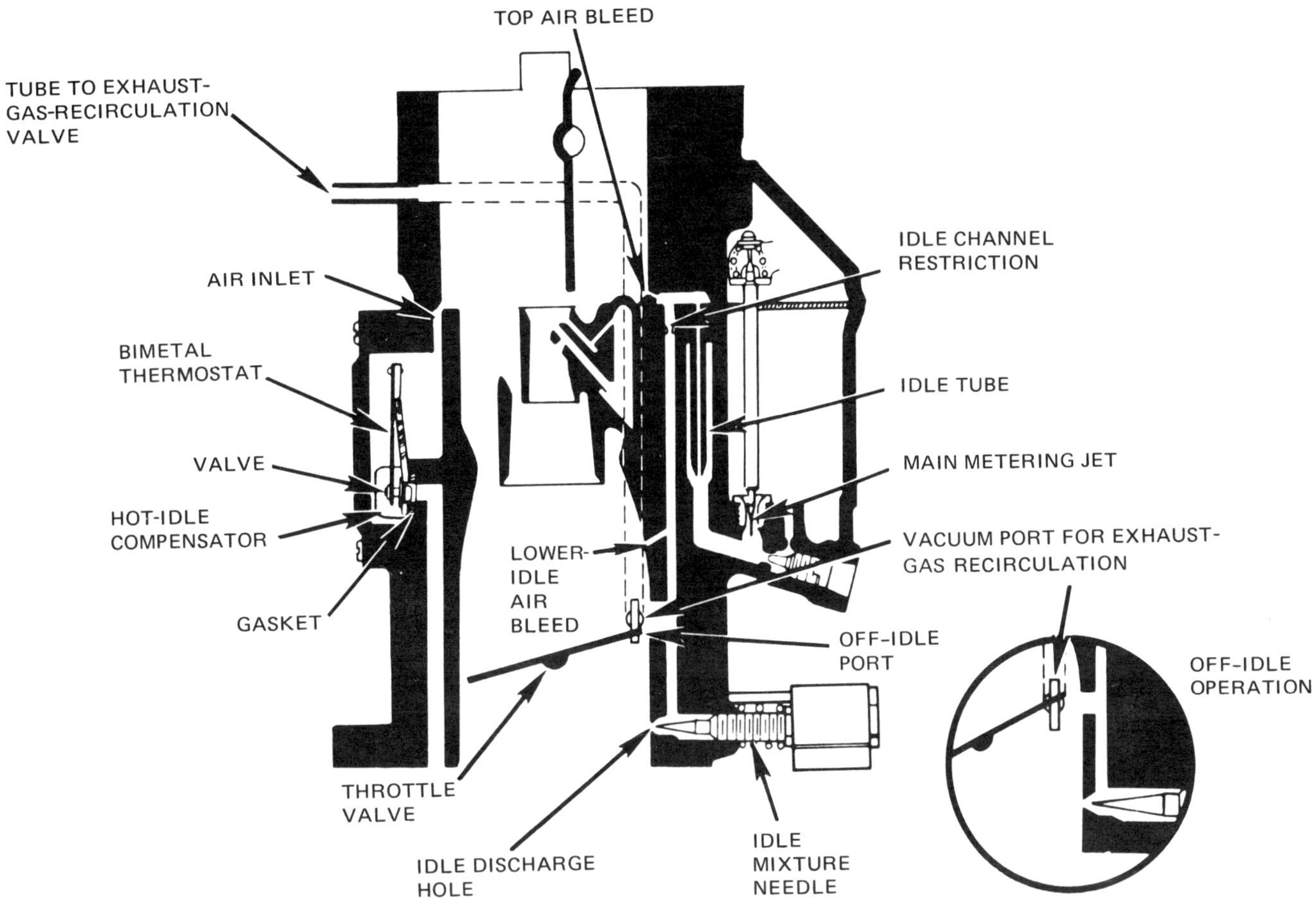

Fig. 12-13. Idle system. Note the passage to the exhaust-gas recirculation system. This passage allows some exhaust gas to feed into the air-fuel mixture when the throttle valve opens past the vacuum port. (*Chevrolet Motor Division of General Motors Corporation*)

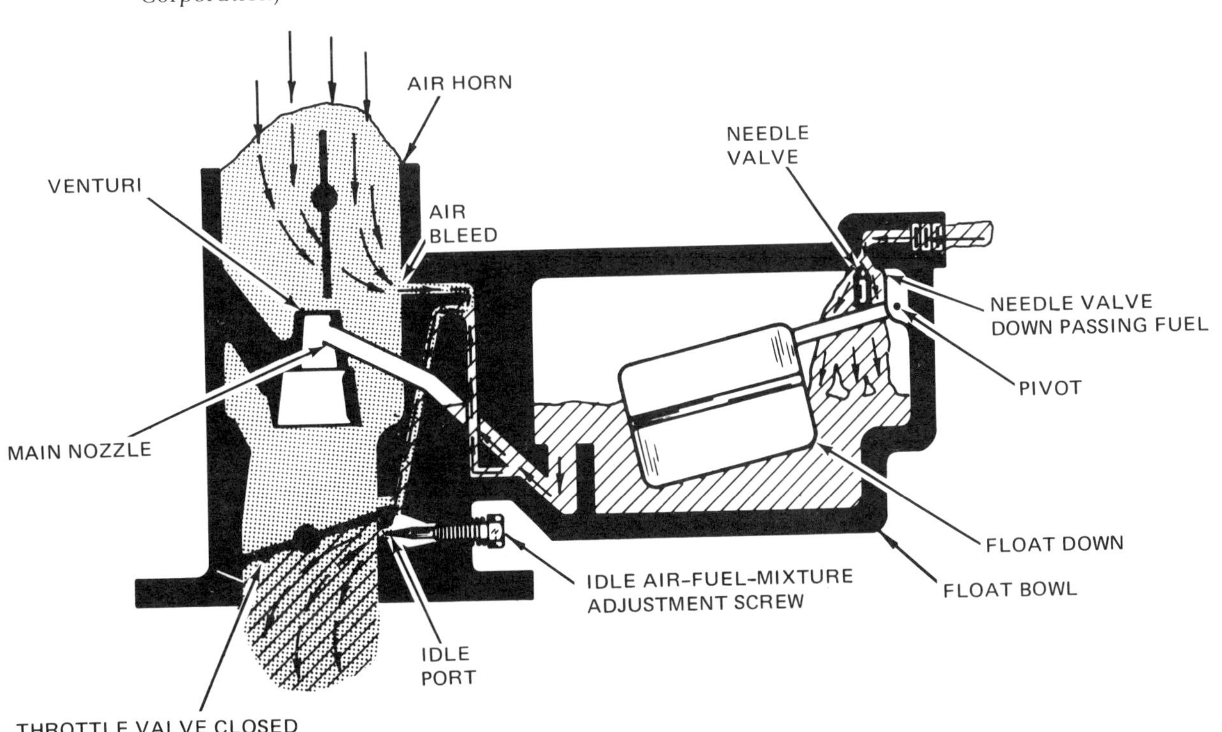

Fig. 12-14. Idle system in a carburetor. The throttle valve is closed so that only a small amount of air can get past it. All fuel is being fed past the idle adjustment screw. The arrows show the flow of air and fuel.

They mix and flow past the tapered point of the idle air-fuel-mixture adjustment screw. The mixture has a high proportion of fuel (is very rich). It leans out somewhat as it mixes with the small amount of air that gets past the closed throttle valve. But the final mixture is still rich enough for good idling (see Fig. 12-7). The richness can be adjusted by turning the idle air-fuel-mixture adjustment screw in or out. This permits less or more air-fuel mixture to flow past the screw.

NOTE: In late-model cars, the idle air-fuel-mixture adjustment screw is fixed or has a locking cap on it. This is because it is illegal to adjust the idle mixture beyond specific limits. The adjustment screw has been set according to federal standards and must not be tampered with.

Figure 12-15 shows a cutaway view of a carburetor with the idle system in operation.

⊘ 12-14 Low-Speed Operation When the throttle is opened slightly (Fig. 12-16), the edge of the throttle valve moves past the low-speed port in the side of the air horn. This port is a vertical slot or a series of small holes, one above the other. Additional fuel is thus fed into the intake manifold through the low-speed port. This fuel mixes with the additional air moving past the slightly opened throttle valve. It provides sufficient mixture richness for part-throttle low-speed operation.

Some air bleeds around the throttle plate, through the low-speed port, when the edge of the throttle is only partway past this port. This air improves the atomization of the fuel coming from the low-speed port.

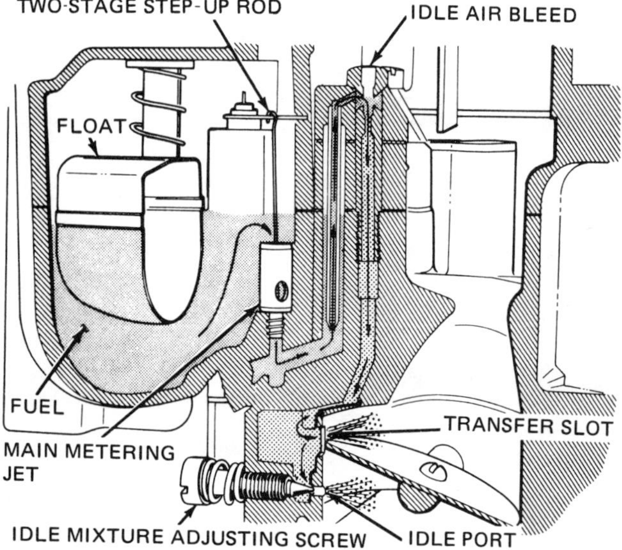

Fig. 12-15. Idle system in a carburetor. The carburetor has been cut away to show the internal arrangement. *(Chrysler Corporation)*

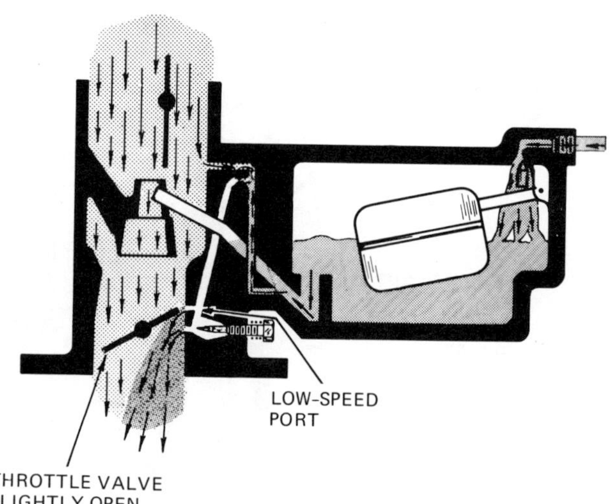

Fig. 12-16. Low-speed operation. The throttle valve is slightly open. The fuel is being fed through the low-speed port as well as through the idle port. The dark color is fuel. The light color is air.

⊘ 12-15 Other Idle Systems There are many varieties of idle systems, in addition to those shown in Figs. 12-14 to 12-16. In two-barrel carburetors, each barrel has its own idle system. In many four-barrel carburetors, only the primary barrels have idle systems (⊘ 12-30).

⊘ 12-16 Main Metering System Suppose the throttle valve is opened enough so that its edge moves well past the low-speed port. Now there is little difference in vacuum between the upper and lower parts of the air horn. Thus, little air-fuel mixture discharges from the low-speed port. However, under this condition, enough air moves through the air horn to produce a vacuum in the venturi. As a result,

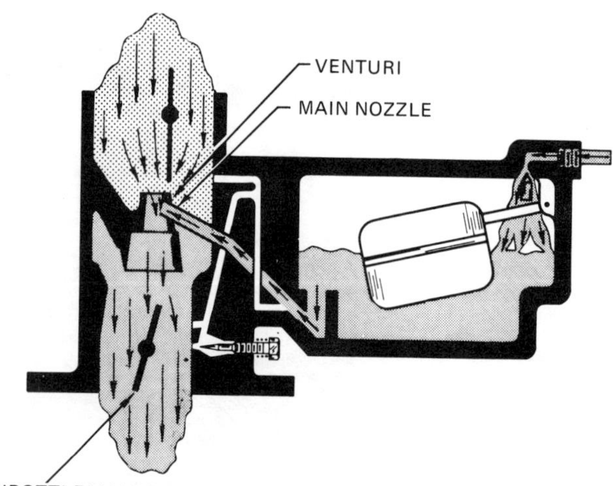

Fig. 12-17. Main metering system in carburetor. The throttle valve is open. Fuel is being fed through the high-speed, or main, nozzle. The dark color is fuel. The light color is air.

the fuel nozzle centered in the venturi (called the *main nozzle* or the *high-speed nozzle*) begins to discharge fuel (as explained in ⊘ 12-6). That is, the main nozzle supplies the fuel when the throttle is partly to fully open. Figure 12-17 shows this action. The fuel path from the float bowl to the main nozzle is called the *main metering system.*

The wider the throttle is opened and the faster the air flows through the air horn, the greater the vacuum in the venturi. The greater vacuum causes additional fuel to be discharged from the main nozzle. As a result, a nearly constant air-fuel ratio is maintained by the main metering system from part-open to wide-open throttle.

⊘ 12-17 Power System For high-speed, full-power, wide-open-throttle operation, the air-fuel mixture must be enriched (see Fig. 12-7). Additional devices in the carburetor provide this enriched mixture during high-speed full-power operation. They are operated mechanically or by intake-manifold vacuum.

⊘ 12-18 Mechanically Operated Power System This system includes a metering-rod jet (a carefully calibrated orifice, or opening) and a metering rod with two or more steps of different diameters (Fig. 12-18). The metering rod is attached to the throttle linkage (Fig. 12-19). When the throttle is opened, the metering rod is lifted. But when the throttle is partly closed, the larger diameter of the metering rod is in the metering-rod jet. This partly restricts fuel flow to the main nozzle. However, enough fuel does flow for normal part-throttle operation. When the throttle is opened wide, the rod is lifted further. This moves the smaller diameter, or step, up into the metering-rod jet. Now the jet is less restricted, and more fuel can flow. The main nozzle is therefore supplied with more fuel, and the air-fuel mixture is enriched.

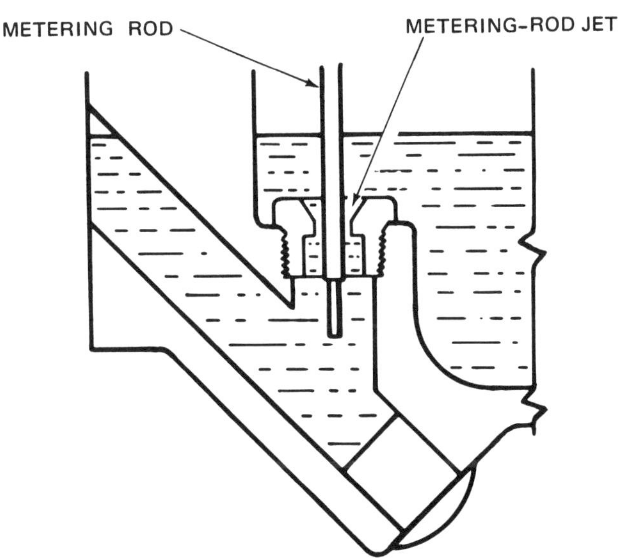

Fig. 12-18. Metering rod and metering-rod jet, for better performance at full throttle.

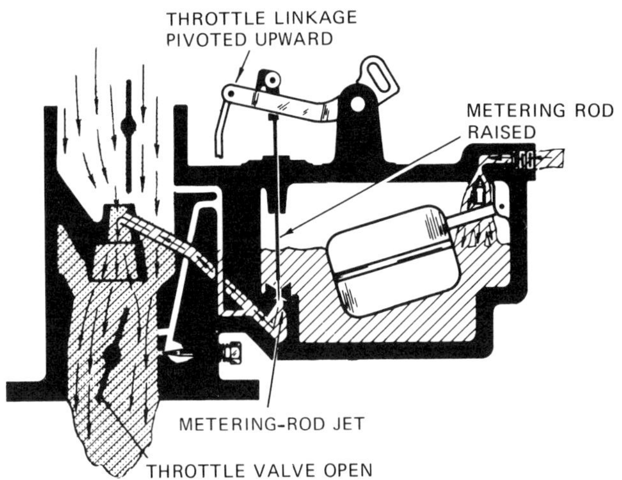

Fig. 12-19. Mechanically operated power system. When the throttle is open, as shown, the metering rod is raised so the smaller diameter of the rod clears the jet. This allows additional fuel to flow.

⊘ 12-19 Vacuum-Operated Power System This system is operated by intake-manifold vacuum. It includes a vacuum piston or diaphragm linked to a valve or a metering rod (similar to the one in Fig. 12-18). One design is shown in Fig. 12-20. During part-throttle operation, the piston is held in the lower position by intake-manifold vacuum. However, when the throttle is opened wide, manifold vacuum is reduced. This allows the spring under the vacuum piston to push the piston upward. This motion raises the metering rod so that the smaller diameter of the rod clears the jet. Now, more fuel can flow to handle the full-power requirements of the engine.

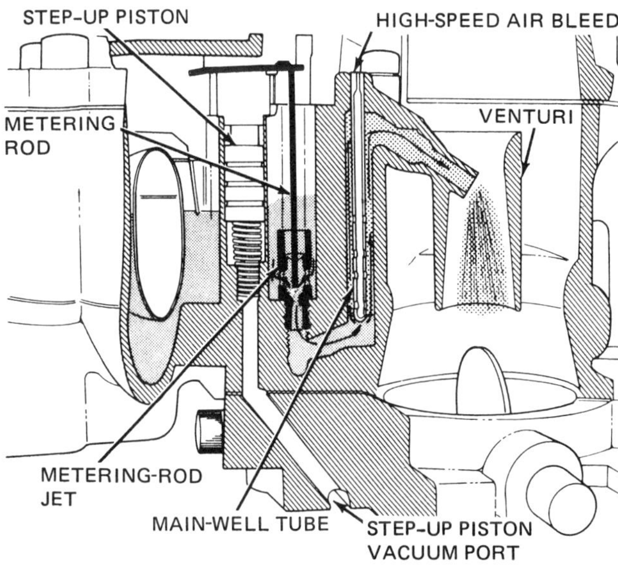

Fig. 12-20. Sectional view of a carburetor using a power or step-up piston, actuated by intake-manifold vacuum, to control the position of the metering rod. (*Chrysler Corporation*)

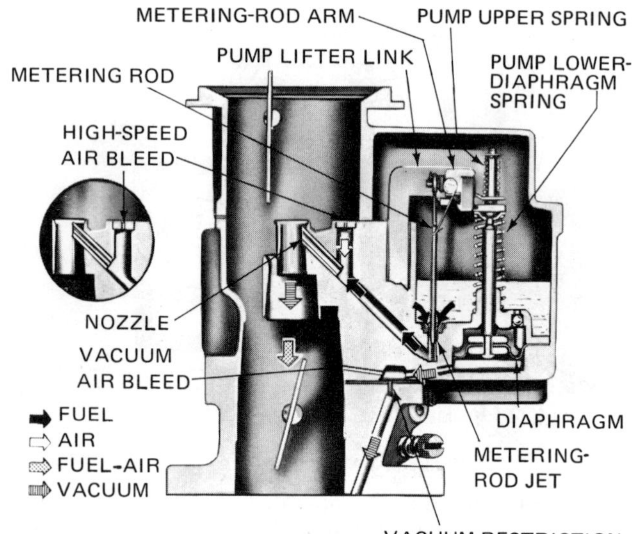

Fig. 12-21. Sectional view of a carburetor using a spring-loaded diaphragm, actuated by intake-manifold vacuum, to control the position of the metering rod. (*Ford Motor Company*)

The carburetor in Fig. 12-21 uses a spring-loaded diaphragm to control the position of the metering rod. The action is similar to that of the carburetor in Fig. 12-20. When the throttle is opened so that intake-manifold vacuum is reduced, the spring raises the diaphragm. This allows the metering rod to be lifted. Its smaller diameter clears the jet, and more fuel can flow.

⊘ 12-20 Combination Power Systems In some carburetors, a combination full-power system is used. It is operated both mechanically and by vacuum from the intake manifold. In one such carburetor, a metering rod is linked to the vacuum diaphragm and to the throttle linkage (Fig. 12-21). Thus, movement of the throttle to "full open" lifts the metering rod to enrich the mixture. Or, loss of intake-manifold vacuum (as during a hard pull up a hill or during acceleration) allows the spring to raise the diaphragm. This lifts the metering rod for an enriched mixture.

Check Your Progress

Progress Quiz 12-1 Here is another chance to find out how well you remember and understand what you have been studying. The following questions deal with the fundamentals of carburetors and carburetor systems. If a question stumps you, reread the last few pages to find the information you need.

Completing the Sentences The sentences that follow are incomplete. After each sentence there are several words or phrases, but only one of them correctly completes the sentence. Write each sentence in your notebook, ending it with the one word or phrase that completes it correctly.

1. The carburetor consists basically of an air horn, a fuel nozzle, and: (*a*) a choke valve, (*b*) a throttle valve, (*c*) an air cleaner.
2. The job of the carburetor is to: (*a*) mix gasoline with air, (*b*) separate gasoline from air, (*c*) increase volumetric efficiency.
3. The throttle valve: (*a*) when closed, allows little or no air to flow through the air horn, (*b*) when open, allows air to flow freely through the air horn, (*c*) both (*a*) and (*b*).
4. A richer mixture must be delivered when a cold engine is being started, because: (*a*) this allows a higher cranking speed, (*b*) only part of the gasoline will vaporize when cold, (*c*) the thick engine oil must be thinned out.
5. An air-fuel ratio of 12:1 means that the mixture has: (*a*) 12 lb [5.4 kg] of gasoline to 1 lb [0.45 kg] of air, (*b*) 12 lb of air to 1 lb of gasoline, (*c*) 1 gallon [4.5 l] of gasoline to 12 gallons [54.6 l] of air.
6. The system that maintains a constant level of gasoline in a bowl is called the: (*a*) power system, (*b*) float system, (*c*) bowl system.
7. The purpose of the float-bowl vent is to: (*a*) prevent engine overheating, (*b*) keep the level of gasoline in the bowl constant, (*c*) equalize the effects of a clogged air cleaner.
8. The purpose of the hot-idle compensator valve is to: (*a*) allow additional air to pass into the idle system, (*b*) supply additional air to prevent a rich mixture when the engine is idling hot, (*c*) increase idle speed when the engine is cold.
9. When the engine is hot and running at 600 rpm, the gasoline is supplied by the: (*a*) idle system, (*b*) low-speed system, (*c*) choke system.
10. The operating mechanism of the vacuum-operated power system includes either a: (*a*) vacuum piston or pump, (*b*) diaphragm or pump, (*c*) vacuum piston or diaphragm.

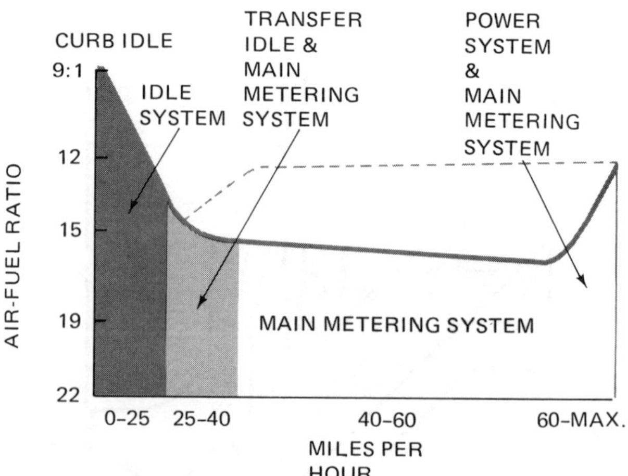

Fig. 12-22. Air-fuel ratios with different carburetor systems operating at various speeds. (*Chevrolet Motor Division of General Motors Corporation*)

⊘ 12-21 Air-Fuel Ratios with Different Systems

Figure 12-22 shows the air-fuel ratios produced by the different carburetor systems. The curve is typical. Actual air-fuel ratios will vary for different carburetors and different operating conditions.

Note that the idle system supplies a very rich mixture to start with. However, as engine speed increases, the mixture leans out. From about 25 to 40 mph [40.24 to 64.37 km/h], the throttle is only partly open; both the idle and main metering systems are supplying air-fuel mixture. Then, in the curve shown, the main metering system takes over at about 40 mph [64.37 km/h]. It continues to supply mixture by itself to about 60 mph [96.56 km/h]. Note that the air-fuel ratio increases somewhat as speed increases (that is, the mixture becomes leaner). Somewhere around 60 mph [96.56 km/h], the power system comes into operation. (Of course, it operates earlier if the throttle is opened wide at a lower speed.) Now, the mixture richness goes up as the speed increases.

⊘ 12-22 Accelerator-Pump System

The carburetor must deliver additional fuel for acceleration. (See ⊘ 12-8.) Rapid opening of the throttle allows a sudden inrush of air. Thus, there is a sudden demand for additional fuel to maintain the air-fuel ratio. Carburetors have accelerator-pump systems to provide this extra fuel. Figure 12-23 shows one type. It includes a pump plunger which can be forced downward by a pump lever that is linked to the throttle. When the throttle is opened, the pump lever pushes the pump plunger down. This forces fuel to flow through the accelerator-pump system and out the pump jet (Fig. 12-24). This additional fuel enters the air passing through the carburetor.

However, when the throttle is opened quickly, fuel may not discharge for a long enough time to prevent stumble. To overcome this problem, most carburetors have a calibrated spring above the plunger cup. This arrangement is used to prolong the fuel discharge. Note, in Fig. 12-25, that the pump plunger is attached to the pump and seal through a spring. This spring applies pressure to the pump. It causes the accelerator-pump system to immediately begin discharging fuel through the jet. The spring maintains its pressure as long as the throttle is held open, and until the pump plunger is all the way down (Fig. 12-24). This allows the accelerator-pump system to discharge fuel for several seconds, or until the power system can take over. It therefore permits smooth acceleration.

Figure 12-25 is a cutaway view of a carburetor with a plunger-type accelerator-pump system. An accelerator-pump system that uses a diaphragm instead of a plunger is shown in Fig. 12-26. When the throttle is opened, the pump lower diaphragm spring lifts the diaphragm. This forces additional fuel from the chamber above the diaphragm, through the accelerator-pump system, and out the pump jet.

An accelerator-pump system for a dual carburetor is shown in Fig. 12-27. This carburetor has two barrels; there is a discharge nozzle for each. The fuel flow from the accelerator pump is split between the two barrels. Regardless of the number of barrels, most carburetors have only one accelerator pump.

⊘ 12-23 Choke System

When an engine is being started, the carburetor must deliver a very rich mixture to the intake manifold. With the engine and carburetor cold, only part of the fuel vaporizes. Thus, extra fuel must be delivered so that enough

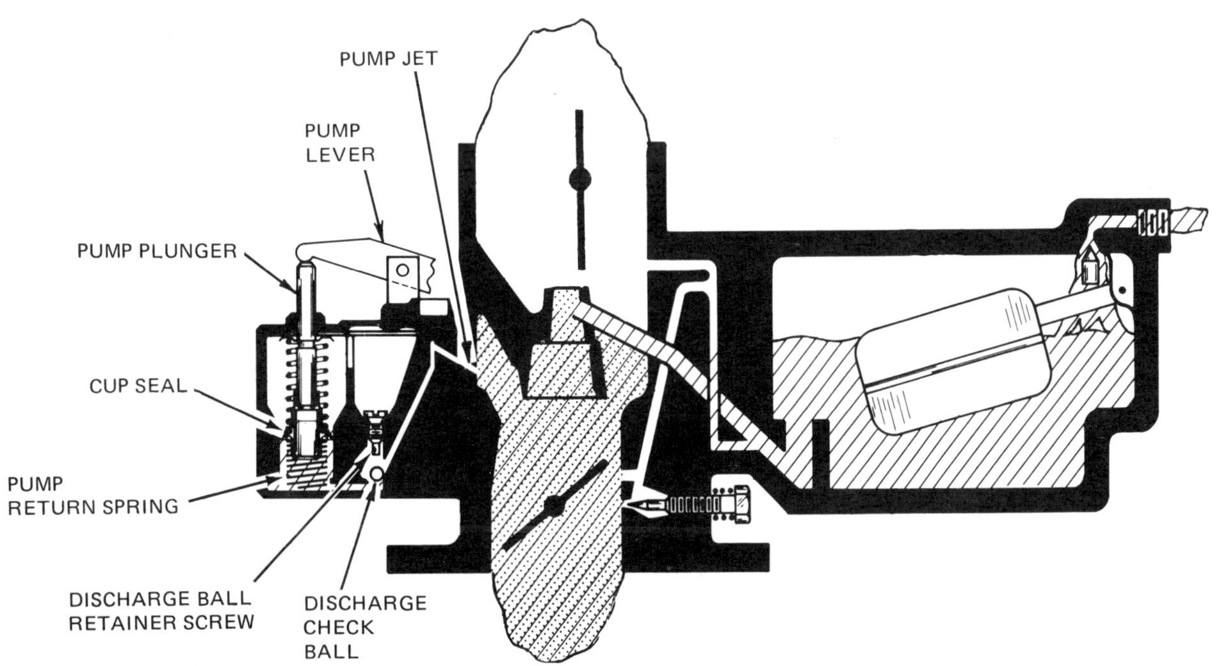

Fig. 12-23. Accelerator-pump system in a carburetor of the type using a pump plunger.

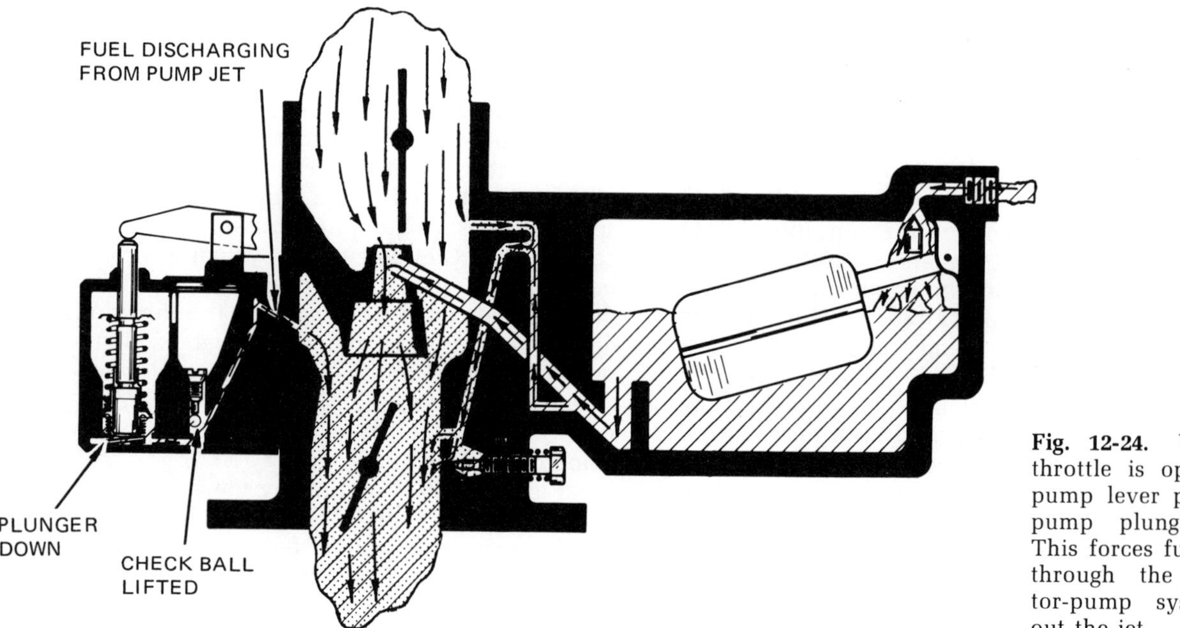

Fig. 12-24. When the throttle is opened, the pump lever pushes the pump plunger down. This forces fuel to flow through the accelerator-pump system and out the jet.

evaporates to make a combustible mixture. Otherwise, the engine cannot start.

During cranking, the airspeed through the carburetor air horn is very low. The venturi vacuum and the vacuum below the throttle do not produce adequate fuel flow for starting. To produce enough fuel flow during cranking, the carburetor has a choke (Fig. 12-28). The choke is a valve in the top of the air horn; it is controlled mechanically or by an automatic device. When the choke valve is closed, only a small amount of air can get past it (the valve "chokes off" the airflow). Then, when the engine is cranked, a fairly high vacuum develops in the air horn. This vacuum causes the main nozzle to discharge a heavy stream of fuel. Enough fuel is delivered to produce the air-fuel mixture needed to start the engine.

As soon as the engine starts, its speed increases from around 300 rpm to over 600 rpm. Now more air (a somewhat leaner mixture) is required. One method of getting more air into the engine as soon as it starts is to mount the choke valve off center on its shaft in the air horn. Then a spring is added to the choke linkage. Now the additional air the engine requires will cause the choke valve to open partly, against the spring pressure. Another arrangement includes a small spring-loaded section in the valve. This section opens to admit the additional air.

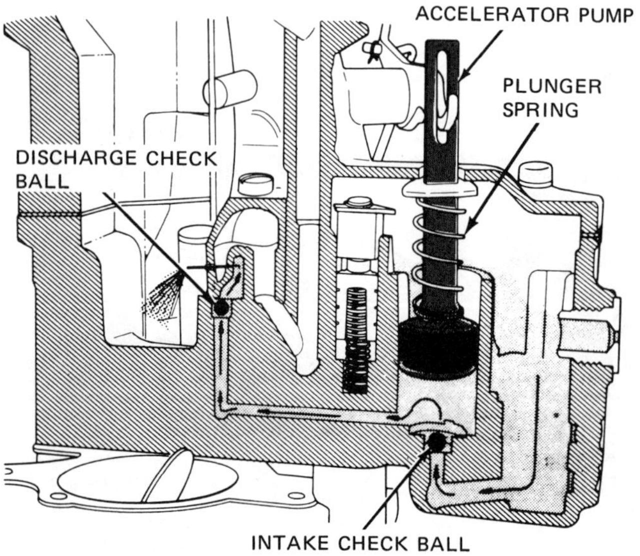

ACCELERATOR PUMP
PLUNGER
SPRING
DISCHARGE CHECK
BALL
INTAKE CHECK BALL

Fig.12-25. Accelerator-pump system using a piston-type pump. (*Chrysler Corporation*)

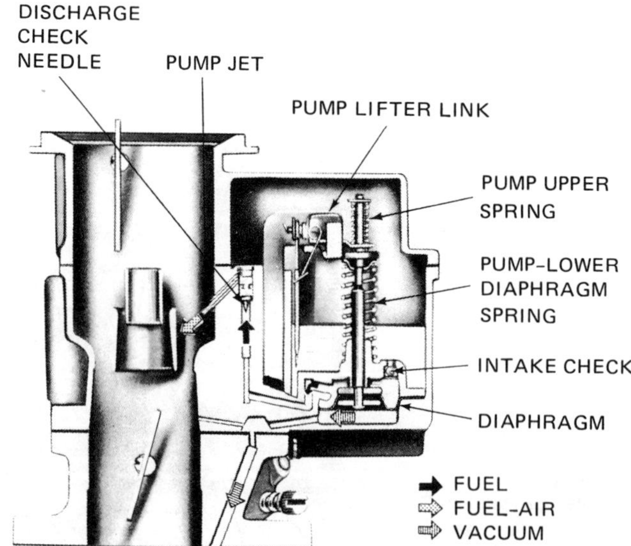

Fig. 12-26. Accelerator-pump system of the type using a spring-loaded diaphragm. Opening of the throttle allows the lower diaphragm spring to lift the diaphragm. This forces fuel through the accelerator-pump system and out the jet. (*Ford Motor Company*)

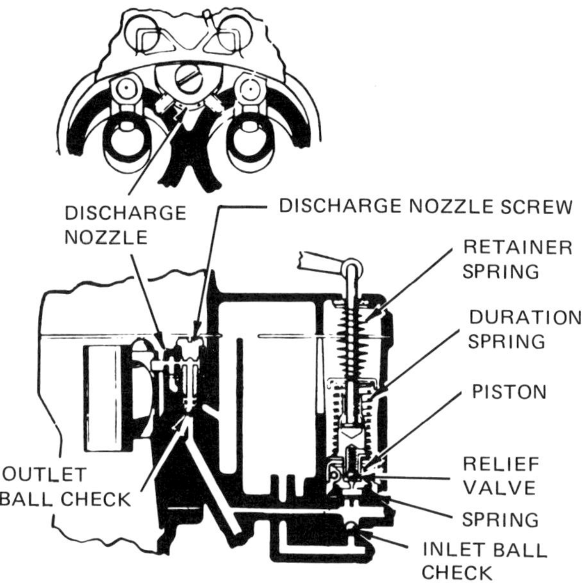

Fig. 12-27. Accelerator-pump system and location of the discharge nozzles in a dual carburetor.

⊘ 12-24 Automatic Chokes

Mechanically controlled chokes are operated by a pullrod on the dash. The pullrod is linked to the choke valve. When it is pulled out, the choke valve is closed. The driver must remember to push the rod in (open the choke) as soon as the engine begins to warm up. If not, the carburetor continues to supply a very rich mixture. The excessive richness causes poor engine performance, high exhaust emissions, fouled spark plugs, poor fuel economy, and many other problems.

To prevent such troubles, most cars now have automatic chokes. Most automatic chokes operate on exhaust-manifold temperature and intake-manifold vacuum. Figure 12-29 shows an automatic choke on a carburetor. It includes a thermostatic spring and a vacuum piston, both linked to the choke valve. The thermostatic spring is made up of two strips of different metals, welded together and formed into a spiral. The two metals have different expansion rates. This causes the thermostatic spring to wind up or unwind as its temperature changes. When the engine is cold, the spring is wound up enough to close the choke valve and spring-load it in the closed position. When the engine is cranked, a rich mixture is delivered to the intake manifold. As the engine starts, air movement through the air horn causes the choke valve to open slightly (working against the thermostatic-spring tension). In addition, the vacuum piston is pulled outward by intake-manifold vacuum. This produces some further opening of the choke valve.

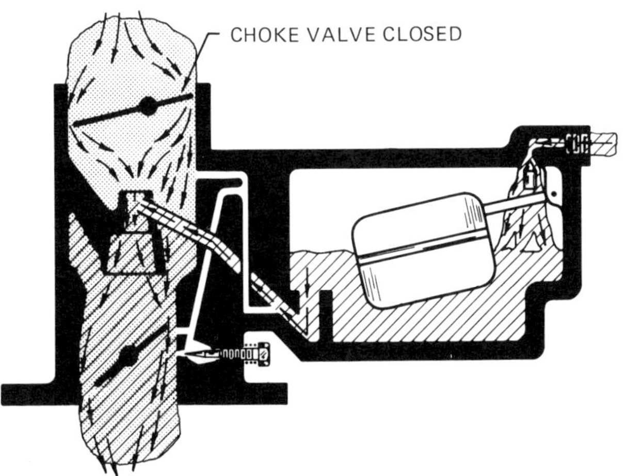

Fig. 12-28. With the choke valve closed, intake-manifold vacuum is introduced into the carburetor air horn. This causes the main nozzle to discharge fuel.

This choke-valve position allows the carburetor to supply the richer mixture needed for cold-engine idling. When the throttle is opened, however, the mixture must be further enriched. The accelerator pump provides some extra fuel, but still more fuel is needed when the engine is cold. This additional fuel is secured by the action of the vacuum piston. When the throttle is opened, intake-manifold vacuum is lost. The vacuum piston releases and is pulled inward by thermostatic-spring tension. The choke valve therefore moves toward the closed position and causes the mixture to be enriched.

Thus, during the first few moments of operation, the choke valve is controlled by the vacuum piston. However, the thermostatic spring begins to take over as the engine warms up. The thermostatic spring is in a housing that is connected to the exhaust manifold through a small tube. Heat passes through this tube and enters the spring housing. The thermostatic spring begins to warm up. As it warms up, the spring unwinds. This causes the choke valve to move toward the open position. When the engine operating temperature is reached, the thermostatic spring has unwound enough to fully open the choke valve. No further choking takes place.

When the engine is stopped and cools down, the thermostatic spring winds up again. This closes the choke valve and spring-loads it in the closed position.

Figure 12-29 is a carburetor, partly cut away to show the construction of the automatic choke. The vacuum passage to the vacuum piston is shown, but the heat tube to the exhaust manifold is not. The heat tube sends heat from the exhaust manifold to the thermostatic-spring housing.

In V-8 engines, the thermostat is located in a well in the intake manifold. There, it can quickly react to the manifold heat as the engine starts (see Figs. 12-30 and 12-33). The thermostat is connected by a link to the carburetor. Some carburetors using this arrangement have vacuum pistons. Others have vacuum diaphragms. Both work with the thermostat, as described, to control the choke-valve position during warm-up.

Some carburetors use heat from the engine coolant to operate the thermostat. That is, the thermostat housing has a passage through which the

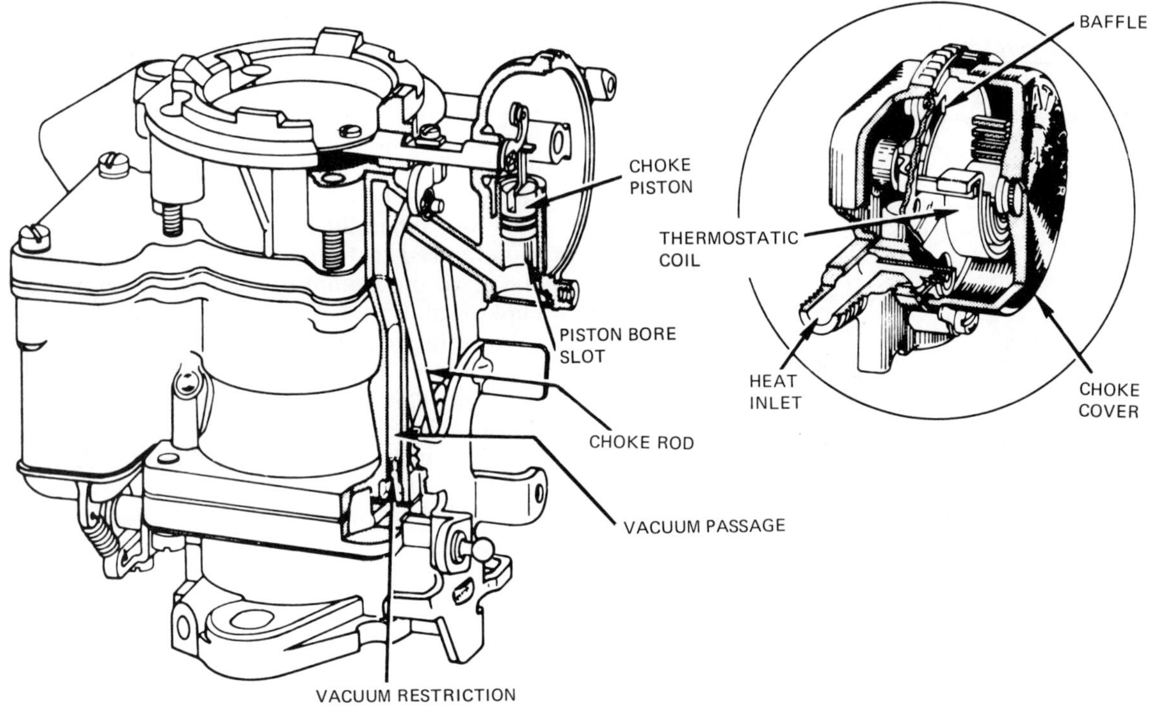

Fig. 12-29. Automatic-choke system on a carburetor. (*American Motors Corporation*)

coolant flows (Fig. 12-31). The action is similar to that of the automatic choke we discussed.

As was mentioned above, instead of a vacuum piston, many automatic chokes now use a vacuum-operated diaphragm (Fig. 12-30). The operation is again similar to that discussed. However, the diaphragm provides more force to break the choke valve loose if it gets stuck. The linkage from the diaphragm to the choke-valve lever rides freely in a slot in the lever. During certain phases of warm-up operation, the changing vacuum causes the linkage to ride to the end of the slot and move the choke valve. For example, when the throttle is opened during cold-engine operation, loss of intake-manifold vacuum causes the diaphragm to move. This movement carries the choke-valve lever around so that the choke valve is moved toward the closed position. This action provides a richer mixture for good acceleration.

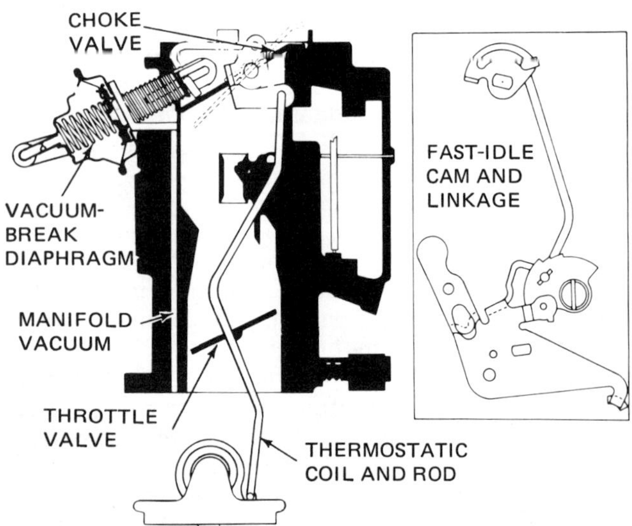

Fig. 12-30. Choke system with the thermostat located in a well in the exhaust manifold. Note the vacuum-break diaphragm. (*Chevrolet Motor Division of General Motors Corporation*)

Many late-model cars have electric automatic chokes. This type of choke includes an electric heating element (Fig. 12-32). The purpose of this heater is to assure faster choke opening. This helps reduce emissions from the engine. Emissions (HC and CO) are relatively high during the early stages of engine warm-up. At low temperatures, the electric heater adds to the heat coming from the exhaust manifold. This reduces the choke-opening time to as little as $1\frac{1}{2}$ min. Figure 12-33 shows the arrangement for a choke mounted in a well in the intake manifold. Figure 12-34 shows the choke and heating element removed from the well.

⊘ 12-25 Manifold Heat Control During initial warm-up of the engine, just after starting, the fuel does not vaporize well. Gasoline vaporizes slowly when it is cold. To improve fuel vaporization and cold-engine operation, a device is used to heat the intake manifold when it is cold. This device, called the *manifold heat-control valve,* is built into the exhaust and intake manifolds. Two arrangements

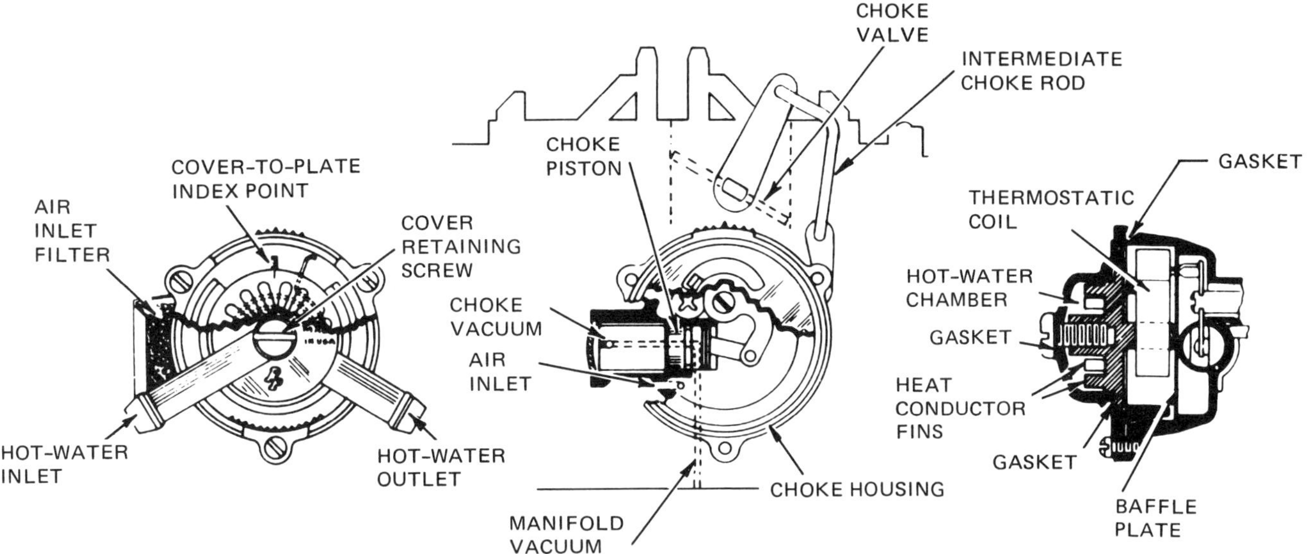

Fig. 12-31. Water-heated choke in cutaway views. (*Buick Motor Division of General Motors Corporation*)

are used, one for in-line engines and another for V-8 engines.

1. *IN-LINE ENGINES* In these engines, the exhaust manifold is located under the intake manifold. At a central point, there is an opening from the exhaust manifold into a chamber, or oven, surrounding the intake manifold (Figs. 12-35 and 12-36). A butterfly valve is placed in this opening. When the valve is turned, the opening is closed or opened. The position of the valve is controlled by a thermostatic spring. When the engine is cold, the thermostatic spring winds up and moves the valve to the closed position (left in Fig. 12-36). Now, when the engine is started, the hot exhaust gases pass through the opening. They circulate through the oven surrounding the intake manifold (Figs. 12-35 and 12-36). Heat from the exhaust gas quickly warms the intake manifold and helps the fuel to vaporize. Thus, cold-engine operation is improved. As the engine warms up, the thermostatic spring unwinds and moves the valve to the opened position (right in Fig. 12-36). Now, the exhaust gases pass directly into the exhaust pipe. They no longer circulate in the oven around the intake manifold.

2. *V-8 ENGINES* In V-8 engines, the intake manifold is placed between the two banks of cylinders. It has a special passage (Fig. 12-37) through which exhaust gases can pass. One of the exhaust mani-

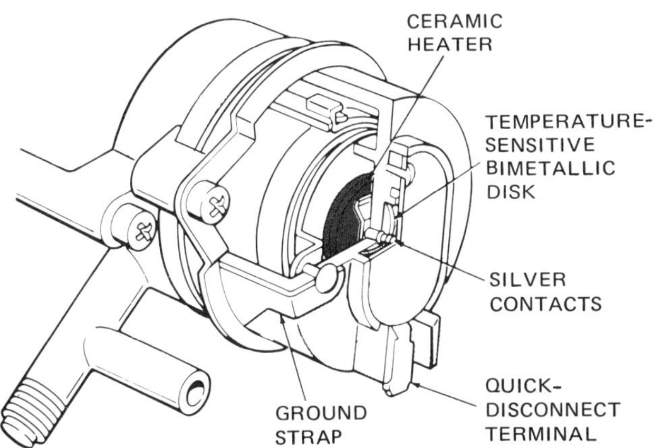

Fig. 12-32. Cutaway view of an electric-assist choke. At low temperature, the ceramic heater is on, adding heat to the choke so it opens more quickly. (*Ford Motor Company*)

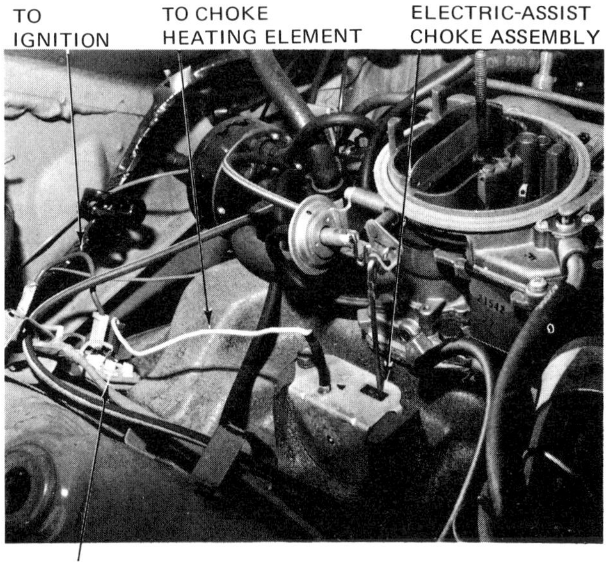

Fig. 12-33. Electric-assist choke mounted in a well in the intake manifold. (*Chrysler Corporation*)

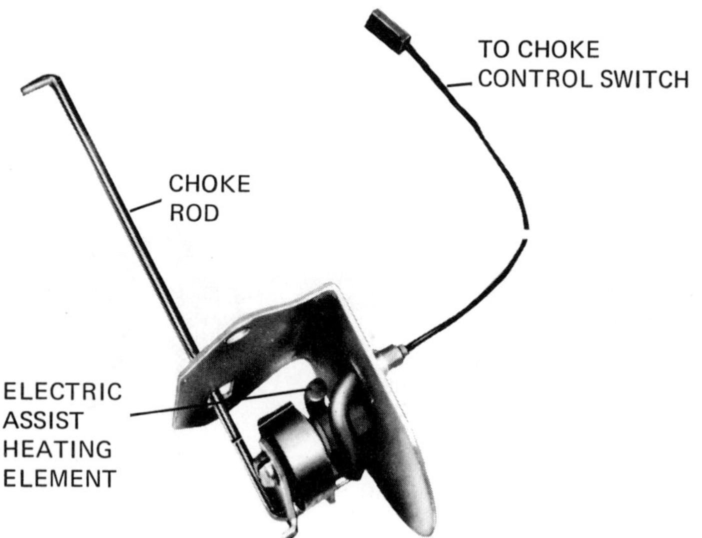

Fig. 12-34. Choke assembly removed from the well in the intake manifold to show the electric-assist heating element. (*Chrysler Corporation*)

folds has a thermostatically controlled valve that closes when the engine is cold. This causes exhaust gases to pass from that exhaust manifold through the special passage in the intake manifold. The exhaust gases then enter the other exhaust manifold. Heat from the exhaust gases thus heats the air-fuel mixture in the intake manifold for improved cold-engine operation. As the engine warms up, the thermostatically controlled valve opens. Then, the exhaust gases from both exhaust manifolds pass directly into the exhaust pipes.

NOTE: Since the introduction of thermostatic air cleaners (heated-air systems, ⊘ 11-11), some engines no longer use a heat-control valve. To do so might add too much heat to the incoming air-fuel mixture. This would reduce the amount of air-fuel mixture entering, and thus reduce engine power.

⊘ 12-26 Anti-Icing When fuel is sprayed into the air passing through the air horn, it evaporates. As it evaporates, the fuel takes on heat. That is, it takes heat from the surrounding air and metal parts. This is the same effect you get when you pour alcohol on your hand. The alcohol evaporates and takes heat from your hand. Your hand feels cold. If you blow on your hand, the alcohol evaporates faster, and your hand feels still colder. The faster the alcohol evaporates and takes heat from your hand, the cooler your hand feels.

Now, let us see how this affects the carburetor. The evaporation of the fuel "robs" the surrounding air and carburetor of heat. Under certain conditions, they get so cold that moisture in the air condenses and actually freezes on the metal parts. If conditions are right, enough ice can build up to cause the engine to stall. This is most likely to occur during the warm-up period following the first startup of the day. It happens most with air temperatures between 40 and 60°F [4.4 and 15.6°C] and high humidity.

To prevent such icing, many carburetors have special anti-icing systems. One arrangement for a V-8 engine is shown in Fig. 12-38. During the warm-up period, the manifold heat-control valve sends hot exhaust gases from one exhaust manifold to the other (see ⊘ 12-25). Part of this hot exhaust gas circulates around the carburetor idle ports and near the throttle-valve shaft. This adds enough heat to guard against ice formation. Another system uses coolant passages in the carburetor. The coolant comes from the engine cooling system. A small amount of the coolant passes through a special coolant manifold in the carburetor throttle body. This adds enough heat to the carburetor to prevent icing.

⊘ 12-27 Fast Idle When the engine is cold, the throttle must be kept open slightly. This allows the cold engine to idle faster than it would if it were warm. Otherwise, with slow idling, the cold engine might stall. With fast idling, enough air-fuel mixture gets through, and airspeeds are great enough, to produce a sufficiently rich mixture.

Fast idle is obtained with a fast-idle cam linked to the choke valve (Fig. 12-39). When the engine is cold, the automatic choke holds the choke valve closed. In this position, the linkage has revolved the fast-idle cam so the adjusting screw rests on the high point of the cam. The adjusting screw prevents the throttle valve from moving to the fully closed position. The throttle valve is held partly open for fast idle. As the engine warms up, the choke valve opens. This rotates the fast-idle cam so the high point moves out from under the adjusting screw. The throttle valve closes for normal hot-engine slow idle.

⊘ 12-28 Air-Bleed and Antisiphon Passages All the carburetor systems except the accelerator-pump system have small openings that permit air to enter,

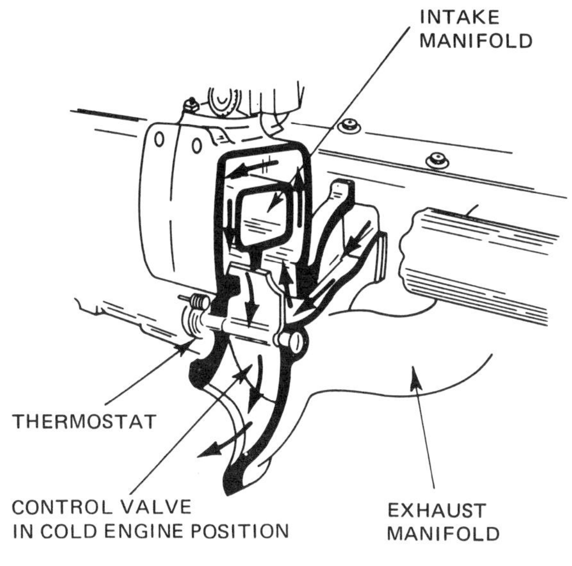

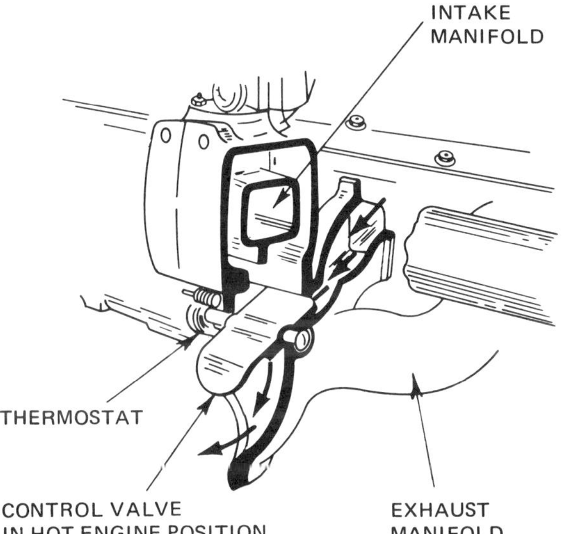

Fig. 12-35. Intake and exhaust manifolds of a six-cylinder incline engine, cut away to show the location and action of the manifold heat control. *Top:* The heat-control valve is in the "heat on" position. It is directing hot exhaust gases up and around the intake manifold, as shown by the arrows. *Bottom:* The valve is in the hot-engine position. (*Ford Motor Company*)

or *bleed* into, the system (Fig. 12-20). This produces some premixing of air and fuel, for better atomization and vaporization. It also helps maintain a uniform air-fuel ratio. At higher speeds, a larger amount of fuel tends to move through the main nozzle. At the same time the faster fuel movement through the main metering system causes more air to bleed into the system. Thus, the air-bleed holes tend to equalize the air-fuel ratio.

Air-bleed passages are also sometimes called *antisiphon* passages. They act as air vents to prevent fuel from siphoning out of the float bowl at intermediate engine speeds.

If the air-bleed passages become plugged, the float bowl may empty itself after the engine shuts off. When the engine is shut off, the intake manifold cools down, and a slight vacuum forms. Normally, air moves in through the air bleeds to satisfy the vacuum. But if the air bleeds are plugged, the vacuum draws fuel out of the float bowl through the idle system. The float bowl can be emptied by this action.

⊘ 12-29 Special Carburetor Devices Other special devices in carburetors include:

1. Vacuum circuits to control the ignition-distributor spark advance.
2. Throttle-return checks and magnetically controlled dashpots to slow throttle closing (on cars with automatic transmissions). Figure 12-40 shows a throttle-return check (also called a dashpot) on a carburetor.
3. Electric kick-down switches (on some cars equipped with automatic transmissions).
4. Governors to control or limit top engine speed.
5. An idle-stop solenoid, which allows the throttle plate to close completely when the ignition is turned off. This prevents "dieseling" or continued running of the engine after the ignition is turned off.

Figure 12-40 shows a throttle-return check on a carburetor. The throttle-return check contains a spring-loaded diaphragm. Air is trapped behind the diaphragm when the throttle is opened. Then, when the throttle is released, the return check causes the throttle to close slowly. This guards against engine stalling due to sudden throttle closing.

The electric kick-down switch is used on some cars with automatic transmissions. It downshifts the transmission, to a lower gear, when the throttle is opened wide (under certain conditions).

Governors are used mostly in heavy-duty vehicles. They prevent overspeeding and rapid wear of the engine. One type controls the throttle valve directly. It tends to close the valve as the maximum set speed is reached. Another type has a throttle plate between the carburetor throttle valve and the intake manifold. The throttle plate moves toward the closed position as the set speed is reached. This prevents the delivery of additional air-fuel mixture and, thus, further increases in engine speed.

⊘ 12-30 Two-Barrel and Four-Barrel Carburetors Carburetors with more than a single barrel, or venturi, are used on many engines. Such carburetors may have two barrels or four barrels. The purpose of the additional barrels is to improve engine "breathing," particularly at high speeds. That is, the extra barrels permit more air and fuel to enter the engine. Of course, if air were the only consideration, then a single large barrel could be used. But with one large barrel, venturi action would be poor. Proper air-fuel ratios would be hard to achieve under varying operating conditions.

1. *TWO-BARREL CARBURETOR* This carburetor

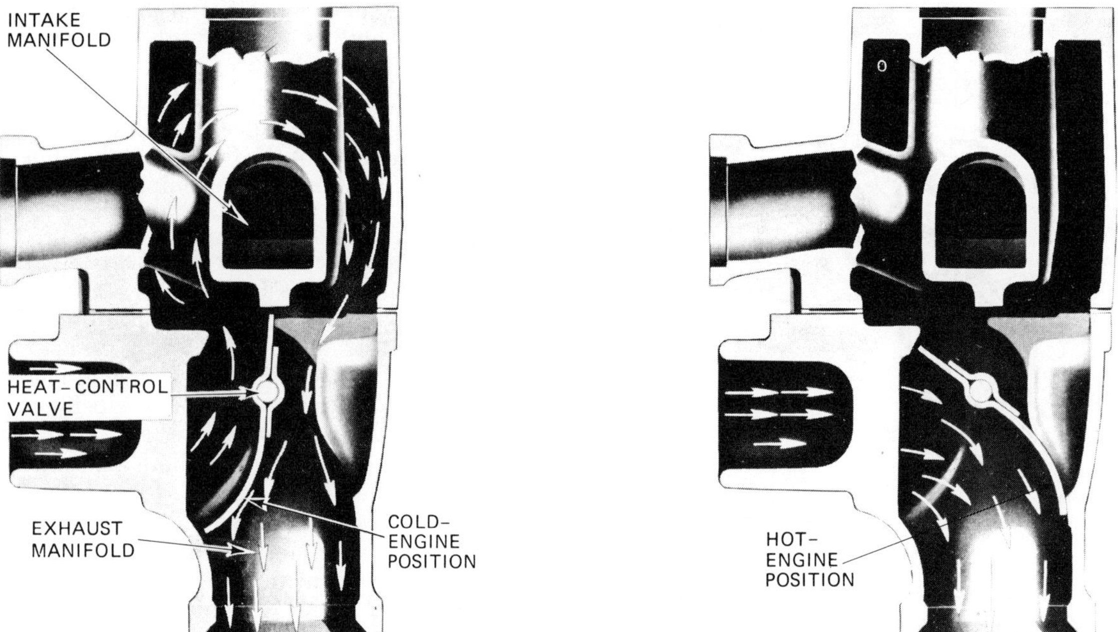

Fig. 12-36. Two extreme positions, in the exhaust manifold, of the manifold heat-control valve. This valve controls the flow of exhaust gases through the intake-manifold jacket. (*Chevrolet Motor Division of General Motors Corporation*)

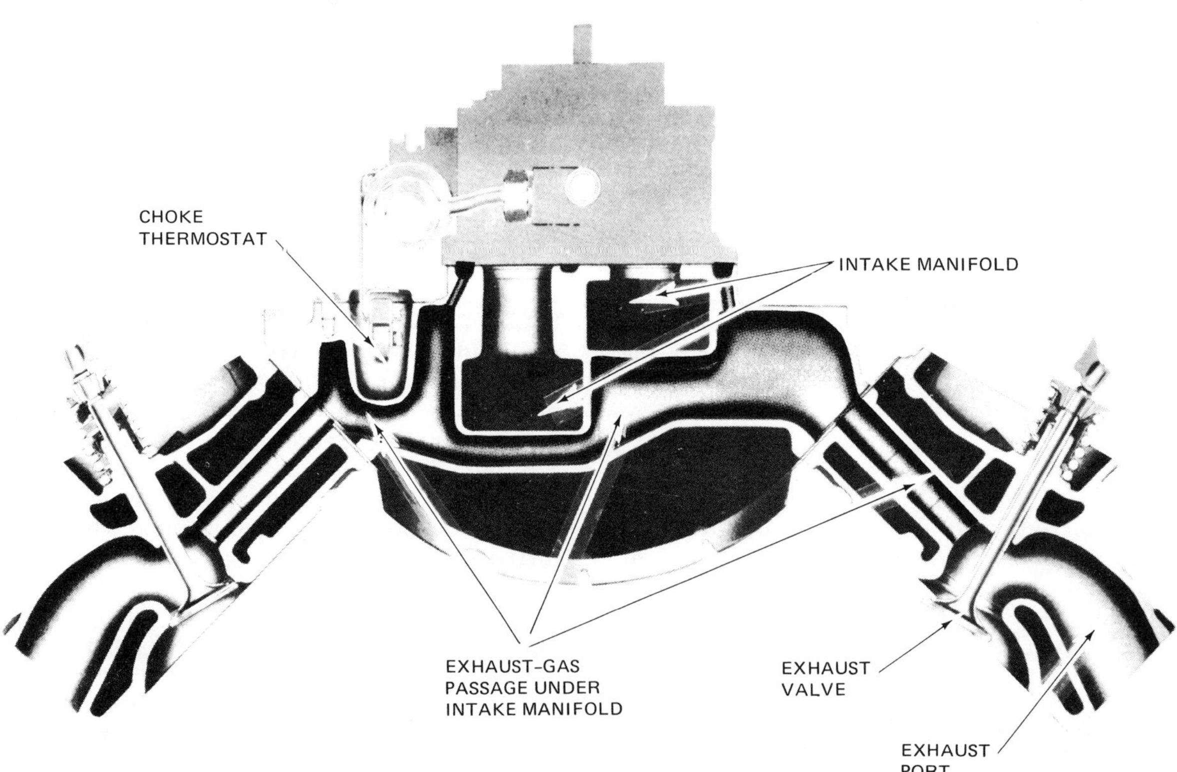

Fig. 12-37. Exhaust-gas passage under the intake manifold in a V-8 engine. Note the well in which the carburetor choke thermostat is located. (*Buick Motor Division of General Motors Corporation*)

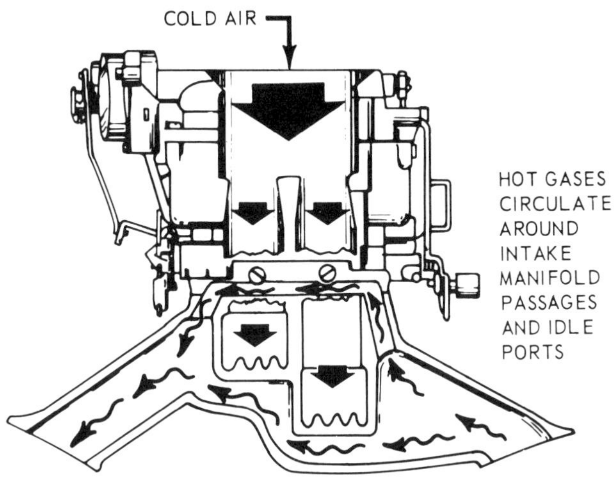

Fig. 12-38. Intake-manifold and carburetor-idle-ports heating passages. Hot exhaust gases heat these areas as soon as the engine starts. (*Cadillac Motor Car Division of General Motors Corporation*)

is essentially two single-barrel carburetors in one assembly (Fig. 12-41). Each barrel handles the air-fuel requirements of half the engine cylinders. Each barrel has a complete set of systems. The throttle valves are fastened to a single throttle shaft, so that both valves open and close together.

2. *FOUR-BARREL CARBURETOR* The four-barrel carburetor (Figs. 12-42 and 12-43) is essentially 2 two-barrel carburetors in one assembly. The carburetor has four barrels and four main nozzles. It is often called a *Quadrajet,* or *quad,* carburetor. One pair of barrels makes up the *primary* side, and the other pair the *secondary* side (Fig. 12-42). Under most operating conditions, only the primary side feeds mixture to the engine. However, when the throttle is moved toward the "wide-open" position for acceleration or full-power operation, the secondary side comes into action. It supplies additional air-fuel mixture, to improve engine breathing. The volumetric efficiency increases, and the engine produces more horsepower.

There are two ways of controlling secondary-barrel action: by a mechanical linkage from the primary-throttle shaft, or by a vacuum device. Figure 12-43 is a sectional view of a carburetor using mechanical linkage. During part throttle, only the primary throttle valves are open. However, when the throttle is opened wide for additional power, the linkage between the primary and secondary throttle valves opens the secondary throttle valves. The secondary barrels then supply air-fuel mixture for full-power engine operation.

In the vacuum-controlled system, there is a vacuum-operated diaphragm. The vacuum is picked up

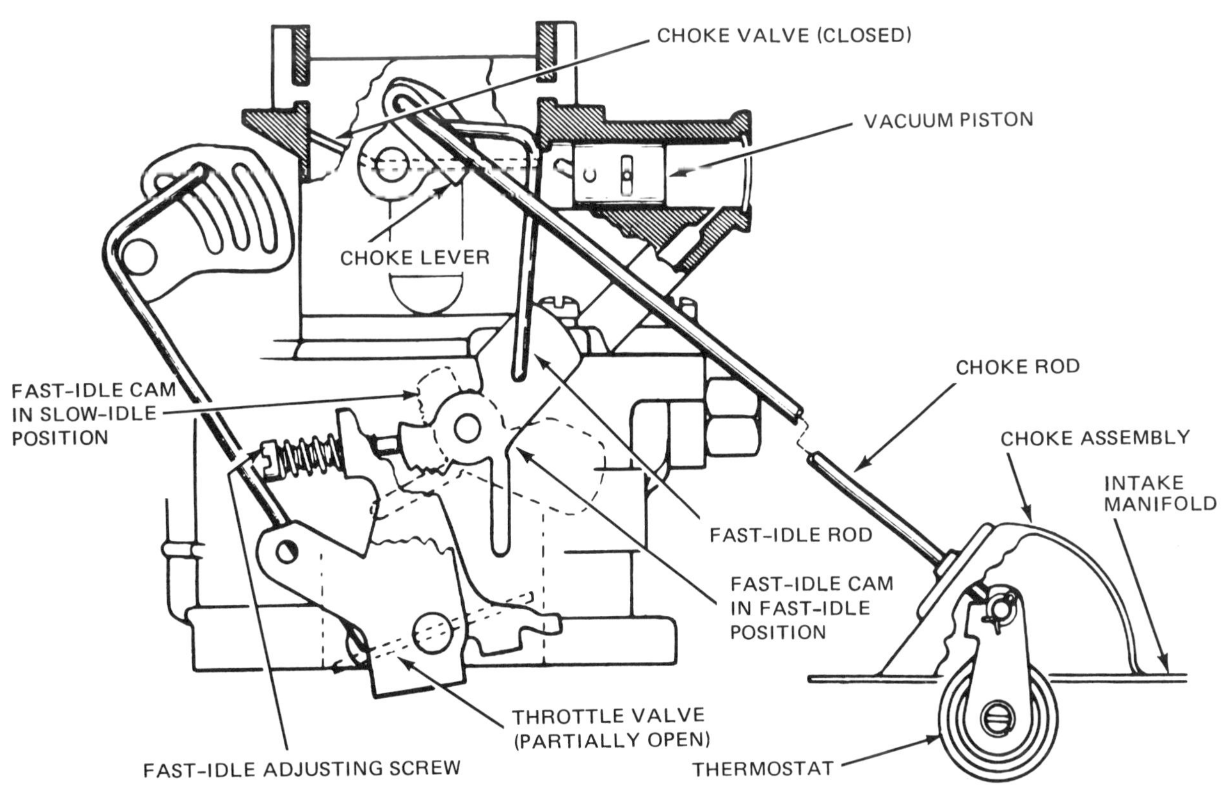

Fig. 12-39. Vacuum and thermostatically operated choke, with the thermostat located in the intake manifold. Note the two positions of the fast-idle cam. (*Chrysler Corporation*)

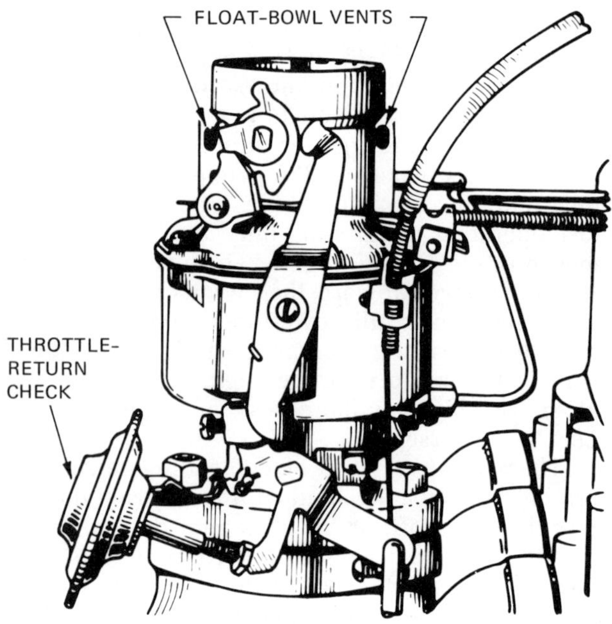

Fig. 12-40. Throttle-return check, or dashpot, on a carburetor. (*Chevrolet Motor Division of General Motors Corporation*)

from one of the primary-barrel venturis. As air speed through the primary barrels increases, so does this vacuum. When the vacuum reaches a preset value—indicating a rather high engine rpm—the vacuum actuates the diaphragm. This opens the secondary throttle valves, and the secondary barrels begin to supply air-fuel mixture.

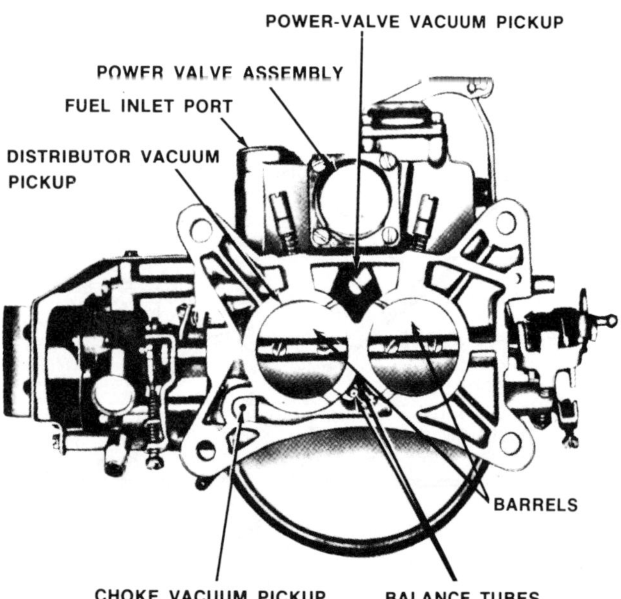

Fig. 12-41. Dual carburetor, showing the location of the two throttle valves.

Fig. 12-42. Four-barrel, or quad, carburetor, showing the locations of the four throttle valves. The small throttle valves are on the primary side.

Check Your Progress

Progress Quiz 12-2 Again, here is a chance to see how well you remember the essential facts. If any of the questions stump you, reread the last few pages to find the information you need.

Completing the Sentences The sentences that follow are incomplete. After each sentence there are several words or phrases, but only one of them correctly completes the sentence. Write each sentence in your notebook, ending it with the one word or phrase that completes it correctly.

1. If the accelerator-pump system is not working, sudden opening of the throttle can cause: (*a*) excessive acceleration, (*b*) engine stumble, (*c*) engine overheating.
2. Most accelerator-pump systems use either a: (*a*) pump or piston, (*b*) plunger or diaphragm, (*c*) throttle valve or plunger.
3. The choke valve is: (*a*) above the throttle valve, (*b*) between the throttle valve and manifold, (*c*) below the throttle valve.
4. When the choke valve is closed, gasoline is delivered from the: (*a*) main nozzle, (*b*) idle system, (*c*) choke nozzle.
5. All automatic chokes use a: (*a*) vacuum piston, (*b*) thermostatic diaphragm, (*c*) thermostatic spring.
6. Two devices that add heat to the air-fuel mixture entering the engine are the heat-control valve and the: (*a*) choke, (*b*) air cleaner, (*c*) thermostatically controlled air-cleaner system.
7. Automatic chokes use either a: (*a*) vacuum piston or thermostatic spring, (*b*) vacuum piston or diaphragm, (*c*) thermostatic spring or electric heater.
8. The fast-idle cam is linked to the: (*a*) accelerator pedal, (*b*) throttle valve, (*c*) choke valve.
9. In the four-barrel carburetor, the secondary bar-

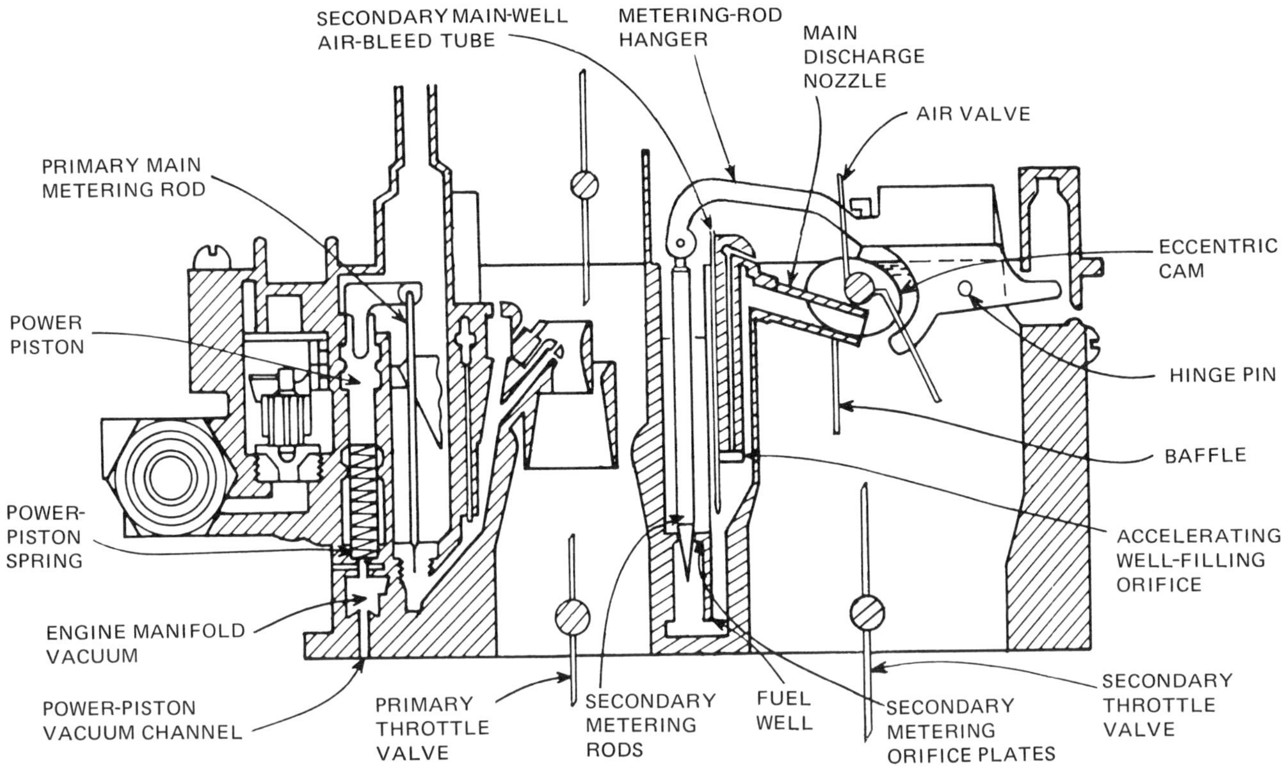

Fig. 12-43. Sectional view of a four-barrel carburetor with mechanical linkage to control the secondary throttle valves. (*General Motors Corporation*)

rels: (*a*) come into operation only during low speed, (*b*) come into operation only for acceleration or full power, (*c*) back up the primary barrels by assisting them at all times.

10. The idle-stop solenoid prevents dieseling by: (*a*) completely closing the throttle plate when the ignition is turned off, (*b*) preventing excessively high idle speed, (*c*) stopping engine idle when the engine gets hot.

CHAPTER 12 CHECKUP

NOTE: Since this is a chapter review test, you should review the chapter before taking the test.

Review Questions In the following, you are asked for some definitions and carburetor actions. Write your answers in your notebook. If you are not sure of an answer, reread the pages in the chapter that will give you the information. The reviewing and writing will help you remember what you need to know to become a carburetor expert.

1. What is carburetion?
2. What is vaporization?
3. What is atomization?
4. What are the three basic parts of the simple carburetor?
5. Describe the venturi effect.
6. What drives the fuel out of the fuel nozzle and into the air passing through the carburetor air horn?
7. Describe the operation of the carburetor float system.
8. Describe the operation of the carburetor idle system.
9. Describe the operation of the carburetor main metering system.
10. Describe the mechanically operated power system. Describe the vacuum-operated power system.
11. Why is the float bowl vented into the carburetor air horn just above the choke?
12. What is the purpose of the float-bowl vent that is connected to the charcoal canister?
13. What is the purpose of the compensator valve in the carburetor?
14. Why is it that the idle adjustment screw is fixed or has a locking cap on it?
15. Why is an accelerator-pump system required?
16. How does an accelerator-pump system work?
17. What is the purpose of the choke? How does the automatic choke work?
18. What is the purpose of the electric choke? How does it work?
19. What is the purpose of the manifold heat-control valve?
20. What is the purpose of using two- and four-barrel carburetors?

SUGGESTIONS FOR FURTHER STUDY

Examine as many carburetors as you can. As you examine each carburetor, write the facts about that carburetor on a separate sheet of paper. At the top of the paper, write the make and model of the car that the carburetor came from, and the model and type of carburetor. Locate the venturi, main nozzle, throttle plate, and so on. Identify all the openings in the air horn. File your carburetor fact sheets in your notebook.

CAUTION: **Be very careful not to spill gasoline when you are examining carburetors which contain gasoline in their float bowls. Remember that gasoline is very explosive, and a spark can set off a blaze or explosion.**

Study the carburetor sections in manufacturers' shop manuals. Make sketches in your notebook of any special features you find.

chapter 13

DIAGNOSING FUEL-SYSTEM TROUBLES

In this chapter, we describe various fuel-system troubles and explain how to track down their causes. Later chapters describe servicing procedures that eliminate troubles.

⊘ 13-1 Tracing Troubles in the Fuel System Usually, it is not difficult to trace a trouble in the fuel system. There are several types of fuel-system troubles; and each type requires its own corrections. However, you will sometimes have to decide whether a trouble is in the fuel system or in some other engine component. Thus, the real problem is often to find the troublesome component. This may sometimes be puzzling, because the trouble could result in several improper conditions. For example, suppose the power valve in a carburetor will not close. This would produce an excessively rich mixture in all running conditions except full-power open-throttle operation. This, in turn, would cause excessive fuel consumption and might foul the spark plugs. Fouled plugs then would cause poor ignition and missing; the carbon deposits might cause defective piston-ring and valve action.

The chart that follows lists the various troubles that might be blamed on the fuel system. Also included are possible causes, checks to be made, and required corrections. This chart supplements the trouble-diagnosis chart in Chap. 34. The various test instruments mentioned in this chapter are described in Chap. 33, which covers all engine testing instruments.

⊘ 13-2 Fuel-System Trouble-Diagnosis Chart Most fuel-system troubles can be listed under a few headings: excessive fuel consumption, poor acceleration, lack of power and high-speed performance, poor idle, engine does not start, hard starting, slow warm-up, stalling, smoky exhaust, and backfiring. The chart that follows lists the possible causes of each of these troubles. The numbered sections following the chart contain more information on how to locate and eliminate the troubles. When a trouble is obviously not in the fuel system, reference is made to the applicable book in the McGraw-Hill Automotive Technology Series.

NOTE: The troubles and possible causes are not listed in the order of frequency of occurrence. That is, item 1 (or item a under "Possible Cause") does not necessarily occur more frequently than item 2 (or item b). Generally, fuel-system troubles and causes are listed first in the chart (even though, in many cases, other automotive components are more likely to cause the troubles listed).

FUEL-SYSTEM TROUBLE-DIAGNOSIS CHART

(See ⊘ 13-3 to 13-15 for detailed explanations of the trouble causes and corrections listed below.)

COMPLAINT	POSSIBLE CAUSE	CHECK OR CORRECTION
1. Excessive fuel consumption (⊘ 13-3)	a. Nervous or "jackrabbit" driver	Drive more reasonably
	b. High speed	Drive more slowly
	c. Short-run and start-and-stop operation	Make longer runs
	d. Excessive fuel-pump pressure or pump leakage	Reduce pressure; repair pump
	e. Choke not opened properly	Open; repair or replace automatic choke
	f. Clogged air cleaner	Clean
	g. High carburetor float level or leaking float	Adjust or replace float
	h. Stuck or dirty float needle valve	Free and clean or replace
	i. Worn carburetor jets	Replace
	j. Stuck metering rod or power piston	Free
	k. Too-rich or too-fast idle	Readjust
	l. Stuck accelerator-pump check valve	Free

FUEL-SYSTEM TROUBLE-DIAGNOSIS CHART (*Continued*)

COMPLAINT	POSSIBLE CAUSE	CHECK OR CORRECTION
	m. Carburetor leaks	Replace damaged parts; tighten loose couplings
	n. Faulty ignition	Check coil, condenser, plugs, contact points, wiring (Chap. 30)
	o. Loss of engine compression	Check compression; repair engine* (Chaps. 33 and 34)
	p. Defective valve action	Check compression; repair engine* (Chaps. 33 and 34)
	q. Excessive rolling resistance from low tires, dragging brakes, wheel misalignment, etc.	Correct cause of rolling resistance†
	r. Clutch slipping	Adjust or repair clutch‡
	s. Transmission slipping or not upshifting	Adjust or repair‡
2. Engine lacks power, acceleration, or high-speed performance (⊘ 13-4)	a. Accelerator pump malfunctioning	Adjust; free; repair
	b. Power step-up on metering rod not clearing jet	Free or adjust
	c. Power piston or valve stuck	Free
	d. Low float level	Adjust
	e. Dirt in filters or in line; clogged fuel-tank-cap vent	Clean; install correct cap
	f. Choke stuck or not operating	Adjust or repair
	g. Air leaks around carburetor	Replace gaskets; tighten nuts or bolts
	h. Antipercolator valve stuck	Free
	i. Manifold heat-control valve stuck	Free
	j. Throttle valves or secondary valves not fully opening	Adjust linkage
	k. Rich mixture due to worn jets, high float level, stuck choke, clogged air cleaner	Adjust; repair; clean; replace worn jets
	l. Vapor lock	Use different fuel or shield fuel line or pump
	m. Fuel pump defective	Service or replace
	n. Clogged exhaust	Clean
	o. Ignition defective	Check timing, coil, plugs, distributor, condenser, wiring (Chap. 30)
	p. Loss of compression	Check engine compression; repair engine* (Chaps. 33 and 34)
	q. Excessive carbon in engine	Clean out*
	r. Defective valve action	Check compression; repair engine* (Chaps. 33 and 34)
	s. Heavy engine oil	Use lighter oil
	t. Cooling system not operating properly	Check system; flush system (Chap. 9)
	u. Engine overheats	Check cooling system (Chap. 9)
	v. Excessive rolling resistance from low tires, dragging brakes, wheel misalignment, etc.	Correct cause of rolling resistance†
	w. Clutch slippage or excessive friction in power train	Adjust or repair‡
	x. Transmission not downshifting or torque converter defective	Check transmission‡
3. Poor idle (⊘ 13-5)	a. Idle mixture or speed not adjusted	Readjust
	b. Automatic-level-control compressor operating	Check vacuum regulator valve
	c. PCV valve stuck	Replace
	d. Other causes listed under item 2	
4. Engine will not start (⊘ 13-6)	a. Ignition defective	Check (Chap. 30)
	b. Fuel line clogged	Clear
	c. Fuel pump defective	Repair or replace
	d. Carburetor jets or lines clogged	Clean
	e. Filter clogged	Clean
	f. Air leaks into intake manifold or carburetor	Replace gaskets; tighten nuts or bolts

FUEL-SYSTEM TROUBLE-DIAGNOSIS CHART *(Continued)*

COMPLAINT	POSSIBLE CAUSE	CHECK OR CORRECTION
5. Hard starting with engine warm (⊘ 13-7)	a. Choke valve closed	Open; adjust or repair
	b. Manifold heat-control valve stuck closed	Open; free valve
	c. Throttle-cracker linkage out of adjustment	Adjust
	d. Vapor lock	Use correct fuel or shield fuel line or pump
	e. Engine parts binding	Repair engine*
6. Slow engine warm-up (⊘ 13-8)	a. Choke valve open	Adjust or repair
	b. Manifold heat-control valve stuck open	Close; free valve
	c. Cooling-system thermostat stuck open	Free; replace if necessary
7. Smoky exhaust (⊘ 13-9)		
a. Blue smoke	Excessive oil consumption	Oil burning in combustion chamber, owing to engine trouble
b. Black smoke	Excessively rich mixture	See item 1 and ⊘ 13-1
c. White smoke	Steam in exhaust	Check cooling-system cylinder-head bolts to eliminate coolant leakage (Chap. 9)
8. Engine stalls cold or as it warms up (⊘ 13-10)	a. Choke valve closed	Open choke valve; free or repair automatic choke
	b. Fuel not getting to or through carburetor	Check fuel pump, lines, filter, float and idle systems
	c. Manifold heat-control valve stuck	Free valve
	d. Engine overheating	Check cooling system (Chap. 9), ignition timing (Chap. 30)
	e. Engine idling speed set too low	Increase idling speed to specified value
	f. Malfunctioning PCV valve	Replace
9. Engine stalls after idling or slow-speed driving (⊘ 13-10)	a. Defective fuel pump	Repair or replace
	b. Overheating	Check cooling system (Chap. 9), ignition timing (Chap. 30)
	c. High float level	Adjust
	d. Idling adjustment incorrect	Adjust
	e. Malfunctioning PCV valve	Replace
10. Engine stalls after high-speed driving (⊘ 13-10)	a. Vapor lock	Use different fuel or shield fuel line*
	b. Carburetor antipercolator valve defective	Check and repair
	c. Engine overheats	Check cooling system (Chap. 9), ignition timing (Chap. 30)
	d. Malfunctioning PCV valve	Replace
11. Engine backfires (⊘ 13-11)	a. Excessively rich or lean mixture	Repair or adjust fuel pump or carburetor
	b. Engine overheating	Check cooling system (Chap. 9), ignition timing (Chap. 30)
	c. Engine conditions such as excessive carbon, hot valves, overheating	Repair engine*
	d. Ignition timing incorrect	Retime (Chap. 30)
	e. Spark plugs of wrong heat range	Install correct plugs (Chap. 30)
12. Engine runs but misses (⊘ 13-12)	a. Fuel pump erratic in operation	Repair or replace
	b. Carburetor jets or lines clogged or worn	Clean or replace
	c. Fuel level not correct in float bowl	Adjust float; clean needle valve
	d. Ignition-system defects such as incorrect timing or defective plugs, coil, points, cap, condenser, wiring	Check ignition system (Chap. 30)
	e. Clogged exhaust	Check tail pipe, muffler; eliminate cause of clogging
	f. Engine overheating	Check cooling system (Chap. 9), ignition timing (Chap 30)
	g. Engine conditions such as valves sticking, loss of compression, defective rings	Check engine*

COMPLAINT	POSSIBLE CAUSE	CHECK OR CORRECTION
13. Engine run-on or dieseling (⊘ 13-13)	a. Idle-stop or solenoid adjustment incorrect	Adjust; fix solenoid
	b. Engine overheating	Check cooling system (Chap. 9)
	c. Hot spots in cylinders	Check engine*
14. Too much HC and CO in exhaust (⊘ 13-14)	a. Carburetor troubles	Check choke, float level, idle-mixture adjustment screw
	b. Ignition troubles	Check for miss; check timing (Chap. 30)
	c. Faulty air injection	Check air-injection system (Chap. 19)
	d. Defective TCS or catalytic system	Check (Chap. 19)

* See *Automotive Engines.*
† See *Automotive Chassis and Body.*
‡ See *Automotive Transmissions and Power Trains.*

⊘ 13-3 Excessive Fuel Consumption The first step in checking a complaint of excessive fuel consumption is to make sure the car really has this trouble. Usually, you would take the word of the owner. However, a fuel-mileage tester (Chap. 34) can be used to measure how much fuel the car is using. The next step is to find the cause of the trouble. It could be in the fuel system, ignition system, engine, or elsewhere in the car.[1] The compression tester and the intake-manifold-vacuum gauge (described in Chap. 33) are used to determine the location of the trouble.

If the trouble appears to lie in the fuel system, the following points should be considered.

1. Nervous drivers, drivers who pump the accelerator pedal when idling, and "jackrabbit" starts use an excessive amount of fuel. Each downward movement of the accelerator pedal causes the accelerator pump to discharge gasoline into the carburetor air horn. This extra fuel is wasted, since it adds nothing to the motion of the car.

2. High-speed operation requires more fuel per mile. A car that will give 20 mpg (miles per gallon) [8.5 km/l] at 30 mph [48.28 km/h] may give less than 15 mpg [6.37 km/l] at 60 mph. At 70 to 80 mph [112.65 to 128.75 km/h], the mileage may drop to well below 10 mpg [4.25 km/l]. Thus, a car operated consistently at high speed shows poorer fuel economy than a car driven consistently at intermediate speed.

3. Short-run, stop-and-start operation uses more fuel. In short-run operation, the engine cools off between runs. It thus operates mostly cold or on warm-up. This means that fuel consumption is high. When the car is operated in heavy city traffic, or under conditions requiring frequent stops and starts, the engine is idling a considerable part of the time. Also, the car is accelerated to traffic speed after each stop. All this uses up a great deal of fuel, and fuel economy is poor.

4. If the fuel pump has excessive pressure, it maintains an excessively high fuel level in the carburetor float bowl. This causes a heavier discharge at the fuel nozzle or jet, producing high fuel consumption. Excessive pump pressure is not a common cause of excessive fuel consumption, however. It results only from installation of the wrong pump or diaphragm spring, or from incorrect reinstallation of the pump diaphragm during repair. However, pumps can develop leaks that will permit loss of gasoline to the outside or into the crankcase. This requires replacement of the diaphragm, tightening of the assembling screws, or replacement of the pump (⊘ 14-12 to 14-14).

5. If a manually operated choke is left partly closed, the carburetor delivers too much fuel for a warm engine. This causes high fuel consumption. On manually operated chokes, it is possible for the choke-valve linkage to get out of adjustment so that the valve will not open fully. This requires readjustment to prevent high fuel consumption (⊘ 14-4). With an automatic choke, the choke valve should move from the closed to the open position during engine warm-up. It should reach the full-open position when the engine reaches operating temperature. This action can be observed by removing the air cleaner and noting the changing position of the choke valve during warm-up. If the automatic choke does not open the choke valve normally, excessive fuel will be used. The choke must be serviced (⊘ 14-5).

6. A clogged air cleaner (on an unbalanced carburetor) acts much like a closed choke valve, since it chokes off the flow of air. The cleaner element should be cleaned or replaced, and fresh oil added (if the cleaner uses oil). See ⊘ 14-2. This is not a problem with a balanced carburetor.

7. In the carburetor itself, the following conditions could cause delivery of an excessively rich air-fuel mixture (see Chap. 15 "Carburetor Service," for corrections):

a. A high float level or a leaking float permits delivery of too much fuel to the float bowl and through

[1] A rough test of mixture richness that does not require any testing instruments is as follows: Install a set of new or cleaned spark plugs of the correct heat range for the engine. Then take the car out on the highway for 15 to 20 min. Stop the car; remove and examine the plugs. If they are coated with a black carbon deposit, the mixture is too rich. See points 4 to 7 in the list in this section.

the fuel nozzle or jet. The float level must be readjusted, or a leaky float replaced.

b. A stuck or dirty float needle valve does not shut off the flow of fuel from the fuel pump. Too much fuel is delivered through the carburetor fuel nozzle or jet. The needle valve should be freed and cleaned or replaced.

c. Worn carburetor jets pass too much fuel, causing the air-fuel mixture to be too rich. Worn jets must be replaced.

d. If the power system operates during part-throttle operation, too much fuel is delivered through the main fuel nozzle. This condition could be due to a stuck metering rod or power piston, which must be freed.

e. An idle that is set too rich or too fast wastes fuel. The idle richness and speed must be reset.

f. If the accelerator-pump check valve sticks open, it may permit the discharge of fuel through the pump system and into the carburetor air horn. This causes excessive fuel consumption. The check valve must be freed and serviced.

g. Carburetor leaks, either internal or external, cause loss of fuel. The correction is to replace damaged gaskets or parts and tighten loose couplings on fuel lines, loose jets or nozzles, and loose mounting nuts or screws.

8. Faulty ignition can also cause excessive fuel consumption. The ignition system could cause engine miss, so that the engine does not utilize all the fuel. Faulty ignition could also cause loss of power and poor acceleration or high-speed performance (see ⊘ 13-4). Conditions in the ignition system that might cause the trouble include a "weak" coil or condenser, incorrect timing, faulty advance-mechanism action, dirty or worn spark plugs or contact points, defective pickup coil or electronic control unit (in an electronic ignition system), and defective wiring.

9. Several conditions in the engine can also produce excessive fuel consumption. Loss of engine compression from worn or stuck rings, worn or stuck valves, or a loose or burned cylinder-head gasket causes loss of power. This means that more fuel must be burned to achieve the same speed or power.

10. Any condition that increases rolling resistance makes it harder for the car to move along the road. This, again, increases fuel consumption. For example, low tires, dragging brakes, and misalignment of wheels increase fuel consumption. So do losses in the power train, as, for instance, from a slipping clutch.

⊘ 13-4 Engine Lacks Power, Acceleration, or High-Speed Performance This type of complaint is usually difficult to analyze, since it is somewhat vague. Almost any component of the engine or car, from the driver to the tires, could cause the problem. As a first step in tracing this sort of complaint, some mechanics take the car out for a road test. The car is accelerated over a good road; a stopwatch is used to determine how long it takes to reach a given speed. The test should be made once in each direction on the same road. The results should then be averaged, so that such variables as wind and road grade are balanced out. The engine can also be checked on the chassis dynamometer (Chap. 33). Or, it can be given a complete tuneup, as detailed in Chap. 35.

Here are some conditions that might cause the complaint. Fuel-system conditions are listed first.

1. Almost any out-of-balance condition in the carburetor could prevent delivery of proper amounts of fuel for good acceleration and full power. Some possibilities are the following (see Chap. 15, "Carburetor Service"):

a. The accelerator pump may not be functioning correctly. This can be checked on many engines by removing the air cleaner and observing the accelerator-pump discharge jet when the throttle is opened. If the pump is functioning correctly, a steady stream of fuel will be discharged from the jet as the throttle is opened. The stream should continue for some moments after the throttle has reached the full-open position. If the pump does not operate correctly, disassembly and servicing are required. Some pumps can be adjusted to change the amount of fuel delivered during acceleration.

b. The power step-up diameter on the metering rod may not be clearing the metering-rod jet during wide-open throttle. In this case, insufficient fuel is delivered for full-power performance. This requires readjustment of the metering-rod linkage.

c. Similarly, if the power piston or valve sticks, the valve cannot open for full power. Then insufficient fuel is delivered. The piston or valve must be freed and cleaned.

d. A low float-level adjustment "starves" the main nozzle or jet. This prevents delivery of normal amounts of fuel and causes a loss of engine power. The float level should be readjusted.

e. Dirt in filters or lines also "starves" the carburetor main nozzle or jet and the engine, by restricting fuel flow. Also, on older cars not equipped with a fuel-vapor recovery system, some fuel-tank caps have a vent to permit air to enter as fuel is withdrawn. If this vent is clogged, no air can enter; a vacuum can develop in the fuel tank. The vacuum can prevent delivery of fuel through the fuel pump to the carburetor. Later-model cars, with fuel-vapor recovery systems, cannot use the old-style cap. The fuel tanks of these cars are sealed. They require a special tank cap with a vacuum valve. The valve opens when fuel is withdrawn, so that air can enter. This prevents a vacuum from forming. If the wrong cap, without a vent or vacuum valve, is installed, a vacuum will form in the fuel tank. The vacuum prevents fuel from being delivered to the carburetor.

f. A stuck or inoperative choke causes loss of power when the engine is cold. It may also cause loss of power when the engine is hot if it is stuck in a partly closed position (since it produces an excessively rich mixture). The choke should be serviced.

g. Air may be leaking into the intake manifold around the carburetor or manifold mounting, or past worn throttle-shaft bearings. This can make the air-fuel mixture too lean for good operation. Gaskets should be replaced, and mounting nuts or screws tightened as necessary. Excessively worn throttle-shaft bearings require carburetor-body replacement.

h. A stuck antipercolator valve may also cause an excessively lean mixture. The valve should be freed or adjusted.

i. A manifold heat-control valve that is stuck in the closed position overheats the air-fuel mixture in the intake manifold with the engine hot. The mixture expands excessively, and the engine becomes "starved." The result is poor performance. If the valve sticks open, warm-up is slowed. The valve should be freed.

j. If the throttle-valve linkage is out of adjustment, the throttle may not open fully. This prevents delivery of full power. The throttle linkage should be adjusted correctly.

k. Most of these conditions produce an excessively lean mixture. However, conditions that produce an excessively rich mixture (see ⊘ 13-3) also cause poor engine performance.

2. Vapor lock also causes engine "starvation." Vaporization (boiling) of the fuel in the fuel pump or fuel line prevents delivery of normal amounts of fuel to the carburetor. Some mechanics check for this condition by inserting a clear plastic tube in the fuel line. They then watch for bubbles to pass through the tube, with the engine hot and running. This is an abnormal condition. The correction is to use a fuel with lower volatility, or to shield the fuel line and pump from engine heat.

3. A defective fuel pump might also "starve" the engine by not delivering sufficient amounts of fuel to the carburetor. The fuel pump should be serviced or replaced (⊘ 14-12 to 14-14).

4. The exhaust system could be clogged by rust, dirt, or mud in the muffler or tail pipe, or a pinched or damaged muffler or tail pipe. This can create sufficient back pressure to prevent normal exhaust from the engine. The result is reduced engine performance, particularly on acceleration or at high speed. Some exhaust systems include exhaust pipes that are laminated. Laminated exhaust pipes consist of a single ordinary exhaust pipe placed tightly inside a second, slightly larger pipe. This combination reduces exhaust noise; the laminated exhaust pipe deadens the "ringing" noise that some engines produce. However, the inner layer of steel can separate from the outer layer, sag or collapse, and partly block the exhaust. This should be checked carefully, since the inner pipe cannot be seen from outside.

5. A defective ignition system can reduce engine performance, just as it can increase fuel consumption (⊘ 13-3, item 8). Conditions in the ignition system that might cause the trouble include a "weak" coil or condenser, incorrect timing, faulty advance-mechanism action, dirty or worn contact points or spark plugs, defective pickup coil or electronic control unit (in an electronic ignition system), and defective wiring.

6. A sluggish engine can result from loss of compression, excessive carbon in the engine cylinders, defective valve action, or heavy engine oil.

7. Failure of the cooling system to operate properly could cause the engine to overheat and lose power (Chap. 9). Also, the cooling-system thermostat may fail to close when the engine cools. It will then prolong the engine warm-up period, the next time the engine is started. This reduces engine performance during warm-up.

8. Any condition that increases rolling resistance reduces acceleration and top speed. These conditions include low tires, dragging brakes, and misaligned wheels.

9. Clutch slippage or excessive friction in the power train reduces acceleration and top speed.

10. An automatic transmission that does not downshift, or a defective torque converter, can reduce performance and acceleration.

⊘ 13-5 Poor Idling If the engine idles roughly, too slowly, or too fast, the idle mixture and idle speed may require adjustment (Chap. 15). In addition, a malfunctioning choke, a high or low float level, vapor lock, clogged idle system, air leaking into the intake manifold, loss of engine compression, improper valve action, an overheating engine, and an improperly operating ignition system can cause poor idling. All these conditions were discussed in the previous section. They can also cause poor engine performance at speeds above idle. Improper idle-mixture or idle-speed adjustment is obvious only when the engine is idling. Another possible cause is the PCV valve being stuck in the open, or high-speed, position. This could allow too much airflow from the crankcase, which would lean out the idle mixture excessively and cause poor idling.

⊘ 13-6 Engine Will Not Start When the engine turns over at normal cranking speed but will not start, the trouble is probably in the ignition or fuel system. The ignition system can be quickly checked as follows: Disconnect the lead from one spark plug (or the coil lead from the center of the distributor cap). Using insulated pliers, hold the lead clip about $^{3}/_{16}$ in [4.763 mm] from the engine block while cranking the engine. If a good spark occurs, the ignition system is probably operating normally, although it could be out of time (see Chap. 30).

If the ignition system operates normally, remove the carburetor air cleaner to check the accelerator-pump system. Open the throttle quickly, and see whether or not the accelerator-pump system is delivering fuel to the carburetor air horn. If it is not, chances are the carburetor is not getting fuel from the fuel pump. The cause could be a defective pump, a clogged filter or fuel line, or an empty fuel tank.

Also, if the car is equipped with a fuel-vapor recovery system, the wrong fuel-tank cap could prevent fuel delivery. The tanks of cars equipped with fuel-vapor recovery systems have special tank caps. The tanks are sealed. When fuel is withdrawn, a vacuum valve on the cap opens to admit air to the tank. If a cap without a vacuum valve is installed, no air can enter to replace the fuel withdrawn. A vacuum develops in the tank and prevents delivery of fuel to the carburetor.

If the accelerator-pump system does deliver fuel to the carburetor air horn, try starting again. If the engine starts when primed by the pump operation, but then stalls, the carburetor idle or main metering system is probably clogged and not functioning normally. If the engine still does not start when primed, there is most likely a problem in the engine.

CAUTION: Reinstall the air cleaner before you attempt to start. If you fail to do this, the engine could backfire through the carburetor. This could burn you and cause a fire. Any fuel in or around the carburetor could be ignited by a backfire.

⊘ 13-7 Hard Starting with Engine Warm If the engine is difficult to start when warm, the problem could be a choke that is sticking closed, improper throttle-cracker linkage, vapor lock (⊘ 13-4, item 2), or engine binding due to overheating. Choke position can be seen with the air cleaner removed. If the choke does not open wide when the engine is hot, the choke should be serviced (⊘ 14-5).

⊘ 13-8 Slow Engine Warm-up If the engine warms up slowly, the trouble could be an open choke (it should be partly closed with the engine cold). This can be checked with the air cleaner removed. Also, the manifold heat-control valve or the cooling-system thermostat could be stuck open.

⊘ 13-9 Smoky Exhaust The color of the smoky exhaust is a clue to what is causing it. If the exhaust is blue, then the engine is burning oil. This engine problem is caused by oil entering the combustion chambers. Oil can enter through the PCV system, through clearances between valve stems and valve guides, and past piston rings.

If the exhaust is black or sooty, the mixture is too rich and is not burning completely. Refer to ⊘ 13-3 for the causes of excessive fuel consumption.

If the smoke is white, coolant from the engine cooling system is probably leaking into the combustion chambers. The water is turned to steam by the heat of combustion; the steam gives the exhaust gas the white color. The remedy is to tighten the cylinder-head bolts or replace the cylinder-head gasket. Those are the most likely places for coolant to leak into the combustion chambers. Less likely, but possibly, the condition could be caused by a cracked cylinder head or cylinder block.

NOTE: If coolant is leaking into the cylinders, there is probably some coolant in the engine oil. To check for this, place a drop of oil from the crankcase on a sheet of aluminum foil. Then apply heat from below the foil, under the drop of oil. If the oil begins to crackle and pop, there is water in it.

⊘ 13-10 Engine Stalls If the engine starts and then stalls, note exactly when the stalling takes place: before or after the engine warms up, after idling or slow-speed driving, or after high-speed or full-load driving. Check the PCV valve. If the PCV valve becomes clogged or sticks, it can cause poor idling and stalling. It should be replaced.

1. *ENGINE STALLS BEFORE IT WARMS UP* This could be due to an improperly set fast or slow idle, or to improper setting of the idle-mixture adjustment screw in the carburetor. It could also be due to a low carburetor float setting or to insufficient fuel entering the carburetor. This condition could result from a faulty float needle valve, dirt or water in the fuel lines or filter, a defective fuel pump, or a plugged fuel-tank vent. Also, the carburetor could be icing (⊘ 12-26). In some instances, certain ignition troubles could cause stalling after starting. However, if the ignition troubles are bad enough to cause stalling, they will probably also prevent starting. Burned contact points or defective spark plugs could permit starting but fail to keep the engine running. Another condition might be an open primary resistance wire. When the engine is cranked, this wire is bypassed. Then, when the engine starts and cranking stops, this wire is inserted into the ignition primary circuit. If the wire were open, the engine would stall at this time.

2. *ENGINE STALLS AS IT WARMS UP* This condition might result from a choke valve that is stuck closed (⊘ 14-4 and 14-5). The mixture would become too rich for a hot engine, and the engine would stall. Also, a stuck manifold heat-control valve might cause the ingoing air-fuel mixture to become overheated and too lean. This would stall the engine. If the hot-idle-speed setting is too low, the engine can stall when it warms up. It is also possible that the engine is overheating (Chap. 9), which could cause vapor lock.

3. *ENGINE STALLS AFTER IDLING OR SLOW-SPEED DRIVING* This can occur if the fuel pump has a cracked diaphragm, weak spring, or defective valve. The pump cannot deliver enough gasoline at low speed to replace the fuel used by the engine. The carburetor float bowl therefore runs dry, and the engine stops. On the other hand, if the float level is set too high or the idle adjustment is too rich, the engine may "load up" with an overrich mixture and stall. A lean idle adjustment also can cause stalling when the engine is hot. Overheating can also cause vapor lock and engine stalling. The engine may overheat during sustained idling or slow-speed driving, because the air movement through the radiator may not be great enough to keep the engine temper-

ature down. If overheating is excessive or abnormal, check for the conditions listed in ⊘ 9-2.

4. *ENGINE STALLS AFTER HIGH-SPEED DRIVING* This may occur if the fuel line or pump gets hot enough to boil the fuel and produce a vapor lock. Shield the fuel line or use a less volatile fuel, to reduce the tendency toward vapor lock. Another condition that might cause stalling after high-speed driving is failure of the antipercolator valve in the carburetor. This causes the mixture to become too rich, and the engine to stall. Stalling might also result from engine overheating (see ⊘ 9-2).

⊘ 13-11 Engine Backfires It is not uncommon for a cold engine to backfire, because of a temporarily improper air-fuel ratio or sluggish intake valves. However, after the engine has started and is warming up, backfiring is more serious. It may be due to an excessively rich or lean mixture which will not ignite properly, causing backfiring through the carburetor. Backfiring may also be due to preignition caused by such engine conditions as hot valves and excessive carbon, as well as such ignition-system conditions as incorrect timing and plugs of the wrong heat range. An engine equipped with the air-injection system of exhaust-emission control will backfire through the exhaust because of a disconnected or defective gulp or diverter valve. Constant backfiring through the carburetor may be caused by burned intake valves, or a clogged exhaust system.

⊘ 13-12 Engine Runs but Misses If the engine runs but misses, it is possible that fuel delivery is not uniform. This could result from clogged fuel lines, clogged nozzles or systems in the carburetor, an incorrectly adjusted or malfunctioning float valve or needle, or an erratic fuel pump. Other conditions that might cause missing include ignition defects such as incorrect timing and defective plugs, coil, points, cap, condenser, or wiring. The exhaust might be clogged, causing back pressure that prevents normal delivery of air-fuel mixture to the cylinders. Also, the engine might be overheating, or it might have sticky valves, loss of compression, defective piston rings, etc.

⊘ 13-13 Engine Run-on, or Dieseling Modern engines, with their emission controls, require a fairly high hot-idle speed for best operation. This makes run-on, or dieseling, possible. If there are hot spots in the combustion chambers, the engine could continue to run if the throttle is not completely closed. The hot spots take the place of the spark plugs. If the throttle valve is slightly open, enough air-fuel mixture can get past it to keep the engine running. Ignition would be produced by the hot spots. Many engines have an idle-stop solenoid to close the throttle completely when the ignition switch is turned off.

If an engine diesels, check the idle-stop solenoid. Chances are it needs adjustment, to allow the throttle valve to close completely when the ignition is turned off. Also, do everything necessary to prevent engine overheating, because this can contribute to the problem of run-on (see ⊘ 9-2).

⊘ 13-14 Too Much HC and CO in Exhaust The exhaust-gas analyzer (Chap. 33) is used to measure the amount of HC and CO in the exhaust gases. Several conditions could cause high readings. In the fuel system, a choke sticking closed, worn jets, high float level, and other conditions listed in ⊘ 13-3 could be the cause. In the ignition system, missing or incorrect timing could be responsible. Also, an emission control such as the air-injection system, transmission-controlled spark system, or catalytic converter could be causing the problem. CO problems generally are easier and cheaper to correct than HC problems. Setting the carburetor and ignition to specifications often corrects a problem with excessive CO emissions. However, excessive HC may be caused by mechanical conditions within the engine that require major engine service or overhaul to correct.

⊘ 13-15 Quick Carburetor Checks Here are several quick carburetor checks. They will give you a rough idea of whether the various carburetor systems are functioning. However, the results of these checks must not be considered as final. They give only a preliminary indication of possible trouble. Accurate analysis requires an exhaust-gas analyzer and an intake-manifold vacuum gauge.

1. *FLOAT-LEVEL ADJUSTMENT* With the engine running at idle speed, remove the air cleaner. Note whether the main metering nozzle is discharging fuel. If it is, chances are the float level is high.

CAUTION: A backfire can occur with the air cleaner off. Removing the air cleaner can lean the air-fuel mixture enough to cause backfiring. Of course, a malfunctioning carburetor can also cause backfiring.

2. *LOW-SPEED (OFF-IDLE) AND IDLE SYSTEM* If the engine does not idle smoothly, the idle system may be malfunctioning. There are other possible causes of poor idling, as noted in ⊘ 13-4 and 13-5. Open the throttle slowly, to increase the engine speed to about 2500 rpm. If the speed does not increase evenly, and the engine runs rough through this speed range, the low-speed system is probably out of order.
3. *ACCELERATOR-PUMP SYSTEM* With the engine not running and the air cleaner off, open the throttle suddenly. Note whether the accelerator-pump jet discharges a flow of fuel. If the accelerator-pump system is functioning normally, the flow should continue for several seconds.
4. *MAIN METERING SYSTEM* With the engine running at approximately 2500 rpm and warmed up, slowly cover part of the air-cleaner air intake with a

piece of stiff cardboard. Do not use your hand! The engine should speed up slightly as the main metering system discharges more fuel.

CHAPTER 13 CHECKUP

NOTE: Since the following is a chapter review test, you should review the chapter before taking the test.

The chapter you have been studying is probably one of the most difficult in the book. At the same time it is perhaps the most important. To be an expert automotive mechanic, you need to know how to find causes of trouble in the engine and fuel system. The fact that you have come this far in the book indicates you have made a fine start toward becoming an expert on fuel systems. The checkup below will help you find out how well you remember the material on fuel-system troubles. It will also help you review the important points, and fix them more firmly in your mind. If any question seems hard, reread the pages that give you the information you need.

Correcting Troubles Lists The purpose of this exercise is to help you to spot unrelated troubles in a list. For example, check through the list "Excessive fuel consumption: high-speed operation, start-and-stop operation, high float level, low-speed operation, worn carburetor jets." You should see that "low-speed operation" does not belong in the list. It is the only condition that would not cause high fuel consumption. Any of the other conditions increases fuel consumption. In each of the following lists, there is one item that does not belong. Write each list in your notebook, but do not write the unrelated item.

1. Engine lacks power: throttle linkage out of adjustment, air leaks into intake manifold, metering rod or power piston stuck, high-octane fuel, low float level.
2. Excessive fuel consumption: clogged air cleaner, short-run operation, high-speed operation, stuck metering rod or power piston, idle speed too low, accelerator-pump check valve stuck open.
3. Poor idle: idle mixture too lean, idle speed too low, loss of engine compression, engine too hot, accelerator pump inoperative.
4. Engine will not start except when primed: fuel line clogged, fuel pump defective, carburetor jets clogged, spark plugs defective, filter clogged.
5. Hard starting with engine warm: choke valve stuck closed, vapor lock, engine parts binding, cooling-system thermostat stuck, manifold heat-control valve stuck.
6. Engine stalls as it warms up: choke valve stuck closed, manifold heat-control valve stuck, engine overheating, heavy engine oil.
7. Engine stalls after idling: defective fuel pump, engine overheating, hot engine valves.
8. Engine stalls after high-speed driving: vapor lock, engine overheating, antipercolator valve malfunctioning, carbon in engine.
9. Engine backfires: lean mixture, rich mixture, engine overheating, excessive carbon, hot valves, high-octane fuel.
10. Engine runs but misses: fuel-pump erratic, carburetor jets clogged, engine overheating, ignition-system defects, excessive rolling resistance, clogged exhaust.

Completing the Sentences The sentences below are incomplete. After each sentence there are several words or phrases, but only one of them correctly completes the sentence. Write each sentence in your notebook, ending it with the one word or phrase that completes it correctly.

1. The fuel-mileage tester measures: (*a*) miles per hour, (*b*) miles per gallon, (*c*) miles per minute, (*d*) the fuel pump.
2. Exhaust-gas analyzers test: (*a*) intake-manifold pressure, (*b*) fuel-pump action, (*c*) exhaust gases, (*d*) intake mixture.
3. Worn carburetor jets or a clogged air cleaner will cause: (*a*) full-power operation, (*b*) high fuel consumption, (*c*) spark knock, (*d*) fast engine warm-up.
4. Excessive rolling resistance will reduce: (*a*) fuel consumption, (*b*) top speed, (*c*) idle speed, (*d*) float-level height.
5. If the engine will not start except when primed, a possible cause is a defective: (*a*) choke, (*b*) accelerator pump, (*c*) fuel pump.
6. If the engine is difficult to start when warm, a possible cause is: (*a*) a defective choke, (*b*) excessive rolling resistance, (*c*) heavy engine oil, (*d*) high-octane fuel.
7. Slow engine warm-up may be due to a stuck: (*a*) accelerator pump, (*b*) fuel pump, (*c*) choke valve.
8. A smoky, black exhaust is due to: (*a*) a lean mixture, (*b*) an overheated engine, (*c*) vapor lock, (*d*) a very rich mixture, (*e*) stuck engine valves.
9. Engine stalling after high-speed driving may be due to: (*a*) vapor lock, (*b*) high compression, (*c*) excessive fuel-pump pressure.
10. Engine backfiring could result from: (*a*) excessive rolling resistance, (*b*) loss of compression, (*c*) improper mixture ratio, (*d*) defective oil pump.
11. Engine missing could be caused by: (*a*) high compression, (*b*) high-octane fuel, (*c*) an erratic fuel pump.
12. An excessively rich mixture will: (*a*) cause excessive rolling resistance, (*b*) cause fouled spark plugs, (*c*) increase engine efficiency, (*d*) damage the fuel pump.
13. The high-speed nozzle in a carburetor air horn discharges gasoline when the engine is running at idling speed. The cause is probably a: (*a*) high float level, (*b*) low float level, (*c*) clogged fuel line, (*d*) defective accelerator pump.
14. Poor fuel economy means: (*a*) less high-speed operation, (*b*) less fuel-pump pressure, (*c*) fewer miles per gallon, (*d*) fewer gallons per mile.

15. If an engine stalls after a period of idling, the cause is probably a defective: (*a*) oil pump, (*b*) water pump, (*c*) fuel pump, (*d*) air pump.

Troubleshooting Fuel-System Complaints As an automotive mechanic, you will hear complaints of high fuel consumption, loss of power, engine stalling, and so on. You will have to know what to do to find the cause and eliminate it. The following questions are "stumpers" that you might actually encounter in the automotive shop. Write down the procedures you would follow to solve each problem. If you are not quite sure of a procedure, reread the pages that give you the information. Then write the procedure in your notebook. Do not copy, but write in your own words. This will help you remember the procedures.

1. A man brings his car into your shop and complains about low gasoline mileage. He is very impatient and keeps "gunning" the accelerator while he talks to you. What might you suspect is the trouble? What other driving conditions increase fuel consumption?

2. How does improper choke action increase fuel consumption?

3. If you suspected that the cause of poor fuel economy was in the carburetor, what are the things you would look for?

4. What are some of the conditions, not in the fuel system, that might increase fuel consumption?

5. A woman drives into your shop and complains that her car will not go faster than about 55 to 60 mph [88.51 to 96.56 km/h]. She used to be able to go 15 to 20 mph [24.14 to 32.19 km/h] faster. What are some of the conditions, in the fuel system as well as elsewhere, that you should consider as the cause of the problem?

6. When an engine turns over but does not start, what ignition-system test should you make? What fuel-system test?

7. You are called to check out a stalled car. You find that the engine, when primed, turns over normally and runs. What would you do to try to find the trouble?

8. If an engine stalls when it warms up, where would you look for the trouble?

9. You are called out to bring in a stalled car. The owner tells you that it had been running all right. However, when the owner stopped, with the engine running, to talk over some business with a client, it stalled. There is fuel in the tank, and the engine does not seem to be overheated. Where would you look for the trouble?

10. An engine is backfiring badly. Where would you look for the trouble?

11. What are some of the causes of missing in an engine?

12. You are called out to bring in a car that will not start. The owner had been out driving all morning, came home, stopped for a moment, and then could not restart the engine. However, when you try, it starts easily. It took you at least an hour to get to the car after the owner called. What do you think might be the trouble?

13. What is a quick check to see whether the carburetor float level is too high?

14. What is a quick check of the main metering system?

15. What is a quick check of the accelerator-pump system?

SUGGESTIONS FOR FURTHER STUDY

Careful observation of checking and trouble-diagnosis procedures in an automotive service shop can be of great value to you. So can examining components and parts that have caused trouble. This will help you link the cause and the effect. For instance, if you examine a fuel pump with a cracked diaphragm, you will see why it cannot deliver enough fuel to the carburetor, so that it starves the engine.

You should get to thoroughly know the trouble-diagnosis procedures given in this chapter. One way of helping yourself remember them is to write the procedures, or the causes and effects, on 3- by 5-in cards. Carry the cards around with you. At odd moments, for instance, when you are riding on a bus, eating a sandwich, or getting ready for work, take out a card and read it over. You will soon know the causes of excessive fuel consumption, loss of power, and other troubles in the engine and the fuel system.

Be sure to talk with expert automotive tuneup specialists, and with your instructor, about the various ways to locate troubles in engines. Ask them about their experiences in locating troubles, how often they find that loss of power is due to defects in the fuel system, whether fuel pumps cause much trouble, and so on.

chapter 14

FUEL-SYSTEM SERVICE

This chapter deals with fuel-system service and covers all fuel-system components except carburetors. It includes servicing information on air cleaners, chokes, fuel filters, fuel tanks, fuel lines, fuel gauges, and fuel pumps. Carburetor service is described in the next chapter. Special tools are required for many fuel-system service jobs; they are described along with the service jobs. In addition, several common hand tools are needed.

⊘ **14-1 Cleanliness** Dirt is the major enemy of good service work. A trace of dirt in the wrong place in a carburetor or fuel pump may cause serious difficulty. For example, dirt in the needle-valve seat in the carburetor float bowl may prevent closing of the needle valve. The float bowl will overfill and cause an excessively rich mixture and high fuel consumption. Similarly, dirt in the idle system or accelerator-pump system may produce carburetor malfunctioning and poor engine operation. Thus, when you repair a fuel pump or a carburetor, make sure that your hands, the repair bench, and your tools are really clean. Here are some other cautions to observe:

CAUTION 1: An air hose is often used to air-dry carburetor and fuel-pump parts after they have been washed in cleaning compound. The air hose is also used to blow out carburetor systems. When using an air hose, remember that the airstream drives dirt particles at high velocity. Flying particles could get into your eyes and injure them. Be very careful where you point the hose. To be safe, wear safety goggles to protect your eyes when you use the air hose.

CAUTION 2: Never forget that gasoline vapor is highly explosive. Use extreme care in handling fuel-system parts that are covered or filled with gasoline. When removing a carburetor, fuel pump, filter, or fuel tank, drain it into a container. Then wipe up all spilled gasoline with cloths. Put the clothes outside to dry. *Never bring an open flame near gasoline!* This could result in a disastrous fire.

CAUTION 3: Never remove a carburetor from a hot engine. Gasoline spilled on hot engine parts could ignite and cause a disastrous explosion and fire.

CAUTION 4: Never prime an engine, with the air cleaner off, by pouring or squirting fuel into the carburetor air horn. The engine could backfire and cause an explosion or fire.

CAUTION 5: Exercise great care if you must run the engine with the air cleaner off. Removing the air cleaner can lean out the air-fuel mixture enough to cause backfiring. Also, a malfunctioning carburetor can cause backfire.

⊘ **14-2 Air-Cleaner Service** A tremendous amount of air passes through the air-cleaner filter element (⊘ 11-10 and 11-11). The filter element removes dirt and dust from the air. This dirt gradually collects in the element, and ultimately clogs it. In oil-bath type cleaners, much of the dirt is washed down into the oil, so the oil gradually gets dirty. At one time, car manufacturers recommended that the air cleaner be removed periodically, and the filter element be cleaned. Today, only Chrysler recommends cleaning. The carburetor on the modern car is balanced. That is, it is internally vented to the air cleaner. With this arrangement, partial clogging of the filter element does not produce a richer mixture.

Because of this, and because of improved filter elements, most manufacturers say only that the filter element should be replaced periodically. They do not give cleaning instructions. Here are typical recommendations.

American Motors Corporation
Replace the filter element every 15,000 mi [24,140 km].

Chrysler Corporation (Chrysler, Dodge, Plymouth)
Inspect and clean the filter element every 12,000 mi [19,312 km] or 12 months. Replace the filter element every 24,000 mi [38,624 km] or 2 years.

Chevrolet (Typical of General Motors)
Replace the filter element every 12,000 mi [19,312 km] on six-cylinder engines, and every 24,000 mi [38,624 km] on V-8 engines. The difference here is that the V-8 has a larger filter element and can run longer without replacement.

Ford Motor Company
Check the filter element every 12,000 mi [19,312 km] and replace it every 24,000 mi [38,624 km].

Exception
All manufacturers say that if the vehicle is operated in dusty conditions, the element should be inspected and replaced twice as often. In other words, replace the element every 12,000 mi [19,312 km], instead of every 24,000 mi [38,624 km].

Figures 14-1 to 14-3 show air cleaners with related parts. In some models, the filter element is removed simply by taking off the wing nut and air-cleaner cap. Then the element is lifted out. In other models (Fig. 14-1), the cap is part of the air-cleaner cover. The assembly includes the snorkel and the connections to the positive crankcase ventilating system and the heat stove for the heated-air intake system. On these, the air-cleaner cover can usually be lifted up enough to remove the element. If it cannot, the hoses have to be disconnected.

Once the element is out, the bottom of the air

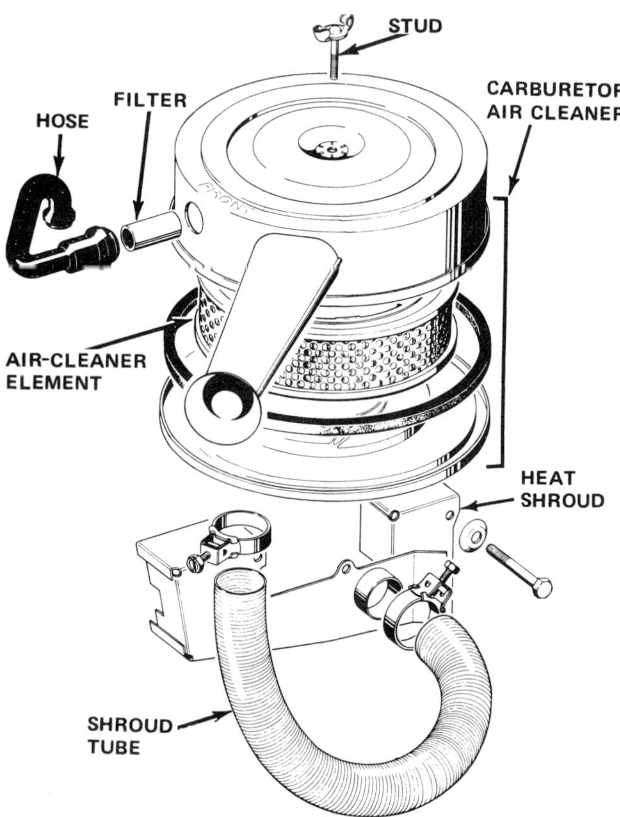

Fig. 14-1. Disassembled view of a carburetor air cleaner and associated parts for a six-cylinder engine. (*American Motors Corporation*)

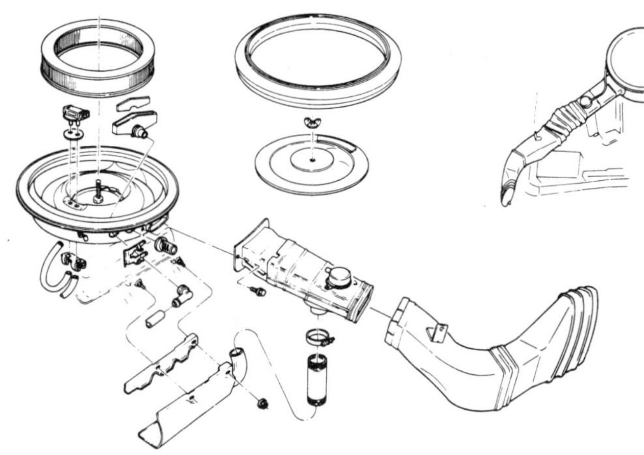

Fig. 14-2. Disassembled view of a carburetor air cleaner and associated parts for a V-8 engine. (*Ford Motor Company*)

cleaner, the gasket surfaces, and the cover should be cleaned. Check the cover seal for tears and cracks. Replace it if it is damaged.

CAUTION: Chrysler adds this caution: If the air cleaner must be loosened from the carburetor for any purpose, it should be removed from under the hood. If the air cleaner rests on or hooks into linkage parts, the parts can be damaged. Cap all carburetor air fittings which could leak air if the engine is to be run without the air cleaner.

1. *CLEANING THE PAPER ELEMENT* Chrysler recommends cleaning the paper element this way: Examine the element; if it is saturated with oil over more than half its circumference, discard it. Check the PCV system, which must have delivered the oil to the air cleaner. Use compressed air to blow out the element, from the inside out (Fig. 14-4). Hold the nozzle at least 2 in [50.8 mm] away from the inside screen.

CAUTION: Do not blow from the outside in! This will embed dust in the paper.

After cleaning, examine the element for punctures. If you can see any pinholes when you hold the element up to the light, discard the element. Make sure the plastic sealing rings on both sides of the element are smooth and uniform. If everything is okay, replace the element. Be sure it seals both top and bottom when the cover is replaced.

2. *CLEANING THE POLYURETHANE ELEMENT* On some Chevrolet models, a polyurethane element is used outside the paper element (Fig. 14-3). After it is removed, inspect it carefully for rips and other damage. Discard it if it is not in good condition. Wash the element in kerosene (Fig. 14-5), squeezing it gently to remove the excess kerosene.

CAUTION: Do not use solvents containing acetone or similar compounds, since they will ruin the ele-

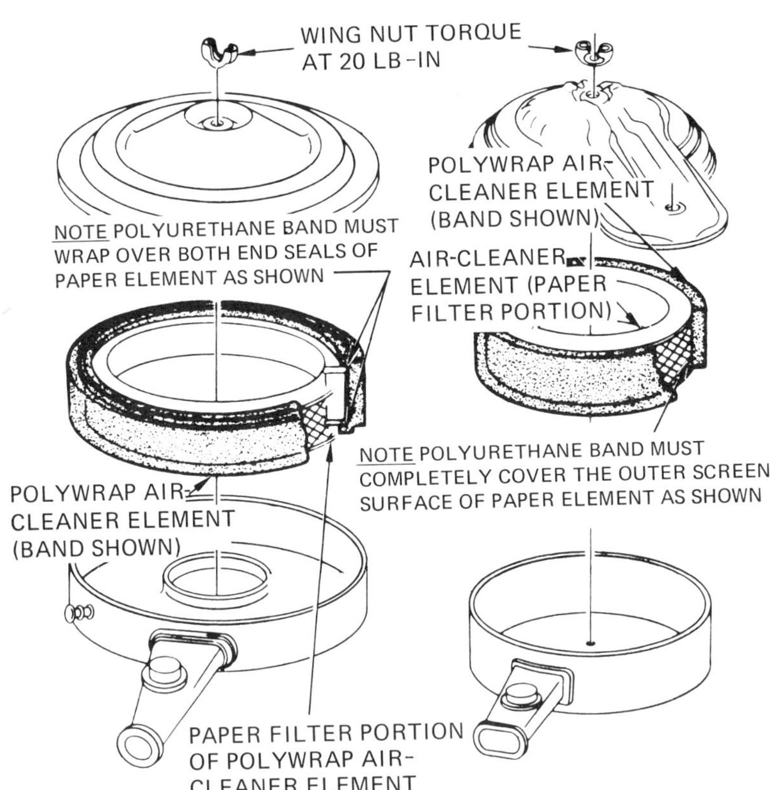

Fig. 14-3. Air cleaners of the type using a polyurethane band, showing the location of the band. *(Chevrolet Motor Division of General Motors Corporation)*

ment. Also, never wring out, shake, or swing the element; this will tear it. Instead, fold over the element and gently squeeze it, as shown in Fig. 14-5.

Dip the cleaned element in engine oil, and squeeze out the excess. Clean the cover and bottom parts of the cleaner. Reinstall the element and its support in the cleaner bottom. Make sure that the element is not folded or creased, and that it seals all the way around the bottom. Replace the cover, mak-

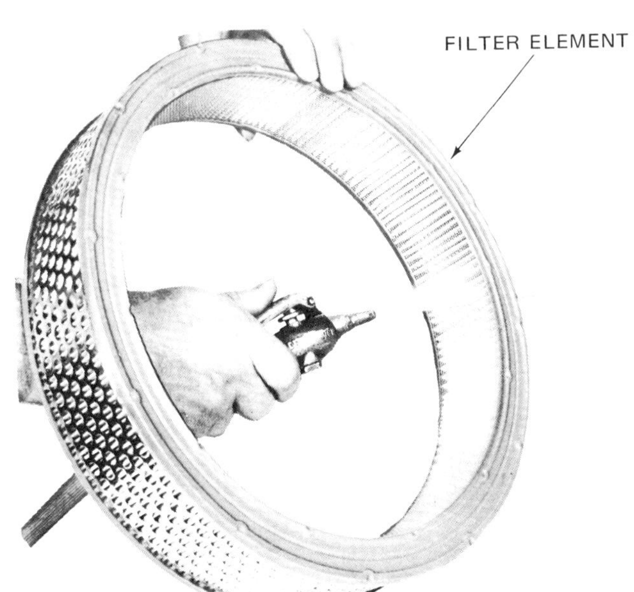

Fig. 14-4. Cleaning the filter element with compressed air blown from inside the element. *(Chrysler Corporation)*

Fig. 14-5. Washing a polyurethane air-cleaner element. *(Chevrolet Motor Division of General Motors Corporation)*

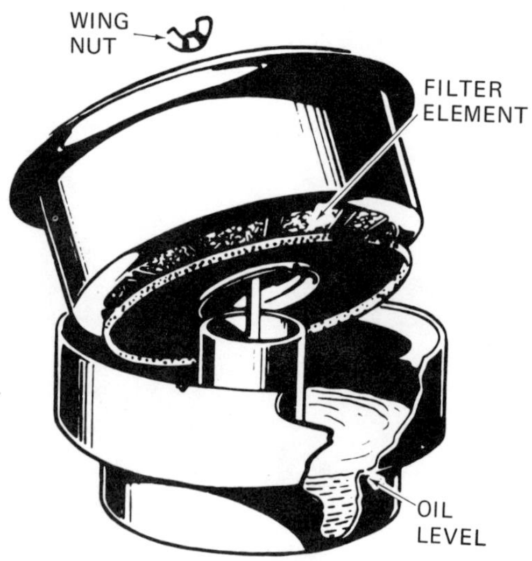

Fig. 14-6. Oil-bath air cleaner. The wing nut and filter element are removed, and the side is partly cut away to show the oil level.

ing sure the element seals all the way around on it. Use a new gasket when installing the air cleaner on the carburetor.

3. *CLEANING THE OIL-BATH CLEANER (FIG. 14-6)* Remove the filter element. Clean it by sloshing it up and down in cleaning solvent. Dry it with compressed air. Dump the old oil from the cleaner body, wash it out with solvent, and dry it. Refill the body to the FULL mark with clean engine oil. Reinstall the filter element and cleaner body on the engine.

CAUTION: Air filters which are not installed directly on the carburetor are connected to the carburetor by a flexible hose. This hose must have an airtight connection to both the filter and the carburetor. Also, the hose must have no tears or punctures, which might admit unfiltered air.

⊘ 14-3 Thermostatically Controlled Air Cleaner

The thermostatically controlled air cleaner (⊘ 11-11) can be checked for proper operation with a temperature gauge or thermometer. Remove the air-cleaner cover, and install the gauge as close as possible to the sensor. Allow the engine to cool to below 85°F [29.4°C] if it is hot. Replace the air-cleaner cover without the wing nut.

Start and idle the engine. When the damper begins to open, remove the air-cleaner cover and note the temperature reading. It should be between 85 and 115°F [29.4 and 46.1°C]. If it is difficult to see the damper, use a mirror.

If the damper does not open at the correct temperature, check the vacuum motor and the sensor, as follows:

With the engine off, the control damper should be in the engine compartment or cold-air-delivery position (see Fig. 11-20). To determine whether the vacuum motor is operating, apply at least 9 in [228.6 mm] of vacuum to the fitting on the vacuum motor. The vacuum can be from the engine or from a vacuum source in the shop. With the vacuum applied, the damper should move to the hot-air-delivery position.

Replace the vacuum motor if it does not work satisfactorily. To do this, drill out the spot welds, and unhook the linkage. The new motor can be installed with a retaining strap and sheet-metal screws.

If the vacuum motor does work okay, the sensor should be replaced. Pry up the tabs on the retaining clip, and remove the old sensor. Install the new sensor, and bend the tabs down again.

⊘ 14-4 Manual-Choke Adjustment

On manual chokes, a choke button on the dash is linked to the choke valve in the carburetor. They are linked by a control wire in a conduit (Fig. 14-7). If the wire kinks or slips in the screw clamp, the choke valve may not open and close properly when the choke button is moved. Loosen the screw clamp, and slide the wire one way or the other to get the proper adjustment. With the choke button in, the choke valve should be open. With the choke button pulled out, the choke valve should be closed. Kinks can be straightened by bending the wire. Sometimes the conduit supports

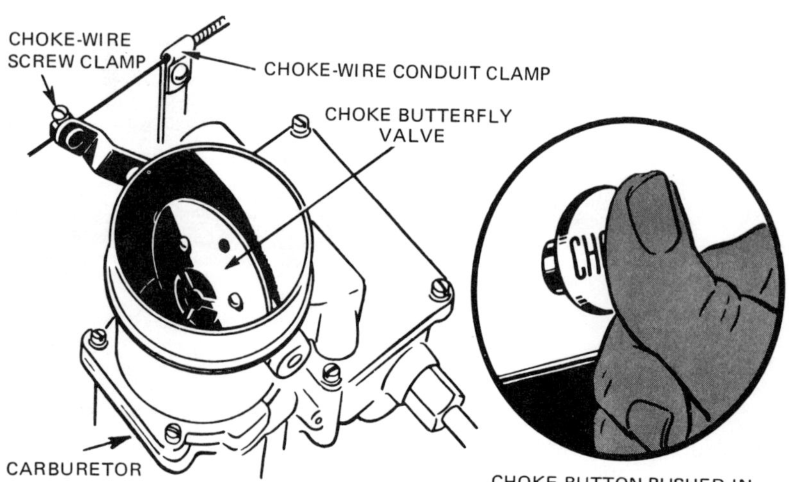

Fig. 14-7. Linkage to the choke valve in a carburetor.

are bent out of line, causing the wire to bind inside the conduit. The supports should be straightened. If the wire still binds, put a few drops of penetrating oil along the conduit. The oil will penetrate to the wire and lubricate it.

⊘ 14-5 Automatic-Choke Adjustment There are several types of automatic chokes. Some can be adjusted, and others require no adjustment. Generally speaking, a properly adjusted choke will not get out of adjustment. It is possible for a choke to become stuck because of collected dirt or gum. Adjustments do not help; the choke requires cleaning, freeing up, and readjustment. If there is difficulty in starting, other possible causes should be considered before the choke is adjusted. If some other condition is causing the trouble (faulty plugs, for example), readjusting the choke could very well make the condition worse (by overenriching the mixture and further fouling the plugs).

Automatic-choke adjustment may be necessary in one case. This is when the car is being operated on an unusual blend of fuel that does not give good warm-up operation with the regular choke setting. For example, if the fuel is excessively volatile, it could cause excessive loading and rolling of the engine on warm-up. That is, the mixture could become too rich, causing the engine to run rough as its speed swings higher and lower. In this case, the choke should be adjusted to provide a leaner mixture to prevent loading.

The automatic choke is either mounted on the carburetor, or it has a thermostatic coil in a well in the intake manifold (⊘ 12-24). Some chokes have an electric-assist coil to speed up the choke action. Others are water-heated. That is, hot coolant from the engine cooling system flows through the choke to hasten choke action.

One electric-assist choke installation is shown in Fig. 14-8. This choke is not adjustable. The choke control switch is thermostatic. It is connected to the battery and to the choke heater. Below 58°F [14.4°C], it connects the choke heater to the battery through a resistance. This allows some current (but not full current) to flow. Above 58°F [14.4°C], the control switch connects the choke heater to the battery directly for fast heating and quick dechoking. At approximately 110°F [43.3°C], it disconnects the choke heater.

The carburetor-mounted choke in Fig. 12-29 can be adjusted. The two or three cover-clamp screws are loosened, and the cover is turned one way of the other, to lean out or enrich the mixture. Some chokes with the thermostatic coil in the intake manifold can be adjusted by bending the rod connecting the coil to the choke. Others cannot be adjusted.

⊘ 14-6 Fuel-Filter Service Fuel filters require no service. They should be checked periodically to make sure they are not clogged, and to replace the

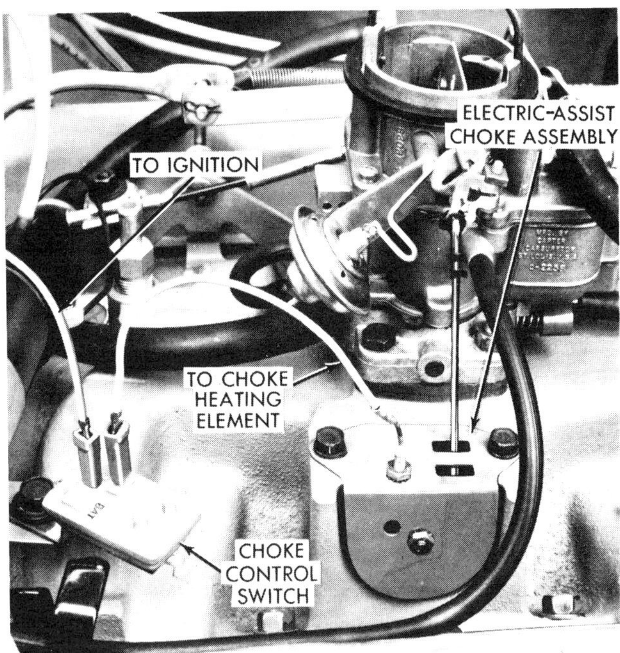

Fig. 14-8. Electric-assist choke assembly, showing the location of the thermostatic choke-control switch. (*Chrysler Corporation*)

filter element or clean the filter, according to type. On some earlier models, the filter is part of the fuel pump (Fig. 14-9). The filter can be removed to replace the element. Another type is the in-line filter (Figs. 11-4 and 11-5). In the type shown in Fig. 11-4, the filter is replaced by first unclamping and detaching the fuel hose from the filter. The filter is then unscrewed from the carburetor and replaced. In the type shown in Fig. 11-5, the fuel line is detached and then the nut is removed. The old filter element is slipped out and replaced with a new element.

⊘ 14-7 Fuel Tank The fuel tank rarely requires attention. If it is damaged, it must, of course, be repaired or replaced. Some car manufacturers recommend that the fuel tank be drained about once a year, to remove deposits of dirt and water. This can be done when the fuel supply is low, so that little gasoline is wasted. Fuel tanks are usually supported by straps bolted to the frame. Removing the straps permits removal of the tank. Before the tank is removed, the fuel-gauge wires and the fuel line must be detached. Naturally, the fuel should be drained from the tank.

CAUTION: Before a tank is repaired, great care must be used to make sure it is absolutely free of gasoline vapor. Even a spark from a hammer blow might cause vapor in the tank to explode.

The fuel filter in the tank (where present) can be cleaned once the tank is removed. It is cleaned by blowing air through it, with an air hose. The air

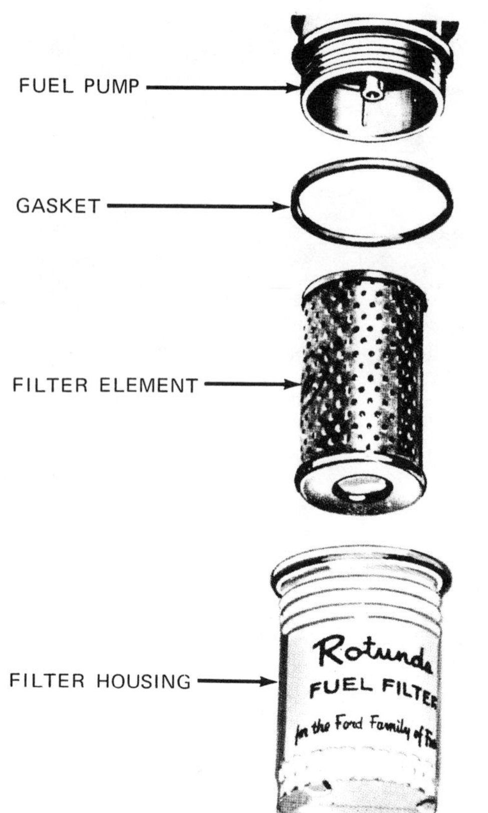

Fig. 14-9. The fuel-filter element is replaced by unscrewing the filter housing. (*Ford Motor Company*)

should be directed through the filter from the fuel outlet.

When replacing a fuel tank, make sure the supports are firmly fastened. Also clean the fuel-gauge terminals well, so they will make good contact when the wires are connected.

⊘ 14-8 Fuel Lines Fuel lines (or pipes, or tubes, as they are also called) are attached to each other and to the carburetor, fuel pump, and tank with different types of couplings. Use two wrenches, as shown in Fig. 14-10, to loosen the type of coupling having two nuts. This will keep the line from twisting and possibly becoming damaged.

When installing a new line of the flared type, it is best to double-flare the tube. The double flaring assures a safer and tighter connection.

Fuel lines should be adequately supported at various points along the frame. A line that is rubbing against a sharp corner should be moved slightly, to avoid wear and a possible leak. Fuel lines must not be kinked or bent unnecessarily. Such treatment is likely to cause a crack and a leak.

If you suspect that the fuel line between the pump and tank is clogged, remove the fuel-tank filler cap. Disconnect the fuel line at the pump, and apply an air hose to it. Do not apply too much air, since this might blow gasoline out of the tank. If the line does not pass air freely, it may be clogged with dirt.

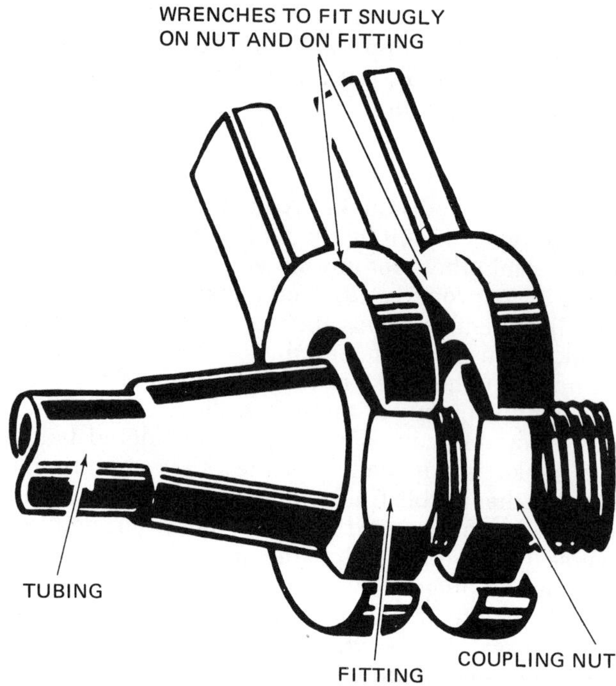

Fig. 14-10. Using two wrenches to loosen or tighten coupling nuts to avoid twisting and damaging the line.

Or, it may have become badly kinked or pinched at a bend or support. Also, on tanks with an internal filter, the filter may have become clogged (but this is extremely rare). Kinked or pinched lines should be replaced. The kinked or pinched place may later crack open and leak, even if it is straightened.

⊘ 14-9 Fuel Gauges Fuel gauges require very little service. Defects in either the dash unit or the tank unit usually require replacement of the defective unit. However, on the type of gauge that has vibrating thermostatic blades (⊘ 11-5), the contact points may get dirty. This can cause needle fluctuation. The points can be cleaned by pulling a strip of clean bond paper between them. Be sure that no particles of paper are left between the points. Never use emery cloth to clean the points. Particles of emery will embed in the points and cause very erratic gauge action.

If a fuel gauge is defective or suspected of malfunctioning, substitute a new tank unit for the old one. This can be done without removing the unit. Disconnect the tank-unit terminal lead from the old unit, and connect it to the terminal of the substitute unit. Then connect a lead from the frame of the substitute unit to any convenient grounding place on the car. Make sure the unit is well grounded. With these connections made, turn on the ignition switch, and operate the float arm of the substitute unit. If the dash unit now works (indicates) as the float arm is moved up and down, then the old tank unit is defective. If the dash unit still does not work, then either it is at fault or the wiring is defective.

NOTE: On the thermostatic type of fuel gauge, the thermostats need a minute or so to heat up before the instrument-panel (dash) unit begins indicating. Therefore, on these, wait a minute or so after turning on the ignition switch.

⊘ **14-10 Fuel-Pump Inspection** The fuel pump can be checked for pressure, capacity, or vacuum with special gauges, as explained in Chap. 33. The vacuum pump of the old-style combination pump can also be tested with the vacuum gauge. Readings should be compared with the manufacturer's specifications for the model of pump being tested. A rather rough test of fuel-pump action can be made by loosening or disconnecting the fuel line from the carburetor, and then cranking the engine. The distributor primary lead should be disconnected from the coil so that the engine does not start. During cranking, the fuel pump should deliver a spurt of gasoline with each rotation of the engine camshaft. Have a container ready to catch the gasoline. Wipe up any spilled gasoline with cloths, and put the cloths outside to dry.

Once its operation is checked, the fuel pump should be checked for leaks. Leaks might occur at fuel-line connections or around sealing gaskets. One example is the joint between the sediment bowl and the cover; another is the joint between the cover and the pump body.

The pump should be replaced if the fuel pressure is too high or too low; if the pump does not deliver fuel normally to the carburetor; if leaks show up in the pump; if the pump has a cracked diaphragm or other defect; or if the pump is noisy. The next section describes various pump troubles and their causes.

⊘ **14-11 Fuel-Pump Troubles** The trouble-diagnosis chart in Chap. 13 lists various fuel-system troubles and their causes. Some of these causes may lie in the fuel pump; many of them are in other fuel-system or engine components. Here are some fuel-system troubles that might be caused by the fuel pump.

1. *INSUFFICIENT FUEL DELIVERY* Insufficient fuel delivery could result from low pump pressure, which in turn could be due to any of the following:

1. A broken, worn-out, or cracked diaphragm
2. Improperly operating fuel-pump valves
3. A broken diaphragm spring
4. A broken or damaged rocker arm
5. A clogged pump-filter screen
6. Air leaking into the sediment bowl, because of a loose bowl or worn gasket

These causes of insufficient fuel delivery all lie within the pump. Many conditions outside the pump could prevent the delivery of normal amounts of fuel. These are listed and described in detail in Chap. 13. They include a clogged fuel-tank-cap vent, a clogged fuel line or filter, air leaks into the fuel line, and vapor lock. In the carburetor, an incorrect float level, a clogged inlet screen, or a malfunctioning inlet needle valve would prevent delivery of adequate fuel to the carburetor.

2. *EXCESSIVE PUMP PRESSURE* High pump pressure causes too much fuel to be delivered to the carburetor. The excessive pressure tends to lift the needle valve off its seat, so that the fuel level in the float bowl is too high. This results in an overrich mixture and excessive fuel consumption. Usually, the pump pressure would be high only after the fuel pump has been removed, repaired, and replaced. If a fuel pump has been operating satisfactorily, its pressure should not increase enough to cause trouble. High pressure could come from installation of an excessively strong diaphragm spring or from incorrect reinstallation of the diaphragm. If the diaphragm is not flexed properly when the cover and housings are reattached, it has too much tension and produces too much pressure.

3. *FUEL-PUMP LEAKS* The fuel pump will leak if any screws have not been properly tightened or if the gasket is damaged or incorrectly installed. If tightening the screws does not stop the leak, the pump must be serviced or replaced. Note also that leaks may occur at fuel-line connections which are loose or improperly coupled.

4. *FUEL-PUMP NOISES* A noisy pump usually has worn or broken internal parts. The problem can be a weak or broken rocker-arm spring, a worn or broken rocker-arm pin or rocker arm, or a broken diaphragm spring. In addition, a loose fuel pump or a scored rocker arm or cam on the camshaft may cause noise. Fuel-pump noise may sound something like engine valve-tappet noise, since its frequency is the same as the camshaft speed. If the noise is bad enough, it can actually be "felt" when the fuel pump is gripped firmly in the hand. Careful listening will usually show that the noise is coming from the fuel pump. Tappet noise is usually distributed along the engine or can be traced to the valve compartment of the engine.

⊘ **14-12 Fuel-Pump Removal** Before removing the fuel pump, wipe off any dirt or grease, to keep it out of the engine. Then take off the heat shield (where present), and disconnect the fuel lines (Fig. 14-10). Remove the attaching nuts or bolts, and lift off the pump. If it sticks, work it gently from side to side. You can also pry lightly under the mounting flange with a screwdriver to loosen it. Do not damage the flange or attaching studs. On engines using a pushrod to operate the fuel pump, remove the rod. Examine it for wear and sticking.

⊘ **14-13 Fuel-Pump Service** Today, many fuel pumps cannot be disassembled for service. They are put together by crimping (Fig. 14-11) and are only serviced by complete replacement. Earlier fuel pumps could be disassembled. For these, you pur-

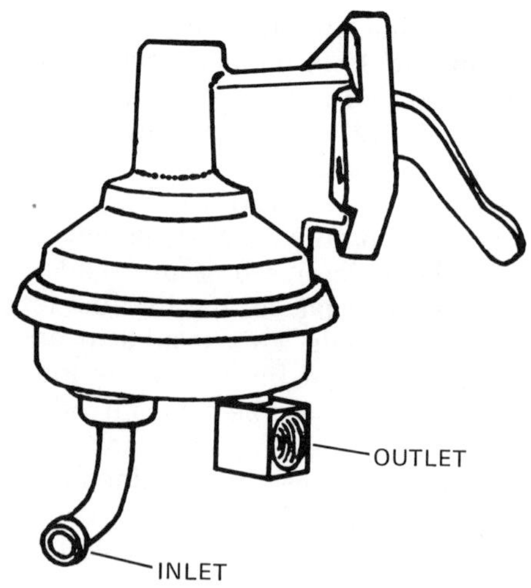

Fig. 14-11. Typical fuel pump. Note that it is assembled by crimping the cover, and that it cannot be disassembled for service. (*GMC Truck and Coach Division of General Motors Corporation*)

chased a repair kit (Fig. 14-12) which had all the parts necessary to rebuild the pump. Now the cost of labor is high, and the cost of a new pump is relatively low. Thus, it is generally cheaper to buy a new pump than to repair an old, defective pump.

⊘ 14-14 Fuel-Pump Installation Make sure the fuel-line connections are clean and in good condition. All gasket material must be scraped off the mounting pads on the engine and on the pump flange. Connect the fuel lines to the pump before attaching the pump to the engine. Then place a new gasket on the studs of the fuel-pump mounting or over the opening in the crankcase. Many automotive manufacturers recommend coating both sides of the new gasket with oil-resistant sealer before installation. The mounting surface of the engine should be clean. Insert the rocker arm of the fuel pump into the opening. Make sure the rocker arm is on the proper side of the camshaft (Fig. 14-13) or is centered over the pushrod. It may be difficult to get the holes in the fuel-pump flange to align with the holes in the crankcase. If so, turn the engine over until the low side of the camshaft eccentric is under the fuel-pump rocker arm. On V-8 engines which use a pushrod, you can use a pair of mechanical fingers (Fig. 14-14) to hold the pushrod up while installing the pump. Attach the pump with the bolts or nuts. Check the pump operation as explained in ⊘ 14-10.

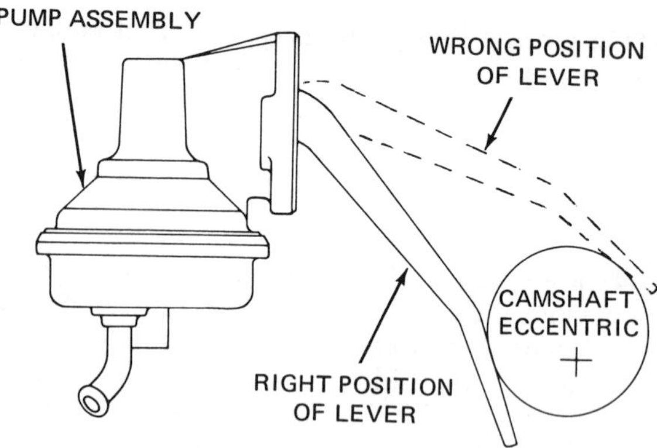

Fig. 14-13. Correct positioning of the fuel-pump lever on the camshaft eccentric. (*Chevrolet Motor Division of General Motors Corporation*)

Check Your Progress

Progress Quiz 14-1 Here is another chance to check your progress. The questions below will help you review the material you have just covered and fix the important points more firmly in your mind. If

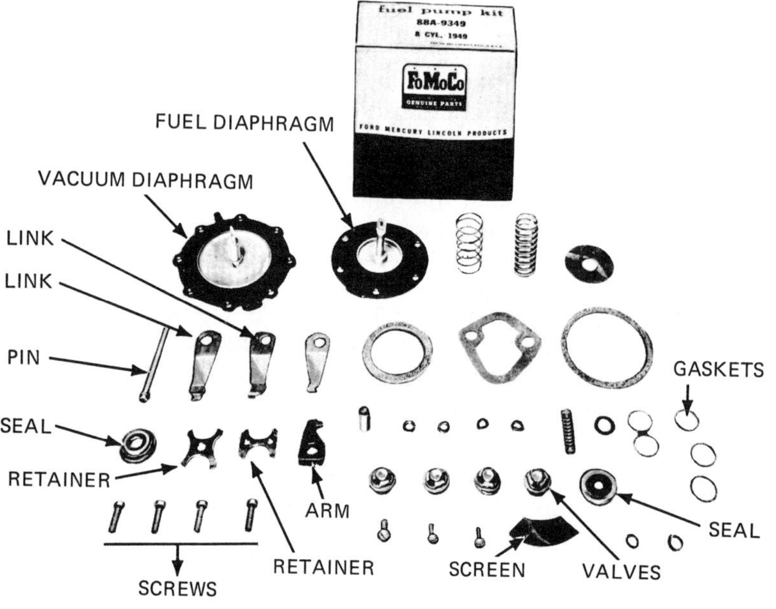

Fig. 14-12. Repair kit for a combination fuel and vacuum pump. (*Ford Motor Company*)

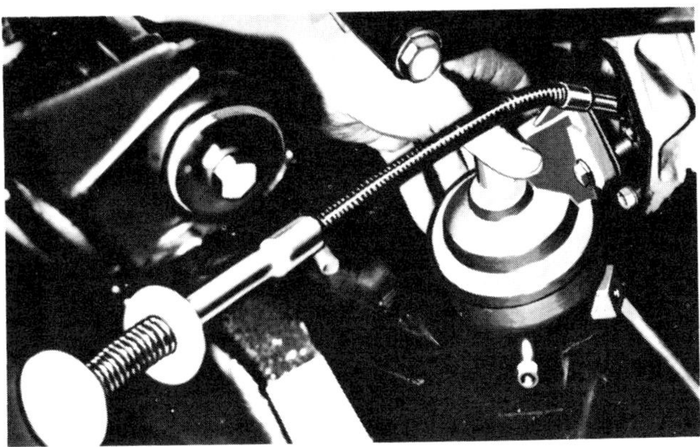

Fig. 14-14. Installing a fuel pump on a V-8 engine, using mechanical fingers to hold the pushrod up. *(GMC Truck and Coach Division of General Motors Corporation)*

any of the questions stump you, reread the pages that give you the information.

Completing the Sentences The sentences below are incomplete. After each sentence there are several words or phrases, but only one of them correctly completes the sentence. Write each sentence in your notebook, ending it with the one word or phrase that completes it correctly.

1. When an oil-bath air cleaner is serviced, the filter element should be: (*a*) replaced, (*b*) washed in oil, (*c*) washed in cleaning fluid.
2. In the manual choke, when the choke button on the dash is pulled all the way out, the choke valve should be: (*a*) closed, (*b*) nearly closed, (*c*) open.
3. To adjust the hot-air choke to get a richer or leaner warm-up mixture, the: (*a*) control wire must be adjusted, (*b*) cover must be turned, (*c*) adjustment screw must be turned.
4. Generally speaking, the automatic choke, if properly adjusted to start with, will: (*a*) require adjustment once a month, (*b*) require adjustment once a year, (*c*) not get out of adjustment.
5. The polyurethane air-filter element should be cleaned by: (*a*) washing in kerosene, (*b*) compressed air, (*c*) vigorous shaking.
6. A fuel line that is kinked or pinched should be: (*a*) straightened by hand, (*b*) replaced, (*c*) straightened with light hammer blows.
7. As a general rule, a defective fuel-guage unit: (*a*) can be readjusted, (*b*) can be rewired, (*c*) should be replaced.
8. The location of a trouble in the fuel gauge can usually be determined by temporarily substituting: (*a*) a new tank unit, (*b*) a new dash unit, (*c*) new wiring.
9. To quick-check the fuel-pump action, you should loosen or disconnect the fuel line from the carburetor: (*a*) with the engine running at medium speed, (*b*) with the engine idling, (*c*) and then crank the engine.
10. A broken diaphragm or spring, stuck valves, clogged screen, or air leaks in the fuel pump can cause: (*a*) high pump pressure, (*b*) low pump pressure, (*c*) high float level, (*d*) a rich mixture.

CHAPTER 14 CHECKUP

NOTE: Since the following is a chapter review test, you should review the chapter before taking the test.

You are now well into the part of the book that discusses actual shopwork on automotive fuel systems. You should know how to service fuel-system components. For this reason, step-by-step procedures on several models of components are included in these pages. As you study the procedures, you will learn the important details of fuel-system service. The following review test gives you a chance to find out how well you remember the essential points covered in this chapter.

Completing the Sentences The sentences below are incomplete. After each sentence there are several words or phrases, but only one of them correctly completes the sentence. Write each sentence in your notebook, ending it with the one word or phrase that completes it correctly.

1. To prevent loss of air-cleaner efficiency, the filter element must be removed from the cleaner periodically and: (*a*) replaced, (*b*) cleaned, (*c*) blown out with compressed air.
2. To adjust the hot-air choke, you loosen the two or three cover-clamp screws and turn the: (*a*) clamp, (*b*) carburetor, (*c*) choke valve, (*d*) cover.
3. If a fuel tank is to be repaired, great care must be used to make sure it is absolutely free of: (*a*) water vapor, (*b*) attaching studs, (*c*) gasoline vapor, (*d*) fuel-gauge wires.
4. Double-flaring the fuel-line tube assures: (*a*) shorter tubing, (*b*) a safer and tighter connection, (*c*) stiffer tubing, (*d*) longer tubing.
5. To locate a trouble in a fuel gauge, you can temporarily substitute, for the old unit, a new: (*a*) instrument-panel unit, (*b*) wire, (*c*) tank unit, (*d*) switch.
6. A broken fuel-pump diaphragm spring, improperly operating pump valves, broken diaphragm, clogged screen, or air leaks could cause: (*a*) high fuel-pump pressure, (*b*) fuel-tank stoppage, (*c*) insufficient fuel delivery to the carburetor.
7. An excessively strong fuel-pump diaphragm spring or an improperly installed diaphragm could cause: (*a*) insufficient fuel delivery, (*b*) high pump pressure, (*c*) a false fuel-gauge reading, (*d*) loose connections.
8. A high fuel level in the float bowl and an excessively rich mixture could result from: (*a*) low pump pressure, (*b*) high pump pressure, (*c*) a cracked diaphragm.
9. Periodically, the PCV valve should be: (*a*) adjusted, (*b*) replaced, (*c*) cleaned.

10. A fuel pump that leaks gasoline should be: (*a*) adjusted, (*b*) soldered, (*c*) replaced.

Service Procedures In the following, you are asked for explanations and lists. Write them in your notebook. Do not copy the procedures from the book; instead, use your own words. Give a step-by-step account of each service job. This will help you remember the procedures when you go into the automotive shop. If possible, study various fuel pumps and instruction manuals on fuel pumps. Base your writeups on these, instead of on the book. This will give you wider experience in servicing fuel pumps.

1. Explain how to adjust a manual choke.
2. Explain how to adjust an electric choke.
3. Explain how to adjust an automatic choke.
4. Explain how to remove and replace an automatic choke.
5. Explain how to remove and replace a fuel line.
6. Explain how to check a defective fuel gauge.
7. Explain how to check a fuel pump for pressure, capacity, and vacuum.
8. Explain how to quick-check a fuel pump.
9. List the conditions that require fuel-pump removal.
10. List conditions in the fuel pump that could cause insufficient fuel delivery.
11. List conditions outside the fuel pump that could cause insufficient fuel delivery.
12. List the causes of excessive fuel-pump pressure.
13. Explain how to remove a fuel pump from an engine.
14. Explain how to install a fuel pump on an engine.

SUGGESTIONS FOR FURTHER STUDY

When you are in an automotive shop, keep your eyes and ears open; learn all you can about how the various fuel-system jobs are done. Study any carburetor and fuel-pump manuals you can get. Carefully examine all the carburetors and fuel pumps you can. If the shop has some old or defective units, see whether you can borrow them. Practice disassembling and reassembling them. The more practice you get in handling the small parts that go into these units, the more skillful you will become. Write, in your notebook, any important facts (or even whole procedures) you find. Writing the facts will help you remember them. At the same time, your notebook will become an increasingly valuable reference.

chapter 15

CARBURETOR SERVICE

This chapter continues the discussion of fuel-system service. It covers the disassembly, repair, reassembly, and adjustment of carburetors. Carburetor service requires a number of special tools; they are described along with the servicing jobs. In addition, several common hand tools are needed.

⊘ **15-1 Cleanliness** It is extremely important to keep carburetor parts and systems as clean as possible. Bits of dirt or dust that get into the carburetor will cause carburetor and engine trouble sooner or later. The jets or nozzles and systems through which gasoline flows are carefully calibrated to within thousandths of an inch. Dirt or gum changes this calibration and affects carburetor and engine performance. On the other hand, careless cleaning of the nozzles or jets may enlarge them slightly. This will result in overrichness, fuel waste, and problems caused by excessive carbon in the engine.

The cautions about use of the air hose and the explosiveness of gasoline vapor (at the end of ⊘ 14-1) also apply to carburetor service. Reread those cautions now. Keep them in mind whenever you work in an automotive shop.

⊘ **15-2 Carburetor Troubles** Various carburetor troubles are outlined in detail in Chap. 13. The trouble-diagnosis chart lists trouble causes in the carburetor and other fuel-system components. In the carburetor, such causes include incorrect fuel level in the float bowl, incorrect idle-speed and idle-mixture adjustments, clogged idle or main metering system, and malfunctioning accelerator-pump system. Quick checks of these systems are outlined in ⊘ 13-15.

Various engine troubles that can be caused by the carburetor are listed below. Remember that many other conditions outside the carburetor can also cause these troubles. See the trouble-diagnosis chart in Chap. 13 and the more comprehensive engine trouble-diagnosis chart in Chap. 34 for more complete information.

1. Excessive fuel consumption can result from:
a. A high float level or a leaky float
b. A sticky or dirty float needle valve
c. Worn jets or nozzles
d. A stuck metering rod or power piston
e. A too-rich or too-fast idle
f. A stuck accelerator-pump check valve
g. A leaky carburetor
h. Excessive fuel-pump pressure

2. Lack of engine power, acceleration, or high-speed performance can result from:
a. The step-up on the metering rod not clearing the jet
b. Dirt or gum clogging the fuel nozzle or jets
c. A stuck power piston or valve
d. A low float level
e. A dirty air filter
f. A stuck or inoperative choke
g. Air leakage into the manifold
h. The throttle valve not fully opening
i. A rich mixture, due to causes listed under item 1 above
j. A heat-control valve stuck closed

3. Poor idling can result from a leaky vacuum hose, stuck PCV valve, or retarded timing. It could also be due to incorrectly adjusted idle mixture or speed, a clogged idle system, or any of the causes listed in item 2 above.

4. Failure of the engine to start unless primed (by the accelerator pump) could be due to: no gasoline in the fuel tank or carburetor, the wrong tank cap (1970 cars and later), or a stopped-up tank or cap vent. The latter causes a vacuum to develop in the tank; the vacuum prevents delivery of fuel to the carburetor. Holes in the fuel-pump flex line allow air leakage, which prevents fuel delivery. In addition, consider clogged carburetor jets or lines, a defective choke, a clogged fuel filter, or air leakage into the manifold as possible causes of this condition.

CAUTION: Never prime the engine by pouring or squirting fuel into the carburetor air horn! If the engine backfires, a disastrous explosion and fire could result.

5. Hard starting with the engine warm could be due to a defective choke, a choke valve stuck closed, or

an improperly adjusted throttle-cracker linkage.
6. Slow engine warm-up could be due to a defective choke valve or manifold heat-control valve.
7. A smoky black exhaust is due to a very rich mixture. Carburetor conditions that could cause this are listed in item *1* above.
8. Engine stalling during warm-up could be due to a defective choke or a choke valve stuck closed.
9. Engine stalling after high-speed driving could be due to a malfunctioning antipercolator.
10. Engine backfiring could be due to an excessively rich or lean mixture. Backfiring in the exhaust system is usually caused by an excessively rich mixture in the exhaust. This may result from a defective air-injection-system antibackfire valve. Lean mixtures may cause a popback in the carburetor.
11. If the engine runs but misses, the most likely cause is a vacuum hose that has come off an intake-manifold fitting. This causes the nearest cylinders to miss. Missing might also be caused by a leaky intake-manifold gasket. In addition, the proper amount and ratio of air-fuel mixture may not be reaching the engine. This could be due to clogged or worn carburetor jets or to an incorrect fuel level in the float bowl.

Some of the conditions noted above can be corrected by carburetor adjustment. Others require removal of the carburetor from the engine so that it can be disassembled, repaired, and reassembled. The rest of this chapter discusses carburetor adjustments and servicing procedures.

⊘ 15-3 Typical Carburetor Adjustments At one time, there were several adjustments that could be made on carburetors. However, automotive emission control laws, passed in recent years, limit the adjustments that can be made. The only adjustment now recommended for late-model cars during tuneup is the idle speed. The idle mixture is preset at the factory, and a limiter cap is installed to prevent tampering (Fig. 15-1). The adjustment procedure is spelled out on a special tuneup decal in the engine compartment (Fig. 15-2). Of course, if some carburetor trouble requires carburetor disassembly, the locking cap or caps may be removed. The idle mixture must then be readjusted, and new limiter caps installed. The procedures are as follows.

1. SETTING THE IDLE SPEED Here is a typical procedure, as given in Fig. 15-2:

1. Disconnect the fuel-tank hose from the vapor canister.
2. Disconnect the vacuum hose to the distributor. Plug the hose.
3. Make sure the distributor contact-point dwell and ignition timing are correct (as described in Chap. 30).
4. Adjust the idle speed by the means provided. In earlier models, this was a screw in the throttle linkage at the carburetor. In later models equipped with idle-speed solenoids, the adjustment screw is in the solenoid. Regardless of the location of the adjustment screw, use a tachometer to measure engine speed. Make the adjustment to get the specified idle speed.
5. Unplug the distributor vacuum hose and reconnect it. Then reconnect the fuel-tank hose.

2. SETTING THE IDLE MIXTURE This adjustment is permissible only if the carburetor has required major service. A typical procedure is:

1. With the limiter caps off, turn the mixture screws in until they lightly touch the seats. Then back them off two full turns.
2. Adjust the idle speed as noted above.

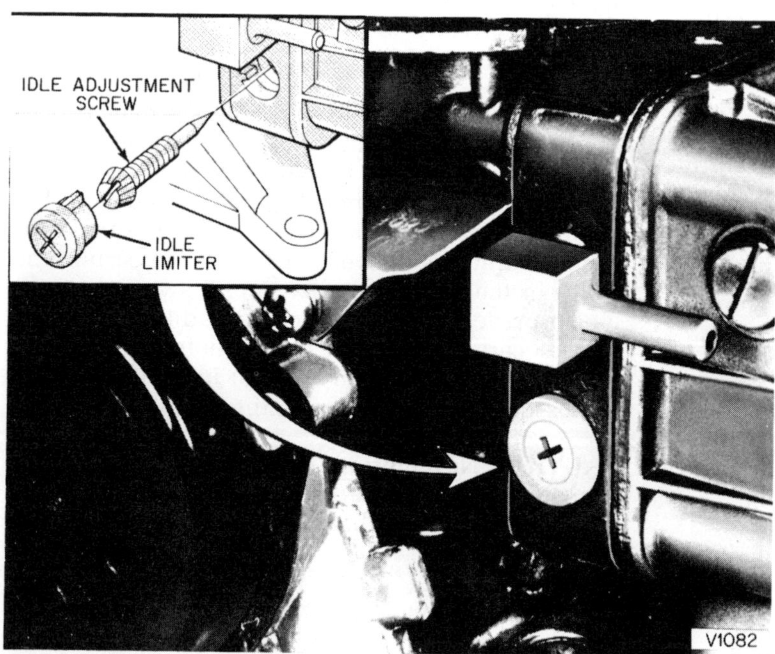

Fig. 15-1. Location of the idle limiter. *(Ford Motor Company)*

XZ
350-400 CU. IN.
2 BBL. CARB.
GM 104-2

VEHICLE EMISSION CONTROL INFORMATION
GENERAL MOTORS CORPORATION GM

MAKE IDLE SPEED AND TIMING ADJUSTMENTS WITH ENGINE AT NORMAL OPERATING TEMP., CHOKE OPEN, AIR COND. OFF, AIR CLEANER INSTALLED, AND DISTR. VACUUM LINE DISCONNECTED AND PLUGGED. RECONNECT DISTR. VACUUM LINE WHEN ADJUSTMENTS ARE COMPLETED.

SET PARKING BRAKE AND BLOCK DRIVE WHEELS.

1. DISCONNECT FUEL TANK HOSE FROM VAPOR CANISTER.
2. ADJUST CARBURETOR SOLENOID SCREW TO SPECIFIED RPM.
3. SET DWELL AND TIMING AT SPECIFIED RPM. RESET IDLE SPEED IF NECESSARY.
4. ADJUST CARBURETOR IDLE CAM SCREW TO SPECIFIED BASE IDLE RPM ON LOW STEP OF CAM WITH SOLENOID WIRE DISCONNECTED. RECONNECT WIRE AFTER ADJUSTMENT.
5. IDLE MIXTURE HAS BEEN SET AT THE FACTORY. IF IDLE MIXTURE ADJUSTMENT IS NECESSARY, SEE SERVICE MANUAL FOR PROCEDURES. IDLE MIXTURE SPECIFICATIONS ARE SHOWN AT RIGHT.
6. REMOVAL OF MIXTURE SCREW CAPS AND/OR ALTERING IDLE MIXTURE TO OTHER THAN SPECIFICATIONS MAY VIOLATE FEDERAL AND OTHER STATE LAWS.
7. RECONNECT FUEL TANK HOSE TO VAPOR CANISTER.

AIR-EGR EXHAUST EMISSION CONTROL	TRANSMISSION	
	AUTOMATIC	MANUAL
DWELL	30°	30°
TIMING (°BTC @ RPM)	8° @ 600	0° @ 900
SOLENOID SCREW (RPM)	600 (DR)	900 (N)
BASE IDLE SCREW (RPM)	500 (DR)	500 (N)
LEAN DROP IDLE MIXTURE (RPM)	650-600 (DR)	1000-900 (N)
MAX. IDLE CO (% @ RPM)	0.5 @ 600 (DR)	0.5 @ 900 (N)

SEE SERVICE MANUAL FOR ADDITIONAL INFORMATION

FUEL REQUIREMENTS—USE 91 OCTANE OR HIGHER.

PRINTED IN U.S.A.

THIS VEHICLE CONFORMS TO U.S. E.P.A. REGULATIONS APPLICABLE TO 1974 MODEL YEAR NEW MOTOR VEHICLES.

PT. NO. 346258

Fig. 15-2. Tuneup decal typical of the decals found in the engine compartments of modern cars.

3. Connect a CO meter to the exhaust system. Adjust the idle-mixture screws to get a satisfactory idle at the specified rpm, and a CO reading at or below the specified maximum. The engine should be running at normal idle, with an automatic transmission in D (drive) or a manual transmission in neutral.
4. After setting the idle mixture, recheck the idle speed as noted above. If everything checks okay, install new limiter caps on the idle-mixture screws.

NOTE: Refer to the manufacturer's service manual covering the model being serviced. It contains detailed instructions and specifications for carburetor adjustments.

⊘ 15-4 Carburetor Removal To remove a carburetor, first disconnect the air and vacuum lines. Remove the air cleaner. Next, disconnect the throttle and choke linkages. Disconnect the hot-air tube to the choke (if present). Disconnect the fuel line and the distributor vacuum-advance line from the carburetor. Use two wrenches, as necessary, to avoid damaging the lines or couplings. Disconnect any wires from switches and other electric controls. Remove the carburetor attaching nuts or bolts, and lift off the carburetor. Try to avoid jarring the carburetor. It may have accumulations of dirt in the float bowl. Rough treatment may stir up this dirt and cause it to get into carburetor jets or systems.

After the carburetor is off, put it in a clean place where dirt and dust cannot get into openings.

CAUTION: Do not remove a carburetor from a hot engine. Fuel could splash onto hot engine parts and ignite, causing a terrible fire. Let the engine cool off before removing the carburetor or fuel pump.

NOTE: If the carburetor is to be off the engine for any length of time, cover the exposed manifold holes with masking tape (Fig. 15-3). Do not use shop cloths, because threads and dirt can drop off and get into the manifold. By protecting the manifold holes, you will keep loose parts from dropping into the manifold. Parts dropped into the manifold can end up in the engine combustion chambers and cause serious damage.

⊘ 15-5 Carburetor Overhaul Procedures Disassembly and reassembly procedures on carburetors vary according to design. The manufacturer's recommendations should be followed carefully. The time required to overhaul a carburetor varies from approximately $\frac{3}{4}$ to 2 hours, depending on type. A few special carburetor tools may be required. The gauges needed to check float clearance, float centering, float height, and choke clearance are usually included in the carburetor overhaul kit.

Overhaul kits are available for many carburetors. The kits contain instructions and all the parts (gaskets, washers, and so forth) required to overhaul the carburetor and restore it to its original condition. Following are some general comments about carburetor service. Later in the chapter, we describe the servicing of typical carburetors in detail.

CAUTION: When removing and handling a carburetor, be extremely careful to avoid spilling any gasoline. Remember that the carburetor float bowl

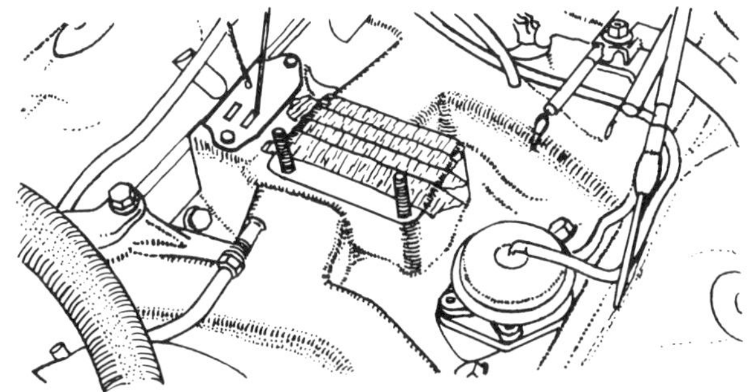

Fig. 15-3. If the carburetor is to be off the engine for any length of time, cover the manifold holes with masking tape. This will keep parts from falling into the manifold.

has gasoline in it. Keep the carburetor upright. Gasoline is extremely flammable. Any gasoline that is spilled should be wiped up immediately. Put gasoline-soaked cloths outside the building, in a safe area, to dry.

NOTE: Disassembly and assembly procedures on carburetors vary greatly, according to their design. The following are general service procedures used on all carburetors.

1. Disassemble the carburetor. Carefully note the position of each part as it is removed. Place the parts in a small pan. A completely disassembled carburetor is shown in Fig. 15-4.

NOTE: This completely disassembled carburetor is shown for reference only. When overhauling a carburetor, disassemble it only as far as necessary for proper cleaning and replacement of defective parts.

2. Thoroughly clean the carburetor castings and metal parts in carburetor cleaner. Be sure that both the inside and outside of each casting are clean.

CAUTION: Do not splash cleaner in your eyes. It can seriously harm them. Wear goggles to protect your eyes.

NOTE: Never soak the pump plunger or any fiber or rubber parts in carburetor cleaner. Wipe these parts clean with a clean, dry shop towel.

3. Wash the parts carefully in hot water or kerosene, as recommended by the cleaner manufacturer. Blow off all parts until they are dry. Blow out all passages in the castings with compressed air. Make sure all jets and passages are clean.

CAUTION: Use the air hose with care. To be completely safe, wear goggles while blowing out the carburetor.

NOTE: Do not use drills or wires for cleaning out fuel passages or air bleeds. (This may enlarge the openings.) Instead, clean out the openings with a chemical cleaner.

4. Check all parts for damage and wear. If damage or wear is noted, replace the part or assembly. Check the float needle and seat for wear. Check the float hinge pin for wear, and the floats for dents and distortion. Shake metal floats to see if they have water or fuel in them. Power pistons that are scored or burned should be replaced. Check the throttle and choke-shaft bores for wear and out of round.
5. Inspect the idle-mixture adjusting needles for burrs and grooves. Either condition requires replacement of the needles. Inspect the accelerator-pump plunger cup. If the cup is damaged, worn, or hard, it must be replaced. Inspect the pump well in the fuel bowl for wear and scoring.

6. Check the fuel filter and fuel screen (if used) for dirt and lint. Check the automatic-choke housing for exhaust deposits and corrosion. Check the choke piston for free movement.

NOTE: A deposit or corrosion in the choke housing indicates a defective choke heat tube.

7. Carefully inspect the cluster assembly. If any parts are loose or damaged, replace the cluster assembly. Inspect all gasket mating surfaces for nicks and burrs. Repair any damage to the gasket mating surfaces. Inspect any remaining carburetor parts for damage and excessive looseness. Replace any parts that are worn, damaged, or excessively loose.
8. Reassemble the carburetor, in the proper order. Install all the gaskets and parts contained in the overhaul kit.

NOTE: Be sure your hands, workbench, and tools are really clean.

CAUTION: Gasoline and other solvents used in carburetor cleaning are highly flammable. Be extremely careful when you work around these flammable liquids.

⊘ 15-6 Carburetor Installation Use a new gasket to ensure a good seal between the carburetor and the mounting pad. Put the carburetor into position on the intake manifold, and attach it with the nuts or bolts. Connect the fuel line and the distributor vacuum-advance line to the carburetor. Use two wrenches, if necessary, to avoid damaging the lines or couplings. Connect the wires to switches and other electric controls (where present). Make the idle-speed, idle-mixture, and other adjustments described later in the chapter, depending on the specific model. Install the air cleaner.

NOTE: Fill the carburetor float bowl before installing the carburetor. This reduces the strain on the starting motor and battery. It also reduces the possibility of backfiring when the engine is started.

Check Your Progress

Progress Quiz 15-1 Now is your chance to stop and check how well you are progressing in Chap. 15. This chapter is an important one, since all automotive tuneup specialists should be familiar with carburetors—even if they don't specialize in carburetor work. The questions below will help you review the material you have just covered.

Completing the Sentences The sentences below are incomplete. After each sentence there are several words or phrases, but only one of them correctly completes the sentence. Write each sentence in your notebook, ending it with the one word or phrase that completes it correctly.

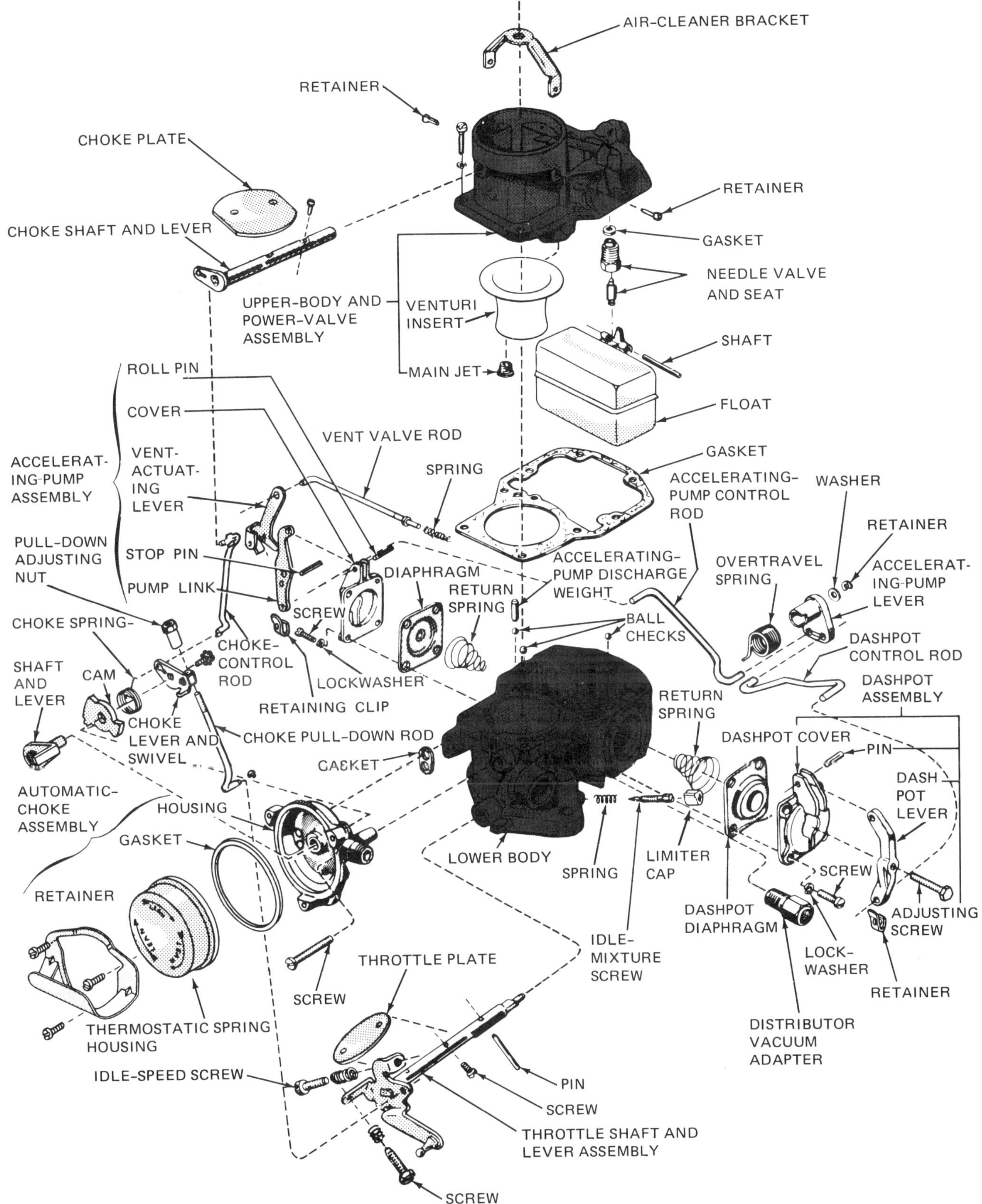

Fig. 15-4. Completely disassembled carburetor. (*Ford Motor Company*)

1. Careless cleaning of fuel nozzles can enlarge them and result in: (*a*) reduced fuel consumption, (*b*) a lean mixture, (*c*) excessive fuel consumption.
2. Dirt or gum in fuel nozzles or jets may cause: (*a*) excessive fuel consumption, (*b*) lack of engine power, (*c*) smoky black exhaust.
3. A high float level may cause: (*a*) excessive fuel consumption, (*b*) a lean mixture, (*c*) failure to start except when primed.
4. A choke valve that is stuck in the closed position may cause an: (*a*) overrich mixture cold, (*b*) overrich mixture hot, (*c*) excessively lean mixture.
5. A clogged fuel nozzle could result in: (*a*) excessive fuel consumption, (*b*) an overrich mixture, (*c*) a high float level, (*d*) failure to start except when primed.
6. A smoky black exhaust is probably due to a: (*a*) low float level, (*b*) very rich mixture, (*c*) very lean mixture, (*d*) clogged idle system.
7. The most common adjustments on the carburetor are: (*a*) idle mixture and idle speed, (*b*) float level and height, (*c*) main-nozzle richness and mixture.
8. When using a carburetor overhaul kit, you should: (*a*) use all the new parts, (*b*) replace only the worn parts, (*c*) replace the carburetor float bowl.

⊘ 15-7 Carburetor Servicing Instructions The carburetor service technician can get servicing instructions on specific carburetor models in two ways. First, the automobile manufacturer issues such instructions; they are found in the shop manual for each automobile. Second, there is an instruction sheet in every carburetor kit. For general servicing and for adjustments that do not require new parts, the service technician should consult the automobile shop manual. When new parts are required, an overhaul kit should be used; the instructions in the kit should be followed. Also, all the new parts in the kit should be used, to restore the carburetor to its original condition.

Figure 15-5 shows a widely used type of carburetor kit, called a "Jiffy Kit" by its manufacturer. The kit shown in Fig. 15-5 fits a Rochester two-barrel carburetor. It contains replacements for all the gaskets and seals, a needle and seat, an accelerator-pump plunger, limiter caps for the idle-mixture adjustment screws, and a package of clips, springs, and other small parts. A disposable gauge is included for making the very important float-level and float-drop adjustments.

To make disassembly and assembly of the carburetor easier, and to simplify making the necessary adjustments in their proper sequence, a detailed instruction sheet is also included. Always read and follow the instructions for the kit you are using. The same basic carburetor, but with some changes, may be used on different engines. Each engine application usually requires its own carburetor settings and specifications. They are all printed on the instruction sheet in the kit.

The following procedures are based on the carburetor servicing instructions found in manufacturers' shop manuals. A decal of the type shown in Fig. 15-2 is located in the engine compartment of every late-model vehicle. It gives specific anti-emission adjustments.

NOTE: Disassemble a carburetor no further than is necessary to clean or replace parts. Some parts, as noted later, should not be removed. They are a permanent part of the assembly.

NOTE: Use a separate clean-parts pan for the parts of each component. Thus, for example, you should put the accelerator-pump parts in one pan, the metering-rod-assembly parts in another, and so on, so as not to mix them up.

⊘ 15-8 Model YF1-V Carburetor Adjustments This carburetor is pictured in Fig. 15-6. Adjustments are as follows.

Fig. 15-5. Contents of a carburetor kit for a widely used two-barrel carburetor. (*Standard Motor Products, Inc.*)

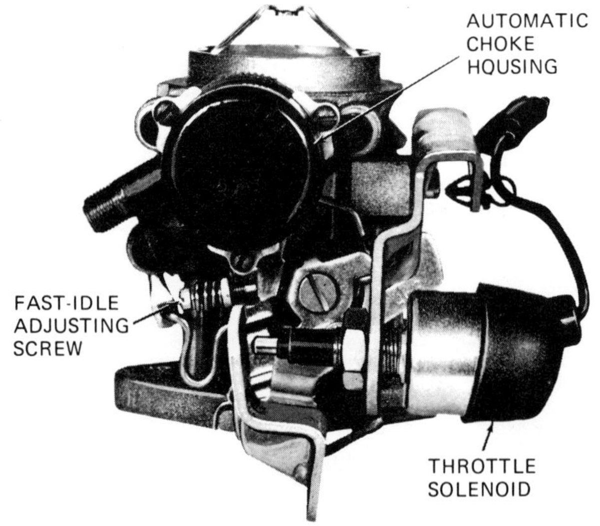

Fig. 15-6. Carburetor with a throttle solenoid. (*Ford Motor Company*)

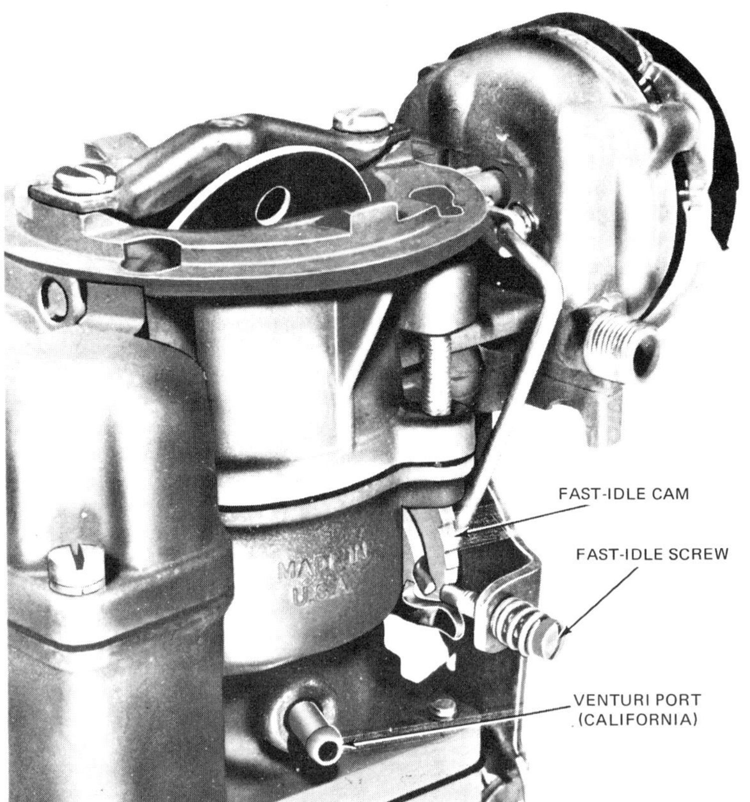

Fig. 15-7. Location of the fast-idle adjusting screw. (*Ford Motor Company*)

1. *FAST-IDLE ADJUSTMENT* Bring the engine to its operating temperature, and remove the air cleaner. Rotate the fast-idle cam to put the fast-idle screw on the high point of the cam (Fig. 15-7). Using a tachometer, adjust the fast idle to specifications by turning the fast-idle screw.
2. *ANTISTALL-DASHPOT ADJUSTMENT* Loosen the dashpot locknut. Hold the throttle in the hot-idle position, and depress the dashpot plunger with a screwdriver blade. Measure the clearance between the throttle lever and plunger tip. Adjust to specifications by turning the antistall dashpot in the correct direction. Tighten the locknut.
3. *AUTOMATIC-CHOKE ADJUSTMENT* This carburetor has the automatic choke mounted on it. Adjustment is made by loosening the clamp screw and turning the spring housing.
4. *DECHOKE ADJUSTMENT* With the air cleaner removed, hold the throttle wide open. Close the choke plate as far as possible without forcing it. Check the clearance between the choke plate and the air horn with a drill of the correct size (Fig. 15-8). Bend the arm on the choke trip lever of the throttle lever to make the adjustment.
5. *CHOKE-PLATE PULLDOWN* Remove the air cleaner and choke-spring housing. Bend a 0.026-in [0.660-mm] wire at a 90° angle, about $\frac{1}{8}$ in [3.175 mm] from one end. Insert the bent end of the wire between the choke-piston slot and the right-hand slot in the choke housing (Fig. 15-9). Rotate the choke-piston lever counterclockwise until the gauge is snug in the piston slot. Press on the choke-piston lever to hold the wire in place. Then check the clearance of

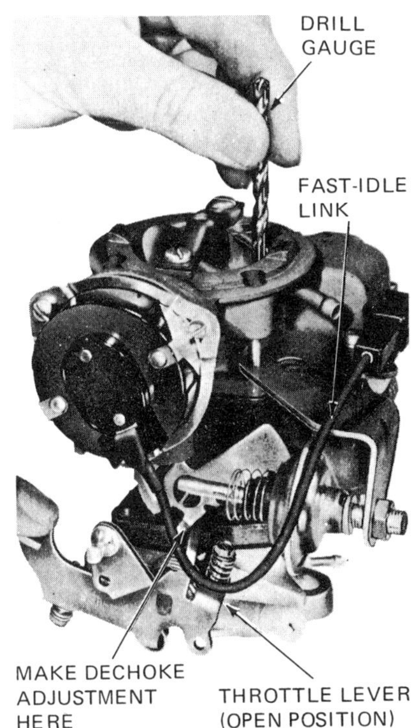

Fig. 15-8. Choke-plate clearance adjustment. (*Ford Motor Company*)

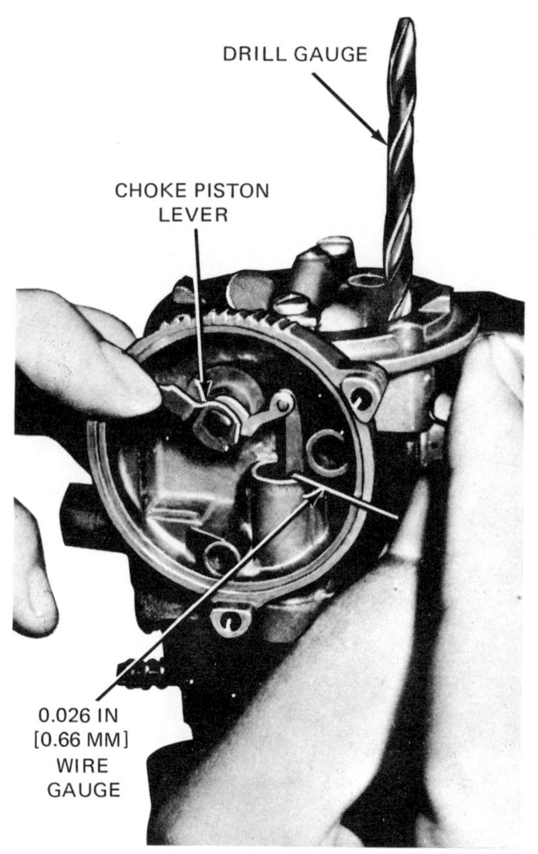

Fig. 15-9. Choke-plate pulldown-clearance adjustment. (*Ford Motor Company*)

the choke plate with a drill of the proper size (Fig. 15-9). To adjust the clearance, bend the choke-piston lever.

6. FAST-IDLE-CAM SETTING Position the fast-idle screw on the kickdown step of the fast-idle cam, against the shoulder of the high step of the cam. Check the clearance between the choke plate and the air horn. Adjust the clearance by bending the choke-plate connecting rod.

7. METERING-ROD ADJUSTMENT Remove the air cleaner, air horn, and gasket. Back out the idle-speed adjusting screw until the throttle plate is closed tightly in the throttle bore. Press down on the end of the pump-diaphragm shaft until the assembly bottoms. Hold the assembly in this position, and turn the rod adjustment screw (Fig. 15-10) until the rod just bottoms in the body casting. Turn the screw one additional turn for final adjustment. Reinstall the air horn, with gasket, and the air cleaner.

8. FLOAT-LEVEL ADJUSTMENT Remove and invert the air horn. Check the clearance between the float and the air horn with a gauge of the proper width (Fig. 15-11). Bend the float arm to adjust the clearance. Do not put any pressure on the needle valve! Do not bend the tab on the float arm.

9. FLOAT-DROP ADJUSTMENT Remove the air horn. Check the clearance between the float and the air horn with the air horn in the upright position. To adjust the clearance, bend the tab on the end of the float arm.

⊘ 15-9 Model YF1-V Carburetor Overhaul Figure 15-12 shows a completely disassembled view of the model YF1-V carburetor. The disassembly procedure is relatively easy if the picture is followed. Several components can be removed from the carburetor without complete disassembly. Here is the

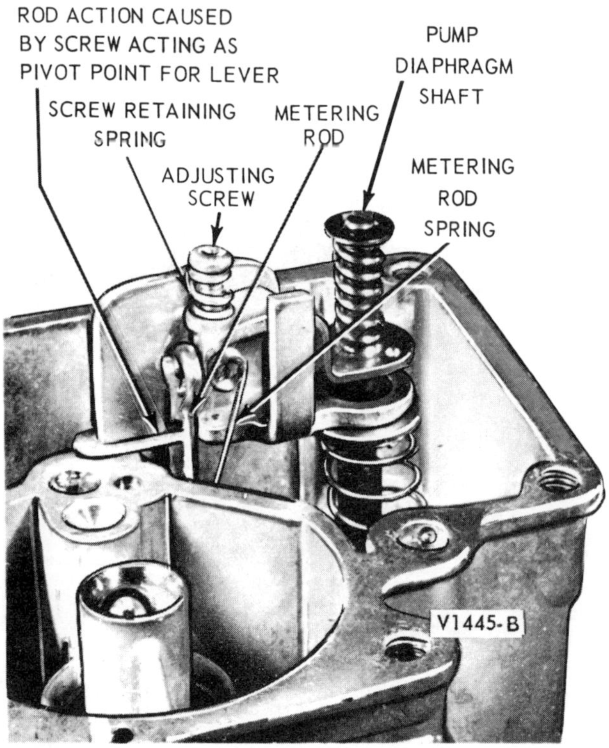

Fig. 15-10. Metering-rod adjustment. (*Ford Motor Company*)

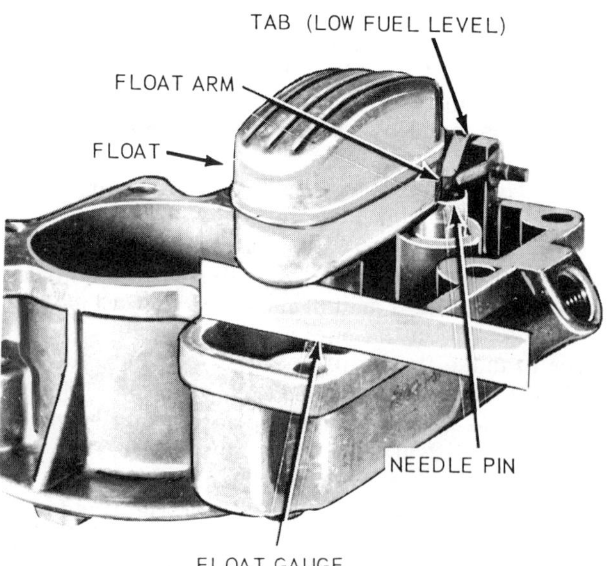

Fig. 15-11. Fuel float-level adjustment. (*Ford Motor Company*)

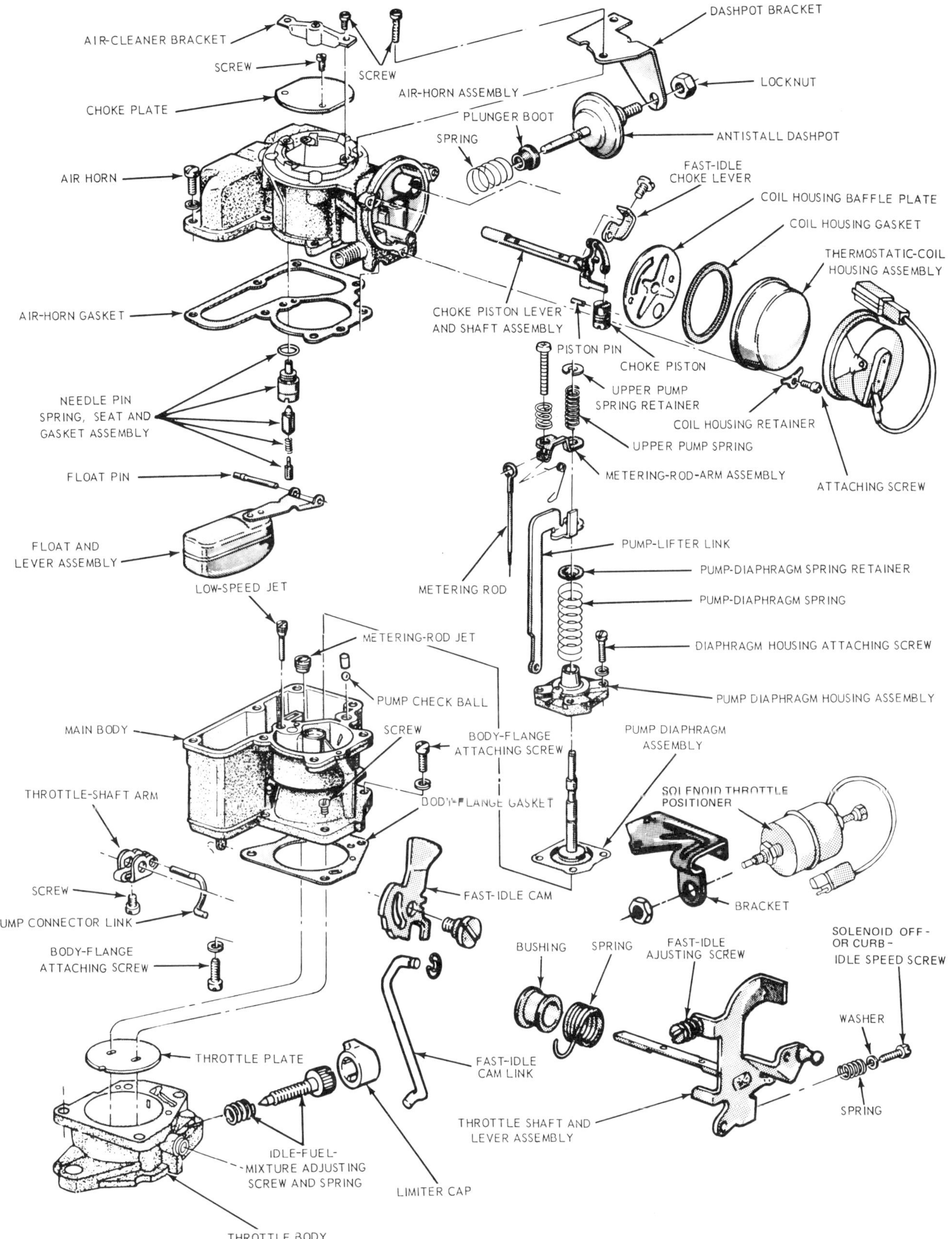

Fig. 15-12. Disassembled view of the model YF1-V carburetor. (*Ford Motor Company*)

order to follow when completely disassembling the carburetor.

1. Remove the thermostatic-spring housing, gasket, baffle, and fast-idle link.
2. Remove the air horn and related parts. Hold the air horn upside down, and remove the float pin and float. Turn the air horn right side up, and catch the needle pin, spring, and needle as they fall out. Remove the needle seat and gasket if necessary.
3. Remove the air-cleaner bracket so you can get to the choke-plate screws (if the choke plate must be removed). Staked screw ends must be filed off; new screws must be used for reassembly.
4. Turn the main body upside down, and catch the accelerator-pump check ball and weight. Remove the throttle-shaft-arm screws, the arm, and the connector link.
5. Remove the fast-idle cam and screw.
6. Remove the accelerator-pump diaphragm-housing screws. Lift out the diaphragm housing and related parts as a unit (Fig. 15-13). Disassemble this, if necessary. Note the positions of the washers shimming either spring, so they can be restored to their original positions. If the main and low-speed jets need replacement, remove them with the proper size screwdriver or jet tool.
7. If necessary, the throttle plate can be removed from the throttle shaft by filing the staked ends off the screws. New screws must be used for reassembly.
8. If you remove the idle-mixture adjustment screw, take off the limiter cap. Then turn the screw in to seat it lightly. Count the exact number of turns required. Then remove the screw.
9. The reassembly procedure is approximately the reverse of disassembly. Follow the picture (Fig. 15-12). If the throttle plate has been removed, reinstall it so that the throttle-plate notch is lined up with the slotted idle port (Fig. 15-14). Make sure the torsion spring is in its original position. Back out the idle-speed adjustment screw so that the throttle can close completely. Count the number of turns required. Make sure the throttle plate is centered in the bore. Tighten and stake the new throttle-plate screws.

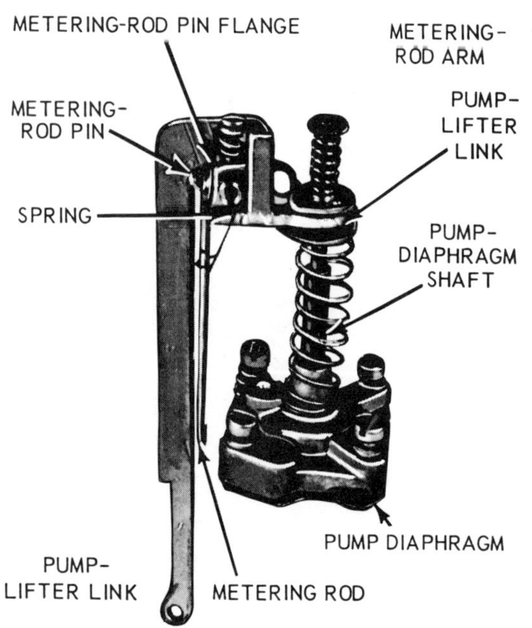

Fig. 15-13. Accelerator-pump and lifter-link assembly. (*Ford Motor Company*)

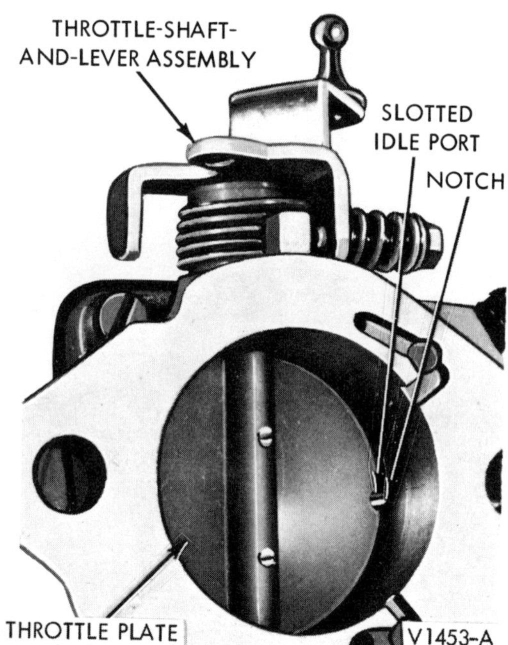

Fig. 15-14. Throttle-plate and shaft-and-lever installation. (*Ford Motor Company*)

Install the idle-mixture screw, turning it in until it is lightly seated. Then back it off the exact number of turns you counted when you removed the screw. Install the limiter cap in its original position.

After completing the assembly, make the adjustments covered in ⊘ 15-8.

⊘ 15-10 Model BBD Carburetor Overhaul The model BBD carburetor is pictured in Fig. 15-15. It is a two-barrel carburetor with a vacuum-choke diaphragm and a thermostatic coil mounted in a well in the intake manifold. In the overhaul procedure that follows, we cover some of the carburetor adjustments.

1. Put the carburetor on a repair stand so that you won't damage the unit. Remove the parts shown in Figs. 15-16 and 15-17. Lift the vacuum piston and rods out as a unit (Fig. 15-18). Remove the vacuum hose.
2. Remove the choke-vacuum diaphragm (dashpot), and set it aside to be cleaned separately. This assembly can be ruined if it is cleaned in a liquid cleaner.
3. Remove the fast-idle cam and linkage. Remove the air horn, lifting it straight up and away from the main body (Fig. 15-19). Discard the gasket.
4. Invert the air horn, and compress the accelera-

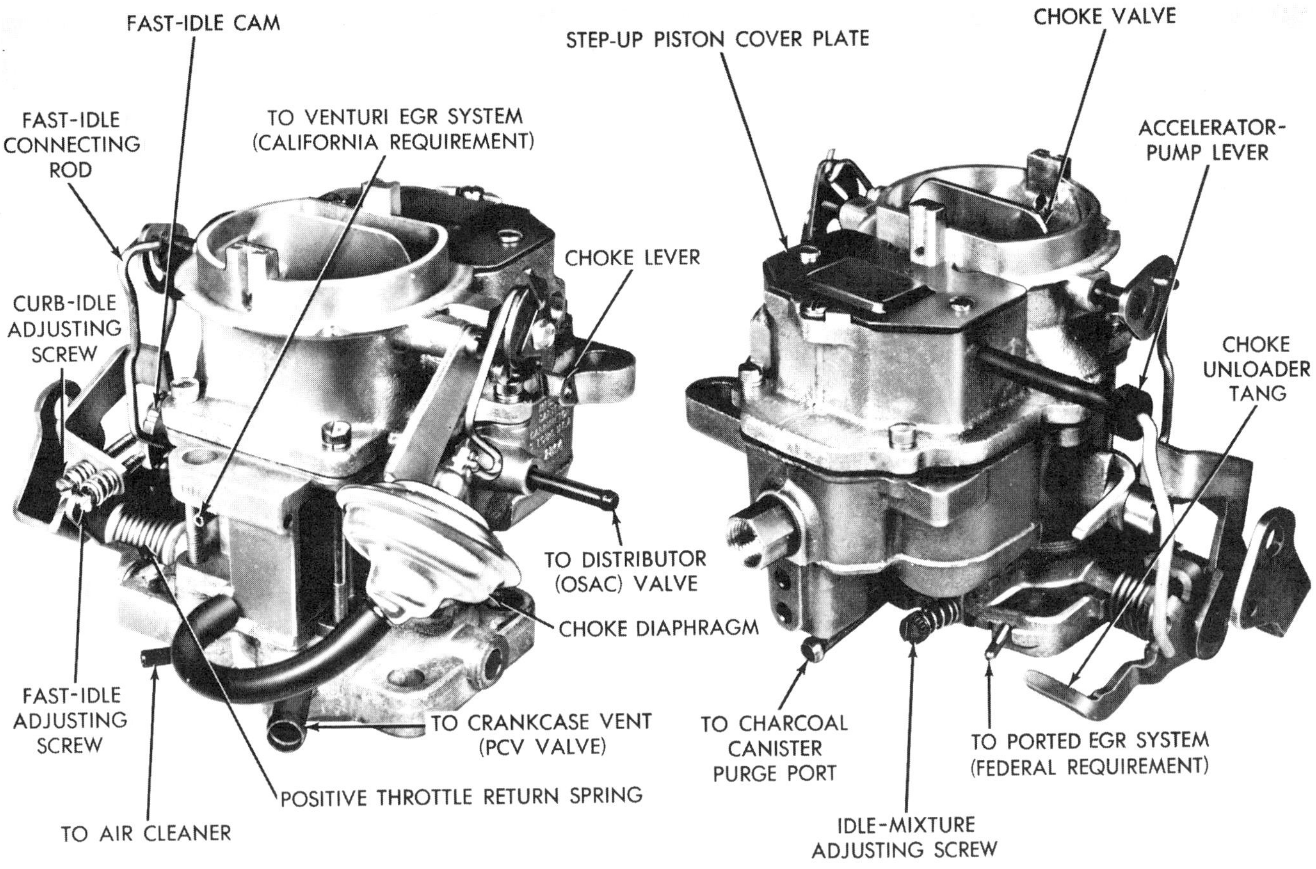

FAST-IDLE CAM
FAST-IDLE CONNECTING ROD
TO VENTURI EGR SYSTEM (CALIFORNIA REQUIREMENT)
CURB-IDLE ADJUSTING SCREW
CHOKE LEVER
TO DISTRIBUTOR (OSAC) VALVE
CHOKE DIAPHRAGM
FAST-IDLE ADJUSTING SCREW
TO CRANKCASE VENT (PCV VALVE)
POSITIVE THROTTLE RETURN SPRING
TO AIR CLEANER
STEP-UP PISTON COVER PLATE
CHOKE VALVE
ACCELERATOR-PUMP LEVER
CHOKE UNLOADER TANG
TO CHARCOAL CANISTER PURGE PORT
TO PORTED EGR SYSTEM (FEDERAL REQUIREMENT)
IDLE-MIXTURE ADJUSTING SCREW

Fig. 15-15. Dual carburetor, Carter Model BBD. (*Chrysler Corporation*)

STEP-UP PISTON ASSEMBLY
PUMP-ARM LOCK SCREW
ACCELERATOR-PUMP SHAFT
ROD-LIFTER LOCK SCREW
GASKET
COVER PLATE

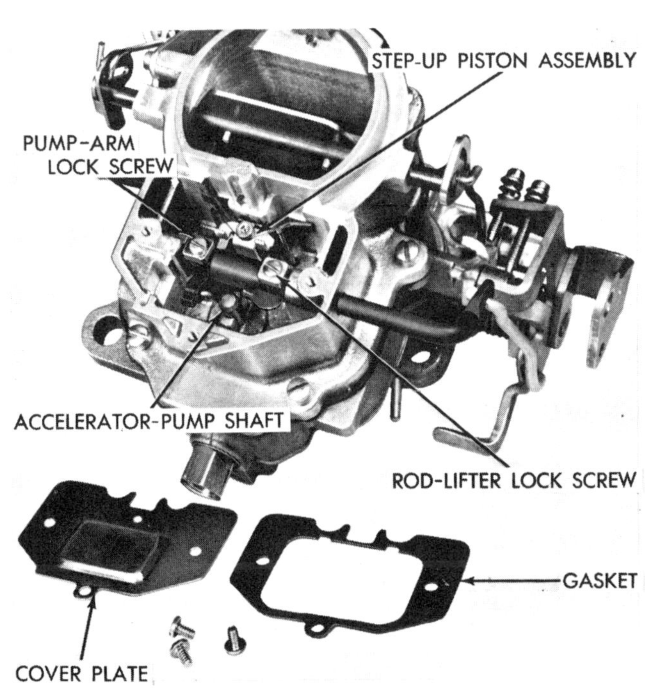

Fig. 15-16. Carter BBD carburetor, partly disassembled. (*Chrysler Corporation*)

ACCELERATOR-PUMP LINK
RETAINER
PUMP ARM
ROD LIFTER
SCREW AND LOCKS
ACCELERATOR-PUMP LEVER

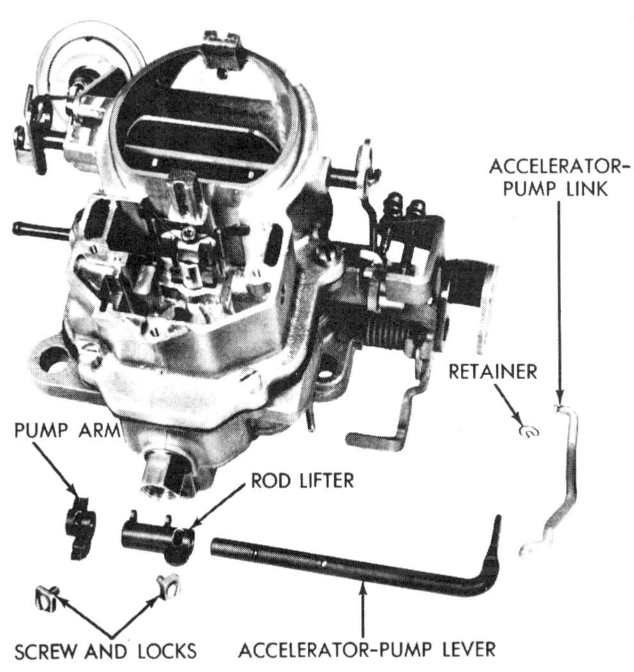

Fig. 15-17. Carter BBD carburetor with accelerator-pump lever and associated parts removed. (*Chrysler Corporation*)

Fig. 15-18. Removing or installing the step-up-piston assembly. (*Chrysler Corporation*)

tor-pump spring. Remove the S link from the pump shaft so that the pump assembly can be removed.
5. Remove the fuel-inlet needle valve, seat, and gasket from the main body. Lift out the floats and pivot pin. Remove the venturi cluster as an assembly (Fig. 15-20). Discard the gaskets. Do not try to disassemble this cluster. It can be cleaned in solvent.
6. Invert the carburetor, and drop out the pump discharge and intake check balls (Fig. 15-21).
7. Turn the idle-mixture limiter cap to stops. Remove the caps. Turn the screws in slowly to seat them gently, counting the number of turns required. Then remove the screws. Separate the throttle body from the main body.

To reassemble the carburetor, reverse the disassembly procedure. Also note the following special points.

If the bearing surfaces for the throttle shaft are worn, the throttle body must be replaced.

To install the idle-mixture screws and springs, turn them in with your fingers to gently seat them. Then back them off the exact number of turns required to seat them during disassembly. Install new limiter caps with the tabs against the stops.

Install the throttle body on the main body. Install the check balls (Fig. 15-21).

Check the accelerator-pump system by pouring about ½ in [12.7 mm] of fuel into the float bowl (Fig. 15-22). Slide the pump plunger down into the pump cylinder. Raise the plunger, and press lightly on the shaft to expel air from the pump passage. Then use a small brass rod (Fig. 15-22) to hold the discharge check ball down on its seat. Again raise the plunger and press it down. No fuel should be emitted from either the intake or the discharge passage. If fuel does discharge, the ball or seat is damaged or dirty. It should be cleaned or replaced.

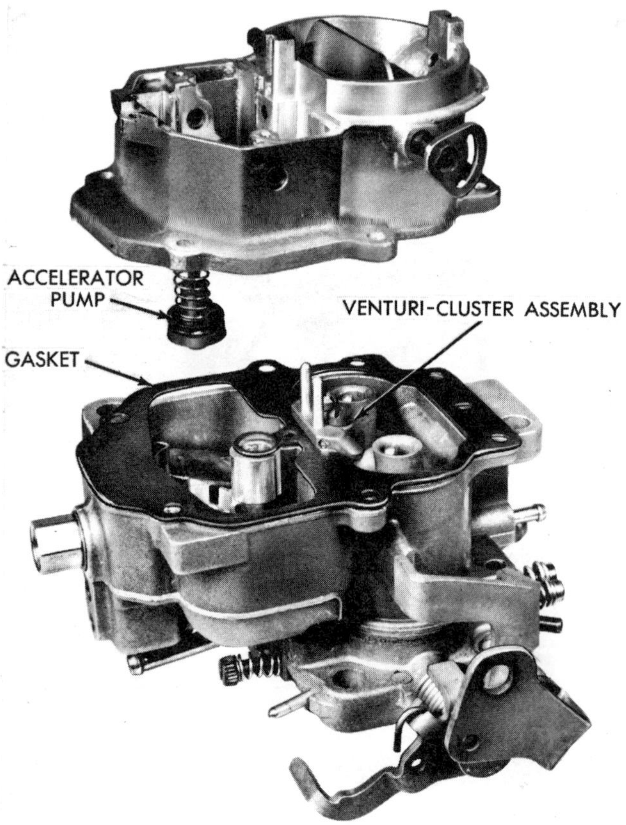

Fig. 15-19. Removing or installing the air horn. (*Chrysler Corporation*)

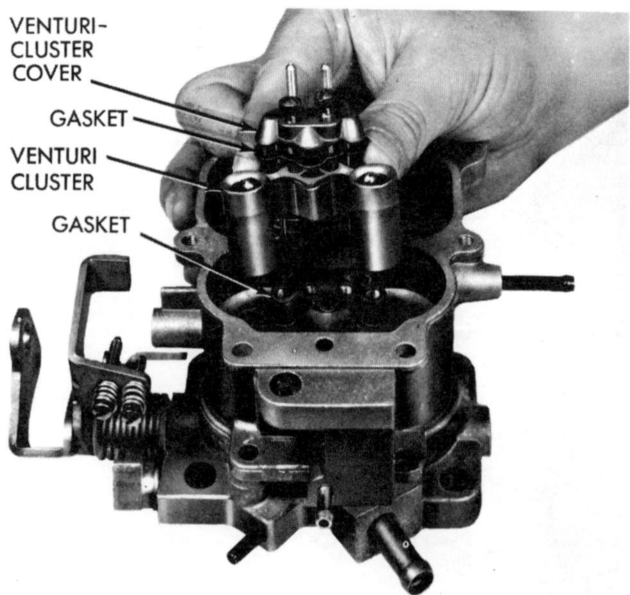

Fig. 15-20. Removing or installing the venturi cluster. (*Chrysler Corporation*)

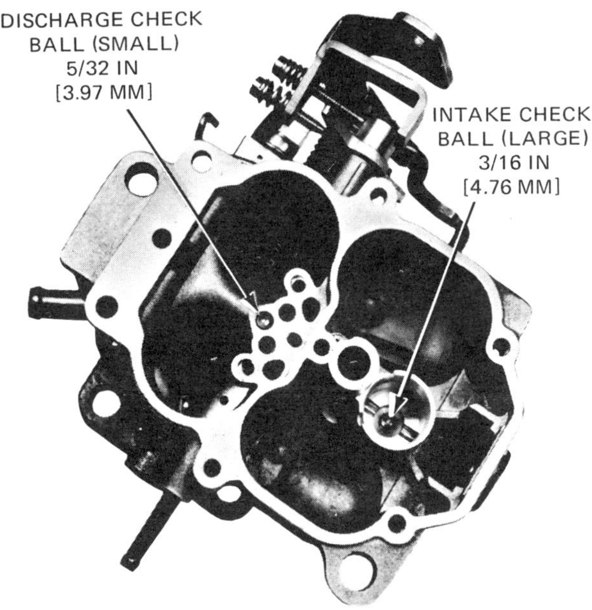

Fig. 15-21. Installing the accelerator-pump intake and discharge check balls. (*Chrysler Corporation*)

Install the venturi cluster with a new gasket.

Check the float setting after installing it and the needle, seat, and gasket (Fig. 15-23). Invert the float bowl as shown, and use the gauge as shown to check the drop. Adjust the drop by bending the float lip.

Install the accelerator pump, with its spring and the S link, in the air horn. Drop the intake ball into the pump bore. Install the step-up piston spring. Using a new gasket, attach the air horn to the main body. Check the gap in the vacuum piston (Fig. 15-24), and adjust it if necessary. Install this assembly, making sure the metering rods are in the metering jets. Now insert the two locks and adjusting screws.

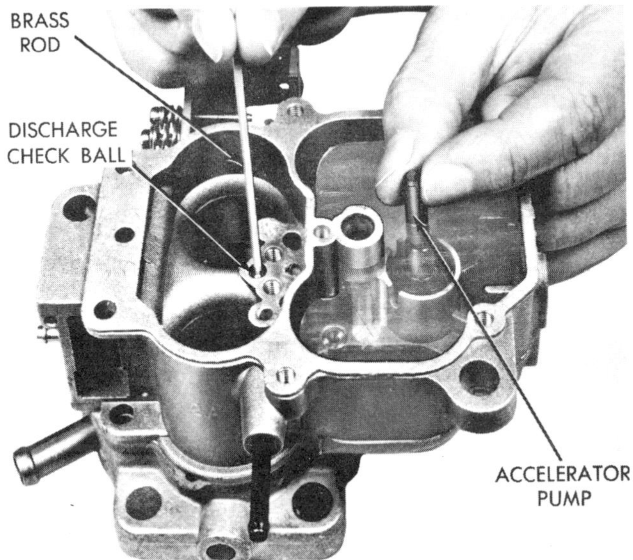

Fig. 15-22. Testing the accelerator-pump intake and discharge check balls. (*Chrysler Corporation*)

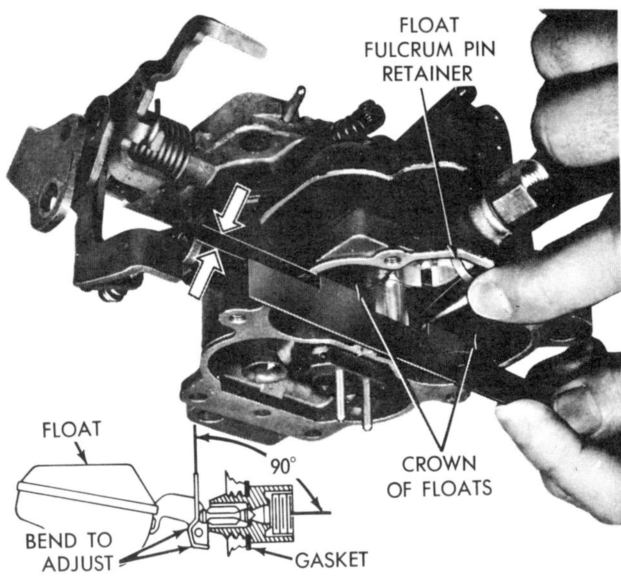

Fig. 15-23. Checking the float setting. (*Chrysler Corporation*)

Install the fast-idle cam and linkage. Connect the accelerator-pump link to the pump lever and throttle lever.

Check the choke-vacuum diaphragm (dashpot) by pushing the stem in and then putting your finger over the vacuum fitting to seal the opening. Release the stem. If the stem moves more than $\frac{1}{16}$ in [1.588 mm] in 10 seconds, the diaphragm is defective. If the diaphragm is okay, install it, first attaching the choke link. Do not attach the hose until the diaphragm is adjusted.

⊘ 15-11 Model BBD Carburetor Adjustments In addition to adjustments made while the carburetor is being assembled, the following adjustments are required.

1. *VACUUM STEP-UP-PISTON ADJUSTMENT* Figure 15-24 shows the preliminary adjustment.

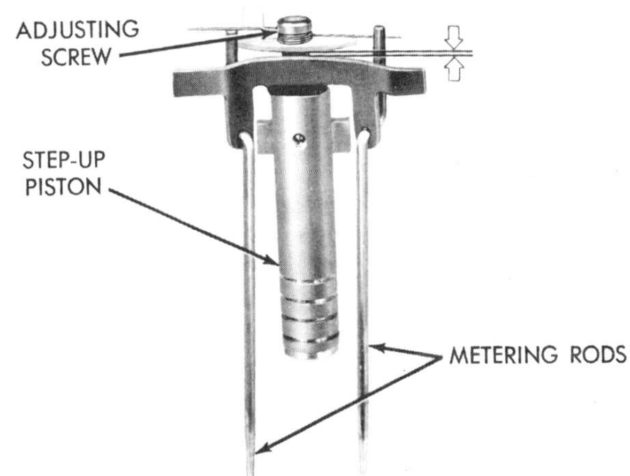

Fig. 15-24. Step-up-piston adjustment. (*Chrysler Corporation*)

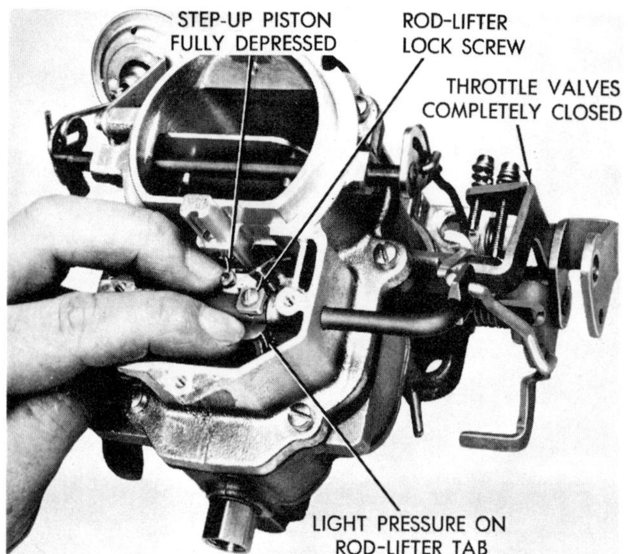

Fig. 15-25. Checking the step-up piston with the piston installed. (*Chrysler Corporation*)

After installation, back off the idle-speed adjustment screw to let the throttle close completely. Count the number of turns. Push the piston down all the way while holding moderate pressure on the lifter tab (Fig. 15-25). Tighten the lockscrew. Return the idle-speed adjustment screw to its original setting.

2. *ACCELERATOR-PUMP ADJUSTMENT* Back off the idle-speed adjustment screw to close the throttle. Open the choke valve so that the fast-idle cam allows the throttle valve to close completely. Turn in the idle-speed adjustment screw, until it just touches the stop. Then turn it in two more turns. Measure the distance between the surface of the air horn and the top of the accelerator-pump shaft. To adjust it, loosen the pump-arm adjusting lockscrew. Rotate the sleeve until the proper adjustment is obtained. Then tighten the lockscrew.

3. *FAST-IDLE-CAM POSITION ADJUSTMENT* Move the idle-speed adjustment screw until it is touching the second highest step on the fast-idle cam. Move the choke valve toward the closed position with light pressure. Insert a gauge of the correct size between the choke valve and the air horn. If adjustment is needed, bend the fast-idle connector rod (Fig. 15-26).

4. *DASHPOT ADJUSTMENT* Connect a vacuum source to the dashpot. Push up on the lever to close the choke valve (Fig. 15-27). Check the clearance between the choke plate and the air horn. Adjust the clearance by bending the link at the point shown. A screwdriver twisted in the U will lengthen the link. Squeezing the U together with pliers will shorten the link.

5. *CHOKE UNLOADER* The choke unloader opens the choke at wide-open throttle. With the throttle wide open, check the choke opening by placing a gauge between the choke plate and the air horn. If necessary, adjust the opening by bending the unloader tang on the throttle lever.

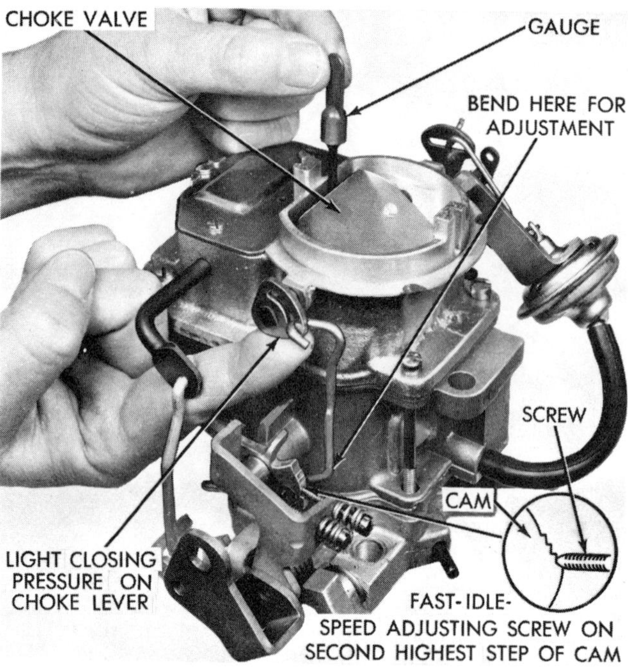

Fig. 15-26. Fast-idle-cam position adjustment. (*Chrysler Corporation*)

6. *IDLE AND FAST-IDLE SPEEDS* These are adjusted in the same way as on other carburetors. The engine must be warmed up.

⊘ 15-12 Rochester 4MV Carburetor Service This section describes the overhaul of the carburetor. The carburetor systems are shown in Fig. 15-28. The car-

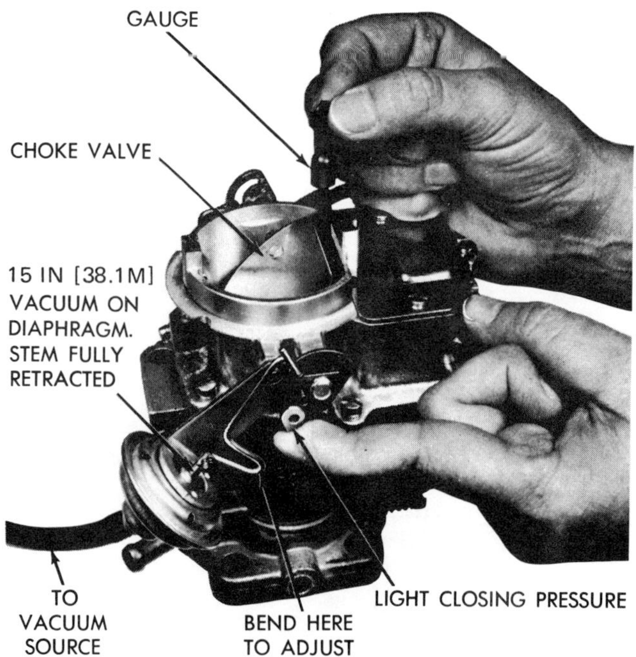

Fig. 15-27. Adjusting the choke vacuum kick. (*Chrysler Corporation*)

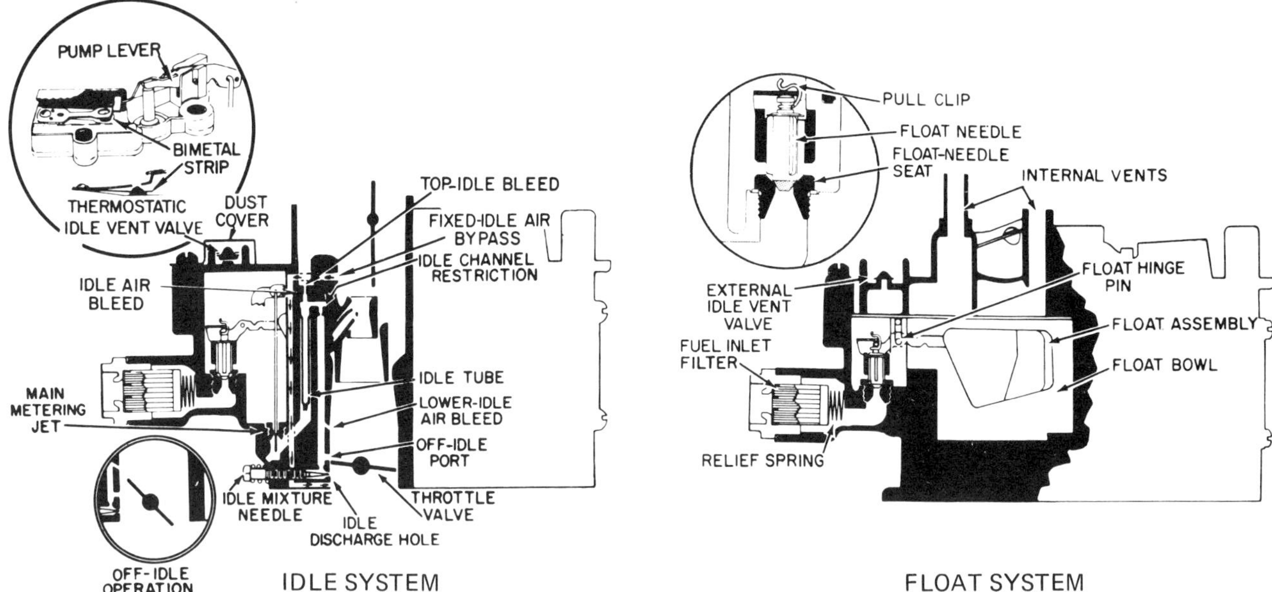

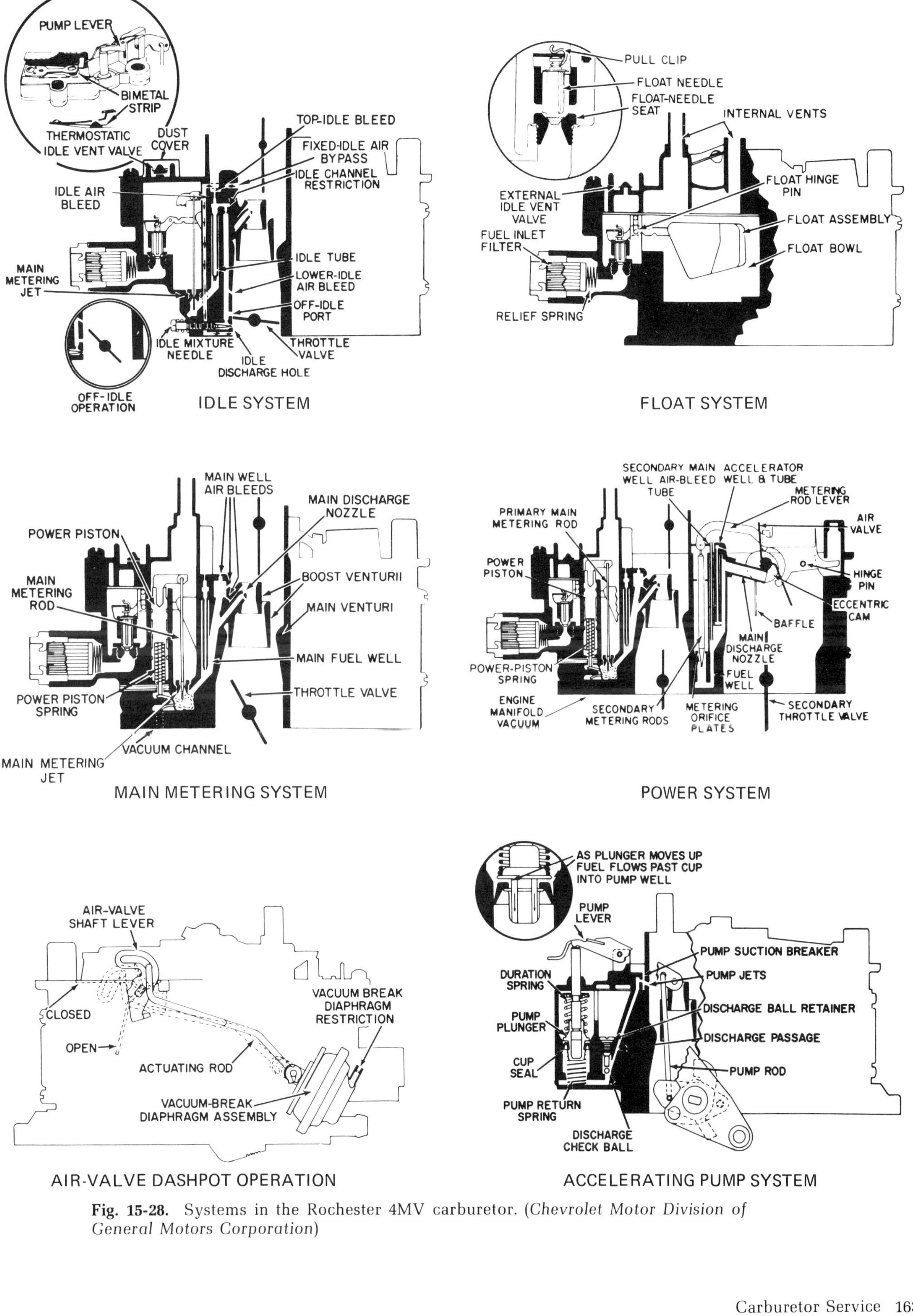

IDLE SYSTEM

FLOAT SYSTEM

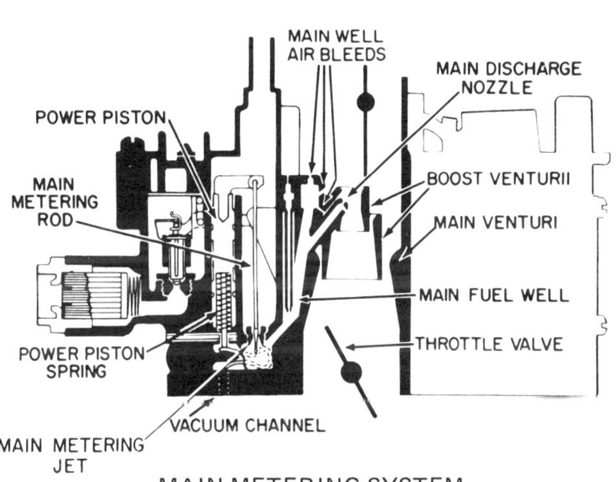

MAIN METERING SYSTEM

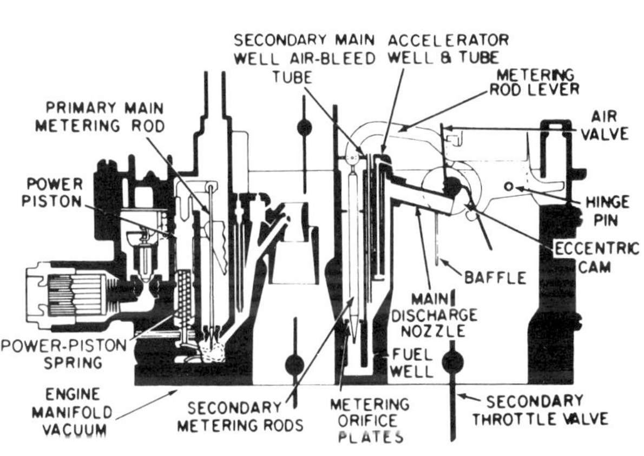

POWER SYSTEM

AIR-VALVE SHAFT LEVER
CLOSED
OPEN
ACTUATING ROD
VACUUM BREAK DIAPHRAGM RESTRICTION
VACUUM-BREAK DIAPHRAGM ASSEMBLY

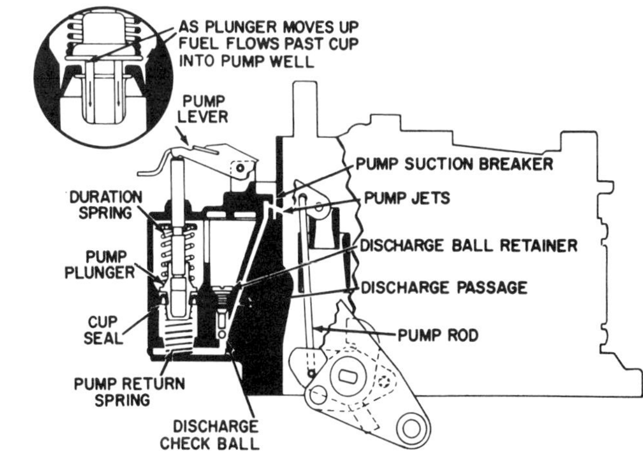

AIR-VALVE DASHPOT OPERATION

ACCELERATING PUMP SYSTEM

Fig. 15-28. Systems in the Rochester 4MV carburetor. (*Chevrolet Motor Division of General Motors Corporation*)

buretor should be mounted in a holding fixture, as shown in Fig. 15-31.

Disassembly

1. *REMOVING THE AIR HORN (FIG. 15-29)* Remove the idle-vent-valve assembly by removing the screw. Remove the choke rod by removing the clips and disconnecting the rod from the shaft lever. Disconnect the pump from the pump lever by removing the spring clip from the upper end of the pump rod. Remove the nine attaching screws (four long, three short, two countersunk). Lift the air horn off the float bowl.

CAUTION: Do not bend the two small main-well air-bleed tubes protruding from the air horn. These are pressed into the casting and must not be removed.

2. *DISASSEMBLING THE AIR HORN* There is very little to the disassembly of the air horn (Fig. 15-29). The secondary metering rods are removed while the air valve is held wide open. Tilt the rods and slide them from the holes. If the choke valve must be removed, remove the screws attaching it to the shaft.

CAUTION: The air valve and air-valve shaft are calibrated and must not be removed.

3. *DISASSEMBLING THE FLOAT BOWL (FIG. 15-30)* Remove the pump plunger from the pump well. Remove the air-horn gasket, the pump-return spring from the pump well, the plastic filler over the float valve, and the power piston and primary metering rods. Use needle-nose pliers, as shown in Fig. 15-31, and pull straight up on the metering-rod hanger. Then remove the power-piston spring from the well.

Detach the metering rods from the power piston (if necessary) by disconnecting the tension springs. Remove the float assembly by pulling up slightly on the retaining pin until the pin can be removed by

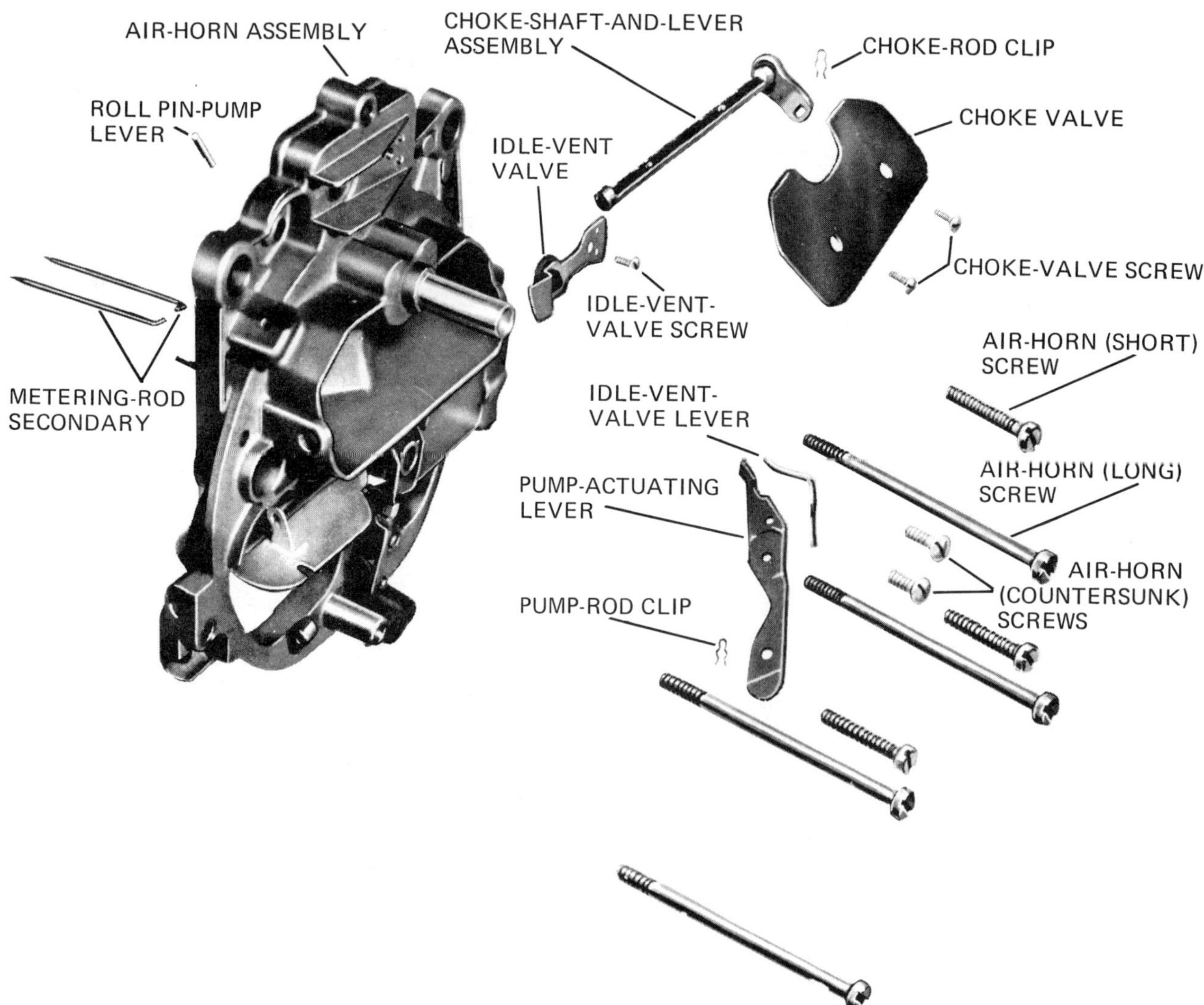

Fig. 15-29. Disassembled view of an air horn. (*Chevrolet Motor Division of General Motors Corporation*)

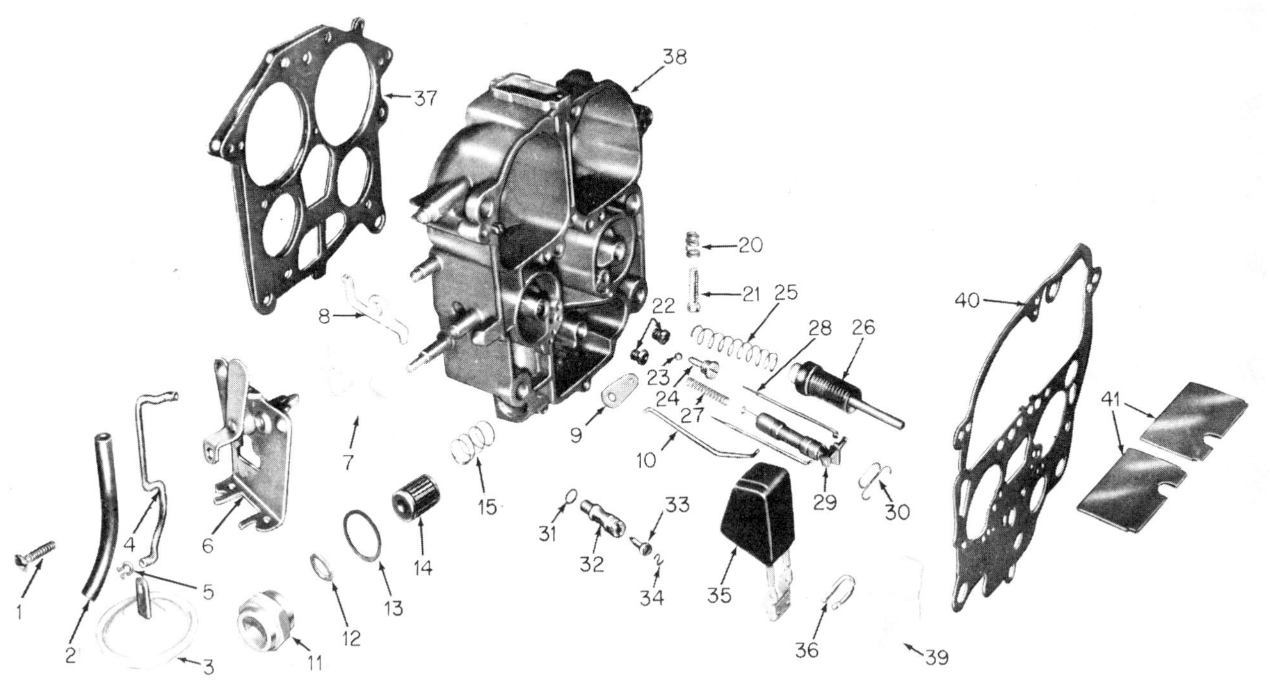

1. CHOKE-CONTROL SCREW
2. VACUUM-BREAK HOSE
3. VACUUM BREAK
4. VACUUM-BREAK LINK
5. VACUUM-BREAK-ROD CLIP
6. CHOKE-CONTROL BRACKET ASSEMBLY
7. FAST-IDLE CAM
8. SECONDARY LOCK-OUT LEVER
9. CHOKE INTERMEDIATE LEVER
10. CHOKE ROD
11. FUEL-INLET NUT
12. FUEL-FILTER GASKET
13. FUEL-INLET-NUT GASKET
14. FUEL-INLET FILTER
15. FUEL-FILTER SPRING
20. IDLE-SPEED-SCREW SPRING
21. IDLE-SPEED SCREW
22. PRIMARY JET
23. PUMP-DISCHARGE BALL
24. PUMP-DISCHARGE-BALL RETAINER
25. PUMP-RETURN SPRING
26. PUMP ASSEMBLY
27. POWER-PISTON SPRING
28. PRIMARY METERING-ROD
29. PRIMARY POWER-PISTON ASSEMBLY
30. METERING-ROD-PRIMARY SPRING
31. FLOAT-NEEDLE-SEAT GASKET
32. FLOAT-NEEDLE SEAT
33. FLOAT NEEDLE
34. FLOAT-NEEDLE PULL CLIP
35. FLOAT ASSEMBLY
36. FLOAT-ASSEMBLY HINGE PIN
37. THROTTLE-BODY GASKET
38. FLOAT-BOWL ASSEMBLY
39. FLOAT-BOWL INSERT
40. AIR-HORN GASKET
41. FLOAT-BOWL BAFFLE

Fig. 15-30. Disassembled view of a float bowl. (*Chevrolet Motor Division of General Motors Corporation*)

sliding it toward the pump well. Then slide the float assembly toward the front of the bowl to disengage the needle pull clip. Do not bend the clip.

Remove the pull clip and float needle. If the seat requires replacement, remove it with a wide-blade screwdriver. Discard the seat gasket. The primary metering jets can be removed, but do not remove the secondary metering disks.

Continue the disassembly by removing the pump-discharge check-ball retainer and ball, the baffles from the secondary side of the bowl, and the vacuum-break hose. Remove the choke-control bracket-assembly retaining screw and choke assembly, and then the secondary lockout link. The fast-idle cam can now be removed from the choke bracket.

Remove the choke rod and lever from the float-bowl well. Remove the fuel-inlet-filter nut and gasket, the filter, and the spring. Finally, detach the throttle body by removing the attaching screws. Remove the gaskets.

4. DISASSEMBLING THE THROTTLE BODY (*FIG. 15-32*) Follow the illustration to remove parts from the throttle body. Use great care to avoid damaging the secondary throttle valves.

Cleaning and Inspection

Clean the metal parts in an approved cold-immersion cleaner. Do not immerse the rubber or plastic parts, diaphragms, vacuum-break assembly, or pump plungers in the cleaner. It could ruin these parts.

Blow out all passages in the castings with com-

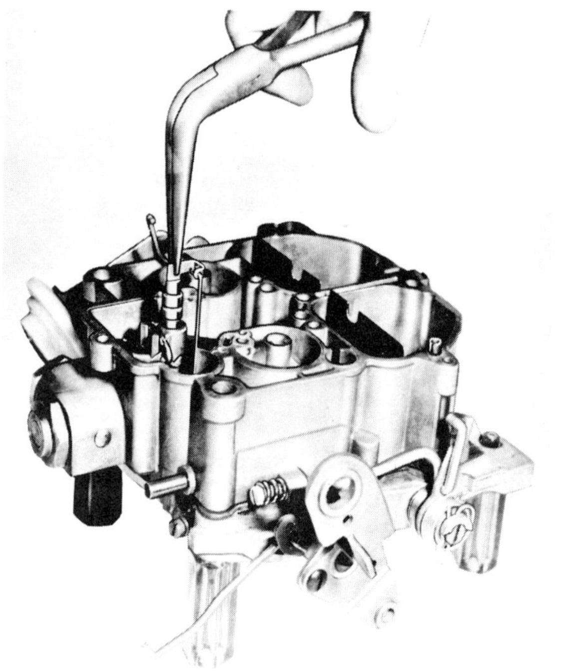

Fig. 15-31. Removing the power piston. (*Chevrolet Motor Division of General Motors Corporation*)

pressed air. Never use drills to clean the jets or passages; this could ruin their calibration. Examine the float needle and seat. If either is worn or damaged, replace both. Make sure the holes in the levers are not worn, and that the air valve is free. If it binds or is damaged, replace the air-horn assembly.

Assembly

1. *THROTTLE BODY* Install the idle-mixture needles and springs. Turn the needles in until they seat; then back them off two turns as a preliminary adjustment. Install the pump rod in the hole in the throttle lever.

2. *FLOAT BOWL (FIG. 15-30)* Install new throttle-body-to-bowl gaskets over the dowels on the bowl. Attach the throttle body with the screws. Place the assembly on the holding fixture (Fig. 15-31). Install the fuel-inlet-filter spring, the filter, a new gasket, and the inlet nut. Tighten the nut securely. Install the fast-idle cam on the vacuum-break assembly. Make sure the fast-idle-cam pickup lever on the intermediate choke shaft is located in the cut-out area of the fast-idle cam.

Connect the choke rod to the choke-rod actuating lever (plain end). Then hold the choke rod with the grooved end pointing inward. Position the choke-rod actuating lever in the well of the float bowl, and install the choke assembly. Be sure to engage the shaft with the hole in the actuating lever

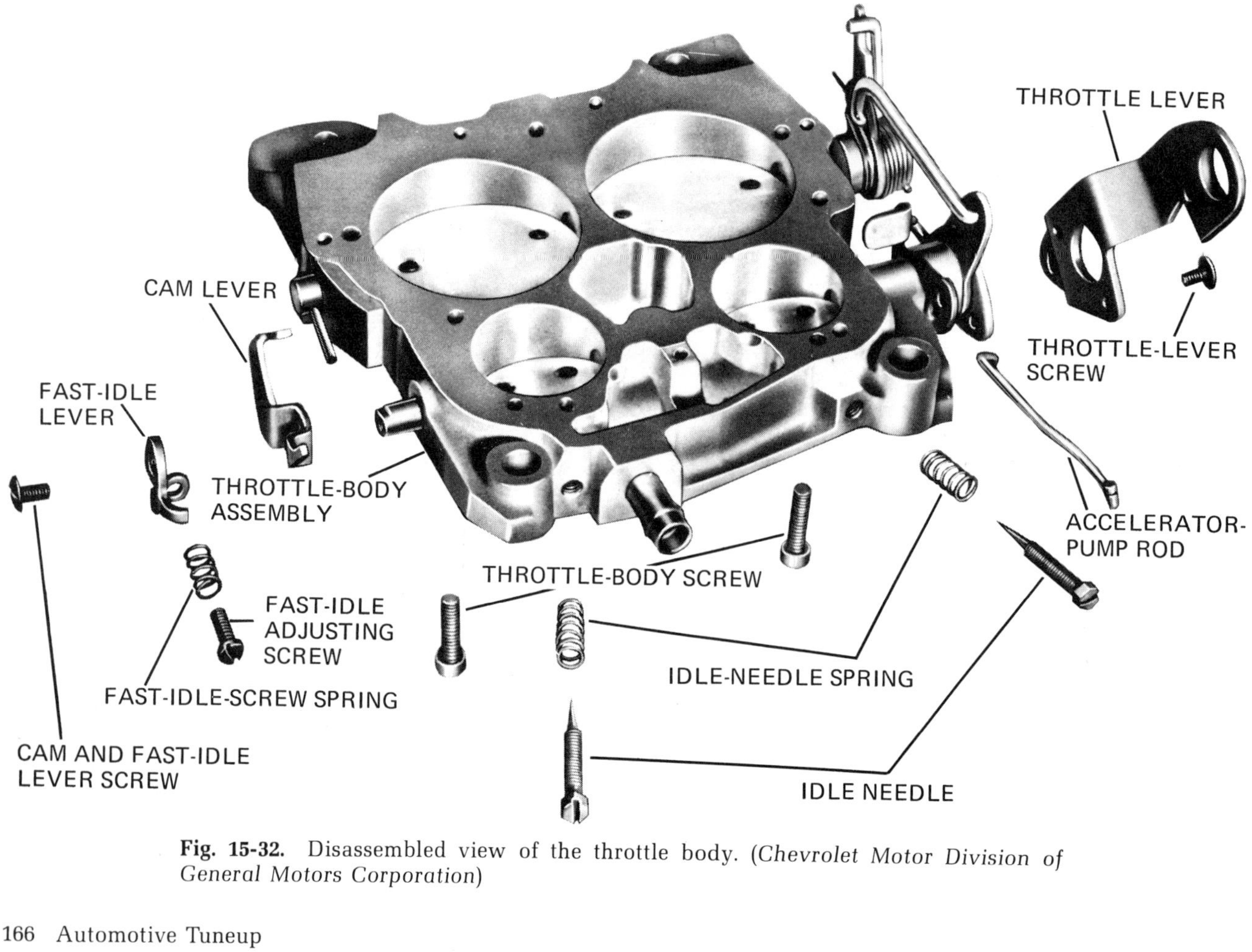

Fig. 15-32. Disassembled view of the throttle body. (*Chevrolet Motor Division of General Motors Corporation*)

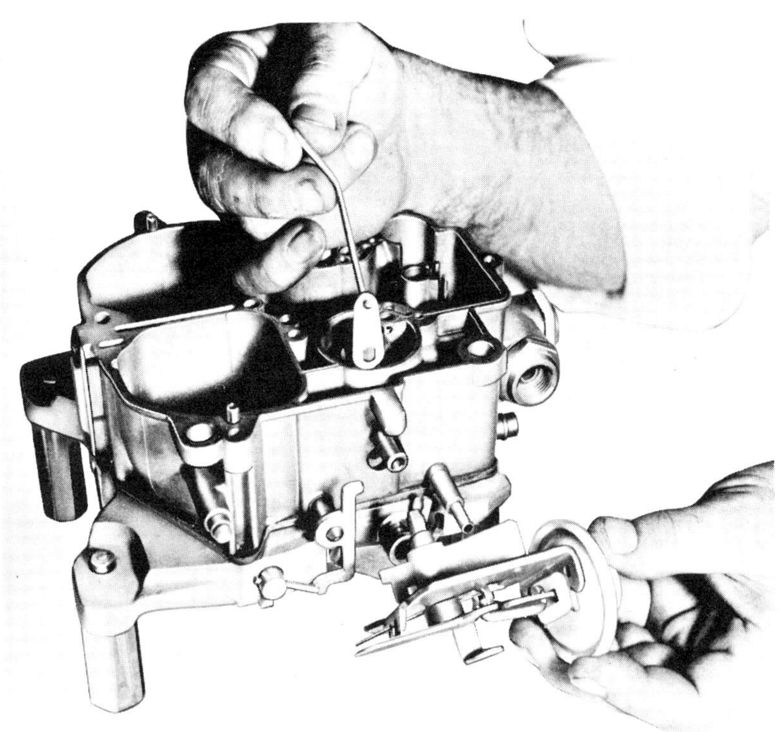

Fig. 15-33. Installing the choke assembly. (*Chevrolet Motor Division of General Motors Corporation*)

(Fig. 15-33). Install the retaining screw, and tighten it. Remove the choke rod from the lever for installation later.

Install the vacuum-break hose, baffles (notches up), pump-discharge check ball and retainer, primary main metering jets, and fuel-inlet-needle seat and gasket. Use a wide-blade screwdriver to avoid damaging the seat. Install the needle.

Use needle-nose pliers to hold the needle pull clip, and install the clip on the needle. Position the clip so that the open end is toward the front of the bowl. Install the float by sliding the float lever under the pull clip from front to back. With the float lever in the pull clip, hold the float assembly at its toe. Install the retaining clip from the pump-well side. Adjust the float level as follows (Fig. 15-34):

1. Use an adjustable T scale to measure from the top of the float-bowl-gasket surface (with the gasket off) to the top of the float at its toe. (The gauging point is $^3/_{16}$ in [4.763 mm] back from the toe.)
2. Bend the float up or down to adjust it.

Continue the assembly by installing the power-piston spring and power-piston assembly. Make sure the metering rods are properly positioned in the jets. Press down on the power-piston retainer to make sure the retaining clip engages. Install the plastic filler over the float needle, pressing it down to seat it properly.

Install the pump-return spring in the pump well. Place the air-horn gasket in position around the primary metering rods and piston and the two dowels on the bowl. Press the power piston down firmly, to ensure correct pin alignment. Install the pump plunger in the pump well.

3. *AIR HORN (FIG. 15-29)* Install the parts that were removed, and install the secondary metering

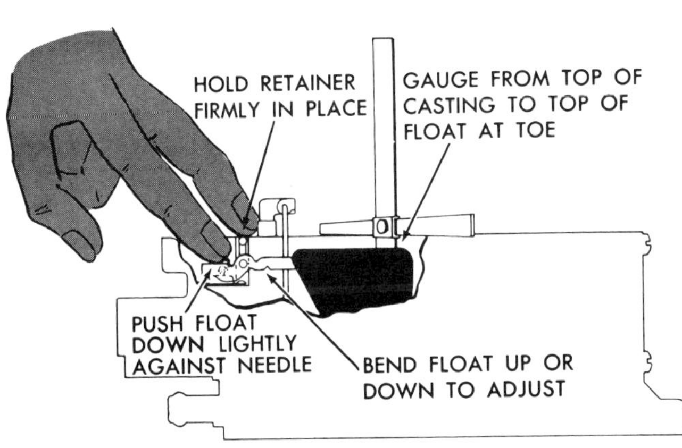

Fig. 15-34. Float-level adjustment. (*Chevrolet Motor Division of General Motors Corporation*)

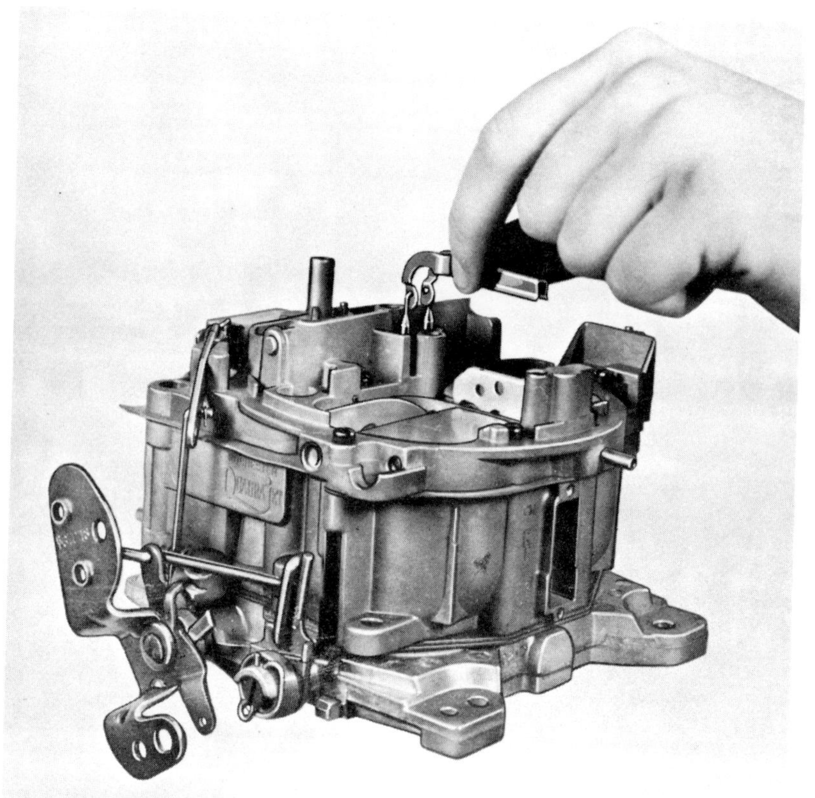

Fig. 15-35. Installing the secondary metering rods. (*Chevrolet Motor Division of General Motors Corporation*)

rods. This is done with the air valves held wide open. Position the rods with their upper ends through the hanger holes and toward each other (Fig. 15-35). Then put the air horn over the bowl. Make sure you position the secondary metering rods, vent tubes, and accelerating-well tubes through the air-horn gasket. Do not force the air-horn assembly onto the float bowl, because this could damage the secondary metering disks. Move the horn slightly sideways to center the metering rods in the disks.

Install the nine screws, tightening them in the sequence shown in Fig. 15-36. Install the idle-vent actuating rod in the pump lever. Connect the pump rod in the pump lever, and secure it with a spring clip. Connect the choke rod in the lower choke lever, and secure it in the upper lever with a spring clip. Install the idle vent valve, engaging the rod. Tighten the attaching screws.

CHAPTER 15 CHECKUP

NOTE: Since the following is a chapter review test, you should review the chapter before taking the test.

You have just completed a chapter on one specialized automotive service—carburetor overhaul and repair. You may not have a great deal to do with carburetors when you work in the service shop. Nevertheless, you should know how typical carburetors are constructed, how they operate, and what services they require. The following checkup will

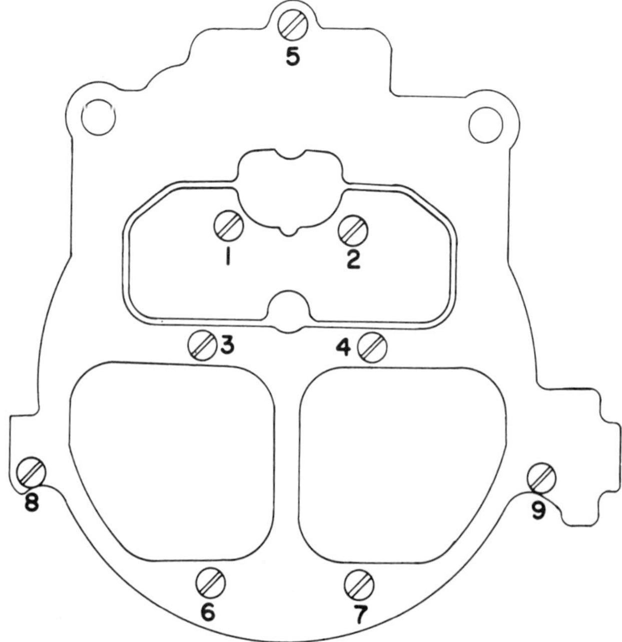

Fig. 15-36. Air-horn attaching-screw tightening sequence. (*Chevrolet Motor Division of General Motors Corporation*)

help you see how well you remember the material on carburetor overhaul. If you are not sure of an answer, reread the pages that clarify it for you.

Unscrambling Carburetor Trouble Causes There are two lists below. One is headed "Troubles," and the other "Causes." Note that the causes are more numerous than the troubles. There usually can be several causes for any particular trouble. To unscramble the lists, write each item in the "Troubles list" in your notebook. Then, after it, write all the items in the "Causes" list that could cause the trouble. Note that a number is given after each trouble. This is the number of causes that should follow the trouble in the unscrambled list. A cause may appear more than once, since a cause can lead to more than one trouble. The lists below are not all-inclusive; they are merely some of the more common troubles and causes.

Troubles
excessive fuel consumption (4)
lack of power (4)
failure to start unless primed (3)
hard starting (engine warm) (2)

Causes
throttle cracker misadjusted
defective choke
clogged jets or nozzles
choke valve closed
high float level
worn jets or nozzles
stuck check valve
low float level
clogged jets or nozzles
stuck metering rod or power piston
dirty air filter
air leakage into manifold
clogged fuel filter

Service Procedures In the following, you are asked for carburetor troubles, service cautions, and overhaul procedures. Write them in your notebook.

1. List the troubles that could result from causes within the carburetor.
2. Make a list of typical carburetor adjustments. Describe briefly how to make each adjustment.
3. Describe a typical carburetor-removal procedure.
4. List the main steps in carburetor overhaul.
5. List the cautions to be observed in repairing carburetors.
6. Prepare a detailed disassembly, inspection, reassembly, and adjustment procedure for one or more carburetors. If possible, do so by using actual carburetors, along with the manuals that apply to them. The best method is to follow the procedure in the manual, step by step, and write down each step as you do it. You will probably want to write the procedure on separate sheets of paper first, and then copy it into your notebook. This will keep your notebook clean.

SUGGESTIONS FOR FURTHER STUDY

Examine various carburetors and carburetor manuals in the shop. If possible, observe carburetor specialists at work overhauling carburetors. Note how they perform each step, the special tools they use, the manuals they refer to for specifications and the part numbers of new parts, the repair kits they need, and the adjustments they make. Handle and overhaul carburetors yourself, if you get the chance. Study all the carburetor manuals you can find. Note the construction of the different types of carburetors, and the procedures used to overhaul and adjust them.

chapter 16

FUEL-INJECTION OPERATION AND SERVICE

In previous chapters, we discussed carburetor fuel systems. These are the most widely used automotive fuel systems. However, another fuel system—fuel injection—is gaining popularity with automotive manufacturers. There are several variations of gasoline fuel-injection systems; we discuss them in this chapter. Fuel-injection systems for diesel engines are covered in greater detail in Automotive Fuel, Lubricating and Cooling Systems, *another book in the McGraw-Hill Automotive Technology Series.*

⊘ 16-1 What is Fuel Injection? For an engine to operate, the combustion chambers must be continuously supplied with a combustible mixture of air and fuel. In most automobile engines, a carburetor provides this mixture (Fig. 16-1). The carburetor is mounted on the intake manifold, which has passages (called *ports*) that are connected to the combustion chambers. Air passes through the carburetor. Fuel is discharged into the air and is mixed, in the carburetor venturi, into the proper air-fuel mixture for the engine. Even while this mixing is taking place, the intake manifold is carrying the mixture through the ports to the cylinders, to be burned.

In a fuel-injection system, the fuel is sprayed under pressure into the airstream going into each combustion chamber. As you can see in Fig. 16-2, only air enters the throttle body and passes through the intake manifold. This important difference eliminates many intake-manifold distribution and carburetion problems. We discuss this further in ⊘ 16-3.

⊘ 16-2 Types of Fuel Injection There are two basic ways to classify fuel-injection systems for automobile engines. One way is according to where, in the engine, the fuel is injected. The second way is according to whether the injection of fuel is continuous or timed.

Fuel can be injected directly into the combustion chambers (Fig. 16-3). The system shown in Fig. 16-3 is the type used in diesel engines. It is called *direct* injection. In a diesel engine, air alone enters the engine cylinders and is compressed. The heat of compression (⊘ 10-5) increases the temperature of the air to 1,000°F [537.8°C] or more. Then the fuel is injected directly into the hot compressed air. It is ignited by the heat of the air.

Fuel can also be injected into the intake port just before the incoming air reaches the intake valve (Figs. 16-2 and 16-4). This system is known as *port* injection. Because it is simpler, it is generally used as the fuel-injection system for gasoline-fueled automobile engines.

Fuel injection can be timed or continuous. The system shown in Fig. 16-3, when used on a diesel engine, must be timed. That is, fuel sprays from the injector for only a short time, toward the end of the compression stroke. Timing the fuel injection in a diesel engine requires an expensive fuel-injection pump and injectors.

⊘ 16-3 Advantages of Fuel Injection In ⊘ 16-1 we mentioned that fuel injection eliminates many intake-manifold distribution and carburetion problems. One of the most difficult problems to overcome with a carburetor is to get the same air-fuel mixture delivered to each cylinder. An intake manifold is a casting with passages, or ports, of different widths and lengths. Because of this, it is very difficult for all cylinders to get the same air-fuel mixture. The air flows around corners and through various shaped passages readily. However, the gasoline, because it is heavier, is unable to make the bends, turns, and corners as it travels through the passages (Fig. 16-5). As a result, some of the gasoline particles continue moving to the end of the manifold. This enriches the mixture going to the end cylinders. In the example shown in Fig. 16-5, the center cylinder, closest to the carburetor, gets a leaner mixture.

Figure 16-6 shows how a fuel-injection system solves the intake manifold distribution problem. A calibrated nozzle, or injector, is placed next to the intake valve of each cylinder. At the right time, fuel under pressure sprays out of the nozzle. Each injec-

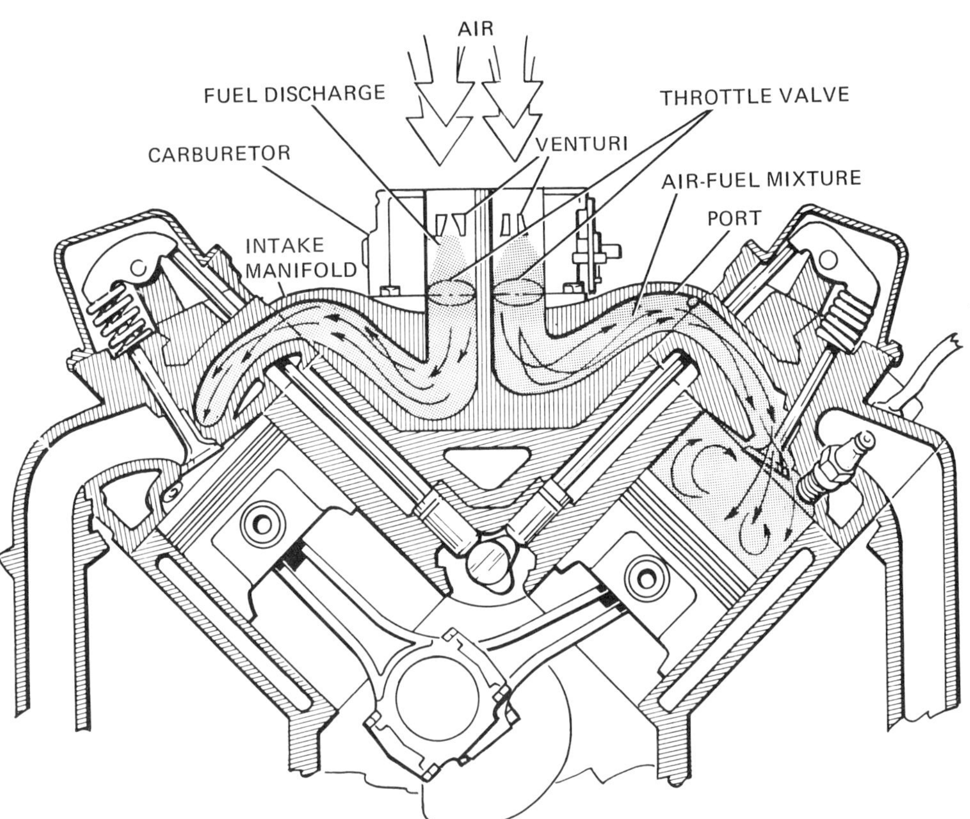

Fig. 16-1. Airflow through a carbureted engine. (*Cadillac Motor Car Division of General Motors Corporation*)

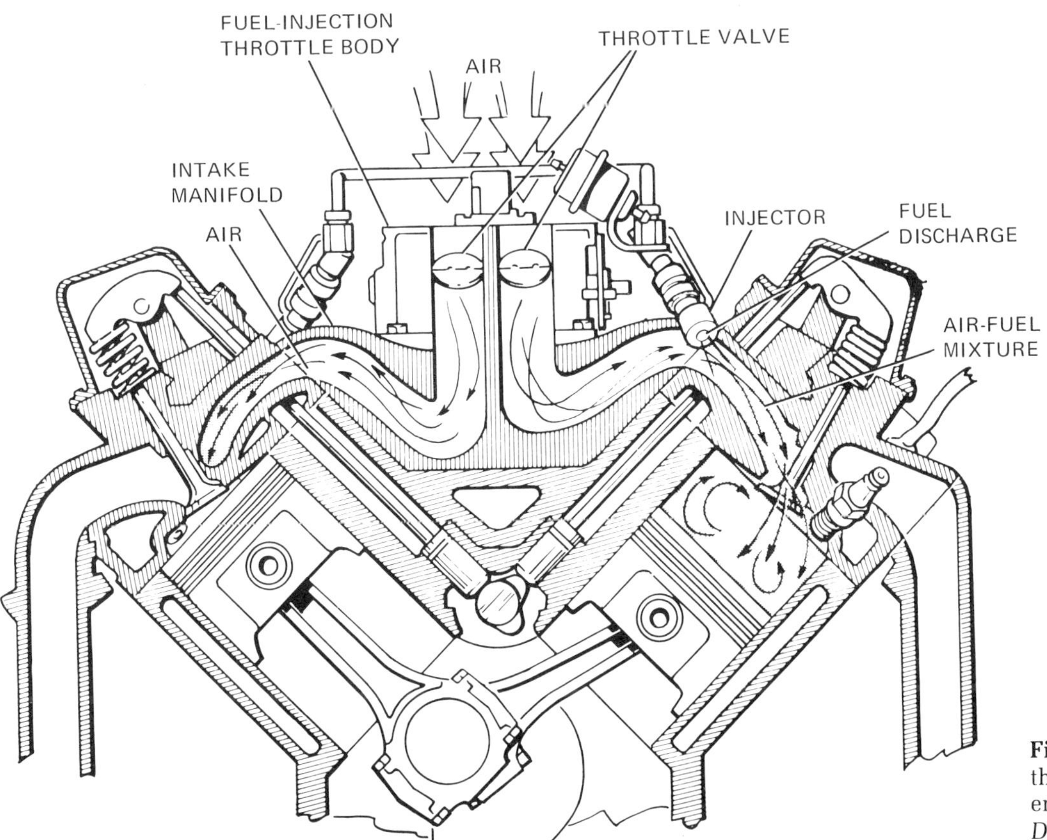

Fig. 16-2. Airflow through a fuel-injected engine. (*Cadillac Motor Division of General Motors Corporation*)

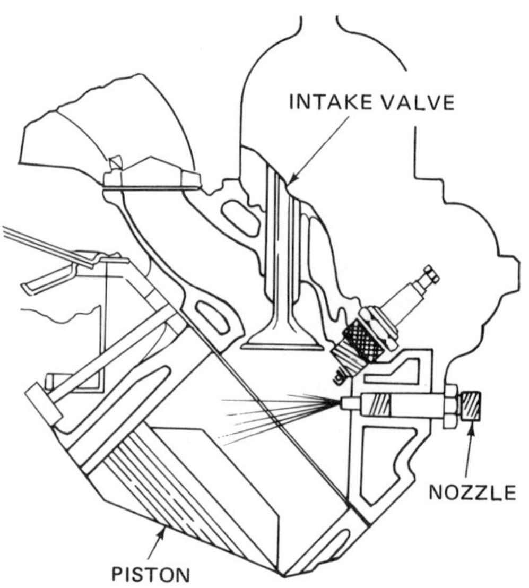

Fig. 16-3. Simplified view showing the method of injecting fuel directly into the combustion chamber of an engine.

tor sprays the same amount of fuel into the same amount of air entering every cylinder. Therefore, the combustion chamber of each cylinder gets the same air-fuel mixture, for all practical purposes. As a result, the engine operates on a leaner overall air-fuel ratio, which reduces HC and CO emissions.

Another advantage of fuel injection is that it allows a more efficient design of intake manifold. This results in improved engine breathing and volumetric efficiency. The hood height of the car can be reduced, with the redesigned intake manifold. With fuel injection, no extra heat is required during warm-up. Engines equipped with fuel injection do not require a manifold heat-control valve or an

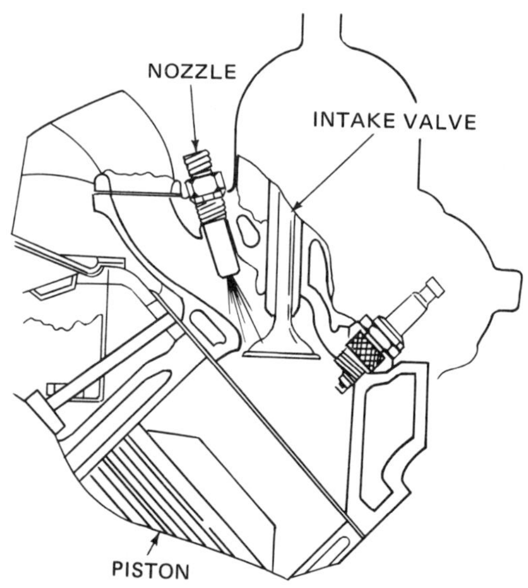

Fig. 16-4. Simplified view showing the method of injecting fuel into the intake manifold just in back of the intake valve.

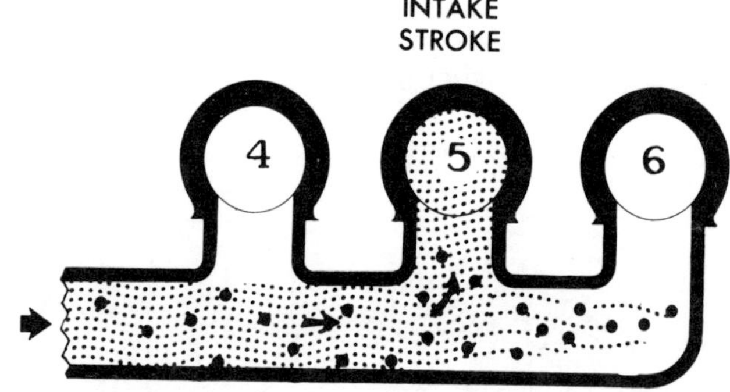

Fig. 16-5. Distribution pattern in an intake manifold. The gasoline particles tend to continue to the end of the manifold, thus enriching the mixture going to the end cylinders. (*Chevrolet Motor Division of General Motors Corporation*)

early-fuel-evaporation (EFE) system. Throttle response is much faster on a fuel-injection engine, because the fuel is under pressure at the injector at all times. All that is needed for acceleration is to open the injector; fuel sprays out instantly. Exhaust emissions during deceleration can be practically eliminated with fuel injection. The system can be designed with a positive, or complete, fuel shutoff for deceleration. In addition to reducing exhaust emissions, this also saves gasoline and improves fuel economy.

⊘ 16-4 Early Mechanical Fuel-Injection Systems

In the late 1950s and early 1960s, Chevrolet and Pontiac offered a continuous-flow fuel-injection system as a high-priced option. It was built by the Rochester Products Division of General Motors Corporation. The system used vacuum signals from the engine to control the air-fuel mixture. Fuel sprayed continuously from a nozzle into the intake port of each cylinder. The nozzle is simply a small calibrated tube, with no valve of any sort. This reduces the cost of the nozzles in the continuous-flow system.

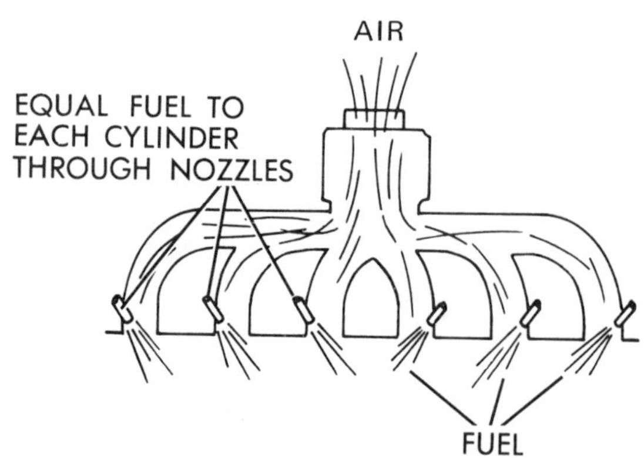

Fig. 16-6. In a fuel-injected engine, the same amount of fuel reaches each cylinder. (*Cadillac Motor Car Division of General Motors Corporation*)

There is always pressure behind the fuel in the nozzle. This comes from the fuel-injection pump. However, on the discharge end of the nozzle, the vacuum can vary from about 22 in [558.8 mm] with the throttle closed and the engine idling, to almost zero at wide-open throttle. This widely varying vacuum affects the fuel spray from the nozzle. For this reason, it was difficult to control fuel flow in the Rochester system, particularly at idle and low speeds.

Figure 16-7 is a schematic view of the Rochester system. It is no longer in use. It consists essentially of a special intake manifold, an air meter, and a fuel meter. The air meter controls the flow of air through the intake manifold to the engine cylinders. The fuel meter controls the flow of fuel to the fuel-injection nozzles in the intake manifold. The system is basically simple. Linkage from the accelerator pedal actuates a throttle valve in the air meter. More air is admitted when more engine power is desired. The fuel meter provides varying amounts of fuel. It supplies more fuel as more air is admitted. Other mechanisms enrich the mixture for acceleration, warm-up, hill climbing, and so on.

⊘ 16-5 Electronic Fuel Injection In the late 1950s, the Chrysler Corporation built a few cars with an early type of electronic fuel-injection system. This system, known as the Bendix Electrojector, was developed and patented by the Bendix Corporation. The electronic part of this system was made with vacuum tubes. It was not widely used.

With the development of solid-state electronics, such as transistors and diodes, a new type of electronic fuel injection appeared. In 1968, Volkswagen began installing a solid-state electronic fuel-injection system built by Bosch on some car models imported into the United States. We discuss the Volkswagen system again in ⊘ 16-10. Now, let's examine the basic Bosch electronic fuel-injection system for gasoline engines.

Figure 16-8 shows the system schematically. The electric fuel-supply pump maintains a high pressure in the fuel line to the injection valves in the intake manifold (Fig. 16-9).

At the proper instant, trigger contact points in the ignition distributor close. Figure 16-10 shows the distributor, cut away so that the trigger contacts can be seen. They are opened and closed by a cam on the distributor shaft. This cam is very different from the cam that opens and closes the ignition contact points.

When the trigger contacts close, they send an electric signal to the electronic control unit (ECU). The ECU then connects half the solenoid injection valves to the battery. (In a four-cylinder engine, this would be two valves; in a six-cylinder engine, three valves; and in an eight-cylinder engine, four valves.) The important point is that the solenoid injection valves are not individually actuated. Half of them are actuated at a time. Figure 16-11 shows three of the valves in operation, spraying fuel into the intake manifold.

The fuel enters just opposite the intake valves, as shown in Fig. 16-8. Figure 16-12 is the injection timing chart for a six-cylinder engine. Note that the individual intake valves open at varying times (crankshaft degrees) after injection. For example, look at the top line, which is for No. 1 cylinder. Injection takes place at 300° of crankshaft rotation. Almost 60° later (near 360°), the No. 1 intake valve opens and the intake stroke starts. Cylinder No. 5 is next in the firing order. Its intake valve opens near 480°, or about 180° after injection. The intake valve for No. 3 cylinder opens about 300° of crankshaft rotation after injection. During these varying intervals between fuel injection and intake-valve opening, the fuel is "stored" in the intake manifold, opposite the intake valves.

Having only two groups of injection valves simplifies the system. No appreciable loss of engine performance results from this storage of the fuel.

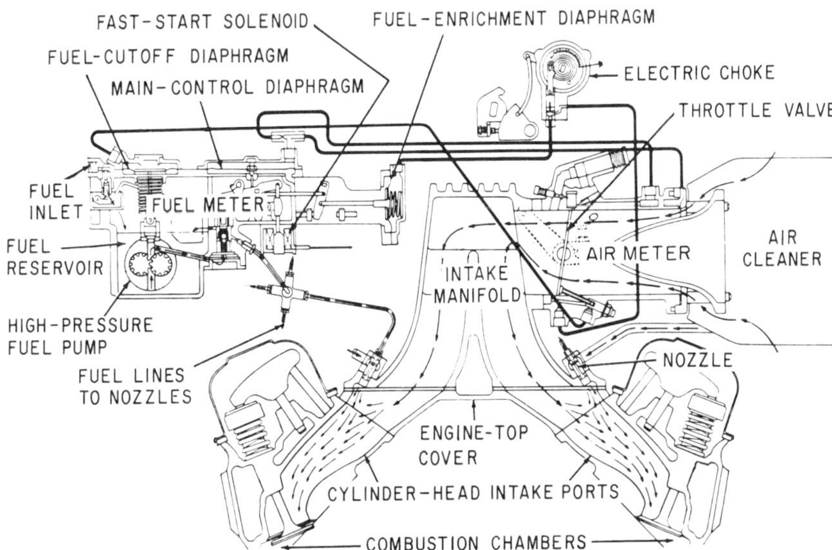

Fig. 16-7. Sectional view of a complete fuel-injection system. (*Chevrolet Motor Division of General Motors Corporation*)

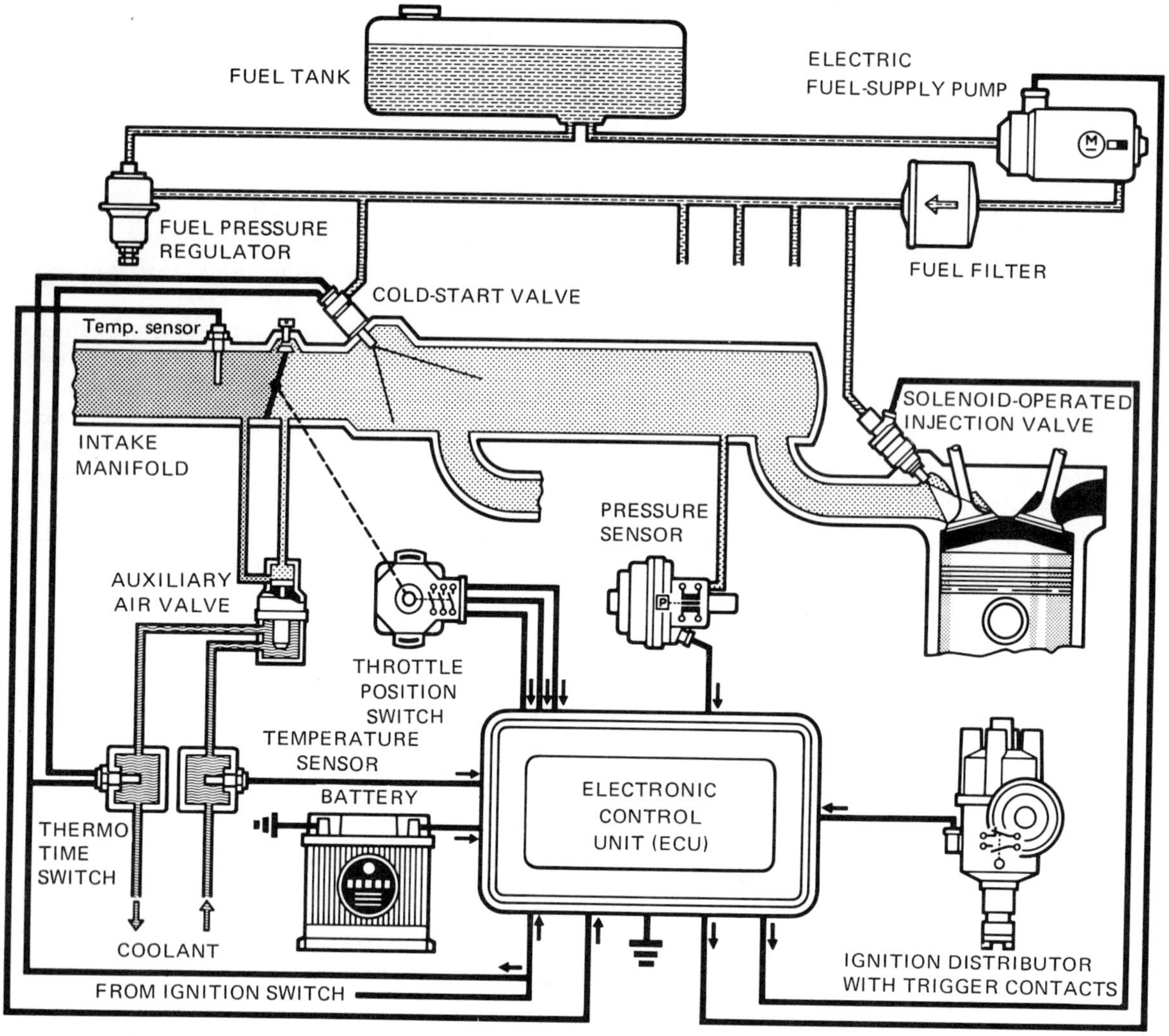

Fig. 16-8. Schematic diagram of an electronic gasoline-injection system. (*Robert Bosch GmbH*)

Remember, the whole action takes place in a small fraction of a second. At highway speed, for example, the time between injection and opening of the intake valve averages only about one hundredth of a second.

The fuel pump is shown in sectional view in Fig. 16-13. It is an electric motor of the "wet-pump" type. This means that the fuel flows through the pump and motor, as shown by the arrows. The pump drives an off-center rotor with a series of notches in which rollers are located (Fig. 16-14). When the pump armature rotates, the rollers are forced out by centrifugal force. They trap fuel between the rotor and the inner face of the pump. This fuel is forced out as the distance between the rotor and inner face decreases, on the outlet or pressure side.

The fuel pressure is controlled by a pressure regulator. The regulator is shown to the upper left in Fig. 16-8. It regulates by dumping some of the fuel back into the fuel tank if the pressure gets too high. Figure 16-15 is a section view of the pressure regulator. If the pressure exceeds a preset value, the diaphragm is pushed back against the spring. This opens the valve, allowing some of the fuel to flow out through the return line to the fuel tank. It is very important to maintain a constant pressure. The amount of fuel injected must depend entirely on how long the solenoid injection valve is open, and not on the fuel pressure.

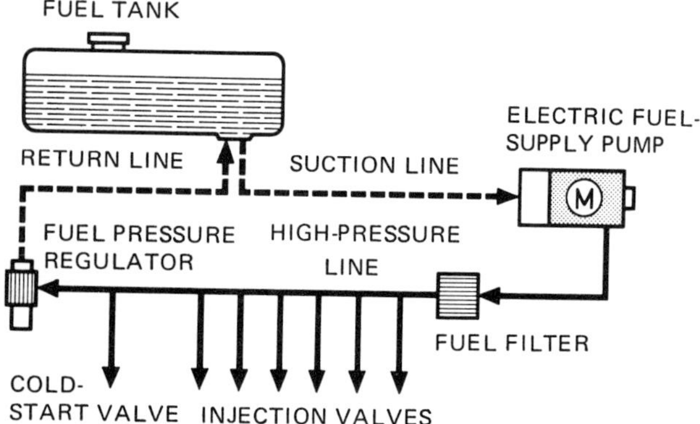

Fig. 16-9. Schematic diagram of the fuel system. (*Robert Bosch GmbH*)

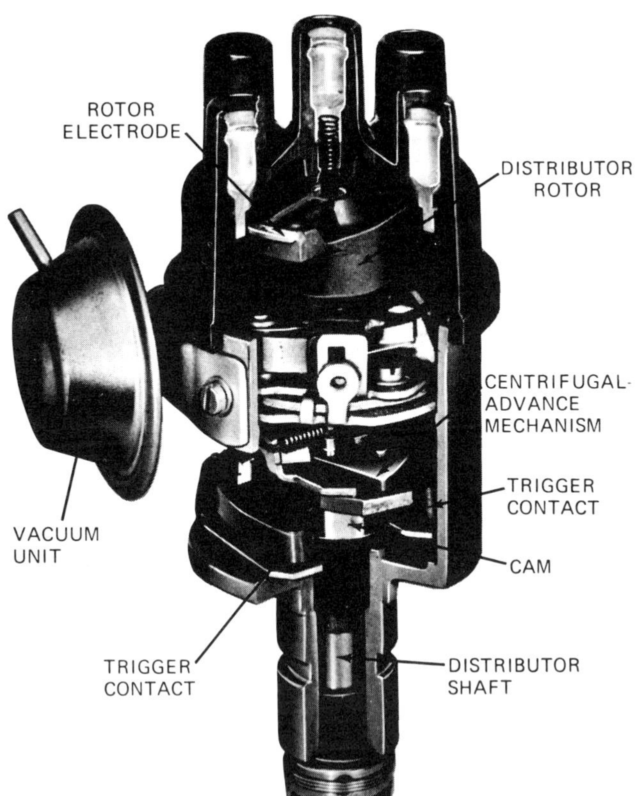

Fig. 16-10. Cutaway view of the distributor, showing the trigger contacts which activate the electronic control. (*Robert Bosch GmbH*)

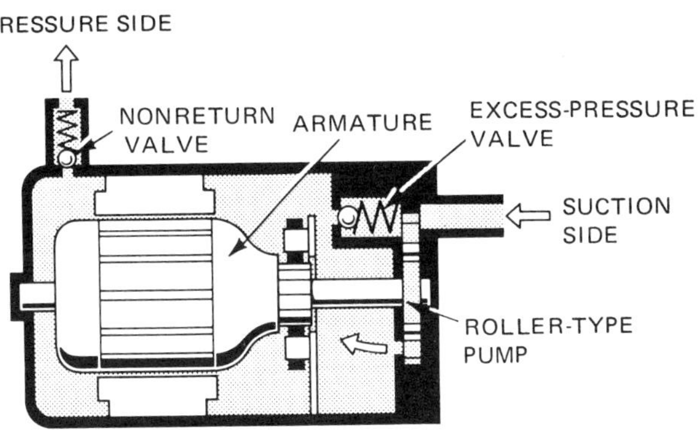

Fig. 16-13. Sectional view of the electric fuel-supply pump. (*Robert Bosch GmbH*)

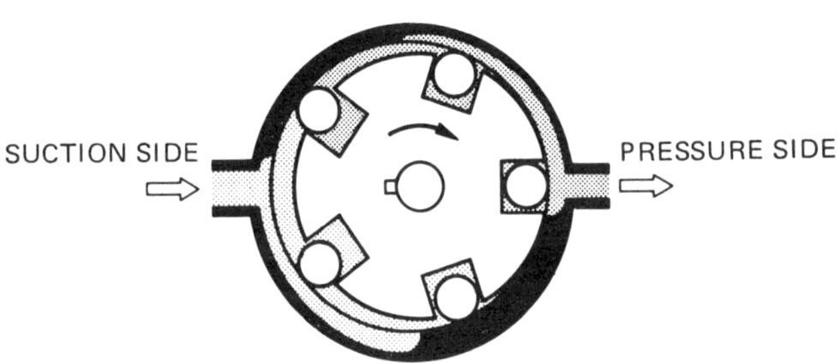

Fig. 16-14. Pumping action of the fuel-supply pump. (*Robert Bosch GmbH*)

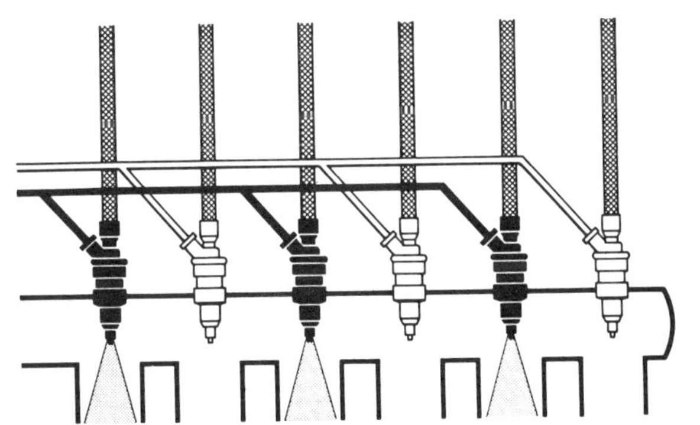

Fig. 16-11. Injection-valve grouping. (*Robert Bosch GmbH*)

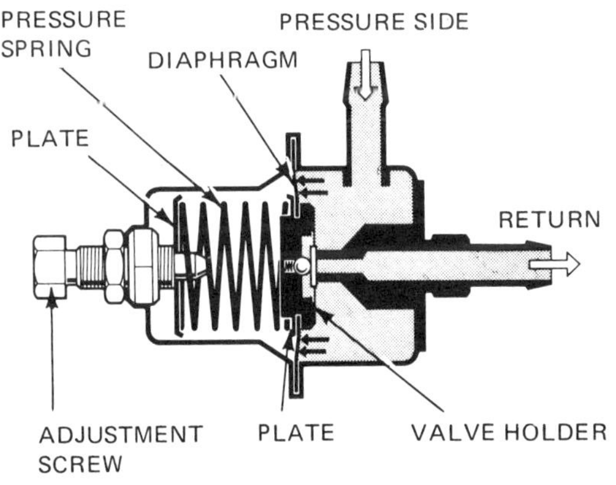

Fig. 16-15. Sectional view of the pressure regulator. (*Robert Bosch GmbH*)

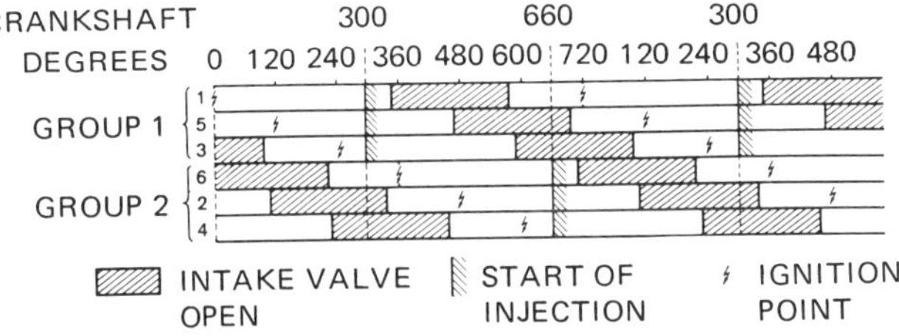

Fig. 16-12. Injection timing chart for a six-cylinder engine. (*Robert Bosch GmbH*)

The solenoid injection valve is shown in sectional view in Fig. 16-16. It simply pulls the plunger and needle away from the nozzle jet when it is connected to the battery. When it is connected, the solenoid produces a magnetic field. This pulls the plunger in toward the solenoid, and the needle is lifted off the nozzle. The fuel can then spray through the nozzle into the intake manifold. The longer the needle is off the nozzle, the more fuel is sprayed.

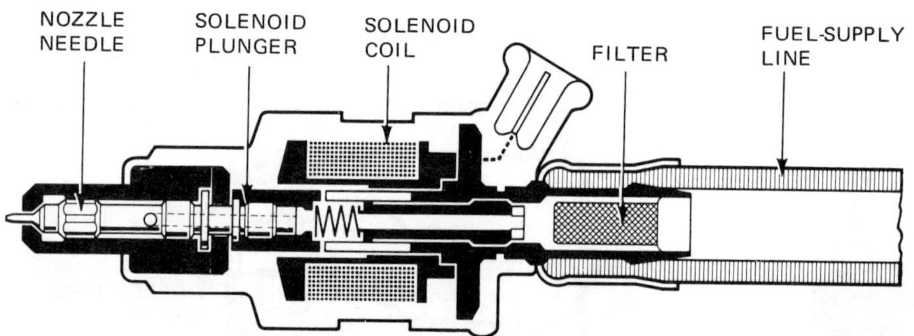

Fig. 16-16. Sectional view of the solenoid-operated injection valve. (*Robert Bosch GmbH*)

⊘ 16-6 Electronic Fuel-Injection Controls

Several factors determine how long an injection valve delivers fuel to the intake manifold. They include the throttle position, intake-manifold vacuum, ingoing-air temperature, and coolant (engine) temperature. See Fig. 16-8. Sensing devices continuously monitor these factors and "report" (electronically) to the ECU. The ECU puts the varying signals together and determines the length of the injection cycle.

For example, consider the intake-air temperature sensor (Fig. 16-17). It constantly measures the temperature of the air entering the intake manifold. The intake-air temperature sensor contains an element that passes varying amounts of electric current as the temperature changes. At low temperatures, for example, it passes more current; it sends a stronger electric signal to the ECU. The ECU then increases the time during which the fuel-injection valves are open. More fuel is delivered to compensate for the colder and denser air.

Similarly, the coolant temperature sensor sends varying amounts of current to the ECU, depending on the temperature of the engine coolant (and thus the engine temperature). When the engine is cold, the engine must receive more fuel, so that the mixture is rich enough. The ECU therefore increases the injection time when the coolant temperature sensor reports that the engine is cold. As the engine warms up, the ECU decreases the injection time.

The intake-manifold pressure sensor (Fig. 16-18) measures intake-manifold pressure and compares it with atmospheric pressure. It contains a pair of *aneroids*. These are flat, hollow disks. In many models, both aneroids are evacuated. That is, they hold a vacuum. As the outside pressure changes, the sides of the aneroid bulge out or in, depending on whether the outside pressure is relatively low or high.

Intake-manifold vacuum is introduced into the end of the pressure sensor. This vacuum acts on the aneroids. For example, if the throttle valve is open and there is little vacuum in the intake manifold, the aneroids are collapsed (Fig. 16-18). But if intake-manifold vacuum is high, the aneroids bulge out (Fig. 16-19). This repositions the plunger in the coils. Changing the position of the plunger in the coils changes the inductance of the coil. What this means is that the coils send a changed electric signal to the ECU. The ECU then changes the injection time so that the correct amount of fuel is injected to meet intake-manifold vacuum conditions. For example, the manifold vacuum is high when the throttle valve is closed or nearly closed. This means that only a little air is getting through to the cylinders. Therefore, only a little fuel should be injected. As a result, the ECU shortens the injection time. This is the same as the carburetor feeding fuel to the air through the idle system.

When the throttle is opened, the vacuum in the intake manifold is reduced. The aneroids collapse somewhat (see Fig. 16-18) and pull the plunger into the coils. The electric signal from the coils then changes. This change causes the ECU to increase the

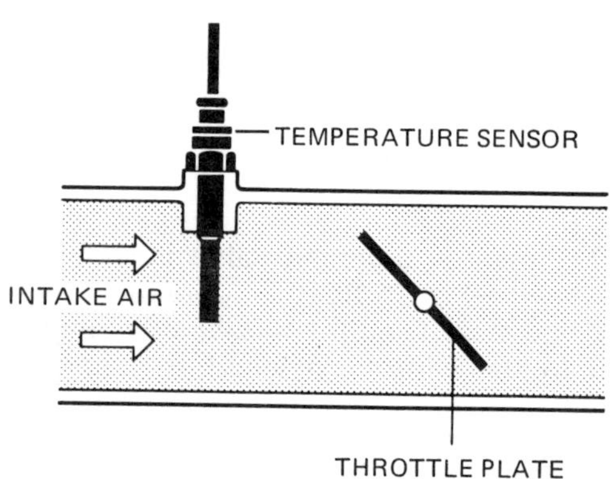

Fig. 16-17. Temperature sensor in the intake manifold. (*Robert Bosch GmbH*)

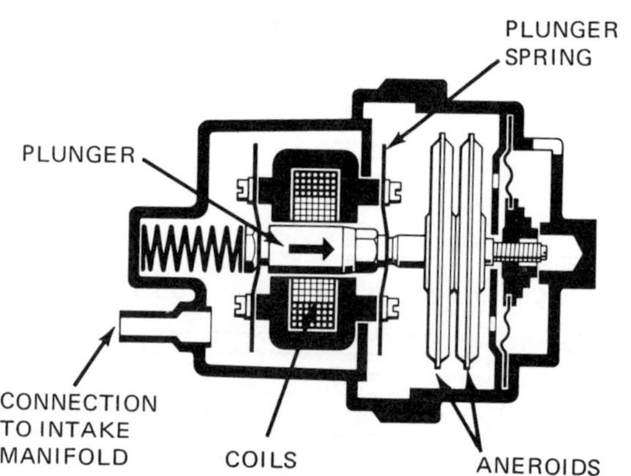

Fig. 16-18. Sectional view of the intake-manifold pressure sensor with the throttle valve open. The aneroid disks are compressed. (*Robert Bosch GmbH*)

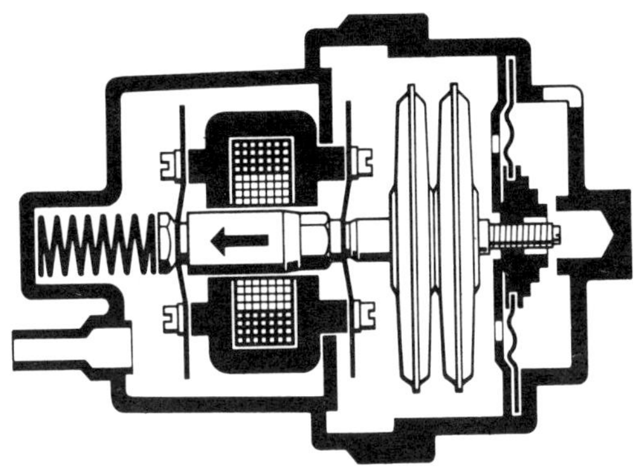

Fig. 16-19. Sectional view of the intake-manifold pressure sensor with the throttle closed. Increased vacuum allows the aneroid disks to expand. (*Robert Bosch GmbH*)

injection time. More fuel is injected so that the air-fuel ratio remains constant.

Remember, however, that other factors also affect the injection time. If the intake air is cold, the injection time is increased, as noted above. Likewise, if the engine (coolant) is cold, the injection time is increased.

⊘ 16-7 Cold Starts In the carburetor fuel system, the choke increases the amount of fuel delivered when the engine is being started cold. In the electronic fuel-injection system, a cold-start valve increases the amount of fuel delivered when the engine is being cold-started. Note the location of the valve in Fig. 16-8. A sectional view is shown in Fig. 16-20. The cold-start valve is triggered by the ECU. The ECU receives information from the engine temperature sensor, the air-intake temperature sensor, and the pressure sensor. If the information indicates that the engine is cold, the ECU connects the cold-start valve to the battery. The solenoid then moves the plunger to allow fuel to spray into the air entering the intake manifold. This results in a sufficiently rich starting mixture.

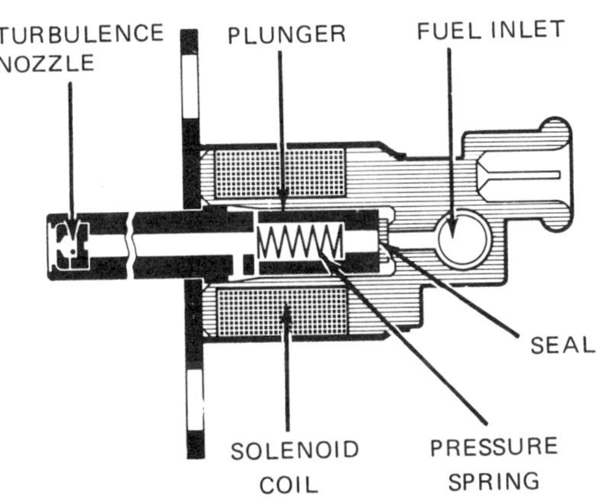

Fig. 16-20. Sectional view of the cold-start valve. (*Robert Bosch GmbH*)

⊘ 16-8 Throttle-Position Switch For more exact control of the injection time, the throttle has a position switch with several contact strips and a sliding contact. As the throttle is opened, the sliding contact connects to the contact strips, one after another. As each connection is made, a different signal is sent to the ECU. This causes the ECU to modify the injection time according to throttle position. For instance, on later models, there is a full-load-enrichment contact strip. When the throttle is opened wide, the sliding contact connects to this contact strip. As a result, the ECU increases the injection time so that additional fuel is injected. This meets the need for a richer mixture at full power.

⊘ 16-9 ECU System Operation Now let us review the operation of the system. When it is first started, the engine is cold. The air going into the intake manifold is cold. The vacuum in the intake manifold is fairly high because the throttle is nearly closed. The ECU gets signals from the air-intake temperature sensor, the coolant temperature sensor, the pressure sensor, and the throttle-position switch. It puts all of these together and "decides" just how long the injection valves should stay open. The ECU also "decides" whether to open the cold-start valve. When the trigger contacts close in the ignition distributor, the ECU opens half the injection valves. A rich mixture is delivered to the intake manifold before the intake valves open.

Then, when the engine starts, the changing intake-air temperature, coolant temperature, throttle position, and intake-manifold vacuum all modify the signals going from the ECU to the injection valves.

The auxiliary air valve, not previously mentioned, senses the temperature of the engine coolant. Note its location in Fig. 16-8, and the sectional view in Fig. 16-21. When the engine is cold, the auxiliary air valve opens to allow some air to flow around the closed throttle valve. This provides the extra air needed when the cold-start valve is open and discharging fuel. However, as the engine (and the coolant) begins to warm up, the auxiliary valve closes, shutting off the flow of extra air.

⊘ 16-10 Volkswagen Electronic Fuel-Injection System The Volkswagen electronic fuel-injection system is similar to the one we just described. It is illustrated in Figs. 16-22 to 16-24. This system was especially designed for the Volkswagen flat-four air-cooled engine. One major reason was to improve the combustion process and reduce the amount of smog-producing substances in the exhaust. (Chapter 17 discusses smog.) The fuel is injected into the intake manifolds behind the intake valves. The injection is timed to coincide with valve opening by triggering contacts in the ignition distributor. The amount of fuel injected is controlled by the length of time the fuel injectors are open. This, in turn, is determined by a number of sensors, which send electric signals to the transistorized control unit (Fig.

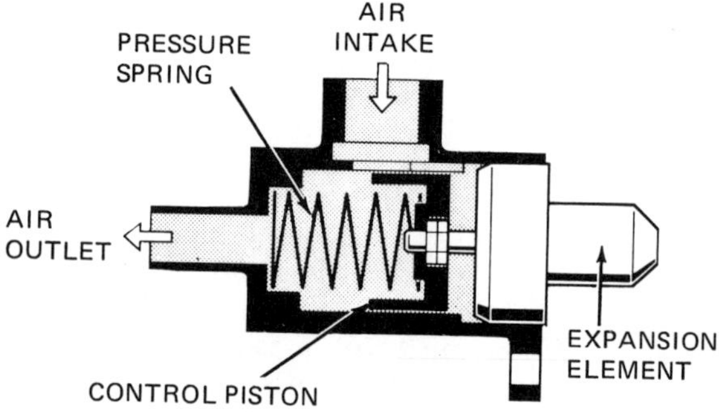

Fig. 16-21. Sectional view of the auxiliary air valve. (*Robert Bosch GmbH*)

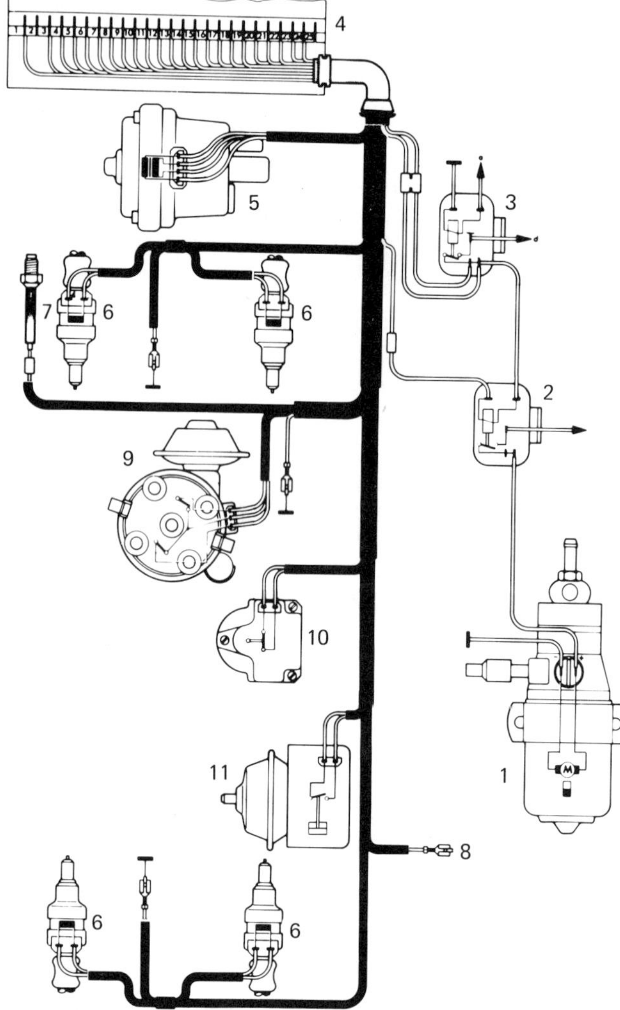

1. Fuel pump
2. Pump relay
3. Main relay
4. Control unit
5. Intake-manifold pressure sensor
6. Injector
7. Cylinder-head temperature sensor
8. Crankcase sensor
9. Ignition distributor
10. Throttle switch
11. Full-load pressure switch

Fig. 16-22. Schematic layout of the control system for the Volkswagen electronic fuel-injection system. The electronic control unit (4) receives signals from various sensors and integrates them to determine the amount of fuel to be injected. (*Volkswagen*)

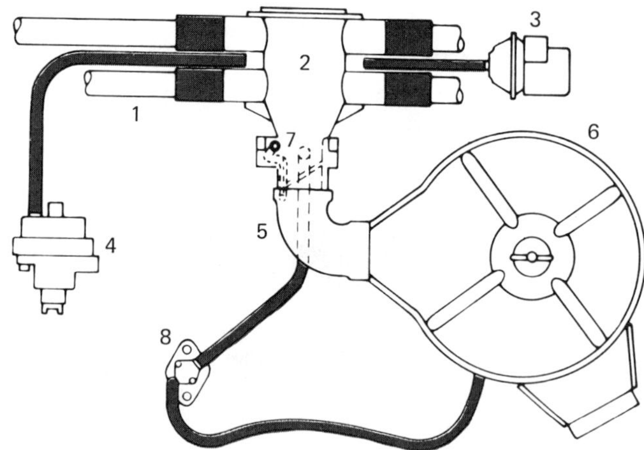

1. Air pipes to cylinders
2. Air distributor
3. Pressure switch
4. Pressure sensor
5. Idling circuit
6. Air cleaner
7. Adjusting screw
8. Auxiliary air regulator (rotary valve)

Fig. 16-23. Air-supply control for the Volkswagen electronic fuel-injection system. (*Volkswagen*)

16-22). Figure 16-23 illustrates the air-supply system and its controls. Figure 16-24 illustrates the fuel-supply system.

⊘ 16-11 Cadillac Electronic Fuel-Injection System

The Cadillac electronic fuel-injection system (Fig. 16-25) is very similar to the Volkswagen system.

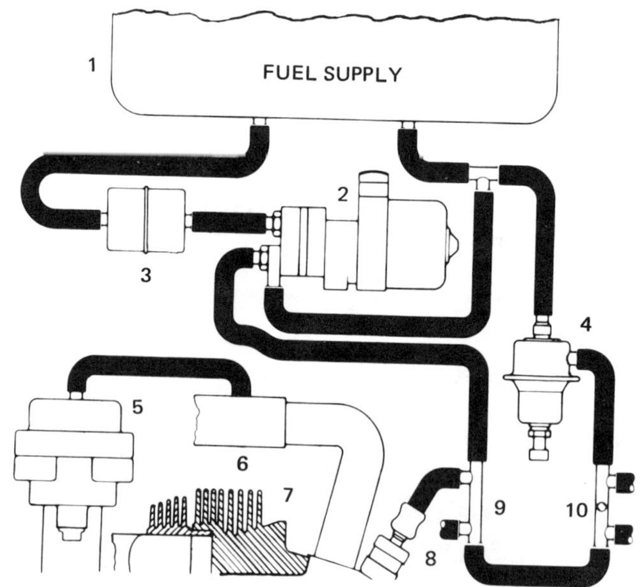

1. Fuel tank
2. Electric fuel pump
3. Filter
4. Pressure regulator
5. Intake-manifold pressure sensor
6. Air pipe
7. Cylinder head
8. Fuel injector
9–10. Distributor pipes to injector

Fig. 16-24. Fuel-supply system for the Volkswagen electronic fuel-injection system. (*Volkswagen*)

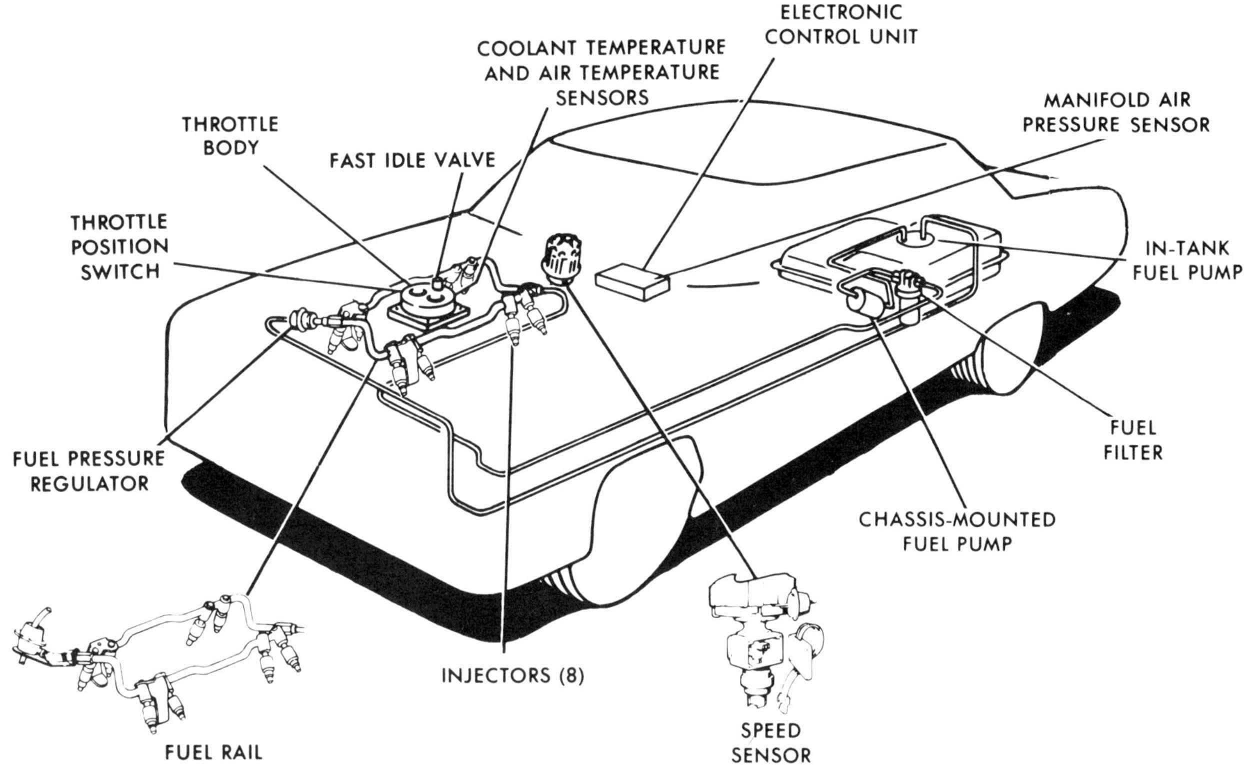

Fig. 16-25. Components of the Cadillac electronic fuel-injection system. (*Cadillac Motor Car Division of General Motors Corporation*)

Cadillac uses a separate fuel-injector valve for each cylinder (Fig. 16-26). The eight injectors on the Cadillac V-8 engine are connected to a fuel rail; they are divided into two groups of four injectors each. Each group of injectors is alternately turned on and off by the electronic control unit. The injectors are turned on once for each two revolutions of the crankshaft. Figure 16-27 is a sectional view of the Cadillac V-8 engine with electronic fuel injection.

Figure 16-28 is a block diagram showing (on the left) the sensors that send information to the ECU. With this and other information (such as engine displacement and volumetric efficiency), the ECU computes the amount of fuel the engine requires. It

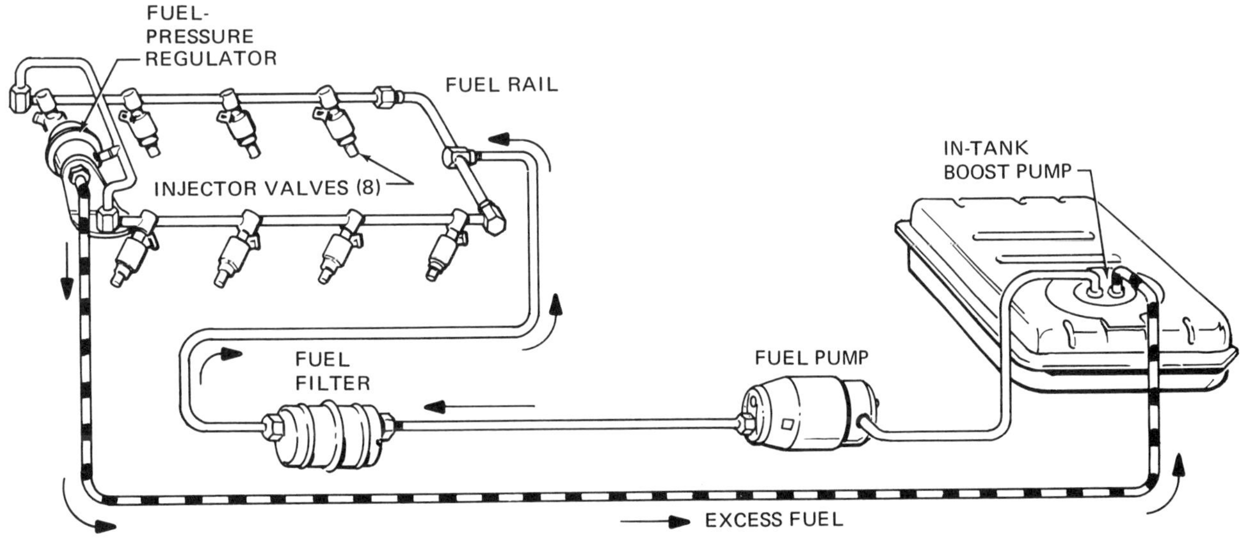

Fig. 16-26. Schematic view of the fuel system used on the Cadillac fuel-injected engine. (*Cadillac Motor Car Division of General Motors Corporation*)

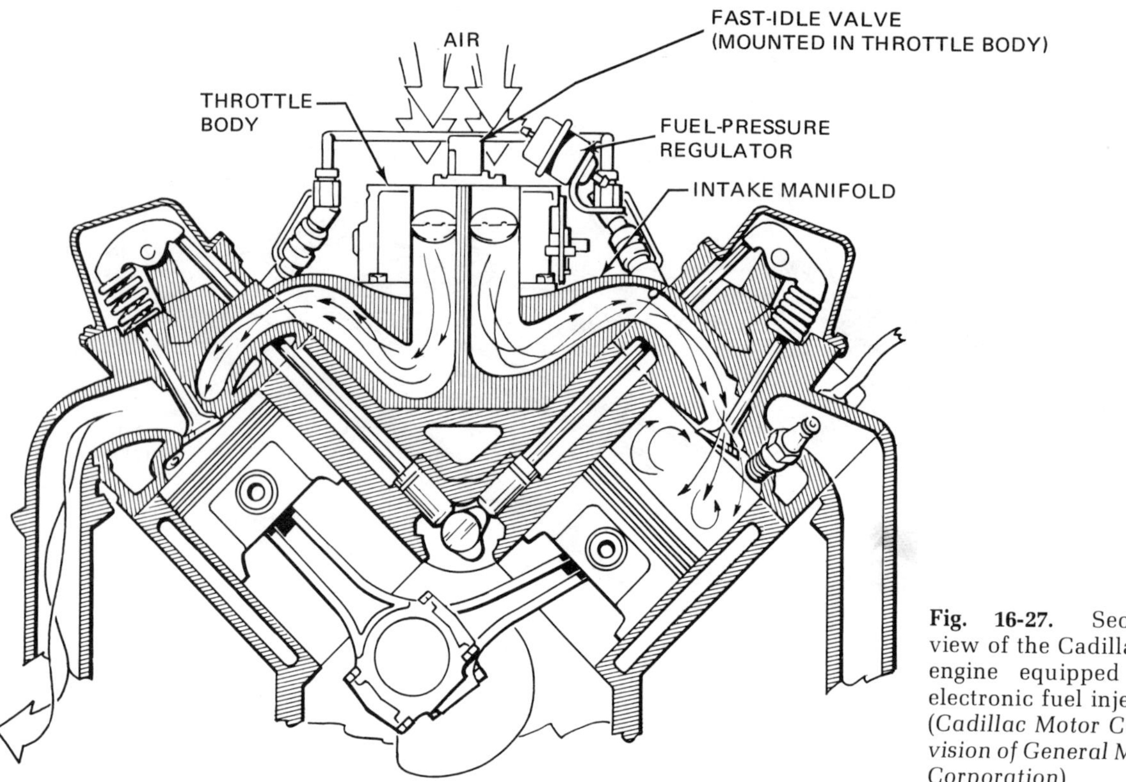

Fig. 16-27. Sectional view of the Cadillac V-8 engine equipped with electronic fuel injection. (*Cadillac Motor Car Division of General Motors Corporation*)

then sends control signals to the injectors and other parts of the system (on the right in Fig. 16-28).

The ECU is a preprogrammed computer installed above the glove box within the passenger compartment. It converts the input information from the sensors into an electric signal which opens the injectors for the proper duration at the proper time. Figure 16-29 shows the size of a similar ECU used in the Chevrolet Cosworth Vega. As you can see by noting the ruler, the ECU is not very large. Figure 16-30 shows the ECU removed from its steel case. The ECU cannot be adjusted or serviced. When a malfunction is traced to the ECU, it is removed from the car and a new one is installed. Accurate diagnosis of ECU operation requires a special tester.

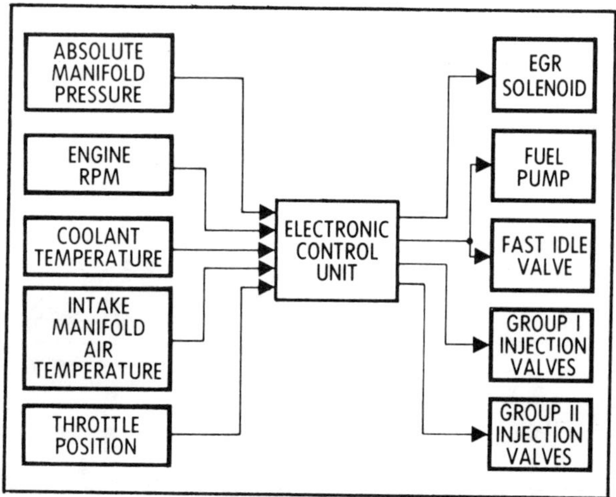

Fig. 16-28. Block diagram showing the sensors (left) that provide information to the electronic control unit. (*Cadillac Motor Car Division of General Motors Corporation*)

⊘ 16-12 Electromechanical Fuel-Injection System for Gasoline Engines Figure 16-31 is a schematic view of a fuel-injection system that is essentially mechanical in nature. Several relays are used to control the system. The system has a two-plunger pump. Each plunger feeds three cylinders through a metering unit. Fuel is injected into the intake manifold, as in the systems described above. The metering units are controlled by a linkage to the accelerator pedal. The amount of fuel delivered by the pump is controlled by a centrifugal governor. Other controls are included to increase the richness of the air-fuel mixture for starting, cold operation, and high-speed, full-power running. There are also pressure cells built into the diaphragm of the injection pump. They alter the amount of fuel delivered, in accordance with the altitude and the density of the air. At higher altitudes, the air is less dense. Therefore, less fuel is required to achieve the normal air-fuel ratio. The pressure cells take care of this automatically.

⊘ 16-13 Late-Model Mechanical Fuel Injection The electronic fuel-injection system is more expensive than the simpler mechanical fuel-injection system. Also, its complicated electronic components cannot be diagnosed except with special testers. To overcome these disadvantages, Bosch has introduced a

Fig. 16-29. Electronic control unit used on the Chevrolet Cogsworth Vega. (*Chevrolet Motor Division of General Motors Corporation*)

Fig. 16-30. Electronic control unit with cover removed. (*Chevrolet Motor Division of General Motors Corporation*)

new continuous type of mechanical fuel-injection system for gasoline-fueled automobile engines (Fig. 16-32). This system uses an electric fuel pump to pressurize the fuel. To control the amount of fuel injected, the volume of intake air is measured by an airflow sensor plate. The sensor plate is placed in the air funnel, through which all air must pass to reach the cylinders.

As the airflow through the funnel increases, it lifts the sensor plate higher in the funnel. This causes a fuel distributor to send, to the cylinder nozzles, precisely the amount of fuel needed to produce the correct air-fuel ratio. The fuel is sprayed continuously, from the injection valves into the port close to the intake valve.

This system is used on some late-model imported cars.

⊘ 16-14 Servicing Electronic Fuel-Injection Systems Before checking for defects in the electronic fuel-injection system, make sure the engine and especially the ignition system are not causing the complaint. If they are not at fault, Cadillac recommends the following visual inspection.

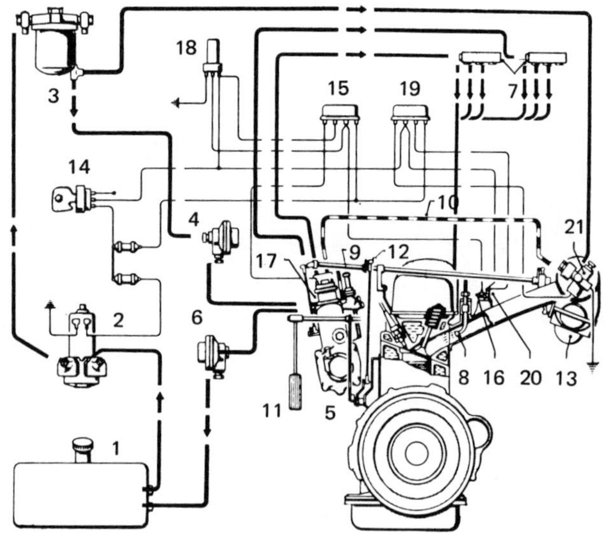

1. Fuel tank
2. Fuel-feed pump
3. Fuel filter
4. Damper container (inlet)
5. Injection pump
6. Damper container (outlet)
7. Fuel-metering units
8. Injection valves
9. Cooling-water thermostat
10. Additional air duct
11. Accelerator
12. Control linkage
13. Throttle connector
14. Ignition-starter switch
15. Relay
16. Thermo switch in cooling-water circuit
17. Magnetic switch for mixture control
18. Time switch
19. Relay
20. Thermo time switch in cooling-water circuit
21. Electromagnetic starter valve with atomizing jet

Fig. 16-31. Schematic layout of a fuel-injection system used on a six-cylinder engine. (*Mercedes-Benz, Daimler-Benz Aktiengesellshaft*)

1. Visually check all wiring-harness connections for:

a. Loose or detached connectors

b. Broken or detached wires

c. Terminals not completely seated in connector housings

d. Partially broken or frayed wires at terminal connections

e. Excessive corrosion

2. Start the engine. Plug the idle bypass passage on top of the throttle body with a clean shop towel, to make it easier to hear any vacuum leaks. Then visually check all vacuum lines:

a. To ensure all vacuum lines are securely connected to their proper fittings (Fig. 16-33)

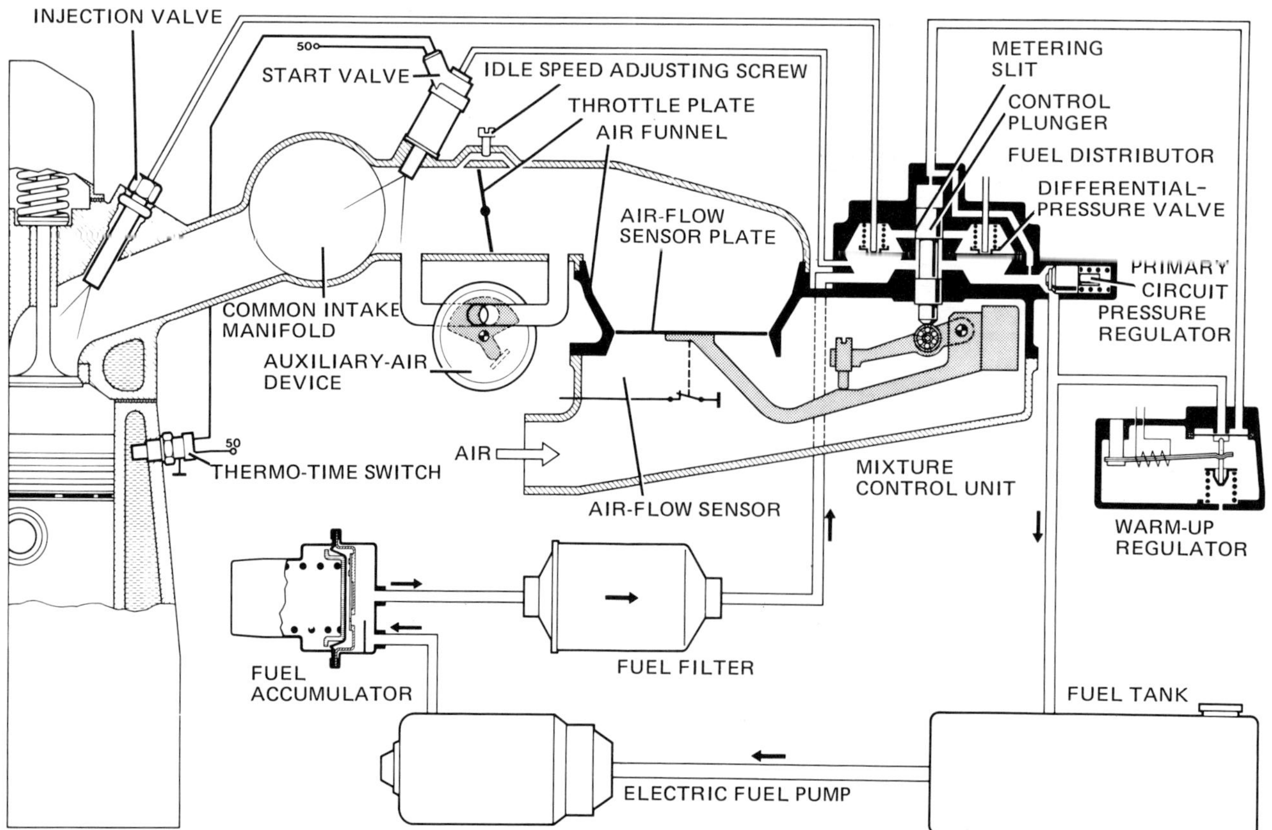

Fig. 16-32. Late-model, mechanical, continuous fuel-injection system used on some imported cars. (*Robert Bosch GmbH*)

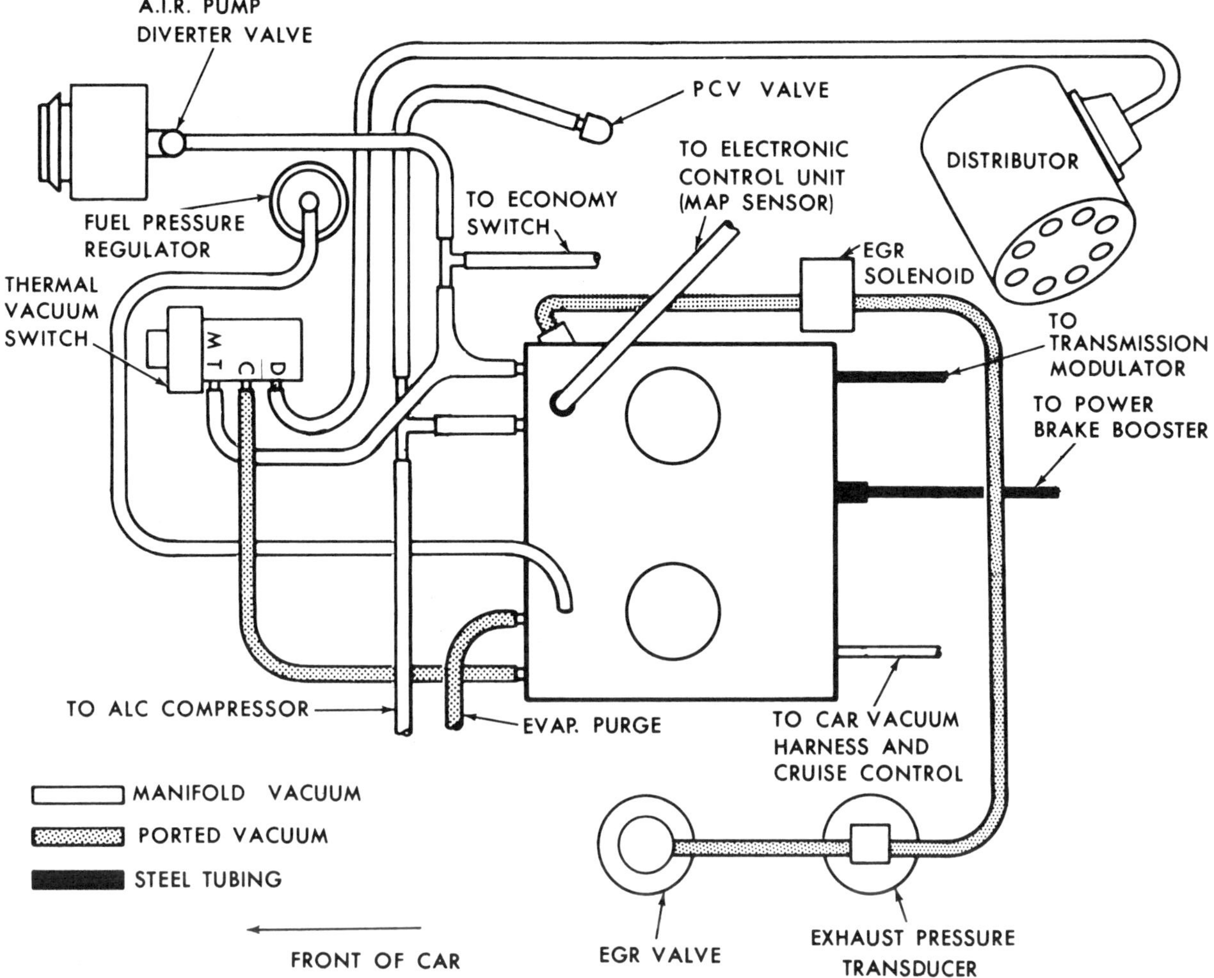

Fig. 16-33. Schematic drawing showing vacuum-hose routing and connections. (*Cadillac Motor Car Division of General Motors Corporation*)

b. For broken, pinched, or cracked lines
3. Visually check the fuel lines for:
a. Leakage
b. Kinks

CAUTION: Do not loosen any fittings in the fuel system until after you have relieved the pressure in the system! Fuel in the system may be pressurized to 41 psi [2.81 kg/cm^2] or more. When loosening a fitting, observe the proper precautions to prevent fuel from spraying out and causing a fire or injuring you. Cover the fitting to be removed with a shop towel, so the fuel will be absorbed. Then place the gasoline-soaked towel in a safety container, or put it in a safe place outside to dry.

If the cause of the problem is not found during the visual inspection, then a preliminary diagnosis is in order. Cadillac lists nine different types of problems that might occur in cars with electronic fuel injection. If the engine and all other systems are operating properly, these problems may be traced to the electronic fuel-injection system. The problems are:

1. Engine cranks but will not start
2. Hard starting
3. Poor fuel economy
4. Engine stalls after start
5. Rough idle
6. Prolonged fast idle
7. No fast idle
8. Engine hesitates or stumbles on acceleration
9. Lack of high-speed performance

After the visual inspection, a special tester, or fuel-injection-system analyzer, must be used to locate the cause of any of these problems.

During the preliminary diagnosis, you should keep in mind certain relationships between parts in the carburetor and components in the electronic fuel-injection system (Fig. 16-34). These relationships can help you to sort out, identify, and pinpoint a defective component.

CARBURETOR	ELECTRONIC FUEL-IGNITION
1. Accelerator pump	1. Throttle position switch
2. Fast-idle cam	2. Electric fast idle valve
3. Float	3. Fuel-pressure regulator
4. Power valve/metering rods	4. Manifold absolute pressure sensor
5. Metering jets and idle fuel system	5. Injection valves, electronic control unit (ECU)

Fig. 16-34. Chart showing the relationship between carburetor components and electronic-fuel-injection components. (*Cadillac Motor Car Division of General Motors Corporation*)

⊘ **16-15 Trouble-Diagnosis Chart** The chart that follows lists various complaints that can be traced to electronic fuel-injection systems, their possible causes, and the checks or corrections to be made. The information in the chart will shorten the time you need to correct a trouble. If you follow a logical procedure, you can usually find the cause of a trouble quickly. On the other hand, haphazard guesswork wastes time and effort.

NOTE: The troubles and possible causes are not listed according to how often they occur. That is, item 1 (or item a under "Possible Cause") does not necessarily occur more often than item 2 (or item b).

ELECTRONIC-FUEL-INJECTION TROUBLE-DIAGNOSIS CHART

COMPLAINT	POSSIBLE CAUSE	CHECK OR CORRECTION
1. Engine will not start; fuel pump does not run	a. Fuse to pump relay terminal blown; cables to pump or pump relay or cables on fuel-pump relay defective	Renew fuse; check whether pump relay energizes (switch ignition on and off, and listen for audible action of relay); if necessary, test with voltmeter; check plug on fuel pump for good connection
	b. No voltage at terminal of pump relay (12 V), because main relay is not operating or cable is defective	Eliminate open circuit
	c. Voltage present at terminal of pump relay, but no ground connection	Fuel pump operates for 1 to 2 seconds after ignition is switched on; check with meter (ground is made by control unit); replace ECU
	d. Open circuit in cable from pump relay to pump plug	Check plug connection; eliminate open circuit
2. Engine will not start; fuel pump runs	a. Connection from cable harness to starter terminal defective	Check with special tester
	b. Pressure-sensor cable not connected; open circuit	Push on pressure-sensor cable; repair
	c. Open circuit in cable connection at temperature sensor (coolant)	Check cables; if necessary, replace temperature sensor
	d. No fuel pressure building up (pipe compressed or pressure regulator defective)	Check pressure with gauge; if necessary, replace pressure regulator
3. Engine starts cold but stalls	a. Cable connector for triggering contacts not pushed on at ignition distributor; open circuit in cable	If necessary, connect special tester and locate the fault; replace trigger contacts or cable harness
	b. Trigger contacts defective	Replace
	c. Pressure sensor defective	Replace
	d. See also item 1, "Engine will not start"	
4. Engine cuts out when driving (usually preceded by misfiring)	a. Trigger contacts have excessive contact resistance or are dirty	Replace trigger contacts
	b. Plug loose	Check
	c. No fuel pressure	Check pressure; determine cause
5. Engine runs irregularly, one cylinder not firing; exhaust white	a. One injector sticking	Replace injector
	b. Connection to injector or injector coil defective	Check connections; replace injector; test system with special tester
6. Engine misfiring, not caused by ignition system	a. Loose connections; main ground cable has poor connection to car body	Check connections; tighten ground connection
7. Engine not reaching full power	a. Fuel pressure low	Check pressure regulator
	b. Pressure sensor defective	Replace
	c. Throttle valve does not open sufficiently	Check throttle valve

ELECTRONIC-FUEL-INJECTION TROUBLE-DIAGNOSIS CHART

COMPLAINT	POSSIBLE CAUSE	CHECK OR CORRECTION
8. Fuel consumption too high	a. Sensors of ECU not functioning correctly; electrical connections have too high resistance	Test system with special tester
	b. Throttle-valve switch incorrectly adjusted	Adjust, using special tester
	c. Fuel pressure incorrect	Check pressure regulator; if necessary, replace it
9. Engine hunts excessively at idle (between 1,000 and 1,800 rpm)	a. Hose between auxiliary air regulator and induction manifold detached or defective	Push hose into position or replace
	b. Throttle-valve stop incorrectly adjusted (open too wide)	Readjust throttle-valve stop
	c. Idling speed set too high	Adjust idling speed
10. Engine misfires when accelerating	Temporary enrichment device in throttle-valve switch not functioning; plug incorrectly connected	Check throttle-valve switch with special tester
11. Too high idling speed; idling speed cannot be adjusted	a. Idling air system leaks	Check idling air system
	b. Rubber sealing ring under the injector	Replace rubber sealing ring
	c. Throttle-valve adjustment incorrect	Readjust throttle valve

For further information on the testing of electronic fuel-injection systems and the use of the special tester, refer to the automobile manufacturer's service manual.

CHAPTER 16 CHECKUP

NOTE: Since the following is a chapter review test, you should review the chapter before taking the test.

You may not run into fuel-injection systems very often, but when you do, you will want to be able to deal with them. Thus, you should remember the facts discussed in this chapter. The following questions will give you a chance to review the material on fuel-injection systems. Write the answers in your notebook.

Completing the Sentences The sentences below are incomplete. After each sentence there are several words or phrases, but only one of them correctly completes the sentence. Write each sentence in your notebook, ending it with the one word or phrase that completes it correctly.

1. In a fuel-injection system, fuel can be sprayed directly into the combustion chamber or into the: (*a*) carburetor, (*b*) intake manifold, (*c*) intake port.
2. Fuel injection can be timed or: (*a*) intermittent, (*b*) continuing, (*c*) pulsed.
3. In a fuel-injection system, the intake manifold carries (*a*) air and fuel, (*b*) only fuel, (*c*) only air.
4. In an electronic fuel-injection system, the injection valves are actuated: (*a*) one by one, (*b*) at all times, (*c*) in groups.
5. In an electronic fuel-injection system, the amount of fuel sprayed into each port is determined by the: (*a*) length of time the injection valve is open, (*b*) trigger contacts in the distributor, (*c*) pressure regulator.
6. The sensors electrically measure and report various conditions to the: (*a*) electronic control unit, (*b*) injection valve, (*c*) trigger contacts.
7. The sensor which contains a pair of aneroid disks is the: (*a*) intake-manifold pressure sensor, (*b*) temperature sensor, (*c*) thermotime switch.
8. In the Cadillac electronic fuel-injection system, the fuel pressure is about: (*a*) 4 psi [0.28 kg/cm^2], (*b*) 14 psi [0.98 kg/cm^2], (*c*) 40 psi [2.81 kg/cm^2].
9. The ECU is best described as a: (*a*) preprogrammed computer, (*b*) complicated ignition distributor, (*c*) precision mechanical fuel pump.
10. The late-model mechanical fuel-injection system determines the amount of fuel needed by measuring: (*a*) engine speed, (*b*) throttle opening, (*c*) the volume of intake air.

Operation of Components In the following, you are asked about operation of certain components of fuel-injection systems. Today, there are several different fuel-injection systsms available. Try to learn as much as you can about all of them, so you will be able to service any vehicle that is brought to you for repair. Also try to learn about diesel fuel-injection systems. Write your answers to the questions, as well as what you learn about other fuel-injection systems, in your notebook.

1. List some of the differences between diesel and gasoline-engine fuel-injection systems.
2. Explain how a typical diesel fuel-injection system operates.

3. Explain how an electronic fuel-injection system operates.
4. Explain how the electronic fuel-injection system varies the amount of fuel injected to suit the operating requirements of the engine.
5. Explain how the late-model mechanical fuel-injection system operates.

SUGGESTIONS FOR FURTHER STUDY

To learn more about diesel-engine fuel systems, refer to the various books that have been written on diesel engines. Check through some diesel-engine manufacturers' servicing and operating manuals. Information on newer developments in fuel injection can be found in automotive trade magazines and in publications of engine manufacturers. You will find it helpful to write, in your notebook, any facts you learn about these systems. This helps fix the information in your mind, and it makes your notebook a valuable reference.

chapter 17

AIR POLLUTION, SMOG, AND THE AUTOMOBILE

In this and the following chapter, we discuss the special devices used to reduce air pollution from automobiles. These devices, called emission controls, *appeared on cars because engineers realized that automobiles were causing atmospheric pollution. Federal and state lawmaking bodies, such as the United States Congress, have now passed laws that make automotive emission control necessary.*

Some of the emission controls were covered in other chapters. For example, the thermostatic air cleaner was discussed in ⊘ 11-11. In this chapter and the next, we review the emission controls discussed previously, and put them together with the rest of the emission controls. Thus, the complete story will be included in the two chapters. In this chapter we look at positive crankcase ventilation and evaporative-control systems. In the next chapter, we look at methods of cleaning up the exhaust gases.

⊘ 17-1 Smog The word "smog" comes from "smoke" and "fog." Smog is a sort of fog with other substances mixed into it. Smog has been around for a long time. Billions of years ago, when our earth was young, there were many volcanoes. They sent millions of tons of ash and smoke into the air. Winds whipped up clouds of dust. Animal and vegetable matter decayed and sent polluting gases into the air.

When humans came along, they began to produce their own kind of air pollution. They discovered fire. In the Middle Ages, people in cities (London, for example) burned soft coal to heat their homes. The smoke from their fires combined with moisture in the air to produce dense layers of smog. The smog would blanket the cities for days, particularly in winter. The heat generated in large cities tends to produce air circulation within a domelike shape (Fig. 17-1). This traps the smog and holds it over the city.

Smog and the substances in it can be harmful—even deadly. Smog blurs vision (Figs. 17-2 and 17-3). It irritates the eyes, the throat, and the lungs. Eyes water, throats get sore, and people cough. Smog can make people ill, and it can make sick people sicker. Air pollution has been linked to such human ills as eczema, asthma, emphysema, cardiovascular difficulties, and lung and stomach cancer. It also has a harmful effect on the environment. Food crops and animals suffer. Paint may peel from houses. It is obvious that we must do everything possible to reduce people-made atmospheric pollutants and smog.

⊘ 17-2 Not All Air Pollution Is Smog Smog, along with smoke, is the most visible evidence at atmospheric pollution. But some atmospheric pollution is not visible and may not become visible until it is mixed with moisture. Lead compounds from leaded gasoline, hydrocarbons (unburned gasoline), carbon monoxide, and other gases may pollute the air without being seen.

⊘ 17-3 Air Pollutants All air is polluted to some extent; that is, all air carries some polluting substances. Many of the pollutants come from natural causes—smoke and ash from volcanoes, dust stirred up by the wind, compounds given off by growing vegetation, gases given off by rotting animal and vegetable matter, salt particles from the oceans, and so on.

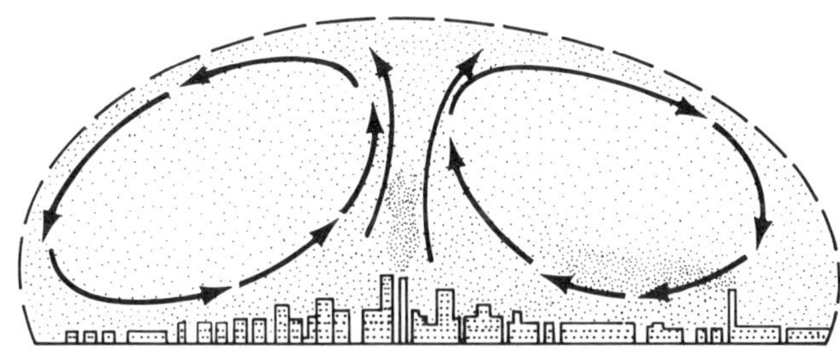

Fig. 17-1. The heat generated within a large city tends to produce a circulatory air pattern which traps smog within a "dome."

Fig. 17-2. View of Los Angeles on a clear day. (*Los Angeles County Air Pollution Control District*)

Fig. 17-3. Same view of Los Angeles on a typical smoggy day. Note that many buildings are hidden. (*Los Angeles County Air Pollution Control District*)

People add to these pollutants by burning coal, oil, gas, gasoline, and many other things. It is these added substances that we are concerned with in this book—especially those that come from the automobile.

Before we discuss the automobile, however, let us review the combustion process. Most fuels, such as coal, oil, gasoline, and wood, contain hydrogen and carbon in various chemical combinations. During combustion, oxygen unites with the hydrogen and carbon to form water (H_2O), carbon monoxide (CO), and carbon dioxide (CO_2).

In addition, many fuels contain sulfur, which produces sulfur oxides (SO_x) when it burns. Also, in the heat of combustion, some of the nitrogen in the air combines with oxygen to form nitrogen oxides (NO_x). Some of the fuel may not burn completely; then, smoke and ash are formed. Smoke is simply particles of unburned fuel and soot (called *particulates*), mixed with air.

All together, it is estimated that 200 million tons of pollutants enter the air every year in the United States alone. This is about 2,000 pounds [907 kg] for every man, woman, and child in the country!

The clean-air laws are aimed at the pollution that is created by people.

⊘ 17-4 Los Angeles Los Angeles is a large city, with about 7 million inhabitants, set in a basin. The city is surrounded on three sides by mountains, and on the fourth by the Pacific Ocean. When the wind blows toward the ocean, it sweeps away pollutants. At other times, the air is stagnant. Smoke and other pollutants from industry and automobiles do not blow away (Figs. 17-2 and 17-3). They just build up into a thick, smelly, foggy layer of smog. The location of Los Angeles, plus all the people and industry there, makes it one of the biggest "smog centers" in the country. It is no surprise that Los Angeles has led in attempts to reduce smog.

Los Angeles has banned unrestricted burning, such as the burning of trash. Incinerators without pollution controls have been outlawed. Industries were forced to change combustion processes, and to add controls to reduce pollution from their chimneys. Laws were passed that required emission controls on automobiles. All these measures have significantly reduced atmospheric pollution in the Los Angeles area.

⊘ 17-5 Pollution from the Automobile If not controlled, the automobile can give off pollutants from four places (Fig. 17-4). Pollutants can come from the fuel tank, the carburetor, the crankcase, and the tail pipe. The fuel tank and carburetor emit gasoline vapor. The crankcase gives off partly burned air-fuel mixture that has blown by the piston rings. The pollutants coming from the tail pipe are partly burned gasoline (HC), carbon monoxide (CO), nitrogen oxides (NO_x), and—if there is sulfur in the gasoline—sulfur oxides (SO_x). In the pages that follow, we discuss the causes of and cures for this pollution.

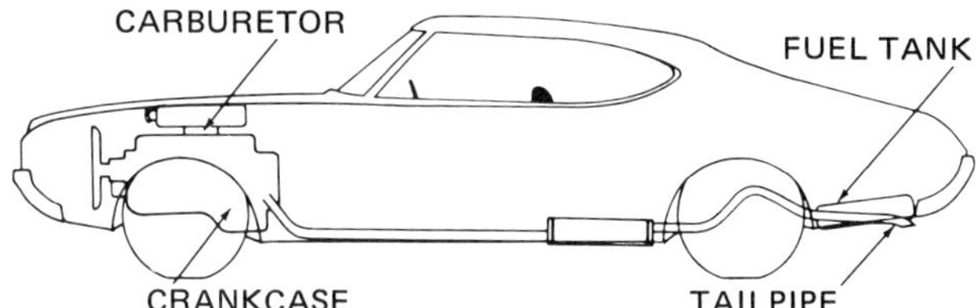

Fig. 17-4. Four possible sources of atmospheric pollution from the automobile.

HC and CO appear in the exhaust gases because of incomplete combustion of the fuel (HC) in the engine cylinders. The high combustion temperature produces the nitrogen oxides (NO_x). We discuss these pollutants in ⊘ 18-6.

⊘ 17-6 Positive Crankcase Ventilation The crankcase is the lower part of the engine, the part that contains the crankshaft. The bottom of the crankcase is the oil pan, which holds the engine oil. In operation, the lubricating system (Chap. 7) sends oil from the oil pan to all moving parts in the engine.

The crankcase must be ventilated. During engine operation, some air-fuel mixture and burned gases leak down into the crankcase past the piston rings. This is called *blow-by* because the gases "blow by" the rings. In addition, water and liquid fuel appear in the crankcase during cold-engine operation. All of these must be cleared from the crankcase before they cause trouble. In earlier engines, the crankcase was ventilated by an opening at the front of the engine and a vent tube at the back. The forward motion of the car and the rotation of the crankshaft caused air to flow through the crankcase. This removed the blowby, water, and fuel (Fig. 17-5). Today, however, closed-crankcase systems, called *positive crankcase ventilating* (PCV) systems, are used on all cars. Air circulates through the crankcase as before, but the air then enters the carburetor and intake manifold. Any blowby, water vapor, or unburned fuel is therefore sent back through the engine. It is not emitted into the air, where it would increase atmospheric pollution.

Unless the water, liquid gasoline, and blowby are removed from the crankcase, sludge and acids will form. Sludge can clog oil lines and prevent oil from getting to the engine parts. This could mean a ruined engine. Acids corrode metal parts, and this, too, can ruin an engine.

NOTE: The engine must first heat up enough to vaporize the liquid water and gasoline in the crankcase. Then the circulating air can remove them, along with the blowby.

A typical PCV system for a six-cylinder engine is shown in Fig. 17-6. A typical system for a V-8 engine is shown in Fig. 17-7. Filtered air from the carburetor air cleaner is drawn through the crankcase. In the crankcase, it picks up the water and fuel vapors and the blow-by. The air then flows back up

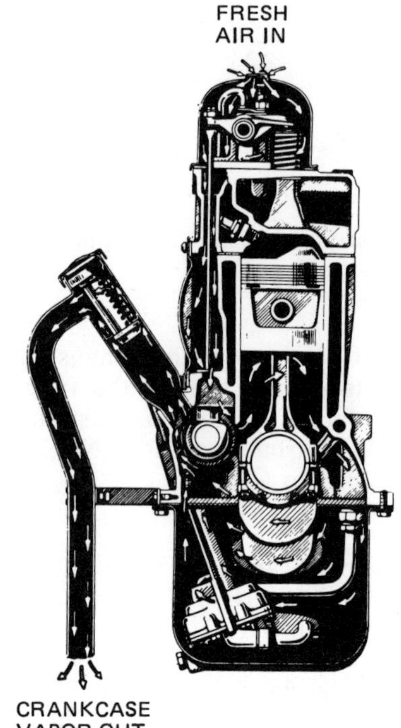

Fig. 17-5. Open-crankcase ventilating system.

Fig. 17-6. Positive crankcase ventilating system for a six-cylinder engine. (*Ford Motor Company*)

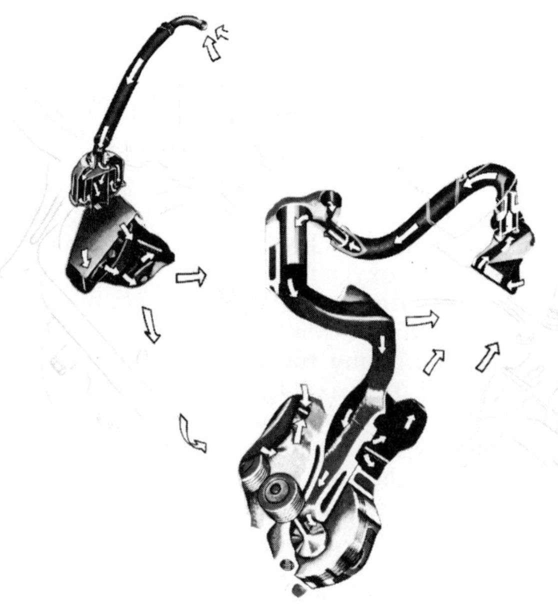

Fig. 17-7. Positive crankcase ventilating system for a V-8 engine. (*Ford Motor Company*)

to the intake manifold and enters the engine. There, the unburned fuel vapor is burned.

Too much air flowing through the intake manifold during idling would upset the air-fuel ratio. This could produce poor idling. To prevent this, a regulator valve is used. The valve is called a positive crankcase ventilating (PCV) valve. The PCV valve allows only a small amount of air to flow through during idle. But as engine speed increases, reduced intake-manifold vacuum causes the valve to open wider. This allows more air to flow through. Figure 17-8 shows the two positions of the valve. Figures 17-9 and 17-10 show the various locations of the PCV valves in six-cylinder and V-8 engines.

Fig. 17-8. The two extreme operating conditions of the PCV valve. (*Ford Motor Company*)

IN A SIX-CYLINDER
ENGINE THE
PCV VALVE IS LOCATED IN:
1. ROCKER-ARM COVER
2. BASE OF CARBURETOR
3. HOSE

Fig. 17-9. Location of the PCV valve on six-cylinder engines.

⊘ 17-7 Need for the Vapor-Recovery System Both the fuel tank and the carburetor can lose gasoline vapor if the car does not have a vapor-recovery system. The fuel tank "breathes" as the temperature changes; that is, the tank heats up, the air inside it expands. Part of the air is forced out through the tank tube, or through the vent in the tank cap. This air is loaded with gasoline vapor. When the tank cools, the air inside it contracts. More air enters the tank from the outside. This tank breathing causes a loss of gasoline. The higher the tank temperature rises (for instance, when the car is parked in the sun), the more gasoline vapor is lost.

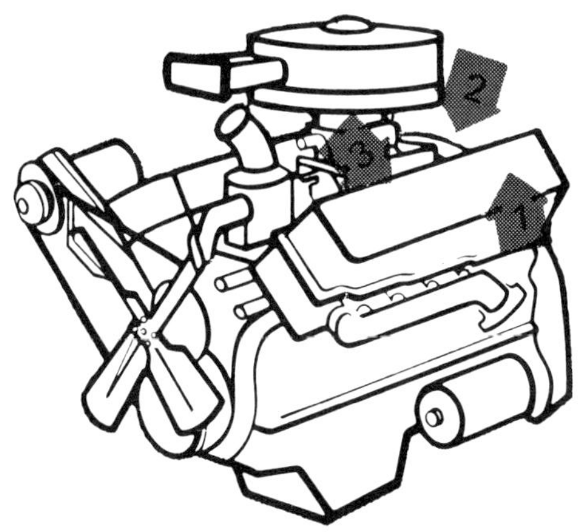

IN A V-8 ENGINE
THE PCV VALVE
IS LOCATED IN:
1. ROCKER-ARM COVER
2. REAR OF ENGINE
3. CARBURETOR BASE

Fig. 17-10. Locations of the PCV valve on V-8 engines.

The carburetor also can lose gasoline by evaporation. The carburetor float bowl is full when the engine is running. When the engine stops, engine heat evaporates some or all of the gasoline stored in the float bowl. Without a vapor-recovery system, this gasoline vapor would pass into the atmosphere.

A vapor-recovery system captures these gasoline vapors and prevents them from escaping into the air. It thus tends to reduce atmospheric pollution. All modern cars are equipped with vapor-recovery systems. They are called by various names: ECS (evaporation-control system), EEC (evaporation emission control), VVR (vehicle vapor recovery), and VSS (vapor-saver system). All work in the same general way.

⊘ 17-8 Vapor-Recovery Systems Figures 17-11 and 17-12 show a typical vapor-recovery system. The canister is filled with activated charcoal. Just after the engine is shut off, heat is still entering the carburetor. Some gasoline is vaporized out of the carburetor float bowl. The vapor passes through the canister and is *adsorbed* by the charcoal. "Adsorbed" means that the gasoline vapor is trapped on the surface of the charcoal particles. Many carburetor float bowls have a special vent (Fig. 12-11) connected by a tube to the charcoal canister. The vent and tube carry the float-bowl vapor directly to the canister.

At the same time, vapor-laden air from the fuel tank is carried by a special emission-control pipe to the canister. As the air passes down through the canister, the gasoline vapor is trapped by the charcoal particles. The air exits from the bottom of the canister, leaving the HC vapor behind. There is a filter at the bottom of the canister. It comes into action during the *purge* phase of operation. This occurs when the engine is started. Then, intake-manifold vacuum draws fresh air up through the canister. This fresh air removes, or purges, the gasoline vapor from the canister. It takes the HC through a purge line to a connection at the carburetor.

⊘ 17-9 Fuel-Return Line Notice, in Fig. 17-11, the fuel-return line that parallels the main fuel line. This fuel-return line connects the pressure side of the fuel pump to the fuel tank. It allows excess gasoline, pumped by the fuel pump, to return to the fuel tank. This action removes any vapor that might develop in the fuel pump. It also maintains a flow of fuel through the fuel pump. This keeps the fuel pump relatively cool and helps prevent vapor lock. There is more on fuel pumps in ⊘ 11-6.

⊘ 17-10 Charcoal Canister A charcoal canister is shown in sectional view in Fig. 17-13. An actual canister is shown in Fig. 17-14. The arrows in Fig. 17-13 show the flow of air and gasoline vapor. When the engine is turned off, vapor from the fuel tank flows into the canister. When the engine is running, intake-manifold vacuum draws air up through the

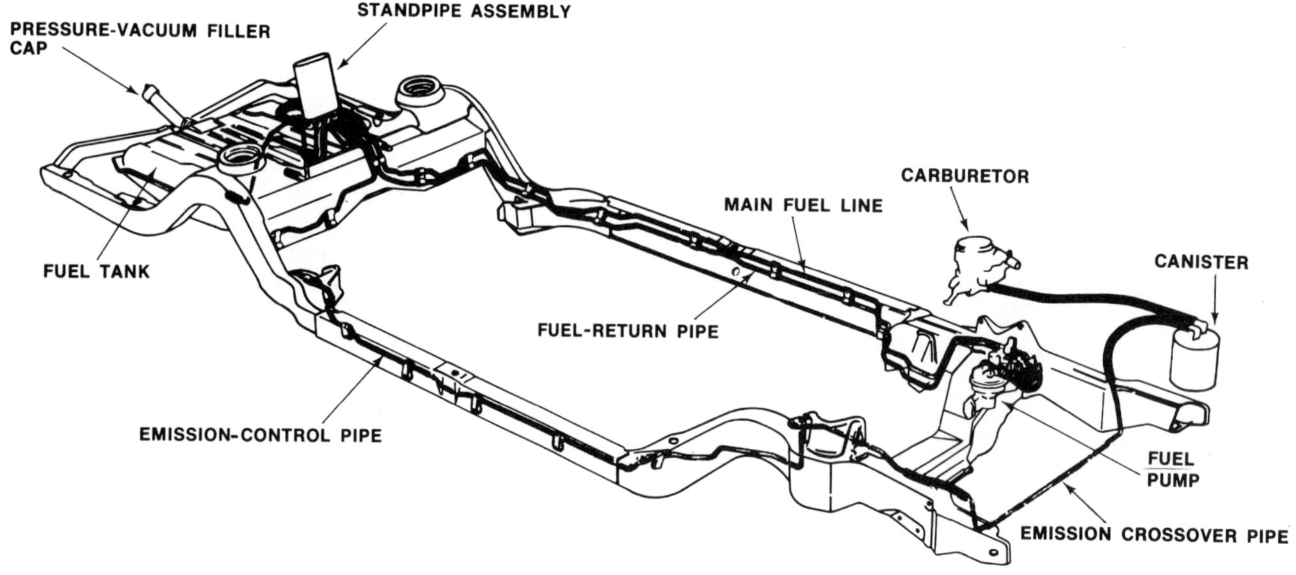

Fig. 17-11. Fuel-evaporation control, or vapor-recovery, system. Vapor goes to the canister. The fuel-return pipe returns excess fuel, not used by the carburetor, to the fuel tank. This constant flow of excess fuel through the fuel pump helps prevent vapor lock.

canister and into the carburetor. This air cleans the gasoline vapor out of the canister.

The charcoal canister in Fig. 17-15 is for a six-cylinder engine. Note that it has a restrictive valve, also known as a purge valve. This valve limits the flow of vapor and air to the carburetor during idling. But it allows full flow of vapor and air during part- to full-throttle operation. In the six-cylinder engine, full flow of vapor and air from the canister could upset engine idling. At higher engine speeds, however, full flow can be tolerated. The valve is operated by a vacuum signal from a drilled hole in the carburetor. This hole is located just below the throttle valve when the throttle valve is closed. With the throttle closed and the engine idling, a high vacuum develops below the throttle. This vacuum causes the purge valve to limit the flow of vapor and air.

On some models, the purge line from the canister is connected to the air cleaner, as in Fig. 17-16. The system operates in the manner described.

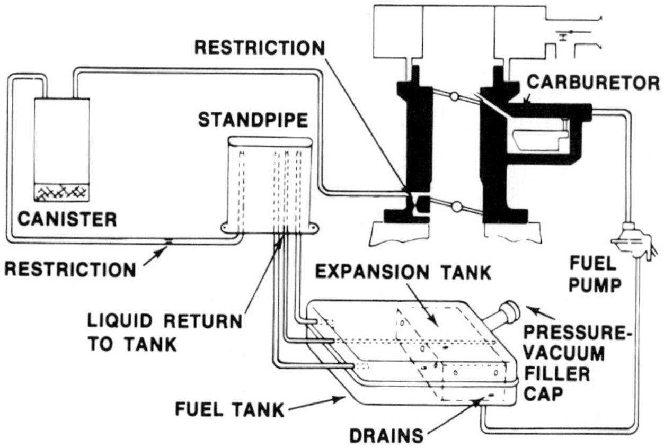

Fig. 17-12. Schematic view of a vapor-recovery system.

⊘ 17-11 Separating Vapor from Fuel The fuel tank must have some way of separating the gasoline vapor from liquid gasoline. Otherwise, liquid gasoline might flow to the canister and then out into the atmosphere. One system uses a standpipe assembly, as shown in Fig. 17-11. Figure 17-17 is a cutaway view of a standpipe assembly. It contains a series of pipes with openings at the top. Three of these pipes are connected to the center and two sides of the fuel

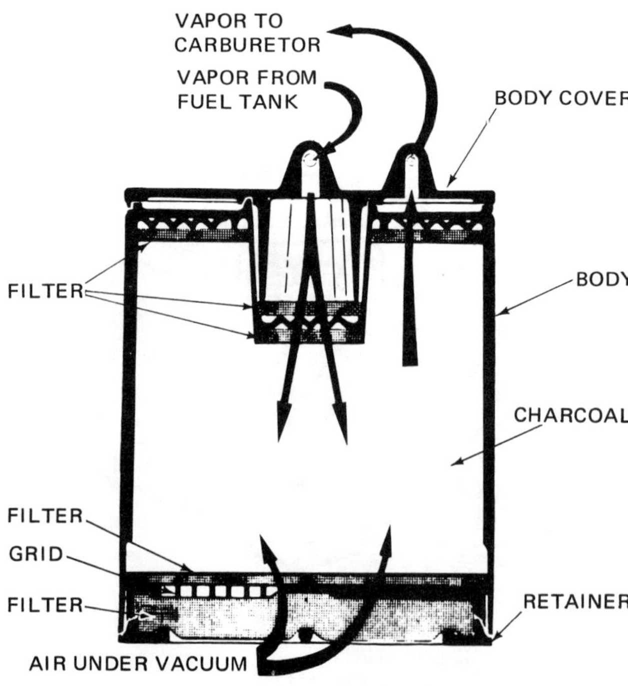

Fig. 17-13. Sectional view of a charcoal canister for a V-8 vapor-recovery system. (*Oldsmobile Division of General Motors Corporation*)

Fig. 17-14. Charcoal canister. Note its size.

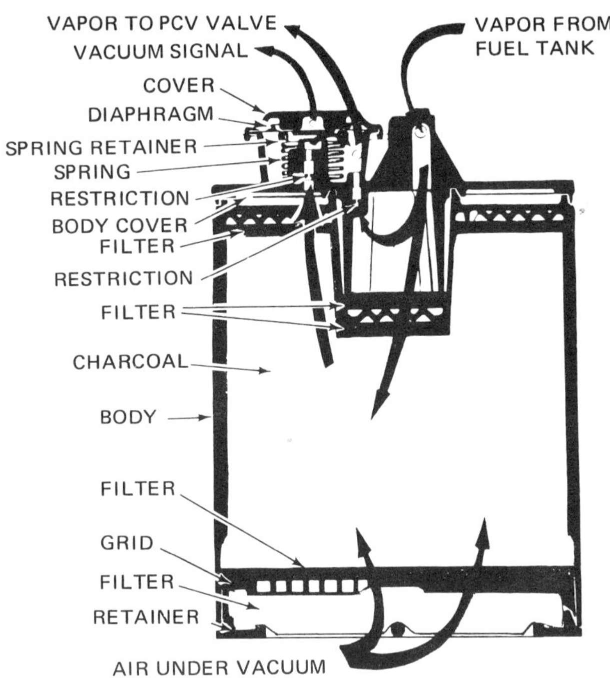

Fig. 17-15. Sectional view of a charcoal canister for a six-cylinder-engine vapor-recovery system. (*Oldsmobile Division of General Motors Corporation*)

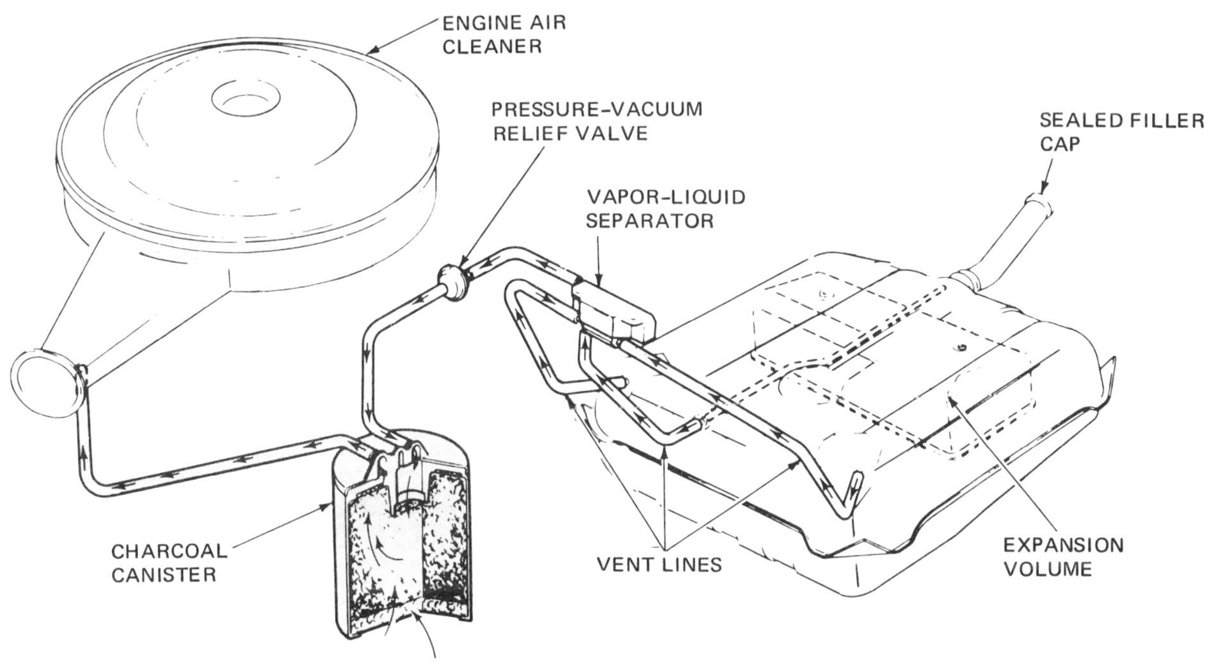

Fig. 17-16. Vapor-recovery system, shown schematically. In this system, the purge line from the canister is connected to the air-cleaner snorkel. (*Buick Motor Division of General Motors Corporation*)

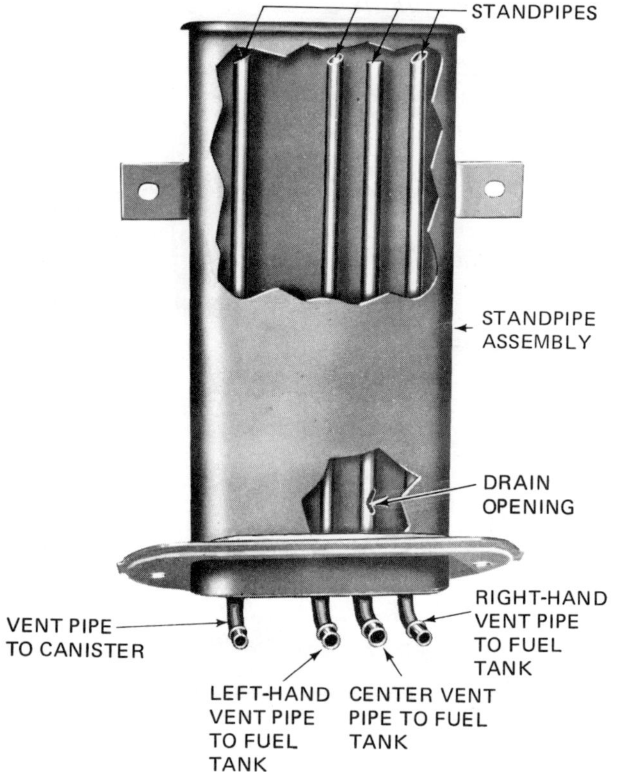

Fig. 17-17. Cutaway view of a standpipe assembly. (*Oldsmobile Division of General Motors Corporation*)

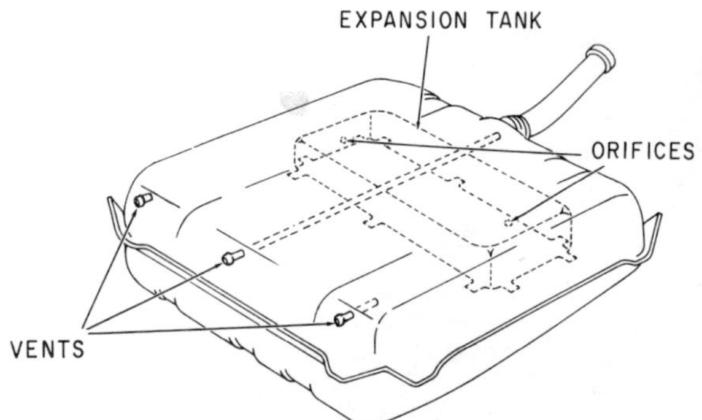

Fig. 17-18. Fuel tank used with a vapor-recovery system. The two side vents are short, but the center vent goes all the way to the rear of the tank. (*Pontiac Motor Division of General Motors Corporation*)

tank. These vents are shown in Fig. 17-18. With this system, at least one of the vents is always above the fuel level, regardless of the tilt of the car. Thus, air and fuel vapor can always pass up into the standpipe and through the vent line to the canister.

Figure 17-19 shows a variation of the standpipe system. Here, a vapor-liquid separator is positioned above the fuel tank. Four vapor vent lines connect the separator to the four corners of the fuel tank.

A still different vapor-liquid separating ar-

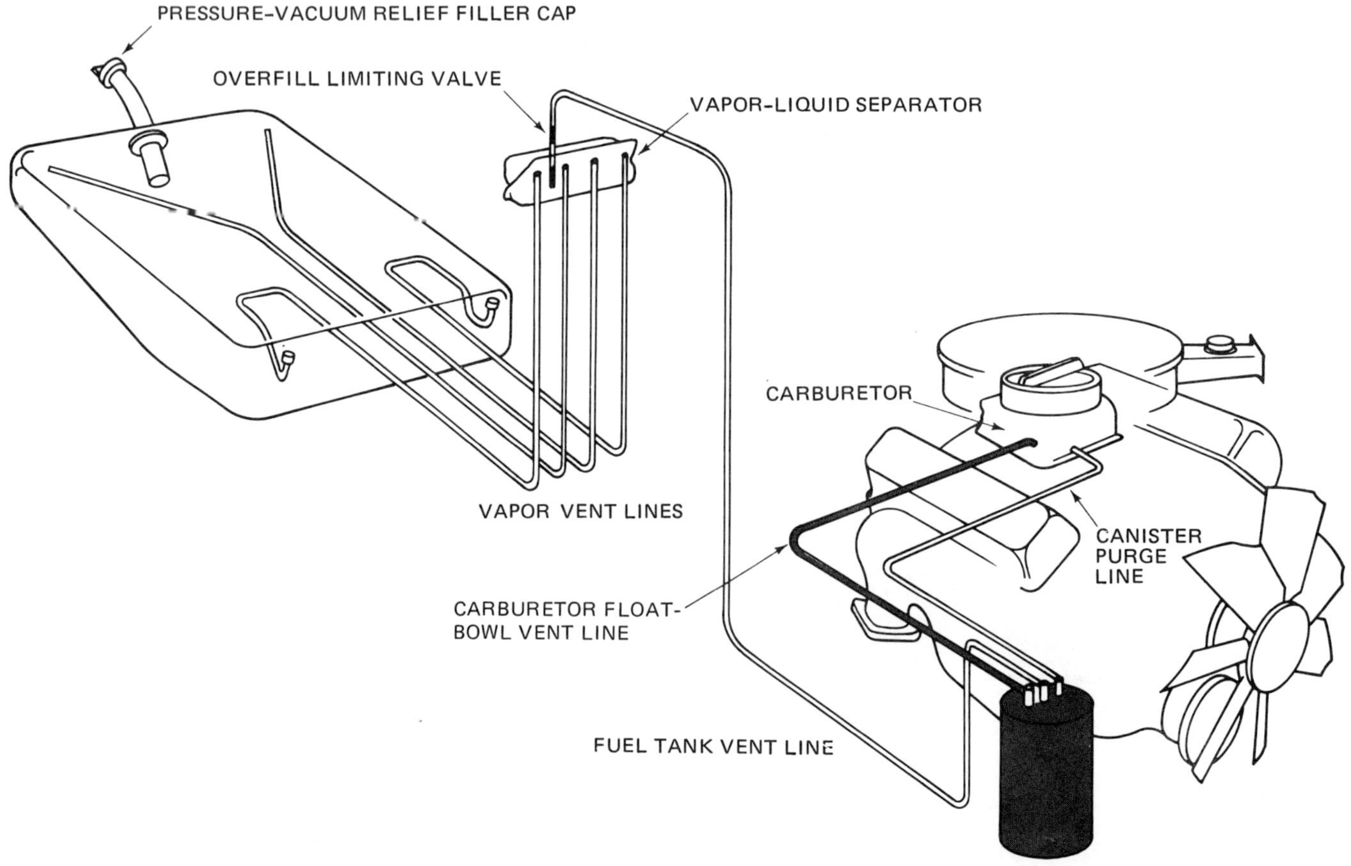

Fig. 17-19. Vapor-recovery system. Note the vent line between the carburetor float bowl and the canister. (*Chrysler Corporation*)

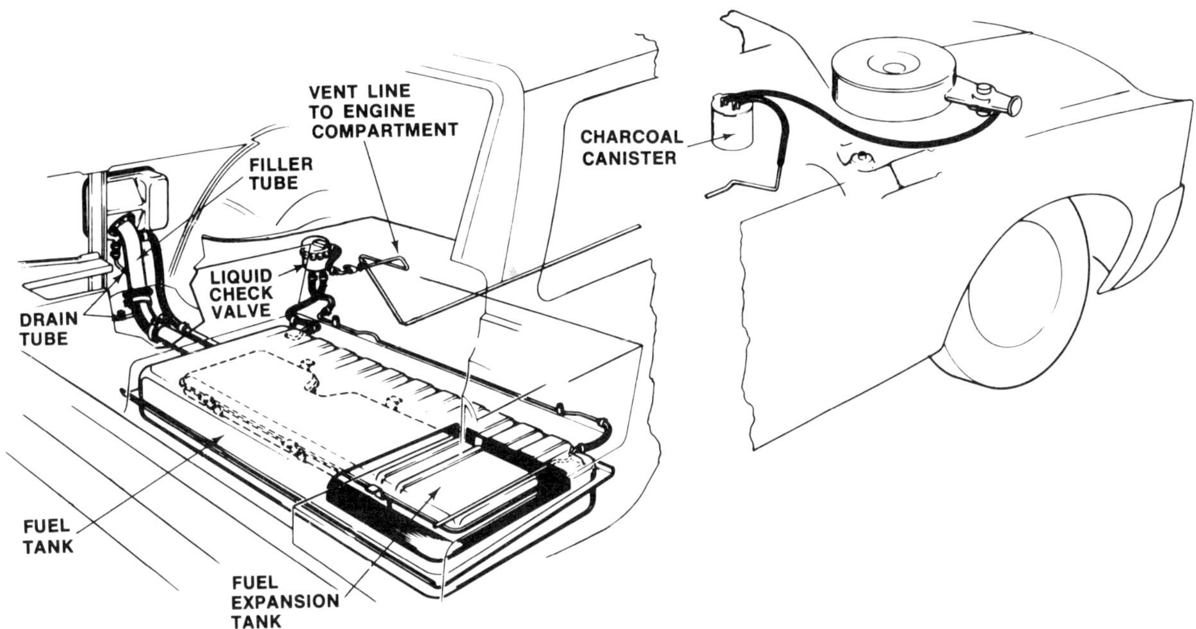

Fig. 17-20. Vapor-recovery system using a liquid check valve. (*American Motors Corporation*)

rangement is shown in Fig. 17-20. In this system, a liquid check valve is used. It is connected by tubes to the two ends of the fuel tank. The liquid check valve passes air but does not pass liquid gasoline.

Another type of vapor separator is shown in Fig. 17-21. This separator is mounted on top of the fuel tank. It is filled with filter material that passes vapor but not liquid gasoline. The vapor separator is mounted at the top center of the fuel tank. This minimizes the chances of liquid gasoline getting directly to the separator.

Some systems use a domed fuel tank (Fig. 17-22). The dome forms the high point of the tank, and the emission-control pipe is connected at this point.

⊘ 17-12 Sealed Fuel Tank

Earlier fuel tanks either had vent pipes or the fuel-tank cap was vented. Modern automobiles, with vapor-recovery systems, use a sealed fuel tank with a special cap. The cap has a pressure-vacuum valve system. It is much like the pressure-vacuum cap used on the radiator of a pressurized cooling system. The cap valve opens if too much pressure develops in the tank. It also opens to admit air when fuel is withdrawn, so that a vacuum does not develop in the tank. Either pressure or a vacuum could damage the tank.

⊘ 17-13 Carburetor Insulator

In some carburetors, an insulator (Fig. 17-23) is used to reduce heat flow

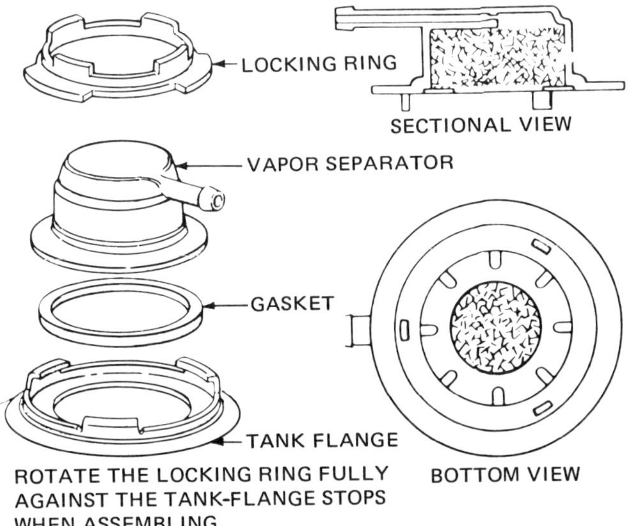

Fig. 17-21. Vapor separator using filter material. (*Ford Motor Company*)

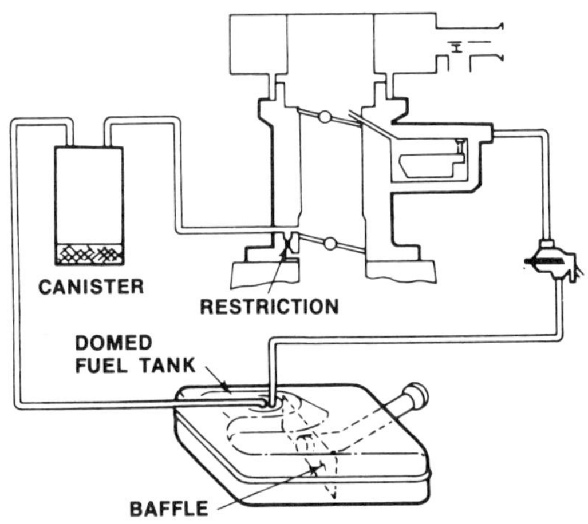

Fig. 17-22. Vapor-recovery system using a domed fuel tank. (*Pontiac Motor Division of General Motors Corporation*)

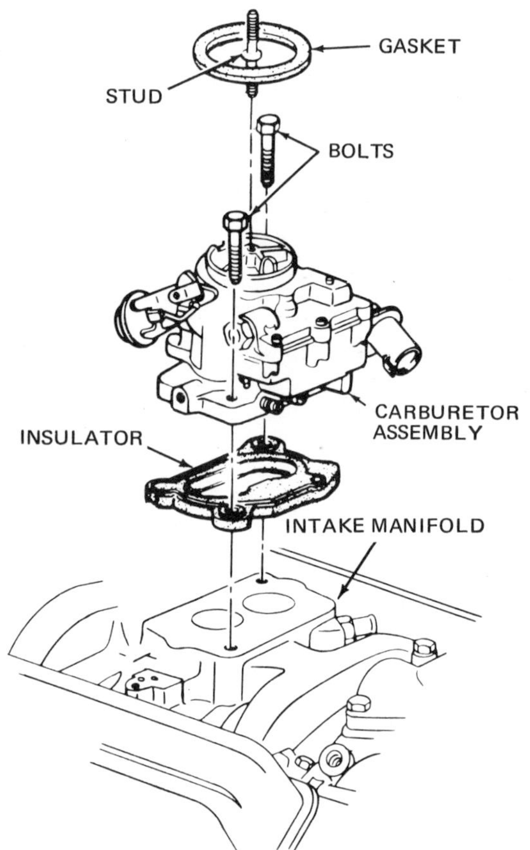

Fig. 17-23. Carburetor insulator placed between the carburetor and the intake manifold. The insulator blocks the passage of heat to the carburetor. It thus reduces fuel evaporation from the float bowl. (*Chevrolet Motor Division of General Motors Corporation*)

from the engine to the carburetor. The insulator is placed between the carburetor and the intake manifold. It forms a heat barrier between them. This reduces fuel evaporation from the float bowl after the engine has been turned off. Another arrangement uses an aluminum heat-dissipating plate which sticks out, as shown in Fig. 17-24.

⊘ 17-14 Vapor Storage in Crankcase Some cars of Chrysler Corporation and some imported cars use the crankcase to store gasoline vapor from the fuel tank and carburetor (Fig. 17-25). When the engine is stopped, gasoline vapor from the fuel tank flows to the crankcase air cleaner. From there, it flows down into the crankcase. At the same time, fuel vapor from the carburetor float bowl flows down into the crankcase. The vapor is two to four times as heavy as air. Thus, it sinks to the bottom of the crankcase. When the engine is started, the positive crankcase ventilating system clears the crankcase of the vapor. The vapor is carried up into the intake manifold and then into the engine, where it is burned.

⊘ 17-15 Expansion Tank You have probably noticed that the fuel tanks in Figs. 17-12 and 17-16 (and other figures) have expansion tanks. These tanks prevent overflow if the fuel temperature rises after the fuel tank has been filled. As the fuel temperature goes up, the fuel expands. The expansion tank gives the fuel a place to go.

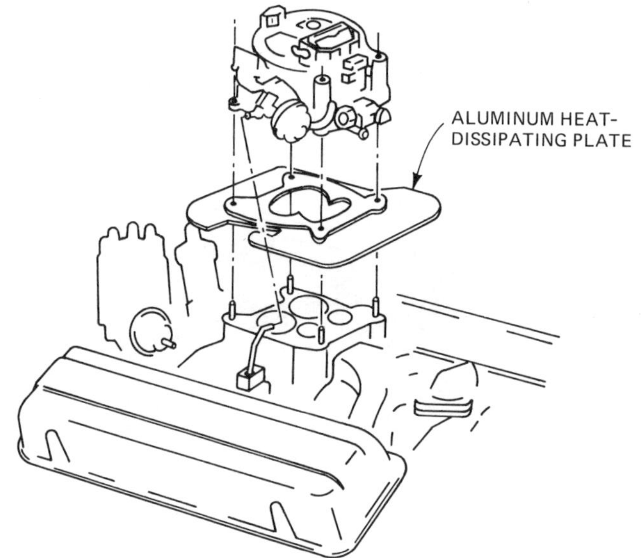

Fig. 17-24. Insulator and aluminum heat-dissipating plate between the carburetor and intake manifold. The insulator and plate reduce heat flow to the carburetor.

CHAPTER 17 CHECKUP

NOTE: Since the following is a chapter review test, you should review the chapter before taking the test.

The following checkup is included so you can review what you have been studying on air pollu-

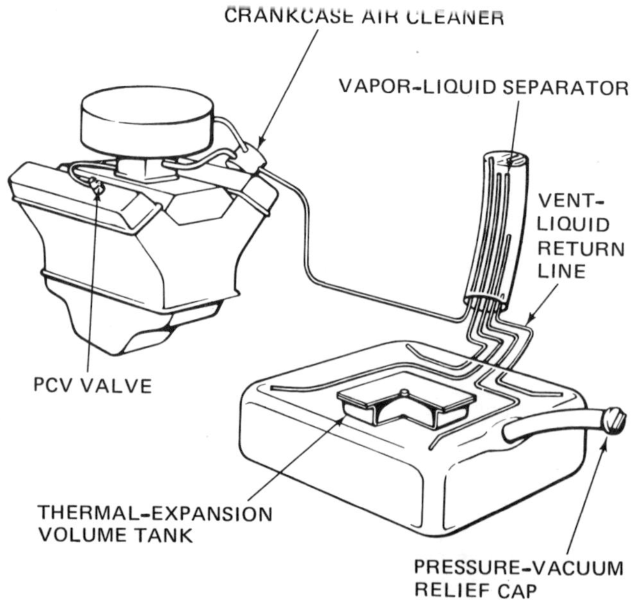

Figure 17-25. Vapor-recovery system using the crankcase for fuel-vapor storage. (*Chrysler Corporation*)

tion, smog, and the automobile. Knowing the fundamentals makes it easier to understand what is being done to reduce atmospheric pollution from the automobile.

Completing the Sentences The sentences that follow are incomplete. After each sentence there are several words or phrases, but only one of them correctly completes the sentence. Write each sentence in your notebook, ending it with the one word or phrase that completes it correctly.

1. The four places from which a car can give off pollutants are the fuel tank, carburetor, and the: (*a*) engine and manifold, (*b*) crankcase and tail pipe, (*c*) crankcase and manifold.
2. Three pollutants that the car gives off are: (*a*) HC, CO, and NO_x, (*b*) HC, CO_2, and H_2O, (*c*) H, C, and CO.
3. The system that picks up blowby and gasoline vapors from the crankcase and sends them through the engine is called: (*a*) a ventilator, (*b*) a positive crankcase ventilating system, (*c*) the antipollution system.
4. The fuel tank breathes as: (*a*) car speed changes, (*b*) temperature changes, (*c*) engine speed increases.
5. Smog is a word made up of the two words: (*a*) smell and fog, (*b*) smell and bog, (*c*) smoke and fog.
6. The vapor-recovery system stores gasoline vapors in: (*a*) a filter, (*b*) the fuel tank, (*c*) a charcoal canister.
7. The modern automobile equipped with a vapor-recovery system uses a: (*a*) sealed fuel gauge, (*b*) pressure-vacuum fuel-tank cap, (*c*) combination vapor and gasoline fuel pump.
8. The purpose of the expansion tank in the fuel tank is to: (*a*) allow the tank to expand to hold more fuel, (*b*) allow the gasoline to expand as its temperature goes up, (*c*) prevent overfilling of the tank.

Review Questions The questions that follow give you a chance to check your general knowledge of smog and the automobile. Write the answers in your notebook. Check back into the chapter if you need to refresh your memory.

1. How did smog first start?
2. What holds smog over big cities?
3. How many tons of people-made pollutants enter the air in the United States each year?
4. What are the four places from which pollutants can come from the automobile?
5. Describe how the positive crankcase ventilating system works.
6. Why is the vapor-recovery system needed? How does it work?
7. What is the purpose of the fuel-return line?
8. Why is a pressure-vacuum fuel-tank cap needed?
9. What is the purpose of the expansion tank?

SUGGESTIONS FOR FURTHER STUDY

Many articles are published, in newspapers and magazines, about atmospheric pollution and what to do about it. Read and save them. Try to decide for yourself whether all the emission controls on automobiles are really necessary. Talk to other people to get their opinions. See if you can come up with some valid answers as to what is really needed.

chapter 18

CLEANING UP THE EXHAUST GAS

In the previous chapter, we described the positive crankcase ventilating system and the fuel-vapor recovery system. These systems reduce pollution from three of the four automotive sources (see Fig. 17-4). In this chapter, we consider the steps that have been taken to clean up the fourth source of pollution—the exhaust gases coming from the tail pipe.

⊘ 18-1 Cleaning up the Exhaust Gas We shall discuss three ways of cleaning up the exhaust gas:

1. Controlling the air-fuel mixture.
2. Controlling combustion
3. Treating the exhaust gas

⊘ 18-2 Controlling the Air-Fuel Mixture Gasoline has been changed to make it burn better. One of the changes is the elimination of lead. Recall from Chap. 10 that tetraethyl lead has been added to gasoline to control detonation and to permit higher compression ratios. Lead is now being removed to permit the use of catalytic converters, which we discuss later in the chapter. Removing the lead has required a reduction of compression ratios. Basically, controlling the air-fuel mixture has meant (1) modifying the carburetor to deliver a leaner air-fuel mixture, and (2) providing faster warm-up and quicker choke action.

⊘ 18-3 Leaner Idling Air-Fuel Mixture Modern carburetors have idle limiters (Fig. 18-1). The idle-mixture adjustment screw is adjusted at the factory. Then the idle-limiter cap is installed. The cap permits limited adjustment of the idle mixture. But it does not permit any adjustment that goes beyond the lean-idle setting required by law. The cap can be removed, of course, if the carburetor requires a major overhaul. But it must then be reinstalled.

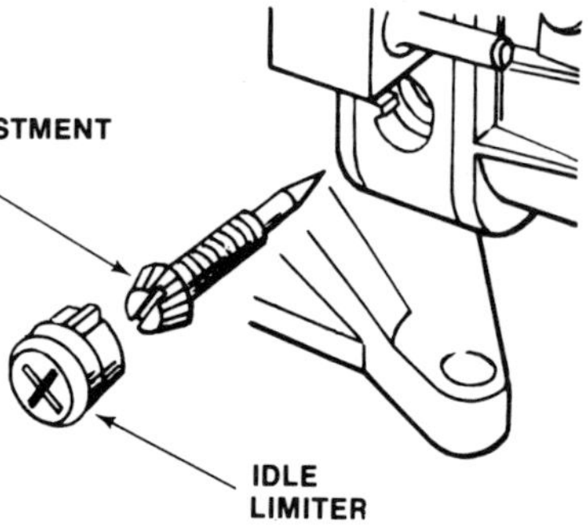

Fig. 18-1. Location of the idle limiter in one model of carburetor. (*Ford Motor Company*)

⊘ 18-4 Faster Warm-up If the air-fuel mixture coming from the carburetor is cold, only part of the fuel vaporizes. This means that an extra-rich mixture is needed. Otherwise, the engine will not get enough gasoline vapor to run properly. Of course, the situation changes as soon as the engine begins to run. Then, the hot exhaust gas circulating around the manifold heat-control valve begins to heat the intake manifold (see ⊘ 12-25). However, this is too slow for

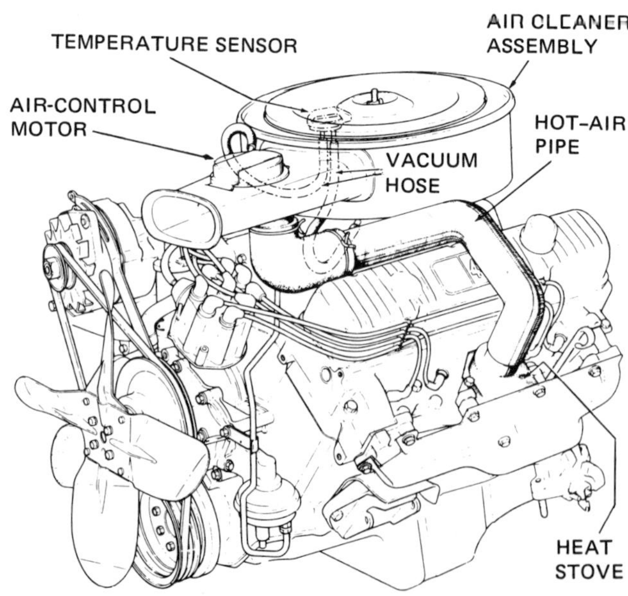

Fig. 18-2. Heated-air system installed on a V-8 engine. (*Buick Motor Division of General Motors Corporation*)

the new systems. So a thermostatically controlled air cleaner is used to quickly provide heated air to the carburetor when the engine is cold. This system, called the *heated-air* system, is discussed in ⊘ 11-11. Figure 18-2 shows the system installed on a V-8 engine.

The system includes a control-damper assembly in the snorkel of the air cleaner. It also includes a heat stove that surrounds the exhaust manifold. When the engine is cold, the temperature sensor in the air cleaner closes the damper. In this position, all air has to come from the heat stove. When the engine starts and the exhaust manifold begins to warm up, hot air is delivered to the carburetor. This action improves cold and warm-up operation.

As the engine begins to warm up, the ingoing air temperature rises above 100°F [37.8°C]. This causes the temperature sensor to admit manifold vacuum to the air-control motor. The air-control motor opens the control-damper assembly. Now air can enter from the engine compartment.

This system allows the engine to start and operate satisfactorily when cold, even though the idle mixture is lean.

⊘ 18-5 Faster-acting Choke In earlier systems, the automatic choke was operated only by engine heat (⊘ 12-24). Late-model cars have electric-assist chokes (Figs. 12-32 to 12-34). The choke thermostat is subjected to heat from both a heating element in the choke and heat from the exhaust gas. This reduces the amount of time during which the engine operates in a choked condition. With the choke valve closed, the engine is fed a very rich air-fuel mixture. The exhaust gas is thus loaded with unburned HC and with CO. The electric-assist choke reduces the length of time during which these pollutants are fed into the atmosphere. There is more information on the electric-assist choke in ⊘ 12-24.

⊘ 18-6 Controlling the Combustion Process The combustion process seems simple at first glance. A mixture of air and gasoline vapor is compressed in the combustion chamber. A spark ignites it. It burns and produces the high pressure that pushes the piston down. However, the process is complicated. Here are some of the factors involved:

1. The layers of air-fuel mixture next to the relatively cool cylinder head and piston head do not burn. The metal surfaces chill these layers below the combustion point. So the unburned fuel is swept out of the cylinder on the exhaust stroke. This adds polluting HC to the atmosphere. There are two methods of combating this problem. One is to use stratified charge or fuel injection. The other is to reduce the surface area surrounding the combustion chamber. We shall come back to these two methods later.
2. Increasing the combustion temperature improves fuel combustion. But the higher temperature produces more nitrogen oxides (NO_x), and these create another problem. More on this later.
3. Vacuum advance gives the air-fuel mixture a longer time to burn when the engine operates at part throttle. But it also allows more time for NO_x to form under certain operating conditions. Therefore, a means must be provided to kill the vacuum advance under these special operating conditions. We cover this in detail later.
4. Carbon buildup in the combustion chambers increases the HC in the exhaust gas. The carbon has pores that fill up during the compression and combustion strokes. During the exhaust stroke, when the pressure is released, the HC in the carbon pores escapes and exits with the exhaust gas.

⊘ 18-7 Reducing the Combustion-Chamber Surface Area Actually, what we are talking about here is reducing the *S/V* ratio (Fig. 18-3). The *S/V* ratio is the ratio between the surface area *S* and the volume *V* of the combustion chamber. A sphere has the lowest possible *S/V* ratio. The wedge combustion chamber (Fig. 18-4) has a higher *S/V* ratio. Thus, for the same volume, the hemispheric combustion chamber has a lower surface area. It has less surface to chill the air-fuel mixture. Therefore, the hemispheric combustion chamber produces a lower percentage of unburned HC in the exhaust.

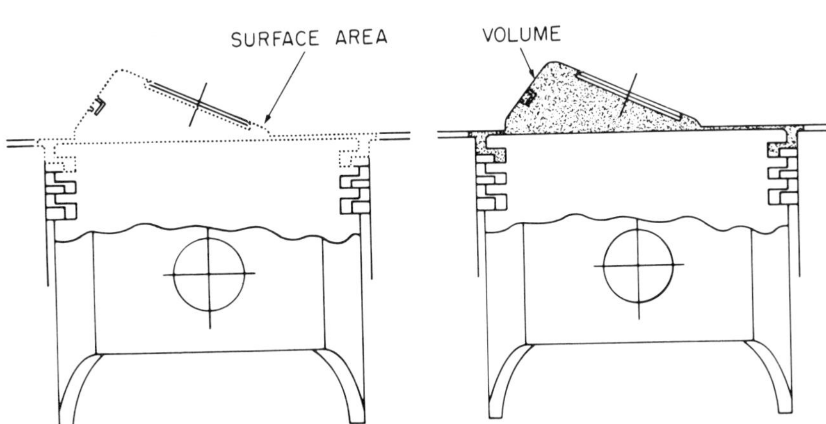

Fig. 18-3. Ratio of the surface area to the volume of the combustion chamber, or *S/V*. This ratio affects the amount of unburned hydrocarbons in the exhaust gas.

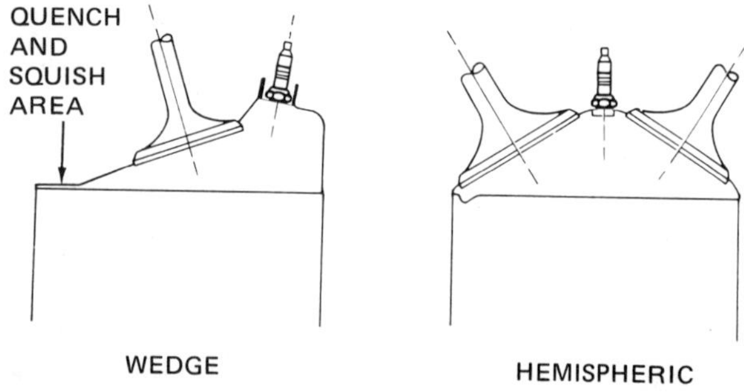

Fig. 18-4. Wedge and hemispheric combustion chambers. (*General Motors Corporation*)

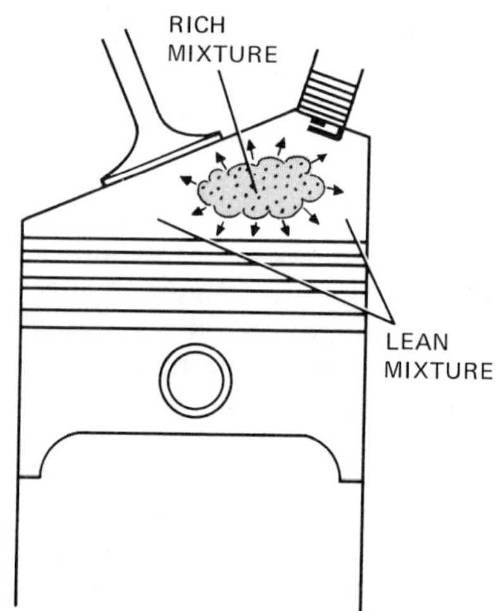

Fig. 18-5. Principle of stratified charging.

⊘ 18-8 Stratified Charge

The stratified-charge engine provides a layer of richer mixture in the center of the compressed air-fuel mixture (Fig. 18-5). The richer mixture is ignited first. During combustion, the burning rich mixture spreads outward. It moves into areas where the mixture is lean and harder to ignite. With stratified charging, a much leaner air-fuel mixture, on the average, can be used. The combustion takes place largely in and around the layer of rich mixture. This means that the fuel is more completely burned. The amounts of pollutants, such as carbon monoxide, unburned gasoline, and nitrogen oxides, are reduced.

One way to achieve stratified charging is to give the air-fuel mixture a swirling motion as it enters the cylinder. This can be done by careful placement of the intake port.

Another method is the so-called Honda system. Here, a separate, small precombustion chamber is used. This precombustion chamber has the spark plug and its own intake valve. Figure 18-6 is an outline view of the engine, showing the valves, the spark plug, and the piston for one cylinder. Figure 18-7 shows how the arrangement works. In operation, the carburetor delivers a very lean mixture to the main combustion chamber, and a very rich mixture to the precombustion chamber. The rich mixture, under the high pressure of combustion, streams out into the main combustion chamber, as shown in 3 and 4 of Fig. 18-7. There it mixes with the lean mixture, and combustion continues. This assures good burning of the fuel so that the polluting gases—carbon monoxide, unburned fuel (HC), and nitrogen oxides—are kept to a minimum.

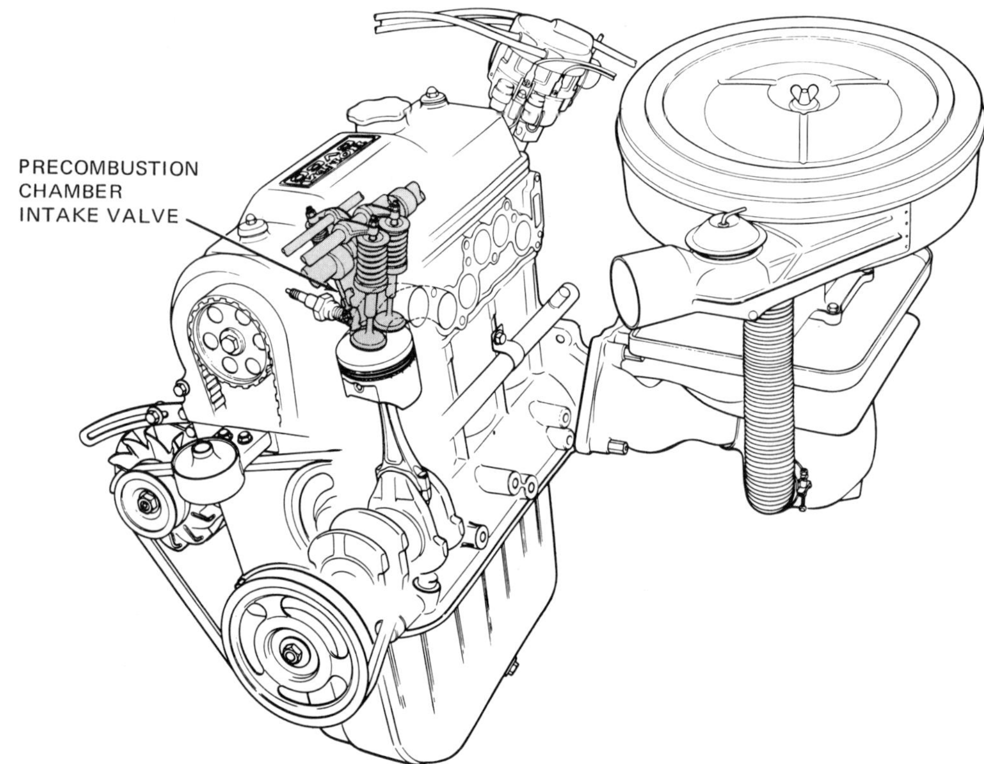

Fig. 18-6. Outline view of the Honda four-cylinder engine, showing the essential working parts of one cylinder. (*Honda*)

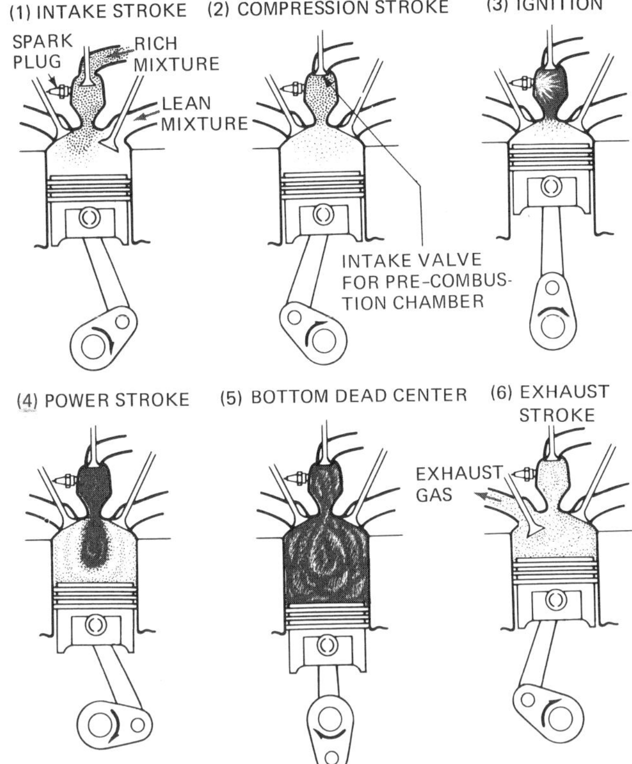

Fig. 18-7. Sequence of actions in the Honda system. (*Honda*)

⊘ 18-9 Fuel Injection

We have already described fuel-injection systems for gasoline engines (Chap. 16). Fuel injection improves combustion and reduces HC and CO in the exhaust. The fuel-injection system more accurately meters the fuel. It supplies the same amount of fuel to all the cylinders. (Contrast this with the carburetor-type system, in which some cylinders get a richer mixture than others.)

⊘ 18-10 Increasing the Combustion Temperature

Increasing the combustion temperature reduces CO and unburned HC in the exhaust. However, it increases the formation of NO_x. One method of reducing NO_x is to reduce the compression ratio. This reduces top combustion temperatures and thus the amount of NO_x that is formed.

Other NO_x reduction methods are used. One of these (the exhaust-gas recirculation, or EGR, system) reduces NO_x during normal running of the engine. Another reduces NO_x during acceleration in lower gears and during part-throttle, high-vacuum conditions. We shall look at both methods.

⊘ 18-11 Exhaust-Gas Recirculation

If a small part of the exhaust gas is sent back through the engine, it lowers the combustion temperature and reduces the formation of NO_x. The amount sent through the engine should vary according to operating conditions. The simplest system of this type is shown in Fig. 18-8. Here, a special passage connects the ex-

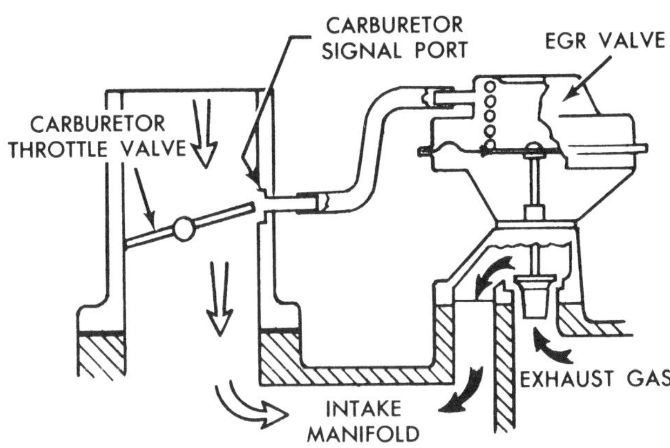

Fig. 18-8. Schematic view of an exhaust-gas recirculation system. (*Chevrolet Motor Division of General Motors Corporation*)

haust manifold with the intake manifold. This passage is opened or closed by a special exhaust-gas recirculation (EGR) valve. The upper part of the valve is sealed. It is connected by a vacuum line to a signal port in the carburetor, as shown. When there is no vacuum at work on the signal port, there is no vacuum in the EGR valve. The spring holds the valve closed. No exhaust gas recirculates. This is the situation during engine idling, when NO_x formation is close to a minimum.

However, when the throttle is opened, it passes the signal port. This allows intake-manifold vacuum to operate the EGR valve. The vacuum raises the diaphragm in the valve. This lifts the valve off the seat. Now exhaust gas can pass into the intake manifold. There, it mixes with the air-fuel mixture and enters the engine cylinders. The exhaust gas lowers the combustion temperature and thus reduces the formation of NO_x. Note that, at wide-open throttle, there is little vacuum in the intake manifold. Thus, the EGR valve is nearly closed. At wide-open throttle, there is less need for exhaust-gas recirculation.

Figure 18-9 shows the EGR valve in the fully open position. On many late-model cars, a thermal vacuum switch prevents exhaust-gas recirculation until the engine temperature reaches about 100°F [37.8°C]. The thermal switch is connected into the vacuum line between the carburetor and the EGR valve. It is mounted in the cooling-system thermostat housing, so that it senses coolant temperature. If this temperature is below 100°F [37.8°C], the thermal switch remains closed. This prevents the vacuum from reaching the EGR valve, so exhaust gas does not recirculate. This improves cold-engine performance for the first few moments of operation. After the engine warms up to where it can tolerate exhaust-gas recirculation, the thermal valve opens. Now vacuum can get to the EGR valve, and exhaust gas can recirculate.

There are several variations of this basic system. For instance, some EGR valves have a second diaphragm. It produces increased exhaust-gas recirculation when the engine is heavily loaded, as during

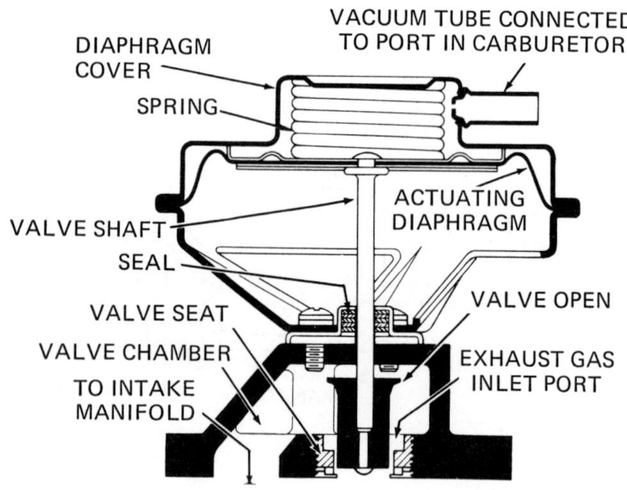

Fig. 18-9. Sectional view of the EGR valve. (*Chevrolet Motor Division of General Motors Corporation*)

hard acceleration. Also, some high-performance engines use a modulator system to provide additional control based on car speed. One system of this type is shown in Fig. 18-10. The modulator system is enclosed in dashed lines. It includes a solenoid valve that is normally open, allowing intake-manifold vacuum to pass through it. When the engine temperature is high enough to open the thermal switch, and the throttle is partly open, intake manifold can operate the EGR valve. The exhaust gas recirculates. However, when the car reaches a set speed, the speed sensor sends a signal to the electronic amplifier. This causes the amplifier to close the solenoid valve. Now the vacuum line is closed, and exhaust-gas recirculation stops.

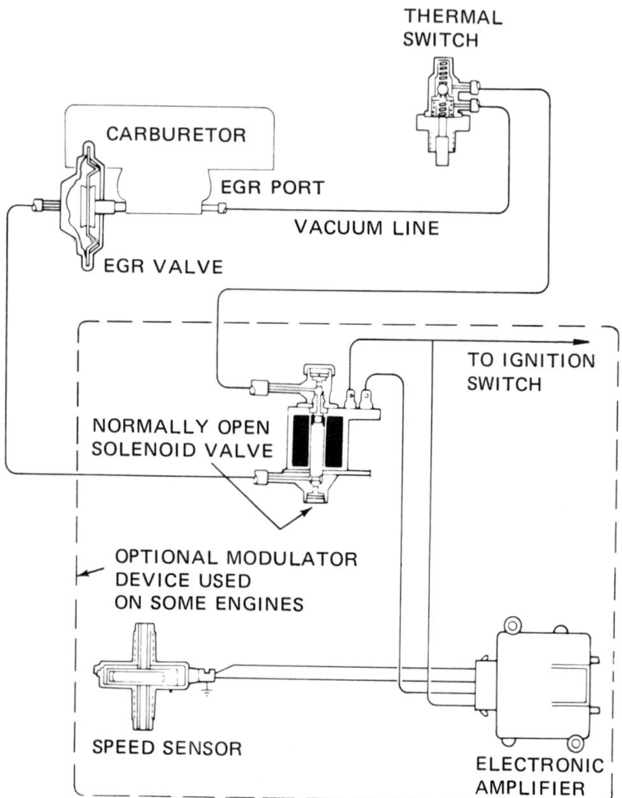

Fig. 18-10. Exhaust-gas recirculation system, showing the optional modulator device for some engines. (*Ford Motor Company*)

⊘ 18-12 Valve Overlap One of the features of the Chrysler complete emission-control systems is additional valve overlap. The complete set of systems is shown in Fig. 18-11. Additional valve overlap does the same thing as the EGR system, but in a different way. Increased valve overlap leaves more of the exhaust gases in the cylinders. The intake valve opens while there is still quite a bit of exhaust gas in the cylinder. Therefore, exhaust gas mixes with the air-fuel mixture in the cylinder. The top combustion temperature is reduced, and less NO_x is formed. However, this increased valve overlap can cause rough idling.

⊘ 18-13 Control of Vacuum Advance—TCS System The distributor vacuum advance is actuated during part-throttle operation. This provides more time for the leaner air-fuel mixture to burn. However, this added time also allows more NO_x to form. Thus, controls are used to prevent vacuum advance under certain conditions. For example, Chevrolet uses a transmission-controlled spark (TCS) system on cars with manual transmissions. The TCS system prevents vacuum advance in reverse, neutral, and low forward gears. Under these special conditions, vacuum advance could greatly increase the formation of NO_x.

Figure 18-12 shows the Chevrolet TCS system for a six-cylinder engine in a manual-transmission car. The diagram also shows the engine temperature switch (lower left), and the idle-stop solenoid. Figure 18-13 shows the situation when the car is first started. Turning on the ignition switch energizes the idle-stop solenoid. The plunger extends to contact the throttle lever. This prevents the throttle from closing completely, so the idle speed stays high enough. When the engine is turned off, the idle-stop solenoid allows the throttle to close completely. This prevents dieseling (the engine running with the ignition off).

Now refer to Fig. 18-13 again. Note that turning on the ignition switch completes the circuit through the vacuum-advance solenoid and temperature-switch cold terminal. At the same time, the circuit to the 20-second time relay is completed. With either of these circuits complete, the vacuum-advance solenoid is energized. Vacuum is admitted to the distributor vacuum-advance mechanism so that vacuum advance is obtained.

Figure 18-14 shows the system in low-gear operation. If the engine temperature has gone up enough, the temperature-switch cold points have opened. Also, after 20 seconds, the time-relay switch opens. Thus, the circuit to the vacuum-advance solenoid is

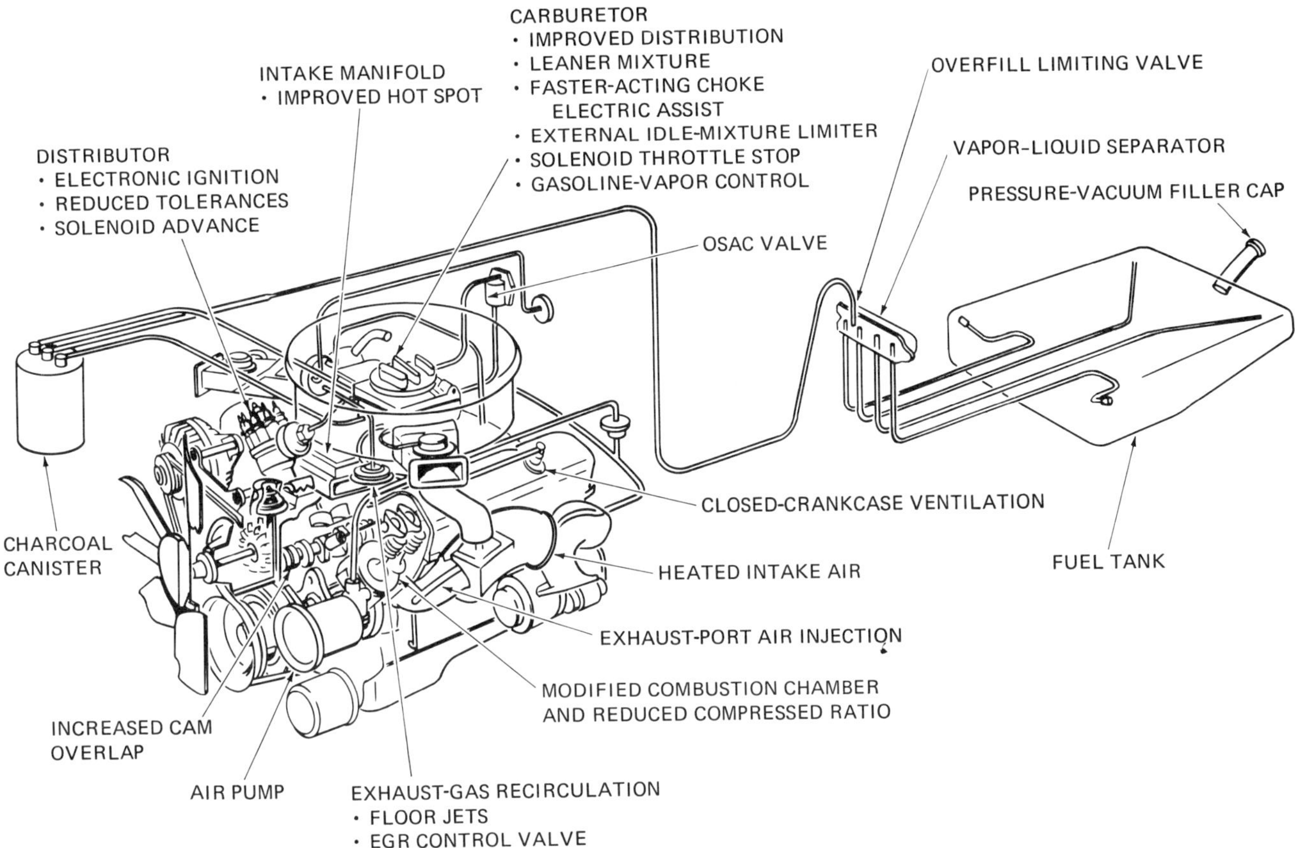

Fig. 18-11. Complete emission-control systems used on Chrysler Corporation V-8 engines. They include a vapor-recovery system, positive crankcase ventilation, exhaust-gas recirculation (plus increased valve overlap), and other features. (*Chrysler Corporation*)

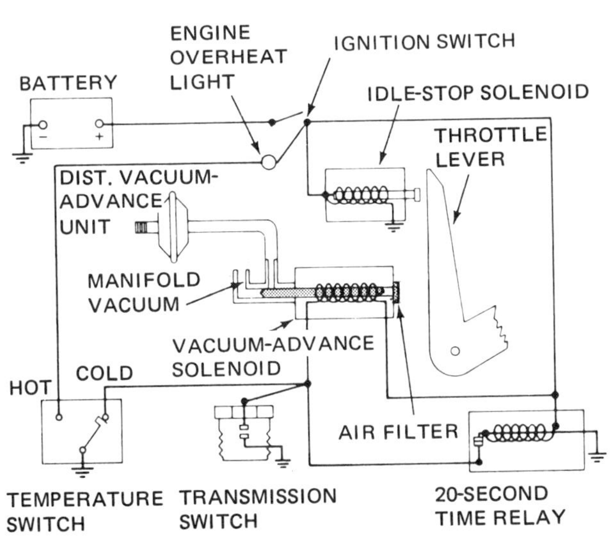

Fig. 18-12. Transmission-controlled spark (TCS) system with the engine off. (*Chevrolet Motor Division of General Motors Corporation*)

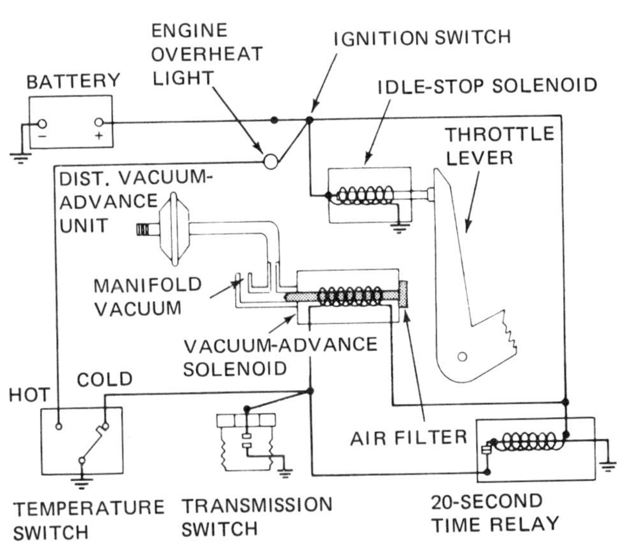

Fig. 18-13. TCS system with a cold engine running. (*Chevrolet Motor Division of General Motors Corporation*)

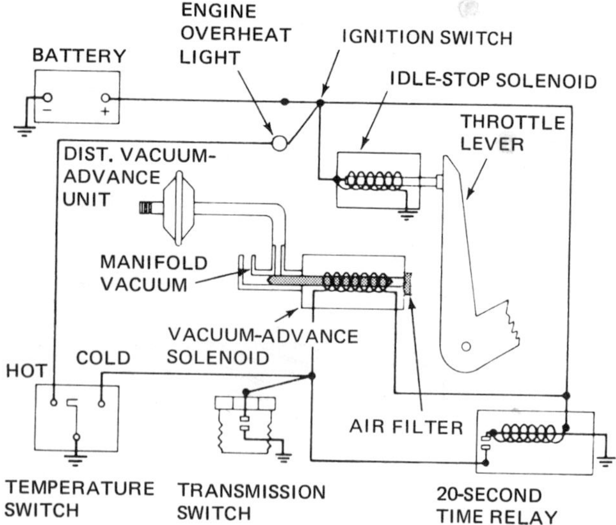

Fig. 18-14. TCS system during low-gear operation. (*Chevrolet Motor Division of General Motors Corporation*)

broken by either of these conditions. The solenoid plunger moves to block vacuum to the distributor vacuum-advance mechanism. No vacuum advance results.

Figure 18-15 shows the system in high gear. The transmission switch closes its points when the transmission is shifted into high. This energizes the vacuum-advance solenoid so that vacuum is admitted to the distributor vacuum-advance mechanism. Vacuum advance can then result.

Some systems have a temperature override switch. This switch provides vacuum advance under any condition if the engine begins to overheat. The system is shown in Fig. 18-16. If the engine becomes too hot, the hot points in the temperature override switch close. This energizes the solenoid so that vacuum is admitted to the distributor vacuum-advance mechanism. With vacuum advance, the engine speed increases and improved cooling results.

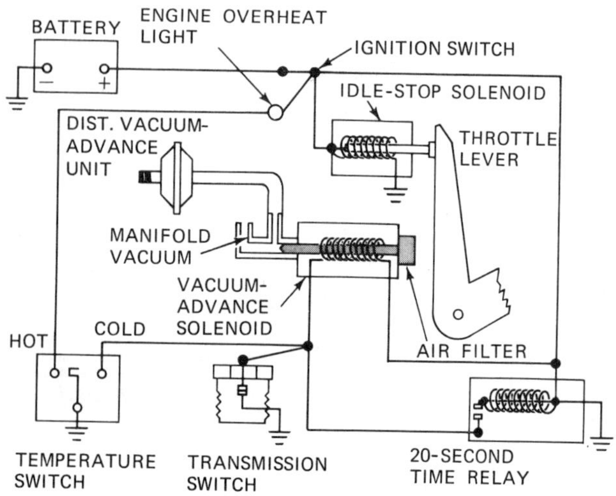

Fig. 18-15. TCS system during operation in high-gear. (*Chevrolet Motor Division of General Motors Corporation*)

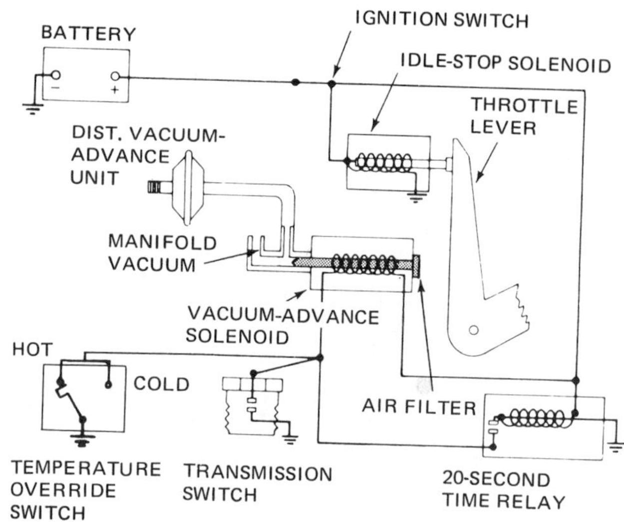

Fig. 18-16. Schematic view of the TCS system which uses a thermostatic temperature override switch. (*Chevrolet Motor Division of General Motors Corporation*)

⊘ 18-14 Control of Vacuum Advance—TRS System

A Ford transmission-regulated spark (TRS) system is shown in Fig. 18-17. It is used for both manual and automatic transmissions. The system works like the Chevrolet TCS system described in ⊘ 18-13. The solenoid valve is normally open, allowing vacuum advance when the transmission is in high gear. In the lower gears, the transmission switch is closed. This closes the solenoid valve. With the solenoid valve closed, vacuum is shut off from the distributor vacuum-advance mechanism. Thus, there is no vacuum advance.

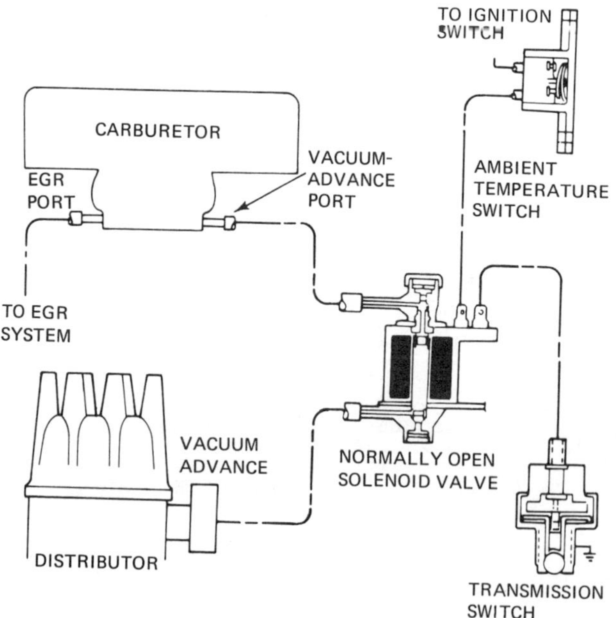

Fig. 18-17. Transmission-regulated spark (TRS) system. (*Ford Motor Company*)

⊘ 18-15 Other Vacuum-Advance Control Systems

There are other vacuum-advance controls. These are specially tailored for the engines and vehicles with which they are used. Late-model cars produced by Chrysler Corporation use an orifice spark-advance control (OSAC). It includes a very small hole, or orifice. This delays, by about 17 seconds, any change in the application of vacuum to the distributor between idle and part throttle. Therefore, there is a delay in vacuum advance until acceleration is well under way. This is a critical time during which vacuum advance could produce high NO_x.

Ford has a somewhat similar system called the spark-delay valve system (Fig. 18-18). This system delays vacuum advance during some vehicle-acceleration conditions. The spark-delay valve is connected between the vacuum-advance port in the carburetor and the distributor vacuum-advance mechanism. During mild acceleration, the vacuum

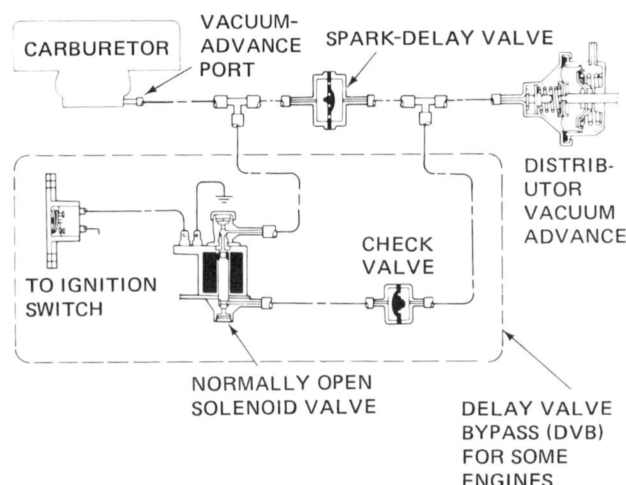

Fig. 18-18. Spark-delay valve system. (*Ford Motor Company*)

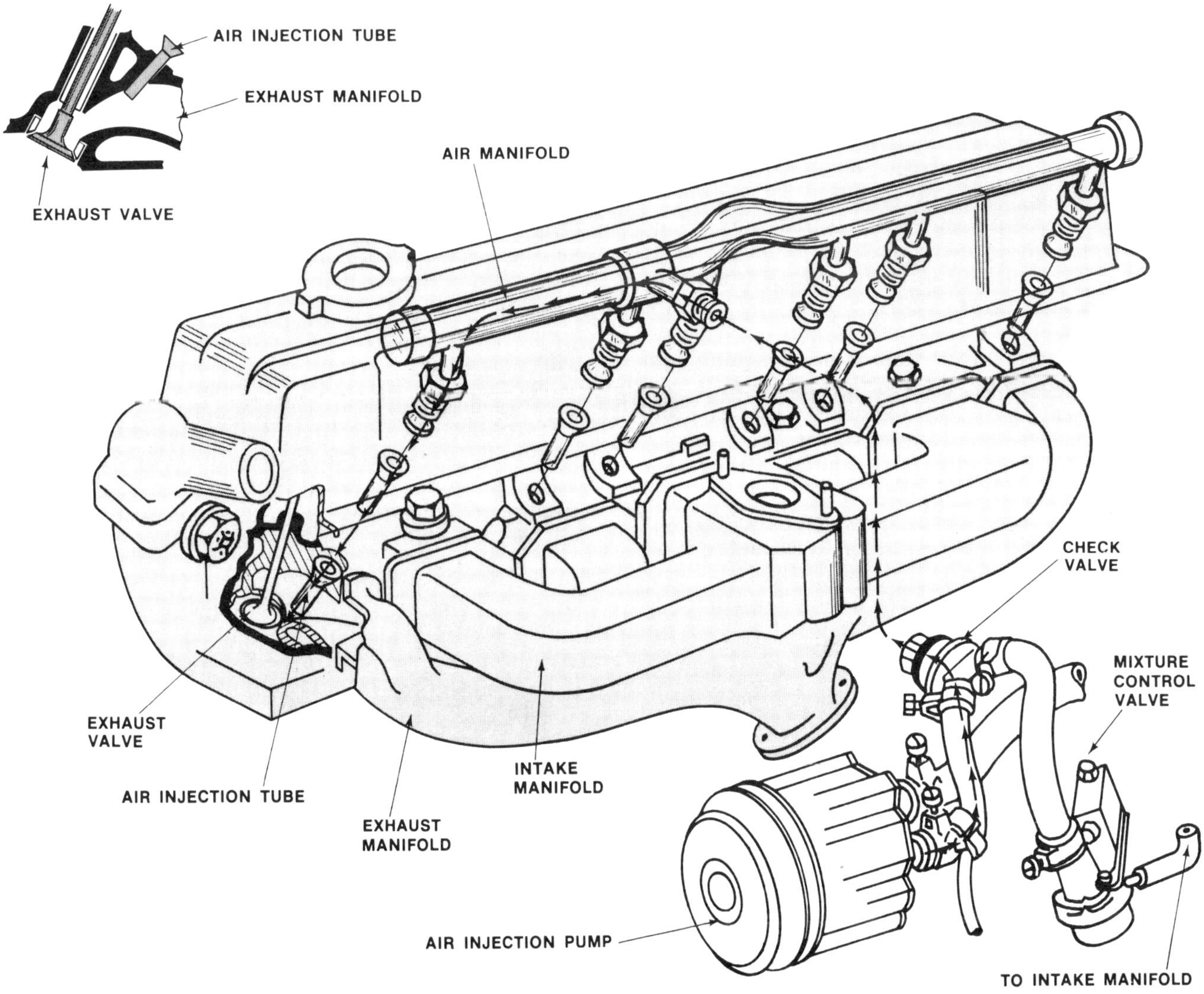

Fig. 18-19. Air-injection system. The air manifold and other parts of the system are shown detached so they can be seen better. The cylinder head has been cut away at the front to show how the air-injection tube fits into the head.

signal to the distributor increases only gradually. This is because the spark-delay valve allows the vacuum to pass through only slowly. During deceleration or heavy acceleration, the change in vacuum is great enough to open a check valve. This valve allows the vacuum to bypass the spark-delay valve. It produces vacuum advance during these critical times, for better engine performance. If the engine temperature is low, the temperature switch actuates the solenoid valve. The valve then passes vacuum directly to the distributor vacuum-advance mechanism (through the check valve). This provides vacuum advance when the engine is cold.

⊘ 18-16 Treating the Exhaust Gases by Air Injection After the exhaust gases leave the engine cylinders, they can be treated to reduce their HC and CO content. One method is to blow fresh air into the exhaust manifolds. This system is called the *air-injection* system. It provides additional oxygen to burn HC and CO coming out of the cylinders. Figure 18-19 shows the details of the system.

The air-injection pump pushes air through the air lines and the air manifold into a series of air-injection tubes. These tubes are located opposite the exhaust valves in the exhaust manifold. The check valve prevents any backflow of exhaust gases to the air pump, in case of backfire. The air-bypass valve operates during engine deceleration. During deceleration, intake-manifold vacuum is high. The bypass valve momentarily diverts air from the air pump to the air cleaner, instead of to the exhaust manifold. This tends to prevent backfiring in the exhaust system.

A variation of this system uses a special chamber, called a *thermal reactor* (Fig. 18-20). In the V-8 system shown, there are two thermal reactors, one for each cylinder bank. These reactors are basically enlarged exhaust manifolds. Being larger, they hold the exhaust gas a little longer. This gives the HC and CO additional time to burn in the pumped-in air.

Note that the system in Fig. 18-20 includes an exhaust-gas recirculation system (⊘ 18-11).

Note also that the air-injection system does nothing to the NO_x in the exhaust gases. NO_x requires a different sort of treatment.

⊘ 18-17 Treating the Exhaust Gases in Catalytic Converters A second method of treating exhaust gas is to use catalytic converters. These convert the pollutants into harmless gases. A system using catalytic converters is shown in Fig. 18-21. Note that this is a dual-exhaust system for a V-8 engine. Each exhaust line has two catalytic converters. One handles HC and CO. The other handles NO_x.

A catalyst is a material that causes a chemical change without entering into the reaction. In effect, the catalyst stands by and encourages two chemicals to react. For example, in the HC/CO catalytic converter, the catalyst encourages the HC to unite with oxygen (O_2) to produce water (H_2O) and carbon dioxide (CO_2). The catalyst in the NO_x converter splits the nitrogen from the oxygen, producing harmless oxygen and nitrogen.

A control system for HC and CO, engineered by General Motors, is shown in Fig. 18-22. The converter is filled with pellets of metal. They are coated with a thin layer of platinum or a similar catalytic metal. The pellets form a matrix through which the exhaust gas must pass. Figure 18-23 shows one design of catalytic converter. As exhaust gas flows through (Fig. 18-24), the platinum or other catalyst produces chemical reactions. Figure 18-25 shows another catalytic-converter design. One advantage of the GM system is that the pellets can be replaced when the catalyst has lost efficiency. In other words, the converter can be recharged with fresh pellets when necessary.

⊘ 18-18 Lead in Gasoline As mentioned in ⊘ 10-12, adding tetraethyl lead to gasoline increases its octane number—that is, its antiknock value. Lead in gasoline, however, can cause a serious problem with catalytic converters. The lead coats the pellets and

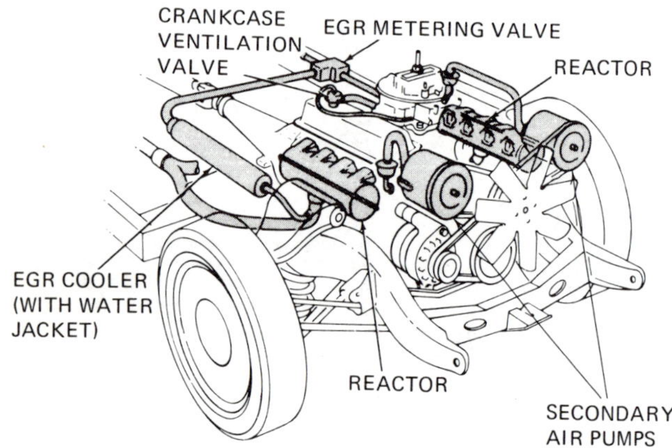

Fig. 18-20. Thermal-reactor system for exhaust-emission control.

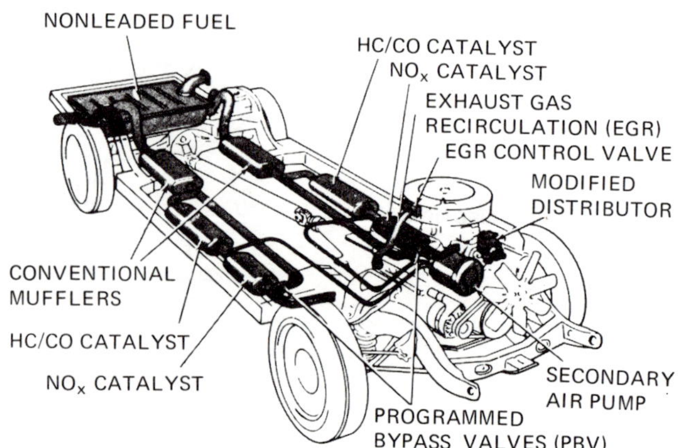

Fig. 18-21. Dual catalytic-converter system for exhaust-emission control. (*Interindustry Emission Control Program*)

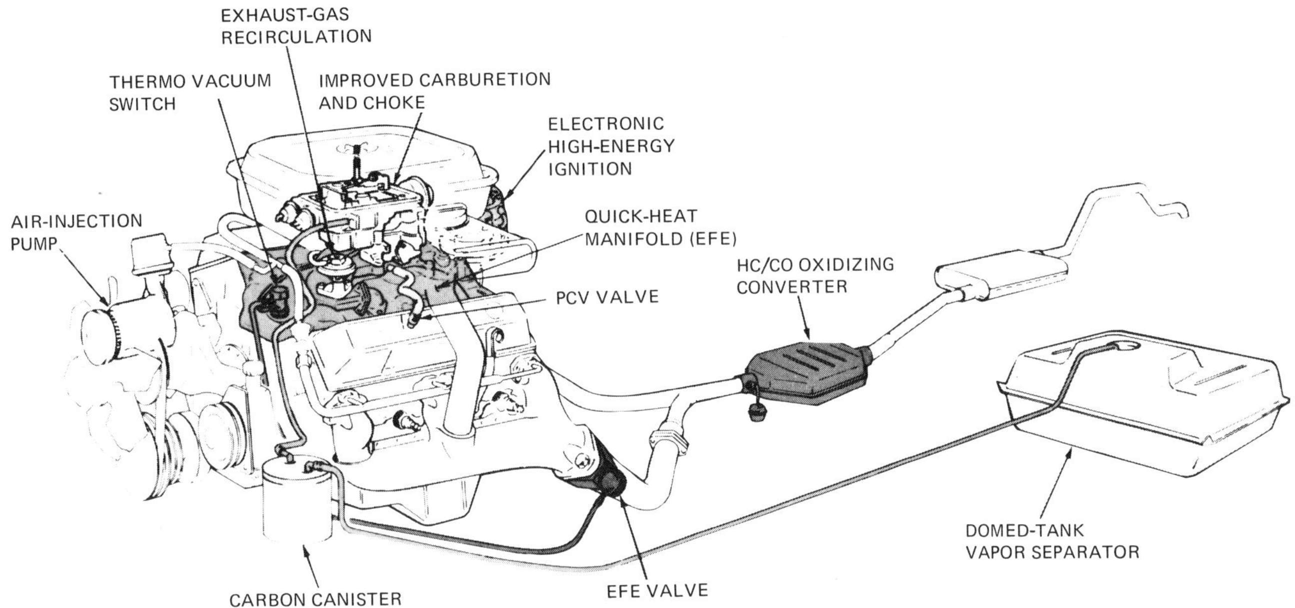

Fig. 18-22. One late-model emission-control system using an under-the-floor catalytic converter. Note that the system uses air injection and other emission-control features described previously. (*General Motors Corporation*)

Fig. 18-23. Cutaway view of the catalytic converter in Fig. 18-22. (*General Motors Corporation*)

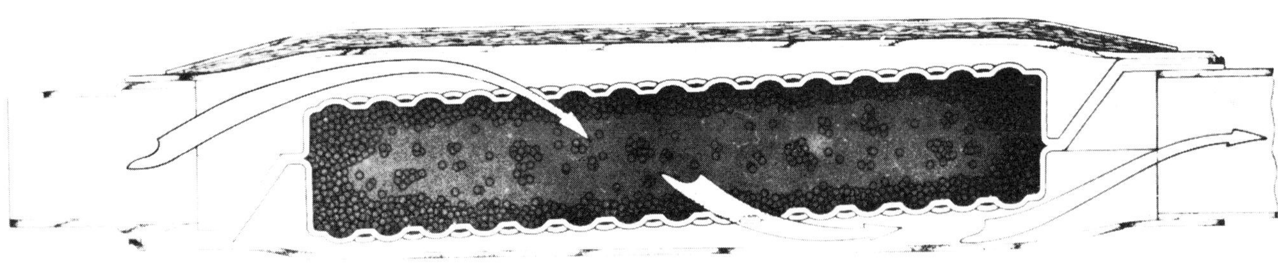

Fig. 18-24. The flow of exhaust gas through the converter is shown by arrows. (*General Motors Corporation*)

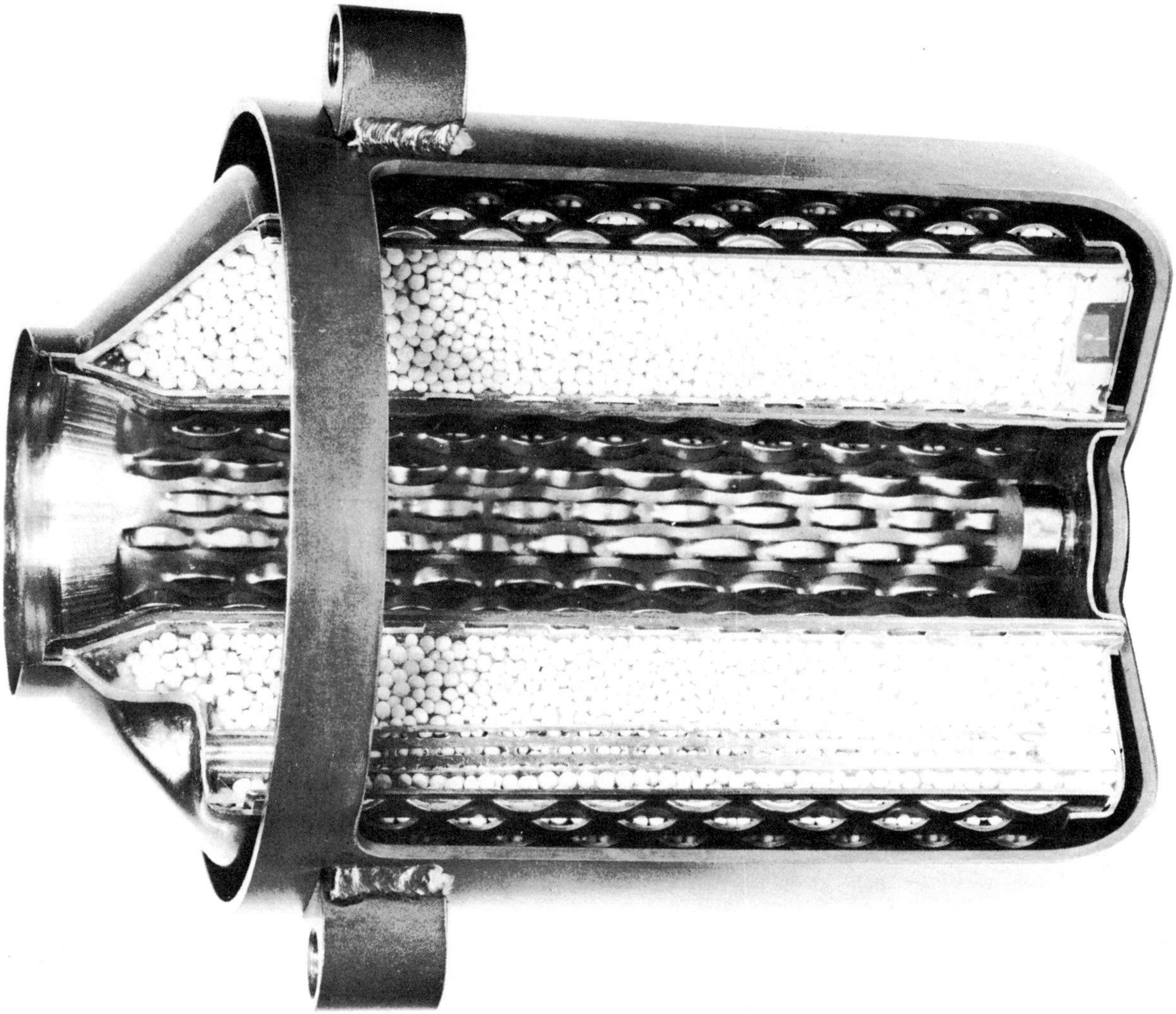

Fig. 18-25. Another design of catalytic converter, cut away so that the pellets can be seen. (*General Motors Corporation*)

reduces their effectiveness. Some authorities state that a tank or two of leaded gasoline will destroy the catalytic action of a converter.

To prevent this from happening, service stations are now dispensing nonleaded gasoline. They have special tanks to hold the nonleaded gasoline, and special pumps to dispense it. In addition, in cars equipped with catalytic converters, the fuel-tank filler neck has a nozzle restriction (Figs. 18-26 and 18-27). The standard pump nozzle will not fit this restriction. Therefore, pumps dispensing nonleaded gasoline have special small-diameter nozzles, as shown. These nozzles fit the restriction. Also, the fuel door on the car carries the warning, "Unleaded Gasoline Only" (Fig. 18-28). Finally, cars with catalytic converters use a different fuel-filler cap (Fig. 18-29). This cap has a special ratchet-tightening device designed to alert the service-station attendant that the car must have unleaded gasoline only.

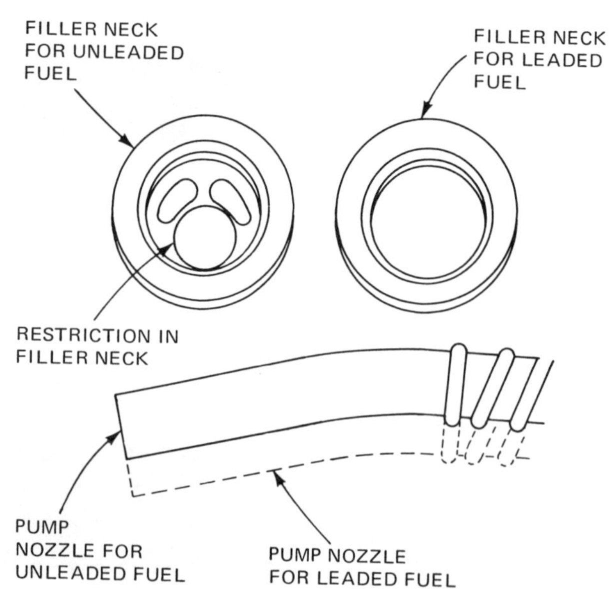

Fig. 18-26. Comparison of the old filler neck and pump nozzle for leaded gasoline with the new filler neck (with restriction) and pump nozzle for unleaded gasoline.

⊘ 18-19 Industry at Work to Reduce Pollution from Cars

The automotive industry has been working to

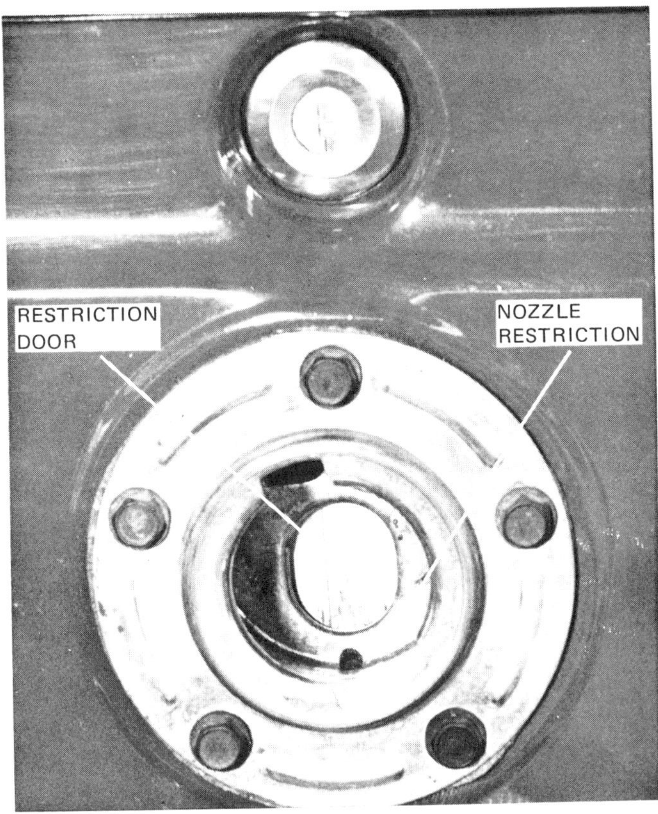

Fig. 18-27. Filler cap removed in readiness to pump gasoline into the tank. (*Ford Motor Company*)

Fig. 18-28. The bumper carries the notice "Unleaded Gasoline Only." (*Ford Motor Company*)

reduce air pollution from automobiles for many years. Many modifications have been made, and several antipollution devices have been added to cars. These include positive crankcase ventilating systems, exhaust-gas recirculation, air-injection systems, fuel-vapor recovery systems, nitrogen-oxides control systems, and catalytic converters.

New testing instruments and procedures have been developed to monitor the effectiveness of these systems. Ford, for example, has developed an emissions test laboratory on wheels (Fig. 18-30). This laboratory can be moved from one part of the country to another, to check cars in different climates and under different operating conditions. For moving,

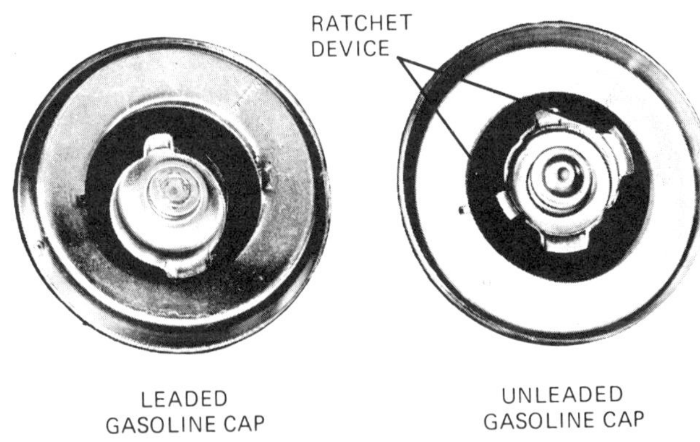

Fig. 18-29. The fuel-tank filler cap has a ratchet-tightening device. It indicates that the tank should have unleaded fuel only. (*Ford Motor Company*)

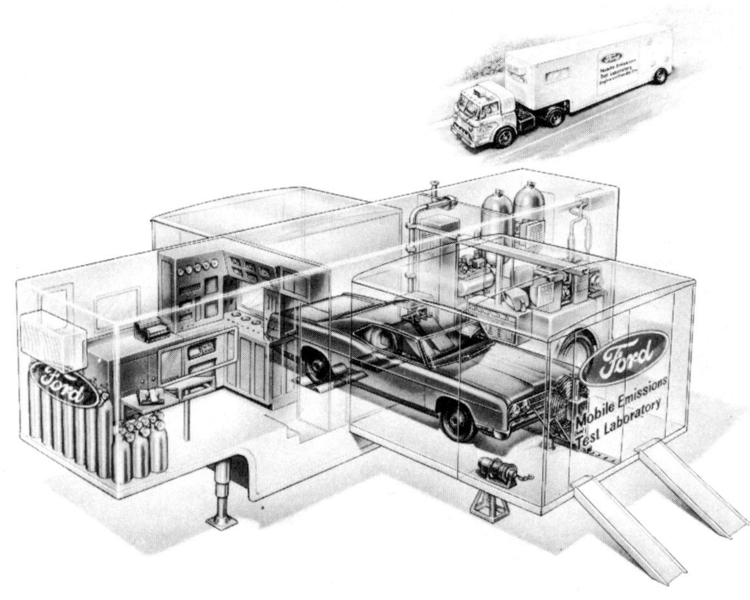

Fig. 18-30. Mobile emissions test laboratory. (*Ford Motor Company*)

the laboratory is folded up into the trailer, as shown to the upper right. When it arrives on location, the center section is expanded (center, in Fig. 18-30), so that there is enough room for a car to be brought in and tested.

CHAPTER 18 CHECKUP

NOTE: Since the following is a chapter review test, you should review the chapter before taking the test.

This chapter concludes our discussion of automotive emission controls. Take the test that follows to make sure you remember the details.

Completing the Sentences The sentences below are incomplete. After each sentence there are several words or phrases, but only one of them correctly completes the sentence. Write each sentence in your notebook, ending it with the one word or phrase that completes it correctly.

1. The pollutant formed at high combustion temperatures is: (*a*) HC, (*b*) CO, (*c*) NO_x.
2. Three ways of cleaning up the exhaust gas are to control the air-fuel mixture, control the combustion, and: (*a*) control the carburetor, (*b*) treat the exhaust gas, (*c*) add tetraethyl lead.
3. Two ways of treating the exhaust gas to reduce pollutants are to supply additional air to the exhaust gas as it leaves the cylinders, and to run the gas through: (*a*) an air injector, (*b*) a catalyst, (*c*) charcoal canisters.
4. One reason why gasoline refiners are getting the lead out of gasoline is that the lead: (*a*) increases NOx, (*b*) can ruin catalysts, (*c*) prevents normal run-on.
5. To control the air-fuel mixture and reduce atmospheric pollution, carburetors have been modified to deliver a leaner air-fuel mixture during: (*a*) idling, (*b*) acceleration, (*c*) high-speed operation.
6. Reducing the compression ratio of an engine reduces the combustion temperature, and this: (*a*) reduces the amount of NO_x formed, (*b*) increases the amount of NO_x formed, (*c*) reduces the amount of HC formed.
7. The transmission-controlled spark (TCS) system permits distributor: (*a*) centrifugal advance in high gear only, (*b*) vacuum advance in high gear only, (*c*) vacuum advance in low gears only.
8. Reducing the combustion-chamber surface area: (*a*) reduces the amount of unburned HC in the exhaust, (*b*) increases the amount of unburned HC in the exhaust, (*c*) reduces the amount of NO_x in the exhaust.
9. One method of reducing NO_x in the exhaust is to: (*a*) increase valve overlap, (*b*) reduce valve overlap, (*c*) prevent valve overlap.

Review Questions The questions that follow give you a chance to check your general knowledge of methods for cleaning up automotive exhaust gases. Write the answers in your notebook. Check back into the chapter if you are not sure about any answers.

1. What are the three ways of cleaning up the exhaust gases?
2. What are the two ways of controlling the air-fuel mixture to achieve lower HC and CO in the exhaust?
3. What is the purpose of the electric heater in the automatic choke?
4. The layer of air-fuel mixture next to the metal surfaces in the combustion chamber does not burn. Why not?
5. What effect does increasing the combustion temperature have on HC, CO, and NO_x in the exhaust?

6. What is the purpose of increasing valve overlap?
7. What is the purpose of the EGR system? How does it work?
8. What is the purpose of the TCS system? How does it work?
9. What is the purpose of the temperature override switch in the TCS system?
10. What is the purpose of injecting air into the exhaust manifold? How does the system work?
11. What is a thermal reactor?
12. What is the purpose of the catalytic converter?

SUGGESTIONS FOR FURTHER STUDY

Continue to look for articles in newspapers and magazines, as suggested at the end of the previous chapter. Go to your local library, and look for material on automotive emissions and emission controls. Keep your eyes and ears open for any information in this field. Much is happening, and new developments are announced periodically. File the articles in your notebook, and be sure to write down any important facts you learn.

chapter 19

SERVICING EMISSION-CONTROL SYSTEMS

In the last two chapters we discussed the emission controls used on modern automotive vehicles. In this chapter, we describe procedures for checking these emission controls.

⊘ **19-1 Emission Tuneup** Soon, we may not be allowed to drive cars that give off excessive amounts of pollutants, whether from the crankcase, the exhaust, the fuel tank, or the carburetor. Stronger antipollution laws, plus more complete state inspection procedures, indicate that such a time is coming. Because low-pollution operation of cars is so important, this chapter discusses the special tuneup procedures for reducing pollutants in the exhaust gases. Chapter 35 outlines the complete tuneup procedure, including checks of the electric and fuel systems and the engine.

There are four systems, on present-day cars, that combat air pollution. These include the positive crankcase ventilating system, the air-injection system, evaporation-control systems which trap gasoline vapors escaping from the carburetor and fuel tank, and various engine modifications (which we shall call the "fourth system"). We cover the servicing of these systems before looking at the antismog tuneup procedure.

⊘ **19-2 Positive Crankcase Ventilating (PCV) System** The PCV valve should be checked periodically. It should be routinely replaced at certain intervals. Recommendations are:

American Motors Corporation
Replace the PCV valve every 15,000 mi [24,140 km].

Chevrolet and Ford
Replace the valve every 24,000 mi [38,624 km] or 24 months, whichever comes first.

Chrysler
Check the valve every 12 months or 12,000 mi [19,312 km]. Replace it every 24,000 mi [38,624 km] or 24 months.

There are special testers that can be used to check the operation of the PCV valve. A simple way to check the system and the valve is to remove the valve or valve connection, with the engine running. Place your hand over the opening. You should feel a slight vacuum pull against your hand. If there is no vacuum, or if you can feel a positive pressure, then something is wrong. Check the PCV valve, hoses, and connections.

Chevrolet offers a different method. With the engine running at idle, remove the PCV valve from the rocker-arm-cover grommet, with hose attached. Block the opening of the valve, and note the change in engine speed. A decrease of less than 50 rpm indicates a plugged PCV valve. You should use a tachometer when making this test, to get an accurate reading of the engine rpm.

Chrysler recommends the following test procedure. Remove the PCV valve from the rocker-arm cover, with the engine idling. The valve should hiss. You should be able to feel a strong vacuum when your finger is placed over the valve inlet. Reinstall the PCV valve, and remove the crankcase inlet air cleaner. Hold a piece of stiff paper over the opening of the rocker-arm cover. After a few moments, the paper should be sucked against the opening. Then stop the engine. Remove the PCV valve from the rocker-arm cover, and shake it. It should click, showing that the valve is free. If the system does not meet these tests, replace the PCV valve and try again. If the system still does not pass the tests, the hose may be clogged. It should be cleaned out or replaced. It may be necessary to remove the carburetor and clean the vacuum passage with a ¼-in [6.35-mm] drill. Also, clean the inlet vent on the crankcase inlet air cleaner that is connected by the hose to the carburetor air cleaner.

⊘ **19-3 Air-Injection System** The filter in the air-injection system should be checked every year or every 12,000 mi [19,312 km] of operation. It should be cleaned or replaced as necessary. The air-pump drive belt should be checked to make sure it is in good condition and is at the right tension. The check valve is designed to prevent backflow of exhaust gases, from the exhaust manifold into the air pump. It can be checked as follows: Blow into it toward the exhaust manifold. It should be free. Attempt to suck air back from the exhaust manifold. It should close. The pump can be tested by temporarily disconnecting the hose from the manifold and then operating the engine at about 1,500 rpm. If the airflow increases as the engine is accelerated, the pump is operating satisfactorily. If it does not, either the belt is too loose or there is trouble in the pump. The pump pressure-relief valve may be stuck open. In this case, you will hear air leaking out. The remedy is to replace the pump.

⊘ 19-4 Evaporation-Control Systems Evaporation-control systems require little in the way of service. About the only troubles that occur are restriction of the fuel flow (so that the engine becomes starved and stalls) and a collapsed fuel tank. The fuel tank can collapse if the venting system in the special fuel-tank cap becomes clogged. A partial vacuum forms inside the tank, causing atmospheric pressure to collapse the tank. About the only periodic service required is to replace the filter (in the bottom of the canister) every year or every 12,000 mi [19,312 km] of operation.

⊘ 19-5 Heated-Air System The heated-air system, with a thermostatically controlled air cleaner, is used on all late-model cars. You can check the operation of this device by starting with the engine cold—below 85°F [29.4°C]. Note first whether the cold-air door in the snorkel is closed or open. It should be wide open. When the engine starts, it should close. As the engine warms up, it should open again. If the door does not work this way, you will need to check further. Checking of the thermostatic action is covered in ⊘ 14-3.

NOTE: You may need a small mirror to see the door in the snorkel clearly.

⊘ 19-6 General Motors Transmission-Controlled Spark (TCS) System The TCS system prevents ignition spark advance in lower gears, to reduce emissions during low-gear operation. If the system fails, vacuum advance is obtained in all gears, and emission of pollutants increases. The system can be checked by connecting a vacuum gauge in the hose between the solenoid and the distributor. In a manual-transmission car, you should get a vacuum only in high gear (third and fourth gears for a four-speed transmission). In an automatic-transmission car, you should get a vacuum only in top gear and in reverse. If there is full vacuum in all gears, the trouble could be any of the following:

1. Blown fuse
2. Disconnected wire or bad connection
3. Defective transmission switch
4. Energized temperature override switch (check by disconnecting the lead to the switch)
5. Solenoid failure

If no vacuum is found in high gear, the trouble could be:

1. Clean-air line and distributor vacuum line reversed at the solenoid
2. Solenoid stuck or not operating the valve properly
3. Vacuum hose broken or plugged
4. Transmission switch or wire shorted to ground

In every case, the solution to the problem is obvious. You have to check each item listed to locate the trouble. Then the defective part should be replaced, and the hoses connected correctly.

⊘ 19-7 Tuning for Low Emissions The essentials of this procedure include setting the distributor contact points correctly; timing the ignition; checking out the carburetor linkage, choke, and idle settings; and checking the condition of the ignition wiring, distributor cap and rotor, and spark plugs. The object is to make sure the air-fuel mixture is right, and the spark is strong enough to ignite the compressed air-fuel mixture at the proper moment. Essentially, that's all there is to it.

NOTE: The ignition-system checking procedure is covered in Chap. 30.

Engineering tests have shown that as many as half the cars on the highway are high polluters because the fuel or ignition system is not properly adjusted or has some defect. That shows how much a good automotive technician can do to reduce air pollution! Besides, gasoline that doesn't burn, or that burns incompletely, is just wasted fuel. Properly tuning an engine to minimize pollution does everyone a favor. It reduces air pollution, saves the car owner money by making the engine run more efficiently, and can greatly improve engine performance.

Here are some things to look for, which have a big effect on pollution.

First, make sure that the choke opens completely as the engine warms up. Naturally, the PCV valve must be working, as noted earlier. Next, remove the distributor cap; check it inside and out for cracks and burn lines. You don't have to remove the high-voltage leads to do this. If you see cracks or burn lines, you can be sure the high voltage is leaking. This means the spark plugs are not getting enough voltage to fire properly. Unburned gasoline is going out the tail pipe. Replace a defective distributor cap by placing the old and new caps side by side, as shown in Fig. 19-1. (This illustration also shows you how to inspect the cap and what to look for.) Transfer one high-voltage lead at a time, from the old cap to the new cap. In this way, you won't mix up the leads.

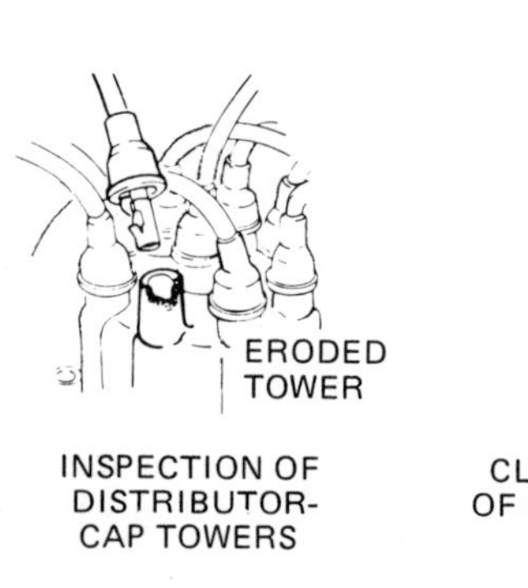

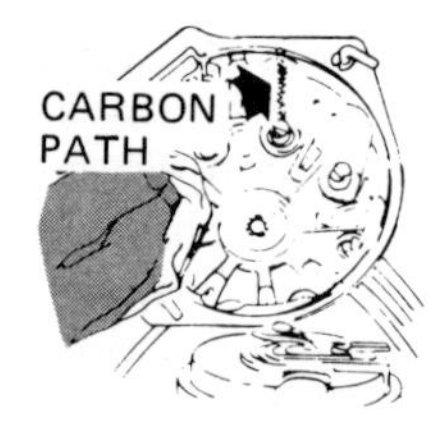

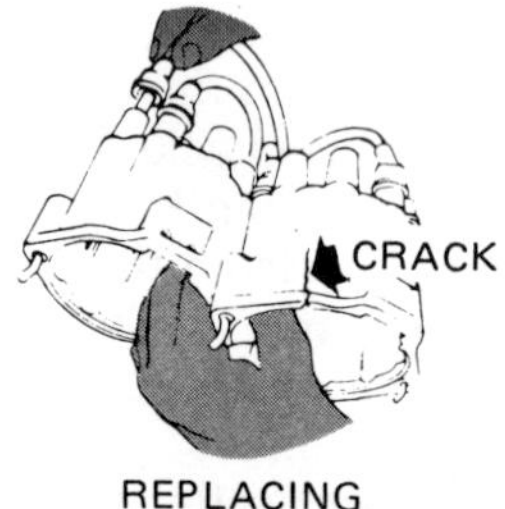

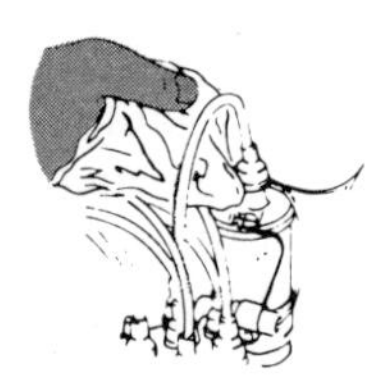

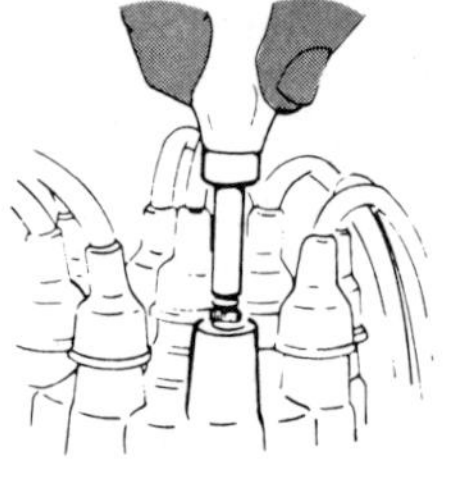

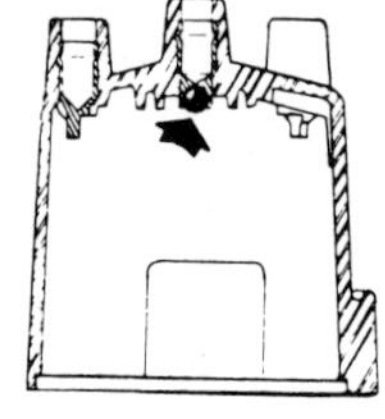

Fig. 19-1. Checking and servicing the distributor cap and rotor. (*Chevrolet Motor Division of General Motors Corporation*)

Examine the high-voltage leads carefully. Cracked insulation and charred ends are indications of high-voltage leaks. If the leads look at all deteriorated, don't take a chance; install new leads. Be sure to use the correct leads for the car.

Look at the distributor rotor. Examine it for cracks and burn lines. They indicate that some of the high voltage is leaking off and not getting to the spark plugs.

Check the spark plugs (Chap. 30). The usual recommendation is to replace the plugs every 10,000 mi [16,093 km].

Check the distributor contact points and the ignition timing. Make any necessary corrections (Chap. 30). Next, check the idle settings.

In late-model cars, the idle-mixture adjustment screw has a limiter, so it cannot be set for an excessively rich mixture. During idling, the engine emits some of its most offensive pollution. Thus, it is important to set the idle mixture as lean as possible. In the past, the mechanic would set the idle mixture to give a very smooth idle. As a rule, this idle mixture was on the rich side. The result was excessive amounts of unburned hydrocarbons in the exhaust.

If the idle-mixture adjustment screw does not have a limiter, here is the way to set it for a lean but satisfactory idle mixture. First, with the engine at operating temperature, connect a vacuum gauge and tachometer to the engine. Start the engine, and back off the idle-mixture screw (or screws) to get a smooth idle. This will give you the maximum rpm and vacuum. Now, slowly turn the screw in, little by little, until the engine begins to misfire and run roughly. At this stage, the vacuum-gauge needle will become erratic. This is a more accurate indication of roughness than the sound of the engine. Now, back off the screw slightly until the engine and needle settle down. Open and close the throttle several times, to make sure the engine returns to the same miss-free idle condition.

The same procedure can be used on carburetors with idle-mixture adjustment-screw limiters. However, do not try to turn the idle-mixture screws beyond the limit. This will break the limiter, and allow anyone to set the idle as rich as they want. Adjust the idle mixture within the limits established by the limiter.

⊘ 19-8 Exhaust-Gas Analyzer

As explained in Chaps. 17 and 18, engine changes and emission-control systems have reduced the amount of HC, CO, and NO_x emitted by the engine. An exhaust-gas analyzer is used to measure the amounts of these pollutants in the exhaust gases. The readings indicate the efficiency of the emission controls.

At one time the major use of the exhaust-gas analyzer was to adjust the carburetor. Changing the carburetor adjustment changes the amount of HC and CO in the exhaust gas. Adjusting the idle-mixture screw, for example, can increase the richness of the idle mixture. This increases the amount of HC

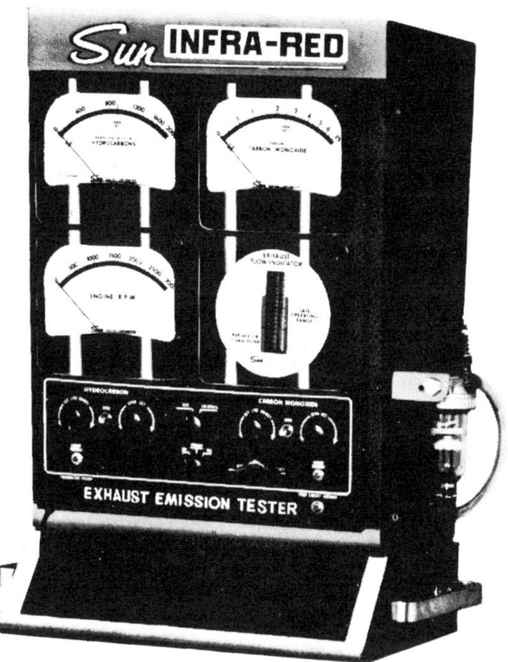

Fig. 19-2. Infrared type of exhaust-gas analyzer. (*Sun Electric Corporation*)

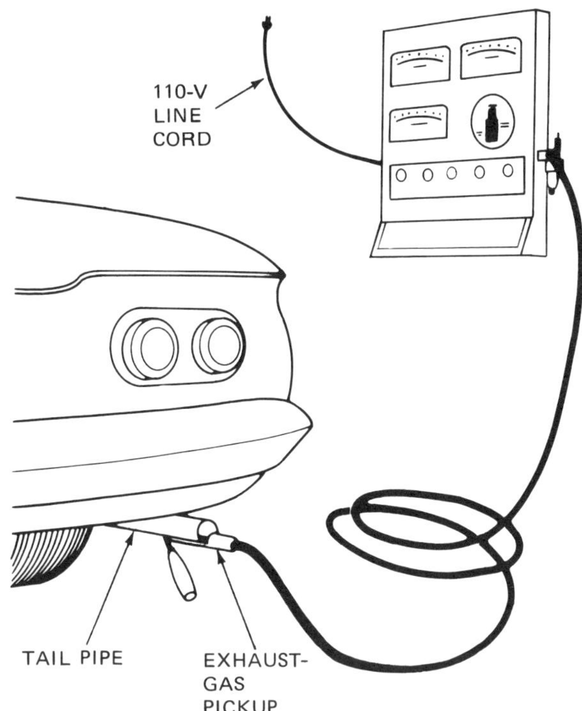

Fig. 19-3. Exhaust-gas analyzer connected for an exhaust-gas test.

and CO in the exhaust gas. As we noted above, one anti-emission step is to set the idle mixture as lean as possible, while still getting a satisfactory idle. This reduces the amount of HC and CO in the exhaust gas.

Today, the exhaust-gas analyzer is used to check the emission controls on the car, as well as the idle adjustment. Figure 19-2 shows one type of exhaust-gas analyzer. To use it, you stick a probe into the tail pipe of the car (Fig. 19-3). The probe draws out some of the exhaust gas and carries it through the analyzer. Two dials on the face of the analyzer (Fig. 19-4) register how much HC and CO are in the exhaust gas. Federal and state laws limit the amount of HC and CO permitted in the exhaust.

A different kind of tester is required for NO_x, but it works in the same general way. It draws exhaust gas from the tail pipe and runs the gas through the analyzer. The meter reports the amount of NO_x in the exhaust gas. Generally, NO_x testers are available only in testing laboratories. They are not widely used in the automotive service shop. Authorities say, however, that someday all well-equipped shops will have them.

⊘ 19-9 Checking Exhaust Gas for HC and CO Unburned gasoline (HC) and carbon monoxide (CO) are

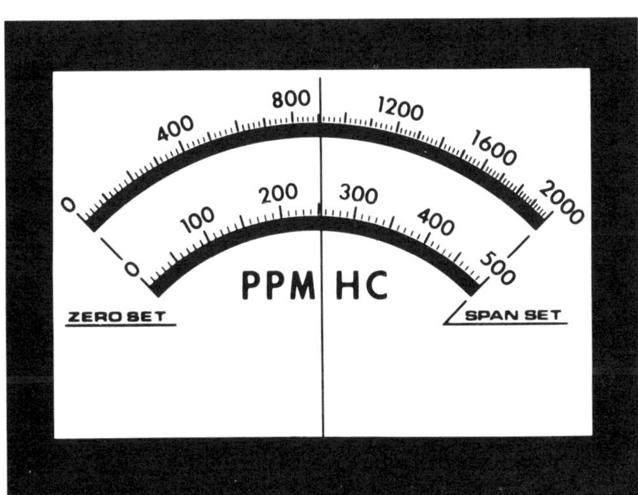

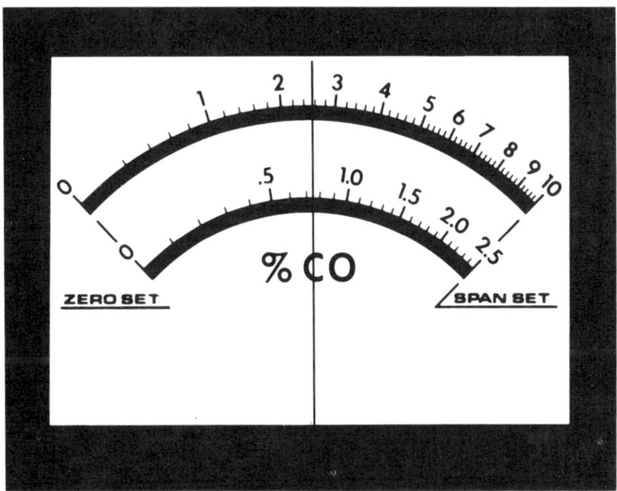

Fig. 19-4. HC and CO meter faces. (*Sun Electric Corporation*)

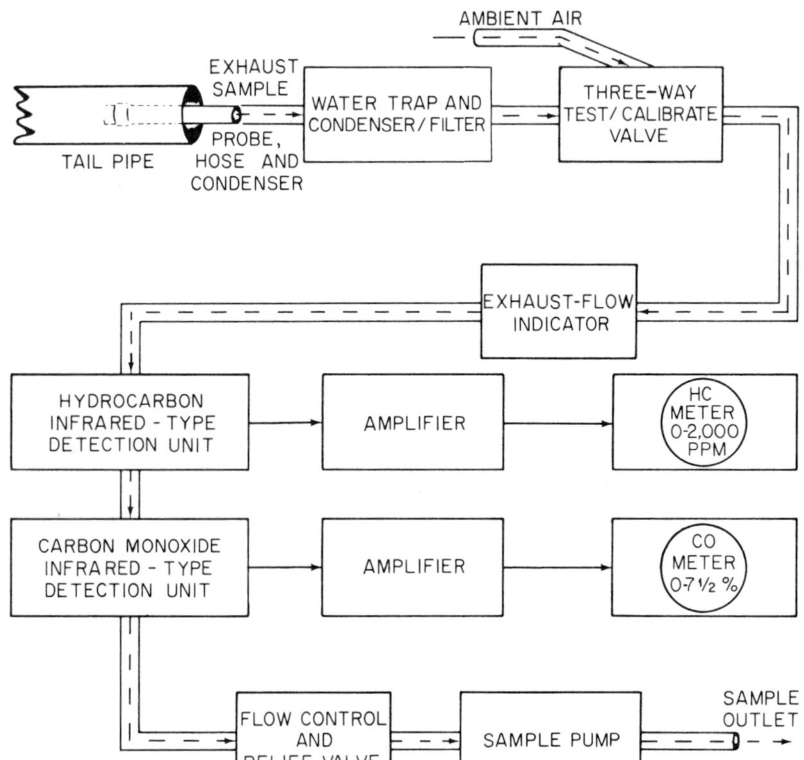

Fig. 19-5. Schematic diagram of the exhaust-emission tester. (*Sun Electric Corporation*)

two of the contaminants found in exhaust gas. Legal limits have been set on the amounts permitted. As previously mentioned, tests for HC and CO are, or will become, part of the state inspection procedure in every state. The HC and CO tester is described in ⊘ 19-8 and illustrated in Figs. 19-2 and 19-4. The circuits of this tester are shown schematically in Fig. 19-5. The meter dials are shown close up in Fig. 19-4. Note that the HC meter registers in parts per million (ppm), and the CO meter registers in percentages. The tester is easy to use. The probe is stuck into the tail pipe of the car while the engine is running. A pump draws some exhaust gas into the tester (Fig. 19-3).

The exhaust gas first passes through a water trap and filter that remove excess moisture. Then it passes through the calibrate valve. This valve is used to adjust the HC and CO meters for the atmospheric conditions surrounding the test area. It prevents any smog in the surrounding air from affecting the test results. Then, after calibration, the exhaust gas flows through the exhaust-flow indicator and the two infrared-type detection units. The exhaust-flow indicator gives a constant check on how the tester is performing. It tells the technician when the tester is not working well, for example, because the filter is clogged or there is water in the line.

The amount of HC in the exhaust-gas sample is detected by one infrared-type detection unit, and the amount of CO is detected by the other unit. The meters register the results. The tester shown in Fig. 19-2 is used as follows:

1. Turn the power-control switch to the TEST position.
2. Clamp the tachometer pickup onto a spark-plug lead.
3. Note the reading on the exhaust-flow indicator. The exhaust-flow ball should remain in the green area and should be quite steady. If it falls into the red area, remove and clean the water trap bowl and filter. Be sure the O ring is in place and properly seated when replacing the bowl. Replace the filter with its open end up. Tighten the bowl-retainer nut finger tight. If the ball bounces rapidly, there is water in the exhaust-sample hose. Drain it, starting at the condensate-filter-assembly connection.
4. Place the sampling probe in the vehicle tail pipe.
5. Check the calibration of the HC and CO meters as follows.
a. Set the TEST/CALIBRATE switches to calibrate. The meter pointers should be within the SET LINE black bar.
b. Depress and hold each SPAN button in turn. The pointers should move to SPAN SET as shown in Fig. 19-4.
c. If the pointers do not indicate as noted, the meters must be recalibrated. To do so, set the TEST/CALIBRATE switches to calibrate. Rotate the HC and CO SET LINE adjusters as necessary to return the pointers to 0 on the SET LINE. Next, hold the SPAN button down for the meter being cali-

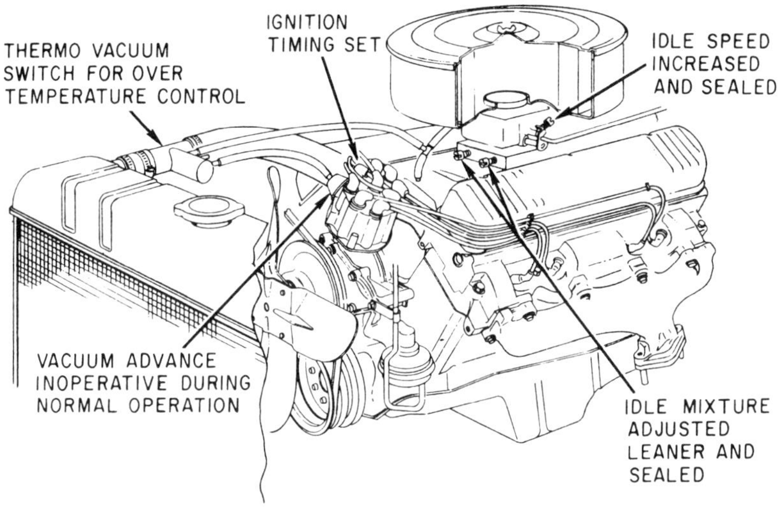

Fig. 19-6. General Motors exhaust-emission control kit for older cars. (*General Motors Corporation*)

brated (HC or CO). Rotate the SPAN SET adjuster to move the pointer to the SPAN SET position on the meter dial. Calibrate both meters.

d. Set the TEST/CALIBRATE switches to TEST, and proceed with the test.

6. Make the emission tests with the engine operating at idle and at the specified rpm. Note the readings on the HC and CO meters.

That's all there is to it. If the readings are high, corrections must be made. Essentially, the correction procedures amount to an engine tuneup job; there are a few additional steps for some of the newer pollution controls. We have covered these procedures on preceding pages.

⊘ 19-10 Used-Car Smog Devices Used-car smog devices, or retrofit kits, are now available. When installed, they reduce pollution from older cars. One advantage of the kits is that a tuneup should be performed at the time of installation. As we noted previously, proper tuneup eliminates a lot of pollution. Even more is eliminated by installing a smog device. There are several types, some produced by the original car manufacturers and some by independent parts suppliers. (One kit is shown in Fig. 19-6.) Some kits are designed to control NO_x, others to control HC and CO. One kit applies sonic waves to the ingoing air-fuel mixture to improve mixing of the air and fuel.

CHAPTER 19 CHECKUP

NOTE: Since the following is a chapter review test, you should review the chapter before taking the test.

You are now well into the part of the book that gives you practical guidance in actual shopwork. We will be discussing servicing procedures through the remainder of the book. The following chapter review test gives you a chance to find out how well you remember the servicing of emission controls.

Completing the Sentences The following sentences are incomplete. After each sentence there are several words or phrases, but only one of them correctly complete the sentence. Write each sentence in your notebook, ending it with the one word or phrase that completes it correctly.

1. Periodically, the PCV valve should be: (*a*) adjusted, (*b*) replaced, (*c*) cleaned.
2. The exhaust-gas analyzer described in the chapter is used to test for (*a*) HC and NO_x, (*b*) HC and CO, (*c*) NO_x and CO_2.
3. The purpose of the emission tuneup is to: (*a*) improve engine performance, (*b*) reduce H_2O, (*c*) reduce HC and CO in the exhaust gas.
4. The air filter in the evaporation-control system should be replaced every: (*a*) 12,000 mi [19,312 km], (*b*) 4 months, (*c*) oil change.
5. A broken drive belt on the engine stops the operation of the: (*a*) heated-air system, (*b*) evaporation-control system, (*c*) air-injection system.

Service Procedures Write, in your notebook, the procedures asked for in the following quiz. Do not copy the procedures from the book, but try to write them in your own words. Give a step-by-step account of how to do each service job. This will help you remember the procedures later, in the automotive shop.

1. List the various systems and items to be checked in an emission tuneup.
2. Explain how to use the exhaust-gas analyzer to check for HC and CO in the exhaust gas.
3. Explain how to service the air-injection system.
4. Explain how to service the evaporation-control system.
5. Explain how to check the heated-air system.

SUGGESTIONS FOR FURTHER STUDY

When you are in the automotive shop, keep your eyes and ears open. Learn all you can about how the various emission controls are serviced. Carefully examine any smog devices you can find. If the shop has some old or defective units, ask to borrow them. Practice disassembling and reassembling the units. The more practice you get in handling the small parts that go into these units, the more skillful you will become. Write, in your notebook, any important facts (or even whole procedures) you find. Writing the facts will help you remember them. At the same time, your notebook will become an increasingly valuable reference.

chapter 20

FUNDAMENTALS OF ELECTRICITY

We use electricity in many ways. It gives us light; it runs much of the machinery around us (refrigerators, factory equipment, television sets, subway trains); and it heats our homes. In the car, electricity does several jobs. It starts the engine when the ignition switch is turned on. It makes the sparks that ignite the compressed air-fuel mixture. It operates the radio, the electric gauges, and the lights. Figure 20-1 shows the major components of the automotive electric system. In this chapter, we describe all these electrical devices. But, first, let's see what electricity is all about.

⊘ 20-1 What is Electricity? Nobody has ever seen electricity, so we rely on the description of the experts who have studied it. Electricity is composed of minute particles. The particles are so tiny that it would take billions of them, all piled together, to make a spot big enough to see through a microscope. These particles are called *electrons*. Electrons are all around us in fantastic numbers. In 1 oz (ounce) [28.35 g (grams)] of iron, for example, there are about 22 million billion billion electrons. Electrons are normally locked into the elements that form everything in our world.

⊘ 20-2 Electric Current If many, many electrons are forced to move together in the same direction (in a wire, for example), we have a flow of electrons. We call this flow an *electric current*. The job of the battery and the generator or alternator is to get electrons to move together in the same direction. When many electrons are moving, we say the current is high. When relatively few electrons are moving, we say the current is low.

⊘ 20-3 Measuring Electric Current The movement of electrons, or electric current, is measured in amperes (A). One ampere (1 A) is a very small amount of electric current. A battery can put out 200 or 300 A as it operates the starting motor. Headlights draw 10 A or more. A single ampere is the flow of 6 billion billion electrons per second.

Obviously, nobody counts electrons to find out how many amperes are flowing in a wire. We use an *ammeter* to measure currents. The ammeter makes use of a strange effect of electron flow. This effect is that a flow of electrons, or electricity, produces magnetism.

⊘ 20-4 Magnetism There are two forms of magnetism: natural and electrical. Natural magnets are made of iron or some other metals. Electrically produced magnets are called *electromagnets*. Natural magnets and electromagnets act in the same way: They attract iron objects. Here are two important facts about magnets:

Magnets can produce electricity.
Electricity can produce magnets.

We shall say more about magnets, electromagnets, and how they act later in this chapter.

⊘ 20-5 The Ammeter Now let's look at how the ammeter measures electric current. The simplest kind of ammeter is shown in Fig. 20-2. This kind of ammeter is found on the instrument panel in many cars. Its purpose is to tell the driver whether the alternator is charging the battery. If the alternator doesn't charge the battery when it should, the battery runs down. If the battery runs down, the car won't start.

Here's how the ammeter works. The conductor is connected at one end to the battery. The pointer is mounted on a pivot. There is a small, oval-shaped piece of iron mounted on the same pivot. This oval piece of iron is called the armature. A permanent magnet, almost circular in shape, is positioned so its two ends are close to the armature. The permanent magnet attracts the armature and tends to hold it in a horizontal position. In this position, the pointer or needle points to 0. Nothing is happening. Now suppose the alternator starts sending current to the battery. This current passes through the conductor. The current produces magnetism. This magnetism attracts the armature and causes it to swing clockwise.

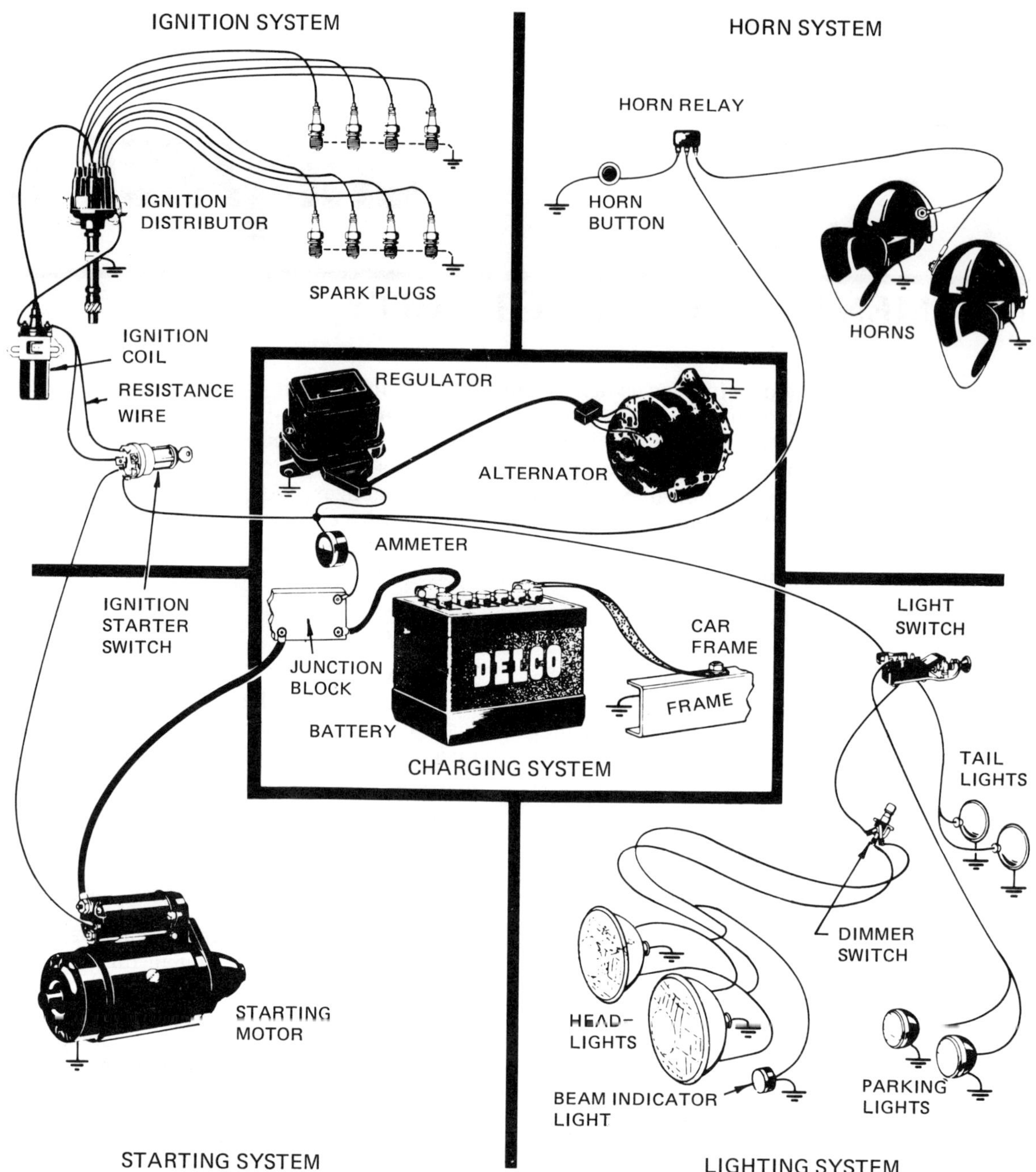

Fig. 20-1. Typical car electric system, showing all major parts and the wiring connections. The symbol ⏚ means ground, or the car frame. Because the car frame is used as the return circuit, only half as much wiring is needed.

This moves the pointer to the CHARGE side. The more current that flows, the stronger the magnetism and the farther the pointer moves. The meter face is marked to show the number of amperes flowing.

Now suppose the alternator is not working, and you turn on the car lights. Current flows from the battery to the lights. The current now flows in the reverse direction through the ammeter conductor. The armature is attracted in the opposite direction. It moves counterclockwise. This moves the pointer to the DISCHARGE side of the ammeter. The more current that flows out of the battery, the further the pointer moves across the DISCHARGE side of the ammeter.

⊘ **20-6 What Makes Electrons Move?** Electrons on the move make up electric current. But what makes the electrons move? Simply this: too many electrons in one spot. When electrons are gathered in one place, they try to move away. The battery and alternator are devices that collect electrons at one terminal and take them away from the other. If the two terminals are connected by a conductor, electrons

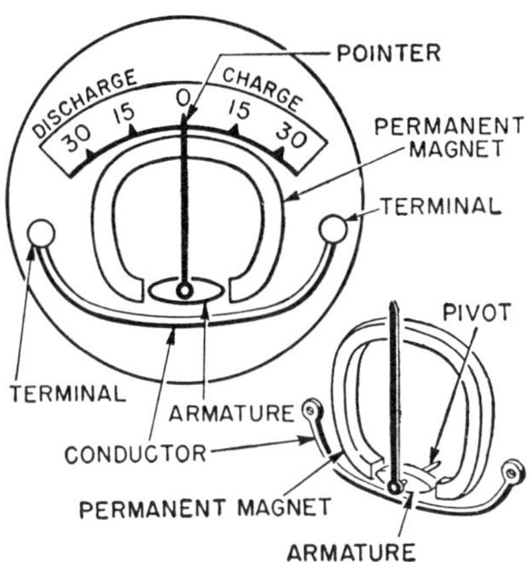

Fig. 20-2. Simplified drawing of a car ammeter, or charge indicator.

flow from the terminal with too many electrons to the terminal with too few.

⊘ 20-7 Voltage Suppose there are a great many electrons at one terminal. And suppose there is a great shortage of electrons at the other terminal. When there is a great excess and a great shortage, we say that the electric pressure is high. We mean that the pressure on electrons to move from the "too-many" terminal to the "too-few" terminal is high.

We measure electric pressure in volts (V). High pressure is high voltage; low pressure is low voltage. Car batteries are 12-V units. Twelve volts (12 V) is considered low pressure. The spark at the spark-plug gap is a flow of electrons at high pressure or voltage. The voltage at the spark-plug gap can be 20,000 V or more. That's high, but not nearly as high as the voltage in the lines that carry electricity from power plants. The voltage in these power lines is in the hundreds of thousands of volts.

⊘ 20-8 Insulation If electrons escape from the wire in which they are flowing, electric power is lost. Insulation keeps the electrons from escaping. That's why wires are covered with insulation. That's also why power lines are hung from long insulators on power poles or towers. In addition, electrons on the loose can be dangerous. For instance, damaged insulation on the wire of a household appliance can cause a fire. Or, anyone who touches the wire or appliance could get an electric shock.

In the car, the wires between the battery, the alternator, and other electrical devices are covered with insulation. The insulation is a *nonconductor*. That means electrons, or electric current, cannot flow through it. But if the insulation goes bad, electric current can go where it is not supposed to. It can take a shortcut through the metal of the car frame and the engine. Such a shortcut is called a *short circuit*. It can cause all sorts of trouble, as you will see later.

Just remember that the insulation keeps the electric current moving in the proper path, or *circuit*. Circuits include the wires and the electrical devices in the car.

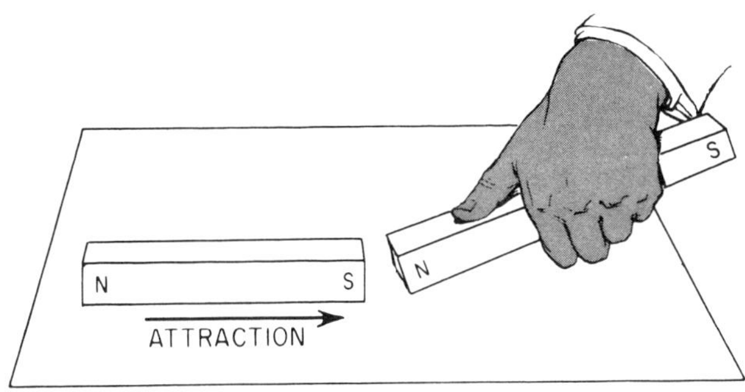

Fig. 20-3. Unlike magnetic poles attract. As the north pole is moved near the south pole, the south pole pulls toward the north pole.

⊘ 20-9 Magnets—Another Look Let's take another look at magnets. A magnet acts through *line of force*. These lines of force stretch between the ends of the magnet. The two ends of the magnet are called the *magnetic poles*, or just the *poles*. One pole is called the *north* pole; the other is the *south* pole. The area surrounding the poles is called a magnetic *field*.

⊘ 20-10 Lines of Force The lines of force have two properties. First, the lines of force tend to shorten up. For example, if you hold the north pole of one magnet close to the south pole of another magnet, the two magnets pull together (Fig. 20-3). The lines of force between the two poles look something like Fig. 20-4. The lines of force, stretching between the two poles, try to shorten up by pulling the two magnets together.

The second property is that the lines of force run more or less parallel to each other. And they try to push away from each other. Suppose we bring like poles together—two north poles, for example (Fig. 20-5). The lines of force run parallel to each other and try to push away (Fig. 20-6). The magnet that is free actually moves away as the like pole of the other magnet is brought closer.

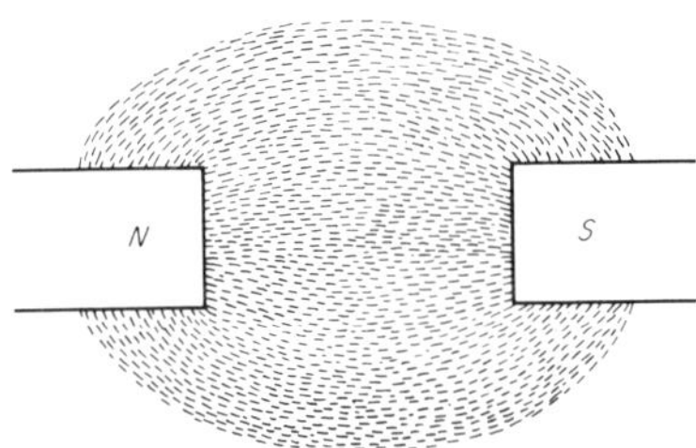

Fig. 20-4. Magnetic lines of force stretching between two unlike magnetic poles try to shorten up. This pulls the two unlike poles together.

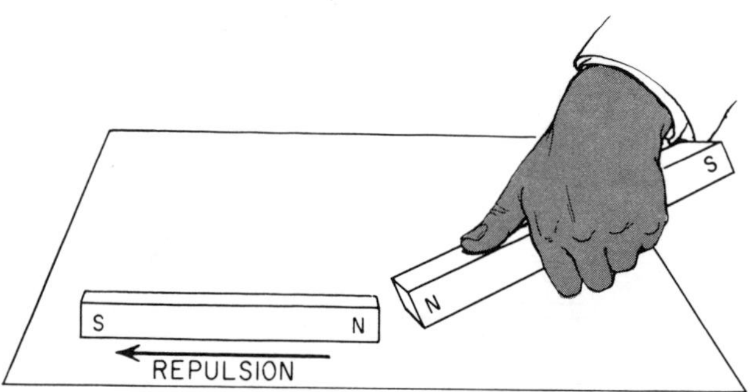

Fig. 20-5. Like magnetic poles repel each other. When a north pole is brought near another north pole, they push away from each other.

We can draw these conclusions:

Like magnetic poles repel each other. North repels north. South repels south.
Unlike magnetic poles attract each other. North attracts south. South attracts north.

⊘ 20-11 Electromagnets

Electromagnets act just like natural magnets. An electromagnet can be made by wrapping wire around a rod. Remember what happens in the ammeter when current flows one way or another through the conductor. The current produced magnetism, or magnetic lines of force.

Current flowing through a single wire, or conductor, does not produce much magnetism. But suppose you wind a wire several times around a rod. Then you connect the ends of the wire to a source of electric current (electrons). Then the turns of wire produce strong magnetism. In other words, a strong magnetic field develops around the coil of wire.

With current flowing through the winding, the winding acts just like a bar magnet (Fig. 20-7). One end of the winding will either attract or repel one pole of a bar magnet. That is, one end of the winding has become a north pole, and the other end a south pole. You can change the poles by reversing the leads to the source of current. Thus, when the electrons flow through in one direction, one of the poles becomes north. But when the electrons flow in the opposite direction the other pole becomes north. The poles reverse. The north pole becomes the south pole, and the south pole becomes the north pole.

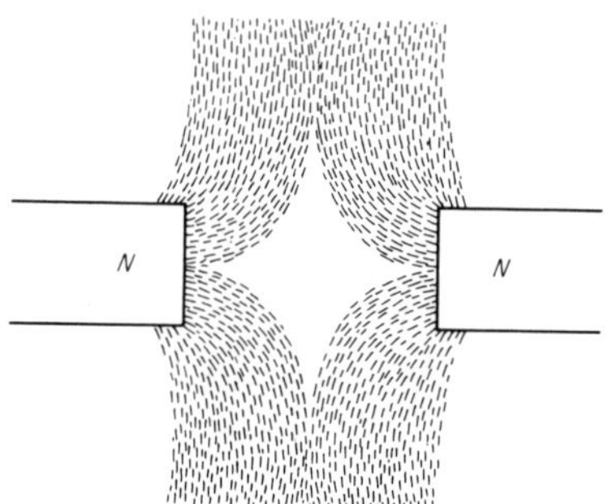

Fig. 20-6. Magnetic lines of force between two like magnetic poles. These magnetic lines of force tend to parallel each other. This forces the two like poles apart.

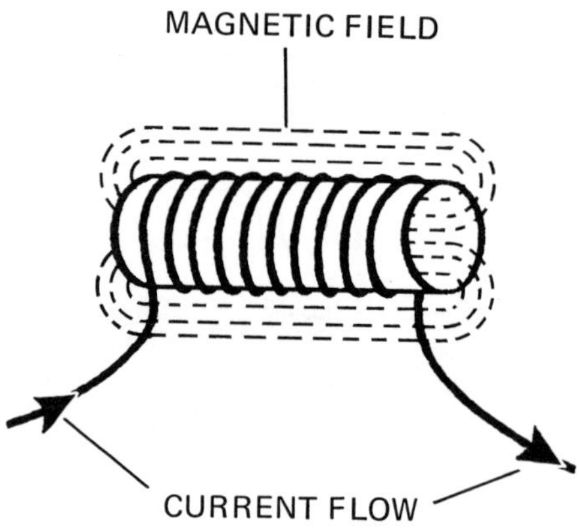

Fig. 20-7. Simple electromagnet.

An electromagnet made by winding wire around a rod is also called a *solenoid*. It is used in several places in the electric system of the automobile. Solenoids are discussed in more detail in Chap. 23.

⊘ 20-12 Resistance

An insulator has a high resistance to the movement of electrons through it. A conductor, such as a copper wire, has a very low resistance. Resistance is found in all electric circuits. In some circuits we want a high resistance, to reduce current flow. In other circuits we want as little resistance as possible, so that a high current can flow.

Resistance is measured in ohms (Ω). A 1,000-ft [304.8-m] length of wire that is about 0.1 in [2.54 mm] in diameter has a resistance of 1 ohm. A 2,000-ft [609.6-m] length of the same wire has a resistance of 2 ohms. In other words, the longer the path, the greater the resistance.

On the other hand, a 1,000-ft [304.8-m] length of wire that is about 0.2 in [5.08 mm] in diameter has a resistance of only $\frac{1}{4}$ ohm. Thus, the thicker the wire, the lower the resistance.

The explanation is simple. The longer the path or circuit, the farther the electrons have to travel, and the more resistance there is to their movement. With the thicker wire, the path is wider; so the resistance is lower.

⊘ 20-13 Ohm's Law

There is a definite relationship between amperes (electron flow), voltage (electrical pressure), and resistance. As the electric pressure goes up, more electrons flow. That is, increasing the voltage increases the amperes of current. However, increasing the resistance decreases the amperes of current. These relationships can be summed up in a formula known as Ohm's law:

Voltage is equal to amperage times ohms.

$$V = IR$$

The main thing to remember about Ohm's law is that increasing the ohms, or resistance, cuts down on the current. We will discuss this again, when we cover the electric system in the car.

Fig. 20-8. Electrical symbol for the ground, or return, circuit.

⊘ 20-14 One-Wire Systems For electricity to flow, there must be a complete path, or circuit. The electrons must flow from one terminal of a battery or alternator, through the circuit, and back to the other terminal. In the automobile, the engine and car frame are used to carry the electrons back to the other terminal. Therefore, no separate wire is required for the return circuit from the electrical device to the battery or the alternator. The return circuit is called the *ground*. It is indicated in wiring diagrams by the symbol shown in Fig. 20-8. Figure 20-1 contains several of these symbols. Just remember that the ground—the engine and car frame—is the return half of the circuit between the source of electricity and the electrical device.

⊘ 20-15 Alternating Current and Direct Current Most of the electricity that is generated and used is *alternating current* (ac). The current flows first in one direction, and then in the opposite direction; it alternates direction in the wire. The current you use in your home is ac. It alternates 60 times each second, and is therefore called 60-cycle ac. See Fig. 20-9.

The automobile cannot use ac. The battery is a direct-current (dc) unit. When you discharge the battery, that is, connect electrical devices to it, you take current out in one direction only. The current does not alternate, or change directions. Likewise, the electrical devices in the car operate on dc only.

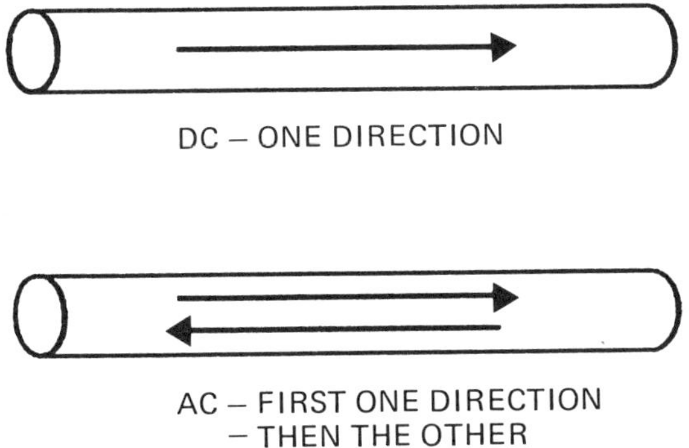

Fig. 20-9. Direct current flows in one direction only. Alternating current flows first in one direction, then in the other.

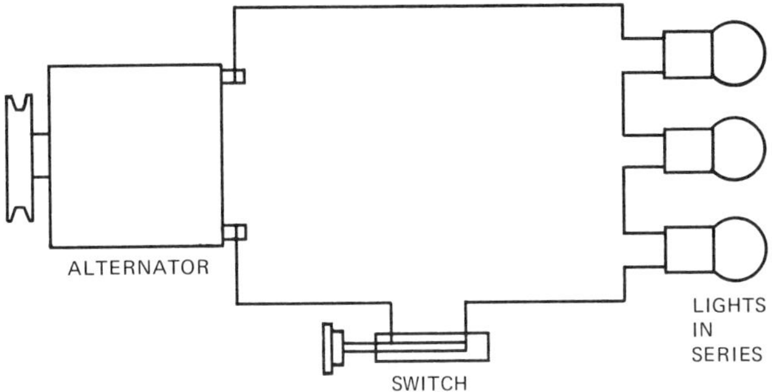

Fig. 20-10. When light bulbs are connected in series, the same current flows through all of them.

⊘ 20-16 Series Circuits In a series circuit, the electrical devices are connected to each other in a line. The current flows from one device to the next device, so that the same current flows through all of them (Fig. 20-10). If one device is turned off, the circuit is broken. No current flows in any device in the circuit.

⊘ 20-17 Parallel Circuits In parallel circuits, the various devices are connected by parallel wires (Fig. 20-11). The current divides; part of it flows into one device, part into another, and so on. Practically the same voltage is applied to each device. Each device can be turned on or off independently of the others.

NOTE: Many automotive circuits are series-parallel circuits. For instance, the headlights are connected to the battery in parallel. However, both are connected in series with a light switch (Fig. 20-13).

⊘ 20-18 Resistance in Parallel and Series Circuits It is simple to figure the resistance of a series circuit. The resistance is the sum of the resistances of the components of the circuit. In Fig. 20-12, the total

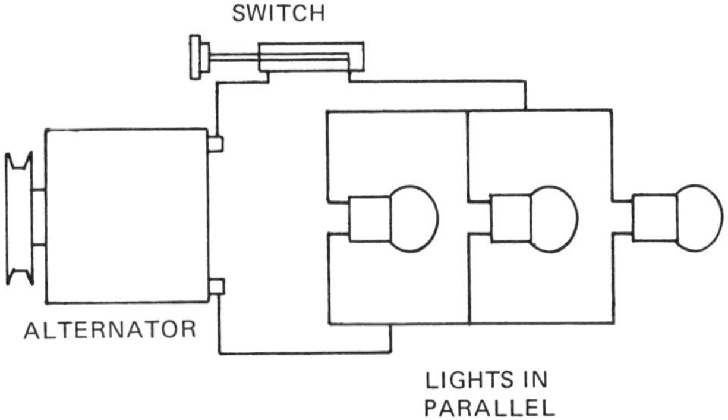

Fig. 20-11. When light bulbs are connected in parallel with the current source, the current divides; part of it flows through each light bulb.

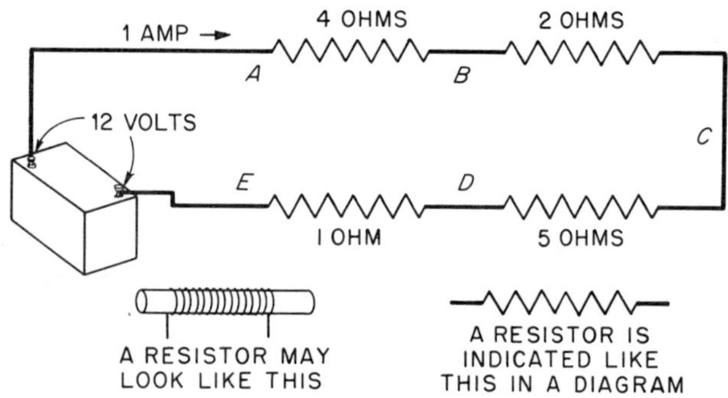

Fig. 20-12. Series circuit made of four resistors with different resistances.

resistance (ignoring the resistance of the wires) is 4 plus 2 plus 5 plus 1, or 12 ohms. Using Ohm's law, we can calculate that 1.0 A flows from the 12-V battery through the 12-ohm circuit.

The resistances of parallel circuits are more difficult to calculate. By paralleling devices, we reduce the total resistance, so that more current flows. For example, the headlights of an automobile are in parallel (Fig. 20-13). To calculate the resistance of a number of circuits in parallel, we use the formula

$$R = \frac{1}{1/r_1 + 1/r_2 + 1/r_3 + 1/r_4 \cdots}$$

in which R is the total resistance in ohms; and r_1, r_2, r_3, r_4, and so on, are the resistances of the individual circuits.

EXAMPLE: Suppose that the resistance of each headlight in Fig. 20-13 is 1 ohm. The total resistance is then

$$R = \frac{1}{1/1 + 1/1}$$
$$= \frac{1}{2/1}$$
$$= \frac{1}{2} = .5 \text{ ohm}$$

⊘ 20-19 Voltage Drop The voltage across each resistor in the circuit in Fig. 20-12 can be measured with a voltmeter. These voltages would add up to 12 V. For instance, the voltage between A and B (across the 4-ohm resistor) would be 4 V. From B to C, the voltage would be 2 V. From C to D, it would be 5 V. From D to E, it would be 1 V. If we did not know the resistance of any resistor, we could measure its voltage and amperage. We could then find its resistance with Ohm's law ($R = V/I$). For instance, the resistance of resistor AB is 4 V divided by 1 A, or 4 ohms.

The voltage is gradually "used up" from one end of the circuit to the other. The voltage drops by 4 V across the 4-ohm resistor. A voltage measurement would show 8 V left between points B and E. From C to E, it would show 6 V; and from D to E, it would show 1 V. Each resistance in a circuit causes a voltage loss, or *voltage drop*. The voltage drop is also called the *IR drop*. This comes from the formula $V = IR$.

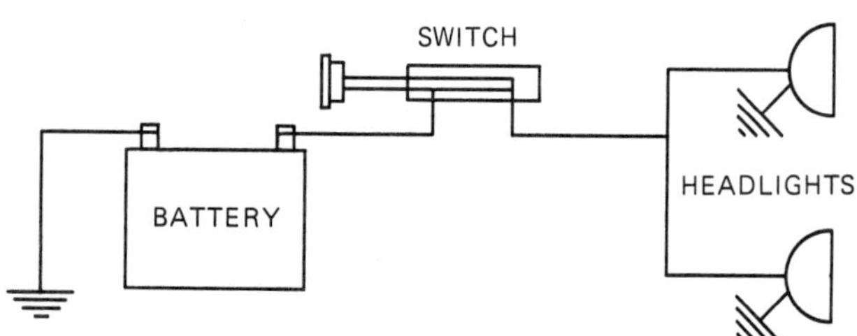

Fig. 20-13. The headlight circuit in an automobile is a series-parallel circuit. The two headlights are in parallel with each other, but are connected in series with the light switch and the battery.

EXPLANATION: The electric pressure, or voltage, is reduced along the circuit. Each component, whether it is the wire itself or a connected electrical device, "uses up" some of the voltage. The electric pressure is reduced as it is used to force electrons through each resistance.

⊘ 20-20 Importance of Voltage Drop The automotive electrician must understand voltage drop. Excessive voltage drop in the headlight circuit, for example, means low voltage at the headlights. This, in turn, means dim headlights. Excessive voltage drop in the charging circuit between the alternator and battery means a low charging voltage at the battery. The battery could very likely become discharged.

Excessive voltage drop can be caused by too small wires, broken strands in a multistrand wire, bad connections, defective contact points (for instance, in the ignition distributor), and other troubles. These conditions increase the resistance of the circuit. The increased resistance "uses up" more of the voltage. Then there is not enough voltage left to operate the headlights, charge the battery, and so on.

There is another way of looking at the excessive resistance caused by a bad connection. Such a bad connection cuts down the width of the electron path, so fewer electrons can get through. Too few electrons reach the headlight, for instance, and it becomes dim.

⊘ 20-21 Resistance Heating As electric current flows through a conductor, it heats up. Normally, the heating is very slight and does no harm. But if the wire is too small, there is considerable heating. Likewise, a bad connection becomes hot.

NOTE: Any connection that becomes abnormally hot when current flows through it is not in good condition.

NOTE: An electric light bulb is simply a tungsten conductor, called the *filament*, in an airtight glass envelope. When the light bulb is connected into an electric circuit, electrons bombard the tungsten atoms. The filament becomes so hot that it glows brilliantly, giving off light.

⊘ 20-22 Temperature Effect on Resistance As current passes through a wire, its resistance may increase along with its temperature. Most metals show this effect. A simple explanation might be this: With increased temperature, the atoms of metal that make up the wire are moving faster. The electrons (current) have a harder time traveling past the faster-moving atoms.

Not all substances show this increase of resistance with increase of temperature. The oxides of some metals, such as manganese, nickel, cobalt, copper, and iron, show the reverse effect. That is, as their temperature goes up, their resistance goes down. This effect is used in electrical devices called *thermistors*. Thermistors have many uses, from temperature measurement to control of many types of mechanisms. In many automobiles, the engine temperature gauge contains a thermistor.

⊘ 20-23 Using Ammeters and Voltmeters Ammeters are used to measure the current flowing through a circuit. Voltmeters are used to measure the voltage between two points in an electric circuit. Suppose we wanted to measure the current flowing in the circuit in Fig. 20-12. We would connect an ammeter into the circuit, in series with the resistance (Fig. 20-14). The current flowing through the circuit would also flow through the ammeter. The ammeter dial would show the amount of current flowing, or the amperage.

To measure the voltage across any resistance, we would connect a voltmeter to the two ends of that resistance (Fig. 20-15).

Remember: The ammeter is connected *into* the circuit, that is, in series. The voltmeter is connected *across* the circuit, in parallel with the component whose voltage is being measured.

⊘ 20-24 Wiring Circuits With the increasing number of electrical devices in modern automobiles, the wiring circuits have become rather complex. Figure

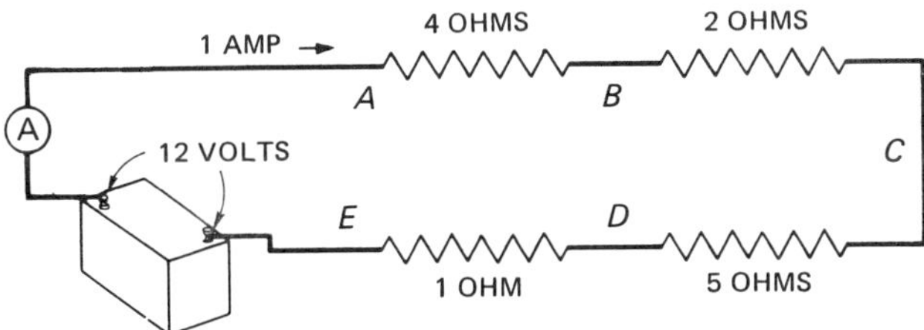

Fig. 20-14. Ammeter connected into the circuit at the battery.

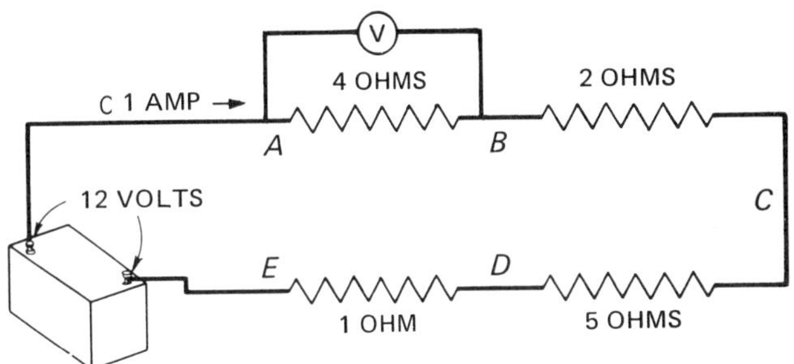

Fig. 20-15. Voltmeter connected across the 4-ohm resistor to measure its voltage drop.

20-16 shows the engine-compartment wiring circuit for one model of automobile. The wires between components are bound together into *harnesses*. Each wire is marked with special colors in the insulation—light green, dark green, red, black with a white tracer, and so on. These markings permit each wire in a harness to be identified.

Circuits that run through the bulkhead (which is between the engine compartment and the instrument panel) are completed by connector plugs and receptacles. Figure 20-17 shows how the wiring harnesses are positioned and how the various connections are made. In this illustration, the instrument-panel cluster has been removed and laid down to show the back of it. As many as a dozen separate wires are gathered together and connected to a receptacle. Then the matching wires are connected to a matching plug. The plug is pushed into the receptacle to complete all these connections at one time. The plugs and receptacles have locking devices that prevent their coming loose in operation.

⊘ 20-25 Printed Circuits The instrument panel carries a number of indicating devices, switches, and controls (Fig. 20-18). These must be interconnected electrically, either with separate wires or with a printed-circuit board. Because there must be a dozen or more connections in a small space, separate wires would be troublesome to connect. Thus, car manufacturers use printed circuits to make the connections. Figure 20-19 shows the location of a printed circuit in the back of an instrument-cluster assembly. The printed circuit is a flat board of insulating material, such as plastic. A series of metallic conducting strips are printed or otherwise applied to the board. Figure 20-20 shows part of a printed circuit. When it is installed as shown in Fig. 20-19, the conducting strips complete the circuits. The contacts on the indicator lights rest on the conducting strips, at the light sockets, when the lights are installed. The strips complete the circuits to the lights.

⊘ 20-26 Fuses, Circuit Breakers, and Fusible Links Most electric circuits have fuses or circuit breakers. They protect the electrical components from damage due to short circuits or grounding.

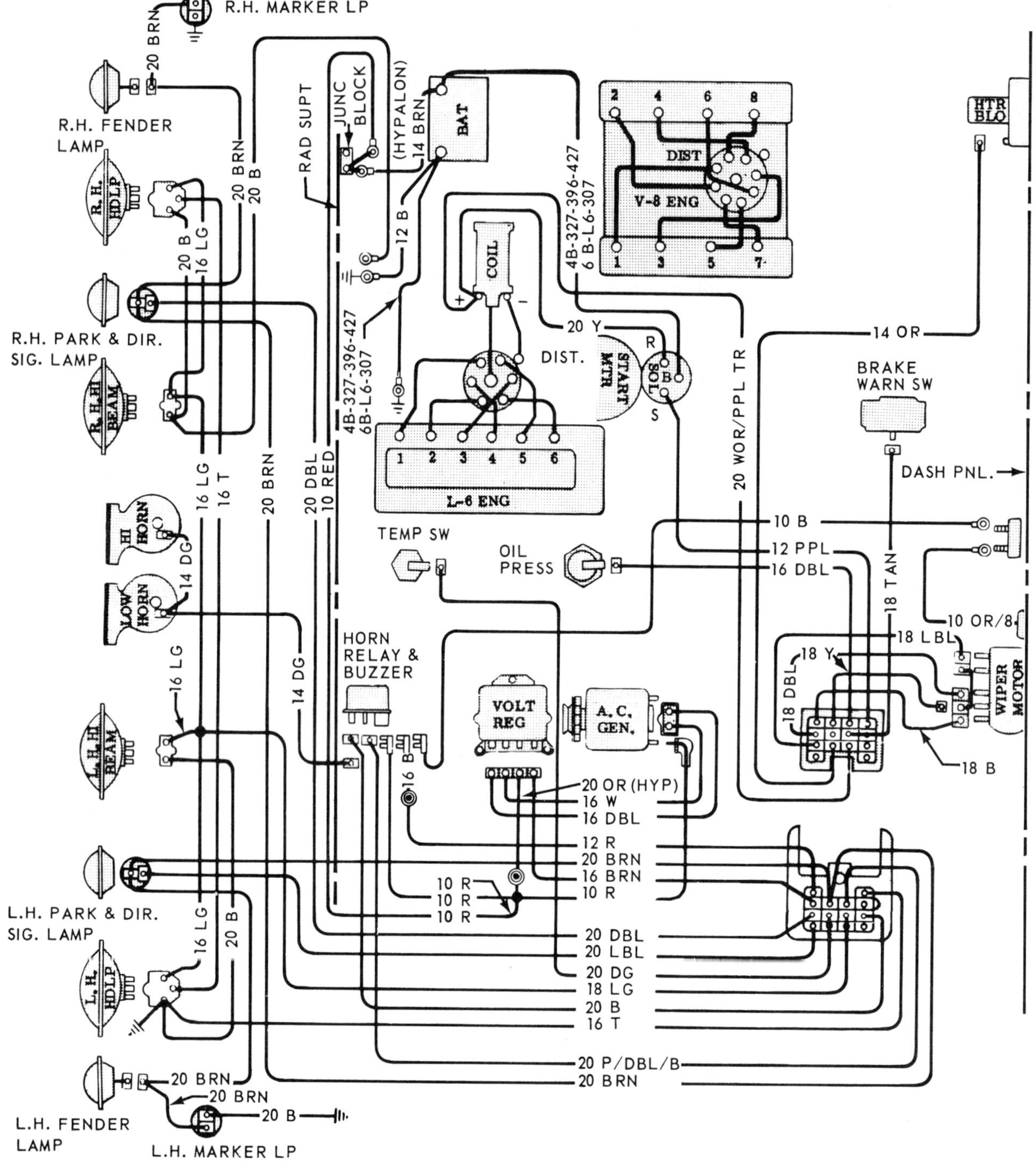

Fig. 20-16. Engine-compartment wiring diagram for one model of Chevrolet. (*Chevrolet Motor Division of General Motors Corporation*)

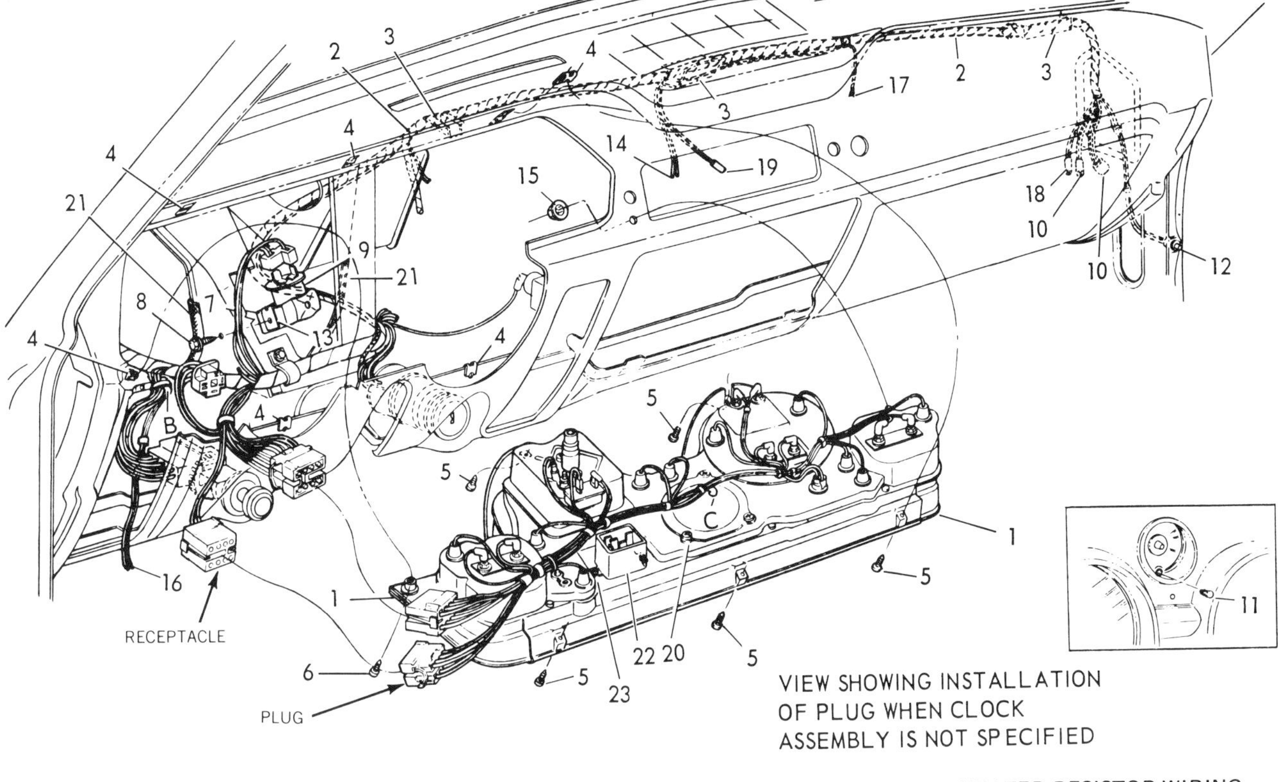

1. CLUSTER ASSEMBLY
2. PART OF WIRING ASSEMBLY
3. LOCATORS FOR PART OF WIRING ASSEMBLY
4. SPRING NUT
5. SCREW
6. SCREW
7. BRACKET
8. SCREW
9. EMERGENCY WARNING FLASHER
10. WIRING ASSEMBLY
11. PLUG
12. DOORJAMB SWITCH (2 REQUIRED). R.H. SHOWN; L.H. SYMMETRICALLY OPPOSITE.
13. NUT
14. BLOWER-MOTOR WIRING
15. STAMPED NUT
16. HEATER-CONTROL-SWITCH WIRING
17. HEATER-RESISTOR WIRING
18. COURTESY-LIGHTS WIRING
19. GLOVE-BOX-LIGHT WIRING
20. SCREW
21. FASTENER
22. WIPER-SWITCH ASSEMBLY
23. SCREW

Fig. 20-17. Instrument-panel wiring for one model of Mustang. (*Ford Motor Company*)

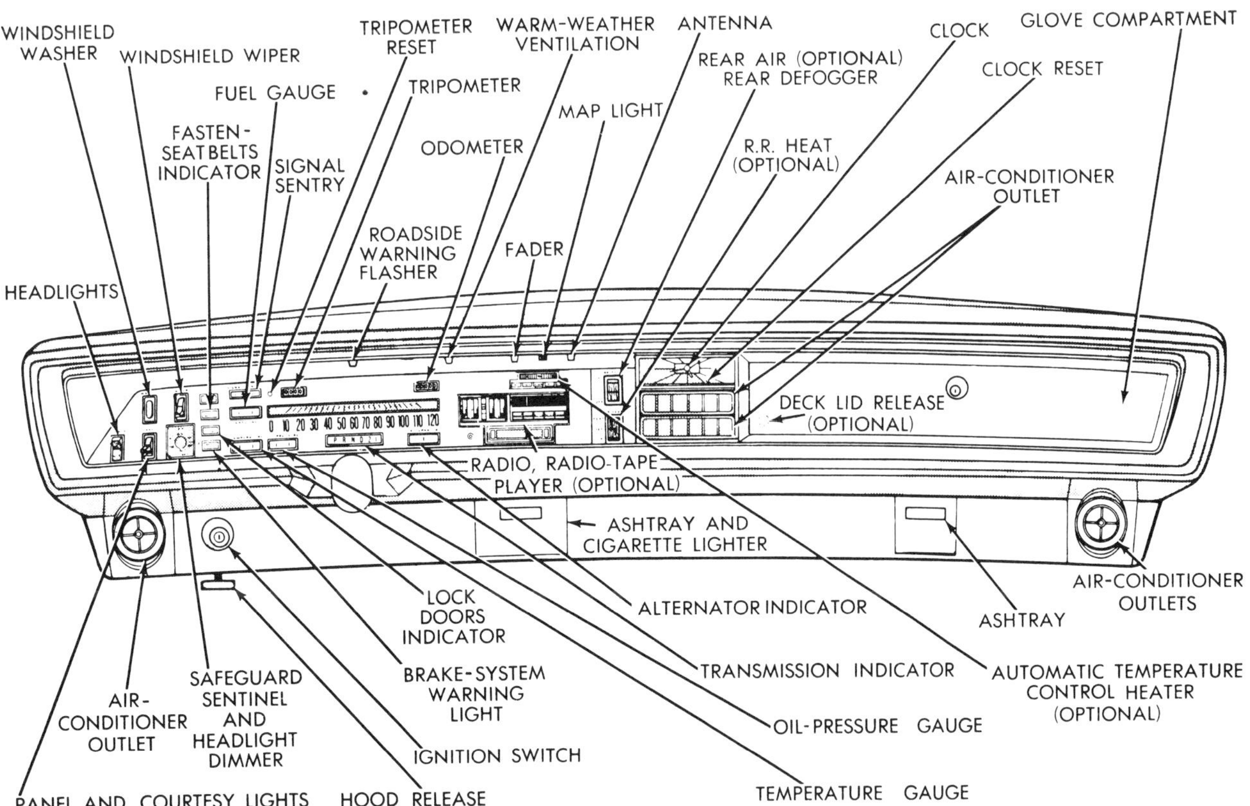

Fig. 20-18. Instrument panel on a fully equipped late-model automobile. (*Chrysler Corporation*)

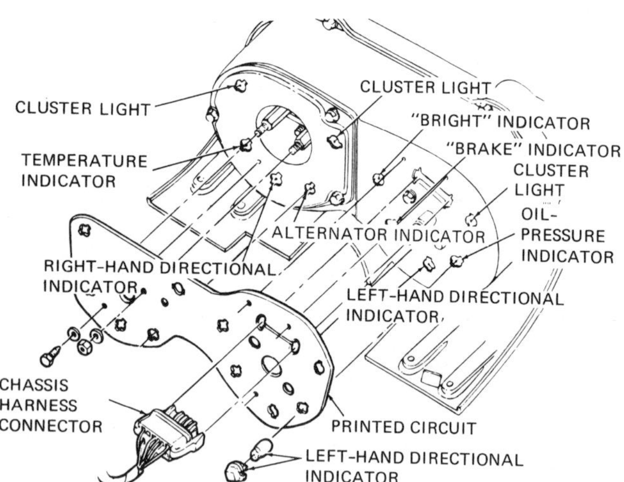

Fig. 20-19. Instrument-cluster assembly. *(Chevrolet Motor Division of General Motors Corporation)*

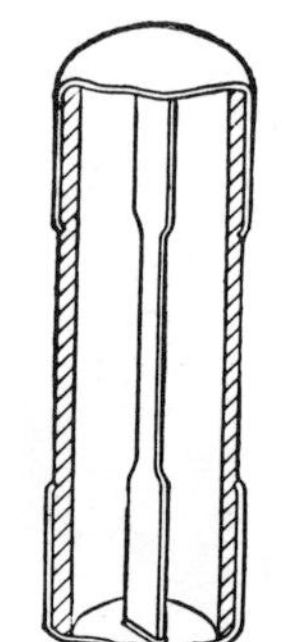

Fig. 20-21. Sectional view of a cartridge fuse.

Typical fuses are of the cartridge type (Fig. 20-21). They consist of a glass envelope, contact caps on each end, and a strip of soft metal connecting the two contact caps. The fuse is connected in series in the circuit. If a short or ground develops in the circuit, excessive current begins to flow. The high current overheats the soft metal strip. This melts the strip (or the fuse "blows"), and the circuit is opened. When this happens, the circuit should be checked, so that the short or ground can be found and eliminated. Then, a new fuse should be installed.

Figure 20-22 is a closeup of a fuse block, showing the fuses in place. Note (in Fig. 20-22) that circuit breakers and the horn relay are also mounted on the fuse block. Circuit breakers perform the same function as fuses, except that they do not "blow" (and thus do not require replacement) when an overload occurs. Instead, they cause contact points to open, interrupting the circuit. When the overload condition is eliminated, the contact points close to complete the circuit again.

Figure 20-23 shows a new type of fuse first installed in 1977 model cars. It works the same way as the cartridge fuse. However, the new fuse, called the mini-fuse, can be plugged in and removed much more easily.

For added protection, many cars have fusible links in the insulated battery cable and in the larger high-current-carrying wires. Figure 20-24 shows how a fusible link is installed. It is simply a wire several gauges smaller than the wire it is protecting. If a short or ground occurs, the fusible link burns apart before the larger wire does. This protects the rest of the circuit from damage.

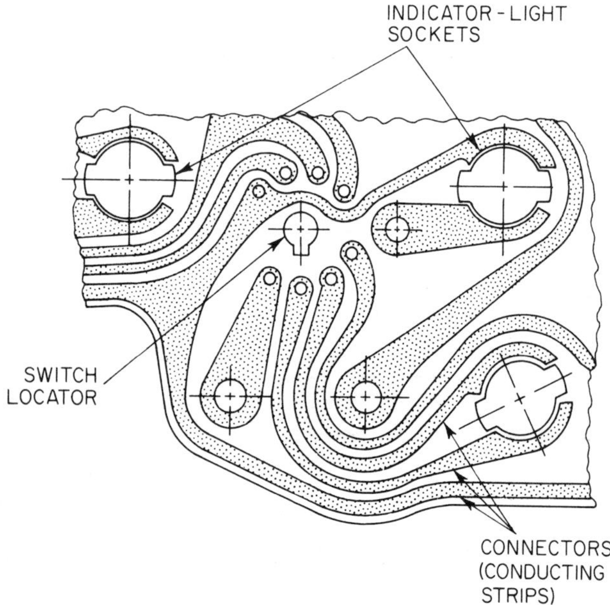

Fig. 20-20. Part of a printed circuit. The connectors are metallic conducting strips printed on the insulating base.

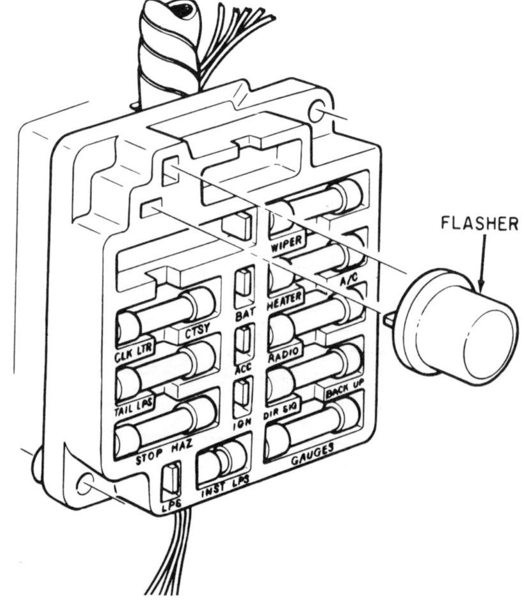

Fig. 20-22. Fuse block, showing fuses in place. *(Chevrolet Motor Division of General Motors Corporation)*

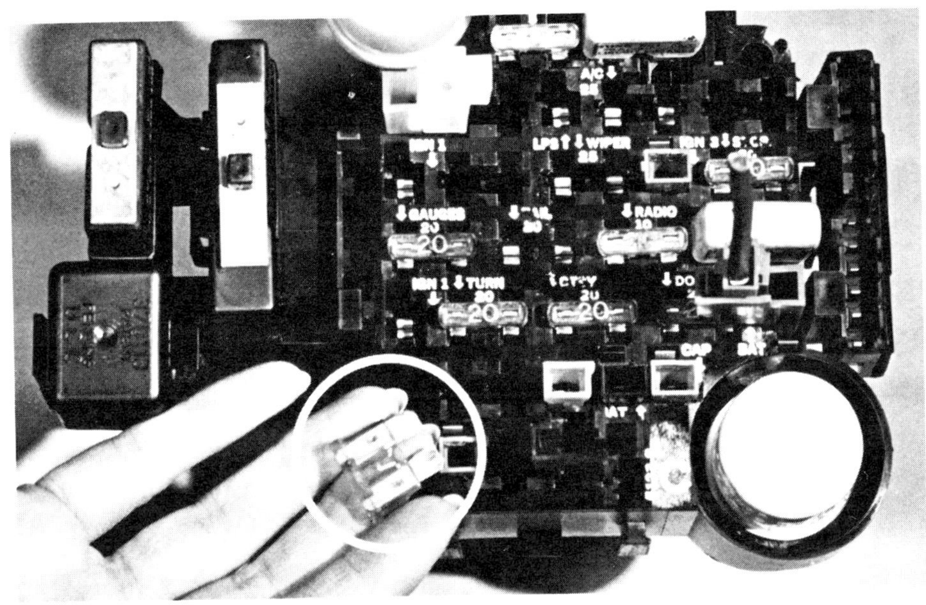

Fig. 20-23. New plug-in type of "mini-fuse" used on late-model cars. (*Oldsmobile Division of General Motors Corporation*)

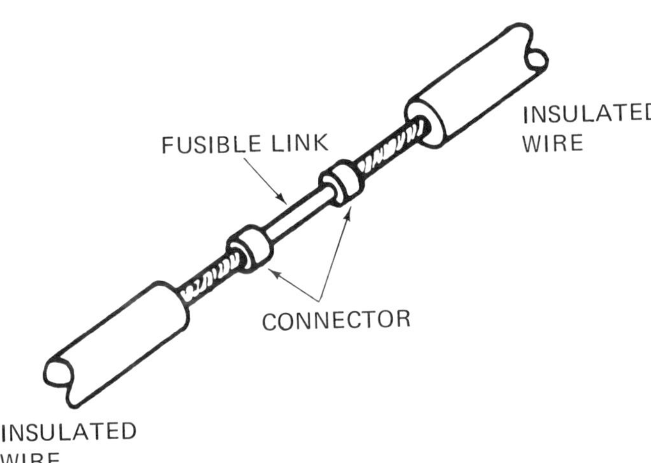

Fig. 20-24. Fusible link connected into an insulated wire circuit.

Check Your Progress

Progress Quiz 20-1 Here is a chance to find out how well you remember the facts you have been studying. In the last few pages, we discussed some fundamentals of electric circuits and magnetism. An understanding of these fundamentals will help you on the job, in the shop or office. Reread the chapter if any question stumps you. Don't get discouraged. Just remember that most good students reread their lessons several times, to retain the essential facts.

Completing the Sentences The sentences below are incomplete. After each sentence there are several words or phrases, but only one of them correctly completes the sentence. Write each sentence in your notebook, ending it with the one word or phrase that completes it correctly.

1. When electrical devices are connected so that the same current flows through all of them, they are in a: (*a*) parallel circuit, (*b*) series circuit, (*c*) series-parallel circuit, (*d*) parallel-series circuit.
2. When electrical devices are connected so that the same voltage is applied to each, they are in a: (*a*) parallel circuit, (*b*) series circuit, (*c*) series-parallel circuit, (*d*) parallel-series circuit.
3. Three resistances, of 2, 3, and 4 ohms, are connected in series. The resistance of the combination is: (*a*) 1 ohm, (*b*) 2 ohms, (*c*) 9 ohms, (*d*) 24 ohms.
4. Three resistances, of 2, 2, and 4 ohms, are connected in parallel. The resistance of the combination is: (*a*) 0.4 ohm, (*b*) 0.8 ohm, (*c*) 8 ohm, (*d*) 16 ohms.
5. Voltage drop is also called (*a*) *VR* drop, (*b*) *VI* drop, (*c*) *IR* drop.

CHAPTER 20 CHECKUP

NOTE: Since the following is a chapter review test, you should review the chapter before taking the test.

You have completed another chapter in the book and have taken a long step toward a better future. The chapter you have just finished may not be as interesting as later chapters, which deal with actual electrical devices in the automobile. However, the fundamentals are important. Once you understand them, you'll be able to answer many puzzling questions about how electric units operate. And you'll do a better job of troubleshooting and repairing electrical devices. The following questions will help you find out how well you remember the fundamentals. Be sure to write your answers in your notebook. Writing the answers helps you to remember them. It also makes your notebook a valuable source of information.

Completing the Sentences The sentences below are incomplete. After each sentence there are several words or phrases, but only one of them correctly completes the sentence. Write each sentence in your notebook, ending it with the one word or phrase that completes it correctly.

1. As described in the book, a flow of electrons is the same as: (*a*) a charge of electricity, (*b*) a current of electricity, (*c*) static electricity.
2. Electrons that are concentrated in an area tend to move away from the area because: (*a*) they repel each other, (*b*) they are very small, (*c*) their electricity is neutralized.
3. An insulator is effective because it: (*a*) does not contain electrons, (*b*) opposes free electron movement, (*c*) has an electron shortage.
4. In an electric circuit, if you increase the resistance without changing the voltage, then the current: (*a*) increases, (*b*) remains the same, (*c*) decreases.
5. If you increase the voltage in an electric circuit without changing the resistance, then the current: (*a*) increases, (*b*) decreases.
6. Generally speaking, it is easier to figure the resistance of: (*a*) parallel circuits, (*b*) series circuits.
7. Generally speaking, increasing the temperature of a wire or a connection: (*a*) increases the resistance, (*b*) increases the current, (*c*) reduces the resistance.
8. Like magnetic poles (north and north, for instance): (*a*) attract each other, (*b*) cancel out, (*c*) repel each other.
9. To use a volmeter, you must connect it into the circuit in: (*a*) series, (*b*) parallel.
10. To use an ammeter, you must connect it into the circuit in: (*a*) series, (*b*) parallel.

Problems Work out the following problems in your notebook.

1. An automobile headlight has a resistance of 1.8 ohms. It is connected to an alternator producing 7.2 V. What current flows through the headlight?
2. A coil of wire has a resistance of 4 ohms. What voltage is required to cause 4 A to flow through it?
3. You connect an ignition coil to a 6-V battery, and it draws 2 A. What is the resistance of the coil?
4. A series circuit is made up of a 4-ohm resistor, a 2.5-ohm resistor, and a 1.5-ohm resistor. What is the total circuit resistance?
5. A parallel circuit is made up of a 2-ohm resistor, a 2.3-ohm resistor, and a 6-ohm resistor. What is the resistance of the combination?

Definitions In the following, you are asked to define certain terms. Write the definitions in your notebook. Writing them down will help you remember them.

1. What is an insulator (in terms of electron activity)?
2. What is a conductor?
3. What is a short circuit?
4. List several reasons why insulation fails.
5. Define "voltage."
6. Define "amperage."
7. Define "electric resistance."
8. State Ohm's law.
9. Define "parallel circuit."
10. Define "series circuit."

SUGGESTIONS FOR FURTHER STUDY

If you are interested in the principles discussed in the chapter, you might like to study them further. Almost any physics book, or a book on basic electricity, will give you much additional information on the subject. Your local library probably has several such books. Also, if you have a chance, you could talk over points of special interest with a science or physics teacher.

chapter 21

AUTOMOTIVE BATTERIES

In this chapter, we describe the construction and operation of automotive storage batteries. The battery is called an electrochemical device. This means that it produces electric current by chemical means, as we explain in the chapter.

⊘ 21-1 Purpose of the Battery The battery (Figs. 21-1 and 21-2) supplies current to operate the starting motor and the ignition system when the engine is being started. It also supplies current for lights, radio, and other electrical accessories when the alternator is not handling the electric load. The amount of current the battery can supply is limited by the "capacity" of the battery. This, in turn, depends on the amount of chemicals it contains.

⊘ 21-2 Chemicals in the Battery The chemicals in the battery are sponge lead (a solid), lead oxide (a paste), and sulfuric acid (a liquid). These three substances react chemically to produce a flow of current. The lead oxide and sponge lead are held in *plate grids;* they form the positive and negative *plates.*

The plate grid (Fig. 21-3) is a framework of antimony-lead alloy with horizontal and vertical bars. The plate grids are made into plates (Fig. 21-4) by applying lead oxide paste. The horizontal and vertical bars hold the paste in the plate.

After the plates are assembled into the battery, the battery is given a "forming" charge. This changes the lead oxide paste in the negative, or minus, plate to sponge lead. It changes the lead oxide paste in the positive, or plus, plate to lead peroxide.

⊘ 21-3 Battery Construction In the battery, several similar plates are spaced and welded (or lead-burned) to a strap. This forms a *plate group* (Fig. 21-5). Plates of two types are used—one type for the positive plate group, the other for the negative plate group. A positive plate group is nested (meshed)

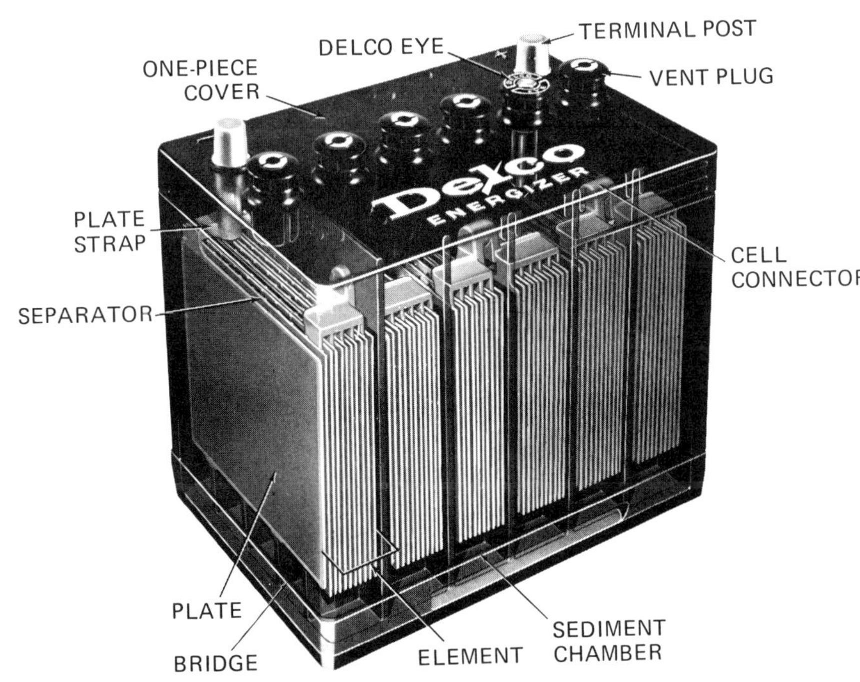

Fig. 21-1. Phantom view of a 12-V battery. The case is shown as though it were transparent, so the inside can be seen. *(Delco-Remy Division of General Motors Corporation)*

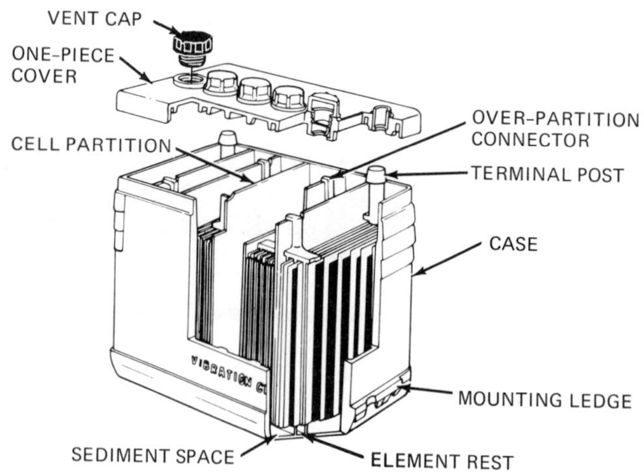

Fig. 21-2. Partly cutaway and disassembled 12-V battery. (*Ford Motor Company*)

with a negative plate group. Separators are placed between the plates to form an *element* (Figs. 21-6 and 21-7). The separators (Fig. 21-8) hold the plates apart so that they do not touch. At the same time, the separators are porous enough to permit liquid to circulate between the plates. Wooden sheets, spun glass matted into sheets, and porous sponge-rubber sheets have been used as separators. Late-model batteries have separators made of acid-resistant polyvinyl chloride or polyethylene-saturated cellulose.

The elements are placed in *cells* in the battery case. Then heavy lead connectors are attached to the cell terminals, to connect the cells in series. Many batteries have connectors that pass through the partitions, as in Fig. 21-9. Others have connectors that go over the partitions, as in Fig. 21-2. After the internal connectors are in place, the cover is put on (Figs. 21-1 and 21-2). The cover has openings through which liquid can be added when the filler plugs or vent caps are removed. After the liquid is added and the battery is given an initial charge, it is ready for operation.

Some batteries have the two main terminals on the battery cover, as in Figs. 21-1 and 21-2. Other batteries have the terminals in the side of the battery case, as in Fig. 21-10. This type of battery is called an ST (for side terminal or sealed terminal) battery by

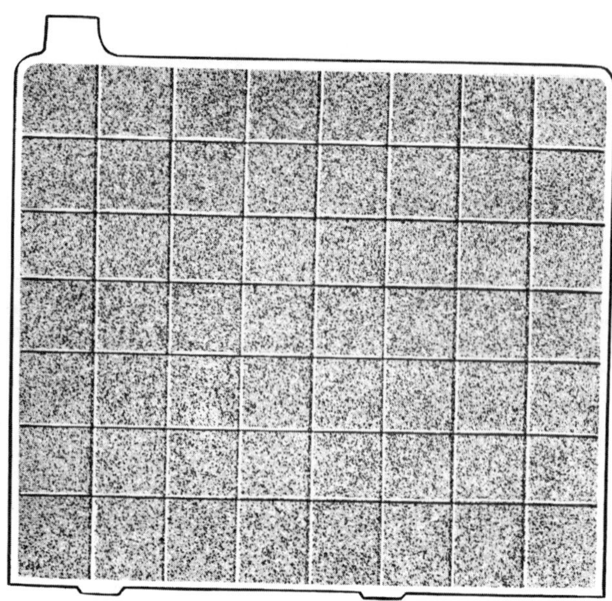

Fig. 21-4. Battery plate.

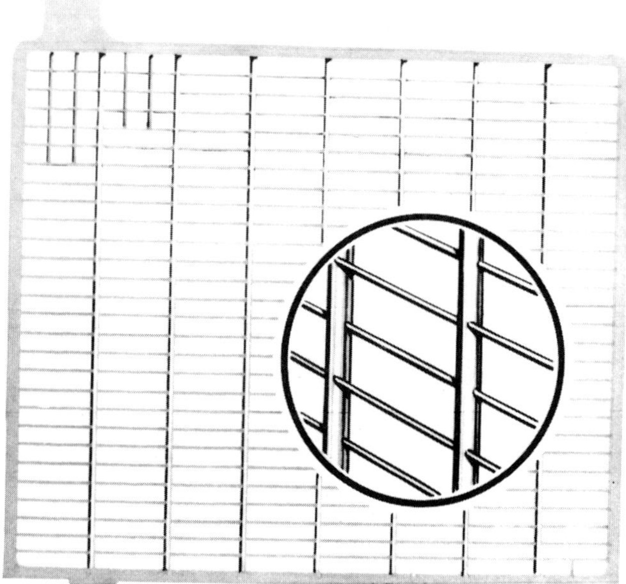

Fig. 21-3. Battery plate grid.

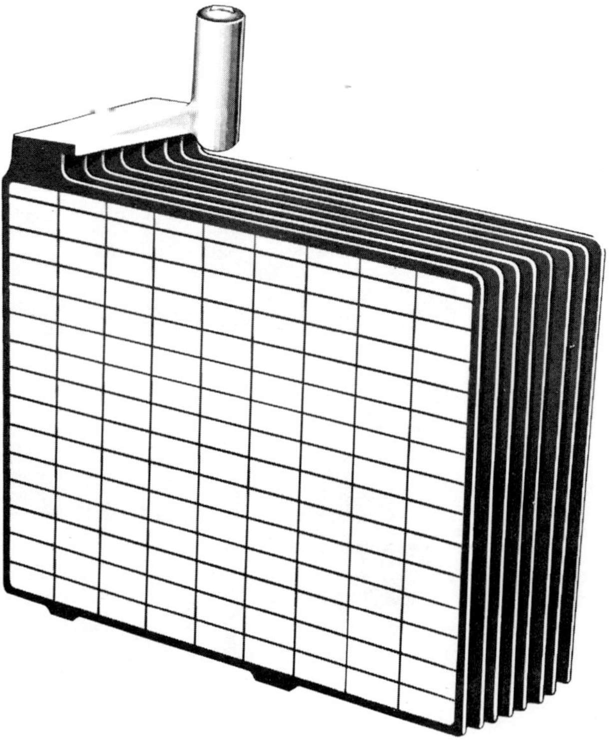

Fig. 21-5. Battery plate group.

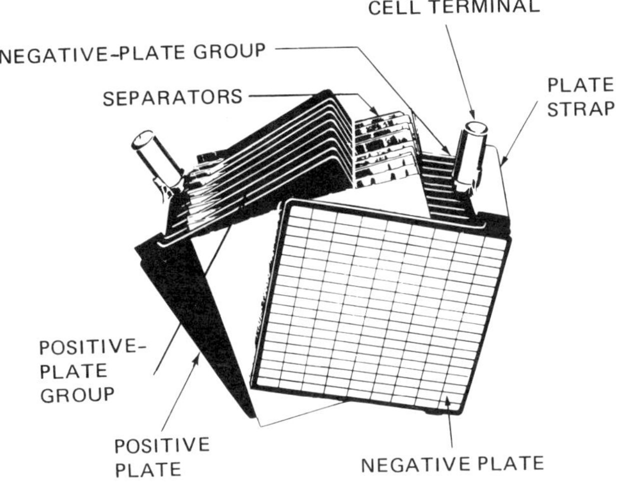

Fig. 21-6. Battery element, partly assembled.

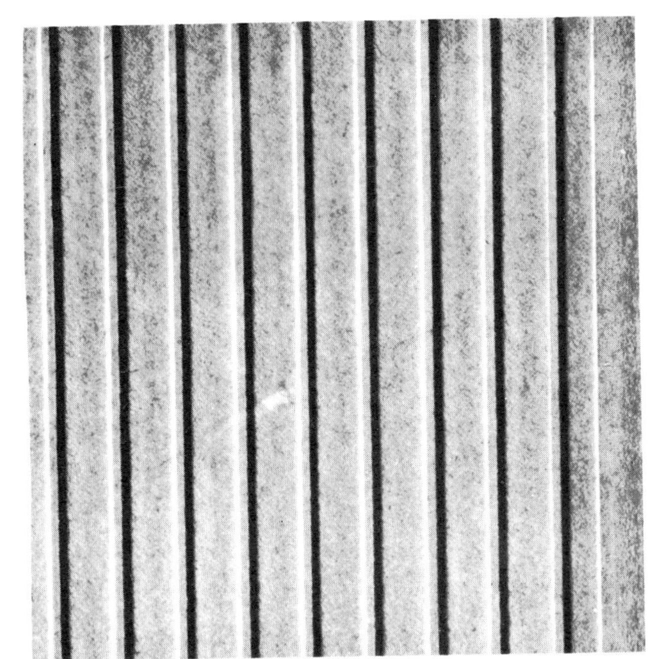

Fig. 21-8. Battery separator.

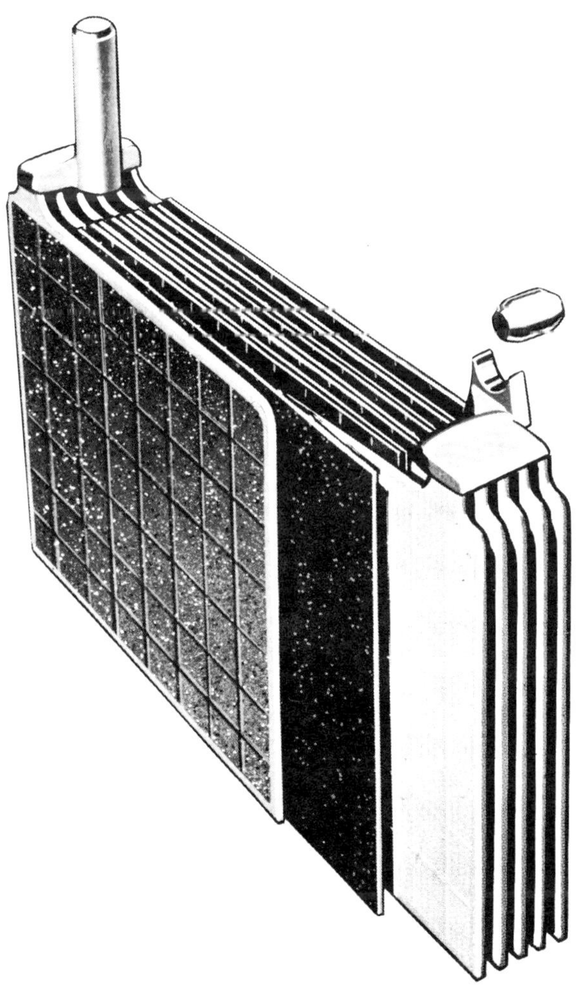

Fig. 21-7. Battery element, partly assembled, for battery with through-the-partition cell connectors. (*Delco-Remy Division of General Motors Corporation*)

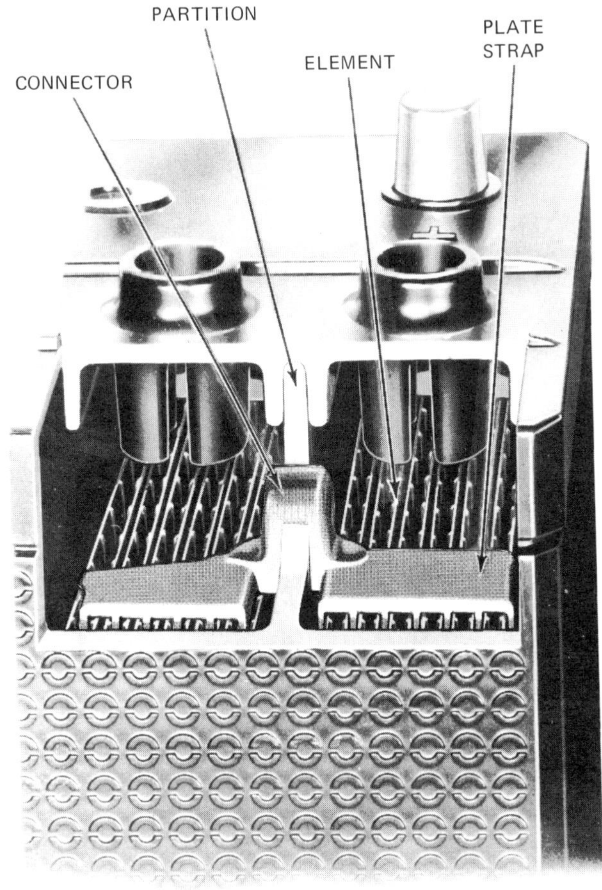

Fig. 21-9. Cutaway view of two cells in a battery which has a one-piece cover and cell connectors that pass through the partitions between the cells. (*Delco-Remy Division of General Motors Corporation*)

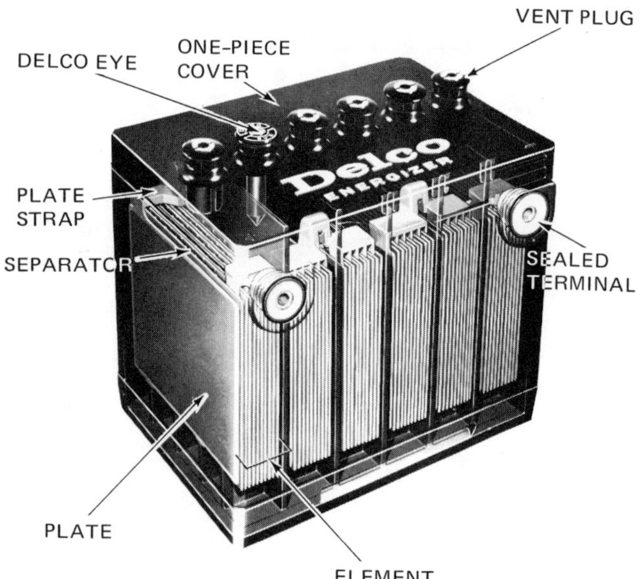

Fig. 21-10. Phantom view of a 12-V battery with the terminals in the side of the battery case. (*Delco-Remy Division of General Motors*)

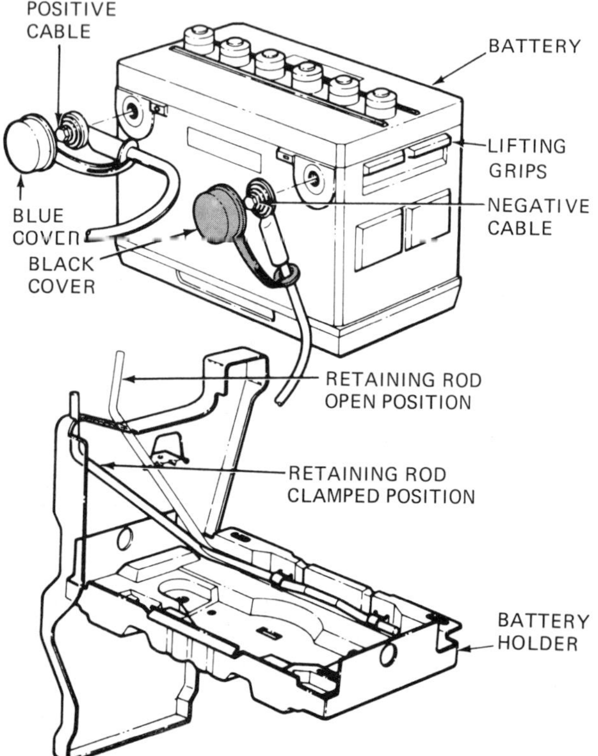

Fig. 21-11. Cable-connection and battery-mounting arrangement. (*Cadillac Motor Car Division of General Motors Corporation*)

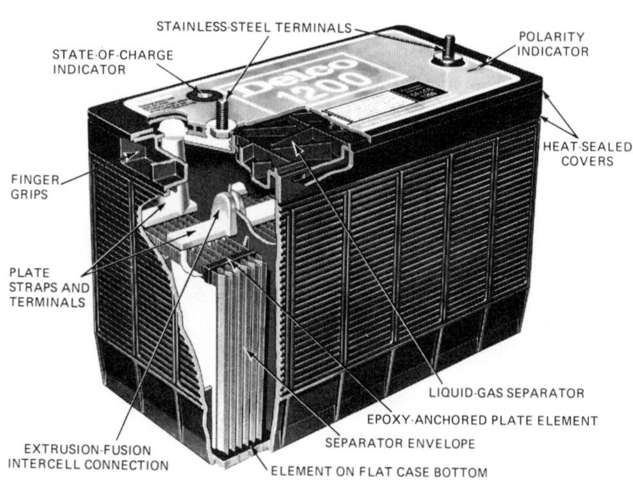

Fig. 21-12. Sealed battery of the type that never requires water. (*Delco-Remy Division of General Motors Corporation*)

the manufacturer. Figure 21-11 shows how the cables are connected to the ST battery. It also shows the battery mounting arrangement.

There is also a "no-service" battery which is sealed (Fig. 21-12). It never requires water, as other batteries occasionally do.

NOTE: Delco-Remy calls their late-model batteries "energizers."

⊘ 21-4 Chemical Activities in the Battery The liquid in a battery is called the *electrolyte*. It is made up of about 40 percent sulfuric acid and about 60 percent water (in a fully charged battery). When sulfuric acid is placed between the plates, chemical actions occur. These actions remove electrons from one group of plates and collect them at the other. This creates a 2.1-V pressure between the two groups of plates. That is, there is a pressure of 2.1 V between the two terminals of the battery cell. If the two terminals are not connected into a circuit, no further chemical activity takes place.

However, when the two terminals are connected in an electric circuit, electrons (current) flow. They flow out of the terminal where chemical activity has collected them. They then flow through the circuit to the other terminal (from which the chemical activity has removed them). Chemical activities now begin again, so the 2.1-V pressure is maintained. The current flow continues. The chemical actions "use up" the sponge lead, lead peroxide, and sulfuric acid. Thus, after a certain amount of current has been withdrawn, the battery becomes discharged (or "run down," or "dead"). It cannot deliver any additional current. When the battery has reached this state, it may be recharged. This is done by supplying it with a flow of current from some external source. The external source forces current back through the battery. This reverses the chemical activities in the battery. The plates are restored to their original composition, and the battery becomes recharged. It is then ready to deliver additional current.

The chemical actions that take place are rather complicated and are not fully understood. The sponge lead (negative plate) and lead peroxide (positive plate) change to lead sulfate as the battery discharges. The sulfate comes from the sulfuric acid. The electrolyte loses acid and gains water as the sulfate goes into the plates. Thus, discharging the battery changes the two different chemicals in the battery plates to a third chemical, lead sulfate. Recharging the battery changes the lead sulfate back to sponge lead in the negative plates, and to lead peroxide in the positive plates. Meantime, the sulfuric acid reappears in the electrolyte.

⊘ 21-5 Connecting Cells

Automotive batteries are usually 12-V units. There are six cells in the 12-V battery. The six cells are connected in series. In series connections, the voltages add. Some special applications require 24-V batteries; these batteries have 12 cells.

NOTE: A battery cell at 80°F [26.7°C] will develop about 2.1 V when fully charged. However, the common practice is to call this 2 V. Thus, a six-cell battery is said to be a 12-V battery, rather than a 12.6-V battery.

⊘ 21-6 Battery Ratings

The amount of current that a battery can deliver depends on the area and volume of the active plate material. It also depends on the amount and strength of electrolyte. Batteries are rated in several ways.

1. *RESERVE CAPACITY* This is the length of time in minutes during which a fully charged battery at 80°F [26.7°C] can deliver 25 A. A typical rating would be 125 min. This figure indicates the ability of a battery to carry the electric load when the alternator is not operating.

2. *COLD CRANKING RATE* There are two cold cranking rates. One is the number of amperes that a battery can deliver for 30 seconds when it is at 0°F [−17.8°C], without the cell voltages falling below 1.2 V. A typical rating for a battery with a reserve capacity of 125 min would be 430 A. This figure indicates the ability of the battery to crank the engine at low temperatures.

The second cold cranking rate is measured at −20°F [−28.9°C]. In this, the final voltage is allowed to drop to 1.0 V per cell. A typical rating for a battery with a reserve capacity of 125 min would be 320 A.

3. *OVERCHARGE LIFE UNITS* This is a measure of how well the battery will stand up when it is overcharged.

4. *CHARGE ACCEPTANCE* This is a measure of how well the battery will accept a charge, under normal operating conditions, from a voltage-regulated automotive charging system.

5. *WATTS* Delco uses an additional rating—watts. This is roughly equivalent to the battery cold-cranking rating.

⊘ 21-7 Battery Efficiency

The ability of a battery to deliver current varies within wide limits. It depends on the temperature and the rate of discharge. At low temperature, chemical activities are greatly reduced; the sulfuric acid cannot work so actively on the plates. Thus the battery is less efficient and cannot supply as much current for as long a time. High rates of discharge do not produce as many ampere-hours as low rates of discharge. At high discharge rates, the chemical activities take place only on the surface of the plates. They do not have time to penetrate the plates and use the materials below the plate surface.

Here are some figures that relate battery efficiency to battery temperature. Note that they are only approximations.

EFFICIENCY, PERCENT	BATTERY TEMPERATURE, °F [°C]
100	80 [26.7]
65	32 [0]
50	0 [−17.8]
10	−45 [−42.8]

⊘ 21-8 Variations in Terminal Voltage

Because the battery produces voltage by chemical means, the voltage varies according to a number of conditions. These conditions and their effects on battery voltage may be summed up as follows.

1. The terminal voltage of a battery that is being charged *increases* with:

a. Increasing charging rate. To increase the charging rate (amperes input), the terminal voltage must be increased.

b. Increasing state of charge. As the state of charge goes up, the voltage must go up to maintain the charging rate. For example, a voltage of approximately 2.6 V per cell is required to force a current through a fully charged battery. Voltage regulators are set to operate at 15 V—slightly below the voltage required to charge a fully charged battery. This setting protects the battery from being overcharged.

c. Decreasing temperature. Lower battery temperatures require a higher voltage to maintain a set charging rate.

2. The terminal voltage of a battery that is being discharged *decreases* with:

a. Increasing discharge rate. As the rate of discharge goes up, chemical activities increase and cannot penetrate the plates so effectively. Therefore, voltage is reduced.

b. Decreasing state of charge. With less of the active

material and sulfuric acid available, less chemical activity takes place. The voltage drops.

c. Decreasing temperature. At lower temperatures, the chemical activities are less effective. The voltage drops.

Check Your Progress

Progress Quiz 21-1 You have now begun your study of automotive electrical components. We shall discuss the construction and operation of each component first, and then its maintenance and repair. If you understand how a device is constructed and operates, it is much easier to maintain and repair the device. We began, in this chapter, with the construction and operation of the battery. Take the quiz that follows to see how well you remember the material. Don't be discouraged if any of the questions stump you. Just reread the last few pages. Even the best students reread their lessons several times. Rereading the pages and taking the quiz will help to fix the facts firmly in your mind.

Completing the Sentences The sentences below are incomplete. After each sentence there are several words or phrases, but only one of them correctly completes the sentence. Write each sentence in your notebook, ending it with the one word or phrase that completes it correctly.

1. A negative plate group and a positive plate group, nested together with separators between, make up: (*a*) a battery, (*b*) a cell, (*c*) an element.
2. The liquid in the battery, a mixture of water and sulfuric acid, is called the: (*a*) electricity, (*b*) electrochemical, (*c*) electrolyte, (*d*) electroliquid.
3. Several plates welded to a plate strap are called a: (*a*) plate element, (*b*) plate group, (*c*) plate cell, (*d*) battery.
4. After the battery plates are formed, they are: (*a*) flattened out, (*b*) changed chemically, (*c*) made thicker.
5. During battery discharge, the sulfuric acid in the electrolyte is replaced by: (*a*) lead sulfate, (*b*) lead peroxide, (*c*) water, (*d*) oxygen.
6. A battery that can deliver 25 A for 2 hr has a reserve-capacity rating of: (*a*) 5 amp-hr, (*b*) 8 amp-hr, (*c*) 120 min.
7. To maintain a constant current input to a battery during charging, as the battery temperature is reduced the voltage must be: (*a*) reduced, (*b*) held constant, (*c*) increased.
8. As the discharge rate of a battery is increased, the voltage of the battery is: (*a*) reduced, (*b*) held constant, (*c*) increased.

CHAPTER 21 CHECKUP

NOTE: Since the following is a chapter review test, you should review the chapter before taking the test.

You are making good progress in the book. Now test your knowledge of the material covered in the chapter you just finished. You may not be able to answer every question the first time. If this happens, don't be discouraged. Instead, do what all expert students do—turn back into the chapter and reread the pages that give you the information you want. By doing this, you, too, will become an expert student. You will find it easier to remember the essential facts. Write your answers in your notebook. This will fill your notebook with valuable information to which you can refer quickly.

Completing the Sentences The sentences below are incomplete. After each sentence there are several words or phrases, but only one of them correctly completes the sentence. Write each sentence in your notebook, ending it with the one word or phrase that completes it correctly.

1. The battery most commonly used for automobiles is the: (*a*) lead-acid type, (*b*) nickel-iron type, (*c*) nickel-cadmium type.
2. As the battery is discharged, the active materials in the negative and positive plates are changed to: (*a*) sulfuric acid, (*b*) lead oxides, (*c*) lead sulfate, (*d*) spongy lead.
3. If you counted the negative and the positive plates in a battery cell, you would find: (*a*) the same number of each, (*b*) one more negative plate, (*c*) one more positive plate.
4. Adding plate area to a battery cell increases the (*a*) voltage, (*b*) current availability, (*c*) cell resistance.
5. Connecting battery cells in series increases the (*a*) voltage, (*b*) current availability, (*c*) cell resistance.

Components of the Battery Below are a list of battery components and a list of the materials of which these components are made (not in order, however). Write, the list of components in your notebook, as is. Next to each component, write the material of which it is made. For example, after "case" you would write "hard rubber or plastic."

Components	*Materials*
case	lead antimony
electrolyte	wood
negative plates	hard rubber or plastic
positive plates	sulfuric acid and water
separator	lead antimony
plate strap	lead
plate grid	lead peroxide

Reviewing the Battery The following questions will help you review battery construction, ratings, and operating characteristics. Write the answers in your notebook.

1. Describe the construction of a battery cell.
2. What is meant by "forming" the plate?
3. What happens to the sulfuric acid in the electrolyte during battery discharge?

4. Describe the chemical actions that take place in the cell during discharge. During recharge.
5. Name several factors that influence battery capacity.
6. List the three conditions that require an increased charging voltage during battery recharging.
7. List the three conditions that result in a lower battery voltage during battery discharge.

SUGGESTIONS FOR FURTHER STUDY

If you are especially interested in the battery, check your local public or school library for books with additional information. In addition, battery manufacturers usually supply manuals describing their batteries.

chapter 22

BATTERY SERVICE

In this chapter, we look at battery maintenance and service. At one time, battery rebuilding was big business. In battery rebuilding, new plates and separators are installed in the old case and cover. Today, however, battery failure means discarding the old battery and installing a new one. Here is how to get full life out of a battery.

⊘ 22-1 Battery Maintenance Most people tend to forget about their car battery. That is, they forget it until, finally, the battery can't do its job and the engine won't start. Battery failure is one of the more common car troubles.

If people would check their batteries once in a while, most battery troubles could be avoided. Here are the things that should be done.

1. Visually inspect the battery.
2. Check the electrolyte level in all cells periodically.
3. Add water if the level is low.
4. Clean off corrosion around the battery terminals and top.
5. Check the battery condition with a testing instrument. (We describe battery test instruments in later sections.)
6. Recharge the battery if it is low.

CAUTION: Sulfuric acid, the active ingredient in battery electrolyte, is very corrosive. It can destroy most things it touches. It will cause painful and serious burns if it gets on the skin. It can cause blindness if it gets into eyes. If you get battery acid (electrolyte) on your skin, flush it off at once with water. Continue to flush for at least 5 min. Put baking soda (if available) on the skin. This will neutralize the acid. If you get acid in your eyes, flush your eyes out with water, over and over again. Get to a doctor at once! Do not wait!

CAUTION: The gases that form above the battery cells during charging are very explosive. Never light a match or a cigarette or cause a spark near a recently charged battery. Never blow off a battery with an air hose. The compressed air could lift the cell cover and splash electrolyte all over you.

⊘ 22-2 Visual Inspection of Battery Look over the battery for signs of leakage, a cracked case or top, corrosion, missing vent plugs, and loose or missing hold-down clamps. Leakage signs could indicate a cracked battery case; they show up as white corrosion on the battery carrier, fender inner panel, or car frame. If the top of the battery is covered with corrosion, and the battery needs water frequently, chances are the battery is being overcharged. This means the charging system should be checked.

The most common cause of a cracked top is improper installation. If the wrong wrench is used to remove or tighten the cable clamps, the battery top probably will be broken. See ⊘ 22-18 on how to remove and replace cable clamps.

The most common cause of a cracked case is excessive tightening of the hold-down clamps. Also, a front-end crash, even if minor (with little damage to the sheet metal), may crack the battery case.

⊘ 22-3 Checking Electrolyte Level and Adding Water To check the battery, remove the vent caps and look down into the cells. If water is needed, add it. Distilled water is recommended, but any water that is fit to drink may be used.

NOTE: You can't check battery cells on sealed batteries, of course. But you can make sure the connections are tight at the terminals.

Many batteries have rings, in the cell covers, which show whether or not the battery needs water. Figure 22-1 shows a ring when the level is too low and when it is correct.

Many batteries have a "Delco Eye," a special vent cap or plug, in one of the six cells (Fig. 22-2). It has a transparent rod extending down into the cell. When the end of the rod is immersed, the exposed top of the rod shows black. When the electrolyte level falls below the rod end, the top of the rod glows. This means water should be added. Thus, the

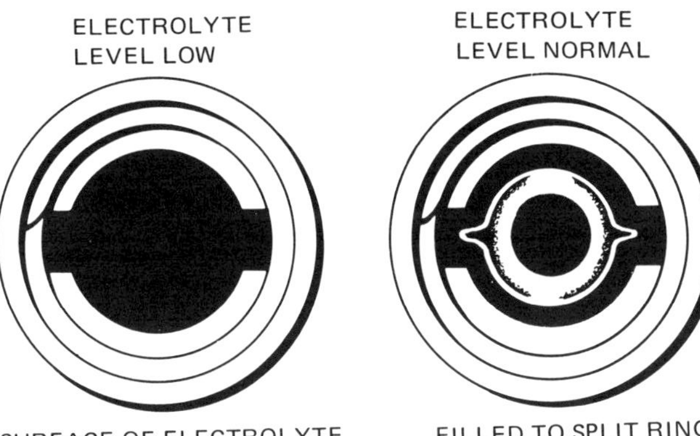

Fig. 22-1. Appearance of the electrolyte and split ring when the electrolyte is too low and when it is correct. (*Delco-Remy Division of General Motors Corporation*)

vent caps do not need to be removed to check the electrolyte level.

CAUTION: Don't add too much water. Too much water will cause the electrolyte to leak out. This will corrode, or eat away, the battery carrier and any other nearby metal. Also, do not add water to a battery when the temperature is below freezing, unless the vehicle is operated for the next 30 minutes. The fresh water may freeze and crack the battery.

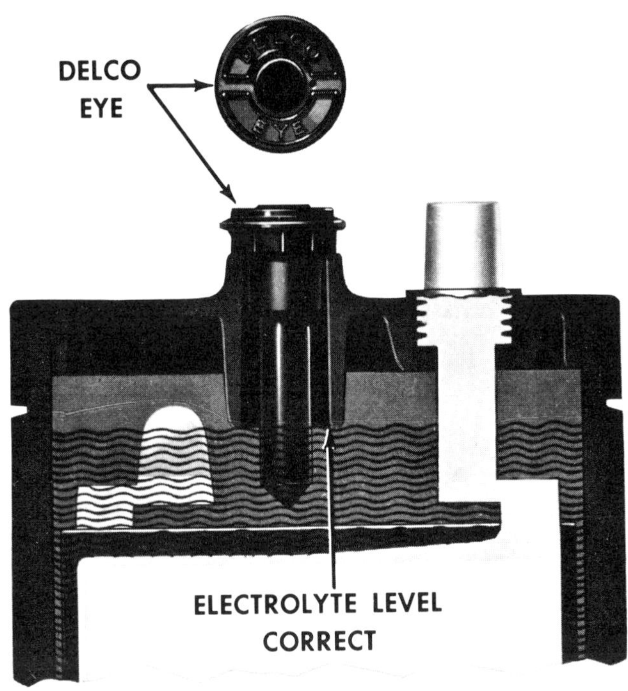

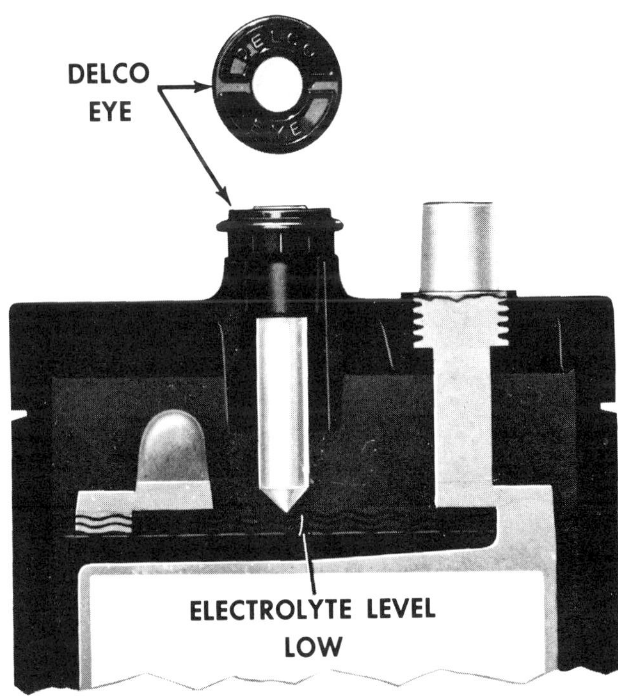

Fig. 22-2. Cutaway views of a battery cell with the Delco Eye. In the top figure, the electrolyte is at the proper level. In the bottom illustration, it is low. (*Delco-Remy Division of General Motors Corporation*)

⊘ 22-4 Cleaning Corrosion off the Battery Battery terminals, especially those located on top of the battery, tend to corrode (Fig. 22-3). Corrosion builds up around the battery, the cable clamp, and, unseen, between the terminal posts and clamps. To get rid of it, and to clean the battery top, mix some common baking soda with water in a can. Brush on the solution, wait until the foaming stops, and then flush off the battery top with water. If the buildup of corrosion around the terminals is heavy, detach the cables from the terminals (as explained later). Then use the special wire brushes shown in Fig. 22-4 to clean the terminal posts and cable clamps. Finally, coat the terminals with an anticorrosion compound to retard corrosion.

⊘ 22-5 Checking Battery Condition There are several ways to test battery condition. The most common way is with a battery hydrometer. Other methods use testing meters. In the shop, you will be shown how to use the instruments that are available, and how to tell a good battery from a bad battery. Here, we cover the highlights of the tests.

⊘ 22-6 Hydrometer Test The hydrometer tests the specific gravity of the battery electrolyte. It has a rubber bulb at the top, a glass tube, a float, and a rubber tube at the bottom (Fig. 22-5). To use it, you squeeze the bulb, put the end of the tube into the battery cell, and then release the bulb. This sucks electrolyte up into the glass tube. The float will float in the electrolyte. The amount the stem of the float sticks out of the electrolyte tells you the battery's state of charge (Fig. 22-6). Take the reading at eye level, as shown.

Fig. 22-3. Corroded battery cables and terminal posts.

CAUTION: Do not drip electrolyte on the car or on yourself! It will ruin the paint on the car and eat holes in your clothes! See the caution in ⊘ 22-1.

If the float sticks out so the reading on the stem is between 1.260 and 1.290, the battery is fully charged. If the reading at the electrolyte level is between 1.200 and 1.230, the battery is only half charged. If the reading is around 1.140, the battery is about run down and needs a recharge. The following table of specific-gravity readings gives a general idea of battery condition.

1.265–1.299 Fully charged battery
1.235–1.265 Three-fourths charged
1.205–1.235 One-half charged
1.170–1.205 One-fourth charged
1.140–1.170 Barely operative
1.110–1.140 Completely discharged

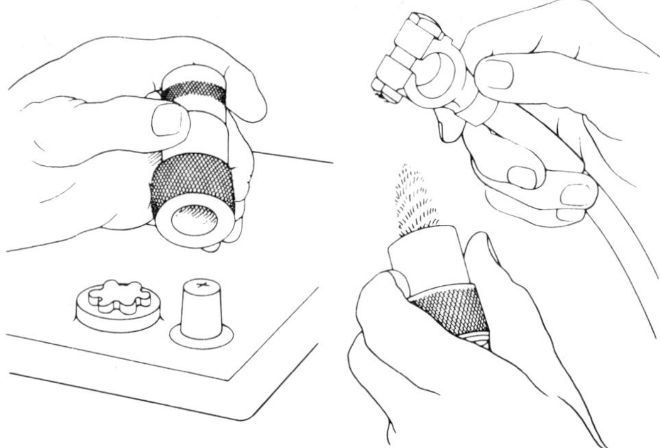

Fig. 22-4. Using special wire brushes to clean battery terminal posts and cable clamps. (*Buick Motor Division of General Motors Corporation*)

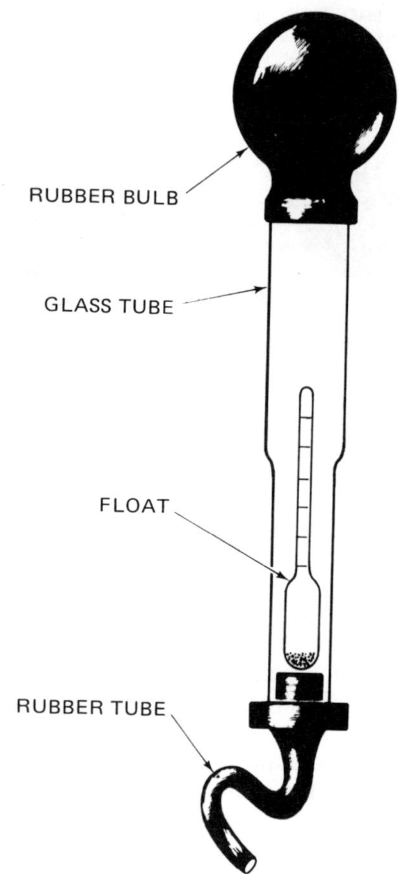

Fig. 22-5. Battery hydrometer. (*Ford Motor Company*)

If a cell tests much lower than the others, there is something wrong with that cell. A cracked case may have allowed electrolyte leakage, or perhaps there is internal damage to the plates or separators. If the variation is only a few specific-gravity points, then there is probably no cause for alarm. But if the cell measures 25 to 50 points lower, it is defective. The battery should be replaced. You could find two or three defective cells in a battery.

NOTE: Some late-model 12-V batteries for passenger-car service have a somewhat lower specific gravity when charged. For instance, one type is fully charged when its specific gravity is 1.270. Other batteries—for example, those used in hot climates—have a specific gravity of 1.225 when fully charged.

The decimal point is not normally mentioned in a discussion of specific gravity. For example, "twelve twenty-five" means 1.225, and "eleven fifty" means 1.150. Also, the word "specific" is often dropped, so that the term becomes just "gravity."

⊘ 22-7 Variation of Gravity with Temperature The temperature also affects the gravity of the electro-

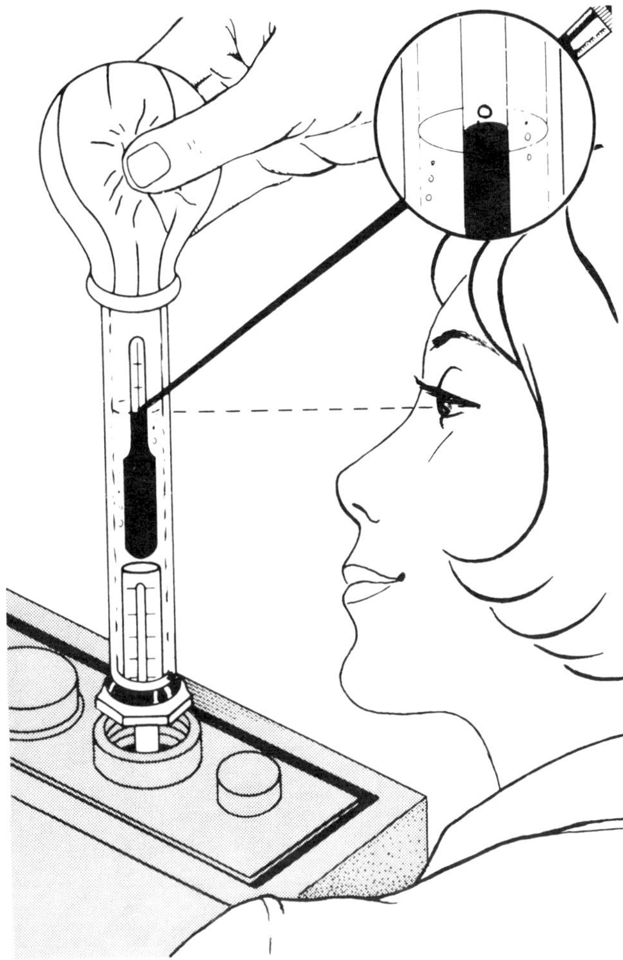

Fig. 22-6. Using a battery hydrometer to check the specific gravity of a battery cell. The reading should be taken at eye level.

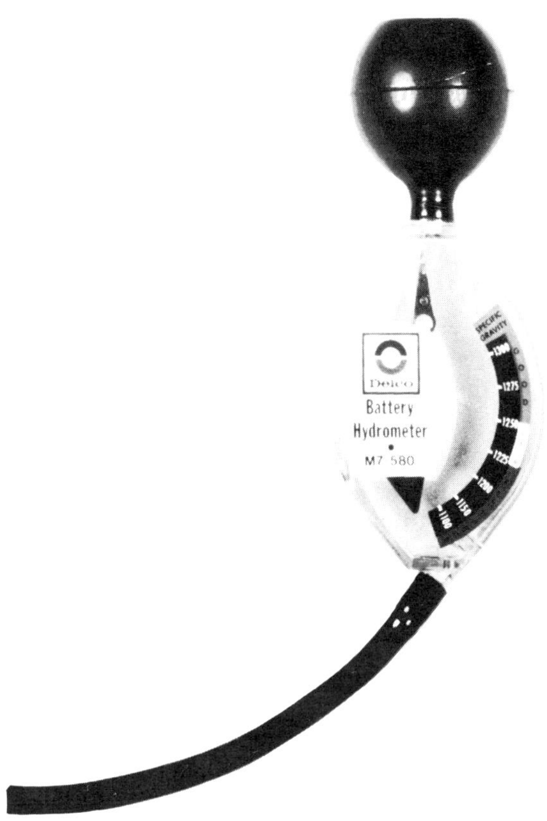

Fig. 22-7. Temperature-compensated hydrometer. *(Delco-Remy Division of General Motors Corporation)*

lyte. This is because a liquid becomes thicker and gains gravity as it cools. As a liquid warms, it becomes thinner and loses gravity. Thus, the temperature must be considered when a gravity reading is taken. A correction must be made if the temperature varies from standard. This correction involves the addition or subtraction of gravity points, according to whether the electrolyte temperature is above or below the 80°F [26.7°C] standard. The gravity of electrolyte changes about four points, or four thousandths (0.004) for every 10°F change in temperature. To make a temperature correction, subtract (or add) four points for every 10°F below (or above) 80°F [26.7°C].

EXAMPLE: The gravity of an electrolyte is 1.250 at 120°F. We add 0.016 (4 × 0.004). The corrected reading is 1.266.

Another gravity is 1.230 at 20°F. We subtract 0.024 (6 × 0.004). The corrected reading is 1.206.

NOTE: The battery hydrometer shown in Fig. 22-7 is compensated for temperature. No temperature corrections have to be made when this hydrometer is used.

⊘ 22-8 Loss of Gravity with Age As a battery ages, the electrolyte gradually loses gravity. This is because of the loss of active material from the plates (as it sheds and drops into the bottom of the cells). Gravity is also lost due to gassing. Over a period of 2 years, for example, battery electrolyte may drop to a top gravity (fully charged) of 1.250. The original top gravity, when new, may have been 1.280. Little can then be done to restore gravity, since the loss is an indication of an aging battery.

⊘ 22-9 Loss of Gravity from Self-Discharge If a battery is allowed to stand idle for a long time, it will slowly self-discharge. This self-discharge results from internal chemical reactions between the battery materials. The higher the battery temperature, the more rapidly self-discharge takes place. The lead sulfate that forms on the battery plates as a result of self-discharge is difficult to convert into active material. Thus, a battery that is badly self-discharged may be ruined.

⊘ 22-10 Battery Gravities for Hot Climates In hot climates, chemical activity takes place more readily in the battery. Thus, it is often desirable to adjust the gravity reading to as low as 1.210 (28.5 percent acid) for a fully charged battery. This reduces the amount of self-discharge and prolongs the life of the battery. On discharge, the electrolyte gravity may get as low

Specific gravity	Freezing temperature, degrees F [C]
1.100	18 [−8.2]
1.160	1 [−17.2]
1.200	−17 [−27.3]
1.220	−31 [−35]
1.260	−75 [−59.4]
1.300	−95 [−70.5]

Fig. 22-8. Table of specific gravities and freezing points.

as 1.075 before the battery stops delivering current. Where there is no danger of freezing, low gravities are okay.

⊘ 22-11 Freezing Point of Electrolyte The higher the gravity of the electrolyte, the lower its temperature must be before it freezes. The battery must be kept sufficiently charged to prevent freezing. Freezing usually ruins the battery (see Fig. 22-8).

⊘ 22-12 Refractometer Test This is the tester described in ⊘ 9-7 and illustrated in Figs. 9-3 to 9-6. It is used to test both the antifreeze strength of engine coolant and the specific gravity of battery electrolyte. Refer to Figs. 9-3 to 9-6 and ⊘ 9-7 for details of the use of the refractometer. The only difference is that, when testing the battery, you use the black dipstick. First, pick up a couple of drops of electrolyte from a battery cell with the black dipstick. Then put the end of the black dipstick into the cover-plate opening. This deposits the drops of electrolyte in the measuring window. Now you can read the electrolyte strength and determine the battery's state of charge. Test all battery cells in this manner. After each test, wipe the black dipstick, the measuring window, and the plastic cover of the refractometer (Fig. 9-3).

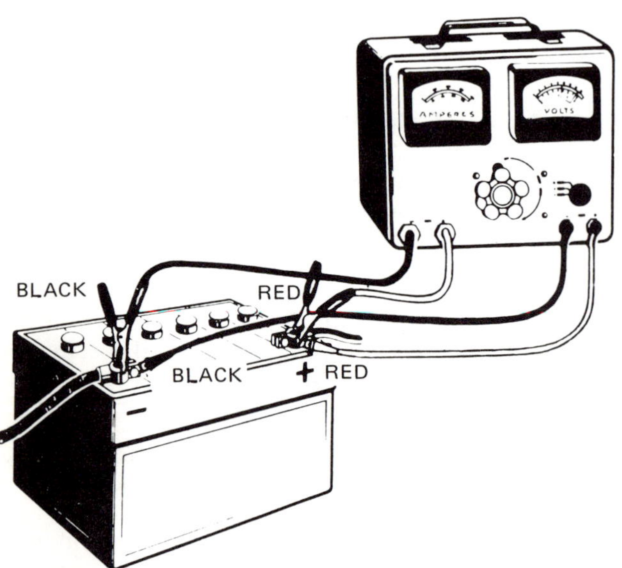

Fig. 22-9. Testing battery voltage under high discharge. *(Chrysler Corporation)*

CAUTION: Be careful not to drip electrolyte on yourself or on the car. Remember that electrolyte contains sulfuric acid, and this acid is very corrosive. It will ruin the paint on the car. And, of course, it will burn your skin (see ⊘ 22-1).

⊘ 22-13 High-Discharge or Capacity Test In this test, the battery voltage is measured during a high discharge. The battery should be in good condition, with no obvious defects such as a broken cover or case. Figure 22-9 shows a battery being given a high discharge while the voltage is measured. Specifications for the amount of high discharge vary. Always check the manufacturer's manual. Figure 22-10 outlines the procedure recommended by the Ford Motor Company.

⊘ 22-14 The 421 Test The 421 test is designed for batteries with a one-piece cover. The test requires a special tester which applies a series of timed discharge and charge cycles to the battery. The battery condition can be determined very accurately within a few minutes. When using the tester, follow the tester manufacturer's instructions carefully.

⊘ 22-15 Cadmium-Tip Test This test requires a special tester. It has cadmium tips that are inserted into the electrolyte of neighboring cells (Fig. 22-11) after the filler plugs are removed. The electrolyte must be up to the proper level. If the car has been operated, or the battery charged, in the last 8 hr, turn on the headlights for 1 min. Then turn the headlights off. Start the test by putting the red probe into the cell nearest the positive terminal. Put the black probe into the next cell. Note the meter reading. Move the probes to cells 2 and 3, and note the meter readings. Continue to the end of the battery. Compare the readings. Figure 22-12 shows various readings and the conditions they indicate. Note the following:

1. If any two cells vary by five scale divisions or more (top scale), the battery is at the point of failure and should be replaced.
2. If all cells vary by less than five scale divisions and all read in the green section, the battery is charged and in good condition.
3. If all cells vary by less than five scale divisions but some fall in the red section, the battery is in good condition but needs charging.
4. If any reading falls in the RECHARGE AND RETEST area, the battery is too low to make a good test. Recharge and retest it.

⊘ 22-16 Battery Service Battery service can be divided into four parts: visual inspection, testing, charging, and care of batteries in stock.

⊘ 22-17 Battery Testing Battery testing includes a check of the condition of the battery, as we have

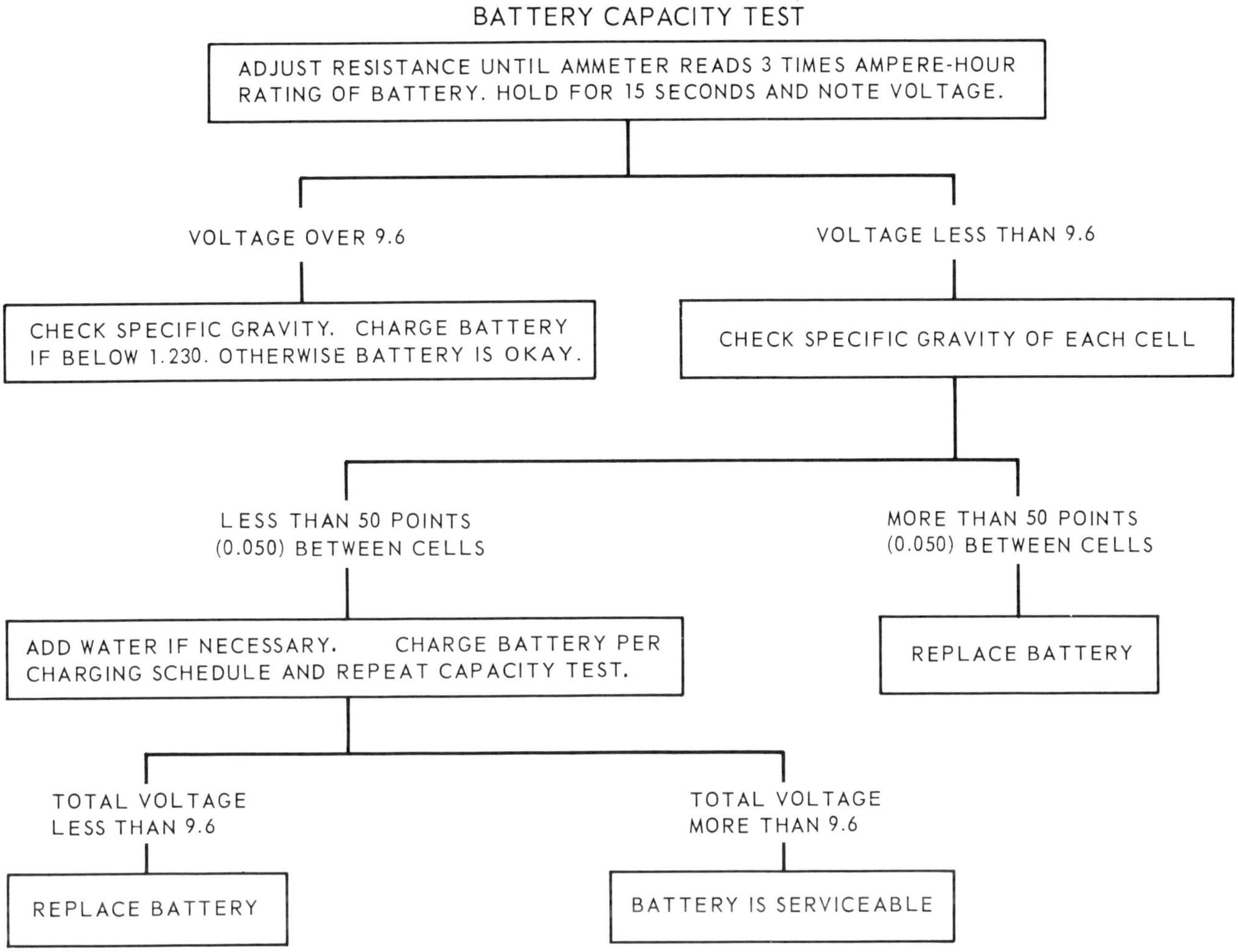

BATTERY CAPACITY TEST

ADJUST RESISTANCE UNTIL AMMETER READS 3 TIMES AMPERE-HOUR RATING OF BATTERY. HOLD FOR 15 SECONDS AND NOTE VOLTAGE.

- VOLTAGE OVER 9.6
  - CHECK SPECIFIC GRAVITY. CHARGE BATTERY IF BELOW 1.230. OTHERWISE BATTERY IS OKAY.
- VOLTAGE LESS THAN 9.6
  - CHECK SPECIFIC GRAVITY OF EACH CELL
    - LESS THAN 50 POINTS (0.050) BETWEEN CELLS
      - ADD WATER IF NECESSARY. CHARGE BATTERY PER CHARGING SCHEDULE AND REPEAT CAPACITY TEST.
        - TOTAL VOLTAGE LESS THAN 9.6
          - REPLACE BATTERY
        - TOTAL VOLTAGE MORE THAN 9.6
          - BATTERY IS SERVICEABLE
    - MORE THAN 50 POINTS (0.050) BETWEEN CELLS
      - REPLACE BATTERY

Fig. 22-10. Battery capacity test recommended by Ford. (*Ford Motor Company*)

seen. It should also include analysis of any abnormality found, so that corrections can be made. This will prevent a repetition of the trouble. Following are various battery troubles and their possible causes.

1. *OVERCHARGING* If the battery requires a considerable amount of water, it is probably being overcharged. That is, too much current is being supplied to the battery. This is a damaging condition that overworks the active materials in the battery and shortens battery life. In addition, overcharging causes more rapid loss of water from the battery electrolyte. Unless this water is replaced frequently, the electrolyte level is likely to fall below the tops of the plates. This exposes the plates and the separators to the air and may ruin them. Also, overcharging causes the battery plates to buckle and crumble. Thus, a battery subjected to severe overcharging will soon be ruined. Where overcharging is experienced or suspected, the charging system should be checked. It should be adjusted if necessary to prevent overcharging (Chap. 27).

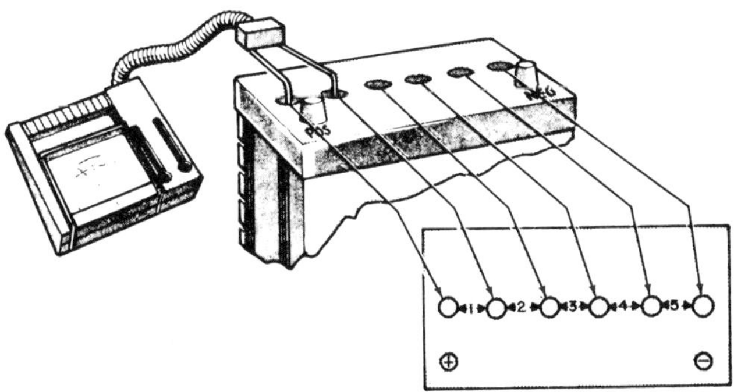

Fig. 22-11. Testing battery cells with a cadmium-tip battery-cell analyzer. (*Chrysler Corporation*)

2. *UNDERCHARGING* If the battery is discharged, it should be recharged as outlined later in this chapter. In addition, an attempt should be made to find out what caused the battery to discharge. It could be:

1. A charging-system malfunction
2. Defective connections in the charging circuit between the alternator and the battery.
3. Excessive load demands on the battery
4. A defective battery
5. Permitting the battery to stand idle for long periods so that it self-discharges excessively

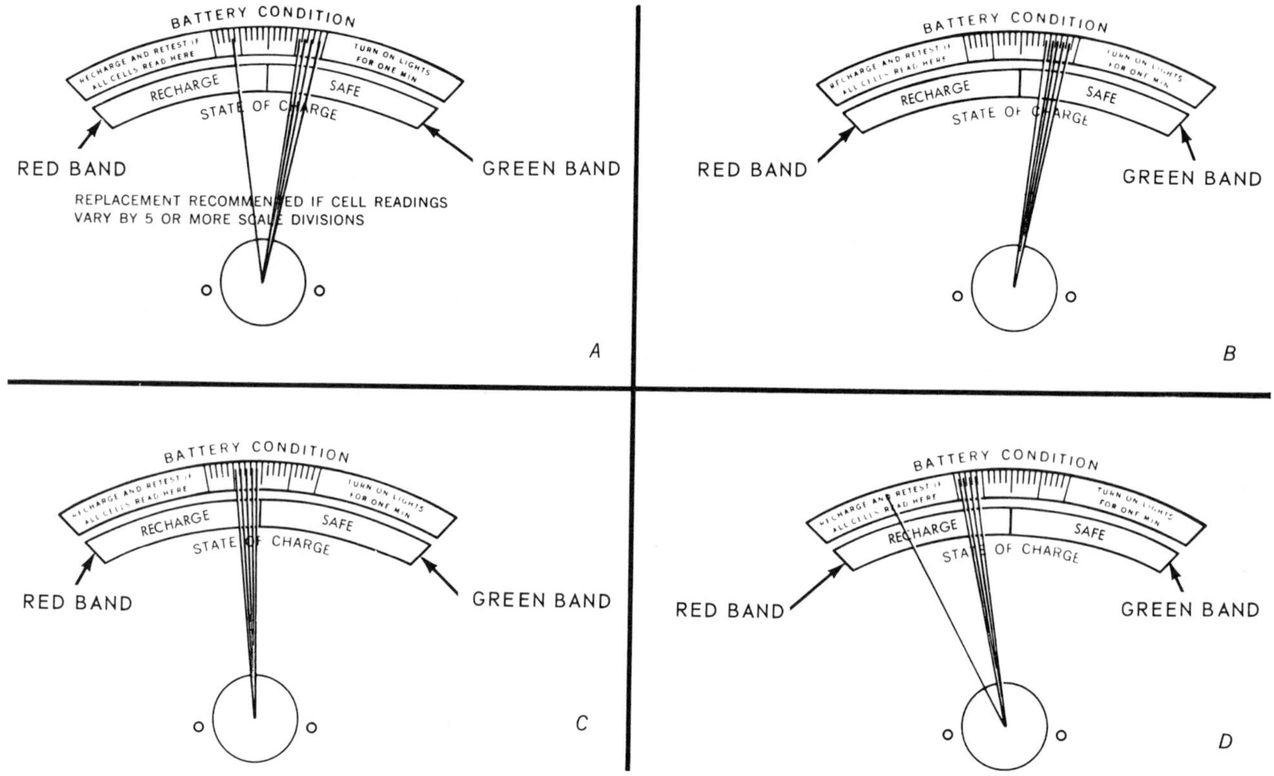

Fig. 22-12. Interpretation of meter readings in the cadmium-tip test. (*Chrysler Corporation*)

In addition, an old battery may have a low specific-gravity reading because it is approaching failure.

3. *SULFATION* The active materials in the plates are converted to lead sulfate during discharge, as already noted. This lead sulfate is reconverted into active material during recharge. However, if the battery stands for long periods in a discharged condition, the lead sulfate is converted into a hard, crystalline substance. This substance is difficult to reconvert into active materials by normal charging methods. Such a battery should be charged at half the normal rate for 60 to 100 hr. Even though this long charging period may reconvert the sulfate to active material, the battery can still be damaged. The crystalline sulfate, as it forms, tends to break the plate grids.

4. *CRACKED CASE* A cracked case may result from excessively loose or tight hold-down clamps, from battery freezing, or from flying stones.

5. *BULGED CASES* Bulged cases result from tight hold-down clamps or from high temperatures.

6. *CORRODED TERMINALS AND CABLE CLAMPS* This condition occurs naturally. You should be prepared to remove excessive corrosion periodically from terminals and clamps. The cable clamps should be disconnected from the terminals, and the terminal posts and cables cleaned as already explained (⊘ 22-4).

7. *CORRODED BATTERY HOLDER* Some spraying of battery electrolyte is natural as the battery is being charged. The battery holder may become corroded from the effects of the electrolyte. Such corrosion may be cleaned off, with the battery removed. Use a wire brush and a baking-soda solution.

8. *DIRTY BATTERY TOP* The top of the battery may become covered with dirt and grime, mixed with electrolyte sprayed from the battery. This should be cleaned off periodically as already explained (⊘ 22-4).

9. *DISCHARGE TO METALLIC HOLD-DOWN* If the hold-down clamps are of the uncovered metallic type, a slow discharge may occur from the insulated terminal to the hold-down clamp. This is more likely to occur with a dirty battery top, across which current can leak. The remedy is to keep the battery top clean and dry.

⊘ 22-18 Removing and Replacing a Battery To remove a battery from a car, first disconnect the grounded-terminal cable clamp. This prevents accidental grounding of the insulated terminal when it is disconnected. To remove a nut-and-bolt type of clamp, loosen the clamp nut about $\frac{3}{8}$ in [9.53 mm]. Use a box wrench or special cable pliers (Fig. 22-13). Do not use ordinary pliers or an open-end wrench. Either of these might break a cell cover when swung around. If the clamp sticks, use a clamp puller (Fig. 22-14). Do not use a screwdriver or bar to pry on the clamp. This could damage the battery cell or cover. To detach the spring-ring type of clamp, squeeze the ends of the rings apart with Vise-grip or Channellock pliers (Fig. 22-15).

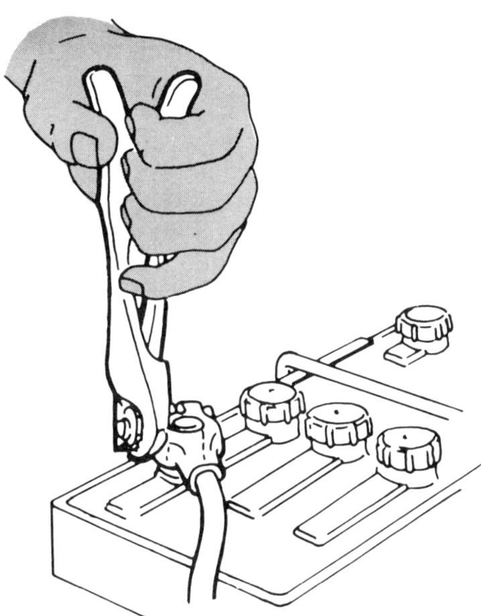

Fig. 22-13. Using battery pliers to loosen the nut-and-bolt type of battery cable clamp.

After the grounded cable is disconnected, disconnect the insulated-terminal cable. Clean both battery terminals and cable clamps with special tools (Fig. 22-4). Loosen the battery hold-downs, and take out the battery. When installing a battery, do not reverse the terminal connections. (Some automobiles have the negative terminal grounded, others the positive terminal.) Reconnect the insulated-terminal cable first. Then reconnect the grounded-terminal cable. Apply corrosion inhibitor to the clamps and terminals. Install and tighten the hold-downs. Avoid overtightening.

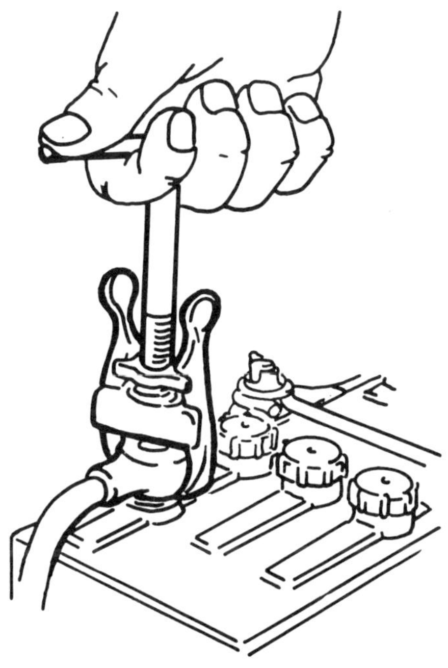

Fig. 22-14. Using a special clamp puller to pull the cable from the battery terminal.

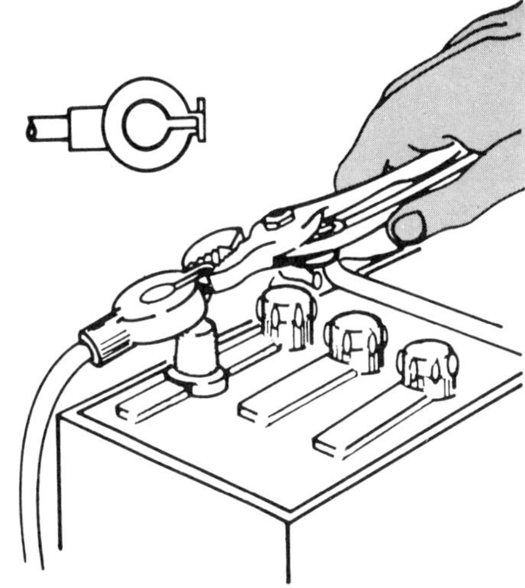

Fig. 22-15. Using pliers to loosen the spring-ring type of cable clamp from a battery terminal.

CAUTION: Make sure the cable clamps are tight and make good connections with the terminal posts. See Fig. 22-16. If the jaws of the clamp come together as shown at the left, chances are the clamp is not tight on the post. This could mean starting trouble. Correct the condition by disconnecting the clamp from the post. Shave the clamp jaws with a file so you get a gap (right, in Fig. 22-16) when the clamp is installed.

⊘ 22-19 Battery "Dopes" "Dopes" is a name for certain chemical compounds that are supposed to restore a battery to the charged condition. Such chemicals should never be added to the battery. Their use may void the battery guarantee and cause battery failure.

⊘ 22-20 Battery Slow Charging There are two methods of slow-charging batteries, the constant-current method and the constant-voltage (constant-potential) method. In the constant-current method, the current input to the battery is adjusted to the manufacturer's specifications. The charging is con-

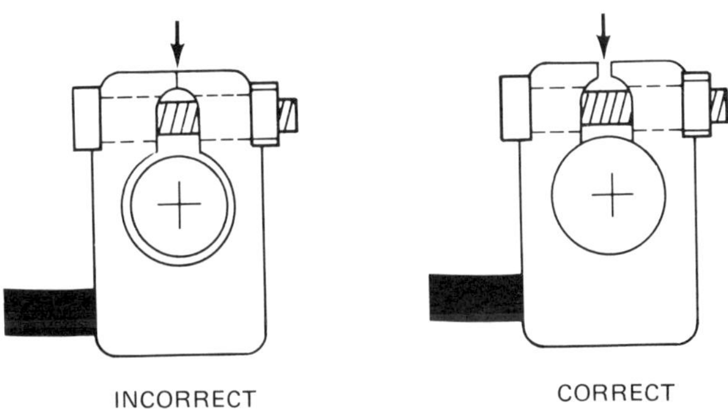

Fig. 22-16. If there is no gap between the jaws of the clamp (left), the clamp is probably loose on the terminal post.

Fig. 22-17. Battery charging room of a large commercial truck garage.

tinued until the battery is gassing freely and there is no rise in gravity for 2 hr.

In the constant-voltage method, the charging voltage is held at a constant value. As the battery approaches a charged condition, its resistance to the charging current increases. At the same time, the current input gradually tapers off. When the battery is fully charged, the current input has been reduced to a few amperes. We assume, in this, that the electrolyte temperature remains within bounds. If the electrolyte temperature increases greatly, the resistance of the battery remains low. Then the battery can be damaged by overcharging, unless it is removed from the charging line in time.

Figure 22-17 shows a battery charging room in a large commercial truck garage. One important thing about the charging room is that there is plenty of ventilation. Batteries give off highly explosive gases when they are charged. Ventilation is necessary to ensure that these gases do not collect and explode.

⊘ 22-21 Quick Charging Quick chargers (Fig. 22-18) charge the battery at a high rate (as much as 100 A) for a short time (30 to 45 min). The battery is thus brought to a fair state of charge before the battery temperature increases excessively. Quick charging does not seem to harm batteries that are not subject to excessive temperatures. However, high charging rates combined with electrolyte temperatures above 120°F [51.7°C] are very damaging to a battery.

Quick chargers cannot, as a rule, bring a battery up to full charge in a short time. However, a battery can be quick-charged for a short time. Then, if the charging operation is finished by a slow-charging method, the battery will come up to full charge.

CAUTION: A battery with discolored electrolyte (from cycling) or with gravity readings more than 25 points apart should not be quick-charged. Likewise, a badly sulfated battery should not be quick-charged. Such batteries may be near failure, but they may give additional service if slow-charged. However, quick-charging might damage them further. During quick-charging, check the color of the electrolyte. Stop charging if it becomes discolored as a result of the stirring up of washed-out active material. Likewise, cell voltages should be checked every few minutes. Charging should be stopped if cell voltages vary by more than 0.2 V.

NOTE: A very low battery may not accept a fast charge. The electrolyte in a very low battery does not have very much sulfuric acid in it. Therefore, the conductivity of the electrolyte is too low to allow a high current to flow through the battery. You might think a battery that refuses to take a high charge is worn out. However, it may be possible to restore the battery to a charged condition as follows: First, slow-charge it for a few minutes to see if it starts coming up to charge. If it does, then it can be put on fast charge. Some fast chargers have a special circuit which will slow-charge a dead battery for a short time and then switch to fast charging.

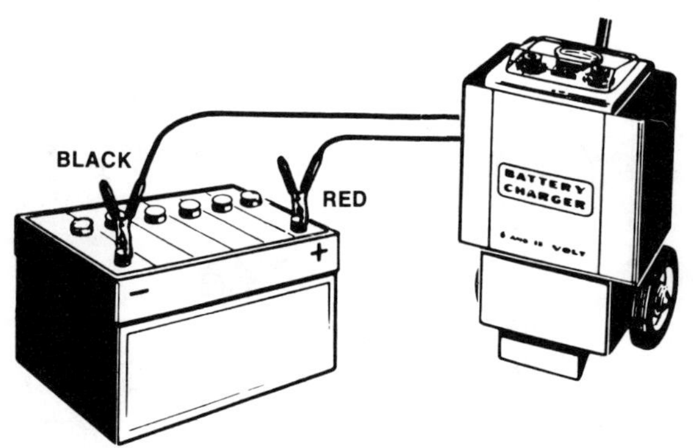

Fig. 22-18. Quick-charger charging a battery.

⊘ 22-22 Care of Batteries in Stock Wet batteries (or batteries with electrolyte in them) are perishable. They are subject to self-discharge. If allowed to self-discharge for too long a time, they can become ruined. To prevent this, batteries in stock should be recharged at 30-day intervals. They should not be stacked on top of each other without some means of individual support. The weight of one battery is enough to collapse the plate assemblies and cause short circuits.

⊘ 22-23 Dry-Charged Batteries Dry-charged batteries contain fully charged positive and negative plates, but no electrolyte. The batteries are sealed with rubber or plastic seals in the vent plugs. Since the batteries contain no moisture, practically no chemical action can take place in them. The manufacturers say they can remain in good condition for as long as 36 months if they are properly stored.

Manufacturers of dry-charged batteries supply ready-mixed electrolyte in a special carton. The carton contains an acidproof plastic bag which holds

Fig. 22-19. Adding electrolyte from a special container to a dry-charged battery. (*Delco-Remy Division of General Motors Corporation*)

the electrolyte. To activate a battery or get it ready for service, all that is necessary is the following:

1. Remove the vent plugs, and take out the plastic seals.
2. Remove the lid from the electrolyte container. Unfold the top of the plastic bag, and cut a small opening in one corner of the bag.
3. Use a glass or acidproof plastic funnel to fill each battery cell (Fig. 22-19). Wear goggles, and observe all the cautions regarding sulfuric acid. Wait a few minutes, and then add more electrolyte if necessary. Some electrolyte will probably be left; do not attempt to use it all. Do not overfill the battery.
4. Before discarding the container, empty it. Rinse the bag thoroughly with water. Otherwise, someone who handles the carton might be severely burned.

Check Your Progress

Progress Quiz 22-1 When a battery is being charged in the automotive shop, it is checked periodically to see how it is taking the charge. Likewise, in this book, we stop periodically so you can find out how you are "taking the charge" of information. The following questions will help you in two ways. First, they review the important points covered in the chapter. Second, they'll tip you off if any of these points are hazy in your mind. This gives you a chance to reread the chapter and fix the facts more firmly in your mind.

Completing the Sentences The sentences below are incomplete. After each sentence there are several words or phrases, but only one of them correctly completes the sentence. Write each sentence in your notebook, ending it with the one word or phrase that completes it correctly.

1. In the 421 test, the open-circuit battery voltage is read after: (*a*) timed discharge and charge cycles, (*b*) cranking for 15 seconds, (*c*) turning the headlights on, (*d*) applying the cadmium tips.
2. During the high-discharge test, a heavy load is placed on the battery, and the (*a*) battery voltage is checked, (*b*) open-circuit voltage is checked, (*c*) individual cell voltages are checked, (*d*) ampere output is checked.
3. During the cadmium-tip test, the tips are placed: (*a*) in the electrolyte of adjacent cells, (*b*) on adjacent cell terminals, (*c*) on the main battery terminals.
4. A battery with a specific gravity of 1.290 can be considered to be: (*a*) fully charged, (*b*) half charged, (*c*) discharged.
5. As the temperature of the electrolyte goes down, its specific gravity: (*a*) goes down, (*b*) remains the same, (*c*) becomes thinner, (*d*) goes up.
6. As a battery ages, the specific gravity of its electrolyte tends to: (*a*) go down, (*b*) remain constant, (*c*) go up.
7. As battery temperature goes up, the rate of self-discharge: (*a*) goes down, (*b*) remains low, (*c*) goes up.
8. As its specific gravity goes down, the freezing temperature of the electrolyte: (*a*) goes down, (*b*) remains low, (*c*) goes up.

CHAPTER 22 CHECKUP

NOTE: Since the following is a chapter review test, you should review the chapter before taking the test.

Once again, you will want to test your knowledge of the chapter you have just finished. Remember, the questions that follow are designed to help you review the chapter, as well as test your knowledge. Thus, if you have difficulty with any question, you should review that part of the chapter that answers it. Be sure to write the answers in your notebook. The act of writing helps you to remember. It also makes your notebook a valuable source of information.

Completing the Sentences The sentences below are incomplete. After each sentence there are several words or phrases, but only one of them correctly completes the sentence. Write each sentence in your notebook, ending it with the one word or phrase that completes it correctly.

1. Two of the most important battery services are: (*a*) adding water and testing, (*b*) adding acid and battery cleaning, (*c*) installing plates and checking voltage, (*d*) replacing the case and recharging.
2. If you have to add water to a battery every few days, you should suspect that the battery is being: (*a*) excessively overloaded, (*b*) overcharged, (*c*) sulfated.
3. A bad connection at the battery could cause: (*a*) battery overcharge, (*b*) excessive battery voltage, (*c*) a rundown battery.

4. Probably the most common battery complaint from the average driver is that the battery has: (*a*) been overcharged, (*b*) run down, (*c*) excessive voltage.
5. One of the damaging effects of overcharging is: (*a*) sulfation of plates, (*b*) oxidation of negative-plate grids, (*c*) oxidation of positive-plate grids.
6. Probably the best thing to do if a fully charged battery varies by more than five scale divisions between cells on the cadmium-tip test is to: (*a*) rebuild it, (*b*) recharge it, (*c*) replace it.
7. A good way to make sure the battery is being installed correctly is to remember that the battery: (*a*) positive post is larger, (*b*) negative post is larger, (*c*) positive cable clamp is smaller.
8. One of the important points to watch in using a quick charger is to avoid: (*a*) taper charging, (*b*) high battery temperatures, (*c*) self-discharging.
9. Wet batteries in stock should be recharged or boosted every: (*a*) week, (*b*) 2 weeks, (*c*) 30 days, (*d*) 90 days.
10. The distinguishing feature of dry batteries is that the: (*a*) battery has no electrolyte, (*b*) plates have been removed, (*c*) separators are dried out.

Analysis of Battery Troubles Various battery troubles are described below. Following each trouble are several possible causes. Only one of the causes listed fits the trouble. Read the descriptions and then decide what has caused the trouble. Write the description and cause in your notebook.

1. You see a battery with the cell covers raised on the positive-terminal sides. You also note a great amount of corrosion around the battery, which indicates considerable spraying of electrolyte. The cause of these conditions is almost surely: (*a*) overcharging, (*b*) undercharging, (*c*) low charging voltage, (*d*) overfilling.
2. You are getting ready to put a battery on a quick charger. In checking the electrolyte, you notice it is brownish in color. The brownish color is due to the presence of: (*a*) positive-plate material, (*b*) negative-plate material, (*c*) separator material.
3. One cell of a battery has a low gravity reading. The other cells and the cell voltages seem normal. There seems to be considerable corrosion around the battery. Your analysis would be that the: (*a*) battery was overcharged, (*b*) battery was overloaded, (*c*) cell-cover seal was leaking.
4. The gravity readings of a battery vary by more then 25 points. Before you reach a decision on what to do with the battery, you should give it a (*a*) high-discharge test, (*b*) high-charge test, (*c*) recharge and a high-discharge test, (*d*) discharge and a high-discharge test.

Battery Maintenance Review Here are some questions on battery maintenance. Write the answers in your notebook.

1. What services does a battery in a car require?
2. What additional services might a battery require after it is removed from the car?
3. Describe the procedure for adding water to a battery.
4. Explain how to remove cable clamps and clean the battery terminals and clamps.
5. Make a list of the main causes of battery trouble.
6. What are the major effects of overcharging a battery?
7. How do you determine the cause of a run-down battery?
8. List the main steps in replacing a battery, including the cautions to be observed.
9. Describe in detail how to quick-charge a battery, listing the special cautions to be observed.
10. List three points to observe in taking care of batteries in stock.

SUGGESTIONS FOR FURTHER STUDY

To learn more about battery maintenance, repair, and trouble causes, spend some time in a local battery shop. Note carefully what the service technician does to analyze and correct battery faults, and to repair batteries. Examine defective batteries that have failed. Don't get electrolyte on your clothes. Be sure to wash your hands carefully afterward. Battery manufacturers often supply complete maintenance and repair manuals on their batteries. Study whatever battery manuals you can find. Write the important facts in your notebook.

chapter 23

STARTING MOTORS

In this chapter, we describe the construction and operation of starting motors. The automotive starting motor is a sturdy, high-capacity electric motor. It is designed to provide the high horsepower required to spin the engine crankshaft and get the engine started. The starting motor is also called a starter *and a* cranking motor. *We begin the chapter by looking into the basic principles of electric motors.*

⊘ **23-1 Basic Motor Principles** When current moves through a conductor, a magnetic field builds up around that conductor. If the conductor is in a magnetic field, as from a horseshoe magnet, force is exerted on the conductor. Figure 23-1 illustrates the conductor in a magnetic field. Figure 23-2 shows the conductor in end view, with the resulting magnetic field indicated. The cross in the center of the conductor indicates that the current is flowing away from the reader. The magnetic field due to the current circles the conductor in a counterclockwise direction. The circular magnetic field to the left of the conductor is in the same direction as the straight-line magnetic field from the magnet. To the right of the conductor, it is in the opposite direction. This weakens the magnetic field to the right of the conductor. It strengthens the magnetic field to the left of the conductor. Thus, the resulting magnetic field distorts around the conductor, as shown in Fig. 23-2.

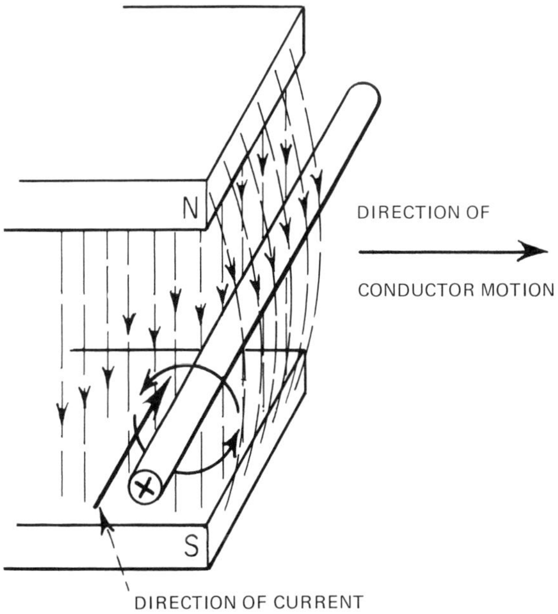

Magnetic lines of force tend to shorten up to a minimum length. Thus, the bent lines of force in the magnetic-field pattern in Fig. 23-2 try to straighten out. As they do, they exert a push to the right on the conductor. The more current flowing, the more the lines of force are distorted around the conductor—and the stronger is the push. Increasing the straight-line magnetic field has a similar effect.

N
DIRECTION OF
CONDUCTOR MOTION
S
DIRECTION OF CURRENT

Fig. 23-1. Conductor held in the magnetic field of a magnet. The direction of current flow and the encircling magnetic field around the conductor are shown by arrows.

⊘ **23-2 Motor Construction** Suppose we bend the conductor into a U and connect the two ends to the two halves of a split copper ring. We now have the

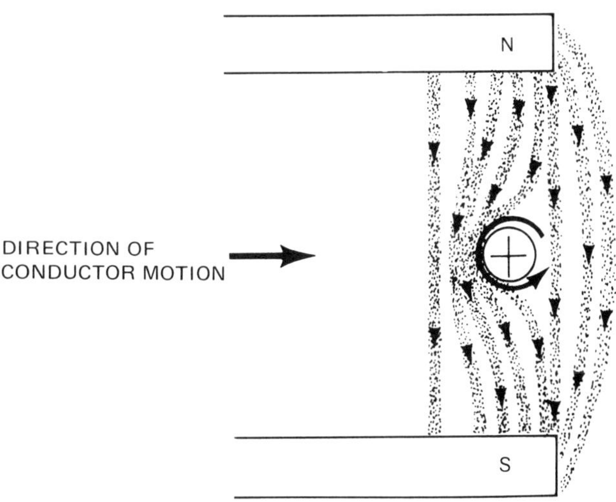

Fig. 23-2. End view of the conductor shown in Fig. 23-1.

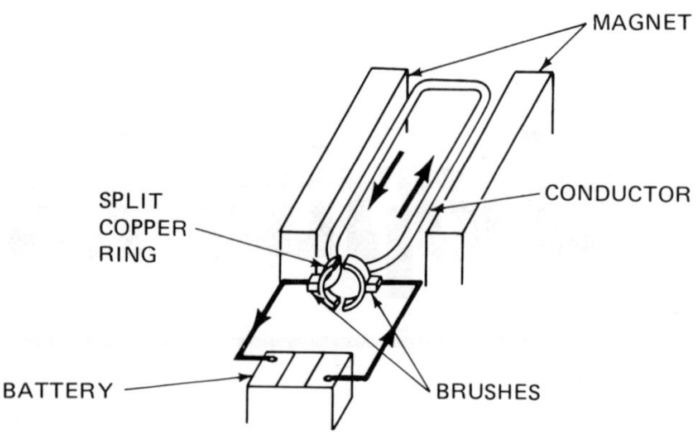

Fig. 23-3. Simple electric motor with a two-segment commutator.

elements of an electric motor (Fig. 23-3). Stationary *brushes,* connected to a battery and resting on the split ring, and two poles of a magnet complete the motor. The brushes are carbon blocks that form sliding contacts with the commutator. The U-shaped conductor and the split ring rotate together. The split ring is called the *commutator.* Current flows from the battery, through the right-hand brush and commutator segment. Then it flows through the conductor and left-hand commutator segment and brush, and back to the battery. This causes the left-hand part of the conductor to be pushed upward, and the right-hand part to be pushed downward (see Fig. 23-2). Thus, the conductor (or loop) rotates in a clockwise direction. As the two sides of the loop reverse positions, the direction of current flow through the loop also reverses. The loop thus continues to be pushed clockwise. It continues to rotate.

A starting motor must have more than one loop to develop enough power. Actually, many loops (or conductors) are used. See Fig. 23-4, which shows a starting-motor armature and field assembly. The ends of the conductors in the armature are connected to the commutator segments.

High magnetic field strength is needed for powerful starting-motor action. The natural magnetic strength of the magnetic poles is aided by field windings. Current flows through the field windings

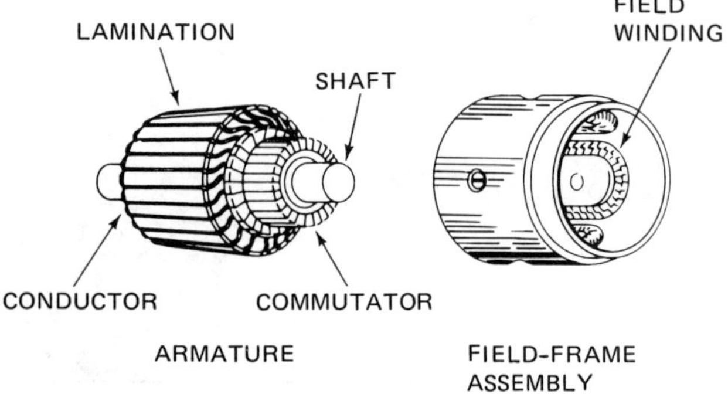

Fig. 23-4. Two major parts of a starting motor, the armature and the field assembly. (*Delco-Remy Division of General Motors Corporation*)

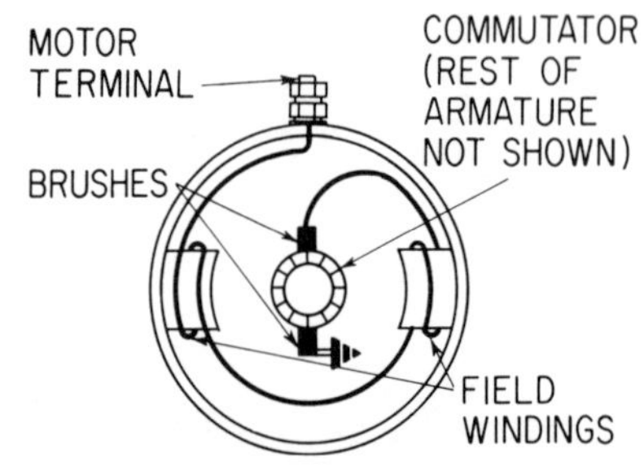

Fig. 23-5. Wiring diagram for a starting motor.

in the proper direction to increase the magnetic field between the two poles.

Figure 23-5 is a simple wiring diagram of a starting motor. Current enters the motor and passes through the two field windings, then through the armature, and back to the battery. If the battery connections were reversed, the current would flow through the armature first, as shown in Fig. 23-6. This is a schematic drawing of a simple motor. This type of motor is called a *series-wound,* or *series,* motor. The armature and field windings are connected in series.

The wiring diagram in Fig. 23-5 is of a two-pole, two-brush starting motor. Many starting motors have four brushes and four poles. Some also have one or two shunt windings (they are called *series-shunt,* or *compound,* units). The shunt windings prevent overspeeding (see Fig. 23-7).

A typical starting motor, with the main parts disassembled, is shown in Fig. 23-8. The motor consists of:

1. The commutator end head, holding the brushes
2. The field frame, into which the field windings are assembled around iron pole shoes
3. The drive housing, which houses the drive assembly and supports the motor on the engine flywheel housing
4. The armature
5. The drive assembly

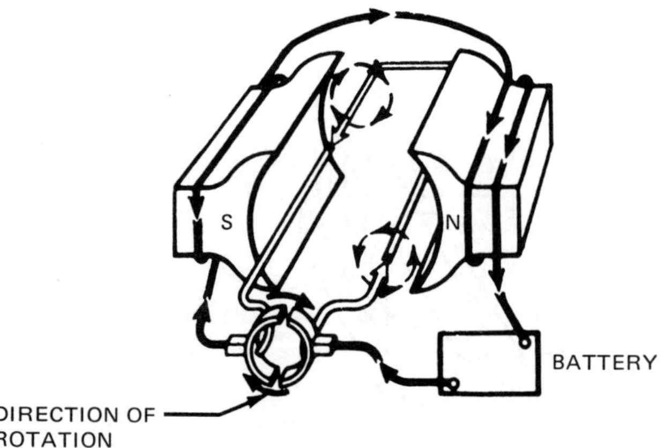

Fig. 23-6. Schematic drawing of a starting motor. The heavy arrows show the direction of current flow. The light circular arrows show the direction of the magnetic field around the conductors. Compare this with Fig. 23-3.

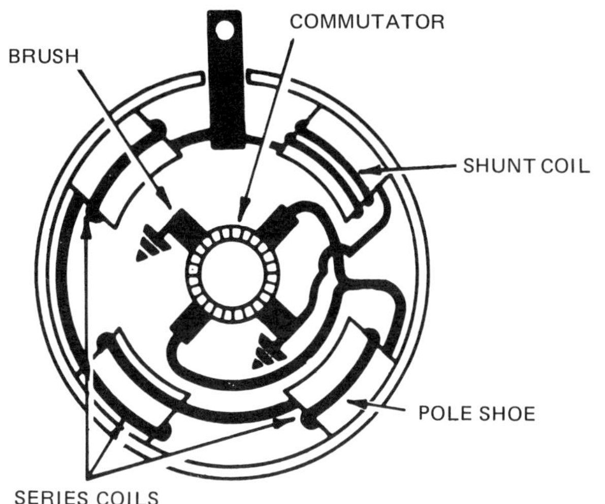

Fig. 23-7. Wiring diagram for a four-pole, series-shunt, or compound, starting motor. (*Delco-Remy Division of General Motors Corporation*)

Most starting motors also have a solenoid that operates the shift lever (⊘ 23-6).

⊘ 23-3 Drive Arrangement The drive assembly contains a small pinion. In operation, the pinion meshes with teeth cut in the flywheel (Fig. 23-9), to provide gear reduction. The armature must rotate about 15 times to rotate the flywheel once. The armature may revolve at 2,000 to 3,000 rpm when the starting motor is operated. The pinion thus spins the flywheel at speeds as high as 200 rpm. This is ample for starting the engine.

After the engine starts, its speed may increase to 3,000 rpm or more. If the drive pinion remained in mesh with the flywheel, it would be spun at 45,000 rpm (because of the 15:1 gear ratio). The starting-motor armature would also be spun at this terrific speed. Centrifugal force would throw the conductors and commutator segments out of the armature, ruining it. To prevent such damage, automatic meshing and demeshing devices are used. For

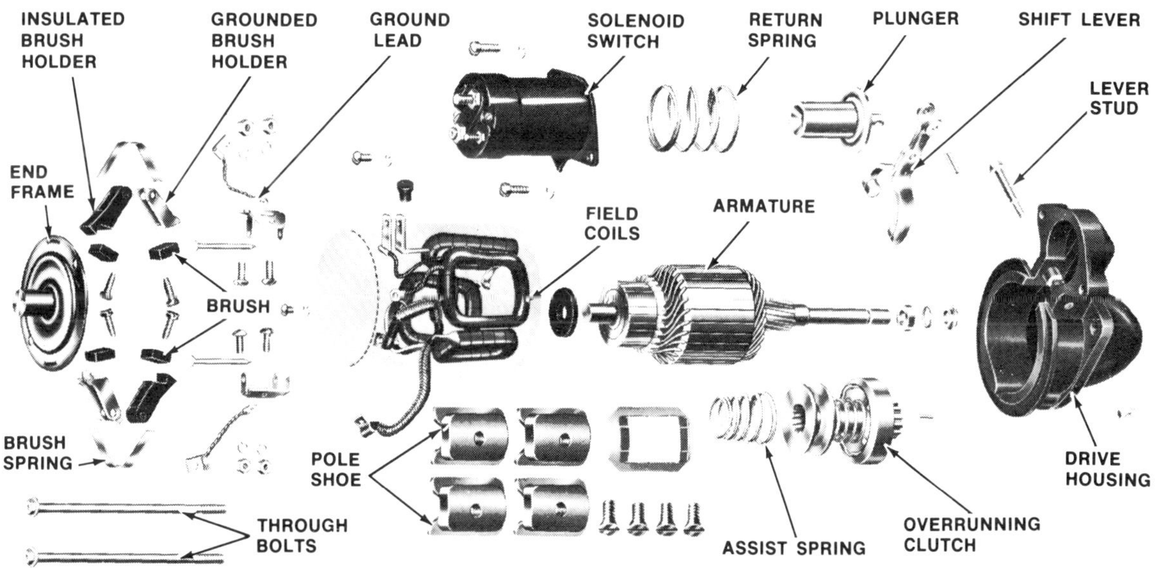

Fig. 23-8. Disassembled view of a starting motor. (*Delco-Remy Division of General Motors Corporation*)

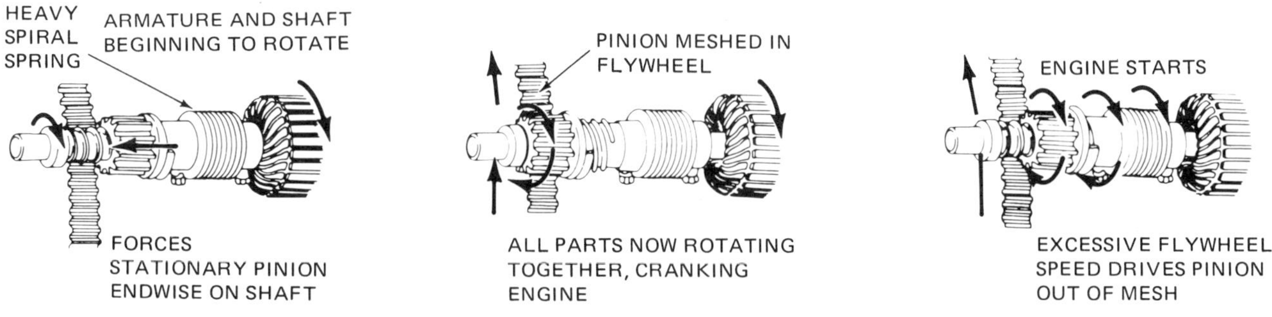

Fig. 23-9. Operation of a Bendix drive. (*Delco-Remy Division of General Motors Corporation*)

passenger cars there are two general types, *inertia* and *overruning clutch.*

⊘ 23-4 Inertia Drive The inertia drive depends on the inertia of the drive pinion to produce meshing. Inertia is the property of all objects to resist changes in their state of motion. When the drive pinion is not rotating, it resists any force that tends to set it into motion. Two types of inertia drive are the Bendix and the Folo-Thru.

1. *BENDIX DRIVE* In the Bendix drive (Fig. 23-9), the drive pinion is mounted loosely on a sleeve. The sleeve has screw threads that match internal threads in the pinion. When the starting motor is at rest, the drive pinion is not meshed with the flywheel teeth. As the starting-motor switch is closed, the armature begins to rotate. This causes the sleeve to rotate also, since it is fastened to the armature shaft through the heavy spiral Bendix spring. Inertia prevents the pinion from instantly picking up speed with the sleeve. The sleeve thus turns within the pinion, just as a screw would turn in a nut that is held stationary. This forces the pinion endwise along the sleeve, so that it meshes with the flywheel teeth. As the pinion reaches the pinion stop, the endwise movement stops. The pinion must now turn with the armature, causing the engine to be cranked. The spiral spring takes up the shock of meshing.

After the engine starts and increases in speed the flywheel rotates the drive pinion faster than the armature. This causes the pinion to be spun back out of mesh from the flywheel. That is, the pinion turns on the sleeve. The screw threads on the pinion and sleeve cause the pinion to be backed out of mesh with the flywheel.

2. *FOLO-THRU DRIVE* This drive (Fig. 23-10) is very similar to the Bendix drive. It has a sleeve attached through a spiral spring to the armature shaft. The sleeve has threads which match internal threads in the pinion base. Also included in the

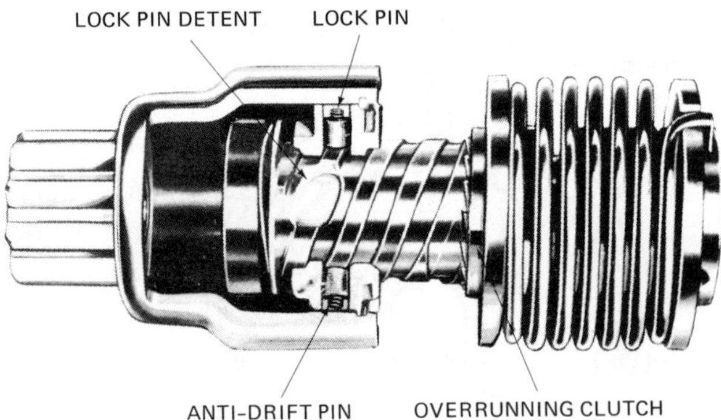

Fig. 23-10. Folo-Thru starting-motor drive. The skirt of the pinion has been cut away to show the lock and the antidrift pin. (*Ford Motor Company*)

pinion base are two small spring-loaded pins. One is an *antidrift* pin. It prevents the pinion from "drifting" into mesh with the flywheel when the engine is running. It imposes a frictional drag that holds the pinion in the demeshed position. The other pin is a *lock* pin. This pin drops into a slot (called a *detent*) in the sleeve thread as the pinion moves out to the cranking position. This holds the pinion in mesh with the engine flywheel during cranking. It prevents the pinion from being kicked out of mesh by a false start (during which the engine might fire a few times and then die). The pinion is thus held in mesh, and cranking continues until the engine really gets started. As the engine speed increases to around 400 rpm, centrifugal force on the lock pin moves it out of the detent. Then, the pinion demeshes from the flywheel in the same manner as in the Bendix drive.

⊘ 23-5 Overrunning Clutch The overrunning clutch (Fig. 23-11) is operated by a shift lever. The lever pushes the drive pinion into mesh with the flywheel teeth. As the shift lever completes its travel,

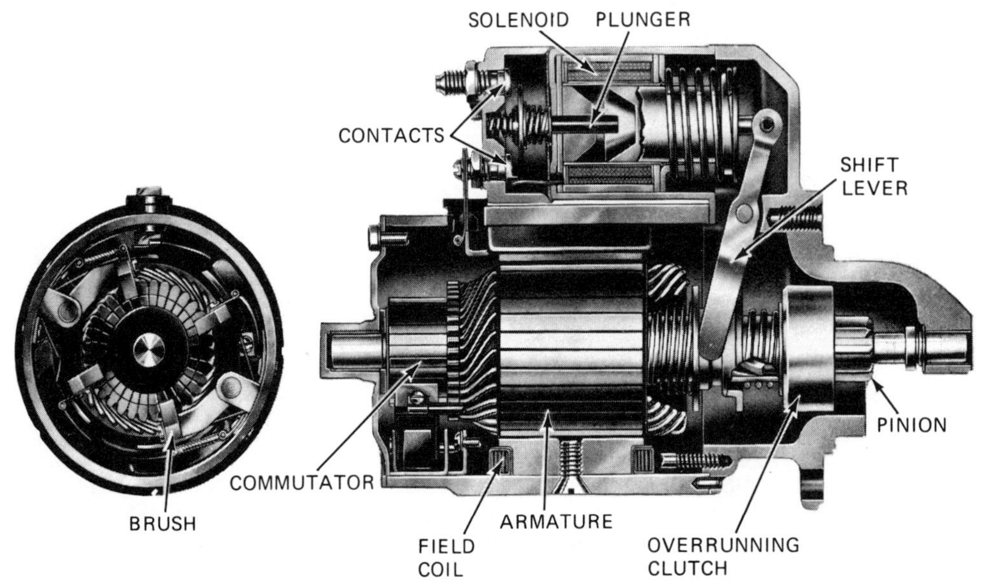

Fig. 23-11. Sectional view of an enclosed shift-lever starting motor with solenoid. (*Delco-Remy Division of General Motors Corporation*)

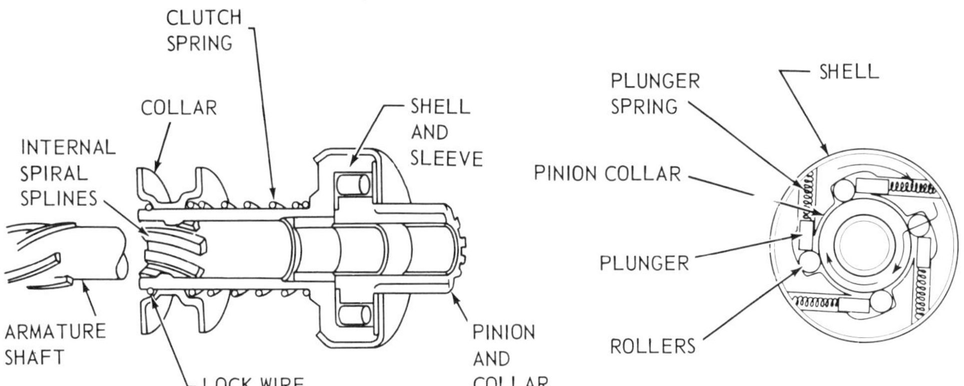

Fig. 23-12. Cutaway and end sectional views of an overrunning clutch. (*Delco-Remy Division of General Motors Corporation*)

it closes the starting-motor switch so that cranking takes place. Straight or spiral splines in the armature shaft and the clutch sleeve cause both to rotate together. A spiral spring is placed between the clutch housing and the shift-lever collar. This spring compresses if the pinion and flywheel teeth happen to butt instead of meshing. Then, after the starting-motor switch is closed and the armature starts to rotate, meshing is completed by the spring pressure.

The clutch (Fig. 23-12) consists of the outer shell and the pinion and collar assembly. The outer shell has four hardened-steel rollers fitted into four notches. The notches are not uniform; they get smaller toward the end opposite the plunger spring (Fig. 23-12). When the armature and shell begin to rotate, the pinion does not. This causes the rollers to rotate into the smaller sections of the notches, where they jam tight. The pinion must now rotate with the armature, cranking the engine. After the engine starts, it spins the pinion faster than the armature. The rollers are rotated into the larger sections of the notches, where they are free. This allows the pinion to spin independently of, or overrun, the remainder of the clutch. A spring on the shift lever pulls the pinion back out of mesh when the shift lever is released.

Gear reduction

The starting motor shown in Fig. 23-13 has a gear reduction which increases cranking torque. The shift

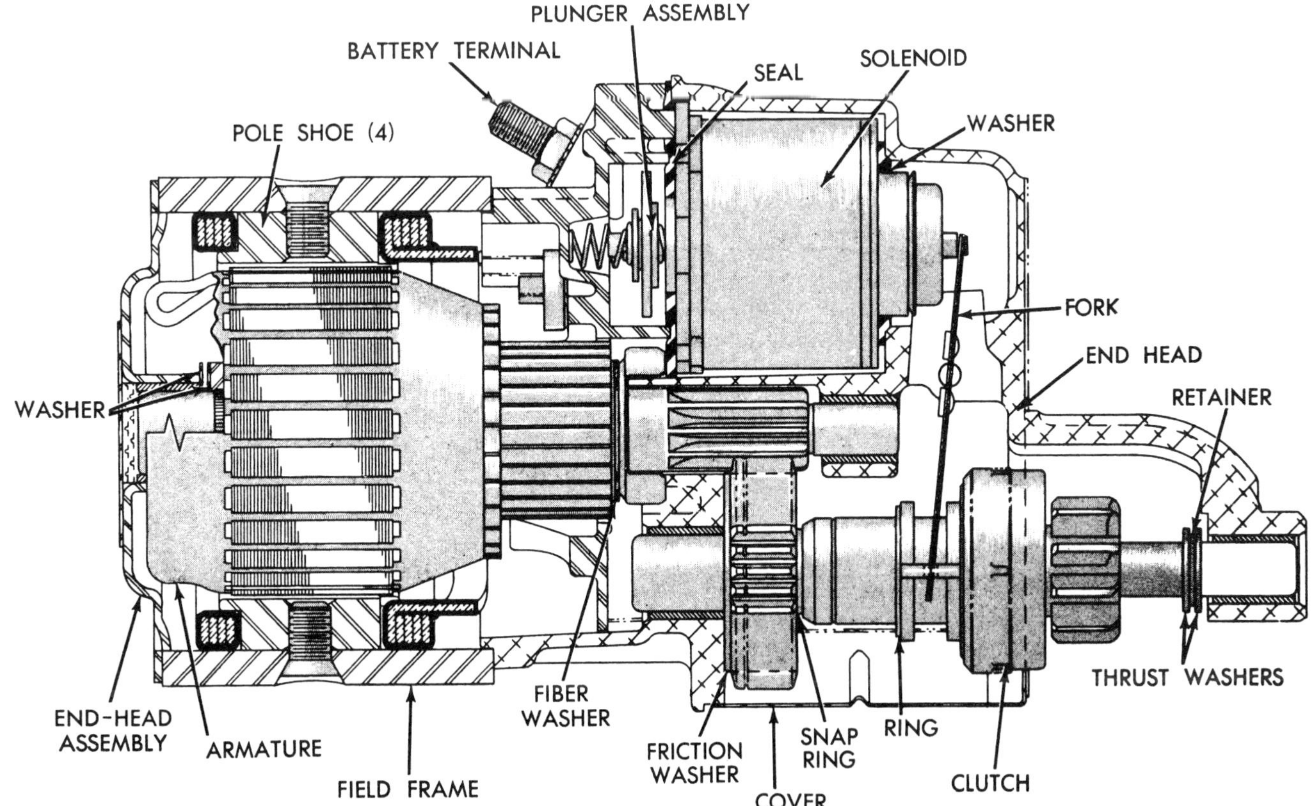

Fig. 23-13. Sectional view of a gear-reduction, overrunning-clutch starting motor. (*Chrysler Corporation*)

lever (or fork) is enclosed. When it is actuated by the solenoid, it shifts the overrunning-clutch pinion into mesh with the flywheel. It also shifts the large driven gear on the clutch shaft into mesh with the smaller gear on the armature shaft. Because of the extra gears in the starting motor, the gear ratio between the armature and the flywheel is 45:1. That is, the armature turns 45 times to turn the flywheel (and the engine crankshaft) once. This provides a high torque (turning force) for starting.

⊘ 23-6 Starting-Motor Controls Starting-motor controls have varied from a simple foot-operated pedal to automatic devices that close the starting-motor circuit when the accelerator pedal is depressed. The system presently used in passenger cars and other vehicles has starting contacts in the ignition switch. When the ignition key is turned past the ON position to START, the starting contacts close. This connects the starting-motor solenoid or magnetic switch to the battery. After the engine starts and the ignition key is released, spring pressure returns the key to the ON position.

Bendix-type starting motors use a magnetic switch. When the starting contacts in the ignition switch are closed, the magnetic-switch winding is connected to the battery. The magnetism produced in the winding pulls the plunger in. This forces the contact disk against the magnetic-switch contacts. Now, current can flow through the contacts and disk to operate the starting motor. After the engine starts, the driver releases the ignition key. The key is returned to the ON position by a spring. This opens the magnetic-switch winding circuit. A spring moves the plunger and contact away from the magnetic-switch contacts. Now, the starting-motor circuit is opened, and the starting motor stops operating.

On starting motors with overrunning clutches, a solenoid is commonly used to produce the clutch-shifting action. The solenoid contains a pair of windings that are connected to the battery when the starting switch is closed. This produces a magnetic field that pulls a plunger in. The plunger movement causes a shift lever to move the overrunning clutch on the armature shaft. This shifts the overrunning-clutch pinion into mesh with the flywheel teeth. At the same time, the plunger movement forces a heavy switch to connect the starting motor directly to the battery. Now, cranking begins. Figure 23-14 shows the sequence of actions. Figure 23-15 is a wiring diagram of a starting-motor system.

Note that the solenoid has two windings, a pull-in winding and a hold-in winding. They work together to pull the plunger in. This combination of windings provides sufficient magnetic strength to mesh the pinion and close the starting-motor switch. After the pinion is meshed and the switch is closed, less magnetism is required to hold the core in. Thus, as the switch closes, the pull-in winding is shorted out, since it is connected between the two solenoid terminals. This reduces the drain on the battery during cranking.

On the Ford starting motor illustrated in Fig. 23-16, there is no separate solenoid. Instead, the starting-motor field windings produce the magnetic field which causes both the shifting action and the rotation of the armature. The magnetic field causes the pole shoe to slide in the frame. This action moves the shift lever so that the drive pinion is forced into mesh with the flywheel teeth. When the ignition switch is turned to START and the automatic-transmission neutral safety switch is closed, the magnetic-switch winding is connected to the battery. This causes the magnetic switch (starter relay) to close its contacts. This connects the starting motor directly to the battery.

One of the field windings acts as the winding to move the pole shoe. It has two parts, as shown—a pull-in winding and a hold-in winding. As the magnetic switch closes its contacts, these two windings are connected directly across the battery (through the contact points). This produces maximum magnetic strength. The other three field windings are connected in series with the armature. The magnetic field of the pole-shoe actuating windings moves the

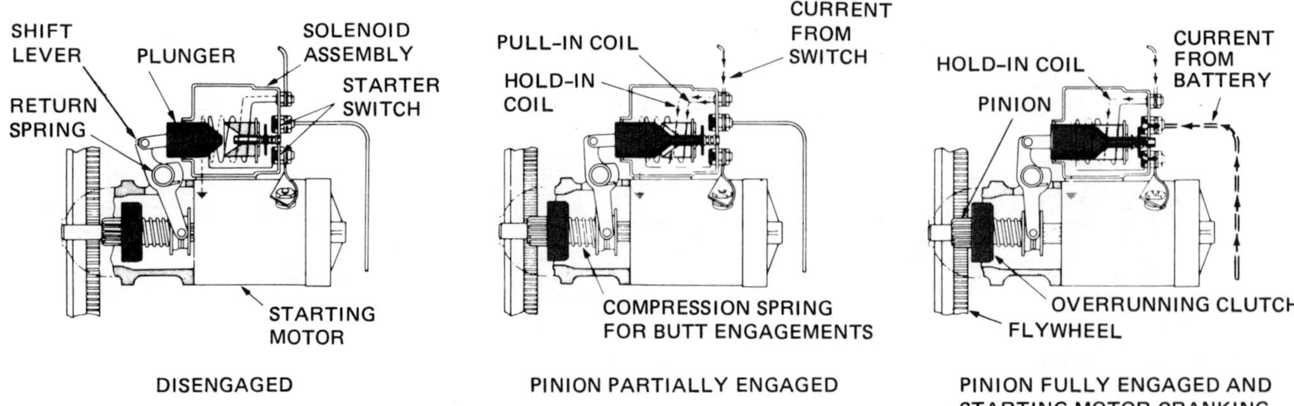

Fig. 23-14. Actions of the solenoid and overrunning clutch as the pinion engages. *(Delco-Remy Division of General Motors Corporation)*

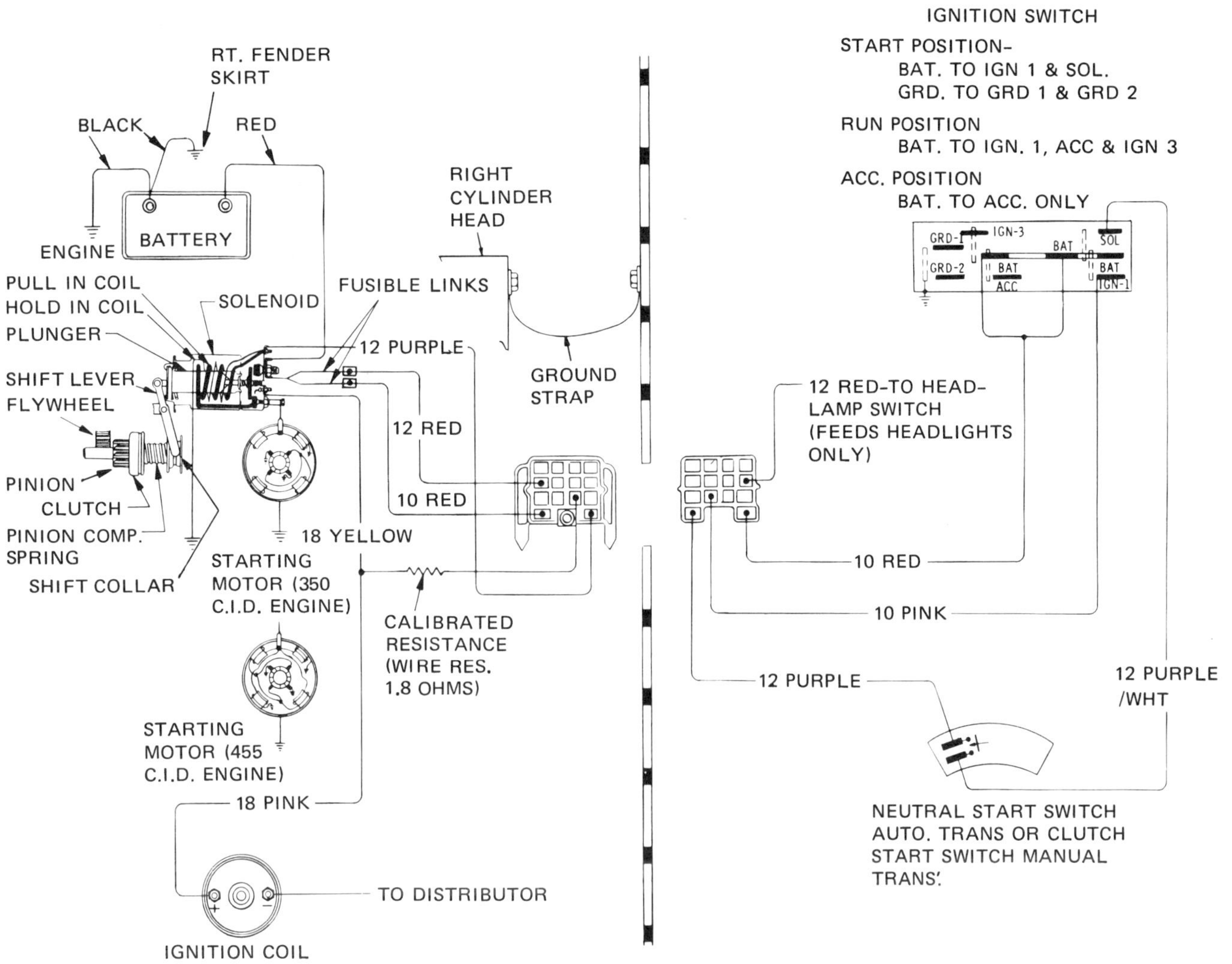

IGNITION SWITCH
START POSITION-
BAT. TO IGN 1 & SOL.
GRD. TO GRD 1 & GRD 2
RUN POSITION
BAT. TO IGN. 1, ACC & IGN 3
ACC. POSITION
BAT. TO ACC. ONLY
GRD-1
IGN-3
SOL
BAT
GRD-2
BAT
ACC
BAT
IGN-1
RT. FENDER
SKIRT
BLACK
RED
ENGINE
BATTERY
RIGHT
CYLINDER
HEAD
PULL IN COIL
HOLD IN COIL
SOLENOID
FUSIBLE LINKS
PLUNGER
12 PURPLE
SHIFT LEVER
FLYWHEEL
GROUND
STRAP
12 RED-TO HEAD-
LAMP SWITCH
(FEEDS HEADLIGHTS
ONLY)
12 RED
PINION
CLUTCH
10 RED
PINION COMP.
SPRING
18 YELLOW
SHIFT COLLAR
STARTING
MOTOR (350
C.I.D. ENGINE)
10 RED
10 PINK
CALIBRATED
RESISTANCE
(WIRE RES.
1.8 OHMS)
12 PURPLE
12 PURPLE
/WHT
STARTING
MOTOR (455
C.I.D. ENGINE)
18 PINK
NEUTRAL START SWITCH
AUTO. TRANS OR CLUTCH
START SWITCH MANUAL
TRANS.
TO DISTRIBUTOR
IGNITION COIL

Fig. 23-15. Wiring diagram for a starting-motor system. (*Buick Motor Division of General Motors Corporation*)

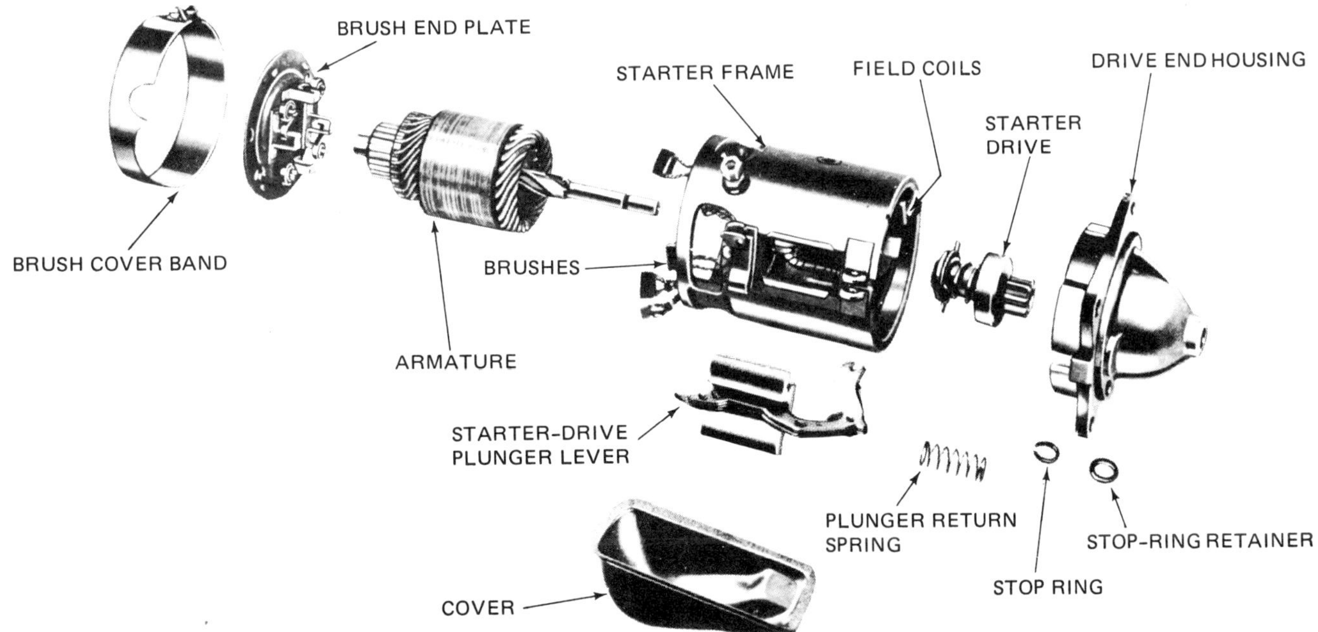

Fig. 23-16. Starting motor with a sliding pole shoe to actuate the shift lever, in disassembled view. (*Ford Motor Company*)

pole shoe and shifts the drive pinion into mesh. At the same time, the armature begins to turn so that the engine is cranked. As the pole shoe and shift lever move, they cause the contact points to open. Now, the pull-in winding is connected in series with the armature. Its magnetism drops. At the same time, however, the hold-in winding retains its full magnetism and keeps the pole shoe in the cranking position. As soon as the ignition switch is released, the magnetic-switch winding is disconnected from the battery. It opens its contacts to disconnect the starting motor from the battery. Cranking stops. The drive pinion is demeshed from the flywheel by the return spring.

1. *AUTOMATIC TRANSMISSIONS* On cars with automatic transmissions, a special switch prevents starting while the car is in gear. As shown in Fig. 23-15, the switch (the neutral safety switch) is connected between the ignition switch and the solenoid. This switch is open at all transmission-lever positions except NEUTRAL (and PARK, in some cars).

2. *IGNITION RESISTANCE* The ignition system includes a resistance wire. The resistance is in series with the ignition-coil primary when the engine is running. This protects the ignition contact points from excessive current. However, during cranking, the ignition switch shorts out the resistance (when the key is turned to START). Now, full battery voltage is imposed on the ignition coil for good performance during cranking. The resistance is also called a *ballast* resistance. On some cars, it is a separately mounted part. But most cars have the resistance in the wiring harness.

3. *OTHER CONTROLS* Other types of controls have been used to prevent starting-motor operation at all times except when starting. Vacuum switches, mounted on the intake manifold or in the carburetor, have been used extensively. This type of vacuum switch closes when the engine is not running. But the switch opens when the engine starts and a vacuum builds up in the intake manifold. Vacuum switches were usually linked to the throttle so that, at part to full throttle, their contacts were open. This was an added safeguard against starting-motor operation while the engine was running. Sometimes a solenoid relay was used. This was a small relay with a single winding and a pair of contacts. When the control switch or circuit was closed, it would connect the relay winding to the battery. Then, the relay would close to connect the solenoid windings to the battery, so that the solenoid would operate.

For heavy-duty applications, a two-step control has been used. This control first imposes a relatively low voltage on the starting motor, to get the armature started. Then, full voltage is imposed to crank the engine. A different heavy-duty system uses a series-parallel switch with two 12-V batteries. During normal operation with the engine running, the two batteries are connected in parallel, and the system is a standard 12-V system. But for starting, the two batteries are connected in series, to supply the starting motor with 24 V. This higher voltage causes the starting motor to develop a higher cranking torque.

Check Your Progress

Progress Quiz 23-1 Here is another chance to check your progress in studying automotive electrical equipment. This chapter covers the fundamentals of starting motors and starting-motor drive mechanisms. You probably realize that this information will be of great value to you. Anyone who plans to have anything to do with automobile service should understand how starting motors operate. Find out how well you remember the material by taking the following quiz.

Completing the Sentences The sentences below are incomplete. After each sentence there are several words or phrases, but only one of them correctly completes the sentence. Write each sentence in your notebook, ending it with the one word or phrase that completes it correctly.

1. To obtain enough cranking power, the starting-motor circuit must have: (*a*) low resistance, (*b*) high resistance, (*c*) welded connections, (*d*) three current paths.
2. A conductor that is carrying current in a magnetic field will: (*a*) resist attempts to move it, (*b*) tend to move, (*c*) move to the north pole.
3. The ring formed of segments, mounted near one end of the armature shaft, and through which current passes to and from the armature windings is called the: (*a*) shaft bearing, (*b*) terminal, (*c*) ring, (*d*) commutator.
4. In the starting motor, the armature windings and the field windings are connected: (*a*) in series, (*b*) in parallel, (*c*) to separate terminals.
5. The flywheel has many more teeth than the starting-motor pinion; the ratio of flywheel teeth to pinion teeth is about (*a*) 2:1 to 6:1, (*b*) 6:1 to 10:1, (*c*) 10:1 to 16:1, (*d*) 16:1 to 30:1.
6. When the armature first starts to rotate, the Bendix pinion moves into mesh with the flywheel teeth because the: (*a*) shift lever moves the pinion, (*b*) sleeve turns in the pinion, (*c*) drive spring pushes the pinion.
7. The drive pinion in the overrunning clutch is moved into mesh for cranking action by: (*a*) pinion inertia, (*b*) the sleeve turning in the pinion, (*c*) a shift lever.
8. The Bendix pinion is moved out of mesh with the flywheel teeth after the engine starts because the: (*a*) sleeve turns faster than the pinion, (*b*) pinion turns faster than the sleeve, (*c*) shift lever is released, (*d*) lever spring retracts the pinion.

CHAPTER 23 CHECKUP

NOTE: Since the following is a chapter review test, you should review the chapter before taking the test.

You are making fine progress in your studies of automotive electric systems. The chapter you have just completed gives you the information you need to understand how starting motors, their drive mechanisms, and their control circuits operate. This will make it much easier for you to service these units, since a vital part of "know-how" is "know-why." Find out how well the essential points have stuck with you by taking the test below. Don't be discouraged if any of the questions stump you. Simply reread the chapter to fix the information more firmly in your mind. Remember, most good students reread their lessons several times.

Completing the Sentences The sentences below are incomplete. After each sentence there are several words of phrases, but only one of them correctly completes the sentence. Write each sentence in your notebook, ending it with the one word or phrase that completes it correctly.

1. Since starting motors draw several hundred amperes from the battery during cranking, starting-motor switches must: (*a*) be mounted on the car floorboard, (*b*) have heavy contacts, (*c*) be operated by foot.
2. As the magnetic switch operates, the contacts in the switch become connected to each other by a: (*a*) heavy wire, (*b*) plunger, (*c*) iron core, (*d*) contact disk.
3. On most cars today, starting-motor control is achieved by a: (*a*) START position on the ignition switch, (*b*) vacuum switch, (*c*) pushbutton on the instrument panel.
4. The neutral safety switch is used on cars with: (*a*) overrunning clutches, (*b*) automatic transmissions, (*c*) automatic clutches.
5. In the starting motor with the sliding pole shoe, the pole shoe is moved by: (*a*) one of the field windings, (*b*) the solenoid, (*c*) the magnetic switch.
6. The solenoid mounted on overruning-clutch starting motors not only closes the circuit between the battery and the starting motor but also: (*a*) demeshes the pinion from the flywheel, (*b*) actuates the vacuum switch, (*c*) meshes the pinion with the flywheel.

Sorting Out the Fundamentals There are two lists below. One item from List 1 combined with one item from List 2 forms a complete statement about starting motors. However, the items in the two lists are not in order. To sort them out, match each item in List 2 with the proper item in List 1. For example, with "Motors operate because" you would match "conductors move in magnetic fields." This forms a complete sentence that states one fundamental of starting motors. Write the combined statements in your notebook.

List 1	*List 2*
Motors operate because	meshes on inertia principle
Starting motors	connects motor to battery
Bendix pinion	connects batteries in series for starting
Overrunning-clutch pinion	conductors move in magnetic fields
Starting-motor switch	are series motors
Series-parallel switch	is meshed by a shift lever

Reviewing the Starting Motor In the following, you are asked to describe the operation of the starting motor, its component parts, and its control circuits. Write your descriptions in your notebook. If you are not sure about an item, turn back into the chapter and reread the pages covering it. Do not copy from the book. Instead, write each description in your own words, just as though you were talking to a friend.

1. Explain, in terms of magnetic lines of force, why a current-carrying conductor moves in a magnetic field.
2. What is the purpose of the commutator?
3. Explain why the starting motor needs a drive mechanism.
4. Explain how a Bendix drive operates.
5. Explain how an overrunning clutch operates.
6. Explain how a magnetic switch operates.
7. Explain how the solenoid used with overrunning-clutch starting motors operates?

SUGGESTIONS FOR FURTHER STUDY

If possible, handle the various parts of different starting motors. This will help you become familiar with the construction of each type of starting motor. If you can find old starting motors to tear down and rebuild, you will be able to study starting-motor construction thoroughly. You may be able to find such old starting motors at your school shop. Or a friendly automotive electrical service shop may have an old starting motor which you can tear down and rebuild. Examine various automobiles, and trace the starting-motor control circuits. Note the different types of switches used on various automobiles. Try to find some detached switches, and examine them carefully. Study service bulletins and manuals issued by the automobile manufacturers to learn more about starting motors and their controls. Be sure to organize the information you get from these bulletins and manuals. Record this information in your notebook.

chapter 24

STARTING-MOTOR TROUBLE DIAGNOSIS

This chapter describes troubleshooting, servicing, and repair procedures for starting motors and starting systems.

⊘ 24-1 Troubleshooting the Starting System The troubleshooting of starting motors can be divided into two parts:

1. Tests made on the car when trouble occurs. These tell you whether the starting motor or some other component is at fault.
2. Tests made on the starting motor after it has been removed from the engine.

⊘ 24-2 Testing the Starting Motor on the Car There are three basic starting troubles:

1. The starting motor does not turn over.
2. The starting motor turns over slowly, but the engine does not start.
3. The starting motor turns over and cranks the engine at normal speed, but the engine does not start.

This last trouble cannot be blamed on the starting motor. If it spins the engine at normal cranking speed, it has done its job. There is some problem in the fuel or ignition system, or the engine, that prevents starting. Let us look at the other two conditions.

⊘ 24-3 The Starting Motor Does Not Turn Over The most likely cause here is a run-down battery. But there could be other causes. Turn on the headlights, and try cranking. There are five possibilities.
1. *NO CRANKING, NO LIGHTS* This is probably due to a completely dead battery. It could also be caused by a bad connection at the battery or starting motor, or an open fusible link (which indicates a short or ground in the system).
2. *NO CRANKING, BUT LIGHTS GO OUT AS YOU CLOSE THE STARTER SWITCH* This is an almost sure sign of a bad connection at the battery. Try wiggling the battery connections to see if this helps.
3. *NO CRANKING, AND LIGHTS DIM ONLY SLIGHTLY AS YOU TRY TO START* Chances are the trouble is in the starting motor. The pinion may not be engaging with the flywheel. Or, there is an open circuit in the solenoid switch or starting motor. If the starting-motor armature spins, then the overrunning clutch is slipping.
4. *NO CRANKING, AND LIGHTS DIM HEAVILY AS YOU TRY TO START* This is most likely due to a run-down battery. It could be low temperature, too. Remember that a battery is much less efficient at low temperatures, and the engine oil is much thicker. The combination could prevent cranking, even though the battery is in fairly good condition. Also, there may be some sort of jam-up in the starting motor or engine.
5. *NO CRANKING, AND LIGHTS STAY BRIGHT* Listen to hear if the solenoid is pulling the plunger in. You can hear this as a definite click. If nothing happens when you try to start, check the solenoid as follows: Connect one end of a jumper to the solenoid battery terminal. Connect the other end to the small terminal on the switch that is connected to the ignition switch. If nothing happens, the trouble is in the solenoid. If the solenoid and starting motor work with the jumper connected, the trouble is in the ignition switch, the transmission switch, or the wires connecting them.

⊘ 24-4 Engine Cranks Slowly but Does Not Start This is very likely due to a run-down or defective battery. The battery is unable to spin the starting motor at normal speed. Low temperature could also be a factor here, as noted in the previous section.

It is possible that the driver may have run the battery down trying to start. That is, some condition in the engine, or the fuel or ignition system, is preventing normal starting. The driver continued to try, however, until the battery ran down.

The procedure here is to test the battery and replace or recharge it if it is low. Or, connect a booster battery, and then try to start. See the caution below about using a booster battery. If the engine cranks normally and starts, the trouble is a low battery. If the engine cranks normally but does not start, the trouble is in the engine. If the engine still cranks

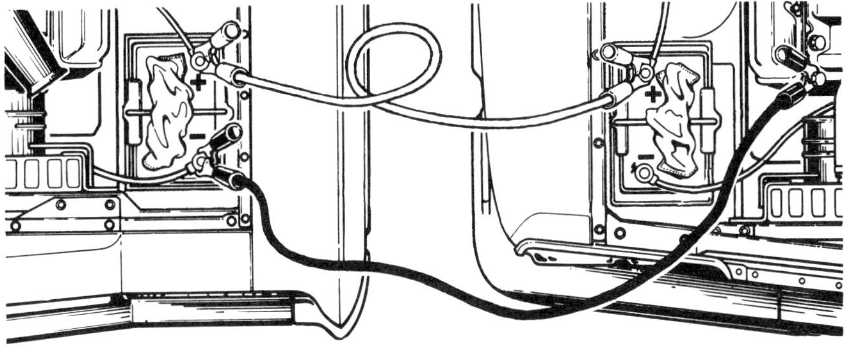

Fig. 24-1. Connections (between the booster battery and the dead battery) for starting a car with a dead battery.

slowly with a good battery, the trouble is in either the starting motor or the engine.

CAUTION: Use care in connecting a booster battery, to avoid hurting yourself or damaging the car's electrical equipment. Here is Ford's recommendation for using jumper cables between two cars (for a negative-ground battery). See Fig. 24-1.

1. **Remove the vent caps from both batteries. Cover the holes with cloths to prevent splashing of the electrolyte in case there is an explosion.**
2. **Shield your eyes.**
3. **Do not allow the two cars to touch each other.**
4. **Make sure all electrical equipment except the ignition is turned off on the car you are trying to start.**
5. **Connect the end of one cable to the positive (+) terminal of the booster battery. Connect the other end of this cable to the positive terminal of the dead battery.**
6. **Connect one end of the second cable to the negative (−) terminal of the booster battery.**
7. **Connect the other end of the second cable to the engine block of the car you are trying to start.** ***Do not connect it to the negative (−) terminal of the car battery!*** **This could damage electrical equipment.**
8. **Now start the car that has the booster battery. Then start the car that has the low battery. After the disabled car is started, disconnect the booster cable from the engine block. Then disconnect the other end of this (the negative) cable. Finally, disconnect the positive cable.**

CAUTION: Never operate the starting motor for more than 30 seconds at a time. Pause for a few minutes to allow it to cool off. Then try again, if necessary. It takes a very high current to crank the engine. This can overheat the starting motor if it is used for too long a time. Overheating can ruin the starting motor.

⊘ 24-5 Bench-testing a Starting Motor No-load and stall tests are made on a starting motor that has been removed from the car. These tests, plus the use of a test light (Fig. 24-2), will tell you the condition of the starting motor.

1. *NO-LOAD TEST* To make the no-load test, connect the starting motor to a battery of the correct voltage, in series with a high-reading ammeter. Measure the rpm and current draw (Fig. 24-3). These should be compared with the manufacturer's specifications for the motor.

2. *STALL TEST* To make this test, lock the drive pinion so that the armature cannot turn. Then apply the specified voltage to see what current the stalled motor draws (Fig. 24-4). A high-reading ammeter is required for this test, as well as a high-capacity carbon-pile rheostat (variable resistance).

3. *INTERPRETING NO-LOAD AND STALL TEST RESULTS* Here are the six most common combinations of conditions found in testing starting motors, along with further tests:

1. Rated current draw and no-load speed indicate a normal starting motor.
2. Low free speed and high current draw may result from:

a. Tight, dirty, or worn bearings; bent armature shaft; or loose field-pole screws, which allow the armature to drag on the pole shoes.
b. Grounded armature or fields. Raise the grounded

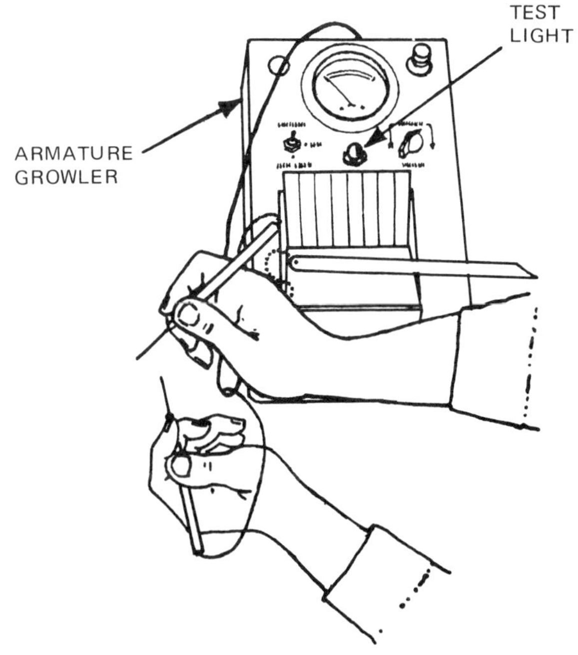

Fig. 24-2. Test light.

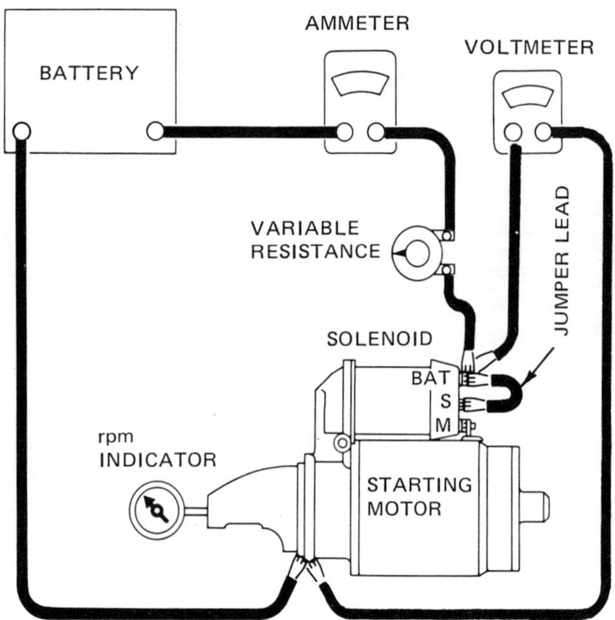

Fig. 24-3. Test setup for a no-load test. The variable resistance is used to adjust the applied voltage to the correct value. (*Delco-Remy Division of General Motors Corporation*)

brushes from the commutator, and insulate them with cardboard. Then check with the test light between the insulated terminal of the starting motor and the frame. If the test lamp lights, indicating a ground, raise the other brushes from the commutator. Check the fields and commutator separately to determine which is grounded. On some units, one end of the field circuit is normally grounded. The ground screw or screws must be removed before the field can be tested for ground.

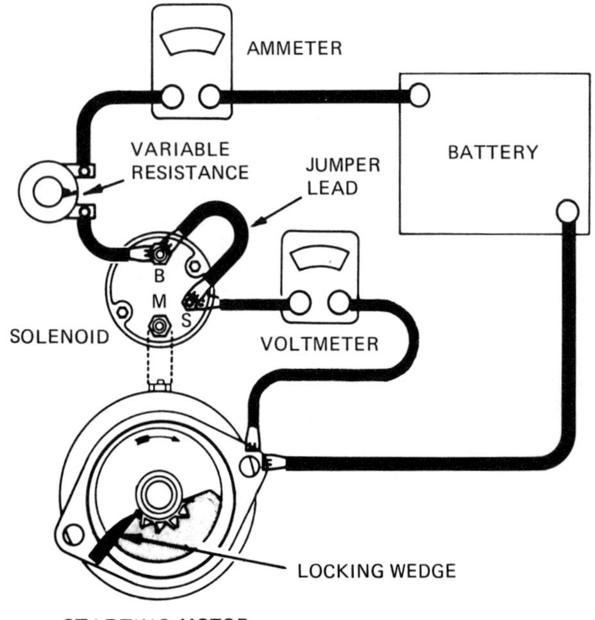

Fig. 24-4. Stall test of a starting motor. (*Delco-Remy Division of General Motors Corporation*)

c. Shorted armature. Check the armature further on a growler (⊘ 25-3).

3. Failure to operate at all with a high current draw indicates:

a. Direct ground in the switch, terminal, or fields. This can be found with a test light by raising the grounded brushes as in item *2b* above.

b. Frozen shaft bearings, which prevent the armature from turning.

c. Grounded armature windings, due, for instance, to thrown windings.

4. Failure to operate with no current draw indicates:

a. Open field circuit. Inspect the internal connections, and trace the circuit with a test light, checking the brushes, armature, and fields.

b. Open armature coils. This condition causes badly burned commutator bars.

c. Broken or weak brush springs; worn brushes; high mica on the commutator; glazed or dirty commutator; or any other condition that prevents good contact between the commutator and the brushes. Most of these can be found by visual inspection.

5. Low no-load speed with low current draw indicates:

a. An open field winding. Raise and insulate the ungrounded brushes from the commutator. Check the fields with a test light. The lamp should light as the leads are connected across each field.

b. High internal resistance due to poor connections; defective leads; dirty commutator; or any other condition listed in item *4c* above.

6. High free speed with a high current draw indicates shorted fields. Since the fields already have a low resistance, there is no practical way to test for this condition. If shorted fields are suspected, replace the fields and check for improvement in performance. But check the other components of the starting motor before going to this trouble.

CHAPTER 24 CHECKUP

NOTE: Since the following is a chapter review test, you should review the chapter before taking the test.

The chapter you have just finished covers the analysis of various starting-motor troubles and outlines methods of locating the causes of troubles. This information is of considerable value, since it will save you much time and effort in the shop. If you know how to analyze troubles, you can find the causes quickly. See how well you remember the trouble-diagnosis procedures by taking the test that follows. If any of the questions stump you, don't be discouraged. Just turn back into the chapter and review the pages that give you the information you need.

If you haven't been keeping a notebook, now is a good time to start one. You will be glad you did after you have finished this book. Your notebook will be a valuable reference when you need to review some point quickly.

Correcting Troubles Lists The purpose of this exercise is to help you spot unrelated troubles in a list. For example, check through the list, "No cranking, no lights: battery dead, open circuit, high battery voltage." You can see that "high battery voltage" does not belong in the list. It is the only condition that would not cause failure to crank. Each of the following lists contains one unrelated item. Write each list in your notebook, but do not write the item that does not belong.

1. No cranking, no lights: battery run down, battery gravity 1.250, open circuit.
2. No cranking, lights go out: poor connection at battery, battery grounded.
3. No cranking, lights dim slightly: pinion not engaging, excessive resistance or open in starting motor, starting motor short-circuited.
4. No cranking, lights dim heavily: engine trouble, battery low, very low temperature, pinion jammed, starting motor open-circuited, frozen shaft bearing or short in starting motor.
5. No cranking, lights stay bright: open circuit in switch, open circuit in starting motor, open in control circuit, battery dead.
6. Engine cranks slowly but does not start: battery run down, solenoid hold-in winding open, very low temperature, starting motor defective, undersized battery cables, mechanical trouble in engine.
7. Engine cranks at normal speed but does not start: ignition system defective, fuel system defective, air leaks in intake manifold or carburetor, battery dead, engine defective.
8. Solenoid plunger chatters: solenoid pull-in winding open, solenoid hold-in winding open, low battery.
9. Pinion disengages slowly after starting: sticky solenoid plunger, overrunning clutch sticks on armature shaft, engine idle high, overrunning clutch defective, shift-lever return spring weak, vacuum switch defective.
10. Lights dim slightly but engine starts in a few seconds: battery dead, normal condition.

Trouble-Diagnosis Procedures In the following, you are asked about starting-motor troubles and their causes. Write your answers in your notebook. If you are not sure about some procedure, turn back into the chapter and review it. Do not copy from the book. Instead, explain the procedures in your own words.

1. Explain how to use the headlights to find the trouble when the starting motor does not operate. List the five possible situations, their causes, and the corrections.
2. List the possible causes and corrections when the engine cranks slowly but does not start.
3. List the possible causes and corrections when the engine cranks at normal speed but does not start.
4. Why might a poor connection at a battery terminal cause the lights to go out when the starting motor is connected to the battery?
5. Why do low temperatures tend to increase starting difficulty?
6. List the possible causes of an open circuit in the starting motor.
7. List the conditions in the starting motor that would cause a heavy current draw without cranking action.
8. Explain why an open-circuited hold-in winding in a solenoid would cause the solenoid plunger to pull in and release repeatedly.

SUGGESTIONS FOR FURTHER STUDY

Often, school automotive shops have samples of damaged starting-motor parts on hand. Examine these parts carefully, to learn how to recognize different types of failures and relate them to their causes. Be sure to write, in your notebook, any important facts you find.

chapter 25

STARTING-MOTOR SERVICE

In the previous chapter we discussed various starting-motor troubles and their possible causes. Now, in this chapter, we describe the services that eliminate starting-motor troubles.

⊘ 25-1 Starting-Motor Service Most starting motors require service only when the engine is overhauled. However, if a starting motor has very heavy use, it may require more frequent service. Also, if a starting motor is damaged or becomes defective, it requires service. Repair and servicing procedures are discussed in the following sections.

⊘ 25-2 Damaged Starting-Motor Parts: Causes and Corrections Several kinds of defects may develop in a starting motor, as follows:

1. *THROWN ARMATURE WINDINGS* Thrown armature windings are normally found only in the overrunning-clutch type of starting motor. This condition results from excessive armature speed that has thrown the windings from the armature. Improper adjustment of the throttle-opening linkage allows the starting motor to operate too long after starting. Opening the throttle too wide puts an excessive burden on the overrunning clutch. It overheats, seizes, and causes the armature to be spun at high speed. A defective overrunning clutch produces the same condition.

2. *BURNED COMMUTATOR BARS* Burned commutator bars usually indicate an open-circuited armature. The open circuit normally will be found at one or more commutator riser bars. It is most often caused by excessively long cranking periods. Such long cranking periods overheat the starting motor and melt the solder at the riser-bar connection. This not only throws solder (thrown solder may be found on the cover band); it also causes the connection to loosen. Arcing then takes place each time the bar with the bad connection passes under the brushes. The bar soon burns. If the bars are not too badly burned, the armature can be repaired. Resolder the connections at the riser bars (using rosin, not acid flux); then turn the commutator on a lathe.

3. *BROKEN OR DISTORTED BENDIX SPRING* The starting motor may have a broken or distorted Bendix spring or a broken drive housing. This is usually caused by an attempted meshing while the engine is on a rockback, or by an engine backfire during cranking. On Bendix-drive starting motors, several seconds should elapse between attempts to start. Then the drive pinion will not go into mesh with the flywheel when the engine is rocking backward. If the ignition is out of time, it may cause the engine to backfire during cranking. This could cause a damaged drive or housing.

4. *DIRTY OR GUMMY COMMUTATOR* The commutator sometimes becomes covered with a film of dirt or gum. This can be cleaned off with No. 00 sandpaper held against the commutator while the starting motor is being operated (for not more than 30 seconds). It is usually best, though, to correct this condition by turning the commutator on a lathe.

⊘ 25-3 Starting-Motor Disassembly, Repair, and Assembly The disassembly of the starting motor is usually simple. The solenoid or switch, where present, is removed first. Next, the cover band (where present) is removed, and the brush leads are disconnected. Where leads are soldered, the brushes are removed from the holders. Then, after the through bolts are taken out, the commutator end frame, field frame, and drive end can be separated. The Bendix drive can be removed from the armature shaft by taking out the drive-head attaching screw. The Folo-Thru drive is removed from the armature shaft by compressing the spring so that the end anchor plate clears the drive pin. The drive pin can then be pushed out of the shaft, and the drive slid off the shaft. On overrunning-clutch starting motors, the overrunning clutch can be slid off the shaft. Some models have a retainer and snap ring. These must be removed before the overrunning clutch can be slid off. Figure 23-8 is a disassembled view of a passenger-car starting motor.

1. *CLEANING STARTING-MOTOR PARTS* The armature and fields should never be cleaned in any solution that dissolves or damages the insulation.

They should be wiped off with a clean cloth. Never clean the overrunning clutch in a solvent tank. The solvent will dissolve the clutch lubrication and ruin the clutch.

2. FIELD-WINDING SERVICE Test for a grounded field with the test-light leads on the terminal stud and frame. If the lamp lights, the field is grounded. Test for open with the test light at the two ends of the field circuit. The lamp should light. If the field windings require replacement, use a pole-shoe screwdriver (Fig. 25-1). The pole-shoe screwdriver prevents damage to the pole-shoe screws and assures tight reassembly of the shoes. Rapping the frame with a plastic hammer while the screws are being tightened helps align the shoes properly. When resoldering connections, use rosin flux. In humid areas, manufacturers recommend that special insulating varnish be applied to the field windings after reassembly. This reduces the effects of moisture.

3. ARMATURE SERVICE The causes and correction of thrown armature windings and burned commutator bars have been discussed. Inspect the armature lamination for rub marks. These mean a worn bearing or a bent shaft has allowed the laminations to rub on the pole shoes. A check for a bent shaft can be made by putting the armature in V blocks. Rotate it while a dial indicator is in position to measure run-out. The run-out, or out-of-roundness, of the commutator can be checked at the same time.

The armature is tested for ground by placing one test-light lead on the laminations and the other on the commutator. If the lamp lights, the armature is grounded. It is tested for short circuits on the growler (Fig. 25-2). The armature is placed on the growler and slowly revolved while a hacksaw blade is held above the armature core. The hacksaw blade vibrates against the core when it is above a slot containing a shorted winding. A shorted or grounded armature should be discarded.

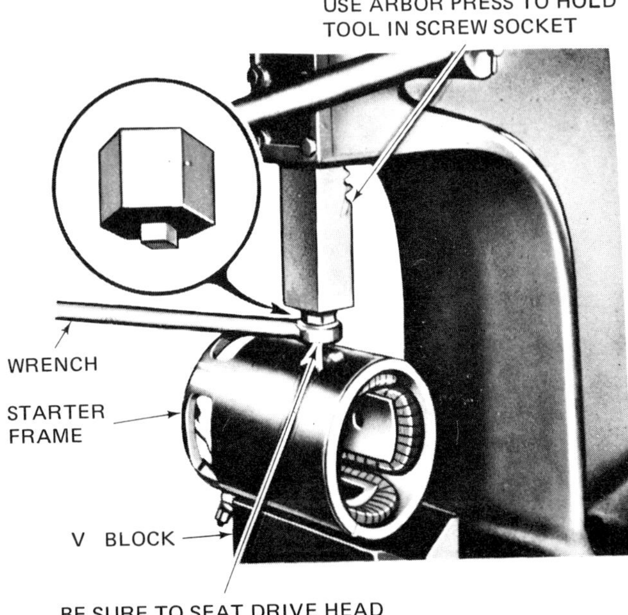

Fig. 25-1. Pole-shoe screwdriver being used on a field frame. (*Ford Motor Company*)

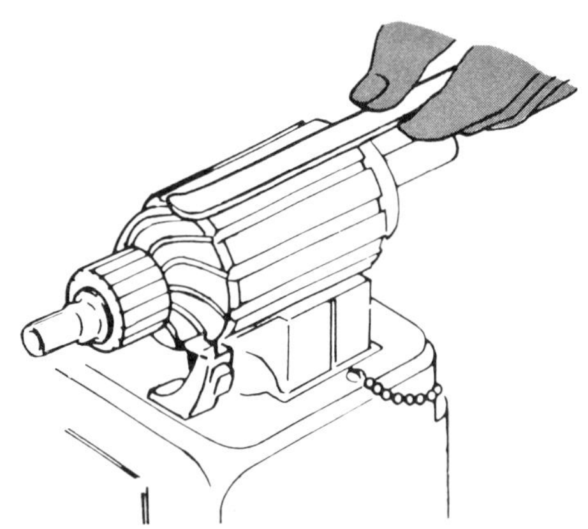
Fig. 25-2. Using a growler to test an armature for short circuits.

If the commutator is out of round or worn, or if it has high mica, it should be turned on a lathe (Fig. 25-3). The cut should be as smooth and as light as possible.

In humid areas, manufacturers recommend that special insulating varnish be applied to the armature to reduce the effects of moisture. The varnish should be kept off the shaft and commutator.

4. BRUSH SERVICE Brushes that are worn to one-half their original length should be replaced. If the brush lead is soldered, unsolder it and unclinch the lead from the connector. Where the lead terminal clip is riveted to the frame, unsolder and unclamp the lead from the clip. Then the lead of a new brush can be clamped and soldered to the clip. With new brushes in place, put the armature into position so that the brushes rest on the commutator. If the brushes do not align with the commutator bars, the brush holders are bent. This requires replacement of the brush holders or the end frame. The brush-spring tension should be checked with a spring scale (Fig. 25-4). Note the pull required to raise the brushes, brush arms, or holders from the contact position. Replace the springs if the tension is not correct.

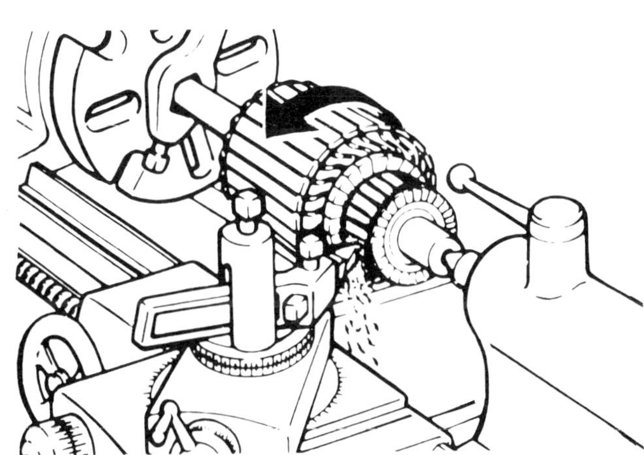
Fig. 25-3. Turning an armature commutator in a lathe.

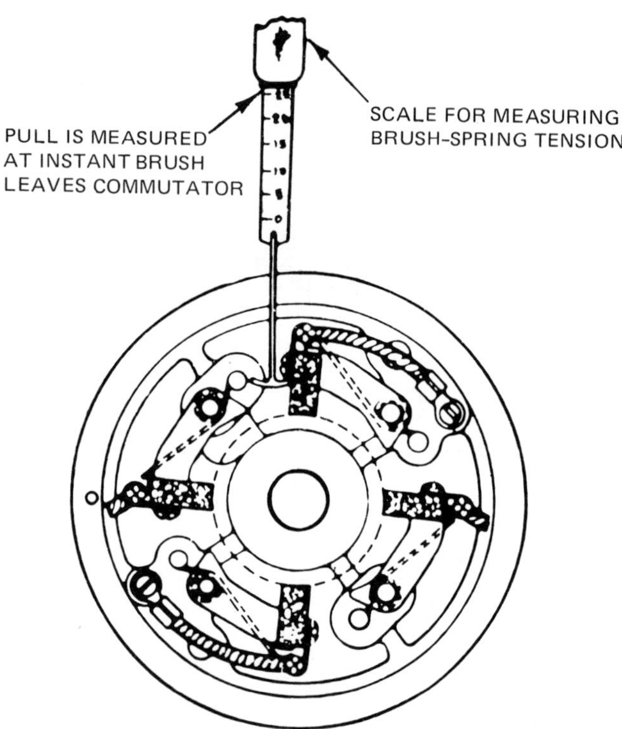

Fig. 25-4. Testing brush-spring tension with a spring scale. (*Delco-Remy Division of General Motors Corporation*)

5. *STARTING-MOTOR-DRIVE LUBRICATION* The Bendix and Folo-Thru drives should be cleaned by washing in kerosene. They should not be lubricated. The overrunning-clutch type of drive must never be cleaned by a high-temperature or grease-dissolving method. This would remove the grease originally packed in the clutch. With the grease removed, the clutch would soon fail.

6. *TESTING THE OVERRUNNING CLUTCH* The overrunning-clutch pinion should turn freely and smoothly in the overrunning direction. It should not slip in the cranking position with normal cranking torque imposed on it. If the pinion turns roughly in the overrunning direction, the rollers are chipped or worn. The clutch should be replaced. If the pinion slips in the cranking direction, the clutch should be replaced.

7. *STARTING-MOTOR LUBRICATION* During reassembly of the starting motor, all bearings should be lubricated with a few drops of light engine oil. Many starting motors have oilless bearings that have no provision for oiling. They should be lubricated, however, before reassembly, with a few drops of light engine oil.

8. *STARTING-MOTOR ASSEMBLY* The assembly procedure is the reverse of disassembly. Soldered connections should be made with rosin, not acid flux.

9. *OVERRUNNING-CLUTCH-PINION CLEARANCE* On the overrunning-clutch type of starting motor, the clearance between the pinion and the thrust washer, retainer, or housing should be measured after assembly. The pinion should be in the cranking position. Refer to the manufacturer's service manual for the detail of the checking procedure.

10. *FOLO-THRU DRIVE* On the Folo-Thru drive, do not turn the pinion out to the extended, or cranking, position. In this position, a lockpin drops into a slot in the sleeve thread to lock the pinion (see Fig. 23-10). The only way the pinion can be unlocked is to mount the starting motor on the engine and start the engine. When the engine speed increases to around 400 rpm, the lockpin will be retracted by centrifugal force. The pinion will then demesh and move back to the retracted position.

11. *TESTING THE ASSEMBLED STARTING MOTOR* The starting motor should be given no-load and torque tests, as outlined above, to make sure it operates according to specifications.

⊘ 25-4 Installing the Starting Motor Whenever a starting motor is being installed or removed, the battery ground cable should be disconnected from the battery terminal. This avoids shorting the battery by an accidental grounding of the insulated cable. When installing the starting motor, connect the leads after the motor is bolted into place in the flywheel housing. Then check the throttle-cracker linkage on cars so equipped. Adjust it as necessary to obtain the proper throttle opening during cranking. This is particularly important on overrunning-clutch starting motors. An excessive throttle opening might spin the overrunning clutch at high speed during initial engine operation. This would cause the overrunning clutch to be overloaded. Figures 25-5 and 25-6 show various starting-motor mounting arrangements.

⊘ 25-5 Checking the Starting-Motor Circuit After the starting motor has been reinstalled on the engine, the cables and connections can be tested. Use a low-reading voltmeter while a high current draw is taken through the circuit. This procedure locates any excessive resistance due to poor connections or bad

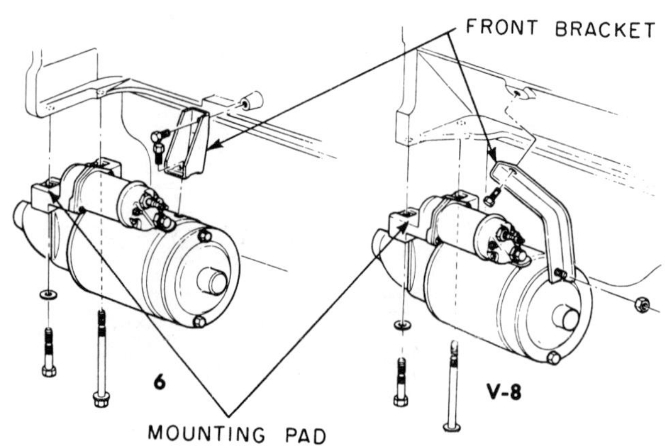

Fig. 25-5. Starting motors that have a mounting pad and a front-brace bracket. (*Chevrolet Motor Division of General Motors Corporation*)

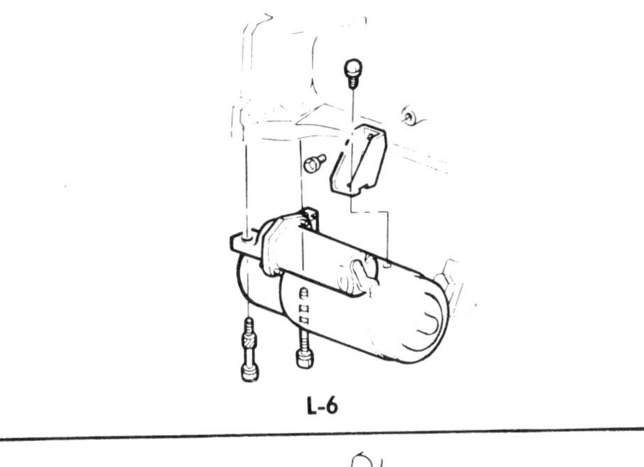

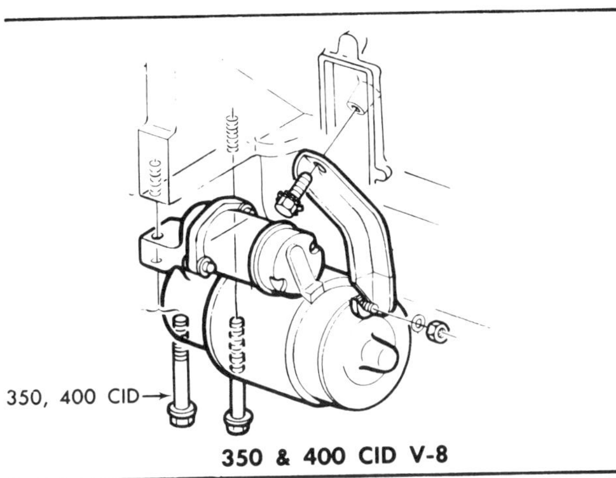

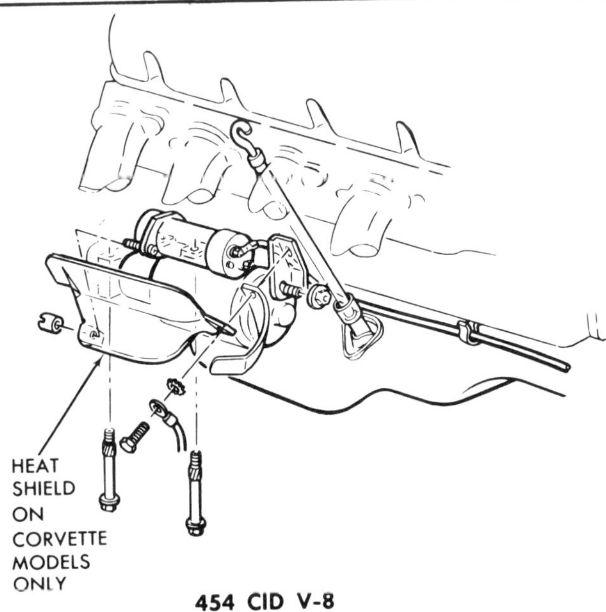

Fig. 25-6. Various methods of attaching the starting motor to the engine. (*Chevrolet Motor Division of General Motors Corporation*)

cables. Excessive resistance prevents the delivery of normal amounts of current to the starting motor.

Two methods can be used to provide high current through the cables. In one method, the starting motor is operated. In the other, a heavy variable resistance is used. With either system, the high amperage flowing through the circuit from the battery shows up excessive resistance in the circuit: There is an excessive voltage drop. Too much voltage drop reduces the voltage at the starting motor, and normal operation is not achieved.

⊘ 25-6 Checking the Circuit with the Starting Motor A low-reading voltmeter is required for this check. Disconnect the ignition primary lead from the ignition distributor to the coil, so that the engine will not start. Operate the starting motor and, very quickly, check the voltage (1) from the insulated battery post to the solenoid battery terminal; (2) from the grounded battery post to the starting-motor housing; and (3) from the solenoid battery terminal to the solenoid motor terminal. Do not run the starting motor for more than 30 seconds. More than a 0.2-volt drop (0.1 volt for 6-volt circuits) at any of these indicates excessive resistance.

The remedy is to disconnect the cables and clean the cable clamps and terminal posts (see ⊘ 22-18). Use new cables if the old ones seem to be in bad condition. Be sure that all connections are clean and tight. Always use cables of adequate size. Undersized cables have too much resistance and may prevent normal cranking, particularly during cold weather. If the excessive resistance is in the solenoid switch, disassemble the switch. Clean or replace the contact disk or contacts.

NOTE: Extra-long battery cables are sometimes required because of the locations of the battery and starting motor. This may result in somewhat higher voltage drops than the recommended 0.1 or 0.2 volt. In such cases, the normal voltage drop should be established by checking several vehicles. When a voltage drop well above this normal value is found, the excessive resistance must be located and eliminated.

CHAPTER 25 CHECKUP

NOTE: Since the following is a chapter review test, you should review the chapter before taking the test.

You are making fine progress in your study of automotive electrical equipment. You have already covered two of the important components of the electric system, the battery and the starting motor. It is obvious that you are working hard and doing a good job; otherwise you would not have come this far in the book. Keep up the good work. You will be glad you did later, when you are in the shop. Knowing the how and why makes the job easier.

When you are asked to write something down, write it in your notebook. By now, your notebook should contain a great deal of valuable information. It will be an excellent reference, and you will be glad you kept it.

Completing the Sentences The sentences below are incomplete. After each sentence there are several words or phrases, but only one of them correctly completes the sentence. Write each sentence in your notebook, ending it with the one word or phrase that completes it correctly.

1. The starting-motor commutator end frame, field frame, and drive housing can be separated by removal of the: (*a*) cover band, (*b*) Bendix drive, (*c*) through bolts, (*d*) head-spring bolt.
2. The Bendix drive normally requires: (*a*) lubrication, (*b*) no lubrication, (*c*) a little grease.
3. A broken or wrapped-up Bendix spring is usually caused by an attempted meshing while the engine is on a rockback, or by: (*a*) high cranking speeds, (*b*) a jammed engine, (*c*) a backfire while cranking.
4. Snapping the brush or brush arm down may cause the: (*a*) brush to crack or chip, (*b*) commutator to dent, (*c*) brush holder to distort.
5. On some later models of overrunning-clutch starting motor, the drive assembly is held on the armature shaft by a thrust collar, retainer, and: (*a*) thrust bolt, (*b*) thrust washer, (*c*) locking nut, (*d*) snap ring.
6. The internal mechanism of the roller-type overrunning clutch: (*a*) should be oiled, (*b*) should be repacked with grease, (*c*) cannot be relubricated.
7. If, when checking an overrunning clutch, you find that the drive pinion slips in the driving direction, you should replace the: (*a*) assembly, (*b*) rollers and pinion, (*c*) shell and rollers.
8. Open circuits in a starting-motor armature will probably produce: (*a*) worn bearings, (*b*) burned commutator bars, (*c*) excessive armature speeds.
9. The growler is used to test the armature for: (*a*) short circuits, (*b*) open circuits, (*c*) excessive armature resistance.
10. Thrown armature windings indicate that the armature was: (*a*) defectively made, (*b*) subject to excessive torque, (*c*) spun at excessive speed.

Correcting Troubles Lists The purpose of the following exercise is to help you spot unrelated troubles on a list. For example, check through the list, "No cranking, no lights: battery dead, open circuit, high battery voltage." You can see that "high battery voltage" does not belong in the list. It is the only condition that would not cause failure to crank. Each of the following lists contains one unrelated item. Write each list in your notebook, but do not write the item that does not belong.

1. Low free speed and high current draw: Tight, dirty, or worn bearings; bent armature shaft; loose pole shoes; open field winding; grounded armature or fields; shorted armature.
2. Failure to operate, with high current draw: direct ground in switch; terminal, field, or armature; frozen shaft bearings; open field winding.
3. Failure to operate, with no current draw: open field circuit; open armature coils; grounded armature or fields; poor contact between brushes and commutator.
4. Low no-load speed and low current draw: open field windings; high internal resistance; commutator bars grounded; commutator dirty; poor internal connections.
5. High free speed and high current draw: shorted fields; open fields.

Starting Motor Service In the following, you are asked to describe various service operations and procedures. Write these in your notebook. The act of writing helps fix the information firmly in your mind. If you are not sure of a procedure, turn back into the chapter and reread the pages that give you the information. Don't copy from the book. Describe each procedure in your own words, just as you would tell it to a friend.

1. Explain how to check overrunning-clutch pinion clearance.
2. Explain how to perform no-load and stall tests on a starting motor.
3. List the abnormal operating conditions that are disclosed by the no-load and stall tests, and what would cause them.
4. Explain how to meter-test the starting-motor circuit.
5. Explain how to disassemble and reassemble a Bendix-drive starting motor. An overrunning-clutch starting motor.
6. Explain how to adjust overrunning-clutch pinion clearance.
7. Explain how to inspect an armature.
8. Explain how to test an armature on a growler. Explain why a short circuit in the starting motor causes the hacksaw blade to vibrate.
9. Explain what could cause commutator bars to burn.
10. Explain how armature windings may be thrown out of their slots.
11. Explain how to remove and replace field windings.
12. List the important points to keep in mind when inspecting or installing starting-motor wiring.

SUGGESTIONS FOR FURTHER STUDY

You will be able to see various types of starting-motor failures, trouble-diagnosis and testing procedures, and overhaul operations in a local automotive electrical service shop. At your school automotive shop, you may be able to examine sample parts from starting motors that have failed. Another source of information is the service bulletins and manuals issued by various electrical-equipment and car manufacturers. Study all of these you can. Be sure to write the important facts in your notebook.

chapter 26

AUTOMOTIVE CHARGING SYSTEMS

This chapter describes the various types of charging systems used on automobiles. The charging system has the job of keeping the battery in a charged condition. The starting motor takes current out of the battery when it cranks the engine. The charging system puts the current back. In addition, the charging system handles electric loads, such as the ignition system and the lights, when the car is running. The charging system includes the generator or alternator, a regulator, and connecting wires.

⊘ 26-1 Function of the Alternator The alternator (or generator) converts mechanical energy from the engine to electric current. As noted, it keeps the battery in a charged condition and handles electric loads when the engine is running. For many years, all cars used direct-current (dc) generators. In recent years, however, manufacturers have switched to alternators, or alternating-current (ac) generators.

NOTE: Direct current (dc) flows in one direction. Alternating current (ac) flows in one direction for a moment, and then flows in the opposite direction. It alternates. The current in your home is ac. It alternates, or changes direction, 120 times per second. It is called 60-cycle current. (One electrical cycle per second is called a *hertz*, abbreviated Hz.) The electric units on the car are all dc units and require direct current.

⊘ 26-2 Generator Principles Both the alternator and the generator produce electric current. But they do so in slightly different ways. Both produce ac inside the unit. The generator uses a commutator and brushes to convert this ac to dc. The alternator uses diodes to make the conversion. We shall explain what these terms mean later in this chapter.

First, let us see how we can make electric current flow in a wire. As explained in Chap. 20, electric current is a flow, or movement, of electrons. We can make electrons move by moving a wire through a magnetic field, as shown in Fig. 26-1. (The dot in the end of the conductor means that the current is moving toward you. If it were moving in the other direction, away from you, there would be a cross in the conductor.) When the conductor is moved through the magnetic field, it cuts through the magnetic lines of force. This cutting of the lines of force causes electrons to move. That is, it produces a flow of electric current. Moving a conductor through a magnetic field is the principle of the dc generator. Actually, the movement of the conductors in the generator is rotary movement. The conductors move in a circle inside the generator.

⊘ 26-3 DC Generators Direct-current (dc) generators have not been used in automobiles for many years. But you will still see dc generators on some small-engine installations. Also, some farm tractors still use dc generators. And, of course, there are some older cars still running with dc generators.

The generator has two major parts, the armature

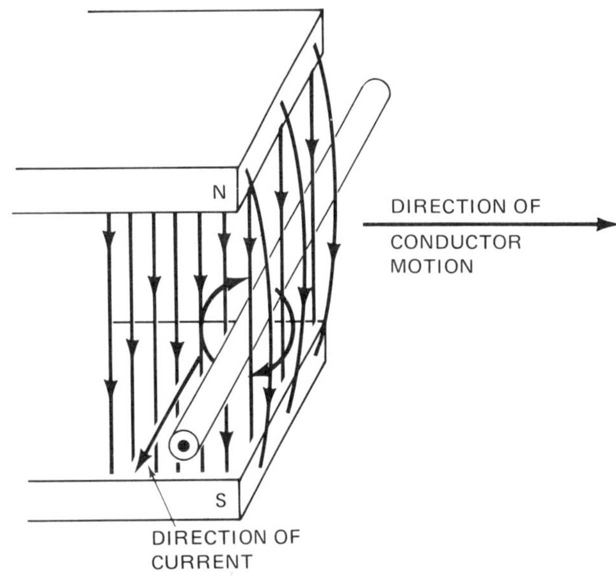

Fig. 26-1. A conductor, moving through a magnetic field as shown, has a flow of current induced in it.

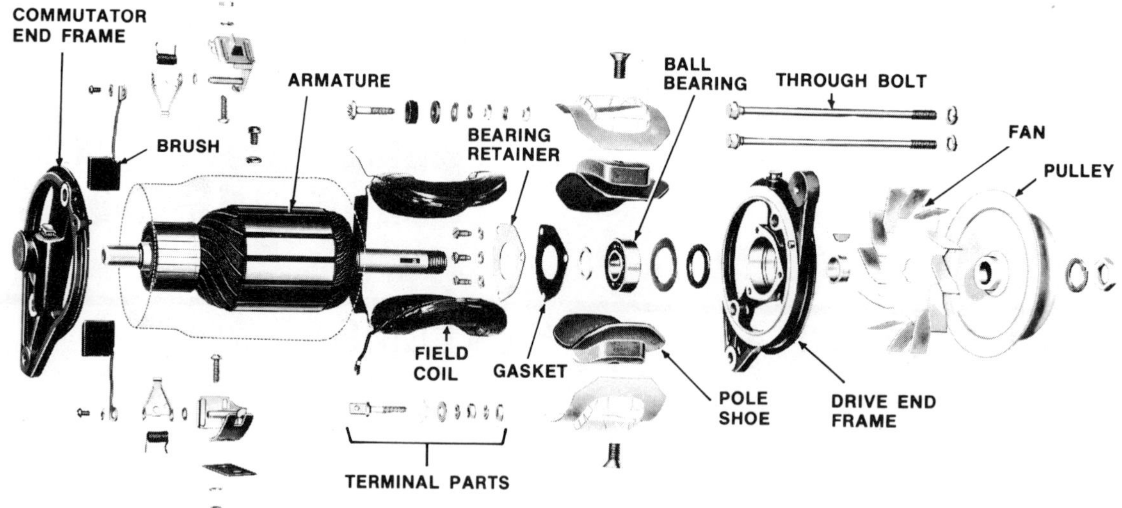

Fig. 26-2. Disassembled view of a passenger-car dc generator. (*Delco-Remy Division of General Motors Corporation*)

and the field-frame assembly (Fig. 26-2). These parts resemble the armature and field-frame assembly in the starting motor (see Fig. 23-4). The main difference is that, in the generator, the conductors in the armature and field coils are much smaller. The generator is mounted on the side of the engine. It is driven by a belt from a pulley on the engine crankshaft. As the armature is rotated, the armature conductors are carried through a magnetic field. Current is thus induced in them. The magnetic field comes from two field coils mounted on the inside of the field frame.

Figure 26-3 shows a dc generator in very simplified form. The armature is shown as a single loop of wire. The two field coils are shown as single turns of wire. The two pole shoes, around which the field coils are assembled, have some magnetism. When the armature starts to rotate, the wire loop cuts through the magnetic field. That action induces some current in the wire. The current flows out through one segment of the commutator. Some of the current flows through the two field coils. But most of the current goes to the "load" (an electric light or other electrical device). It passes through the load, and then goes back to the other segment of the commutator. So the current from the armature loop flows in two complete circuits—the field-coil circuit and the load circuit.

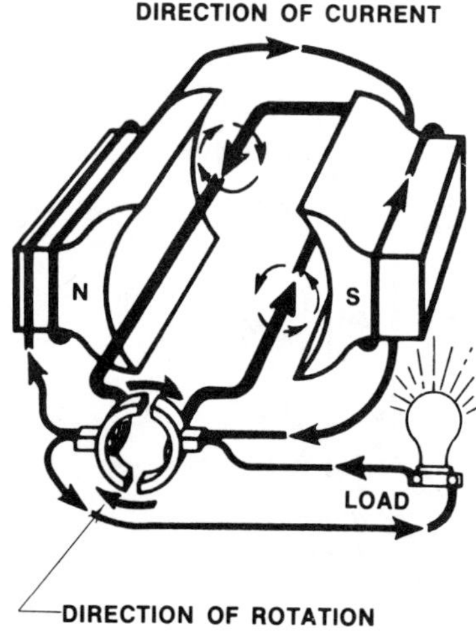

Fig. 26-3. Simplified schematic diagram of a generator. The heavy arrows show the direction of current flow. The light circular arrows show the directions of magnetic fields around the conductors.

The current flowing in the field coils increases the magnetism. The increased magnetism increases the amount of current induced in the armature loop. This is how large amounts of current are obtained from the generator. Many loops are added to the armature; they all work together to produce current.

⊘ 26-4 Commutation

Study Fig. 26-3 for a moment. Notice that, as the loop rotates, the two sides cut the magnetic field. They cut it first in one direction, and then in the other. Thus, the current flows through the loop first one way, and then the other. The current alternates.

The commutator is used to turn the alternating current into direct current. Notice, in Fig. 26-3, that the commutator, which has two segments in the simple example, also rotates. The side of the loop that moves down through the magnetic field is always connected, through its commutator segment, to the right-hand brush. So, every time the current reverses in the loop, the commutator segments also reverse positions. The current always flows out of the same brush and always flows back through the other brush.

In this way, the commutator and the brushes turn the ac of the armature loops into dc.

⊘ 26-5 Regulators for DC Generators

Generators have to be regulated. Otherwise, they would con-

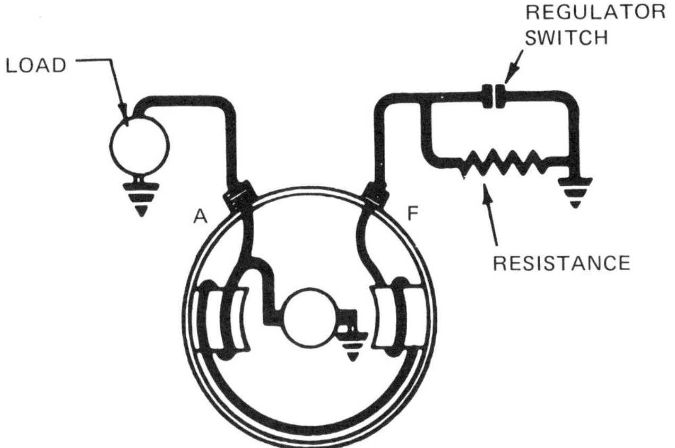

Fig. 26-4. Simplified wiring diagram for a dc generator with an externally grounded field circuit.

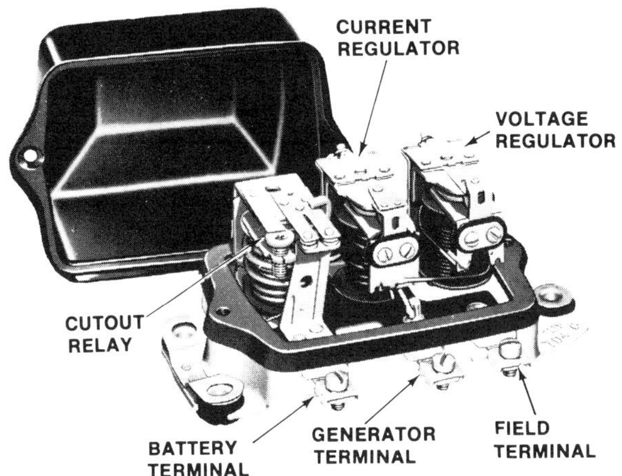

Fig. 26-5. Current and voltage regulator for a dc generator, with the cover removed. (*Delco-Remy Division of General Motors Corporation*)

tinue to increase the current output until they burned up. Look at Fig. 26-3 again. Part of the current from the armature loop goes through the field coils. This increases the magnetic strength of the field coils. The stronger the magnetic field, the more current the armature produces. And the more current the armature produces, the stronger the magnetic field gets. Thus, the current could continue to increase until the generator burned up.

To prevent this, generators have regulators. The principle of the regulator is simple. The regulator puts a resistance into the field circuit when the current gets too high (Fig. 26-4). The resistance cuts down the amount of current flowing. This reduces the strength of the magnetic field. The resistance is controlled by a pair of contact points. When the points are closed, there is no resistance in the field circuit. When the points are open, the resistance is connected into the field circuit. In operation, the points vibrate, or open and close. They stay closed just the right amount of time to feed the field coils the amount of current they need.

⊘ 26-6 Three-Unit Regulator The regulator most commonly used with dc generators has three units (Fig. 26-5). Let's review them quickly.

1. *CUTOUT RELAY* The cutout relay closes the circuit to the battery when the generator is running. This allows the generator to charge the battery. The cutout relay opens the circuit when the generator stops. This prevents the battery from discharging back through the generator.
2. *CURRENT REGULATOR* The current regulator has a pair of contact points and a resistance. When the generator current output gets too high, the contact points open. When the contact points open, the resistance is connected into the generator field circuit, and it reduces the current. Actually, the points vibrate—open and close—hundreds of times a second. This keeps the resistance in the field circuit just long enough to prevent too much generator current.
3. *VOLTAGE REGULATOR* The voltage regulator works on voltage. Voltage, you remember, is electric pressure. The higher the pressure, or voltage, the more current is pushed through electrical equipment.

When a battery is low, it will accept a lot of current. But when a battery is fully charged, it will take only a very small current. The small current requires a high pressure, or voltage. Therefore, when the generator is working against a fully charged battery, it keeps increasing its voltage to get current through the battery.

If this voltage were allowed to increase, the battery would be overcharged and ruined. At the same time, all the electrical equipment would have too much current pushed through it by the high voltage. Excess current could ruin the electrical equipment. For example, high voltage will burn out the headlights.

To prevent this, the voltage regulator has a pair of contact points and a resistance. When the voltage gets too high, the points open. The resistance is connected into the generator field circuit. The magnetic field is weakened, and the generator voltage is held to a safe amount. Actually, the points vibrate, just as in the current regulator. This keeps the resistance in the field circuit just the right amount of time to prevent the generator voltage from going too high.
4. *COMBINED ACTION* Remember that the current regulator prevents the generator from exceeding its rated output. For example, if the generator is rated at 40 A, the current regulator keeps the output from going above this valve. Remember also that the voltage regulator prevents too much voltage. When it operates, it cuts down the generator output to suit the battery and the connected electric load. For example, suppose the battery is charged, and nothing is turned on but the ignition. In this case the voltage regulator cuts the generator output down to a few amperes.

Remember this: Either the current regulator is working, holding output to a safe maximum, or the

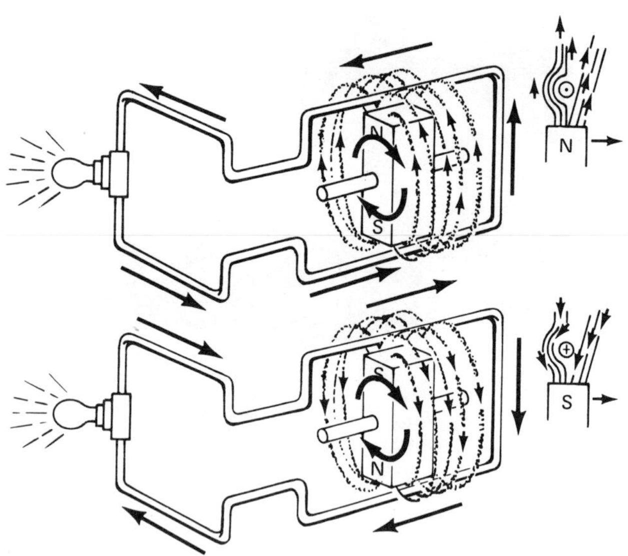

Fig. 26-6. Simplified alternator, consisting of a single stationary loop of wire and a rotating bar magnet. The distortion of moving lines of force around a leg of the loop (conductor), and the direction of current (electron) flow, are shown at the right.

voltage regulator is working, holding the voltage down and thereby cutting output down. They do not both work at the same time.

⊘ 26-7 Alternator (AC Generator) Principles The dc generator rotates the conductors in a stationary magnetic field. The alternator rotates a magnetic field so that stationary conductors are cut by the moving magnetic lines of force.

Let's look at a simple alternator (Fig. 26-6). In the simple one-loop unit shown, the rotating bar magnet supplies the moving field. At the top, the north pole of the bar magnet passes the upper leg of the loop, and the south pole passes the lower leg of the loop. As the loop cuts the magnetic field, current (electron flow) is induced in the loop in the direction shown by the arrows. At the bottom, the magnet has rotated half a turn. Its south pole is now passing the upper leg of the loop, and its north pole is passing the lower leg. Now, magnetic lines of force are being cut by the two legs in the opposite direction. So current (electron flow) is induced in the loop in the opposite direction. Thus, as the magnet spins and the two poles alternately pass the two legs of the loop, electrons in the loop are pushed first in one direction, and then in the other. In other words, the electrons alternate in direction; alternating current flows.

Three things can increase the current (the number of electrons) moving in the loop: The first is increasing the strength of the magnetic field. The second is increasing the speed with which the magnetic field rotates. The third is increasing the number of loops.

In the actual alternator, both the strength of the magnetic field and the number of loops are increased. Instead of a simple bar magnet, the rotating part of the alternator is made up of two or more pole pieces. They are assembled on a shaft over an electromagnetic winding. The electromagnet is made up of many turns of wire. When current flows in the electromagnetic winding, a strong magnetic field is created. The pointed ends of the two pole pieces become, alternately, north and south poles (Fig. 26-7). The winding is connected to the battery through a pair of insulated rings that rotate with the shaft. A pair of stationary brushes ride on the rings. The two ends of the winding are attached to the rings, and the brushes make continuous sliding (or slipping) contact with the slip rings (Fig. 26-8).

Figure 26-9 shows the stationary loops of an alternator assembled into a frame. The assembly is called a *stator*. The loops are interconnected as explained below so that the current produced in all loops adds together. Since this current is alternating, it must be *rectified*, or converted, into direct current.

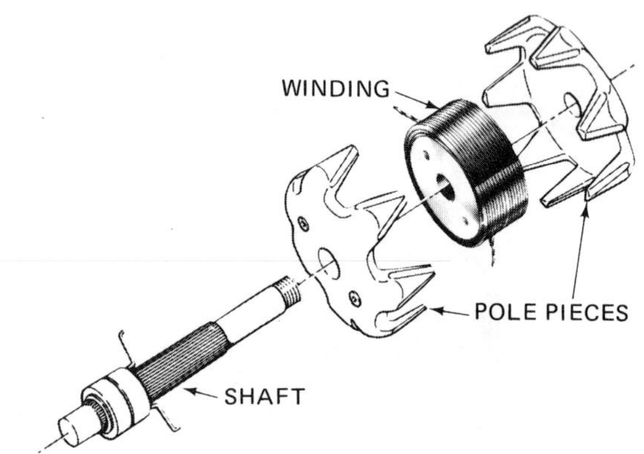

Fig. 26-7. Rotor of an alternator, in partly disassembled view. (*Delco-Remy Division of General Motors Corporation*)

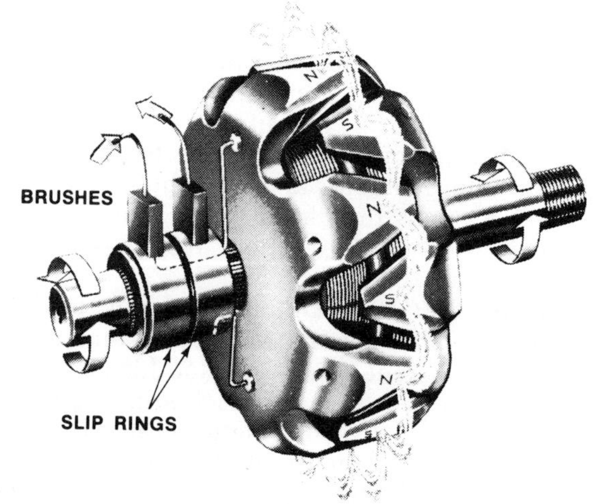

Fig. 26-8. Rotor of an alternator, showing the brushes in place on the slip rings. (*Delco-Remy Division of General Motors Corporation*)

Fig. 26-9. Stator of an alternator. (*Delco-Remy Division of General Motors Corporation*)

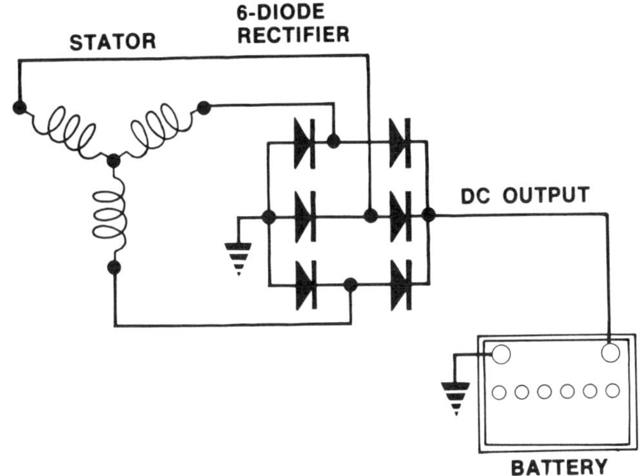

Fig. 26-11. Wiring diagram for an alternator with a six-diode rectifier and a Y-connected stator.

26-8 The Alternator The ac generator, or alternator, produces alternating current. The battery, ignition system, and other electrical components on the automobile cannot use ac, however. They are all dc units. The ac output must therefore be rectified, or changed to dc.

1. *RECTIFYING ac* Automotive alternators have built-in diode rectifiers. The diode is an electronic device that permits current to flow through it in one direction only. Figure 26-10 illustrates how four diodes can be used to change ac to dc. The four diodes are numbered 1 to 4 in the illustration. To the left, the current from the ac source moves through the conductors shown solid. Diodes 1 and 3 permit the current to flow through. But diodes 2 and 4 do not, since the current is flowing in the wrong direction for them. However, when the direction of the current has reversed, as shown to the right in Fig. 26-10, diodes 2 and 4 pass the current. But diodes 1 and 3 do not.

2. *THREE-PHASE* The circuit in Fig. 26-10 is termed *single-phase*, since there is only a single ac source. Such a source produces a pulsating current. This is like a single-cylinder engine. It does not provide a smooth flow of power. Its output is a series of peaks, between which no power is delivered. To provide a much smoother flow of current, alternators are built with three stator circuits. These, in effect, give overlapping pulses of ac. When these are rectified, a smooth flow of dc is obtained.

The three stator circuits can be interconnected in either of two ways, with "Y" connections or with "delta" connections (Figs. 26-11 and 26-12). They operate similarly and are serviced similarly. The ac generated in the three legs of the stator passes through six diodes and is converted into dc.

3. *DIODE HEAT SINKS* Diodes are usually mounted in the slip-ring end of the alternator, in a metal bracket called a *heat sink*. The heat sink takes heat from the diodes, which can become rather hot in operation. The heat sink has large radiating surfaces. They radiate the heat into the air surrounding the alternator. This keeps the diodes from overheating.

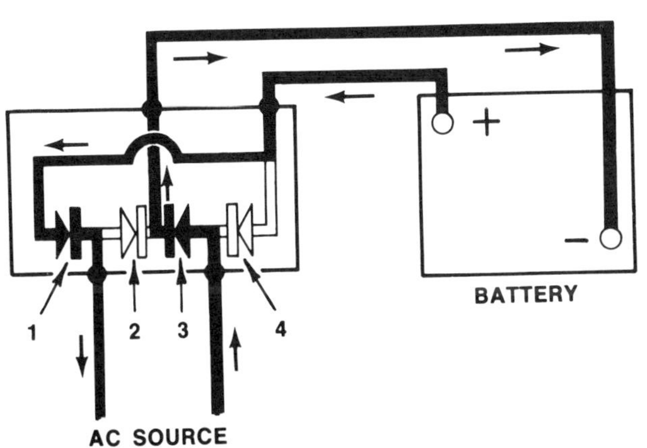

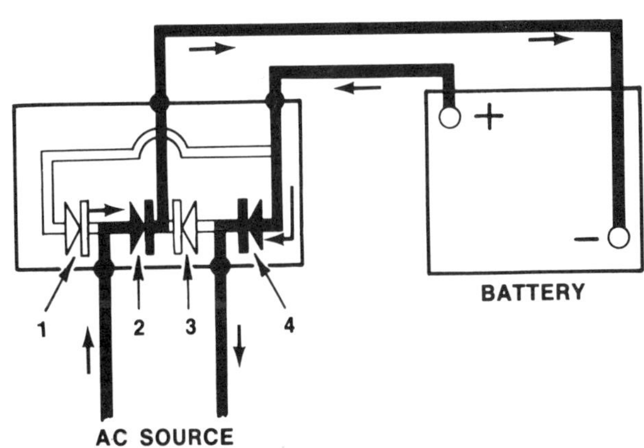

Fig. 26-10. Four diodes connected to an ac source. The diodes rectify the alternating current (change it to direct current) to charge the battery.

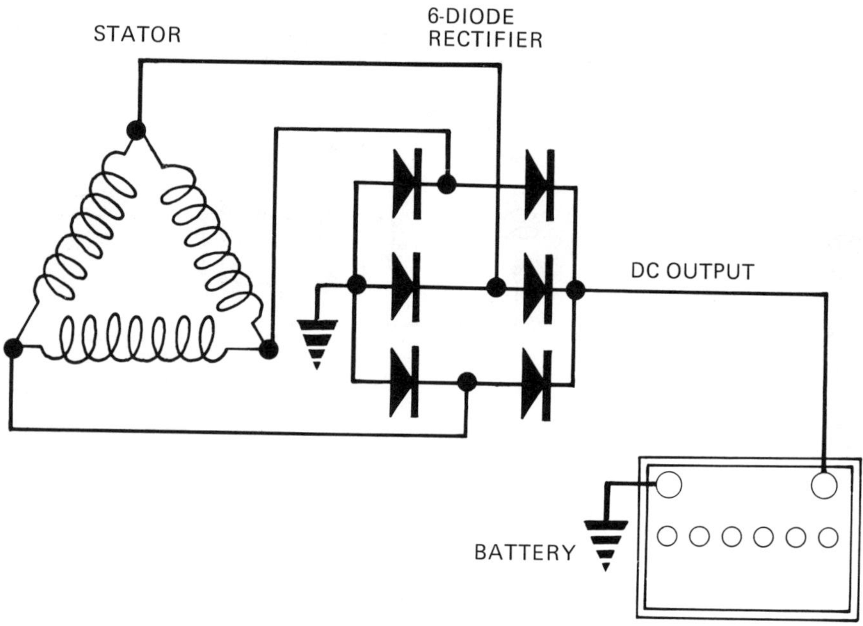

Fig. 26-12. Wiring diagram for an alternator with a six-diode rectifier and a delta-connected stator.

4. *TYPES OF ALTERNATORS* Several types of alternators are in use. Figure 26-13 shows an alternator of the type used on Chrysler-built cars, mounted on an engine. Figure 26-14 shows an alternator with built-in voltage regulator.

⊘ 26-9 Alternator Regulator A variety of devices has been used to regulate alternators. When alternators were first introduced, many of the regulators were very complex. They included a field relay, an indicator-light relay, and a voltage regulator. Recently, alternator-regulator systems have been much simplified. For instance, the latest types have the regulator built into the alternator, so that the circuit looks like Fig. 26-15. Basically, the regulator limits the alternator field current as necessary to prevent excess alternator voltage. The stator remains permanently connected to the battery. The diodes prevent the battery from discharging back through the stator when the alternator is not operating. The field (rotor) is connected to the battery only when the alternator is operating. The connection is made through either the field relay or the ignition switch.

Fig. 26-13. Alternator installed on an engine in a car. (*Chrysler Corporation*)

⊘ 26-10 External Regulators for Alternators There are two basic types of alternator regulators, the built-in type (Fig. 26-15) and the external type. Let us look at the external type first. The wiring diagram for a recent external alternator-regulator system, used on Ford cars, is shown in Fig. 26-16. The system includes a field relay and a voltage limiter (or regulator). The system shown has a charge indicator light which comes on when the engine is started. It goes off when the alternator begins to charge the battery. If the light fails to go off, something is wrong. Here is how it all works.

1. *FIELD RELAY* The purpose of the field relay is to connect the alternator field to the battery when the engine is first started. This supplies the alternator field windings (in the rotor) with current so the rotor can build up a magnetic field. When the engine stops, the field relay disconnects the rotor from the battery. This prevents the battery from discharging through the rotor.

The contact points of the field relay are connected in series with a resistance. The resistance is in parallel with the indicator light. When the igni-

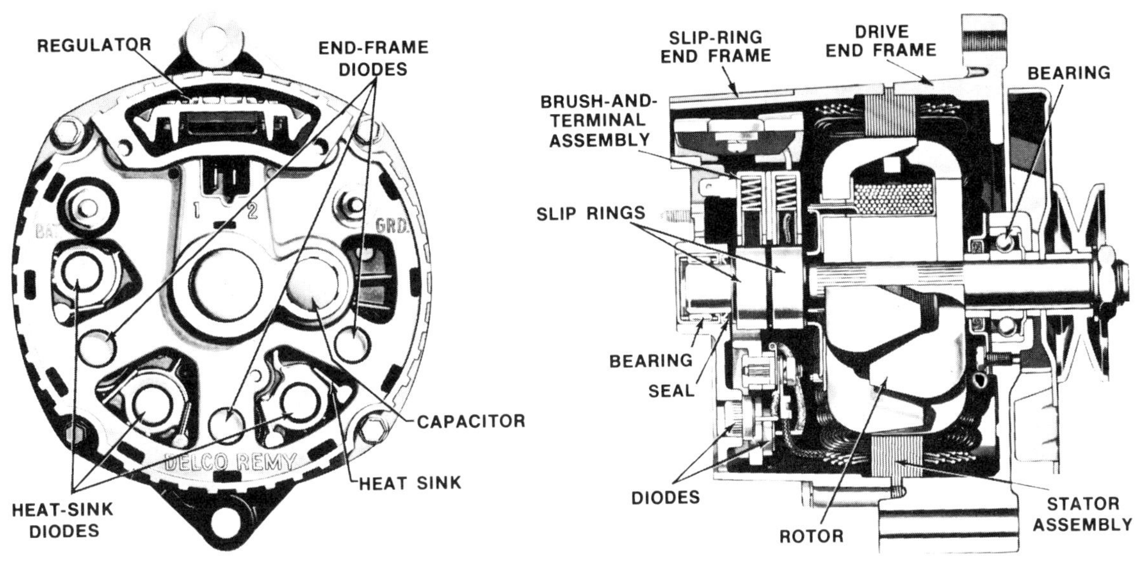

Fig. 26-14. End and sectional views of an alternator with built-in diodes and voltage regulator. The manufacturer calls this a "Delcotron." (*Delco-Remy Division of General Motors Corporation*)

tion switch is turned on, the accessory terminal of the ignition switch is connected to the battery. Now, current can flow through the resistance and the charge indicator light. The indicator light comes on. At the same time, current flows to the rotor, so a magnetic field builds up. As the engine starts, the alternator is driven; it begins to build up voltage. This voltage goes through the field-relay winding. The field-relay winding builds up a magnetic field. This pulls the upper point of the field relay down. The points close. Now, the voltage is the same on both sides of the indicator light. This is because both sides are connected through the closed points. Therefore, no current flows through the light, and the light goes out. This indicates that the alternator is charging the battery.

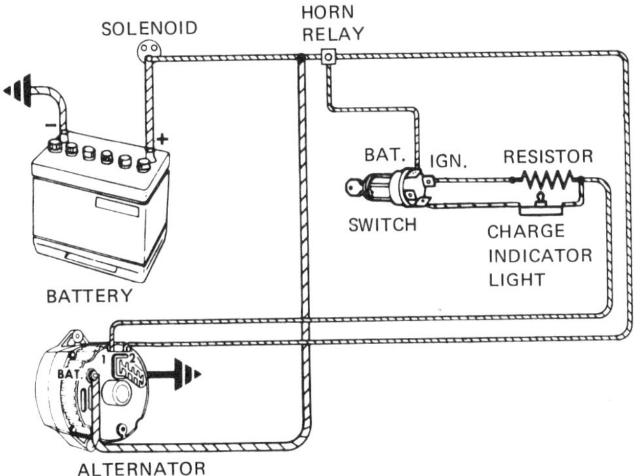

Fig. 26-15. Wiring diagram for a charging system using an alternator with an integral voltage regulator and a charge-indicator light. (*Chevrolet Motor Division of General Motors Corporation*)

2. *FIELD RELAY WITH AMMETER* Figure 26-17 shows the same system with an ammeter instead of a charge indicator light. Notice that the ingition switch is connected differently. It is connected directly to terminal S of the regulator. When the ignition switch is closed, it connects the field relay to the battery. The relay closes and connects the battery to the field terminal of the alternator. (The connection is made through a resistance in the regulator.) This is the same action that takes place in the system shown in Fig. 26-16. The only difference is that the ignition switch in Fig. 26-16 is connected to terminal I. The end effect is the same, however. The alternator field is connected to the battery through a resistance in the regulator. In Fig. 26-17, output from the alternator flows through the ammeter, which indicates the current going to the battery.

3. *VOLTAGE LIMITER* The voltage limiter has a winding that is connected through a resistance across the alternator. Notice that one end of the winding is grounded. The other end is connected through the resistance and the ignition switch (in Fig. 26-16) to the battery. Suppose the voltage increases to the specified maximum. The magnetism of the winding is then great enough to separate the upper contact points. When this happens, a resistance is inserted into the alternator field circuit. The resistance cuts down the field current and, thus, the alternator voltage. As the voltage falls, the magnetic field of the voltage-limiter winding decreases. The upper contacts close, and the whole cycle repeats. The points open and close several hundred times per second to maintain a safe voltage. Suppose now that the voltage creeps up, even with the resistance in the field circuit. Then the magnetism of the winding becomes great enough to close the lower contacts. When this happens, both ends of the field winding

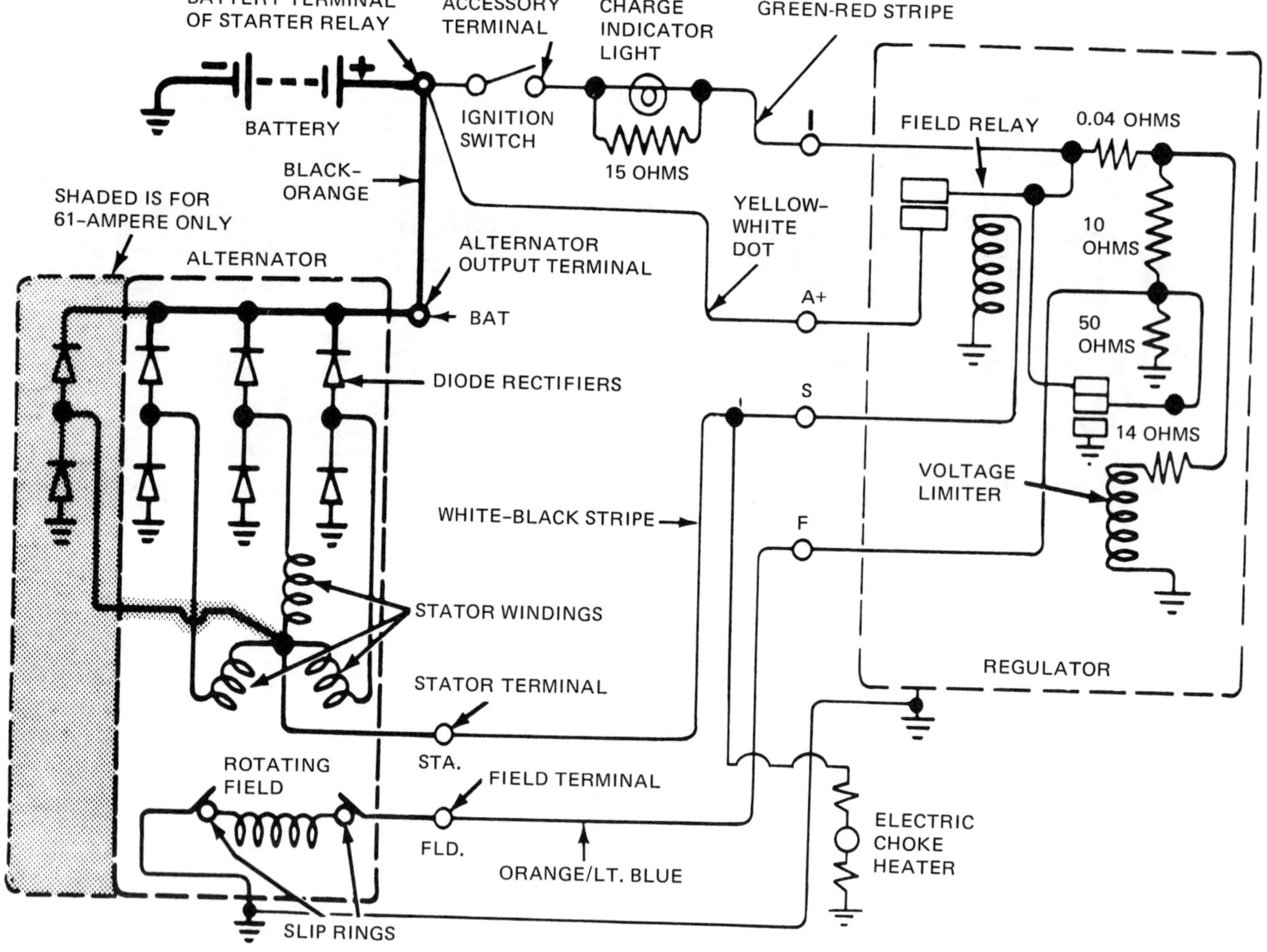

Fig. 26-16. Wiring diagram for a charging system using an alternator, a separately mounted voltage regulator with field relay, and a charge-indicator light. (*Ford Motor Company*)

are grounded. This lowers the alternator field magnetism enough to prevent any further increase in alternator voltage.

When the alternator is running at high speed, its voltage can creep up—even with the resistance in the alternator field. This is the reason for the added point, which grounds both ends of the alternator field circuit. So there are two regulating conditions. For low or medium speed, when only light regulation is required, the upper points open and close. This inserts and removes resistance in the field circuit. At high speeds, with no load applied, the lower points open and close. They ground both ends of the field when they are closed. Figure 26-18 shows the regulator with the cover in place. This regulator is not adjustable. If it does not operate properly, it should be replaced with a new unit.

⊘ 26-11 Alternator with Internal Regulator

Figure 26-15 shows the exterior wiring system for an alternator with a built-in voltage regulator. Figure 26-19 shows the same wiring system with an ammeter instead of the charge indicator light. Because the regulator is built into these alternators (see Fig. 26-14), the external wiring is simple. The regulator is of the solid-state type, using transistors.

Transistors are used in radios, television sets, computers, and many other electronic devices. They are a form of electric valve that can be opened by very small electric currents. When they open, they let a large current through. In the voltage regulator, transistors are used to control the alternator field current. When the alternator voltage is below the maximum, the transistors allow full field current to flow. But when the voltage increases to the maximum, the transistors shut off the field-current flow. As the field current drops, the alternator voltage falls. This falling voltage is a signal to the transistors to let the field current flow again. The action takes place many times each second. It holds the field current to the correct value so the alternator maintains the specified voltage.

Figure 26-20 shows the complete circuit of an alternator and solid-state voltage regulator. The diode trio to the middle right provides direct current

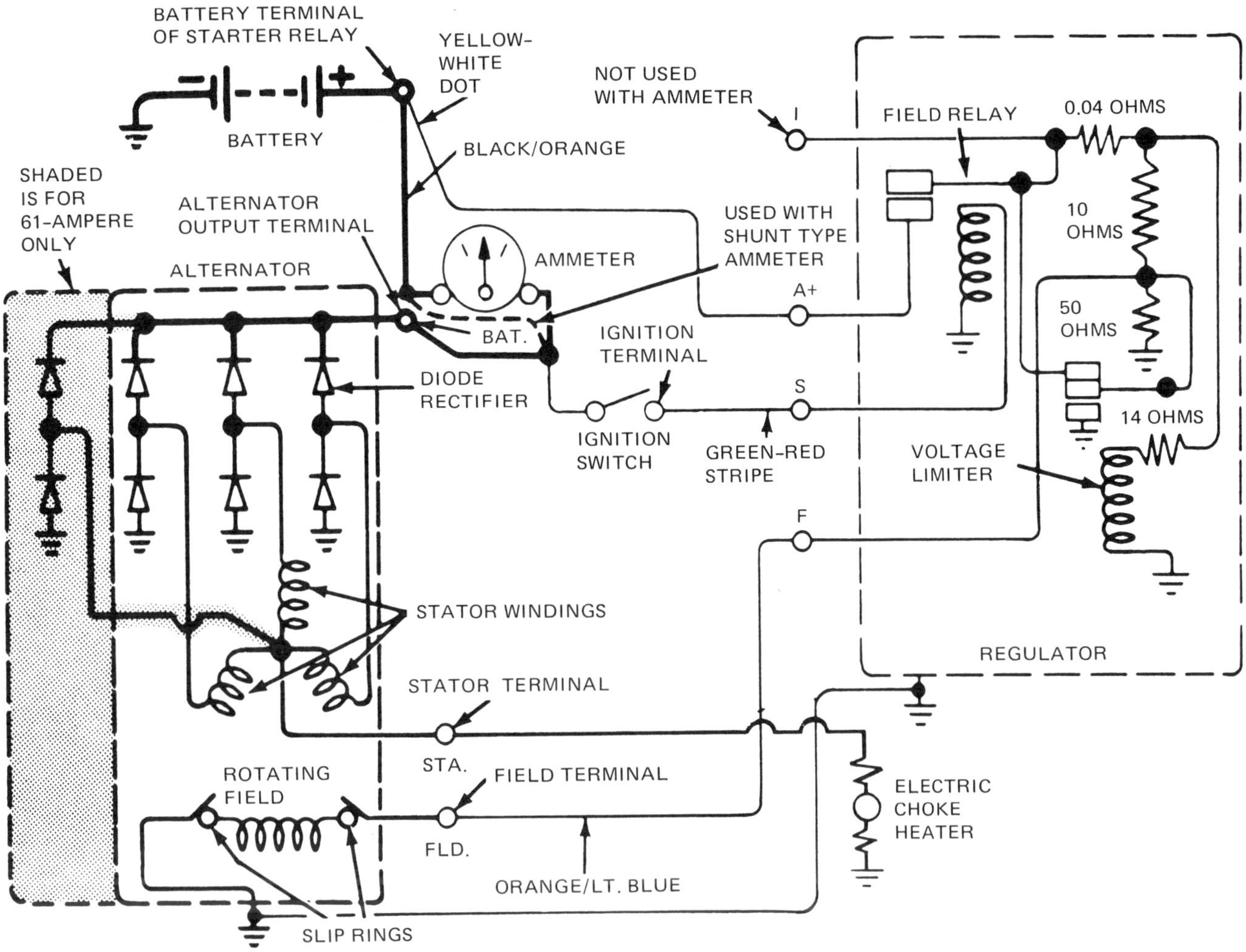

BATTERY TERMINAL OF STARTER RELAY
YELLOW-WHITE DOT
BATTERY
BLACK/ORANGE
NOT USED WITH AMMETER
I
FIELD RELAY
0.04 OHMS
SHADED IS FOR 61-AMPERE ONLY
ALTERNATOR OUTPUT TERMINAL
ALTERNATOR
AMMETER
USED WITH SHUNT TYPE AMMETER
A+
10 OHMS
50 OHMS
BAT.
IGNITION TERMINAL
DIODE RECTIFIER
S
IGNITION SWITCH
GREEN-RED STRIPE
14 OHMS
VOLTAGE LIMITER
F
STATOR WINDINGS
REGULATOR
STATOR TERMINAL
STA.
ROTATING FIELD
FIELD TERMINAL
ELECTRIC CHOKE HEATER
FLD.
ORANGE/LT. BLUE
SLIP RINGS

Fig. 26-17. Wiring diagram for a charging system using an alternator, a separately mounted voltage regulator with field relay, and an ammeter. (*Ford Motor Company*)

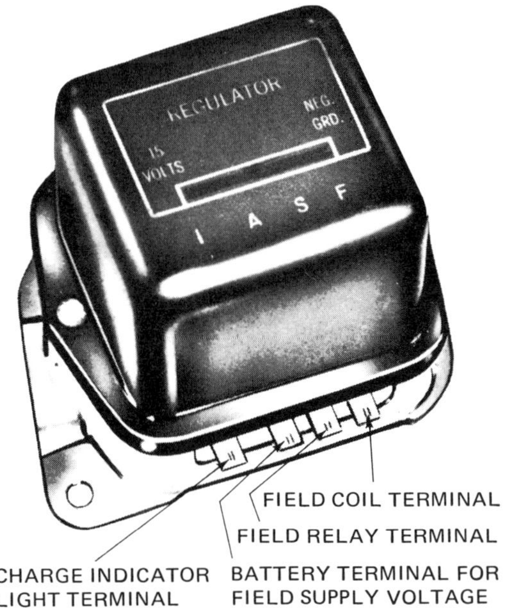

Fig. 26-18. Voltage limiter for the charging system in Fig. 26-17. (*Ford Motor Company*)

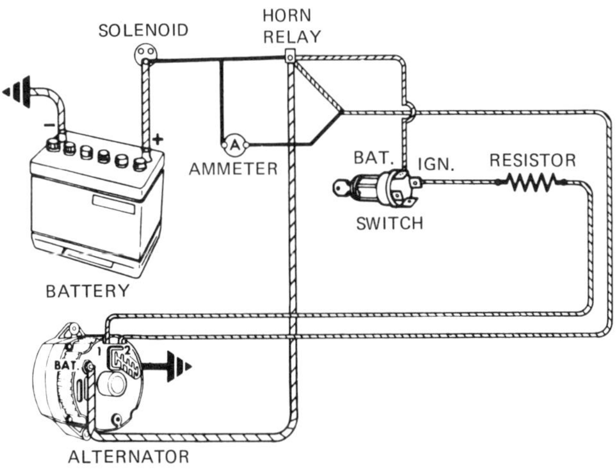

Fig. 26-19. Wiring diagram for a charging system using an alternator with an integral voltage regulator and an ammeter. (*Chevrolet Motor Division of General Motors Corporation*)

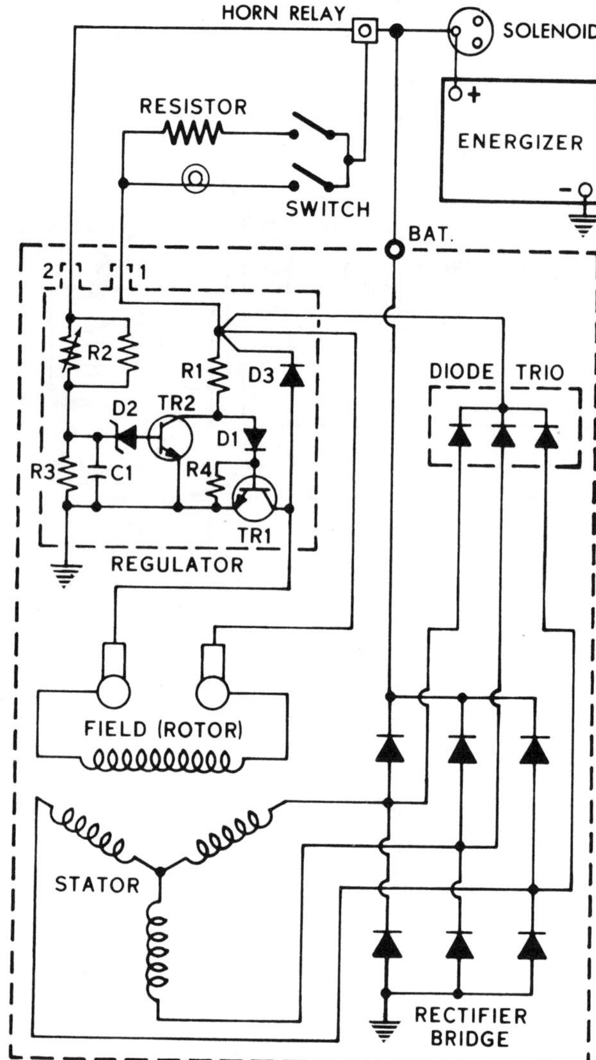

Fig. 26-20. Internal wiring diagram for an alternator with an integral voltage regulator. The external charging circuit is also shown. (*Chevrolet Motor Division of General Motors Corporation*)

to the regulator and alternator field. The regulator is not adjustable. If it becomes defective, it is replaced with a new unit.

CHAPTER 26 CHECKUP

NOTE: Since this is a chapter review test, you should review the chapter before taking the test.

The chapter you have just completed brings you up to date on the latest types of automotive charging systems. The chapters that follow explain how to troubleshoot and service alternators and ac regulators. A good understanding of these units will help you in your service work. Find out how well you remember the essential details of alternator and ac regulator theory by taking the test below.

Completing the Sentences The sentences below are incomplete. After each sentence there are several words or phrases, but only one of them correctly completes the sentence. Write each sentence in your notebook, ending it with the one word or phrase that completes it correctly.

1. No cutout relay is needed to prevent battery discharge through the alternator when the engine is not running. This is taken care of by (*a*) transistor action, (*b*) diode action, (*c*) ignition-switch action.
2. The alternators described in the chapter do not need current regulators because they are: (*a*) controlled by the field relay, (*b*) connected through the ignition switch, (*c*) self-limiting.
3. Alternating current is produced in both the dc generator and the alternator. In the alternator, this ac is changed to dc by: (*a*) diodes, (*b*) the field relay, (*c*) the voltage regulator, (*d*) the current regulator.
4. One difference between dc generators and alternators is that, in the alternator, the conductors in which current is induced: (*a*) are in the armature, (*b*) rotate, (*c*) are stationary.
5. In most alternators, the magnetic field is produced by: (*a*) stationary field coils, (*b*) the stator windings, (*c*) field coils in the rotor.
6. In the alternator, output regulation is achieved by varying the: (*a*) field current, (*b*) speed, (*c*) stator current.
7. The usual number of diodes in the alternator is: (*a*) two, (*b*) three, (*c*) four, (*d*) six.
8. The heat sink is located in the: (*a*) rotor, (*b*) stator, (*c*) end frame.
9. The typical automotive alternator is: (*a*) one-phase, (*b*) two-phase, (*c*) three-phase, (*d*) four-phase
10. In the alternator with stationary field coils, magnetic-field movement is achieved by: (*a*) the vibrating contacts, (*b*) magnets in the rotor, (*c*) stator action.
11. The alternator field is connected to the battery through the field relay or: (*a*) the ignition switch, (*b*) an indicator relay, (*c*) the regulator.
12. The ac vibrating voltage regulators described in the chapter have: (*a*) one set of contacts, (*b*) two sets of contacts, (*c*) no contacts.
13. When the upper contacts close in the ac voltage regulator described in the chapter, the: (*a*) stator is grounded, (*b*) resistance is shorted out, (*c*) field circuit is grounded.
14. In the fully transistorized regulator, field current is controlled by: (*a*) contact points, (*b*) diodes, (*c*) transistors.
15. The alternator with the built-in regulator requires, in addition to a good ground connection: (*a*) only one lead, (*b*) two leads, (*c*) three leads.

Reviewing the Alternator and Regulator In the following, you are asked for descriptions relating to the construction and operation of alternators and ac regulators. If any question stumps you, turn back into the chapter and reread the pages that clear up the problem. Write your descriptions in your notebook, but don't copy from the book. Write as though you were talking to a friend.

1. Describe the operation of the alternator, and point out the difference between the alternator and the dc generator.
2. What is a heat sink, and what is its purpose?
3. Explain how a diode rectifies.
4. Make a drawing of a three-phase Y-connected alternator with six diodes. Explain how the diodes rectify the ac from the stator.
5. Explain why the alternator requires a regulator.
6. The charging circuit using an alternator does not require a cutout relay. Why not?
7. The alternator does not require a current regulator. Why not?
8. Explain how the ac voltage regulator works. What is the purpose of the lower contacts? Of the upper contacts?
9. What is the purpose of the field relay? How does it work?
10. Explain how the regulator with a transistor and contact points works.

SUGGESTIONS FOR FURTHER STUDY

You can learn more about alternators and ac regulators by studying the actual units and the shop manuals put out by their manufacturers. Either your school automotive shop or a local friendly automotive service station will probably have units that you can examine. They should also have service manuals describing how the units work. Be sure to write, in your notebook, any important facts you find.

chapter 27

CHARGING-SYSTEM SERVICE

Several simple checks can be made on alternators and charging circuits to locate troubles. They are covered in this chapter, along with the servicing procedures for alternators.

⊘ 27-1 Testing Alternator-Regulator Systems Many late-model cars use solid-state alternator regulators. As we mentioned in ⊘ 26-11, General Motors cars now have built-in solid-state voltage regulators (see Fig. 26-14). Chrysler cars have separately mounted solid-state voltage regulators. Such regulators use transistors to control alternator voltage. The late-model cars manufactured by the Ford Motor Company have electromechanical regulators. These are sealed and cannot be adjusted. Thus, regulator adjustments, once an important part of automotive service, are not required on late-model cars. However, basic checks of the charging system are still necessary to pinpoint troubles.

Most charging-system troubles show up as faulty indicator lamps, undercharged batteries, or overcharged batteries. Let us now look at typical testing procedures, as outlined by car manufacturers.

⊘ 27-2 Chevrolet Charging-System Diagnosis This procedure is typical for General Motors cars using alternators with built-in voltage regulators. Figures 26-15 and 26-19 show the two circuits for this system. One includes an indicator light, and the other an ammeter. Observe the following precautions when working on the charging system:

1. Never attempt to polarize the alternator. This can cause serious damage to the system.
2. Do not short across or ground any of the terminals in the charging circuit. (Exceptions are given in the instructions that follow.)
3. Never operate the alternator with the output terminal disconnected. The alternator voltage could go high enough to burn out the alternator.
4. Make sure the alternator and battery are connected correctly, according to their polarity.
5. When connecting a booster battery, connect negative to negative and positive to positive, as explained in ⊘ 24-4. Observe the cautions outlined in ⊘ 24-4.

As a final step in the checking procedure, look the system over carefully. Check all connections, the wiring, and the alternator mounting. Check the drive belt for condition and tension (see ⊘ 27-9). The procedures for checking for indicator-light, undercharge, and overcharge troubles follow.

⊘ 27-3 Indicator-Lamp Circuit Check In normal operation, the lamp should light when the engine is being cranked. It should go off when the engine starts. The lamp should be off when the ignition switch is off. There are three troubles that require checking.

1. *SWITCH OFF, LAMP ON* Disconnect the two leads from the alternator No. 1 and No. 2 terminals. If the lamp stays on, there is a short between these two leads. If the lamp goes off, the short is inside the alternator, in the diodes. Replace the rectifier bridge which carries the diodes. This requires disassembly of the alternator.

2. *SWITCH ON, LAMP OFF, ENGINE STOPPED* This can be caused by a burned-out indicator light bulb. If the bulb is ok, the condition also can be caused by diode defects, by a short between the leads to the No. 1 and No. 2 terminals, by reversal of the two leads to the terminals, or by an open in the circuit. An open can cause a run-down battery. To find the trouble if an open is suspected, proceed as follows.

   1. Connect a voltmeter from the No. 2 terminal to ground. If your reading is zero, there is an open between the terminal and the battery. If a reading is obtained, go to step 2.
   2. With ignition switch on and No. 1 and No. 2 terminal leads disconnected, momentarily ground the No. 1 terminal lead.

CAUTION: Do not ground the No. 2 terminal lead. This directly grounds the positive terminal of the battery. It is a direct short across the battery terminals.

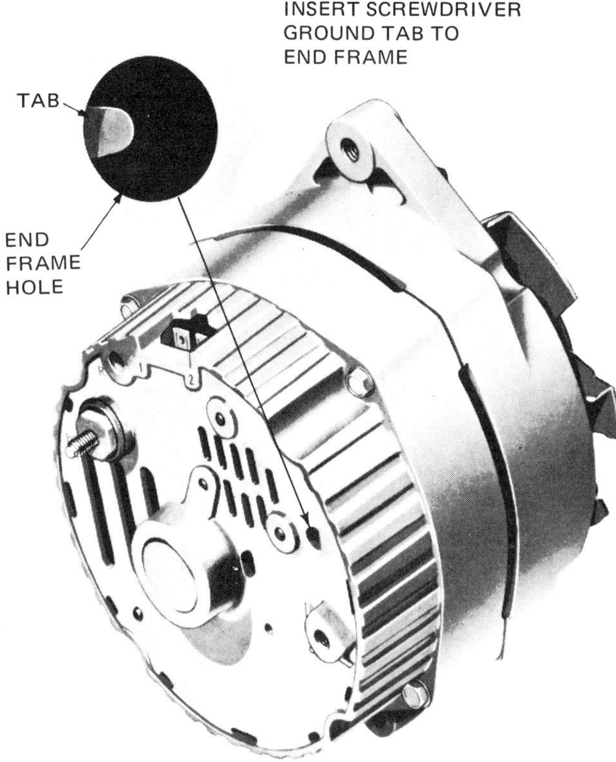

Fig. 27-1. Alternator, showing the test hole. A screwdriver is inserted in the test hole to ground the field circuit. The screwdriver should be pushed in only far enough to touch the tab. If pushed in too far, it could damage the alternator. (*Chevrolet Motor Division of General Motors Corporation*)

3. If the lamp does not light with No. 1 terminal lead grounded, check for a blown fuse or fusible link, a burned-out bulb, or an open in the No. 1 terminal lead.
4. If the lamp lights, unground the No. 1 terminal lead. Reconnect the two leads to the No. 1 and No. 2 terminals. Insert a screwdriver into the test hole shown in Fig. 27-1. This grounds the field winding, and the lamp should come on.
5. If the lamp does not light, check the connection between the wiring harness and the No. 1 terminal of the alternator. Other possible troubles could be with the brushes, slip rings, and field winding in the rotor. Checking these requires removal and disassembly of the alternator.
6. If the lamp lights and a voltmeter reading was obtained in step 1, replace the regulator in the alternator.

3. *SWITCH ON, LAMP ON, ENGINE RUNNING* There is a problem in the alternator. Check it as outlined in ⊘ 27-4.

⊘ 27-4 Battery Undercharged This can be caused by frequent stops and starts, accessories or lights left on, a loose drive belt (see ⊘ 27-9), an old battery that will not accept a charge normally, or defects in the wiring or connections. If all these check out correctly, check the alternator output as follows:

1. Disconnect the battery ground cable. Connect an ammeter into the circuit at the BAT (battery) terminal of the alternator. Reconnect the ground cable.
2. Turn on some accessories to load the battery. The radio, high-beam headlights, windshield wipers, and heater motor at high speed all add to the load. Connect a carbon pile (a heavy variable resistance) across the battery.
3. Operate the engine at moderate speed. Adjust the carbon pile to get the maximum alternator output.
4. If the output is within 10 percent of the rated output stamped on the alternator, the alternator is okay. Recheck the circuit connections, wiring, etc.
5. If the output is not within 10 percent of the rated value, ground the field winding by inserting a screwdriver into the test hole (Fig. 27-1). If the output now increases, the trouble is in the regulator. It must be replaced. If the output does not increase, the trouble is in the diodes, field winding, or stator. The alternator must be removed from the engine and disassembled to find the trouble.

⊘ 27-5 Battery Overcharged This condition requires frequent additions of water to the battery. Overcharging shortens the life of the battery and the electrical accessories. Connect a voltmeter from the alternator No. 2 terminal to ground. If the reading is zero, this lead circuit is open. If the voltmeter reads okay (battery voltage), the problem is in the alternator. It must be removed from the engine for further checking. This involves disassembly, so the field winding in the rotor can be checked for shorts.

⊘ 27-6 Plymouth-Chrysler Checking Procedures Three test are outlined in the Plymouth-Chrysler service manual. They are the charging-circuit test, alternator-output test, and voltage-regulator test.

1. *CHARGING-CIRCUIT RESISTANCE TEST* A voltmeter, an ammeter, and a carbon-pile resistor are connected as in Fig. 27-2. Then the engine speed and carbon pile are adjusted to maintain a 20-A flow in the circuit. The voltmeter reading should not exceed 0.7 V. If it is higher, there is excessive resistance, due to bad connections or wiring.

2. *CURRENT-OUTPUT TEST* Connect a voltmeter, an ammeter, and a carbon-pile resistor as in Fig. 27-2. Start the engine, and operate it at idle. Increase the engine speed, and adjust the carbon pile a little at a time. Continue this until a speed of 1,250 rpm and a voltmeter reading of 15 V are obtained.

CAUTION: Do not allow the voltage to go above 16 V.

If the ammeter reads within the specified limits for the alternator being checked, the alternator is satisfactory. If the reading is low, remove the alternator from the engine for further checking.

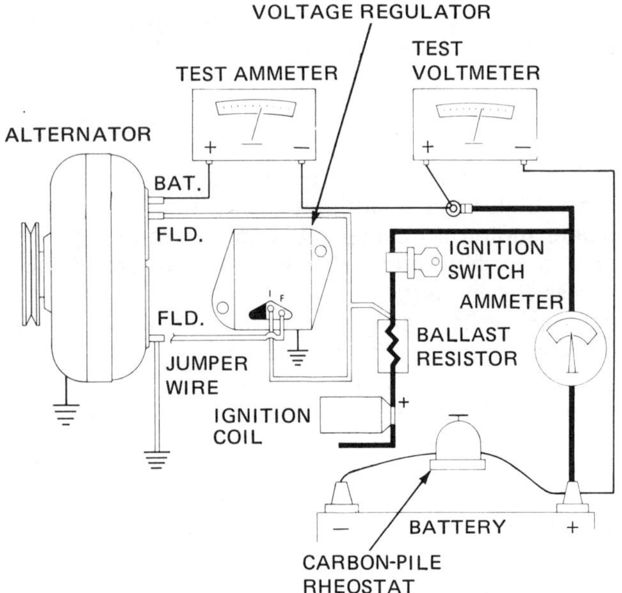

Fig. 27-2. Test meters and carbon-pile rheostat connected for a resistance test of the charging circuit. Note that the lead has been disconnected from the alternator field terminal (FLD). The terminal has been grounded with a jumper wire. (*Chrysler Corporation*)

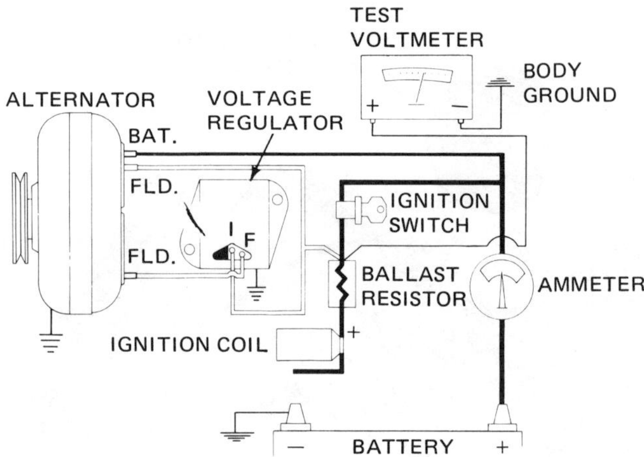

Fig. 27-3. Voltmeter connected for a test of the voltage regulator. (*Chrysler Corporation*)

3. *VOLTAGE-REGULATOR TEST* Connect a voltmeter as shown in Fig. 27-3. Make sure the battery is in good condition and charged. Start and run the engine at 1,250 rpm (as measured with a tachometer, which is described in Chap. 33) with all lights and accessories turned off. Compare the voltmeter reading with the specifications for the alternator being checked.

If the voltage is low or fluctuates, check the regulator ground to make sure it is good. Then turn off the ignition switch, and disconnect the voltage-regulator connectors. Check the battery voltage at the wiring-harness terminal. If it tests okay, the trouble is in the regulator. It should be replaced.

If the voltage is high, turn off the ignition switch. Then disconnect the voltage-regulator connector. Check the battery voltage with a voltmeter at the wiring-harness terminal. If the voltage reads okay, replace the regulator.

NOTE: Plymouth has a special electronic voltage-regulator tester (Tester Tool C-4133) that simplifies the testing procedure.

⊘ 27-7 Ford Checking Procedures The charging circuit can be checked either with meters or with the special Ford tester (ARE 20-22 tester) shown in Fig. 27-4. To use the tester, first disconnect the wiring-harness plug from the regulator. Connect the tester into the circuit at the regulator. The tester has a plug to connect to the wiring harness, and a plug to connect to the regulator. With the tester connected, start the engine and operate it at about 2,000 rpm. Then make two tests, one with the test switch at A, and one with the switch at B. Then compare the pattern of lights on the tester with the test chart. Figure 27-5 shows some of the light patterns and what they mean. The complete test chart, showing all light patterns, is given in the Ford shop manual.

Ford outlines a second procedure in their shop manual. It uses a tester that has a voltmeter, an ammeter, and a carbon pile (master control). This tester is shown in Fig. 27-6, connected for an alternator-output test.

⊘ 27-8 Chrysler-Plymouth Alternator Service If the checks outlined earlier point to alternator trouble, the alternator should be removed for further checks and service.

CAUTION: Always disconnect the battery ground strap from the battery terminal before disconnecting the leads from the alternator.

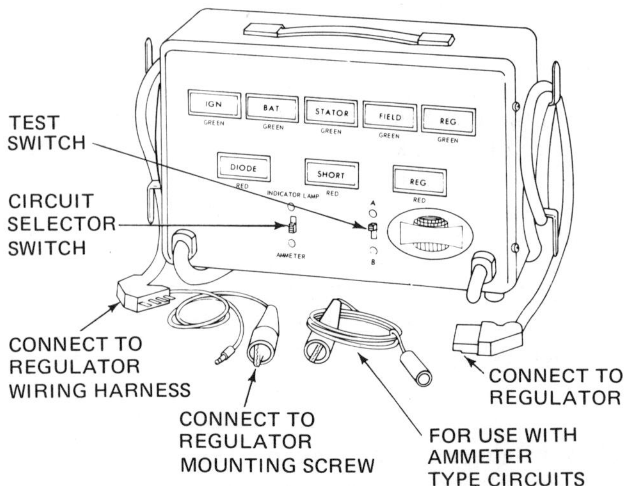

Fig. 27-4. The ARE 20-22 tester, used to test the alternator. (*Ford Motor Company*)

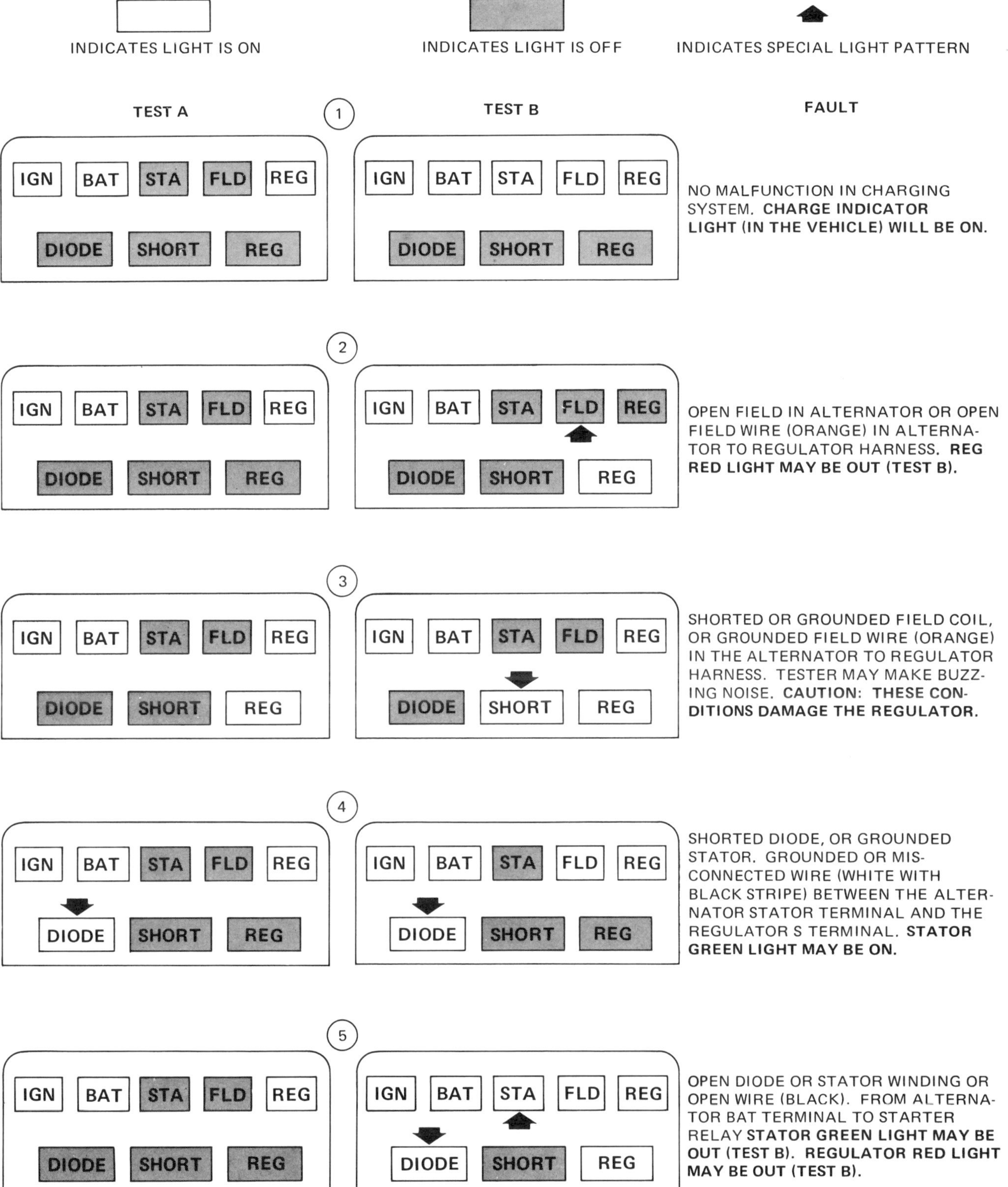

Fig. 27-5. Part of the ARE 20-22 tester test chart. (*Ford Motor Company*)

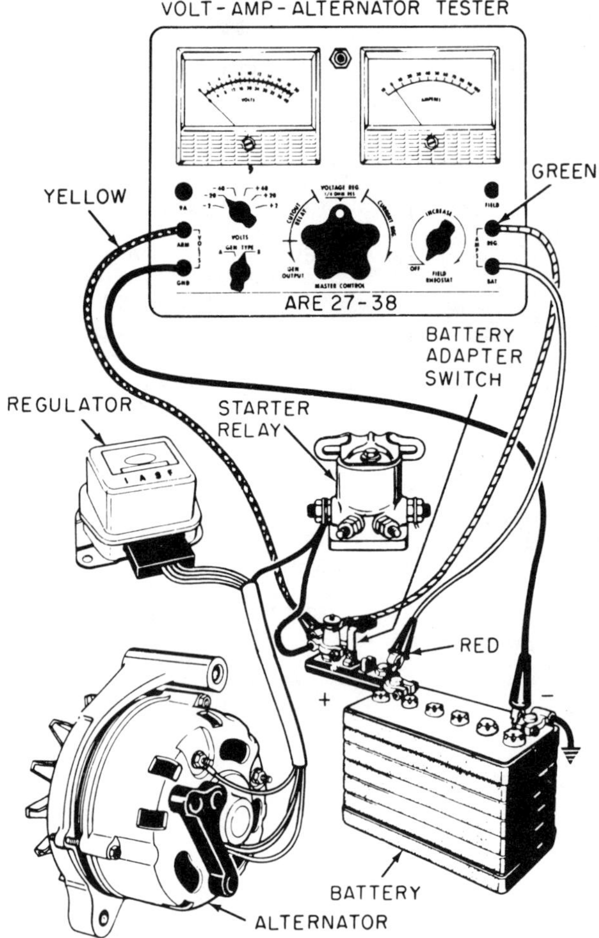

Fig. 27-6. Voltage-amperage alternator tester connected to make an output test of the alternator. (*Ford Motor Company*)

1. *BENCH TESTS* Rotor field-coil draw, field-circuit-ground check, and diode checks are three tests to be made with the alternator on the bench.

a. *Field-Coil Draw* Connect the test-ammeter positive lead to the positive terminal of a fully charged battery. Connect the negative lead of the ammeter to the field terminal of the alternator. Connect a jumper lead to the negative terminal of the battery and to the end shield of the alternator. On units with two field terminals, connect the second field terminal to the negative [grounded] terminal of the battery. Slowly turn the rotor by hand. The field coil should be 2.3 to 2.7 amps (at 12 volts). A low current draw indicates high resistance in the field circuit. This may be due to brushes not seating well on slip rings, dirty or worn slip rings, or poor connections in the field coils. Excessive current draw indicates a possible shorted field coil or grounded field circuit.

b. *Testing Field Circuit for Grounds* Remove the ground brush (Fig. 27-7) on earlier models (on late models, both brushes are insulated). Use a test light and check with prods from the insulated-brush terminal to the end shield. If the light goes on, there is a ground. Check further by removing the insulated-brush assembly (Fig. 27-8). Then separate the end shields by taking out the three through bolts and prying between the stator and drive-end shield with a screwdriver (Fig. 27-9). Check with test-light prods between one slip ring and the end shield. If the light goes on, the rotor has an internal ground. If the light does not go on, the ground is in the insulated-brush assembly.

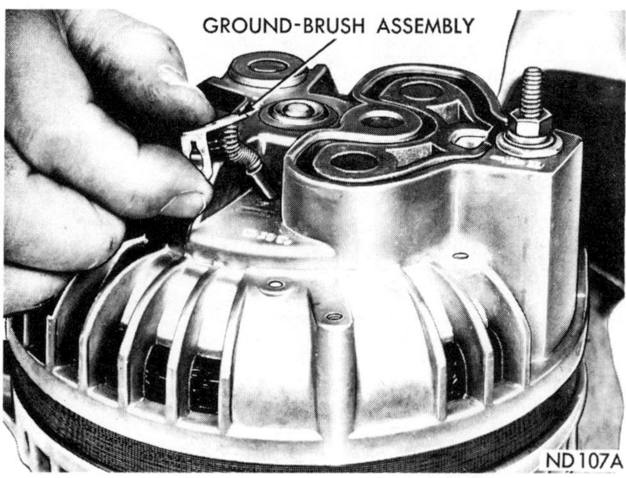

Fig. 27-7. Removing the ground brush from an alternator. The later-model, isolated-field alternator does not have a ground brush. Instead, both brushes are insulated. (*Chrysler Corporation*)

NOTE: The later model of the Chrysler-Plymouth alternator has an isolated field. That is, it has two field terminals, and neither of the brushes is grounded in the alternator. This alternator is used

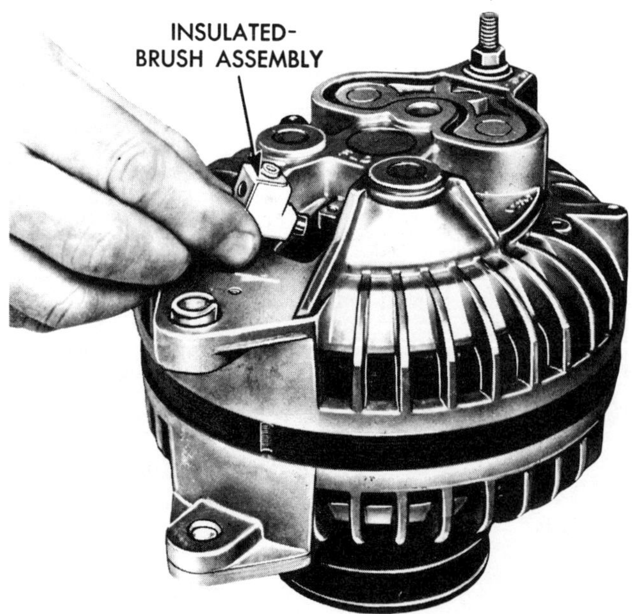

Fig. 27-8. Removing the insulated brush from an alternator. (*Chrysler Corporation*)

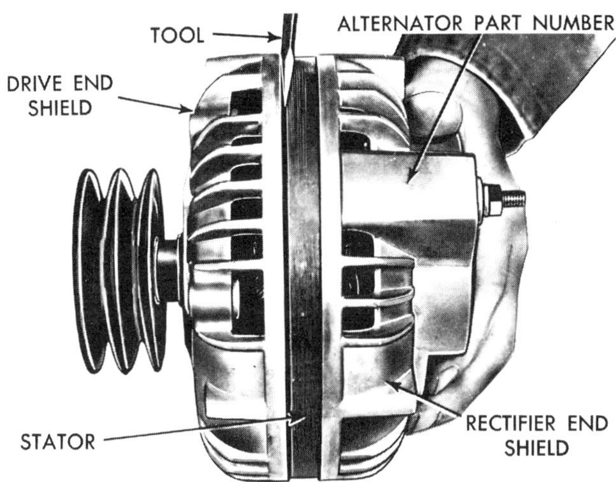

Fig. 27-9. Separating the drive end shield from the stator. (*Chrysler Corporation*)

with a transistorized voltage regulator which is not adjustable. To test the field circuit for grounds, it is not necessary to remove either brush because both are insulated.

c. *Testing Diodes with C-3829 Tester* If the special Chrysler testing tool C-3829 is available (Fig. 27-10), the diodes may be tested without disconnecting the leads. The rectifier end shield, which contains the diodes, must be removed to check the diodes. First, the ground and insulated brushes must be removed (Figs. 27-7 and 27-8). Then, the three through bolts must be taken out and the end shields separated (Fig. 27-9). Next, plug the tester into a 110-volt source and place the rectifier end shield on an insulated surface. Clip the test lead to the alternator battery terminal and touch the exposed bare metal connections of each of the positive case rectifiers (diodes) with the test prod (Fig. 27-10).

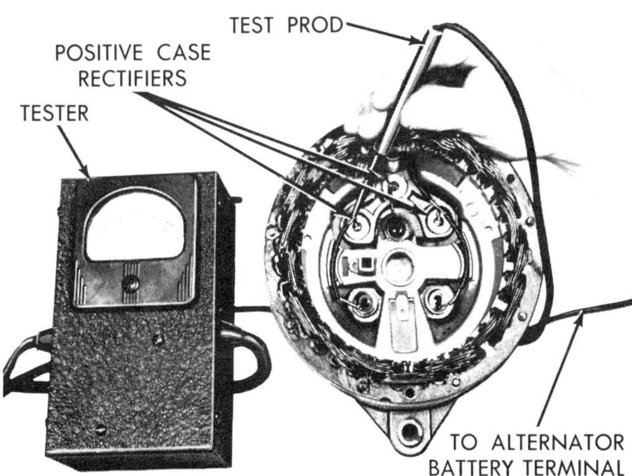

Fig. 27-10. Testing positive diodes with a special tester. (*Chrysler Corporation*)

CAUTION: Do not break the sealing around the rectifier lead wires. This sealing protects against corrosion. Touch the prod to the exposed metal connection nearest the rectifier.

Meter readings should be $1\frac{3}{4}$ amps or more. Readings should be about the same for all three rectifiers. With two good diodes and one shorted diode, the readings at the good ones will be low, and the shorted diode will read zero. If one diode is open, it will read about 1 amp, with the other two reading okay.

Use the tester to check the negative rectifiers (diodes). The same procedure is used, but the meter will read on the opposite side of the scale from its reading when checking the positive diodes.

NOTE: Locations of the diodes are different in different alternator models. For example, Fig. 27-11 shows their location in the alternator that uses the electronic control unit. This alternator has two field terminals, both insulated.

d. *Testing Diodes with Test Light* If the C-3829 tester is not available, the stator leads at the Y connections must be cut as close to the Y as possible. Then each diode should be checked with a 12-volt battery and a number 67 bulb (4 candlepower), as shown in Fig. 27-12. Touch one probe to the outer case of the diode and the other to the wire in the center of the diode, as shown. Then reverse the probes. The light should go on in one direction but not in the other. If it lights in both directions, the diode is shorted. If it does not light in either direction, the diode is open. Replace-

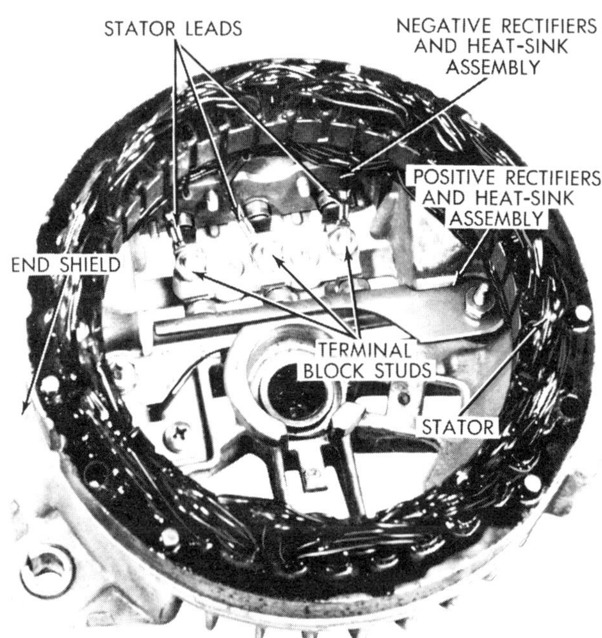

Fig. 27-11. Rectifier end shield and stator assembly. (*Chrysler Corporation*)

Fig. 27-12. Testing diodes with a low-voltage test light and battery. (*Chrysler Corporation*)

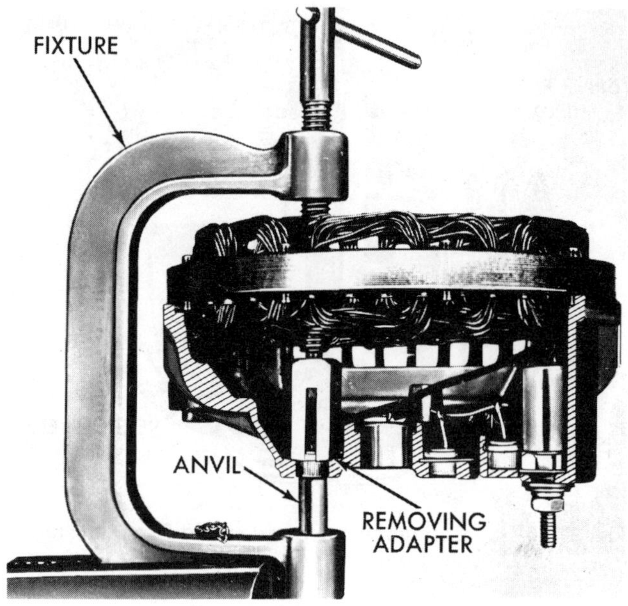

Fig. 27-14. Removing a diode with a special adapter. The shield has been cut away in the picture so that the adapter can be seen. (*Chrysler Corporation*)

ment of diodes is explained in a following paragraph.

e. *Testing Stator* To test the stator with a test light, unsolder the diode leads. Do not blow off melted solder with air. Particles could get into the diodes and short them out.

Use a low-voltage test light as shown in Fig. 27-12, touching one lead to the stator pole frame and checking with a test prod to each of the three stator leads (Fig. 27-13). If the light goes on, the stator is grounded and must be replaced.

Test stator windings for continuity, or complete circuit, by connecting one test prod to all three stator leads at the Y connection, and touch each of the other stator leads with the test prod. If the light fails to go on, the circuit is open and the stator will require replacement.

f. *Replacing Diodes* A special tool (removing adapter) must be used to remove the diodes on the earlier alternator models. Clamp the tool in a vise (Fig. 27-14). Support the end shield on the clamp anvil under the rectifier to be removed, as shown. Make sure the bore of the tool completely surrounds the diode. Turn the screw to force the diode out. To install a new diode, make sure it is squarely in the mounting hole and use the special

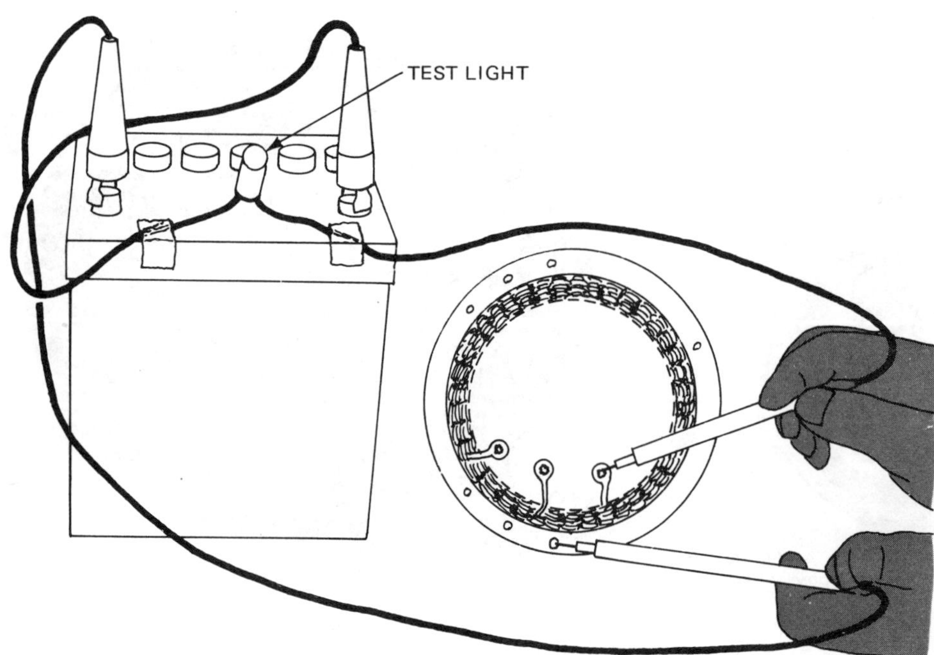

Fig. 27-13. Testing a stator with a low-voltage test light. (*Chrysler Corporation*)

installing support (in place of the removing adapter) with the same clamp shown in Fig. 27-14. Apply pressure with the screw to force the diode in until the collar of the diode bottoms against the casting.

CAUTION: Never drive the diode in with a hammer. Any mechanical shock—even dropping the diode—could ruin it.

Resolder the connections with rosin-core solder. Avoid overheating the diode, as this could ruin it. Quickly cool the soldered connection with a cloth dampened with water.

On later alternator models with two insulated field terminals, the two heat sinks, holding three diodes each, are removed as assemblies. (Figure 27-15 shows the removal of the negative rectifier (with three diodes) and heat-sink assembly from the end shield.) This means that four hex-head screws must be removed. Then two nuts and washers are removed to take off the positive rectifier (with three diodes) and the heat-sink assembly.

2. *ALTERNATOR DISASSEMBLY AND REASSEMBLY* We have already described most of the steps required to disassemble the alternator. Additional steps include removing the pulley and bearings and replacing the old rotor slip rings with new ones.

a. *Disassembly* (*Fig. 27-16*) Further disassembly steps, after the rectifier end shield has been removed (Fig. 27-9), follow:

Remove the pulley with a puller (Fig. 27-17). Pry the drive-end-bearing spring retainer from the end shield with a screwdriver (Fig. 27-18). Support the end shield and tap the rotor shaft with a plastic hammer to remove the rotor. The drive-end bearing must be removed, if it is to be replaced, with a puller.

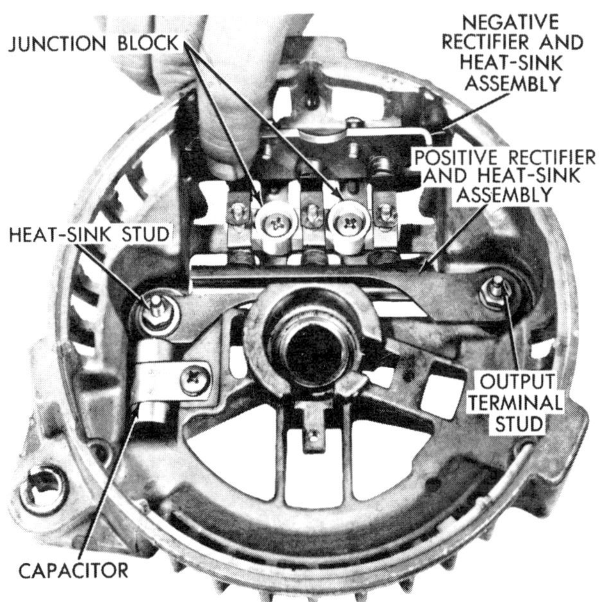

Fig. 27-15. Removing the negative rectifiers and heat-sink assembly. (*Chrysler Corporation*)

The output terminal, capacitor, heat-sink insulator, and heat sink are held in place by the terminal nuts and washers. Remove these nuts to separate the parts.

If the needle bearing in the rectifier end shield requires replacement, support the shield and press the bearing out with special tools.

b. *Inspecting Parts* Electrical checking of the various parts has already been covered. Inspect the various parts for damage and wear. Worn or pitted slip rings should be replaced as noted in a following paragraph. Worn bearings should be replaced. Check for burned insulation, poor soldering at connections, and cracked or damaged housings. Replace all damaged parts.

CAUTION: Never clean the rotor, stator, bearings, or rectifier parts with solvent. This would probably ruin them. Instead, wipe them with a clean cloth.

c. *Replacing Slip Rings* If the slip rings require replacement, remove the plastic grease retainer from the rotor and unsolder and unwind the field-coil leads from the slip-ring lugs (Fig. 27-19). Do not break the leads. Use a chisel to cut the slip rings at opposite points (180 degrees apart). Break the plastic insulator and remove the old rings. Clean the rotor of all old ring parts. Move the leads out of the way and position new slip rings in proper alignment with the leads. Use a special tool to press the rings down into place. The field lead to the insulated slip ring should be clear at the access hole through the fan and pole piece. Tin the leads and wrap them around the slip-ring lugs, starting from the lug shoulders and winding outward. Solder with rosin-core solder.

Test for grounds with a low-voltage test light, placing one prod against a ring and the other against the rotor pole piece. If the light goes on, the slip rings are grounded and must be replaced. Test the rotor for complete circuit by putting prods on the two rings. The light should go on. If it does not, the circuit is open. Check for broken leads. If the open is not evident and repairable, replace the rotor assembly.

d. *Reassembly* On reassembly, use special bearing tools to install new bearings if required. After the drive-end shield—with bearing-spring retainer and bearing—has been installed on the rotor, press the pulley onto the rotor shaft. Support the lower end of the rotor shaft on the press table so pressure is applied to the shaft through the pulley and not through the end shield.

Install the heat-sink insulator, capacitor, and terminal screw with insulating washer, lock washers, and nuts. Put the stator and rectifier-end shield into place on the rotor and drive-end shield, pushing the rotor shaft through the rectifier-end-shield bearing. Put the through bolts, washers, and nuts into

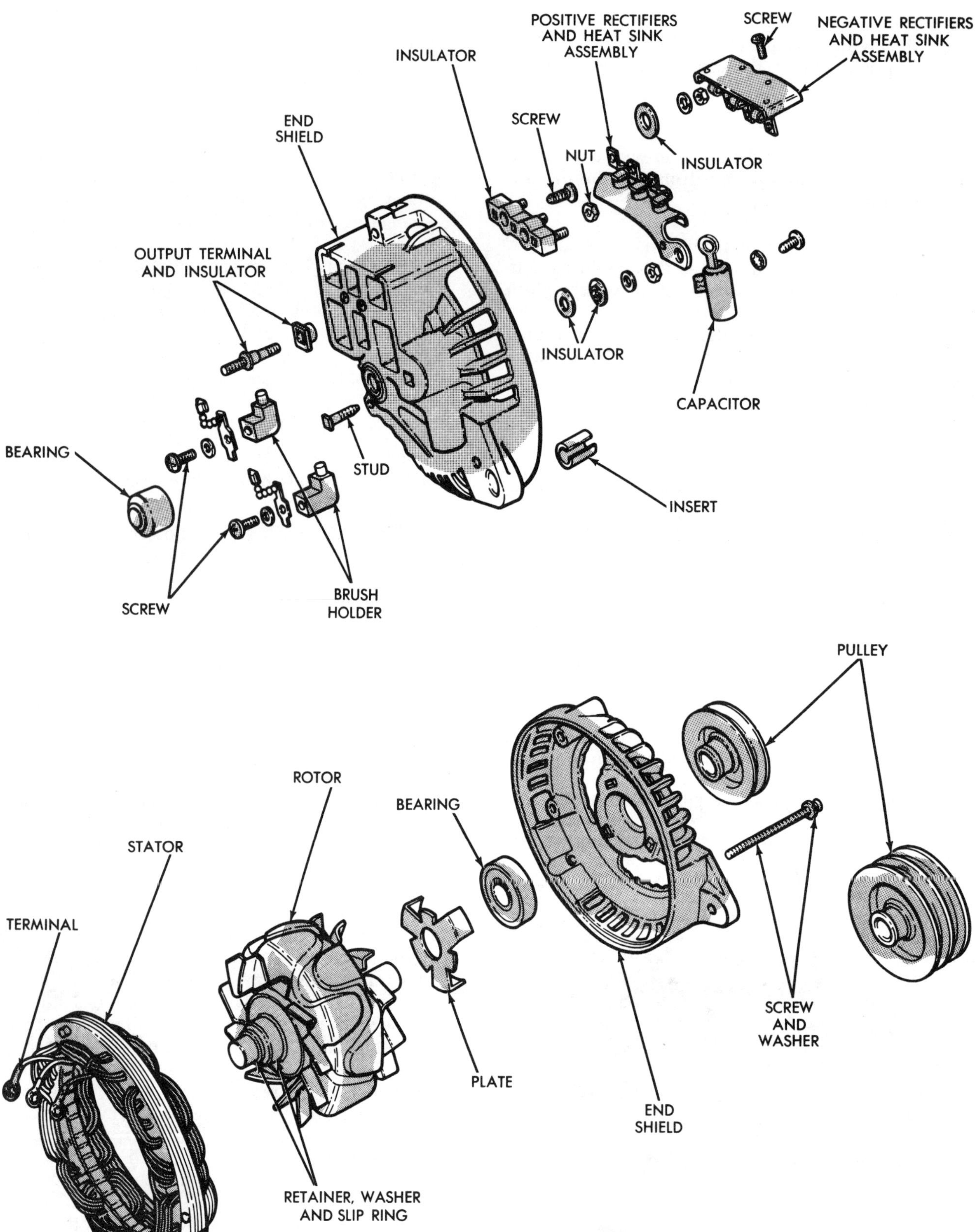

Fig. 27-16. Disassembled view of a late-model alternator. (*Chrysler Corporation*)

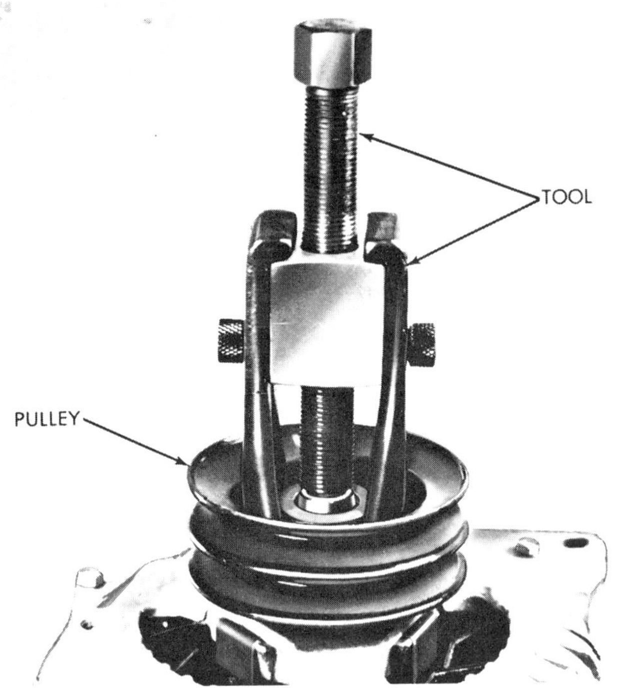

Fig. 27-17. Using a puller to remove the pulley. Turning the screw pulls the pulley off the shaft. (*Chrysler Corporation*)

place and tighten them evenly to 20 to 30 pound-feet [2.8 to 4.2 kg-m].

Install the insulated brush in the end shield, and put the bronze terminal on the plastic holder with the tab of the terminal in the holder recess. Put the nylon washer on the terminal and install the lock washer and attaching screw. Install the ground brush and the attaching screw.

Rotate the pulley slowly by hand to make sure the rotor fans do not hit the diodes, capacitor leads, or stator connections.

Install the alternator on the car, and connect the leads and ground wire. Reconnect the battery

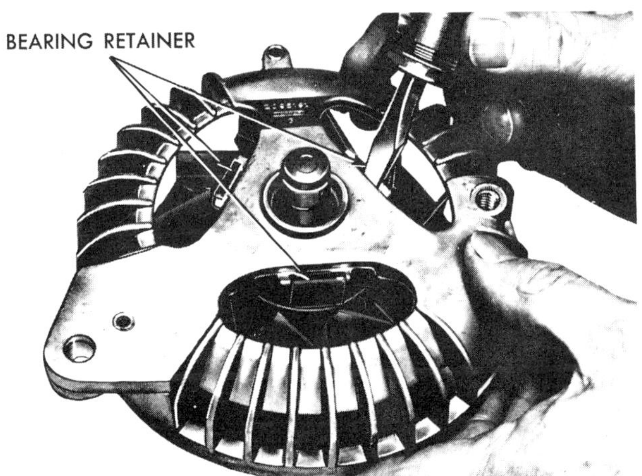

Fig. 27-18. Disengaging the bearing retainer from the end shield. (*Chrysler Corporation*)

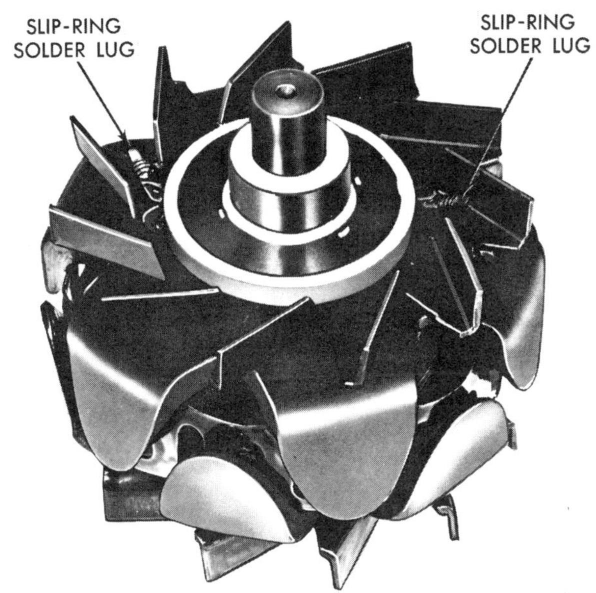

Fig. 27-19. Solder points on the slip rings. (*Chrysler Corporation*)

ground cable, start the engine, and check the alternator output as already described in ⊘ 27-6.

⊘ 27-9 Ford Alternator Service If the checks described earlier indicate alternator trouble, the alternator should be removed for further checking.

NOTE: Always disconnect the battery ground strap from the battery before disconnecting the leads from the alternator.

1. *ALTERNATOR DISASSEMBLY* Figure 27-20 is a disassembled view of the alternator discussed herein. Ford also supplies higher-output alternators. The alternator shown in Fig. 27-20 is disassembled as follows:

1. Mark both end housings with scribe marks so they can be properly realigned on reassembly. Remove the three through bolts and separate the front-end housing and rotor from the stator and rear-end housing.
2. Remove nuts and washers from the rear-end housing and separate the housing from the stator and rectifier assembly.
3. Remove brush-holder mounting screws and take off the holder, brushes, springs, insulator, and terminal.
4. If the bearing requires replacement, support the housing on the inner boss to press it out.
5. If the rectifier assembly is being replaced or the stator is being tested, unsolder the stator leads, using a small (100-watt) soldering iron. Avoid excessive heat.
6. If the rectifier has a molded circuit board, remove the screws from the rectifier by rotating the bolt

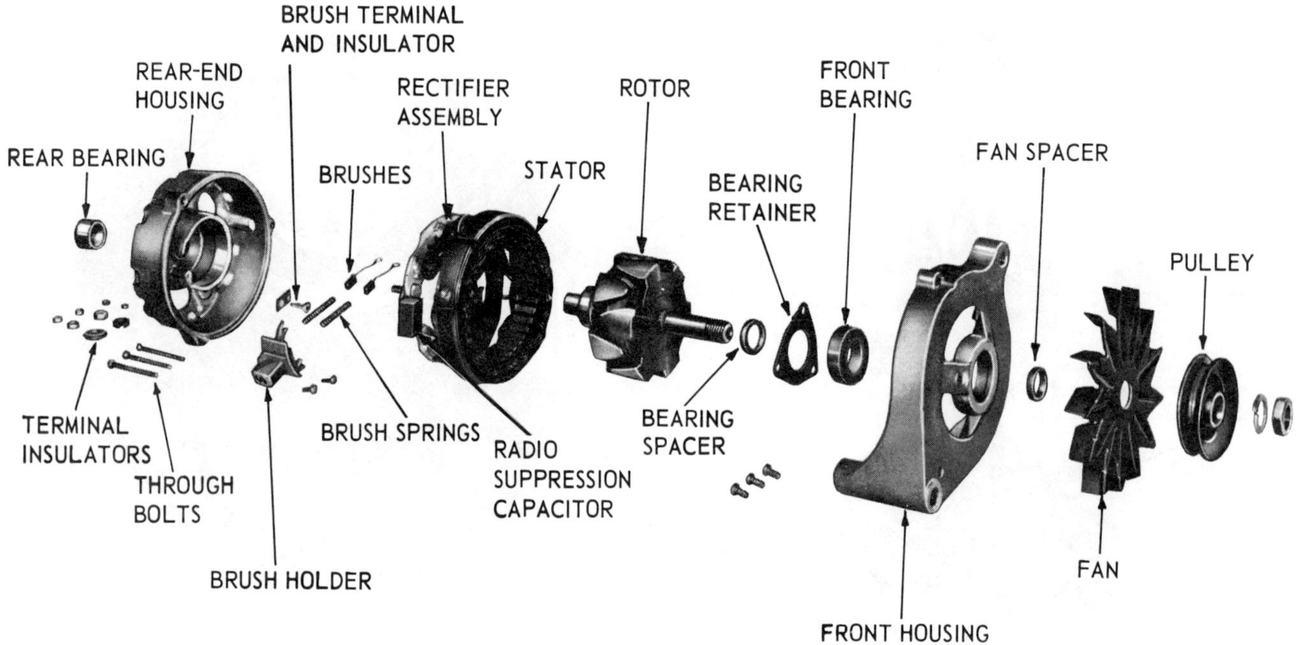

Fig. 27-20. Disassembled view of an alternator. (*Ford Motor Company*)

heads one-quarter turn clockwise to unlock them and then removing the screws (Fig. 27-21). On the type with a fiber circuit board, push the screws out.

7. Remove the drive pulley nut, lock washer, pulley, fan, spacer, rotor, and rotor stop (Fig. 27-22).
8. If the old front bearing is defective, remove the three screws that hold the retainer and remove the retainer. Then support the housing near the boss and press the bearing out.

2. *CLEANING AND INSPECTING PARTS* Never use solvent to clean the rotor, stator, bearings, or rectifier assembly. This could ruin them. Instead, wipe the parts with a clean cloth. Check bearings for wear or loss of lubricant, either of which would require bearing replacement.

Check rear of rotor shaft for roughness or chatter marks. These indicate slippage in the bearing, which would call for rotor replacement.

Replace the pulley if it is out of round or bent.

If the slip rings are rough or pitted, they can be turned down. But do not turn them down below 1.220 inch [31 mm]. These slip rings are not replaceable. If they are damaged, the rotor must be replaced.

Check for stripped threads, poor soldered connections, burned insulation, and cracked housings. Replace defective parts. Resolder poor connections. Avoid excessive heat on diodes.

3. *ELECTRICAL CHECKS* Both before and after the alternator is disassembled, the various components—diodes, rotor, and stator—should be electri-

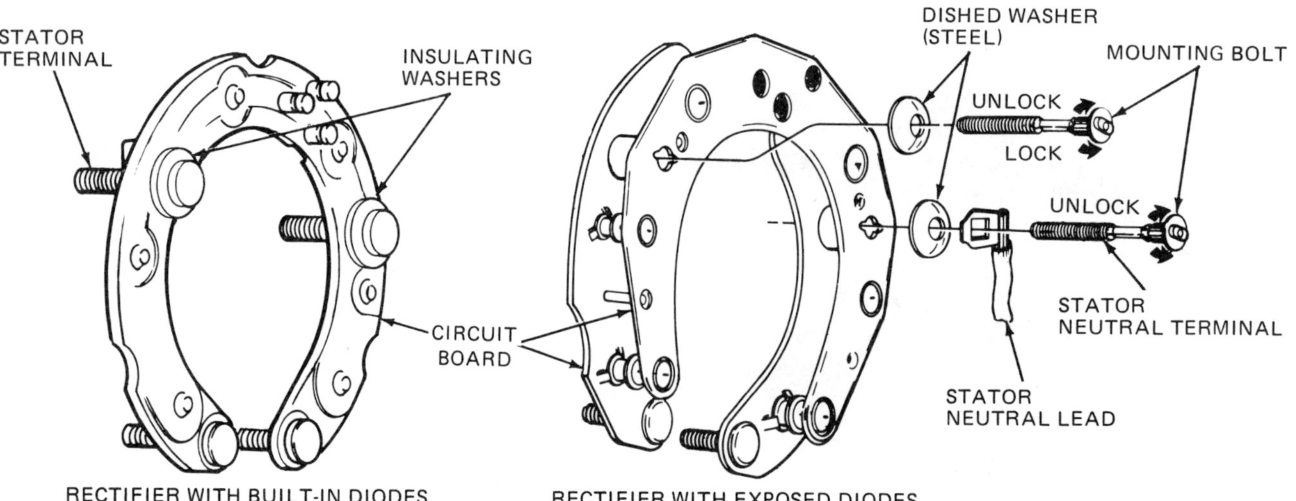

Fig. 27-21. Rectifier assemblies. (*Ford Motor Company*)

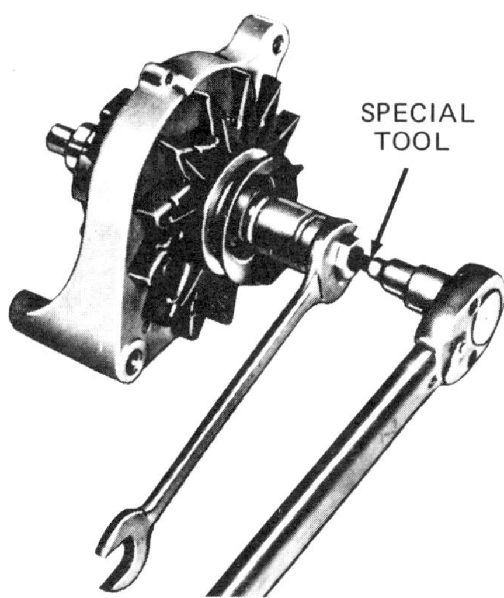

Fig. 27-22. Removing the pulley. (*Ford Motor Company*)

cally checked, as follows:

a. *Rectifier-Short or Ground and Stator-Ground Test* Use the ARE 27-42 ohmmeter. Set the MULTIPLY BY knob at 10, and calibrate the ohmmeter as explained inside the instrument cover. Touch the probes to the BAT (battery) and STA (stator) terminals as shown in Fig. 27-23. Then reverse the probes and repeat the test. The ohmmeter should read about 60 ohms in one direction and infinity (no needle movement) in the other. A reading in both directions indicates a bad positive diode, a grounded diode plate, or a grounded BAT terminal.

Fig. 27-23. Testing with an ohmmeter for a shorted or grounded rectifier or a grounded stator. (*Ford Motor Company*)

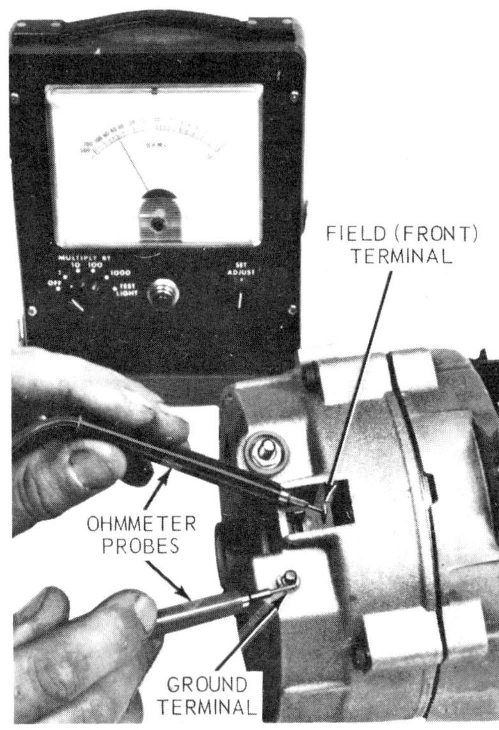

Fig. 27-24. Testing with an ohmmeter for an open or short-circuited field. (*Ford Motor Company*)

Perform the same test on the STA (stator) and GND (ground) terminals of the alternator. A reading in both directions indicates a bad negative diode, a grounded stator winding, a grounded positive diode plate, or a grounded BAT terminal.

Infinite readings on all four tests indicates an open STA terminal lead inside the alternator.

b. *Field-Open or Short-Circuit Test* Use the ohmmeter with MULTIPLY BY knob set at 1. Calibrate. Probe the alternator field terminal and ground terminal (Fig. 27-24). Now, spin the alternator pulley. The ohmmeter reading should be between 3.5 and 250 ohms and should fluctuate while the pulley is turning. No needle movement indicates an open brush lead, worn or stuck brushes, or a bad rotor assembly. A reading of less than 3.5 ohms indicates a grounded brush assembly or field terminal or a bad rotor.

c. *Diode Test on Bench* Disassemble the alternator and remove the rectifier assembly, as explained above. Set the ohmmeter MULTIPLY BY knob at 10 and calibrate the meter. Check each diode first in one direction and then in the other (Fig. 27-25). Diodes should show about 60 ohms in one direction and infinity in the other. If any diode does not, replace the rectifier assembly.

d. *Stator-Coil-Open or Ground Test on Bench* Disassemble the alternator to separate the stator assembly. Set the ohmmeter MULTIPLY BY knob at 1000. Probe from one of the stator leads to the stator laminated core. Repeat for each of the stator leads. Reading should be infinite for each (no needle movement). Do not touch the metal probes

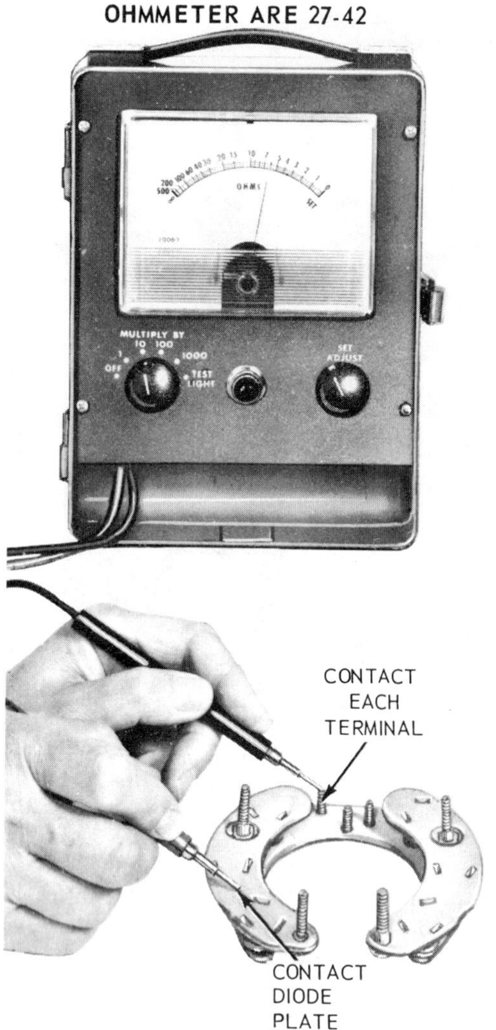

Fig. 27-25. Testing diodes in the assembly used in the rear-terminal alternator (except 61-amp unit). (*Ford Motor Company*)

or the stator leads with your hands. This will cause an incorrect reading.

e. *Open-Rotor or Short-Circuit Test on Bench* Disassemble the alternator to separate the rotor. Set the ohmmeter MULTIPLY BY knob at 1. Touch the two probes to the two rotor slip rings. The meter should read 3.5 to 4.5 ohms. A higher reading indicates a bad connection at the slip ring or a broken wire. A lower reading indicates a shorted winding. If the defect is not obvious or not easily repairable, discard the rotor.

Touch one probe to the rotor shaft and the other to one ring and then the other. There should be no reading. If there is, the rotor winding is grounded to the shaft. Unless the ground can be easily fixed, replace the rotor.

4. *REASSEMBLY*

1. Press in new bearings if the old have been removed. Support the housing at the boss.
2. If the stop ring on the rotor drive shaft is damaged, remove it. Install a new ring by pushing it onto the shaft and into the groove. Do not use snap-ring pliers, because this will damage the ring.

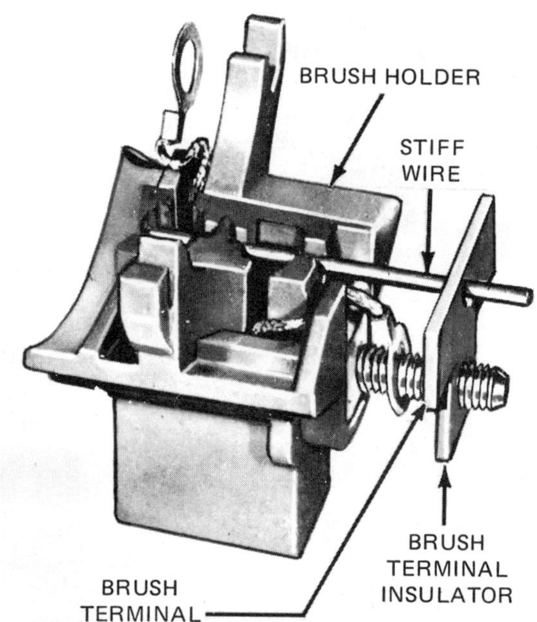

Fig. 27-26. Brush-holder assembly, showing a stiff wire being used to hold brushes in place during assembly of the alternator. (*Ford Motor Company*)

3. The rotor stop goes on the shaft with the recessed side against the stop ring. Put the front-end housing, fan spacer, fan, pulley, and lock washer on the shaft and install the retaining nut, tightening it to specifications (Fig. 27-22).
4. Use a piece of stiff wire, as shown in Fig. 27-26, to hold the brushes in position after placing the brushes, the springs, the terminal, and the insulator in the brush holder.
5. Install the brush-holder assembly in the rear-end housing and attach with mounting screws. Place the brush leads as shown in Fig. 27-27.
6. Wrap the three stator-winding leads around the printed-circuit-board terminals and solder them, using a 100-watt iron and rosin-core solder. Avoid excessive heat on diodes. Position the stator neutral-lead eyelet on the stator terminal insulators (Fig. 27-28) and put the diode assembly in place as shown.
7. The molded-circuit-board rectifier is attached with the mounting bolts (Fig. 27-21). Note the position of dished washers and stator neutral lead.
8. If the alternator uses a fiber circuit board, push the screws straight through into the holes.

CAUTION: Do not use the metal dished washers on the fiber circuit board. This will cause a short circuit.

9. Install the STA and BAT terminal insulators (Fig. 27-28). Put the stator and diode-plate assembly

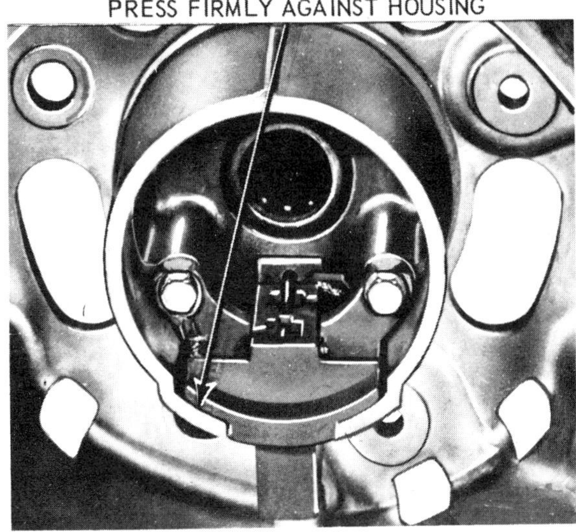

Fig. 27-27. Brush-lead positions in an alternator. (*Ford Motor Company*)

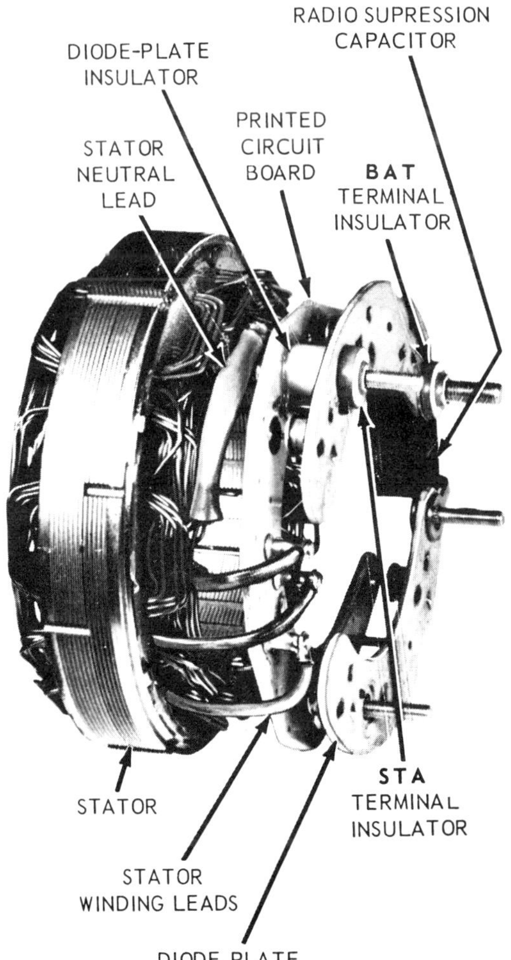

Fig. 27-28. Stator-lead connections in an alternator. (*Ford Motor Company*)

into the rear-end housing. Put insulators on the terminal bolts (black on STA, red on BAT, and white on FLD), and install five retaining nuts.

10. Position the rear-end housing and stator marks. Bring the housings together, seating the stator core in the steps in the housings. Install the through bolts. Remove the stiff wire holding the brushes (Fig. 27-26), and put a daub of waterproof cement over the hole to seal it.
11. Test the alternator for output.

⊘ 27-10 General Motors (Delco-Remy) Alternator Service The diodes and field may be checked with an ohmmeter as shown in Fig. 27-29. The alternator must be disconnected.

CAUTION: Always disconnect the ground strap from the battery before disconnecting alternator or regulator leads.

Tests A and B are diode tests (Fig. 27-29). Prods should be tried one way and then the other in each test. The meter should read high one way and low the other. If the meter reads the same in either direction (high or low), a diode is defective.

Test C is a field test for open. The meter should be connected between the field terminal and ground and should read within specifications. If it does not, the field is open or grounded.

1. ALTERNATOR DISASSEMBLY If the tests described earlier or the checks above show the alternator to be defective, it must be disassembled as follows:

1. Clamp the alternator in a vise by the mounting flange and use box and allen wrenches (Fig. 27-30) to remove the pulley retaining nut. Then remove the washer, pulley, fan, and spacer from the shaft.

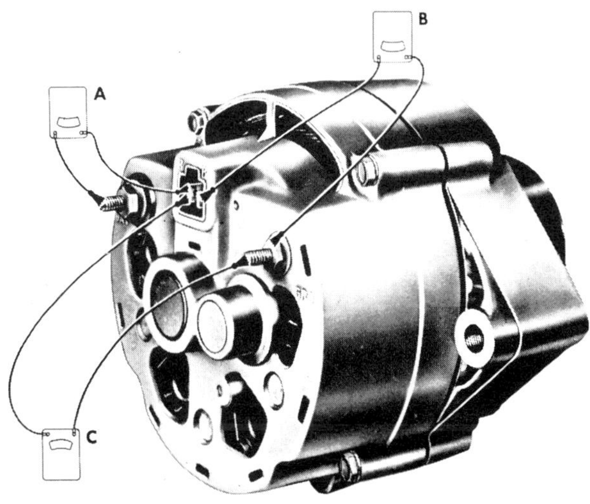

Fig. 27-29. Using an ohmmeter to check the diodes and field (rotor) in an alternator. (*Delco-Remy Division of General Motors Corporation*)

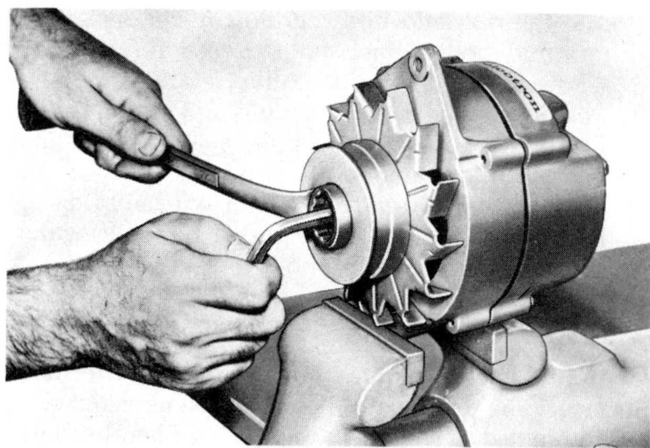

Fig. 27-30. Using box and allen wrenches to remove a pulley retaining nut. (*Delco-Remy Division of General Motors Corporation*)

2. Remove four through bolts and loosen the end frames by prying at the bolt locations.
3. Remove the slip-ring end frame and stator, as an assembly, from the drive end and rotor assembly. Put a piece of tape (pressure-sensitive and not friction, which would leave a gummy deposit) over the slip-ring end-frame bearing to prevent dirt from entering.

NOTE: If the brushes drop onto the rotor shaft and become contaminated with bearing lubricant, they should be cleaned, prior to reinstallation, with a chemical cleaner such as trichloroethylene.

4. Remove the three stator-lead attaching nuts and separate the stator from the end frame.
5. Remove screws, brushes, and holder assembly.
6. Remove the heat sink from the end frame by removing BAT and GRD terminals and one attaching screw (Fig. 27-31).
7. Remove the slip-ring end bearing, if necessary, by removing the inner seal.
8. Take the rotor from the drive-end frame and take out the bearing, if necessary, by removing the retainer plate.

2. *CLEANING AND INSPECTING PARTS* Clean all parts with a cloth, but do not wash the rotor, stator, diodes, or bearings in cleaning solvent. This could ruin them. If bearings are worn or rough, discard them.

Slip rings are not replaceable. If slightly worn, they may be cleaned up with 400-grain polishing cloth. If they are out of round, they may be turned down in a lathe. They should be true to 0.001 inch [0.0254 mm]. If excessive material must be removed or if rings are damaged, discard the rotor assembly.

If brushes are worn down halfway, replace them. Make sure the brush springs have the proper tension and are not distorted. Brushes must move freely in the holders.

a. *Rotor Tests* With an ohmmeter, check from either slip ring to the shaft and from one slip ring to the other to check for grounds or opens (Fig. 27-32). The rotor is checked for shorts by connecting a 12-volt battery and ammeter in series with the two slip rings. Excessive current draw indicates a short. A grounded, open, or shorted rotor must be discarded.

b. *Stator Tests* Connect an ohmmeter as shown in Fig. 27-33 to check for opens or grounds in the stator. Shorts are hard to find in the stator because of the low resistance of the winding. Usually, if all other tests are okay but the alternator does not supply rated output, the trouble is due to a shorted stator.

c. *Diode Checks* The stator must be disconnected for a diode check. The diodes may be checked with an ohmmeter connected first in one direction and then in the other across each diode. If both readings are the same (high or low), the diode is defective and should be discarded.

On later models of this alternator, the diodes are permanently assembled into diode trios (Fig. 27-34). Two trios are used, one for the positive and

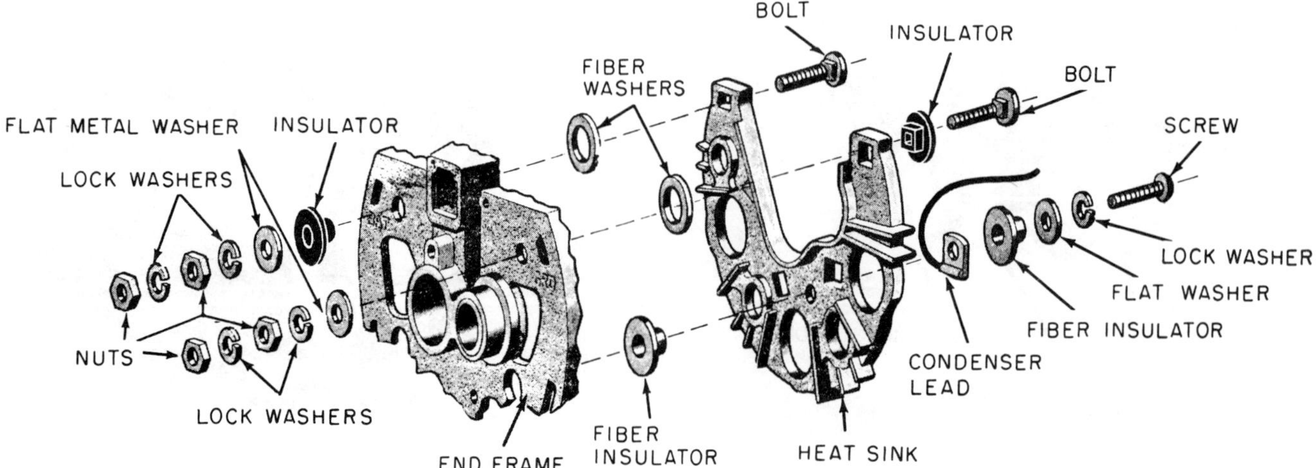

Fig. 27-31. Locations of heat-sink parts in a 5.5-inch Delcotron alternator. (*Chevrolet Motor Division of General Motors Corporation*)

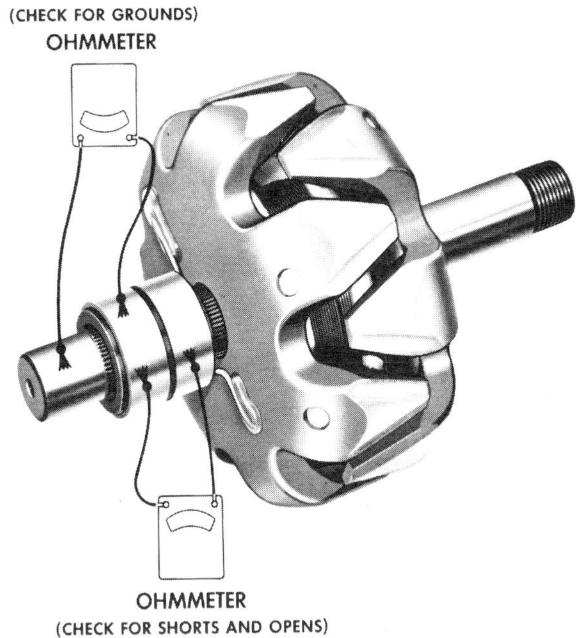

Fig. 27-32. Using an ohmmeter to check a rotor for grounds or opens. (*Chevrolet Motor Division of General Motors Corporation*)

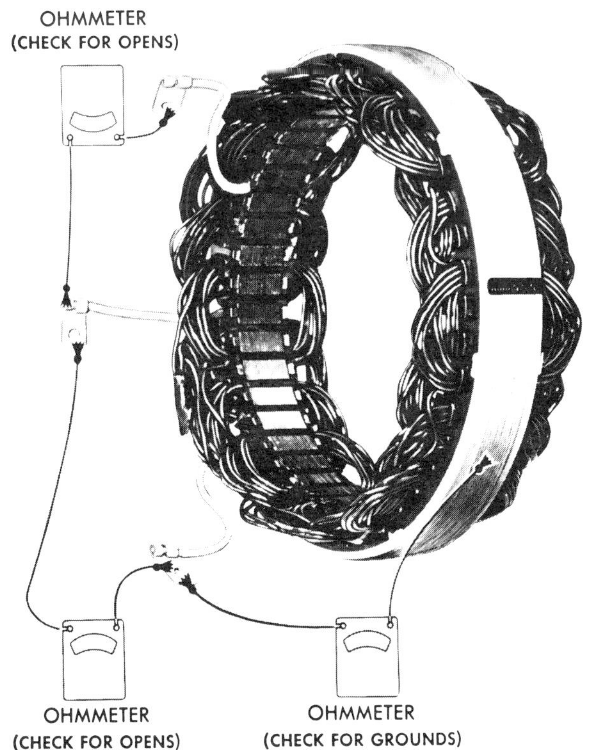

Fig. 27-33. Using an ohmmeter to check a stator for opens or grounds. (*Chevrolet Motor Division of General Motors Corporation*)

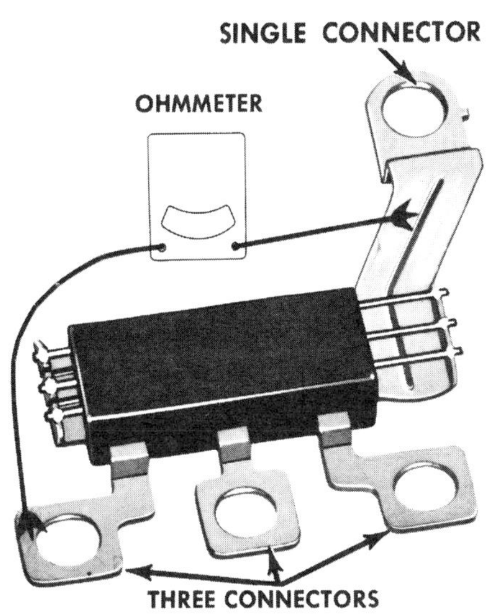

Fig. 27-34. Diode-trio checks. (*Chevrolet Motor Division of General Motors Corporation*)

one for the negative diodes. On these, remove the diode trios from the slip-ring end frame and check each diode as shown.

NOTE: A 12-volt test light can also be used to check diodes. As the test prods are put across each diode, first in one direction and then in the other, the light should go on one way but not the other.

d. Rectifier-Bridge Check Later models require a rectifier-bridge check (Fig. 27-35). Connect the

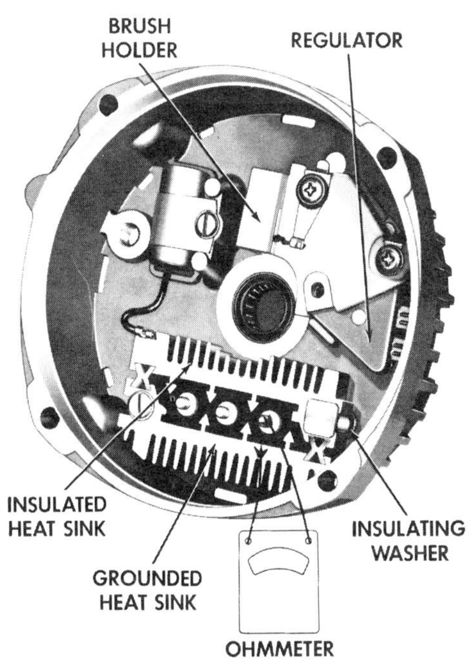

Fig. 27-35. Rectifier-bridge checks. (*Chevrolet Motor Division of General Motors Corporation*)

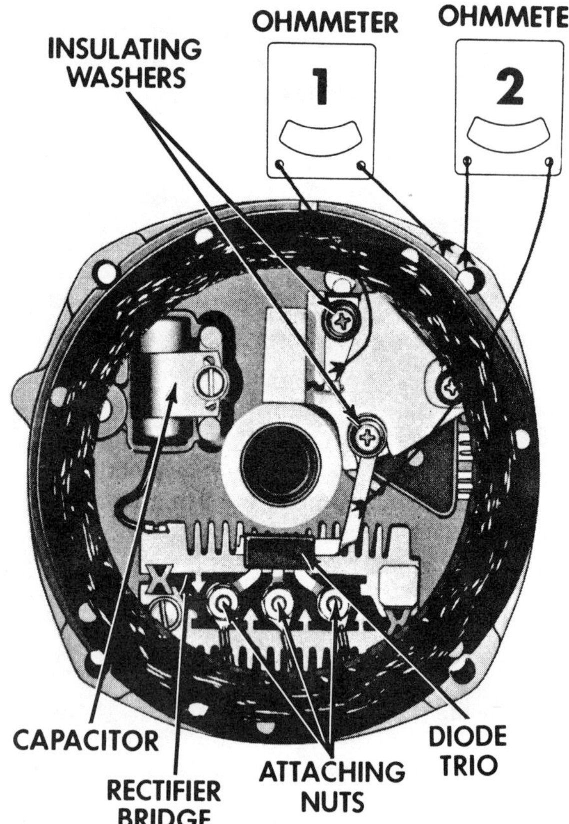

Fig. 27-36. Brush-lead-clip checks. (*Chevrolet Motor Division of General Motors Corporation*)

ohmmeter, as shown. Then reverse connections. If both readings are the same, replace the rectifier bridge. Repeat at each of the three terminals.

e. *Voltage-Regulator and Brush-Lead-Clip Check* Connect an ohmmeter from the brush-lead clip to the end frame as shown in Fig. 27-36. Reverse the connections. If both readings are zero, either the brush-lead clip is grounded or the voltage regulator is defective. The brush-lead clip will be grounded if, on reassembly, the insulating sleeve or washer is omitted.

3. *ALTERNATOR REASSEMBLY*

1. *Diode Replacement* If a diode requires replacement on the older-model alternator, support the heat sink with a special tool and press out the diode with the tool as shown in Fig. 27-37. Press in the new diode with the same tool.

CAUTION: Do not strike the diode, as any shock could ruin it. Also, do not bend the diode stem, as this could cause internal damage.

On the later-model alternator which uses diode trios (Fig. 27-34), if one diode tests bad, discard the trio.

2. Replace the heat sink, noting proper relationship of parts as shown in Fig. 27-31. Before putting the heat sink in place, install the brush holder and brushes in the end frame (Fig. 27-38). Use a bent

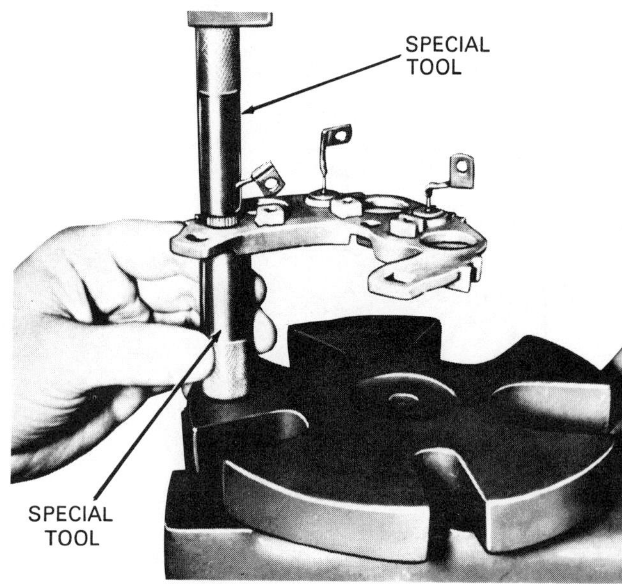

Fig. 27-37. Installing a diode with an arbor press and special tools. (*Chevrolet Motor Division of General Motors Corporation*)

paper clip or stiff wire to hold the brushes down in place in the holder (Fig. 27-39). Then attach the holder to the end frame. (The paper clip or wire is removed after the alternator assembly is completed.) Finally, install the heat sink.

3. If a new bearing is installed in the drive-end frame, pack it about one-fourth full with Delco-Remy #1948791 grease or equivalent. Then press the bearing into the end frame and install a new retainer plate. Stake retainer-plate bolts to the plate so they will not loosen.
4. If the slip-ring end bearing requires replacement, press the old one out and press a new one in with a flat plate over the bearing so it is pressed down flush with the outside of the end frame. Support the end frame from the inside around the bearing boss to avoid damage to the end frame. Saturate the felt seal with SAE20 oil and install the seal and the retainer at the inner end of the bearing.
5. To finish the reassembly, install the stator assembly in the slip-ring end frame and locate the diode connectors over the relay, diode, and stator leads, and tighten terminal nuts. Then install the rotor,

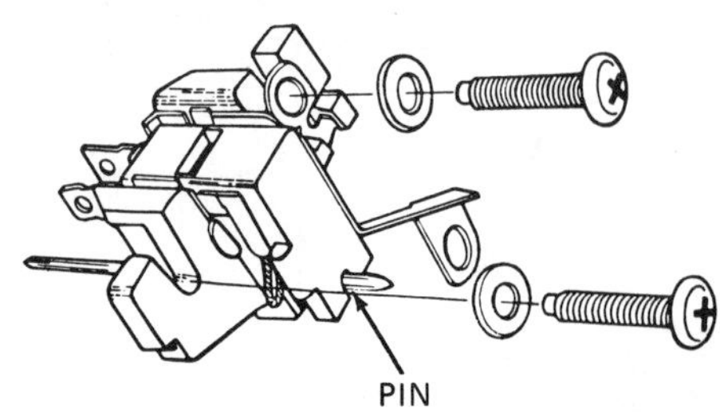

Fig. 27-38. Relation of parts in a brush-holder assembly. (*Chevrolet Motor Division of General Motors Corporation*)

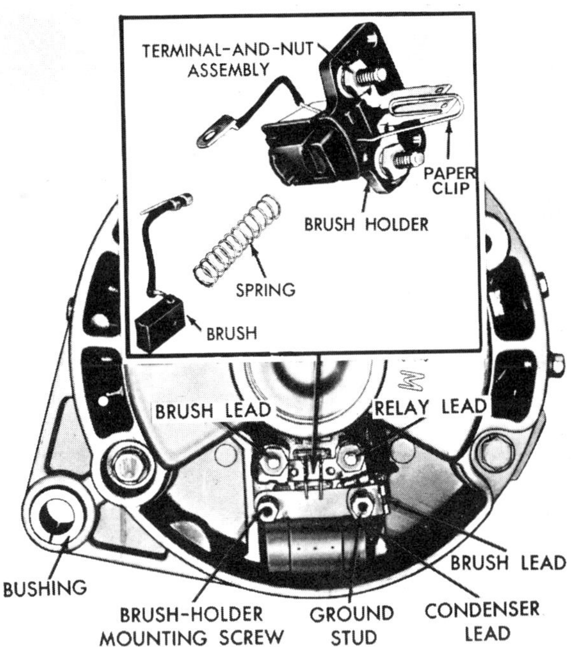

Fig. 27-39. Brush-holder assembly in an alternator, showing a paper clip being used to hold brushes in place during reassembly. (*Chevrolet Motor Division of General Motors Corporation*)

fan, spacer, pulley, washer, and nut. Tighten with a torque wrench (Fig. 27-40).

6. Assemble the slip-ring end frame and stator assembly to the drive-end frame and rotor assembly. Secure with four through bolts. Remove the brush-holding wire to allow brushes to seat on the slip rings.
7. Check alternator output after assembly.

⊘ 27-11 Belt-Tension Adjustment The drive belt must be properly tightened. A loose belt slips and soon wears out. It does not drive the alternator fast enough to keep the battery charged. An excessively tight belt causes rapid bearing wear. Figure 9-12 shows a belt-tension tool in use. This tool applies a measured amount of tension to the belt to check the amount of deflection. If the deflection is too great, the belt tension is low and should be increased. To do this, loosen the alternator-mounting and adjusting-bracket bolts. Move the alternator outward to increase the tension. Tighten the bolts after adjustment is complete.

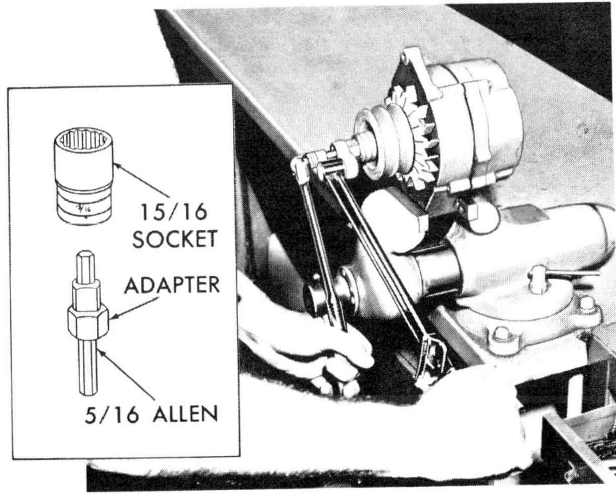

Fig. 27-40. Torquing a pulley nut to the proper tightness during reassembly. (*Chevrolet Motor Division of General Motors Corporation*)

CHAPTER 27 CHECKUP

NOTE: Since the following is a chapter review test, you should review the chapter before taking the test.

You are now moving along well in your study of automotive electrical equipment. With a little more effort you will finish the book. Then you will have the background information you need to be an automotive tuneup technician. Take the test below to find out how well you remember the key points covered in this chapter.

Completing the Sentences The sentences that follow are incomplete. After each sentence there are several words or phrases, but only one of them correctly completes the sentence. Write each sentence in your notebook, ending it with the one word or phrase that completes it correctly.

1. Alternators should: (*a*) not be polarized, (*b*) be polarized.
2. Three tests are made on the Chrysler-Plymouth charging system using the electronic control unit. In these tests, you measure the charging-circuit resistance, alternator output, and: (*a*) current setting, (*b*) voltage-regulator setting, (*c*) regulator air gaps.
3. To start the disassembly of the Chrysler alternator, you remove the: (*a*) brushes, (*b*) rotor, (*c*) stator.
4. If the slip rings on the Chrysler alternator are damaged, you replace the: (*a*) rotor, (*b*) alternator, (*c*) slip rings.
5. On Delco-Remy and Ford alternators, if the slip rings are damaged, you replace the: (*a*) slip rings, (*b*) stator, (*c*) rotor.

Reviewing Regulator Adjustments In the following, you are asked about checks and adjustments on the regulators used with alternators. You need to know about alternator regulators to be up to date; therefore the checks and adjustments should be of interest to you. Write your answers in your notebook.

1. Describe how to check the current output of the Chrysler alternator. What are possible causes of low output?
2. Explain how to check the charging system using the Delco-Remy alternator with built-in voltage regulator.
3. Explain how to check a charging system on a Ford.

Reviewing Alternator Service In the following, you are asked about the procedures for overhauling alternators. Write each description or explanation in your notebook, in your own words.

1. Describe the procedure for checking diodes.
2. Explain how to check a stator.
3. Explain how to check a rotor.
4. Why must diodes be handled with care?
5. Write step-by-step disassembly and reassembly procedures for one model of alternator.

SUGGESTIONS FOR FURTHER STUDY

Your school automotive shop or a local service station may have defective alternators that you can practice on. If you can get one, try to disassemble it. You will find the procedure very interesting. Write down each of the steps. Also, study the manufacturer's shop manuals which describe the servicing procedures on alternators. Be sure to write, in your notebook, any important facts you pick up.

chapter 28

IGNITION SYSTEMS

This chapter describes the construction and operation of automotive ignition systems and their components. The typical ignition system includes the battery, ignition coil, ignition distributor, switch, spark plugs, and wiring.

⊘ 28-1 Function of Ignition System The ignition system supplies high-voltage surges (as high as 35,000 V) of current to the spark plugs in the engine cylinders. These surges produce electric sparks at the spark-plug gaps. The sparks ignite, or set fire to, the compressed air-fuel mixture in the combustion chambers. Each spark appears at the plug gap just as the piston approaches top dead center on the compression stroke, when the engine is idling. At higher speed or during part-throttle operation, the spark is *advanced.* It occurs somewhat earlier in the cycle. The mixture thus has ample time to burn and deliver its power. The ignition system consists of the battery, switch, ignition distributor, ignition coil, spark plugs, and wiring (Fig. 28-1)

Some systems use transistors to reduce the load on the distributor contact points. Other systems do not have contact points. Instead they use a combination of transistors and a magnetic pickup in the distributor. These are explained in the sections that follow.

⊘ 28-2 Ignition Distributor The ignition distributor has two jobs. First, it closes and opens the circuit between the battery and the ignition coil. When the circuit closes, current flows in the ignition coil and builds up a magnetic field. When the circuit opens, the magnetic field in the coil collapses. The coil produces a high-voltage surge of current. (How the coil does this is explained later.) The distributor's second job is to distribute each high-voltage surge to the correct spark plug at the correct instant. It does this by means of the distributor rotor and cap and secondary wiring.

There are two basic types of distributor: (1) the type using contact points to close and open the coil primary circuit; (2) the type using a magnetic pickup and a transistor control unit to interrupt the current flow in the coil primary circuit. This second type is used in electronic ignition systems.

⊘ 28-3 Distributor with Contact Points This distributor (Figs. 28-2 and 28-3) consists of a housing, a drive shaft with breaker cam, and advance mechanism, a breaker plate with contact points and a condenser, a rotor, and a cap. The shaft is usually driven by the engine camshaft through spiral gears (Fig.

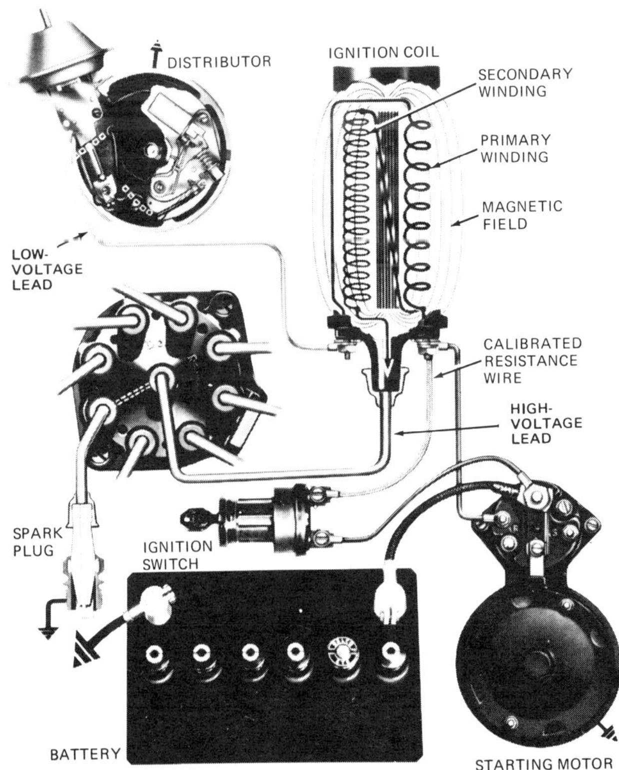

Fig. 28-1. Typical ignition system. It consists of the battery (source of power), ignition switch, ignition coil (shown schematically), distributor (shown in top view with its cap removed and placed below it), spark plugs (one shown in sectional view), and wiring. The coil is shown schematically, with magnetic lines of force indicated. (*Delco-Remy Division of General Motors Corporation*)

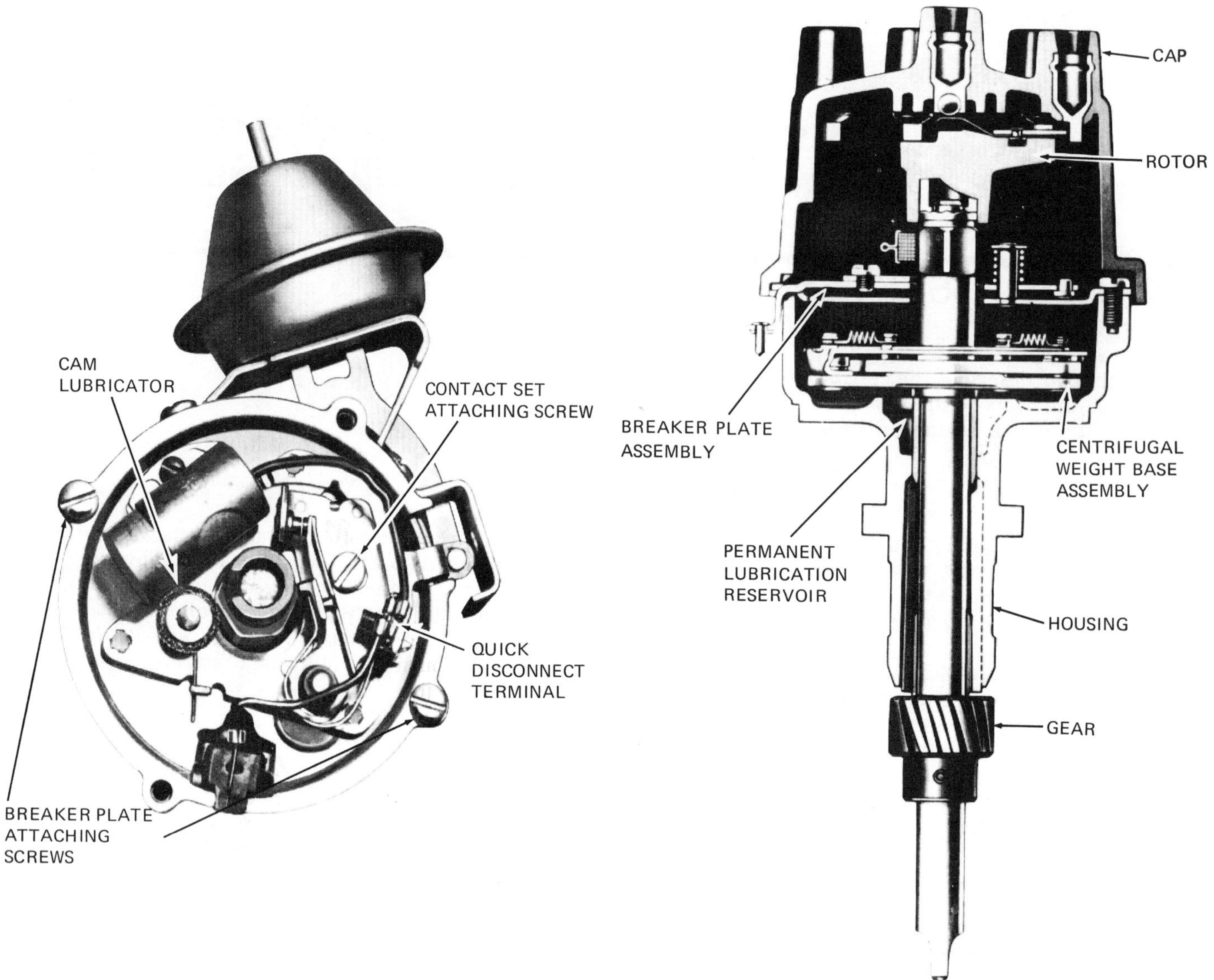

Fig. 28-2. Sectional and top views of an ignition distributor. In the top view, the cap and the rotor have been removed so that the breaker plate can be seen. (*Delco-Remy Division of General Motors Corporation*)

2-15). It rotates at one-half the crankshaft speed. Usually, the distributor drive shaft is coupled with a shaft that drives the oil pump.

Rotation of the shaft and breaker cam causes the distributor contact points to open and close. The breaker cam usually has the same number of lobes as there are cylinders in the engine.[1] It rotates at one-half the crankshaft speed. The contact points close and open once for each cylinder with every breaker-cam rotation. Thus, the coil produces one high-voltage surge for each cylinder every two crankshaft revolutions. This ignites the air-fuel mixture compressed in each cylinder every other crankshaft revolution.

The rotor rotates with the breaker cam on which it is mounted. As it does, a metal spring and segment (or blade) on the rotor connect the center terminal of the cap with each outside terminal in turn. Thus the high-voltage surges from the coil are directed first to one spark plug, then to another, and so on, according to the firing order.

⊘ 28-4 Electronic Ignition System The electronic ignition system does not use contact points. Instead, it uses a magnetic pickup device in the distributor and an electronic amplifying device with transistors. With the cap on, the distributor looks the same as the contact-point distributor. However, when the caps are removed, the difference between the two is apparent. There are various kinds of electronic igni-

[1] In some designs, the breaker cam has only one-half as many lobes as there are engine cylinders. Then there are two sets of contact points that are arranged to close and open alternately. This produces the same effect as the breaker-cam-and-contact-point arrangement discussed above.

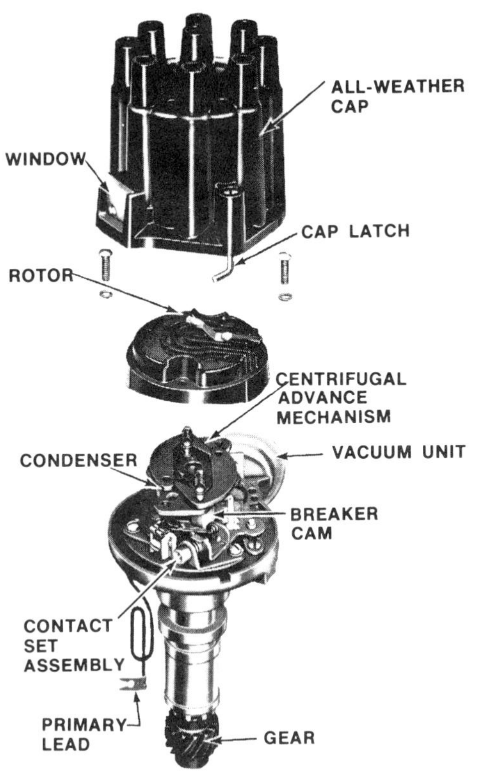

Fig. 28-3. Partly disassembled distributor. (*Delco-Remy Division of General Motors Corporation*)

tion systems. We shall describe two of them: the Chrysler system and the General Motors system.

⊘ 28-5 Chrysler Electronic Ignition System

An electronic ignition system has been used in all Chrysler Corporation cars made in the United States since 1973. In this system, the distributor has a metal rotor with a series of tips on it. This rotor, called the *reluctor*, is shown in Fig. 28-4. The reluctor takes the place of the breaker cam in the contact-point distributor previously discussed. Notice that the reluctor in Fig. 28-4 has six tips. It is for a six-cylinder engine, so there is one for each cylinder. Notice also that the distributor has a permanent magnet and a pickup coil.

The principle of operation is simple. The reluctor provides a path for the magnetic lines of force from the magnet. Every time a tip of the reluctor passes the pickup coil, it carries the magnetic field through the coil. This magnetic field produces a pulse of electric current in the coil. The current is very small, but it is enough to trigger the control unit into action.

The control unit uses electronic devices—diodes and transistors—to control the flow of current to the ignition coil. When the pulse of current from the pickup coil arrives at the control unit, the control unit stops the flow of current to the ignition coil. This is the same job the contact points do in the other type of distributor. When the current stops flowing in the ignition coil, the magnetic field in the

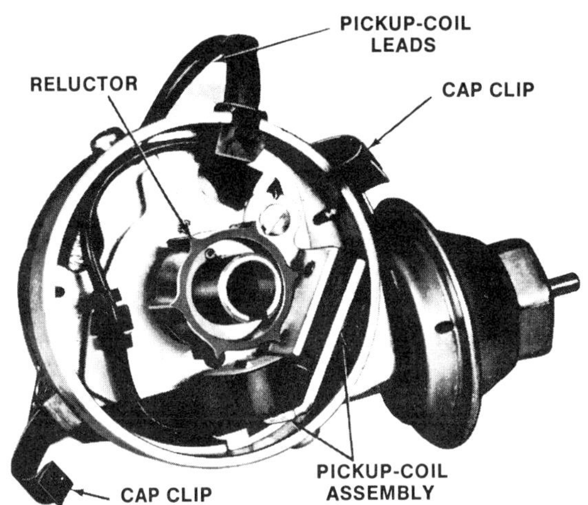

Fig. 28-4. Top view of the Chrysler electronic ignition distributor. The cap and rotor have been removed to show the reluctor and the pickup coil. (*Chrysler Corporation*)

coil collapses. This causes the coil to produce a high-voltage surge. The high-voltage surge is led through the distributor rotor, cap, and wiring, to the spark plug that is ready to fire.

The tip of the reluctor now rotates past the pickup coil. The pulse of current from the pickup coil ends. This allows the control unit to close the circuit from the battery to the ignition coil. Primary current flows again, and a magnetic field builds up once more in the ignition coil. Then the next tip of the reluctor passes the pickup coil, and the whole series of events is repeated.

In this system there are no contact points to adjust or wear out. Everything is automatic. The only adjustment required is the ignition timing, which we shall discuss later.

Figure 28-5 shows the wiring for the Chrysler

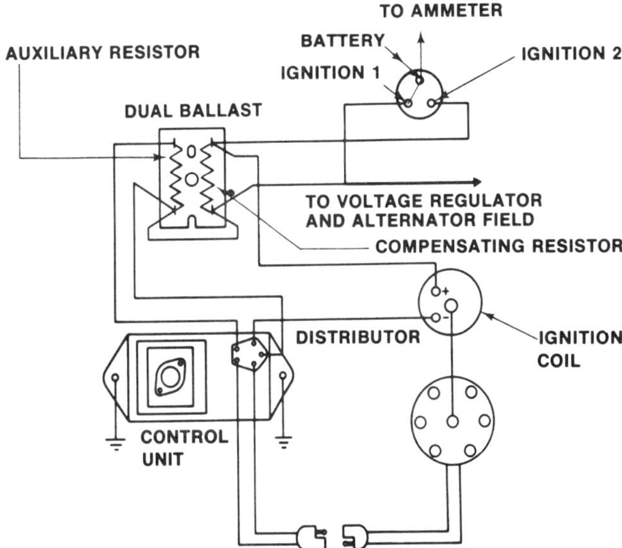

Fig. 28-5. Schematic wiring diagram for the Chrysler electronic ignition system. (*Chrysler Corporation*)

electronic ignition system. The dual ballast is a two-resistor unit that protects the system from overload. But it allows maximum current to flow during cranking. This assures a strong spark for good starting performance.

⊘ 28-6 General Motors Electronic Ignition System General Motors calls the distributor used in their electronic ignition system a *magnetic-pulse* distributor. Figure 28-6 shows the distributor. It looks much like the Chrysler unit, and it works in about the same way. The General Motors distributor has a pole piece in the form of a ring. The pole piece has a series of teeth, pointing inward. There is one tooth for each cylinder in the engine. Under the pole piece is a permanent magnet with a pickup coil. The timer core, made of iron, is placed on top of the distributor shaft. It is placed exactly the same way as the cam in the contact-point distributor. The timer core also has one tooth for each cylinder in the engine.

When the engine is running, the teeth on the timer core align with the teeth on the pole piece. They align the same number of times per timer-core rotation as there are cylinders in the engine. Suppose we had an eight-cylinder engine. Then there would be eight teeth on the pole piece and eight teeth on the timer core. The teeth would align eight times for every revolution of the timer core. Every time the teeth align, magnetic lines of force are carried through the pickup coil. This produces a pulse of current that flows to the ignition-pulse amplifier (Fig. 28-7). There, the pulse electronically opens the circuit to the ignition-coil primary. The magnetic field in the coil collapses, and a high-voltage surge is produced. This surge is carried by the high-voltage leads, the distributor cap, and the rotor to the spark plug that is ready to fire.

⊘ 28-7 General Motors High-Energy Ignition (HEI) System In 1973, General Motors introduced an ignition distributor that has the ignition coil assembled into it (for V-6 and V-8 engines) and that produces voltages of up to 35,000 V. The wiring for this unit is greatly simplified, as shown in Fig. 28-8. Note that there is one lead from the battery (which Delco-Remy calls an *energizer*). This lead goes through the ignition switch to the electronic distributor. No primary resistance is used. The only other leads are the high-voltage cables going to the spark plugs. Because of the higher voltage, special silicone-insulated spark-plug wires are used. These wires have a larger diameter (8 mm) than standard spark-plug wires. They are gray in color, have more heat resistance, and deteriorate less. However, the silicone insulation is soft and must not be mishandled or allowed to rub against other parts. Special wiring-harness connectors are used to hold the spark plug wires securely in place on top of the distributor cap.

Figure 28-9 shows the distributor assembled. It looks different from the ignition distributor in older cars, but it works the same way. All connections between the coil and distributor are inside the HEI

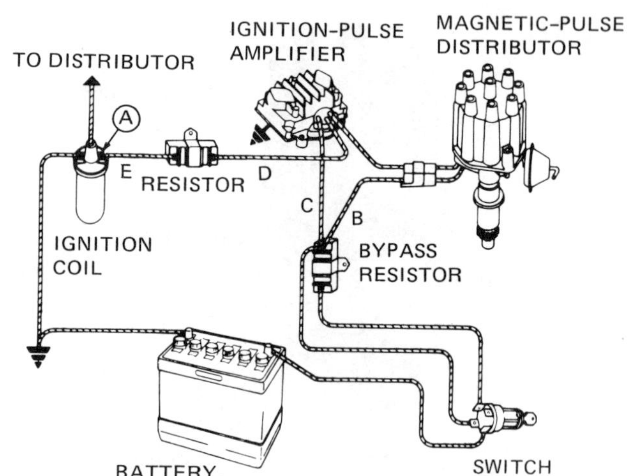

Fig. 28-7. Wiring diagram for an ignition system using a magnetic-pulse distributor and a transistor control unit (ignition pulse amplifier) to amplify the ignition pulse. (*Delco-Remy Division of General Motors Corporation*)

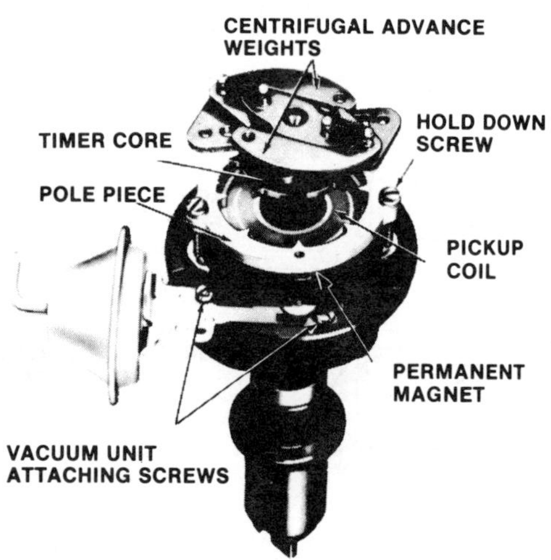

Fig. 28-6. Magnetic-pickup distributor with the cap and rotor removed. (*Delco-Remy Division of General Motors Corporation*)

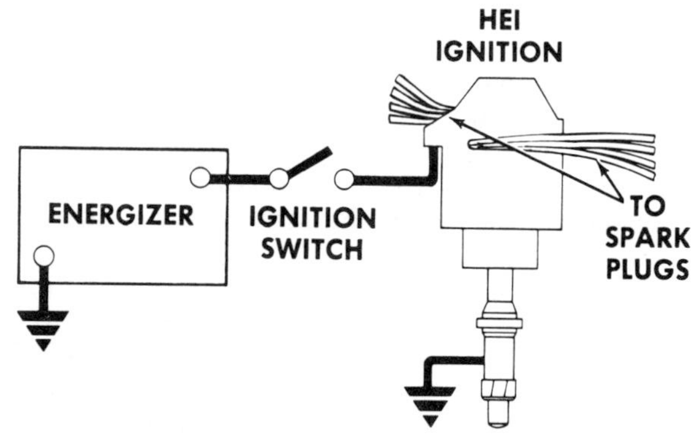

Fig. 28-8. Basic wiring diagram for the General Motors High-Energy Ignition (HEI) System. (*Delco-Remy Division of General Motors Corporation*)

Fig. 28-9. HEI distributor, which includes the ignition coil. Wiring-harness connectors hold the silicone-insulated spark-plug wires in place. (*Delco-Remy Division of General Motors Corporation*)

distributor. Also, the electronic amplifier, which Delco-Remy calls the *electronic module,* is mounted inside the distributor. Figure 28-10 shows the HEI distributor with cap, rotor, and electronic module removed. The capacitor (condenser) in the distributor is for control of radio noise. It has no function in the High-Energy Ignition System. As you can see, the wiring in the High-Energy Ignition System is much simplified. The distributor uses the magnetic-pulse principle. This is explained in ⊘ 28-6. The special procedures required to test these units are covered in Chap. 30.

Figure 28-11 and 28-12 show the HEI distributor in assembled and partly disassembled views. Tachometer connections to the HEI distributor are shown in Fig. 28-11.

For a short time prior to the introduction of the HEI system, General Motors installed a *unit distributor* on some cars. The unit distributor was an early version of the HEI distributor, and they share many features. However, the unit distributor did not have

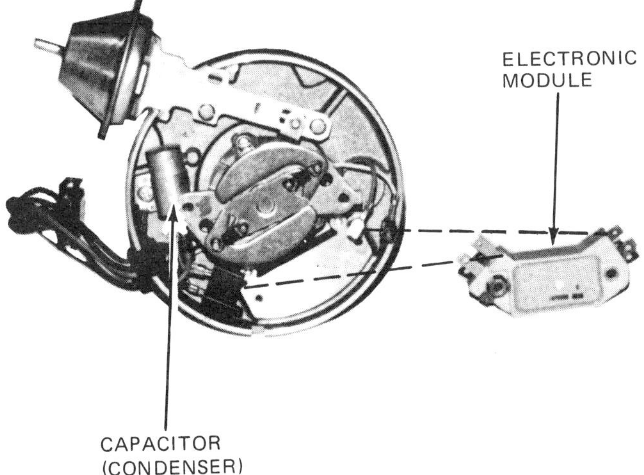

Fig. 28-10. HEI distributor with the electronic module removed. (*Delco-Remy Division of General Motors Corporation*)

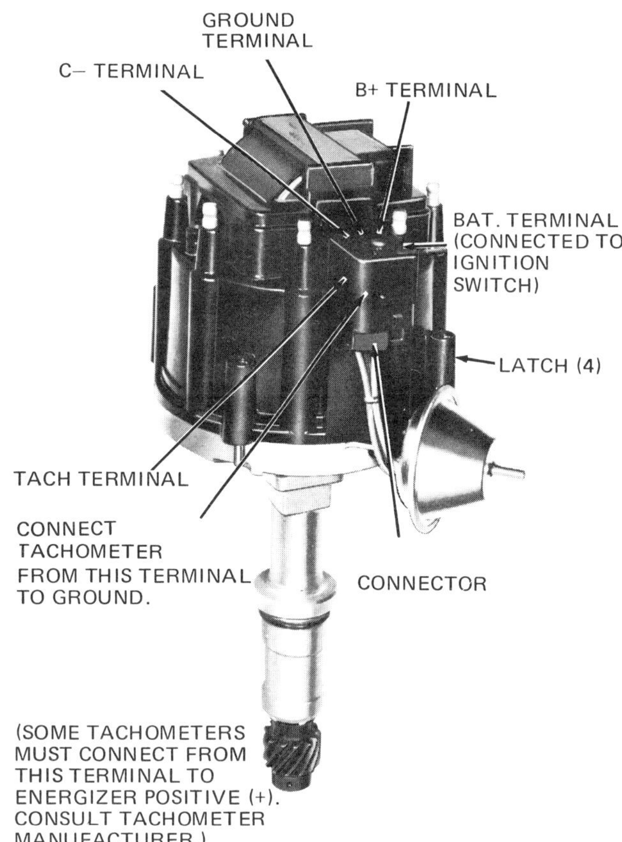

Fig. 28-11. Distributor of the High-Energy Ignition (HEI) System, which includes the ignition coil. (*Delco-Remy Division of General Motors Corporation*)

the higher secondary-voltage characteristic of the High-Energy Ignition System. The testing of the unit distributor is covered in Chap. 30.

NOTE: The High-Energy Ignition System uses spark plugs with a wider gap—as wide as 0.080 in [2.03 mm]. A standard plug cannot be used with this system because, to get the wide gap, the side electrode would have to be bent at a severe angle. Instead, plugs made especially for the HEI system must be used.

⊘ 28-8 Spark Plugs The spark plug (Fig. 28-13) is a metal shell in which a porcelain insulator is fastened. An electrode extends through the center of the insulator. A second electrode is attached to one side of the shell. This electrode is bent in toward the center electrode. Threads on the metal shell allow it to be screwed into a tapped hole in the cylinder head. This grounds the electrode that is attached to the shell. The two electrodes are made of special heavy wire. There is a gap of up to 0.040 in [1.02 mm] between them. The electric spark jumps this gap to ignite the air-fuel mixture in the combustion chamber. The spark jumps from the center, or insulated, electrode to the grounded, or outer, electrode.

Some spark plugs have a built-in resistor (Fig. 28-13) which is part of the center electrode. This

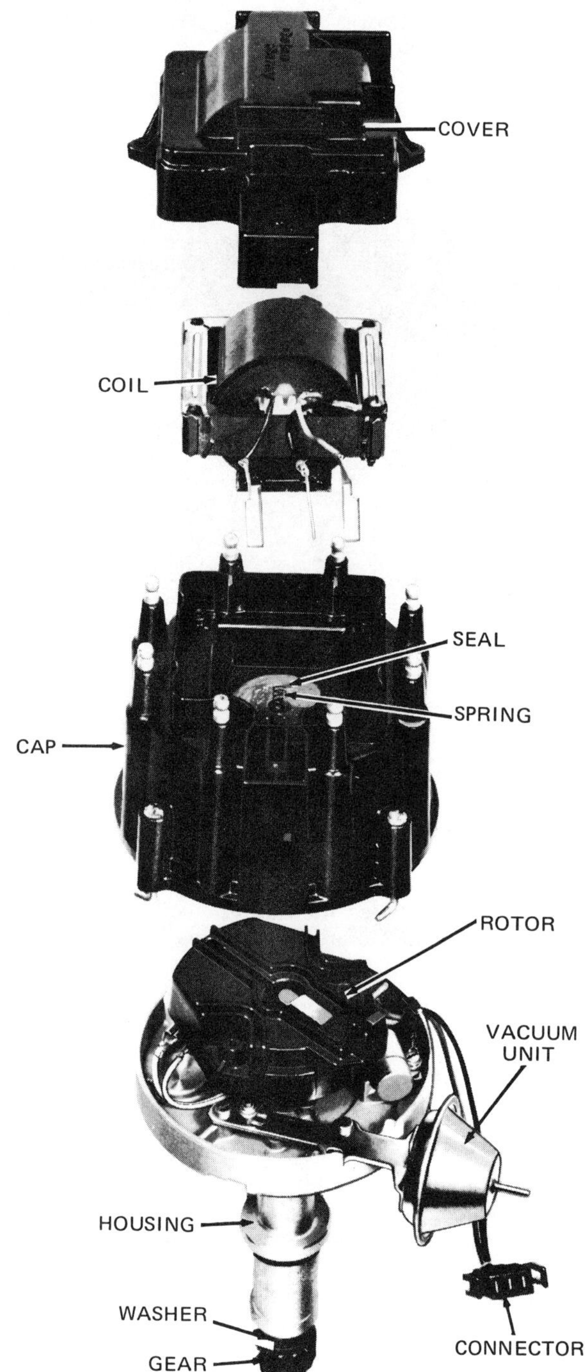

Fig. 28-12. Partly disassembled view of the HEI distributor. (*Delco-Remy Division of General Motors Corporation*)

resistor reduces radio and television interference from the ignition system. It also reduces electrode erosion caused by over-long sparking. We have been describing the high-voltage surge from the ignition-coil secondary as if it were a single powerful surge. Actually, it is more complex than that. There may be a number of early surges before a full spark forms. At the end of the sparking cycle, the spark may die and re-form several times. All this takes place in only a few ten-thousandths of a second. The effect is

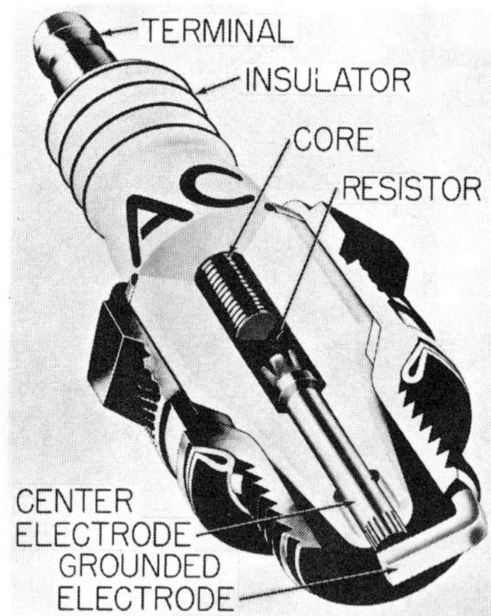

Fig. 28-13. Cutaway view of a resistor-type spark plug. (*AC Spark Plug Division of General Motors Corporation*)

that the ignition wiring acts like a radio transmitting antenna. The surges of high voltage send out static that causes radio and television interference. The resistors in the spark plugs tend to reduce the number of surges. They thus reduce the interference and the wear on the electrodes.

⊘ 28-9 Spark-Plug Heat Range The heat range of a spark plug tells how hot the plug gets in operation (Fig. 28-14). The temperature that a plug reaches depends on how far the heat must travel. The heat path is from the center electrode to the cooler outer shell of the plug and then to the cylinder head. If the path is long, the plug runs hotter than with a short path. When a plug runs too cold, sooty carbon collects on the insulator, around the center electrode. A hotter-running plug burns this carbon away or prevents its formation. Carbon deposits can also be caused by too-rich air-fuel mixtures or by too much oil in the cylinder.

If the plug runs too hot, the insulator may take on a white or grayish cast and may appear blistered. A plug that runs too hot wears more rapidly. The higher temperatures cause the electrodes to burn away more quickly. In addition, with a hot-running plug, there is always a danger of preignition (see ⊘ 10-9).

⊘ 28-10 Secondary Wiring The secondary wiring consists of the high-voltage cables connected be-

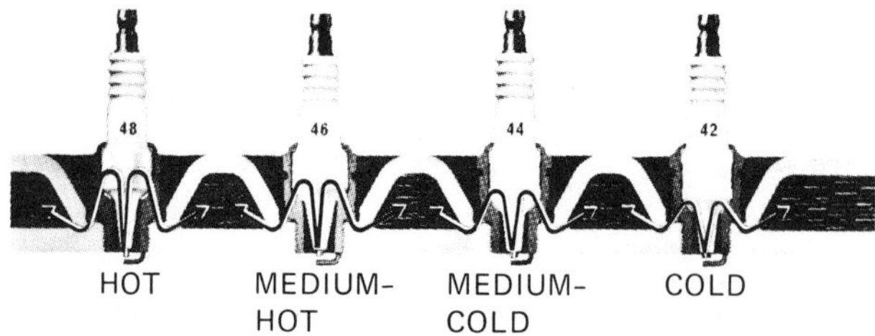

Fig. 28-14. Heat range of spark plugs. The longer the heat path (indicated by arrows), the hotter the plug runs. (*AC Spark Plug Division of General Motors Corporation*)

tween the distributor cap, the spark plugs, and the high-voltage terminal of the ignition coil. These cables carry the high-voltage surges that produce the spark at the plug gaps. Thus, they must be heavily insulated to contain the high voltage. The insulation must be able to withstand the effects of high temperature, oil, and high voltage.

Before 1961, the cores of the cables were of copper or aluminum wire. However, in 1961, automotive manufacturers in the United States began to use carbon-impregnated linen cores. The carbon-impregnated linen forms a resistance path for the high-voltage surges. It produces the same effect as the resistors in the spark plugs (⊘ 28-8). These cables thus prevent the ignition system from interfering with radio and television.

In 1963, manufacturers began using cables with graphite-saturated fiber-glass cores. These worked like the carbon-impregnated linen-core cables. However, it is claimed that they resist breakage when pulled off spark plugs. Also, they have less tendency to char from high temperatures.

⊘ 28-11 Ignition Coil The ignition coil transforms, or steps up, the 6 or 12 V of the battery to the high voltage required to make the current jump the spark-plug gap. The air-fuel mixture between the two electrodes presents a high resistance to the passage of current. The voltage (pressure) must be very high to push current (electrons) from the center electrode to the outside electrode.

The ignition coil has two circuits, a primary circuit and a secondary circuit (Fig. 28-1). The secondary circuit is made up of many thousands of turns of fine wire. The primary circuit is made up of a few hundred turns of heavier wire. The primary wire is wound around the outside of the secondary winding (Fig. 28-15). When the distributor contact points close and current flows in the primary circuit, a magnetic field builds up. When the distributor contact points open and current stops flowing, the magnetic field collapses. The collapsing magnetic field induces high voltage in the secondary winding. This creates the high-voltage surge that is conducted through the distributor rotor and cap to a spark plug.

⊘ 28-12 Primary and Secondary Circuits To get a clearer picture of the two circuits in the ignition system, let us look at each one separately. Figure 28-16 shows the primary circuit. It consists of the battery, the contact points in the distributor, the primary winding in the ignition coil, the ignition switch, and the wiring.

Figure 28-17 is the same illustration with the secondary circuit added. The secondary circuit includes the secondary winding in the ignition coil, the distributor cap and rotor, the spark plugs, and the connecting wires.

⊘ 28-13 Distributor-Cap and Rotor Action As you can see from Figs. 28-2 and 28-3, the rotor sits on top

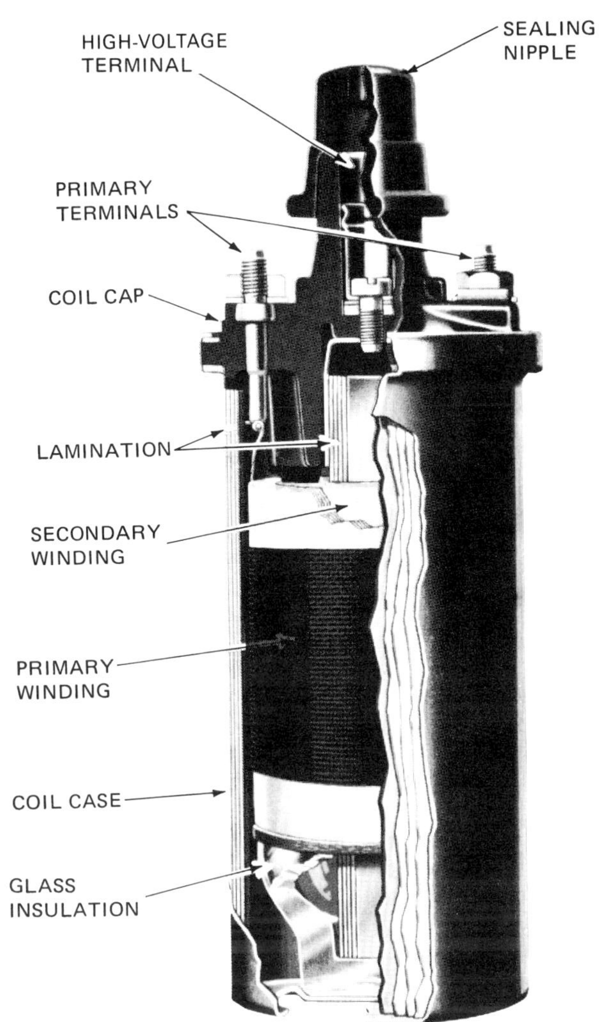

Fig. 28-15. Ignition coil. The case is cut away to show how the primary winding is wound around the outside of the secondary winding. (*Delco-Remy Division of General Motors Corporation*)

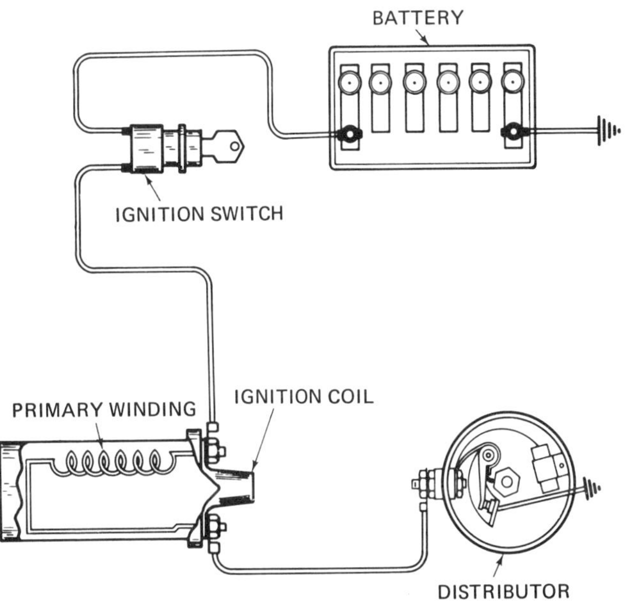

Fig. 28-16. Simplified primary circuit of the ignition system.

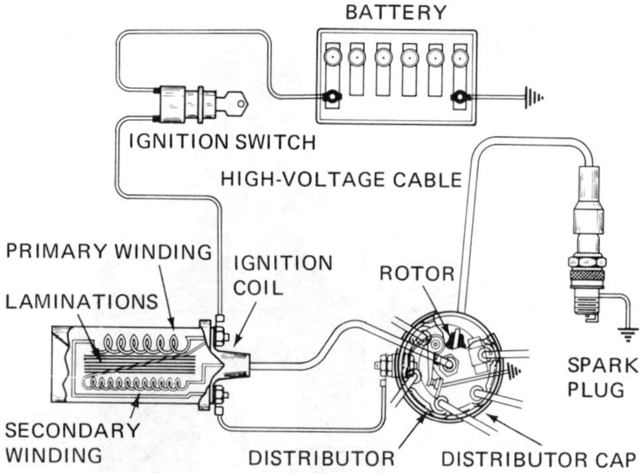

Fig. 28-17. Secondary circuit added to the primary circuit of the ignition system. Only one spark plug is shown.

of the cam in the distributor. Figure 28-18 shows several rotors. The purpose of the rotor is to connect the center terminal of the distributor cap to the outside terminals of the cap.

The terminals are insulated from one another and are held in place in the cap. You can see three of them cut away in Fig. 28-19. The center terminal of the cap has a carbon button on its lower end. This button rests on one end of the rotor blade. A small spring holds the carbon button and rotor blade in continuous contact. Therefore, the rotor blade is always connected to the secondary winding of the ignition coil. Whenever the coil secondary winding produces a high-voltage surge, the rotor blade is pointing at the side terminal which is connected to the spark plug that is ready to fire (Fig. 28-17).

Let's review the actions: The contact points open (or the control unit in the electronic system stops the flow of primary current). The magnetic field (that was created by current flowing in the coil primary winding) collapses. This collapse produces a high-voltage surge in the coil secondary winding.

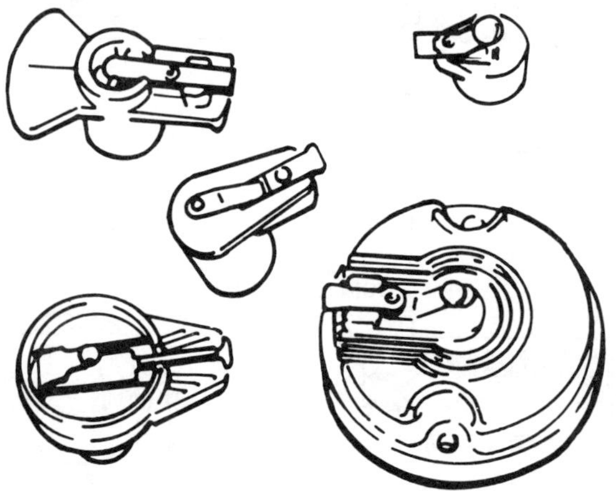

Fig. 28-18. Types of distributor rotors. The one at the lower left has a carbon resistor. The one at the lower right is attached to the advance mechanism by screws.

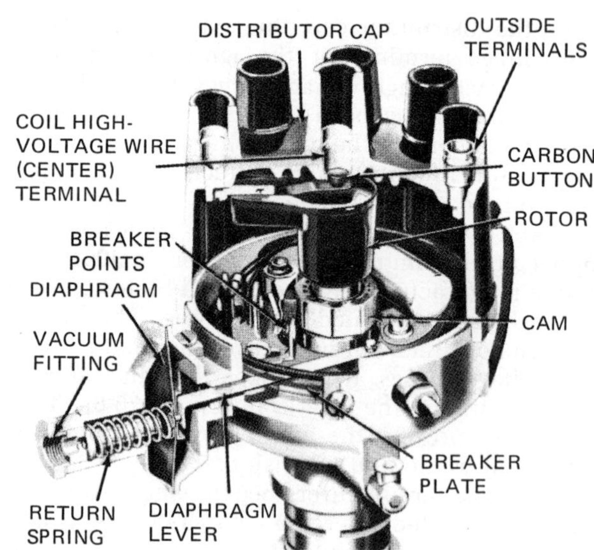

Fig. 28-19. Cutaway view of a distributor, showing how the rotor is mounted on top of the cam. This picture also shows the construction of the vacuum-advance mechanism. (*Ford Motor Company*)

The high-voltage surge is led from the center terminal of the ignition coil to the center terminal of the distributor cap. From there it goes through the rotor blade and to one side terminal. The side terminal is connected to the spark plug in the cylinder whose compression stroke is ending. The spark produced at the spark plug by the high-voltage surge ignites the compressed air-fuel mixture. It burns, and the power stroke follows.

Now, let us review in more detail how the magnetic field is produced, what happens when it collapses, and how the condenser enters into the action.

⊘ 28-14 Producing the Magnetic Field Current flowing through a winding causes a magnetic field. The magnetic field does not, however, spring up instantly when the circuit is closed to the battery. It takes a small fraction of a second (called the *buildup time*) for this to occur. The reason for this lies in the fact that the winding has *self-induction*. This term expresses the effect of each turn of wire in the winding on nearby turns. Figure 28-20 illustrates the magnetic fields surrounding two neighboring turns of wire in the winding. The wires are shown in end view, as current flows in them. The current is flowing into the page, as indicated by the crosses. When

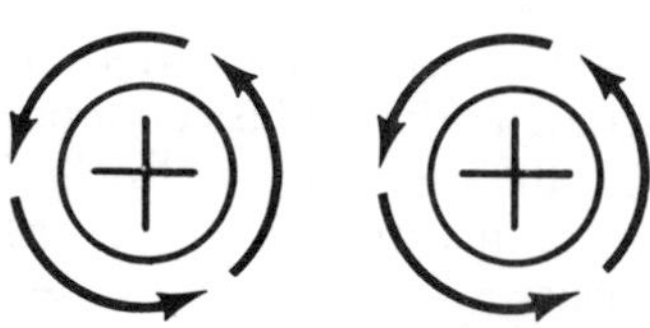

Fig. 28-20. Magnetic fields, surrounding two neighboring turns of wire, in a winding through which current is passing.

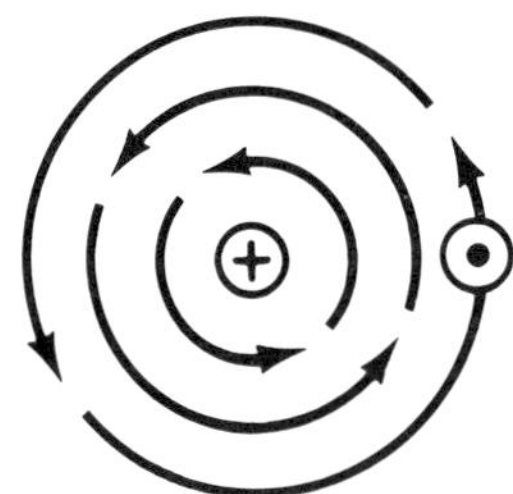

Fig. 28-21. Effect, on the neighboring wire, of an increasing magnetic field from one wire.

the current first starts to flow, the encircling magnetic fields begin to move outward from the wires. This is somewhat like ripples on a pool of water, moving out from where a stone has been dropped. Figure 28-21 illustrates the effect of this action on the right-hand wire. The moving magnetic field attempts to induce, in that wire, a flow of current in the opposite direction, which is called a counter-voltage. This is indicated by the dot, which means the current is flowing toward the reader. To understand how current can be induced in the wire, consider the alternator.

As explained in ⊘ 26-7, the alternator rotates a magnetic field through the stator, which has stationary conductors. The movement of the magnetic field produces a flow of current in the conductors. In the ignition coil, there is movement of the current and movement of the magnetic field. The moving magnetic field induces current in the stationary conductors. This is the effect illustrated in Fig. 28-21. The turns of wire are stationary. But the expanding magnetic field from the left-hand conductor cuts across the right-hand conductor and induces current flow in the opposite direction. The current tends to flow out of the page, as shown by the dot.

Actually, the current cannot flow in this direction in the right-hand wire. The battery is already forcing current through the winding (and every turn of wire) in the opposite direction, as shown in Fig. 28-20. But there is a tendency for current to be induced in the reverse direction in every turn of wire. The tendency is brought about by the expanding magnetic fields from nearby turns of wire. This tendency combats any increase in current flow through the winding. The battery voltage must overcome this tendency before it can build up the magnetic field in the winding. This takes a fraction of a second.

⊘ 28-15 Effect of Collapsing Magnetic Field on Primary Winding When the distributor contact points open, the current stops flowing. The magnetic field from the primary winding begins to collapse. This means that the magnetic field surrounding each turn of wire begins to collapse back toward the wire. Thus, instead of the field moving to the right, as in Fig. 28-21, the field moves to the left. This induces a flow of current in the right-hand wire in a direction opposite to that shown—that is, in the direction in which it flowed when the winding was connected to the battery. Such action, again, is self-induction.

⊘ 28-16 Condenser Effect As the distributor contact points open, the current from the battery through the primary winding of the coil is stopped. Instantly, the magnetic field begins to collapse. This collapse tends to reestablish the flow of current. If it were not for the *condenser* (also called a *capacitor*), the flow of current would be reestablished. A heavy electric arc would move across the contact points as they separated. The points would burn, and the energy stored in the ignition coil as magnetism would be consumed by the arc. The condenser prevents this, however. It provides a place for the current to flow as the points begin to move apart.

The condenser (or capacitor) is made up of two thin metallic plates separated by an insulator. The plates are two long, narrow strips of lead or aluminum foil. They are insulated from each other by special condenser paper and wrapped to form a winding. The winding is then installed in a container. A condenser is shown in Fig. 28-22. The two plates provide a large surface area onto which the electrons (flow of current) can move at the instant the contact points separate. Remember, it is the massing of electrons in one place in a circuit that causes them to move and produce a current. The condenser provides a large surface area. Thus, many electrons can flow into it without all collecting in one spot.

The number of electrons the condenser can accept is, however, limited. It quickly becomes charged. But, by this time, the contact points are sufficiently far apart to prevent an arc from forming between them. In effect, the condenser acts as a reservoir into which electrons flow at the instant the points begin to separate. By the time the reservoir is filled, the points are too far apart for the electrons to jump across them. The electrons, or current, must stop flowing in the primary circuit. It is a current flow that induces the magnetic field. Thus, the quick stoppage of the current causes the magnetic field to collapse rapidly. It is this rapid collapse that induces

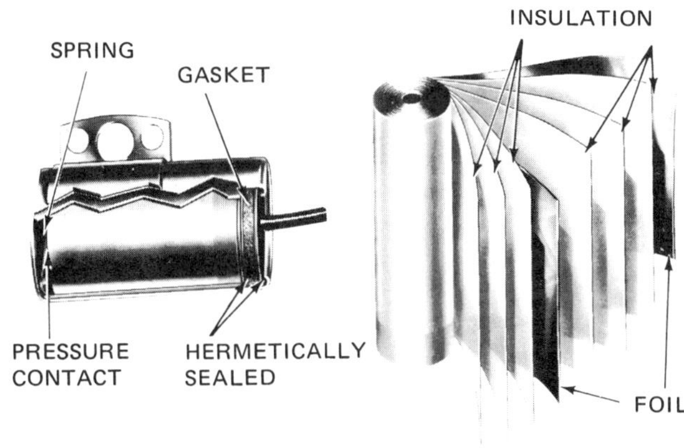

Fig. 28-22. Condenser, assembled and partly unwound.

the high voltage in the secondary winding of the ignition coil. About $\frac{1}{10,000}$ of a second after the points begin to open, the induced voltage in the primary circuit has charged the condenser with a voltage of up to 300 volts. Then the condenser discharges itself into the primary winding of the coil in a series of diminishing oscillations. Because the condenser is used, the magnetic field collapses about 20 times faster. The importance of the condenser in speeding the collapse of the magnetic field explains why an engine will not run without a condenser, or with a defective condenser.

⊘ 28-17 Effect of Magnetic-Field Collapse on Secondary Winding The rapid collapse of the magnetic field causes the magnetic lines of force to move rapidly across the thousands of turns of wire in the secondary winding. This means that each turn has a voltage induced in it. All turns are connected in series, so the total voltage induced is the sum of the voltages in all the turns. Thus, the winding supplies a high voltage during the magnetic-field collapse. One end of the secondary winding is connected through ground (by way of the cylinder block and head) to the side electrode in the spark plug. The other end of the secondary winding is connected through the distributor cap and rotor, and through the wiring, to the center electrode in the spark plug. This high voltage, suddenly imposed on the spark plug, causes electrons (current) to jump across the gap, producing an electric spark. The spark is timed by the spark-advance mechanisms located in the distributor (⊘ 28-20).

NOTE: The ignition-coil voltage output varies with different operating conditions. The coil produces only enough voltage to jump the spark-plug gap. The different plugs in an engine have different voltage requirements if their gaps are different. Also, air-fuel mixture richness, and the amount of mixture compressed during each compression stroke, will vary. These variations result from changes in throttle opening and engine speed. Thus, the coil voltage must change to meet these different conditions.

⊘ 28-18 Summary of Actions Let us review briefly the actions taking place in the ignition system. The piston in one of the engine cylinders starts up on the compression stroke. At the same time, one of the distributor breaker-cam lobes moves away from the contact-point breaker arm. The contact points close. Current flows through the primary winding of the ignition coil, and a magnetic field builds up. Then, the piston reaches the position in the cylinder at which ignition of the compressed air-fuel mixture should take place. At this instant the next cam lobe has moved around to where it strikes against the contact-point breaker arm, so that the contact points separate. The current stops flowing in the primary circuit, and the magnetic field collapses. This induces high voltage in the secondary winding. The rotor on top of the breaker cam, in the meantime, has moved into position. It is now opposite the outside distributor-cap terminal connected to the cylinder spark plug. The spark plug is thus connected to the secondary winding of the ignition coil, through the cap and rotor, at the instant that the high voltage is induced. A spark therefore occurs at the spark-plug gap.

⊘ 28-19 Ignition-Coil Resistor In many passenger cars with 12-V systems, there is a resistance wire in the ignition-coil primary circuit (see Figs. 23-15 and 28-1). This wire is shorted out by the ignition switch when it is turned to START. Now, full battery voltage is imposed on the ignition coil for good cranking performance. After the engine is started, the ignition switch is moved to ON. The resistance is then connected in the ignition primary circuit. It thus protects the contact points from excessive current.

⊘ 28-20 Spark-Advance Mechanisms There are two general types of spark-advance mechanisms—centrifugal and vacuum. These mechanisms vary the spark timing for different engine operating conditions.

⊘ 28-21 Centrifugal Advance When the engine is idling, the spark is timed to occur just before the piston reaches top dead center on the compression stroke. At higher speeds, it is necessary to deliver the spark to the combustion chamber somewhat earlier. This gives the mixture time to burn and deliver its power to the piston. To provide this advance, a centrifugal-advance mechanism is used (Fig. 28-23). It consists of two weights that are thrown out against spring tension as engine speed increases. This movement is transmitted through a toggle arrangement to the breaker cam (or to the timer core or reluctor of magnetic-pickup distributors). This causes the cam (or timer core or reluctor) to advance, or move ahead, with respect to the distributor drive shaft. On the contact-point distributor, this advance causes the cam to open and close the contact points earlier in the compression stroke at high speeds. On the magnetic-pickup distributor, the timer core is advanced so that the pickup coil advances the timing of its signals to the transistor control unit. Since the rotor, too, is advanced, it comes into position earlier in the cycle. The timing of the spark to the cylinder thus varies from no advance at low speed to full advance at high speed (when the weights have reached the outer limits of their travel). The maximum advance may be as much as 45° of crankshaft rotation before the piston reaches top dead center. It varies with different makes of engines. The toggle arrangement and springs are designed to give the correct advance for maximum engine performance.

⊘ 28-22 Vacuum Advance Under part throttle, a partial vacuum develops in the intake manifold. This

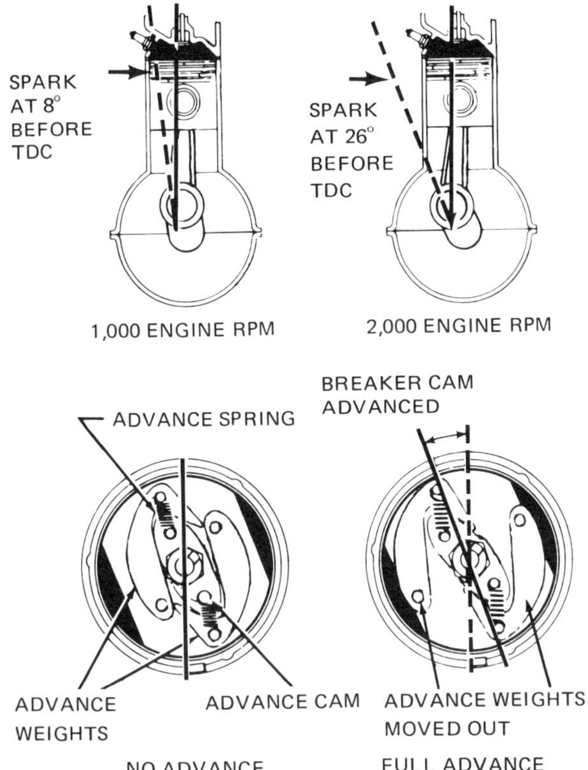

Fig. 28-23. Centrifugal-advance mechanism in the no-advance and full-advance positions. In the typical example shown, the ignition is timed at 8° before top dead center on idle. There is no centrifugal advance at 1,000 engine rpm. There is 26° total advance (18° centrifugal plus 8° of original timing) at 2,000 engine rpm. (*Delco-Remy Division of General Motors Corporation*)

means that less air and fuel are admitted to the cylinder (the volumetric efficiency is lowered). Thus, the mixture is compressed less. The mixture burns more slowly when ignited. To give it more time to burn, the spark should be somewhat advanced. To obtain this spark advance, a vacuum-advance mechanism is used.

Figure 28-19 shows a type of vacuum-advance mechanism used on contact-point distributors. It contains a spring-loaded, airtight diaphragm. The diaphragm is connected by a linkage, or lever, to the breaker plate. The breaker plate is supported on a bearing so it can turn with respect to the distributor housing. It actually turns only a few degrees. The linkage to the spring-loaded diaphragm prevents any greater rotation than this.

The spring-loaded side of the diaphragm is connected through a vacuum line to an opening in the carburetor (Fig. 28-24). This opening is on the atmospheric side of the throttle valve when the throttle is in the idling position. There is no vacuum advance in this position.

As soon as the throttle is opened, however, it moves past the vacuum-line opening. The intake-manifold vacuum can then draw air from the vacuum line and the airtight chamber in the vacuum-

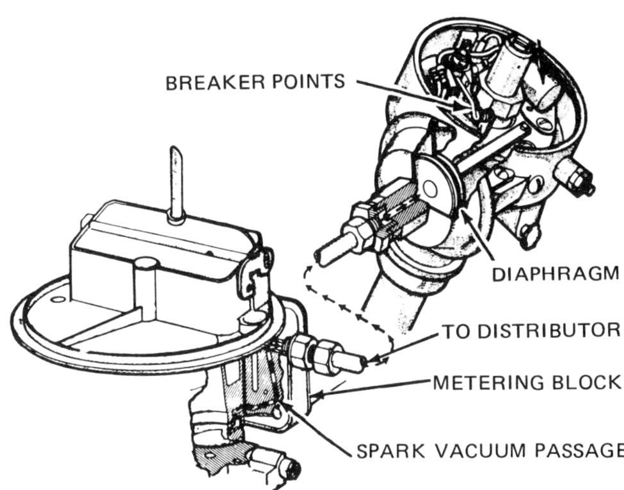

Fig. 28-24. Connection of the vacuum line between the carburetor and the vacuum-advance mechanism on the distributor. (*Ford Motor Company*)

advance mechanism. This causes the diaphragm to move against the spring. The linkage to the breaker plate then rotates the breaker plate. This movement carries the contact points around. Thus, the cam, as it rotates, closes and opens the points earlier in the cycle. The spark then appears at the spark-plug gap earlier in the compression stroke. As the throttle is opened wider, there is less vacuum in the intake manifold, and less vacuum advance. At wide-open throttle, there is no vacuum advance at all. The spark advance under this condition is provided entirely by the centrifugal-advance mechanism.

On the magnetic-pickup distributor, the vacuum-advance mechanism is attached to the magnetic-pickup assembly (Fig. 28-6). This assembly is rotated to provide the vacuum advance.

⊘ 28-23 Combination of Centrifugal and Vacuum Advances At any particular engine speed, there will be some centrifugal advance due to engine speed. There may be an additional spark advance due to the operation of the vacuum-advance mechanism. Figure 28-25 illustrates this. At 40 mph [64 km/h], the centrifugal-advance mechanism provides 15° of spark advance in this example. The vacuum-advance mechanism can supply up to 15° of additional advance under part-throttle conditions. However, if the engine is operated at wide-open throttle, no vacuum advance is obtained. The advance usually varies between the straight line (centrifugal advance) and the curved line (centrifugal advance plus total possible vacuum advance) as the throttle is closed and opened.

⊘ 28-24 Full Vacuum Control The distributor in Fig. 28-26 does not contain a centrifugal-advance mechanism. Instead, it utilizes vacuum from the carburetor venturi and intake manifold to produce the proper advance. Full control by vacuum alone is

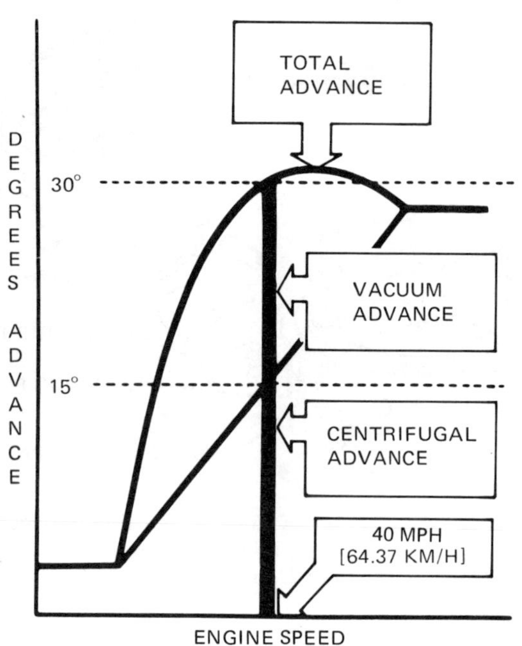

Fig. 28-25. Centrifugal-advance and vacuum-advance curves for one particular application.

possible because airspeed through the carburetor air horn, and thus the vacuum in the venturi, is directly related to engine speed. Let us see how the system works.

In the carburetor shown in Fig. 28-26, there are two vacuum openings in the air horn. One is at the venturi, and the other is just above the throttle when it is closed. The lower, or throttle, vacuum-takeoff opening may have two ports on some models, as in Fig. 28-26. These openings are connected to each other by vacuum passages. They are connected to the distributor vacuum-advance mechanism by a vacuum line. Vacuum imposed on the diaphragm in the vacuum-advance mechanism causes the breaker-plate assembly to rotate. This is very similar to the action of the vacuum-advance devices discussed earlier. Rotation of the breaker-plate assembly causes an advance of the spark.

As engine speed increases, the vacuum at the venturi in the carburetor increases. This is due to the increase of air speed through the venturi. This causes an increasing spark advance which is related to engine speed. At the same time, under part-throttle operating conditions, there is a vacuum in the intake manifold. This acts at the throttle vacuum ports in the carburetor to produce a further vacuum advance. Thus, the vacuum conditions at the two points in the carburetor produce, in effect, a combined speed advance (as with a centrifugal device) and vacuum advance.

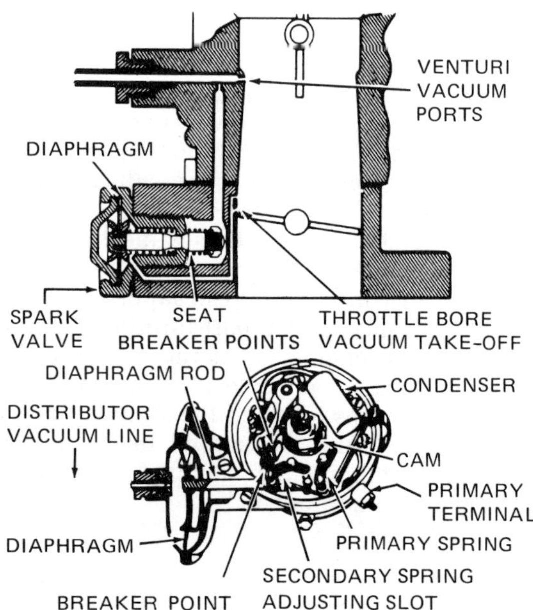

Fig. 28-26. Vacuum-line connections between a carburetor and a distributor having full vacuum control. (*Ford Motor Company*)

⊘ 28-25 Vacuum-Advance Controls for Emission Reduction

Reduction During some operating conditions, vacuum advance can increase the formation of nitrogen oxides during combustion. As explained in Chap. 18, nitrogen oxides (NO_x) form during combustion at high temperatures. Thus, part-throttle operation in the lower gears can cause an increase of NO_x in the exhaust gases. To prevent this, automobiles are equipped with control systems that prevent vacuum advance under some conditions.

Car manufacturers achieve vacuum-advance control by different methods. Figure 28-27 shows one system. It allows vacuum advance only in high gear—with certain exceptions noted below. The system includes a transmission switch, a solenoid vacuum switch, and a temperature override system. For normal operation in any gear but high, the transmission switch is closed. This connects the solenoid vacuum switch to the battery. The solenoid pulls in its plunger, closing off the vacuum connection to the lower part of the carburetor (that is, to manifold

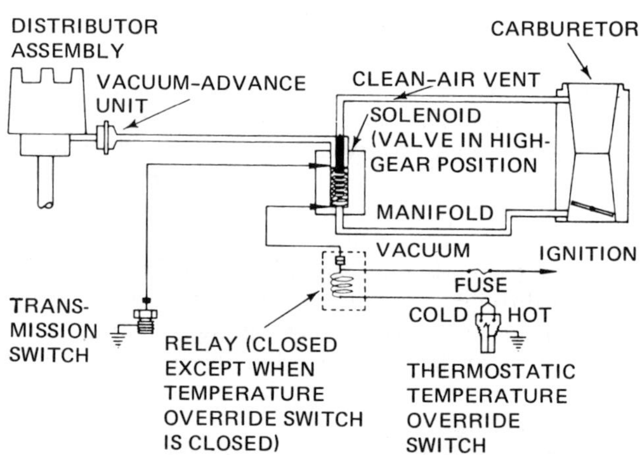

Fig. 28-27. Schematic view of the transmission-controlled spark (TCS) system. (*Chevrolet Motor Division of General Motors Corporation*)

vacuum). At the same time, the solenoid opens a connection to the upper part of the carburetor through a clean-air vent. This releases any vacuum on the vacuum-advance mechanism at the distributor. There is no vacuum advance.

When the transmission goes into high gear, the transmission switch is opened. This allows the solenoid plunger to be pushed up by a spring. This shuts off the clean-air vent. It opens the line from the manifold vacuum vent to the vacuum-advance unit. Now, normal vacuum advance can take place.

The temperature override system provides full advance for better performance in all gears when the engine is cold. A thermostatic coolant-temperature switch is closed when the engine is cold. This connects the relay winding to the battery (through the ignition switch). The relay contact points open, thus opening the circuit to the solenoid. Now, regardless of the position of the transmission switch, the solenoid cannot operate. The vacuum-advance unit remains connected to the manifold vacuum vent in the carburetor. Thus, the system provides normal vacuum advance.

When the engine warms up, the thermostatic override switch opens. This opens the relay winding. The relay points close. The system now operates so that vacuum advance is obtained only in high gear, as explained above.

The system also has a hot override position. This provides vacuum advance at all gear positions if the engine is overheating. The vacuum advance improves engine cooling. See Chap. 18 for the details of this and other vacuum-advance control systems.

⊘ 28-26 Ignition Switch In late-model cars, the ignition switch is mounted on the steering column, as shown in Fig. 28-28. This arrangement locks the steering shaft when the ignition switch is turned off and the ignition key is removed. A small gear on the end of the ignition switch rotates and releases a plunger. The plunger enters a notch in a disk on the steering shaft, to lock the shaft. If a notch is not lined up with the plunger, the plunger rests on the disk. When the steering wheel, shaft, and disk are turned slightly, the plunger drops into a notch.

When the ignition key is inserted and the ignition switch is turned on, the plunger is withdrawn from the disk. This unlocks the steering shaft.

The ignition switch has an extra set of contacts that are used when the switch is turned past ON to START. The contacts connect the starting-motor solenoid to the battery so that the starting motor can operate. As soon as the engine is started and the key is released, it returns to ON. The starting motor is then disconnected from the battery.

The alternator field circuit is connected to the battery through the ignition switch when it is turned to ON. When the ignition switch is turned to OFF, the alternator field circuit is disconnected. This keeps the battery from running down through the field circuit.

The ignition switch also operates a buzzer if the key is in the lock when the driver's car door is open. This reminds the driver to remove the key from the lock when the car is parked. It helps guard against theft of the car.

Such accessories as the radio and the car heater are connected to the battery through the ignition switch. This ensures that these units are off when the driver turns off the engine and leaves the car.

CHAPTER 28 CHECKUP

NOTE: Since this is a chapter review test, you should review the chapter before taking the test.

The ignition system may seem very complex when you look at it for the first time. But if you have followed the explanations in this chapter, you know that it is really rather simple. In operation, the ignition-coil primary winding is connected to the battery momentarily (through the distributor contact points or electronic control unit). This loads the ignition coil with magnetism. Then, when the ignition coil is disconnected, it discharges this magnetism and pro-

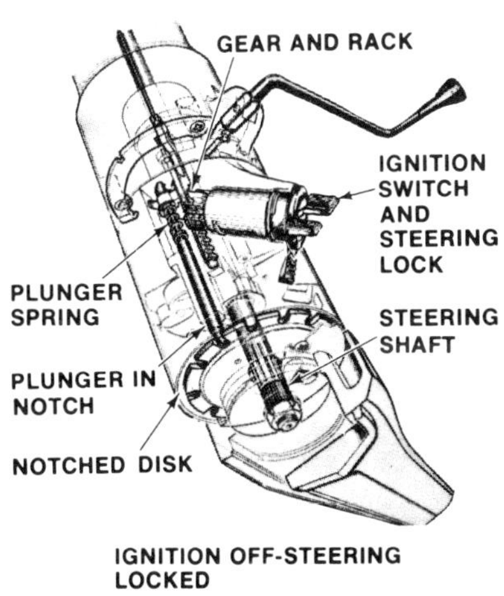

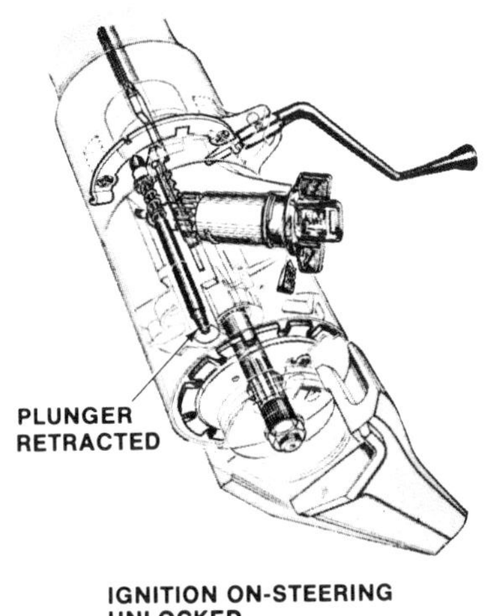

Fig. 28-28. Combination ignition switch and steering-wheel lock in phantom views, showing the two positions of the lock. (*General Motors Corporation*)

duces a high-voltage surge. The surge is led through the distributor cap and rotor and the wiring, to a spark plug.

Find out how well you remember the details of the ignition system by taking the test that follows. If you cannot answer all the questions, or if you are confused about any ignition-system action, study the chapter again. You should know the answers before you proceed to the next chapter.

Completing the Sentences The sentences below are incomplete. After each sentence there are several words or phrases, but only one of them correctly completes the sentence. Write each sentence in your notebook, ending it with the one word or phrase that completes it correctly.

1. The ignition coil has: (*a*) one winding, (*b*) two windings, (*c*) three windings, (*d*) four windings.
2. The primary winding of the ignition coil is connected to the battery through the: (*a*) spark-plug wiring, (*b*) distributor cap and rotor, (*c*) distributor gearing, (*d*) distributor contact points.
3. The voltage induced in a winding by self-induction is called: (*a*) reverse voltage, (*b*) reduced voltage, (*c*) counter-voltage, (*d*) maximum voltage.
4. The spark-producing high voltage is developed in the secondary winding during: (*a*) magnetic buildup, (*b*) magnetic collapse, (*c*) the time the points are closed.
5. The ignition condenser is connected: (*a*) across the points, (*b*) in series with the points, (*c*) in the secondary circuit.
6. The main function of the ignition condenser is to protect the contact points and produce: (*a*) quick magnetic collapse, (*b*) slow magnetic collapse, (*c*) high voltage on the points.
7. The rotating switch that connects the various spark plugs to the ignition-coil secondary in regular firing order is formed by the distributor: (*a*) points and condenser, (*b*) cap and rotor, (*c*) switch and contact points.
8. The device in many distributors that pushes the breaker cam ahead as engine speed increases is called the: (*a*) vacuum-advance mechanism, (*b*) centrifugal-advance mechanism, (*c*) full-advance mechanism, (*d*) vacuum-brake mechanism.
9. The device in many distributors that shifts the position of the breaker plate or magnetic-pickup assembly to produce a change in the timing of the spark is actuated by: (*a*) intake-manifold vacuum, (*b*) engine speed, (*c*) centrifugal advance.
10. With wide-open throttle, vacuum advance is: (*a*) at a maximum, (*b*) part to full, (*c*) at a minimum.

Reviewing the System In the following, you are asked for explanations of the actions that take place in the ignition system, as well as the purpose and operation of various components. If you are not clear about some explanation, carefully review the pages that clear up the matter. Then write each explanation in your notebook, in your own words.

1. Describe briefly the construction of an ignition coil.
2. Explain briefly what takes place in the ignition-coil primary circuit when the distributor contacts close and open.
3. What is meant by self-induction?
4. Explain how self-induction takes place between two nearby turns of wire in a winding.
5. What happens in the secondary winding during magnetic-field buildup?
6. Explain the effect of self-induction in the primary winding after the contact points open.
7. What is meant by buildup in the ignition coil? About how long is the normal buildup time?
8. Describe the construction of a condenser.
9. Describe briefly the action of a condenser during the short interval after the contact points open.
10. Describe the action in the ignition-coil secondary winding during magnetic collapse.
11. Describe the action in the ignition-coil primary winding during magnetic collapse.
12. Briefly summarize the actions in the ignition system. Begin when the breaker-cam lobe moves out of the way so that the contacts can close, and end the summary when the spark occurs at the spark-plug gap.
13. Why are spark advances needed?
14. Why is centrifugal advance desirable? Vacuum advance?
15. Describe two types of vacuum-advance mechanisms.
16. Explain the operation of the magnetic-pickup ignition system.
17. Explain the operation of the control unit in the electronic ignition system.

SUGGESTIONS FOR FURTHER STUDY

Study the ignition-equipment sections of various shop manuals and bulletins issued by automobile and electrical-equipment manufacturers. If you have a chance, examine this equipment in a local automotive electrical service shop or your school shop. Note especially the provisions for driving the distributor, and the different types of advance mechanisms that distributors use. Be sure to write any important facts in your notebook.

chapter 29

IGNITION-SYSTEM TROUBLE DIAGNOSIS

This chapter lists the causes of ignition failure and describes trouble-diagnosis methods. The next chapter describes several instruments that can be used to check the ignition system and its components. Chapter 31 describes distributor service.

⊘ 29-1 Causes of Ignition Failure Ignition-system failures can be grouped into three categories, as follows:

1. Loss of energy in the primary circuit. This, in turn, may be caused by several conditions:
a. Resistance in the primary circuit due to defective leads, bad connections, poor distributor ground, burned distributor contact points or switch, or open coil primary
b. Points not properly set
c. Discharged battery or defective alternator
d. Defective condenser (shorted, low insulation resistance, or high series resistance)
e. Grounded primary circuit in coil, wiring, or distributor
f. Defective electronic-amplifier unit or pickup-coil circuit
2. Loss of energy in the secondary circuit, owing to:
a. Plugs fouled, broken, or out of adjustment
b. Defective high-voltage wiring which allows high-voltage leaks
c. High-voltage leakage across coil head, distributor cap, or rotor
d. Defective connections in high-voltage circuits
3. Out of time owing to:
a. Timing not set properly
b. Distributor bearing or shaft worn, or shaft bent
c. Defective centrifugal-advance mechanism
d. Preignition, due to plugs of wrong heat range, fouled plugs, etc.

⊘ 29-2 Ignition-System Trouble-Diagnosis Chart The chart that follows lists (1) various ignition-system troubles and possible engine troubles that might originate in the ignition system; (2) possible causes of these troubles; and (3) checks or corrections to be made.

IGNITION-SYSTEM TROUBLE-DIAGNOSIS CHART

(See ⊘ 29-3 to 29-14 for detailed explanations of the trouble causes and corrections listed below.)

CONDITION	POSSIBLE CAUSE	CHECK OR CORRECTION
1. Engine cranks normally but will not start (⊘ 29-4)	a. Open primary circuit	Check connections, coil, contact points, and switch for open
	b. Coil primary grounded	Replace coil
	c. Points not opening	Adjust
	d. Points burned	Clean or replace
	e. Out of time	Check and adjust timing
	f. Condenser defective	Replace
	g. Coil secondary open or grounded	Replace coil
	h. High-voltage leakage	Check coil head, distributor cap and rotor, and leads
	i. Spark plugs fouled	Clean and adjust or replace
	j. Defects in electronic amplifier or pickup-coil circuit	Replace defective part
	k. Fuel system faulty	See Chap. 14
	l. Engine faulty	See Chap. 34
2. Engine runs, but misses on one cylinder (⊘ 29-5)	a. Defective spark plug	Clean or replace
	b. Defective distributor cap or lead	Replace

IGNITION-SYSTEM TROUBLE-DIAGNOSIS CHART (cont)

CONDITION	POSSIBLE CAUSE	CHECK OR CORRECTION
	c. Engine defect such as stuck valve, defective rings, piston, gasket	See Chap. 34
3. Engine runs but misses on different cylinders (⊘ 29-6)	a. Points dirty, worn, or out of adjustment	Clean, replace, or adjust as necessary
	b. Condenser defective	Replace
	c. Advance mechanisms defective	Repair or replace distributor
	d. Defective high-voltage wiring	Replace
	e. Defective (weak) coil	Replace
	f. Bad connections	Clean and tighten connections
	g. High-voltage leakage	Check coil head, distributor cap and rotor, and leads
	h. Defective spark plugs	Clean; adjust or replace
	i. Defective fuel system	See Chap. 14
	j. Defects in engine, such as loss of compression or faulty valve action	See Chap. 34
4. Engine lacks power (⊘ 29-7)	a. Timing off	Retime ignition
	b. Exhaust system clogged	Clear
	c. Excessive rolling resistance	Check tires, brakes, wheel bearings, and alignment
	d. Heavy engine oil	Use correct oil
	e. Wrong fuel	Use correct fuel
	f. Engine overheats	See item 5 below
	g. Other defects listed under item 3 above	
5. Engine overheats (⊘ 29-8)	a. Late ignition timing	Retime ignition
	b. Lack of coolant or other trouble in cooling system	See Chap. 14
	c. Late valve timing or other engine conditions	See Chap. 34
6. Engine backfires (⊘ 29-9)	a. Ignition timing off	Retime ignition
	b. Ignition crossfiring	Check high-voltage wiring, cap, and rotor for leakage paths
	c. Spark plugs of wrong heat range	Install correct plugs
	d. Engine overheating	See item 5 above
	e. Fuel system not supplying proper air-fuel ratio	See Chap. 14
	f. Engine defects such as hot valves or carbon	See Chap. 34
7. Engine detonates or pings (⊘ 29-10)	a. Improper timing	Retime engine
	b. Advance mechanisms faulty	Rebuild or replace distributor
	c. Points out of adjustment	Adjust
	d. Distributor bearing worn, or shaft bent	Rebuild or replace distributor
	e. Spark plugs of wrong heat range	Replace with correct plugs
	f. Low-octane fuel	Use fuel of proper octane
	g. Conditions listed under item 6 above	
8. Rapid wear of centrifugal-advance mechanism (⊘ 29-11)	a. Loose or worn valve timing gears	See Chap. 34
	b. Worn oil pump	See Chap. 34
9. Pitted contact points (⊘ 29-12)	a. Transfer of point material to positive points	Install new condenser with higher capacity; separate leads or move closer to ground; shorten condenser lead
	b. Transfer of point material to negative points	Install new condenser with lower capacity; move leads closer together or away from ground; lengthen condenser lead
10. Burned or oxidized contact points (⊘ 29-13)	a. Excessive resistance in condenser circuit	Tighten condenser mounting and connection; replace condenser if bad
	b. High voltage	Adjust voltage regulator
	c. Excessive contact angle	Reset contacts
	d. Weak spring tension	Adjust contact-spring tension
	e. Oil or crankcase vapors entering distributor	Clear engine PCV system; avoid overlubricating distributor
11. Spark plugs defective (⊘ 29-14)	a. Cracked insulator	Careless installation; install new plug

CONDITION	POSSIBLE CAUSE	CHECK OR CORRECTION
	b. Plug sooty	Install hotter plug; correct condition (in fuel system or engine) causing oil burning or high fuel consumption
	c. Plug white or gray, with blistered insulator	Install cooler plug

⊘ 29-3 Quick Checks to Locate Trouble There are several quick checks that can be made when certain types of troubles are reported. These quick checks often immediately indicate the cause of a trouble. On the other hand, it may be necessary to use special testing instruments (as explained on following pages) to find the cause. Often, the first step is to replace the battery, since the driver may have run it down attempting to start. Quick checks to be made, as well as causes and corrections of various ignition troubles, are described below.

NOTE: If an oscilloscope is available (see ⊘ 30-6 to 30-9) and the engine can be started, the oscilloscope can pinpoint many trouble causes in the ignition system.

⊘ 29-4 Engine Cranks Normally but Will Not Start If the starting motor cranks the engine at normal cranking speed but the engine will not start, the trouble is probably in the ignition system or the fuel system. First test the ignition system by trying the spark test, as follows: Disconnect the lead from one spark plug. Use insulated pliers and hold the lead clip about $\frac{3}{16}$ in [4.76 mm] from the engine block while cranking the engine. Or, pull the lead from the center terminal of the distributor cap, and using insulated pliers, hold it close to the engine block. If a good spark jumps to the block, the primary and secondary circuits are probably in good condition. These circuits must both function normally to produce a good spark. If they do, then failure to start could be due to badly fouled spark plugs or out-of-time ignition. However, many other conditions (including faulty fuel-system action, malfunctioning valves, and loss of engine compression) could prevent normal starting. Most often, though, failure to start (with normal cranking) is due to troubles in the ignition or fuel system.

One condition that sometimes prevents starting on humid or rainy days is moisture collecting on the spark-plug insulators. The moisture allows the high-voltage current to leak to ground instead of jumping the spark gap. Thus, no ignition occurs and the engine does not start. However, if the moisture is wiped from the spark-plug insulators, a normal start can be made.

NOTE: Another way of checking for a spark is to remove the distributor cap and snap the contact points open and closed. The ignition switch should be on, and the lead from the coil high-voltage terminal should be held close to the engine block. This check does not, of course, test the distributor drive or the secondary wiring.

If a spark does not occur when the spark test is made, the ignition system is not doing its job of producing high voltage. Check further by watching the instrument-panel ammeter while cranking.

NOTE: If the car does not have an ammeter, connect a test ammeter into the ignition primary circuit to make this test.

1. A small reading which fluctuates somewhat during cranking indicates that the primary circuit is probably okay. The trouble is most likely in the secondary; it is due to a defective coil secondary, defective secondary connections or leads, or high-voltage leakage across the coil head, cap, or rotor. An open or "weak" condenser can also prevent high-voltage buildup in the secondary.
2. A fairly high and steady ammeter reading, with no fluctuations during cranking, indicates that the trouble is probably in the primary circuit. The points may not be opening because they are out of adjustment or the condenser is grounded. Or, the primary circuit is grounded in the coil or primary wiring.
3. If there is no ammeter reading, the primary circuit is open. The open could be due to a loose connection, defective wiring or switch, distributor contact points out of adjustment or burned, or an open coil primary. A voltmeter can be used to find the open by checking from various terminals in the primary to ground to see where voltage is available. First, check from the distributor primary-lead terminal on the coil to ground. If there is voltage here, the trouble is inside the distributor. If there is no voltage at the distributor primary-lead terminal on the coil, check from the other ignition-coil primary terminal to ground. If you now get a reading, the trouble is in the coil primary winding. If you get no reading, the trouble is in the wiring or the switch. Disassemble the switch extension if the coil has one, so that the coil and switch may be checked separately.

⊘ 29-5 Engine Runs but Misses on One Cylinder On some engines, you can locate a missing cylinder by using a screwdriver to short out each cylinder spark plug in turn. The engine should be running, at various speeds. The screwdriver should have an insulated handle so you do not get shocked. Short out the spark plug by touching the screwdriver blade to the spark-plug terminal and the cylinder block. This prevents a spark from occurring in the spark plug and causes the cylinder to miss. On late-model cars, the spark plugs have neoprene boots over the spark-plug terminals. It is difficult to short these plugs out. Instead, remove the cables from the distributor cap one by one, and note any change in engine speed.

If the engine rhythm or speed changes when a plug is shorted out or its circuit is opened, then that cylinder was delivering power before being shorted out. However, if no change in engine operation is noted when a spark plug is shorted out or its circuit is opened, then the cylinder is not delivering power; it is missing. If you locate a missing cylinder, remove the lead from the spark plug (with the other cylinders operating) and hold it close to the engine block to see if a good spark occurs. If it does not, the cause of the trouble is in the secondary circuit of the ignition system. It could be defective cable insulation or a cracked or burned distributor cap. Either of these could allow high-voltage leakage to ground. But if a good spark occurs, then that spark plug probably is defective. Install a new plug. If the cylinder now performs normally, the trouble was a defective plug. If changing the plug does not help, then the trouble is in the engine cylinder (stuck valve, defective rings, piston, head gasket, and so on).

CAUTION: On the High-Energy Ignition System, use rubber gloves or insulated pliers to handle spark-plug cables on a running engine. You can get a severe shock from this system because of the high voltage it produces

NOTE: A quick way to locate the cause of engine-missing trouble is to check the system with an oscilloscope (⊘ 30-9).

⊘ 29-6 Engine Runs but Misses on Different Cylinders A miss that seems to jump around from cylinder to cylinder could be due to any of several conditions in the ignition system, fuel system, or engine. The distributor contact points could be worn, dirty, or out of adjustment. The condenser or ignition coil could be "weak," so that the spark is not uniform and erratic missing occurs. The advance mechanisms might be erratic in action and thus cause uneven timing and missing. Distributors with the breaker plate supported by balls running in a ball track in the distributor housing may have the following troubles: The ball track wears, or the balls get dirty or worn; this causes the breaker plate to hang up or tilt when the vacuum-advance mechanism operates. This then causes a momentary erratic miss.

Bad ignition-circuit connections or defective wiring can also cause missing. If high-voltage leakage occurs across the coil head, distributor cap, or rotor, or if there is leakage through secondary-wiring insulation, missing may occur. After a while, continued leakage across the coil head or the rotor etches a visible path. If this occurs, the part requires replacement. Otherwise, wiping dirt from the part and keeping it clean and dry will prevent such leakage. If the insulation on the secondary wiring has deteriorated (is cracked or rotting), it may allow high-voltage leakage. This condition requires replacement of the wiring.

Connecting a coil incorrectly, so that the secondary polarity is reversed, could increase the voltage requirement so much that missing results. The reversed connections mean that electrons must jump from the cooler outside spark-plug electrode to the center electrode. This requires a much higher secondary voltage. It increases the possibility of engine missing, especially at high speeds. Normally, the coil is connected so that electrons jump from the hot center electrode to the outer electrode. When the *emitting* electrode is hot, voltage requirements are much lower.

To test for reversed polarity, hold an ordinary pencil tip between the high-voltage-wire clip and the spark-plug terminal (Fig. 29-1). The spark should flare out between the pencil tip and the spark plug, as shown. If it flares out between the pencil tip and the wire clip, the polarity is reversed. Another test is

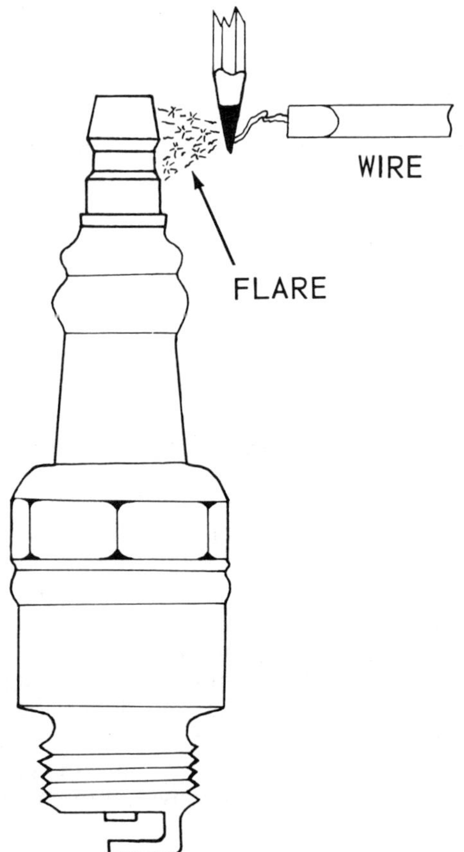

Fig. 29-1. Using a pencil tip to check the polarity of the ignition coil. If the flare is between the pencil tip and the high-voltage-lead clip, and not as shown, the coil is connected backward.

to connect a neon bulb (NE-2 or similar) between the spark-plug terminal (high-voltage lead connected) and ground. With the engine running, the neon-bulb electrode that is connected to the spark-plug terminal should glow. If the terminal connected to ground glows, the polarity is reversed.

Worn or fouled spark plugs will miss, especially during a hard pull or on acceleration.

Remember also that many other conditions in the engine and fuel system could cause missing. If the fuel system fails to deliver an air-fuel mixture of the proper proportions, or if the engine has faulty valve action or loss of compression, missing will occur.

⊘ 29-7 Engine Lacks Power Many conditions can cause lack of power. With the timing off or with any of the conditions discussed in ⊘ 29-6, the engine does not deliver normal power. In addition, if the exhaust system is clogged, if heavy engine oil or the wrong fuel is being used, or if there is excessive rolling resistance due to underinflated tires, dragging brakes, and so on, then the engine will seem sluggish and lack power.

⊘ 29-8 Engine Overheats Engine overheating may be caused by many conditions in the engine cooling system or in the engine itself. It can also be caused by late ignition timing.

⊘ 29-9 Engine Backfires Backfiring can be caused by several conditions in the ignition system. If the ignition timing is considerably off, or if ignition crossfiring occurs (owing to sparks jumping from one terminal or lead to another), ignition may occur before the intake valve closes. This causes a backfire.

If a spark plug runs too hot, it may glow enough to ignite the air-fuel mixture before the intake valve closes. Here, the remedy is to use a cooler-running plug.

Preignition, and possibly backfiring, also occurs if valves run red hot, or if carbon in the combustion chambers gets so hot it glows. Incorrect air-fuel ratio may also cause backfiring.

⊘ 29-10 Engine Detonates or Pings Detonation or pinging is often blamed on the ignition system (it is often called a "spark knock"). But many other conditions can cause detonation. In the ignition system, detonation may result from such conditions as excessively advanced timing, faulty advance mechanisms (which cause excessive advance), out-of-adjustment points, a worn distributor bearing or bent shaft (which causes erratic point opening and possible excessive advance to some cylinders), and spark plugs of the wrong heat range (which glow and cause preignition). Other causes of detonation include fuel with an octane rating too low for the engine and the type of operation, excessive carbon in the engine combustion chambers, and conditions listed in ⊘ 29-9. Actually, of all these conditions, the most usual causes of pinging are excessive ignition advance and gasoline with an octane rating too low for the engine and operating conditions.

⊘ 29-11 Rapid Wear of Centrifugal-Advance Mechanism Rapid wear of the centrifugal-advance mechanism occurs on certain engines as a result of loose or worn valve-timing gears or a worn oil pump. These conditions cause backlash and torsional vibration in the distributor drive. This, in turn, wears the centrifugal-advance mechanism rapidly.

⊘ 29-12 Pitted Contact Points Some arcing across the contact points occurs in spite of condenser action. Under some conditions, this arcing may cause point pitting. Pitting is due to the transfer of point material from one contact to the other. A pit is left in one contact, and there is a matching buildup of material on the other contact. Normally, the system is balanced, so pitting is at a minimum. But under certain unusual conditions, it does occur. To correct point pitting, note the following.

If material is being transferred from the negative point to the positive point, then one or all three of the following steps should be taken.

1. Install a new condenser with a higher capacity.
2. Separate the low- and high-voltage leads, or move these leads closer to ground. This reduces the capacitive effect between these leads.
3. Shorten the condenser lead, if possible.

If the positive point is losing material to the negative point, install a new condenser with a lower capacity, move the leads closer together or away from ground, or lengthen the condenser lead.

⊘ 29-13 Burned or Oxidized Contact Points Burning or oxidizing of contact points can be caused by several conditions, as follows:

1. Excessive resistance in the condenser circuit. This is detectable with a high-frequency condenser tester. It is corrected by either tightening the condenser mounting and connections or replacing the condenser, according to where the resistance is.
2. High voltage, which causes excessive current draw through the points. This can be detected by making a voltmeter check with the engine operating at medium speed. Correction normally requires readjustment of the voltage-regulator setting or reduction of alternator output.
3. Contact angle too large (point opening too small). The points remain closed too much of the total operating time, so they burn rapidly. This requires checking of the cam angle or point opening and readjustment as necessary.
4. Weak spring tension, which causes the points to flutter, bounce, and arc at high speeds. Measure the spring tension; readjust or replace the points.

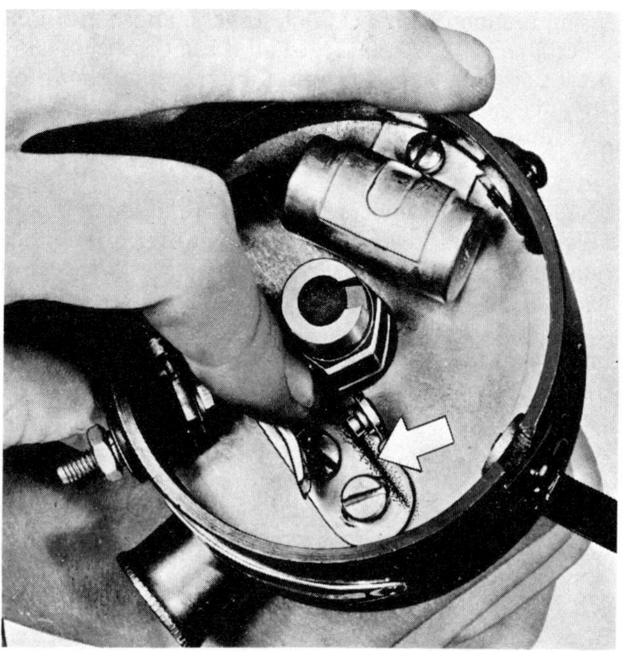

Fig. 29-2. A smudgy line under the contact points indicates that oil or crankcase vapor is getting between the contact points, causing rapid burning of the points.

5. Oil or crankcase vapors entering the distributor housing and depositing on the point surfaces, causing them to burn rapidly. A glance at the breaker plate usually discloses this condition. The oil on the point surfaces burns, and leaves a black smudge on the breaker plate under the point (Fig. 29-2). A clogged engine PCV system (which forces oil into the distributor), excessive oiling of the distributor, or worn distributor bearings can produce this trouble.

⊘ 29-14 Spark Plugs Defective Spark plugs may fail for a variety of reasons. They are subjected to high temperature, high pressure, and high voltage. Spark plugs must withstand these conditions and operate at the proper temperature. If a plug becomes too hot, it wears rapidly and may burn. If it does not get hot enough, it may become fouled as oil, fuel soot, or carbon deposits on it. If enough material collects, then the high-voltage current leaks to ground through the deposit, instead of jumping the spark gap. The plug cannot fire, and the engine misses.

The temperature the plug reaches is governed by the heat range of the plug. Heat range is determined by the shape of the plug and the distance heat must travel from the center electrode of the plug to reach the cylinder head (Fig. 29-3). If the heat must travel a long path, then the plug runs hot. If the path is short, the plug runs cool.

You can tell from its appearance whether a plug is of the correct heat range for the engine. Figure 29-4 illustrates several spark-plug conditions and explains their causes. If a plug is operating too cold, there will be a sooty deposit on the insulator around the center electrode. The plug is not hot enough to burn away this deposit. Even with a plug of the heat range specified for the engine, a deposit may form if (1) the air-fuel mixture is excessively rich (from excessive choking, worn carburetor jets, and so on), or (2) excessive amounts of oil enter the combustion chamber (due to worn rings or cylinder walls, excessive intake-valve-stem clearance, and so on). In such cases, a hotter plug would help to prevent formation of excessive deposits on the plug. But it would not, of course, cure the basic trouble.

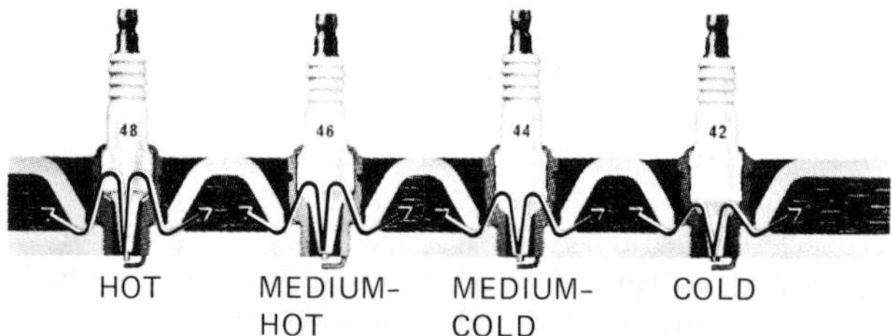

Fig. 29-3. Heat range of spark plugs. The longer the heat path (indicated by arrows), the hotter the plug runs. (*AC Spark Plug Division of General Motors Corporation*)

If the plug runs too hot, a white or grayish cast will appear on the insulator; the insulator may also appear blistered. A plug that runs too hot wears more rapidly; the electrodes burn away more rapidly. One cause of high plug temperature, aside from improper heat range, is incorrect installation of the plug in the engine. If the plug is not tightened to the correct tension, the plug gasket is not sufficiently compressed. In such a case, the heat path may be somewhat restricted. The plug therefore runs hotter. This may also result if the plug seat in the cylinder head is not cleaned before the plug is installed. Dirt could block off the heat path and cause a hot-running plug. On many late-model cars, the plugs do not use gaskets. On these, the seating faces (on plug and head) must be clean and smooth to form a good seal and heat path.

Cracked insulators are caused, as a rule, by careless installation or by improper adjustment of the plug gap.

CHAPTER 29 CHECKUP

NOTE: Since the following is a chapter review test, you should review the chapter before taking the test.

While this chapter is short, it is very important. You may want to refer to it often. As a tuneup technician, you must have a good understanding of ignition troubles, what causes them, and how to find and eliminate them with a minimum of lost time. Take the quiz that follows to find out if you remember the information on ignition-system trouble diagnosis.

Correcting Troubles Lists The purpose of this exercise is to help you spot unrelated troubles in a list.

NORMAL

Brown to grayish tan color and slight electrode wear. Correct heat range for engine and operating conditions.

RECOMMENDATION: Properly service and reinstall. Replace if over 10,000 miles of service.

SPLASHED DEPOSITS

Spotted deposits. Occurs shortly after long-delayed tune-up. After a long period of misfiring, deposits may be loosened when normal combustion temperatures are restored by tune-up. During a high-speed run, these materials shed off the piston and head and are thrown against the hot insulator.

RECOMMENDATION: Clean and service the plugs properly and reinstall.

CARBON DEPOSITS

Dry soot.

RECOMMENDATION: Dry deposits indicate rich mixture or weak ignition. Check for clogged air cleaner, high float level, sticky choke or worn breaker contacts. Hotter plugs will temporarily provide additional fouling protection.

HIGH-SPEED GLAZING

Insulator has yellowish, varnish-like color. Indicates combustion chamber temperatures have risen suddenly during hard, fast acceleration. Normal deposits do not get a chance to blow off, instead they melt to form a conductive coating.

RECOMMENDATION: If condition recurs, use plug type one step colder.

OIL DEPOSITS

Oily coating.

RECOMMENDATION: Caused by poor oil control. Oil is leaking past worn valve guides or piston rings into the combustion chamber. Hotter spark plug may temporarily relieve problem, but positive cure is to correct the condition with necessary repairs.

MODIFIER DEPOSITS

Powdery white or yellow deposits that build up on shell, insulator, and electrodes. This is a normal appearance with certain branded fuels. These materials are used to modify the chemical nature of the deposits to lessen misfire tendencies.

RECOMMENDATION: Plugs can be cleaned or, if replaced, use same heat range.

TOO HOT

Blistered, white insulator, eroded electrodes and absence of deposits.

RECOMMENDATION: Check for correct plug heat range, overadvanced ignition timing, cooling system level and/or stoppages, lean air-fuel mixtures, leaking intake manifold, sticking valves, and if car is driven at high speeds most of the time.

PREIGNITION

Melted electrodes. Center electrode generally melts first and ground electrode follows. Normally, insulators are white, but may be dirty due to misfiring or flying debris in combustion chamber

RECOMMENDATION: Check for correct plug heat range, overadvanced ignition timing, lean fuel mixtures, clogged cooling system, leaking intake manifold, and lack of lubrication.

Fig. 29-4. Appearance of spark plugs related to causes. (*Champion Spark Plug Company*)

For example, check through the list, "Engine runs but misses on one cylinder: defective spark plug, distributor cap or lead defective, engine defects, fuel system faulty." You should see that "fuel system faulty" does not belong in the list. With a faulty fuel system, missing would not be confined to one cylinder; it would occur in different cylinders. Each of the following lists contains one unrelated item. Write each list in your notebook, but do not write the item that does not belong.

1. Engine cranks normally but will not start: open

primary circuit, coil primary grounded, points burned, battery run down, out of time, condenser defective, secondary open or grounded, high-voltage leakage, plugs fouled, fuel system or engine faulty.
2. Engine runs but misses on one cylinder: defective spark plug, condenser shorted, distributor cap or lead defective, engine defects.
3. Engine runs but misses on different cylinders: points defective or out of adjustment, condenser defective, advance mechanisms defective, high-voltage wiring or coil defective, bad connections, excessive engine compression, defective plugs, fuel-system or engine troubles.
4. Engine lacks power: timing off, exhaust system clogged, run-down battery, excessive rolling resistance, heavy engine oil, wrong fuel, engine overheating.
5. Engine overheats: ignition timing late, lack of coolant, cooling-system troubles, late valve timing, engine troubles, burned contact points.
6. Engine backfires: ignition timing off, ignition crossfiring, spark plugs of wrong heat range, centrifugal advance not operating, air-fuel mixture incorrect, engine defects.
7. Engine detonates or pings: improper timing, advance mechanism faulty, excessive resistance in condenser circuit, distributor bearing worn or shaft bent, spark plugs of wrong heat range, low-octane fuel.
8. Centrifugal-advance mechanism wears rapidly: loose or worn valve timing gears, improper timing, worn oil pump.
9. Contact points pitted: condenser of wrong capacity, leads improperly arranged, timing late.
10. Contact points burned: excessive resistance in condenser circuit, high voltage, excessive contact angle, weak spring tension, plugs running too hot, crankcase vapors entering distributor.

SUGGESTIONS FOR FURTHER STUDY

Each time you diagnose a trouble in an ignition system, write the important facts in your notebook. Enter the year, make, and model of car, the type of engine, and the type of ignition system. Then list the condition or customer complaint, the cause of the condition, and the correction you made to restore the engine to proper operating condition.

chapter 30

IGNITION-SYSTEM SERVICE

In the last two chapters, we discussed the construction and operation of ignition systems, and possible troubles in the ignition system. Now, in this chapter, we describe ignition-system testers and explain how to use them to service the ignition system. The next chapter describes distributor service.

⊘ 30-1 Ignition-Coil Testers Two general types of ignition-coil testers are widely used. One type makes use of a spark gap or neon tube. The coil to be tested is connected to the spark gap, and the spark it can produce is measured. A coil known to be good is then tested, and its performance is compared with that of the coil in question. Any variation between the two tests can lead to wrong conclusions. Thus, great care must be taken in making connections, adjusting the gap, and selecting the proper coil for comparison (it should have the same number of turns of wire, and be connected in same manner). Then, too, this type of tester does not always detect such problems as shorted primary windings in a coil.

Most engineers now recommend the use of a scope-type coil tester (Figs. 30-1 and 30-2). This type of tester measures coil performance and gives an accurate picture of coil condition.

⊘ 30-2 Ignition-Condenser Testers Ignition condensers are relatively inexpensive. Ignition technicians often simply replace the condenser on any ignition job. Yet it is sometimes desirable to test the condenser, particularly where trouble is being traced. Four factors are important in the operation and testing of an ignition condenser. These are:

1. Grounding or shorting of the condenser, caused by a breakdown of the insulation between the two condenser plates. This condition prevents condenser action. It can be detected with a test light.
2. Low insulation resistance, which prevents the condenser from holding a charge, so that the condenser is said to be "weak." The insulation permits the charge to leak from one plate to the other. The presence of moisture weakens the insulation and is one cause of low insulation resistance. One method that has been used to check for this condition is to charge the condenser from a 110-V test light, and then hold the condenser clip close to the condenser case to see if a spark occurs. This method is not very accurate, and the results are not conclusive. A good condenser tester usually includes a more reliable means of testing for this condition.
3. High series resistance, which results from a defective condenser lead or poor connection within the condenser. No means of testing for this condition is available, except by high frequency. Condenser testers usually have a high-frequency test for checking the condenser for high series resistance.
4. Capacity, which determines the amount of charge that the condenser can take. The capacity of any condenser depends on the area of the plates and on the insulating and impregnating materials. It will not normally change in service.

Condenser testers for checking all these conditions are available. They should be used whenever a condenser must be tested (Fig. 30-2).

⊘ 30-3 Distributor Testers Distributor testers, or *synchroscopes*, are variable-speed devices into which the distributor is clamped to check the centrifugal-advance mechanism (Fig. 30-3). As the distributor speed is increased, the synchroscope indicates the distributor rpm and the amount of centrifugal advance. Many such testers include vacuum-advance testers. In these, a source of vacuum is applied to the vacuum-advance mechanism on the distributor. The degree of vacuum advance and the amount of vacuum required to secure it are then checked. These testers also detect shaft eccentricity caused by worn bearings and bent shafts. (⊘ 31-14 and 31-15 cover the disassembly and repair of distributors.) Usually, the tester includes a dwell meter for measuring contact-point settings. If it does not, then a separate meter, a feeler gauge, or a dial indicator should be used to measure point opening.

The distributor tester must include a source of vacuum to test and adjust full-vacuum-control distributors.

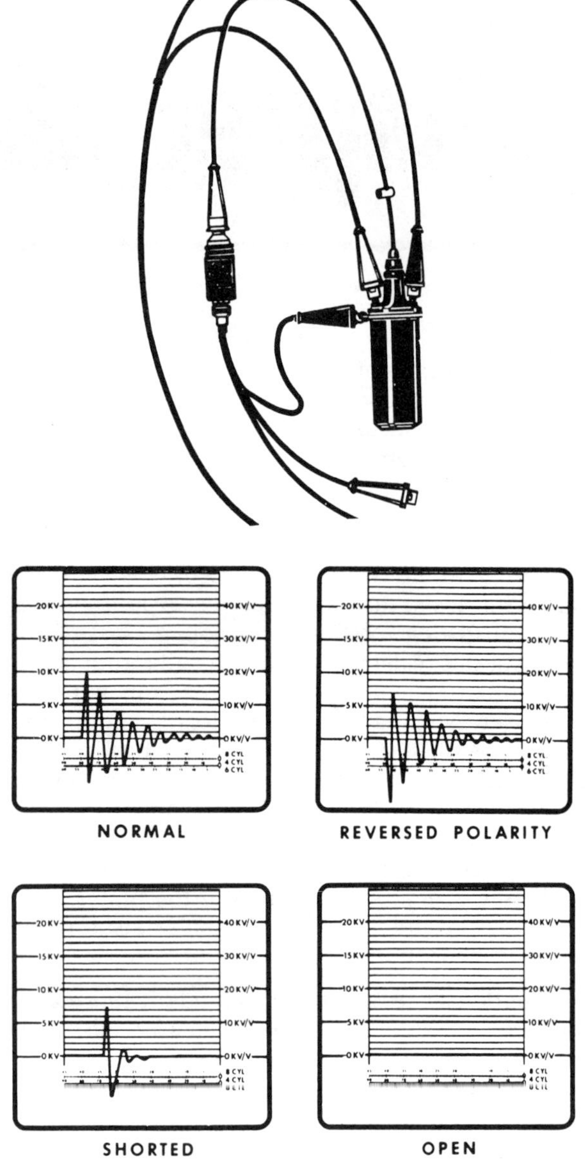

Fig. 30-1. *Top:* Leads from the scope to the test coil. *Bottom:* Scope patterns for various coil conditions. (*Sun Electric Corporation*)

NOTE: To test electronic distributors on the tester, a special "distributor pulse amplifier" must be fitted to the tester. This takes the place of the pulse amplifier, which is left on the car.

⊘ 30-4 Contact-Point-Opening Checking Devices

Two general types of devices are used to check contact-point opening: dial indicators and dwell meters. Before the contact-point opening is measured, the contacts should be inspected for alignment and general condition. If they are worn or burned, they should be replaced (⊘ 31-7). As a rule, alignment is a possible problem only on new contacts; they will not go out of alignment in service. See ⊘ 31-8 for the alignment procedure. We discuss the contact-point-opening checking devices here.

Fig. 30-2. Combination coil and condenser tester. (*Sun Electric Corporation*)

1. *DIAL INDICATOR* This method of checking the contact-point opening is no longer widely used. It is included here in case you happen to run across a dial indicator in a service shop. The dial indicator clamps to the distributor housing and measures the movement of the movable contact point, in thousandths of an inch. The movement registers on a dial. At the speeds at which the ignition system operates, a small error in point-opening adjustment

Fig. 30-3. Ignition-distributor tester. (*Sun Electric Corporation*)

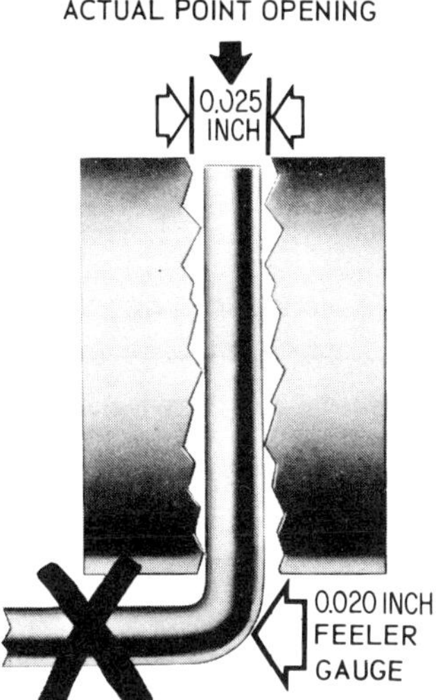

Fig. 30-4. Why a feeler gauge may not accurately measure the point opening of used and roughened points. The roughness of the points is exaggerated.

can cause poor ignition performance. For instance, if the point opening is too wide, the points remain closed too short a time. This does not allow sufficient energy (in magnetic form) to be stored in the coil. As a result, the high-voltage surge (from the secondary winding) is too weak. The engine does not perform properly, and may develop a "miss"—particularly at high speed. Adjustment is made as explained in ⊘ 31-8.

A feeler gauge can be used to check contact-point openings, but it is not always accurate—especially if the points are not new. On used points that have become rough, the feeler gauge measures from high point to high point on the contacts, so that the true point opening cannot be obtained (Fig. 30-4).

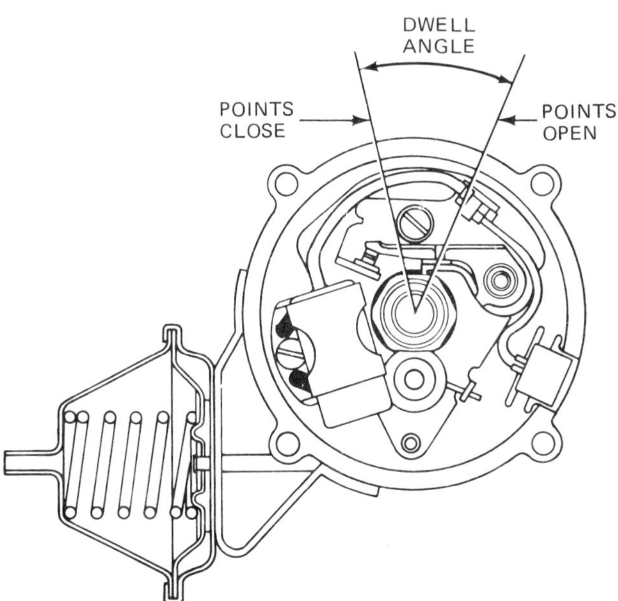

Fig. 30-5. Dwell angle.

With new points, accurate point-opening settings can be made with a feeler gauge. The feeler gauge can be used when no other means of setting the point opening is available. However, some authorities prefer not to use this method.

2. *DWELL METER* Another method of setting the point opening is by using a dwell meter. The dwell angle is the number of degrees the distributor cam rotates from the instant the points close until they open again (Fig. 30-5). As the point opening is increased, the dwell angle is reduced, and vice versa. Since this is a definite relationship between point opening and dwell angle, only one of them need be checked. If one is correct, then the other is correct—provided the points are properly aligned. Point adjustment is covered in ⊘ 31-8.

The dwell meter electrically measures the percentage of the total time, per cam revolution, that the points remain closed. It records the dwell angle on a meter face. Engine analyzers and distributor testers have dwell meters, so that the dwell angle may be tested along with the advance mechanism.

⊘ 30-5 Contact-Pressure Gauge If the contact-point pressure is not correct, trouble may result. Low point pressure causes point bouncing and chattering at high speed, with a resulting high-speed miss. Excessive pressure causes rapid cam, contact-point, and breaker-lever rubbing-block wear. The pressure is measured with a spring gauge hooked to the breaker-lever arm. You measure the amount of pull, in a line perpendicular to the point faces, required to separate the points. Figure 30-6 shows how to take the measurement on three types of breaker-lever arms. Figure 30-7 shows a spring scale being used to check the contact pressure. See ⊘ 31-9 for the adjustment procedure.

⊘ 30-6 Oscilloscope Testers In recent years, many service facilities have adopted the oscilloscope ignition tester (Fig. 30-8) as a diagnostic device. It can quickly pinpoint troubles in the ignition system. The oscilloscope is a type of voltmeter that uses a televisionlike picture tube to show ignition voltages. Figure 30-8 shows an electronic engine tester which includes an oscilloscope. The oscilloscope, or "scope," is to the upper left in the picture.

The oscilloscope draws a picture of the ignition voltages on the face of the tube. The picture shows

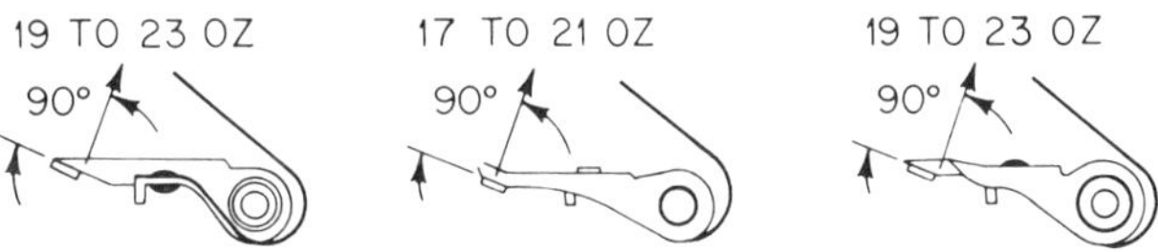

Fig. 30-6. Places at which the spring gauge should be hooked on three types of breaker arms to measure contact-point pressure. Pull should be exerted in the direction shown by the arrows. (*Delco-Remy Division of General Motors Corporation*)

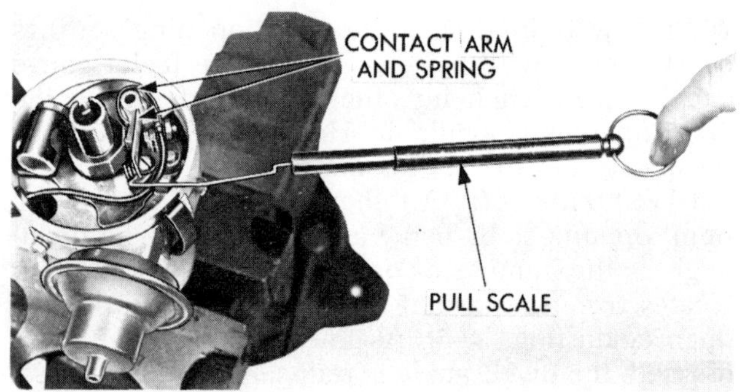

Fig. 30-7. Using a spring gauge to check contact pressure. (*Chrysler Corporation*)

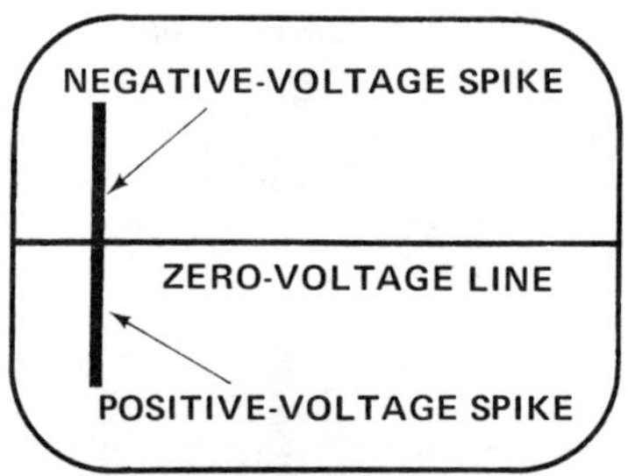

Fig. 30-9. The oscilloscope draws a horizontal zero-voltage line until a negative or positive voltage pulse enters. This causes the trace to kick up or down, as shown. The higher the voltage, the further the trace moves up or down. The sharp up-and-down movements of the trace are called *spikes*.

what is happening in the ignition system. If something is wrong, the picture shows what it is.

To understand the pictures, we shall first review the ignition system. When the ignition-coil primary circuit is opened (either by opening of the contact points or by the electronic amplifier), the voltage in the secondary winding jumps up. It can go up to 35,000 V. This high voltage surges to a spark plug and produces a spark. That is, the high voltage jumps the gap between the insulated and grounded electrodes of the spark plug. It takes a high voltage to start the spark. But after the spark is established, much less voltage is needed to keep the spark going. The scope can, among other things, draw a picture of how and when this voltage goes up and then drops down.

The picture is drawn on the face of the tube by a stream of electrons. This is exactly how the picture tube works in a television set. In the scope, however, the stream of electrons draws a picture of just one thing—the ignition-system voltages feeding into the scope. Figure 30-9 shows the face of the picture tube and helps to explain its use.

When a voltage, such as the voltage that fires a spark plug, is detected by the scope, a "spike," or vertical line, appears on the face of the tube. This is shown in Fig. 30-9. The higher the voltage, the higher the spike. If the voltage spike points down, it indicates that the ignition coil or the battery is connected backward.

To see how the scope picks up the voltages and what the scope pictures mean, first look at the *basic pattern* (see Fig. 30-10). The basic pattern is what the scope would show if it were drawing the voltage pattern for one spark plug. To start with, the contact points have opened (or the electronic amplifier has opened the primary circuit). The high-voltage surge from the coil has arrived at the spark plug. The voltage goes up, from A to B, as shown. This is called the *firing line*. After the spark is established, the voltage drops off considerably and holds fairly steady, from C to D. Of course, this is a very short time, measured in hundred-thousandths of a second. But the spark lasts for as long as 20° of crankshaft rotation. This is long enough to ignite the compressed air-fuel mixture in the cylinder.

After most of the magnetic energy in the coil has been converted into electricity to make the spark, the spark across the spark-plug gap dies. However, there is still some energy left in the coil, and this produces a wavy line, from D to E. This line is called the *coil-condenser oscillation line*. This wavy line means that the remaining energy is pushing electricity back and forth in the ignition secondary circuit. The voltage alternates, but it is no longer high enough to produce a spark. After a very short time,

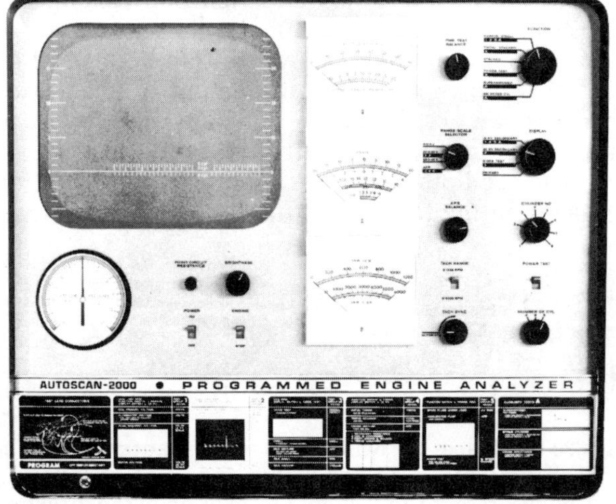

Fig. 30-8. Electronic engine tester with an oscilloscope. (*Autoscan, Inc.*)

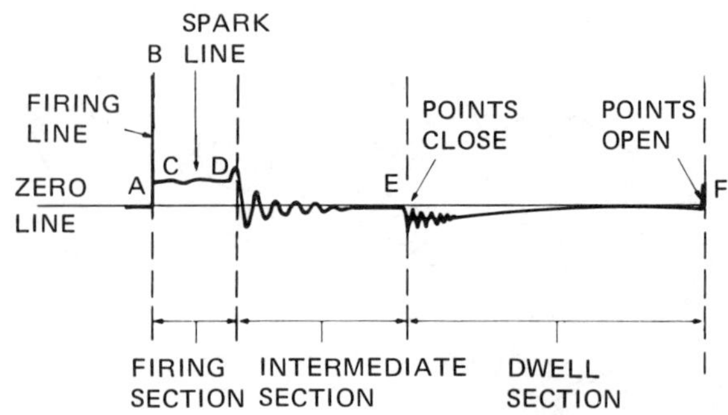

Fig. 30-10. Waveform, or trace, showing one complete spark-plug firing cycle. (*Sun Electric Corporation*)

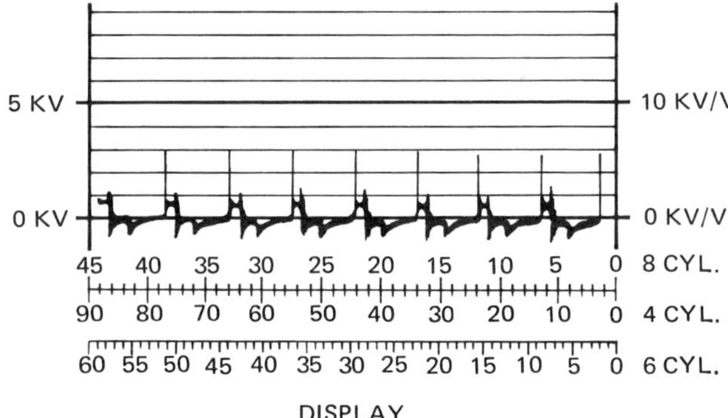

Fig. 30-11. Parade, or display, pattern of the ignition secondary voltages in an eight-cylinder engine. (*Sun Electric Corporation*)

the voltage dies out. Then, at E, the points close, sending current to the primary winding of the ignition coil. Now an alternating voltage is produced in the secondary. This is the result of the buildup of current in the coil primary winding. This is shown by the oscillations following E. The section from E to F is called the *dwell section*. This is the time during which the contact points are closed. During this time, the magnetic field is building up in the ignition-coil primary. Then, when the points open at F, we are back to A again. The magnetic field collapses, and the whole process is repeated.

Figure 30-10 is the complete voltage picture of the secondary voltage in a normally operating ignition system. Any change from this normal picture indicates trouble. To the expert, the type of change indicates where the trouble is and what is causing it.

⊘ 30-7 Oscilloscope Patterns The curves that the scope draws on the tube face are called *patterns*. The patterns can be drawn on the tube face in different ways. For example, the scope can be adjusted to draw a *parade* pattern, as shown in Fig. 30-11. It is called a parade pattern because the traces for the separate cylinders follow one another across the tube face, like marchers in a parade. Note that they follow from left to right across the screen, in normal firing order, with No. 1 cylinder on the left.

By adjusting the scope in a different way, the traces can be stacked one above the other, as shown in Fig. 30-12. Stacking the traces this way produces a *raster* pattern. It lets you compare the traces, so you can see if something is wrong in a cylinder. The pattern is read from the bottom up in the firing order, with No. 1 cylinder at the bottom.

A third way to display the traces is to superimpose them (Fig. 30-13), that is, put them one on top of another. This gives a quick comparison and shows whether the voltage pattern from any one cylinder differs from those of the others. If everything is okay in the cylinders, only one curve appears on the tube face. This is because all the curves fall on top of each other.

⊘ 30-8 Using the Scope There are several makes of oscilloscopes. Many are combined in consoles with the instruments for testing the separate ignition components, the engine rpm, the intake-manifold vacuum, and so on. Figure 13-8 shows a complete tester of this type. Figure 30-14 shows a similar tester. Scopes have pickup sensors that can be clamped onto the ignition wires, as shown in Fig. 30-15. Thus, it is not necessary to disconnect and reconnect the ignition circuits. The pattern-pickup sensor is clamped onto the wire that goes from the ignition coil to the distributor-cap center terminal. The sensor senses the high-voltage surges going to all

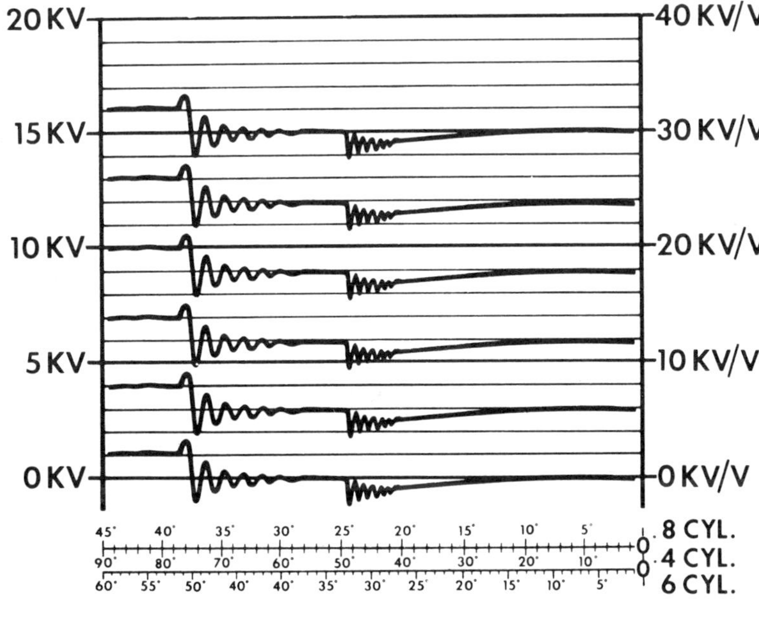

Fig. 30-12. Stacked, or raster, pattern of the ignition secondary voltages in a six-cylinder engine. (*Sun Electric Corporation*)

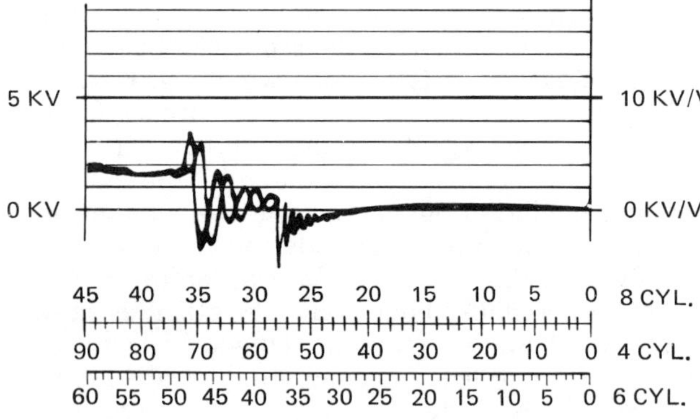

Fig. 30-13. Superimposed pattern of the ignition secondary voltages in a six-cylinder engine. (*Sun Electric Corporation*)

Fig. 30-14. Electronic-diagnosis engine tester. This tester includes an oscilloscope (at top center) and other testing devices to check the condenser, distributor contact-point dwell, engine speed, and other items. (*Sun Electric Corporation*)

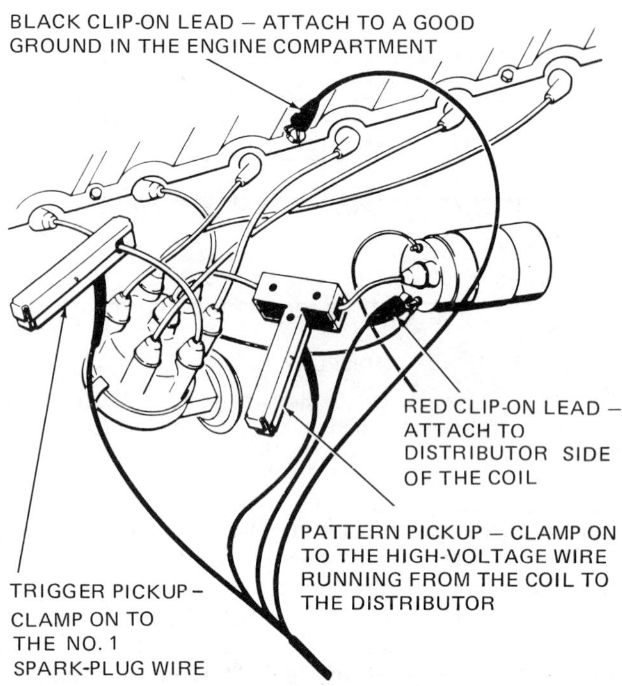

Fig. 30-15. To connect an oscilloscope to the ignition system, test leads are clipped to terminals, and pickup sensors are clamped on high-voltage leads. (*Autoscan, Inc.*)

the spark plugs. The trigger-pickup sensor is clamped onto the wire that goes to the plug in the No. 1 cylinder. The trigger pickup senses when the plug fires. This is the signal to the scope to start another round of traces.

⊘ 30-9 Reading the Patterns The patterns in Fig. 30-16 show different troubles that occur in the ignition system. The scope pattern for any cylinder's ignition-circuit voltage shows what voltages are occurring in that circuit. The way that the voltage varies from normal shows you where the electrical problem exists. For example, the scope can detect wide or narrow spark-plug gaps, open spark-plug wires, shorted coils or condensers, arcing contact points, improper contact-point dwell, and other problems. Many abnormal engine conditions change the voltage required to fire the plug. This, too, shows up on the scope. When you work in a shop that has an oscilloscope, you will be given detailed instructions on how to use it.

⊘ 30-10 Electronic-Ignition Testers Electronic ignition systems, such as those described in ⊘ 28-4 to 28-7, require special testing procedures and equipment. Figure 30-17 shows the special electronic-ignition tester recommended by Chrysler Corporation. It is simple to use. You plug the tester into the wiring harness between the distributor connector and the electronic-control-unit connector. Then, with the ignition switch turned on, you check the ignition system with the tester. The green light comes on if

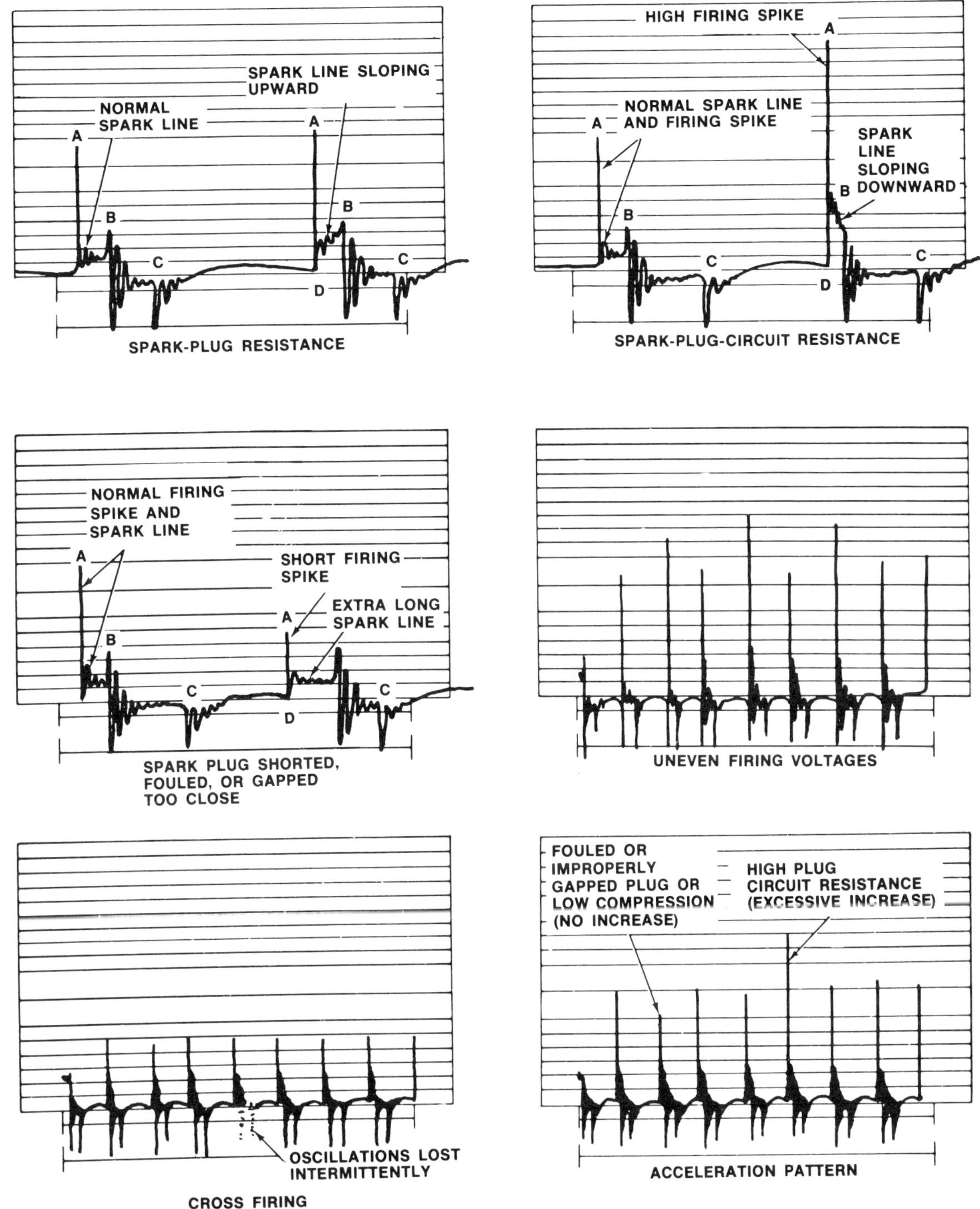

Fig. 30-16. Abnormal traces and their causes. (*Ford Motor Company*)

everything is okay. The red light comes on to signal trouble. When you use the tester, follow the special instructions that explain the testing procedure. Typical electronic-distributor and electronic-amplifier testing procedures are covered in Chap. 31.

⊘ 30-11 Ignition Timing There are various devices for timing the engine. As mentioned in ⊘ 28-1, the spark must occur at the spark-plug gap as the piston reaches some definite position in the compression stroke. Adjusting the distributor on the engine so the spark occurs at this correct instant is called *ignition timing*. You adjust the distributor by turning it in its mounting. If you rotate the distributor in the direction opposite to normal distributor-shaft rotation, you move the timing ahead. That is, the contact points open earlier (or the electrical pulse from the pickup coil occurs earlier). This advances the spark, so the sparks appear at the spark plugs earlier. Turning the distributor in the opposite direction, or in the direction of distributor-shaft rotation, retards the sparks. The sparks appear at the plugs later.

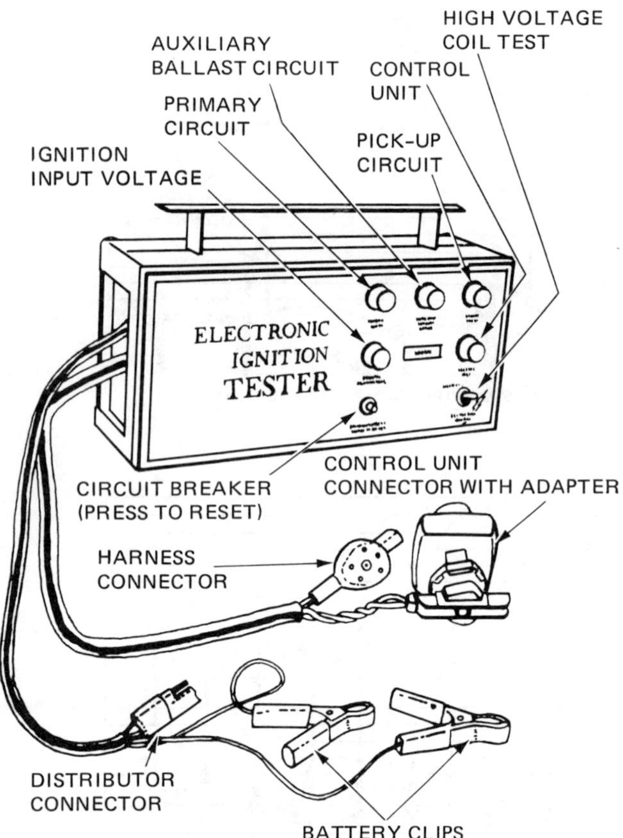

Fig. 30-17. Electronic-ignition tester. (*Chrysler Corporation*)

1. *TIMING WITH A TIMING LIGHT* To time the ignition, check the markings on the crankshaft pulley with the engine running. Since the pulley turns rapidly, you cannot see the markings in normal light. But by using a special timing light, you can make the pulley appear to stand still. The timing light is a stroboscopic light. You use it by connecting the timing-light lead to the No. 1 spark plug, as shown in Fig. 30-18. Every time the plug fires, the timing light gives off a flash of light (Fig. 30-19). The light lasts only a fraction of a second. The repeated flashes of light make the pulley seem to stand still.

To connect the timing light, the spark-plug nipple must be removed from the spark plug. A metal adapter is then installed between the spark-plug clip inside the nipple and the spark plug. The clip on the timing-light lead is then attached to this adapter. However, some timing lights do not require the use of a metal adapter. These timing lights have a type of spark-plug-lead connector that clamps around the spark-plug cable. Ice picks, pins, or wires should never be forced through the spark-plug cable or nipple to connect the timing light. This damages the cable or the nipple and permits high-voltage leakage through the hole. It causes engine miss.

To set the ignition timing, the engine must be running at the specified idle speed. Disconnect and plug the vacuum line at the distributor. Loosen the clamp screw that holds the distributor in its mounting. Then turn the distributor one way or the other. As you turn the distributor, the marking on the pulley will move ahead or back. When the ignition timing is correct, the markings will align with a timing pointer, or timing mark, as shown in Fig. 30-20. Tighten the distributor clamp.

2. *MONOLITHIC TIMING* Monolithic timing is a relatively new timing method developed by Ford.

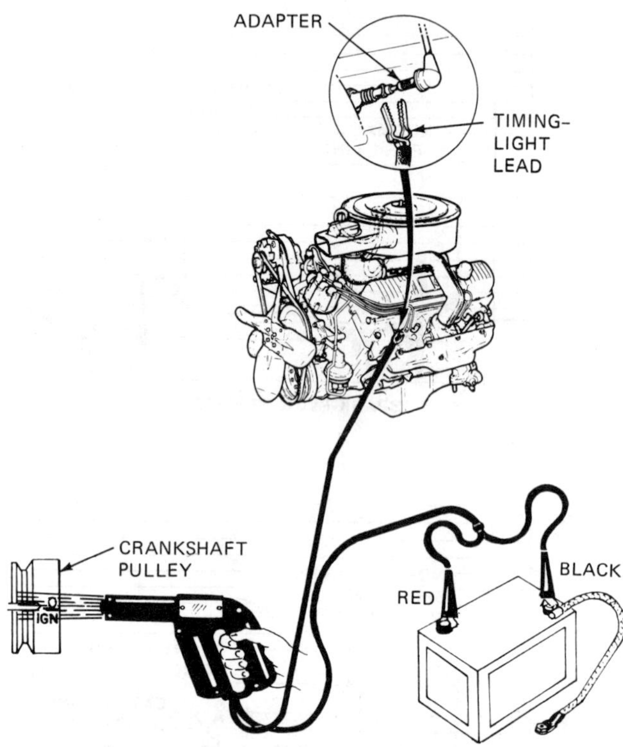

Fig. 30-18. A timing light is used to check the ignition timing.

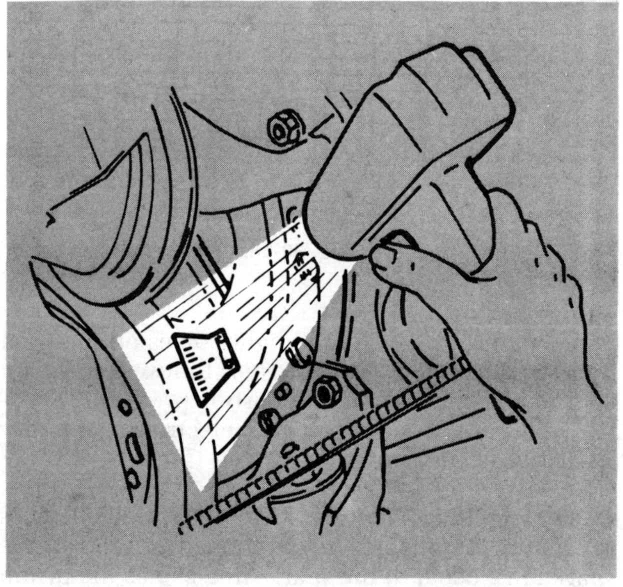

Fig. 30-19. The timing light flashes every time the No. 1 spark plug fires.

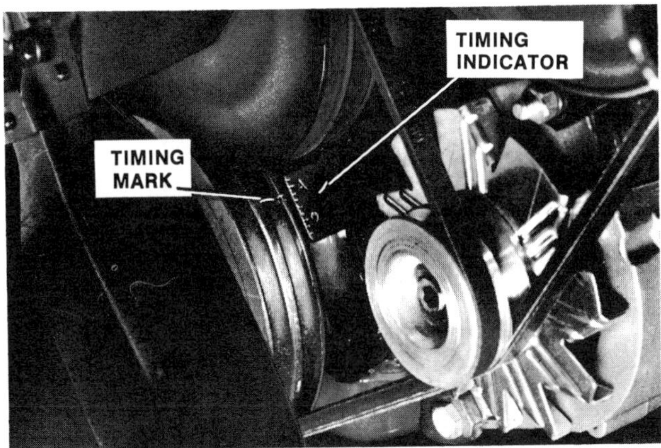

Fig. 30-20. Ignition timing marks on the crankshaft pulley.

The method requires a special location indicator on the front end of the crankshaft (Fig. 30-21). As the crankshaft rotates, this indicator produces an electromagnetic pulse in the monolithic timing equipment installed on the engine. The pulse triggers the timing light, and adjustments are made as already described.

The advantage claimed for the monolothic timing procedure is that the timing is done on the crankshaft, not on a pulley that is driven through a rubber ring. Here's how it operates. The crankshaft pulley includes a torsional-vibration damper to reduce crankshaft vibrations. This damper works through a rubber ring that is between the driving flange on the crankshaft and the pulley itself. The rubber ring can reduce the accuracy of the setting because it allows the pulley to shift away from normal alignment with the crankshaft. Since the triggering device in the monolithic timing system is on the crankshaft itself, more accurate timing is claimed.

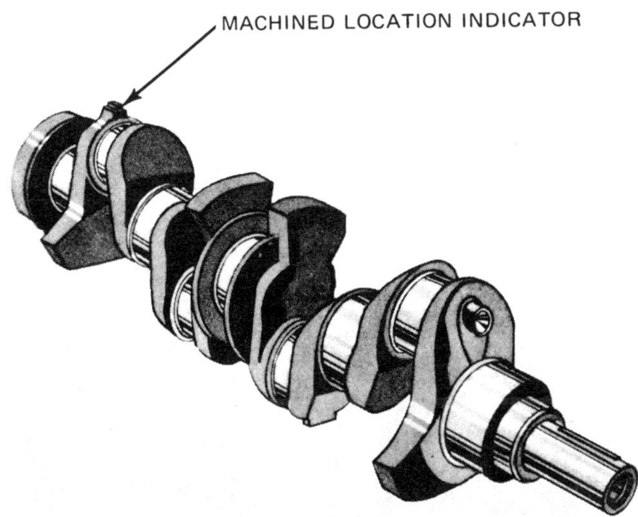

Fig. 30-21. Crankshaft with location indicator for monolithic timing. (*Ford Motor Company*)

CAUTION: When connecting a timing light, always connect the leads to the battery first. Then make the connection to the No. 1 spark plug. When disconnecting the timing light, always disconnect the timing-light lead from the No. 1 spark plug first. Then disconnect the battery leads. If you disconnect the battery leads first, you may get a high-voltage shock when you touch the battery connections.

NOTE: There are other timing methods. Late-model Cadillacs can be timed without a timing light. A special probe-type advance meter is used. Another method, seldom used today, employs a test light connected across the points. With the engine not running but the timing marks aligned, the distributor is turned so that the points just open. This is shown by the test light coming on. Then the distributor clamp is tightened. Another method uses a piston-position gauge. It is inserted into the spark-plug hole to determine the exact position of the piston in the No. 1 cylinder.

⊘ 30-12 Spark-Plug Service Spark plugs will foul or the electrodes will wear rapidly if their heat range is wrong for the engine. (See Fig. 29-3, which illustrates spark-plug heat range.) Figure 29-4 relates spark-plug appearance to various conditions in the engine. Figure 30-22 shows a spark-plug cleaner. The spark plug is put into the cleaner. The cleaner sends a blast of grit against the electrodes and insulator, to clean them. After the cleaning, the spark-plug electrodes should be filed flat with an ignition file. Then a special tool is used to adjust the electrode gap (Fig. 30-23).

NOTE: The cost of labor is high, and the cost of spark plugs is relatively low. Thus many service experts insist that it is cheaper and more efficient to install new plugs than to clean and regap the old ones. One manufacturer (of small engines) strongly opposes the use of cleaned and regapped plugs in the

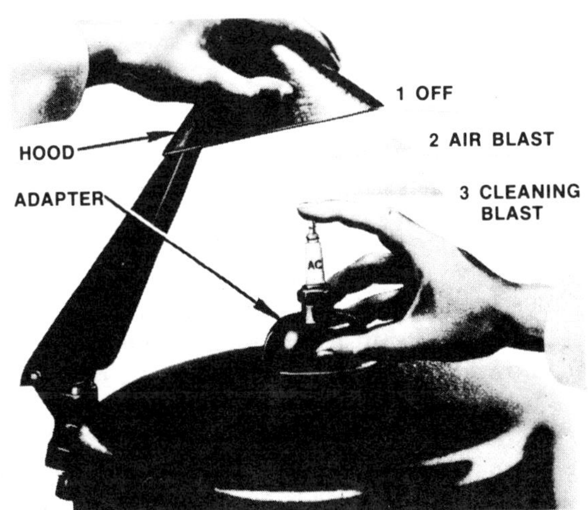

Fig. 30-22. Spark-plug cleaner and tester. (*AC Spark Plug Division of General Motors Corporation*)

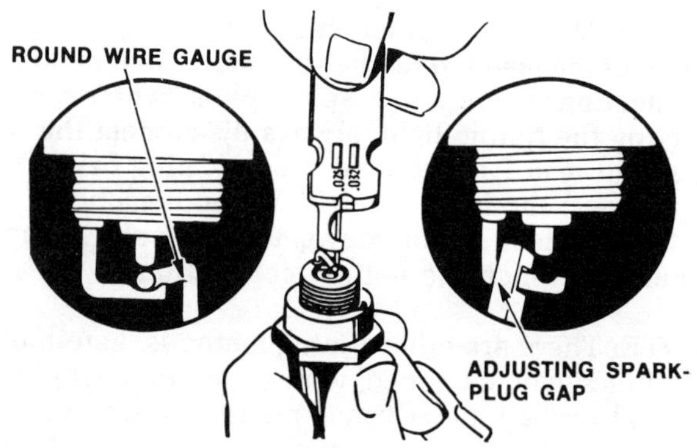

Fig. 30-23. Using a special gauge and adjusting tool to adjust the spark-plug gap.

engines they make. They say that if the plug is not perfectly cleaned, particles of grit get into the engine. This can severely damage pistons, rings, and the cylinder.

CAUTION: The General Motors High-Energy Ignition System (see ⊘ 28-7) requires special wide-gap spark plugs. The gap specified for some applications is 0.080 in [2.03 mm]. A standard plug cannot be satisfactorily adjusted to this wide a gap, because it requires bending the outer electrode at a sharp angle. Always use the special plugs specified for the High-Energy Ignition System.

⊘ 30-13 Removing Spark Plugs from the Engine Spark-plug manufacturers recommend installing new spark plugs at intervals of 10,000 mi [16,093 km]. This avoids loss of engine operating economy and atmospheric pollution; both are caused by worn plugs. Before the plugs are removed, the area surrounding them should be cleaned thoroughly so that dirt will not fall into the cylinders. One method of doing this is to blow the dirt away with a compressed-air hose. Another is to loosen the plugs a little and then start the engine. Running the engine for a few moments allows the leakage of compression to blow dirt away from around the plugs.

NOTE: See ⊘ 30-14 on the proper way to disconnect the high-voltage cables from the spark plugs. This must be done properly, to avoid damaging the cables.

Some engines, such as the Chrysler hemi (hemispheric) engine, have the spark plugs mounted in wells (Fig. 30-24). On these, the spark-plug covers must first be pulled out, with the cables. Then a special tool or a thin-walled socket must be used to reach down into the wells to loosen and remove the plugs.

⊘ 30-14 Ignition Wiring An important part of ignition service is to inspect the wiring to make sure it is in good condition. Cracks or punctures in the secondary-wiring insulation can allow high-voltage

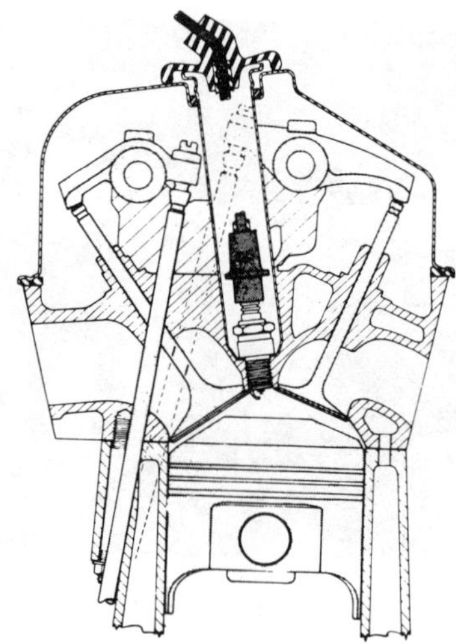

Fig. 30-24. Location of a spark plug in the Chrysler hemispherical engine. (*Chrysler Corporation*)

leakage and engine miss, particularly under heavy load.

Visually inspect the secondary wiring for cracks, burned spots caused by being too close to the exhaust manifold, and brittleness. Feel the wiring to see if it is hard or crumbly. You can make a secondary-insulation check with the oscilloscope. If you do not have an oscilloscope, you can check secondary-wiring insulation as follows: With the engine not running, connect the one end of a test probe to a good ground such as the engine block. Leave the other end, with the test point, free to probe. Disconnect the cable from a spark plug, and insulate the clip end from ground. Now start the engine, and move the test probe along the entire length of the cable. If there are punctures or cracks, a spark will jump through the insulation to the end of the test point.

An ohmmeter can be used to check the condi-

Fig. 30-25. Installing a cable and nipple on a distributor-cap tower. (*Chrysler Corporation*)

tion of the conductor in a spark plug cable. Place one ohmmeter lead on each end of the cable. Resistance should be between 3,000 to 7,000 ohms per foot of cable length. No reading indicates an open, or break, in the cable conductor, and the cable must be replaced. High resistance readings should be checked with the manufacturer's specifications before condemning the cable. Some types of spark plug cable are used that have a maximum allowable resistance of 5,000 ohms per inch.

Here is one recommended way to install new cable assemblies: Grasp the nipple and clip end of the cable, as shown in Fig. 30-25. Gently push the cable clip into the cap tower. Pinch the larger diameter of the nipple to release trapped air. Then push the cable and nipple until the cable clip is fully entered into the cap terminal and the nipple is all the way down around the terminal. Ford provides a special tool to remove the wires from spark plugs. Figure 30-26 shows the tool and how to use it. If the connectors become loose on the coil terminals, the fit can be improved by squeezing the connector as shown in Fig. 30-27.

If you are replacing a set of ignition cables, replace one cable at a time. See Fig. 31-3 (upper right). This avoids getting mixed up and connecting a cable from the distributor cap to the wrong spark plug. If all the cables have been removed, first determine which direction the rotor turns and the firing order. From these, you will be able to figure out how the cables should be connected.

Never remove cable and nipple assemblies from the distributor or coil towers unless (1) the nipples are damaged or (2) cable testing shows the cables are bad and must be replaced. You can ruin a cable by careless removal and installation.

NOTE: Do not puncture cables or nipples with test probes. Puncturing the cable insulation or a nipple can ruin the cable. The probe can separate the conductor and cause high resistance. Also, breaking the insulation can result in high-voltage leakage to ground. Either of these can cause engine miss.

⊘ 30-15 Location of Secondary Wiring The high-voltage cables, or secondary wiring, must be connected correctly between the distributor cap and the spark plugs. Also, the secondary wiring must be

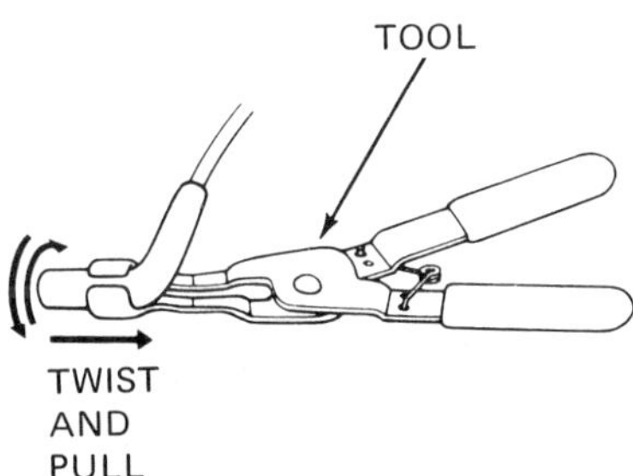

Fig. 30-26. Removing cables from spark plugs with a special tool. (*Ford Motor Company*)

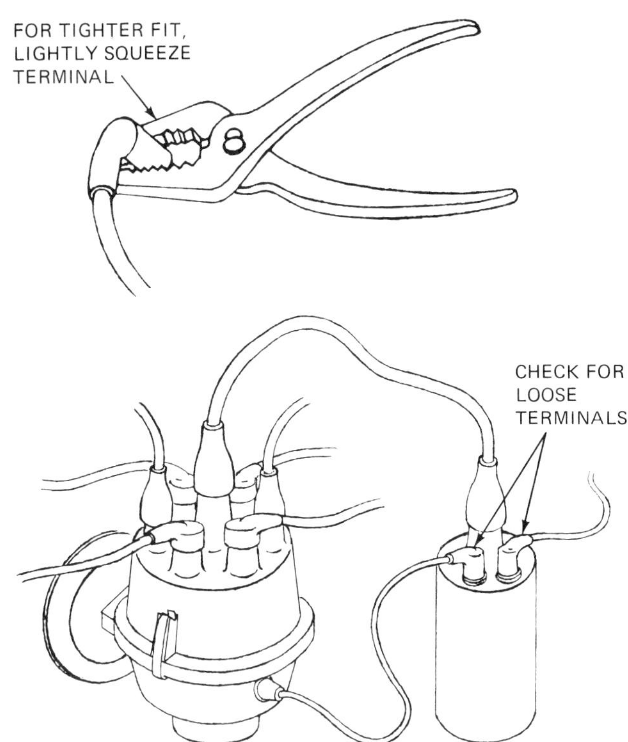

Fig. 30-27. Squeezing the connectors to original size to reestablish good fit. (*Ford Motor Company*)

positioned correctly, and held apart by the plastic looms provided (see Figs. 30-28 and 30-29). Note how the cables are positioned and separated. Improper placement or bundling together of cables can cause crossfiring. That is, the high-voltage surge can leak from one cable to another, causing the wrong spark plug to fire. This can cause engine missing or backfire (see ⊘ 29-9).

CHAPTER 30 CHECKUP

NOTE: Since the following is a chapter review test, you should review the chapter before taking the test.

You are moving along in your study of automotive electrical equipment. With this chapter, you have almost finished the major components of the electric system (except for ignition-distributor service) and have only the lights and electrical devices to study. Then, you will have all the essential background information in automotive electric systems. If you have been able to get practical experience along with your studies, you are about ready to begin actual shopwork. To find out how well you remember the information in this chapter, take the following test. If you have trouble with any of the questions, restudy the chapter.

Reviewing Ignition Troubles In your notebook, write down the answers to the following questions. Do not copy from the book, but try to write in your

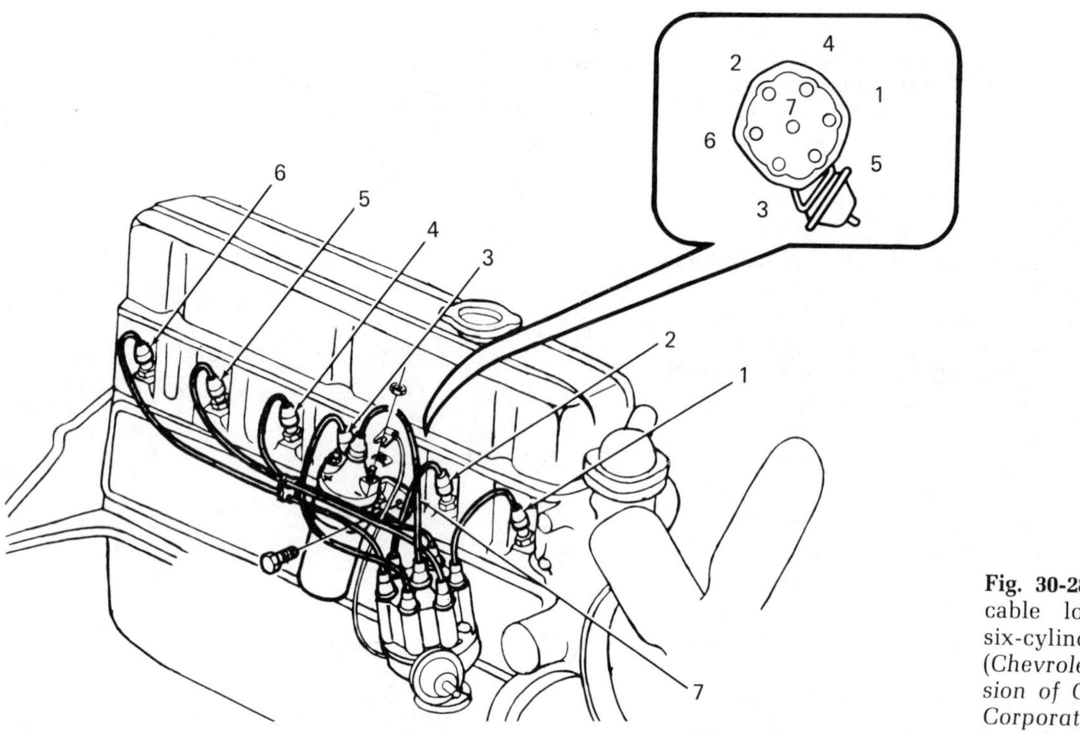

Fig. 30-28. Spark-plug-cable locations on a six-cylinder engine. (*Chevrolet Motor Division of General Motors Corporation*)

own words, just as you would explain things to a friend. This will help you remember the procedures and explanations.

1. List the possible causes of ignition failure.
2. List the various engine troubles that might originate in the ignition system. Give the ignition-trouble causes under each.
3. Explain how to make the spark test. Explain how to use the ammeter if no spark occurs, and the significance of the various ammeter readings.
4. Explain how to correct pitting of points.
5. List the causes of burned contact points.
6. Explain what is meant by "heat range" in spark plugs.
7. Describe the appearance of a plug that has been running too hot. Running too cold.
8. Explain the four factors that should be tested when a condenser is checked.
9. What is the purpose of an oscilloscope? Describe how it is used.
10. What is wrong with using a feeler gauge to check the point opening of worn points?
11. What is dwell angle?

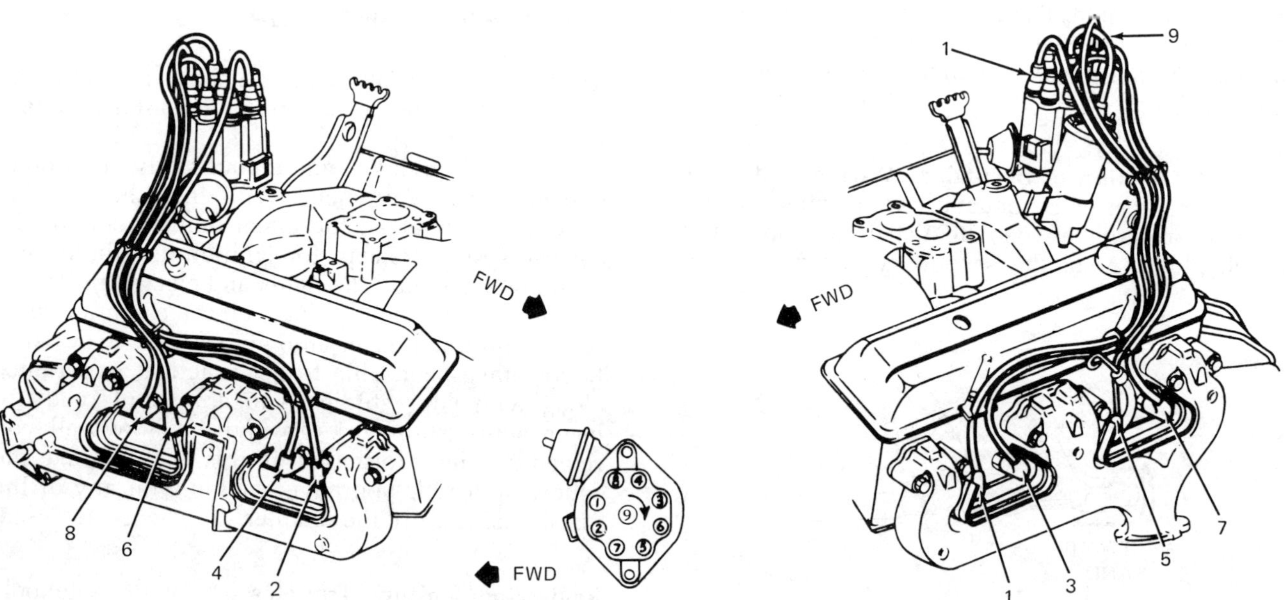

Fig. 30-29. Spark-plug-cable locations on a V-8 engine. (*Chevrolet Motor Division of General Motors Corporation*)

12. What is the purpose of checking contact-point pressure? How is it checked?
13. What is meant by "timing the ignition"? In general, how is this accomplished?
14. Explain how a stroboscopic light is used to check ignition timing.
15. Explain how an oscilloscope tester works.
16. What is a parade pattern? A stacked pattern?
17. Describe several ignition-system troubles and the effect they have on the scope pattern.

Grouping Ignition Troubles There are two lists below. The first list includes the three basic ignition troubles. The second list includes the conditions causing these troubles. Your job here is to put these two lists together properly. To do this, write the three basic causes in your notebook, leaving spaces under each. Then write each condition under the proper cause. For example, "defective high-voltage wiring" would go under "loss of energy in secondary circuit."

Causes
loss of energy in primary circuit
loss of energy in secondary circuit
out of time

Conditions
defective high-voltage wiring
timing incorrectly set
centrifugal advance defective
points improperly set
discharged battery or defective alternator
excessive resistance in primary circuit
leakage across distributor cap or rotor
condenser shorted
vacuum advance defective
plugs fouled or broken
coil primary grounded
distributor bearing or shaft worn

Completing the Sentences The sentences below are incomplete. After each sentence there are several words or phrases, but only one of them correctly completes the sentence. Write each sentence in your notebook, ending it with the one word or phrase that completes it correctly.

1. Failure to start with normal cranking is usually due to troubles in the: (*a*) ignition or starting system, (*b*) ignition or engine, (*c*) ignition or fuel system.
2. If you cannot get a spark during the spark test, chances are the trouble is in the: (*a*) engine, (*b*) fuel system, (*c*) ignition system, (*d*) spark plugs.
3. If no spark occurs during the spark test and the ammeter shows a small fluctuating reading, chances are the trouble is in the: (*a*) secondary circuit, (*b*) primary circuit, (*c*) ignition switch.
4. If no spark occurs during the spark test and the ammeter shows a fairly high and steady reading, chances are the trouble is in the: (*a*) secondary circuit, (*b*) primary circuit, (*c*) spark plugs.
5. If no spark occurs during the spark test and the ammeter shows no reading, the trouble is in the: (*a*) secondary circuit, (*b*) primary circuit, (*c*) alternator.
6. If no change in the operation of the engine is noted when a spark plug is shorted out, then that: (*a*) spark plug is okay, (*b*) cylinder is delivering power, (*c*) cylinder is missing.
7. Ignition crossfiring or hot plugs or valves are apt to cause: (*a*) late ignition timing, (*b*) burned contact points, (*c*) engine backfiring.
8. Excessively advanced ignition timing can cause: (*a*) burned contacts, (*b*) pinging, (*c*) loss of energy in the primary, (*d*) crossfiring.
9. Excessive resistance in the condenser circuit, high voltage, large dwell angle, or crankcase vapors in the distributor can cause: (*a*) pitted contact points, (*b*) ignition crossfiring, (*c*) burned plugs, (*d*) burned contact points.
10. In regard to the heat range of spark plugs, the longer the heat path, the: (*a*) hotter the plug, (*b*) colder the plug.
11. A plug that runs too cold usually is: (*a*) blistered, (*b*) sooty, (*c*) blue.
12. The oscilloscope tester reacts to high-voltage surges from the: (*a*) distributor high-voltage terminal, (*b*) coil high-voltage terminal, (*c*) contact points closing.
13. If the firing voltage of one cylinder is considerably higher than that of the others, it is likely that: (*a*) the plug gap is excessive, (*b*) there is a short in the circuit, (*c*) voltage is leaking from the high-voltage lead.
14. A feeler gauge or a dwell meter is recommended for setting the distributor: (*a*) vacuum advance, (*b*) contact-point opening, (*c*) ignition timing.
15. On many distributors, contact-point opening is adjusted by: (*a*) shifting the stationary point, (*b*) moving the breaker cam, (*c*) changing the spring tension.

SUGGESTIONS FOR FURTHER STUDY

Every testing-equipment manufacturer issues, with each instrument, detailed instructions on how to use it. In automotive electrical service shops or the school automotive shop, study these instructions whenever you have a chance. Watch how the instruments are used. Another source of information on the use of testing instruments is automobile manufacturers' shop manuals. Study these manuals at every opportunity. Write, in your notebook, any important facts you learn.

chapter 31

IGNITION-DISTRIBUTOR SERVICE

In Chaps. 28 to 30, we described how the ignition system works, various causes of ignition-system trouble, and ignition testing instruments. In addition, we described servicing procedures for all ignition-system components except distributors. In this chapter, we cover distributors.

⊘ 31-1 Distributor Service In this chapter, we look at the various checks and services required for distributors, both the contact-point type and the electronic type. The contact-point distributor is a little more complicated to service, because it requires installation and adjustment of the contact points. Both distributors require checking of the centrifugal- and vacuum-advance mechanisms and of the cap and rotor. The distributors for electronic ignition systems (⊘ 28-4 to 28-6), as well as HEI and unit distributors (⊘ 28-7), require different testing procedures which we shall cover later.

⊘ 31-2 Checking Cap and Rotor The cap with the spring-loaded screw clamps (Fig. 31-1) is removed by pressing down on the screw and then turning the screw either way. The cap with the spring clamps (Fig. 31-2) is removed by prying with a screwdriver. Do not apply pressure to this cap, as it might break. Check the cap and rotor as shown in Fig. 31-3. Wipe the cap with a cloth dampened in solvent. Discard the cap if it is cracked, broken, or has carbonized paths inside or out that could permit high-voltage leakage. Also replace the cap if the rotor button is worn or broken.

To replace a defective cap, place the old and new caps side by side (Fig. 31-3, upper right). Change the leads, one by one, from the old cap to the new cap. In this way, you will not get the leads mixed up. When removing a lead, grasp it through the rubber boot, as close to the tower as possible. Twist slightly to break the seal of the boot on the tower, and then pull straight out. When inserting the lead, be sure to push it all the way down into the high-voltage towers. On the type that enters the towers vertically (Fig. 31-3), push the lead down first. Then slip the rubber boot down snugly over the tower. On the type that has a right-angle bend (Fig. 31-4), push the terminal clip down into place through the rubber boot. Pinch

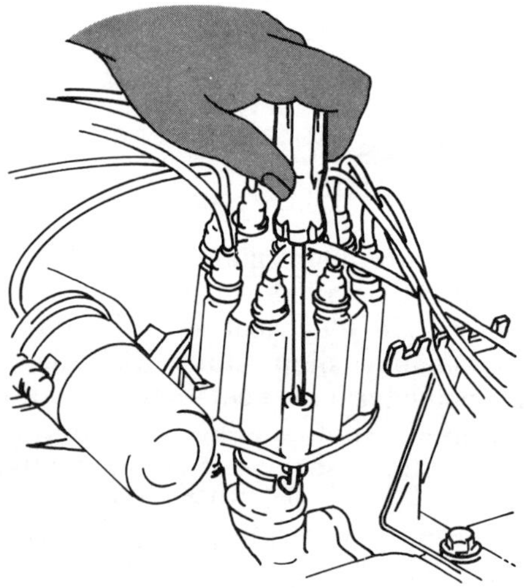

Fig. 31-1. Removing a distributor cap that has spring-loaded screw clamps. (*Delco-Remy Division of General Motors Corporation*)

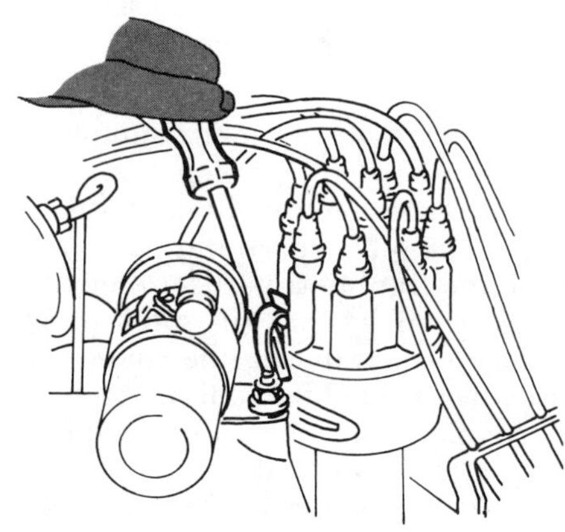

Fig. 31-2. Removing a distributor cap that has spring clamps. (*Delco-Remy Division of General Motors Corporation*)

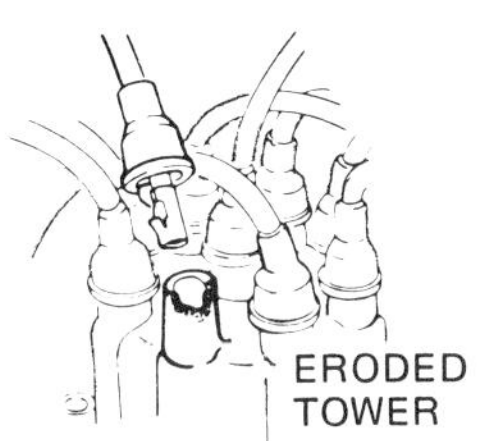

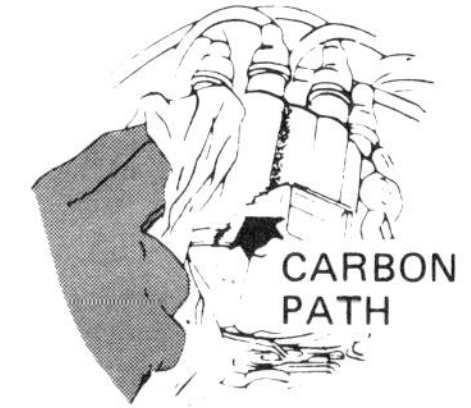

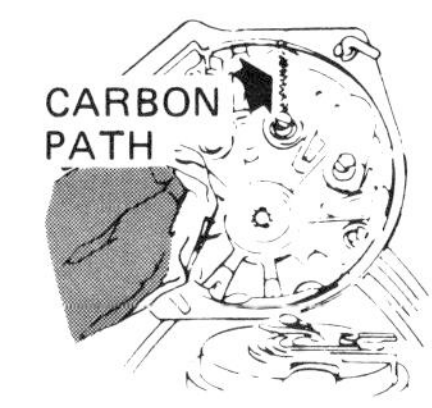

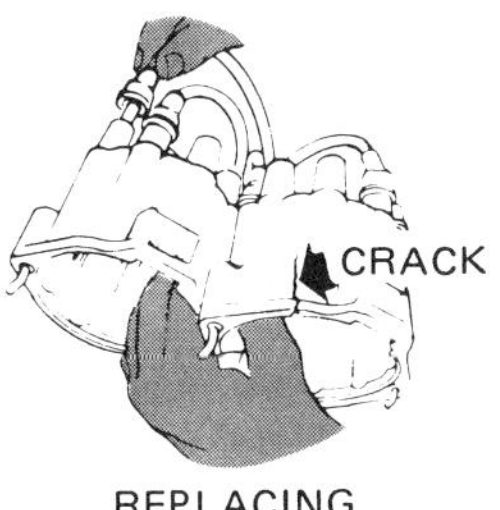

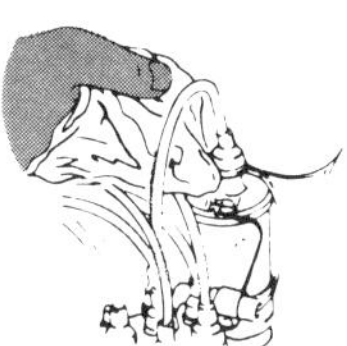

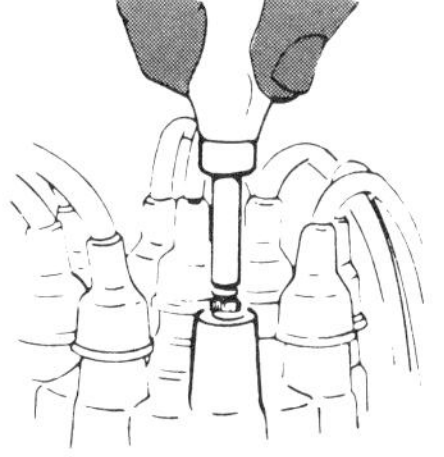

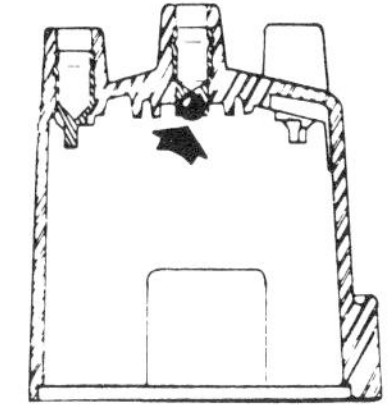

Fig. 31-3. Checking and servicing a distributor cap and rotor. (*Chevrolet Motor Division of General Motors Corporation*)

the larger part of the boot to squeeze out the trapped air. Then push the boot all the way down into place.

NOTE: See also ⊘ 30-14 (and Figs. 30-25 and 30-27) on ignition-wiring inspection and replacement.

Various types of rotors are shown in Fig. 31-5. Most of these rotors will slip off the breaker cam. The one at the lower right in the illustration, however, is attached to the advance mechanism with screws. Examine the rotor for wear and erosion of the metal segment, and for cracks and carbonized paths that could permit high-voltage leakage. Discard any rotor that is in doubtful condition. If the rotor has a carbon resistor (Fig. 31-5), discard the rotor when the resistor is damaged.

⊘ 31-3 Checking the Advance Mechanisms On some distributors, the centrifugal- and vacuum-advance mechanisms can be checked for freeness of action. The centrifugal-advance mechanism ad-

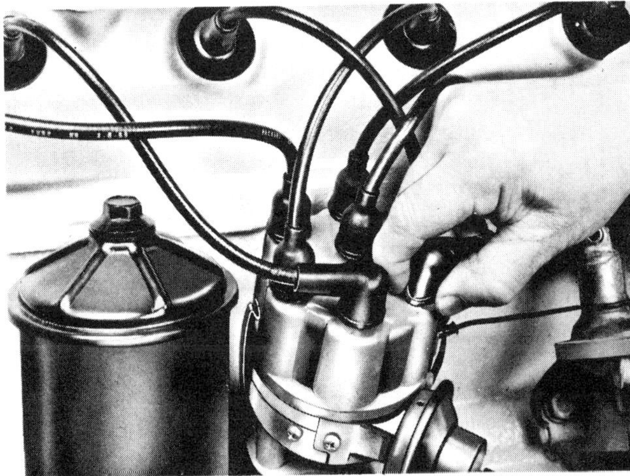

Fig. 31-4. Installing a high-voltage lead and rubber boot on a distributor cap. (*Chrysler Corporation*)

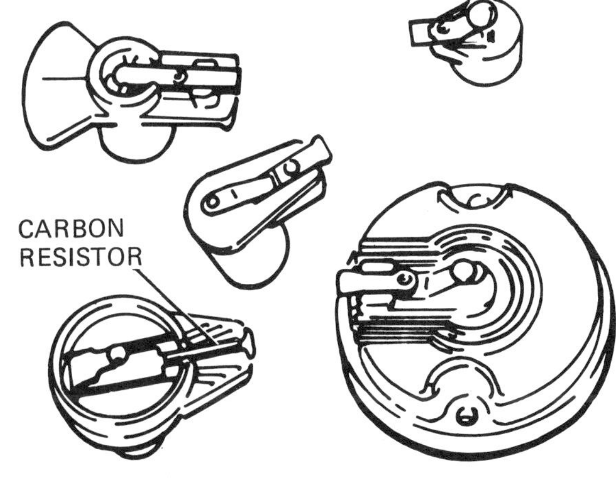

Fig. 31-5. Types of distributor rotors. The one at the lower left has a carbon resistor. The one at the lower right is attached to the advance mechanism by screws. (*Delco-Remy Division of General Motors Corporation*)

vances the breaker cam or reluctor. The vacuum-advance mechanism advances the breaker plate or pickup-coil assembly. Thus, if the advance springs are not too strong, it is possible to turn the cam or reluctor to see if the centrifugal advance is free. Likewise, on some distributors, it is possible to turn the breaker plate or pickup-coil assembly to check the freeness of the vacuum advance.

NOTE: Do not put too much pressure on the parts to turn them! You can damage the reluctor or pickup-coil assembly. Also, do not try to turn the breaker cam or reluctor by putting pressure on the rotor. You can break it.

The proper way to check the advance mechanism is to remove the distributor from the engine (see ⊘ 31-16) and put it in a distributor tester (Fig. 30-3). You can then drive the distributor in the direction of its rotation and check out the advance curve. That is, you start out at low speed and gradually increase the speed, noting when the advance starts and how the advance increases with speed. On some distributors, the centrifugal advance can be adjusted (⊘ 31-4). On others, if the advance is not within specifications, the distributor must be disassembled for replacement of the advance springs and other parts.

Vacuum advance is checked with the distributor driven at a specified speed. Vacuum is then applied to the vacuum-advance mechanism, and the amount of advance obtained is noted. Some distributors have provision for adjusting vacuum advance (⊘ 31-5). On others, the advance unit is replaced when it does not provide the proper advance.

⊘ 31-4 Adjusting Centrifugal Advance We noted that some distributors have provision for adjusting centrifugal advance. Figure 31-6 shows how to adjust the centrifugal advance on Ford six- and eight-cylinder distributors. Bend the adjustment bracket out to increase the spring tension and thus decrease centrifugal advance. Bend the adjustment bracket in to decrease the spring tension and thus increase centrifugal advance.

Other distributors have different adjustment procedures. Refer to the manufacturer's shop manual for the specifications and procedures.

⊘ 31-5 Adjusting Vacuum Advance Some distributors also have provision for adjusting vacuum advance. Figure 31-7 shows how this is done on some late-model Ford distributors. Use an allen wrench of the proper size to turn the socket-head screw in the vacuum-advance mechanism. Turn it clockwise to increase the vacuum advance, or counterclockwise to decrease it. Some earlier models were adjusted by installing or removing spacing washers under the plug in the vacuum-advance unit (Fig. 31-8).

⊘ 31-6 Inspecting Contact Points Use a screwdriver to carefully separate the contact points. Note their color and roughness. The points should be uniform and gray in color. If they are blue or

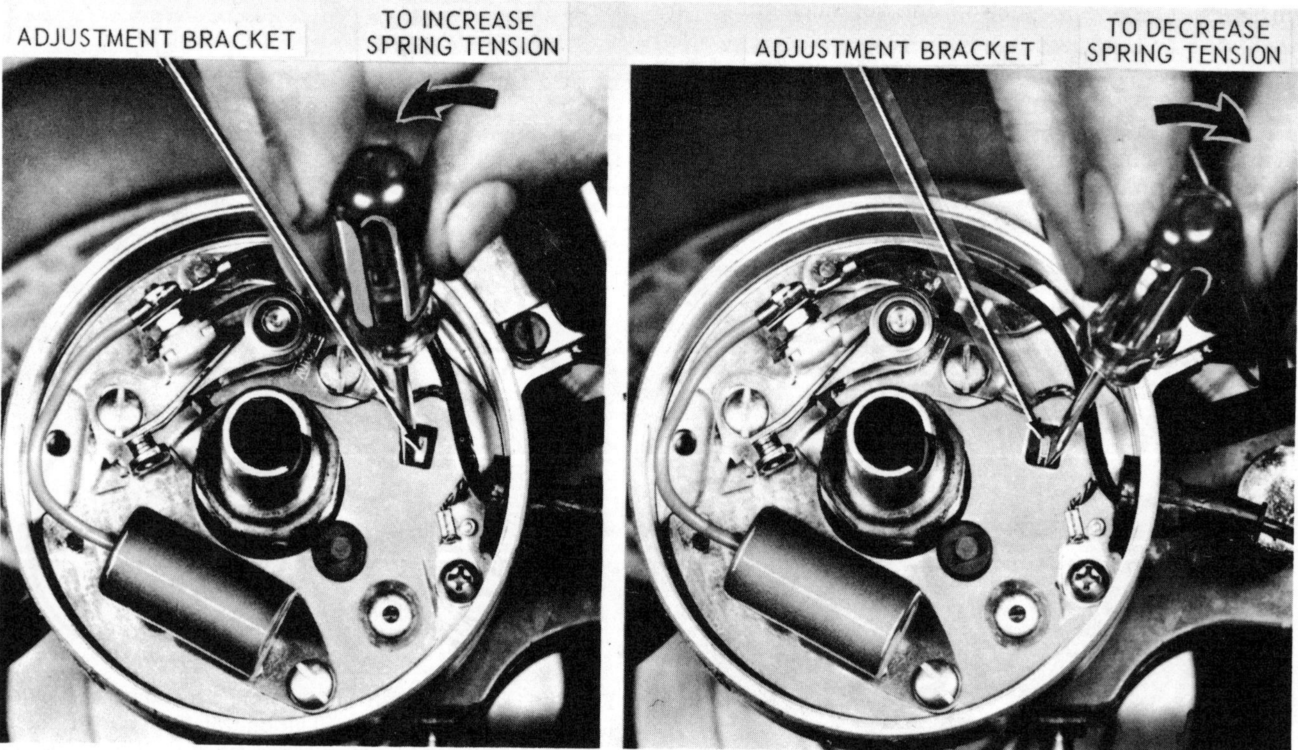

Fig. 31-6. Adjusting centrifugal advance. (*Ford Motor Company*)

Fig. 31-7. Adjusting vacuum advance. (*Ford Motor Company*)

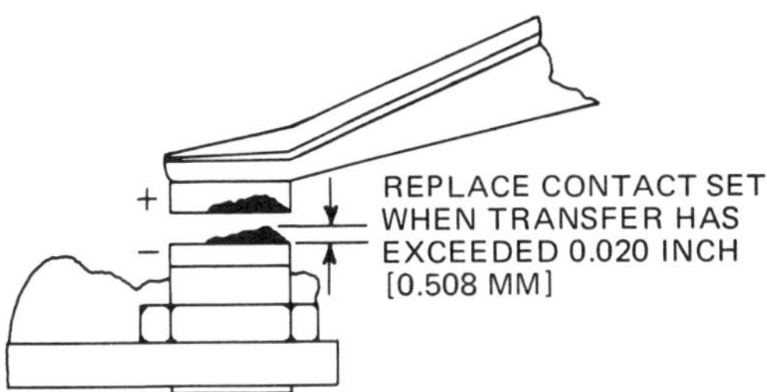

Fig. 31-9. If contact-material transfer exceeds 0.020 in [0.508 mm], the contact points should be replaced. (*Delco-Remy Division of General Motors Corporation*)

burned, there may be excessive current in the primary. This could be due to a high voltage-regulator setting. Points get rather rough in service. Actually, rough points may have a greater contact area than new contacts. However, if the contacts are burned or are too rough, they should be replaced. For example, if contact-material transfer has produced a buildup on one point of 0.020 in [0.508 mm], the contact set should be replaced (see Fig. 31-9). See ⊘ 29-12 and 29-13 for the causes of contact-point pitting and burning.

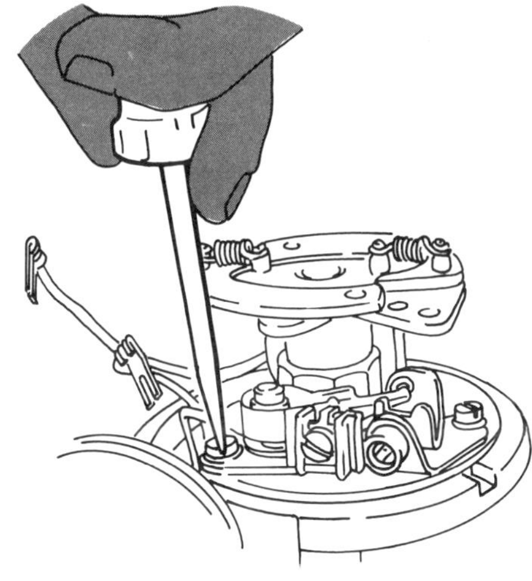

Fig. 31-10. Loosening a screw to remove the contact-point set. (*Delco-Remy Division of General Motors Corporation*)

⊘ 31-7 Replacing Contact Points Some contact points are supplied as assembled sets. On these, the stationary contact and the movable contact are replaced as a unit. On others, the breaker arm and then the stationary-contact base are removed. The removal of a contact-point set is shown in Figs. 31-10 and 31-11. After the lead screw is loosened and the leads are detached, the two screws holding the con-

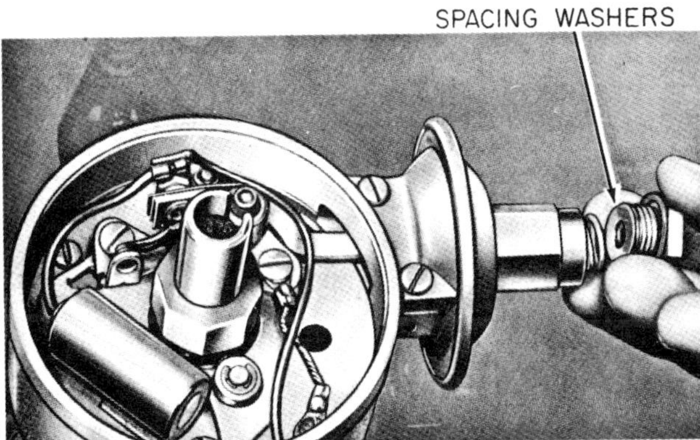

Fig. 31-8. Vacuum advance can be adjusted on some distributors by installing or removing spacing washers. (*Ford Motor Company*)

Fig. 31-11. Lifting a contact set from a breaker plate. (*Delco-Remy Division of General Motors Corporation*)

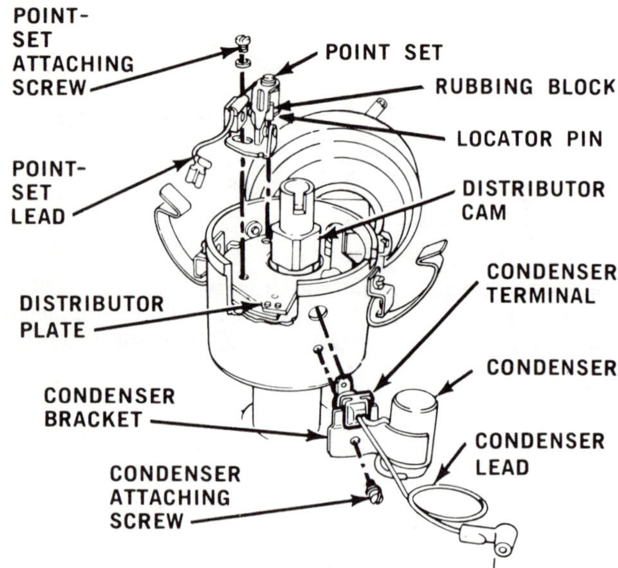

Fig. 31-12. Partly disassembled distributor, showing the proper locations of the contact-point set and condenser. (*Ford Motor Company*)

tact set to the breaker plate are loosened. The contact set will then slip out from under the screws. Figure 31-12 shows a contact-point set removed from a distributor.

To replace the set, first wipe the breaker plate clean. If the distributor does not have a cam lubricator, apply a bit of high-temperature grease to the cam. Install the new contact set, attach the leads, and adjust the contacts as explained in ⊘ 31-8.

NOTE: Many contact sets are now supplied with the condenser as part of the assembly (Fig. 31-13). These are called Unisets by the manufacturer, Delco-Remy.

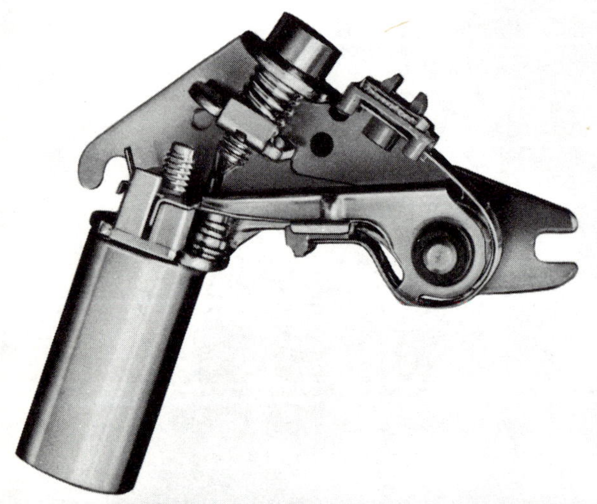

Fig. 31-13. Contact set with attached condenser. With this set, called a "Uniset" by the manufacturer, the points and condenser are replaced as a unit. (*Delco-Remy Division of General Motors Corporation*)

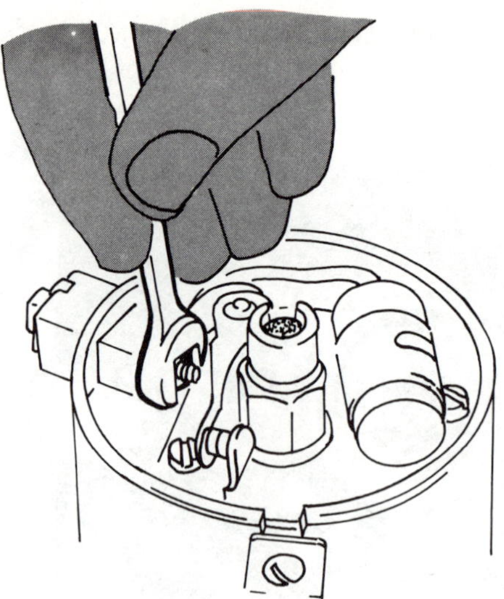

Fig. 31-14. Loosening the nut that attaches the spring of the contact lever. (*Delco-Remy Division of General Motors Corporation*)

The installation procedure is the same as for other sets, except that it is not necessary to install a separate condenser. Many automotive technicians routinely replace the condenser when new points are installed.

The separately mounted contact lever and stationary contact are removed by loosening the lever-spring attaching nut. Then the screw that holds the stationary contact to the breaker plate is removed. The lever and stationary point can then be lifted off separately (see Figs. 31-14 and 31-15). Adjust the new contacts after they have been installed (⊘ 31-8).

⊘ 31-8 Adjusting Contact-Point Opening Before adjusting the point opening or dwell angle, align the

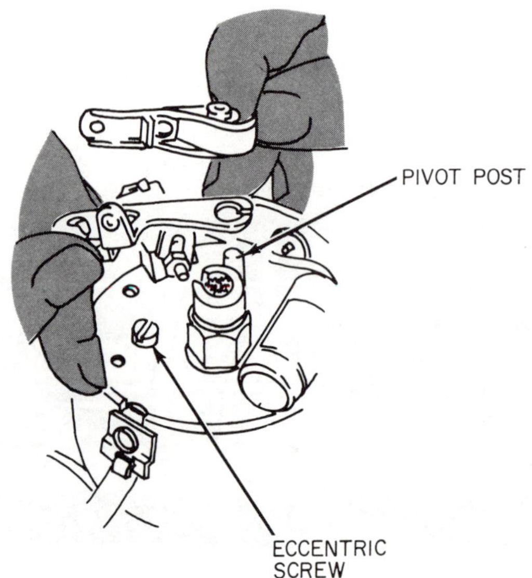

Fig. 31-15. Removing the lever and stationary point. (*Delco-Remy Division of General Motors Corporation*)

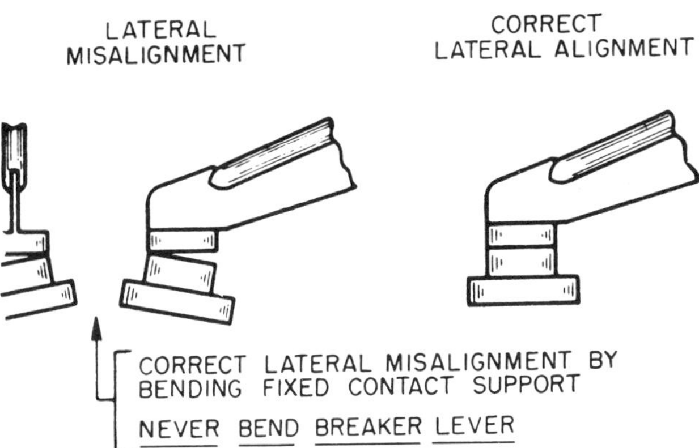

Fig. 31-16. Correct and incorrect lateral alignment of flat contact points.

points. Figures 31-16 and 31-17 show the right and wrong ways to align points. Figure 31-18 shows an alignment tool provided by Ford. Note that twisting the tool one way or the other bends the stationary-point support. See also Fig. 31-19. Never bend the lever arm! This can break it. After the points are aligned, adjust the point opening or dwell angle.

New contact points can be adjusted with a feeler gauge. Turn the distributor shaft until the peak of a cam lobe is under the center of the lever rubbing block (Fig. 31-20). If the distributor is on the engine, rotate the distributor in its mounting. With the lever as shown in Fig. 31-20, measure the gap between the lever contact and the stationary contact (Fig. 31-21). Figures 31-21 to 31-23 show how to adjust the contact-point opening on different distributors. The stationary-contact support is moved to make the adjustment. Then the lockscrew is tightened.

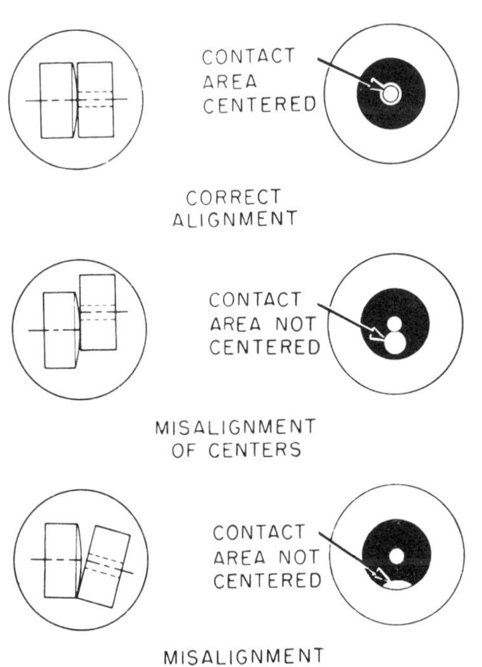

Fig. 31-17. Correct and incorrect alignment of vented contact points.

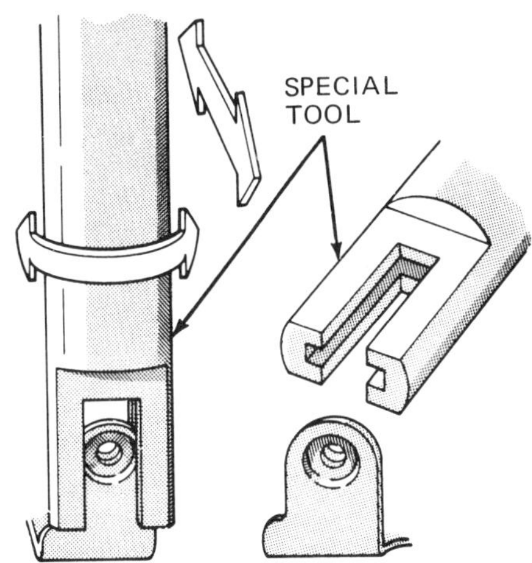

Fig. 31-18. Special tool to align the stationary contact point. (*Ford Motor Company*)

Some contact-point kits come with special disposable tools. For example, Fig. 31-24 shows a special plastic tool for contact-point and spark-plug-gap adjustment. This tool comes in a tuneup kit, with the contact-point set. It is used as shown in Fig. 31-25. First, you break off the feeler gauge (see the break-off point in Fig. 31-24). Then, you slip the sleeve over the cam as shown in Fig. 31-25. Note that the position of the cam lobes makes no difference. The sleeve and the special feeler gauge, used together, provide the proper spacing for the contact points. Insert the feeler gauge as shown (Fig. 31-25), and adjust the points. Figure 31-26 shows how round feeler gauges are used to check spark-plug gaps. (See ⊘ 30-12).

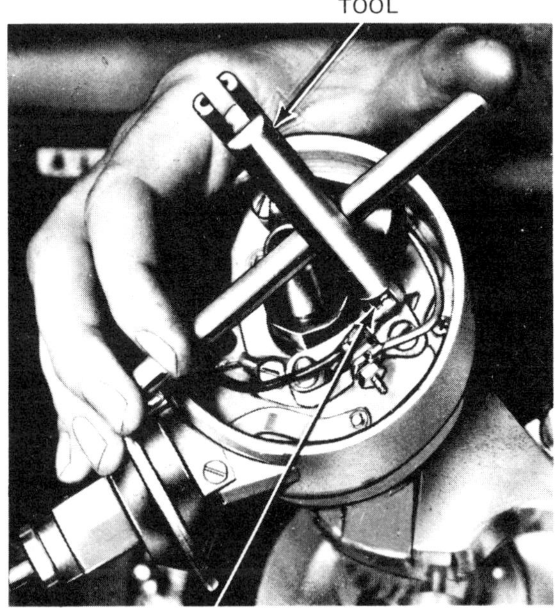

Fig. 31-19. Aligning contact points with a special tool. Note that the bracket on which the stationary contact is mounted is being bent to attain alignment. (*Ford Motor Company*)

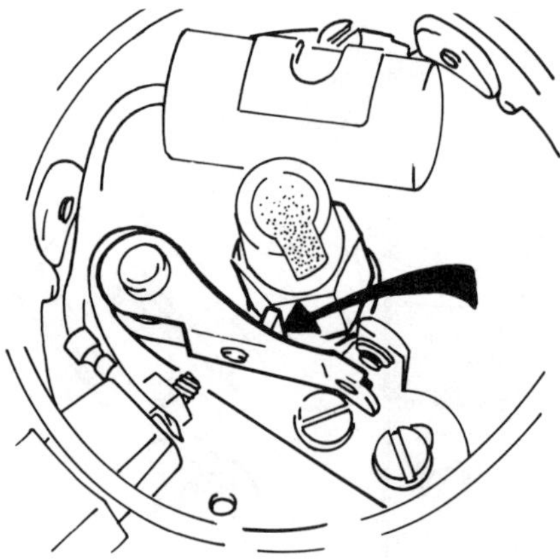

Fig. 31-20. The cam lobe must be under the rubbing block to check the point opening. (*Delco-Remy Division of General Motors Corporation*)

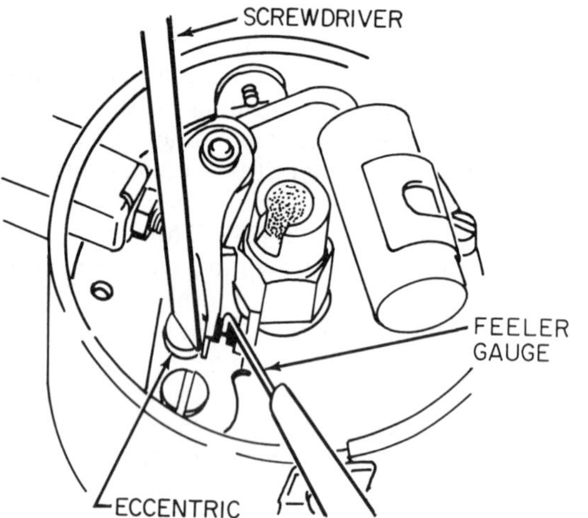

Fig. 31-21. On some distributors, the eccentric is turned with a screwdriver to adjust the point opening. (*Delco-Remy Division of General Motors Corporation*)

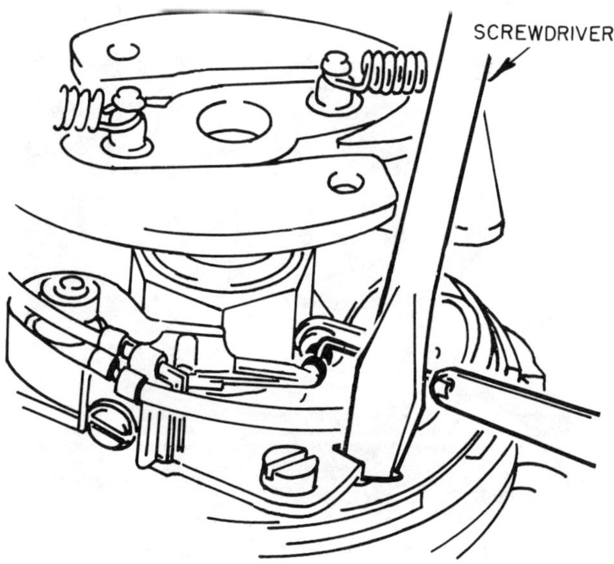

Fig. 31-22. On some distributors, the stationary point base is pried back or forth with a screwdriver to adjust the point opening. (*Delco-Remy Division of General Motors Corporation*)

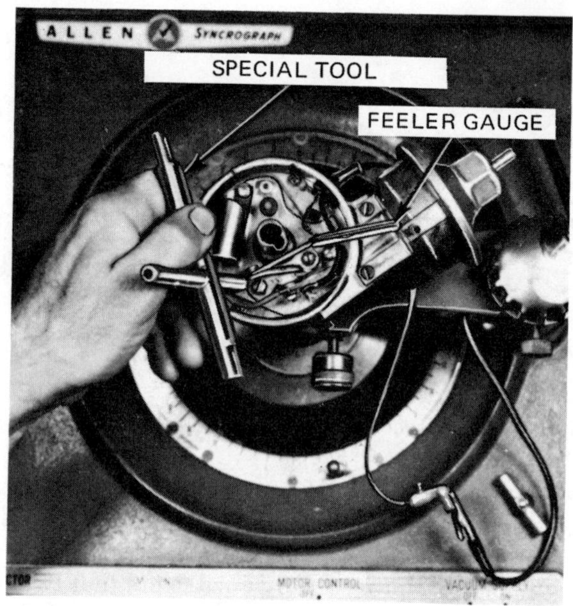

Fig. 31-23. Adjusting contact-point gap. (*Ford Motor Company*)

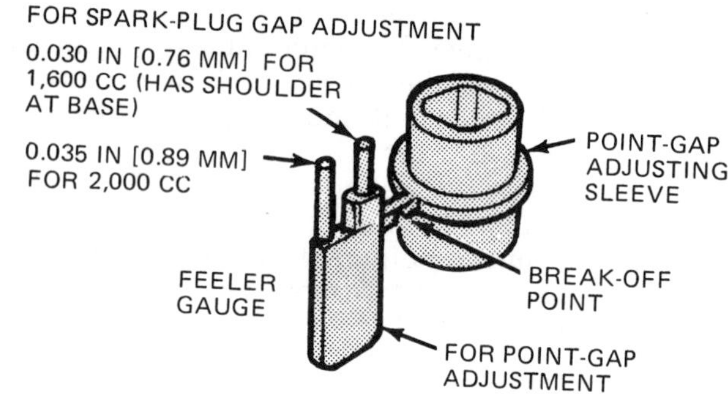

Fig. 31-24. Plastic throw-away tool included in a tuneup kit. The tool is used to adjust the contact-point opening and the spark-plug gap. (*Ford Motor Company*)

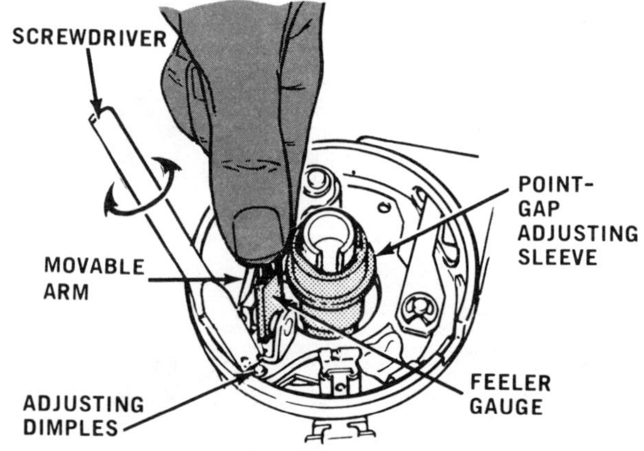

Fig. 31-25. Using the special plastic tool to adjust the contact-point opening. The sleeve is placed over the breaker cam. Then the feeler gauge is used to gauge the opening while the stationary-point base is adjusted to get the proper gap. (*Ford Motor Company*)

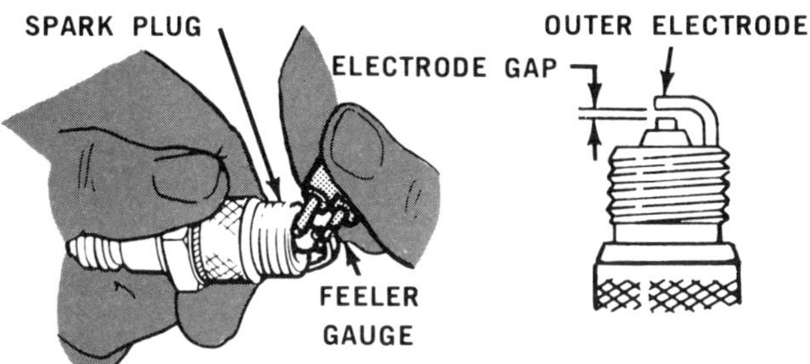

Fig. 31-26. Using the feeler gauge from the plastic throw-away tool to check the spark-plug gap. (*Ford Motor Company*)

Figure 30-4 shows you why you should not attempt to adjust used contacts with a feeler gauge. The roughness of the contact surfaces makes it impossible to get an accurate setting. A dwell meter can be used to get an accurate setting on new or used contacts (⊘ 30-4). The dwell meter permits adjustment of the contact points in the type of distributor with the cap window (Fig. 31-27), without removing the cap.

⊘ 31-9 Adjusting Contact-Point Spring Tension In the preassembled contact set (Figs. 31-10 and 31-11), the spring tension is checked at the factory and does not require adjustment. On other contact sets, the spring tension must be measured as shown in Figs. 30-6 and 30-7. Figure 31-28 shows how to make the adjustment. First disconnect the primary lead wire and the condenser lead. Loosen the nut holding the spring in position. Then move the spring toward the breaker-arm pivot to decrease the tension. Move it in the opposite direction to increase the tension. Finally, tighten the locknut, and recheck the tension. Repeat the procedure until the tension is right. Then reconnect the primary lead wire and the condenser lead.

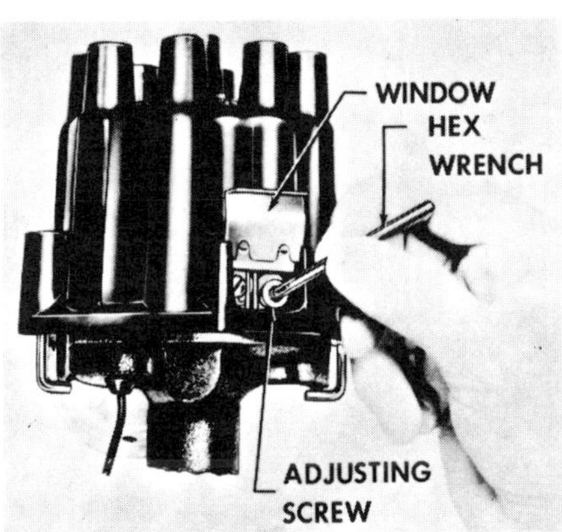

Fig. 31-27. The contact points of the distributor which has a metal window in the cap can be adjusted by raising the window and using a hex wrench. (*Delco-Remy Division of General Motors Corporation*)

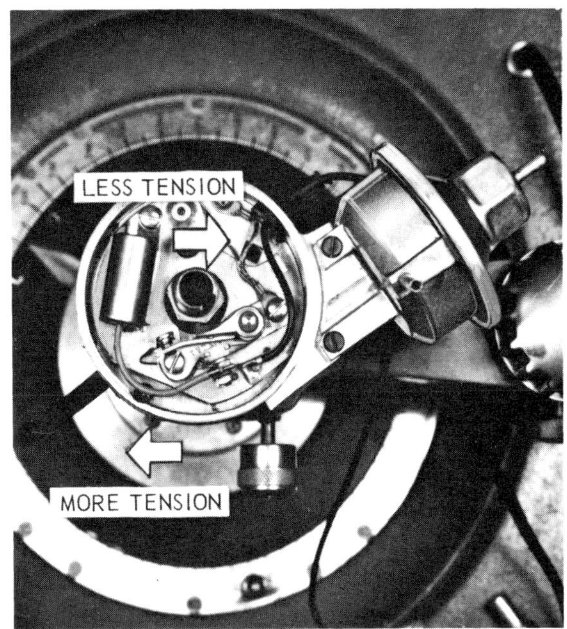

Fig. 31-28. Adjusting the contact-point spring tension. (*Ford Motor Company*)

⊘ 31-10 Synchronizing Dual-Contact Distributors On dual-contact distributors, first adjust the point opening of each set separately. Then, with the distributor mounted in a distributor tester (Fig. 30-3), check the dwell angles. Then check the total dwell. Adjust to get the proper dwell by moving the adjustable plate. Tighten the locking screws after the adjustment is completed.

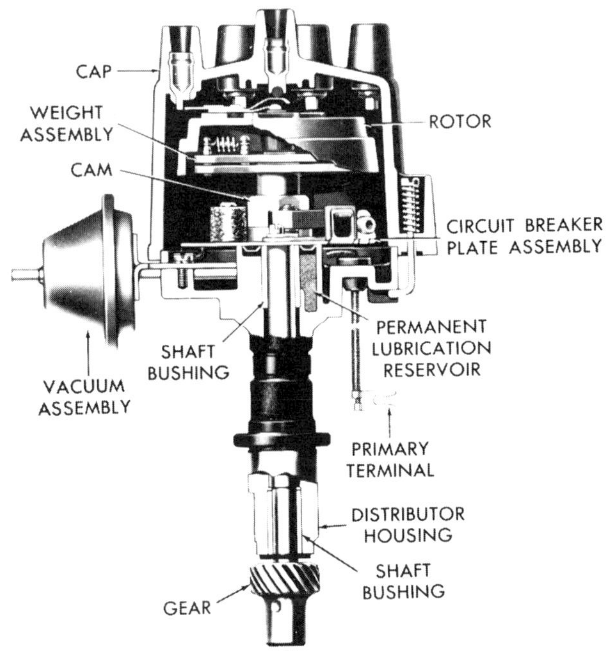

Fig. 31-29. Sectional view of a distributor for an eight-cylinder engine. Note the permanent lubrication reservoir. This distributor needs no periodic lubrication. (*Chevrolet Motor Division of General Motors Corporation*)

⊘ 31-11 Distributor Lubrication Most distributors now have built-in oil reservoirs to lubricate the shaft bushings (Fig. 31-29). They also have a cam lubricator (Fig. 31-30). These distributors usually require no lubrication, except during overhaul. However, the cam lubricator must be turned or replaced at periodic intervals if it is of the type shown in Fig. 31-30. Every 12,000 mi [19,312 km], the cam lubricator should be turned 180°. It should be replaced every 24,000 mi [38,624 km]. Also, on some distributors, the cam should be lightly lubricated periodically (or during overhaul). See the manufacturer's shop manual for specific recommendations.

⊘ 31-12 Testing the Electronic Distributor and Control Unit We mentioned in ⊘ 30-10 (and illustrated in Fig. 30-17) the tester recommended by Chrysler Corporation for checking their electronic ignition systems. The tester is connected into the ignition system at the wiring harness. First, the connector between the distributor and control unit is unplugged. Then, the tester connectors are plugged into the male and female halves of the wiring-harness-circuit connector. Figure 31-31 shows the circuit and where the tester is plugged in.

The Ford testing procedure requires a voltmeter and an ohmmeter. Figure 31-32 shows the circuit. Figure 31-33 shows the two connectors in the wiring harness from the electronic control module (or electronic amplifier, as it is called by other manufacturers). The tables in Fig. 31-34 show where the voltage should be checked (from pin to pin in the connectors). They also show what the resistance should be in various parts of the circuit. If a voltage or resistance varies from the specifications, replace the unit or the wire that does not test properly.

⊘ 31-13 Testing HEI and Unit Distributors The unit distributor includes the ignition coil (see ⊘ 28-

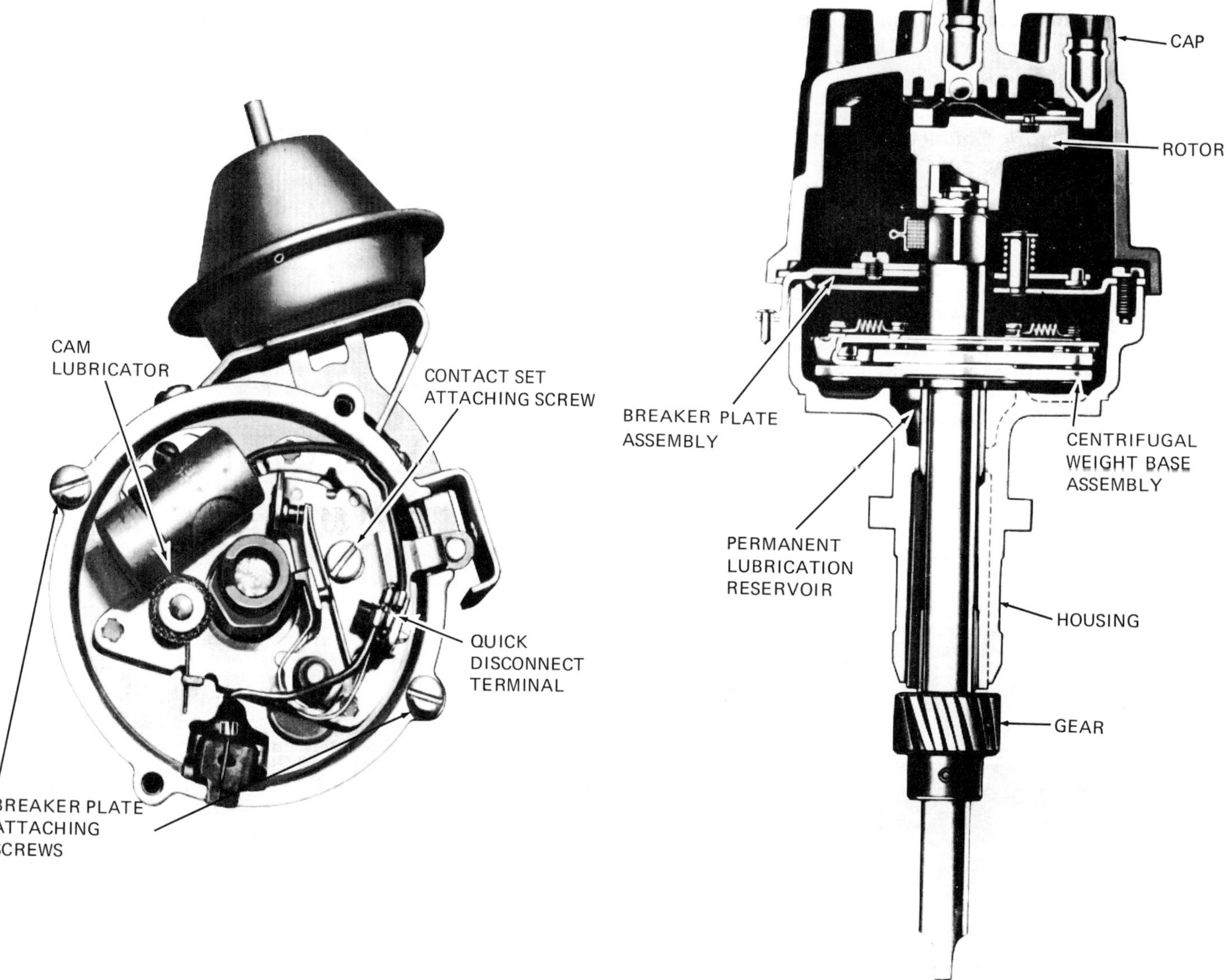

Fig. 31-30. Top and side sectional views of a distributor for a six-cylinder engine. Note the cam lubricator. (*Chevrolet Motor Division of General Motors Corporation*)

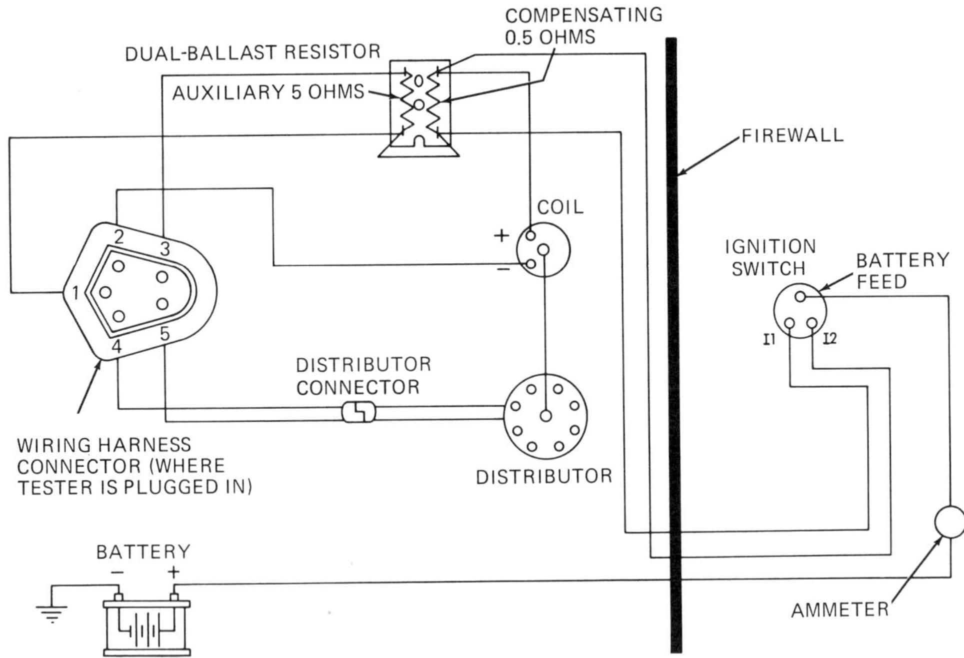

Fig. 31-31. Wiring circuit for an electronic ignition system, showing the point where the tester is plugged in. (*Chrysler Corporation*)

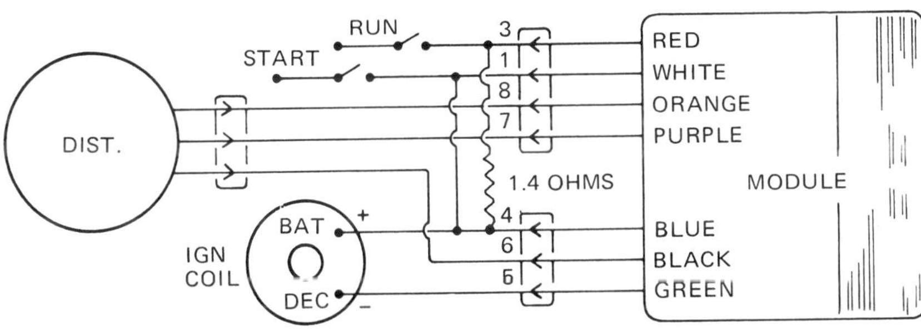

Fig. 31-32. Schematic wiring diagram for an electronic ignition system. (*Ford Motor Company*)

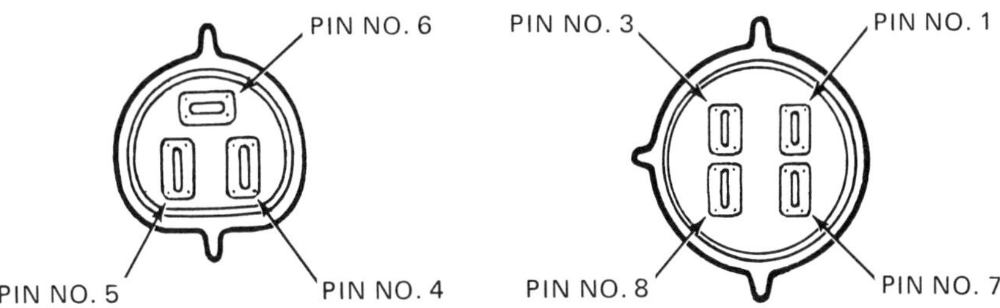

Fig. 31-33. Connectors in the harness that connects the electronic module with the electronic distributor. The pin numbers correspond to the numbers in Fig. 31-32. (*Ford Motor Company*)

7). Figure 31-35 shows the distributor with the cap and main shaft removed. Figure 31-36 shows the four ohmmeter checks of the ignition coil. Readings A and B should be practically zero. If either reading is infinity, replace the coil. Reading C should be 6,000 to 9,000 ohms. If it is outside that range, replace the coil. Reading D should be infinity. If it is not, replace the coil.

Figure 31-37 shows the two ohmmeter checks of the pickup-coil assembly. The reading at A should be between 650 and 850 ohms. If it falls outside this range, replace the pickup-coil assembly. The test should be made with a vacuum gradually applied to the vacuum-advance unit, so that the vacuum advance moves the pickup coil from no advance to full advance. If reading B is anything other than infinity at any time, replace the pickup-coil assembly.

NOTE: If the engine does not run (or runs and misses), the ignition coil and pickup coil should be

TROUBLE ISOLATION TESTS

	TEST VOLTAGE BETWEEN	SHOULD BE	IF NOT, CONDUCT
KEY ON	Pin #3 and engine ground	Battery voltage	Module bias test
	Pin #5 and engine ground	Battery voltage	Battery source test
CRANKING	Pin #1 and engine ground	8–12 volts	Cranking test
	Pin #5 and engine ground	8–12 volts	Starting circuit test
	Pin #7 and pin #8	½ volt ac or dc volt wiggle	Distributor hardware test

	TEST RESISTANCE BETWEEN	SHOULD BE	IF NOT, CONDUCT
KEY OFF	Pin #7 and pin #8 Pin #6 and engine ground Pin #7 and engine ground Pin #8 and engine ground	400–800 ohms 0 ohms more than 70,000 ohms more than 70,000 ohms	Magnetic pickup (stator) test
	Pin #3 and coil tower Pin #5 and pin #4	7,000–13,000 ohms 1.0–2.0 ohms	Coil test
	Pin #5 and engine ground	more than 10.0 ohms	Short test
	Pin #3 and pin #4	1.0–2.0 ohms	Resistance wire

Fig. 31-34. Trouble-isolation tests with voltmeter and ohmmeter. (*Ford Motor Company*)

checked as noted above. Then, if they check out okay and all connections, wiring, and spark plugs are in good condition, the fault must lie in the electronic module (Fig. 31-35). Replace it.

The High-Energy-Ignition-System distributor is shown in Figs. 31-38 and 31-39. To test the ignition coil disconnect the wiring harness. Turn the four latches, and remove the cap. Connect an ohmmeter as at 1 in Fig. 31-40. This connection is to the BAT (battery) and TACH (tachometer) terminals. The ohmmeter reading should be zero or nearly zero. If it is not, replace the coil. Then connect the ohmmeter as at 2 in Fig. 31-40. The reading should not be infinite. If it is, the coil is open and should be replaced.

Next, disconnect the two leads from the electronic module (Fig. 31-41). Connect the ohmmeter from one of these leads to ground, as shown at 1.

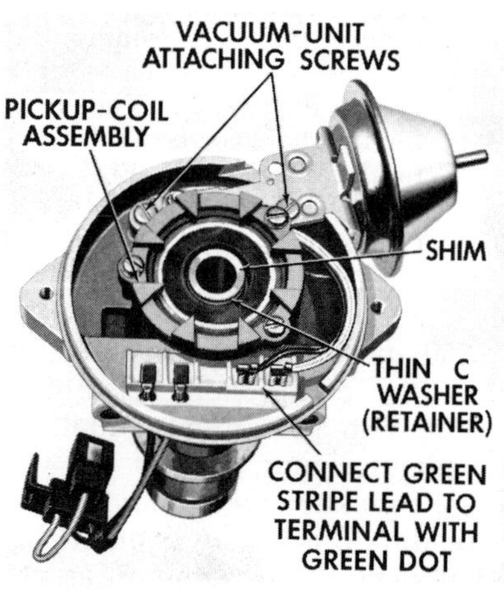

Fig. 31-35. Unit distributor with the cap, rotor, and shaft assembly removed. (*Pontiac Motor Division of General Motors Corporation*)

Fig. 31-36. Ignition-coil check in the unit distributor, using an ohmmeter. (*Pontiac Motor Division of General Motors Corporation*)

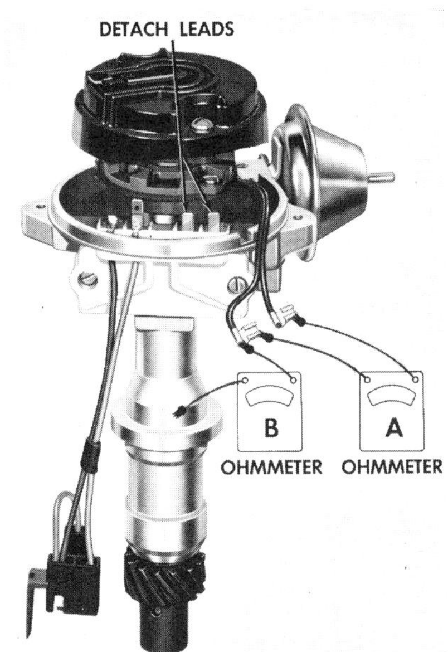

Fig. 31-37. Pickup-coil check in the unit distributor, using an ohmmeter. (*Pontiac Motor Division of General Motors Corporation*)

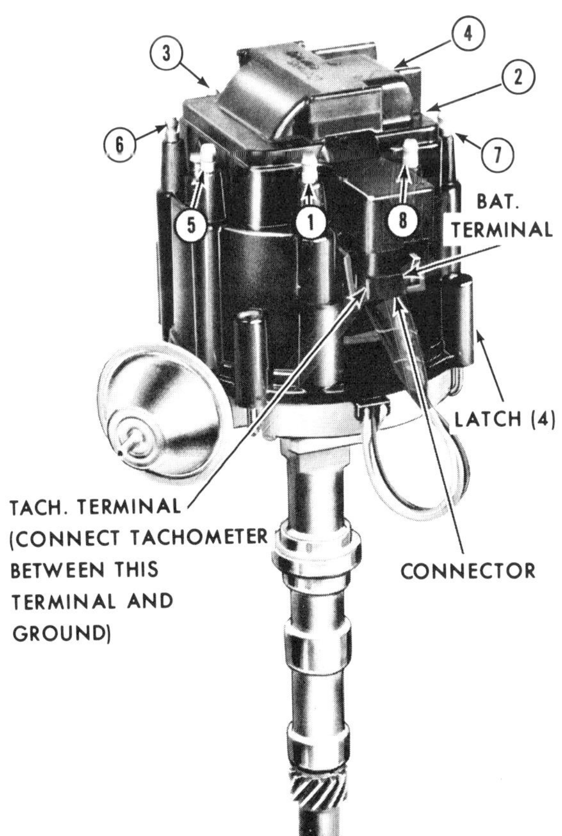

Fig. 31-38. High-Energy Ignition System. (*Cadillac Motor Car Division of General Motors Corporation*)

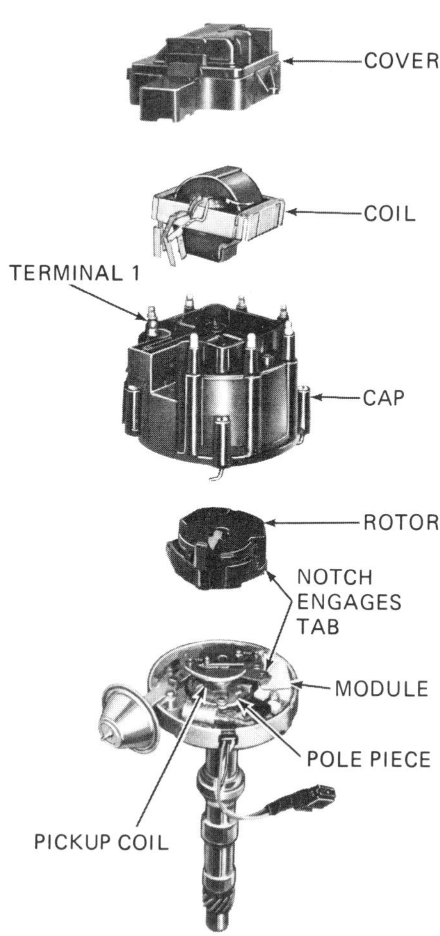

Fig. 31-39. High-Energy Ignition System disassembled. (*Cadillac Motor Car Division of General Motors Corporation*)

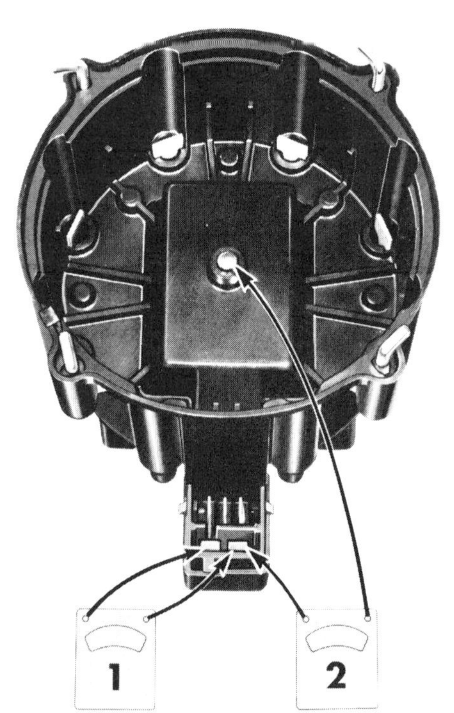

Fig. 31-40. Checking the ignition coil in the High-Energy Ignition System. (*Cadillac Motor Car Division of General Motors Corporation*)

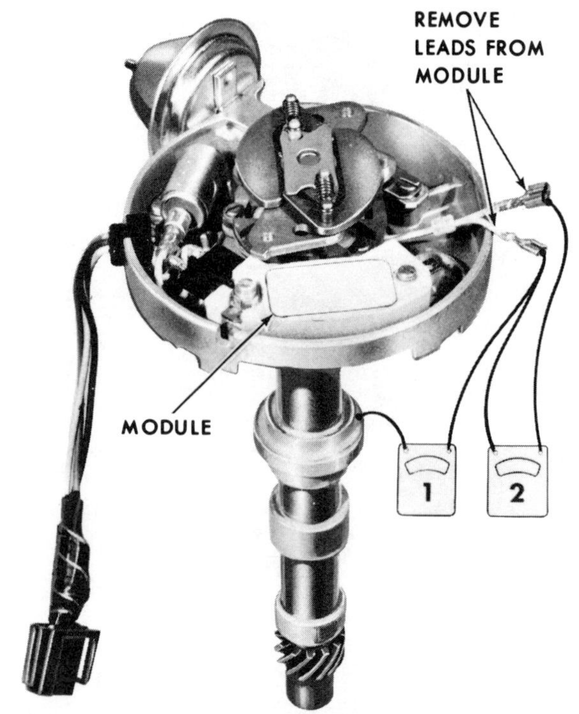

Fig. 31-41. Checking the pickup coil in the High-Energy Ignition System. (*Cadillac Motor Car Division of General Motors Corporation*)

Apply vacuum to the vacuum advance gradually, so that the pickup-coil assembly is moved. The ohmmeter should register infinity at all times. If it does not, replace the pickup-coil assembly. Check the other pickup-coil lead in the same way. It should give an infinite reading. Now connect the ohmmeter as shown at 2 in Fig. 31-41. Apply vacuum, and note the ohmmeter reading. It should be between 650 and 850 ohms. If it is outside these limits, replace the pickup-coil assembly.

If everything else checks okay but the engine still misses or will not run, replace the electronic module.

A quick check of the electronic module can be made with a dwell meter. At idle, the HEI distributor will show about 12° dwell. At about 2,500 rpm, the dwell should be about 30°. If the dwell does not increase as the engine is accelerated, the module is defective and should be replaced.

⊘ 31-14 Distributor Disassembly The procedure for disassembling a distributor varies somewhat, because different distributors are constructed differently (see Figs. 31-42 to 31-44). On the typical ignition distributor, the cap, rotor, and dust seal or radio-frequency interference shield are first taken off. Then the terminal (where present) is disassembled, and the breaker plate is taken out. Then the coupling or gear is removed. This is done by grinding or filing off the peened-over head of the pin, and driving out the pin. Next, the shaft and advance-mechanism assembly are lifted out of the distributor housing.

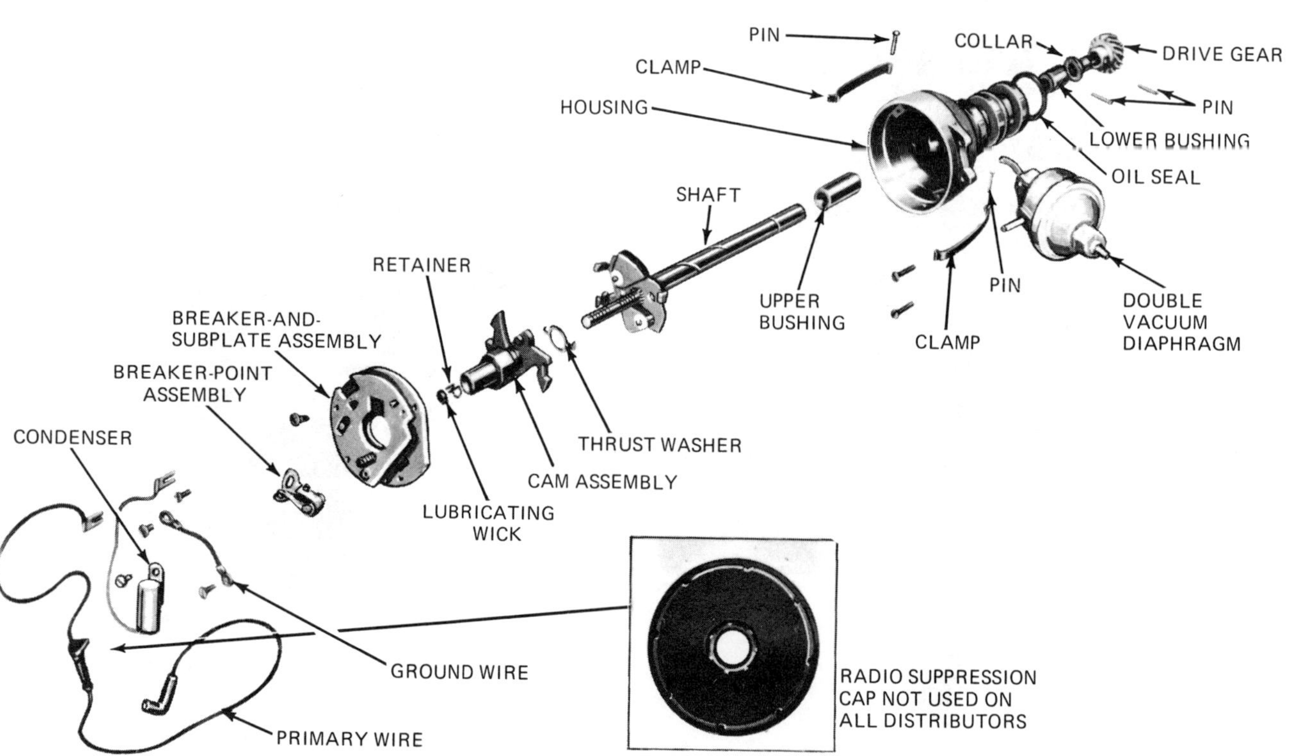

Fig. 31-42. Disassembled view of a distributor for a V-8 engine. (*Ford Motor Company*)

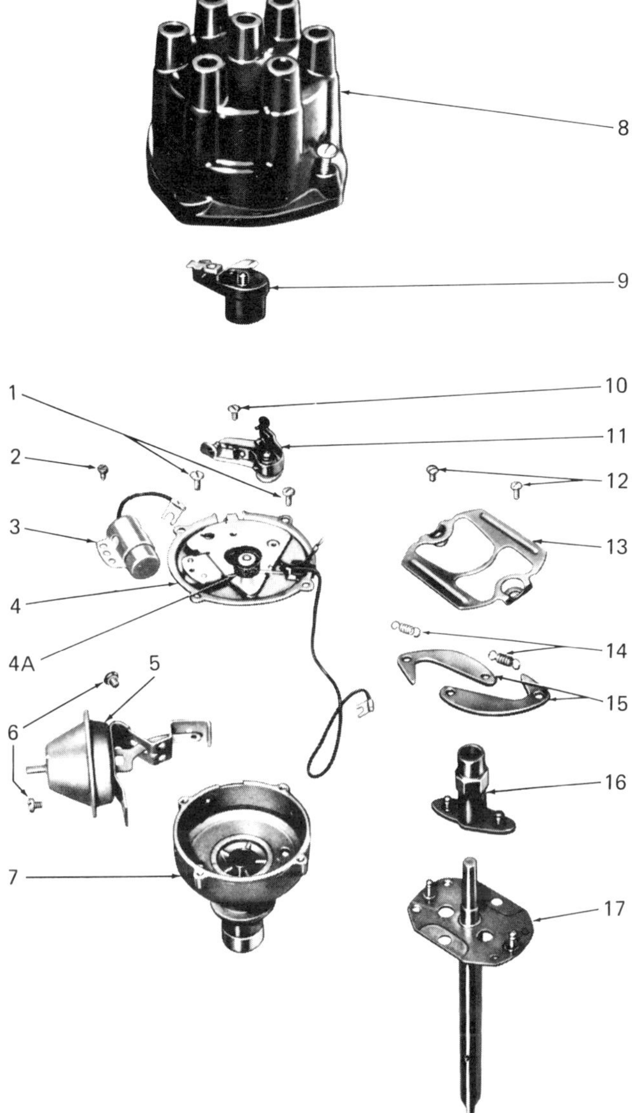

1. Breaker-plate attaching screws
2. Condenser attaching screw
3. Condenser
4. Breaker-plate assembly
4A. Cam lubricator
5. Vacuum-control assembly
6. Vacuum-control attaching screws
7. Housing
8. Cap
9. Rotor
10. Contact-point attaching screw
11. Contact-point assembly
12. Weight-cover attaching screws
13. Weight cover
14. Weight springs
15. Advance weights
16. Cam assembly
17. Main-shaft assembly

Fig. 31-43. Disassembled view of an ignition distributor for a six-cylinder engine. (*Chevrolet Motor Division of General Motors Corporation*)

CAUTION: Before attempting to take out the shaft, be sure that there are no burrs around the pinhole. Burrs might damage the distributor bearing when the shaft is removed from the housing. File down any burrs before removing the shaft.

The advance mechanism can be disassembled by taking off the nuts or screws holding the weight hold-down plate in place. Note the condition of the bearing in the distributor housing; replace it if it is excessively worn (see ⊘ 31-15).

NOTE: Some distributors have a flexible drive-gear arrangement. It includes rubber cushions that prevent engine vibration from reaching the distributor. On such units, the old driving blocks, cushions, retainers, and pin should be discarded, and new ones installed. If the old ones are used again, they will probably fit too loosely to protect against vibration.

Some heavy-duty and special-application distributors have special features. These include two-piece housings, ball bearings, dual contacts, and engine-governor drives or tachometer drives. On such units, the disassembly procedure is more complex than that given above. However, these units can

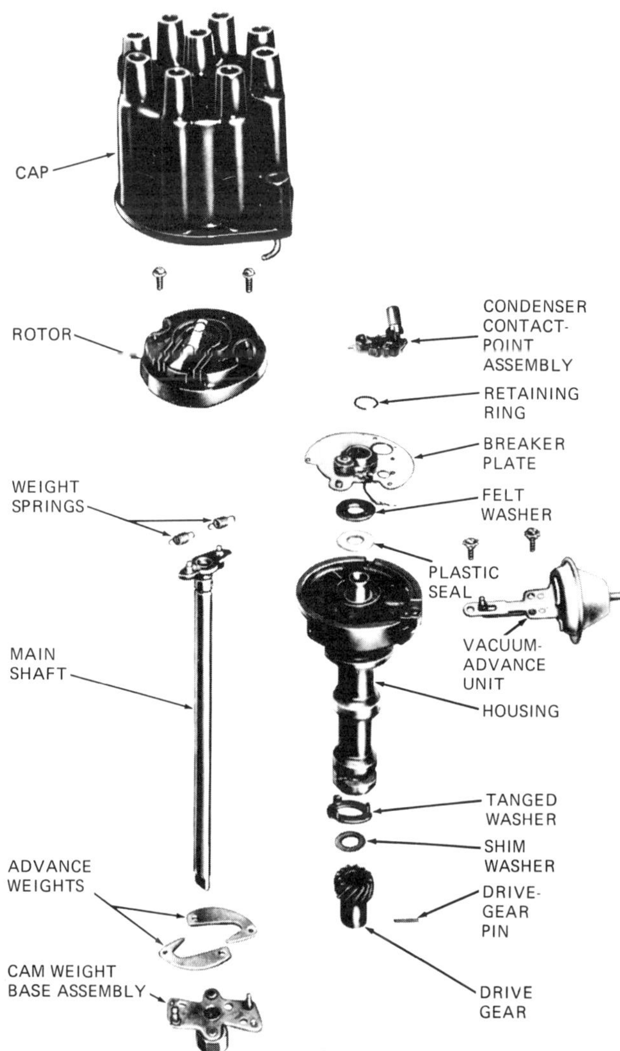

Fig. 31-44. Disassembled view of a distributor for an eight-cylinder engine. (*Chevrolet Motor Division of General Motors Corporation*)

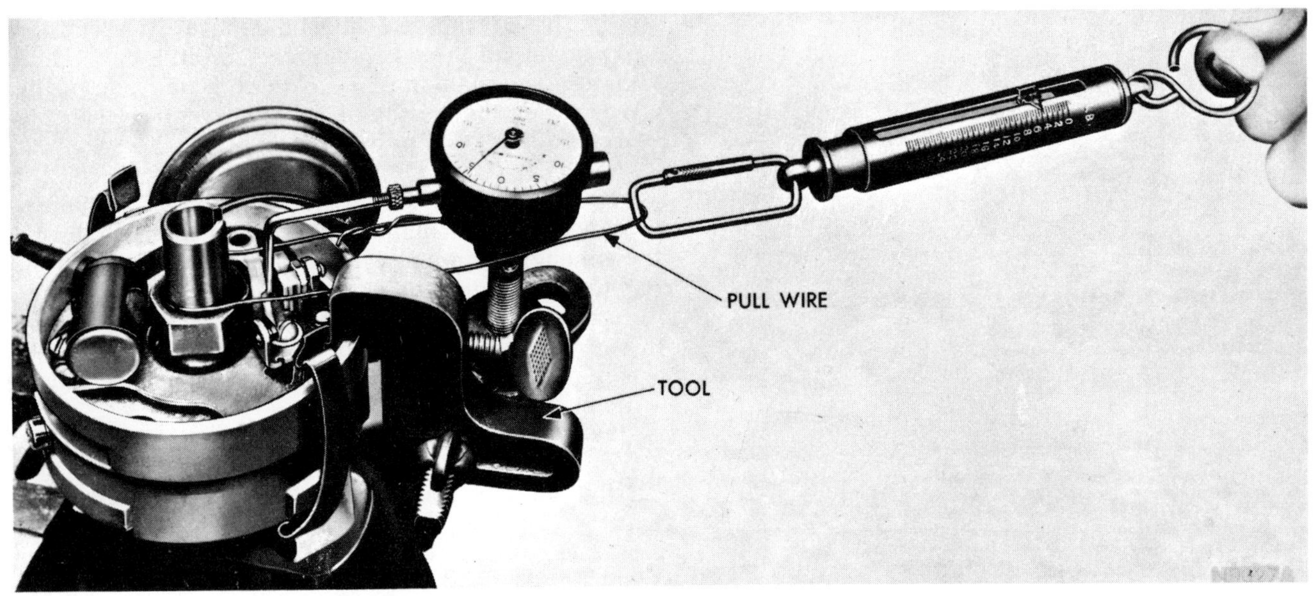

Fig. 31-45. Using a dial indicator and spring gauge to check the side movement of the shaft, and thus the amount of wear of the bearing. (*Chrysler Corporation*)

be easily serviced, provided you carefully note the locations and relationships of the parts *before* you begin to remove them. If you have any doubt about the reassembly procedure, always refer to the manufacturer's service manual.

⊘ 31-15 Distributor Reassembly During reassembly, several checks should be made, and the following points kept in mind.

1. *CHECKING FOR BEARING WEAR* Note the condition of the bearing in the distributor housing, and replace it if it is worn. A worn bearing causes variations in contact-point opening, sometimes enough to result in engine missing. To check the bearing for wear, place the shaft in its normal position in the bearing, and then try to move the shaft sideways. A dial indicator can be attached to the housing, so that the actual side movement of the shaft can be measured. One manufacturer recommends that the bearing be replaced if the side play is more than 0.006 in [0.15 mm] when 5 lb [2.27 kg] of side pull is applied with a spring gauge (see Fig. 31-45). An arbor press should be used to press out the old bearing and press in a new one. A special arbor is required to install the new bearing. The extension on the special arbor is sized to maintain the proper bearing inside diameter when the bearing is pressed into the housing.

NOTE: Some bearings may require reaming to size after they are installed.

On some distributors, the bushings are not replaceable. If the bushings are worn, the distributor housing and the bushing should be replaced as a unit.

2. *INSTALLING THE SHAFT* When installing the gear or the coupling, be sure that the shaft end play is correct. It varies with different distributors, so check the manufacturer's specifications. On some distributors, end play is adjusted by adding or removing shims on the lower end of the shaft, between the coupling or gear and the distributor housing. On other distributors, end play is established by drilling a new hole through the shaft if necessary. During reassembly, the shaft is put into position in the distributor housing or base and pushed down as far as it will go. Then the gear or coupling is slipped onto the shaft and up against a feeler gauge held between the gear and housing (or washer, if used). Finally, a hole is drilled through the gear and shaft, and the pin is installed. The end play should be checked after the pin has been put into place, but before it has been peened over. The end play should be rechecked after peening, to ensure that it is still within specifications.

3. *BALL-SUPPORTED BREAKER-PLATE INSTALLATION* On distributors in which the breaker plate is supported by three balls, place a small amount of petroleum jelly in the ball seats in the breaker plate. Then put the balls in the seats. (The jelly keeps the balls in place while the plate is being installed.) Then align the balls with the vertical grooves in the housing. The spring seat should be on the plate next to the vacuum-control-link slot in the housing. Finally, push the plate down and turn it slightly to bring it into position.

4. *BEARING-SUPPORTED BREAKER-PLATE INSTALLATION* The bearing arrangement that supports the breaker plate in Delco-Remy external-adjustment distributors is shown in Fig. 31-46. On this type distributor, the breaker plate is supported on the outer diameter of the upper bearing (Fig. 31-46). To install the breaker plate, put it in place on the bushing. Then install the retainer ring (Fig. 31-46) to hold the breaker plate in position.

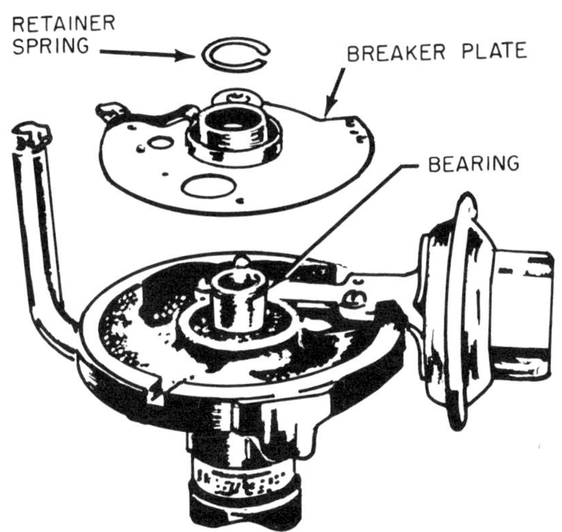

Fig. 31-46. Disassembled view of the type of breaker support used in an external-adjustment distributor. (*Delco-Remy Division of General Motors Corporation*)

5. *CONTACT-POINT ADJUSTMENT* The installation and adjustment of the contact points was described in ⊘ 31-7 to 31-9.
6. *ADJUSTMENT OF ADVANCES* In some models, the advance mechanisms can be adjusted, as explained in ⊘ 31-4 and 31-5.
7. *LUBRICATION* During reassembly, lubricate the distributor by the means provided. Refill oil reservoirs with oil of the specified type. (See also ⊘ 31-11.)

⊘ 31-16 Distributor Removal and Installation Distributor removal and replacement is simple if the engine is left undisturbed while the distributor is out. However, if the engine is cranked so that the crankshaft and camshaft are turned with the distributor out, replacement is a little more complicated.
1. *DISTRIBUTOR REMOVAL* Remove the air cleaner. Disconnect the vacuum hose or hoses from the distributor. Disconnect the primary lead running from the ignition coil to the distributor. Remove the distributor cap, and push the cap-and-wire assembly aside.

Scratch a mark on the distributor housing. Scratch another mark on the engine block, such that the two marks line up. These marks locate the position of the distributor housing in the block. Scratch a third mark on the distributor housing exactly under the rotor tip. This mark locates the position of the rotor in the housing.

Remove the distributor hold-down bolt and clamp. Lift the distributor out of the block.

NOTE: If the engine is not cranked while the distributor is out, the distributor can easily be installed in the correct position. Simply align the rotor tip with the marks on the distributor housing and cylinder block during installation.

2. *DISTRIBUTOR INSTALLATION* If the engine has been cranked with the distributor out, timing has been lost. The engine must be retimed. This is necessary to establish the proper relationship between the distributor rotor and the No. 1 piston.

Remove the No. 1 spark plug from the cylinder head. Place a shop towel over your fingers, and cover the spark-plug hole. Crank the engine until you feel compression pressure on your finger.

Bump the engine with the starting motor until the timing marks on the crankshaft pulley and timing cover are aligned. This means that the No. 1 piston is in firing position.

Now the distributor can be installed in the cylinder block. Make sure to align the marks you made on the distributor housing and cylinder block. Check to make sure that the distributor gasket or rubber 0 ring is in place when you install the distributor.

NOTE: Three different distributor drives are shown in Fig. 31-47. You may have to turn the rotor slightly to engage the drive. Also, when the distributor goes down into place on the spiral-gear drive, the rotor will turn. So you must start with the rotor back of the proper position. Then it will turn into the correct position as the distributor goes down into place.

Make sure the distributor housing is fully seated against the cylinder block. If it is not, the oil-pump shaft is not engaging. Hold the distributor down firmly, and bump the engine a few times until the distributor housing drops into place.

Install, but do not tighten, the distributor clamp and bolt. Rotate the distributor until the contact points just start to open to fire No. 1 cylinder. Hold the distributor cap in place above the distributor. Make sure that the rotor tip lines up with the No. 1 terminal on the cap. Install the cap and wires. Connect the primary wire from the ignition coil to the distributor.

Start the engine. Set the ignition timing (⊘ 30-11). Connect the vacuum hose or hoses to the distributor. Replace the air cleaner.

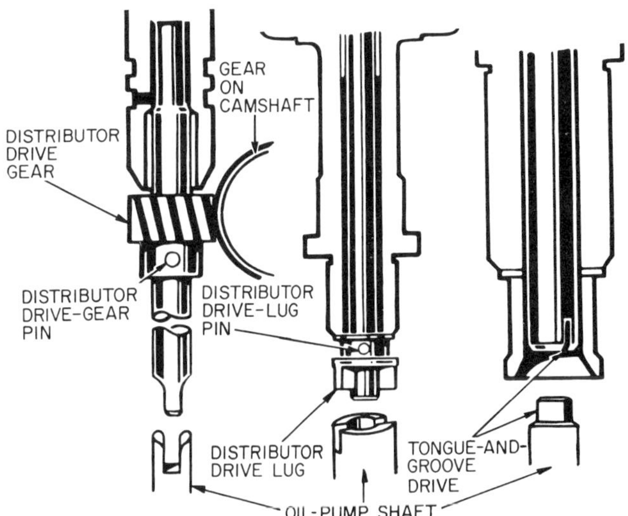

Fig. 31-47. Distributor installation methods.

CHAPTER 31 CHECKUP

NOTE: Since the following is a chapter review test, you should review the chapter before taking the test.

You have now completed your study of ignition systems. Chapters 28 to 31, supplemented by manufacturers' shop manuals, give you everything you need to know to perform ignition service. You will, of course, need practical experience in the shop. But you have now covered the theory which you will apply in performing actual shopwork. Take the following test to see how well you remember what you studied in this chapter. If you have trouble with any of the questions, study the chapter again.

Reviewing Ignition Service Write the answers to the following questions in your notebook.

1. Describe the procedure for replacing a defective distributor cap.
2. Explain how to remove and replace a distributor on an engine (engine not cranked while distributor is out).
3. Describe the procedure for removing and replacing a set of contact points in a distributor.
4. Write disassembly and reassembly procedures for a typical distributor.
5. Explain how to adjust (1) the contact-point opening and (2) the spring pressure.
6. If the engine has been disturbed with the distributor off, how do you reinstall the distributor?
7. Explain how to adjust (1) centrifugal advance and (2) vacuum advance.
8. Explain how to check the components in an electronic ignition system.
9. Explain how to check the components of an HEI distributor.

SUGGESTIONS FOR FURTHER STUDY

When you are in an automotive electrical service shop, note how ignition systems and their parts are serviced. Notice the methods of checking the complete system and the coil, condenser, distributor, and plugs. Study the operating manuals supplied with the various testing instruments. Also, study the bulletins and manuals issued by the automobile and equipment manufacturers. Be sure to write, in your notebook, any important facts you learn.

chapter 32

AUTOMOTIVE ELECTRONICS

In earlier chapters, we described semiconductors, diodes, and transistors. We explained that these are called solid-state devices; they work electronically, with no moving parts. In various chapters in the book, we explained how diodes and transistors are used in specific automotive equipment. For instance, we discussed alternators with built-in diodes and voltage regulators. We described electronic ignition systems which use pickup coils and electronic pulse amplifiers instead of contact points. Now we review the various ways in which solid-state devices are used in the automobile.

⊘ 32-1 Automotive Electronics and the Computer Electronic computers are used almost everywhere today. Huge computers solve problems of interstellar distances and keep astronauts on course as their spaceships head out to the moon or beyond. Small pocket-size computers solve difficult engineering problems in a few seconds. On-board electronic computers also solve operating problems in automotive electric circuits. The pulse amplifier in the electronic ignition system, for example, repeatedly has to decide when to cut off the flow of current to the ignition-coil primary winding. The electronic voltage regulator that controls the alternator is constantly monitoring the alternator voltage. It has to decide when and how often to cut the current flowing to the alternator field (rotor) winding. The basic actions of these two devices are exactly the same as the actions in a computer. That is, the computer receives signals and then turns circuits on or off. The electronic voltage regulator and ignition electronic pulse amplifier do the same thing.

The electronic circuits that control the electronic ignition system and alternator are simple, at least as far as the automotive mechanic is concerned. They perform so well that many other uses are being found for solid-state devices in the automobile. We shall get to these later in the chapter.

⊘ 32-2 Electronics—the Mechanic's Friend Many mechanics were somewhat fearful about the introduction of electronics into the automobile. It seemed to some that they would have to learn a whole new technology. But it did not turn out that way. An electronic circuit is a "go no-go" circuit. Either it works or it does not work. If it does not work, you replace the electronic component. There are no adjustments. The testers are simple to use. They are plugged in and, by a series of lights or meter readings, they tell you if the circuit is working properly. If it is not, they tell you which component needs replacement.

Another advantage is that transistors and diodes, theoretically at least, never wear out. Connections may deteriorate, but the solid-state device itself continues to do its job as long as it is not overheated or jarred excessively. The voltage regulator inside the alternator, for example, is encapsulated in plastic. That means it is sealed in so that dust and moisture cannot get to it. If it fails for any reason, it is serviced by complete replacement; this takes only a few moments. Contrast this with the long procedure required to replace or adjust the regulators for dc generators.

Many more electronic devices are being used, or will be used, on the automobile than most people suspect. Later, we shall list them and describe where they fit into the electric system.

⊘ 32-3 Integrated Circuits "Integrated circuit" is a term that used to scare the automotive electrician. But no more. "Integrated" means "put together." So an integrated circuit is simply a circuit in which many separate devices have been put together. Take the alternator voltage regulator, for example. Figure 32-1 shows the circuit. It includes two transistors and three diodes as well as a capacitor and several resistances. All this is packed into a disk about the size of a silver dollar. If you cut into the disk, you would have a hard time trying to determine what was a diode and what was a transistor. Actually, much of the regulator's bulk is the protective plastic coating on the outside.

The regulator's size can be reduced much further. By using new methods of manufacture, engi-

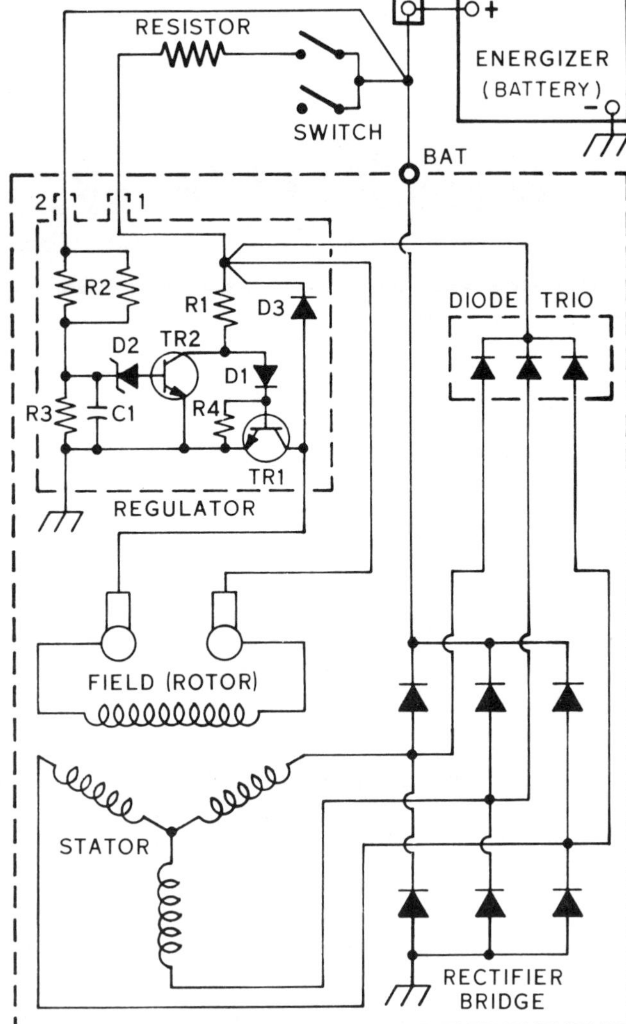

Fig. 32-1. Wiring diagram for an alternator with a built-in solid-state voltage regulator. (*Delco-Remy Division of General Motors Corporation*)

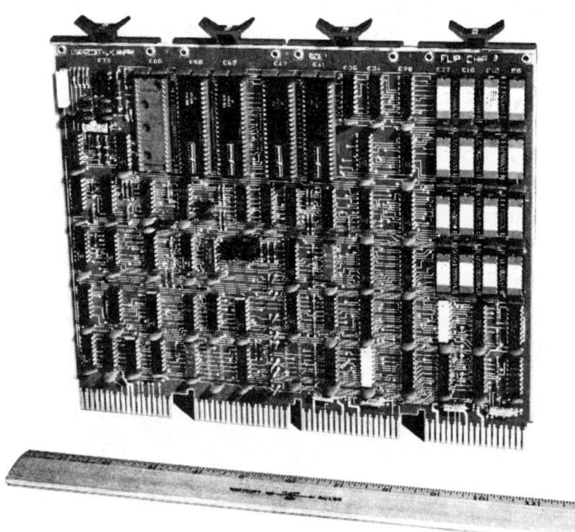

Fig. 32-2. Integrated circuit, showing how many separate devices can be put together into a single component. Note its size. It has 65,000 bits of memory and contains more than 110,000 transistors. (*Digital Equipment Corporation*)

neers have been able to squeeze many components, including transistors, resistors, and diodes, into almost incredibly small spaces (see Fig. 32-2). Today, the solid-state art has progressed so far that a hundred thousand components can be crowded into a case the size of a half dollar.

But the automotive electrician need not worry. Even if such complex circuits appear in automobiles, the checks will be simple. The service will be still simpler: Replace the complete solid-state device if it does not test up to specifications.

⊘ 32-4 Electronic Devices in the Automobile Here is a list of the electronic devices used in automobiles today. After each item, we give the section in the book that covers the device.

1. Alternator voltage regulator (⊘ 26-11)
2. Electronic ignition system (⊘ 28-4)
3. Seat-belt-starter interlock system
4. Sensor panel or warning system (⊘ 35-4)
5. Air bags (⊘ 32-5)
6. Anticollision radar (⊘ 32-6)
7. Antiskid system (⊘ 32-7)
8. Electronic fuel injection (⊘ 16-5)
9. Accessories, including solid-state clocks, radio and tape controls, headlight dimmer, automatic on-off headlight control, speed controls, automatic temperature controls, and antitheft systems (⊘ 32-9)

⊘ 32-5 Air-Bag Controls Air bags are designed to protect the driver and passenger during a front-end crash (Fig. 32-3). In case of a crash, the air bags inflate in a fraction of a second. The driver and passengers are cushioned as they are thrown forward during the crash. Figure 32-4 shows the complete system for the passenger side of the front seat. The controls for this system are electronic. The action is triggered by a *deceleratometer*—a device that measures how rapidly the car is decelerating, or slowing down. The car slows down very quickly during a front-end crash. This causes the deceleratometer to signal the electronic control. Almost instantly, this control releases the compressed gas in the container to inflate the air bags.

NOTE: Another book in the McGraw-Hill Automotive Technology Series, *Automotive Chassis and Body,* describes the air-bag system in detail.

⊘ 32-6 Anticollision Radar Radar works by sending out bursts of short radio waves. These waves bounce off any object at which the radar is pointed. The waves then come back to the radar. The time it takes for the waves to reach the object and return is measured electronically. A computer then calculates the distance between the object and the radar. In highway-patrol work, the patrolling officer sets up the radar, or it is mounted on the patrol car. The radar then measures both the distance between the radar and the oncoming car, and how rapidly that distance is being reduced. In other words, it measures how fast the car is coming.

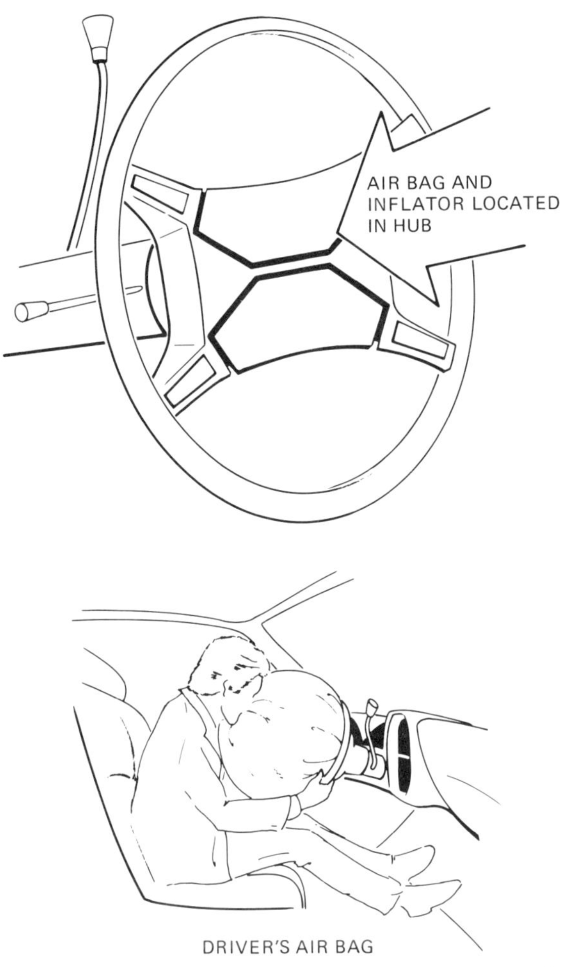

Fig. 32-3. Location of the air bag in the steering wheel. The lower picture shows the action when the air bag is inflated and the driver is thrown forward into it. (*General Motors Corporation*)

This same principle is put to work in the anticollision radar system (Fig. 32-5). The anticollision radar constantly measures the distance to the car ahead, and how fast that distance is decreasing. If the between-car distance becomes dangerously small, the radar signals the throttle and brake. They automatically slow down or stop the car. Similarly, if the car is headed into a stationary barrier or a wall, the anticollision radar applies the brakes far quicker than the driver could. In other words, the electronic system works much faster than a human being.

⊘ 32-7 Antiskid Braking System When the brake pedal is pushed down, brake fluid is sent to the brake mechanism of the car wheels. This slows or stops the wheels so the car is slowed or stopped. During hard braking, the tires may skid on the pavement. The squeal that results may sound like a quick stop is being made, but a quicker stop could be made if the tires did not actually skid. A skidding tire cannot stop the car as rapidly as a tire that is just below the skidding point. In other words, the best braking is achieved when the tire is almost but not quite skidding.

To take advantage of this fact, many trucks and buses are now equipped with antiskid devices. Also, an increasing number of passenger cars have antiskid systems installed as optional equipment. The antiskid braking system uses alternator-like devices at the car wheels. That is, each wheel has a magnetic wheel attached to the brake disk (Fig. 32-6). A sensor coil, much like the stator winding in an alternator, is located near the magnetic wheel. As the wheel rotates, it carries a magnetic field through the sensor

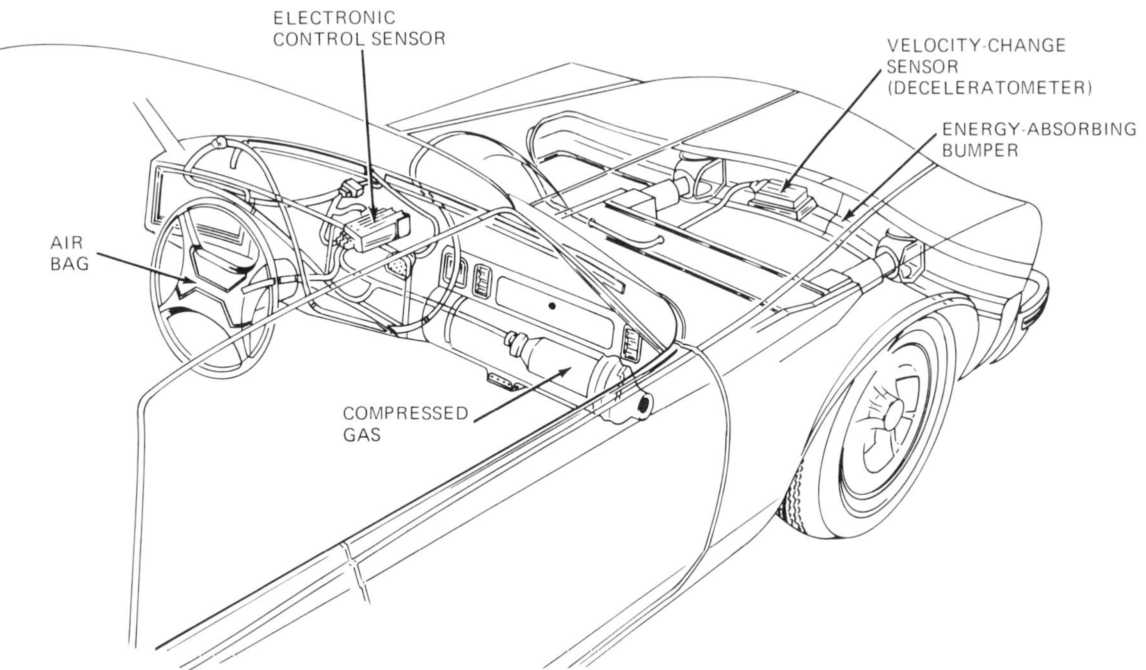

Fig. 32-4. Locations of the components in an air-bag system. (*General Motors Corporation*)

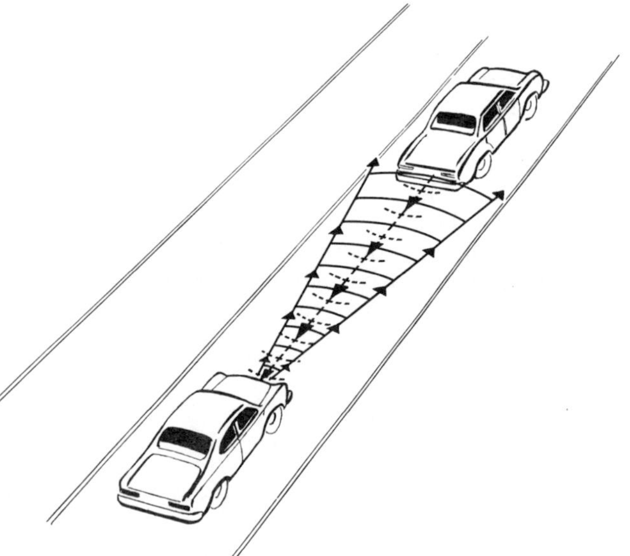

Fig. 32-5. The on-board radar in the car behind senses how fast the gap between cars is being narrowed. When the danger point is reached, the radar triggers electronic devices to slow the car.

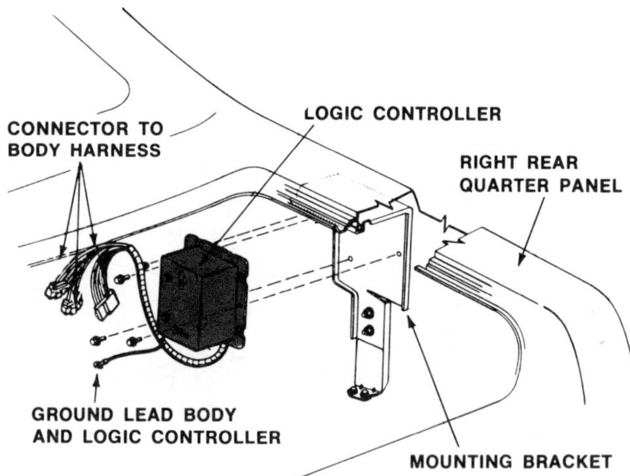

Fig. 32-7. Location of the logic control unit. (*Chrysler Corporation*)

coil. This produces an alternating current in the sensor coil. The alternations are proportional to the speed of the wheel—that is, to how fast the wheel is turning. The ac is fed into the logic control unit (Fig. 32-7). The logic control unit also receives ac signals from the other car wheels. It continually compares these signals. If one of the ac signals suddenly drops in frequency, that wheel is slowing down rapidly. In other words, it is about to skid. In this case, the logic control unit signals the modulators (Fig. 32-8). The modulator controlling the brake at the wheel which is about to skid reduces brake-fluid pressure to that brake. The braking at the wheel eases up just enough to prevent a skid; it provides the maximum braking possible without a skid.

⊘ 32-8 Electronic Fuel Injection Most automotive engines have carburetors. Carburetors mix air with fuel and send the resulting air-fuel mixture into the engine cylinders. The mixture is highly combustible. It burns in the engine cylinders, and this is what produces the engine power.

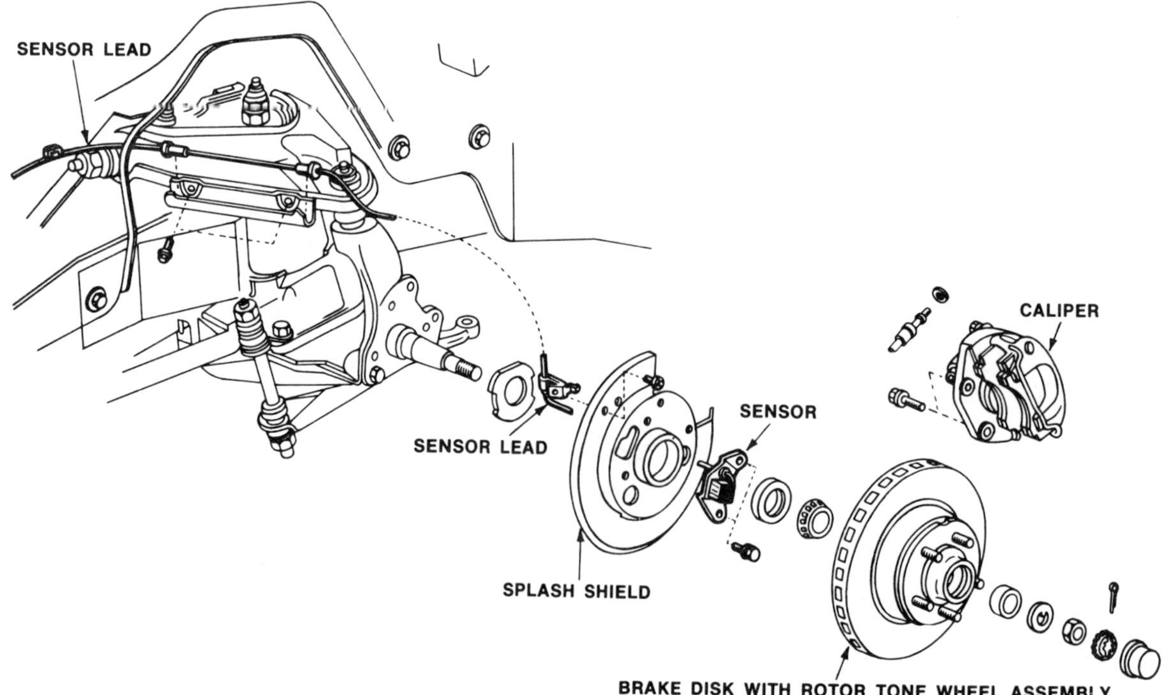

Fig. 32-6. Antiskid mechanism for the Chrysler Sure-Brake system at a front wheel. (*Chrysler Corporation*)

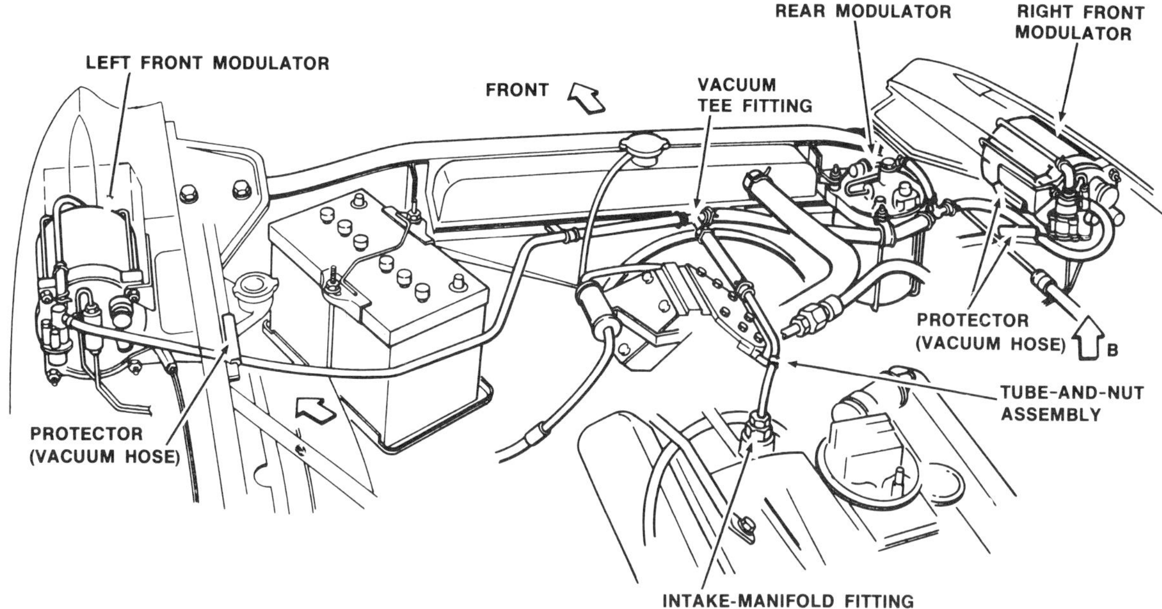

Fig. 32-8. Locations of the modulators in the Chrysler Sure-Brake antiskid system. (*Chrysler Corporation*)

Fuel-injection systems do the job somewhat differently. As we discussed in detail in Chap. 16, air going into the engine cylinders is mixed with fuel by means of the fuel-injection system. In gasoline engines, the fuel is injected into the intake manifold, just opposite the intake valves. The fuel is not injected continuously. It is injected periodically, just before the intake valves open.

The amount of fuel injected must be very carefully controlled. More fuel must go in when the engine is operating cold, is being accelerated, or is operating at wide-open throttle. To provide this con-

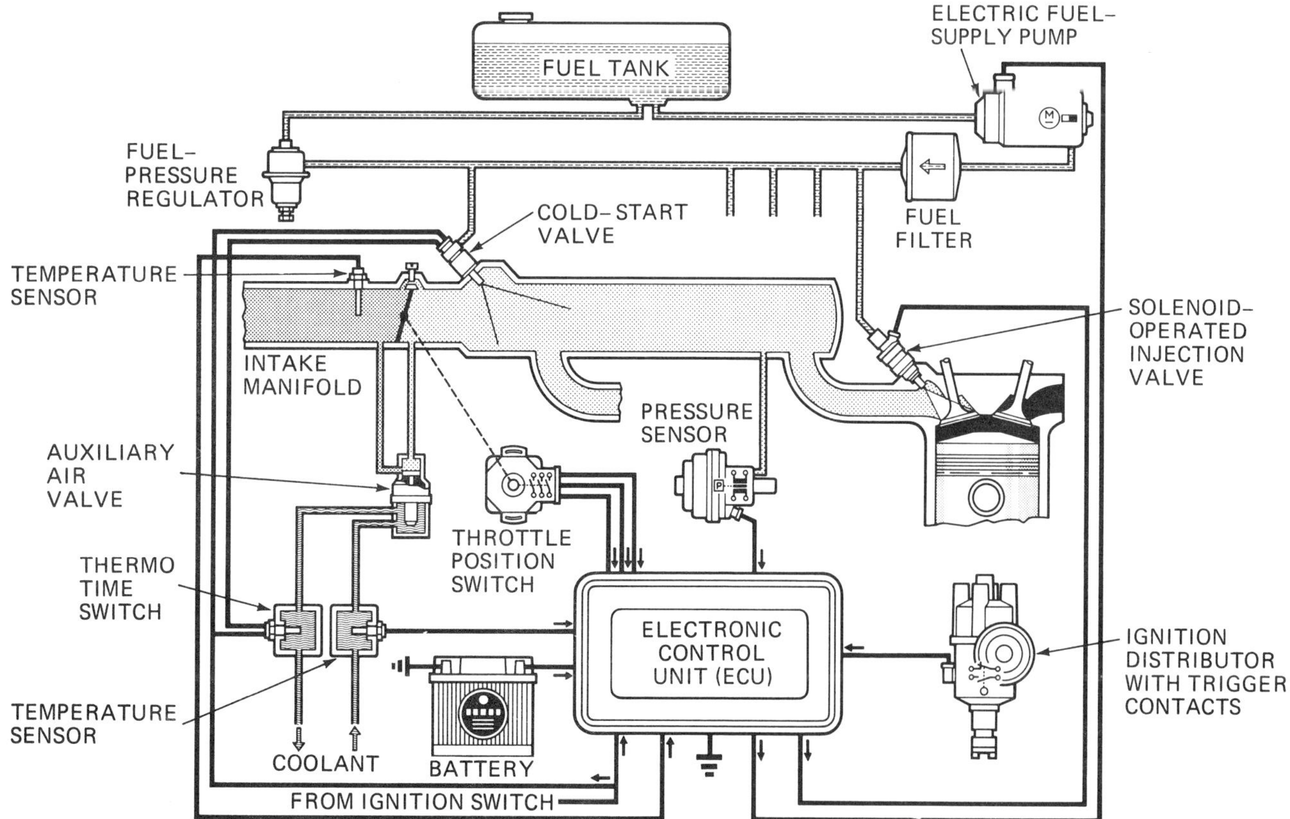

Fig. 32-9. Schematic diagram of the electronically controlled fuel-injection system for liquid-cooled engines. (*Robert Bosch GmbH*)

trol, which must be exact and almost instantaneous, an electronic control unit is used. Figure 32-9 shows the complete system. The electronic control unit has up to 300 components, including about 30 transistors and 40 diodes. This combination controls the solenoid-operated injection valves, which are positioned in the intake manifold opposite the intake valves.

⊘ 32-9 Other Electronic Devices As previously mentioned, other electronic devices are appearing on automobiles. Many automotive clocks are solid-state devices. Radios and tape decks have transistors and diodes as the working parts. Headlight dimmers and on-off headlight controls are other examples of electric devices used in the automobile. Speed controls also operate electronically. The driver selects the speed, and the electronic control holds the car at that speed, opening the throttle more or less to do so. Automatic temperature controls use electronic devices to actuate the car heater or air conditioner, as necessary. Antitheft systems also use electronic devices.

Automotive testing equipment is making increased use of electronics. The oscilloscope and the timing light operate electronically. Exhaust-gas analyzers have electronic devices that sniff out and measure the pollutants in engine exhaust gas. Some dynamic wheel balancers are electronic. They use electronic circuits to spot out-of-balance wheels and to indicate how much weight to apply and where to apply it. Now undergoing tests in research laboratories are engine testers that can be hooked to operating engines to measure main-bearing clearances. We shall soon see many other applications of electronics to automotive testing and operation.

⊘ 32-10 The Electronic Automobile The day of the electronic car is here. As we have shown, there are dozens of electronic devices on the modern car. There are still more coming. For instance, work is now going on with electronically controlled ignition spark-advance mechanisms. These are designed to provide an exactly correct spark advance for every operating condition. This improves engine operation, increases power output, and reduces pollutants coming from the engine. Sensor devices, such as the sensor panel described in Chap. 35, will become common. They will tell the driver and the automotive mechanic when service is needed and what service to perform.

Farther down the road is the one-wire automotive electric system. That is, instead of a great many wires running to individual components, there will be a single wire connecting all. An electric control module will monitor the system and see that the proper amount of current is sent to each operating device. It may be a few years until this becomes a reality. However, we mention it to show you how far ahead engineers and scientists are planning. They take into account, in their planning, the jobs of the automotive electrician and the automotive mechanic. They know that equipment must work—and it must be serviced with reasonable ease. But electronic service is usually a snap. That is, if trouble occurs, you snap out the old module and snap in a new one.

CHAPTER 32 CHECKUP

NOTE: Since the following is a chapter review test, you should review the chapter before taking the test.

Here is your chapter review test on the electronic automobile. As you have seen, there is nothing to fear in the electronic revolution in automotive controls. Fortunately, you do not have to be an expert in solid-state theory to determine whether or not the amplifier unit in an electronic ignition system is working. It is a simple matter of making a test or two and, if the amplifier is not doing its job, replacing it. Now see how well you remember the electronic devices discussed in the chapter. Answer the following questions in your notebook.

1. Why is electronics called the mechanic's friend?
2. What is an integrated circuit?
3. What would you say is the most complicated integrated circuit discussed in the chapter?
4. Name ten electronic devices used on automobiles.
5. Explain how the air-bag system works.
6. Explain how the anticollision radar system works.
7. Explain how the antiskid braking system works.
8. Explain how the electronic fuel-injection system works.

SUGGESTIONS FOR FURTHER STUDY

Other books in the McGraw-Hill Automotive Technology Series cover, in detail, some of the devices and systems discussed in this chapter. Refer to these books for additional information. Manufacturers' shop manuals describe the systems and devices that are now being installed on cars. You can pick up a great deal of information from these manuals. Your science teacher or librarian can help you select books that will fill you in on the fundamentals of electronics and integrated circuits. Be sure to write any important facts in your notebook.

chapter 33

ENGINE TESTING PROCEDURES AND TOOLS

The purpose of this chapter is to describe engine testing procedures, and the instruments used to make the tests. Later chapters discuss engine troubles or faulty conditions disclosed by the engine tests, and the methods for correcting these conditions.

⊘ 33-1 Engine Testing Procedures Engine testing procedures are of two types. One type is used when there is an obvious trouble that seems related to the engine. For example, suppose there is a miss in the engine, or a customer complains of excessive fuel or oil consumption. Then there are definite checks that can be made to pinpoint the cause of the trouble. This is called troubleshooting, or trouble-diagnosis.

The second type of engine testing procedure is a general approach. Every engine component is tested as the procedure is carried out. Any worn condition, subnormal operation, or other defect is detected. This general approach is often referred to as "engine tuneup." The correction of troubles found during the testing procedure "tunes up" the engine; that is, it improves engine performance.

Actually, both types of engine testing procedures have their place in the automotive business. When you encounter a specific trouble, you want to follow a specific procedure to find its cause so you can correct it. On the other hand, it is often proper to make a complete check of the engine and its components. For example, many automotive authorities recommend that the engine and its components be checked periodically (about every 10,000 mi [16,093 km] or at least once a year). Such an engine analysis shows up worn units and parts, and improper adjustments that soon might cause real trouble. Corrections can then be made before serious trouble develops. In other words, the general procedure eliminates trouble before it happens. This is called *preventive maintenance*. You prevent trouble by maintaining the engine in good operating condition.

⊘ 33-2 Engine Testing Instruments The engine testing instruments we cover in this chapter are as follows:

1. Tachometer, which measures engine speed in revolutions per minute (rpm)
2. Cylinder compression tester, which measures the ability of the cylinders to hold compression
3. Cylinder leakage tester, which finds any places where there is compression leakage
4. Engine vacuum gauge, which measures intake-manifold vacuum
5. Exhaust-gas analyzer, which measures the amount of pollutants in the exhaust gas
6. Ignition timing light, which is used to set the ignition timing and check the spark advance
7. Oscilloscope, which shows the overall operating condition of the ignition-system circuits
8. Chassis dynamometer, which checks the engine and its components under actual operating conditions

There are also instruments to test the battery, starting motor, charging system, and cooling system. There are other instruments to test ignition coils, condensers, spark plugs, distributor contact-point dwell, and distributor advance mechanisms.

⊘ 33-3 Tachometer The tachometer is connected to the ignition system and operates electrically. The tachometer measures engine speed in revolutions per minute (rpm). It actually measures the number of times the primary circuit is interrupted, and then translates this into engine rpm. It is a necessary instrument because the idle speed must be adjusted to a specific rpm. Also, many tests must be made at specific engine speeds. The tachometer has a selector knob that can be turned to 4, 6, or 8, according to the number of cylinders in the engine being tested. Figure 33-1 shows a tachometer connected to an engine.

Many high performance cars have tachometers mounted on the instrument panel (Fig. 33-2). They tell the driver how fast the engine is turning. The driver can then keep the rpm within the range at which the engine develops maximum torque. This lets the driver get the best performance from the engine. Many of these tachometers have a red line at

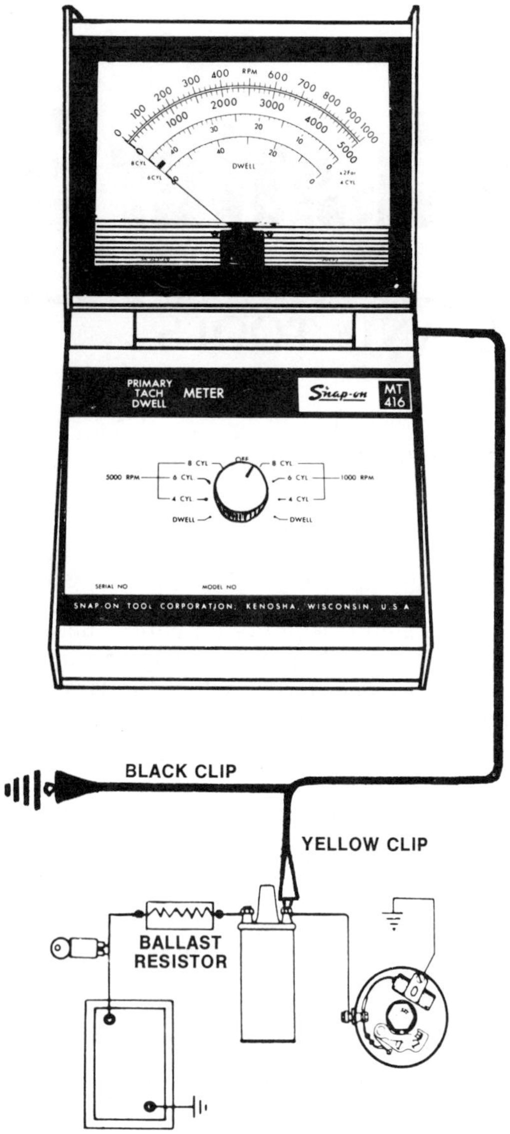

Fig. 33-1. Tachometer connected to an engine. (*Snap-on Tools Corporation*)

the top rpm on the dial. The red line marks the danger point for engine speed.

Some tachometers are mechanical instead of electrical. They are driven off a gear on the ignition-distributor shaft. They operate somewhat like the speedometer.

⊘ 33-4 Cylinder Compression Tester The cylinder compression tester measures the ability of the cylinders to hold compression. The pressure operates on a diaphragm in the tester. It causes the needle on the face of the tester to move around to indicate the pressure being applied. Figure 33-3 shows a compression tester being used to measure the pressure in an engine cylinder. When making a compression test, the engine should be at normal operating temperature.

To use the tester, first remove all the spark plugs. A recommended way to do this is to disconnect the wires and loosen the plugs one turn. Next, reconnect the wires and start the engine. Then run the engine for a few moments at 1,000 rpm. The combustion gases will blow any dirt out of the plug wells. (Otherwise, the dirt could fall into the cylinders when the spark plugs are removed.) The gases will also blow out any loosened carbon that is caked around the exposed threaded ends of the plugs. This procedure prevents carbon and dirt particles from lodging under a valve and holding the valve open during the compression test.

Next, hold the compression-tester fitting into the spark-plug hole of the No. 1 cylinder, as shown in Fig. 33-3. To protect the coil from high voltage, disconnect the lead from the negative terminal of the coil. (This is the lead that goes to the distributor.) Then hold the throttle wide open, and operate the starting motor to crank the engine. The needle will

Fig. 33-2. Engine tachometer mounted in a car center console. (*Chrysler Corporation*)

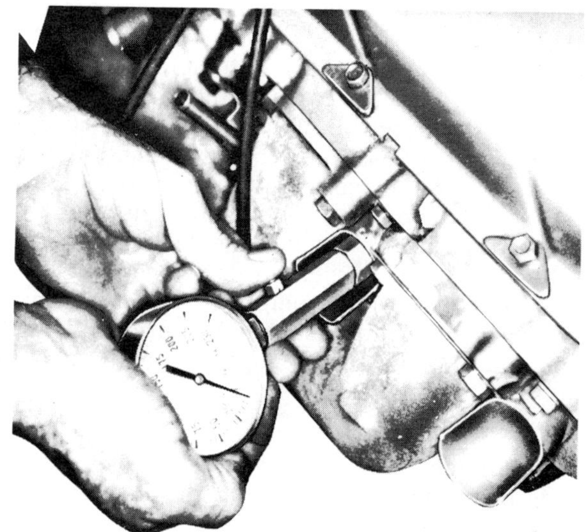

Fig. 33-3. Cylinder compression tester in use. (*Chevrolet Motor Division of General Motors Corporation*)

move around to show the maximum compression pressure the cylinder is developing. Write down this figure. Test the other cylinders in the same way.

⊘ 33-5 Results of the Compression Test The engine manufacturer's specifications tell you what the compression pressure of the cylinders should be. If the results of the compression test show that compression is low, there is leakage past the piston rings, valves, or cylinder-head gasket. To correct the trouble, you must remove the cylinder head and inspect the engine parts.

Before you do this, however, you can make one more test to pinpoint the trouble. Squirt a small quantity of engine oil into the cylinder through the spark-plug hole. Then retest the compression. If the pressure increases to a more normal figure, the low compression is due to leakage past the piston rings. Adding the oil helps seal the rings temporarily, so that they hold the compression pressure better. The trouble in this case is caused by worn piston rings, a worn cylinder wall, or a worn piston. The trouble could also be caused by rings that are broken or stuck in the piston-ring grooves.

If adding oil does not increase the compression pressure, the leakage is probably past the valves. This could be caused by:

1. Broken valve springs
2. Incorrect valve adjustment
3. Sticking valves
4. Worn or burned valves
5. Worn or burned valve seats
6. Worn camshaft lobes
7. Dished or worn valve lifters

It may also be that the cylinder-head gasket is "blown." This means the gasket has burned away so that compression pressure is leaking between the cylinder head and the cylinder block. Low compression between two adjacent cylinders is probably caused by the head gasket blowing between the cylinders.

Whatever the cause—rings, pistons, cylinder walls, valves, or gasket—the cylinder head must be removed so that the trouble can be fixed.

⊘ 33-6 Cylinder Leakage Tester The cylinder leakage tester does approximately the same job as the compression tester but in a different way. It applies air pressure to the cylinder with the piston at top dead center (TDC) on the compression stroke. In this position, both valves are closed. Very little air should escape from the combustion chamber. Figure 33-4 shows a cylinder leakage tester. Figure 33-5 shows the tester connected to an engine cylinder and how it pinpoints places where leakage can occur.

To use the cylinder leakage tester, first remove all plugs, as explained previously. Then remove the air cleaner, crankcase filler cap or dipstick, and radiator cap. Set the throttle wide open, and fill the radiator to the proper level. You are now ready to begin.

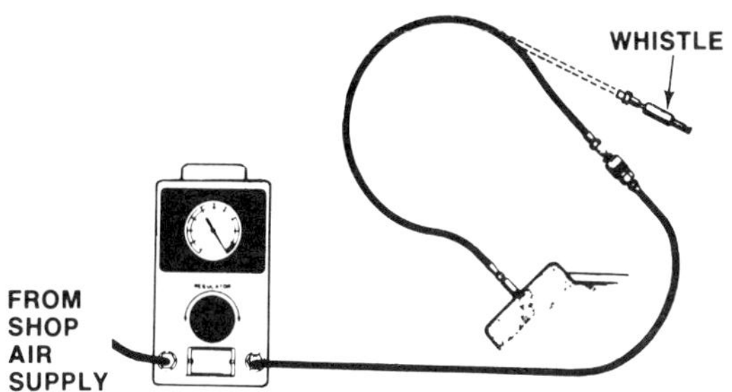

Fig. 33-4. Cylinder leakage tester. The whistle is used to locate TDC in No. 1 cylinder. (*Sun Electric Corporation*)

Connect the adapter, with the whistle, to the spark-plug hole of the No. 1 cylinder. Turn the engine over until the whistle sounds. When the whistle sounds, the piston is moving up on the compression stroke. Continue to rotate the engine until the timing marks on the engine are aligned. When the marks align, the piston is at TDC. Disconnect the whistle from the adapter, hose and connect the tester as shown in Figs. 33-4 and 33-5.

Next, apply air pressure from the shop supply. Note the gauge reading, which shows the percentage of air leakage from the cylinder. Specifications vary, but a reading above 20 percent means there is excessive leakage. If the air is blowing out of an adjoining spark-plug hole, the head gasket is blown between the cylinders. If the air leakage is excessive, check

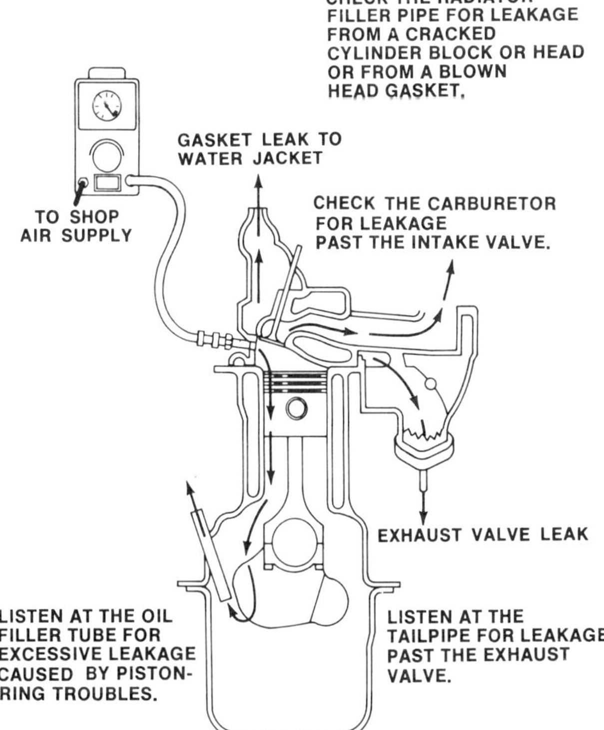

Fig. 33-5. How the cylinder leakage tester works. It applies air pressure to the cylinder through the spark-plug hole, with the piston at TDC and both valves closed. Places where air is leaking can then be pinpointed, as shown. (*Sun Electric Corporation*)

further by listening at three places: the carburetor, tail pipe, and crankcase filler pipe.

Figure 33-5 shows what it means when you can hear air escaping at any of the three listening places. If air bubbles up through the radiator, then the trouble is a blown cylinder-head gasket or a cracked cylinder head. These conditions allow leakage from the cylinder to the cooling system.

Check the other cylinders in the same manner. A special adapter supplied with the tester lets you quickly find TDC on the other cylinders. The tester instructions explain how to use the adapter.

⊘ 33-7 Engine Vacuum Gauge The engine vacuum gauge is used to track down troubles in an engine that does not run as well as it should. This gauge measures intake-manifold vacuum. The intake-manifold vacuum changes with different operating conditions and with different engine defects. The way the intake-manifold vacuum varies from normal indicates what is wrong inside the engine.

Figure 33-6 shows the vacuum gauge connected to the intake manifold. With the gauge connected, start the engine. The test must be made with the engine at operating temperature. Operate the engine on idle and at other speeds as detailed in the following list. The list includes the meanings of the various readings (see Fig. 33-7).

1. A steady and fairly high reading on idle indicates normal performance. Specifications vary with different engines, but a reading somewhere between 17 and 22 in [432 and 559 mm] Hg indicates the engine is okay. The reading will be lower at higher altitudes, because of the lower atmospheric pressure. For every 1,000 ft [305 m] above sea level, the reading will be reduced about 1 in [25.4 mm] Hg.

NOTE: "Inches or millimeters Hg" (mercury) refers to the way the vacuum gauge is scaled. There is no mercury in the gauge.

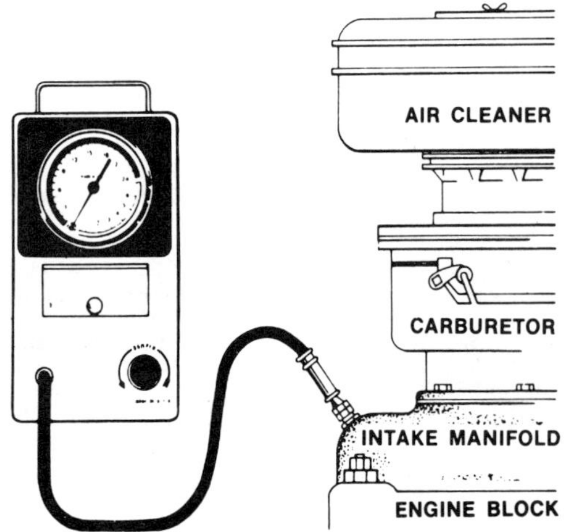

Fig. 33-6. Vacuum gauge connected to the intake manifold for a manifold-vacuum test. (*Sun Electric Corporation*)

2. A steady and low reading on idle indicates late ignition or valve timing, or possibly leakage around the pistons. Leakage around pistons (excessive blow-by) could be due to worn or stuck piston rings, worn cylinder walls, or worn pistons. Each of these conditions reduces engine power. With reduced power, the engine does not "pull" as much vacuum.
3. A very low reading on idle indicates a leaky intake-manifold or carburetor gasket, or possibly leakage around the carburetor throttle shaft. Air leakage into the manifold reduces the vacuum and engine power.

NOTE: Late-model engines, with high-lift cams and more valve overlap, are likely to have a lower and more uneven intake-manifold vacuum. Also, certain automotive emission controls lower the intake-manifold vacuum.

4. Back-and-forth movement of the needle that increases with engine speed indicates weak valve springs.
5. Gradual falling back of the needle toward zero with the engine idling indicates a clogged exhaust line.
6. Regular dropping back of the needle indicates that a valve is sticking open or a plug is not firing.
7. Irregular dropping back of the needle indicates that valves are sticking only part of the time.
8. Floating motion or slow back-and-forth movement of the needle indicates that the air-fuel mixture is too rich.

A test can be made for loss of compression due to leakage around the pistons. This condition would result from stuck or worn piston rings, worn cylinder walls, or worn pistons. Race the engine for a moment, and then quickly release the throttle. The needle should swing around to 23 to 25 in [584 to 635 mm] Hg as the throttle closes. This indicates good compression. If the needle fails to swing around this far, there is loss of compression. Further checks should be made.

⊘ 33-8 Exhaust-Gas Analyzer At one time the major use of the exhaust-gas analyzer was to adjust the carburetor. It is still used for that purpose, but today it has the added job of checking the emission controls on the automobile. We covered emission controls in Chaps. 17 to 19. We explained that their main purpose is to cut down on carbon monoxide (CO), hydrocarbons (HC), and nitrogen oxides (NO_x) in the exhaust gas. Refer to ⊘ 19-8 for the details of the modern exhaust-gas analyzer and how it is used.

⊘ 33-9 Ignition Timing Light The sparks must reach the spark plugs in the cylinders at exactly the right time. They must arrive a specific number of degrees before TDC (top dead center) on the compression stroke. Adjusting the distributor to make the sparks arrive at the right time is called *ignition*

LOW AND STEADY READING INDICATES LOW COMPRESSION, AIR LEAKS, OR LATE IGNITION TIMING

RAPID VIBRATION WHEN ENGINE IS ACCELERATED INDICATES WEAK VALVE SPRINGS

INTERMITTENT DROP OF NEEDLE INDICATES STICKY VALVES

FLOATING MOTION OF NEEDLE INDICATES RICH MIXTURE

TYPICAL VACUUM-GAUGE READING

Fig. 33-7. Vacuum-gauge readings and their meanings.

timing. The adjustment is made by turning the distributor in its mounting. If you rotate the distributor in the direction opposite to normal cam rotation, you move the contact points ahead. That is, the points close and open earlier. This action advances the sparks, and the sparks appear at the spark plugs earlier. Rotating the distributor in the direction of normal cam rotation retards the sparks. The sparks appear at the spark plugs later. Ignition timing and the use of the timing light are covered in ⊘ 30-11.

⊘ 33-10 Oscilloscope The oscilloscope, or "scope," is a high-speed voltmeter. It uses a televisionlike picture tube to show the ignition voltages. Figure 30-14 shows an electronic engine tester which includes an oscilloscope (upper center).

The oscilloscope displays a picture of the ignition-system voltages on the tube. The picture shows what is happening in the ignition system. If something is wrong, the picture shows what it is. In ⊘ 30-6 to 30-9, we explain how the oscilloscope works and how to use it.

⊘ 33-11 Dynamometer The chassis dynamometer can test the engine power output under various operating conditions. It can duplicate any kind of road test at any load or speed desired. The part of the dynamometer that you can see consists of two heavy rollers mounted at or slightly above floor level (Fig. 33-8). The car is driven onto these rollers, as shown in Fig. 33-9, so that the car wheels can drive the rollers. Next, the engine is started, and the transmission is put into gear. The car is then operated as though it were out on an actual road test.

Under the floor is a device that can place various loads on the rollers. This allows the technician to test the engine under various operating conditions. For example, the technician can find out how the engine would do during acceleration, cruising, idling, and deceleration. The test instruments, such

Fig. 33-8. Chassis dynamometer of the flush floor type. The rollers are set at floor level. (*Sun Electric Corporation*)

Fig. 33-9. Automobile in place on a chassis dynamometer. The rear wheels drive the dynamometer rollers, which are flush with the floor. At the same time, instruments on the test panel measure car speed, engine power output, engine vacuum, and so on. (*Sun Electric Corporation*)

as the scope, dwell-tachometer, and vacuum gauge, are hooked into the engine. These instruments then show the condition of the engine during actual operating conditions.

The dynamometer can also be used to check the transmission and the differential. For example, the shift points and other operating conditions of an automatic transmission can be checked. Special diagnostic dynamometers are becoming more popular. These units include many of the instruments discussed above. They have motorized rollers that permit testing of wheel alignment, suspension, brakes, and steering.

⊘ 33-12 Cooling-System Testers There are three basic types of testers for the cooling system: coolant antifreeze testers, pressure testers, and belt-tension testers.

1. *COOLANT ANTIFREEZE TESTER* Antifreeze protects the engine from damage due to coolant freeze-up. Thus, it is important to check the coolant during cold weather, to find out how well it is protected against freezing. That is, you measure the concentration of antifreeze in the coolant.

There are three types of coolant antifreeze testers: the hydrometer (Fig. 9-2), the refractometer (Fig. 9-3), and the kind with several balls in a glass tube. The use of these testers is covered in Chap. 9, together with cooling-system service.

2. *PRESSURE TESTER* The pressure tester is a small pump with a pressure gauge (Fig. 9-10). The tester is attached to the radiator filler neck, as shown, and the pump is operated to apply pressure. If the pressure holds steady and there are no signs of leaks, the cooling system is tight. (See Chap. 9.)

3. *BELT-TENSION TESTER* If there is not enough tension, the belt slips. The fan and water pump are not driven fast enough, and the engine can overheat. Also, the belt wears out rapidly. One type of belt-tension tester is shown in Fig. 9-12. Adjustment is made by moving the alternator out slightly. But the belt should not be overtightened. Excessive belt tension can cause failure of the water-pump or alternator bearing.

⊘ 33-13 PCV-Valve Testers In Chap. 17 we mentioned that modern engines are equipped with a positive crankcase ventilating (PCV) system. This system passes air through the crankcase and then up to the intake manifold. The air passing through picks up any blowby or hydrocarbon that has leaked down past the piston rings. The unburned and partly burned gasoline then passes through the engine again, where it has another chance to burn.

The PCV valve is designed to prevent too much air from flowing during idle. If the valve sticks open, too much air will flow into the intake manifold. The air-fuel mixture may become too lean at idle, and the engine will idle roughly or stall. On the other hand, if the valve sticks closed, not enough air will get through; the blowby and HC can accumulate in the crankcase. This could seriously damage the engine. These products can form corrosive acids and goo that could plug oil lines and cause the engine to fail from oil starvation.

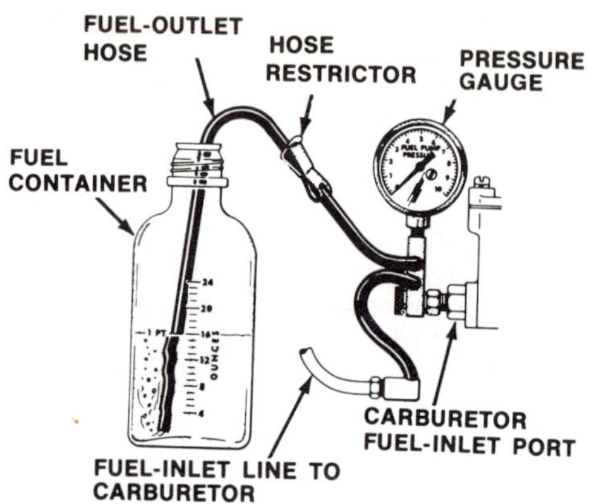

Fig. 33-10. Fuel-pump pressure and capacity tests.

The PCV valve should be checked periodically. It should be routinely replaced at stated intervals. See Chap. 19 for recommended service intervals.

⊘ 33-14 Fuel-System Testers The exhaust-gas analyzer, engine vacuum gauge, oscilloscope, and other instruments are used to check engine performance. These test instruments also report on the fuel system. In addition, fuel-pump pressure and capacity testers (Fig. 33-10) are used to check on how well the fuel pump is doing its job. Figure 33-11 shows a fuel-mileage tester. It is used to determine accurately how many miles per gallon the vehicle is delivering.

⊘ 33-15 Electrical-System Testers A variety of instruments are required to test the automotive electrical equipment. These include distributor, coil, and condenser testers for the ignition-system components. To check the charging system, ammeters and voltmeters are required. Any of several instruments

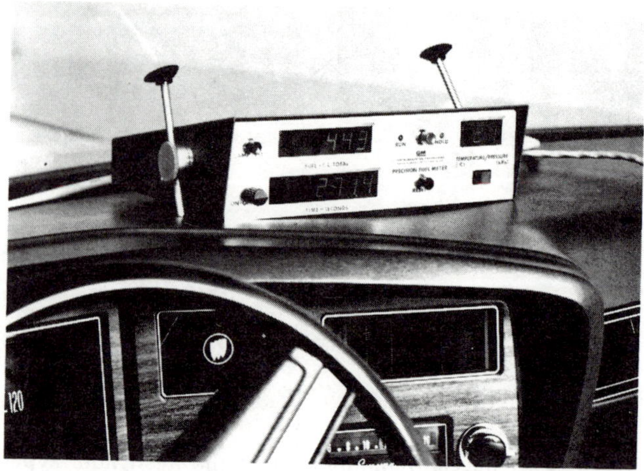

Fig. 33-11. Precision fuel-mileage indicator. (*Fluidyne Instrumentation*)

can be used to check the battery, including the hydrometer, voltmeter, 421 tester, and cadmium-tip tester. For the details on how to use these instruments and how to service electrical components, refer to Chaps. 22, 25, 27, and 30.

CHAPTER 33 CHECKUP

NOTE: Since the following is a chapter review test, you should review the chapter before taking the test.

The material in this chapter is designed to acquaint you with the procedures and instruments used to test engines. Find out how well you remember this material by taking the following test. If you cannot answer any question, turn back and reread the pages that give you the information you need.

Completing the Sentences The sentences that follow are incomplete. After each sentence there are several words or phrases, but only one of them correctly completes the sentence. Write each sentence in your notebook, ending it with the one word or phrase that completes it correctly.

1. Two types of engine testing procedures are: (*a*) trouble diagnosis and fault-finding, (*b*) trouble diagnosis and tuneup, (*c*) preventive maintenance and tuneup.
2. The general procedure which eliminates trouble before it happens is called: (*a*) preventive maintenance, (*b*) trouble diagnosis, (*c*) a timing test.
3. When the tachometer is connected between the distributor primary terminal and ground, it indicates: (*a*) engine speed, (*b*) engine vacuum, (*c*) engine compression.
4. If pouring heavy oil into the cylinder increases the compression pressure, then the loss of compression is probably due to leakage: (*a*) past the valves, (*b*) past the head gasket, (*c*) past the piston rings.
5. If the vacuum-gauge needle swings around to 23 to 25 in [584 to 635 mm] Hg as the throttle is quickly closed after the engine has been raced, it indicates: (*a*) stuck valves, (*b*) low compression, (*c*) satisfactory compression, (*d*) leaky valves.
6. A steady but low vacuum reading with the engine idling indicates that the engine: (*a*) is losing power, (*b*) has a stuck valve, (*c*) exhaust line is clogged.
7. A very low vacuum reading with the engine idling indicates: (*a*) stuck valves, (*b*) air leakage into the manifold, (*c*) loss of compression, (*d*) faulty piston rings.
8. A valve that sticks open or a plug that is not firing will cause the vacuum-gauge needle to: (*a*) oscillate slowly, (*b*) drop back regularly, (*c*) fall back slowly to zero, (*d*) read too high.
9. The device which can give a very close approximation of a road test in the garage is called the: (*a*) engine dynamometer, (*b*) chassis dynamometer, (*c*) tachometer, (*d*) engine tester.

Unscrambling the Test Instruments Following are two lists. The first includes various test instruments discussed in the chapter. The second list gives the purposes of these instruments, but not in the same order. To unscramble the lists, match each test instrument with its purpose. Put the two together, and write the result in your notebook. For instance, the first test instrument listed is "compression tester." When you look down the purposes list, you come to "checks cylinder compression." So you put the two together and write "compression tester checks cylinder compression."

Test Instruments	*Purposes*
compression tester	analyzes exhaust gas
tachometer	checks intake-manifold vacuum
vacuum gauge	checks ignition timing
combustion tester	checks engine speed
timing light	checks cylinder compression

SUGGESTIONS FOR FURTHER STUDY

Test-instrument manufacturers publish information on how to use their instruments and what the test results mean. If you can borrow this information from your local service station or your school shop, you will find it of considerable interest. Also examine test instruments in the shop, and note carefully how they are used. Here is a word of caution: These instruments can be damaged by careless handling or by connecting them improperly. You must know what you are doing before you attempt to use them. Carefully study the information on how to use the instruments. Make sure you know how to use any instrument before you attempt to do so.

chapter 34

DIAGNOSING ENGINE TROUBLES

This chapter discusses various engine troubles and relates them to possible causes and corrections. That is, it describes engine trouble-diagnosis procedures. It is not an easy chapter to study, but at the same time it is probably the most important chapter in the book. It gives you the information you need to understand how engine troubles develop, how to determine the cause of a trouble, and how to correct it. Regardless of what you plan to do in the automotive field—whether you want to work in the service shop, plant, office, or laboratory—a knowledge of engine troubles and corrections will be of great value to you.

⊘ 34-1 How to Study This Chapter There are different ways to study this chapter. You could go through it page by page, just as you have studied the previous chapters. Perhaps a better way would be to take one complaint at a time (as listed in the Engine Trouble-Diagnosis Chart), read through the possible causes and checks or corrections, and then study the section later in the chapter that discusses the complaint. For example, you would begin with complaint 1, "Engine will not turn over." After reading the causes and checks or corrections listed in the second and third columns in the chart, you would turn to ⊘ 34-4 (referred to in the first column) and study it.

Since a knowledge of trouble causes and corrections is so helpful, you will probably be referring to the Engine Trouble-Diagnosis Chart many times. One way to help yourself remember the information is to write each complaint, with its causes and corrections, on a separate 3- by 5-in card. You can also get a deck of the McGraw-Hill *Automotive Trouble-shooting Cards* which list troubles and their possible causes. Carry the cards around with you. At odd moments, when you are riding a bus, eating a sandwich, or getting ready for bed, you can take out a card and read it over. Soon you will know the troubles, their causes, and the checks or corrections "backward and forward."

⊘ 34-2 Need for a Logical Procedure After a trouble has been located in an engine, it is usually not too difficult to eliminate the conditions causing the trouble. *Automotive Engines,* another book in the McGraw-Hill Automotive Technology Series, discusses the various engine services. It explains, in detail the corrections to be made to eliminate different causes of engine trouble. Other books in the Automotive Technology Series cover the operation and servicing of all other automotive components. These books are *Automotive Electrical Equipment; Automotive Fuel, Lubricating and Cooling Systems; Automotive Chassis and Body; Automotive Transmissions and Power Trains; Automotive Emission Control;* and *Automotive Air Conditioning.*

This chapter is devoted to trouble diagnosis—the detective work that a mechanic must do when dealing with engine trouble. Careful analysis and straight thinking are often needed to find the cause of the trouble. If a logical procedure is followed, the cause can usually be spotted without delay. But haphazard guesswork wastes time, and may allow you to overlook the basic cause of the trouble. For example, suppose you tell a driver that the battery needs to be recharged or replaced. That is, you blame the run-down battery for the trouble. But you should search further, to find out why the battery ran down. Perhaps it was old, or possibly the alternator or regulator was not operating properly. On the other hand, the driver might have been driving mostly at night with the lights and radio on. The trouble could also be due to hard starting or frequent starts and stops. These cause the driver to use the starting motor excessively, so that the battery runs down. The point is this: Unless the real cause of the trouble is found and corrected, the driver will soon be in trouble again.

⊘ 34-3 Engine Trouble-Diagnosis Chart A variety of complaints can bring a driver to a mechanic. However, the driver rarely has a clear idea of what is causing the trouble. Most complaints, however, can be grouped under a few basic headings. These include: engine will not turn over; engine turns over but will not start; engine runs but misses; engine lacks power, acceleration, or high-speed performance; engine overheats; engine uses excessive oil or gasoline; and engine is noisy. The chart that follows lists the various engine troubles, together with their possible causes, checks to be made, and corrections. (The section whose number is given under each conplaint contains fuller explanations of how the trouble can be located and eliminated.) Some causes of trouble will be found in the engine itself. Other trouble causes may be traced to the fuel, cooling, lubricating, or electric system.

NOTE: The troubles and possible causes are not listed in the chart in the order of frequency of occurrence. That is, item 1 (or item a under "Possible Cause") does not necessarily occur more frequently than item 2 (or item b).

ENGINE TROUBLE-DIAGNOSIS CHART

(See ⊘ 34-4 to 34-21 for detailed explanations of the trouble causes and corrections listed below.)

COMPLAINT	POSSIBLE CAUSE	CHECK OR CORRECTION
1. Engine will not turn over (⊘ 34-4)	a. Run-down battery	Recharge or replace battery; start engine with jumper battery and cables (see Chap. 22)
	b. Starting circuit open	Find and eliminate the open; check for dirty or loose cables (see Chap. 25)
	c. Starting-motor drive jammed	Remove starting motor, and free drive (see Chap. 25)
	d. Starting motor jammed	Remove starting motor for teardown and correction (see Chap. 25)
	e. Engine jammed	Check engine to find trouble
	f. Transmission not in neutral, or neutral switch out of adjustment	Check and adjust neutral switch if necessary
	g. Seat belt not fastened, or interlock faulty	Check interlock
	h. See also causes listed under item 3; driver may have run battery down trying to start	
2. Engine turns over slowly but does not start (⊘ 34-5)	a. Run-down battery	Recharge or replace battery; start engine with jumper battery and cables (see Chap. 22)
	b. Defective starting motor	Repair or replace (see Chap. 25)
	c. Bad connections in starting circuit	Check for loose or dirty cables; clean and tighten (see Chap. 25)
	d. See also causes listed under item 3; driver may have run battery down trying to start	
3. Engine turns over at normal speed but does not start (⊘ 34-6)	a. Defective ignition system	Try spark test; check timing, ignition system (see Chap. 30)
	b. Defective fuel pump or overchoking	Prime engine; check accelerator-pump discharge, fuel pump, fuel line, choke carburetor (see Chap. 14)
	c. Air leaks in manifold or carburetor	Tighten mounting; replace gaskets as needed
	d. Defect in engine	Check compression or leakage (⊘ 34-7), valve action, timing
	e. Burned-out ignition resistor	Replace
	f. Plugged fuel filter	Clean or replace
	g. Plugged or collapsed exhaust system	Replace collapsed parts
4. Engine runs but misses on one cylinder (⊘ 34-8)	a. Defective spark plug	Clean or replace (see Chap. 30)
	b. Defective distributor cap or spark-plug cable	Replace (see Chap. 30)
	c. Valve stuck open	Free valve; service valve guide
	d. Broken valve spring	Replace
	e. Burned valve	Replace
	f. Bent pushrod	Replace
	g. Flat cam lobe	Replace camshaft
	h. Defective piston or rings	Replace; service cylinder wall as necessary
	i. Defective head gasket	Replace
	j. Intake-manifold leak	Replace gasket; tighten manifold bolts

COMPLAINT	POSSIBLE CAUSE	CHECK OR CORRECTION
5. Engine runs but misses on different cylinders (⊘ 34-8)	a. Defective distributor advance, coil, condenser	Check distributor, coil, condenser (see Chap. 30)
	b. Defective fuel system	Check fuel pump. flex line, carburetor (see Chap. 14)
	c. Crossfiring plug wires	Replace or relocate
	d. Loss of compression	Check compression or leakage (⊘ 33-4 to 33-6)
	e. Defective valve action	Check compression, leakage, vacuum (⊘ 33-4 to 33-7)
	f. Worn pistons and rings	Check compression, leakage, vacuum (⊘ 33-4 to 33-7)
	g. Overheated engine	Check cooling system (see Chap. 9)
	h. Manifold heat-control valve stuck	Free valve
	i. Restricted exhaust	Check exhaust, tail pipe, muffler; eliminate restriction
6. Engine lacks power, acceleration, or high-speed performance hot or cold (⊘ 34-10)	a. Defective ignition	Check timing, distributor, wiring, condenser, coil, plugs (see Chap. 30)
	b. Defective fuel system; secondary throttle valves not opening	Check carburetor, choke, filter, air cleaner, fuel pump (see Chap.14)
	c. Throttle valve not opening fully	Adjust linkage (see Chap. 14)
	d. Restricted exhaust	Check tail pipe, muffler; eliminate restriction
	e. Loss of compression	Check compression or leakage (⊘ 33-4 to 33-6)
	f. Excessive carbon in engine	Clean
	g. Defective valve action	Check with compression, leakage, vacuum testers (⊘ 33-4 to 33-7)
	h. Excessive rolling resistance from low tires, dragging brakes, wheel misalignment, etc.	Correct the defect causing rolling resistance
	i. Heavy oil	Use correct oil
	j. Wrong or bad fuel	Use good fuel or correct octane
	k. Transmission not downshifting; defective torque converter	Check transmission
7. Engine lacks power, acceleration, or high-speed performance hot only (⊘ 34-10)	a. Engine overheating	Check cooling system (see Chap. 9)
	b. Choke stuck partly open	Repair or replace (see Chap. 15)
	c. Sticking manifold heat-control valve	Free valve
	d. Vapor lock	Use different fuel or shield fuel line
8. Engine lacks power, acceleration, or high-speed performance cold only (⊘ 34-10)	a. Automatic choke stuck open	Repair or replace (see Chap. 15)
	b. Manifold heat-control valve stuck open	Free valve
	c. Cooling-system thermostat stuck open	Repair or replace (see Chap. 9)
	d. Engine valves stuck open	Free valves; service valve stems and guides as needed
9. Engine overheats (⊘ 34-12)	a. Lack of coolant	Add coolant; look for leak
	b. Ignition timing late	Adjust timing (see Chap. 30)
	c. Loose or broken fan belt	Tighten or replace (see Chap. 9)
	d. Thermostat stuck closed	Replace (see Chap. 9)
	e. Clogged water jackets	Clean (see Chap. 9)
	f. Defective radiator hose	Replace (see Chap. 9)
	g. Defective water pump	Repair or replace (see Chap. 9)
	h. Insufficient oil	Add oil
	i. High-altitude, hot-climate operation	Drive more slowly; keep radiator filled
	j. Defective fan clutch	Replace (see Chap. 9)
	k. Valve timing late; slack timing chain has allowed chain to jump a tooth	Retime; adjust or replace
	l. No vacuum advance in any gear	TCS system or distributor defective (see Chap. 19)
10. Rough idle (⊘ 34-13)	a. Incorrect carburetor idle adjustment	Readjust idle mixture and speed (see Chap. 15)
	b. PCV valve stuck open	Replace
	c. See also other causes listed under items 6 through 8	

COMPLAINT	POSSIBLE CAUSE	CHECK OR CORRECTION
11. Engine stalls cold or as it warms up (⊘ 34-14)	a. Choke valve stuck closed or will not close	Open choke valve; free or repair automatic choke (see Chap. 15)
	b. Fuel not getting to or through carburetor	Check fuel pump, lines, filter, float, and idle systems (see Chap. 14)
	c. Manifold heat-control valve stuck	Free valve
	d. Throttle solenoid improperly set	Adjust
	e. Idling speed set too low	Increase idling speed to specified value (see Chap. 15)
	f. PCV valve stuck open	Replace
	g. Damper in thermostatic air cleaner stuck closed	Free; repair or replace control motor
12. Engine stalls after idling or slow-speed driving (⊘ 34-14)	a. Defective fuel pump	Repair or replace fuel pump (see Chap. 14)
	b. Overheating	See item 9
	c. High carburetor float level	Adjust (see Chap. 15)
	d. Incorrect idling adjustment	Adjust (see Chap. 15)
	e. Malfunctioning PCV valve	Replace
	f. Throttle solenoid improperly set	Adjust
13. Engine stalls after high-speed driving (⊘ 34-14)	a. Vapor lock	Use different fuel or shield fuel line (see Chap. 14)
	b. Carburetor venting or idle-compensator valve defective	Check and repair (see Chap. 15)
	c. Engine overheating	See item 9
	d. PCV valve stuck open	Replace
	e. Improperly set throttle solenoid	Adjust
14. Engine backfires (⊘ 34-15)	a. Ignition timing off	Adjust timing (see Chap. 30)
	b. Spark plugs of wrong heat range	Install correct plugs (see Chap. 30)
	c. Excessively rich or lean mixture	Repair or adjust fuel pump or carburetor (see Chaps. 14 and 15)
	d. Engine overheating	See item 9
	e. Carbon in engine	Clean
	f. Valves hot or stuck	Adjust, free, clean; replace if bad
	g. Cracked distributor cap	Replace
	h. Inoperative antibackfire valve	Replace
	i. Crossfiring plug wires	Replace
15. Engine run-on or dieseling (⊘ 34-16)	a. Incorrect idle-stop or solenoid adjustment	Adjust; fix solenoid
	b. Engine overheating	See item 9
	c. Hot spots in cylinders	Check plugs, pistons, cylinders for carbon; check valves for defects and faulty seating
	d. Timing advanced	Adjust (see Chap. 30)
16. Too much HC and CO in exhaust gas (⊘ 34-17)	a. Ignition miss	Check plugs, wiring, cap, coil, etc. (see Chap. 30)
	b. Incorrect ignition timing	Time ignition (see Chap. 30)
	c. Carburetor troubles	Check choke, float level, idle-mixture adjustment screw, etc., as listed in item 20
	d. Faulty air injection	Check pump, hoses, manifold
	e. Defective TCS system	Check system
	f. Defective catalytic converters	Replace converters or catalyst
17. Smoky exhaust		
a. Blue smoke	Excessive oil consumption	See item 18 and ⊘ 34-18
b. Black smoke	Excessively rich mixture	See item 20 and ⊘ 34-20
c. White smoke	Steam in exhaust	Replace cylinder-head gasket; tighten cylinder-head bolts to eliminate coolant leakage into combustion chambers
18. Excessive oil consumption (⊘ 34-18)	a. External leaks	Correct seals; replace gaskets
	b. Burning oil in combustion chamber	Check valve-stem clearance, piston rings, cylinder walls, rod bearings, vacuum-pump diaphragm
	c. High-speed driving	Drive more slowly

COMPLAINT	POSSIBLE CAUSE	CHECK OR CORRECTION
19. Low oil pressure (⊘ 34-19)	a. Worn engine bearings	Replace
	b. Engine overheating	See item 9
	c. Oil dilution or foaming	Replace oil
	d. Lubricating-system defects	Check oil lines, oil pump, relief valve (see Chap. 7)
20. Excessive fuel consumption (⊘ 34-20)	a. Jackrabbit starts	Drive more reasonably
	b. High-speed driving	Drive more slowly
	c. Short-run operation	Drive longer distances
	d. Excessive fuel-pump pressure or pump leakage	Reduce pressure; repair or replace pump (see Chap. 14)
	e. Choke partly closed after warm-up	Open; repair or replace automatic choke (see Chap. 15)
	f. Clogged air cleaner	Clean (see Chap. 14)
	g. High carburetor float level	Adjust (see Chap. 15)
	h. Stuck or dirty carburetor float needle level	Free and clean (see Chap. 15)
	i. Worn carburetor jets	Replace (see Chap. 15)
	j. Stuck metering rod or power piston	Free (see Chap. 15)
	k. Idle too rich or too fast	Adjust (see Chap. 15)
	l. Stuck accelerator-pump check valve	Free (see Chap. 15)
	m. Carburetor leaks	Replace gaskets; tighten screws, etc. (see Chap. 15)
	n. Cylinder not firing	Check coil, condenser, timing, plugs, contact points, wiring (see Chap. 30)
	o. Automatic transmission slipping or not upshifting	Check transmission
	p. Loss of engine compression (worn engine)	Check compression or leakage (⊘ 33-4 to 33-6)
	q. Defective valve action (worn camshaft, chain slack, or jumped tooth)	Check with compression, leakage, or vacuum tester (⊘ 33-4 to 33-7)
	r. Excessive rolling resistance from low tires, dragging brakes, wheel misalignment, etc.	Correct the defects causing the rolling resistance
	s. Clutch slippage	Adjust or repair
21. Engine noises (⊘ 34-21)		
a. Regular clicking	Valve and tappet	Readjust valve clearance or replace noisy hydraulic lifters
b. Ping or detonation on load or acceleration	Detonation due to low-octane fuel, carbon, advanced ignition timing, or causes listed under item 14	Use higher-octane fuel; remove carbon; adjust ignition timing
c. Light knock or pound with engine floating	Worn connecting-rod bearings or crankpin; misaligned rod; lack of oil	Replace bearings; service crankpins; replace rod; add oil
d. Light, metallic double knock, usually most audible during idle	Worn or loose pin or lack of oil	Service pin and bushing; add oil
e. Chattering or rattling during acceleration	Worn rings or cylinder walls, low ring tension, or broken rings	Service walls; replace rings
f. Hollow, muffled bell-like sound (engine cold)	Piston slap due to worn pistons or walls, collapsed piston skirts, excessive clearance, misaligned connecting rods, or lack of oil	Replace or resize pistons; service walls; replace rods; add oil
g. Dull, heavy, metallic knock under load or acceleration, especially when cold	Regular noise means worn main bearings; irregular noise is worn thrust bearing knock (on clutch engagement or on hard acceleration)	Replace or service bearings and crankshaft
h. Miscellaneous noises (rattles, etc.)	Loosely mounted accessories: alternator, horn, oil pan, front bumper, water pump, etc.	Tighten mounting

⊘ 34-4 Engine Will Not Turn Over If the engine will not turn over when starting is attempted, make sure the control lever is in neutral (N) or park (P). Or, if the car has a manual transmission, make sure the clutch pedal is depressed. Check the battery and cables. A low battery can cause the solenoid plunger to repeatedly pull in and release (making a clattering noise) but will not crank the engine.

If the starter spins and the drive pinion engages, the starting-motor overrunning clutch is slipping. If the solenoid plunger pulls in (a loud click) but nothing else happens, there is trouble in the solenoid (poor contacts), starting motor, or circuit. If the solenoid plunger does not pull in, the solenoid circuit is at fault. Connect a jumper lead between the solenoid battery terminal and solenoid switch terminal. If the starting motor now operates, the solenoid is okay. The trouble is in the ignition switch, the neutral starting switch, or the circuit between them. If the starting motor still does not operate, remove it for service.

Another method of checking for the cause of trouble when the engine will not turn over uses the headlights or dome light. This is a preliminary, or "instant," check. It is not as accurate as the preceding method, but some technicians use it as a first step in the diagnosis. Here is how to do the check: Turn on the headlights or dome light, and try to start the engine. The lights will (1) stay bright, (2) dim considerably, (3) dim slightly, (4) go out, or (5) not burn at all.

1. If the lights stay bright, there is an open circuit in the starting motor or starting-motor circuit. Check as outlined in Chapter 24. Also, the transmission may not be in neutral, or the neutral switch may need adjustment. In addition, on some late-model cars, the ignition-interlock safety belts may not be fastened properly, or the system may be defective.
2. If the lights dim considerably, the battery may be run down. Or, there may be mechanical trouble in the starting motor or engine. If the battery tests okay, remove the starting motor for further checks. Try to turn the engine flywheel in the normal direction of rotation to see if the engine is jammed.
3. If the lights dim only slightly, listen for cranking action (sound of an electric motor running). If the starting motor runs, the pinion is not engaging the flywheel (Bendix type) or the overrunning clutch is slipping. If the solenoid clicks but the starting motor does not rotate, the cause could be a low battery. However, it is probably trouble in the starting motor. Remove the starting motor for service.
4. If the lights go out as cranking is attempted, there may be a bad connection in the main circuit, probably at a battery terminal.
5. If the lights burn dimly or not at all when they are turned on, even before cranking is attempted, the battery is probably run down.

⊘ 34-5 Engine Turns Over Slowly but Does Not Start The cause of this condition could be a rundown battery, a defective starting motor, or mechanical trouble in the engine. Check the battery, starting motor, and starting circuit. (See Chaps. 22 and 25, and *Automotive Electrical Equipment*, another book in the McGraw-Hill Automotive Technology Series.) If they are normal, the trouble probably is in the engine (defective bearings, rings, etc., which could produce high friction). Remember that, in cold weather, cranking speed is reduced by thickening of the engine oil and reduction of battery efficiency.

NOTE: If the battery is run down, the driver may have discharged it while attempting to start. The cause of starting failure could be as noted in the following sections.

⊘ 34-6 Engine Turns Over at Normal Cranking Speed but Does Not Start This means that the battery and starting motor are in normal condition. The cause of the trouble is probably in the ignition or fuel system. The difficulty could be overchoking.[1] Try cranking with the throttle wide open. If the engine does not start, disconnect the lead from one spark plug (or from the center distributor-cap terminal). Hold the lead clip about $^3/_{16}$ in [4.76 mm] from the engine block. Crank the engine to see if a good spark occurs. If a good spark does occur, the ignition system is probably okay (the timing could be off, however).

If the ignition system seems to be operating normally, the fuel system should be analyzed. First, prime the engine by operating the carburetor accelerator pump several times.

CAUTION: Gasoline is highly explosive. Stay back, out of the way, while priming the engine because the engine might backfire through the carburetor. Replace the air cleaner before cranking.

If the engine now starts and runs for a few seconds, the fuel system is probably faulty. It is not delivering fuel to the engine. First make sure there is gasoline in the fuel tank. Temporarily disconnect the fuel inlet to the carburetor. Hold a container under the fuel line to catch fuel, and crank the engine to see whether fuel is delivered. If fuel is not delivered, the fuel pump is defective or the fuel line is clogged. If fuel is delivered, the fuel filter is probably at fault, the automatic choke is not working correctly, or possibly there are air leaks into the intake manifold or carburetor.

If the fuel and ignition systems seem to be okay on the preliminary checks, check the mechanical condition of the engine. Use cylinder compression and leakage testers (⊘ 34-7) for this. Also, note that a

[1] This analysis applies to a cold engine. Failure to start with a hot engine may be caused by a defective choke that fails to open properly as the engine warms up. This condition causes flooding of the engine (delivery of too much gasoline). Open the throttle wide while cranking (this dechokes the engine), or open the choke valve by hand and then crank the engine.

plugged or collapsed exhaust system can build up back pressure. This could prevent normal exhaust and intake, so that the engine will not start.

⊘ 34-7 Cylinder Compression and Leakage Testers These testers are used to determine whether the cylinder can hold compression, and whether there is excessive leakage past the rings, valves, or head gasket. The compression tester (Fig. 33-3) has been a basic engine testing instrument for many years. Recently, the cylinder leakage tester has come into use. Some mechanics believe it is more accurate in pinpointing cylinder defects.

The use of compression and leakage testers has been described in detail (compression tester in ⊘ 33-4 and 33-5, and leakage tester in ⊘ 33-6).

⊘ 34-8 Engine Runs But Misses A missing engine is a rough engine. If one or more cylinders fail to fire, the engine is thrown out of balance. The result is roughness and loss of power. It is sometimes hard to track down a miss. The miss might occur at some speeds and not others. Also, the miss may skip around. The modern method of checking out a missing engine is to use an oscilloscope and a dynamometer. (The oscilloscope is discussed in ⊘ 30-6 to 30-8. The dynamometer is discussed in ⊘ 33-11.) If these testing instruments are not available, then proceed as follows.

Use insulated pliers to disconnect each spark-plug cable in turn, one at a time. (Disconnecting the cable prevents the spark from reaching the spark plug, and the spark plug does not fire.) If disconnecting the cable changes the engine speed or rhythm, then the cylinder was delivering power before you disconnected the cable. But if there is no change in engine speed or rhythm, then that cylinder was missing before you disconnected the cable.

Check a missing cylinder further by holding the spark-plug-lead clip close to the engine block while the engine is running. If no spark occurs, there is probably a high-voltage leak. It is due to a bad lead or a cracked or burned distributor cap. If a good spark occurs, install a new spark plug in the cylinder (or swap plugs between two cylinders). Then reconnect the lead, and see whether the cylinder still misses. If it does, the cause of the trouble is probably defective engine parts, such as valves or rings.

If the miss is hard to locate, perform a general tuneup (Chap. 35). A tuneup will disclose and possibly eliminate various causes of missing. These could include defects in the ignition system or fuel system, loss of engine compression, sticky or damaged engine valves, overheating engine, sticky manifold heat-control valve, and clogged exhaust.

With most oscilloscopes, you can make a power-balance test that will quickly pinpoint the missing cylinder. When the oscilloscope is connected to the running engine, you turn a knob or push a button. This shorts out the cylinders, one by one, in the firing order. The scope shows which cylinder is shorted out. If shorting out a cylinder changes the engine rpm as registered on the tachometer, you know that cylinder was delivering power. But if no change in rpm takes place, then you know that cylinder was not delivering power.

⊘ 34-9 Engine Vacuum Gauge The vacuum gauge is important for tracking down troubles in an engine that runs but does not perform satisfactorily. It measures intake-manifold vacuum. The intake-manifold vacuum varies with different operating conditions and with different engine defects. The manner in which the vacuum varies from normal indicates the type of engine trouble (⊘ 33-7 explains how to use the vacuum gauge.)

⊘ 34-10 Engine Lacks Power This is a general complaint that is often difficult to analyze. The best procedure is to do a tuneup (Chap. 35). This will disclose various engine conditions that could cause loss of power. To get some idea of the cause, find out whether the engine lacks power both when hot and cold, only when hot, or only when cold. Also, find out if the problem developed suddenly or if the power fell off over a period of many months or many miles of operation. A chassis dynamometer (⊘ 33-11) or an oscilloscope (⊘ 30-6 to 30-8) can be used to help locate the cause of the trouble.

1. ENGINE LACKS POWER WHEN HOT OR COLD The fuel system may not be enriching the mixture as the throttle is opened. This condition could be due to a faulty accelerator pump, or a defective main metering or power system in the carburetor. Also, the fuel system could be supplying an excessively lean or rich mixture. This could be due to a defective fuel pump, clogged lines, clogged filter, worn carburetor jets or lines, air leaks at the carburetor or manifold joints, malfunctioning PCV valve, and other causes. Carburetors and fuel-system action can be checked with an exhaust-gas analyzer (⊘ 19-8).

Another condition could cause lack of power when the engine is hot or cold. This condition is an improper linkage adjustment that prevents full throttle opening. Also, the ignition system may be causing trouble, owing to incorrect timing, a "weak" coil, reversed polarity, wrong spark-plug heat range, and other causes. The wrong fuel or oil for the engine could reduce performance. Numerous other engine conditions could cause loss of power: deposits (carbon), lack of compression (faulty valves or rings, worn cylinder walls or pistons), and defective bearings. A clogged exhaust (bent or collapsed exhaust or tail pipe or clogged muffler) could create back pressure that would cause poor engine performance. Also, any excessive rolling resistance would absorb engine power and hold down engine acceleration and speed. This would include dragging brakes, underinflated tires, misaligned wheels, and excessive friction in the transmission or power train. Finally, the automatic transmission may not be downshifting, or the torque converter may be defective.

2. *ENGINE LACKS POWER ONLY WHEN HOT* The engine may be overheating (⊘ 34-12). Also, the automatic choke may not be opening normally as the engine warms up. The manifold heat-control valve may be stuck. Or there may be a vapor lock in the fuel pump or line.

3. *ENGINE LACKS POWER ONLY WHEN COLD (OR REACHES OPERATING TEMPERATURE TOO SLOWLY)* The automatic choke may be leaning out the mixture too soon (before the engine warms up). The manifold heat-control valve may not be closed (so that not enough heat reaches the intake manifold). Or the cooling-system thermostat may be stuck open. In this case, coolant circulates between the engine and radiator even with the engine cold, so warm-up is delayed. Occasionally, engine valves may stick open when the engine is cold; then, as the engine warms up, the valves become free and work normally.

⊘ 34-11 Exhaust-Gas Analyzer At one time the main use of the exhaust-gas analyzer was to adjust the carburetor. Today, its major job is to check automotive emission controls. If the emission controls are not working properly, there are excessive amounts of HC and CO in the exhaust gas. The exhaust-gas analyzer measures the amount of HC and CO in the exhaust gas coming out the tail pipe. The exhaust-gas analyzer is discussed in ⊘ 19-8.

⊘ 34-12 Engine Overheats Most engine overheating is caused by loss of coolant through leaks in the cooling system. Other causes include a loose or broken fan belt, a defective water pump, clogged water jackets, a defective radiator hose, and a defective thermostat or fan clutch. Also, late ignition or valve timing, lack of engine oil, overloading the engine, or high-speed, high-altitude, or hot-climate operation can cause engine overheating. Freezing of the coolant could cause lack of coolant circulation, resulting in local hot spots and boiling. Also, if a faulty TCS system prevents vacuum advance in any gear, or if the distributor vacuum advance is defective, overheating may result.

⊘ 34-13 Rough Idle If the engine idles roughly but runs normally above idle, the idle speed and idle mixture are probably incorrectly adjusted. A rough idle could also be due to a loose vacuum hose (or one that is disconnected from the intake manifold) or a PCV valve that is stuck open.

⊘ 34-14 Engine Stalls If the engine starts and then stalls, note when the stalling takes place. It may be before the engine warms up, as it warms up, after idling or slow-speed driving, or after high-speed or full-load driving. Special note should be made of the PCV valve. If this valve becomes clogged or sticks, it causes poor idling and stalling.

1. *ENGINE STALLS BEFORE IT WARMS UP* This condition could be due to an improperly set fast or slow idle, or to improper adjustment of the idle-mixture screw in the carburetor. It could also be due to a low carburetor float setting or to insufficient fuel entering the carburetor. This could result from a defective thermostatic air cleaner, dirt or water in the fuel lines or filter, a defective fuel pump, or a plugged fuel-tank vent. Also, the carburetor could be icing.

Certain ignition troubles could cause stalling after starting. But, as a rule, if ignition troubles are bad enough to cause stalling, they also prevent starting. However, burned contact points might permit starting but fail to keep the engine going. One other condition that could cause stalling before the engine warms up is an open primary resistance wire. When the engine is cranked, this wire is bypassed. Then, when the engine starts and cranking stops, this wire is inserted into the ignition primary circuit. If this wire were open, the engine would then stall.

2. *ENGINE STALLS AS IT WARMS UP* This condition could result if the choke valve sticks closed. The mixture becomes too rich for a hot engine, and the engine stalls. If the manifold heat-control valve sticks closed, the air-fuel mixture might become overheated and too lean, causing the engine to stall. If the hot-idle speed is too low, the engine may stall as it warms up because the idling speed drops too low. Also, stalling may be caused by overheating of the engine, which could cause vapor lock. In addition, if the damper in the thermostatic air cleaner sticks closed, the air-fuel mixture can become overheated and too lean, causing the engine to stall.

3. *ENGINE STALLS AFTER IDLING OR SLOW-SPEED DRIVING* This condition could occur if the fuel pump has a cracked diaphragm, weak spring, or defective valve. The pump fails to deliver enough fuel for idling or slow-speed operation (although it could deliver enough for high-speed operation); the engine stalls. If the carburetor float level is set too high or the idle adjustment is too rich, the engine may "load up" and stall. A lean idle adjustment may also cause stalling. The engine may overheat during sustained idling or slow-speed driving. With this condition, the air movement through the radiator may not be sufficient to keep the engine cool. Overheating, in turn, could cause vapor lock and engine stalling. (See ⊘ 34-12 for causes of overheating.)

4. *ENGINE STALLS AFTER HIGH-SPEED OR FULL-LOAD DRIVING* This condition could occur if enough heat collects to cause vapor lock. The remedy here is to shield the fuel line and fuel pump or use a less volatile fuel. Failure of the venting or idle-compensator valve in the carburetor may also cause stalling after high-speed or full-load operation. Excessive overheating of the engine is also a primary cause of stalling (⊘ 34-12).

⊘ 34-15 Engine Backfires Most backfiring is caused by a faulty antibackfire valve. It could also be caused by late ignition timing or ignition crossfiring (caused by the high voltage jumping across the distributor cap or through the cable insulation). In addition, backfiring could be due to spark plugs of the wrong heat range (which overheat and cause preignition); excessively rich mixtures (caused by fuel-pump or carburetor troubles); overheating of the engine (⊘ 34-12); carbon in the engine; hot valves; or intake valves that stick open or seat poorly.

Carbon in the engine, if excessive, may retain enough heat to preignite the air-fuel mixture as it enters the cylinder. Backfiring would occur. Carbon also increases the compression ratio and thus the tendency for detonation and preignition. Hot plugs may cause preignition (cooler plugs should be installed). If intake valves hang open, combustion may be carried back into the carburetor. Valves that have been ground excessively so that they have sharp edges, valves that seat poorly, or valves that are carboned so that they overheat often produce backfiring.

⊘ 34-16 Engine Run-on, or Dieseling Modern engines, with their emission controls, require a fairly high, hot idle for best operation. This makes run-on, or dieseling, possible. With hot spots in the combustion chambers, the engine could continue to run if the throttle is not completely closed. Enough air-fuel mixture can get past the slightly open throttle to keep the engine running. The hot spots act as the spark plugs, igniting the mixture in the combustion chambers.

Modern engines have an idle-stop solenoid to close the throttle completely when the ignition switch is turned off. If an engine runs on, or diesels, check the idle-stop solenoid (if present). Make sure it is releasing when the ignition is turned off. It could require adjustment to permit the throttle to close completely. Be sure the engine idle speed is not set too high. Engine run-on could also be caused by advanced ignition timing. Correction of engine overheating is covered in ⊘ 34-12. Correction of hot spots may require spark-plug service or removing the cylinder head for cleaning and valve service.

⊘ 34-17 Too Much HC and CO in Exhaust Gas If the exhaust-gas analyzer (⊘ 19-8) shows that there is too much HC and CO in the exhaust, correction must be made. Excessive CO can usually be brought within specifications by proper adjustment of the carburetor. Excessive HC usually can be corrected by proper service and adjustment of the ignition system, and by replacement of worn parts in the engine. Some states require exhaust-gas testing of all cars during state inspection. Cars that emit too much HC and CO must be repaired and adjusted before they can be licensed. This restriction is designed to get the "smoggers" off the highways. Here are the possible causes (the corrections are obvious):

1. Missing due to ignition problems such as faulty plugs, high-voltage wiring, distributor cap, ignition coil, condenser, or contact points. (High HC and CO emissions can also be caused by excessive carbon deposits in the combustion chamber or stuck or burned valves.)
2. Incorrect ignition timing.
3. Carburetor troubles such as the choke sticking closed, worn jets, high float level, and other conditions listed in ⊘ 34-20.
4. Faulty air-injection system, which does not inject enough air into the exhaust manifold to completely burn the HC and CO. (This could be caused by a faulty air pump or a leaking hose or air manifold.)
5. Defective transmission-controlled spark system, which permits vacuum advance in all gear positions instead of high and reverse only.
6. Defective catalytic converters, which must be replaced or serviced to restore the catalytic action.

⊘ 34-18 Excessive Oil Consumption Oil may be lost from the engine in three ways: by leakage in liquid form; by burning in the combustion chamber; and by leaving the crankcase through the crankcase ventilating system, in the form of mist or vapor.

External leakage can often be detected by inspecting the seals around the oil pan, cylinder-head cover, and timing-gear housing and at oil-line and filter connections.

Burning of oil in the combustion chamber gives the exhaust gas a bluish tinge. Oil can enter the combustion chamber through the PCV system, through the clearance between intake-valve or exhaust-valve stems and valve guides, and past the piston rings.

If the intake-valve stem clearance is excessive, oil is "pulled" through the clearance and into the combustion chamber on each intake stroke. The appearance of the intake-valve stem often indicates that this is occurring. Some oil remains on the underside of the valve and stem to form carbon. Oil can also seep down past the exhaust-valve stem if the clearance is excessive. The remedy is to install valve seals or a new valve guide, and possibly a new valve.

Probably the most common cause of excessive oil consumption is passage of oil into the combustion chamber between the piston rings and cylinder walls. This is often called "oil pumping." It is due to worn, tapered, or out-of-round cylinder walls or worn or carboned rings. In addition, when engine bearings are worn, excessive oil is thrown on the cylinder walls. The rings are not able to control all of it, and too much oil works up into the combustion chamber.

High speed must also be considered if there is excessive oil consumption. High speed means high temperatures and thus thin oil. More oil is thrown on the cylinder walls because it is thin. The piston rings, moving at high speed, cannot function so effectively. More oil works up into the combustion chamber. In addition, the churning effect of the oil in the crankcase creates more oil vapor and mist at high speed. More oil is thus lost through the crankcase ventilating system. Tests show that an engine uses several times as much oil at 60 mph [97 km/h] as at 30 mph [48 km/h].

There is one misleading thing about high-speed operation and oil consumption. For example, suppose a car is driven around town in start-and-stop driving, so the engine never really gets warmed up. Some oil will be used up, but the remaining oil may be diluted with water and unburned gasoline (see ⊘ 17-6). Thus, even though some oil is gone, the crankcase will still measure full, owing to the addition of the water and fuel. However, suppose the car is now taken out onto the highway and driven at high speed. The water and fuel will boil off rapidly. The car can appear to lose as much as a quart [0.95 liter] of oil in 100 mi [161 km] or less.

⊘ 34-19 Low Oil Pressure Low oil pressure is often a warning of a worn oil pump or engine bearings. The bearings pass so much oil that the oil pump cannot maintain oil pressure. Further, the end bearings are probably oil-starved, and may fail. Other causes of low oil pressure are a weak relief-valve spring, worn oil pump, broken or cracked oil line, and clogged oil line. Oil dilution, or foaming, sludge, insufficient oil, or oil made too thin by engine overheating also cause low oil pressure.

⊘ 34-20 Excessive Fuel Consumption This condition can be caused by almost anything in the car, from the driver to underinflated tires or a defective choke. A fuel-mileage tester can be used to accurately check fuel consumption (Fig. 33-11). The compression or leakage tester and the vacuum gauge (⊘ 33-4 to 33-7) will help determine whether the trouble is in the engine, fuel system, ignition system, or elsewhere.[2] Also, the exhaust-gas analyzer, dynamometer, and fuel-flow meter are useful in analyzing the problem.

If the trouble seems to be in the fuel system, consider the following:

1. A driver who pumps the accelerator when idling, and insists on being the first to move when the stoplight changes, uses excessive amounts of fuel.
2. Operation with the choke partly closed after warm-up uses excessive amounts of fuel.
3. Short-run operation means that the engine operates on warm-up most of the time. This means high fuel consumption.

These three conditions are due to the type of operation: Changing operating conditions is the only cure. If excessive fuel consumption is not due to any of these conditions, however, then the fuel pump should be checked for excessive pressure. High fuel-pump pressure causes a high float-bowl level and a rich mixture. Special gauges are used to check fuel-pump pressure.

4. If excessive fuel consumption is not due to operating conditions or high fuel-pump pressure, the trouble is likely to be in the carburetor. It could be any of the following conditions:
   a. If the car is equipped with an automatic choke, the choke may not be opening rapidly enough during warm-up, or may not open fully. The automatic choke should be checked by removing the air cleaner and observing choke operation during warm-up.
   b. A clogged air cleaner that does not admit sufficient air can act somewhat like a partly closed choke valve. The cleaner element should be cleaned or replaced.
   c. If the float level in the float bowl is high, it causes flooding and delivery of excessive fuel to the carburetor air horn. The needle valve may be stuck open or may not be seating fully. The float level should be checked and adjusted.
   d. If the idle mixture is set too rich, or the idle speed too high, excessive fuel consumption results. These should be checked and adjusted as necessary.
   e. Where the accelerator-pump system has a check valve, failure of the check valve to close properly may allow fuel to feed into the carburetor air horn. The carburetor should be disassembled for repair.
   f. A metering rod stuck in the high-speed full throttle position, or an economizer valve stuck open, permits the power system to function. This supplies an excessively rich mixture. The carburetor should be disassembled for repair.
   g. Worn jets permit the discharge of too much fuel. The jets should be replaced during carburetor rebuilding.
5. Faulty ignition can also cause excessive fuel consumption; the ignition system could cause engine miss and thus failure of the engine to use all the fuel. This trouble would also be associated with loss of power, acceleration, or high-speed performance (⊘ 34-10). Conditions in the ignition system that might contribute to the trouble include a "weak" coil or condenser, incorrect timing, faulty advance-mechanism action, dirty or worn plugs or contact points, and defective wiring.
6. Inferior engine action can produce excessive fuel consumption. Examples include loss of engine compression from worn or stuck rings, worn or stuck valves, or a loose or burned cylinder-head gasket. Power is lost under these conditions, and more fuel must be burned to reach the same speed. (Refer to ⊘ 33-4 to 33-6 for compression- and leakage-checking procedures.)
7. Excessive fuel consumption can also result from

[2]Here is a rough test of mixture richness that does not require any testing instruments. Install a set of new or cleaned spark plugs of the correct heat range for the engine, and operate the car for 15 to 20 min. Then stop the car, and remove and examine the plugs. If the spark plugs are coated with a black carbon deposit, the mixture is too rich. (See item 20, points *a* to g.) Black exhaust smoke is another indication of an excessively rich mixture. The mixture is too rich to burn fully, and so the exhaust gas contains "soot," or unburned fuel.

conditions that make it hard for the engine to move the car along the road. Such factors as low tires, dragging brakes, defective automatic transmission, and misalignment of wheels increase the rolling resistance of the car. The engine must use up more fuel to overcome this excessive rolling resistance.

⊘ 34-21 Engine Noises Some engine noises may have little significance. Other noises may indicate serious trouble that requires prompt attention to prevent major damage to the engine.

A listening rod, or stethoscope, is helpful in locating the source of a noise. The rod acts like the stethoscope that a doctor uses to listen to a patient's heartbeat or breathing. When one end is placed at the ear, and the other end at some part of the engine, noises from that part of the engine are carried along the rod to the ear. A long screwdriver or one of the engine stethoscopes now available can be used.

When using the listening rod to locate the source of a noise, touch the engine end to various places on the engine. Move it around until the noise is loudest. You can also use a piece of garden hose (about 4 ft [1.2 m] long) to locate engine noises. Hold one end of the hose to your ear, and move the other end of the hose around the engine until the noise is loudest. By determining the approximate position of the noise, you can locate such defects as a broken and noisy ring in a particular cylinder, and a main-bearing knock.

CAUTION: Keep away from the moving fan belt and fan when using the listening rod.

Here is a list of engine noises, along with tests that may be necessary to confirm a diagnosis.

1. *VALVE AND TAPPET NOISE* This is a regular clicking sound that gets louder as engine speed increases. The cause is usually excessive valve clearance or a defective hydraulic valve lifter. A feeler gauge inserted between the valve stem and lifter or rocker arm will reduce the clearance. If the noise also is reduced, then the cause is excessive clearance. The clearance should be readjusted. If inserting the feeler gauge does not reduce the noise, it may be the result of such conditions in the valve mechanism as weak springs, worn lifter faces, lifters loose in the block, rough adjustment-screw face, and rough cams. (The noise may not be coming from the valves at all; see the conditions listed below.)

2. *DETONATION* Spark knock, or detonation, is a pinging or chattering sound. It is most noticeable during acceleration or when the car is climbing a hill. Some spark knock is normal. But when it becomes excessive, it may be due to such conditions as fuel with too low an octane rating for the engine, carbon deposits in the engine (which increase the compression ratio), and advanced ignition timing. (The conditions described in ⊘ 34-15 also may cause detonation.)

3. *CONNECTING-ROD NOISES* Connecting-rod noise usually has a light knocking or pounding character. The sound is most noticeable when the engine is "floating" (not accelerating or decelerating). The sound becomes more noticeable as the accelerator is eased off, with the car running at medium speed. To locate connecting-rod noise, short out the spark plugs, one at a time. The noise will be considerably reduced when the cylinder that is responsible is not delivering power. A worn bearing or crankpin, a misaligned connecting rod, inadequate oil, or excessive bearing clearances can cause connecting-rod noise.

4. *PISTON-PIN NOISE* Piston-pin noise is similar to valve and tappet noise, but it has a unique metallic double knock. It is usually most audible during idle with the spark advanced. However, on some engines, the noise becomes most audible at car speeds of around 30 mph [48 km/h]. A check can be made by running the engine at idle with the spark advanced, and then shorting out the spark plugs. Piston-pin noise is reduced somewhat when the plug in a noisy cylinder is shorted out. Causes of this noise are a worn or loose piston pin, a worn bushing, and lack of oil.

5. *PISTON-RING NOISE* Piston-ring noise is also similar to valve and tappet noise. It is a clicking, snapping, or rattling sound. This noise, however, is most evident on acceleration. Low ring tension, broken rings, worn rings, or worn cylinder walls produce this noise. Since the noise can sometimes be confused with other engine noises, make a test as follows: Remove the spark plugs, and add 1 to 2 fluid ounces [30 to 60 cc] of heavy engine oil to each cylinder. Crank the engine for several revolutions, to work the oil down past the rings. Then replace the plugs and start the engine. If the noise has been reduced, the rings probably are at fault.

6. *PISTON SLAP* Piston slap is a muffled, hollow, bell-like sound. It is caused by the piston rocking back and forth in the cylinder. If it occurs only when the engine is cold, it is not serious. When it occurs under all operating conditions, further investigation is required. Piston slap is caused by inadequate oil, worn cylinder walls, worn pistons, collapsed piston skirts, excessive piston clearances, or misaligned connecting rods.

7. *CRANKSHAFT KNOCK* Crankshaft knock is a heavy, dull, metallic knock. It is most noticeable when the engine is under a heavy load or accelerating, particularly when cold. When the noise is regular, it probably results from worn main bearings. When the noise is irregular and sharp, it is probably due to a worn end-thrust bearing. The latter condition, when unusually bad, causes the noise each time the clutch is released and engaged, and when accelerating.

8. *MISCELLANEOUS NOISES* Other noises result from loosely mounted parts, such as the alternator, starting motor, horn, water pump, manifolds, flywheel, crankshaft pulley, and oil pan. In addition, other automotive components, such as the clutch, transmission, and differential, may develop noises.

CHAPTER 34 CHECKUP

NOTE: Since the following is a chapter review test, you should review the chapter before taking the test.

The chapter you have just completed is probably one of the hardest chapters in the book. At the same time, it is one of the most important chapters. To be an expert automotive tuneup technician, you must know what troubles an engine might have, the causes of these troubles, and how to find the causes. That is, you need to be a good troubleshooter. The fact that you have come this far in the book shows that you have made an earnest start toward becoming an engine expert. You have done well. The checkup that follows will help you determine how well you understand and remember the information you studied in this chapter. If a question stumps you, reread the pages that give you the answer.

Correcting Troubles Lists In each of the following lists, there is one item that does not belong. For example, check through the list, "Engine will not turn over: run-down battery, worn rings, starting circuit open, engine jammed, starting motor jammed." You should see that "worn rings" does not belong. It is the only condition that does not directly cause failure of the engine to turn over. Write each list in your notebook, but do not write the item that does not belong.

1. Engine turns over slowly but does not start: run-down battery, undersized battery cables, bad connections in the starting circuit, defective starting motor, stuck cooling-system thermostat.
2. Engine will not turn over: engine jammed, starting motor or drive jammed, starting circuit open, run-down battery, excessive carbon in the engine.
3. Engine runs, but one cylinder misses: defective spark plug, stuck valve, defective fuel pump, defective rings, defective distributor cap.
4. Engine turns over at normal speed but does not start: defective ignition system, defective engine, defective fan belt, defective fuel system.
5. Engine runs, but different cylinders miss: clogged exhaust, defective rings, overheated engine, defective valve action, loss of compression, excessive vacuum in intake manifold, defective ignition.
6. Engine lacks power, acceleration, or high-speed performance when cold: stuck valves, stuck manifold heat-control valve, vapor lock, stuck automatic choke.
7. Engine lacks power, acceleration, or high-speed performance when hot or cold: defective valve action, defective ignition system, defective fuel system, loss of compression, excessive carbon in the engine, run-down battery.
8. Engine lacks power, acceleration, or high-speed performance when hot only: overheating engine, defective choke, vapor lock, stuck manifold heat-control valve, incorrect idle-mixture adjustment.
9. Engine overheats: ignition timing late, loose fan belt, defective water pump, high altitude, clogged water jackets, defective radiator hose, defective fuel pump, defective thermostat, lack of coolant.
10. Engine stalls as it warms up: closed choke valve, stuck manifold heat-control valve, overheating engine, idling speed too low, defective head gasket.
11. Engine stalls after idling or slow-speed driving: defective fuel pump, overheating, high float level, overcharged battery.
12. Engine stalls after high-speed driving: carburetor antipercolator defective, vapor lock, run-down battery.
13. Engine backfires: spark plugs of wrong heat range, overheating engine, hot valves, carbon in the engine, vapor lock, rich or lean mixture, ignition timing off.
14. Excessive oil consumption with blue exhaust smoke: burning oil in combustion chamber, clogged air cleaner, worn rings, worn valve guides, worn bearings.
15. Excessive fuel consumption with black exhaust smoke: clogged air cleaner, rich idle, worn carburetor jets, loss of engine compression, run-down battery, faulty ignition, defective valve action.
16. Light knock or pound with engine floating: worn connecting-rod bearing, spark knock, worn crankpin, misaligned rod, lack of oil.
17. Dull, heavy knock under load or acceleration: worn main bearings, loose piston pin, worn crankshaft end-thrust bearings.
18. Light double knock during idle: worn piston pin, lack of oil, broken rings, loose piston pin, worn piston-pin bushing.
19. Hollow, muffled, bell-like sound with engine cold: worn piston, collapsed piston skirt, worn cylinder walls, worn piston-pin bearings, lack of oil.
20. Chattering or rattling during acceleration: worn rings, worn cylinder walls, low ring tension, broken rings, misaligned rods.

Completing the Sentences The sentences that follow are incomplete. After each sentence there are several words or phrases, but only one of them correctly completes the sentence. Write each sentence in your notebook, ending it with the one word or phrase that completes it correctly.

1. An engine will not turn over if it has: (*a*) a defective ignition coil, (*b*) a run-down battery, (*c*) a defective fuel pump, (*d*) valves that hang open.
2. An engine will turn over slowly because of: (*a*) a defective water pump, (*b*) vapor lock, (*c*) undersized battery cables, (*d*) excessive fuel-pump pressure.
3. Failure of an engine to start even though it turns over at normal cranking speed could be due to a: (*a*) run-down battery, (*b*) defective starting motor, (*c*) sticking engine valve, (*d*) defective ignition.
4. Missing in one cylinder is likely to result from: (*a*) a clogged exhaust, (*b*) an overheating engine, (*c*) vapor lock, (*d*) a defective spark plug.
5. Irregular missing in different cylinders may result

from: (*a*) a defective starting motor, (*b*) a defective carburetor, (*c*) an open cranking circuit.

6. Loss of engine power as the engine warms up is most likely caused by: (*a*) vapor lock, (*b*) excessive rolling resistance, (*c*) the throttle valve not closing fully, (*d*) heavy oil.

7. An engine will lose power (hot or cold) if it has: (*a*) an incorrect idle adjustment, (*b*) an automatic choke valve that is stuck open, (*c*) worn rings and cylinder walls.

8. An engine may stall as it warms up if the: (*a*) ignition timing is off, (*b*) choke valve sticks closed, (*c*) battery is run down, (*d*) throttle valve does not open fully.

9. An engine will overheat if the: (*a*) automatic choke sticks, (*b*) fan belt breaks, (*c*) fuel pump is defective, (*d*) battery is run down.

10. The most probable cause of an engine stalling after idling or slow-speed driving is (*a*) loss of compression, (*b*) a defective fuel pump, (*c*) sticking engine valves.

11. Stalling of an engine after high-speed driving is likely to be caused by: (*a*) vapor lock, (*b*) incorrect ignition timing, (*c*) worn carburetor jets.

12. Engine backfiring may result from: (*a*) spark plugs of the wrong heat range, (*b*) vapor lock, (*c*) a run-down battery, (*d*) worn piston rings.

13. A smoky blue exhaust may be due to: (*a*) an excessively rich mixture, (*b*) burning oil in the combustion chamber, (*c*) a stuck choke valve, (*d*) incorrect valve adjustment.

14. A smoky black exhaust may be due to: (*a*) worn piston rings, (*b*) worn carburetor jets, (*c*) spark plugs of the wrong heat range.

15. A light knock or pound with the engine floating can result from worn: (*a*) main bearings, (*b*) connecting-rod bearing, (*c*) rings.

16. A light double knock during idle can result from: (*a*) piston slap, (*b*) spark knock, (*c*) incorrect ignition timing, (*d*) a loose or worn piston pin.

17. A rattling or chattering sound during acceleration may be due to: (*a*) worn main bearings, (*b*) loose valve and tappet adjustment, (*c*) worn or broken rings.

18. A hollow, muffled, bell-like sound, with the engine cold, is likely to be due to: (*a*) worn or collapsed pistons, (*b*) worn main bearings, (*c*) a loose oil pan, (*d*) sticking engine valves.

19. A dull, heavy knock under load or acceleration is likely to be due to worn: (*a*) rings, (*b*) main bearings, (*c*) piston pins, (*d*) pistons.

20. Loss of engine compression can result from: (*a*) worn rings or cylinder walls, (*b*) loose valve and tappet adjustment, (*c*) a defective fan belt.

Troubleshooting Engine Complaints As an engine expert, you will hear complaints of loss of power, high fuel consumption, knocking, and so on. You must know what to do to find the causes of these troubles. The following questions are stumpers that you might actually encounter in an automotive shop. In your notebook, write the procedures you would follow to find the causes of the various engine troubles. Do not copy. Write the procedures in your own words. This will help you remember them. If you are not quite sure of a procedure, turn back to the pages that give you the necessary information.

1. You are called to check a car in which the engine will not turn over when the starting-motor switch is closed. You turn on the headlights and try to start the car. What are the five things that might happen to the headlights? List the probable causes of each.

2. What are the possible causes of the trouble when an engine turns over slowly but will not start? How would you locate the actual cause?

3. A car that will not start is pulled into your shop. On testing it, you find that the engine turns over at normal speed but will not start. What ignition and fuel-system checks should be made?

4. An engine misses. What check can you make to locate the missing cylinder?

5. You find that one particular engine cylinder is missing. What further checks can you make on this cylinder? What are possible causes of the trouble?

6. What are the possible causes of the trouble when an engine miss is irregular and cannot be traced to any one cylinder?

7. List the possible causes of the trouble, and how to locate them, when an engine loses power as it warms up.

8. An engine lacks power hot and cold, What are the possible causes of the trouble, and how would you diagnose the trouble?

9. An engine lacks power only when cold, but seems to run normally when hot. What could the trouble be, and what would you do to make sure?

10. What would you look for if an engine overheated?

11. What are three basic conditions under which an engine will stall? What are the causes of each condition? How can you tell which is the trouble?

12. List the possible causes of engine backfiring. Describe how to locate the actual cause.

13. In what three ways can engine oil be lost?

14. List the causes of excessive oil consumption due to burning of oil in the combustion chamber.

15. What are some causes of excessive fuel consumption resulting from troubles in the fuel system?

16. Describe various types of car operation that increase fuel consumption.

17. What are causes of excessive fuel consumption due to high rolling resistance?

18. List the various engine noises, and explain their causes.

19. List the causes of loss of compression.

20. Explain how to use the engine vacuum gauge. Make a list of the various vacuum-gauge readings, along with their causes.

SUGGESTIONS FOR FURTHER STUDY

Carefully observe trouble-diagnosis procedures in the automotive shop. Examine all the engine components you can, after engines are torn down. Both of these will be of great value to you in linking the causes and effects of engine troubles. For instance, see if you can examine the pistons, rings, and cylinder walls of an engine which has lost compression and is using too much oil. You will quickly see why the engine lost compression, and why it used too much oil.

The trouble-diagnosis procedures outlined in this chapter will be of great help to you in the automotive shop. Thus, you will want to study these procedures carefully, and refer to the Engine Trouble-Diagnosis Chart over and over again. At the beginning of this chapter, we suggested that you write the trouble-diagnosis procedures on 3- by 5-in cards, and carry the cards around with you. Also, you may obtain a deck of the McGraw-Hill *Automotive Troubleshooting Cards,* which list troubles and their possible causes. Whenever you get a chance, as, for instance, when you are listening to music on the radio, eating lunch, or getting ready for bed, you can take out one of the cards and read it. Soon you will know the procedures thoroughly.

Be sure to discuss, with expert automotive mechanics and your teacher, the various methods of locating engine troubles. Ask them about their experiences in locating troubles: how often they find that loss of compression is due to worn rings, whether they find much valve-guide wear, and so on.

chapter 35

ENGINE TUNEUP

This chapter describes the procedure known as engine tuneup. Tuneup includes testing the various components and accessory systems involved in engine operation. It also includes readjusting or replacing parts as required to restore engine performance. Sometimes, a tuneup will uncover serious problems that require major repair work. Automotive Engines, *another book in the McGraw-Hill Automotive Technology Series, describes the service jobs that may be performed on engines. In this chapter, we shall not repeat any of the engine testing procedures described in Chap. 34. When we refer to a specific test or repair operation, turn to the sections that describe the procedure.*

⊘ 35-1 What is Tuneup? Engine tuneup means different things to different people. To some, it means a quick once-over check of the obvious trouble spots in an engine. To others, it means use of the proper test instruments to do a careful, complete analysis of all engine components. In addition, it means adjusting everything to "specs" and repairing or replacing all worn parts. The latter is the proper meaning of engine tuneup. It is the basis for the procedure outlined in this chapter.

NOTE: In this chapter, we combine two separate programs: engine tuneup and complete car-care inspection. Engine tuneup includes checking and servicing the engine and its systems. Car-care inspection includes checking all other components on the car, such as brakes, steering, and tires. Together, engine tuneup and car-care inspection cover everything in and on the car that could cause trouble. Most automotive shops find that a customer who comes in for an engine tuneup can also be sold a car-care inspection. Likewise, a customer who comes in for a car-care inspection can also be sold a tuneup.

See the other books in the McGraw-Hill Automotive Technology Series for the details of servicing automotive components other than the engine. These books include *Automotive Electrical Equipment; Automotive Fuel, Lubricating and Cooling Systems; Automotive Chassis and Body; Automotive Transmissions and Power Trains; Automotive Air Conditioning,* and *Automotive Emission Control.*

⊘ 35-2 Tuneup Procedure An engine tuneup follows a fairly set procedure. Many mechanics use a printed form supplied by automotive or test-equipment manufacturers (Fig. 35-1). The mechanic follows the form and checks off the listed items, one by one. This ensures that every part of the procedure is performed. However, not all tuneup forms are the same. Different companies have different ideas about what should be done, and the order in which it should be done. In addition, the tuneup procedure depends on the equipment available. If the shop has an oscilloscope or a dynamometer, it is used as part of the tuneup procedure. If these test instruments are not available, then the tuneup is performed differently.

The procedure that follows includes car-care inspection. It lists all essential checks and adjustments, in what authorities believe is the most logical sequence.

⊘ 35-3 Tuneup and Car Care The tuneup procedure restores driveability, power, and performance that have been lost through wear, corrosion, and deterioration of engine parts. Such changes take place gradually in many parts, during normal car operation. Because of federal and state laws limiting automotive emissions, the tuneup procedure must include checks of all emission controls. Here is the procedure.

1. If the engine is cold, operate it for at least 20 min at 1,500 rpm, or until it reaches operating temperature.
2. Connect the oscilloscope, if available, and perform an electronic diagnosis. Check for any abnormal ignition-system conditions that appear on the pattern. Make a note of any abnormality and the cylinder(s) in which it appears.

CUSTOMER ______________________ PHONE __________ DATE __________

MAKE-YEAR-MODEL ______________________ MILEAGE __________

SIGNATURE ______________________

PLEASE CHECK DESIRED SERVICES

Complete Infra-Red Engine Tune-Up

(CONSISTS OF ALL ITEMS LISTED BELOW)

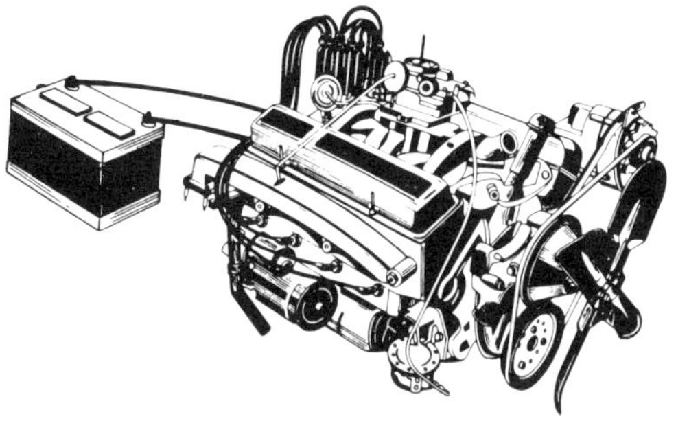

1 ☐ USE INFRARED EXHAUST GAS ANALYSIS & VISUAL INSPECTION TO TEST & ADJUST CARBURETOR & CHOKE
(Needed for smooth idle, economy, good performance & low exhaust emissions)

2 ☐ TEST CYLINDER BALANCE & COMPRESSION FACTORS
(Needed for smooth idle, economy & good performance)

3 ☐ CLEAN OR REPLACE SPARK PLUGS AS NEEDED

4 ☐ REMOVE DISTRIBUTOR FROM ENGINE FOR SERVICE—TEST MECHANICAL & ELECTRICAL CONDITION—CALIBRATE ADVANCE MECHANISM
(Has direct bearing on gasoline mileage, exhaust emissions & performance—also permits proper installation of ignition points)

5 ☐ REPLACE IGNITION POINTS IF NEEDED & SET INITIAL TIMING

6 ☐ SERVICE MANIFOLD HEAT CONTROL VALVE
(Affects warm-up & running performance)

7 ☐ REPLACE FUEL FILTER ELEMENT IF NEEDED & TEST FUEL PUMP OPERATION
(To guard against unpredictable road failures)

8 ☐ SERVICE AIR POLLUTION CONTROL MECHANISM—P.C.V.
(Affects fuel air ratio and idle performance)

9 ☐ CLEAN, TEST & SERVICE SPARK PLUG WIRES, IGNITION COIL, DISTRIBUTOR CAP & ROTOR
(Helps prevent starting & missing problems due to dampness and/or resistance)

10 ☐ TEST GENERATOR OR ALTERNATOR & REGULATOR—REPLACE DRIVE BELTS IF NEEDED
(To insure battery will be kept fully charged for starting)

11 ☐ SERVICE & TEST BATTERY—CLEAN BATTERY TOP & CABLES—RECHARGE IF NEEDED—TEST STARTER
(Helps prevent unpredicted starting failures)

12 ☐ SERVICE AIR FILTER—REPLACE IF NEEDED
(Affects general performance of engine)

13 ☐ USE CYLINDER & CRANKCASE CHEMICAL TUNE-UP ADDITIVES
(Helps prevent sticking valves, rings & lifters)

14 ☐ ROAD TEST
(For over-all automobile performance & general condition)

15 ☐ TELEPHONE IF ADDITIONAL SERVICES ARE FOUND NECESSARY

Sun SERVICE CONTROL SYSTEM

Fig. 35-1. Printed tuneup form. (*Sun Electric Corporation*)

3. Remove all spark plugs. Fully open the throttle and choke valves. Disconnect the distributor lead from the coil primary terminal to prevent engine starting.
4. Check the compression of each cylinder. Record the readings. If one or more cylinders read low, squirt about a tablespoonful of engine oil through the spark-plug hole. Recheck the compression. Record the new readings.

NOTE: If the compression is low, indicating either bad rings or valves, tell the owner the engine is not tunable without overhaul or repair.

5. Clean, inspect, file, gap, and test the spark plugs. Discard worn or defective plugs. (Many shops install new plugs instead of servicing the old ones.) Gap all plugs, old and new. Install the plugs.
6. Inspect and clean the battery case, terminals, cables, and hold-down brackets. Test the battery. Add water, if necessary. If severe corrosion is present, clean the battery and cables with brushes and a solution of baking soda and water.
7. Test the starting voltage. If the battery is in good condition but cranking speed is low, test the starting system.
8. If the battery is low or the customer complains that the battery keeps running down, check the charging system (alternator and regulator). If the battery is old, it may have worn out. A new battery is required.
9. Check the drive belts, and replace any that are in poor condition. If you have to replace one belt of a two-belt drive, replace both belts. Tighten the belts to the correct tension, using a tension gauge.
10. Inspect the distributor rotor and cap, and the primary and high-voltage (spark-plug) wires (Fig. 35-2).

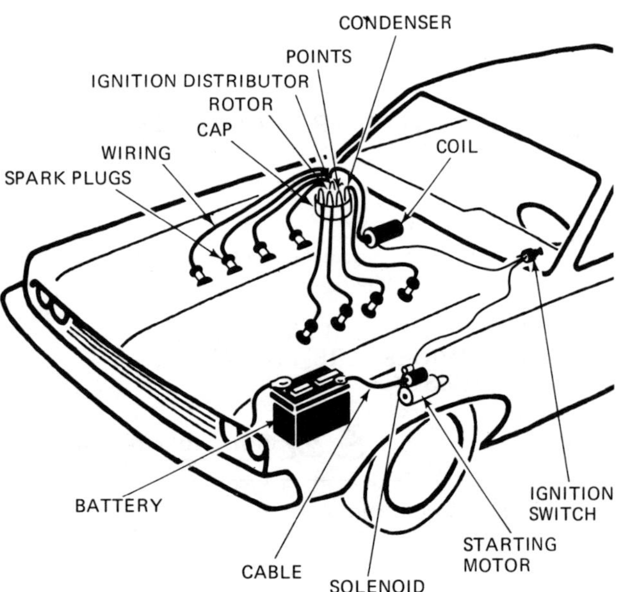

Fig. 35-2. Simplified drawing of an engine ignition system.

11. Clean or replace the distributor contact points. Adjust the points (by setting the point gap). Lubricate the distributor breaker cam if specifications call for this. On distributors with round cam lubricator, turn the cam lubricator 180° every 12,000 mi [19,312 km]. Replace the cam lubricator every 24,000 mi [38,624 km].
12. Check the distributor cap and rotor (Fig. 35-3). Check the centrifugal and vacuum advances. Set the contact dwell, and then adjust the ignition timing. Make sure the idle speed is not excessive because this could produce centrifugal advance during timing adjustment.
13. Use the oscilloscope to recheck the ignition system. Any abnormal conditions that appeared in step 2 should now have been eliminated.
14. Check the manifold heat-control valve. Lubricate it with heat-valve lubricant. Free up or replace the valve if necessary.
15. Check fuel-pump operation with a fuel-pump tester. Replace the fuel filter. Check the fuel-tank cap, fuel lines, and connections for leakage and damage.
16. Clean or replace the air-cleaner fiter. If the engine is equipped with a thermostatically controlled air cleaner, check the operation of the control damper.
17. Check the operation of the choke and the fast-idle cam. Check the throttle valve for full opening, and the throttle linkage for free movement.
18. Inspect all engine vacuum fittings, hoses, and connections. Replace any brittle or cracked hose.
19. Clean the engine oil-filler cap if a filter-type oil-filler cap is used.
20. Check the cooling system (Fig. 35-4). Inspect all hoses and connections, and the radiator, water pump, and fan clutch (if used). Check the strength of the coolant, and record the reading. Pressure-check the cooling system and radiator cap. Squeeze the hoses to check them. Replace any defective hose (collapsed, soft, cracked, etc.).
21. Check and replace the PCV valve if necessary (see Fig. 35-5). Clean or replace the PCV filter, if required. Inspect the PCV hoses and connections. Replace any cracked or brittle hose.
22. If the engine is equipped with an air-pump type of exhaust-emission control, replace the pump inlet air filter (if used). Inspect the system hoses and connections. Replace any brittle or cracked hose.
23. If the vehicle is equipped with a fuel-vapor recovery system, replace the charcoal-canister filter.
24. Check the transmission-controlled vacuum spark-advance system if the vehicle is so equipped.
25. On engines equipped with an EGR system, inspect and clean the EGR valve. Inspect and clean the EGR discharge port.
26. Tighten the intake-manifold and exhaust-manifold bolts to the proper tension in the proper sequence.
27. Adjust the engine valves, if necessary.
28. Adjust the carburetor idle speed. Use an exhaust-gas analyzer to adjust the idle-mixture screw.

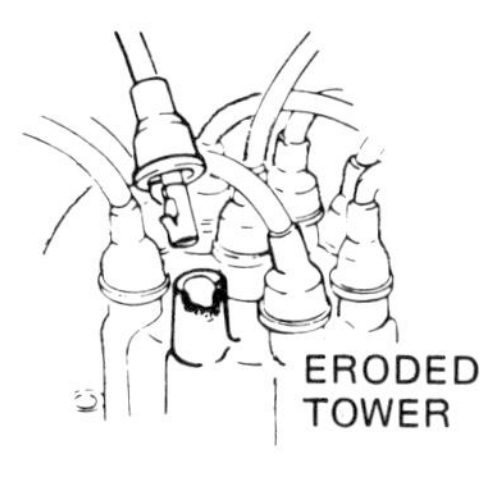

INSPECTION OF DISTRIBUTOR-CAP TOWERS

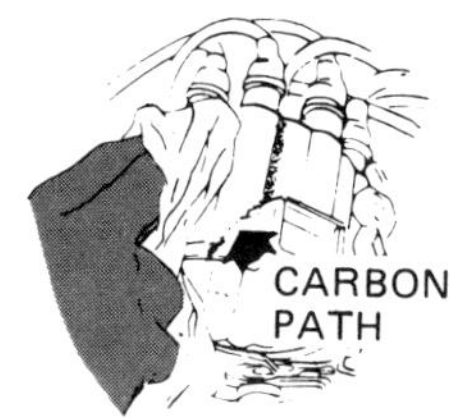

CLEANING AND INSPECTION OF OUTSIDE OF DISTRIBUTOR CAP

CLEANING AND INSPECTION OF INSIDE OF DISTRIBUTOR CAP

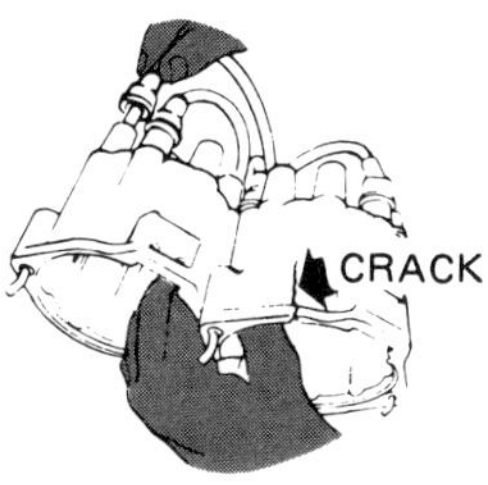

REPLACING DISTRIBUTOR CAP

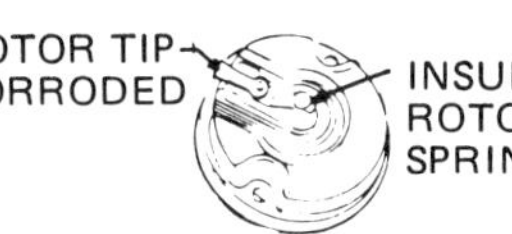

ROTOR INSPECTION

BLOWING OUT INSIDE OF DISTRIBUTOR CAP AND INSPECTION OF INSERT TERMINALS

CLEANING IGNITION COIL

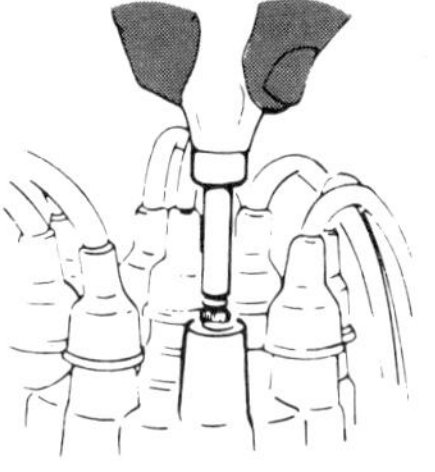
CLEANING TOWER INSERT

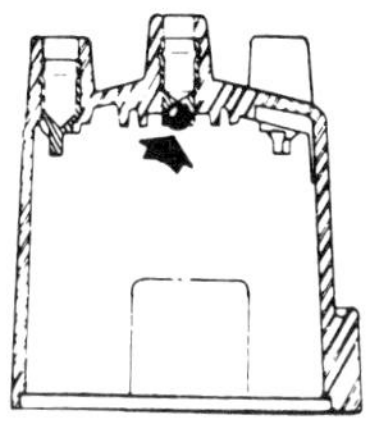
INSPECTION OF CARBON ROTOR BUTTON

Fig. 35-3. Inspection and service of distributor cap and rotor. (*Chevrolet Motor Division of General Motors Corporation*)

Check the amounts of CO and HC in the exhaust gas. (Many mechanics check the CO and HC both before and after the tuneup job, to show how much the tuneup has reduced these pollutants.)

29. Road-test the car on a dynamometer or on the road. Check for driveability, power, and idling. Note any abnormal condition on the repair order before you return the car to the customer.

30. Check the door-jamb sticker to determine if oil and oil-filter changes are due. Also note the schedule for chassis lubrication. Recommend an oil change and a lube job if they are due. (See Figs. 7-14 and 35-6). Note that car manufacturers recommend changing the oil filter every time (or every other time) the oil is changed.

31. Whenever the car is on the lift, check the exhaust system for leaks which could admit CO into the car. Also check for loose bolts, rust spots, and other under-the-car damage.

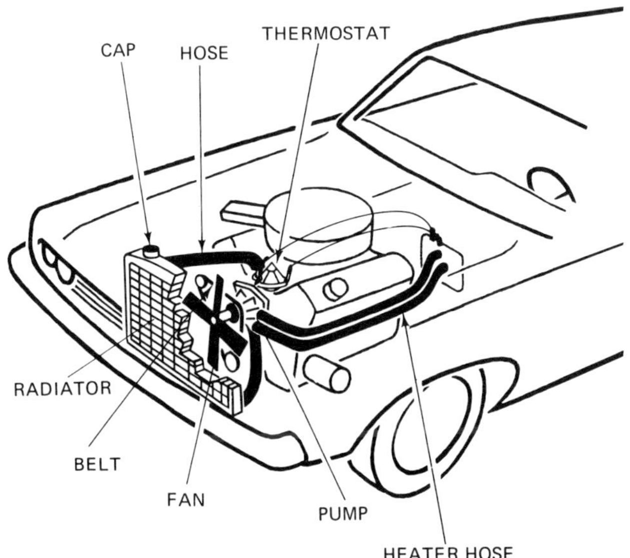

Fig. 35-4. Engine cooling system.

NOTE: Items 32 to 37 that follow are not actually part of the tuneup job. They are included here so you will have the complete car-care program all in one place.

32. Check the brakes for even braking and adequate braking power.

33. Check the steering system for ease and smoothness of operation. Check for excessive play in the system. Record any abnormal conditions.

34. Check the tires for inflation and for abnormal wear. Abnormal wear can mean suspension trouble; for this, a front-end alignment job should be recommended.

35. Check the suspension system for looseness, excessive play, and wear.

36. Check the front wheels and ball joints for excessive wear and loose bearings. Adjust the bearings, if necessary.

37. Check the headlights and horns to make sure

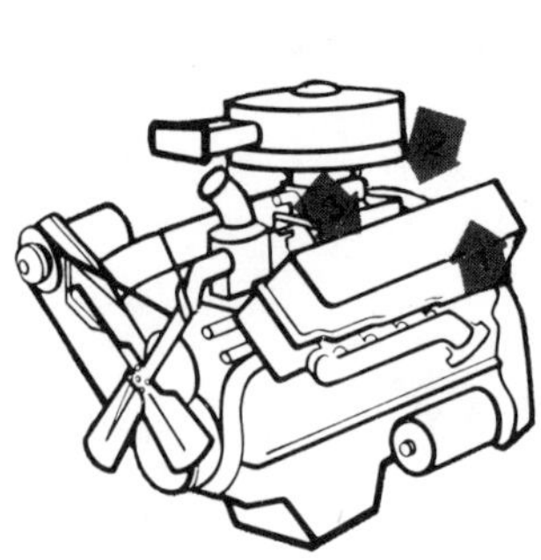

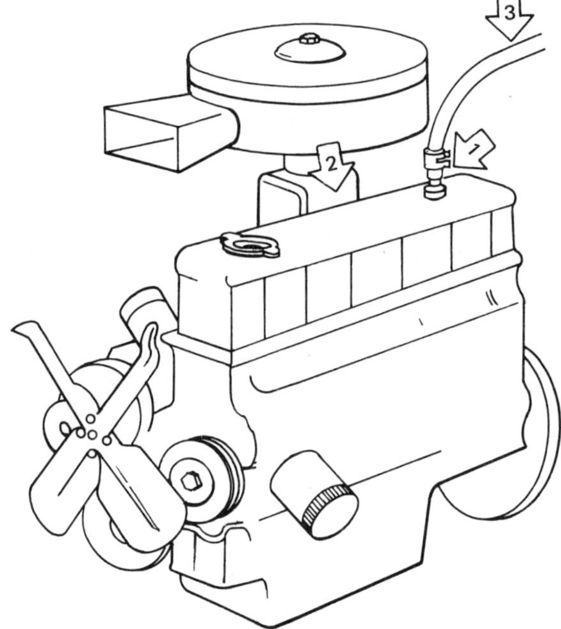

Fig. 35-5. PCV-valve locations.

they are in good working order. Check all other lights. Replace any burned-out lights. Check headlight alignment, if possible.

NOTE: As you can see, the preceding tuneup and car-care procedure covers about everything on the vehicle that could cause trouble. The complete procedure will uncover any problems that might affect driveability and performance. If all necessary corrections are made, new-car performance will be restored to the vehicle.

Fig. 35-6. Engine oil is changed by placing the container under the oil-pan drain hole and then removing the drain plug.

⊘ 35-4 Engine Analyzers and Computer Testers

Figure 35-7 shows an engine analyzer. It includes an oscilloscope and other instruments for making comprehensive tests of all engine components. Once you learn how to use this equipment, you can perform a complete engine analysis in a very short time.

In addition, there are testers that run many of

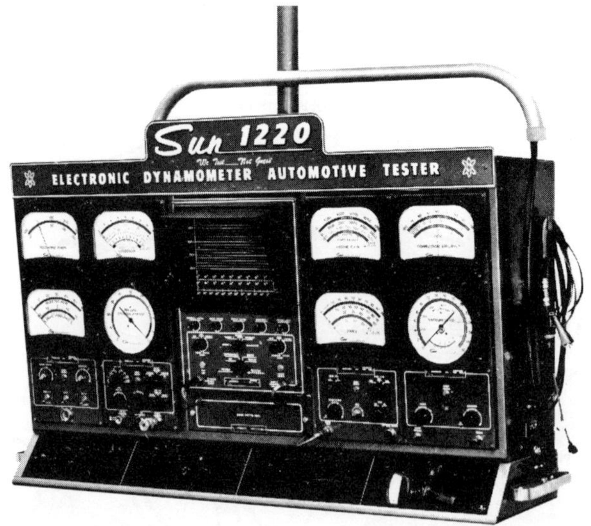

Fig. 35-7. Electronic-diagnosis engine tester, or engine analyzer. This tester includes an oscilloscope (top center) and devices that check the condenser, distributor contact-point dwell, engine speed, and so on. (*Sun Electric Corporation*)

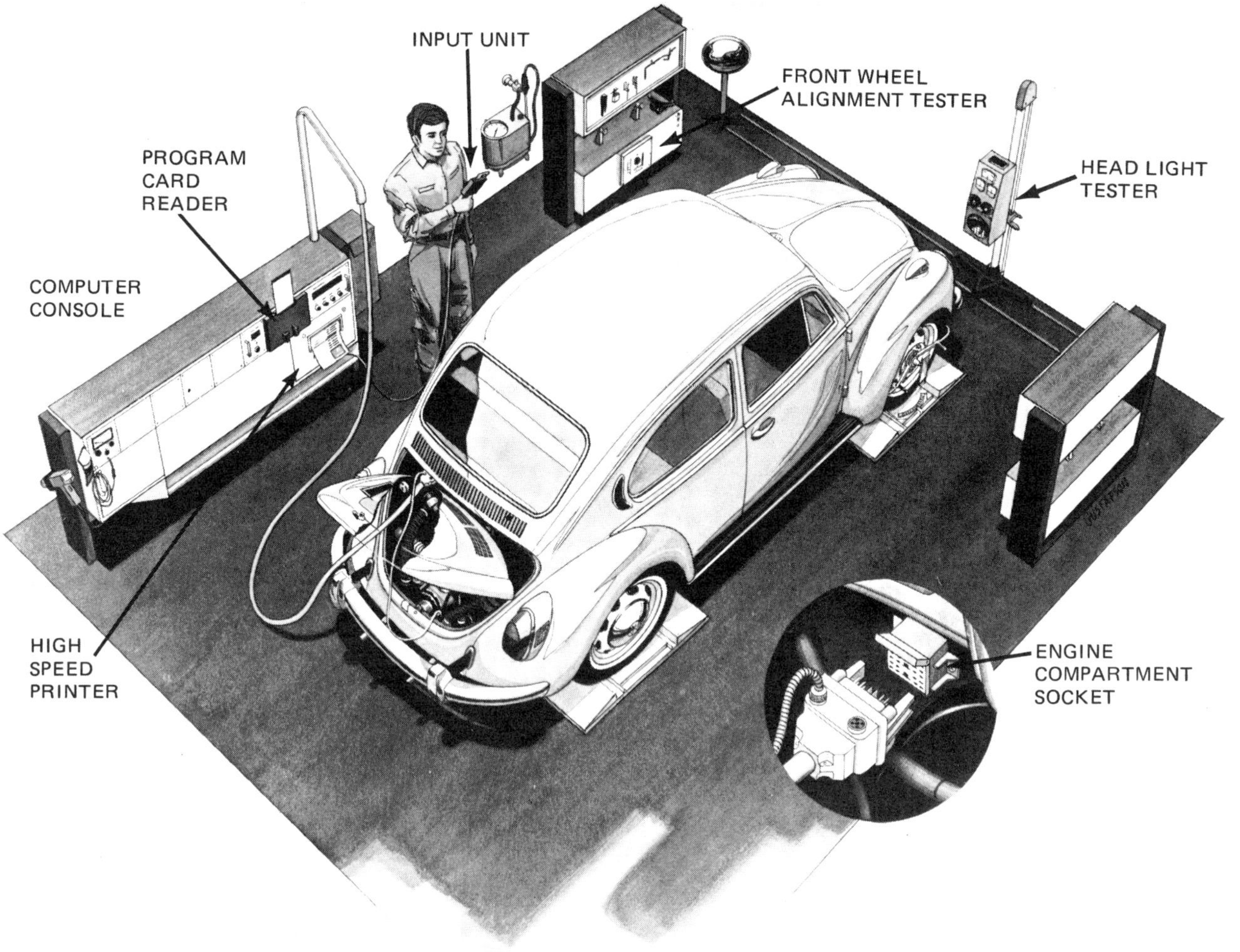

INPUT UNIT
FRONT WHEEL ALIGNMENT TESTER
PROGRAM CARD READER
HEAD LIGHT TESTER
COMPUTER CONSOLE
HIGH SPEED PRINTER
ENGINE COMPARTMENT SOCKET

Fig. 35-8. Computerized automobile diagnostic system. (*Volkswagen of America, Inc.*)

the tests almost automatically. They produce a printed record of the tests and the test results.

Figure 35-8 shows a computerized diagnostic system introduced by Volkswagen. Wiring and sensors built into the car are connected to the computer through a socket in the engine compartment. The system checks more than 70 items. A special program card contains the specifications for the year and model of car being checked. One type of card is shown in Fig. 35-9. The computer compares the operation of components on the car with values it reads from the program card. The electrical system and engine compression are among the items checked. The results of the tests are recorded by a high-speed printer.

Figure 35-10 shows the printout from another type of engine diagnostic computer. This printed record tells the mechanic and the customer what work is needed to bring the car up to specifications.

One further refinement has been suggested. This is to put into the computer information on the costs of parts and repair operations. Then the computer could print out, along with the test information, the cost of correcting any troubles. That is, it would print out the cost of parts and labor. The computer

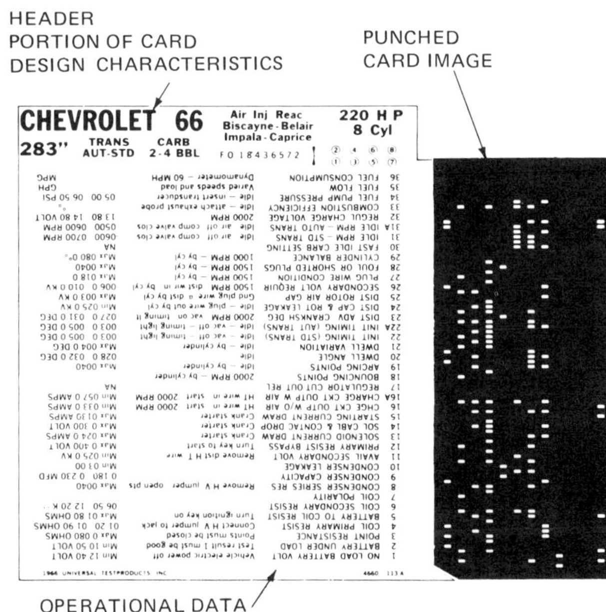

Fig. 35-9. Computer program card listing the specifications for a certain car. (*Universal Testproducts, Incorporated*)

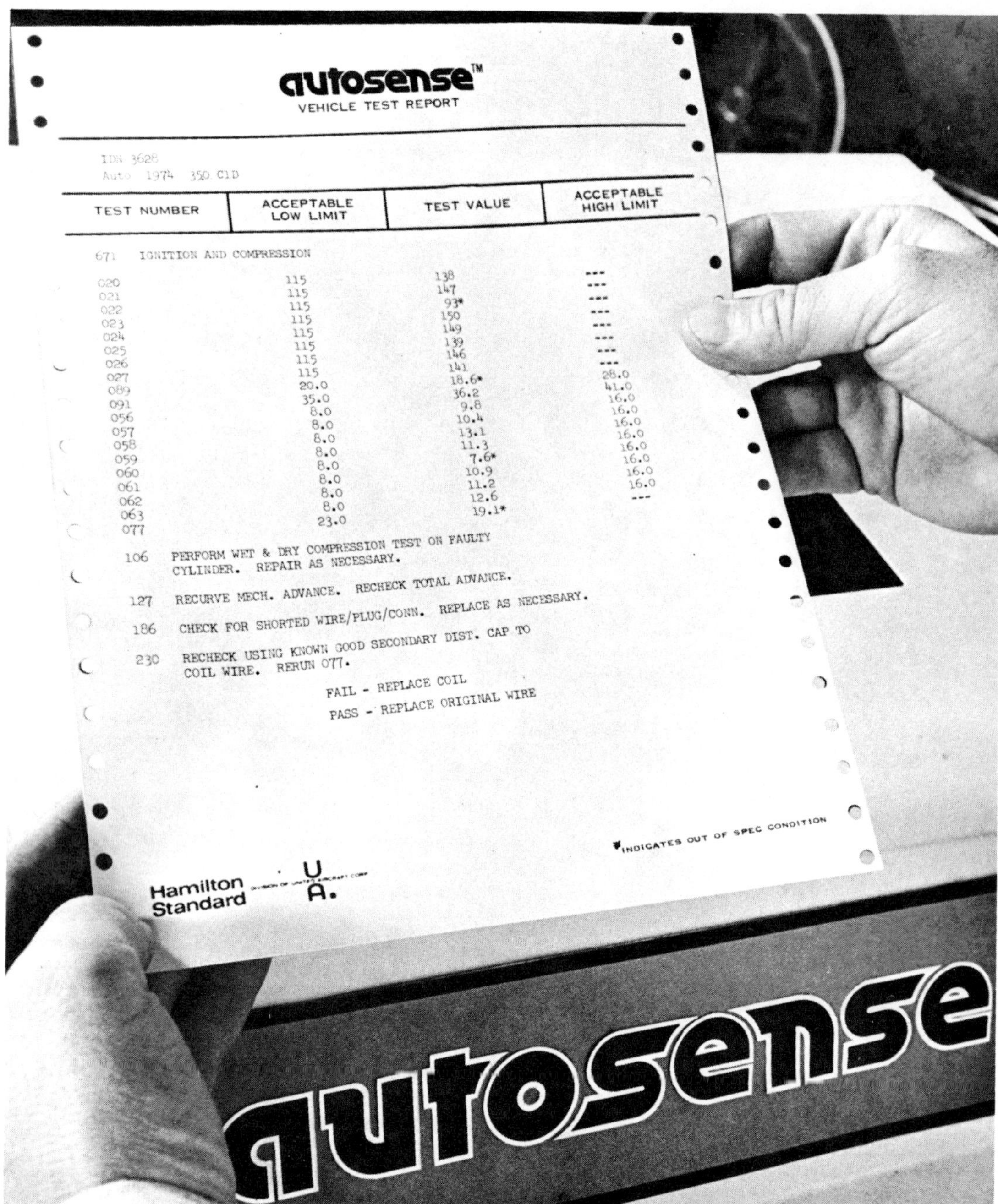

autosense™
VEHICLE TEST REPORT

IDN 3628
Auto 1974 350 CID

TEST NUMBER	ACCEPTABLE LOW LIMIT	TEST VALUE	ACCEPTABLE HIGH LIMIT
671 IGNITION AND COMPRESSION			
020	115	138	---
021	115	147	---
022	115	93*	---
023	115	150	---
024	115	149	---
025	115	139	---
026	115	146	---
027	115	141	---
089	20.0	18.6*	28.0
091	35.0	36.2	41.0
056	8.0	9.8	16.0
057	8.0	10.4	16.0
058	8.0	13.1	16.0
059	8.0	11.3	16.0
060	8.0	7.6*	16.0
061	8.0	10.9	16.0
062	8.0	11.2	16.0
063	8.0	12.6	16.0
077	23.0	19.1*	---

106 PERFORM WET & DRY COMPRESSION TEST ON FAULTY CYLINDER. REPAIR AS NECESSARY.

127 RECURVE MECH. ADVANCE. RECHECK TOTAL ADVANCE.

186 CHECK FOR SHORTED WIRE/PLUG/CONN. REPLACE AS NECESSARY.

230 RECHECK USING KNOWN GOOD SECONDARY DIST. CAP TO COIL WIRE. RERUN 077.

FAIL - REPLACE COIL

PASS - REPLACE ORIGINAL WIRE

*INDICATES OUT OF SPEC CONDITION

Hamilton Standard

Fig. 35-10. The computer printout tells the mechanic and the customer what work is needed. (*Hamilton Standard Division of United Aircraft Corporation*)

might also be programmed to schedule the work, depending on the availability of technicians and space in the shop.

Some car manufacturers are beginning to use on-the-car diagnostic or trouble-indicating devices. One such device is the sensor panel introduced by Toyota in 1974 (Fig. 35-11). This panel is installed on the roof of the car, above the driver (Fig. 35-12). It is connected to sensors in the light circuits, brakes, windshield washer, battery, cooling-system radiator, and engine crankcase (see Fig. 35-11). The sensor panel has 11 warning lights to indicate when something needs attention. For example, if any of the four lights at the top of the panel (LICENSE, BRAKE, TAIL, HEAD) come on, it indicates trouble in that light circuit. If one headlight burns out, HEAD comes on to warn the driver of the trouble. The four FLUID LEVEL lights (W-WASHER, BATTERY, RADIATOR, ENGINE OIL) indicate low fluid levels in these four areas. That is, if the car needs engine oil, the ENGINE OIL light comes on. The BRAKE section of the panel warns of low brake fluid, loss of vacuum in the power-brake unit, or excessive brake-lining wear. Figure 35-13 shows how the 11 warning lights are connected to sensors in the areas they serve.

According to some experts, the day is coming

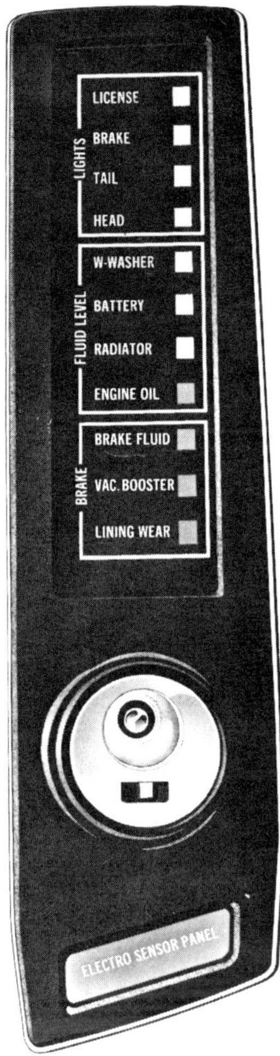

Fig. 35-11. Sensor panel, called the "Electro Sensor Panel," or ESP, by the manufacturer. (*Toyota Motor Sales, Limited*)

when a general tuneup procedure, as discussed in this chapter, will not be used. They see preventive maintenance, as part of a complete vehicle maintemance schedule (Fig. 35-14), evolving to *predictive* maintenance. That is, on-the-car indicating devices will automatically tell the driver when a part or system needs service.

CHAPTER 35 CHECKUP

NOTE: Since the following is a chapter review test, you should review the chapter before taking the test.

Engine tuneup and car-care inspection are very important to the "health" of the automobile. Many service stations and automotive shops specialize in tuneup and car-care, so it is important to know the essentials of these procedures. Check how well you remember what you have just studied by taking the following test. If any of the questions stump you, reread the pages that give you the information you need.

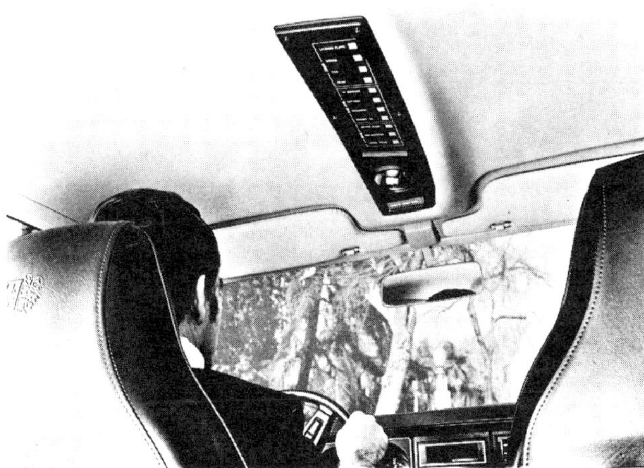

Fig. 35-12. Location of the sensor panel in the car. (*Toyota Motor Sales, Limited*)

Completing the Sentences The sentences that follow are incomplete. After each sentence there are several words or phrases, but only one of them correctly completes the sentence. Write each sentence in your notebook, ending it with the one word or phrase that completes it correctly.

1. You determine when the engine oil was last changed by: (*a*) asking the driver, (*b*) inspecting the oil, (*c*) looking at the door-jamb sticker.
2. A tuneup includes: (*a*) checking the air cleaner, spark plugs, and ignition system, (*b*) checking the manifold heat-control valve, PCV valve, and carburetor, (*c*) both (*a*) and (*b*).
3. If you have to replace one belt of a two-belt drive, you should: (*a*) tighten both belts to the tension of the new belt, (*b*) replace both belts, (*c*) check the pulleys to see what is wrong.
4. When the car is up on the lift, you should check the exhaust system for leaks that could cause: (*a*) carbon monoxide leaking into the car, (*b*) excess noise, (*c*) exhaust smoke.

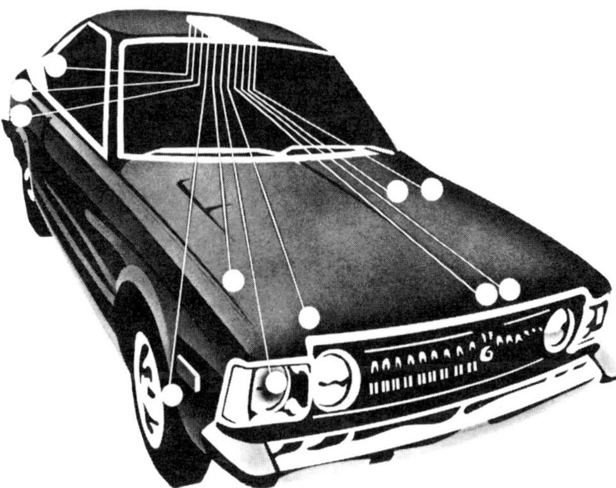

Fig. 35-13. Connections from the sensor panel to the 11 service areas. (*Toyota Motor Sales, Limited*)

1976 CADILLAC — COMPLETE VEHICLE MAINTENANCE SCHEDULE

When To Perform Services (Months or Miles whichever occurs first)	Item No.	Services (For Details, See Numbered Paragraphs)	Mileage When Service Is To Be Performed					
			7.5	15.0	22.5	30.0	37.5	45.0
Section A – Lubrication and General Maintenance								
Every 6 Months or 7,500 Miles	A-1	*Chassis Lubrication	X	X	X	X	X	X
	A-2	•*Fluid Levels Check	X	X	X	X	X	X
	A-3	*Engine Oil Change	X	X	X	X	X	X
At 1st Oil Chg. – Then Every 2nd	A-4	*Oil Filter Change	X		X		X	
See Explanation	A-5	Tire Rotation (Steel Belted Radial)	X		X		X	
	A-6	Rear Axle Lube Change						
Every 12 Months	A-7	Air Conditioning Check		yrly.		yrly.		yrly.
Every 12 Months or 15,000 Miles	A-8	*Cooling System Check		X		X		X
		*–Coolant Change				X		
See Explanation	A-9	Wheel Bearing Repack				X		
Every 30,000 Miles	A-10	Final Drive Boots & Seals Check (Eldorado)				X		
Every 100,000 Miles	A-11	*Auto. Trans. Fluid & Filter Change						
Section B – Safety Maintenance								
Every 6 Months or 7,500 Miles	B-1	Owner Safety Checks	X	X	X	X	X	X
	B-2	Tire, Wheel and Disc Brake Inspection	X	X	X	X	X	X
	B-3	*Exhaust System Check	X	X	X	X	X	X
	B-4	Suspension and Steering Check	X	X	X	X	X	X
	B-5	Brake and Power Steering Check	X	X	X	X	X	X
Every 12 Months or 15,000 Miles	B-6	*Drive Belt Check		X		X		X
	B-7	Drum Brake and Parking Brake Check		X		X		X
	B-8	Throttle Linkage Check		X		X		X
	B-9	Underbody Flush & Check		X		X		X
	B-10	Bumper Check		X		X		X
Section C – Emission Control Maintenance								
At First 6 Months or 7,500 Miles – Then at 18 Month/ 22,500 Mile Intervals as Indicated in Log	C-1	Air Cleaner Check	X		X			X
	C-2	Carburetor Choke (Except Fuel Injection)	X		X			X
	C-3	Engine Idle Speed Adjustments	X		X			X
	C-4	EFE System Check (Except Fuel Injection)	X		X			X
	C-5	Carburetor (Or Fuel Injection Throttle Body) Mounting Torque	X		X			X
	C-6	Vacuum Advance System & Hoses Check	X		X			X
Every 12 Months or 15,000 Miles	C-7	Fuel Filter Replacement		X		X		X
	C-8	PCV System Check & Filter Service		X		X		X
		– PCV Valve Replacement				X		
Every 18 Months or 22,500 Miles	C-9	Spark Plug Wires Check			X			X
Every 22,500 Miles	C-10	Spark Plug Replacement			X			X
	C-11	Engine Timing Adjustment & Dist. Check			X			X
Every 24 Months or 30,000 Miles	C-12	ECS System Check & Filter Replacement				X		
	C-13	Fuel Cap, Tank and Lines Check				X		
Every 30,000 Miles	C-14	Air Cleaner Element Replacement				X		

•Also A Safety Service *Also An Emission Control Service

Fig. 35-14. Complete vehicle maintenance schedule for a new car having the latest emission controls. (*Cadillac Motor Car Division of General Motors Corporation*)

5. A quick way to check the radiator hose is to: (*a*) squeeze the hose, (*b*) look under the car for coolant, (*c*) remove and inspect the hose.
6. As part of the tuneup procedure, you should: (*a*) clean and reinsulate the spark plugs, (*b*) clean, gap, and replace old plugs, (*c*) install all new plugs, (*d*) either (*b*) or (*c*).
7. If the vehicle is equipped with a fuel-vapor recovery system, you should: (*a*) replace the charcoal canister, (*b*) replace the canister filter, (*c*) replace the vapor-recovery valve.
8. To see how much the tuneup has reduced pollutants in the exhaust gases, many mechanics check for HC and CO: (*a*) after the tuneup is done, (*b*) before the tuneup is done, (*c*) both (*a*) and (*b*).

SUGGESTIONS FOR FURTHER STUDY

Make a collection of the printed tuneup forms supplied by automotive and test-equipment manufacturers (see Fig. 35-1). Note the similarities and differences among the forms. Keep in mind that some of these forms have a dual purpose: They not only list the checks to be made, but also list them in a way that can attract potential customers. That is, they are sales sheets also. This means that the checks may not be listed in the order in which they will actually be done. Rather, they are listed in a way that puts the most important items first.

Also, refer to automotive manufacturers' shop manuals, and make lists of the key steps in the tuneup procedures they recommend. Then compare these, to see what is common among them.

As you do all this, you will learn the basic steps in the tuneup procedure. And that is important information for any automotive tuneup technician to know.

GLOSSARY

This glossary of automotive terms used in the book provides a ready reference for the student. The definitions may differ somewhat from those given in a standard dictionary. They are not intended to be all-inclusive but to refresh the memory on automotive terms. More complete definitions and explanations of the terms are found in the text.

ABDC Abbreviation for *after bottom dead center;* any position of the piston between bottom dead center and top dead center, on the upward stroke.

accelerator A foot-operated pedal, linked to the throttle valve in the carburetor; used to control the flow of gasoline to the engine.

accelerator pump In the carburetor, a pump (linked to the accelerator) which momentarily enriches the air-fuel mixture when the accelerator is depressed at low speed.

A.C.I.D. Abbreviation for a four-mode driving-test cycle used to test exhaust emissions or vehicle driveability; the modes are accelerate, cruise, idle, and decelerate.

additive A substance added to gasoline or oil to improve some property of the gasoline or oil.

adsorb To collect in a thin layer on the surface of another material.

advance The moving ahead of the ignition spark in relation to piston position; produced by centrifugal or vacuum devices in accordance with engine speed and intake-manifold vacuum.

afterboil Boiling of fuel in the carburetor or coolant in the engine immediately after the engine is stopped.

A.I.R. Abbreviation for *air-injection reactor,* part of a system of exhaust-emission control. See **air-injection system.**

air bleed An opening into a gasoline passage through which air can pass, or bleed, into the gasoline as it moves through the passage.

air cleaner A device, mounted on or connected to the carburetor, for filtering dirt and dust out of air being drawn into the engine.

air filter A filter that removes dirt and dust particles from air passing through it.

air-fuel mixture The air and fuel traveling to the combustion chamber after being mixed by the carburetor.

air-fuel ratio The proportions of air and fuel (by weight) supplied for combustion.

air gap A small space between parts that are related magnetically, as in an alternator, or electrically, as the electrodes of a spark plug.

air horn In the carburetor, a tubular passage on the atmospheric side of the venturi through which the incoming air must pass, and which contains the choke valve.

air-injection system An exhaust-emission control system; injects air at low pressure into the exhaust manifold or thermal reactor to complete the combustion of unburned hydrocarbons and carbon monoxide in the exhaust gas.

air pollution Contamination of the air by natural and people-made pollutants.

air pump Any device for compressing air. In the air-injection system of exhaust-emission control, an engine-driven (belt-driven) pump incorporating a rotor and vanes.

alternating current Electric current flowing first in one direction and then in the opposite direction.

alternator In the vehicle electric system, a device that converts mechanical energy into electric energy for charging battery and operating electrical accessories. Also known as an ac **generator.**

ammeter A meter for measuring amount of current (in amperes) flowing through an electric circuit.

amperage the amount of current, in amperes.

ampere A unit of measure for current; one ampere corresponds to a flow of 6.28×10^{18} electrons per second.

antibackfire valve A valve used, in the air-injection system, to prevent backfiring in the exhaust system during deceleration.

antifreeze A chemical, usually ethylene glycol, that is added to the engine coolant to raise the coolant boiling point and lower its freezing point.

antiknock compound An additive put into gasoline to suppress spark knock or detonation—usually a lead compound (which becomes an air pollutant in engine exhaust, according to some authorities.)

arcing Name given to the spark that jumps the air gap between two electrical conductors; for example, the arcing of the distributor contact points.

armature A part moved by magnetism, or a part moved through a magnetic field to produce current.

ATDC Abbreviation for *after top dead center;* any position of the piston between top dead center and bottom dead center, on the downward stroke.

atmospheric pressure The weight of the atmosphere, per unit area. Atmospheric pressure at sea level is 14.7 psi absolute [1.03 kg/cm^2 (kilograms per square centimeter)]; it decreases as altitude increases.

atom The smallest particle into which an element can be divided.

atomization The spraying of a liquid through a nozzle so that the liquid is broken into a fine mist.

automotive air pollution Evaporated and unburned fuel and other undesirable by-products of combustion which escape from a motor vehicle into the atmosphere; mainly carbon monoxide (CO), hydrocarbons (HC), nitrogen oxides (NO_x), sulfur oxides (SO_x), and particulates.

backfiring Preexplosion of the air-fuel mixture so that the explosion passes back around the opened intake valve and through the intake manifold and carburetor. Also applied to the loud explosion of overly rich exhaust gas in the exhaust manifold which exits through the muffler and tail pipe with a loud popping or banging noise.

back pressure Pressure in the exhaust manifold of a running engine; affects volumetric efficiency.

balanced carburetor Carburetor in which the float bowl is vented into the air horn to compensate for the possible effects of a clogged air filter.

ballast resistor Same as **ignition resistor.**

barrel Term sometimes applied to the cylinders in an engine; used in referring to the number of throttle bores in a carburetor.

battery An electrochemical device for storing energy in chemical form so that it can be released as electricity; a group of electric cells connected together.

battery acid The electrolyte used in a battery, a mixture of sulfuric acid and water.

battery cell A battery element that is covered with electrolyte; a cell has a specific gravity of about 1.300 and a voltage of about 2 volts when fully charged.

battery charge Restoration of chemical energy to a battery by supplying a measured flow of electric current to it over a specified period of time.

BDC Abbreviation for **bottom dead center.**

bellows A device, usually metal, that can lengthen or shorten much like an accordion. Some cooling-system thermostats are of the bellows type.

Bendix drive A type of starting-motor drive which screws into mesh with the flywheel teeth as the starting-motor armature begins to turn. It demeshes automatically as the engine speed increases when the engine starts.

bhp Abbreviation for **brake horsepower.**

bimetal A thermostatic element made up of two metals with different heat expansion rates. Temperature changes produce a bending or distortion of the element.

Bloc-Chek A special measuring device that, when inserted in the radiator filler neck of a running engine, can detect leakage of exhaust gas into the cooling system.

blowby Leakage of compressed air-fuel mixture and burned gases (from combustion) past the piston rings into the crankcase.

boiling Conversion from the liquid to the vapor state, taking place throughout the liquid. The conversion is accompanied by bubbling as vapor rises from below the surface.

bore An engine cylinder, or any cylindrical hole. Also used to describe the process of enlarging or accurately refinishing a hole, as "to bore an engine cylinder." The bore size is the hole diameter.

bottom dead center The piston position at the lower limit of its travel in the cylinder, such that the cylinder volume is at its maximum.

brake horsepower Power delivered by the engine and available for driving the vehicle; bhp = torque × rpm/5,252.

breaker cam See **distributor cam.**

breakerless system An electronic ignition system which utilizes conventional breaker contacts to time and trigger the system; may be a conventional system or an electronic ignition system.

breather On engines without emission-control devices, the opening that allows air to circulate through the crankcase and thus produces crankcase ventilation.

brush A block of conducting substance, such as carbon, which rests against a rotating ring or commutator to form a continuous electric circuit.

BTDC Abbreviation for *before top dead center;* any position of the piston between bottom dead center and top dead center, on the upward stroke.

bulb An indivisible assembly which contains a source of light; normally used in a lamp.

bushing A one-piece sleeve placed in a bore as a bearing surface.

butterfly A type of valve used for the choke and throttle valve in a carburetor; a movable flat plate that governs the flow of air into the carburetor.

bypass A separate passage which permits a liquid, gas, or electric current to take a path other than that normally used.

cables Stranded conductors, usually covered with insulating material, used for connections between electrical devices.

cadmium-tip tester A battery tester with two cadmium tips which are inserted into the electrolyte of adjacent battery cells to determine cell voltage.

calibrate To check or correct the initial setting of a test instrument.

cam A rotating lobe or eccentric which can be used with a cam follower to change rotary motion to reciprocating motion.

cam angle See **dwell.**

camshaft The shaft in the engine which has a series of cams for operating the valve mechanisms. It is driven by gears or sprockets and a toothed belt or chain from the crankshaft.

canister A special container, in an evaporative control system, that contains charcoal to trap vapors from the fuel system.

capacitor See **condenser**

capacitor-discharge ignition system An ignition system which stores its primary energy in a capacitor; available for automobiles, but standard on some outboard engines and motorcycles.

carbon (C) A black deposit left on engine parts such as pistons, rings, and valves by the combustion of fuel, and which inhibits their action.

carbon dioxide (CO_2) A colorless, odorless gas resulting from complete combustion; usually considered harmless. The gas absorbed from air by plants in photosynthesis; used to carbonate beverages.

carbon monoxide (CO) A colorless, odorless, tasteless, poisonous gas which results from incomplete combustion. A pollutant contained in engine exhaust gas.

carbon pile A pile, or stack, of carbon disks enclosed in an insulating tube. When the disks are pressed together, the electrical resistance of the pile decreases.

carburetion The actions that take place in the carburetor: converting liquid fuel to vapor and mixing it with air to form a combustible mixture.

carburetor The device in an engine fuel system which mixes fuel with air and supplies the combustible mixture to the intake manifold.

carburetor heated air A system in which heated air, radiated from the exhaust manifold, is routed to the carburetor for more complete combustion and better engine performance with a leaner air-fuel mixture.

carburetor insulator A spacer, or insulator, used to prevent excess engine heat from reaching the carburetor.

catalyst A substance that can speed or slow a chemical reaction between substances, without itself being consumed by the reaction. In the catalytic converter, platinum and palladium are the active catalysts.

catalytic converter A mufflerlike device for use in an exhaust system; it converts harmful exhaust gases into harmless gases by promoting a chemical reaction between a catalyst and the pollutants.

cc Abbreviation for **cubic centimeter.**

cell Formed by suspending an element of unlike positive and negative plates in electrolyte in a compartment of a battery. The cell produces about 2 volts.

Celsius see **centigrade.**

centigrade A thermometer scale on which water boils at 100° and freezes at 0°. The formula $°C = \frac{5}{9}(°F - 32)$ converts Fahrenheit readings to centigrade (Celsius) readings.

centimeter (cm) A unit of linear measure in the metric system; equal to approximately 0.39 in.

centrifugal advance A rotating-weight mechanism in the distributor; advances and retards ignition timing through centrifugal force resulting from changes in engine distributor rotational speed.

cetane number An indicator of the ignition quality of diesel fuel. A high-cetane fuel ignites more easily (at a lower temperature) than a low-cetane fuel.

change of state Transformation of a substance from solid to liquid, from liquid to vapor, or vice versa.

charcoal canister A container filled with activated charcoal, used to trap gasoline vapor from the fuel tank and carburetor while the engine is off.

charging rate The amperage flowing from the alternator into the battery.

check To verify that a component, system, or measurement complies with specifications.

choke In the carburetor, a device used when starting a cold engine; it "chokes off" the air flow through the air horn, producing a partial vacuum in the air horn for greater fuel delivery and a richer mixture. Operates automatically on many newer cars.

choke plate In the carburetor, a valve that "chokes off" the air flow through the air horn, producing a partial vacuum in the carburetor for greater fuel delivery and a richer mixture.

CID Abbreviation for **cubic inch displacement.**

circuit The complete path of an electric current, including the current source. When the path is continuous, the circuit is closed and current flows. When the path is broken, the circuit is open and no current flows. Also used to refer to fluid paths, as in refrigerant and hydraulic systems.

circuit breaker A protective device that opens an electric circuit to prevent damage when overheated by excess current flow. One type contains a thermostatic blade that warps to open the circuit when the maximum safe current is exceeded.

closed-crankcase ventilation system A system in which the crankcase vapors (blowby gases) are discharged into the engine intake system and pass through to the engine cylinders rather than being discharged into the air.

CO See **carbon monoxide**

CO_2 See **carbon dioxide**

coil In an automobile ignition system, a transformer used to step up the battery voltage (by induction) to the high voltage required to fire the spark plugs.

cold-cranking rate A battery rating; the minimum amperage maintained by a battery for 30 seconds with a minimum voltage of 1.2 volts per cell, check at a battery temperature of 0°F [−17.8°C] and at −20°F [−28.9°C].

cold rate A battery rating; the number of minutes a battery will deliver 300A at 0°F [−17.8°C] before the cell voltage drops below 1.0 volt.

combustion Burning; fire produced by the proper combination of fuel, heat, and oxygen. In the engine, rapid burning of air-fuel mixture in the combustion chamber.

combustion chamber The space between the top of the piston and the cylinder head, in which the air-fuel mixture is burned.

commutation In a dc generator, the effect produced by the commutator and brushes, in which the alternating current developed in the armature windings is changed to direct current.

commutator A series of copper bars at one end of a generator or starting-motor armature, electrically insulated from the armature shaft and insulated from each other by mica. The brushes rub against the bars of the commutator, which form a rotating connector between the armature windings and brushes.

compound vortex-controlled combustion engine A type of stratified-charge engine built by Honda. See **Honda system.**

compression Reducing the volume of a gas by squeezing it into a smaller space. Increasing the pressure reduces the volume and increases the density and temperature of the gas.

compression ignition The ignition of fuel solely by the heat generated when air is compressed in the cylinder; the method of ignition in a diesel engine.

compression pressure The pressure in the combustion chamber at the end of the compression stroke.

compression ratio The volume of the cylinder and combustion chamber when the piston is at BDC, divided by the volume when the piston is at TDC.

compression stroke The piston movement from BDC to TDC immediately following the intake stroke, during which both the intake and exhaust valves are closed while the air-fuel mixture in the cylinder is compressed.

compression tester An instrument for testing the amount of pressure, or compression, developed in an engine cylinder during cranking.

condenser In the ignition system, a device that is also called a capacitor; connected across the contact points to reduce arcing by providing a storage place for electricity (electrons) as the contact points open. In an air-conditioning system, the radiatorlike heat exchanger in which refrigerant vapor loses heat and returns to the liquid state.

conductor Any material or substance that allows current or heat to flow easily.

constant-current charging A battery-charging method in which an unchanging amount of current is made to flow into the battery.

constant-voltage charging A charging method in which a constant voltage is applied to the battery. The charging current decreases as the battery approaches the charged condition.

contact points In the conventional ignition system, the stationary and the movable points in the distributor which open and close the ignition primary circuit.

controlled-combustion system An exhaust-emission control system used by General Motors; regulates engine combustion efficiency through special settings of the carburetor, distributor, and vacuum advance, by heating the carburetor intake air, and with a higher engine operating temperature. Also known as the engine modification system, and used by other manufacturers under other names.

coolant The liquid mixture of about 50 percent antifreeze and 50 percent water used to carry heat out of the engine.

cooling system The system that removes heat from the engine by the forced circulation of coolant, and thereby prevents engine overheating. It includes the water jackets, water pump, radiator, and thermostat.

crankcase dilution Dilution of the lubricating oil in the oil pan; caused by liquid gasoline condensing from the blowby in a cold engine and seeping down the cylinder walls.

crankcase ventilation The circulation of air through the crankcase of a running engine to remove water, blowby, and other vapors; prevents oil dilution, contamination, sludge formation, and pressure buildup.

cranking motor See **starting motor.**

cross-firing Jumping of a high-voltage surge in the ignition secondary circuit to the wrong high-voltage lead, so that the wrong spark plug fires. Usually caused by improper routing of the spark-plug wires, faulty insulation, or a defective distributor cap or rotor.

cross-flow radiator A radiator in which the coolant flows horizontally from the input tank on one side of the radiator, through the individual coolant passages, to the output tank on the opposite side of the radiator.

cubic centimeter (cucm or cc) A unit of volume in the metric system; equal to approximately 0.061 in^3.

cubic inch displacement The cylinder volume swept out by the pistons of an engine as they move from BDC to TDC, measured in cubic inches.

current A flow of electrons, measured in amperes.

cut out In a running engine, to miss momentarily but not stall.

cutout relay A device in the charging circuit between the generator and battery; closes when the generator charges the battery, and opens when the generator stops.

CVCC See **compound vortexcontrolled combustion;** also, **Honda system.**

cycle Any series of events which repeat continuously. In the engine, the four (or two) piston strokes that together produce the power.

cylinder A circular tubelike opening in an engine cylinder block or casting in which a piston moves up and down.

cylinder leakage tester A testing device that forces compressed air into the cylinder through the spark-plug hole, when the valves are closed and the piston is at TDC on the compression stroke. The percentage of compressed air that leaks out is measured, and the source of the leak accurately pinpoints the defective part.

dashpot A device on the carburetor that prevents the throttle valve from closing too suddenly.

DC or dc Abbreviation for **direct current.**

deceleration A decrease in velocity or speed. Also, allowing the car or engine to coast to idle speed from a higher speed with the accelerator at or near the idle position.

Delco Eye A type of battery vent cap that shows a low electrolyte level in the cell without being removed from the battery.

detergent A chemical added to engine oil; helps keep internal parts of the engine clean by preventing the accumulation of deposits.

detonation Commonly referred to as spark knock or **ping.** In the combustion chamber, an uncontrolled second explosion (after the spark occurs at the spark plug) with spontaneous combustion of the remaining compressed air-fuel mixture, resulting in a pinging noise.

diagnosis A procedure followed in locating the cause of a malfunction.

diaphragm A thin dividing sheet or partition which separates an area into compartments; used in fuel pumps, modulator valves, vacuum-advance units, and other control devices.

diesel cycle An engine operating cycle in which air is compressed, and fuel oil is injected into the compressed air at the end of the compression stroke. The heat produced by the compression ignites the fuel oil, eliminating the need for spark plugs or a separate ignition system.

dieseling A condition in which an automobile engine continues to run after the ignition is off. Caused by carbon deposits or hot spots in the combustion chamber growing sufficiently to furnish heat for combustion.

dimmer switch A two-position switch, usually mounted on the car floor; operated by driver to select high or low headlight beam.

diode A solid-state electronic device which allows the passage of an electric current in one direction only. Used in the alternator to convert alternating current to direct current for charging battery.

direct current Electric current that flows in one direction only.

directional signal A device on the car that flashes lights to indicate the direction in which the driver intends to turn.

dispersant A chemical added to oil to prevent dirt and impurities from clinging together in lumps that could clog the engine lubricating system.

displacement In an engine, the total volume of air-fuel mixture an engine is theoretically capable of drawing into all cylinders during one operating cycle. Also, the volume swept out by the piston in moving from one end of a stroke to the other.

distributor Any device that distributes. In the ignition system, the rotary switch that directs high-voltage surges to the engine cylinders in the proper sequence. See **ignition distributor.**

distributor cam The cam on the top end of the distributor shaft which rotates to open and close the contact points.

distributor advance See **centrifugal advance, ignition advance,** and **vacuum advance.**

distributorless ignition An electronic ignition system which does not utilize breaker contacts to time or trigger the system, and does not utilize a distributor for distribution of the secondary voltage. One type is crankshaft-triggered.

distributor plate The plate in the ignition distributor that is fastened to the distributor housing and does not move.

distributor timing See **ignition timing.**

diverter valve In the air-injection system of exhaust-emission control, a valve that diverts air-pump output into the air cleaner or the atmosphere during deceleration; prevents backfiring and popping in the exhaust system.

DOHC See **double-overhead-camshaft engine.**

double-overhead-camshaft (DOHC) engine An engine with two camshafts in each cylinder head to actuate the valves; one camshaft operates the intake valves, and the other operates the exhaust valves.

downdraft carburetor A carburetor in which the air horn is so arranged that air passes down through it on its way to the intake manifold.

down-flow radiator A radiator in which coolant enters the radiator at the top, and loses heat as it flows down through passages to the bottom of the radiator.

driveability The general operation of an automobile, usually rated from good to poor; based on characteristics of concern to the average driver, such as smoothness of idle, even acceleration, ease of starting, quick warmup, and tendency to overheat at idle.

dry-charged battery A new battery that has been charged, and then stored with the electrolyte removed. Electrolyte must be added to activate the battery at the time of sale.

dual carburetors Two carburetors mounted on one engine.

dual-diaphragm advance A vacuum-advance mechanism with two diaphragms; attaches to the engine distributor to control spark timing. One diaphragm provides normal ignition timing advance for starting and acceleration; the other diaphragm retards the spark during idling and part-throttle operation.

dual-point system A system that controls spark timing by electromechanical selection of separate advance and retard distributor points; used on Chevrolet LUV light trucks. Sometimes used to refer to any ignition system which has two sets of contact points in the distributor.

duct A tube or channel used to convey air or liquid from one point to another. In emission systems, a tube on an air cleaner that has a vacuum motor mounted on it to help regulate the temperature of the carburetor intake air.

dwell The number of degrees the distributor shaft or cam rotates while the distributor points are closed.

dwell meter A precision electrical instrument used to measure the cam or dwell or number of degrees the distributor points are closed while engine is running.

dynamometer A device for measuring the power output, or brake horsepower, of an engine. An engine dynamometer measures the power output at the flywheel; a chassis dynamometer measures power output at the drive wheels.

efficiency The ratio between the power of an effect and the power expended to produce the effect; the ratio between an actual result and the theoretically possible result.

EGR system Abbreviation for **exhaust-gas recirculation system.**

electric-assist choke A choke in which a small electric heating element warms the choke spring, causing it to release more quickly. This reduces exhaust emissions during the startup of a cold engine.

electric current A movement of electrons through a conductor such as a copper wire; measured in amperes.

electric system In the automobile, the system that electrically cranks the engine for starting; furnishes high-voltage sparks to the engine cylinders to fire the compressed air-fuel charges; lights the lights; and powers the heater motor, radio, and other accessories. Consists, in part, of the starting motor, wiring, battery, alternator, regulator, ignition distributor, and ignition coil.

electrode In a spark plug, the spark jumps between two electrodes. The wire passing through the insulator is the center electrode. The small piece of metal welded to the spark-plug shell (and to which the spark jumps) is the side, or ground, electrode.

electrolyte The mixture of sulfuric acid and water used in lead-acid storage batteries. The acid enters into chemical reaction with active material in the plates to produce voltage and current.

electromagnet A coil of wire (usually around an iron core) which produces magnetism as electric current passes through it.

electromagnetic induction The characteristic of a magnetic field that causes an electric current to be created in a conductor if it passes through the field, or if the field builds and collapses around the conductor.

electron A negatively charged particle that circles the nucleus of an atom. The movement of electrons is an electric current.

electronic fuel-injection system A system that injects gasoline into a spark-ignition engine, and that includes an electronic control to time and meter the fuel flow.

electronic ignition system A transistorized ignition system which does not have mechanical contact points in the distributor, but uses the distributor for distributing the secondary voltage to the spark plugs. Also called a *solid-state* ignition system.

electronic spark control A system that controls the vacuum to the distributor, preventing vacuum advance below a selected speed; generally used by Ford on cars with automatic transmission.

emission control Any device or modification added onto or designed into a motor vehicle for the purpose of reducing air-polluting emissions.

energy The capacity or ability to do work. Usually measured in work units of pound-feet [kilogram-meters], but also expressed in heat-energy units (Btus [joules]).

engine A machine that converts heat energy into mechanical energy. A device that burns fuel to produce mechanical power; sometimes referred to as a *power plant*.

engine tune-up A procedure for inspecting, testing, and adjusting an engine, and replacing any worn parts, to restore the engine to its best performance.

ethyl See **tetraethyl lead.**

ethylene glycol Chemical name of a type of permanent antifreeze.

evaporation control system A system which prevents the escape of gasoline vapors from the fuel tank or carburetor to the atmosphere while the engine is off. The vapors are stored in a charcoal canister or in the engine crankcase until the engine is started.

exhaust emissions Pollutants emitted into the atmosphere through any opening downstream of the exhaust ports of an engine.

exhaust-gas analyzer A device for sensing the amounts of air pollutants in the exhaust gas of a motor vehicle. The analyzers used in automotive shops check HC and CO; those used in testing laboratories can also check NO_x.

exhaust-gas recirculation system An NO_x control system that recycles a small part of the inert exhaust gas back through the intake manifold at all throttle positions except idle and wide open, to lower the combustion temperature.

exhaust manifold A device with several passages through which exhaust gases leave the engine combustion chambers and enter the exhaust piping system.

exhaust pipe The pipe connecting the exhaust manifold with the muffler.

exhaust stroke The piston stroke (from BDC to TDC) immediately following the power stroke, during which the exhaust valve opens so that the exhaust gases can escape from the cylinder to the exhaust manifold

exhaust system The system through which exhaust gases leave the vehicle. Consists of the exhaust manifold, exhaust pipe, muffler, tail pipe, and resonator (if used).

exhaust valve The valve that opens during the exhaust stroke to allow burned gases to flow from cylinder to exhaust manifold.

fan The bladed device on the front of the engine that rotates to draw cooling air through the radiator, or around the engine cylinders; an air blower such as the heater fan and the A/C blower.

fast-idle cam A mechanism on the carburetor, connected to the automatic choke, that holds the throttle valve slightly open when the engine is cold; causes the engine to idle at a higher rpm as long as the choke is applied.

field coil A coil, or winding, in a generator or starting motor which produces a magnetic field as current passes through it.

field-frame assembly The round, soft-iron frame in a generator or motor into which the field coils are assembled.

field relay A relay that is part of some alternator charging systems; connects the alternator field to the battery when the engine runs, and disconnects it when the engine stops.

field winding See **field coil.**

filter A device through which air, gases, or liquids are passed to remove impurities.

fins On a radiator or heat exchanger, thin metal projections over which cooling air flows to remove heat from hot liquid flowing through internal passages. On an air-cooled engine, thin metal projections on the cylinder and head which greatly increase the area of the heat-radiating surfaces and help cool the engine.

firing line The high-voltage vertical spike, or line, that appears on the oscilloscope pattern of the ignition-system secondary circuit. The firing line shows when the spark plug begins to fire. It also shows the voltage required to fire it.

firing order The order in which the engine cylinders fire, or deliver their power strokes, beginning with No. 1 cylinder.

flasher An automatic-reset circuit breaker used in directional-signal and emergency-signal circuits.

flat spot Lack of normal acceleration or response to throttle opening; implies no loss of power but also no increase in power.

float bowl In a carburetor, the reservoir from which gasoline is metered into the passing air.

float level The float position at which the needle valve closes the fuel inlet to the carburetor, to prevent further delivery of fuel.

float system In the carburetor, the system that controls the entry of fuel and the fuel level in the float bowl.

flooded Term used to indicate that the engine cylinders received "raw" or liquid gasoline, or an air-fuel mixture too rich to burn.

fluid Any liquid or gas

force Any push or pull exerted on an object; measured in units of weight, such as pounds, ounces, kilograms, or grams.

four-barrel carburetor A carburetor with four throttle valves. In effect, two two-barrel carburetors in a single assembly.

four-cycle See **four-stroke cycle.**

four-stroke cycle The four piston strokes—intake, compression, power, and exhaust—that make up the complete cycle of events in the four-stroke-cycle engine. Also called *four-cycle* and *four-stroke*.

421 tester A tester for batteries with a one-piece cover; applies timed discharge-charge cycles to battery to determine its condition.

friction The resistance to motion between two bodies in contact with each other.

fuel Any combustible substance. In an automobile engine, the fuel (gasoline) is burned, and the heat of combustion expands the resulting gases, which force the piston downward and rotate the crankshaft.

fuel filter A device located in the fuel line, ahead of the float bowl; removes dirt and other contaminants from fuel passing through.

fuel gauge A gauge that indicates the amount of fuel in the fuel tank.

fuel-injection system A system which delivers fuel under pressure into the combustion chamber, or into the air flow just as it enters each individual cylinder. Replaces the conventional carburetor.

fuel line The pipe or tubes through which fuel flows from the fuel tank to the carburetor.

fuel nozzle The tube in the carburetor through which gasoline feeds from the float bowl into the passing air. In a fuel-injection system, the tube that delivers the fuel into the compressed air or the passing air stream.

fuel pump The electrical or mechanical device in the fuel system which forces fuel from the fuel tank to the carburetor.

fuel system In an automobile, the system that delivers the combustible mixture of vaporized fuel and air to the engine cylinders. Consists of the fuel tank and lines, gauge, fuel pump, carburetor, and intake manifold.

fuel tank The storage tank for fuel on the vehicle.

full-flow filter Type of oil filter designed so that all the oil from the oil pump flows through it.

full throttle Wide-open throttle position, with the accelerator pressed all the way down to the floorboard.

fuse A device designed to open an electric circuit when the current is excessive, to protect equipment in the circuit. An open, or "blown," fuse must be replaced after the circuit problem is corrected.

fuse block A boxlike unit that holds the fuses for the various electric circuits in an automobile.

fusible link A type of fuse in which a special wire melts to open the circuit when the current is excessive. An open or "blown" fusible link must be replaced after the circuit problem is corrected.

gap The air space between two electrodes, as the spark-plug gap or the contact-point gap.

gas A state of matter in which the matter has neither a definite shape nor a definite volume; air is a mixture of several gases. In an automobile, the discharge from the tail pipe is called the *exhaust gas*. Also, gas is a slang expression for the liquid fuel, gasoline.

gasket A layer of material, usually made of cork or metal or both, that is placed between two machined surfaces to provide a tight seal between them.

gasoline A liquid blend of hydrocarbons, obtained from crude oil; used as the fuel in most automobile engines.

gassing Hydrogen gas escaping from a battery; the gas is formed during battery charging.

gauge pressure A pressure read on a scale which ignores atmospheric pressure. Thus, the atmospheric pressure of 14.7 psi absolute is equivalent to 0 psi gauge.

generator A device that converts mechanical energy into electrical energy; can produce either ac or dc electricity. In automotive usage, a dc generator (now seldom used).

grommet A device, usually made of hard rubber or a like material, used to encircle or support a component. In emission systems, a grommet is located in the valve-cover assembly to support and help seal the PCV valve.

grounding Connection of an electric unit to the vehicle engine or frame to provide a return path for electric current.

ground-return system Common system of electric wiring in which the chassis and frame of a vehicle are used as part of the electric return circuit to the battery or alternator; also known as the *single-wire system*.

growler An electrical test instrument for checking starting motors and generator armatures.

Guide-Matic An electronic device that automatically controls the headlights, shifting between upper and lower beams as conditions require.

gulp valve In the air-injection system, a type of antibackfire valve which allows a sudden intake of fresh air through the intake manifold during deceleration; prevents backfiring and popping in the exhaust system.

hazard system Also called the *emergency signal system;* a driver-controlled system of flashing front and rear lights, used to warn approaching motorists when a car has broken down.

HC abbreviation for **hydrocarbon.**

headlights Lights at the front of a vehicle; designed to illuminate the road ahead of the vehicle.

heat A form of energy; released by the burning of fuel. In an engine, heat energy is converted to mechanical energy.

heat-control valve In the engine, a thermostatically operating temperature.

heat of compression Increase of temperature brought about by the compression of air or air-fuel mixture.

heat sink A device for absorbing heat from one medium and transferring it to another. The diodes in alternators are usually mounted in heat sinks which remove the heat from the diodes and thus prevent them from overheating.

HEI See **high-energy ignition (HEI) system.**

hesitation Momentary pause in the rate of acceleration; momentary lack of throttle response at some car speed other than acceleration from a standing start.

high-compression Term used to refer to the increased compression ratios of modern automotive engines, as compared to engines built in the past.

high-discharge test A battery test in which the battery is discharged at a high rate while the cell voltages are checked.

high-energy ignition system A General Motors electronic ignition system without contact points, and with all ignition-system components contained in the distributor. Capable of producing 35,000 volts.

high-speed system In the carburetor, the system that supplies fuel to the engine at speeds above about 25 mph [40 km/h]. Also called the *main metering system*.

high-voltage cables The secondary (or spark-plug) cables or wires that carry high voltage from the ignition coil to the spark plugs.

Honda system A type of controlled-combustion system for spark-ignition engines. Has a small chamber that surrounds the spark-plug electrodes with a rich mixture; once the rich mixture ignites, it enters the main chamber, igniting the leaner air-fuel mixture in that chamber.

horn An electrical noise-making device on a vehicle; used for signaling.

horn relay A relay connected between the battery and the horns. When the horn button is pressed, the relay is energized; it then connects the horns to the battery.

horsepower A measure of mechanical power, or the rate at which work is done. One horsepower equals 33,000 ft-lb (foot-pounds) of work per minute; it is the power necessary to raise 33,000 lb a distance of 1 ft in 1 minute.

Hydrocarbon (HC) An organic compound containing only carbon and hydrogen, usually derived from fossil fuels such as petroleum, natural gas, and coal; an agent in the formation of photochemical smog. Gasoline is a blend of liquid hydrocarbons refined from crude oil.

hydrometer A device used to measure specific gravity. In automotive servicing, a device used to measure the specific gravity of battery electrolyte to determine the state of the battery charge; also a device used to measure the specific gravity of coolant to determine its feezing temperature.

IC See **internal combustion engine.**

idle Engine speed when the accelerator pedal is fully released, and there is no load on the engine.

idle limiter A device that controls the maximum richness of the idle air-fuel mixture in the carburetor; also aids in preventing overly rich idle adjustments. Limiters are of two types: the external plastic-cap type, installed on the head of the idle-mixture adjustment screw, and the internal-needle type, located in the idle passages of the carburetor.

idle-limiter cap A plastic cap placed over the head of the idle-mixture adjustment screw, to limit its travel and prevent the idle mixture from being set too rich.

idle mixture The air-fuel mixture supplied to the engine during idling.

idle-mixture adjustment screw The adjustment screw (on some carburetors) that can be turned in or out to lean out or enrich the idle mixture.

idle port The opening into the throttle body through which the idle system in the carburetor discharges fuel.

idle speed The speed, or rpm, at which the engine runs without load when the accelerator pedal is released.

idle-stop solenoid An electrically operated two-position plunger used to provide a predetermined throttle setting at idle.

idle system In the carburetor, the passages through which fuel is fed when the engine is idling.

ignition The action of the spark in starting the burning of the compressed air-fuel mixture in the combustion chamber.

ignition advance The moving forward, in time, of the ignition spark relative to the piston position. TDC or 1° ATDC is considered advanced as compared to 2° ATDC.

ignition coil The ignition-system component that acts as a transformer to step up (increase) the battery voltage to many thousands of volts; the high-voltage surge from the coil is transmitted to the spark plug to ignite the compressed air-fuel mixture.

ignition distributor The ignition-system component that closes and opens the primary circuit to the ignition coil at the proper times and distributes the resulting high-voltage surges from the ignition coil to the proper spark plugs.

ignition resistor A resistance connected into the ignition primary circuit to reduce the battery voltage to the coil during engine operation.

ignition retard The moving back, in time, of the ignition spark relative to the piston position. TDC or 1° BTDC is considered retarded as compared to 2° BTDC.

ignition switch The switch in the ignition system (usually operated with a key) that opens and closes the ignition-coil primary circuit. May also be used to open and close other vehicle electric circuits.

ignition system In the automobile, the system that furnishes high-voltage sparks to the engine cylinders to fire the compressed air-fuel mixture. Consists of the battery, ignition coil, ignition distributor, ignition switch, wiring, and spark plugs.

ignition timing The delivery of the spark from the coil to the spark plug at the proper time for the power stroke, relative to the piston position.

I-head engine An overhead-valve (OHV) engine; an engine with the valves in the cylinder head.

IMCO Abbreviation for *improved combustion system,* an exhaust-emission control system used by Ford and comprised mainly of carburetor and distributor modifications. See also **controlled-combustion system.**

indicator A device used to make some condition known by use of a light or a dial and pointer; for example, the temperature indicator or oil-pressure indicator.

induction The action of producing a voltage in a conductor or coil by moving the conductor or coil through a magnetic field, or by moving the field past the conductor or coil.

inductive-type semiconductor ignition system An ignition system in which the primary energy is stored in an inductor or coil. This is the type now used in Chrysler, Ford, and General Motors HEI systems.

infrared analyzer A nondispersive test instrument used to measure very small quantities of pollutants in exhaust gas. See **exhaust-gas analyzer.**

injector The tube or nozzle through which fuel is injected into the intake airstream or the combustion chamber. Also, a performance term used for an engine equipped with fuel injection.

insulated-return system System of vehicle electrical wiring in which a separate insulated wire is used to provide the electric return circuit to the battery or alternator; also known as the *two-wire system.*

insulation Material that stops the travel of electricity (electrical insulation) or heat (heat insulation).

insulator A poor conductor of electricity or of heat.

intake manifold A device with several passages through which the air-fuel mixture flows from the carburetor to the ports in the cylinder head or cylinder block.

intake stroke The piston stroke from TDC to BDC immediately following the exhaust stroke, during which the intake valve opens and the cylinder fills with air-fuel mixure from the intake manifold.

international-combustion (IC) engine An engine in which the fuel is burned inside the engine itself, rather than in a separate device (as is the case for a steam engine).

jet A calibrated passage, in the carburetor, through which fuel flows.

kilogram (kg) In the metric system, a unit of weight and mass; approximately equal to 2.2 lb.

kilometer (km) In the metric system, a unit of linear measure; equal to 0.621 mi.

kilowatt (kW) A unit of power, equal to about 1.34 hp.

knock A heavy metallic engine sound which varies with engine speed; usually caused by a loose or worn bearing. Name also used for detonation, pinging, and spark knock. See **detonation.**

kW Abbreviation for **kilowatt.**

laminated Made up of several thin sheets or layers.

lamp A divisible assembly that provides light; contains a bulb or other light source and sometimes a lens and reflector.

lead (pronounced *leed*) A cable or conductor to carry electrical current. A heavy metal; used in lead-acid storage batteries.

leaded gasoline Gasoline to which small amounts of tetraethyl lead are added to improve engine performance and reduce detonation.

lean mixture An air-fuel mixture that has a relatively high proportion of air and a relatively low proportion of fuel. An air-fuel ratio of 16:1 indicates a lean mixture, compared to an air-fuel ratio of 13:1.

light A gas-filled bulb enclosing a wire that glows brightly when an electric current passes through it; a lamp. Also, any visible radiant energy.

lines of force See **magnetic lines of force.**

linkage An assembly of rods, or links, used to transmit motion.

liquefied petroleum gas (LPG) A hydrocarbon suitable for use as an engine fuel, obtained from petroleum and natural gas; a vapor at atmospheric pressure but becomes a liquid under sufficient pressure. Butane and propane are the liquefied gases most frequently used in automotive engines.

liquid-cooled engine An engine that is cooled by the circulation of liquid coolant around the cylinders.

liter (1) In the metric system, a measure of volume; approximately equal to 0.26 gal (U.S.), or about 61 in^3. Used as a metric measure of engine-cylinder displacement.

loading An enrichment of the air-fuel mixture to the point of rough engine idle; sometimes causes missing and is usually accompanied by the emission of black smoke from the tail pipe.

load test A starting-motor test in which the current draw is measured under normal cranking load.

lobe A projecting part; for example, the rotor lobe or the cam lobe.

low-lead fuel Gasoline which is low in tetraethyl lead, containing no more than 0.5 g per gallon.

low-speed system The system in the carburetor that supplies fuel to the air passing through during low-speed, part-throttle operation.

lubricating system The system in the engine that supplies engine parts with lubricating oil to prevent actual contact between any two moving metal surfaces.

lugging Low-speed, full-throttle engine operation in which the engine is heavily loaded and overworked; usually caused by failure of the driver to shift to a lower gear when necessary.

magnetic Having the ability to attract iron. This ability may be permanent, or it may depend on a current flow, as in an electromagnet.

magnetic field The area (or field) of influence of a magnet, within which it will exhibit magnetic properties; extends from the "north" pole of the magnet to its "south" pole. The strength of the field of an electromagnet increases with the number of turns of wire around the iron core and the current flow through the wire.

magnetic lines of force The imaginary lines by which a magnetic field may be visualized.

magnetic pole The point where magnetic lines of force enter or leave a magnet.

magnetic switch A switch with a winding (a coil of water); when the winding is energized, the switch is moved to open or close a circuit.

magnetism The ability, either natural or produced by a flow of electric current, to attract iron.

magneto An engine-driven device that generates its own primary current, transforms that current into high-voltage surges, and delivers them to the proper spark plugs.

main jet The fuel nozzle, or jet, in the carburetor that supplies fuel when the throttle is partially to fully open.

malfunction Improper or incorrect operation.

manifold vacuum The vacuum in the intake manifold that develops as a result of the vacuum in the cylinders on their intake strokes.

meter (m) A unit of linear measure in the metric system, equal to 39.37 inches. Also, the name given to any test instrument that measures a property of a substance passing through it, as an ammeter measures electric current. Also, any device that measures and controls the flow of a substance passing through it, as a carburetor jet meters fuel flow.

metering rod and jet A device consisting of a small, movable, cone-shaped rod and a jet; increases or decreases fuel flow according to engine throttle opening, engine load, or a combination of both.

mica An insulating material used to separate the copper bars of commutators.

millimeter (mm) In the metric system, a unit of linear measure, approximately equal to 0.039 inches.

misfire In the engine, a failure to ignite the air-fuel mixture in one or more cylinders. This condition may be intermittent or continuous in one or more cylinders.

miss See **misfire.**

mode Term used to designate a particular set of operating characteristics.

monolithic Made as a single unit. In catalytic-converter construction, a substrate or supporting structure for the catalyst, made as a single unit (usually in the shape of a honeycomb), is monolithic; however, the coated-bead or pellet-type catalytic converter is not.

monolithic timing Making accurate spark-timing adjustments with an electronic timing device which can be used with the engine running.

motor A device that converts electric energy into mechanical energy; for example, the starting motor.

Motor Octane Number (MON) Laboratory octane rating of a fuel-established on single-cylinder, variable-compression-ratio engines.

mph Abbreviation for *miles per hour*, a unit of speed.

multiple-viscosity oil An engine oil which has a low viscosity when cold (for easier cranking) and a higher viscosity when hot (to provide adequate engine lubrication).

mutual induction The condition in which a voltage is induced in one coil by a changing magnetic field caused by a changing current in another coil. The magnitude of the induced voltage depends on the number of turns in the two coils.

negative One of the two poles of a magnet, or one of the two terminals of an electrical device.

negative terminal The terminal from which electrons flow in a complete electric circuit. On a battery, the negative terminal can be identified as the battery post with the smaller diameter; the minus sign (−) is often also used to identify the negative terminal.

neoprene A synthetic rubber that is not affected by the various chemicals that are harmful to natural rubber.

neutral-start switch A switch wired into the ignition switch to prevent engine cranking unless the transmission shift lever is in NEUTRAL.

nitrogen oxides (NO_x) Any chemical compound of nitrogen and oxygen. Nitrogen oxides result from high temperature and pressure in the combustion chambers of automobile engines and other power plants during the combustion process. When combined with hydrocarbons in the presence of sunlight, nitrogen oxides form smog. A basic air pollutant; automotive exhaust-emission levels of nitrogen oxides are controlled by law.

no-load test A starting-motor test in which the starting motor is operated without load, and the current draw and armature speed at specified voltages are noted.

nonconductor Same as **insulator.**

nonleaded gasoline See **unleaded gasoline.**

north pole The pole from which the lines of force leave a magnet.

NO_x Abbreviation for any **nitrogen oxides.**

NO_x control system Any device or system used to reduce the amount of NO_x produced by an engine.

nozzle The opening, or jet, through which fuel passes when it is discharged into the carburetor venturi.

octane number The number used to indicate octane rating of gasoline.

octane rating A measure of the antiknock properties of gasoline. The higher the octane rating, the more resistant the gasoline is to spark knock or detonation.

ohm The unit of electrical resistance.

ohmmeter An instrument used to measure electrical resistance.

OHV See **overhead-valve engine.**

oil A liquid lubricant; made from crude oil and used to provide lubrication between moving parts. In a diesel engine, oil is used for fuel.

oil dilution Thinning of oil in the crankcase; caused by liquid gasoline leaking past the piston rings from the combustion chamber.

oil filter A filter which removes impurities from crankcase oil passing through it.

oil-level indicator The indicator that is removed and inspected to check the level of oil in the crankcase of an engine or compressor. Usually called the *dipstick*.

oil-pressure indicator A gauge that indicates (to the driver) the oil pressure in the engine lubricating system.

oil seal and shield Two devices used to control oil leakage past the valve stem and guide, and into the ports or the combustion chamber of an engine.

one-wire system On automobiles, use of the car body, engine, and frame as a path for the grounded side of the electric circuits; eliminates the need for a second wire as a return path to the battery or alternator.

open circuit In an electric circuit, a break, or opening, which prevents the passage of current.

open system A crankcase emission-control system which draws air through the oil-filter cap, and does not include a tube from the crankcase to the air cleaner.

orifice A small opening, or hole, into a cavity.

orifice spark-advance control A system used on some engines to aid in the control of NO_x. Consists of a valve which delays the change in vacuum to the distributor vacuum-advance unit between idle and part throttle.

o ring A type of sealing ring, made of a special rubberlike material; in use, the O ring is compressed into a groove to provide the sealing action.

oscilloscope A high-speed voltmeter which visually displays voltage variations on a television-type picture tube. Widely used to check engine ignition systems; can also be used to check charging systems and electronic fuel-injection systems.

overcharging Continued charging of a battery after it has reached the charged condition. This action damages the battery and shortens its life.

overhead-camshaft (OHC) engine An engine in which the camshaft is mounted over the cylinder head, instead of inside the cylinder block.

overhead-valve (OHV) engine An engine in which the valves are mounted in the cylinder head above the combustion chamber, instead of in the cylinder block; in this type of engine, the camshaft is usually mounted in the cylinder block, and the valves are actuated by pushrods.

overheat To heat excessively; also, to become excessively hot.

overrunning clutch drive A type of clutch drive which transmits rotary motion in one direction only; when rotary motion attempts to pass through in the other direction, the then driving member overruns and does not pass the motion to the other member. Widely used as the drive mechanism for starting motors.

parade pattern An oscilloscope pattern showing the ignition voltages on one line, from left to right across the scope screen in engine firing order.

parallel circuit The electric circuit formed when two or more electrical devices have their terminals connected together, positive to positive and negative to negative, so that each may operate independently of the others, from the same power source.

passage A small hole or gallery in an assembly or casting, through which air, coolant, fuel, or oil flows.

PCV Abbreviation for **positive crankcase ventilation.**

PCV valve The valve that controls the flow of crankcase vapors in accordance with ventilation requirements for different engine speeds and loads.

percolation The condition in which a bowl vent fails to open when the engine is turned off, and pressure in the fuel bowl forces raw fuel through the main jets into the manifold.

permanent magnet A piece of steel that retains its magnetism without the use of an electric current to create a magnetic field.

petroleum The crude oil from which gasoline, lubricating oil, and other such products are refined.

photochemical smog Smog caused by hydrocarbons and nitrogen oxides reacting photochemically in the atmosphere. The reactions take place under low wind velocity, bright sunlight, and an inversion layer in which the air mass is trapped (as between the ocean and mountains in Los Angeles). Can cause eye and lung irritation.

pickup coil In an electronic ignition system, the coil in which voltage is induced by the reluctor.

ping Engine "knock" that occurs only during accerleration. Usually associated with medium to heavy throttle acceleration or lugging at relatively low speeds, especially with a manual transmission. However, it may occur in higher speed ranges under heavy-load conditions. Caused by too much advance of ignition timing or low-octane fuel.

piston A movable part, fitted to a cylinder, which can receive or transmit motion as a result of pressure changes in a fluid. In the engine, the cylindrical part that moves up and down within a cylinder as the crankshaft rotates.

piston displacement The cylinder volume displaced by the piston as it moves from the bottom to the top of the cylinder during one complete stroke.

plate In a battery, a rectangular sheet of spongy lead. Sulfuric acid in the electrolyte chemically reacts with the lead to produce an electric current.

polarity The quality of an electrical component or circuit that determines the direction of current flow.

polarizing a generator Correcting the generator field polarity so the generator will build up polarity in the proper direction to charge the battery.

pole See **magnetic pole.**

pole shoe The curved metal shoe around which a field coil is placed.

pollutant Any substance that adds to the pollution of the atmosphere. In a vehicle, any such substance in the exhaust gas from the engine, or evaporating from the fuel tank or carburetor.

pollution Any gas or substance, in the air, which makes it less fit to breathe. Also, noise pollution is the name applied to excessive noise from machinery or vehicles.

polyurethane A synthetic substance used in filtration materials; normally associated with the filtering of carburetor inlet air.

pop-back Condition in which the air-fuel mixture is ingited in the intake manifold. Because combustion takes place outside the combustion chamber, the combustion may "pop back" through the carburetor.

port In the engine, the opening in which the valve operates and through which air-fuel mixture or burned gases pass; the valve port.

positive One of the two poles of a magnet, or one of the two terminals of an electrical device.

positive crankcase ventilation (PCV) A crankcase ventilation system; uses intake-manifold vacuum to return the crankcase vapors and blowby gases from the crankcase to the intake manifold to be burned, thereby preventing their escape into the atmosphere.

positive terminal The terminal to which electrons flow in a complete electric circuit. On a battery, the positive terminal can be identified as the battery post with the larger diameter; the plus sign (+) is often also used to identify the positive terminal.

post A point at which a cable is connected to the battery.

pour point The lowest temperature at which an oil will flow.

power stroke The piston stroke from TDC and BDC immediately following the compression stroke, during which both valves are closed and the air-fuel mixture burns, expands, and forces the piston down to transmit power to the crankshaft.

ppm Abbreviation for *parts per million;* the unit used in measuring the level of hydrocarbons in exhaust gas with an exhaust-gas analyzer.

precombustion chamber In some diesel engines, a separate small combustion chamber into which the fuel is injected and where combustion begins.

preignition Ignition of the air-fuel mixture in the combustion chamber, by any means, before the ignition spark occurs at the spark plug.

premium gasoline The best or highest-octane gas available to the motorist.

pressure Force per unit area, or force divided by area. Usually measured in pounds per square inch (psi) and kilograms per square centimeter (kg/cm^2).

pressure cap A radiator cap, with valves, which causes the cooling system to operate under pressure and thus at a somewhat higher and more efficient temperature.

pressure tester An instrument that clamps in the radiator filler neck; used to pressure-test the cooling system for leaks.

pressurize To apply more than atmospheric pressure to a gas or liquid.

preventive maintenance The systematic inspection of a vehicle to detect and correct failures, either before they occur or before they develop into major defects. A procedure for economically maintaining a vehicle in a satisfactory and dependable operating condition.

primary The low-voltage circuit of the ignition system.

primary winding The outer winding, of relatively heavy wire, in an ignition coil.

printed circuit An electric circuit made by applying a conductive material to an insulating board in a pattern that provides current paths between components mounted on or connected to the board.

progressive linkage A carburetor linkage used with multiple-carburetor installations to progressively open the secondary carburetors.

psi Abbreviation for *pounds per square inch,* a unit of pressure.

psig Abbreviation for *pounds per square inch* of **gauge pressure.**

pulley A metal wheel with a V-shaped groove around the rim; drives, or is driven by, a belt.

pump A device that transfers gas or liquid from one place to another.

quad carburetor A four-barrel carburetor.

quench The removal of heat during combustion from the end gas or outside layers of air-fuel mixture by the cooler metallic surfaces of the combustion chamber, thus reducing the tendency for detonation to occur.

quench area The area of the combustion chamber near the cylinder walls which tends to cool (quench) combustion through the effect of the nearby cool water jackets.

quick charger A battery charger which produces a high charging current and thus substantially charges, or boosts, a battery in a short time.

radiator In the cooling system, the device that removes heat from coolant passing through it; takes hot coolant from the engine and returns the coolant to the engine at a lower temperature.

radiator pressure cap See **pressure cap.**

raster pattern An oscilloscope pattern showing the ignition voltages one above the other, from the bottom to the top of the screen in the engine firing order.

recharging The action of forcing electric current into a battery in the direction opposite that in which current normally flows during use. Reverses the chemical reaction between the plates and electrolyte.

rectifier A device which changes alternating current to direct current; in the alternator, a diode.

refractometer An instrument used to measure the specific gravity of a liquid such as battery electrolyte or engine coolant; gives a reading that is already adjusted for the temperature of the liquid being tested.

regulator In the charging system, a device that controls alternator output to prevent excessive voltage.

relay An electrical device that opens or closes a circuit or circuits in response to a voltage signal.

reluctor In an electronic ignition system, the metal rotor (with a series of tips) which replaces the conventional distributor cam.

required voltage The voltage required to fire a spark plug.

research octane number A number used to describe the octane rating of a marketed gasoline. See also **Motor Octane Number.**

reserve capacity A battery rating; the number of minutes a battery can deliver a 25-amp current before the cell voltages drop to 1.75 volts per cell.

residual magnetism The magnetism that remains in a material after the electrical current producing the magnetism has stopped flowing.

resistance The opposition to a flow of current through a circuit or electrical device; measured in ohms. A voltage of 1 volt will cause 1 ampere to flow through a resistance of 1 ohm. This is known as Ohm's law, which can be written in three ways: amperes = volts/ohms; ohms = volts/amperes; and volts = amperes × ohms.

retard Usually associated with the spark-timing mechanisms of the engine; the opposite of spark advance. Also, to delay the introduction of the spark into the combustion chamber.

rich mixture An air-fuel mixture that has a relatively high proportion of fuel and a relatively low proportion of air. An air-fuel ratio of 13:1 indicates a rich mixture, compared to an air-fuel ratio of 16:1.

road-draft tube A method of scavenging the engine crankcase of fumes and pressure, used prior to the introduction of crankcase emission control systems. The tube, which was connected into the crankcase and suspended a few inches from the ground, depended on venturi action to create a partial vacuum as the vehicle moved. The method was ineffective below about 20 mph [32 km/h].

RON Abbreviation for **research octane number.**

rotary Term describing the motion of a part that continually rotates or turns.

rotor A revolving part of a machine, such as an alternator rotor, disk-brake rotor, distributor rotor, or Wankel-engine rotor.

rpm Abbreviation for *revolutions per minute,* a measure of rotational speed.

SA Designation for lubricating oil that is acceptable for use in engines operated under the mildest conditions.

SAE Abbreviation for *Society of Automotive Engineers.* Used to indicate a grade or weight of oil measured according to Society of Automotive Engineers standards.

sag A momentary decrease in acceleration rate; does not occur immediately after throttle application (as in a hesitation), but after the vehicle has acquired some speed.

SB Designation for lubricating oil that is acceptable for minimum-duty engines operated under mild conditions.

SC Designation for lubricating oil that meets requirements for use in the gasoline engines in 1964 to 1967 passenger cars and trucks.

schematic A pictorial representation, most often in the form of a line drawing. A systematic positioning of components and their relationship to each other or to the overall function.

scope Short for **oscilloscope.**

SD Designation for lubricating oil that meets requirements for use in the gasoline engines in 1968 to 1971 passenger cars and some trucks.

SE Designation for lubricating oil that meets requirements for use in the gasoline engines in 1972 and later cars, and in certain 1971 passenger cars and trucks.

seal A material, shaped around a shaft, used to close off the operating compartment of the shaft, preventing oil leakage.

sealed-beam headlight A headlight that contains the filament, reflector, and lens in a single sealed unit.

secondary circuit The high-voltage circuit of the ignition system;

consists of the coil, rotor, distributor cap, spark-plug cables, and spark plugs.

segments The copper bars of a commutator.

self-discharge Chemical activity in the battery which causes the battery to discharge even though it is furnishing no current.

self-induction The inducing of a voltage in a current-carrying coil of wire because the current in that wire is changing.

semiconductor A material that acts as an insulator under some conditions and as a conductor under other conditions.

semiconductor ignition system See **electronic ignition system.**

separator A thin sheet of wood, rubber, or glass mat that is placed between positive and negative plates in a battery cell to insulate them from each other.

series circuit An electric circuit in which the devices are connected end to end, positive terminal to negative terminal. The same current flows through all the devices in the circuit.

series-parallel system A starting system using two batteries, connected differently for different functions. For example, a system with a 24-volt starting motor, two 12-volt batteries, and a 12-volt alternator. For starting, the two batteries are connected in series to produce 24 volts; for charging, they are connected in parallel to produce 12 volts.

service rating A designation that indicates the type of service for which an engine lubricating oil is best suited. See **SA, SB, SC, SD,** and **SE.**

short circuit A defect in an electric circuit which permits current to take a short path, or circuit, instead of following the desired path.

smog A term coined from the words *smoke* and *fog*. First applied to the foglike layer that hangs in the air under certain atmospheric conditions; now generally used to describe any condition of dirty air and/or fumes or smoke. Smog is compounded from smoke, moisture, and numerous chemicals which are produced by combustion.

smoke Small gasborne or airborne particles, exclusive of water vapor, that result from combustion; such particles emitted by an engine into the atmosphere in sufficient quantity to be observable.

smoke in exhaust A visible blue or black substance often present in the automotive exhaust. A blue color indicates excessive oil in the combustion chamber; black indicates excessive fuel in the air-fuel mixture.

snap ring A metal fastener, available in two types; the *external* snap ring fits into a groove in a shaft; the *internal* snap ring fits into a groove in a housing. Snap rings must be installed and removed with special snap-ring pliers.

soldering Joining pieces of metal with solder, flux, and heat.

solenoid An electromechanical device which, when connected to an electrical source such as a battery, produces a mechanical movement. This movement can be used to control a valve or to produce other movements.

solenoid relay A relay that connects a solenoid to a current source when its contacts close; specifically, the starting-motor solenoid relay.

solenoid switch A switch that is opened and closed electromagnetically, by the movement of a solenoid core. Usually, the core also causes a mechanical action, such as the movement of a drive pinion into mesh with flywheel teeth for cranking.

solid-state regulator An alternator regulator encapsulated in a plastic material and mounted in the alternator.

south pole Pole at which magnetic lines of force enter a magnet.

spark advance See **advance.**

spark duration The length of time a spark is established across a spark gap, or the length of time current flows in a spark gap.

spark knock See **detonation.**

spark line Part of the oscilloscope pattern of the ignition secondary circuit; the spark line shows the voltage required to sustain the spark at the spark plug, and the number of distributor degrees through which the spark exists.

spark plug A device that screws into the cylinder head of an engine; provides a spark to ignite the compressed air-fuel mixture in the combustion chamber.

spark-plug heat range The distance heat must travel from the center electrode to reach the outer shell of the spark plug and enter the cylinder head.

spark test A quick check of the ignition system; made by holding the metal spark-plug end of a spark-plug cable about $\frac{3}{16}$ inch [4.76 mm] from the cylinder head, or block; cranking the engine; and checking for the existence and intensity of a spark.

squish The actions in some combustion chambers in which the last part of the compressed air-fuel mixture is pushed, or squirted, out of a decreasing space between the piston and cylinder head.

stacked pattern See **raster pattern.**

stall test A starting-motor test in which the current draw is measured with the motor stalled.

starter See **starting motor.**

starting motor The electric motor that cranks the engine, or turns the crankshaft, for starting.

starting-motor drive The drive mechanism and gear on the end of the starting-motor armature shaft; used to couple the starting motor to, and disengage it from, the flywheel ring-gear teeth.

static friction The friction between two bodies at rest.

stator In the torque converter, a third member (in addition to the turbine and pump) which changes the direction of fluid flow under certain operating conditions (when the stator is stationary). In an alternator, the assembly that includes the stationary conductors.

steering-and-ignition lock A device that locks the ignition switch in the OFF position and locks the steering wheel so it cannot be turned.

stoplights Lights, at the rear of a vehicle, which indicate that the brakes are being applied by the driver to slow or stop the vehicle.

storage battery A device that changes chemical energy into electrical energy; that part of the electric system which acts as a reservoir for electric energy, storing it in chemical form.

stratified charge In a gasoline-fueled spark-ignition engine, an air-fuel charge with a small layer of very rich air-fuel mixture; the rich layer is ignited first, after which ignition spreads to the leaner mixture filling the rest of the combustion chamber. The diesel engine is a stratified-charge engine.

stroke In an engine cylinder, the distance that the piston moves in traveling from BDC to TDC to BDC.

stumble A condition related to vehicle driveability; the tendency of an engine to falter, and then catch, resulting in a noticeable hesitation felt by the driver. A momentary abrupt deceleration during an acceleration.

sulfation The lead sulfate that forms on battery plates as a result of the battery action that produces electric current.

sulfuric acid See **electrolyte.**

sulfur oxides (SO_x) Acids that can form in small amounts as the result of a reaction between hot exhaust gas and the catalyst in a catalytic converter.

supercharger In the intake system of the engine, a device that pressurizes the ingoing air-fuel mixture. This increases the amount of mixture developed to the cylinders and thus increases the engine output. If the supercharger is driven by the engine exhaust gas, it is called a **turbocharger.**

superimposed pattern On an oscilloscope, a pattern showing the ignition voltages one on top of the other, so that only a single trace, and variations from it, can be seen.

surface ignition Ignition of the air-fuel mixture, in the combustion chamber, by hot metal surfaces or heated particles of carbon.

surge Condition in which the engine speed increases and decreases slightly but perceptibly, in spite of the fact that the driver has not changed the throttle position.

S/V ratio The ratio surface area s of the combustion chamber to its volume V, with the piston at TDC. Often used as a comparative indicator of hydrocarbon emission levels from an engine.

switch A device that opens and closes an electric circuit.

tachometer A device for measuring engine speed, or revolutions per minute.

tank unit The part of the fuel-indicating system that is mounted in the fuel tank.

TCS See **transmission-controlled spark system.**

TDC Abbreviation for **top dead center.**

temperature The measure of heat intensity or concentration, in degrees. Temperature is not a measure of heat quantity.

temperature-sending unit A device, in contact with the engine coolant, whose electrical resistance changes as the coolant temperature increases or decreases; these changes control the movement of the indicator needle of the temperature gauge.

tetraethyl lead A chemical which, when added to engine fuel, increases its octane rating, or reduces its knocking tendency. Also called *ethyl.*

thermistor A heat-sensing device with a negative temperature coefficient of resistance; that is, as its temperature increases, its electrical resistance decreases. Used as the sensing device for engine-temperature indicating instruments.

thermostat A device for the automatic regulation of temperature; usually contains a temperature-sensitive element that expands or contracts to open or close off the flow of air, a gas, or a liquid.

thermostatically controlled air cleaner An air cleaner in which a thermostat controls the preheating of intake air.

throttle A disk valve in the carburetor base that pivots in response to accelerator-pedal position; allows the driver to regulate the volume of the air-fuel mixture entering the intake manifold, thereby controlling the engine speed. Also called the *throttle plate* or **throttle valve.**

throttle-return check Same as **dashpot.**

throttle solenoid positioner An electric solenoid which holds the throttle plate open (hot-idle position), but also permits the throttle plate to close completely when the ignition is turned off, to prevent "dieseling."

throttle valve A round disk valve in the throttle body of the carburetor; can be turned to admit more or less air, thereby controlling engine speed.

timing In an engine, delivery of the ignition spark or operation of the valves (in relation to the piston position) for the power stroke. See **ignition timing** and **valve timing.**

timing chain A chain that is driven by a sprocket on the crankshaft and that drives the sprocket on the camshaft.

timing gear A gear on the crankshaft; drives the camshaft by meshing with a gear on its end.

timing light A light that can be connected to the ignition system to flash each time the No. 1 spark plug fires; used for adjusting the timing of the ignition spark.

top dead center The piston position when the piston has reached the upper limit of its travel in the cylinder, and the center line of the connecting rod is parallel to the cylinder walls.

torque Turning or twisting effort; usually measured in pound-feet or kilogrammeters. Also, a turning force such as that required to tighten a connection.

torque test A starting-motor test in which both the torque developed and the current drawn are measured while the specified voltage is applied.

transducer Any device which converts an input signal of one form into an output signal of a different form. For example, the automobile horn converts an electric signal to sound.

transistor An electronic device that can be used as an electric switch; used to replace the contact points in electronic ignition systems.

transmission-controlled spark (TCS) system A General Motors NO_x exhaust-emission control system; makes use of the transmission-gear position to allow distributor vacuum advance in high gear only.

transmission-regulated spark (TRS) system A Ford exhaust-emission control system, similar to the General Motors transmission-controlled spark system; allows distributor vacuum advance in high gear only.

trouble diagnosis The detective work necessary to find the cause of a trouble.

tuneup A procedure for inspecting, testing, and adjusting an engine, and replacing any worn parts, to restore the engine to its best performance.

turbocharger A supercharger driven by the engine exhaust gas.

turbulence The state of being violently distrubed. In the engine, the rapid swirling motion imparted to the air-fuel mixture entering a cylinder.

twenty-five-ampere rate A battery rating; the length of time a battery can deliver 25 amps before the cell voltage drops to 1.75 volts, starting with the electrolyte at 80° [26.7°C].

twenty-hour rate A battery rating; the amount of current a battery can delivery for 20 hours before the cell voltage drops below 1.75 volts, starting with an electrolyte temperature of 80°F [26.7°C].

two-barrel carburetor A carburetor with two throttle valves.

two-stroke cycle The two piston strokes during which fuel intake, compression, combustion, and exhaust take place in a two-stroke-cycle engine.

unit distributor A General Motors ignition distributor that uses a magnetic pickup coil and timer core instead of points and a condenser. The ignition is assembled into the distributor as a unit.

unleaded gasoline Gasoline to which no lead compounds have been intentionally added. Gasoline that contains 0.05 g or less of lead per gallon; required by law to be used in 1975 and later vehicles equipped with catalytic converters.

vacuum Negative gauge pressure, or a pressure less than atmospheric pressure. Vacuum can be measured in psi, but is usually measured in inches or millimeters of mercury (Hg); a reading of 30 inches [762 mm] Hg would indicate a perfect vacuum.

vacuum advance The advancing (or retarding) of ignition timing by changes in intake-manifold vacuum, which reflect throttle opening and engine load. Also, a mechanism on the ignition distributor that uses intake-manifold vacuum to advance the timing of the spark to the spark plugs.

vacuum gauge In automotive-engine service, a device that measures intake-manifold vacuum and thereby indicates actions of engine components.

valve A device that can be opened or closed to allow or stop the flow of a liquid or gas.

valve float A condition in which the engine valves do not close completely, or fail to close at the proper time.

valve overlap The number of degrees of crankshaft rotation during which the intake and exhaust valves are open together.

valve timing The timing of the opening and closing of the valves in relation to the piston position.

vapor A gas; any substance in the gaseous state, as distinguished from the liquid or solid state.

vapor-liquid separator A device in the evaporative emission control system; prevents liquid gasoline from traveling to the engine through the charcoal-canister vapor line.

vapor lock A condition in the fuel system in which gasoline vaporizes in the fuel line or fuel pump; bubbles of gasoline vapor restrict or prevent fuel delivery to the carburetor.

vapor-return line A line from the fuel pump to the fuel tank; allows vapor that has formed in the fuel pump to return to the fuel tank.

vehicle identification number (VIN) The number assigned to each vehicle by its manufacturer, primarily for registration and identification purposes.

venturi In the carburetor, a narrowed passageway or restriction which increases the velocity of air moving through it; produces the vacuum responsible for the discharge of gasoline from the fuel nozzle.

VIN Abbreviation for **vehicle identification number.**

viscosity The resistance to flow exhibit by a liquid. A thick oil has greater viscosity than a thin oil.

viscosity rating An indicator of the viscosity of engine oil. There are separate ratings for winter driving and for summer driving. The winter grades are SAE5W, SAE10W, and SAE20W. The summer grades are SAE20, SAE30, SAE40, and SAE50. Many oils have multiple-viscosity ratings, as, for example, SAE10W-30.

volatility A measure of the ease with which a liquid vaporizes; has a direct relationship to the flammability of a fuel.

voltage The force which causes electrons to flow in a conductor. The difference in electrical pressure (or potential) between two points in a circuit.

voltage drop The reduction (drop) in voltage across an electrical device or a cricuit; due to the resistance of the device or circuit.

voltage regulator A device that prevents excessive alternator or generator voltage by alternately inserting and removing a resistance in the field circuit.

voltmeter A device for measuring the potential difference (voltage) between two points, such as the terminals of a battery or alternator, or two points in an electric circuit.

volumetric efficiency The ratio of the amount of air-fuel mixture that actually enters an engine cylinder to the theoretical amount that could enter under ideal conditions.

Wankel engine A rotary engine in which a three-lobe rotor turns eccentrically in an oval chamber to produce power.

wedge combustion chamber A combustion chamber resembling a wedge in shape.

wiring harness A group of individually insulated wires, wrapped together to form a neat, easily installed bundle.

WOT Abbreviation for *wide-open throttle.*

INDEX

Ac (alternating current), 223
Ac generator (*See* Alternator)
Accelerator-pump system, 117
Additives, oil, 53–55
Air-bag controls, 350
Air bleed, carburetor, 112–114, 122–123
Air-bypass valve, 206 (*See also* Air-injection system)
Air cleaners, 97–99, 139–142
servicing of, 139–142
thermostatically controlled, 98–99, 142
Air-cooled engines, 33
Air-fuel mixture, 198–199
Air-fuel ratios, 110, 117
Air-injection system, 100, 206, 212–213
air-bypass valve in, 106
air pump in, 100
servicing of, 212–213
Air pollution, 187–196, 208–210
Air pump, 100
Alternating current (ac), 223
Alternator, 267–276, 280–295
belt tension for, 295
diode heat sinks in, 271
external regulators for, 272–273
function of, 267
internal regulator for, 274–276
principles of, 270–271
rectifying ac from, 271–272
regulators for, 272–276
servicing of, 280–295
stator circuits in, 271
types of, 272
Alternators, Chrysler, 280–295
servicing of 280–295
Alternators, Delco-Remy, 291–295
servicing of, 291–295
Alternators, Ford, 287–291
servicing of, 287–291
Ammeter, 219–220, 225
Anticollision radar, 350–351
Antifreeze, 66, 72, 360
tester for, 360
Anti-icing system, carburetor, 122
Antiknock value, 85–87 (*See also* Detonation)
Antisiphon passages, carburetor, 122–123
Antiskid braking system, 351–352
Armature, servicing of, 262
Atomization, 108
Automatic chokes, 119–120, 143
adjustment of, 143
Automobile, pollution from, 189
Automotive electronics, 349–354
on-car devices, 350–354
Automotive-emission controls, 187–196, 198–210, 212–217
cleaning exhaust gas with, 198–210
controlling air pollution with, 198–210
servicing of, 212–217
Automotive-engine fuels, 84–89

Batteries, 231–236, 238–247
adding water to, 238–239
cadmium-tip test of, 242
capacity test of, 242
cells in, 232–235
chemical action in, 231, 234–235
cleaning corrosion from, 239
construction of, 231–234
dry-charged, 246–247
efficiency of, 235
electrolyte in, 238–239, 246
421 test of, 242

Batteries (*Cont.*):
freezing point of, 242
high-discharge test of, 242
hydrometer test of, 239–242
overcharging of, 243
purpose of, 231
ratings of, 235
refractometer test of, 242
removing and replacing of, 244–245
self-discharge of, 241
service of, 238–247
side-terminal, 232–234
specific gravity of, 239–242
sulfation of, 244
testing of, 239–244
visual inspection of, 238–239
voltage variations in, 235–236
wet type of, 246
BDC (bottom dead center), 4
Belt-tension adjustment, 295, 360
Bendix drive, 252
Bloc-Chek tester, 78
Blowby, 100
Bore, cylinder, 19
Bosch electronic fuel-injection, 173–180 (*See also* Fuel injection)
Bottom dead center (BDC), 4
Brake horsepower, 24–25
Braking system, antiskid, 351–352
Brushes, starting motor, 250, 263
Butane, 89

Cadillac electronic fuel-injection system, 178–180
Cadmium-tip test, 242
Cam lobe, 11–12
Camshaft bearings, lubrication of, 60
Canister, charcoal, 191–192
Capacitor (*See* Condenser)
Capacity test, 242
Carbon dioxide (CO_2), 84
Carbon monoxide (CO), 47, 84, 89
Carburetor, 8, 108–125, 149–168
accelerator-pump system in, 117
adjustments of, 150–151
air bleeds in, 112–114, 122–123
air cleaner for, 97–99
air-fuel mixture of, 198–199
air-fuel ratios in, 110–117
anti-icing system in, 122
antisiphon passages in, 122–123
choke in, 117–120 (*See also* Choke, carburetor)
fast idle in, 122
float-bowl vents in, 111–112
four-barrel, 123–125
fuel nozzle action in, 109–110
fundamentals of, 108–110
governor on, 123
idle limiter on, 198
installation of, 152
insulator for, 195–196
main metering system in, 114–115
manifold heat control for, 120–122
overhaul procedures for, 151–152
Quadrajet, 123–125
removal of, 151
servicing of, 149–168
systems in, 110–118
throttle valve in, 108–110
two-barrel, 123
vacuum piston in, 115–116
venturi in, 108–109

Carburetor, Carter BBD, 158–162
Carburetor, Carter YF1-V, 154–158
Carburetor, Rochester 4MV, 162–168
Carburetor, Rochester Quadrajet, 123–125
Carter BBD carburetor, 158–162
Carter YF1-V carburetor, 154–158
Catalysts, 101, 206–208
Catalytic converter, 78, 101, 206–208
Cells, battery, 232, 235
Centrifugal advance, 306, 315
wear of, 315
(*See also* Distributor, ignition)
Charcoal canister, 191–192
Charging systems, 267–276, 278–295
diagram of, 278–280
servicing of, 278–295
testing of, 278–280
(*See also* Alternator; Generator; Regulator)
Choke, carburetor, 117–120, 142–143, 199
adjustment of, 142–143
automatic, 119–120
electric, 120
fast-acting, 199
Chrysler electronic ignition system, 299–300
Circuit breakers, 225–229
Circuits, electric, 223–224
resistance in, 223–224
Clearance volume, 20–21
CO (carbon monoxide), 47, 84, 89
CO_2 (carbon dioxide), 84
Coil, ignition, 303–306, 319
testers for, 319
Combustion, 85–89, 104–105, 199–201
chemistry of, 89
controlling of, 199
heat of compression in, 85
Honda system of, 104–105
stratified charge type of, 104–105
Combustion chamber, 9, 41–42, 78, 88, 199
Commutator, generator, 268
starting motor,250
Compression ratio, 8–9, 20–21, 85
Compression stroke, 8–9
Compression tester, cylinder, 356–357
Condenser, ignition, 305–306, 319
testers for, 319
Connecting rod, 1–3, 59
oil holes in, 59
Contact points, 320–321, 334–339
adjusting of, 320–321, 336–339
Continuous-flow fuel injection, 172–173
Coolant, engine, 66, 75–77
Cooling system, engine, 32, 66–72, 74–83, 360
antifreeze solutions for, 72 (*See also* Antifreeze)
servicing of, 74–83
Corvair engine, 30–31
Crankcase, dilution in, 85
vapor storage in, 196 (*See also* Vapor-recovery system)
ventilation of, 100 (*See also* Positive crankcase ventilation)
Cranking motor (*See* Starting motor)
Crankpin, 1–4
Crankshaft, 1–4
Current,
alternating, 223
direct, 225
Current regulator, 269–270
Cutout relay, 269
Cylinders, engine, 1, 11, 28, 39, 356–358
arrangements of, 28
numbering of, 39

Dc generator (*See* Generator, dc)
Detonation, 21, 85–89, 372
chemical control of, 87
factors affecting, 88
Diesel engine, 36–39, 54, 89, 101
two-cycle type of, 39
Diodes, 271, 283–294
testing of, 283–292
Dipstick, 59
Direct-current (dc), 225
Displacement, piston, 19–20
Distributor, ignition, 297–301, 319–320, 332–347
checking advance mechanism in, 333–334
contact-point type of, 297–298
disassembly of, 344–345
installation of, 347
installing shaft in, 346
lubrication of, 340
reassembly of, 345–346
removal and installation of, 347
synchronizing dual-contact in, 339
testers for, 319–320
DOHC (double-overhead camshaft) engines, 14
Double-overhead camshaft (DOHC) engines, 14
Dry-charged batteries, 246–247
Dual-contact distributors, 339
Dual exhaust systems, 100
Dwell, 321, 336–339
adjusting of, 336–339
Dynamometer, 24–25, 359–360

Efficiency, engine, 22–25
volumetric, 22–23
EGR (exhaust-gas recirculation), 99–100 (*See also* Exhaust-gas recirculation)
EGR valve, 201–202 (*See* Exhaust-gas recirculation)
Electric choke, 120
Electric fuel gauges, 97
Electric fuel pumps, 96–97
Electrical-system testers, 360–361
Electricity, 219–229
electrons, 219–221
fundamentals of, 219–229
magnetism, 219–220
measuring of, 219
Ohm's law for, 222–223
one-wire system, 223
resistance, 222–223
Electrolyte, 234–235, 238–246
checking specific gravity of, 239–242
freezing point of, 242
Electromagnets, 219, 222
Electromechanical fuel-injection, 180
ECU (electronic control unit), 173, 176–177
Electronic control unit (ECU), 173, 176–177
Electronic fuel injection, 102–103, 173–185, 352–354
Cadillac type of, 178–180
cold start valve in, 177
electronic control unit for, 173, 176–177
controls for, 176–177
coolant temperature sensor in, 176
intake-air temperature sensor in, 176–177
intake-manifold pressure sensor in, 176
operation of, 177
servicing of, 181–184
throttle-position switch in, 177
trouble diagnosis chart for, 184–185
visual inspection of, 181–183
Volkswagen type of, 177–178
Electronics, automotive, 349–354
computers in, 349
integrated circuits for, 349–350
(*See also* Electronic fuel injection)
Electrons, 219–221
movement of, 220–221
Electronic ignition system, 298–301, 324–325, 340–344
Electronic ignition system (*Cont.*):
Chrysler, 299–300
General Motors, 300–301
high-energy ignition, 300–301
testers for, 324–325
testing of, 340–344
Emergencies, shop, 45–46
Emission controls, automotive:
air-injection system, 100, 206, 212–213
catalytic converter, 78, 101, 206–208
evaporative control systems, 191–196
exhaust-gas recirculation, 99–100, 201–202
orifice spark-advance control (OSAC), 205
positive crankcase ventilation, 59, 89, 100, 189–190, 212, 360
servicing of, 212–217
spark-delay valve system, 205–206
thermal reactor, 206
transmission-controlled spark (TCS), 202–204
transmission-regulated spark (TRS), 204
unleaded gasoline, 87–88
used-car smog devices, 217
vacuum-advance controls, 308–309
valve overlap, 100
vapor-recovery system, 191–196
Emissions, tuneup for reducing, 212–214
Energizer (*See* Batteries)
Engine analyzers, 380–383
Engines, 1–25, 33–42, 50–63, 66–72, 84–89, 355–372, 376–383
air-cooled, 33
analyzers for, 380–383
computer testers for, 380–383
cooling systems for, 66–72
cycles of, 34–39
cylinders in, 1
diesel, 36–39 (*See also* Diesel engine)
efficiency of, 25
fan on, 67–68
firing order of, 39
flat-head, 11–12
fuels for, 84–89
fundamentals of, 1–6
gas turbine, 40–41
high compression, 21
horsepower of, 22
I-head, 12–14
L-head, 11–12
liquid-cooled, 33–34, 66
lubricating system in, 53–63
measurements of, 19–25
multiple-cylinder, 10
noises in, 372
oil, 53–56 (*See also* Oil)
oil coolers for, 56
oil pump in, 56–58
operation of, 8–17
overhead camshaft, 14
overheating of, 369
performance of, 22
power of, 21–22
reciprocating, 1–6
rotary, 1, 40–42
(*See also* Gas turbine; Rotary engine; Wankel engine)
servicing safety cautions for, 50
testing instruments for, 355–361
torque of, 23–24
trouble diagnosis of, 362–372
tuneup of, 376–383
two-cycle, 34–39
two-cycle vs. four-cycle, 36
types of, 1–6, 28–42
vacuum gauge for, 358, 368
valves in, 5
Wankel, 1, 41–42
Ethyl gasoline, 87
(*See also* Leaded gasoline)
Ethylene glycol, 72
Evaporation-control systems, 191–196
servicing of, 213
Exhaust gas, 78, 99–100, 198–210, 214–217, 358, 369–370
air-injection for, 206
analyzer for, 214–217, 358, 369–370
catalytic converters for, 206
cleaning of, 198–210
exhaust manifolds for, 100
leakage test for, 78
recirculation of, 99–100, 201–202
(*See also* Exhaust system)
Exhaust-gas analyzer, 214–217, 358, 369–370
checking for HC and CO with, 215–217
Exhaust-gas recirculation (EGR), 99–100, 201–202
EGR valve in, 201–202
Exhaust manifolds, 100
Exhaust stroke, 9–10
Exhaust system, 100–101
catalytic converter in, 101
(*See also* Catalytic converter)
laminated exhaust pipes in, 100
Expansion-core plugs, 81–83
Expansion tank, 71, 196
External-combustion engines, 1

Fan, engine, 67–68
Fan belt, testing of, 79
Fast idle, 122
Field relay, alternator, 272–273
Filament, light bulb, 225
Filter, air, 97–99, 139–142
Filter, fuel, 92
Fire prevention, 46
Firing order, engine, 39
Flat-four engine, 29–30
Flat-head engine, 11–12
Flat-six engine, 30–32
Float-bowl vents, 111–112
Float system, carburetor, 110–112
Folo-thru drive, 164, 252
Four-barrel carburetor, 123–125
Four-stroke-cycle engine, 1–6, 10, 36
421 test, battery, 242
Friction, 24
Friction horsepower, 24–25
Fuel, automotive-engine, 84–89, 371–372
excessive consumption of, 371–372
Fuel filter, 92, 143
Fuel gauges, 92–93, 97, 144–145
electric, 97
Fuel injection, 101–103, 170–185, 201
advantages of, 170–172
electromechanical, 180
electronic, 102–103, 173–185
fuel-supply pump in, 174
gasoline engines with, 101–103
mechanical, 172–173, 180–181
types of, 170
(*See also* Electronic fuel injection; Diesel engine)
Fuel lines, 144
Fuel-nozzle, carburetor, 109–110
Fuel pump, 93–97, 145–146
electric, 96–97
installation of, 146
removal of, 145
servicing of, 145–146
troubles in, 145
Fuel-return line, 191
Fuel screen, 92
Fuel system, 8, 84, 91–107, 108–125, 129–137, 139–147, 149–168, 173–185
air cleaner in, 97–99
carburetor in, 8, 108–125, 149–168 (*See also* Carburetor)
choke adjustment in, 142–143
cleanliness in, 139

Fuel system (*Cont.*):
components of, 91
diesel engine, 39 (*See also* Diesel engine)
electric fuel pumps in, 96–97
electronic fuel injection for, 173–185
filter in, 92, 143
fuel injection in, 170–185
fuel lines in, 144
fuel pump in, 93–94, 145–146
fuel tank in, 143–144
gauges in, 144–145
low fuel indicator in, 93
purpose of, 91
screens in, 92
troubles in, 129–137
vapor lock in, 84
vapor-return line in, 94–96
testers for, 360
servicing of, 139–147
Fuel tank, 91–92, 143–144, 195–196
domed type of, 195
expansion tank in, 196
pressure-vacuum cap for, 195
sealed type of, 195
Fuel-vapor recovery system, 95–96, 112, 191–196
(*See also* Vapor-recovery system)
Fuels, automotive engine:
butane, 89
propane, 89
(*See also* Gasoline)
Fuses, 225–229
Fusible links, 225–229

Gas turbines, 40–41
Gasoline, 46, 84–89, 206–208
additives in, 84–89
antiknock value of, 85
lead in, 206–208
scavengers in, 87
source of, 84
storage of, 46
volatility of, 84
Gasoline engine fuel injection, 101–103
Gauges, fuel, 92–93
General Motors electronic ignition system, 300–301
high-energy ignition (HEI), 300–301
unit distributor in, 301
Generator, dc, 267–270
commutator in, 268
principles of, 267
regulator for, 268–270
Governor, 123
Ground, electrical, 223

HC (hydrocarbon), 84
(*See also* Gasoline)
Heat of compression, 36–39, 85
Heat-control valve, manifold, 100
Heat range, spark plug, 302
Heated air system, 98–99, 199, 213
servicing of, 213
Heater, car, 71–72
Hemispheric combustion chamber, 88
Heptane, 86
High-discharge test, battery, 242
High-energy ignition (HEI), 300–301
testing of, 340–344
Honda combustion system, 104–105, 200
Horsepower (hp), 21–25
brake, 24–25
friction, 24–25
Hot-idle compensator valve, 112
Hydraulic valve lifter, 16–17
Hydrocarbon (HC), 84
(*See also* Gasoline)
Hydrometer test, battery, 239–242
coolant, 75

I-head engine, 12–14
Idle-stop solenoid, 202
Idle system, carburetor, 112–114
Ignition coil, 303, 306, 319
resistor for, 306
testers for, 319
Ignition condenser, 305–306, 319
testers for, 319
Ignition distributor, 297–301, 332–347
servicing of, 332–347
(*See also* Distributor, ignition)
Ignition switch, 309
Ignition system, 297–309, 311–316, 319–329
advance mechanism in, 306–309
centrifugal advance in, 306
coil in, 303, 306, 319
condenser in, 305–306
distributor in, 297–301
distributor cap and rotor action in, 303–304
electronic, 298–301 (*See also* Electronic ignition system)
electronic-ignition testers, 324–325
function of, 297
magnetic field in, 306
oscilloscope for, 321–324
primary and secondary circuits in, 303
resistor in, 306
secondary wiring in, 302–303
servicing of, 319–329
spark plugs in, 301–303
switch for, 309
timing of, 325–327
trouble diagnosis of, 311–316
vacuum advance in, 306–309
wiring in, 328–329
Ignition timing, 325–327
monolithic, 326–327
Ignition timing light, 326, 358–359
Ignition wiring, 328–329
In-line engines, 28–30
Indicator-lamp, checks of, 278–279
Inertia drive, 252
Insulation, electrical, 221–222
Insulator, carburetor heat, 195–196
Intake-manifold vacuum, 99
Intake stroke, 8
Integrated circuits, 349–350
Internal-combustion engine, 1–6
IR drop, 224
Iso-octane, 86

L-head valve train, 11–12
Laminated exhaust pipes, 100
Leaded gasoline, 206–208
Leakage tester, cylinder, 357–358
Light bulb, 225
Lines of force, 221–222
Liquefied petroleum gas (LPG), 89, 105–107
Liquid-cooled engines, 33–34, 66
Liters, 20
Los Angeles smog, 189
Low fuel-level indicator, 93
LPG (liquefied petroleum gas), 89, 105–107
Lubricating system, engine, 53–63
changing oil and filter, 61–63
oil filter in, 58–59
oil in, 53–56
operation of, 59–63
servicing of, 61–63

Magnetic field, 221, 305–306
collapsing of, 305
Magnetic poles, 221
Magnetic switch, starting motor, 254–256
Magnetism, 219–222
electromagnets, 222
lines of force, 221–222
magnetic field, 221
magnetic poles, 221

Magnetism (*Cont.*):
natural magnets, 221–222
Main metering system, carburetor, 114–115
Maintenance, predictive, 383
Manifold heat control, 100, 120–122
Mazda, 42
Mechanical fuel injection, 180–181
Metering rod, carburetor, 115
Modified borderline procedure, 86–87
MON (motor octane number), 87
Monolithic timing, 326–327
Motor octane number (MON), 87
Muffler, 100
Multiple-viscosity oils, 53

Neutral safety switch, 256
Nitrogen oxides (NO_x), 84, 99–100, 308–309
vacuum advance controls for, 308–309
Nonconductor (*See* Insulation, electrical)
Nonleaded gasoline, 208
pump nozzle for, 208
NO_x (nitrogen oxides), 84, 99–100, 308–309

Octane number, 85
Octane ratings, 87–88
OHC (overhead-camshaft) engines, 14
Ohm's law, 222–223
Ommeter, 328–329
Oil, engine, 53–56, 61–63, 370–371
additives in, 53–55
changing of, 61–63
detergent dispersants in, 55
excessive consumption of, 370–371
extreme-pressure compounds in, 55
multiple viscosity, 53
oxidation inhibitor in, 55
pour-point depressants in, 55
service ratings of, 53–54
viscosity of, 53–55
viscosity improver in, 55
Oil coolers, 56
Oil filters, 58–63
changing of, 62–63
Oil-level indicators, 59
Oil-pressure indicators, 59
Oil pump, engine, 56–58
gear type of, 57
relief valve in, 58
rotor type of, 57–58
One-wire system, 223
Orifice spark-advance control (OSAC), 205
OSAC (orifice spark-advance control), 205
Oscilloscope, 321–324, 359
basic pattern, 322–323
coil-condenser line, 322
dwell section, 323
firing line, 322
patterns shown on, 323–324
use of, 323–324
Overhead-camshaft (OHC) engine, 14
Overhead-valve engine, 12–14
Overrunning clutch, starting motor, 252–253, 264
testing of, 264

Parallel circuits, 223–224
PCV system (*See* Positive crankcase ventilation)
Pinging, 21
Piston, engine, 1, 4, 10, 19–20, 34, 372
displacement of, 19–20
rings for, 10
slap in, 372
stroke of, 4, 34
Poppet valves, 5
Positive crankcase ventilation (PCV), 59, 89, 100, 189–190, 196, 212–213, 360
crankcase vapor storage in, 196
servicing of, 212–213
testers for, 360

Positive crankcase ventilation (PCV) (*Cont.*):
valve in, 190, 212
Power, engine, 21–22
Power equipment safety, 48
Power stroke, 9
Power system, carburetor, 115–116
Precombustion chamber, 104–105, 200
Predictive maintenance, 383
Preignition, 87
Pressure cap, fuel tank, 195
radiator, 71
Printed circuits, 225
Propane, 89
Pump, fuel, 93–94 (*See also* Fuel pump)
Pushrods, 12–14

Quad carburetor, 123–125
Quench, combustion, 88
Quick-charger, battery, 246

Radiator, 67–69, 81–82
cross-flow, 69
down-flow, 69
locating and repairing leaks in, 81–82
Radiator pressure cap, 71, 79
pressure-testing of, 79
RC engine (*See* Wankel engine)
Reciprocating engine, 1–6
Rectifier-bridge, checks of, 293–294
Refractometer, 75–77, 242
testing electrolyte with, 242
Regulator, alternator, 272–276
diode trio in, 274–276
external type of, 272–273
field relay in, 272–273
internal type of, 274–276
transistors in, 274–276
voltage limiter in, 273–274
Regulator, dc generator, 268–270
Relief valve, oil pump, 58
Research octane number (RON), 87
Resistance, electrical, 222–225
heating of, 224–225
temperature effect on, 225
Road test, 48
Rochester 4MV carburetor, 162–168
Rochester fuel injection system, 172–173
Rocker arms, 12–14
Rod, connecting, 1–3
RON (research octane number), 87
Rotary combustion engine (*See* Wankel engine)
Rotary engine, 1, 40–42
Rotary motion, 1–4
Rotor, alternator, 290
Rumble, combustion, 87

Safety, shop, 45–48
Screen, fuel, 92
Seat belt, use of, 48
Secondary wiring, 302–303, 329
location of, 329
Self-induction, coil, 304–306
Series circuits, 223–224
Shop, driving cars in, 48
emergencies, 45–46
layouts of, 45
safety in, 45–48
Short circuit, 221
Single-overhead camshaft (SOHC) engines, 14
Six-cylinder engine, 30, 60–61, 189–190
Slant-six engine, 30
Slip rings, replacing of, 285
(*See also* Alternator)
Smog, 88, 99–100, 187–196
Smog devices, used-car, 217

SOHC (single-overhead camshaft) engine, 14
Solenoid, 222, 254–256
starting motor, 254–256
Solenoid injection valve, 173–175
Spark-advance mechanisms, 306–309
Spark-delay valve system, 205–206
Spark knock, 21, 85–89
Spark plugs, 301–303, 316, 327–328
cables for, 302–303
heat range of, 302
removing of, 328
servicing of, 327–328
trouble diagnosis of, 316
Specific gravity, battery, 239–242
Starter (*See* Starting motor)
Starting motor, 249–260, 262–265
bench-testing of, 259–260
Bendix drive for, 252
brushes in, 250
circuit checks of, 264–265
commutator in, 250
compound, 250
construction of, 249–251
controls for, 254–256
drive arrangement in, 251–252
drive lubrication in, 264
Folo-thru drive for, 252
gear reduction in, 253–254
inertia drive for, 252
installing of, 264
lubrication of, 264
magnetic switch for, 254–256
neutral safety switch for, 256
no-load test of, 259–260
overrunning clutch for, 252–253
principles of, 249–251
series-shunt, 250
series-wound, 250
servicing of, 262–265
stall test of, 259–260
testing of, 264
trouble diagnosis of, 258–260
two-step control of, 256
vacuum control of, 256
Stator, 270, 284, 289–290
testing of, 284, 289–290
Stratified charge, 104–105, 200
Stroke, piston, 4, 19
Sulfation, battery, 244
Sulfur, in gasoline, 89
Superchargers, 103–104
Surface ignition, 87
Surface/volume (S/V) ratio, 199
S/V (surface/volume) ratio, 199
Switch, ignition, 309
Synchroscope (*See* Distributor, testers for)

Tachometer, 355–356
Tank, fuel, 91–92
TCS (transmission-controlled spark) system, 202–204
TDC (top dead center), 4
Tel, 87
Temperature indicators, 72
Testing instruments, engine, 355–361
Tetraethyl lead, 87–88
Thermal reactor, 206
Thermistor, 93, 225
Thermostat, cooling system, 69–71, 77–78
testing of, 77–78
Thermostatically controlled air cleaner, 98–99, 142
Throttle valve, carburetor, 108–110
Time-relay switch, TCS, 202–204
Timing chain, engine, 15
Timing light, ignition, 326, 358–359

Tools, care of, 47–48
Torque, engine, 23–24
Transfer port, 36
Transistors, 274–276
Transmission controlled spark, 202–204
TRS (transmission-regulated spark) system, 204
Tuneup, engine, 213–214, 376–383
for low emissions, 213–214
procedure for, 376–380
Turbochargers, 103–104
Two-barrel carburetor, 123
Two-cycle diesel engine, 39
Two-cycle engine, 34–39

Unit distributor, 301, 340–342
testing of, 340–342
Unburned gasoline (*See* HC)
Uniset contact points, 336
Unleaded gasoline, effect on catalytic converters, 87
effect on valves and valve seats, 87–88
Used-car smog devices, 217

Vacuum, 8
Vacuum advance, 202–206, 306–309
control of, 202–206
for emission reduction, 308–309
Vacuum-advance solenoid, 202–204
Vacuum gauge, engine, 358
Vacuum piston, carburetor, 115
Valve guide, 5
Valve-in-head engine, 12–14
Valve lifter, 11, 16–17
Valve overlap, 100, 202
Valve port, 5
Valve tappet, 11
Valve timing, 14–15
Valve train, 10–17, 60–61
Valves, 5, 10–17, 32, 50–51
servicing of, 50–51
Vapor-liquid separator, 192–195
Vapor lock, 84, 95–96
Vapor-recovery system, 191–196
charcoal canister in, 191–192
fuel-return line in, 191
vapor-liquid separator in, 192–195
Vapor-return line, fuel pump, 94–96
separator in, 95–96
Vapor storage in crankcase, 196
Vaporization, 108
Variable-speed fan drive, 68
V-8 engines, 32
Venturi effect, in carburetor, 108–109
V-4 engines, 28–29
Volkswagen electronic fuel-injection system, 177–178
Volkswagen engine, 29–30
Voltage, 221
Voltage drop, 224
Voltage limiter, 273–274
Voltage regulator, alternator, 273–274
dc generator, 269–270
Voltmeter, use of, 225
Volumetric efficiency, 22–23
V-6 engines, 30

Wankel engine, 1, 41–42
Water jackets, engine, 66
Water pump, 66–67, 77–82
servicing of, 82
testing of, 77–78
Wedge combustion chamber, 88
Wiring circuits, 225, 328–329
ignition, 328–329
Work, 21

ANSWERS TO QUESTIONS

The answers to questions in the progress quizzes and chapter checkups are given below. In some questions, you are asked to list parts, describe the purpose and operation of components, define terms, and so on. The answers to such questions cannot be given here, since that would mean repeating most of the book. Therefore, you are asked to refer to the book and to the glossary to check those answers.

If you want to figure your grade on any quiz, divide the number of questions in the quiz into 100. This gives you the value of each question. For instance, suppose there are 8 questions. Since 100 divided by 8 is 12.5, each correct answer is worth 12.5 points. If you got 6 correct out of the 8, then your grade is 75 (that is, 6 × 12.5).

If you are not satisfied with the grade you make on a quiz or checkup, restudy the chapter or section and then take the quiz again. This review will help you remember the important facts.

Remember this: When you are taking a course in a school, you can pass and graduate even though you make a grade of less than 100. But in servicing automotive air conditioners, you must be 100 percent right all the time. If you make one error out of a hundred service jobs, for example, your average is 99. In school, that is a fine average. But in the automotive shop, that one error could cause such serious trouble (a ruined compressor, inoperative valve) that it would outweigh all the good jobs you performed. Therefore, always proceed carefully in performing any service job. Make sure you know exactly what you are supposed to do, and how you are to do it.

CHAPTER 1

Progress Quiz 1-1
Matching

internal-combustion engine	burns fuel inside engine
external-combustion engine	burns fuel outside engine
reciprocating	up-and-down motion
piston	fits in cylinder
connecting rod and crankshaft	converts reciprocating to rotary motion
TDC	top dead center
valve	moves up and down in valve guide
valve port	opened and closed by valve
BDC	bottom dead center
connecting rod	attaches piston to crankpin

Chapter 1 Checkup
Completing the Sentences 1. (c) 2. (a) 3. (b) 4. (a) 5. (a) 6. (c) 7. (a)

CHAPTER 2

Progress Quiz 2-1
Correcting Lists 1. reverse 2. flywheel 3. underslung camshaft 4. intake manifold 5. electric motor

Completing the Sentences 1. (b) 2. (d) 3. (c) 4. (a) 5. (a)

Chapter 2 Checkup
Completing the Sentences 1. (c) 2. (c) 3. (a) 4. (b) 5. (a)

CHAPTER 3

Progress Quiz 3-1
Completing the Sentences 1. (b) 2. (a) 3. (b) 4. (c) 5. (b) 6. (c) 7. (a) 8. (a) 9. (b) 10. (a)
Problems 1. 28.27 in^3 2. 8.5:1 3. 10:1

Chapter 3 Checkup
Completing the Sentences 1. (b) 2. (b) 3. (a) 4. (a) 5. (b) 6. (a) 7. (a)

CHAPTER 4

Progress Quiz 4-1
Completing the Sentences 1. (b) 2. (c) 3. (c) 4. (a) 5. (b)

Chapter 4 Checkup
Completing the Sentences 1. (c) 2. (a) 3. (b) 4. (c) 5. (a) 6. (b) 7. (d) 8. (b) 9. (c) 10. (a)
Questions 1. in-line 2. Volkswagen 3. shrouds 4. the water pump 5. water jackets 6. four 7. the piston 8. A full piston stroke clears the cylinder of burned gases. 9. up to 1,000°F [538.7°C] 10. the heat of compression 11. gas turbine and Wankel 12. gasifier and power 13. movement of high-pressure burned gas through the power-turbine blades 14. three 15. Neither has valves; in both, the valve ports are opened and closed by movement of the piston or rotor.

Chapter 5 Checkup
Completing the Sentences 1. (b) 2. (a) 3. (c) 4. (c) 5. (b) 6. (a) 7. (b) 8. (d) 9. (d) 10. (a)

Chapter 6 Checkup
Completing the Sentences 1. (b) 2. (a) 3. (d) 4. (a) 5. (c)

CHAPTER 7

Progress Quiz 7-1
Completing the Sentences 1. (a) 2. (b) 3. (a) 4. (b) 5. (a) 6. (b) 7. (a) 8. (a) 9. (b) 10. (a)

Chapter 7 Checkup
Completing the Sentences 1. (c) 2. (b) 3. (c) 4. (b) 5. (b) 6. (a) 7. (c) 8. (c) 9. (a) 10. (a)
Unscrambling the Purposes of Oil

Jobs	*Reasons*
lubricate	to minimize wear
lubricate	to minimize power loss
act as cooling agent	to remove heat from engine parts
resist squeezing out	to absorb shock loads in bearings
cover rings	to form seal between rings and walls
pick up dirt	to serve as cleaning agent

Chapter 8 Checkup
Completing the Sentences 1. (a) 2. (c) 3. (a) 4. (b) 5. (a) 6. (c) 7. (b) 8. (d) 9. (c) 10. (b)

Chapter 9 Checkup
Completing the Sentences 1. (c) 2. (a) 3. (a) 4. (b) 5. (a) 6. (b) 7. (d) 8. (c) 9. (c) 10. (a)
Correcting Lists 1. thermostat stuck open 2. thermostat stuck closed 3. fuel pump 4. filter 5. thermostat stuck open

Chapter 10 Checkup
Completing the Sentences 1. (a) 2. (b) 3. (c) 4. (a) 5. (b) 6. (a) 7. (b) 8. (a) 9. (c) 10. (b)

Chapter 11 Checkup
Completing the Sentences 1. (b) 2. (a) 3. (a) 4. (b) 5. (c) 6. (b) 7. (b) 8. (b) 9. (b) 10. (a)

CHAPTER 12

Progress Quiz 12-1
Completing the Sentences 1. (b) 2. (a) 3. (c) 4. (b) 5. (b) 6. (b) 7. (c) 8. (b) 9. (a) 10. (c)

Progress Quiz 12-2
Completing the Sentences 1. (b) 2. (b) 3. (a) 4. (a) 5. (c) 6. (c) 7. (b) 8. (c) 9. (b) 10. (a)

Chapter 13 Checkup
Correcting Troubles Lists 1. high-octane fuel 2. idle speed too low 3. accelerator pump inoperative 4. spark plugs defective 5. cooling-system thermostat stuck 6. heavy engine oil 7. hot engine valves 8. carbon in engine 9. high-octane fuel 10. excessive rolling resistance
Completing the Sentences 1. (b) 2. (c) 3. (b) 4. (b) 5. (c) 6. (a) 7. (c) 8. (d) 9. (a) 10. (c) 11. (c) 12. (b) 13. (a) 14. (c) 15. (c)

CHAPTER 14

Progress Quiz 14-1
Completing the Sentences 1. (c) 2. (a) 3. (b) 4. (c) 5. (a) 6. (b) 7. (c) 8. (a) 9. (c) 10. (b)

Chapter 14 Checkup
Completing the Sentences 1. (a) 2. (d) 3. (c) 4. (b) 5. (c) 6. (c) 7. (b) 8. (b) 9. (b) 10. (c)

CHAPTER 15

Progress Quiz 15-1
Completing the Sentences 1. (c) 2. (b) 3. (a) 4. (b) 5. (d) 6. (b) 7. (a) 8. (a)

Chapter 15 Checkup
Unscrambling Carburetor Trouble Causes

Troubles	*Causes*
excessive fuel consumption	high float level
	worn jets or nozzles
	stuck metering rod or power piston
	stuck check valve
lack of power	clogged jets or

	nozzles low float level dirty air filter air leakage into manifold
failure to start unless primed	clogged jets or nozzles clogged fuel filter defective choke
hard starting (engine warm)	choke valve closed throttle cracker misadjusted

Chapter 16 Checkup
Completing the Sentences 1. (c) 2. (b) 3. (c) 4. (c) 5. (a) 6. (a) 7. (a) 8. (c) 9. (a) 10. (c)

Chapter 17 Checkup
Completing the Sentences 1. (b) 2. (a) 3. (b) 4. (b) 5. (c) 6. (c) 7. (b) 8. (b)

Chapter 18 Checkup
Completing the Sentences 1. (c) 2. (b) 3. (b) 4. (b) 5. (a) 6. (a) 7. (b) 8. (a) 9. (a)

Chapter 19 Checkup
Completing the Sentences 1. (b) 2. (b) 3. (c) 4. (a) 5. (c)

CHAPTER 20

Progress Quiz 20-1
Completing the Sentences 1. (b) 2. (a) 3. (c) 4. (b) 5. (c)

Chapter 20 Checkup
Completing the Sentences 1. (b) 2. (a) 3. (b) 4. (c) 5. (a) 6. (b) 7. (a) 8. (c) 9. (b) 10. (a)
Problems 1. 4 A 2. 16 V 3. 3 ohms 4. 8 ohms 5. 1 ohm

CHAPTER 21

Progress Quiz 21-1
Completing the Sentences 1. (c) 2. (c) 3. (b) 4. (b) 5. (c) 6. (c) 7. (c) 8. (a)

Chapter 21 Checkup
Completing the Sentences 1. (a) 2. (c) 3. (b) 4. (b) 5. (a)
Components of the Battery

case	hard rubber or plastic
electrolyte	sulfuric acid and water
negative-plate material	lead
positive-plate material	lead peroxide
separator	plastic, rubber, or wood
plate strap	lead antimony
plate grid	lead antimony

CHAPTER 22

Progress Quiz 22-1
Completing the Sentences 1. (a) 2. (c) 3. (a) 4. (b) 5. (a) 6. (a) 7. (b) 8. (b)

Chapter 22 Checkup
Completing the Sentences 1. (a) 2. (b) 3. (c) 4. (b) 5. (c) 6. (c) 7. (a) 8. (b) 9. (c) 10. (a)
Analysis of Battery Troubles 1. (a) 2. (a) 3. (c) 4. (c)

CHAPTER 23

Progress Quiz 23-1
Completing the Sentences 1. (a) 2. (b) 3. (d) 4. (a) 5. (c) 6. (b) 7. (c) 8. (b)

Chapter 23 Checkup
Completing the Sentences 2. (b) 2. (d) 3. (a) 4. (b) 5. (a) 6. (c) 7. (c)
Sorting Out the Fundamentals

List 1	*List 2*
Motors operate because	conductors move in magnetic fields
Starting motors	are series motors
Bendix pinion	meshes on inertia principle
Overrunning-clutch pinion	is meshed by shift lever
Starting-motor switch	connects motor to battery
Series-parallel switch	connects batteries in series for starting

Chapter 24 Checkup
Correcting Troubles Lists 1. battery gravity 1.250 2. battery grounded 3. starting motor short-circuited 4. starting motor open-circuited 5. battery dead 6. solenoid hold-in winding open 7. battery dead 8. solenoid pull-in winding open 9. engine idle high 10. battery dead

Chapter 25 Checkup
Completing the sentences 1. (c) 2. (b) 3. (c) 4. (a) 5. (d) 6. (c) 7. (a) 8. (b) 9. (a) 10. (c)
Correcting Troubles Lists 1. open field winding 2. open field winding 3. grounded armature or fields 4. commutator bars grounded 5. open fields

Chapter 26 Checkup
Completing the Sentences 1. (b) 2. (c) 3. (a) 4. (c) 5. (c) 6. (a) 7. (d) 8. (c) 9. (c) 10. (b) 11. (a) 12. (b) 13. (c) 14. (c) 15. (a)

Chapter 27 Checkup
Completing the Sentences 1. (a) 2. (b) 3. (a) 4. (c) 5. (c)

Chapter 28 Checkup
Completing the Sentences 1. (b) 2. (d) 3. (c) 4. (b) 5. (a) 6. (a) 7. (b) 8. (b) 9. (a) 10. (c)

Chapter 29 Checkup
Correcting Troubles Lists 1. battery run down 2. condenser shorted 3. excessive engine compression 4. run-down battery 5. burned contact points 6. centrifugal advance not operating 7. excessive resistance in condenser circuits 8. improper timing 9. timing late 10. plugs running too hot

Chapter 30 Checkup
Grouping Ignition Troubles Loss of energy in primary circuit: points improperly set, discharged battery or defective alternator, excessive resistance in primary circuit, condenser shorted, coil primary grounded
Loss of energy in secondary circuit: defective high-voltage wiring, leakage across distributor cap or rotor, plugs fouled or broken
Out of time: timing incorrectly set, centrifugal advance defective, vacuum advance defective, distributor bearing or shaft worn
Completing the Sentences 1. (c) 2. (c) 3. (a) 4. (b) 5. (b) 6. (c) 7. (c) 8. (b) 9. (d) 10. (a) 11. (b) 12. (b) 13. (a) 14. (b) 15. (a)

Chapter 33 Checkup
Completing the Sentences 1. (b) 2. (a) 3. (a) 4. (c) 5. (c) 6. (a) 7. (b) 8. (b) 9. (b)
Unscrambling the test Instruments

Test instruments	*Purposes*
compression tester	checks cylinder compression
tachometer	checks engine speed
vacuum gauge	checks intake-manifold vacuum
combustion tester	analyzes exhaust gas
timing light	checks ignition timing

Chapter 34 Checkup
Correcting Troubles Lists 1. stuck cooling-system thermostat 2. excessive carbon in engine 3. defective fuel pump 4. defective fan belt 5. excessive vacuum in intake manifold 6. vapor lock 7. run-down battery 8. incorrect idle-mixture adjustment 9. defective fuel pump 10. defective head gasket 11. overcharged battery 12. run-down battery 13. vapor lock 14. clogged air cleaner 15. run-down battery 16. spark knock 17. loose piston pin 18. broken rings 19. worn piston-pin bearings 20. misaligned rods
Completing the Sentences 1. (b) 2. (c) 3. (d) 4. (d) 5. (b) 6. (a) 7. (c) 8. (b) 9. (b) 10. (b) 11. (a) 12. (a) 13. (b) 14. (b) 15. (b) 16. (d) 17. (c) 18. (a) 19. (b) 20. (a)

Chapter 35 Checkup
Completing the Sentences 1. (c) 2. (c) 3. (b) 4. (a) 5. (a) 6. (d) 7. (b) 8. (c)